Computer Fundamentals and Programming in C

THIRD EDITION

Reeema Thareja

Assistant Professor
Department of Computer Science
Shyama Prasad Mukherji College for Women
University of Delhi

OXFORD
UNIVERSITY PRESS

OXFORD
UNIVERSITY PRESS

Oxford University Press is a department of the University of Oxford. It furthers the University's objective of excellence in research, scholarship, and education by publishing worldwide. Oxford is a registered trade mark of Oxford University Press in the UK and in certain other countries.

Published in India by
Oxford University Press
22 Workspace, 2nd Floor, 1/22 Asaf Ali Road, New Delhi 110002

First Edition published in 2012
Third Edition published in 2023
Second impression 2024

ISBN-13: 978-93-5497-789-3
ISBN-10: 93-5497-789-8

Typeset in Times New Roman
by Ideal Publishing Solutions, Delhi
Printed in India by Rakmo Press, New Delhi 110 020

For product information and current price, please visit www.india.oup.com

Preface

In today's digital age, computer technology has become an integral part of our lives. It has revolutionized the way we communicate, work, and even entertain ourselves. Whether you are a student, a professional, or simply someone interested in learning about computers and programming, this book is for you. *Computer Fundamentals and Programming in C* is designed to provide a comprehensive understanding of the basics of computer systems and programming using the C programming language. The book is written in a simple and easy-to-understand language, making it accessible to readers with little to no prior knowledge of the subject.

The first part of the book covers the fundamental concepts of computer systems such as hardware, software, operating systems, and computer networks. The second part of the book focuses on programming in the C language. It covers topics such as functions, arrays, strings, pointers, and file handling. It also explains the basics of computer programming such as data types, variables, operators, and control structures. The book also includes numerous examples and exercises to help readers practice and reinforce their understanding of the concepts discussed.

ABOUT THE BOOK

This third edition of *Computer Fundamentals and Programming in C* has been designed as a textbook for the undergraduate students of engineering, computer science, and computer applications. The objective of this book is to introduce the readers to the elements of computing, computer hardware and software, and C programming.

PEDAGOGICAL FEATURES

The following are the salient features of the book:

Notes and Programming Tips Highlight important terms and concepts, and programming tips educate the readers about common programming errors and how to avoid them

Points to Remember Summary points at the end of each chapter help readers to revise all the important concepts explained in the chapter

Glossary Includes a list of key terms along with their definitions for a quick recapitulation of important terms learned in all chapters

Case Studies Select chapters on C include case studies that show how C can be used to create programs demonstrating real-life applications

Programming Examples About 250 C programs are included, which demonstrate the applicability of the concepts learned

Objective Questions Includes comprehensive exercises at the end of each chapter to facilitate revision – Answers to these questions are provided in Appendix F at the end of the book

Exercises Includes plenty of program code-related programs at the end of relevant chapters, which require the readers to find the output of a given code, the functionality of a given loop, or errors in a given program code

CONTENT AND COVERAGE

The book is divided into two parts spanning 18 chapters and five appendices.

Part I: Computers in Fundamentals

Chapter 1, *Introduction to Computers*, provides an introduction to computers. The chapter explains the generations, classifications, applications, and the basic organization of a computer system.

Chapter 2, *Input and Output Devices*, presents a detailed description of the different types of input and output devices.

Chapter 3, *Computer Memory and Processors*, explains the significance of memory hierarchy and discusses the different types of primary and secondary memory that are widely used to store data. It also discusses the basic processor architecture (including RISC and CISC) and the instruction set.

Chapter 4, *Number Systems and Computer Codes*, discusses binary, octal, and hexadecimal number systems. The chapter enables the reader to perform arithmetic operations on different number systems. Important codes such as ASCII, EBCDIC, Excess 3, Gray code, and Unicode are also discussed in the chapter.

Chapter 5, *Boolean Algebra and Logic Gates*, introduces the concepts of digital computing systems such as Boolean algebra, Boolean functions, Boolean expressions, and logic gates.

Chapter 6, *Computer Software*, provides a thorough overview of computer software. It discusses different types of system software and application software packages that are widely used.

Chapter 7, *Computer Networks and the Internet*, talks about different types of computer networks, wired and wireless media, network devices and topologies, area networks, and data transmission mode. It also discusses the Internet, TCP/IP protocol, and different services provided by the Internet.

Chapter 8, *Designing Efficient Programs*, details the different steps in software development process, which are performed for creating efficient and maintainable programs. It also explains the different tools, which are used to obtain solution(s) of a given problem at hand.

Part II: Programming in C

Chapter 9, *Introduction to C*, discusses the building blocks of the C programming language. It includes descriptions on identifiers, constants, variables, and operators supported by the language.

Annexure 1 shows the steps to write, compile, and execute a C program in Unix/Linux and Ubuntu environments.

Chapter 10, *Decision Control and Looping Statements*, deals with special types of statements such as decision control, iterative, break, control, and jump.

Case Study 1 includes two programs which harness the concepts learnt in Chapters 9 and 10.

Chapter 11, *Functions*, deals with declaring, defining, and calling functions. It also discusses the storage classes as well as variable scope in C. The chapter ends with the concept of recursion and a discussion of the Tower of Hanoi problem.

Annexure 2 discusses how to create user-defined header files.

Chapter 12, *Arrays*, provides a detailed explanation of arrays that includes one-dimensional, two-dimensional, and multi-dimensional arrays. Towards the end of the chapter, the operations that can be performed on such arrays are also explained.

Case Study 2 provides an introduction to sorting and various sorting techniques such as bubble sort, insertion sort, and selection sort.

Chapter 13, *Strings*, discusses the concept of strings, which are better known as character arrays. The chapter not only focuses on reading and writing strings but also explains various operations that can be used to manipulate them.

Chapter 14, *Pointers*, presents a detailed overview of pointers, pointer variables, and pointer arithmetic. The chapter also relates the use of pointers with arrays, strings, and functions. This helps readers to understand how pointers can be used to write better and efficient programs.

Annexure 3 explains the process of deciphering pointer declarations.

Case Study 3 includes a program which demonstrates how pointers can be used to access and manipulate strings.

Chapter 15, *Structure, Union, and Enumerated Data Type*, introduces user-defined data types – structures and unions. It includes the use of structures and unions with pointers, arrays, and functions so that the inter-connectivity between the programming techniques can be well understood.

Annexure 4 provides an explanation about bit fields and slack bytes.

Chapter 16, *Files*, discusses how data can be stored in files. The chapter deals with opening, processing, and closing of files through a C program. These files are handled in text mode as well as binary mode for better clarity of the concepts.

Chapter 17, *Preprocessor Directives*, deals with preprocessor directives. It includes small program codes that illustrate the use of different directives in a C program.

Chapter 18, *Introduction to Data Structures*, provides an introduction to different data structures such as linked lists, stacks, queues, trees, and graphs.

Appendix A, *Bitwise Operations*, discusses bit-level programming and some of the bitwise operators.

Appendix B, *ANSI C Library Functions*, lists some of the ANSI C library functions and their descriptions.

Appendix C, *Advanced Type Qualifiers and Inline Functions in C*, introduces some advanced type qualifiers as well as inline functions.

Appendix D, *Interview Questions with Solutions*, includes about 100 frequently asked interview questions along with their solutions.

Appendix E, *Linux: A Short Guide* discusses the basics of Linux kernel and shell and describes the most commonly used Linux commands.

Appendix F, *Emerging Technologies, gives an insight on new emerging areas in the field of computer science such as Artificial Intelligence, Blockchain Technology, Metaverse, etc.*

NEW TO THE EDITION

In this edition, we have added the following new topics in the appropriate chapters:

- A section on Type-C (Or USB-C Port) and comparison between RAM and ROM
- Wireless input devices like speaker, printer, 3D printers
- Lab Activities on working with Google drive to store data on cloud
- Updates on MS Office 2019 and Windows 11
- Types of computer software and customized software
- Generic software development vs specific-purpose software
- Latest updates in versions of C

Topics on emerging technologies including Artificial Intelligence, Metaverse, Immersive Experience, Robotics, Big Data, Internet of Things have been added to Appendix F. For additional reading, topics like 5G, Augmented Reality, Virtual Reality, Mixed Reality, Internet of Things, Machine Learning, Deep Learning, Blockchain, Computer Vision, Drones, NLP and Robotics are added on the Online Resource Centre. The reader can access these topics by using the link given on the back cover of this book.

ACKNOWLEDGEMENTS

The writing of this textbook was a mammoth task for which a lot of help was required from many people. Fortunately, I have had wholehearted support of my family, friends, and fellow members of the teaching staff and students at Shyama Prasad Mukherji College, New Delhi.

My special thanks would always go to my parents, Mr Janak Raj Thareja and Mrs Usha Thareja, and my siblings, Pallav, Kimi, and Rashi, who were a source of abiding inspiration and divine blessings for me. I am especially thankful to my son, Goransh, who has been very patient and cooperative in letting me realize my dreams. My sincere thanks go to my uncle, Mr B.L. Theraja, for his inspiration and guidance in writing this book.

I would also like to thank the following reviewers for their valuable feedback and their contribution in enhancing the content: Dr Santosh Singh, Banasthali Vidyapith, Jaipur; and Dr. S. Radhika, R.M.K. Engineering College, Kavaraipettai, Tamil Nadu.

Last but not the least, I would like to thank the editorial team at Oxford University Press, India for their help and support over the past few years. Comments and suggestions for the improvement of the book are welcome. Please send them to me at reemathareja@gmail.com.

Reema Thareja

Brief Contents

Detailed Contents

PART I

COMPUTER FUNDAMENTALS

1 Introduction to Computers

TAKEAWAYS

- Characteristics of computers
- Stored program concept
- Generations of computers
- Generations of computers
- Types of computers
- Applications of computers
- Basic organization of a computer

1.1 DEFINITION

We all have seen computers in our homes, schools, and colleges. In fact, in today's world, we find computers in most aspects of our daily lives. For some of us, it is hard to even imagine a world without them. A computer, in simple terms, can be defined as an electronic device that is designed to accept data, perform the required mathematical and logical operations at high speed, and output the result.

Nowadays, computers come in different sizes. Their size may vary from very small to very large. In the past, computers were extremely large in size and often required an entire room for installation. These computers consumed enormous amounts of power and were too expensive to be used for commercial applications. Therefore, they were used only for limited tasks, such as computing trajectories for astronomical and military applications. However, with technological advancements, the size of computers became smaller and their energy requirements reduced immensely. This opened the way for adoption of computers for commercial purposes.

These days, computers have become so prevalent that interactive devices such as cellular phones, global positioning system (GPS) units, portable organizers, automated teller machines (ATMs), and gas pumps, all work with computers. Computers are basically meant to solve problems quickly and accurately.

1.2 CHARACTERISTICS OF COMPUTERS

A computer is an electronic device that performs mathematical and logical operations based on a given set of instructions known as a *program*. A computer accepts data, processes it, and produces information. Here, data refers to some raw fact or figure, and information implies the processed data. For example, if 12-12-95 is the date of birth of a student, then it is data (a raw fact/figure). However, when we process this data (subtract it from the present-date) and say that the age of the student is 23 years, then the outcome is information.

Before going into details, let us learn some key terms that are frequently used in association with computers.

Data is a collection of raw facts or figures.

Information comprises processed data to provide answers to *'who'*, *'what'*, *'where'*, and *'when'* type of questions.

Knowledge is the application of data and information to answer the *'how'* part of the question (refer Figure 1.1).

Instructions are the commands given to the computer which tell it what to do.

Program is a set of instructions in a language understood by computers.

Software is a set of programs.

Hardware refers to computer and all its physical parts.

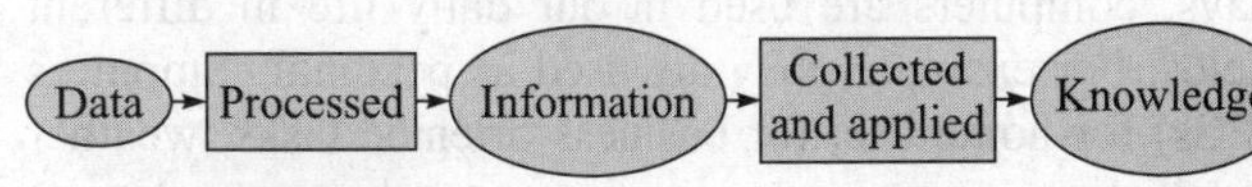

Figure 1.1 Data, information, and knowledge

The important characteristics of a computer (refer to Figure 1.2) are:

Speed Computers can perform millions of operations per second, which means that data that may otherwise take many hours to process is output as information in the fraction of a second. The speed of computers is usually given in nanoseconds and picoseconds, where 1 nanosecond = 1×10^{-9} seconds and 1 picosecond = 1×10^{-12} seconds.

Accuracy Computers are very fast, reliable, and robust devices. They always give accurate results, provided that correct data and set of instructions are input to them. Hence,

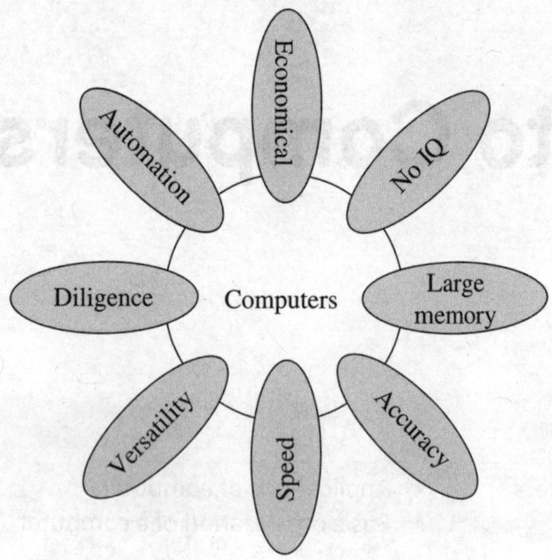

Figure 1.2 Characteristics of computers

in the event of an error, it is the user who has fed the incorrect data/program is responsible. This clearly means that the output generated by a computer depends on the given instructions and input data. If the input data is wrong, then the output will also be erroneous. In computer terminology, this is known as *garbage-in, garbage-out (GIGO)*.

Automation Besides being very fast and accurate, computers are automatable devices that can perform a task without any user intervention. The user just needs to assign the task to the computer, after which it automatically controls different devices attached to it and executes program instructions.

Diligence Unlike humans, computers never get tired of a repetitive task. They can continually work for hours without generating errors. Even if a large number of executions needs to be executed, each and every execution requires the same duration, and is executed with the same accuracy.

Versatile Versatility is the quality of being flexible. These days, computers are used in our daily life in different fields. For example, they are used as personal computers (PCs) for home use, for business-oriented tasks, weather forecasting, space exploration, teaching, railways, banking, medicine, and so on. On the PC that we use at home, we may play a game, compose and send e-mails, listen to music, etc. Therefore, computers are versatile devices as they can perform multiple tasks of different nature at the same time.

Memory Similar to humans, computers also have memory. Just the way we cannot store everything in our memory and need a secondary medium, such as a notebook, to record certain important things, computers also have internal or primary memory (storage space) as well as external or secondary memory. While the internal memory of computers is very expensive and limited in size, the secondary storage is cheaper and of bigger capacity.

Computers store a large amount of data and programs in the secondary storage space. The stored data and programs can be retrieved and used whenever required. Some examples of secondary devices include optical disks (CDs and DVDs), hard disk drives, and pen drives.

When data and programs have to be used, they are copied from the secondary memory into the internal memory, often known as random access memory (RAM). The concept of computer memory is discussed in detail in Chapter 3.

No IQ Although the trend these days is to make computers intelligent by inducing artificial intelligence (AI) in them, they still do not have any decision-making abilities of their own. They need guidance to perform various tasks.

Economical Today, computers are considered as short-term investments for achieving long-term gains. Using computers also reduces manpower requirements and leads to an economical and efficient way of performing various tasks. Hence, computers save time, energy, and money. When compared to other systems, computers can do more work in lesser time. For example, using the conventional postal system to send an important document takes at least two to three days, whereas the same information when sent using the Internet (e-mail) will be delivered instantaneously.

1.3 STORED PROGRAM CONCEPT

All digital computers are based on the principle of stored program concept, which was introduced by Sir John von Neumann in the late 1940s. The following are the key characteristic features of this concept:

- Before any data is processed, instructions are read into the memory.
- Instructions are stored in the computer's memory for execution.
- Instructions are stored in binary form (using binary numbers—only 0s and 1s).
- Processing starts with the first instruction in the program, which is copied into the control unit circuit. The control unit executes the instructions.
- Instructions written by users are performed sequentially until there is a break in the current flow.
- Input/Output and processing operations are performed simultaneously. While data is being read/written, the central processing unit (CPU) executes another instruction in the memory that is ready for execution.

Note

A stored program architecture is a fundamental computer architecture wherein the computer executes the instructions that are stored in its memory.

John W. Mauchly, an American physicist, and J. Presper Eckert, an American engineer, further contributed to the stored program concept to make digital computers much

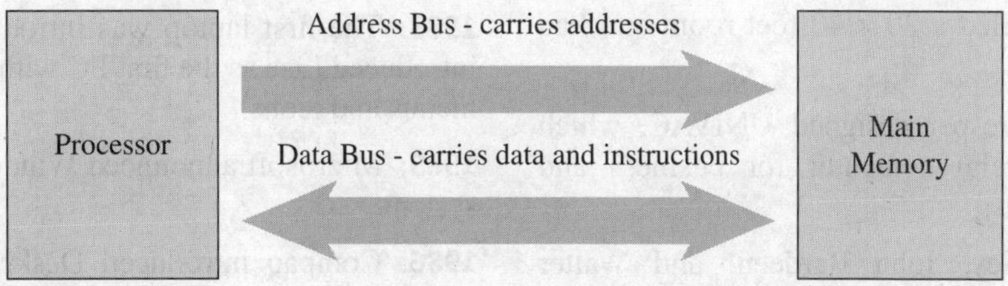

(a)

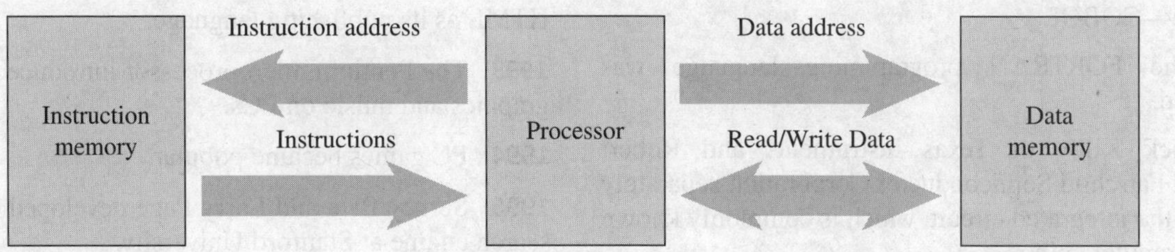

(b)

Figure 1.3 Von Neumann architecture: (a) Shared memory for instructions and data; (b) Separate memories for instructions and data

more flexible and powerful. As a result, engineers in England built the first stored program computer, Manchester Mark I, in the year 1949. They were shortly followed by the Americans who designed EDVAC in the very same year.

1.3.1 Types of Stored Program Computers

A computer with a von Neumann architecture stores data and instructions in the same memory (refer Figure 1.3(a)). This is a serial machine in which data and instructions are selected one at a time. Data and instructions are transferred to and from memory through a shared data bus. Since there is a single bus to carry data and instructions, process execution becomes slower.

Later Harvard University proposed a stored program concept in which there is a separate memory to store data and instructions (refer Figure 1.3(b)). Instructions are selected serially from the instruction memory and executed in the processor. When an instruction needs data, it is selected from the data memory. Since there are separate memories, execution becomes faster.

1.4 HISTORY OF COMPUTERS

Early computers were mainly designed for solving number-crunching problems. These computers were punch-card based machines that took up entire rooms. Today, our smartphones have much more computing power than that was available in those early computers.

In this section, we will read about history of computers way back from the invention of abacus and take a look at the remarkable achievements in computing technology till the current time.

Timeline of Developments

300 BC: The abacus was an early aid for mathematical computations and was designed to aid human's memory while performing calculations. A skilled abacus operator can add and subtract with the same speed as that of a person performing the same calculation using a hand calculator. The invention of abacus is often wrongly attributed to China. It was used by the Babylonians even in 300 BC and is still in use today (in the Far East).

1822: English mathematician Charles Babbage designed a steam-driven calculating machine that could compute tables of numbers. Though the project failed as he could not complete the construction of the engine, it laid the foundation for the first computer.

1890: Herman Hollerith, an American inventor, designed a punched card system to calculate the 1880 census. The system completed the task in three years saving the US government $5 million. Later Herman established a company that we today know as IBM.

1936: British mathematician Alan Turing conceptualized a universal machine called the Turing machine capable of computing anything that is computable. The central concept of the modern computer is based on this machine.

1941: John Vincent Atanasoff, a Bulgarian-American physicist, and his graduate student, Clifford Berry, at Iowa State College designed Atanasoff–Berry computer (ABC) that could solve 29 equations simultaneously. It was the first time a computer could store information in its main memory.

1943–1944: John W. Mauchly and J. Presper Eckert built Electronic Numerical Integrator and Calculator (ENIAC), which is considered as the grandfather of digital computers. It filled a 20 × 40 feet room and had 18,000 vacuum tubes.

1946: Mauchly and Presper designed UNIVAC, which was the first commercial computer for business and government applications.

1947: William Shockley, John Bardeen, and Walter Brattain of Bell Laboratories invented the transistor. Soon vacuum tubes in computers were replaced by transistors.

1953: Grace Hopper developed the first computer language—COBOL.

1954: The FORTRAN programming language was developed.

1958: Jack Kilby of Texas Instruments and Robert Noyce at Fairchild Semiconductor Corporation separately invented the integrated circuit, which is commonly known as the computer chip.

1964: Douglas Engelbart developed a prototype of the modern computer, with a mouse and a graphical user interface (GUI). This was a remarkable achievement as this shifted computers from a specialized machine for scientists and mathematicians to a machine that can be used by general public.

1969: Unix operating system was developed at Bell Labs. It was written in the C programming language and was designed to be portable across multiple platforms. Soon it became the operating system of choice among mainframes at large companies and government entities.

1970: DRAM chip was introduced by Intel.

1971: Alan Shugart with his team in IBM invented the floppy disk which allowed data to be shared among computers.

1973: Robert Metcalfe, a research member at Xerox, developed Ethernet for connecting multiple computers and other hardware.

1974–1977: Personal computers started becoming popular.

1975: Paul Allen and Bill Gates started writing software for the Altair 8800 using the new BASIC language. On April 4, they both formed their own software company, Microsoft.

1976: Steve Jobs and Steve Wozniak started Apple Computers and developed Apple I, the first computer with a single-circuit board.

1977: Apple II was launched that offered colour graphics and incorporated an audio cassette drive for storage.

1978: WordStar, a word processor application, was released by MicroPro International.

1979: VisiCalc, the first computerized spreadsheet program for personal computers, was unveiled.

1981: The first IBM personal computer was introduced that used Microsoft's MS-DOS operating system. The term PC was popularized.

1983: The first laptop was introduced. Moreover, Apple introduced Lisa as the first PC with a GUI with drop-down menus and icons.

1985: Microsoft announced Windows as a new operating system.

1986: Compaq introduced Deskpro 386 in the market, which was a 32-bit architecture machine that provided speed comparable to mainframes.

1990: Tim Berners-Lee invented World Wide Web with HTML as its publishing language.

1993: The Pentium microprocessor introduced the use of graphics and music on PCs.

1994: PC games became popular.

1996: Sergey Brin and Larry Page developed the Google search engine at Stanford University.

1999: The term Wi-Fi was introduced when users started connecting to the Internet without wires.

2001: Apple introduced Mac OS X operating system, which had protected memory architecture and pre-emptive multitasking, among other benefits. To stay competitive, Microsoft launched Windows XP.

2003: The first 64-bit processor, AMD's Athlon 64, was brought into the consumer market.

2004: Mozilla released Firefox 1.0 and in the same year Facebook, a social networking site, was launched.

2005: YouTube, a video sharing service, was launched. In the same year, Google acquired Android, a Linux-based mobile phone operating system.

2006: Apple introduced MacBook Pro, its first Intel-based, dual-core mobile computer.

2007: Apple released iPhone, which brought many computer functions in the smartphone.

2009: Microsoft launched Windows 7 in which users could pin applications to the taskbar.

2010: Apple launched iPad, which revived the tablet computer segment.

2011: Google introduced Chromebook, a laptop that runs on the Google Chrome operating system.

2015: Apple released the Apple Watch. In the same year, Microsoft launched Windows 10.

2016: First reprogrammable quantum computer was created.

2017: The Defense Advanced Research Projects Agency (DARPA), U.S. Department of Defense, started a project to develop "Molecular Informatics" programme that uses molecules as computers. This is based on the idea that millions of molecules exist, and each molecule has a unique 3D structure and properties such as shape, size, and colour. This can be used to encode and process data beyond the 0s and 1s of current binary-based, digital architectures. If the project is successful, future computers may be minuscule molecular machines.

2018: Launches of the first AI-powered smart speakers with virtual assistants, such as Amazon Echo Dot and Google Home, advancements in autonomous vehicles and drone technology, widespread adoption of blockchain technology, the introduction of foldable smartphones, such as the Samsung Galaxy Fold.

2019: The rollout of 5G networks, the increasing popularity of smart home devices, the launch of foldable smartphones from several major manufacturers, advancements in virtual and augmented reality technologies.

2020: The rapid growth of telemedicine and online education due to the COVID-19 pandemic, advancements in AI, including improved natural language processing and computer vision, the increasing use of cloud computing and data analytics, the launch of new gaming consoles, such as the PlayStation 5 and Xbox Series X.

2021: The introduction of new and improved smart wearable devices, such as smartwatches and fitness trackers, the increasing use of AI in various industries, including finance, healthcare, and retail, advancements in quantum computing and cryptography, the rollout of advanced robotics and automation technologies

2022: The increasing integration of AI and machine learning in various devices, such as smartphones and home appliances, the growth of the Internet of Things (IoT) and connected devices, advancements in biotechnology, including gene editing and synthetic biology, the increased use of virtual and augmented reality in various industries, such as gaming and retail

2023: Continued advancements in AI, robotics, and automation, the widespread adoption of autonomous vehicles and drones, the increasing use of blockchain and cryptocurrencies, the growth of the edge computing and 5G networks.

1.4.1 Generations of Computers

After reading these interesting developments in computing technology, let us also understand the evolution of computers through different generations.

First Generation (1942–1955)

Hardware technology First generation computers were manufactured using thousands of vacuum tubes (see Figure 1.4); a vacuum tube is a device made of fragile glass.

Memory Electromagnetic relay was used as primary memory and punched cards were used to store data and instructions.

Software technology Programming was done in machine or assembly language.

Used for Scientific applications

Examples ENIAC, EDVAC, EDSAC, UNIVAC I, IBM 701

Highlights

- Fastest calculating device of those times
- Too bulky and required a complete room for storage
- Highly unreliable as vacuum tubes emitted a large amount of heat and burnt frequently
- Required air-conditioned rooms for installation
- Costly
- Difficult to use
- Required constant maintenance because vacuum tubes used filaments that had limited lifetime. Therefore, these computers were prone to frequent hardware failures

Figure 1.4 Vacuum tube

Second Generation (1955–1964)

Hardware technology Second generation computers were manufactured using transistors (see Figure 1.5). Transistors were reliable, powerful, cheaper, smaller, and cooler than vacuum tubes.

Memory Magnetic core memory was used as primary memory; magnetic tapes and magnetic disks were used to store data and instructions. These computers had faster and larger memory than the first generation computers.

Software technology Programming was done in high-level programming languages. Batch operating system was used.

Used for Scientific and commercial applications

Examples Honeywell 400, IBM 7030, CDC 1604, UNIVAC LARC

Highlights

- Faster, smaller, cheaper, reliable, and easier to use than the first generation computers
- Consumed 1/10th the power consumed by the first generation computers
- Bulky in size and required a complete room for installation
- Dissipated less heat than the first generation computers but still required air-conditioned rooms
- Costly
- Difficult to use

Figure 1.5 Transistors

Figure 1.6 Integrated circuits

Third Generation (1964–1975)

Hardware technology Third generation computers were manufactured using integrated chips (ICs) (shown in Figure 1.6). ICs consist of several components such as transistors, capacitors, and resistors on a single chip to avoid wired interconnections between components. These computers used *SSI* and *MSI* technology. Minicomputers came into existence.

Note

Initially, ICs contained 10–20 components. This technology was called Small Scale Integration (SSI). Later, it was enhanced to contain about 100 components. This was called MSI (Medium Scale Integration).

Memory Larger magnetic core memory was used as primary memory; larger capacity magnetic tapes and magnetic disks were used to store data and instructions.

Software technology Programming was done in high-level programming languages such as FORTRAN, COBOL, Pascal, and BASIC. Time sharing operating system was used. Software was separated from the hardware. This allowed users to invest only in the software they need.

Used for Scientific, commercial, and interactive online applications

Examples IBM 360/370, PDP-8, PADP-11, CDC6600

Highlights

- Faster, smaller, cheaper, reliable, and easier to use than the second generation computers
- Consumed less power than the second generation computers
- Bulky in size and required a complete room for installation
- Dissipated less heat than the second generation computers but still required air-conditioned rooms
- Costly
- Easier to use and upgrade

Fourth Generation (1975–1989)

Hardware technology Fourth generation computers were manufactured using ICs with LSI (Large Scale Integration) and later with VLSI (Very Large Scale Integration) technology (see Figure 1.7). Microcomputers came into existence. Use of PCs became widespread. High-speed computer networks in the form of LANs, WANs, and MANs started growing. Besides mainframes, supercomputers were also used.

Memory Semiconductor memory was used as primary memory, and large capacity magnetic disks were used as built-in secondary memory. Magnetic tapes and floppy disks were used as portable storage devices.

Note

LSI circuits contained 30,000 components on a single chip and VLSI circuits have about one million electronic components on a single chip.

Software technology Programming was done in high-level programming languages such as C and C++. GUI-based operating system (e.g. Windows) was introduced. It had icons and menus among other features to allow computers to be used as a general purpose machine by all users. UNIX was also introduced as an open source operating system. Apple Mac OS and MS-DOS were also released during this period. All these operating systems had multi-processing and multi-programming capabilities.

Used for Scientific, commercial, interactive online, and network applications

Examples IBM PC, Apple II, TRS-80, VAX 9000, CRAY-1, CRAY-2, CRAY-X/MP

Highlights Faster, smaller, cheaper, powerful, reliable, and easier to use than the previous generation computers

Fifth Generation (1989–Present)

Hardware technology Fifth generation computers are manufactured using ICs with ULSI (Ultra Large Scale Integration) technology (see Figure 1.8). The use of Internet became widespread and very powerful mainframes, desktops, portable laptops, and smartphones are being used commonly. Supercomputers use parallel processing techniques.

Figure 1.7 VLSI chip

Figure 1.8 ULSI chip

Note

ULSI circuits contain about 10 million electronic components on a single chip.

Memory Semiconductor memory is used as primary memory; large capacity magnetic disks are used as built-in secondary memory. Magnetic tapes and floppy disks were used as portable storage devices, which have now been replaced by optical disks and USB flash drives.

Software technology Programming is done in high-level programming languages such as Java, Python, and C#. GUI-based operating systems such as Windows, Unix, Linux, Ubuntu, and Apple macOS are being used. These operating systems are more powerful and user-friendly than the ones available in the previous generations.

Used for Scientific, commercial, interactive online, multimedia (graphics, audio, video), and network applications

Examples IBM notebooks, Pentium PCs, SUM workstations, IBM SP/2, Param supercomputer

Highlights

- Faster, smaller, cheaper, powerful, reliable, and easier to use than the previous generation computers
- Speed of microprocessors and the size of memory are growing rapidly
- High-end features available on mainframe computers in the fourth generation are now available on the microprocessors
- Consume less power than computers of prior generations
- Air-conditioned rooms required for mainframes and supercomputers but not for microprocessors

1.5 CLASSIFICATION OF COMPUTERS

Computers can be broadly classified into four categories based on their speed, amount of data that they can process, and price (refer to Figure 1.9). These categories are as follows:

- Supercomputers
- Mainframe computers
- Minicomputers
- Microcomputers

1.5.1 Supercomputers

Among the four categories, the supercomputer is the fastest, most powerful, and most expensive computer (see Figure 1.10). Supercomputers were first developed in the 1980s to process large amounts of data and to solve

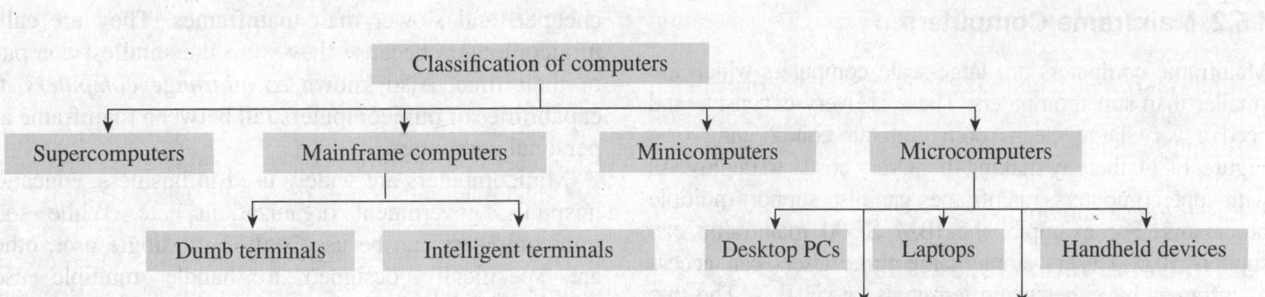

Figure 1.9 Classification of computers

Figure 1.10 Supercomputer

© Carol Gauthier/Shutterstock

complex scientific problems. Supercomputers use parallel processing technology and can perform more than one trillion calculations in a second.

A single supercomputer can support thousands of users at the same time. Such computers are mainly used for weather forecasting, nuclear energy research, aircraft design, automotive design, online banking, controlling industrial units, etc. Some examples of supercomputers are CRAY-1, CRAY-2, CYBER 205, and ETA A-10.

1.5.2 Mainframe Computers

Mainframe computers are large-scale computers which are smaller than supercomputers. These are very expensive and need a very large clean room with air conditioning (see Figure 1.11), thereby making them very costly to deploy. As with supercomputers, mainframes can also support multiple processors. For example, the IBM S/390 mainframe can support 50,000 users at the same time. Users can access mainframes by either using terminals or via PCs. The two types of terminals that can be used with mainframe systems are as follows:

Figure 1.11 Mainframe computer

© MOAimage/Shutterstock

Dumb Terminals

Dumb terminals consist of only a monitor and a keyboard (or mouse). They do not have their own CPU and memory and use the mainframe system's CPU and storage devices.

Intelligent Terminals

In contrast to dumb terminals, intelligent terminals have their own processor and thus can perform some processing operations. However, just like the dumb terminals, they do not have their own storage space. Usually, PCs are used as intelligent terminals to facilitate data access and other services from the mainframe system.

Mainframe computers are typically used as servers on the World Wide Web. They are also used in organizations such as banks, airline companies, and universities, where a large number of users frequently access the data stored in their databases. IBM is the major manufacturer of mainframe computers. Some examples of mainframe computers include IBM S/390, CYBER 176, and Amdahl 580.

1.5.3 Minicomputers

As the name suggests, minicomputers are smaller, cheaper, and slower than mainframes. They are called minicomputers because they were the smallest computer of their time. Also known as *midrange computers*, the capabilities of minicomputers fall between mainframe and personal computers.

Minicomputers are widely used in business, education, hospitals, government organizations, etc. While some minicomputers can be used only by a single user, others are specifically designed to handle multiple users simultaneously. Usually, single-user minicomputers are used for performing complex design tasks.

As with mainframes, minicomputers can also be used as servers in a networked environment, and hundreds of PCs can be connected to it.

The first minicomputer was introduced by Digital Equipment Corporation (DEC) in the mid-1960s. Other manufacturers of minicomputers include IBM Corporation (AS/400 computers), Data General Corporation, and Prime Computer.

1.5.4 Microcomputers

Microcomputers, commonly known as PCs, are very small and inexpensive. The first microcomputer was designed by IBM in 1981 and was named IBM PC. Later on, many computer hardware companies copied this design and termed their microcomputers as *PC-compatible,* which refers to any PC that is based on the original IBM PC design.

Another type of popular PC is designed by Apple. PCs designed by IBM and other PC-compatible computers have a different architecture from that of Apple computers. Moreover, PCs and PC-compatible computers commonly use the Windows operating system, while Apple computers use the Macintosh operating system (macOS). PCs can be classified into the following categories:

Desktop PCs

A desktop PC is the most popular model of PCs. The system unit of the desktop PC can be placed flat on a desk or a table. It is widely used in homes and offices.

Laptops

Laptops (Figure 1.12) are small microcomputers that can easily fit inside a briefcase. They are very handy and can easily be carried from one place to another. They may also be placed on a user's lap (thus the name). Hence, laptops are very useful, especially when going on long journeys. Laptops operate on a battery and do not always have to be plugged in like desktop computers.

Figure 1.12 Laptop

The memory and storage capacity of a laptop is almost equivalent to that of a desktop computer. As with desktop computers, laptops also have hard disk drives, USB drives, etc. For input, laptops have a built-in keyboard and a trackball/touchpad, which is used as a pointing device (as a mouse is used for a desktop PC).

Today, laptops have the same features and processing speed as the most powerful PCs. However, a drawback is that laptops are generally more expensive than desktop computers.

Workstations

Workstations are single-user computers that have the same features as PCs, but their processing speed matches with that of a minicomputer or a mainframe computer. Workstation computers have advanced processors, and more memory and storage capacity than PCs. Therefore, they are more expensive and powerful than a normal desktop computer.

Although workstation computers are widely used as powerful single-user computers by scientists, engineers, architects, and graphics designers, they can also be used as servers in a networked environment.

Network Computers

Network computers are specially designed to be used as terminals in a networked environment. For example, some network computers are specifically designed to access data stored on a network (including the Internet and intranet). They have less processing power, memory, and storage than a desktop computer.

Some network computers do not have any storage space and merely rely on the network's server for data storage and processing tasks. The concept of network computers had become popular in the mid-1990s when several variations of computers such as Windows terminals, NetPCs, and diskless workstations were widely used.

Network computers that are specifically designed to access only the Internet or intranet are often known as Internet PCs or Internet boxes. Some network computers used in homes do not even have a monitor. Such computers may be connected to a television, which serves as the output device. The most common example of a home-based network computer is Web TV, which enables a user to connect a television to the Internet. The Web TV is equipped with a special set-top box that is used to connect to the Internet. The set-top box also provides controls to enable the user to navigate the Internet, send and receive e-mails, and perform other tasks on the network while watching television. The other reason for the popularity of network computers is that they are cheaper to purchase and maintain than PCs.

Handheld Computers

The mid-1990s witnessed a range of small personal computing devices that are commonly known as handheld computers, or mobile computers. These computers are called handheld computers because they can fit in one hand, while users can use the other hand to operate them.

Figure 1.13 Tablet
© ecco/Shutterstock

Handheld computers are very small in size, and hence they have small-sized screens and keyboards.

Some examples of handheld computers are as follows:

Smartphones These days, cellular phones are web-enabled telephones. Such phones are also known as smartphones because, in addition to basic phone capabilities, they also facilitate users to access the Internet and send e-mails, edit Word documents, create an Excel sheet, prepare a presentation, and lots more.

Smartphones run an advanced mobile operating system that enables them to run various applications. The four major mobile operating systems are iOS, Android, BlackBerryOS, and Windows Mobile. Smartphones also have a processor, more storage space, more memory, and a larger screen than a regular cell phone.

In a nutshell, a smartphone refers to a multi-functional mobile phone handset that has varied functionalities from a camera to a web browser to a high-density display.

Tablet PCs A tablet PC (see Figure 1.13) is a computing device that is smaller than a laptop, but bigger than a smartphone. Features such as user-friendly interface, portability, and touch screen have made them very popular in the recent years. These days, a wide range of high-performance tablets are available in the market. While all of them look similar from outside, they may differ in features such as operating system, speed of data connectivity, camera specifications, size of the screen, processing power, battery life, and storage capability.

Some operating systems that are used in tablets are Android Jellybean (an open-source operating system built by Google), Windows 8, and iOS (developed by Apple). Each operating system has its own advantages and disadvantages and a proprietary app store, from which users can download applications, extending the tablet's functionality. These apps range from games to specialized word processors to e-book readers.

While users can easily type directly on the surface of a tablet, some users prefer a wireless or bluetooth-connected keyboard. These days, tablets also offer an optional docking station with keyboards which transforms the tablet into a full-featured netbook.

Uses The following are the uses of Tablet PCs:

- Video conferencing
- Reading e-books, e-newspaper
- Watching movies
- Playing games
- Sharing pictures, video, songs, documents, etc.
- Browsing the Internet
- Sending e-mails
- Business people use them to perform tasks such as editing a document, exchanging documents, taking notes, and giving presentations
- Tablets are best used in crowded places such as airports and coffee shops, where size and portability become more important

Note

Tablets are preferably used when one does not have to perform heavy processing tasks.

1.6 APPLICATIONS OF COMPUTERS

SCAN THE PAGE TO KNOW MORE

When the first computers were developed, they were used only in the fields of mathematics and science. In fact, the first effective utilization of computers was for decoding messages in military applications. Later on, computers were used in real-time control systems, like for landing on the moon. However, with the advancement of technology, the cost of computers and their maintenance declined. This opened the way for computers to be extensively used in the business and commercial sector for information processing. Today, computers are widely used in fields such as engineering, health care, banking, and education. Let us discuss how computers are being effectively utilized to perform important tasks.

Word processing Word processing software enables users to read and write documents. Users can also add images, tables, and graphs for illustrating a concept. The software automatically corrects spelling mistakes and includes copy–paste features (which is very useful where the same text has to be repeated several times).

Internet The Internet is a network of networks that connects computers all over the world. It gives a user access to a vast amount of information, much more than that available in any library. Using e-mail, the user can communicate in seconds with a person who is located thousands of miles away. Chat software enables users to chat with another person in real time (irrespective of the physical location of that person). Video conferencing tools are becoming popular for conducting meetings with people who are unable to be present at a particular place.

Digital video or audio composition Computers make audio or video composition and editing very simple. This has drastically reduced the cost of equipment to compose music or make a film. Graphics engineers use computers for developing short or full-length films and creating 3D models and special effects in science fiction and action movies.

Desktop publishing Desktop publishing software enables users to create page layouts for entire books.

Let us now have a look at the different areas where computers are being widely utilized.

1.6.1 Application Areas of Computers

e-Business

e-Business or electronic business is the process of conducting business via the Internet. This may include buying and selling of goods and services using computers and the Internet. Use of e-mail and video conferencing technology has revolutionized the way business is being conducted these days.

While an e-mail is a service that delivers messages from a sender to one or more receivers via computer, voice mail systems capture, store, and transmit spoken messages. Video conferencing, which is an advanced form of teleconferencing, provides a complete simulation of a normal meeting environment in which all concerned parties can see, hear, and present material, just as if they were in the same room. These meetings not only speed up business process but also save the cost of travel and the cost of time wasted during travel.

Note

Both the terms—e-Commerce and e-Business—are often used interchangeably.

Companies today use e-commerce applications for marketing, transaction, and product and customer services processing. For example, the website of a company can perform activities such as interactive marketing, ordering, payment, and customer support process.

e-commerce used to perform transactions between business partners or customers has several applications such as home banking, electronic shopping, renting a house, finding a job, conducting an auction, marketing and advertising products or services, and providing customer service. e-commerce helps users to conduct business transactions in the following forms:

Business-to-consumer or B2C In this form of electronic commerce, business companies deploy their websites on the Internet to sell their products and services to customers. On their websites, they provide features such as catalogues, interactive order processing system, secure electronic payment system, and online customer support.

Business-to-business or B2B This type of electronic commerce involves business transactions performed between business partners (customers are not involved). For example, companies use computers and networks to order raw materials from their suppliers. Companies can also supply their products to their dealers.

Consumer-to-consumer or C2C This type of electronic commerce enables customers to carry business transactions among themselves. For example, on auction websites, a customer sells his/her product which is purchased by another customer.

Electronic banking Electronic banking, also known as cyberbanking or online banking, supports various banking activities, such as opening accounts and funds transfer, conducted from any place instead of a physical bank location.

Bioinformatics

Bioinformatics is an interdisciplinary field of molecular biology, computer science, statistics, and mathematics. It involves analyses of genomic information to understand human diseases and thus discover new drugs to treat those diseases. Computers are used to collect, store, analyse, and integrate biological and genetic information to facilitate gene-based drug discovery and development.

We know that DNA is made up of smaller pieces of molecules and the sequence of molecules along a string of DNA contains all information about an organism. This information can be used to grow new organisms. For example, scientists are using this information to grow better variety of crops, to generate a genome that will enable cows to yield more milk, so and so forth.

Computers help scientists to store the DNA information in huge databases, retrieve it as and when required, and analyse it to grow and develop new organisms.

Scientists also use bioinformatics to identify diseases and develop drugs for them. This is done by writing special programs that compare the sequence of molecules in the DNA of a healthy person with that of the patient's. These analyses help them to identify what is missing in a patient and to determine drugs that can make the molecules in the DNA of the patient look similar to that of a healthy person. For example, one of the drugs to treat AIDS was designed using bioinformatics techniques.

Health care

Like in our daily lives, computers have also become a necessary device in the healthcare industry. The following are areas in which computers are extensively used in the healthcare industry:

Storing records To begin with, computers are first and foremost used to store the medical records of patients. Earlier, patient records were kept on paper, with separate records dealing with different medical issues. With time, the number of prescriptions, medical reports, etc., grow in volume making it difficult to maintain and analyse. Use of computers to store patient records has led to great improvement in the efficiency and accuracy of the entire process.

Now, the entire medical history of patients is easily accessible. Since the records are electronically stored, they can be easily shared between different doctors (in same or different healthcare organizations) who are treating the same patient.

Surgical procedures Computers are used for certain surgical procedures. They enable surgeons to use computers to control and move surgical instruments in the patient's body for a variety of surgical procedures. In such surgeries, a small incision is made, and then a small surgical tool with an attached camera is placed inside the patient's body. This reduces the risk of complications from a larger surgical wound, and minimizes damage done to the patient's body. In such a scenario, computers are not only used to drive the tools but also used to relay images from inside the patient's body out to the doctors.

Computers also help to determine the cause of an affliction or illness. For example, computers can combine ultrasonography and imaging in fields like cardiology to check the functionality of the heart. In case of a serious ailment, the causes can be detected in less time and treatment can be started at the earliest, thereby saving a number of lives.

Today, tablets and computers are being used in surgical consultations and video conferencing between doctors.

Better diagnosis and treatment Computers help physicians make better diagnoses and recommend treatments. Moreover, computers can be used to compare expected results with actual results in order to help physicians make better decisions.

Doctors sitting in hospitals can monitor their patients sitting in their homes by using computer-based systems. As soon as warning signs of serious illnesses are spotted, they alert the concerned doctor quickly.

Geographic Information System and Remote Sensing

A geographic information system (GIS) is a computer-based tool for mapping and analysing earth's features. It integrates database operations and statistical analysis to be used with maps. GIS manages location-based information and provides tools for display and analysis of statistics such as population count, types of vegetation, and economic development opportunities. Such type of information helps to predict outcomes and plan strategies.

Remote sensing is the science of taking measurements of the earth's features using sensors on airplanes or satellites. These sensors collect data in the form of images, which are then analysed to derive useful information.

The key feature of remote sensing is that it acquires information about an object without making physical contact with it. Remote sensing is a sub-field of geography, which can be applied in the following areas:

- Monitoring deforestation in areas like the Amazon Basin
- Studying features of glaciers in Arctic and Antarctic regions
- Analysing the depth of coastal and ocean areas
- Studying land usage in agriculture
- Examining the health of indigenous plants and crops
- Determining the prospect for minerals
- Locating and measuring intensity of earthquakes (after they had occurred) by comparing the relative intensity and precise timings of seismograms collected from different locations

Meteorology

Meteorology is the study of the atmosphere. This branch of science observes variables of Earth's atmosphere such as temperature, air pressure, water vapour, and the gradients and interactions of each variable, and how they change over time. Meteorology has applications in many diverse fields such as the military, energy production, transport, agriculture, and construction. Some of the applications include the following:

Weather forecasting It includes application of science and technology to predict the state of the atmosphere (temperature, precipitation, etc.) for a future time and a given location. Weather forecasting is done by collecting quantitative data about the current state of the atmosphere and analysing the atmospheric processes to predict weather patterns.

Weather forecasts are especially made to generate warnings regarding heavy rainfall, snowfall, storms, etc. They are also important to agriculturists and also to commodity traders within stock markets. Temperature forecasts are used by utility companies to estimate demand over coming days.

Aviation meteorology Aviation meteorology studies the impact of weather on air traffic management. It helps cabin crews to understand the implications of weather on their flight plan as well as their aircraft.

Agricultural meteorology Agricultural meteorology deals with the study of effects of weather and climate on plant distribution, crop yield, water-use efficiency, and plant and animal development.

Nuclear meteorology Nuclear meteorology studies the distribution of radioactive aerosols and gases in the atmosphere.

Maritime meteorology Maritime meteorology is the study of air and wave forecasts for ships operating at sea.

Multimedia and Animation

One of the most powerful aspects of computing technology is multimedia and animation which combines still images, moving images, text, and sound in meaningful ways.

Using animation software, we can reproduce real-world phenomena such as fire, smoke, fluids, movement of chemicals through the air and ground, and the respiratory system to name a few. Animation is an easy and effective way to show complex interactions or events. Thus, it is an excellent tool for educating an audience.

Note

Displaying a number of still images within a fraction of a second gives an animation effect. For example, displaying at least 30 still images in a second gives an effect of a moving image.

A dynamic multimedia presentation (created using tools like MS PowerPoint) can make the message not only easily understood but also effective. Multimedia presentation helps corporate people to share information or their ideas and graphically present information in a more understandable and persuasive manner. Multimedia presentations can be recorded and played or displayed dynamically depending on a user's inputs. Multimedia and animation is used to create computer games. A laser show is also an example of a multimedia application. Multimedia and animation is used to add special effects in movies.

In education, multimedia is used to prepare training courses. Students find it difficult to learn complex computer algorithms and data structures by reading only a textual explanation. However, they find it interesting to learn through interacting with an animation of the algorithm.

Note

Edutainment is the combination of education with entertainment.

Legal System

Computers are used by lawyers to search for legal precedent and case research. Lawyers use computers to look through millions of individual cases and find whether similar or parallel cases have been approved, denied, criticized, or overruled in the past. This enables lawyers to formulate strategies based on past case decisions. Moreover, computers are also used to keep track of appointments and prepare legal documents and briefs.

Retail Business

Computers are used in retail shops to enter orders, calculate costs, and print receipts. They are also used to keep an inventory of the products available and their complete description.

Sports

In sports, computers are used to compile statistics, identify weak players and strong players by analysing statistics, sell tickets, create training programmes and diets for athletes, and suggest game plan strategies based on the competitor's past performance. Computers are also used to generate most of the graphic art displays flashed on scoreboards.

Television networks use computers in the control room to display action replays and insert commercial breaks as per schedule.

In addition, there are simulation software packages available that help sportspersons to practice their skills as well as identify flaws in the technique.

Simulation

Supercomputers that can process enormous amount of data are widely used in simulation tests. Simulation of automobile crashes or airplane emergency landings is done to identify potential weaknesses in designs without risking human lives. Supercomputers also enable engineers to design aircraft models and simulate the effects that winds and other environmental forces have on those designs. Astronauts are trained using computer-simulated problems that could be encountered during launch, in space, or upon return to earth.

Aerospace

Spacecrafts are usually monitored using computers that not only keep a continuous record of the voyage and speed, direction, fuel, and temperature, but also suggest corrective action if the vehicle makes a mistake. The remote stations on earth compare all these quantities with the desired values, and in case these values need to be modified to enhance the performance of the spacecraft, signals are immediately sent that set in motion the mechanics to rectify the situation. With the help of computers, all this is done within a fraction of a second.

Education

A computer is a powerful teaching aid and can act as another teacher in the classroom. Teachers use computers to develop instructional material. Teachers may use pictures, graphs, and graphical presentations to easily illustrate an otherwise difficult concept. Moreover, teachers at all levels can use computers to administer assignments and keep track of grades. Students can also give exams online and get instant results.

Industry and Engineering

Computers are found in all kinds of industries, such as thermal power plants, oil refineries, and chemical industries, for process control, computer-aided designing (CAD), and computer-aided manufacturing (CAM).

Computerized process control (with or without human intervention) is used to enhance efficiency in applications such as production of various chemical products, oil refining, paper manufacturing, and rolling and cutting of steel to customer requirements.

In CAD, computers and graphics-oriented software are integrated for automating the design and drafting process. It helps an engineer to design a 3D machine part, analyse its characteristics, and then subject it to simulated stresses. In case a part fails the stress test, its specifications can be modified on the computer and retested. The final design specifications are released for production only when the engineer is satisfied that the part meets strength and other quality considerations.

The CAM phase begins when the CAD phase is complete. In this phase, the metal or other materials are manufactured while complying with their specifications. This computer-controlled manufacturing helps to produce high-quality products.

Robotics

Robots are computer-controlled machines mainly used in the manufacturing process in extreme conditions where humans cannot work. For example, in high temperature, high pressure conditions or in processes that demand very high levels of accuracy. The main distinguishing feature between a robot and other automated machines is that a robot can be programmed to carry out a complex task and then reprogrammed to carry out other complex tasks.

Decision Support Systems

Computers help business managers to analyse their organization's data to understand the present scenario of their business, view the trends in the market, and predict the future of their products. Managers also use decision support systems to analyse market research data, to study the competition, and to plan effective strategies for penetrating their markets.

Expert Systems

Expert systems are used to automate the decision-making process in a specific area, such as analysing the credit histories for loan approval and diagnosing a patient's condition for prescribing an appropriate treatment. Expert systems analyse the available data in depth to recommend a course of action. A medical expert system might provide the most likely diagnosis of a patient's condition.

To create an expert system, an extensive amount of human expertise in a specific area is collected and stored in a database, also known as a knowledge base. A software called an interface engine analyses the data available in the knowledge base and selects the most appropriate response.

Publishing

Computers play a very important role in designing and printing books/magazines, journals, brochures, etc. Publishing software, such as Adobe InDesign, CorelDraw, and QuarkXpress, offer predefined templates using which a user can easily add text, images, or other symbols to a document. Documents created using computers are easy to edit. Word-processing software automatically checks and corrects spelling and grammar mistakes. Moreover, publishing by computer takes less time to create and share with others.

It is because of all these reasons that digital books make up about 30% of the book publishing market. Several magazines for niche markets are especially designed for the online market. It has become very convenient for first-time writers to self-design and publish their works using these tools than approaching traditional publishers to publish their books.

Data Analysis

Researchers and data scientists are increasingly using computers for data analysis for doing market research. Even in the academic world, data analysis is applied in fields such as sociology, psychology, political science, medicine, and educational science. Computers and relevant software enables users to gain a deeper insight into data not only efficiently and effectively but also in very less time. Computers can easily handle very large amounts of data. It can not only store data but also perform repetitive calculations rapidly and accurately. Results of analysis can be presented in the form of charts which are easy to read and interpret.

Note

MATLAB, MS Excel, and SPSS are some commonly used software packages for performing data analysis.

Accounting

Before computers, several books of accounts such as journals, cash books, special purpose books, and ledger were maintained manually. These books helped users to prepare summary of transactions and financial statements. However, with increase in the number and complexity of transactions, computers are now being used to store and process accounting data with greater speed and accuracy.

Preparing financial statements such as balance sheet, income statement, sales ledger, purchases ledger, and stock records requires the processing of innumerable business transactions without any error. A computer can maintain records of all such transactions very effectively and economically. Among other benefits of using computers in accounting are labour saving, time saving, accuracy, minimization of frauds, and better customer relationship.

Note

Computerized accounting system gives businesses greater transparency in day-to-day transactions and provides access to vital information.

Railway and Airline Reservation

In railways and airlines, apart from maintaining train/flight schedules, tracking traffic and monitoring their movements in real time, computers are also used by customers to reserve tickets. Computers along with the power of Internet has made it easy to maintain a record of number of seats booked, passengers' names and other details, number or name of train or flight, number of seats in first, second and general class, number of seats available on a particular date, present status of a ticket using its PNR number, concessions availed, etc.

The reservation system also allows customers to do cancellation. The ease of booking and cancellation of tickets has made it very convenient for people, especially in countries such as India, which has the largest railway network in the world since handling all the reservation manually is beyond anyone's imagination.

1.7 BASIC ORGANIZATION OF A COMPUTER

A computer is an electronic device that performs five major operations:

- Accepting data or instructions (input)
- Storing data
- Processing data
- Displaying results (output)
- Controlling and coordinating all operations inside a computer

In this section, we will briefly discuss all these functions and see how one unit of a computer interacts with another to perform these operations. Refer to Figure 1.14, which shows the interaction between the different units of a computer system.

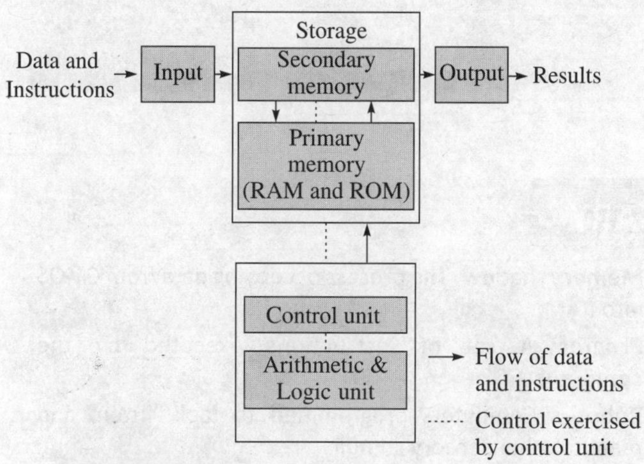

Figure 1.14 Block diagram of a computer

Input This is the process of entering data and instructions (also known as *programs*) into the computer system. The data and instructions can be entered by using different input devices such as keyboard, mouse, scanner, and trackball.

> **Note**
>
> Computers understand binary language, which consists of only two symbols (0 and 1), so it is the responsibility of the input devices to convert the input data into binary codes.

Storage Storage is the process of saving data and instructions permanently in the computer so that they can be used for processing. The computer storage space not only stores data and programs that operate on that data but also stores the intermediate results and the final results of processing.

A computer has two types of storage areas:

Primary storage Primary storage, also known as *main memory*, is the storage area that is directly accessible by the CPU at very high speeds. It is used to store data and parts of programs, the intermediate results of processing, and the recently generated results of jobs that are currently being worked on by the computer. Primary storage space is very expensive and therefore limited in capacity. Another drawback of main memory is that it is volatile in nature; that is, as soon as the computer is switched off, the information stored gets erased. Hence, it cannot be used as a permanent storage of useful data and programs for future use. Both random access memory (RAM) and read-only memory (ROM) are examples of primary storage.

Secondary storage Also known as *auxiliary memory*, this memory is just the opposite of primary memory. It overcomes all the drawbacks of the primary storage area. It is cheaper, non-volatile, and used to permanently store data and programs of those jobs that are not being currently executed by the CPU. Secondary memory supplements the limited storage capacity of primary memory. An example is the magnetic disk used to store data, such as C and D drives, for future use.

Processing The process of performing operations on the data as per the instructions specified by a user (program) is called processing. Data and instructions are taken from the primary memory and transferred to the arithmetic logic unit (ALU), which performs all sorts of calculation. The intermediate results of processing may be stored in the main memory, as they might be required again. When the processing completes, the final result is then transferred to the main memory. Hence, the data may move from the main memory to the ALU multiple times before the processing is over.

Output Output is the process of giving the result of data processing to the outside world (external to the computer system). The results are given through output devices such as monitors and printers. Since the computer accepts data only in binary form and the result of processing is also in binary form, the result cannot be directly given to the user. The output devices, therefore, convert the results available in binary codes into a human-readable form before displaying it to the user.

Control The control unit (CU) is the central nervous system of the entire computer system. It manages and controls all the components of the computer system. It is the CU that decides the manner in which instructions will be executed and operations performed. It takes care of the step-by-step processing of all operations that are performed in the computer.

Note that the CPU is a combination of the ALU and the CU. The CPU is better known as the brain of the computer system because the entire processing of data is done in the ALU, and the CU activates and monitors the operations of other units (such as input, output, and storage) of the computer system.

> **Note**
>
> ALU, CU, and CPU are the key functional units of a computer system.

POINTS TO REMEMBER

- A computer is an electronic machine that accepts data and instructions and performs computations on the data based on the instructions.
- Computers are used in all interactive devices, such as cellular telephones, GPS units, portable organizers, ATMs, and gas pumps.
- Modern-day computers are based on the principle of the stored program concept, which was introduced by Sir John von Neumann in the late 1940s.
- The speed of the computer is usually given in nanoseconds and picoseconds.
- The term computer generation refers to the different advancements in computer technology. With each new generation of computers, the circuitry has become smaller and more advanced than that in the previous generation.
- First generation computers used a very large number of vacuum tubes for circuitry and magnetic drums for memory.
- Second generation computers were manufactured using transistors rather than vacuum tubes.
- The development of the integrated circuit was the hallmark of the third generation of computers.
- The microprocessor started the fourth generation of computers, with thousands of integrated circuits built into a single silicon chip.
- Fifth generation computers are manufactured using integrated chips built with ultra-large scale integration (ULSI) technology.
- The CPU is a combination of the ALU and the CU. The CPU is known as the brain of the computer system.
- The CU is the central nervous system of the entire computer system. It manages and controls all the components of the computer system.

GLOSSARY

Computer A computer is an electronic machine that takes instructions and performs computations based on those instructions.

Expert systems Expert systems are custom-writt en computer programs that are 'expert' in a particular problem area, and embody a human expert's knowledge, experience, and problem-solving strategies. They are being used in many areas such as medicine, chemistry, geology, meteorology, and computer systems.

Garbage-in, garbage-out If input data is wrong, then the output will also be erroneous.

GUI A GUI is a type of user interface that enables users to interact with programs in more ways than typing. A GUI offers graphical icons and visual indicators to display the information and actions available to a user. The actions are performed by direct manipulation of the graphical elements.

Input The process of entering data and instructions into the computer system.

Integrated circuit Also called a chip or microchip, an IC is a semiconductor wafer on which thousands or millions of tiny resistors, capacitors, and transistors are fabricated. It can be used as an amplifier, oscillator, ti mer, counter, computer memory, or microprocessor.

Internet It is a network of networks that connects computers all over the world.

Memory shadow The process of copying data from CMOS into RAM.

Program A set of instructions executed by the computer.

Robotics Computers programmed to look, listen, and react to other sensory stimuli.

Semiconductor devices Semiconductor devices are electronic components that make use of the electronic properties of semiconductor materials (such as silicon and germanium). The conductivity of such devices can be controlled by introducing an electric field, by exposure to light, and even pressure and heat, thereby making such devices excellent sensors.

Storage The process of saving data and instructions permanently in the computer so that it can be used for processing.

Stylus A stylus is an electronic pen that looks like a small ballpoint pen.

Transistor A transistor is a semiconductor device that is used to amplify and switch electronic signals. Although some transistors are packaged individually, others are usually found embedded in ICs.

Vacuum tube A vacuum tube is a device used to amplify electronic signals.

EXERCISES

Fill in the Blanks

1. A program is the ________.
2. Computers operate on ________ based on ________.
3. Computers can perform ________ calculations in a second.
4. The speed of computers is expressed in ________ or ________.
5. Raw facts or figures are called ________.
6. ________ is an example of primary memory.
7. ________ and ________ are examples of first generation computing devices.
8. Second generation computers were first developed for the ________ industry.
9. ________ packages allow easy manipulation and analysis of data organized in rows and columns.
10. CRAY-1, CRAY-2, CYBER 205, and ETA A-10 are ________.
11. ________ concept was introduced by Sir John von Neumann in the late 1940s.
12. Android Jellybean, Windows, and iOS are all examples of popular operating systems used in ________ and ________.
13. First generation computers were manufactured using ________.
14. The intermediate results of processing are stored in ________ memory.
15. ________ is a mathematical model of computation that defines an abstract machine.

Multiple-choice Questions

1. Which was the first commercial computer delivered to a business client?
   (a) UNIVAC (b) ENIAC
   (c) EDSAC (d) None of these
2. Which technology was used to manufacture second generation computers?
   (a) Vacuum tubes (b) Transistors
   (c) ICs (d) None of these
3. Time sharing operating systems were used in which generation of computers?
   (a) First (b) Second
   (c) Third (d) Fourth
4. Choose the computer languages that are specially designed for the fifth generation of computers.
   (a) ALGOL (b) SNOBOL
   (c) LISP (d) Prolog
5. Web TV is an example of
   (a) supercomputer (b) minicomputer
   (c) network Computer (d) laptop
6. The brain of the computer is the
   (a) control unit (b ALU
   (c) CPU (d) All of these

State True or False

1. Computers work on the GIGO concept.
2. 1 nanosecond = 1 × 10 – 12 seconds.
3. Floppy disks and hard disks are examples of primary memory.
4. First-generation computers used a very large number of transistors.
5. First-generation computers could be programmed only in binary language.
6. ALGOL is used in the third generation of computers.
7. Fifth-generation computers are based on AI.
8. Network computers have more processing power, memory, and storage than a desktop computer.
9. RAM stores the data and parts of program, the intermediate results of processing, and the recently generated results of jobs that are currently being worked on by the computer.
10. A serial port is used to connect old printers.

Review Questions

1. Define a computer.
2. Differentiate between data and information.
3. Differentiate between primary memory and secondary memory.
4. Write a short note on the characteristics of a computer.
5. Computers work on the garbage-in, garbage-out concept. Comment.
6. Explain the evolution of computers. Further, state how computers in one generation are better than their predecessors.
7. Broadly classify computers based on their speed, the amount of data that they can hold, and price.
8. Discuss the variants of microcomputers that are widely used today.
9. Explain the areas in which computers are being applied to carry out routine and highly specialized tasks.

LAB ACTIVITY 1: UNDERSTANDING COMPUTER HARDWARE

As part of this activity, the instructor must show the parts of the computer to the students, as illustrated in Figure A.1.

Figure A.1 Computer case and its parts
© Kitch Bain/Shutterstock

Figure A.2 RAM memory
© Chutchawarn/Shutterstock

Figure A.3 Hard disk drive
© Vladimir Arndt/Shutterstock

Activity I: Parts of a Computer

The following are some of the major parts of the computer:

CPU The CPU is the brain of the computer. It performs all calculations and controls the devices connected to the computer system. The faster the CPU, the quicker programs can process the instructions.

RAM A fast CPU is of no use if the computer does not have sufficient RAM. As discussed earlier, RAM is the computer's memory which stores information used by applications that are currently being executed by the CPU (see Figure A.2). More memory means more applications can be executed at the same time without decreasing the system's performance.

Hard disk drive (HDD) The HDD of the computer is the secondary memory of the computer system where information is stored permanently (see Figure A.3). All types of data, documents, and programs are stored on the HDD. The larger the HDD, the more the amount of data that can be stored on the drive. Though the size of the HDD does not affect the speed of execution of a program, it does affect the speed at which a user can access his/her files.

Figure A.4 Video card
© Leo Shoot/Shutterstock

Video card The video card is a board that plugs into the motherboard of the computer and generates images for display (see Figure A.4). Many video cards these days have their own RAM and processor to enhance the speed of the graphics display. Many computers come with an in-built video chip. In such a computer, a separate video card is used only if the computer has to be used for high-end multimedia work or to play video games.

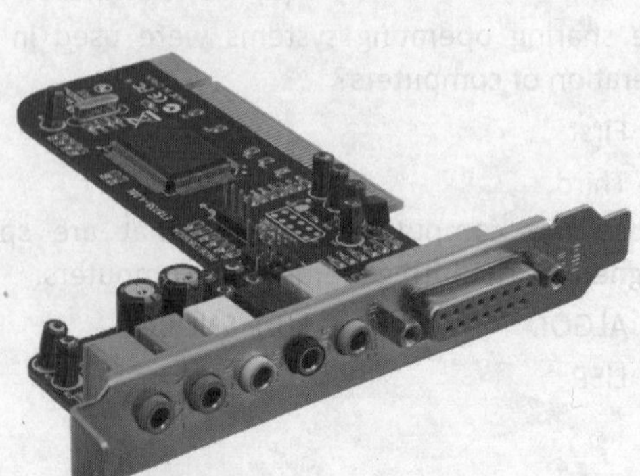

Figure A.5 Sound card
© bogdandimages/Shutterstock

Sound card Like video cards, sound cards are expansion boards that are used to enable a computer to manipulate sound (see Figure A.5). For example, sound cards allow users to plug in speakers and a microphone. Some sound cards also provide jacks for connecting the computer to a common stereo. These days, many computers come with a built-in sound chip, which makes it unnecessary to buy a separate card unless a higher quality of sound is needed.

Network card A network card is used to connect the computer either to other computers or to the Internet (in case we are using a fast Internet connection such as cable or DSL).

Fans There are one or more fans inside the computer to keep the air moving and the computer cool.

Cables There are multiple wires inside the computer that are flat, ribbon-like cables. They are used to provide power and communication to the various parts inside the computer.

Activity II: Motherboard

The motherboard, also known as the mainboard or the parent board (refer Figure A.6), is the primary component of a computer. It is used to connect all the components of the computer. The motherboard is a printed circuit that has connectors for expansion cards, memory modules, the processor, etc.

Characteristics of a Motherboard

A motherboard can be classified depending on the following characteristics:.

- Form factor
- Chipset
- Type of processor socket used
- Input–Output connectors

Form factor Form factor refers to the motherboard's geometry, dimensions, arrangement, and electrical requirements. The industry has defined a few standards for form factors, so that they can be used in different brands of cases.

Integrated components Some of the motherboard's components are integrated into its printed circuitry. These include the following:

- Chipset
- CMOS clock and battery
- BIOS
- System bus and expansion bus

In addition to these, the latest motherboards also have a number of onboard multimedia and networking devices (which can be disabled), such as integrated network card, integrated graphics card, integrated sound card, and upgraded hard drive controllers.

Chipset It is an electronic circuit that coordinates data transfers between the different components of the computer (such as the processor and memory). In order to enhance the computer's upgradeability, one must choose a motherboard that has the latest chipset integrated in it. Some chipsets may include a graphics or audio chip, which makes it unnecessary to install a separate graphics card or

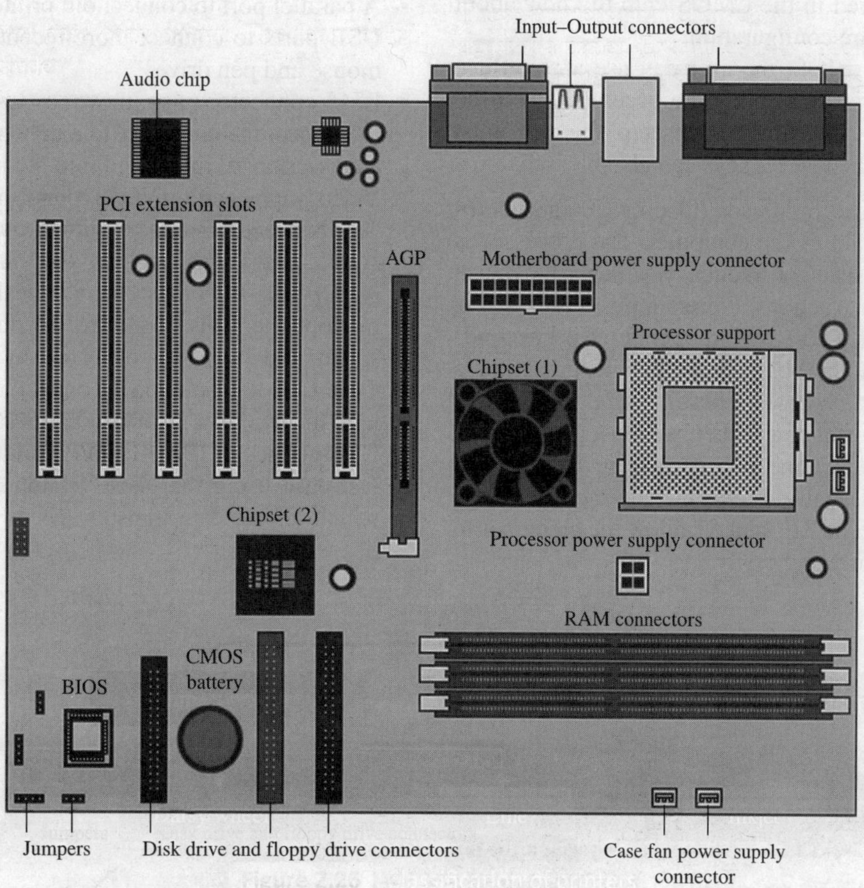

Figure A.6 Computer's motherboard

sound card. However, in case we need very high quality of audio and visual capabilities, then we must disable the graphics/audio chip in the BIOS setup and install high-quality expansion cards in the appropriate slots.

CMOS clock and battery The real-time clock (or RTC) is a circuit that is used to synchronize the computer's signals. When the computer is switched off, the power supply stops providing electricity to the motherboard. You must have observed that when we turn on the system, it always displays the correct time. This is because an electronic circuit, called the complementary metal-oxide semiconductor (CMOS) chip, saves some system information, such as time, date, and other essential system settings.

The CMOS chip is powered by a battery located on the motherboard. Information about the hardware installed in the computer (such as the number of tracks or sectors on each hard drive) is stored in the CMOS chip. Since the CMOS chip is quite slow, some systems prefer to copy the CMOS chip's content into RAM, which is a comparatively faster storage. This process of copying data into RAM is known as *memory shadow*.

Have you noticed that, at times, the system time gets reset automatically, or the clock runs late? This indicates that you need to change the battery.

BIOS The basic input/output system (BIOS) is an interface between the operating system and the motherboard. The BIOS is stored in ROM, which cannot be rewritten. The BIOS uses data stored in the CMOS chip to know about the system's hardware configuration.

To configure the BIOS, the user can use an interface known as *BIOS setup*, which can be accessed when the computer is booting. To enter BIOS setup, the user must press the DEL key. F1 and F2 keys can also be used.

Processor socket The processor (also called the *micro-processor*) is the brain of the computer. The processor is characterized by its speed or frequency, which is the rate at which it executes instructions. For example, an 800-MHz processor can perform 800 million operations per second.

The slot on the motherboard into which the processor is inserted is called the *processor socket* or *slot*. Irrespective of whether we use a slot or a socket, we must gently insert the processor, so that none of its pins are bent (it has hundreds of them). Usually, a concept called *zero insertion force* (ZIF) is used. The ZIF sockets allow the processor to be inserted very gently and easily.

When the computer is on, the processor is working and it releases heat, which must be dissipated to keep the circuits from melting. Therefore, the processor is generally mounted on a cooler that is made of metal (such as copper or aluminum), which conducts heat well. In addition to the cooler, there is also a fan to improve air circulation around it and to improve the heat transfer. The fan vents hot air from the case and lets fresh air come in from outside.

RAM connectors RAM is the primary storage area that stores data while the computer is running. However, its contents are erased when the computer is turned off or restarted. While the hard disk can store data permanently, we still need RAM because it is extremely fast when compared to mass storage devices such as hard drives. Therefore, the fast processor accesses data from RAM and not from the hard disk. The data is transferred from the hard disk to the RAM, from where it is used by the processor. RAM is available in the form of modules that plug into motherboard connectors.

Expansion slots Expansion slots are compartments into which expansion cards can be inserted. Such cards render new features or enhance the computer's performance. For example, the AGP slot (also known as Accelerated Graphics Port) is a fast port used for graphics cards.

I/O connectors The motherboard has a number of input–output sockets (Figure A.7) on its rear panel, some of which include:

- A serial port to connect some old peripherals
- A parallel port to connect old printers
- USB ports to connect more recent peripherals such as mouse and pen drive
- RJ45 connector (also known as LAN or Ethernet port) to connect the computer to a network. It corresponds to a network card integrated into the motherboard
- Video graphics array (VGA) connector to connect a monitor. This connector interfaces with the built-in graphics card
- Audio plugs that include the *line in*, *line out*, and *microphone* to connect sound speakers, hi-fi system, or microphone. This connector interfaces with the built-in sound card
- Type C is a 24-pin USB connector system. The port is half the width and one-third the height of a standard USB connector. Type-C ports can transfer data at a very fast pace using the latest version of the USB protocol which allows data transfer speeds of up to 10 gigabits per second.

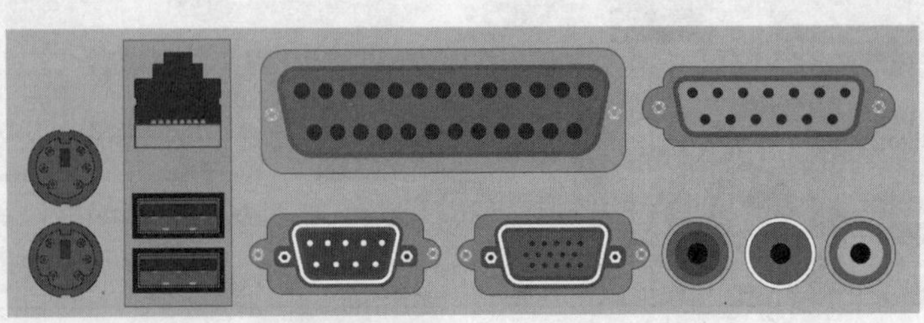

Figure A.7 I/O connectors

2 Input and Output Devices

TAKEAWAYS

- Keyboard
- Pointing devices
- Handheld devices
- Optical devices
- Audiovisual input devices
- Electronic card readers
- Digitizers
- Soft copy devices
- Hard copy devices
- Voice response systems
- Biometric devices

2.1 INPUT DEVICES

An input device is used to feed data and instructions into a computer. In the absence of an input device, a computer is only a display device. In this section, we will read about some of the widely used input devices. Figure 2.1 categorizes input devices into different groups.

2.1.1 Keyboard

A keyboard is the main input device for computers. Computer keyboards look very similar to the keyboards of typewriters, with some additional keys, as shown in Figure 2.2.

Using a keyboard, a user can type a document, use keystroke shortcuts, access menus, play games, and perform numerous other tasks. Most keyboards have between 80 and 110 keys, which include the following:

Alphabetic keys These include the letters of the English alphabet. The layout of the keyboard is known as QWERTY for its first six letters. The QWERTY pattern has been a standard right from the time computer keyboards were introduced.

Numeric keys These include Arabic numerals (0–9), arranged in the same configuration found on calculators to speed up data entry of numbers. When the Num Lock key is set to ON, the user can type numbers, dot, or input the symbols /, *, –, and +. When the Num Lock key is set to OFF, the numeric keys can be used to move the cursor on the screen.

Function keys These are used by applications and operating systems to input specific commands. They are often placed on the top of the keyboard in a single row. Function keys can be programmed so that their functionality varies from one program to another.

Control keys These are used to handle control of the cursor and the screen. Four arrow keys are arranged in an inverted *T*-type fashion between the alphabetic and the numeric keys, and are used to move the cursor on the screen in small increments. In addition to the arrow keys, there are other cursor keys (or navigational keys), such as:

- *Home* and *End* to move the cursor to the beginning and end of the current line, respectively
- *PageUp* and *PageDown* to move the cursor up and down by one screen at a time, respectively
- *Insert* to enter a character between two existing characters
- *Delete* to delete a character at the cursor position

Other common control keys on the keyboard include *Control* (Ctrl), *Alternate* (Alt), *Escape* (Esc), *Print Screen*, *Pause*, the *Windows* or *Start* key (Microsoft Windows logo), and a shortcut key. The shortcut key is used to access the options available by pressing the right mouse button. The Esc key cancels the selected option, and the Pause key suspends a command/process in progress. Finally, the Print Screen key captures everything on the screen as an image. The image can be pasted into any document.

Note

Keys such as Shift, Ctrl, and Alt are called *modifier keys* because they are used to modify the normal function of a key. For example, Shift + character (lowercase) makes the computer display the character in upper case.

Inside the Keyboard

A keyboard is like a miniature computer that has its own processor and circuitry to carry information to and from that processor. The circuitry consists of a *key matrix*, which is a grid of circuits underneath the keys. Each circuit is broken at a point below each key. When a key is pressed, it corresponds to pressing a switch, thereby completing the circuit.

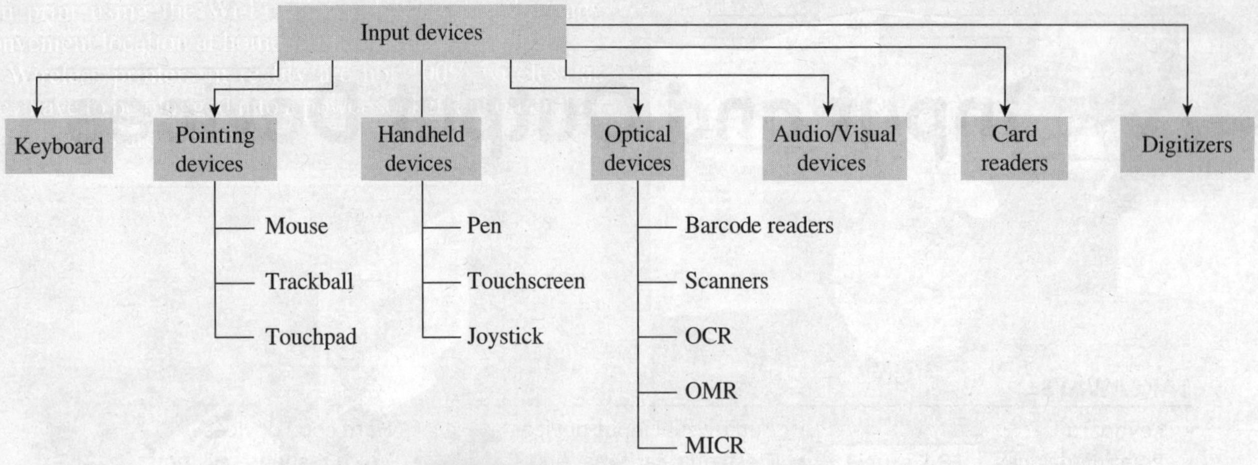

Figure 2.1 Categories of input devices

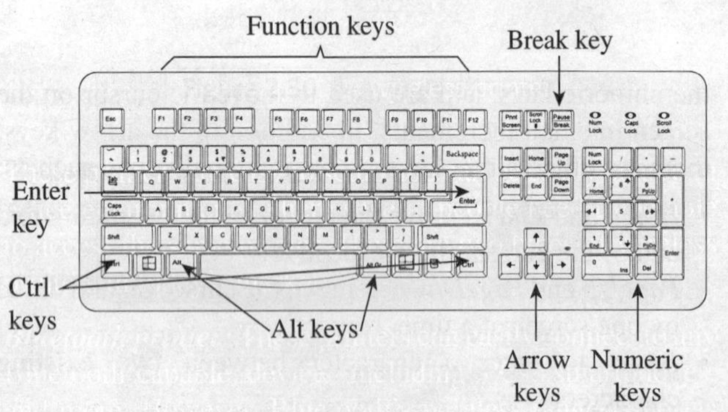

Figure 2.2 Keyboard

When the processor finds a closed circuit, it compares the location of that circuit on the key matrix to the character map in its read-only memory (ROM). A character map is a lookup table that tells the processor what each keystroke or a combination of keystrokes represents. For example, the character map tells the processor that pressing the key 'c' corresponds to the small letter 'c' but the keys 'Shift' and 'c' pressed together is a 'C'.

Note that a computer can also use separate character maps, overriding the one found in the keyboard. This is usually done when the user is typing in a language that uses letters that do not have equivalents on a keyboard with English letters.

Advantage

- The keyboard is easy to use and inexpensive.

Disadvantages

- The keyboard cannot be used to draw figures.
- The process of moving the cursor to another position is very slow. Mouse and other pointing devices are more suitable for this purpose.

Wireless Keyboard

Wireless keyboards connected to computers without wire is useful when users cannot sit close to the computer monitor for a long time or when tangled wires behind the computer become difficult to organize. Wireless technology facilitates users to position the wireless keyboard in ways that are not possible with the corded version.

A wireless keyboard is the same as a normal computer keyboard. The only difference is that it transfers typing data to the computer wirelessly using infrared, Bluetooth or wi-fi. When the user types using a wireless keyboard, the receiver connected to the computer accepts it and passes it further for processing.

Figure 2.3 Wireless keyboard

Bluetooth wireless keyboard Bluetooth is one of the most popular methods of syncing a wireless keyboard with a computer. Such a keyboard is well-suited for offices as it creates a reliable connection without cluttering the desk.

Advantages

- High data transfer speed
- No need for a direct line-of-sight for connection

Disadvantage

- Effective over a short range

Radio frequency (RF) keyboard Radio frequency wireless keyboards work well for long-range use. They use a broadcast method similar to the Wi-Fi standard used in wireless networking to communicate with a computer or other device. An RF receiver or a Bluetooth antenna, receives the information transmitted to it from the keyboard. The information or commands sent wirelessly are then translated by the computer's operating system.

Advantage

- Some models of RF wireless keyboards can work at distances up to 100 feet.

Disadvantages

- More expensive than wired and Bluetooth wireless keyboards
- Can interfere with other wireless devices in close proximity

Infrared keyboard Infrared keyboards use light waves to communicate with computers. We all are familiar with infrared light that we use to connect our TV remote with the TV set. The same technology can be used to connect a wireless keyboard with a computer system.

Advantage

- High data transfer rate

Disadvantage

- This keyboard requires direct line-of-sight. That is, the infrared keyboard will lose its connection if a solid object passes between it and the computer.

Projection keyboard Like infrared keyboards, projection wireless keyboards use light to communicate with a computer. However, unlike the infrared keyboard, a projection keyboard does not have any physical component other than a small projector unit. The projector unit is used to cast an image of a keyboard onto a flat surface. Breaks in the light beams are used to work out what the operator is typing. Such keyboards are especially beneficial for those who travel regularly, as they have limited space to use a full-size real keyboard.

2.1.2 Pointing Devices

A pointing input device enables users to easily control the movement of the pointer to select items on a display screen, to select commands from commands menu, to draw graphics, etc. Some examples of pointing devices include mouse, trackball, light pen, joystick, and touchpad.

Mouse

A mouse is an input device that was invented by Douglas Engelbart in 1963. It is the key input device used in a graphical user interface (GUI). It can be used to handle the pointer on the screen to perform various functions such as opening an application or a file. With the mouse, users no longer need to memorize commands, which was earlier a necessity when working with text-based command line environments like MS-DOS.

A mouse has two buttons and a scroll wheel. It can be held in the hand and easily moved, without lifting, along a hard flat surface to move the cursor to the desired location—up, down, left, or right. Once the mouse is placed at an appropriate position, a user may perform the following operations:

Point Placing the pointer over a word or an object on the screen by moving the mouse on the desk is termed as pointing.

Click Pressing either the left or the right button of the mouse is known as clicking. Clicking a mouse button initiates some action; for example, when we click the right button by pointing the mouse on a word, a menu pops up on the screen. When we move the pointer over the icon of an application, say Internet Explorer, and double-click on it, then it opens that application for us.

Drag Dragging means pointing to a desired location while pressing the left button.

Scroll The scroll wheel, which is placed in between the left and right buttons of the mouse, is used to vertically scroll through long documents.

Today, the mouse has become so important that every user buys a mouse when he or she buys a computer. It is specially used to create graphics such as lines, curves, and freehand shapes on the screen. It is connected to a serial or a universal serial bus (USB) port on the system unit. Some of the popular mouse types are as follows:

Mechanical mouse This type of mouse has a rubber or metal ball at its bottom and an electronic circuit containing sensors. When the mouse is moved over a flat surface, the sensors detect the direction of movement of the ball. The electronic circuit translates the movement into signals and feeds them as input to the computer.

Optical mouse An optical mouse is more advanced than a mechanical mouse. It contains a ball inside. The movement of the mouse is detected using laser technology, by using optical sensors.

Wireless mouse As the name suggests, a wireless mouse does not use wires to send signals to the computer. Users can use it on multiple surfaces to point and click on a computer screen from across the room.

Majority of wireless mouse use radio frequencies (RF) to send signals from the mouse to the computer. This requires a transmitter and a receiver. The communication takes place as follows:

- The mouse transmits radio signals to a receiver
- The receiver is connected to the computer with a wire.

Besides RF, it can also interact with computers through a Bluetooth dongle rather than a cable. The range on a Bluetooth mouse is comparable to other RF computer mice.

Given their mobility and flexibility, wireless mice can be conveniently used with laptops and are well-suited for presentations. Some of them are equipped with laser pointers that helps in directing audience's attention. A wireless mouse may also have multiple buttons to play and stop programs on the computer. A wireless mouse is shown in Figure 2.4.

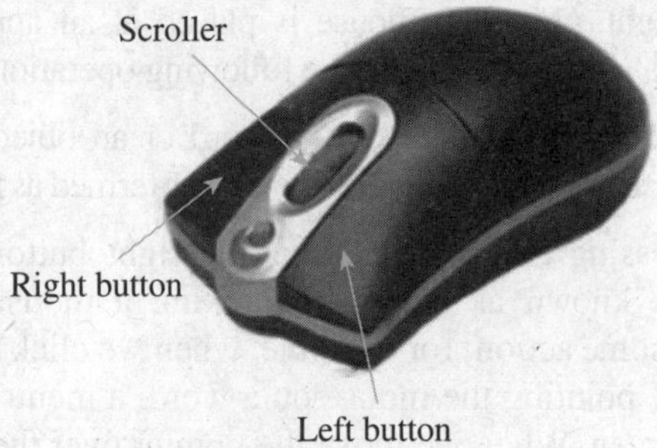

Figure 2.4 A wireless mouse

Advantages

- The mouse is easy to use and can be used to quickly place the cursor anywhere on the screen.
- It also helps to quickly and easily draw figures.
- It is inexpensive.
- Its point-and-click capabilities make it unnecessary to remember and type in commands.

Disadvantages

- The mouse needs extra desk space to be placed and moved easily.
- The ball in the mechanical mouse must be cleaned to remove dust from it.

Trackball

A trackball is a pointing device that is used to control the position of the cursor on the screen. It is usually used in notebook computers, where it is placed on the keyboard, as shown in Figure 2.5.

Figure 2.5 Trackball on keyboard

© Eugene Sergeev/Shutterstock

A trackball is nothing but an upside-down mouse where the ball rotates in place within a socket. A user rolls the ball to position the cursor at an appropriate position on the screen and then clicks one of the buttons (identical to mouse buttons) near the trackball, either to select objects or to position the cursor for text entry. This is shown in Figure 2.6.

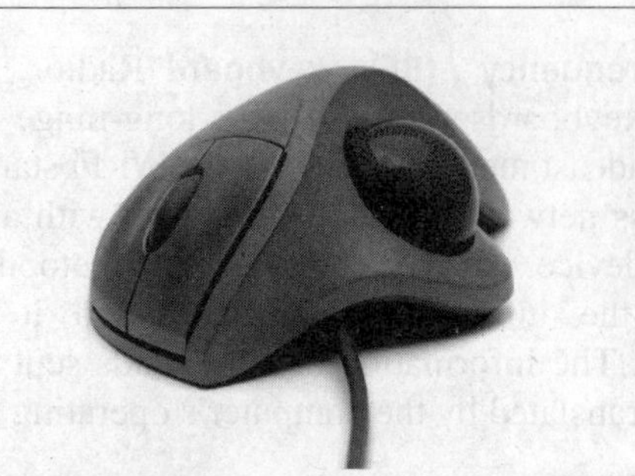

Figure 2.6 Trackball used like a mouse

© Andrew Buckin/Shutterstock

To move the pointer, the ball is rotated with the thumb, fingers, or the palm of the hand. The advantage of a trackball over a mouse is that the former is stationary, and so it does not require much space to use. Moreover, trackballs can be placed on any type of surface, including the user's lap. These advantages make trackballs very popular pointing devices for portable computers and mobile phones.

Note that the working of a trackball is identical to that of a mouse.

Advantages

- The trackball provides better resolution.
- It occupies less space.
- It is easier to use as compared to a mouse as its use involves less hand-and-arm movements.

Disadvantage

- The trackball chamber is often covered with dust, so it must be cleaned regularly.

Touchpad

A touchpad (or trackpad), as shown in Figure 2.7, is a small, flat, rectangular stationary pointing device with a sensitive surface of 1.5–2 square inches. A user has to slide his or her fingertips across the surface of the pad to point to a specific object on the screen. The surface translates the motion and position of the user's fingers to a relative position on the screen. There are also buttons around the edge of the pad which work like mouse buttons. Touchpads are widely used in laptops, and are in-built on laptop keyboards. They can also be attached to a PC and can be used with personal digital assistants (PDAs) and iPads.

Figure 2.7 Touchpad

© Yulia Nikulyasha Nikitina/Shutterstock/OUP Picture Bank

The working of a touchpad is similar to that of a mouse or a trackball. The pressure of the finger on the surface leads to capacitance effect, which is detected by the sensors. The sensors send appropriate signals to the processor, which interprets them and displays the pointer on the screen.

Advantages

- The touchpad occupies less space.
- It is easier to use as compared to a mouse as its use involves less hand-and-arm movements.
- It is in-built in the keyboard, and hence negates the need to carry an extra device.

2.1.3 Handheld Devices

A handheld device is a pocket-sized computing device with a display screen and touch input and/or a miniature keyboard. Some common examples of handheld devices include smartphones, PDAs, handheld gaming consoles, and portable media players (e.g., iPods). In this section, we will read about joystick, stylus (pen), and touchscreen, which are used to input data to handheld devices.

Joystick

A joystick (refer Figure 2.8) is a cursor control device widely used in computer games and computer-aided design (CAD)/computer-aided manufacturing (CAM) applications. It consists of a handheld lever that pivots on one end and transmits its coordinates to a computer. The joystick has one or more push buttons, called switches, whose position can also be read by the computer. The lever of a joystick moves in all directions to control the movement of the pointer on the computer screen. A joystick is similar to a mouse, but with the mouse, the cursor stops moving as soon as we stop moving the mouse. However, in the case of the joystick, the pointer continues moving in the direction to which the joystick is pointing. To stop the pointer, the user must return the joystick to its upright position.

Figure 2.8 Joystick

© Viktor Kunz/Shutterstock

Stylus

A stylus (shown in Figure 2.9) is a pen-shaped input device used to enter information or write on the touchscreen of a handheld device. It is a small stick that can also be used to draw lines on a surface as input into a device, choose an option from a menu, move the cursor to another location on the screen, take notes, and create short messages. The stylus usually slides into a slot built into the device for that purpose.

Figure 2.9 Stylus

© Photodisc/OUP Picture Bank

Touchscreen

A touchscreen (shown in Figure 2.10) is a display screen that can identify the occurrence and position of a touch inside the display region. A user can touch the screen by using either a finger or a stylus. The touchscreen facilitates the user to interact with what is displayed on the screen in a straightforward manner, rather than in an indirect way by using a mouse or a touchpad. Such touchscreen displays are available on computers, laptops, PDAs, and mobile phones.

Figure 2.10 Touchscreen

© Gareth Boden/OUP Picture Bank

Touchscreen monitors are an easy way of entering information into computers (or mobile phones). Touchscreen monitors have become more and more commonplace as their price has steadily dropped over the past decade. These days, touchscreen monitors are widely used in different applications including point-of-sale (POS) cash registers, automated teller machines (ATMs), car navigation screens, mobile phones, gaming consoles, and any other type of appliance that requires users to input and receive information instantly.

2.1.4 Optical Devices

Optical devices, also known as data-scanning devices, use light as a source of input for detecting or recognizing different objects such as characters, marks, codes, and images. These devices convert these objects into digital data and send it to the computer for further processing. Some optical devices that are discussed in this section include barcode readers, image scanners, and optical character recognition (OCR), optical mark recognition (OMR), and magnetic ink character recognition (MICR) devices.

Barcode Reader

A barcode reader (also price scanner or POS scanner) is a handheld input device that is used to capture and read information stored in a barcode (see Figure 2.11). It consists of a scanner, a decoder, and a cable used to connect the reader to a computer. The function of the barcode reader is to capture and translate the barcode into numerals and/or letters. It is connected to a computer for further processing of the captured information. This connection is achieved through a serial port, keyboard port, or an interface device called a wedge.

A barcode reader works by directing a beam of light across the barcode and measuring the amount of light reflected back. The dark bars reflect less light as compared to the amount of light reflected by the white spaces between those bars. The scanner converts this light energy into electrical signals. The decoder then converts these signals into data and sends it to the computer for processing.

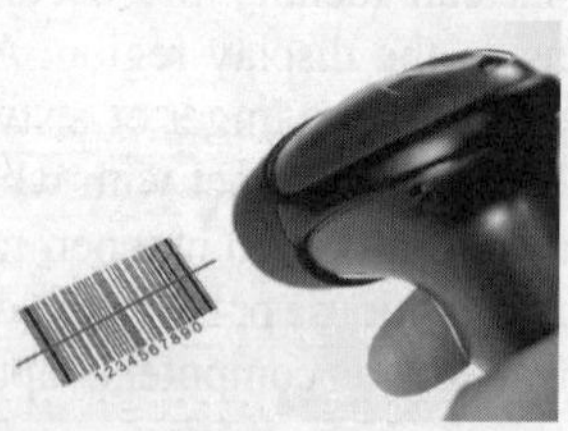

Figure 2.11 Barcode reader
© florin oprea/Shutterstock

These days, barcode readers are widely used to:

- Generate bills in supermarkets and retail stores
- Take stock of inventory in retail stores
- Check out books from a library
- Track manufacturing and shipping movement
- Keep track of employee login
- Identify hospital patients
- Tabulate the results of direct mail marketing returns
- Tag honeybees used in research

Advantages

- Barcode readers are inexpensive.
- They are portable.
- They are handy and easy to use.

Disadvantages

- Barcode readers must be handled with care. If they develop a scratch, users may not be able to read the code.
- They can interpret information using a limited series of thin and wide bars. To interpret other unique identifiers, the bar display area must be widened.

Image Scanner

A scanner (shown in Figure. 2.12) is a device that captures images, printed text, and handwritten text, from different sources such as photographic prints, posters, and magazines and converts them into digital images for editing and display on computers. Scanners come in handheld, feed-in, and flatbed types, and can be used for scanning either colour images, black-and-white images, or both. While lower resolution scanners are adequate for capturing images for computer display, very high-resolution scanners, on the other hand, are used for scanning of high-resolution printing. Some scanners have graphics software such as Adobe Photoshop to help users resize or modify captured images.

The basic types of image scanners are flatbed, hand, film, and drum scanners. The scanners that we see in our colleges or offices are flatbed scanners. In this type, the document to be scanned is placed on a glass pane and an opaque cover is lowered over it. A sensor and light move along the pane, reflecting off the image placed on the glass. The cover is used to prevent other light from interfering, and the image becomes visible to the detector.

Figure 2.12 Flatbed image scanner
© Mile Atanasov/Shutterstock

A handheld image scanner has to be manually moved across the image to be scanned. The scanner produces light from green light emitting diodes (LEDs), which highlight and scan the image onto a computer for further processing. However, these days, 3D image scanners have become the most popular form of hand scanners, as they are able to compensate for jerky hand movements during scanning.

Film scanners are usually used in photography. The slide or negative film is first inserted in strips of six or less frames into the film scanner, and then moved across a lens and a sensor to capture the image.

While handheld and film scanners use charge coupled device (CCD) arrays, drum scanners, on the other hand, use photo multiplier tubes (PMTs). Drum scanners are mounted on an acrylic cylinder that rotates while passing the object in front of precision optics, which in turn transfers the image information to the PMTs. Most drum scanners use three matched PMTs that are capable

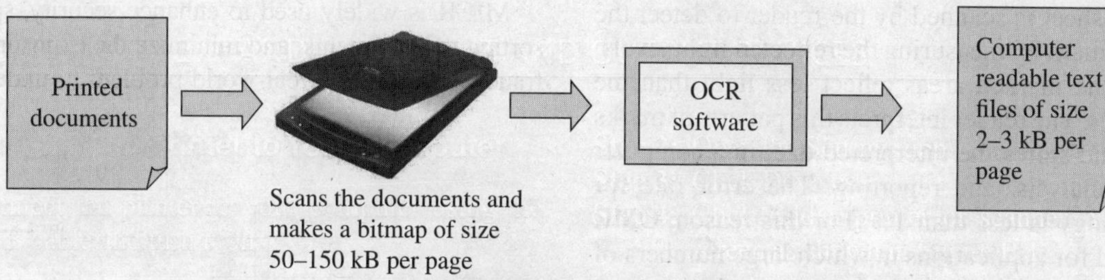

Figure 2.13 OCR system

of detecting red, blue, and green light. The light of the object being scanned is separated into red, blue, and green beams. Drum scanners are very expensive and are often used for high-end applications.

Advantages

- Any printed or handwritten document can be scanned and stored in a computer for further processing.
- The scanned and stored document will never deteriorate in quality with time. The document can be displayed and printed whenever required.
- There is no fear of loss of documents. Users can scan important documents and store them permanently in the computer.

Disadvantages

- Scanners are usually costlier than other input devices.
- The documents that are scanned and stored as images are bigger in size as compared to other equivalent text files.
- Text documents are scanned and stored as images. Therefore, they occupy more space and are also uneditable because computers cannot interpret individual characters in images.

Optical Character Recognition (OCR)

Optical character recognition is the process of converting printed materials into text or word processing files that can be easily edited and stored. The steps involved in OCR include (refer Figure 2.13):

- Scanning the text character by character
- Analysing the scanned image to translate the character images into character codes (e.g., ASCII)

In OCR processing, scanned images are analysed to detect light and dark areas so as to identify each character. When a character is recognized, it is converted into an ASCII code.

OCR has facilitated users to store text documents as text files (rather than as images, as in case of scanners). Hence, the text files occupy much less storage space and can be easily edited. These days, OCR is widely used to:

- Digitize and preserve ancient texts
- Process cheques and credit card slips
- Sort letters for speeding up mail delivery

Let us take a real-world example to understand the power of OCR. The police department usually has all the criminal records stored in large file cabinets. Scanning millions of pages to find a particular record is not only tedious and error-prone but also an expensive process. However, if OCR is used to convert the pages into computer-readable text, the police can easily search through the entire history in a few seconds.

Advantages

- Printed documents can be converted into text files.
- Advanced OCR can recognize handwritten text and convert it into computer-readable text files.

Disadvantages

- OCR cannot recognize all types of fonts.
- Documents that are poorly typed or have strikeover cannot be recognized.
- Very old documents when passed through OCR may not convert into an exact copy of the text file. This is because some characters may not have been recognized properly. In such cases, the user has to manually edit the file.

Optical Mark Recognition (OMR)

Optical mark recognition is the process of electronically extracting data from marked fields, such as checkboxes and filled-in fields, on printed forms. An optical mark reader, as shown in Figure 2.14, is fed with an OMR sheet that has pen or pencil marks in pre-defined positions to indicate each selected response (e.g., answers for multiple-choice questions in an entrance examination).

Figure 2.14 Optical mark reader

© BonNontawat/Shutterstock

The OMR sheet is scanned by the reader to detect the presence of a mark by measuring the reflected light levels. The dark or the marked areas reflect less light than the unmarked ones. The reader interprets this pattern of marks and spaces, and stores the interpreted data in a computer for storage, analysis, and reporting. The error rate for OMR technology is less than 1%. For this reason, OMR is widely used for applications in which large numbers of hand-filled forms have to be quickly processed with great accuracy, such as surveys, reply cards, questionnaires, ballots, or answer sheets for multiple-choice questions.

Advantage

- Optical mark readers work at very high speeds. They can read up to 9000 forms per hour.

Disadvantages

- It is difficult to gather large amounts of information using optical mark readers.
- Some data may be missing in the scanned document.
- They are sensitive devices that reject an OMR sheet if it is folded, torn, or crushed.

Magnetic Ink Character Recognition (MICR)

Magnetic ink character recognition is used to verify the legitimacy of paper documents, especially bank cheques. It consists of magnetic ink printed characters (refer Figure 2.15) that can be recognized by high-speed magnetic recognition devices. The printed characters provide important information (such as cheque number, account number, and, in some cases, the amount on the cheque) for processing to the receiving party.

MICR characters are usually printed in E-13B or CMC-7 fonts. Each font is made up of a series of numbers and symbols specifically designed for readability on high-speed cheque-sorting machines. The symbols provide beginning and end points for each group of numbers in order to enable the machines to determine what each series of numbers mean. To print the magnetic characters on the cheque is a critical task, and the line placement, character placement, skew, quality, and the positioning of the line in the MICR band area are important features which should not be altered.

MICR is widely used to enhance security, speed up the sorting of documents, and minimize the exposure to cheque fraud. Let us take a real-world problem to understand how

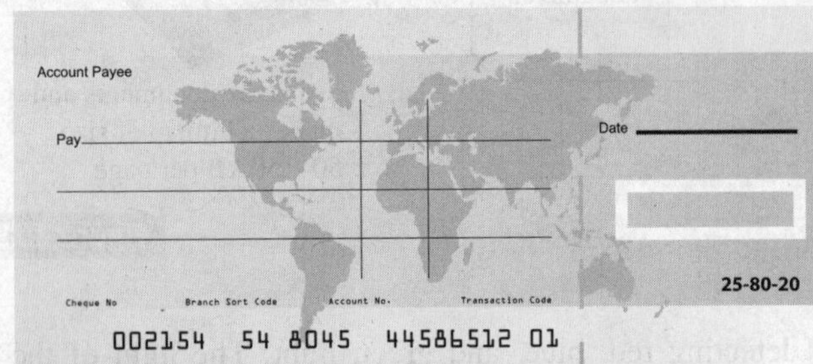

Figure 2.15 Cheque containing magnetic ink characters printed on it

© nicemonkey/Shutterstock

MICR reduces the risk to fraud. If a person gives a cheque produced using a colour photocopying machine, the magnetic ink line will either not respond to the magnetic fields, or will produce an incorrect code when scanned using an MICR reader. The MICR device even rejects cheques issued by an account owner who has a history of writing bad cheques.

2.1.5 Audiovisual Input Devices

Today, all computers are multimedia-enabled, that is, computers not only allow one to read or write text, but also enable a user to record songs, view animated movies, etc. Hence, in addition to having a keyboard and a mouse, audio–video devices have become a necessity today.

Audio Input Devices

Audio input devices are used to either capture or create sound. They enable computers to accept music, speech, or sound effects for recording and/or editing. Microphones and CD players are examples of two widely used audio input devices.

A microphone feeds audio input to a computer. However, the audio input must be converted into digital data before being stored in the computer. For this, the computer must

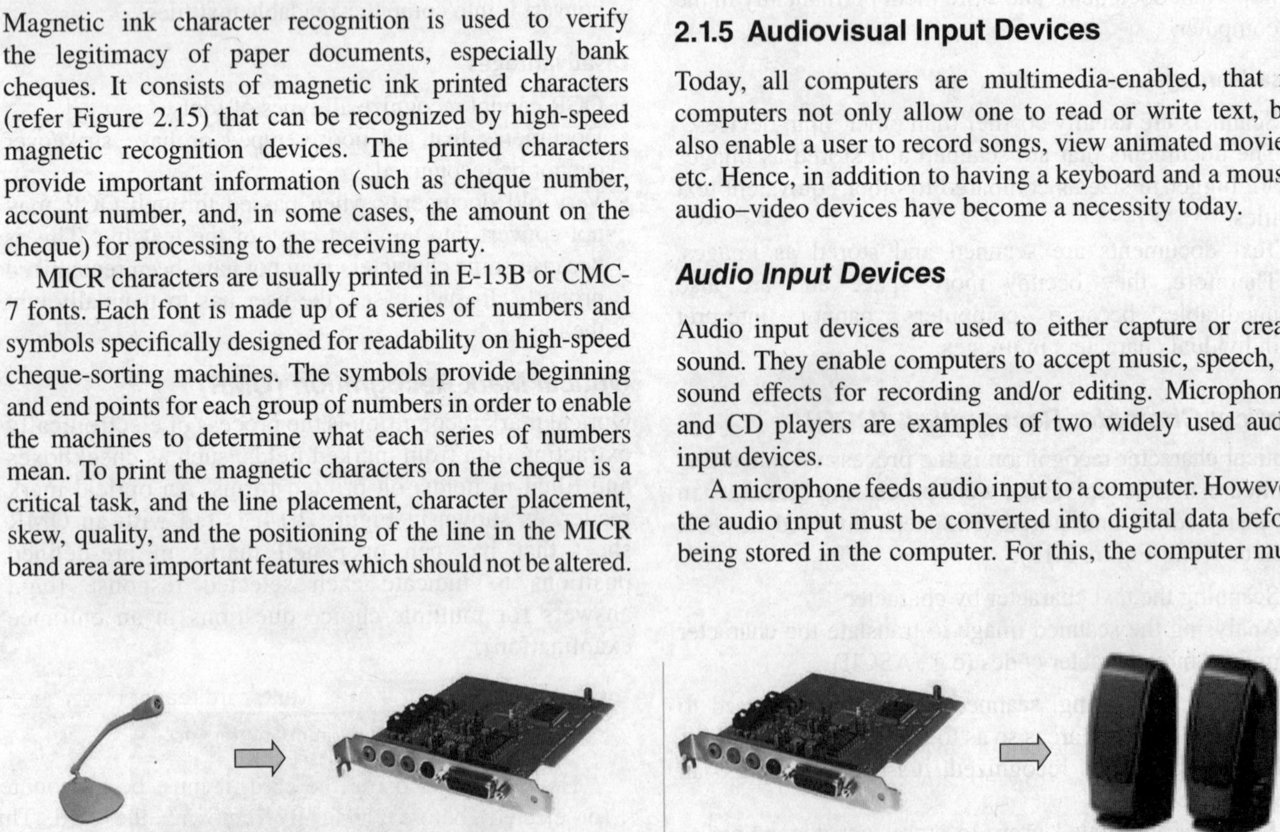

Figure 2.16 Recording and retrieving audio data

have a sound card. The sound card is a hardware unit that converts analog signals generated through the microphone into digital data, so that it can be stored in the computer. When the user wants to hear pre-recorded audio input, the sound card converts the digital data into equivalent analog signals and sends them to speakers. This process is depicted in Figure 2.16.

A computer with a microphone and speakers can be used to make telephone calls and do video conferencing (using a web camera or 'webcam') over the Internet.

Video Input Devices

Video input devices are used to capture video from the outside world into a computer. Here, the term *video* means a moving picture along with sound (as in television). As we have sound cards to convert analog audio signals into digital data and vice versa, we also have video cards to convert analog video signals to digital data to store it in the computer (and vice versa). Digital cameras and web cameras are popular examples of video input devices.

A digital camera as shown in Figure 2.17(a) is a handheld and easily portable device used to capture images and videos. The digital camera digitizes images and videos (converts them into 1s and 0s) and stores them in a memory card. The data can then be transferred to a computer using a cable that connects the computer to the digital camera. Once the images or videos are transferred to the computer, they can be easily edited, printed, or transmitted (e.g., through e-mails).

As with digital cameras, web cameras (also called *webcams*) too capture videos that can be transferred via the Internet in real time. Web cameras are widely used for video conferencing. They are not very costly, and this is one reason they are so widely used for security and privacy purposes. Webcams are also used as security cameras, since PC-connected cameras can be used to watch for movement and sound, recording both when they are detected. These recordings can then be saved in a computer and used to detect or investigate theft or any other crime. A web camera is shown in Figure 2.17(b).

(a) (b)

Figure 2.17 Video input devices: (a) Digital camera; (b) Web camera

Advantages

- Audio input devices can be used by people who are visually impaired.
- They are best used in situations where users want to avoid input through keyboard or mouse.
- Video input devices are very useful for applications such as video conferencing.
- They can be used to record memorable moments in one's life.
- They can also be used for security purposes.

Disadvantages

- Audio input devices are not effective in noisy places.
- With audio input devices, it is difficult to clearly distinguish between two similar sounding words such as 'sea' and 'see'.
- Videos and images captured using video input devices have very big file sizes, and they must be compressed before being stored on computers.

2.1.6 Card Reader

A card reader is an electronic device which is used to read flash memory cards and smart cards. While in some computers, a card reader is already integrated, it can also be used as a standalone device and can be connected to a computer using a USB port.

> **Note**
> These days, computers and other multi-function devices such as printers, scanners, and copiers have built-in card readers.

When a memory card is inserted into the card reader, the computer will show it as a mounted disk. The user can then view the contents of the memory card by double-clicking the card's icon which appears on the desktop of Macintosh computers or inside 'My Computer' on Windows machines. Once the card is mounted, users can conveniently copy-paste or work with files as they work with files in any other drive on their computer. A multi-card reader is shown in Figure 2.18.

Figure 2.18 Multi-card reader

However, after using the card, it must be unmounted (or ejected) before physically removing the card. This prevents the data on the card from getting corrupted.

> **Note**
> Smart cards are a type of plastic technology with a built-in chip used for processes such as personal identification, access control, authentication, and financial transactions.

Different types of card readers include contact, contactless, and a combination of contact and contactless smart cards.

Contact smart card readers In this type, smart cards must be manually inserted into the card reader. This is especially used for applications that require more security, such as e-commerce transactions, verifying admission IDs, network security, loyalty cards, electronic cash, and healthcare cards.

Contactless smart card readers They do not require cards to be placed into the card reader. Rather, it uses radio frequency for communication between the card and the card reader. Undoubtedly, contactless card readers offer more convenience to users and process information with a greater speed as there is no need for inserting the card into the reader. Some common applications of contactless card readers include resource access, electronic passports, parking, vending, and tollbooth fares.

2.1.7 Digitizer

The term 'digitization' means converting analog information (such as text, image, and sound) into a digital format for storage, transmission and processing. Correspondingly, a digitizer is a device that performs digitization. Scanners which we have discussed earlier are a well-known example of a digitizer. Other examples of commonly used digitizers include:

Digital camera In a digital camera, light enters through the lens, and the hardware and software inside the camera converts that information into the form of 1s and 0s so that this digital data can be stored as an image file. This file can then be transferred to a computer for permanent storage, editing, printing or sharing online.

Note

As of 2018, more than 300 exabytes of data is stored digitally worldwide.

Audio digitizer Microphones when connected to a computer (or even a smartphone) capture analog audio input. This input is then converted into a digital format for storage or processing either by a discrete sound card, or by an audio hardware on the motherboard itself.

Digital tablet A tablet is a computing device that is smaller than a computer but larger than a smartphone. Tablets have a touch screen that allows users to work on them either using their fingers or with a digital pen-like device called stylus. Users can write, draw, and paint by touching the tablet. All tablets have a software that converts the analog touch input to lines or pressure-sensitive brush strokes in a document. The software also has handwriting recognition capability which allows it to convert handwritten text to typewritten words.

Tablets typically use a stylus as a pointing device, but some also use a mouse-like device known as a puck, which offers more precision than a mouse does. These tablets are typically designed for professional applications such as CAD/CAM.

2.2 OUTPUT DEVICES

Any device that outputs information from a computer can be called an output device. Output devices are electromechanical devices that accept digital data (in the form of 0s and 1s) from a computer and convert them into human-understandable language.

Since these days all computers are multimedia-enabled, the information from computers is usually output in either visual or auditory format. Monitors and speakers are two widely used output devices. These devices provide instant feedback to a user's input. For example, monitors display characters as they are typed. Similarly, speakers play a song instantly when a user selects one from a playlist. Other examples of output devices include printers, plotters, and projectors.

In the following sections, we will discuss these output devices. However, before going into their details, let us classify the output devices based on whether they give a hard copy or a soft copy output (refer Figure 2.19).

2.3 SOFT COPY DEVICES

Soft copy output devices are those that produce an electronic version of an output—for example, a file that is stored on a hard disk, a CD, or a pen drive—and is displayed on the computer screen (monitor). Features of a soft copy output include the following:

- Output can be viewed only when the computer is on.
- Users can easily edit soft copy output.

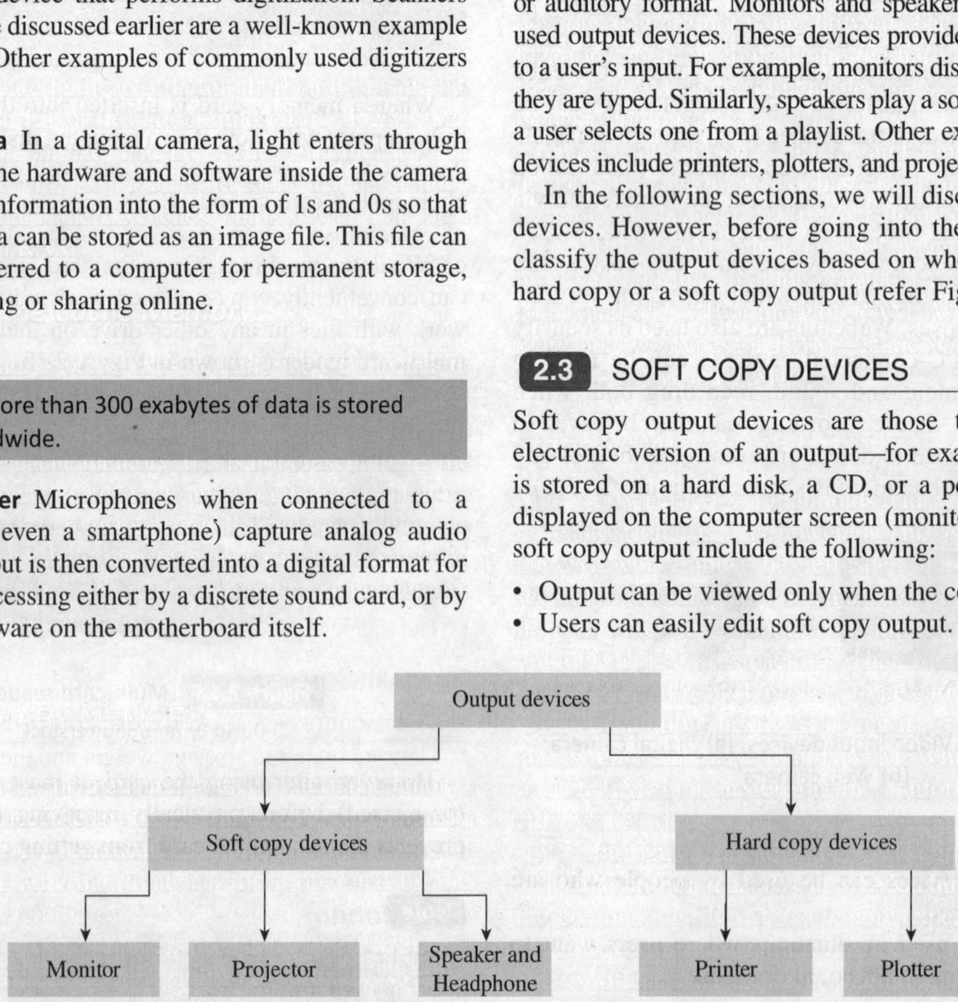

Figure 2.19 Classification of output devices

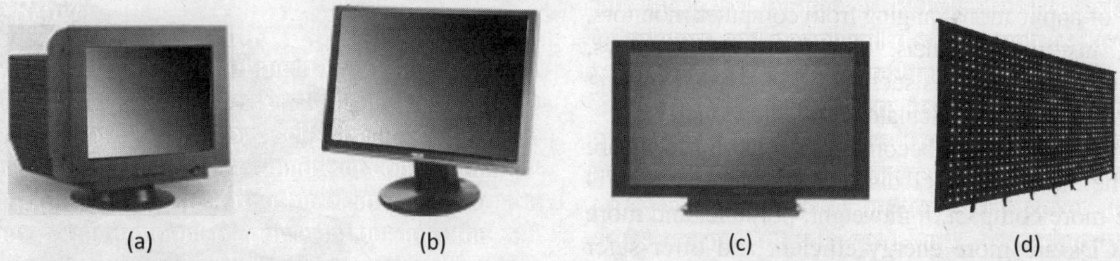

Figure 2.20 Types of monitors: (a) CRT; (b) LCD; (c) Plasma display; (d) LED

- Soft copy cannot be used by people who do not have a computer.
- Searching for data in a soft copy is easy and fast.
- Distribution of material can be done easily and quickly.

2.3.1 Monitors

A monitor is a soft copy output device used to display text and graphics information generated by a computer. Computer monitors are similar to television screens but they display information at a much higher quality. The monitor is connected to either the video graphics array (VGA) or the digital video interface (DVI) port on the video card (on the motherboard or separately purchased).

Monitors come in four variants—cathode ray tube (CRT), liquid crystal display (LCD), plasma display panel, and light emitting diode (LED) (refer Figure 2.20). While CRT monitors look much like traditional televisions and are very huge in size, LCD monitors on the other hand are thinner, offering equivalent graphics quality. However, these days, LCD monitors are replacing CRT monitors as they are cheaper and occupy less space on the desk. Most monitors have a size range of 15′ to 21′ or more (where size is defined as a diagonal measurement from one corner of the screen to the other).

CRT Monitor

CRT monitors work by firing charged electrons at a phosphor-coated film (refer Figure 2.21). When electrons hit the screen, they glow, thereby enabling the viewer to see the output.

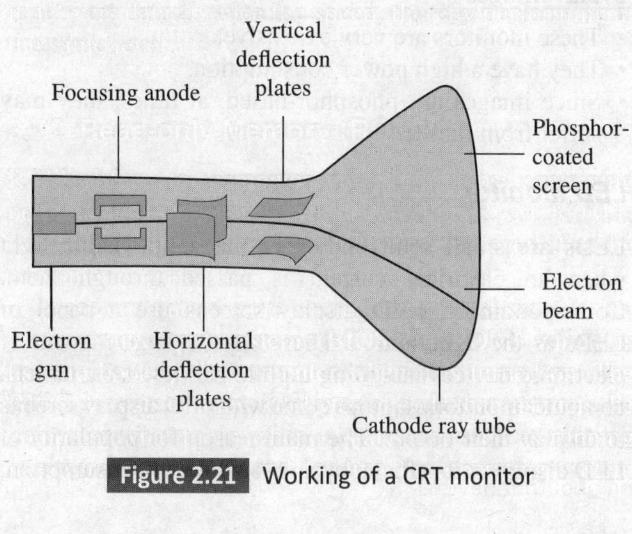

Figure 2.21 Working of a CRT monitor

In a CRT, the cathode (negative terminal) is a heated filament that is placed in a vacuum created inside a glass tube. The ray is a stream of electrons that come out from the heated cathode into the vacuum. While electrons are negative, the anode, on the other hand, is positive, so it attracts the electrons coming out of the cathode. That is, the anode focuses the stream of electrons to form a tight beam that is then accelerated by an accelerating anode. This tight, high-speed beam of electrons flies through the vacuum in the tube and hits the flat screen at the other end of the tube. This screen is coated with phosphor, which glows when struck by the beam, thereby displaying a picture, which the viewer sees on the monitor.

Note

Note that colour CRT monitors contain three electron guns (one each for red, blue, and green).
Each pixel or dot on the screen has three phosphors (red, blue, and green). When the beam from these guns is focused on the phosphors, they light up. By varying the intensities of the beam, the viewer can see different colours.

Advantages

- CRT monitors provide images of good quality (bright as well as clear).
- CRT monitors are cheapest when compared to other monitors.
- The images are clear even when viewed from an angle.

Disadvantages

- CRT monitors occupy a large space on the desk.
- They are bigger in size and weight and therefore difficult to move from one place to another when compared with other types of monitors.
- Power consumption is higher than in other monitors.

LCD Monitor

An LCD monitor is a thin, flat, electronic visual display that uses the light modulating properties of liquid crystals, which do not emit light directly. LCD screens are used in a wide range of applications ranging from computer monitors, televisions, instrument panels, aircraft cockpit displays, signage to consumer devices such as video players, gaming devices, clocks, watches, calculators, and telephones.

These days, LCDs have become so popular that they are replacing the traditional CRT displays at a fast pace. LCD screens are more compact, lightweight, portable, and more reliable. LCDs are more energy efficient and offer safer disposal than CRTs. It is because of their low electrical power consumption that they are being widely used in battery-powered electronic equipment.

LCD technology is based on the principle of blocking light. The LCD consists of two pieces of polarizing filters (or substrates) that contain a liquid crystal material between them (see Figure 2.22). A backlight creates light, which is made to pass through the first substrate. Simultaneously, electrical currents cause the liquid crystal molecules to align, thus allowing varying levels of light to pass through the second substrate and create colours, and hence images are seen on the screen.

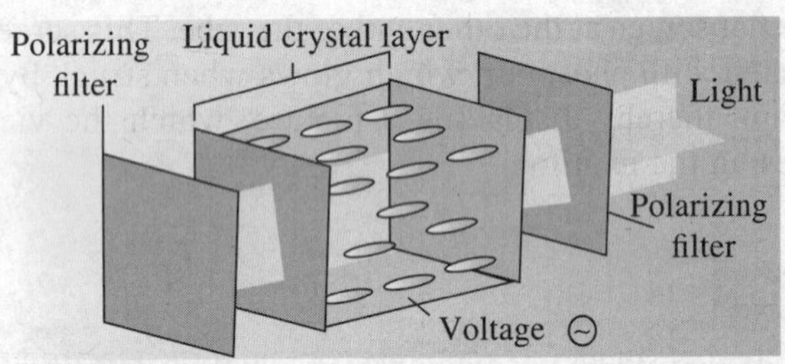

Figure 2.22 Working of an LCD monitor

Advantages

- LCD monitors are very compact and lightweight.
- They consume less power.
- They do not suffer from geometric distortion.
- There is little or no flicker of images (depending on the backlight technology used).
- They are more reliable than CRTs.
- They can be made in almost any size or shape.
- They cause less eye fatigue.

Disadvantages

- They are more expensive than CRTs.
- Images are not very clear when viewed from an angle.

Plasma Monitor

Plasma monitors are thin and flat monitors widely used in televisions and computers. They contain two glass plates that have hundreds of thousands of tiny cells filled with xenon and neon gases. An address electrode and a transparent display electrode are sandwiched between the glass plates. The display electrode is covered by a magnesium oxide protective layer and is arranged in a horizontal row along the screen, while the address electrode is arranged in a vertical column, thereby forming a grid-like structure as shown in Figure 2.23.

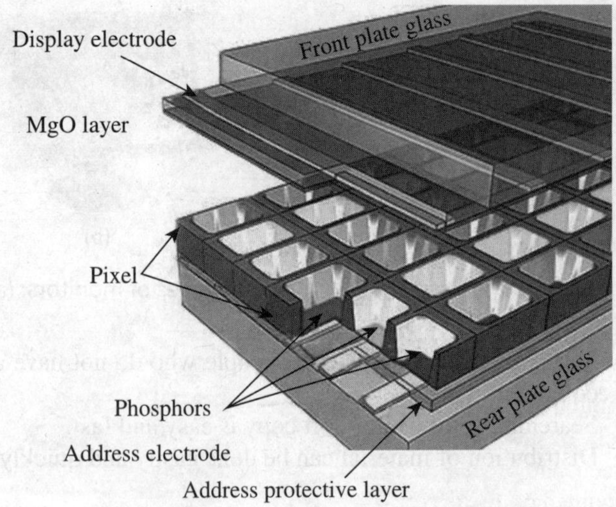

Figure 2.23 Working of a plasma monitor

To ionize the gas in a particular cell, the electrodes that intersect at that cell are charged at least thousands of times within a small fraction of a second (charging each cell in turn).

Once the intersecting electrodes are charged, an electric current begins to flow through the gas in the cell. This current creates a rapid flow of charged particles, thereby stimulating the gas atoms to release ultraviolet photons. When these UV photons hit a phosphor atom in the cell, one of phosphor's electrons jumps to a higher energy level, and the atom heats up. When the electron falls back to its normal level, it releases energy in the form of a visible light photon.

Advantages

- The technology used in plasma monitors allows producing a very wide screen using extremely thin materials.
- Very bright images are formed which look good from almost every angle.
- These monitors are not heavy and are thus easily portable.

Disadvantages

- These monitors are very expensive.
- They have a high power consumption.
- Since images are phosphor-based, at times, they may suffer from flicker.

LED Monitor

LEDs are small semiconductors that emit visible light when an electrical current is passed through them. Correspondingly, LED display screens use a panel of LEDs as the light source. These days, a large number of electronic devices including mobile phones, TVs, tablets, computer monitors, laptops come with LED display screens to display their output. The main reason for popularity of LED display is its efficiency and low-energy consumption.

These features make them best suited for handheld and chargeable devices. LEDs are also used outdoors in store signs, billboards, destination signs on public transport vehicles. There are two types of LED panels. The first category of LED panels is the conventional one that uses discrete LEDs. The second category comprises of surface-mounted device (SMD) panels. Most outdoor screens and some indoor screens are built with discrete LEDs (or individually mounted LEDs). In such a screen, a cluster of red, green, and blue diodes which together form a full-colour pixel are spaced evenly apart.

Most indoor screens are built using SMD technology. Though this technology is now used for outdoor devices as well. In such a screen, a single SMD pixel consists of red, green, and blue diodes mounted on a chipset, which is then mounted on the driver PC board. These diodes are smaller than a pinhead and are set very close together.

Advantages of LEDs over LCDs

- Produce more brilliant light with higher intensity
- Less expensive
- Have a broader dimming range
- More reliable
- Power efficient as they use very less power (even 20 watts)
- Can easily work at lower temperatures
- Longer lifespan
- Less impact on the environment

2.3.2 Projectors

A projector (Figure 2.24) is a device that takes an image from a video source and projects it onto a screen or another surface. These days, projectors are used for a wide range of applications, varying from home theater systems for projecting movies and television programmes onto a screen much larger than even the biggest available television, to projectors used by organizations for projecting information and presentations onto screens large enough for rooms filled with many people. Projectors also allow users to change/adjust some features of images such as brightness, sharpness, and colour settings, similar to the features available in a standard television. Projectors are now available in a variety of different shapes and sizes, and are produced by many different companies.

Figure 2.24 Projector

© olegbush/Shutterstock

A projector works by receiving a video signal from some external device such as a DVD player or a computer and projects that signal onto a screen. To display the image on a big screen, the projector first displays that image (represented in the video signal) onto a small screen inside the projector itself, which is then projected onto the final screen using bright light and a lens. The lens is shaped in such a way that it takes the small image and turns it into a dramatically larger one.

Projectors can be broadly classified into two categories depending on the technology they use.

LCD Projector

LCD projectors make use of their own light to display the image on the screen/wall. These projectors are based on LCD technology. To use these projectors, the room must be first darkened, else the image formed will be blurred.

Digital Light Processing (DLP) Projector

DLP projectors use a number of mirrors to reflect the light. When using a DLP projector, the room may or may not be darkened because it displays a clear image in both situations.

2.3.3 Speakers, Microphones and Headphones

Initially, computers were designed to be used only for scientific purposes, but later, with the advances in technology, computers became so popular and inexpensive that they are now used in almost every sphere of our day-to-day lives. Today, all business and home users demand audio capabilities from their computers. For this purpose, speakers were developed in different sizes and shapes, and with different powers and sound quality. With all these types of speakers, a user can enjoy music, movies, or games, and the sound will be spread through the entire room. With good quality speakers, the sound will also be audible even to people sitting in another room or even to neighbours!

However, in case a user wants to enjoy loud music without disturbing the people nearby, a headphone can be used. Headphones are small devices that fit in or on the ear, and give about the same quality and power of the sound, as speakers, only to the listener. Most of today's headphones feature some noise-cancelling technologies, so that the listener may listen to only the sound from the speakers and not anything else from the surrounding environment.

Users often use headphones to chat with people over the Internet. With headphones, they are assured that the conversation is heard only by them. However, in addition to the headphones, they are also required to use a separate microphone to talk to the other person. Hence, another device called the headset was developed to allow users to talk and listen at the same time, using the same device. Headsets are widely used in call centres and other telephone-intensive jobs, and for personal use on computers to facilitate comfortable simultaneous conversation and typing. Figure 2.25 shows the various audio devices used with computers.

Although every computer has a built-in speaker, an external speaker disables this lower-fidelity built-in speaker. Speakers available in the market have a wide range of quality and prices. The normal computer speakers are small and have mediocre sound quality. Other speakers are available that have equalization features such as bass and treble controls. Users can also use a lead to connect their computer's sound output to an existing stereo system to give much better results than the small, low-cost computer speakers.

(a) (b) (c)

Figure 2.25 Audio devices: (a) Speaker; (b) Headphone; (c) Headset

Wireless Speakers, Microphones and Headphones

Wireless speakers connected to the computer without any wire comes in three variants- Bluetooth, Wi-Fi, and Proprietary Speakers.

Bluetooth speakers are widely used with smartphones and tablets. Once the two devices are paired, they are connected by a short-range link through which audio data can be transferred. Best suited for portability, these speakers' run-on battery power and are smaller than other kinds of speakers. Top selling Bluetooth speakers include Boss, Boat, FUGOO, JBL, Bose, and UE.

Wi-Fi speakers connect to a home network and communicate over TCP/IP. They can connect over longer distances than Bluetooth. Therefore, they are used for whole-house audio systems. Wi-fi speakers consume power. Unlike Bluetooth speakers, they do not run-on batteries.

> **Note**
>
> AirPlay speakers use Apple's proprietary wireless multimedia technology. They connect only to Apple i-devices

Advantages of Wireless speakers

- No wires needed
- Speakers can be placed anywhere within transmission range
- Very useful in home-theatre systems and in outdoor speaker systems

Disadvantages of Wireless Speakers

- Gives uneven sound quality
- Prone to signal interference from other household gadgets. This can further degrade the sound quality and (in extreme cases) causes the audio to drop out completely.
- Except for the smaller Bluetooth models, wireless speakers must be plugged into wall outlets, making them not truly wireless. It requires more power so you need to plug each speaker into a power source. Battery-operated wireless speakers exist, but may not have the quality as expected. This makes it less wireless.
- If the transmitter or receiver stops working or drops out, it will affect the listening experience.
- Limited bandwidth issues. Wired speakers can carry more information in the form of electrical signals as compared to wireless ones.

A wireless microphone transmits user's voice to its receiver. The sound system receives the signal from the receiver, amplifies it and outputs it through the speakers.

A wireless mic system has three main parts that together operate as low powered, individual radio station.

Microphone connected to the transmitter.

Transmitter that converts the audio from the microphone to radio waves and then transmits them to the receiver.

Receiver connected to the computer by a short audio cable, receives the radio transmission from the transmitter. It then converts the transmission back to an audio signal so that it can be amplified.

The paired audio sources wirelessly transmit encoded audio signals either using radio frequencies or infrared carriers. Wireless headphones wirelessly receive these signals and decode it to audio. The wireless headphones with built-in receivers are designed to accept the wireless waves that carry the audio signal. These audio signals are therefore known as the carrier wave.

Transmitters effectively encode the audio signal into a wireless format (the carrier wave) and propagate the wireless signal through the air. The intended audio signal is known as the modulating signal. This modulating signal is encoded into a carrier wave that is transmitted wirelessly to the receiver.

Audio signals are generally made up of frequencies within the audible range of 20 Hz – 20,000 Hz. The wireless receiver reads the carrier wave and decodes the modulating signal (audio signal) from the wave. Wireless receivers must be tuned to accept the specified carrier wave frequency.

If the audio signal is digital, it is converted into an analog audio signal. The analog audio signal is then amplified to drive the headphone drivers properly. There are different types of wireless headphones.

***Radio Frequency (RF)* headphones** can transmit through walls and solid objects (unlike most Bluetooth devices) without degrading the signal. They can work with minimal audio compression, thereby providing better sound quality with less delay.

IR headphones use infrared light waves to transfer the audio signal to the headphones. So, they need a line-of-sight (LOS) connection between the transmitter and the headphones. The have a lower risk of interference with other wireless devices.

***Bluetooth-enabled* headphones** work by transmitting audio signals through a low-powered 2.4Ghz.

Kleer headphones use a proprietary wireless connection technology that can operate in 2.4GHz, 5.2GHz, and 5.8GHz ranges. They deliver CD-quality audio to allow users to hear the true quality of the content. Kleer headphones have longer battery life and lower audio latency than Bluetooth and other wireless technologies.

Regardless of the type of wireless headphone, the steps of transmitting audio remain the same. These steps are:

1. The audio source transmits the audio signal that is received by a wireless transmitter.
2. The wireless transmitter encodes the audio signal (modulating signal) into a carrier wave.
3. The carrier wave is propagated through space.
4. The wireless receiver receives the wireless signal and decodes it.
5. Digital audio signals are converted to analog signals and amplified using an internal amplifier.
6. The amplified audio signal is sent to the headphone receivers.
7. The headphone converts the audio signal into sound.

2.4 HARD COPY DEVICES

Hard copy output devices are those that produce a physical form of output. For example, the content of a file printed on a paper is a form of hard copy output. The features of hard copy output include:

- A computer is not needed to see the output.
- Editing and incorporating edits in a hard copy is difficult.
- Hard copy output can be easily distributed to people who do not have a computer.
- Searching for data in a hard copy is a tiring and difficult job.
- Distribution of hard copy is not only costly but slower as well.

2.4.1 Printers

A printer is a device that takes the text and graphics information from a computer and prints it on a paper. Printers are available in the market in various sizes, speeds, sophistication, and costs. Usually, more expensive printers are used for higher resolution colour printing. The qualities of printers that are of interest to users include:

Colour Colour printouts are needed for presentations, maps, and other pages where colour is part of the information. Colour printers can also be set to print only in monochrome. These printers are more expensive, so if users do not have a specific need for colour printouts, they will find a black-and-white printer cheaper to operate.

Resolution The resolution of a printer means the sharpness of text and images rendered on paper. It is usually expressed in dots per inch (dpi). Even the least expensive printer provides sufficient resolution for most purposes at 600 dpi.

Speed Speed means the number of pages that are printed in one minute. The speed of a printer is an important factor for users who have a large number of pages to print. While high-speed printers are quite expensive, inexpensive printers, on the other hand, can print only about 3–6 sheets per minute. Colour printing is even slower.

Memory Most printers have a small amount of memory (for example, 1 MB), which can be expanded by users. Having more memory enhances the speed of printing.

Printers can be broadly classified into two groups: impact and non-impact printers as shown in Figure 2.26.

Impact Printer

These printers print characters by striking an inked ribbon against a paper. Examples of impact printers include dot matrix printers, daisy wheel printers, and most types of line printers.

Advantages

- These printers enable users to produce carbon copies.
- They are cheap.

Disadvantages

- Impact printers are slow.
- They offer poor print quality, especially in the case of graphics.
- They can be extremely noisy.
- They can print only using the standard font.

Figure 2.26 Classification of printers

Non-impact Printer

Non-impact printers are much quieter than impact printers, as their printing heads do not strike the paper. They offer better print quality, faster printing, and the ability to create prints that contain sophisticated graphics. Non-impact printers use either solid or liquid cartridge-based ink, which is either sprayed, dripped, or electrostatically drawn onto the page. The main types of non-impact printers are inkjet, laser, and thermal printers.

Advantages

- Non-impact printers produce prints of good quality, and hence render sophisticated graphics.
- They are noiseless.
- They are fast.
- They can print text in different fonts.

Disadvantages

- These printers are expensive.
- The ink cartridges used by them are also costly.

Now we will read about the different types of printers.

Dot Matrix Printer

A dot matrix printer (shown in Figure 2.27) prints characters and images of all types as a pattern of dots (hence the name). This printer has a printhead (or hammer) that consists of pins representing a character or image. The printhead runs back and forth, or in an up-and-down motion on the page and prints by striking an ink-soaked cloth ribbon against the paper, much like the print mechanism of a typewriter. From the 1970s to 1990s, dot matrix impact printers were the most common type of printers used with PCs.

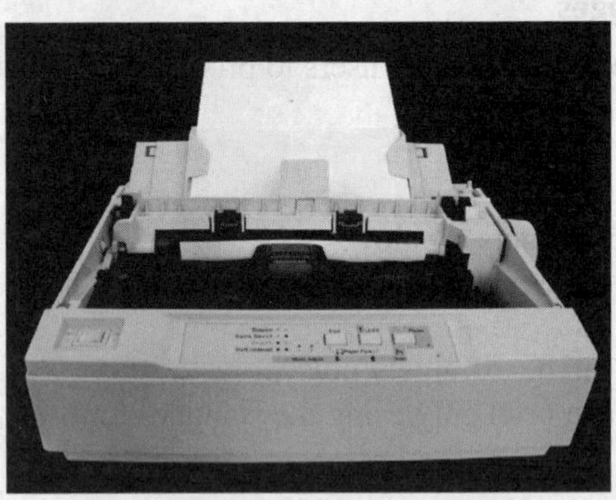

Figure 2.27 Dot matrix printer

© burnel1/Shutterstock

Several dot matrix printer manufacturers implemented colour printing through a multi-colour ribbon. Colour was obtained through a multi-pass composite printing process. In each pass, the printhead struck a different section of the ribbon (one primary colour). However, because of poor colour quality and increased operating expense, colour dot matrix printers could never replace their monochrome counterparts. Moreover, the black ink section would gradually contaminate the other three colours (RGB), thereby changing the consistency of printouts over the life of the ribbon. Colour dot matrix printers were therefore suitable only for abstract illustrations and pie charts, but not for photo-realistic reproduction.

The speed of dot matrix printers varies in the range of 50–500 cps (characters per second).

Advantages

- The dot matrix printer can produce carbon copies.
- It offers the lowest printing cost per page.
- It is widely used for bulk printing where the quality of the print is not of much importance.
- It is inexpensive.
- When the ink is about to be exhausted, the printout gradually fades rather than suddenly stopping midway through a job.
- It can use continuous paper rather than individual sheets, making it useful for data logging.

Disadvantages

- This printer creates a lot of noise when the pins strike the ribbon against the paper.
- It can only print lower resolution graphics, with limited quality.
- It is very slow.
- It has poor print quality.

Daisy Wheel Printer

Daisy wheel printers use an impact printing technology to generate high-quality output comparable to typewriters, and are three times faster. However, today, daisy wheel technology is found only in some electronic typewriters.

The printhead of a daisy wheel printer is a circular wheel, about 3 inches in diameter with arms or spokes. The shape of the printer wheel resembles the petals of a daisy flower, and hence its name. The characters are embossed at the outer ends of the arms.

To print a character, the wheel is rotated in such a way that the character to be printed is positioned just in front of the printer ribbon. The spoke containing the required character is then hit by a hammer, thereby striking the ribbon to leave an impression on the paper placed behind the ribbon. The movement of all these parts is controlled by a microprocessor in the printer.

The key benefit of using a daisy wheel printer is that the print quality is high, as the exact shape of the character hits the ribbon to leave an impression on the paper.

Line Printer

A line printer is a high-speed impact printer in which one typed line is printed at a time. The speed of a line printer usually varies from 600 to 1200 lines per minute, or approximately 10–20 pages per minute. Because of their high speed, line printers are widely used in data centres and in industrial environments. Band printer is a commonly used variant of line printers.

Band Printer

A band printer (loop printer) is an impact printer with a printing mechanism that uses a metal loop or band to produce typed characters. A set of characters is permanently embossed on the band, and this set cannot be changed unless the band is replaced. The band itself revolves around hammers that push the paper against the ribbon, allowing the desired character to be produced on the paper.

The main advantage of using a band printer is its high speed. This type of printer can print 2000 lines per minute, and is, therefore, perfect for high-volume printing in businesses, schools, and other organizations. Band printers are normally attached to mainframes and used for industrial printing.

However, band printers cannot be used for any graphics printing, as the characters are predetermined and cannot be changed unless the band is changed. Band printers were very popular in the 1970s and 1980s; however, today, laser printers have replaced band printers.

Note

Band printers are often confused with band printing. Band printing is the process of sending output to a printer and is not associated with this type of printers.

Inkjet Printer

Inkjet printers, shown in Figure 2.28, came in the market in the 1980s, but it was only in the 1990s that their prices reduced enough to bring the technology to a bigger user base. Inkjet printers have made rapid technological advances in recent years. Colour inkjet printers have succeeded in making colour printing an affordable option even for home users.

Figure 2.28 Inkjet printer
© Iakov Filimonov/Shutterstock

The printhead of inkjet printers has several tiny nozzles, also called jets. As the paper moves past the printhead, these nozzles spray ink onto it, forming characters and images. If we observe a printout that has just come out from an inkjet printer, we will see that the dots are extremely small (usually between 50 and 60 microns in diameter) and are positioned very precisely, with resolution of up to 1440 × 720 dpi. To create a coloured image, the dots can have different colours combined together.

An inkjet printer can produce from 100 to several hundred pages (depending on the nature of the hard copy), before the ink cartridges must be replaced. There is usually one black ink cartridge and one colour cartridge containing ink in primary pigments (cyan, magenta, and yellow).

While inkjet printers are cheaper than laser printers, they are more expensive to maintain. The cartridges of inkjet printers have to be changed more frequently, and the special coated paper required to produce high-quality output is very expensive. Hence, the cost per page of inkjet printers becomes ten times more than laser printers. Therefore, inkjet printers are not well suited for high-volume print jobs.

Laser Printer

A laser printer, shown in Figure 2.29, is a non-impact printer that works at very high speeds and produces high-quality text and graphics. It uses the technology used in photocopier machines. When a document is sent to the printer, the following steps take place:

- A laser beam 'draws' the document on a drum (which is coated with a photoconductive material) using electrical charges.
- After the drum is charged, it is rolled in a toner (a dry powder type of ink).
- The toner sticks to the charged image on the drum.
- The toner is transferred onto a piece of paper and fused to the paper with heat and pressure.
- After the document is printed, the electrical charge is removed from the drum and the excess toner is collected.

Figure 2.29 Laser printer
© restyler/Shutterstock

While colour laser printers are also available in the market, users mostly prefer monochrome printers, because the former is up to ten times more expensive than the latter.

Wireless Printer or Wi-Fi Printers

Wi-Fi printers can connect to a network without using wires. Once connected to a Wi-Fi network, any computer, smartphone, and tablet connected to the same network can print using the Wi-Fi printer that is placed at any convenient location at home.

Wireless printers in reality are not 100% wireless as they have to be plugged into a power socket, but other than that no wires are required.

Figure 2.30 A wireless printer

These printers are easy to setup and can be easily shared in office environments where several people need to be able to access the same printer. There are two types of wireless printers in today's market.

Bluetooth printer: These printers can easily connect to any Bluetooth-capable device, including PCs, smartphones, and more. However, Bluetooth's wireless range is not as strong as compared to Wi-Fi printer. So, the devices need to be fairly close to each other.

Wi-Fi printer: Wi-Fi printers can connect to the internet router and provide its services to other devices on that router's network or even an external network (if so configured). In case of network congestion, Wi-Fi printers can have slower print times.

3D Printers

3D printing, the latest buzzword, is a process in which a digital model is turned into a tangible, solid, three-dimensional object, usually by laying down many successive, thin layers of a material.

3D printers have become popular because they have made manufacturing easily accessible owing to its low cost and small size.

How does a 3D printer works?

The working process of a 3D printer can be explained with the help of following four steps:

Step 1: A virtual design of the object is made. This design is like a blueprint for the 3D printer to read and is created using a computer-aided design (CAD) software or using a 3D scanner, which creates a copy of an existing object by basically taking pictures of it from different angles.

Figure 2.31 3D printer

Step 2: Prepare the virtual model for printing. This is done by breaking down the model into many layers using a process called slicing. Slicing takes the model and slices it into hundreds or even thousands of thin, horizontal layers using special software.

Step 3: Upload the slices to the 3D printer using a USB cable or Wi-Fi connection.

Step 4: The 3D printer reads every slice of the model and prints it layer by layer.

Advantages of 3D Printers

- 3D printed materials easier to manufacture
- 3D objects can be printed quickly
- These objects are less expensive as they provide ways to reduce the total number of parts that need to be welded together while also significantly reducing weight and increasing strength. For example, GE Aviation's LEAP engine uses 3D printed Cobalt-chrome fuel nozzles that weigh 25% less and are five times as strong as traditionally manufactured nozzles. 3D printers are affordable
- 3D printers use low-cost plastics and concrete that are easily accessible.
- 3D printers are fast and thus ideal for quick prototyping of products as it can be done in house in small runs. This makes making any sort of changes to products faster and easier as these changes are done through CAD software.
- 3D printers can work with a variety of specialty materials including plastics, metals, nitinol, gold and carbon fiber. These materials have high heat resistance, water repellency and strength.

Disadvantages of 3D Printers

- Objects created by 3D printers may not provide enough strength and be durable. Though the strength of 3D printing relies heavily on materials being used, creating objects layer-by-layer may not always produce tough objects.
- 3D printers may vary with time. Moreover, accuracy with 3D printing is dependent on the techniques and

printer used. For example, some smaller 3D printers (like desktop models) can wear out easily.

- 3D printers may require post-processing activities like sanding or smoothing out an object, heat treatment or removing support struts. These post-processing add to the costs involved.

Note

Tinkercad is a free CAD software that can be used in the browser without installing it. The model creates and the model as a printable file (.STL or .OBJ file). This file is fed to the printer via USB, SD or Wi-Fi.

2.4.2 Plotters

A plotter as shown in Figure 2.32 is a printing device that is usually used to print vector graphics with high print quality. They are widely used to draw maps, in scientific applications, and computer-aided engineering (CAE). Architects use plotters to draw blueprints of the structures they are working on.

A plotter is basically a printer that interprets commands from a computer to make line drawings on paper with one or more automated pens. Since plotters are much more expensive than printers, they are used only for specialized applications. There are two different types of plotters: drum and flatbed.

Figure 2.32 Plotter

© Michal Vitek/Shutterstock

Drum Plotter

A drum plotter is used to draw graphics on a paper that is wrapped around a drum. This type of plotter is usually used with mainframe and minicomputer systems. The drum plotter works by rotating the drum back and forth to produce vertical motion. The pen, which is mounted on a carriage, is moved across the width of the paper. Hence, the vertical movement of the paper and the horizontal movement of the pen create the required design under the control of the computer.

Drum plotters can make multicolour drawings by using pens with different coloured inks. Moreover, drum plotters support very large plot sizes with paper widths of up to 1 metre.

Flatbed Plotter

In a flatbed plotter, the paper is spread on the flat rectangular surface of the plotter, and the pen is moved over it. Flatbed plotters are less expensive, and are used in many small computing systems. The size of the plot is limited only by the size of the plotter's bed. In this type of plotter, the paper does not move; rather, plotting is done by moving an arm that moves a pen over the paper.

In case of flatbed plotters, pens of different colours are mounted in the pen-holding mechanism that moves on the surface. The microprocessor in the plotter selects the desired pen and controls its movement.

2.5 VOICE RESPONSE SYSTEM (VRS)

A voice response system in simple terms is a computer interface which responds to voice commands, instead of responding to inputs from a mouse or a keyboard. This system has a limited vocabulary and organizes sentences by combining pre-recorded words saved in a database. As VRS promotes voice-activated data entry, operators have to no longer enter data manually.

Uses of VRS

- VRS is best suited for visually impaired people. Since they cannot use a mouse or a keyboard, they can use voice response systems to instruct a computer.
- VRS is used to provide customer service. It is an automated telephony system that interacts with callers, gathers information, and routes calls to the appropriate recipients. A user gives input by a combination of voice telephone input and touch-tone keypad selection and gets the output in the form of voice, fax, callback, e-mail, and other contact methods.
- With the help of a VRS system, users can use their voices to activate and operate software applications. For example, turning on/off lights and fans, closing and opening a garage door, etc.
- Public transport (bus/train/airplane/metro) uses VRS to notify passengers of next destination, schedule, or other vital information.
- VRS enables customers to fill out sales order forms with a phone keypad. The completed form is then forwarded to a salesperson.

Advantages

- Saves time and money as VRS can replace humans to answer frequently asked questions (FAQs). Saves cost of a telephone operator who would be appointed just to answer users' commonly asked queries.

- Greater customer satisfaction as VRS eliminates wait time by responding to a caller immediately. Businesses use VRS to enhance their customer satisfaction by ensuring that their customers are heard and guided instantly.
- VRS is available 24×7 so that uninterrupted service is provided to the callers whenever they need it.

Disadvantages

- VRS can recognize only those words that are in its vocabulary.
- When VRS is used to handle calls, it does not permit responses outside the parameters programmed in the software. So many a times, customers get frustrated.
- Installing the VRS comes with an initial cost.

However, as with all technology, the VRS is evolving and improving with time to address these limitations.

2.6 BIOMETRIC DEVICES

The word 'biometric' is derived from the Greek words 'bio' and 'metric', where bio means 'life' and metric means 'to measure'. Thus, biometric means identifying a person using his/her biological features (or measures). Correspondingly, any device which uses biometrics to identify a person is known as a biometric device. Biometric devices capture raw biometric samples in a form that can be digitized and stored in a database for matching the patterns for identification and authentication. All modern smartphones come with fingerprint and face identification capability to provide access to the phone. In this case, the smartphone is acting like a biometric device. We all know that as compared to a password, this type of identification system is more difficult to fake as biological features are unique to a person. Other commonly used techniques for biometric identification include identification by a person's hand geometry, iris, voice, and retina. Some banks have initiated using fingerprint readers for approval at ATMs. Social networking sites such as Facebook use face recognition software to tag users in photographs. Some commonly used biometric devices include:

> **Note**
>
> There are two types of biometric sensors. One that measures physiological features (such as face, fingerprint, and palm print). The other uses behavioural metrics (such as keystroke, signature, and voice).

Face scanner A face scanner identifies a person by taking measurements of his/her face. For example, the distance between the person's chin, eyes, nose, and mouth. For facial identification, a high-definition camera is used.

Hand scanner the palm of a person's hand is also unique to the person. A biometric hand scanner identifies the person by the palm of his/her hand.

Finger scanner A biometric finger scanner identifies a person by his/her fingerprint as it is unique to every individual.

Retina or iris scanner A biometric retina or iris scanner identifies a person by scanning the iris or retina of his/her eyes. Such a device has sensors that use infrared light to identify a person.

Voice scanner A voice scanner mathematically breaks down a person's voice to identify it. The most important characteristics used for identification include nasal tone, fundamental frequency, inflection, and cadence.

Vein scanner This device scans the vein pattern under the skin to identify a person. Some biometric scanners also match DNA pattern for identification.

Signature recognition While some signature recognition devices analyse and measure the pressure applied, stroke order, and speed, others do the same thing by comparing visual images of signatures.

Though biometric devices are reliable, they can still produce false negatives (when an authorized user is not recognized or authenticated) and false positives (when an unauthorized user is recognized and authenticated).

POINTS TO REMEMBER

- An input device is used to feed data and instructions into a computer.
- A keyboard is an electromechanical device which is used to input alphanumeric data into a computer.
- A wireless keyboard can be connected to a computer using Bluetooth, radio frequency, or infrared technology.
- A pointing input device enables users to easily control the movement of the pointer. It is connected to the serial or USB port on the system unit.
- A mouse is an input device which enables users to control the movement of the pointer in a graphical user interface.
- A trackball is a pointing device which is usually used in notebook computers.
- A touchpad is a small, flat, rectangular stationary pointing device with a sensitive surface of 1.5–2 square inches.
- A joystick is a cursor control device widely used in computer games and CAD/CAM applications.
- A stylus is a pen-shaped input device used to enter information or write on the touchscreen of a phone.
- A touchscreen is a display screen that can identify the occurrence and position of a touch inside the display region.
- A barcode reader is a handheld input device used to capture and read information stored in a barcode.
- A scanner is a device that captures images, printed text, and handwritten text, from different sources

such as photographic prints, posters, and magazines, and converts them into digital images for editing and display on computers.
- Audio input devices are used to either capture or create sound. Microphones and CD players are examples of two widely used audio devices.
- A sound card is a hardware unit that converts analog signals generated through a microphone into digital data, so that it can be stored in a computer.
- Video input devices are used to capture video from the outside world into a computer.
- An electronic card reader is used to read flash memory cards or smart cards.
- A digitizer is a device which receives analog data and creates its digital equivalent.
- Any device that outputs information from a computer can be called an output device. Basically, output devices are electromechanical devices that accept digital data from a computer and convert them into a human understandable language.
- A monitor is a soft copy output device used to display text and graphics information generated by a computer through a video card. It is connected to either the VGA or the DVI port on the video card (which is on the motherboard or separately purchased).
- A projector is a device that takes an image from a video source and projects it on a screen or another surface.
- Impact printers print characters by striking an inked ribbon against a paper, whereas non-impact printers use either solid or liquid cartridge-based ink, which is either sprayed, dipped, or electrostatically drawn onto a page.
- A dot matrix printer is an impact printer which prints characters and images as a pattern of dots.
- An inkjet printer is a non-impact printer. The printhead consists of tiny nozzles and as the paper moves past the printhead, nozzles spray ink onto it, forming characters and images.
- A laser printer is a non-impact printer which uses a laser beam to produce an image on a negatively charged cylindrical drum.
- A voice response system (VRS) is an interface that responds to voice commands, instead of responding to inputs from a mouse or a keystroke.
- Biometric devices capture raw biometric data, such as fingerprints and voice, in a form that can be digitized and stored in a database for matching the patterns for identification and authentication.

GLOSSARY

3D printing The process in which a digital model is turned into a tangible, solid, three-dimensional object, usually by laying down many successive, thin layers of a material

Impact printer A printer that works by striking an inked ribbon against the paper

Input device A device that is used to feed data and instructions into the computer

Optical character recognition The process of converting printed materials into text or word processing files that can be easily edited and stored

Optical device A device that uses light as a source of input for detecting or recognizing different objects

Optical mark recognition The process of electronically extracting data from marked fields, such as checkboxes and fill in fields, on printed forms

Output device A device that is used to present information from the computer to the user

Pointing device A device that enables the users to easily control the movement of the pointer to select items on a display screen, to select commands from the command menu, to draw graphics, etc.

Printer A device that takes the text and graphics information obtained from a computer and prints it on paper

Slicing The process of breaking down a virtual model into many layers for printing using a 3D printer.

EXERCISES

Fill in the Blanks

1. _______ is used to feed data and instructions into the computer.
2. _______ captures everything on the screen as an image.
3. The movement of an optical mouse is detected using ________ waves.
4. _______ is used to enter information or write on the touchscreen of a phone.
5. A barcode reader is connected to the computer through a ________ port.
6. _______ technology is used for electronically extracting data from marked fields.

7. _______ converts analog signals generated through a microphone into digital data.
8. _______ capture videos that can be transferred via the Internet in real-time.
9. _______ allow the users to talk and listen at the same time.
10. The resolution of a printer means _______.
11. Any wireless device require a _______ and a _______.
12. _______ keyboards need a direct line-of-sight for connection.
13. A wireless _______ transmits user's voice to its receiver.
14. Wi-Fi printers can connect to the internet _______ to provide its services to other devices.
15. _______ which is a combination of living cells and polymergel.
16. _______ headphones deliver CD-quality audio.
17. 3D printer accepts the design model from a _______ or a _______.

Multiple-choice Questions

1. Which keys are used by applications and operating systems to perform specific commands?
   (a) Typing keys (b) Arrow keys
   (c) Control keys (d) Function keys
2. Select the optical devices from the following options:
   (a) MICR (b) Barcode reader
   (c) Scanner (d) All of these
3. Select the printer that uses impact printer technology from the following options:
   (a) Daisy wheel (b) Laser
   (c) Band (d) Inkjet
4. Select the pointing devices from the following options:
   (a) Keyboard (b) Barcode reader
   (c) Joystick (d) Touchscreen
5. Which type of screen is used in gaming devices, clocks, watches, calculators, and telephones?
   (a) LCD (b) Plasma
   (c) CRT (d) All of these

State True or False

1. Home and End keys move the cursor to the previous and next page, respectively.
2. Pointing devices can be connected to the USB port of a computer.
3. The movement of the cordless mouse is detected using laser technology.
4. OCR is used to verify the legitimacy or originality of paper documents.
5. The monitor is a soft copy output device.
6. Non-impact printers create characters by striking an inked ribbon against the paper.
7. A laser printer uses the same technology used in photocopier machines.
8. A plotter is used to print vector graphics.
9. A mouse cannot be used with a laptop computer.
10. Soft copy output devices are those that produce a physical form of output.
11. The receiver for a wireless mouse is connected to the computer wirelessly.
12. Bluetooth keyboard is only effective over a short range.
13. Wired speakers are prone to signal interference from other household gadgets.

Review Questions

1. How does a keyboard work?
2. Explain the working of different types of mouse.
3. How is OCR technology better than an ordinary image scanner?
4. How does MICR technology help to detect fraud in cheque payments?
5. Web cameras can be used to check security in a bank. Comment.
6. How are projectors used to display information to a user?
7. How are headsets better than speakers and headphones?
8. Differentiate between impact and non-impact printers.
9. Can characters of different fonts be printed with a band printer?
10. Why is a line printer preferred over a dot matrix printer? If you have an image to be printed, which out of the two will you use and why?
11. Under which situation, will you prefer to use an inkjet printer over a laser printer?
12. How is a plotter different from a printer?
13. Explain the variants of plotters.
14. What are input devices? Discuss the different types of input devices in detail.
15. Give a detailed note on different output devices.
16. How is a touchpad better than a trackball?
17. Which pointing input device would you prefer to use, mouse or trackball? Justify your answer.
18. List the applications of touchscreen.
19. What are optical input devices? Where are they used and for what purpose?
20. Differentiate between a soft copy and a hard copy output.
21. Which factors will you consider while purchasing a monitor for your personal computer? After considering the factors, which monitor will you buy?
22. What is a data projector? How is it different from a computer screen?
23. How does a wireless mouse communicate with the computer?
24. Give the advantages and limitations of wireless keyboard.
25. Explain the main components of a wireless mic system.
26. Compare different types of wireless headphones present in the market.
27. List the steps involved in the process of transmitting-receiving audio signals through wireless headphones. Write a short note on 3D printers.

LAB ACTIVITY 2: HANDLING INPUT AND OUTPUT DEVICES

Activity I: Adding a Printer to Your Computer

Step 1: Connect the printer to your computer using the USB cable and turn it on.

Step 2: Open the Settings app from the Start menu.

Step 3: Click Devices.

Step 4: Click Add a printer or scanner. You will get a screen as shown in Figure B.1.

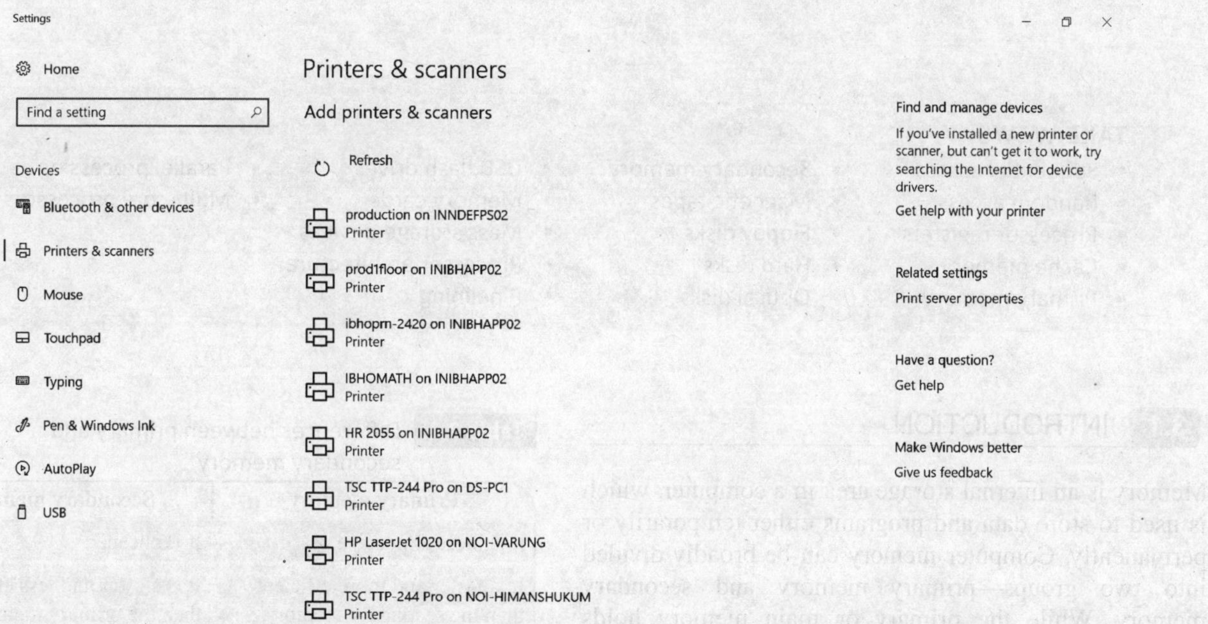

Figure B.1

Step 5: Click on the name of the printer and select Add device.

Step 6: If the printer is not in the list, select The printer that I want isn't listed.

Step 7: Select Add a local printer or network printer with manual settings button and click Next.

Step 8: Choose a printer port. (You can use an existing port and click on Next.)

Step 9: Select the manufacturer and model of the printer and click Next. The printer will be installed.

Activity II: Customizing Mouse Settings in Windows 10

Step 1: Click on the Search button (🔍) and type Control Panel.

Step 2: Click on Mouse option. The Mouse Properties window will open.

Step 3: In the Buttons tab:

(a) Under the Button configuration, click on Switch primary and secondary buttons checkbox to swap the functionality of left and right mouse buttons.

(b) To increase or decrease the Double-click speed, move the Speed slider towards either Slow or Fast. With this you can change how quickly you must click the buttons to perform a double-click.

(c) To drag the mouse without holding the mouse button, check the Turn on ClickLock.

(d) Click on Apply and Ok to save the changes

Click Pointers tab to customize the mouse pointer:

(a) To give your pointers a new look, click on a new mouse pointer scheme from the dropbox.

(b) To change an individual pointer, click on the pointer you want to change in the Customize list. Then click on Browse, select the pointer you want to use, and click Open.

(c) Click on Apply and Ok to save the changes.

Click Pointer Options tab:

(a) In the Motion option, move the slider to increase or decrease the pointer speed.

(b) To speed up the process of selecting a choice when a dialog box appears, use the Snap To option and select the Automatically move pointer to the default button in a dialog box checkbox.

(c) To make the pointer work more accurately when it is moved slowly, under Motion, click on the Enhance pointer precision checkbox.

(d) To find a misplaced pointer by pressing the CTRL key, under Visibility, click on the Show location of pointer when I press the CTRL key checkbox.

(e) Click on Apply and Ok to save the changes.

3 Computer Memory and Processors

TAKEAWAYS

- Sequential access
- Random access
- Processor registers
- Cache memory
- Primary memory
- Secondary memory
- Magnetic tapes
- Floppy disks
- Hard disks
- Optical disks
- USB flash drives
- Memory cards
- Mass storage devices
- Processor architecture
- Pipelining
- Parallel processing
- Multi-core processors

3.1 INTRODUCTION

Memory is an internal storage area in a computer, which is used to store data and programs either temporarily or permanently. Computer memory can be broadly divided into two groups—primary memory and secondary memory. While the primary or main memory holds instructions and data when a program is executing, the secondary or auxiliary memory holds data and programs that are not currently in use and provides long-term storage.

To execute a program, all the instructions and data that have to be used by the CPU are loaded into the main memory. However, the primary memory is volatile and it can retain data only when the power is on. Moreover, it is very expensive and therefore limited in capacity.

On the contrary, the secondary memory stores data and instructions permanently, even when the power is turned off. It is cheaper and can store large volumes of data. Moreover, data stored in the auxiliary memory is highly portable, as users can easily move it from one computer to another. The only drawback of the secondary memory is that data can be accessed from it at very low speeds as compared with the data access speed of the primary memory. Table 3.1 lists the differences between primary and secondary memory.

Table 3.1 Differences between primary and secondary memory

Primary memory	Secondary memory
It is more expensive.	It is cheaper.
It is faster and more efficient than the secondary memory.	It is slower and less efficient than the primary memory.
It is directly accessed by the CPU.	It cannot be accessed directly by the CPU.
It is volatile in nature.	It is non-volatile in nature.
Storage capacity is limited.	It has large storage capacity.
It has no moving parts.	It has moving parts.
The memory is power-dependent.	The memory is power independent.
Memory is integrated, circuit based.	Memory is magnetic or optical-based.
It consumes less power.	It consumes more power.
It stores data temporarily.	It stores data permanently.

3.2 MEMORY ORGANIZATION

The internal structure of the main memory is made of storage units which can store a binary digit (either 0 or 1). This smallest unit of data is known as a *bit* (short for binary digit). A group of four bits is called a *nibble*, and a group of eight bits is called a *byte*. The main memory can be best considered as a matrix of words, where a *word* is the smallest unit of memory that has an independent address. The number of bits in a word depends on the processor design. Most modern processors have a word size of 8, 16, 24, 32, or 64 bits. Memory could be either byte-addressable or word-addressable. In a byte-addressable memory unit, every addressable unit (or location) can store a byte (or 8 bits). Similarly, in a word-addressable memory unit, every addressable unit can store a word (16 bits). This means that every 16 bits have a unique address. Present-day computers, however, use double-word (32 bit) or quad-word (64 bit) addressable memory units.

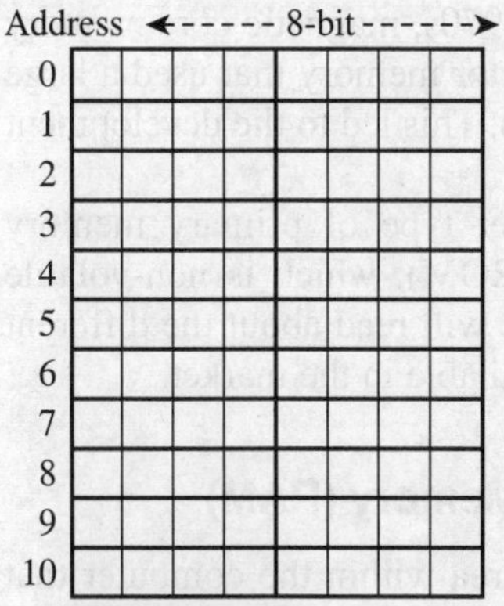

Figure 3.1 Memory organization

Figure 3.1 shows a 2D organization of byte-addressable memory. Every cell stores a bit and every row stores a byte (or a group of 8 bits). In a byte-addressable memory, 8 bits can be read or written simultaneously. Similarly, in a 64-bit (quad-word) memory organization, 64 bits can be read or written simultaneously. This clearly indicates that more the number of bits in each addressable unit, faster is data access.

3.3 MEMORY HIERARCHY

In contemporary usage, *memory* usually refers to random access memory (RAM), typically dynamic RAM (DRAM), but it can also refer to other forms of data storage. In computer terminology, the term *storage* refers to storage devices that are not directly accessible by the CPU (i.e. secondary storage). Examples of secondary storage include hard disk drives, optical disk drives, and other devices that are slower than RAM but are used to store data permanently.

These days, computers use different types of memory, which can be organized in the hierarchy as shown in Figure 3.2. As we can see from the figure, there is a trade-off between performance and cost. Memory at the higher levels in the storage hierarchy have lesser capacity to store data, are more expensive, and are faster to access.

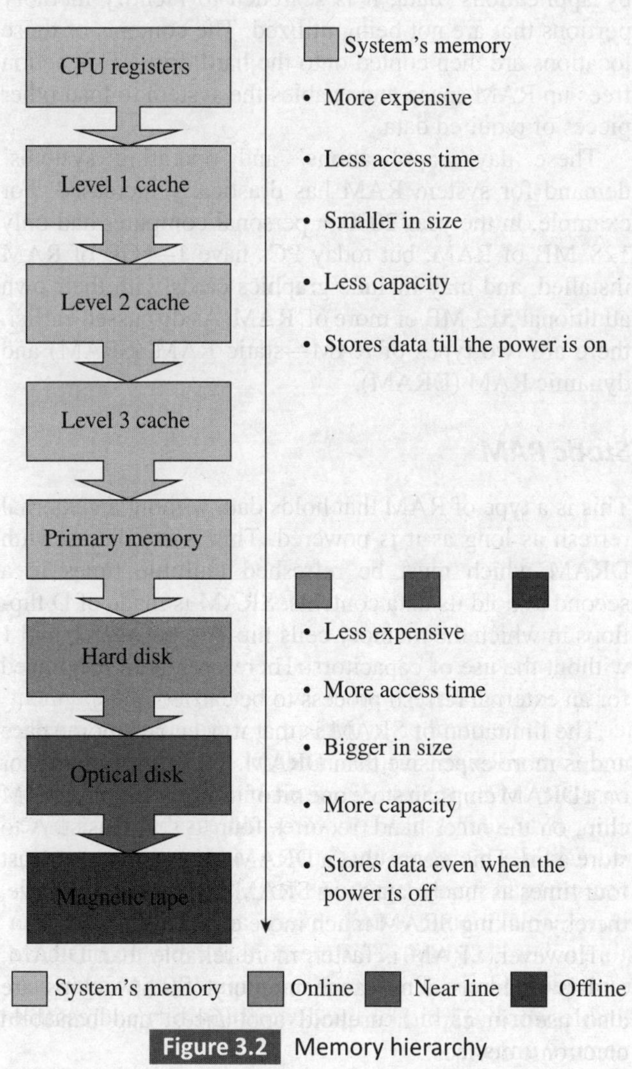

Figure 3.2 Memory hierarchy

3.4 SEQUENTIAL AND RANDOM ACCESS

Memory devices can be accessed either randomly or sequentially. The method of access has a great impact on application efficiency in terms of disk usage. Therefore, we must understand the differences between these two access methods which are listed in Table 3.2.

Table 3.2 Differences between sequential and random access

Sequential access	Random access
Data is read sequentially in a specified order. 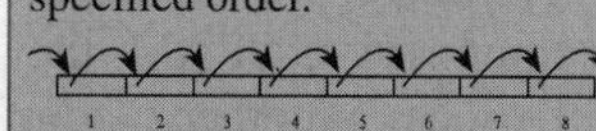	Data is read in an arbitrary manner. 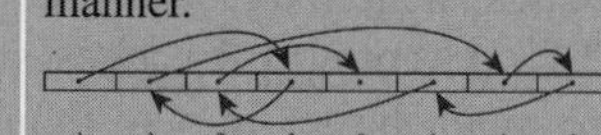
If the 99th record is desired after the 1st one, then all the records have to be traversed to reach the desired one. Therefore, the time required to return data varies depending on the position of the record.	Random access always returns data in constant time.
Sequential access devices can store a large number of records at a very low cost.	Random access devices are expensive than sequential access devices.
Magnetic tapes support sequential access.	RAM supports random access.
Sequential access is faster if records are to be accessed in the same order.	Random access is faster if records are to be accessed in a random order.

Note

If the need of an application is to access all the records in order then sequential access is the preferred choice.

3.5 PROCESSOR REGISTERS

Processor registers are located inside the processor and are therefore directly accessed by the CPU. Each register stores a word of data (which is either 32 or 64 bits in present-day computers). CPU instructions instruct the arithmetic and logic unit (ALU) to perform various calculations or other operations on the data. Registers are the fastest among all types of computer data storage.

3.6 CACHE MEMORY

Cache memory is an intermediate form of storage between the ultra-fast CPU registers and the primary memory. The CPU uses cache memory to store instructions and data that are repeatedly required to execute programs, thereby improving the overall system speed and increasing the performance of the computer.

Cache memory is widely used for memory caching. It is a portion of memory made of high-speed static RAM (SRAM) instead of the slower and cheaper dynamic RAM (DRAM) which is used for main memory. Maintaining frequently accessed data and instructions in the cache helps in avoiding the need to access the slower DRAM repeatedly.

Some memory caches are in-built in the architecture of microprocessors. For example, the Intel 80486 microprocessor has an 8K memory cache, and the Pentium E2160 has a 1 MB cache. Such *internal caches* are often called level 1 (L1) caches. However, modern PCs also come with external cache memory, called level 2 (L2) caches, which are built onto the motherboard outside the CPU. Although L2 caches are composed of SRAM, they are much larger in size than L1 caches. Another type of cache, called level 3 (L3), is an extra cache that has a much larger size than L1 and L2 caches, but is slower than them (but faster than RAM).

Working of the Cache Memory

When a program is being executed and the CPU wants to read data or instructions, the following steps are performed:

The CPU first checks whether the data or instruction is available in the cache memory. If it is not present there, the CPU reads the data or instructions from the main memory into the processor registers and also copies it into the cache memory. When the same piece of data/instruction is needed again, the CPU reads it from the cache memory instead of the main memory.

3.7 PRIMARY MEMORY

Primary memory (or main memory or internal memory) can be directly accessed by the CPU. The CPU continuously reads instructions stored in the primary memory and executes them. Any data that has to be operated by the CPU is also stored there.

Historically, early computers used delay lines, William's tubes, or rotating magnetic drums as primary storage. From 1954 to 1970s, magnetic core memory became the dominant technology to be used as the primary memory of computers. Later, in the 1970s, magnetic core memory was replaced by semiconductor memory that used a large number of integrated circuits. This led to the development of modern RAM.

However, there is another type of primary memory called read-only memory (ROM), which is non-volatile in nature. In this section, we will read about the different types of RAM and ROM available in the market.

3.7.1 Random Access Memory (RAM)

RAM is a volatile storage area within the computer that is typically used to store data temporarily, so that it can be promptly accessed by the processor. The information stored in the RAM is loaded from the computer's hard disk, and includes data related to the operating system and applications that are currently being executed by the processor.

RAM is called *random access* because any memory cell can be directly accessed if its address is known. When the RAM gets full, the computer system operates at a slow speed. When multiple applications are being executed simultaneously and the RAM gets fully occupied by applications' data, it is searched to identify memory portions that are not being utilized. The contents of those locations are then copied onto the hard drive. This action frees up RAM space and enables the system to load other pieces of required data.

These days, applications' and operating systems' demand for system RAM has drastically increased. For example, in the year 2000, a personal computer had only 128 MB of RAM, but today PCs have 1–4 GB of RAM installed, and may include graphics cards with their own additional 512 MB or more of RAM. As discussed earlier, there are two types of RAM—static RAM (SRAM) and dynamic RAM (DRAM).

Static RAM

This is a type of RAM that holds data without an external refresh as long as it is powered. This is in contrast with DRAM which must be refreshed multiple times in a second to hold its data contents. SRAM is made of D flip-flops in which the memory cells flip-flop between 0 and 1 without the use of capacitors. Therefore, there is no need for an external refresh process to be carried out.

The limitation of SRAM is that it occupies more space and is more expensive than DRAM. While each transistor on a DRAM chip can store one bit of information, an SRAM chip, on the other hand, requires four to six transistors to store a bit. This means that a DRAM chip can hold at least four times as much data as an SRAM chip of the same size, thereby making SRAM much more expensive.

However, SRAM is faster, more reliable than DRAM, and is often used as cache memory. SRAM chips are also used in cars, household appliances, and handheld electronic devices.

Dynamic RAM

This is the most common type of memory used in personal computers, workstations, and servers today. A DRAM chip contains millions of tiny memory cells. Each cell is made up of a transistor and a capacitor, and can contain one bit of information—0 or 1. To store a bit of information in a DRAM chip, a tiny amount of power is put into the cell to charge the capacitor. Hence, while reading a bit, the transistor checks for a charge in the capacitor. If a charge is present, then the reading is 1; if not, the reading is 0.

However, the problem with DRAM is that the capacitor leaks energy very quickly and can hold the charge for only a fraction of a second. Therefore, a refresh process is required to maintain the charge in the capacitor so that it can retain the information. This refresh process is carried out multiple times in a second and requires that all cells be accessed, even if the information is not needed.

However, the advantage of DRAM over SRAM is that it is cheaper, can hold more data per chip, and generates less heat than SRAM. DRAM is widely used to build main memory. The following are the different types of DRAM:

Synchronous DRAM (SDRAM) SDRAM synchronizes itself with the clock speed of the microprocessor to enable faster access to memory.

Enhanced SDRAM (ESDRAM) This version of SDRAM, though not widely used, includes a small SRAM cache to reduce delays in data access and to speed up operations.

Double data rate SDRAM (DDR) DDR allows data transfers on both the rising and falling edges of the clock cycle, which doubles the data throughput. DDR SDRAM chips are available in capacities of 128 MB to 1 GB. Although DDR memory is very common, the technology is becoming outdated and is being replaced by DDR2.

DDR2 These chips are the next generation of DDR SDRAM memory. They can hold 256 MB to 2 GB of memory and can operate at higher bus speeds. Although DDR2 has twice the latency (data access delays) of DDR, it delivers data at twice the speed, thereby performing at the same level.

3.7.2 Read-only Memory (ROM)

ROM refers to computer memory chips containing permanent or semi-permanent data. Unlike RAM, ROM is non-volatile; that is, the data is retained in it even after the computer is turned off.

Most computers store critical programs such as the basic input/output system (BIOS) in ROM, which is used to boot up the computer when it is turned on. The BIOS consists of a few kilobytes of code that instructs the computer what to do when it starts up, such as running hardware diagnostics and loading the operating system into the RAM. Moreover, ROMs are used extensively in calculators and peripheral devices such as laser printers, whose fonts are often stored in ROMs.

Originally, ROMs were read-only. Thus, in order to update the programs stored in them, ROM chips had to be removed and physically replaced by another that had a newer version of the programs. However, today ROM chips are not literally read-only, as updates to the chip are possible. The process of updating a ROM chip is a bit slower, as memory must be erased in large portions before it can be rewritten. Rewritable ROM chips include PROMs, EPROMs, and EEPROMs.

Programmable Read-only Memory (PROM)

It is also called one-time programmable ROM, and can be written to or programmed using a special device called a PROM programmer. The PROM programmer uses high voltages to permanently destroy or create internal links (fuses or anti-fuses) within the chip. The working of a PROM programmer is similar to that of a CD-ROM recorder, which enables users to burn programs onto blank CDs. The recorded or the burnt data can be read multiple times. Therefore, programming a PROM is also called *burning*, just like burning a CD-R.

Erasable Programmable Read-only Memory (EPROM)

It is a type of ROM that can be erased and re-programmed. EPROM can be erased by exposing the chip to strong ultraviolet light, typically for 10 minutes or longer, and can then be rewritten with a process that again needs the application of high voltages. Repeated exposure to ultraviolet light wears out the chip. EPROM is much more useful than PROM and can be compared with a reusable CD-RW.

Electrically Erasable Programmable Read-only Memory (EEPROM)

It is based on a semiconductor structure similar to EPROM, but allows the entire or selected contents to be electrically erased, then rewritten electrically, so that they need not be removed from the computer. The process of writing an EEPROM is also known as *flashing*.

Flash memory is also a type of EEPROM in which the contents can be erased under software control. This is the most flexible type of ROM, and is widely used to store BIOS programs. It is primarily used in memory cards, USB flash drives, laptop computers, digital audio players, digital cameras, and mobile phones. EEPROM blurs the difference between read-only and read-write. However, EEPROM is rewritten only once a year or so, compared to real read–write memory (RAM), where rewriting is often done many times per second.

Table 3.3 differentiates between RAM and ROM.

Table 3.3 Differences between RAM and ROM

RAM	ROM
Data can be read as well as written.	Data can only be read.
Data bus connecting RAM is bi-directional.	Data bus connecting ROM is unidirectional.
Stores data temporarily.	Stores data permanently.
Data is stored while computer is being used by users to hold their data.	Data is stored during the time of fabrication.
It is required while computer is being used to run applications.	It is required for booting or starting the computer and for storing important drivers and system software.

Note

(a) By applying write protection, some types of reprogrammable ROMs may temporarily become read-only memory. .
(b) In practice, both RAM and ROM support random access of memory.

3.7.3 Finding Required Data from Main Memory

The main memory is organized as a matrix of bits, as shown in Figure 3.1. A matrix of bits means a combination of rows and columns storing bits. The main memory, which holds data and programs for execution, is directly or indirectly connected to the processor via a *bus*. There are two buses, an address bus and a data bus. The CPU first sends a number through the address bus. This number denotes the memory address of the desired data. Then it reads or writes the data using the data bus.

3.8 SECONDARY STORAGE DEVICES

Secondary memory (also known as external memory or auxiliary memory) differs from main memory in that it is not directly accessible by the CPU. Secondary storage devices hold data even when the computer is switched off. An example of such a device is a hard disk.

The computer usually uses its input/output channels to access data from secondary storage devices to transfer the data to an intermediate area in the main memory. Secondary storage devices are non-volatile in nature, cheaper than the primary memory, and can be used to store huge amounts of data. While the CPU can read the data stored in the main memory in nanoseconds, the data from the secondary storage devices can be accessed in milliseconds.

Secondary storage devices are formatted according to a file system that organizes the data into files and directories. The file system also provides additional information such as the owner of a certain file, the access time, the access permissions, and other information.

3.8.1 Offline Storage

Offline storage devices are those on which data is recorded and then they are physically removed or disconnected (off the computer, hence the name). Such devices include magnetic tapes, floppy disks, optical disks, flash memory devices, and external hard disks. In order to access data from an offline storage device, it must first be connected to a computer.

Offline storage devices are widely used to store a backup of important data. For example, if the original data gets destroyed in case of a system crash, the data can be recovered from the offline devices, which are usually stored in another distant place. Moreover, offline storage also provides security of critical data since these devices are physically inaccessible by a computer, and therefore data confidentiality or integrity cannot be affected by malicious software.

3.9 MAGNETIC TAPES

Figure 3.3 Magnetic tape

Magnetic tapes (shown in Figure 3.3) are mass storage devices capable of backing up and retaining large volumes of data. A magnetic tape, which resembles an audio tape, is a thin strip of plastic coated with magnetic recording material. These storage devices are used as sequential access secondary storage devices.

Magnetic tapes are available in the form of cassettes, reels, and cartridges, with reels being most widely used. Reels that are used with mini and mainframe computers are 1/2 inch wide and 2400 feet long. Such a tape can store 1600 characters per inch of the tape length.

Storage capacity of magnetic tape
= Data recording density × Length of the tape

Here, data recording density is the amount of data that can be stored on a given length of tape. It is measured in bytes per inch (bpi), and usually varies from 800 to 77,000 bpi. For example, a tape of length 2400 feet with 1000 bpi as its storage density has a storage capacity of $2400 \times 12 \times 1000 = 2,88,00,000 = 28 \times 10^6 = 28$ MB.

However, as of now, magnetic tapes with storage capacity of up to 35 trillion bytes (terabytes) of data are easily available in the market.

Data representation On a magnetic tape, data is recorded in the form of tiny non-magnetized and magnetized spots, where the presence of a spot represents 1 and its absence represents 0. This means that data is stored in the form of 0s and 1s. For example, 'A' is stored as 1011 on the tape. Data on a tape is represented using the EBCDIC standard. (We will read about computer codes in Chapter 4.) However, the data stored on a tape can be accessed only in a sequential fashion. Unlike magnetic disks, flash drives, optical disks, and floppy disks, magnetic tapes do not support random access of data.

On a tape, data is stored in terms of records, with individual records separated by a gap known as the inter-record gap. In addition, when records are short, they may be grouped to form blocks. The data stored in the form of blocks will then have inter-block spacing.

Magnetic tape drive A tape drive is used to read and write data on a magnetic tape. The tape drive unit consists of a supply reel, a take-up reel, a read/write (R/W) head, and an erase head. When a user has to edit/rewrite the pre-recorded data on a tape, the previously recorded data is erased by the erase head and the new data is recorded. The process of recording data is much similar to that of recording on an audio tape or audio cassette.

Usage A magnetic tape can store large amounts of information and is therefore used in the regular backing up of hard disks.

Advantages

- A magnetic tape is compact in size, light in weight, and can store large amounts of data. Therefore, tapes are easily portable and can be used to transfer data from one computer to another.
- Magnetic tapes are economical. The cost of storing data is very less as compared to other storage devices.
- Copying of data on a magnetic tape is easy and fast.
- Magnetic tapes can be used for long-term data storage and retrieval.
- Tape drives use less power.
- Tape drives can easily be stored offsite, allowing data to survive even if the computer itself is destroyed or stolen.

Disadvantages

- Data stored on tapes can be accessed only sequentially.
- As compared to other storage devices, data on tapes is accessed at very slow speeds because of sequential access.
- Special hardware is required to read the data stored on tapes, and most standard PCs available today do not come with such hardware.
- With advancements in technology, hard drives have become cheaper than tapes and are therefore being increasingly used for backups.
- Magnetic tapes are easily susceptible to degradation due to heat, humidity, dust, mishandling, electromagnetic surfaces, and ordinary wear.
- Magnetic tapes are best suited for full-system restores and not for restoring of individual files. This is because finding and restoring individual files can be a long, slow, and cumbersome process.

3.10 FLOPPY DISKS

Floppy disks (shown in Figure 3.4) are data storage devices which consist of a thin magnetic storage medium encased in a square plastic shell lined with fabric that removes dust particles. The storage capacity of floppy disks is very limited as compared to optical disks and flash drives. Although floppy disks are inexpensive, they are much slower than other data storage devices. Moreover, floppy disks must be handled with utmost care as they are vulnerable to damage from mishandling. For example, data stored on a floppy disk can be lost if the disk is bended, removed while in use, or exposed to excessive temperature, dust, or smoke.

Figure 3.4 Floppy disk

© Photodisc/OUP Picture Bank

Floppy disks were widely used from the mid-1970s till early 2000s to distribute software, transfer data, and create backups. They are no longer used as they have been superseded by flash drives, external hard drives, optical disks, and memory cards.

The mechanism of a floppy disk involves two motors. While one motor in the drive rotates the diskette at a regulated speed, the second motor moves the magnetic R/W head (or heads, if a double-sided drive) along the surface of the disk. To read/write data on the disk media, there must be physical contact between the R/W head and the disk media. Figure 3.5 shows the internal parts of a floppy disk.

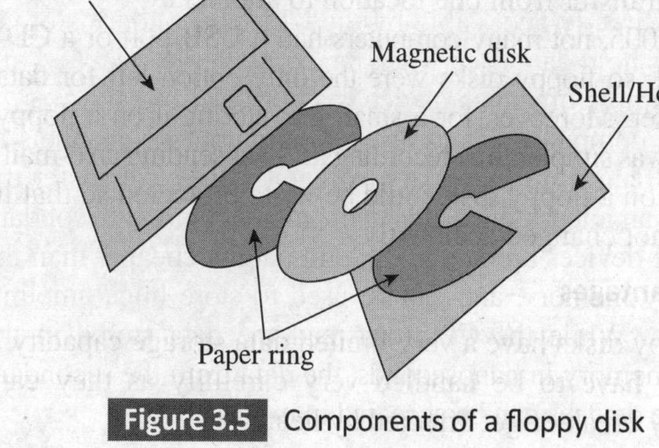

Figure 3.5 Components of a floppy disk

Reading/writing data In order to write data on a floppy disk, current is passed through a coil in the head. The magnetic field of the coil magnetizes spots on the disk as it rotates. The change in magnetization encodes the digital data.

Similarly, to read data from the floppy disk, a small amount of current is induced in the head coil to detect the magnetization on the disk. The floppy drive controller separates the data from the stream of pulses coming from the floppy drive, decodes the data, tests for errors, and sends the data to the host computer system.

Tracks and sectors A blank floppy disk has a pattern of magnetized tracks, each broken into sectors. The tracks on the floppy disk have some spaces between the tracks where no data is written. Similarly, there are spaces between the sectors and at the end of the track to allow for slight speed variations in the disk drive. Usually some padding bytes are written on these spaces, which are discarded by the floppy disk controller.

Moreover, each data sector has a header that stores the sector location on the disk. An error checking code is also written into the sector headers and at the end of the user data, so that the diskette controller can detect errors when reading the data.

Storage capacity All 3.5 inch floppy disks are double-sided. They have 80 sectors, 18 sectors/track, and can store 512 bytes/sector.

Therefore the storage capacity of a floppy disk

$= 2 \times 80 \times 18 \times 512$ bytes

$= 14{,}74{,}560$ bytes $= 1.47$ MB

At the time of their introduction, floppy disks had many advantages over the existing storage technologies, such as tapes and hard disks.

Advantages

- Floppy disks were cheaper.
- Once data or files were written, users could access the data several times.
- Because of their small size, they were easily portable and easy to handle.
- Unlike magnetic tapes, floppy disks provided random access.
- Unlike hard disks, floppy disks could be easily used for data transfer from one location to another.
- Till 2005, not many computers had a USB port or a CD-ROM, so floppy disks were the only option left for data transfer. Moreover, for a small file, storing it on a floppy disk was simpler than recording a CD or sending an e-mail.
- Data on a floppy disk could be write protected so that it was not changed accidently.

Disadvantages

- Floppy disks have a very limited data storage capacity.
- They have to be handled very carefully as they can easily break or get affected by heat.
- Data on a floppy disk gets easily corrupted if there are some scratches on the disk. So they are not very reliable.
- Data access from a floppy disk is done at a very slow speed.
- Data can be erased if the disk comes into contact with another magnetic device.

3.11 HARD DISKS

A hard disk drive is a secondary storage device that stores all the programs and files and provides relatively quick access to large amounts of data stored on an electromagnetically charged surface or a set of surfaces (refer Figure 3.6). Today, PCs come with hard disks that can store 1 TB (where 1 TB = 1000 GB) of data. A hard disk is basically a set of disks, stacked together like phonograph records.

Figure 3.6 Hard disk drive

© Zadorozhnyi Viktor/Shutterstock

The parts of a hard disk are shown in Figure 3.7. A single hard disk includes several *platters* (or disks) that are covered with a magnetic recording medium. Each platter requires two R/W heads, one for each side. Note that in the figure, all the R/W heads are attached to a single access arm so they cannot move independently.

A R/W head can move back and forth over the platters to read or write data on them. Data is actually stored on the surface of a platter in *sectors* and *tracks* (refer Figure 3.8). While tracks are concentric circles, sectors on the other

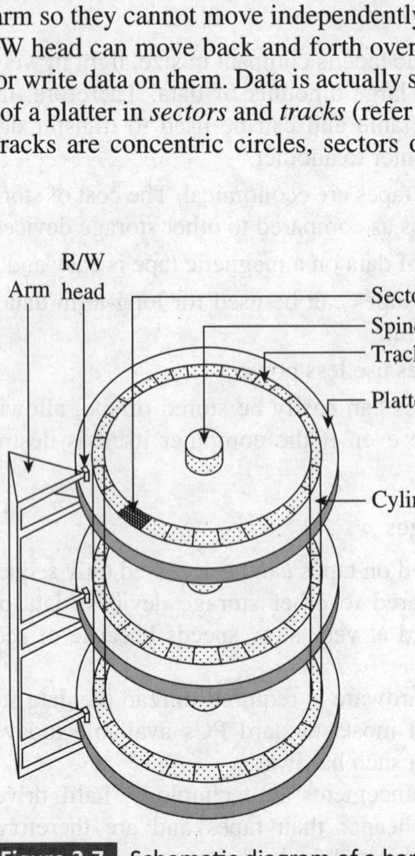

Figure 3.7 Schematic diagram of a hard disk

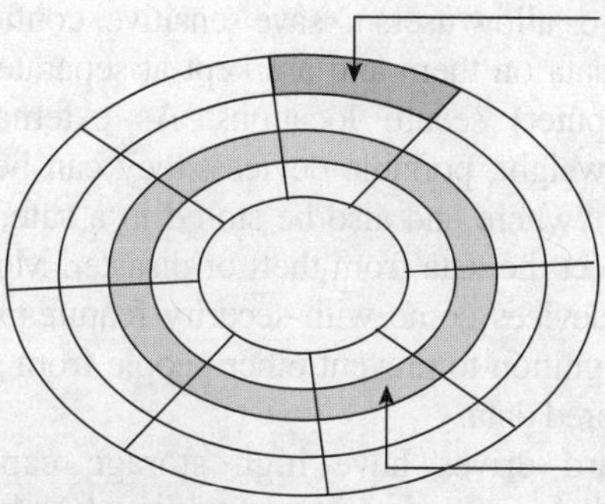

Figure 3.8 Cross-section of a cylinder

hand are pie-shaped wedges on a track. Thus, a track is divided into a number of sectors (also called segments) that can store a fixed number of bytes—for example, 256 or 512. Tracks are numbered consecutively from outermost to innermost, starting from zero. The number of tracks on a disk can vary from 40 on low-capacity disks to several thousands on high-capacity disks.

Moreover, each platter has the same number of tracks, and a track location that cuts across all platters is called a *cylinder*. In simple terminology, a cylinder is vertically formed by tracks. For example, track 2 on platter 0, plus track 2 on platter 1, plus track 2 on platter *n* is cylinder 2. The number of cylinders of a disk drive is equal to the number of tracks on a single platter of the disk.

When a computer is turned on, platters in the hard disk drive immediately begin to spin. While the platters in a desktop computer's hard disk drive rotate 7200 times per minute, the hard drives in laptop computers usually make 5400 rotations per minute (rpm). The steady hum that we hear when a computer is turned on is the noise of a hard disk spinning. Even when we are not retrieving from or writing anything to the hard disk, the platters spin. However, the arm with the R/W head moves only when we run a program or open, save, or delete a file. The arm can move back and forth across the surface of the platters as many as 50 times in a second.

Note

A typical hard disk drive has two electric motors—a disk motor to spin the disks and an actuator (motor) to position the R/W head assembly across the spinning disks.

The R/W head does not actually touch the platters, instead it just barely skims above them, supported by a cushion of moving air that is generated by the spinning of the platters. The rapid motion of the platters and heads inside the hard disk drive makes it susceptible to head crash. Head crash can also occur if dust settles on the hard drive, thereby resulting in bouncing of the arm when the disk operates. During a head crash, the fragile magnetic recording medium gets ruined, resulting in a loss of the data stored in it. A user must very carefully move his or her laptop as moving it abruptly when it is switched on can lead to head crash.

The performance of a hard disk depends on its access time, which is the time required to read or write on the disk. Access time is a combination of the following three components:

Seek time This is the time taken to position the R/W head over the appropriate cylinder (usually around 8 ms on an average). Seek time varies depending on the position of the access arm when the R/W command is received. Its value will be maximum when the access arm is positioned over the innermost track while the data that has to be accessed is stored on the outermost track. Similarly, it will be zero if the access arm is already positioned over the desired track. On an average, the seek time varies from 10 to 100 ms.

Rotational delay This is the time taken to bring the target sector to rotate under the R/W head. Assuming that the hard disk spins at 7200 rpm, or 120 rotations per second, a single rotation is done in approximately 8 ms. The average rotational delay is around 4 ms.

Transfer time The time to transfer data or read/write to a disk is called the transfer rate.

Thus, the overall time required to access data = seek time + rotational delay + transfer time.

The sum of the seek time and the rotational delay is also known as *disk latency*. Disk latency is the time taken to initiate a transfer.

Note

The key to using hard drives effectively is to minimize disk latency. Ideally, this can be done by defragmentation, which moves related data to physically close areas on disks. Some computer operating systems perform defragmentation automatically.

To access data from a hard disk, a disk address has to be specified. The disk address represents the physical location of a record on the disk, and comprises the following components:

- Sector number
- Track number
- Surface number (when data is recorded on both sides of the disk)

The storage capacity of a disk with multiple recording surfaces can be calculated as:

Storage capacity = No. of recording surfaces × No. of tracks per surface × No. of sectors per track × No. of bytes per sector

Example 3.1

A hard disk has 10 disk plates, 2000 tracks per surface, 125 sectors per track, and 512 bytes of data can be stored per sector. Using this information, calculate the storage capacity of the disk.

Solution

The disk has 10 plates, which means 20 recording surfaces. However, in a double-sided disk, the upper surface of the first disk and the lower surface of the last disk are normally not used for recording data because these surfaces may be scratched easily.

Therefore, the storage capacity can be calculated as:

Storage capacity = 18 × 2000 × 125 × 512
= 2,30,40,00,000 bytes
= 2 × 10^9 bytes = approximately 2 GB

Advantages

- Magnetic disks enable random access of data, which is useful for all types of real-world applications.
- They can be used as a shared device in a multi-user environment.
- They are preferred for both online and offline storage of data.
- They can store large amounts of data. If required, multiple disks can be used.
- The cost of data storage is very low. With advancement in technology, the cost of magnetic disks has reduced and the capacity of data they can store has constantly increased.
- Data transfer rate of magnetic disks is much higher than that of the magnetic tapes.

Disadvantages

- They must be stored in a dust-free environment.
- They are larger in size and heavier in weight when compared to flash drives and optical disks.

3.12 EXTERNAL HARD DISKS

As the name suggests, an external hard disk (see Figure 3.9) is a drive that is located outside the computer case. It is used in addition to internal hard drives to store data. It has become quite popular because of its portability and high-storage capacity. It is connected to a computer system with a high-speed interface cable, usually with plug-and-play interfaces such as USB and FireWire, and may also contain a fan for cooling. While with USB connections, data can move at a rate of 12 to 480 Mbps (megabits per second), FireWire on the other hand can transfer data at speeds ranging from 400 to 800 Mbps. External hard drives can also be connected to computers wirelessly.

Figure 3.9 External hard disk
© Audrius Merfeldas/ Shutterstock

External drives allow users to save sensitive, confidential, and important data on them and are kept at separate (away from the computer) secure locations. As external hard drives are lightweight, portable devices, they can be easily carried away anywhere and also be stored in a safe, secure location to protect the data from theft or disaster. Moreover, some external devices come with security features such as fingerprint recognition to prevent other people from gaining access to the stored data.

External hard drives have high storage capacities. External hard disks with a storage capacity of 1–4 TB are very common these days. Therefore, they are often used to back up numerous computer files or serve as a network drive to store shared content.

They are extensively used by people who do audio/video editing. These media files require high-quality settings, and therefore consume a large amount of disk space.

Note

External hard disks are also called removable hard disks.

3.13 OPTICAL DISKS

Optical storage refers to storing data on an optically readable medium by making marks in a pattern that can be read using a beam of laser light precisely focused on a spinning disk. Optical storage devices are the most widely used and reliable storage devices. The most popular optical storage devices are CD-ROM, DVD-ROM, CD-Recordable, CD-Rewritable, etc.

Today, every computer contains a CD/DVD drive. A single CD or a DVD can hold a large amount of data, including software packages, movies, and songs. While some optical storage media are read-only, others are read- and write-enabled.

An optical storage medium consists of a flat, round, portable metal disk, which is usually 0.75 inches in diameter and less than $\frac{1}{20}$th of an inch thick. The disk is coated with a thin metal, or plastic, or other material that is highly reflective.

An optical disk stores information in the form of pits and lands (shown in Figure 3.10). Pits are tiny reflective

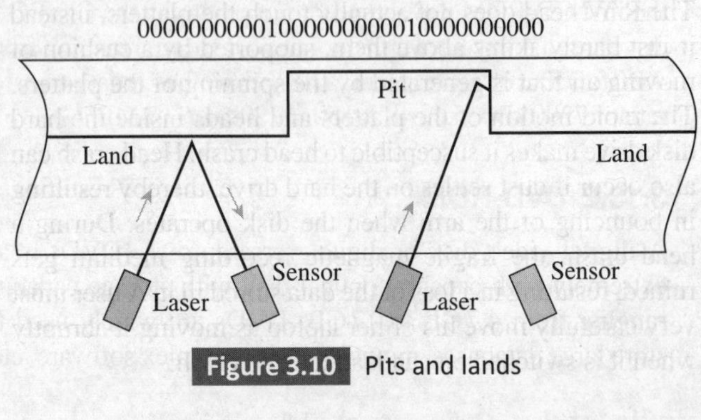

Figure 3.10 Pits and lands

bumps created with a laser beam and lands are flat areas separating the pits. While a land reflects the laser light and is read as binary digit 1, a pit on the other hand absorbs the light and is read as binary digit 0.

Similar to magnetic disks, optical disks also have tracks that are divided into sectors, but the shape of these sectors is different from that of sectors in magnetic disks. Different types of optical storage devices are explained in this section.

3.13.1 CD-ROM

Compact disk read-only memory (CD-ROM), shown in Figure 3.11, is a type of optical disk that uses laser technology to read data from and write data to the disk. A single CD-ROM can store a large amount of data, but once the information is stored, it becomes permanent and cannot be altered. This means that the stored information can only be read for processing, hence the name.

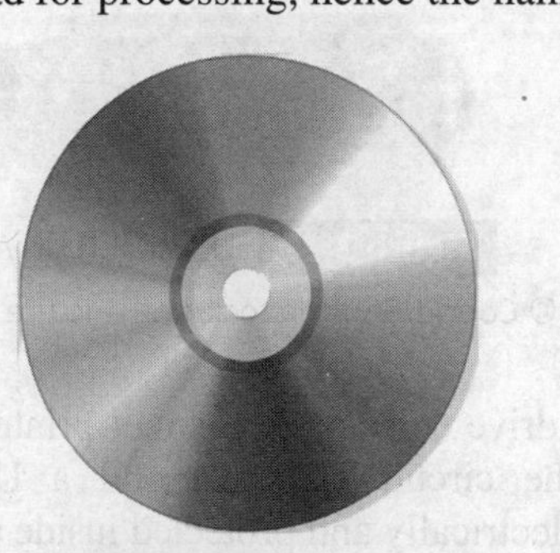

Figure 3.11 CD-ROM

© Italianphoto/Shutterstock/OUP Picture Bank

CDs are easily portable from one computer to another and are therefore used to transfer data from one computer to another (similar to a floppy disk). The storage capacity of a CD-ROM varies from 650 MB to 1 GB, which is 1000 times greater than that of a floppy disk. Most software products (such as Microsoft Office and Windows operating system) are available on CD-ROMs.

CD-ROM drive A CD-ROM drive is used to read the information stored on a CD-ROM. The data transfer rate of the first CD-ROM drive was 150 kB/s (kilobytes per second), and is denoted as X. The data transfer rate of a CD-ROM is much slower than that of a typical hard disk drive, which reads data at a rate of 5–15 MB/s (megabytes per second). The speeds of all CD-ROM drives are calculated relative to the first CD-ROM drive's speed. For example, the CD-ROM drives used today have transfer rates (or speeds) ranging from 48X to 75X, or more. Here, a 48X drive has a data transfer rate of 7200 kB/s (i.e., 48 × 150 = 7200) or 7.2 MB/s.

3.13.2 DVD-ROM

A digital video disk or digital versatile disk (DVD) is an extremely high-capacity optical disk with storage capacity ranging from 4.7 GB to 17 GB. DVDs are widely used to store large databases, movies, music, complex software, etc.

Most of the DVD-ROMs are double-sided disks, as they can store data on both the sides of the disk. Although a DVD-ROM resembles a CD-ROM in size and shape, it stores information in a different manner. A DVD-ROM drive is compatible with CD-ROM drives and can therefore read CDs.

A standard DVD can store seven times more data than a CD because of its multi-layer storage technique and the fact that the size of its pits and tracks is smaller. When data is recorded on a DVD, the laser starts on the inside of the disk and moves outward. The laser beam has a smaller wavelength and can be focused on two different layers on the disk. Data can be recorded on each of the layers, thereby doubling the storage capacity of the disk.

In a double-sided DVD-ROM, two such disks are stuck back-to-back to allow recording on both sides. However, such DVD-ROMs must be handled very carefully, as both sides have data stored on them and this data can be damaged accidentally due to mishandling.

3.13.3 CD-R

Compact disk recordable (CD-R) is a blank disk that can be used to store information. For example, users can use it to store their databases, software, projects, assignments, etc.

The process of writing data on an optical disk is called burning. A CD-R can be used in any CD-ROM drive and is functionally equivalent to a pre-recorded CD-ROM. However, once data is written on the CD-R, it cannot be changed. Moreover, users can continue to store data on other parts of the disk until it is full. However, each part of the CD-R can be written only once and can be read many times.

Today, many utility programs such as Nero Burning ROM are available in the market to write data on CD-Rs. CD-Rs are widely used to back up critical data. However, to record information on a CD-R, users must have a CD writer. A CD writer or recorder (or simply CD-R drive) can also read information from a CD. The speed of these drives is up to 48X or more, and they are more expensive than ordinary CD-ROM drives.

3.13.4 CD-RW

Compact disk rewritable (CD-RW) is a new generation of erasable optical disks. Users can write and overwrite data on CD-RW disks multiple times. However, the reliability of disks tends to decrease, each time we rewrite data. Both CD-Rs and CD-RWs can be used for taking backup of important data. Moreover, CD-RWs are also used to create audio CDs, so that users can record their own music or movies on purchased CDs.

A CD-RW drive is used to write data on a CD-RW. Such drives have read and write speeds up to 48X or more, but the re-write speed is 10X or more. A CD-RW drive is advanced and more expensive than a CD-R drive. A CD-RW drive is compatible with both CD-R and CD-RW, and can therefore read or write data on both CD-R and CD-RW disks.

3.13.5 Blu-Ray Disks

A Blu-ray disk is an optical disk developed by the Blu-ray Disc Association (BDA), which includes leading companies such as Apple, Dell, Hitachi, HP, JVC, LG, Mitsubishi, Panasonic, Pioneer, Philips, Samsung, Sharp, Sony, TDK, and Thomson. The format of a Blu-ray disk was specifically developed to bring forward a recordable, rewritable disk that can store large amount of data and display high-definition videos.

Although a Blu-ray disk has the same size as that of a CD or a DVD, it can store much more data than a DVD. A single-sided Blu-ray disk can store 25 GB of data and a dual-layer disk can store 50 GB of data. While CDs and DVDs use a red laser to read and write data, Blu-ray disks on the other hand use a blue-violet laser, hence the name Blu-ray. The advantage of using a blue laser with a shorter wavelength of 405 nm than a red laser (650 nm) is that it allows to focus the laser spot with even greater precision. This means that data can be packed more tightly and therefore stored in less space. Moreover, the storage capacity of this disk is enough to store a continuous backup copy of most people's hard drives on a single disk.

A Blu-ray disk player is backwards compatible with CDs and DVDs and can therefore play a CD or a DVD despite the differences between the types of laser used. However, Blu-ray disks cannot play on CD and DVD players, because those players lack the blue-violet laser required to read the disks.

Advantages

- Blu-ray disks have larger storage capacity as compared to CDs and DVDs.
- Data stored on Blu-ray disks can be copied only a certain number of times to help prevent piracy.
- They provide backward compatibility as Blu-ray drives can work with CDs as well as DVDs.
- Blu-ray disks can store HD video and thus provide a better picture quality than DVDs.

Disadvantages

- Blu-ray disks are more expensive than CDs or DVDs.
- To take advantage of the enhanced viewing experience offered by Blu-ray, users must connect the Blu-ray disk player to a HD television. Without HDTV, a Blu-ray video would be played with the same picture and sound quality as that provided by a DVD. Thus, a user has to spend more money when using a Blu-ray disk.
- A Blu-ray disk is not very durable as a slight scratch to the surface makes the disk unreadable. For this reason, newer Blu-ray disks come with a protective coating that helps to prevent surface scratches.
- Failure to install a Blu-ray firmware update on the Blu-ray player may result in the inability to play some new Blu-ray disks.

3.14 USB FLASH DRIVES

Universal Serial Bus (USB) flash drives or pen drives (Figure 3.12) are removable, rewritable, and are physically much smaller drives, weighing less than 30 g. The storage capacity of the USB flash drives available in the market varies from 8 GB to 1 TB. These devices are a good substitute for floppy disks and CD-ROMs as they are smaller, faster, have thousands of times more capacity, and are more durable and reliable. Until 2005, most desktop and laptop computers had floppy disk drives, but nowadays floppy disk drives have been completely replaced by USB ports.

Figure 3.12 USB flash drive

© Coprid/Shutterstock/OUP Picture Bank

A flash drive consists of a small printed circuit board carrying the circuit elements and a USB connector, insulated electrically and protected inside a plastic, metal, or rubberized case. The USB connector is often protected inside a removable cap, although it is not likely to be damaged if unprotected. USB flash drives draw power from the computer via external USB connection.

USB flash drives are useful in several ways:

Personal data transport Flash drives are used to transport and store personal files such as documents, pictures, and videos.

System administration Flash drives are widely used by system and network administrators to store configuration information and software used for system maintenance, troubleshooting, and recovery. They are also used to transfer recovery and antivirus software to infected PCs. As these drives have much larger storage capacity, they have also replaced CD-ROMs, which were earlier needed when reinstalling or updating a system.

Booting operating systems These days, PC firmware allows booting from USB drives. Such a configuration is known as a live USB.

Music storage and marketing Digital audio files stored on a USB flash drive can be easily transported from one computer to another and played on a compatible media player. Moreover, many home hi-fi and car stereo head units are now equipped with a USB port, so that flash drives can be connected to them.

Backup Many users (especially involved in business) use flash drives as a backup medium. However, one must remember that it is easy to lose them and easy for people without a right to the data to make illicit copies.

Newer flash drives have much higher estimated lifetimes and are therefore available with warranties of five years, or more. Moreover, flash drives have experienced an exponential growth in their storage capacity over time. Today, flash drives of 1 TB are not uncommon. This has made them a very good substitute for magnetic disks.

Advantages

- Data stored on flash drives is impervious to damages due to scratches and dust.
- Flash drives are mechanically very robust and computers these days come with a USB port, so they can be easily used to transfer data from one computer to another.
- Flash drives have higher data capacity than any other removable media.
- Compared to hard drives, flash drives use very little power and have no fragile moving parts.
- Flash drives are small and lightweight devices.
- Operating systems can read from and write to flash drives without installing device drivers.
- Specially manufactured flash drives have a tough rubber or metal casing designed to be waterproof and virtually unbreakable. The data stored in these flash drives does not get destroyed even when submerged in water. Leaving such a drive out to dry completely before allowing current to run through it has been known to recover the drive, with no further problems in the future.

Disadvantages

- Flash drives can sustain only a limited number of write and erase cycles before the drive fails. Therefore, flash drives are usually not a good option to run application software or operating systems.
- Most flash drives do not have a write-protect mechanism to prevent the host computer from writing or modifying data on the drive. Write-protection devices are highly recommended when repairing a virus-contaminated host computer as there is a risk of infecting the USB flash drive itself.
- Flash drives are very small devices that can easily be misplaced, left behind, or otherwise lost. This can at times be a serious problem, especially if the data is sensitive.
- The cost per unit of storage of a flash drive is higher than that of hard disks.

3.15 MEMORY CARDS

A memory card (sometimes called a *flash memory card* or a *storage card*; shown in Figure 3.13) is a small device that can store digital files. They are easily portable from one place to another. A user can take a memory card, insert it into portable electronic devices such as a laptop, store files such as text documents, pictures, audio files, and video files, and then remove the card and take it to another device where it can be again inserted to copy the files onto the local disk of that computer. PCs can access the data stored on flash memory cards using a memory card reader.

Figure 3.13 Memory card

© Ilya Akinshin/ Shutterstock/OUP Picture Bank

Technically, a memory card uses flash memory, which enables users to add/delete files multiple times. Initially, when flash cards were first introduced in the market, they were incredibly expensive. However, with advancements in technology, memory cards have become cheaper. Today, different types of memory cards are available in the market. These include compact flash memory (which is the largest in size but has the smallest capacity to store data), secure digmemory card (SD), miniSD card, microSD card, memory stick, and the multimedia card (MMC). As these cards have evolved, they have become smaller in size and larger in data capacity.

Most of these cards have constantly powered non-volatile memory, which means that data is retained on these cards even when there is no power supply to the computer, and they do not need to be periodically refreshed. Memory cards have no moving parts; therefore, they are unlikely to suffer from mechanical difficulties.

Since newer memory cards are smaller, require less power, have higher storage capacity, are completely silent, are less prone to mechanical failures, allow immediate access to data, and are portable among a greater number of devices, they are being widely used in the production of an increasing number of small, lightweight, and low-power devices.

Advantages

- Memory cards have non-volatile memory; thus they can store data permanently.
- There is no need of data refresh.
- They are smaller, lighter, and compact; thus they are highly portable.
- They have high data storage capacity.
- They require less amount of power.
- They can be easily used in small, lightweight, and low-power devices including cameras, smartphones, tablets, to name a few.
- They do not produce any noise while transferring data.

Disadvantages

- Memory cards can easily break.
- Because of their small size, they can get lost, misplaced, or smashed.

- Memory cards have a limited life. After a certain number of read-write cycles, their performance may gradually degrade.
- The cost per MB is more than that of a CD, DVD, or hard disk.

3.16 MASS STORAGE DEVICES

Mass storage refers to storing enormous amounts of data. Mass storage devices can store up to several trillion bytes of data and hence are used to store large databases, such as the data of customers of a big retail chain and library transactions of students in a college.

Mass storage devices have the following features:

- Sustainable transfer speed
- Low cost
- High data storage capacity
- Less weight
- Better tolerance of physical stress caused by shaking or dropping
- Low power consumption
- Easily portable

All these features make it convenient to use these devices with mobile phones, laptops, and desktops. Some of the commonly used mass storage devices are discussed in this section.

3.16.1 Disk Array

A disk array, commonly known as a redundant array of independent disks (RAID), is a group of one or more physically independent and high-capacity hard disk drives, which can be used in place of larger, single disk drive systems. The benefit of such a system is that it helps reduce costs because having several medium-sized hard disks is cheaper than having a single large hard disk.

As shown in Figure 3.14, a disk array contains several disk drive trays to improve speed and increase protection against loss of data. The storage capacity of a disk array is several terabytes. The disk array unit allows data to be read from or written to any disk in the array. Disk arrays are a vital component of high-performance storage systems, and their importance is continuously growing with the increase in demand to access information for the day-to-day operation of modern businesses.

Figure 3.14 Disk array

3.16.2 Automated Tape Library

An automated tape library, also known as a *tape silo*, *tape robot*, or *tape jukebox*, is a storage device that contains one or more tape drives. As shown in Figure 3.15, a tape library consists of a number of slots to hold tape cartridges, a barcode reader to identify tape cartridges, and an automated method called *robot* for loading the appropriate tape on one of the tape drives for processing. After processing, the robot automatically returns the tape to the library.

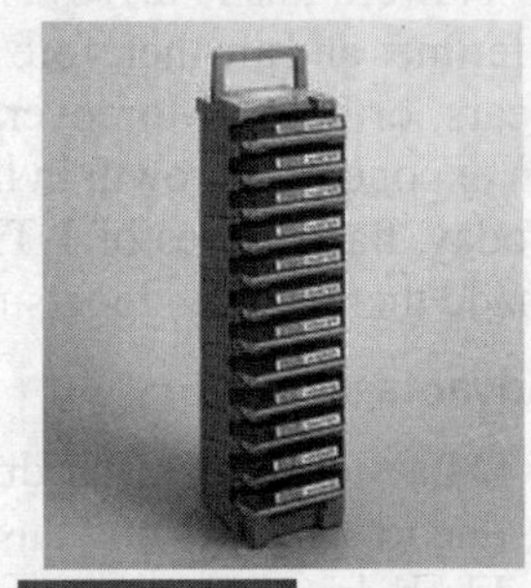

Figure 3.15 Automated tape library

Tape libraries can store large amounts of data ranging from 20 terabytes to more than 411 petabytes of data (1 petabyte = 1000 terabytes). They offer a cost-effective solution to the problem of storing large volumes of data, with the cost per gigabyte being at least 60 per cent less than when using most hard drives. In addition, multiple drives also lead to improved reliability because even when one of the drives fails, the unit can still continue to function with the other devices at a slower speed.

Though tape drives provide systematic access to very large quantities of data, the access is slow, varying from several seconds to several minutes. A tape library is commonly used for data backups as the final stage of digital data archiving. In organizations, it is extensively used for recording daily transactions or data auditing.

3.16.3 CD-ROM Jukebox

A CD-ROM jukebox, also known as an *optical jukebox*, an *optical disk library*, or a *robotic drive*, is a data storage device that can automatically load and unload optical disks such as CDs and DVDs to provide terabytes and petabytes of tertiary storage (Figure 3.16). It can have up to 2000 slots for disks and usually has a robot that traverses the slots and drives for loading the appropriate CD-ROM. After processing, the robot automatically returns it back to the library.

CD-ROM jukeboxes are extensively used for creating backups and in disaster recovery situations. They can be used for archiving data (data is stored on media that will last up to 100 years). Generally archival data is usually written on disks of write-once, read-many (WORM) type so that

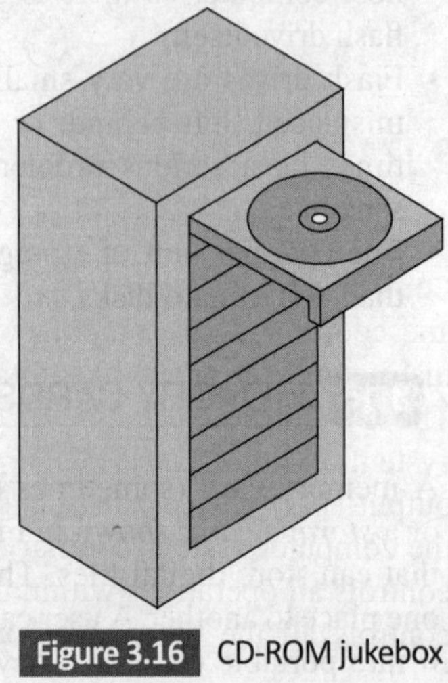

Figure 3.16 CD-ROM jukebox

DATA BACKUP

Data backup is the process of making one or more copies of data from an online storage device (hard disk) and storing them on a tertiary storage device such as a magnetic tape. The copy of data acts as an offline storage so that if the system loses the original data, it can be retrieved from the backup device and restored in the online storage device.

The online storage system may lose its data because of a disk crash, a virus attack, a hardware malfunction, an accidental deletion of a file, or a natural disaster like an earthquake. In such cases, re-creating all the files would take a lot of time, and at times, it might not even be possible. Therefore, it is a good practice to take regular data backups so that the data can be retrieved within a short time. There are two types of data backups, which can be compared as follows:

Data backup

Full data backup
- It copies all the data on a tertiary device.
- The process takes from few minutes to hours.
- It is an expensive process in terms of both time taken and storage space occupied.
- It is slower.
- It is simple.

Incremental data backup
- It copies only newly created files or files changed since the last backup.
- It needs less backup time and storage space.
- It is faster.
- It is complex when compared to full data backup.

they can never be erased or changed. Moreover, jukeboxes are effectively used for archiving data in systems such as online digital libraries, online encyclopaedias, and online museums.

Note

Hierarchical storage management is a strategy that moves less frequently used or unused documents from a fast magnetic disk to optical jukebox devices in a process called *migration*. If the files are needed, they are migrated back to the magnetic disk.

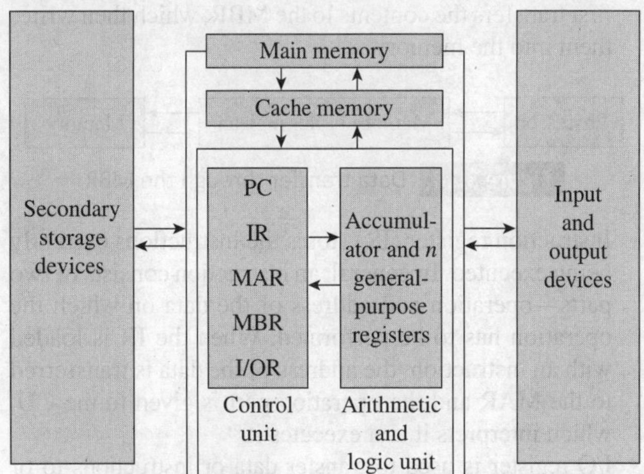

Figure 3.17 Basic computer organization

3.17 BASIC PROCESSOR ARCHITECTURE

As discussed in Chapter 1, a processor consists of two main parts— airthmetic and logic unit (ALU) and control unit (CU). Besides these components, it also consists of registers and a bus interface unit (BIU) as shown in Figure 3.17.

3.17.1 Execution Unit

The execution unit mainly consists of the CU and the ALU.

Control unit The main function of the CU is to direct and coordinate the computer operations. It interprets the instructions (program) and initiates action to execute them. The CU controls the flow of data through the computer system and directs the ALU, registers, buses, and input/output (I/O) devices. It is, therefore, called the brain of the computer system. Similar to the human brain, the CU controls all operations within the processor, which in turn controls all the other parts of the computer system. In addition, the CU is responsible for fetching, decoding, and executing instructions, as well as storing results.

Arithmetic and logic unit The ALU performs arithmetic (add, subtract, multiply, divide, etc.), comparison (less than, greater than, or equal to), and other operations.

3.17.2 Registers

A processor register is a computer memory that provides quick access to the data currently being used for processing. The ALU stores all the temporary results and the final result in processor registers. As mentioned earlier, registers are at the top of the memory hierarchy and are always preferred to speed up program execution.

Registers are also used to store the instructions of the program currently being executed. There are different types of registers, each with a specific storage function.

Accumulator and general-purpose registers These are frequently used to store the data brought from the main memory and the intermediate results during program execution. The number of general-purpose registers varies from processor to processor.

Special-purpose registers These include the following:

- Memory address register (MAR) stores the address of the data or the instruction to be fetched from the main memory. The value stored in the MAR is copied from the program counter.
- Memory buffer register (MBR) stores the data or the instruction fetched from the main memory (Figure 3.18). If an instruction is fetched from the memory, then the contents of the MBR are copied into the instruction register. If a data is fetched from the memory, the contents are either transferred to the accumulator or to the I/O register. The MBR is also used while writing contents to the main memory. In this case, the processor first transfers the contents to the MBR, which then writes them into the memory.

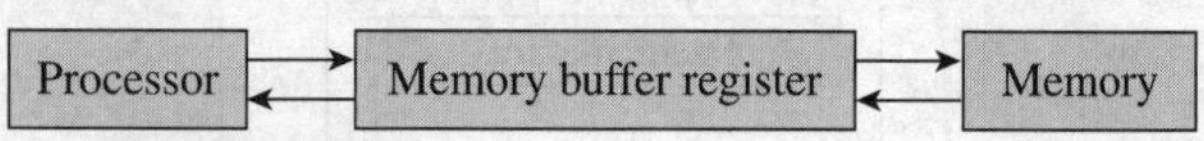

Figure 3.18 Data transfer through the MBR

- Instruction register (IR) stores the instructions currently being executed. In general, an instruction consists of two parts—operation and address of the data on which the operation has to be performed. When the IR is loaded with an instruction, the address of the data is transferred to the MAR and the operation part is given to the CU, which interprets it and executes it.
- I/O register is used to transfer data or instructions to or from an I/O device. An input device transfers data to the I/O register for processing. Correspondingly, any data to be sent to an output device is written to this register.
- Program counter stores the address of the next instruction to be executed.

The size of a register is usually specified by the number of bits it can store. For example, a register can be of 8 bits, 16 bits, 32 bits, or 64 bits. Bigger the register size, more the data that can be stored in it.

To execute an instruction, a processor normally follows a set of basic operations that are together known as an instruction cycle (Figure 3.19). The operations performed in an instruction cycle involve the following:

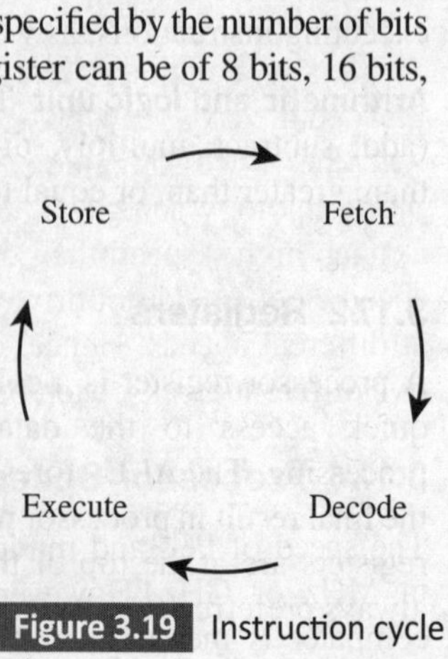

Figure 3.19 Instruction cycle

Fetch Retrieving an instruction or a data from memory.

Decode Interpreting the instruction.

Execute Running the corresponding commands to process the data.

Store Writing the results of processing into memory.

This instruction cycle is repeated continuously until the power is turned off.

3.17.3 Bus Interface Unit (BIU)

BIU provides functions for transferring data between the execution unit of the CPU and other components of the computer system that lie outside the CPU. Every computer system has three different types of buses to carry information from one part to the other. These are the data bus, control bus, and address bus (Figure 3.20).

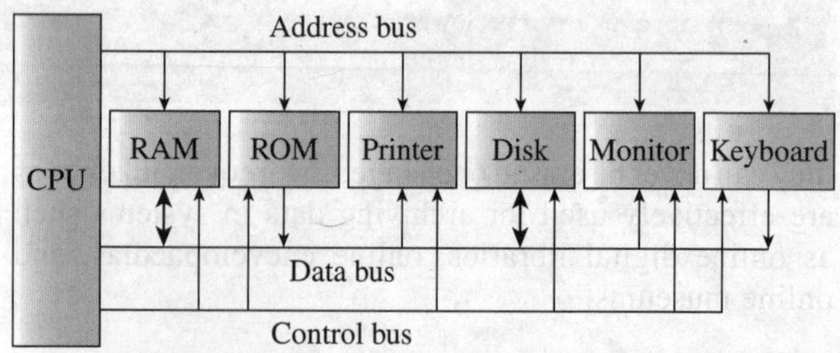

Figure 3.20 Buses within a computer system

The BIU puts the contents of the program counter on the address bus. Note that the content of the program counter is the address of the next instruction to be executed. Once the memory receives an address from the BIU, it places the contents at that address on the data bus, which is then transferred to the IR of the processor through the MBR. At this time, the contents of the program counter are modified (i.e., incremented by 1) so that it now stores the address of the next instruction.

3.17.4 Instruction Set

An instruction set is a set of commands that instructs the processor to perform specific tasks. It tells the processor what it needs to do, from where to find the data (register, memory, or I/O device), from where to find the instruction, and so on. Nowadays, computers come with a large set of instructions, and each processor supports its own instruction set. Although the instructions across processors are almost the same, they may vary in their internal design. A basic set of instructions that is supported by most processors is given in Table 3.4.

An instruction set can be built into the hardware of the processor or it can be emulated in the software, using an interpreter. The hardware design is more efficient and faster for running programs than the emulated software version.

Table 3.4 Basic instruction set

Instruction	Purpose	Example	Comment
ADD	To add two numbers	ADD AX, BX	AX and BX are processor registers that hold data.
SUB	To subtract two numbers	SUB AX, BX	AX and BX are processor registers that hold data.
MUL	To multiply two numbers	MUL AX, BX	AX and BX are processor registers that hold data.
DIV	To divide two numbers	DIV AX, BX	AX and BX are processor registers that hold data.
CMP	To compare two numbers	CMP AX, BX	AX stands for the accumulator.
IN	To input data from a device	INP DX	DX is a processor register.
OUT	To output data to a device	OUT DX	Data to be output is in DX.
JMP	To jump to another address in memory	JMP MAIN	MAIN is the name of a location.
JMPIF	To jump to another address in memory only when the specified condition is true	JMPZ MAIN (Jump if zero)	The program will go to MAIN if the value is equal to zero.
LOAD	To load data in the processor from memory	LOAD AX	The data will be loaded from memory in the accumulator.
STORE	To load data in memory from the processor	STORE AX	The data in the accumulator will be stored in memory.
CALL	To call a subroutine	CALL PROC	Call a subroutine named Proc.
RET	To return from a subroutine	RET	—

Note

Every instruction contains two parts—opcode and operand. Opcode specifies the instruction to be performed (e.g., ADD, SUB) and operand is the data (e.g., data in register, in memory, or available through I/O device) on which the instruction is to be applied.

3.17.5 System Clock

A small quartz crystal circuit called the system clock controls the timing of all operations within a computer system. The system clock regularly generates ticks to control the functioning of the computer. Every processor has a system clock to synchronize various operations that take place within the computer system. Many modern computers even have multiple system clocks that vibrate at a specific frequency. When we talk of the system clock, two important questions need to be answered. First, how does the system clock affect the speed of the processor? Second, why is there a need for multiple clocks within a single computer system?

Clock speed is measured by the number of ticks per second, where a tick is the smallest unit of time in which processing is done. A processor can perform some operations in a single clock tick, whereas others may require more ticks. The ticking of the clock drives the circuits in the computer. Therefore, faster the clock ticks, more is the number of operations that can be performed (considering other factors to be the same).

Nowadays, processors have system clocks with speeds in the gigahertz range, where *giga* stands for billion and *hertz* means one cycle per second. Therefore, a computer that operates at 3 GHz has three billion clock cycles in one second, which means that the computer can perform more than one billion operations in a second. Hence, clock speed is one of the factors that have a profound effect on a computer's performance.

Note

Other factors that can affect a computer's performance include the type of processor, availability of cache memory, memory access time, and speed of BIU.

Initially, computers had a single unified system clock that operated at a very low speed. This clock was connected with the processor, memory, and other components. As the technology advanced, some devices could operate at a much higher speed than others. However, a single slow speed clock could not drive the components that operated at different speeds. Hence, computers today have four or five different clocks, each operating at a different speed.

3.17.6 Processor Speed

The speed of PCs and minicomputers is usually specified in MHz or GHz. However, the speed of a mainframe computer is measured in MIPS (millions of instructions per second) or BIPS (billions of instructions per second) and that of a supercomputer is measured in MFLOPS (millions of floating-point operations per second), GFLOPS (giga or billions of floating-point operations per second), or TFLOPS (10^{12} floating-point operations per second). The reason for the variations in speed is that personal or minicomputers use a single processor to execute instructions, whereas mainframes and supercomputers employ multiple processors to speed up their overall performance.

3.17.7 Processor-to-Memory Communication

To execute a program, the CPU reads instructions from memory. These instructions can be of two types:

1. Those that *load* values from memory to registers and those that *store* values from registers to memory.
2. Those that operate on values stored in registers. For example adding values stored in two registers.

To execute the instructions, the CPU communicates with memory using the processor registers – MAR and MBR.

To read data from memory: The address of the location from which the value is to be read is placed in the MAR. The control unit of CPU then enables memory and, finally, memory places the requested value in the MBR.

To write data to memory: The address of the location is put in the MAR and the data is put in the MBR. Memory is then enabled for a write operation. Finally, memory writes that value in the specified location.

3.17.8 Processor Communication with I/O

The information received from an I/O device is stored in the memory unit. Similarly, any information transferred from the CPU to an I/O device is originated from memory. The role of the CPU is to just process the information; the source and the destination of information is always the memory unit.

Data transfer between the CPU and I/O devices can be done in the following modes:

- Programmed I/O
- Interrupt-initiated I/O
- Direct memory access (DMA)

Programmed I/O This mode is used when I/O instructions are written in a computer program. This means that each data transfer is initiated by an instruction in the program. Usually the transfer is done from a CPU register and memory.

When data has to be transferred between the I/O device and memory, the data is first transferred to the CPU. The CPU then transfers it to memory or the IO device. In this mode, the CPU constantly monitors I/O devices. Though this technique seems to be quite simple, it is very time-consuming as it needlessly keeps the CPU busy. To improve CPU utilization, we need to switch to interrupt-initiated mode.

Interrupt-initiated I/O The interrupt-driven I/O significantly improves CPU performance by eliminating the need of waiting unnecessarily for I/O devices to transfer data. In this mode, instead of constantly monitoring I/O devices for data transfer, the CPU performs some other task. Whenever the device has to initiate a transfer, it sends an interrupt to the CPU.

On receipt of the interrupt, the CPU temporarily leaves the current task to perform the I/O transfer. After data transfer is complete, the CPU resumes the task it was doing.

Direct memory access (DMA) To speed up data transfer, the DMA mode is preferred. In this mode, data is directly transferred between a fast storage medium such as a magnetic disk and memory unit without any intervention of the CPU. That is, instead of sending data to the CPU so that it can be transmitted to the memory or the I/O device, the two entities can directly communicate with each other using the memory buses. During DMA, the CPU is idle and it has no control over memory buses.

3.18 PIPELINING AND PARALLEL PROCESSING

Most of the modern PCs support pipelining, which is a technique with which the processor can fetch the second instruction before the execution of the first instruction is complete. Initially, a processor had to wait for an instruction to complete all stages before it could fetch the next instruction, thereby wasting its time. However, with pipelining, processors can operate at a faster pace as they no longer have to wait for one instruction to complete before fetching the next instruction. Such processors that can execute more than one instruction per clock cycle are called *superscalar processors.* Instruction execution without pipelining and with pipelining are shown in Figure 3.21.

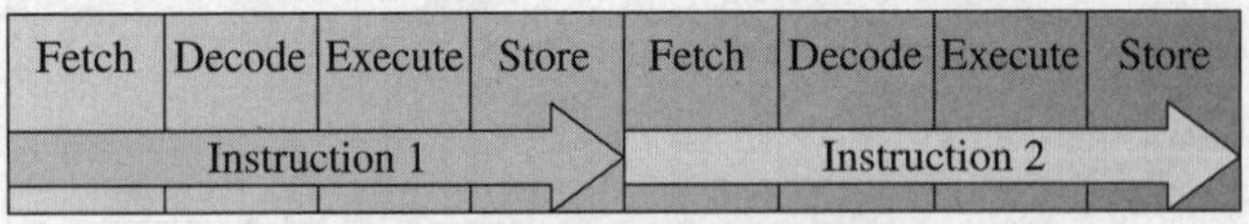

(a) Machine cycle (without pipeline)

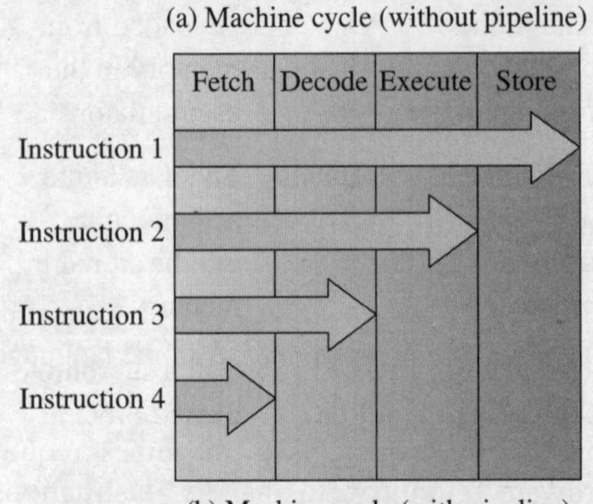

(b) Machine cycle (with pipeline)

Figure 3.21 Instruction execution without and with pipelining

The other technique which enhances a computer's performance is *parallel processing*. With this method, multiple processors can be used simultaneously to execute a single program or task. In parallel processing, a complex and large task is divided into smaller tasks in such a way that each task can be allocated to a processor. Thus, multiple processors work together simultaneously on the sub-parts of the task assigned to them.

Parallel processing systems need a special software to determine how the problem will be divided and then, at a later stage, how the sub-solutions will be combined to form the final solution of the problem. Modern-day PCs implement parallel processing by using dual-core processors or multi-core processors (discussed in next section).

Computers working on high-end applications, such as artificial intelligence and weather forecasting, go a step further by implementing the concept of *massively parallel processing*, that is, large-scale parallel processing.

3.19 TYPES OF PROCESSORS

A computer is a combination of hardware and software. However, companies often argue about the role that hardware and software should play in the design of processor architecture. Companies such as Intel want the hardware to bear more responsibility than the software so that the software can be simple and easy; companies such as Apple, on the other hand, want the software to lead. Based on these entirely contrasting opinions, there are two major processor architectures—complex instruction set computer (CISC) and reduced instruction set computer (RISC).

3.19.1 Complex Instruction Set Computer

Intel's hardware-oriented approach has given rise to CISC architecture in which more complexities have been added in the hardware to allow the software to be simpler. In CISC machines, most of the instructions are implemented using hardware. The hardware in such machines is capable of understanding and executing the instructions. For example, in a CISC machine, when multiplication needs to be performed, the programmer just has to write the name of the instruction and its operands (e.g., MUL 2, 3). The processor will automatically load the data values in processor registers, multiply them in the execution unit, and store the result. The advantages of CISC processors include the following:

- Programs can be very simple and short and require less memory space.
- Less effort is required by the translator (discussed in Chapter 6) to convert the program into machine language.
- Faster execution of instructions is possible.

However, on the downside, CISC machines require additional hardware circuitry to handle instructions. This adds to the complexity and cost of the processor's hardware circuitry. Therefore, CISC processors are more expensive than RISC processors.

Note

Majority of the PCs use CISC processors.

3.19.2 Reduced Instruction Set Computer

Apple's software-oriented approach has led to RISC architecture, which utilizes a small but highly optimized set of instructions. A research done by IBM found that 20 per cent of the instructions perform 80 per cent of the work in computers. Programmers rarely used all the instructions, and so companies wanted to reduce the number of instructions and to have only frequently used instruction in the hardware. Others could be implemented in the software using the basic instruction set. The main principle of RISC is that it takes long and complex instructions from a CISC design and reduces it to multiple shorter instructions, which can execute faster. The simplicity of RISC gave more freedom to computer companies to decide on the efficient use of space in a microprocessor.

Although RISC machines are less complex and less expensive, they place extra demand on programmers to implement complex computations by combining simple instructions. Unlike CISC machines, programs developed for RISC machines have more lines of code. Therefore, they require more memory space and more effort from a translator to convert the code into machine language.

Note

Whether RISC or CISC is used depends on the application. For some applications, RISC performs better, whereas for others, CISC will be preferable.

Since both RISC and CISC have their own advantages, the recent trend is the convergence of these two technologies. The lines between the two architectures have begun to blur as both the architectures have started adopting each other's strategy. For example, pipelining, which is an important concept of RISC machines, is now being implemented in CISC machines. Similarly, RISC machines are adopting superscalar execution and are also moving towards having more transistors on a single chip to incorporate more complicated, CISC-like commands.

3.19.3 Multi-Core Processors

A multi-core processor, as the name suggests, has two or more processors installed in the same chip. For example, a dual-core processor has a set of two processors that are connected into the same socket. Ideally, a dual-core processor should be nearly twice as powerful as a single-core processor. But, in reality, performance gain is about 50 per cent. This means that a dual-core processor is about one-and-a-half times as powerful as a single-core processor.

Most present-day computers are multi-core processors. Computer systems with tens or even hundreds of processors are referred to as many-core or massively multi-core systems. In a multi-core architecture, a single physical processor bundles more than one processor as a single processor. The objective is to create a system that can perform more tasks at the same time, thereby obtaining improved overall system performance. Multicore-based processors are used in mobile devices, desktops, workstations, and servers.

Note

Multicore processors were first produced by Intel and AMD in the early 2000s. Since then, processors have been created with two cores (dual core), four cores (quad core), six cores (hexa core), and eight cores (octo core). Processors have also been made with as many as 100 physical cores, as well as 1000 effective independent cores.

Thus, we see that a multi-core processor implements the concept of parallel processing. The architecture of such a processor enables communication between all the cores to ensure that the processing tasks are divided and assigned accurately. The completed task from each core is delivered back to the motherboard using shared memory.

A multi-processor system enhances computer's speed and efficiency, reduces the system's heat and power consumption to give better performance with less or the same amount of energy. Multicore technology is widely used in applications such as encoding, 3D gaming, and video editing.

Note

Since multi-core processors generate less heat and consume less power, they are also called energy-efficient or power-aware processors.

3.20 CLOUD STORAGE

Cloud storage allow users to store their data and files on the internet by using a cloud computing provider. The service provider securely stores, manages, and maintains the storage servers, infrastructure, and network to ensure that every user is able to access the data whenever required. Cloud storage eliminates the need for the buyers to buy and manage data storage infrastructure, giving them the agility, scalability, and durability, with anytime, anywhere data access.

Cloud storage delivers cost-effective, scalable and secure storage to the users. They do not have to worry about running out of capacity, maintaining storage area networks (SANs), replacing failed devices, adding infrastructure to scale up with demand, or using underutilized hardware when demand decreases. Cloud storage is said to be elastic as you can increase or decrease the infrastructure with demand and pay only for what they are actually using.

Even big and small organizations having billions of files and petabytes of data are opting for cloud storage to leverage the benefits of scalability, durability, and cost savings to create centralized data that is accessible anytime and anywhere.

Access to data stored on cloud is provided using traditional storage protocols or directly using an application programming interface (API). The cloud storage provider might also offer services designed to help collect, manage, secure, and analyze data at a massive scale.

Advantages

Cost effective With cloud storage, there is no need to purchase additional hardware to store and manage data.

Elasticity Users can add or remove storage capacity on demand, and only pay for storage that is currently in use. If data is less frequently used then users can move it to a lower-cost storage, thus save more money

Ease of access With cloud storage, resources are only a click away. Users can start using them or quit using them in just few minutes. This drastically increases the agility for the organization. There is no longer the need to procure, install, administer, and maintain the resources.

Fuel innovation Cloud storage integrates a wide range of analytics tools to give users more insights from the stored data.

Enhanced productivity Since IT staff can quickly avail the exact amount of storage needed, as and when required, they can focus on solving complex application problems rather than managing storage systems.

Efficient data management Cloud storage provides global storage for distributed teams. Users can organize and manage data in ways that support specific use cases, create cost efficiencies, enforce security, and meet compliance requirements.

Security Cloud storage providers store data in highly secured data centers. They are designed to handle concurrent device failure by quickly detecting and repairing any lost data (that is replicated at several machines) to ensure business continuity. Data is further protected by using version control and replication tools to more easily recover data in case of application failures. Most importantly, all data is encrypted, both at rest and in transit. Permissions and access controls work just as well in the cloud as they do for on-premises storage.

Durability and availability Cloud storage stores data redundantly on multiple devices across one or more data centers. This is helpful to ensure availability and durability as data can still be accessed even if one or more sites are unable to provide services due to an attack or failure.

Disadvantages

Security Data security is a big concern while going for cloud storage as once data leaves a company›s premises, it cannot control it will be handled and stored. Though service providers always try to enhance their security capabilities with encryption, multifactor authentication (MFA) and replicating data storage at multiple locations, data is still vulnerable to security breaches.

Data access To transmit/receive huge volumes of data stored on cloud, company must have a good and fast internet connection that in turn significantly increases the cost of using cloud storage.

Performance degradation A company may face performance issues if its in-house applications need to frequently access the data stored in the cloud. In such a situation, either the server (and applications) have to be moved in to the same cloud or bring back the necessary data in-house.

Cost Frequently accessing data on the cloud significantly increases the cost of access. in this situation, it is better to deploy the storage in-house as the ongoing costs would eventually exceed the cost of implementing and maintaining the on-premises system.

POINTS TO REMEMBER

- Computer memory is an internal storage area in a computer that is used to store data and programs either temporarily or permanently.
- While the main memory holds instructions and data when a program is being executed, the secondary memory holds data and programs not currently in use and provides long-term storage.
- To execute a program, all the instructions or data that has to be used by the CPU has to be loaded into the main memory. However, the primary memory is volatile and the data can be retained in it only when the power is on. Moreover, it is very expensive and therefore limited in capacity.
- On the contrary, the secondary memory stores data or instructions permanently, even when the power is turned off. It is cheaper and can store large volumes of data. Moreover, data stored in auxiliary memory is highly portable.
- Processor registers are located inside the processor and are therefore directly accessed by the CPU. Each register stores a word of data (which is either 32 or 64 bits in most present-day computers). Registers are the fastest of all forms of computer data storage.
- Cache memory is an intermediate form of storage between the ultra-fast registers and the main memory. It is basically a portion of memory made of high-speed SRAM instead of the slower and cheaper DRAM, which is used for main memory.
- RAM is a volalite storage area within the computer that is used to store data temporarily. There are two types of RAM—SRAM and DRAM.
- Most computers contain ROM that stores critical programs such as the BIOS which is used to boot up the computer when it is turned on. The BIOS consists of a few kilobytes of code that tells the computer what to do when it starts up, e.g., running hardware diagnostics and loading the operating system into the RAM.
- Magnetic tapes are mass storage devices capable of backing up and retaining large volumes of data. They are available in form of cassettes, reels, and cartridges.
- Floppy disks are data storage devices that consist of a thin magnetic medium encased in a square plastic shell.
- A hard disk drive is a storage device, which is a part of the general-purpose computer and is used for storing data on a set of disks that are stacked together like phonograph records.
- An external hard disk is a drive that is located outside the computer case and can be connected to a computer system using plug-and-play interfaces such as USB.
- An optical disk stores information in form of pits and lands. Pits are the tiny reflective bumps created with a laser beam, and lands are flat areas separating the pits. While a land reflects the laser light and is read as binary digit 1, a pit on the other hand absorbs the light and is read as binary digit 0.
- USB flash drives or pen drives are removable, rewritable, and physically small devices which have the storage capacity from 8 GB to 1 TB.
- A flash memory card is a small, portable device used to store digital files. Though most laptop computers come with a memory card reader, most desktop computers use a memory card reader to access the files.
- The main components of a processor are: arithmetic logic unit (ALU), control unit, registers, and a bus interface unit (BIU).
- The CU directs and coordinates the computer operations.

- The BIU provides functions for transferring data between the execution unit and other components of the computer system that lie outside the CPU.
- Pipelining is a technique with which the processor can fetch the second instruction before completing the execution of the first instruction.
- In parallel processing, multiple processors can be used simultaneously to execute a single program.
- CISC architecture is hardware oriented in which more complexities have been added to the hardware to allow the software to be simpler.
- RISC machines are less complex and less expensive, but require programmers to implement complex computations by combining simple instructions.
- Multi-core processors implement the concept of parallel processing by enabling communication between all the cores to ensure that the processing tasks are divided and assigned accurately.
- Cloud storage allow users to store their data and files on the internet by using a cloud computing provider.

GLOSSARY

Basic input output system (BIOS) Program that tells the computer what to do when it starts up, e.g., running hardware diagnostics and loading the operating system into RAM.
Cache memory An intermediate form of storage between the ultra-fast registers and the RAM.
Computer memory An internal storage area in the computer used to store data and programs either temporarily or permanently.
Data transfer rate The time taken to transfer data or the time taken to read/write to a disk.
Disk latency The sum of the seek time and the rotational delay. It is actually the time taken to initiate a transfer.
DRAM A type of RAM that must be refreshed multiple times in a second to retain its data contents.
Erasable programmable read only memory A type of ROM that can be erased and re-programmed. The EPROM can be erased by exposing the chip to strong ultraviolet light.
Flash memory A type of EEPROM in which the contents can be erased under soft ware control. The most flexible type of ROM.
Hard disk A set of disks stacked together like phonograph records, which have data recorded electromagnetically in concentric circles known as tracks.
Instruction set A set of commands that instructs the processor to perform specific tasks.
Offline storage Data storage device on which the data is recorded and then physically removed or disconnected (off the computer). For example, magnetic tapes, floppy disks, optical disks, flash memory, and external hard disks.
Optical storage Storing data on an optically readable medium by making marks in a pattern that can be read using a beam of laser light precisely focused on a spinning disk. The most popular optical storage devices are CD-ROM, DVD-ROM, CD-R, and CD-RW.
Primary memory It is also known as main memory or internal memory; the only type of memory that is directly accessed by the CPU, which continuously reads and executes instructions stored in the primary memory.
Programmable read-only memory A type of ROM that can be programmed using high voltages.
Rotational delay The time taken to bring the target sector to rotate under the R/W head.
Seek time The time taken to position the R/W head over the appropriate cylinder.
SRAM A type of RAM that holds data without an external refresh as long as it is powered. It is made of D flip-flops in which the memory cells flip-flop between 0 and 1 without the use of capacitors.
Superscalar processors Processors that can execute more than one instruction per clock cycle.
System clock A small quartz crystal circuit that controls the timing of all operations within the computer system.

EXERCISES

Fill in the Blanks

1. The ________ memory holds data and programs that are currently being executed by the CPU.
2. _______ memory is volatile.
3. _______ memory stores data or instructions permanently.
4. _______ are the fastest of all forms of computer data storage.
5. A processor register can store ________ bytes.
6. Static RAM is made of ________.
7. _______ is a one-time programmable ROM.
8. The flash memory is also a type of ________.
9. Digital cameras and mobile phones have ________ memory.
10. The number of cylinders of a disk drive is equal to the number of ________.

11. The process of writing data to a optical disk is called ________.
12. The most popularly used soft ware for writing data on CD-Rs is ________.
13. Data on a magnetictape is represented using the ________ code.
14. ________ are concentric circles and ________ are pieshaped wedges on a track.
15. The ti me taken to R/W data to a disk is called ________.
16. ________ unit directs and coordinates the computer operations.
17. Intermediate results during program execution are stored in ________.
18. ________ stores the address of the data or instruction to be fetched from memory.
19. An instruction consists of ________ and ________.
20. The instruction cycle is repeated continuously until ________.
21. Buses in a computer system can carry ________, ________, and ________.
22. In an instruction, ________ specifies the computation to be performed.
23. A ________ is the smallest unit of ti me in which processing is done.
24. The speed of PCs and minicomputers is specified in ________ or ________.
25. Giga is ________ and tera is ________.
26. ________ processors are power-efficient processors.
27. ________ storage is extensively used by applications that need to store data in a hierarchical file and folder format.

Multiple-choice Questions

1. The memory used by the CPU to store instructions and data that are repeatedly required to execute programs to improve overall system performance is
   (a) primary memory (b) auxiliary memory
   (c) cache memory (d) flash memory
2. Magnetic tapes, floppy disks, optical disks, flash memory, and hard disks are examples of
   (a) primary memory (b) auxiliary memory
   (c) cache memory (d) flash memory
3. The ti me taken to initiate a transfer is called
   (a) seek time (b) rotational delay
   (c) data transfer rate (d) disk latency
4. Disk address is specified using
   (a) sector number (b) track number
   (c) surface number (d) all of these
5. The memory used in MP3 players, PDAs, laptops, and digital audio players is
   (a) primary memory (b) optical memory
   (c) cache memory (d) flash memory
6. The component of the processor that controls the flow of data through the computer system is
   (a) BIU (b) execution unit
   (c) CU (d) ALU
7. While transferring data from memory into the processor, the register that is used as an intermediate placeholder of the data is
   (a) MAR (b) program counter
   (c) MBR (d) IR
8. The speed of supercomputers is specified by
   (a) GHz (b) GIPS
   (c) GFLOPS (d) all of these
9. Which of the following is usually not done by the cloud service provider?
   (a) Storing data
   (b) Managing data
   (c) Accessing data
   (d) Developing infrastructure for data
10. Which of the following is a big concern in context of cloud storage?
    (a) Security (b) Accessibility
    (c) Durability (d) Availability
11. ______ data refers to data that is rarely accessed
    (a) Hot (b) Cold
    (c) Active (d) Inactive

State True or False

1. Primary memory is faster than secondary memory.
2. Cache memory is made of DRAM.
3. L2 caches are built into the motherboard outside the CPU.
4. An SRAM chip can hold more data than a DRAM chip of the same size.
5. EPROM can be erased by exposing the chip to strong ultraviolet light.
6. PROM allows its entire or selected contents to be electrically erased.
7. Seek ti me is the ti me taken to bring the target sector to rotate under the R/W head.
8. CD-Rs can be written only once and can be read as many times.
9. Operating systems can read and write to flash drives without installing device drivers.
10. Memory cards use flash memory to store data.
11. The ALU initiatesaction to execute the instructions.
12. The value stored in the program counter is copied from the MAR.
13. The program counter stores the address of the next instruction to be executed.
14. The executing unit provides functions for data transfer.
15. A processor can perform all operations in a single clock tick.

16. Computers can have at most one clock.
17. The speed of a mainframe computer is measured in MHz or GHz.
18. Personal computers support pipelining.
19. Pipelining needs replication of components.
20. Parallel processing can be implemented only on server machines.
21. In RISC machines, most of the instructions are implemented using hardware.
22. An instruction set can be implemented only using an opcode.
23. Object storage is a data storage architecture for large stores of structured data.
24. Software test and development environments should be separate ideally.

Review Questions

1. What do you understand by computer memory?
2. Differentiate between primary memory and secondary memory.
3. Give the characteristics of the memory hierarchy chart.
4. What is a BIOS? Which kind of memory is preferred in it, and why?
5. Differentiate between static RAM and dynamic RAM.
6. Give the organization of computer memory. How does the CPU access a memory cell?
7. Explain the working of a magnetic disk.
8. How is data stored on optical storage devices?
9. A DVD-ROM can store more data than a CD-ROM of the same size. Comment.
10. What is a USB flash drive?
11. Write a short note on memory cards.
12. Give the formulas used to calculate the storage capacity of magnetic disks, floppy disks, and magnetic tapes. Which of these have the highest storage capacity? Explain with the help of relevant examples.
13. What is a head crash? How does it occur?
14. Briefly discuss the importance of cache memory.
15. What do you understand by re-programmable ROM chips?
16. Discuss the different types of optical storage devices.
17. Draw and explain the basic architecture of a processor.
18. 'Control unit is the brain of the computer.' Justify.
19. What are special-purpose registers?
20. Define instruction cycle.
21. Differentiate between pipelining and parallel processing.
22. How can pipelining improve processor performance?
23. What are multi-core processors?
24. Differentiate between RISC and CISC.
25. Differentiate between private and public cloud. Which one would you prefer?
26. Explain any three ways in which you use cloud computing in your daily life.

LAB ACTIVITY 3: HANDLING MEMORY STORAGE DEVICES

Activity I: Transferring Files from a USB Flash Drive to a Computer

Files can be transferred to and from a USB flash drive once it is inserted into the USB port of the computer. Follow the steps given below to transfer the files from the flash drive into your computer:

Step 1: Insert the flash drive into any USB port on your computer.

Step 2: Open File Explorer (press the Windows logo key + E).

Step 3: Select the pen drive icon in the right pane (see Figure C.1).

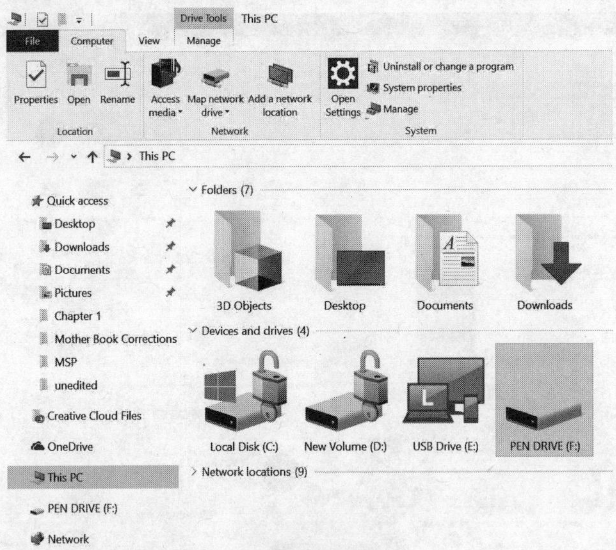

Figure C.1

Step 4: Select the folder that contains the files to be transferred.

Step 5: Copy the required files.

Step 6: Paste the files in the desired folder on your computer.

Note

Do not transfer files to and from a flash drive while it is being scanned.

Activity II: Optimizing a Drive

Optimization (defragmentation) is a process that physically organizes the contents of a storage device such as a hard disk so that the files are stored into contiguous locations. This helps to improve the storage device's performance by reducing the loading time. Follow the steps given below to optimize a local drive on your computer system:

Step 1: Select the folder icon on the taskbar.

Step 2: Right click on the drive that you want to optimize and click Properties.

Step 3: In the drive's Properties dialog box, click on the Tools tab.

Step 4: Click on the Optimize button.

Step 5: Click on the Analyze button (see Figure C.2). After the disk is analysed, check the percent of fragmentation in the Current status column. If it is less than 10%, there is no need to optimize the drive. Click on the Close button.

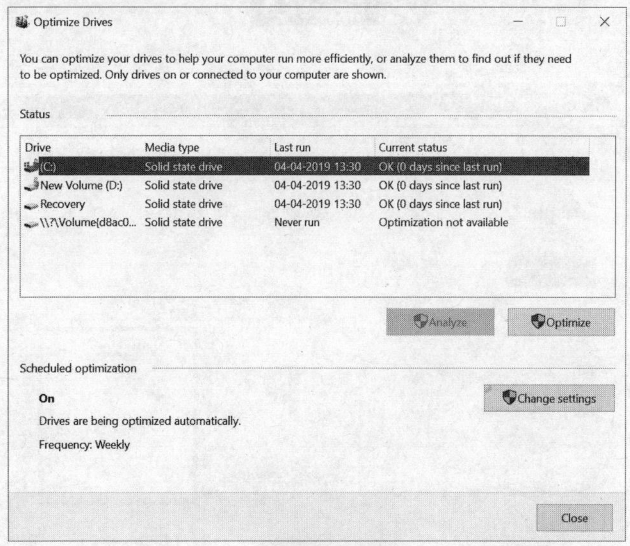

Figure C.2

Step 6: If the percent of fragmentation is more than 10%, click on the Optimize button. Depending on the size and degree of fragmentation of the drive, the process may take from few minutes to few hours.

Activity III: Using Google Drive

Google Drive is a free cloud storage service provided by Google. It serves you a place where you can store your files online (on the Internet) in the cloud so that they could be accessed anywhere (even far away from your home computer). Google Drive also gives you access to free web-based applications for creating documents, spreadsheets, presentations, and more. Today, Google Drive has become a popular cloud storage service offering **15 Giga Bytes** (15GB) of free storage space to all the users having a Gmail account.

The steps for uploading a file on the Google Drive are given below:

Step 1: Open the web browser and type drive.google.com.

Step 2: Use your Gmail account to sign in the Google Drive.

Step 3: Click on New button in the top left corner.

Step 4: A menu will be displayed.

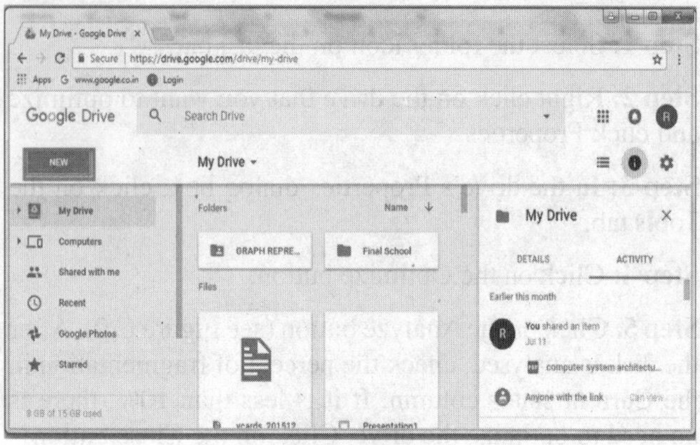

Figure C.3

Click on File Upload to upload a file or Folder Upload to upload the entire Folder on your computer.

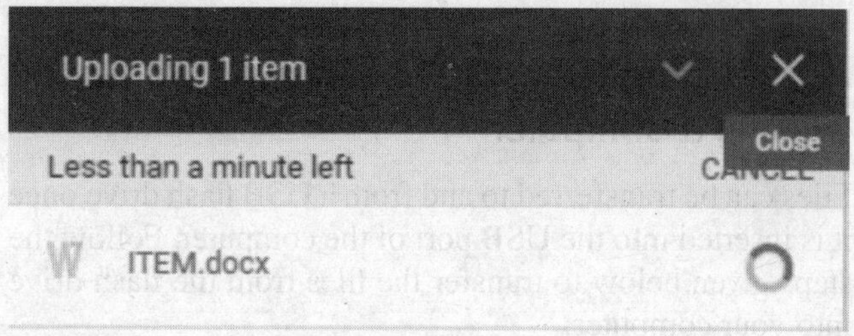

The Word File- Item. docx is being uploaded

Figure C.4

Step 5: Browse the file and click on Open. On the bottom right corner of the window, you will see that the file is being uploaded.

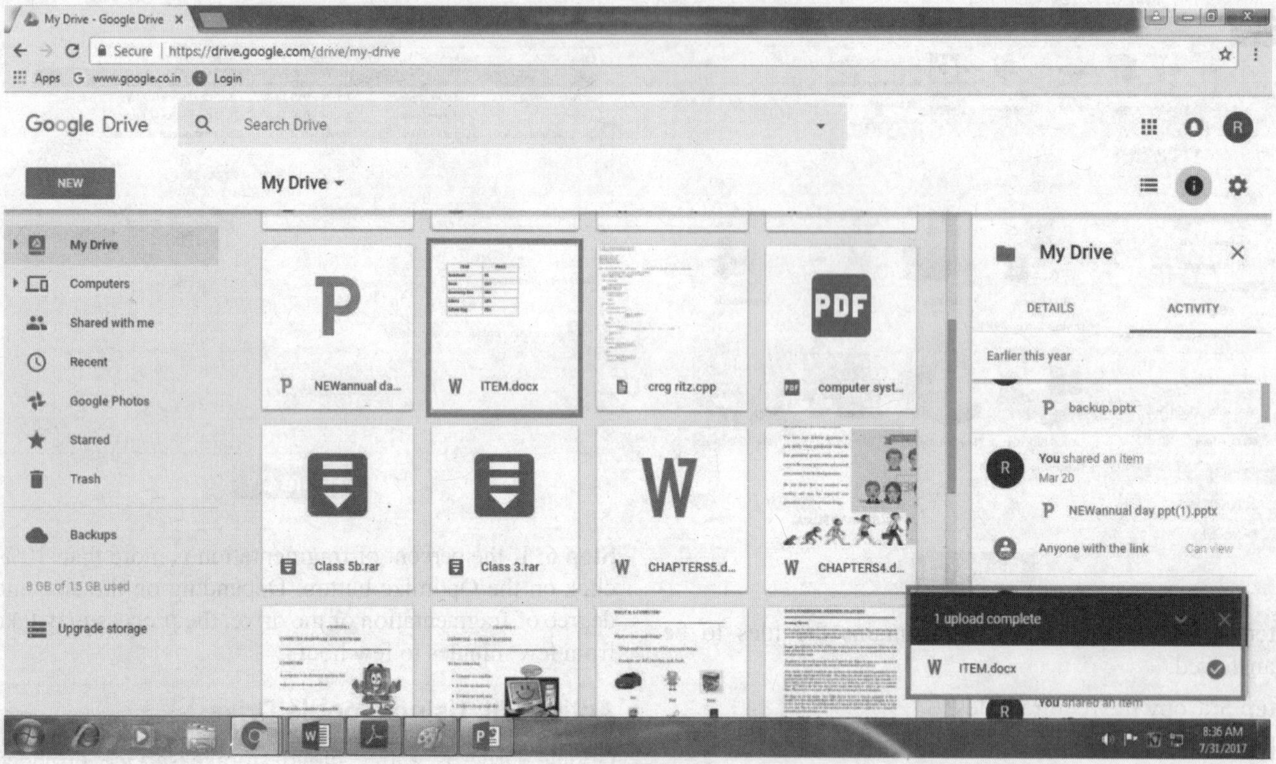

Figure C.5

Once the file is uploaded, you can see it added in your drive.

The steps for organizing files on the Google Drive are given below:

In Google Drive, the links on the left pane allow you to organize your files under different categories.

My Drive is where all of your uploaded files and folders are stored.

Shared with Me are all files and folders that have been shared with you by others.

Starred files are files that you have marked as important.

Recent includes files and folders that you have most recently edited.

The steps for sharing a file on the Google Drive are given below:

Step 1: Open the web browser and type drive.google.com.

Step 2: Use your Gmail account to sign in the Google Drive.

Step 3: Right click on the file that you want to share.

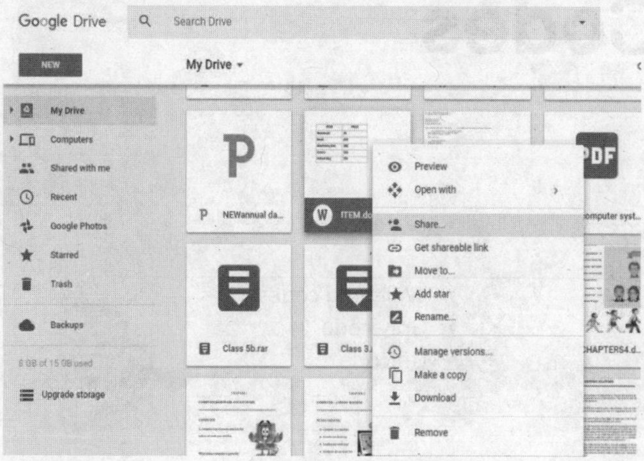

Step 4: From the pop-up menu, click on Share.

Step 5: Enter the email address of the recipient(s).

Step 6: Choose what recipient(s) can do with your file. The options are,

View: Recipient(s) can see, but cannot change or share the file with others.

Comment: Recipient(s) can make comments and suggestions, but cannot change or share the file with others.

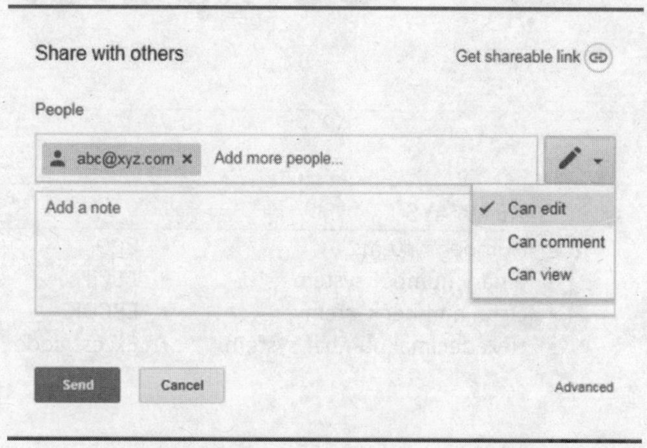

Edit: Recipient(s) can make changes, accept or reject suggestions, and share the file with others.

Step 9: Click on Send.

> You can also click on Get Sharable Link and share with other people so that they can share it on social networking websites like Google+, Facebook, Twitter, etc.

The steps for searching a file on the Google Drive are given below:

Step 1: Type the entire name or part of the file name in the Search Drive box.

Step 2: A list of files matching the name entered in the Search Drive box is displayed.

Step 3: Click on the desired file.

> Google Drive will search through titles, content, and owners.

More Activities on Google Drive

There are actually some more things that you can do on Google drive. These things include:

Download files or folders: To download files or folders from Google Drive to your computer, right click on the file, and select Download.

Delete files or folders: To delete files or folders from Google Drive, right click on the file, and select Remove.

Create Files: Google Drive also allows you to **create and share** files. These files can be created with various Microsoft Office programs. Some types of files that you can create and share on Google Drive include:

- **Documents: It is similar to Microsoft Word document and can be used** for composing letters, flyers, essays, and other text-based files.
- **Spreadsheets: It is similar to Microsoft Excel workbook and is used** for storing and organizing information.
- **Presentations: It is similar to Microsoft** PowerPoint presentation and is used for creating slideshows.
- **Forms:** For collecting and organizing data.
- **Drawings:** For creating simple vector graphics or diagrams.

4 Number Systems and Computer Codes

TAKEAWAYS

- Number systems
- Binary number system
- Octal number system
- Hexadecimal number system
- BCD
- ASCII
- EBCDIC
- Excess code
- Weighted codes
- Gray code
- Unicode

4.1 INTRODUCTION TO NUMBER SYSTEMS

Data is stored in a computer in the form of 0s and 1s. This is because computers understand only binary language (which consists of just two digits, 0 and 1). Therefore, for a computer, all data and information is reduced to numbers. Whether a user stores songs, pictures, numbers, or documents, all information is treated as binary numbers.

In this chapter, we will learn about the different types of number systems used in computers as well as different types of codes that convert human language, consisting of alphanumeric and special characters, into machine language (in binary code) which the computer understands.

Representation of Numbers in Radix r

Before discussing number systems, let us first understand the *base* or *radix* of a number system. The number of unique digits used to form numbers within a number system is called radix of that system. For example, in the decimal number system we use digits 0–9 to form numbers; thus, its radix is 10.

A general number system $(N)r$ of radix r can be represented as follows:

$$(N)r = d_{n-1}\, r^{n-1} + \ldots + d_0 r^0 + d_{-1} r^{-1} + \ldots + d_{-m} r^{-m}$$

where r = radix

d_i = Digit at position i, $-m \le i \le n-1$

r^i = Weight of position i, $-m \le i \le n-1$

n = Number of integral digits in N

m = Number of fractional digits in N

Digits in radix r number system include $0, \ldots, r-1$.

Example 4.1

Let us consider the decimal number 234.56. Form the number using the aforegiven radix representation.

Solution

At position 2, $d_2 = 2$, $r^2 = 10^2 = 100$

At position 1, $d_1 = 3$, $r^1 = 10^1 = 10$

At position 0, $d_0 = 4$, $r^0 = 10^0 = 1$

At position –1, $d_{-1} = 5$, $r^{-1} = 10^{-1} = 0.1$

At position –2, $d_{-2} = 6$, $r^{-2} = 10^{-2} = 0.01$

We can form the number using the aforementioned representation as follows:

$(N)r = d_{n-1}\, r^{n-1} + \ldots + d_0 r^0 + d_{-1} r^{-1} + \ldots + d_{-m} r^{-m}$

$= 100 \times 2 + 10 \times 3 + 1 \times 4 + 0.1 \times 5 + 0.01 \times 6$

$= 200 + 30 + 4 + 0.5 + 0.06$

$= 234.56$

Positional and Non-positional Number Systems

In a positional number system, each digit has a different value depending on its position in the number. For example, value of 2 in 123 is 20 but in 231 it is 200. Moreover, the total value that a number represents is the sum of the resultant value of all positions. For example, in the number 123, the value 123 is obtained by adding 100, 20, and 3.

The above logic is not applicable to non-positional number systems such as the Roman number system. In a non-positional number system, each symbol represents the same value regardless of its position. For example, in number XXXI, X always stands for 10 irrespective of its position.

Since it was very difficult to perform arithmetic operations with non-positional number systems, positional number systems had to be developed.

4.2 BINARY NUMBER SYSTEM

Computers are electronic machines that operate using binary logic. These devices use two different voltage levels to represent the two binary values (0 V for logic 0 and +5 V for logic 1). Therefore, the two values, 0 and 1, correspond to the two digits used by the binary number system.

The binary number system works like the decimal number system, with the following exceptions:

- While the decimal number system uses base 10, the binary number system uses base 2.
- The decimal number system uses digits 0 to 9, whereas the binary number system uses only two digits, 0 and 1.

Some important terms in the binary number system include the following:

- *Bit* is the short form of 'binary digit'. It is,the smallest possible unit of data. In computerized data, a bit can be either 0 or 1.
- *Nibble* is a group of four bits.
- *Byte* is a group of eight bits. A nibble is a half byte. Bits 0–3 are called the low-order nibble, and bits 4–7 form the high-order nibble.
- *Word* is a group of two bytes. Bits 0–7 form the low-order byte and bits 8–15 form the high-order byte. However, these days, depending on the computer architecture, a word could be a group of four bytes (32 bits) or eight bytes (64 bits).

Table 4.1 lists these terms in the binary number system with examples.

Table 4.1 Important terms in the binary number system

Term	Size (bits)	Example
Bit	1	0
Nibble	4	1010
Byte	8	0101 1100
Word	16	0101 1100 0101 1100

Now let us understand how much data can be encoded in the binary form using different numbers of bits. If we have a single bit, we can represent only $2^1 = 2$ values, 0 and 1. With two bits, we can represent $2^2 = 4$ values, namely 00, 01, 10, and 11. Tables 4.2–4.4 illustrate this concept better.

Table 4.2 Binary representation with two bits

Number of bits: 2 Data values that can be represented = $2^2 = 4$	
Decimal value	Binary value
0	00
1	01
2	10
3	11

Table 4.3 Binary representation with three bits

Number of bits: 3 Data values that can be represented = $2^3 = 8$			
Decimal value	Binary value	Decimwwal value	Binary value
0	000	4	100
1	001	5	101
2	010	6	110
3	011	7	111

Table 4.4 Binary representation with four bits

Number of bits: 4 Data values that can be represented = $2^4 = 16$			
Decimal value	Binary value	Decimal value	Binary value
0	0000	8	1000
1	0001	9	1001
2	0010	10	1010
3	0011	11	1011
4	0100	12	1100
5	0101	13	1101
6	0110	14	1110
7	0111	15	1111

Applications of Binary Numbers

- Binary number system is best suited to be used with computers, as mechanical and electronic relays recognize only two states of operation—on/off or closed/open. In the binary number system, character 1 = on = closed circuit = true and character 0 = off = open circuit = false.
- Binary numbers can be easily translated into electrical impulses.
- Binary numbers can be effectively used to encrypt messages.
- Binary number system is the backbone of the development of computer science and many forms of electronics. It led to the development of devices such as typewriter, cathode ray tube, telegraph, and transistor.
- Binary number system is also used in statistical investigations and probability studies to explain strategy, prove mathematical theorems, and solve puzzles.

4.3 WORKING WITH BINARY NUMBERS

We all are very familiar with how decimal numbers operate. The same concept can be applied to binary numbers (base 2), octal numbers (base 8), and hexadecimal numbers (base 16). So before discussing other number systems, let us first take a look at how we form a number in the decimal number system.

Suppose we have a decimal number 123, what do we call this number? How did we get its value? The answer is that we first arrange individual digits into columns and then multiply each digit with the value of its position. Figure 4.1 illustrates this concept.

	Hundreds (10^2)	Tens (10^1)	Ones (10^0)
Decimal	1	2	3

Figure 4.1 Position of the digits of 123 using the decimal number system

Here, $123 = 1 \times 100 + 2 \times 10 + 3 \times 1$
or $123 = 1 \times 10^2 + 2 \times 10^1 + 3 \times 10^0$

The same concept is applicable to the binary number system, the only difference being that wherever 10 is used, it is replaced by 2 as shown in Table 4.5.

4.3.1 Converting a Binary Number into Decimal Form

In a binary number, all the columns are powers of 2. Table 4.5 shows the five least significant digit place holders.

Table 4.5 Five least significant digit place holders

Sixteen's column	Eight's column	Four's column	Two's column	One's column (LSB)
2^4	2^3	2^2	2^1	2^0

Note that, in Table 4.5, all the columns are specified in powers of 2. Hence, in order to convert a binary number into its decimal equivalent, multiply that place holder value (power of 2) with the bit, and then add all the products.

Example 4.2

Convert 1101 into a decimal number.

Solution

Use Table 4.5 to form the decimal number.

Decimal number $= 1 \times 2^3 + 1 \times 2^2 + 0 \times 2^1 + 1 \times 2^0$
$= 1 \times 8 + 1 \times 4 + 0 \times 2 + 1 \times 1$
$= 8 + 4 + 0 + 1$
$= 13$

Example 4.3

Convert 1010 1001 into a decimal number.

Solution

Decimal number $= 1 \times 2^7 + 0 \times 2^6 + 1 \times 2^5 + 0 \times 2^4 + 1 \times 2^3 + 0 \times 2^2 + 0 \times 2^1 + 1 \times 2^0$
$= 1 \times 128 + 0 \times 64 + 1 \times 32 + 0 \times 16 + 1 \times 8 + 0 \times 4 + 0 \times 2 + 1 \times 1$
$= 128 + 0 + 32 + 0 + 8 + 0 + 0 + 1$
$= 169$

The following steps summarize the procedure to convert a binary number into a decimal number.

Step 1: Start with the least significant bit (LSB) and multiply that bit with 2^0. Note that any number raised to 0 is always 1.

Step 2: Continue working from right to left. Multiply each bit with an incremental power of 2 (i.e., 2^1, 2^2, 2^3, 2^4, etc).

Step 3: Repeat Step 2 until all the bits have been multiplied.

Step 4: Add the end result of the multiplication carried out in steps 1 and 2 to get the decimal number.

4.3.2 Converting a Decimal Number into Binary Form

To convert a decimal number into its binary equivalent, simply divide the decimal number by 2 and then write down the remainder; repeat this process until the number cannot be divided by 2 anymore.

Example 4.4

Convert decimal 13 or $(13)_{10}$ into its binary equivalent.

Solution

2	13	R
2	6	1
2	3	0
2	1	1
	0	1

Now write the result starting from the last remainder obtained.

Therefore, $(13)_{10} = (1101)_2$.

Example 4.5

Convert 169 into its binary equivalent.

Solution

2	169	R
2	84	1
2	42	0
2	21	0
2	10	1
2	5	0
2	2	1
2	1	0
	0	1

Now write the result starting from the last remainder obtained.

Therefore, $(169)_{10} = (1010\ 1001)_2$.

4.3.3 Adding Two Binary Numbers

Addition of binary numbers is similar to the addition of decimal numbers. While performing binary addition, start by adding the bits (digits) in one column at a time, from right to left as we do in the case of adding decimal numbers. However, to perform binary addition, one must remember the rules of addition.

Rules of Binary Addition

- 0 + 0 = 0
- 0 + 1 = 1
- 1 + 0 = 1
- 1 + 1 = 0, and carry 1 to the next more significant bit.

Example 4.6

Add the following binary numbers.

Solution

```
  0001010          1010101
+ 0100100        + 0101010
  -------          -------
  0101110          1111111

   11 — Carry     1111 — Carry
  1011            1010101
+ 0001          + 0101110
  ----            --------
  1100            10000011
```

4.3.4 Subtracting Two Binary Numbers

Now that we have learnt to perform addition on two binary numbers, subtraction will also be an easy task to perform. As with binary addition, there are certain rules to be followed for binary subtraction. These rules can be summarized as:

- 0 – 0 = 0
- 1 – 0 = 1
- 1 – 1 = 0
- 0 – 1 = 1, and borrow 1 from the next more significant bit.

Note

Note that the value borrowed from the next more significant bit depends on the base of the number system and is always the decimal equivalent of the base. Hence, in the decimal number system, 10 is borrowed, in binary 2 is borrowed, in octal 8 is borrowed, and in hexadecimal 16 is borrowed.

Example 4.7

Perform subtraction on the following binary numbers.

Solution

```
                                0 10 0 10
  1011       10110111          1 0 1 0 1 1 0
-1001      -00110010         - 0 1 0 1 0 1 0
 ----       --------           -------------
 0010       10000101           0 1 0 1 1 0 0

         10                   1  1                     10
      0  0 10              0 10 10 10               0  0 10
  1 0 1 1 0 1            1 0 0 0 1 0 1          1 0 1 1 0 1
- 1 0 0 1 1 1          - 0 0 1 1 0 0 0        - 1 0 0 1 1 1
  -----------            -------------          -----------
  0 0 0 1 1 0            0 1 0 1 1 0 1          0 0 0 1 1 0

     10  1 10 10
   0  0 10  0  0 10
 1 1 1 0 1 1 0
-1 0 1 0 1 1 1
 -------------
 0 0 1 1 1 1 1
```

4.3.5 Subtracting Two Binary Numbers Using Two's Complement

Though the previously discussed technique of subtracting two binary numbers is simple, there is another way to perform subtraction. In this technique, subtraction is done through addition. Do you recall having learnt in school that a positive number subtracted from another positive number is the same as a negative number added to a positive number? This fundamental concept can be used to restructure the subtraction problem into an addition problem. This is called subtraction by the two's complement method.

Step 1: To subtract two binary numbers using two's complement, first find the two's complement of the number to be subtracted (subtrahend). Two's complement is calculated in the following two steps:

- Complement each bit of the number. That is, change 1 to 0 and 0 to 1. The resultant number is said to be in *one's complement* form.
- Add 1 to the resultant number in one's complement form to get the corresponding *two's complement*.

Step 2: Add the minuend and subtrahend (which is now in two's complement form). Take care of the carries in each column, and discard any carry bit that extends beyond the number of bits of the original number or the two's complement.

However, an important point to note here is that when subtracting binary values, it is important to maintain the same number of bits for each number (minuend and subtrahend). For this, we may pad the number with extra zeroes to the left of the value.

We should also remember to discard the carry obtained after adding the last bits. Observe the following examples, which will help make the concept clear.

Example 4.8

Calculate 1011 – 1001 using two's complement method.

Solution

Step 1: Find the two's complement of the subtrahend.

Subtrahend = 1001

One's complement of subtrahend = 0110

Two's complement of subtrahend = 0110 + 1 = 0111

Step 2: Add the minuend and the two's complement of the subtrahend.

```
  1011
+ 0111    Now discard the carry from the last bit;
1 0010    hence the result = 0010.
```

Example 4.9

Calculate 10110111 – 00110010 using two's complement method.

Solution

Step 1: Find the two's complement of the subtrahend.

Subtrahend = 00110010

One's complement of subtrahend = 11001101

Two's complement of subtrahend = 11001101 + 1 = 11001110

Step 2: Add the minuend and the two's complement of the subtrahend.

```
  10110111
+ 11001110
1 10000101
```

Now discard the carry from the last bit; hence the result = 10000101.

Example 4.10

Calculate 1010110 – 0101010 using two's complement method.

Solution

Step 1: Find the two's complement of the subtrahend.

Subtrahend = 0101010

One's complement of subtrahend = 1010101

Two's complement of subtrahend = 1010101 + 1 = 1010110

Step 2: Add the minuend and the two's complement of the subtrahend.

```
  1010110
+ 1010110    Now discard the carry from the last
1 0101100    bit; hence the result = 0101100
```

4.3.6 Multiplying Two Binary Numbers

Binary numbers are multiplied in the same manner as we multiply two decimal numbers.

Two numbers *A* and *B* are multiplied using partial products. For each bit in *B*, the product of that bit with the corresponding bit in *A* is calculated and written on a new line (shifted leftward). The partial products are added together to get the final result.

The rules of multiplication of binary numbers are the same as that of decimal numbers, that is:

- $0 \times 0 = 0$
- $0 \times 1 = 0$
- $1 \times 0 = 0$
- $1 \times 1 = 1$

Example 4.11

Multiply the following binary numbers.

Solution

```
 1010
  ×11
 1010
10100
11110
```

```
   1011
  ×1001
   1011
  00000
 000000
1011000
1100011
```

```
  111010
    ×101
  111010
 0000000
11101000
100100010
```

4.3.7 Dividing Two Binary Numbers

Binary division is again similar to dividing two decimal numbers. According to the long division method, the divisor is multiplied with the quotient, and the result is then subtracted from the dividend.

Example 4.12

Divide the following binary numbers.

Solution

```
     0011
11 ) 1001 (
     0
     10
     0
     100
      11
      11
      11
       0
```

```
     011101
10 ) 111011 (
     0
     11
     10
      11
      10
       10
       10
        01
         0
         11
         10
          1
```

```
      00101111
101 ) 11101110 (
      0
      11
      0
      111
      101
       100
         0
       1001
        101
        1001
         101
         1001
          101
          1000
           101
            11
```

4.4 OCTAL NUMBER SYSTEM

The octal number system is the base 8 number system which uses digits 0–7. This number system was used extensively in early mainframe computer systems, but has become less popular in comparison with binary and hexadecimal number systems.

Octal decimals operate in the same manner in which decimal and binary numbers operate. In the octal number system, each column is a power of 8 as shown in Table 4.6.

Table 4.6 Four least significant digit place holders in the octal number system

	Fourth digit	Third digit	Second digit	First digit
Octal	8^3	8^2	8^1	8^0

4.4.1 Converting an Octal Number into Decimal Form

Try to recall what we did to convert a binary number into its decimal equivalent; the same steps can be applied to convert an octal number into decimal. The only difference is that we will use base 8 instead of base 2.

In order to convert an octal number into its decimal equivalent, multiply that place holder value (power of 8) with the digit, and then add all the products.

Example 4.13

Convert $(123)_8$ into its decimal equivalent.

Solution

Use Table 4.6 to form the decimal number.

Decimal number = $1 \times 8^2 + 2 \times 8^1 + 3 \times 8^0$

$= 1 \times 64 + 2 \times 8 + 3 \times 1$

$= 64 + 16 + 3$

$= 83$

Example 4.14

Convert $(10567)_8$ into its decimal equivalent.

Solution

Decimal number = $1 \times 8^4 + 0 \times 8^3 + 5 \times 8^2 + 6 \times 8^1 + 7 \times 8^0$

$= 1 \times 4096 + 0 \times 512 + 5 \times 64 + 6 \times 8 + 7 \times 1$

$= 4096 + 0 + 320 + 48 + 7$

$= 4471$

The following steps summarize the procedure to convert an octal number into a decimal number.

Step 1: Start with the least significant digit and multiply that digit with 8^0. Note that any number raised to 0 is always 1.

Step 2: Continue working from right to left. Multiply each digit with an incremental power of 8 (i.e., 8^1, 8^2, 8^3, 8^4, etc.).

Step 3: Repeat Step 2 until all digits have been multiplied.

Step 4: Add the end result of the multiplication carried out in steps 1 and 2 to get the decimal number.

4.4.2 Converting a Decimal Number into Octal Form

To convert a decimal number into its octal equivalent, simply divide the decimal number by 8 and then write down the remainder; repeat this process until it cannot be divided by 8 anymore.

Example 4.15

Convert decimal 786 or $(786)_{10}$ into its octal equivalent.

Solution

8	786	R
8	98	2
8	12	2
8	1	4
	0	1

Now write the result starting from the last remainder obtained.

Therefore, $(786)_{10} = (1422)_8$.

Example 4.16

Convert $(9890)_{10}$ into its octal equivalent.

Solution

8	9890	R
8	1236	2
8	154	4
8	19	2
8	2	3
	0	2

Now write the result starting from the last remainder obtained.

Therefore, $(9890)_{10} = (23242)_8$.

4.4.3 Converting an Octal Number into Binary Form

To convert an octal number into its binary equivalent, replace each octal digit with its binary equivalent.

Example 4.17

Convert $(63)_8$ into its binary equivalent.

Solution

$(63)_8$ can be converted into its binary equivalent using the following steps:

Step 1: Write the binary equivalent of 6, which is equal to 110.

Step 2: Write the binary equivalent of 3, which is equal to 011.

Step 3: Merge the two values. Therefore, $(63)_8 = (110011)_2$.

Example 4.18

Convert $(175)_8$ into its binary form.

Solution

Step 1: Write the binary equivalent of 1, which is equal to 001.

Step 2: Write the binary equivalent of 7, which is equal to 111.

Step 3: Write the binary equivalent of 5, which is equal to 101.

Step 4: Merge the values. Therefore, $(175)_8 = (001111101)_2$.

4.4.4 Converting a Binary Number into Octal Form

To convert a binary number into its octal equivalent, divide the binary number into groups of bits, where each group consists of exactly three bits (except the last). Convert each group into its equivalent octal number. Combine these individual octal numbers to get the final result.

Example 4.19

Convert $(1101\ 100)_2$ into its octal equivalent.

Solution

The steps to convert $(1101\ 100)_2$ into octal form are as follows:

Step 1: Divide the number into groups of three bits each, starting from the LSB. Therefore,

1 101 100

Step 2: Convert each group of binary bits into its equivalent octal number. Thus, we have 1 5 4.

Step 3: Merge the octal values to get the final result. Hence, $(1101100)_2 = (154)_8$.

Example 4.20

Convert $(10100110)_2$ into its octal equivalent.

Solution

Step 1: Divide the number into groups of three bits each. Therefore,

10 100 110

Step 2: Convert each group of binary bits into its equivalent octal number. Thus, we have 2 4 6.

Step 3: Merge the octal values to get the final result. Hence, $(10100110)_2 = (246)_8$.

4.4.5 Adding Two Octal Numbers

When we add two decimal numbers, there can be two cases:

Case 1: The sum is less than 10. In this case, we just write the digit obtained after addition.

$$\begin{array}{r} 4 \\ +5 \\ \hline 9 \end{array} \qquad \begin{array}{r} 3 \\ +2 \\ \hline 5 \end{array}$$

Case 2: The sum is greater than or equal to 10. In this case, 10 is subtracted from the sum and the result is written at that position. Moreover, a carry is given to the next digit.

$$\begin{array}{r} 1 \\ 1\ 4 \\ +2\ 7 \\ \hline 4\ 1 \end{array} \qquad \begin{array}{r} 1 \\ 3\ 6 \\ +4\ 8 \\ \hline 8\ 4 \end{array}$$

Now, 4 + 7 = 11 which is greater than 10. Subtracting 10 from 11, we get 1. Write 1 at that position and add a carry to the next digit.	Now, 6 + 8 = 14 which is greater than 10. Subtracting 10 from 14, we get 4. Write 4 at that position and add a carry to the next digit.

The same concept can be applied while doing octal addition. When we add two octal numbers there can be two cases:

Case 1: The sum is less than 8. In this case, we just write the digit obtained after addition.

$$\begin{array}{r} 4 \\ +3 \\ \hline 7 \end{array} \qquad \begin{array}{r} 3 \\ +2 \\ \hline 5 \end{array}$$

Case 2: The sum is greater than or equal to 8. In this case, 8 is subtracted from the sum and the result is written at that position. Moreover, a carry is given to the next digit.

1 1 4 +2 7 4 3	1 1 3 6 5 +4 5 7 1 0 4 4
Now, 4 + 7 = 11 which is greater than 8. Subtracting 8 from 11, we get 3. Write 3 at that position and add a carry to the next digit.	Now, 5 + 7 = 12 which is greater than 8. Subtracting 8 from 12, we get 4. Write 4 at that position and add a carry to the next digit.

4.4.6 Subtracting Two Octal Numbers

When we subtract two decimal numbers, there can be two cases:

Case 1: If the digit in the minuend is greater than the digit in the subtrahend, subtract the digits and write the result at that position.

9 −5 4	8 −6 2

Case 2: If the digit in the minuend is smaller than the digit in the subtrahend, borrow 1 from the immediate higher place. When a digit is borrowed, the minuend digit at the current place gets 10 and 1 is subtracted from the minuend digit at the immediate higher place.

8 12 ~~9~~ ~~2~~ − 4 8 4 4	6 14 ~~7~~ ~~4~~ − 6 5 0 9
Since 2 is less than 8, we borrow 1 from the next immediate digit. So 9 now becomes 8. Moreover we get 10, so now it's not 2 but 10 + 2 = 12. 8 is finally subtracted from 12 and the result is written.	Since 4 is less than 5, we borrow 1 from the next immediate digit. So 7 now becomes 6. Moreover we get 10, so now it's not 4 but 10 + 4 = 14. 5 is finally subtracted from 14 and the result is written.

The same concept can be applied while doing octal subtraction. When we subtract two octal numbers, there can be two cases:

Case 1: The digit in the minuend is greater than the digit in the subtrahend. In this case, we just subtract the digits and write the result.

7 6 5 4 − 2 3 4 1 5 3 1 3

Case 2: The digit in the minuend is smaller than the digit in the subtrahend. In this case, borrow 1 from the immediate higher place. When a digit is borrowed, the minuend digit at the current place gets 8 and a 1 is subtracted from the minuend digit at the immediate higher place.

13 8 ~~4~~ ~~5~~ ~~0~~ 10 ~~5~~ ~~6~~ ~~1~~ ~~2~~ − 2 7 5 6 2 6 3 4	7 5 ~~8~~ 9 ~~6~~ ~~0~~ ~~1~~ 5 − 3 7 6 2 2 0 3 3	9 8 3 ~~1~~ ~~0~~ 8 ~~4~~ 2 ~~1~~ ~~0~~ − 3 6 5 4 0 3 3 4

4.5 HEXADECIMAL NUMBER SYSTEM

The hexadecimal number system is the base 16 number system. It uses sixteen distinct symbols—symbols 0–9 represent values zero to nine, and A, B, C, D, E, F (or a–f) represent values 10–15. Figure 4.2 shows numbers from 0 to 15 and their values in binary as well as hexadecimal number systems.

The main problem with binary numbers is that for larger values binary numbers quickly become too unwieldy. The hexadecimal (base 16) number system overcomes this problem as hexadecimal numbers are very compact. Moreover, it is very easy to convert from hexadecimal to binary and vice versa.

In the hexadecimal system, just like in the binary, octal, and decimal number systems, we start counting from the first column, which represents the smallest unit. Then, working from right to left, we move to a 16's column, a 256's column, a 4096's column, a 65,536's column, and so on. In programming languages, prefix '0x' is used to indicate a hexadecimal number.

4.5.1 Converting a Hexadecimal Number into Decimal Form

To convert a hexadecimal number to decimal, multiply the value in each position by its hex weight and add all the values.

Dec	0	1	2	3	4	5	6	7	8	9	10	11	12	13	14	15
Bin	0000	0001	0010	0011	0100	0101	0110	0111	1000	1001	1010	1011	1100	1101	1110	1111
Hex	0	1	2	3	4	5	6	7	8	9	A	B	C	D	E	F

Figure 4.2 Hexadecimal number system and its binary and decimal equivalents

Example 4.21

Convert 0x312B into its equivalent decimal value.

Solution

Decimal number = $3 \times 16^3 + 1 \times 16^2 + 2 \times 16^1 + B \times 16^0$
= $3 \times 4096 + 1 \times 256 + 2 \times 16 + B \times 1$
= 12288 + 256 + 32 + 11
= 12587

Example 4.22

Convert hexadecimal 123 into decimal.

Solution

Decimal number = $1 \times 16^2 + 2 \times 16^1 + 3 \times 16^0$
= $1 \times 256 + 2 \times 16 + 3 \times 1$
= 256 + 32 + 3
= 291

4.5.2 Converting a Decimal Number into Hexadecimal Form

To convert a decimal number into its hexadecimal equivalent, simply divide the decimal number by 16 and then write down the remainder; repeat this process until it cannot be divided by 16 anymore.

Example 4.23

Convert decimal 1239 into its hexadecimal equivalent.

Solution

16	1239	R	
16	77	7	Now write the result starting from the last
16	4	D	remainder obtained.
	0	4	Therefore, $(1239)_{10} = (4D7)_{16}$.

Example 4.24

Convert $(56789)_{10}$ into its hexadecimal equivalent.

Solution

16	56789	R	
16	3549	5	
16	221	D	Now write the result starting from the
16	13	D	last remainder obtained.
	0	D	Therefore, $(56789)_{10} = (DDD5)_{16}$

4.5.3 Converting a Hexadecimal Number into Binary Form

Figure 4.2 can be used to easily convert a hexadecimal number into its binary equivalent. Simply substitute the corresponding four bits in binary for each hexadecimal digit in the number.

Example 4.25

Convert 0xABCD into its binary equivalent.

Solution

From Figure 4.2, we have, $(ABCD)_{16} = (1010\ 1011\ 1100\ 1101)_2$.

Example 4.26

Convert $(F1E2)_{16}$ into binary.

Solution

$(F1E2)_{16} = (1111\ 0001\ 1110\ 0010)_2$

4.5.4 Converting a Binary Number into Hexadecimal Form

Figure 4.2 can also be used to convert a binary number into its hexadecimal form. The first step is to pad the binary number with leading zeroes (if necessary), so that it contains multiples of four bits.

Example 4.27

Convert the binary number 01101110010110 into its hexadecimal equivalent.

Solution

Note that the given binary number contains 14 bits. Pad the number with two zeroes on the left so that the number has 16 bits (multiple of four bits).

Now, the binary number = 0001 1011 1001 0110.

The next step is to look up these binary values in Figure 4.2 and substitute the appropriate hexadecimal digits. The equivalent hexadecimal number = 1B96.

4.5.5 Converting a Hexadecimal Number into Octal Form

To convert a hexadecimal number into its octal equivalent, first convert the hexadecimal number into its binary equivalent. Then convert the binary number into its equivalent octal number.

Example 4.28

Convert $(A1E)_{16}$ into octal form.

Solution

Perform the following steps:

Step 1: Write the binary equivalent of A, which is equal to 1010.

Step 2: Write the binary equivalent of 1, which is equal to 0001.

Step 3: Write the binary equivalent of E, which is equal to 1110.

Step 4: Merge the individual values. Thus, $(A1E)_{16}$ = $(1010\ 0001\ 1110)_2$.

Step 5: Divide the binary number into groups of three binary bits. Therefore,

101 000 011 110

Step 6: Convert each group of binary bits into its equivalent octal number. Thus, we have 5 0 3 6.

Step 7: Merge the octal values to get the final result. Hence, $(A1E)_{16} = (5036)_8$.

Example 4.29

Convert $(6B0)_{16}$ into its octal equivalent.

Solution

Step 1: Write the binary equivalent of 6, which is equal to 0110.

Step 2: Write the binary equivalent of B, which is equal to 1011.

Step 3: Write the binary equivalent of 0, which is equal to 0000.

Step 4: Merge the individual values. Thus, $(6B0)_{16}$ = $(0110\ 1011\ 0000)_2$.

Step 5: Divide the binary number into groups of three binary bits. Therefore,

011 010 110 000

Step 6: Convert each group of binary bits into its equivalent octal number. Thus, we have 3 2 6 0.

Step 7: Merge the octal values to get the final result. Hence, $(6B0)_{16} = (3260)_8$.

4.5.6 Converting an Octal Number into Hexadecimal Form

To convert an octal number into its equivalent hexadecimal number, first convert the octal number into its binary equivalent and then convert the binary number into its hexadecimal form.

Example 4.30

Convert $(567)_8$ into its hexadecimal equivalent.

Solution

The steps to be performed to convert $(567)_8$ into its hexadecimal equivalent are as follows:

Step 1: Write the binary equivalent of 5, which is equal to 101.

Step 2: Write the binary equivalent of 6, which is equal to 110.

Step 3: Write the binary equivalent of 7, which is equal to 111.

Step 4: Merge the individual values. Thus, $(567)_8$ = $(101\ 110\ 111)_2$.

Step 5: Divide the binary number into groups of four binary bits. (Left pad the binary number with zeroes if there are not enough bits to be grouped.) Therefore,

0001 0111 0111

Step 6: Convert each group of binary bits into its equivalent hexadecimal number. Thus, we have 1 7 7.

Step 7: Merge the octal values to get the final result. Hence, $(567)_8 = (177)_{16}$.

Example 4.31

Convert $(134)_8$ into its hexadecimal equivalent.

Solution

Step 1: Write the binary equivalent of 1, which is equal to 001.

Step 2: Write the binary equivalent of 3, which is equal to 011.

Step 3: Write the binary equivalent of 4, which is equal to 100.

Step 4: Merge the individual values. Thus, $(134)_8$ = $(001\ 011\ 100)_2$.

Step 5: Divide the binary number into groups of four binary bits. Therefore,

0000 0101 1100

Step 6: Convert each group of binary bits into its equivalent hexadecimal number. Thus, we have 5C.

Step 7: Merge the hexadecimal values to get the final result. Hence, $(134)_8 = (5C)_{16}$.

4.5.7 Adding Two Hexadecimal Numbers

We can add two hexadecimal numbers in the same way as we add decimal and octal numbers. When we add two hexadecimal numbers, there can be two cases:

Case 1: The sum is less than 16. In this case, we just write the digit obtained after addition.

```
  1 A 2 B
+ 2 3 6 1
  3 D 8 C
```

Case 2: The sum is greater than or equal to 16. In this case, 16 is subtracted from the sum and the result is written at that position. Moreover, a carry is given to the next digit.

```
     1         1 1 1        1 1 1
  2 C 4 A     5 C 8 D     6 E 8 C
+ D 2 8 7   + 9 6 7 6   + B 3 A D
  F E D 1     F 3 0 3   1 2 2 3 9
```

4.5.8 Subtracting Two Hexadecimal Numbers

When we subtract two hexadecimal numbers, there can be two cases:

Case 1: The digit in the minuend is greater than the digit in the subtrahend. In this case, we just subtract the digits and write the result.

```
  6 A 7 B
 –2 3 6 1
  4 7 1 A
```

Case 2: The digit in the minuend is smaller than the digit in the subtrahend. In this case, borrow 1 from the immediate higher place. When a digit is borrowed, the minuend digit at the current place gets 16 and a 1 is subtracted from the minuend digit at the immediate higher place.

```
                       F                    23
   D 21  8 16        E 16 17        E  7  7 28
   E  5  9  0        F  0  1  D     E  8  8  C
 – 3  A  8  7      – 9  6  7  6   – B  3  A  D
   A  B  0  9        5  9  A  7     3  4  D  F
```

4.6 WORKING WITH FLOATING POINT NUMBERS

In computer's terminology, a floating point number is a number that contains a decimal point. For example, the numbers 2.3, 0.05, and –1234.567 are all floating point numbers. Numbers that do not have a decimal point are called integers. An arithmetic operation that includes one or more floating point number is called floating point arithmetic.

A floating point number has four parts—a sign, a mantissa, a radix, and an exponent. The sign is either a 1 or –1. The mantissa, which is always a positive number, holds the significant digits of the floating point number. The exponent indicates the positive or negative power of the radix which should be multiplied with the mantissa and sign. The four components are combined as follows to get the floating point value:

$$\text{sign} \times \text{mantissa} \times \text{radix}^{\text{exponent}}$$

Floating point numbers have multiple representations because one can always multiply the mantissa of any floating point number by some power of the radix and change the exponent to get the original number. For example, number –5 can be represented equally by any of the following forms in radix 10:

Forms of –5

Sign	Mantissa	Radix^{exponent}
–1	50	10^{-1}
–1	5	10^{0}
–1	0.5	10^{1}
–1	0.05	10^{2}

For each floating point number there is one representation that is said to be *normalized.* A floating-point number is normalized if its mantissa is within the range defined by the following relation:

$$1/\text{radix} <= \text{mantissa} < 1$$

A normalized radix 10 floating point number has its decimal point just to the left of the first non-zero digit in the mantissa. The normalized floating point representation of –5 is $-1 \times 0.5 \times 10^1$. In other words, a normalized floating point number's mantissa has no non-zero digits to the left of the decimal point and a non-zero digit to the right of the decimal point. Any floating point number that does not fit into this category is said to be *denormalized.* Note that the number zero has no normalized representation because it has no non-zero digit which can be put to the right of the decimal point.

In general, for a fractional number *a*, in any number system of base *b*, the position values can be written as:

Position	5	4	3	2	1	0	.	–1	–2	–3	–4	–5
Position value	b^5	b^4	b^3	b^2	b^1	b^0		b^{-1}	b^{-2}	b^{-3}	b^{-4}	b^{-5}

The generalized table when used with specific base systems can be given as in Table 4.7.

Now let us use Table 4.7 to convert the following numbers of base *b* into decimal.

1. Convert $(10110.1110)_2$ into decimal:

$$\begin{aligned}(10110.1110)_2 &= 1 \times 2^4 + 0 \times 2^3 + 1 \times 2^2 + 1 \times 2^1 + 0 \times 2^0 + 1 \times 2^{-1} + 1 \times 2^{-2} + 1 \times 2^{-3} + 0 \times 2^{-4} \\ &= 1 \times 16 + 0 \times 8 + 1 \times 4 + 1 \times 2 + 0 \times 1 + 1 \times 1/2 + 1 \times 1/4 + 1 \times 1/8 + 0 \times 1/16 \\ &= 16 + 0 + 4 + 2 + 0 + 0.5 + 0.25 + 0.125 + 0 \\ &= 22.875\end{aligned}$$

2. Convert $(127.35)_8$ into decimal:

$$\begin{aligned}(127.35)_8 &= 1 \times 8^2 + 2 \times 8^1 + 7 \times 8^0 + 3 \times 8^{-1} + 5 \times 8^{-2} \\ &= 1 \times 64 + 2 \times 8 + 7 \times 1 + 3 \times 1/8 + 5 \times 1/64 \\ &= 64 + 16 + 7 + 0.375 + 0.078125 \\ &= 87.453125\end{aligned}$$

3. Convert $(21F.DE)_{16}$ into decimal:

$$\begin{aligned}(21F.DE)_{16} &= 2 \times 16^2 + 1 \times 16^1 + F \times 16^0 + D \times 16^{-1} + E \times 16^{-2} \\ &= 2 \times 256 + 1 \times 16 + 15 \times 1 + 13 \times 1/16 + 14 \times 1/256 \\ &= 512 + 16 + 15 + 0.8125 + 0.0546875 \\ &= 543.8671875\end{aligned}$$

Now that we have converted a fractional binary/octal/hexadecimal number into its decimal equivalent, let us learn how the fractional part of a decimal number can be converted into its equivalent binary/octal/hexadecimal number.

Example 4.32

Convert the decimal number 92.25 into its equivalent binary number.

Solution

Break the number into two parts. The first part consists of digits before the decimal point, and the second part contains digits

Table 4.7 Position values of digits in various number systems

Position	5	4	3	2	1	0	.	–1	–2	–3	–4	–5
Position value in decimal	10^5	10^4	10^3	10^2	10^1	10^0		10^{-1}	10^{-2}	10^{-3}	10^{-4}	10^{-5}
Position value in binary	2^5	2^4	2^3	2^2	2^1	2^0		2^{-1}	2^{-2}	2^{-3}	2^{-4}	2^{-5}
Position value in octal	8^5	8^4	8^3	8^2	8^1	8^0		8^{-1}	8^{-2}	8^{-3}	8^{-4}	8^{-5}
Position value in hexadecimal	16^5	16^4	16^3	16^2	16^1	16^0		16^{-1}	16^{-2}	16^{-3}	16^{-4}	16^{-5}

after the point. A separate procedure is applied to convert these individual parts of the decimal number into binary. While the whole number part (before the decimal) is converted using repeated division by 2 and considering the remainders, the fractional part, on the other hand, is converted by repeated multiplication of the fractional part with 2 and considering only the whole number part of the result.

Number = 92.25	
Whole number part = 92	Fractional part = 0.25
2 | 92 | R 2 | 46 | 0 2 | 23 | 0 2 | 11 | 1 2 | 5 | 1 2 | 2 | 1 2 | 1 | 0 | 0 | 1 $(92)_{10} = (1011100)_2$ Note down the remainders starting from the last obtained.	0.25 ×2 0.50 ×2 1.00 ×2 0.00 $(0.25)_{10} = (0.010)_2$ Note the digit before the decimal point obtained from the first multiplication to the last.
Hence $(92.25)_{10} = (1011100.010)_2$	

Example 4.33

Convert the decimal number 178.92 into its equivalent octal number.

Solution

Number = 178.92	
Whole number part = 178	Fractional part = 0.92
8 | 178 | R 8 | 22 | 2 8 | 2 | 6 | 0 | 2 $(178)_{10} = (262)_8$ Note down the remainders starting from the last remainder obtained.	0.92 ×8 7.36 ×8 2.88 ×8 7.04 ×8 0.32 $(0.92)_{10} = (0.7270)_8$ Note the whole number part of the result obtained from the first multiplication to the last.
Hence $(178.92)_{10} = (262.7270)_8$	

Example 4.34

Convert the decimal number 12345.48 into its equivalent hexadecimal number.

Solution

Number part = 12345	
Whole number part = 12345	Fractional part = 0.48
16 | 12345 | R 16 | 771 | 9 16 | 48 | 3 16 | 3 | 0 | 0 | 3 $(12345)_{10} = (3039)_{16}$ Note down the remainders starting from the last remainder obtained.	0.48 ×16 7.68 ×16 A.88 ×16 E.08 ×16 1.28 $(0.48)_{10} = (0.7AE1)_{16}$ Note the whole number part of result obtained from the first multiplication to the last.
$(12345.48)_{10} = (3039.7AE1)_{16}$	

4.7 SIGNED NUMBER REPRESENTATION IN BINARY FORM

Signed number representation is required to encode negative numbers in the binary number system. Basically, negative numbers in any base system are written by preceding the number with a – sign (minus sign). However, the binary system, which the computer understands, does not support the minus sign to write negative numbers.

Hence, a different technique is required to encode the minus sign in terms of 0s and 1s. There are three widely used techniques for extending the binary number system to represent signed numbers. These techniques are sign-and-magnitude, one's complement, and two's complement. Out of the three, the two's complement method is the most popular for representing signed numbers in the binary number system.

4.7.1 Sign-and-magnitude

Sign-and-magnitude is the simplest technique in which the most significant bit (MSB) is set to 0 for a positive number and to 1 for a negative number. The other bits denote the value or the magnitude of the number.

Hence, a byte having eight bits can use only seven bits to denote the magnitude, and one bit is used to denote the sign of the number. Using seven bits, numbers from –127 to +127 can be represented (i.e., 2^7 combinations).

For example, consider Table 4.8 which illustrates how signed numbers are represented using sign-and-magnitude method.

Table 4.8 Representation of signed numbers in sign-and-magnitude method

Decimal number	Binary equivalent in sign-and-magnitude form							
	Sign bit	7th bit	6th bit	5th bit	4th bit	3rd bit	2nd bit	1st bit
+36	0	0	1	0	0	1	0	0
–45	1	0	1	0	1	1	0	1
+117	0	1	1	1	0	1	0	1
–108	1	1	1	0	1	1	0	0

4.7.2 One's Complement

The one's complement representation of a negative number is obtained by taking the complement of its positive counterpart (in binary). For example, to represent –45 in the binary number system using one's complement method, perform the following steps:

- Write the binary representation of the number's positive counterpart, that is, the binary equivalent of +45.
- Negate each bit in the binary representation of the positive number (+45 in this case).

So, +45 in binary form is 0010 1101. Now negate each bit to obtain the binary representation of –45.

Hence, –45 in binary = 1101 0010.

The PDP-1 and UNIVAC 1100/2200 series use one's complement arithmetic. The range of signed numbers that can be represented using one's complement in a byte is from -127_{10} to $+127_{10}$.

4.7.3 Two's Complement

In one's complement method, +0 is represented as 00000000 and –0 is represented as 11111111. In sign-and-magnitude method, –0 is represented as 10000000. These different representations sometimes become problematic. Therefore, to avoid such a situation, the two's complement representation is generally used. This representation is obtained in the following two steps:

- Complement or negate the bits in the binary representation of the positive number.
- Add 1 to the result of the first step.

In two's complement –54 can be given as:

Binary representation of +54 is 0011 0110

Complement each bit: 1100 1001

Add 1 to this result. Therefore,

```
 1 1 0 0 1 0 0 1
             +1
 ---------------
 1 1 0 0 1 0 1 0    (–54 in two's complement)
```

The main advantage of using two's complement is that there is only one zero (0000 0000). For example, when converting –0 in two's complement form, complementing the bits gives 11111111 and adding 1 gives 0000 0000 and a carry bit of 1. In two's complement, we discard the carry from the last bit. Hence, the result is only 0000 0000.

Note

Similar to the one's and two's complements, there is also nine's complement and ten's complement.

To find the nine's complement of a number, subtract each digit of the number from 9. For example, the nine's complement of 12345 is 87654.

To find the ten's complement of a number, first find the nine's complement of that number and then add 1 to it.

For example, the nine's complement of 314700 is 685299 and ten's complement is 685300.

4.8 BCD CODE

Binary coded decimal (BCD) is a very simple technique used for encoding decimal numbers. In this scheme, each digit is represented by its own binary sequence. The main advantage of using BCD is that it allows easy conversion to decimal numbers for printing or display, and allows faster decimal calculations.

Consider Figure 4.2 in which the binary representation of numbers 0–15 is shown. In BCD representation the digits 0–9 are used. Each decimal digit (0–9) is represented by four binary digits. For example, decimal 7 = 0111 in BCD. There are two types of BCD numbers—unpacked BCD and packed BCD.

In *unpacked BCD* representation, only one decimal number is represented per byte. The number is stored in the lower nibble, and the higher nibble is not relevant to the value of the represented number. For example,

```
Decimal 17 = 0000 0001 0000 0111 (in BCD)
                  ↓         ↓
                  1         7
```

Hence, to convert a decimal number into an unpacked BCD number, assign each decimal digit, its eight-bit binary equivalent.

In *packed BCD* representation, two decimal numbers are stored in a single byte. For example,

Decimal 17 = 0001 0111 (in BCD)

0001 → 1, 0111 → 7

Hence, to convert a decimal number into a packed BCD number, assign to each digit of the decimal number its four-bit equivalent, padding the upper nibble with zeroes, if necessary. For example,

Decimal 7 = 0111 (in packed BCD) or 0000 0111 (in packed BCD, if padding is required).

To convert a number from BCD to decimal, just reverse the process, that is, perform the following steps:

- Start with the least significant byte.
- Group the binary digits into groups of four if it is a packed BCD number, otherwise in groups of eight bits if it is an unpacked BCD number.
- Convert each set into its decimal equivalent.

For example, consider the packed BCD number, 0010 1001. Convert it into its equivalent decimal number. Now, in the number, identify the LSB to start with. So, 0010 1001_{LSB}. Group the binary digits into sets of four because the number is in packed BCD format.

0010 1001

0010 → 2, 1001 → 9

Hence, the decimal equivalent of the packed BCD number 0010 1001 = 29.

Now, let us discuss another example. Consider the unpacked BCD number, 0000 0011 0000 0110. Convert it into its equivalent decimal number. Now, in the number, identify the LSB. So, 0000 0011 0000 0110_{LSB}. Group the binary digits into sets of eight because the number is in unpacked BCD format.

0000 0011 0000 0110

0000 0011 → 3, 0000 0110 → 6

Hence, the decimal equivalent of the unpacked BCD number 0000 0011 0000 0110 = 36.

The following are the advantages and disadvantages of BCD codes:

Advantages

- Similar to the decimal number system
- One must remember binary equivalent of only 0–9 decimal numbers
- It is easy to use BCD codes for input and output operations in digital systems

Disadvantages

- BCD addition and subtraction has different rules
- BCD arithmetic is more complex than binary arithmetic
- BCD is less efficient than binary numbers because it requires more number of bits to store the same decimal number

4.9 OTHER CODES

In this section, we will read about other coding techniques that are widely used to convert data into the form of 0s and 1s.

4.9.1 ASCII Code

ASCII stands for American Standard Code for Information Interchange. It is a seven-bit character code (refer Figure 4.3) that was introduced by the American National Standards Institute (ANSI) and is used by personal and workstation computers.

ASCII characters are examples of unpacked BCD numbers. Values in ASCII codes are represented as their four-bit binary equivalents stored in the lower nibble, while the upper nibble contains 011 and has no bearing on the value of the represented number. ASCII is the most common format for text files in computers and on the Internet. It can define 128 different characters because it is a seven-bit code, and can support 2^7 combinations. The various ASCII characters are listed in Figure 4.3.

4.9.2 Extended Binary Coded Decimal Interchange Code

Extended binary coded decimal interchange code (EBCDIC) is an eight-bit character-encoding technique used on IBM mainframe operating systems. It supports a wider range of control characters than ASCII because it supports eight-bit character codes that can encode 2^8 or 256 characters.

EBCDIC is easier to use on punched cards. Although it is considered to be an obsolete coding system, it is still used in some equipment to allow for continued use of software written many years ago that requires an EBCDIC communication environment.

EBCDIC characters are similar to ASCII characters. While the lower nibble contains the four-bit binary equivalent (as in ASCII), the upper nibble on the other hand is padded with 1111, instead of 011.

4.9.3 Excess-3 Code

In the excess-3 (XS3) coding method, each decimal digit is the four-bit binary equivalent with 3 (0011) added.

4.9.4 Weighted Codes

In weighted binary codes, each position of the number represents a specific weight. For example, we have 8421, 2421, 5211, and 4221 codes.

8421 BCD Code

BCD codes are also known as 8421 codes because each of the four bits is given a 'weighting' according to its column value in the binary system. The LSB has the weight or value $2^0 = 1$, the next bit has value $2^1 = 2$, the next bit has value $2^2 = 4$, and the MSB has the value $2^3 = 8$, as shown in Table 4.9.

<table>
<tr><th>Dec Hx Oct Char</th><th>Dec Hx Oct Html Chr</th><th>Dec Hx Oct Html Chr</th><th>Dec Hx Oct Html Chr</th></tr>
<tr><td>0 0 000 NUL (null)</td><td>32 20 040   Space</td><td>64 40 100 @ @</td><td>96 60 140 ` '</td></tr>
<tr><td>1 1 001 SOH (start of heading)</td><td>33 21 041 ! !</td><td>65 41 101 A A</td><td>97 61 141 a a</td></tr>
<tr><td>2 2 002 STX (start of text)</td><td>34 22 042 " "</td><td>66 42 102 B B</td><td>98 62 142 &#98 b</td></tr>
<tr><td>3 3 003 ETX (end of text)</td><td>35 23 043 # #</td><td>67 43 103 C C</td><td>99 63 143 c c</td></tr>
<tr><td>4 4 004 EOT (end of transmission)</td><td>36 24 044 $ $</td><td>68 44 104 D D</td><td>100 64 144 d d</td></tr>
<tr><td>5 5 005 ENQ (enquiry)</td><td>37 25 045 % %</td><td>69 45 105 E E</td><td>101 65 145 e e</td></tr>
<tr><td>6 6 006 ACK (acknowledge)</td><td>38 26 046 & &</td><td>70 46 106 F F</td><td>102 66 146 f f</td></tr>
<tr><td>7 7 007 BEL (belll)</td><td>39 27 047 ' '</td><td>71 47 107 G G</td><td>103 67 147 g g</td></tr>
<tr><td>8 8 010 BS (backspace)</td><td>40 28 050 ((</td><td>72 48 110 H H</td><td>104 68 150 h h</td></tr>
<tr><td>9 9 001 TAB (horizontal tab)</td><td>41 29 051))</td><td>73 49 111 I 1</td><td>105 69 151 i i</td></tr>
<tr><td>10 A 012 LF (NL line feed, new line)</td><td>42 2A 052 * *</td><td>74 4A 112 J J</td><td>106 6A 152 j j</td></tr>
<tr><td>11 B 013 VT (vertical tab)</td><td>43 2B 053 + '</td><td>75 4B 113 K K</td><td>107 6B 153 k k</td></tr>
<tr><td>12 C 014 FF (NP form feed, new page)</td><td>44 2C 054 , ,</td><td>76 4C 114 L L</td><td>108 6C 154 l l</td></tr>
<tr><td>13 D 015 CR (carriage return)</td><td>45 2D 055 - -</td><td>77 4D 115 M M</td><td>109 6D 155 m m</td></tr>
<tr><td>14 E 016 SO (shift out)</td><td>46 2E 056 . .</td><td>78 4E 116 N N</td><td>110 6E 156 &#110 n</td></tr>
<tr><td>15 F 017 SI (shift in)</td><td>47 2F 057 / /</td><td>79 4F 117 O O</td><td>111 6F 157 &#ll 1; 0</td></tr>
<tr><td>16 10 020 DLE (data link escape)</td><td>48 30 060 0 0</td><td>80 50 120 P P</td><td>112 70 160 p p</td></tr>
<tr><td>17 11 021 DC1 (device control 1)</td><td>49 31 061 1 1</td><td>81 51 121 Q Q</td><td>113 71 161 q q</td></tr>
<tr><td>18 12 022 DC2 (device control 2)</td><td>50 32 062 2 2</td><td>82 52 122 R R</td><td>114 72 162 r r</td></tr>
<tr><td>19 13 023 DC3 (device control 3)|</td><td>51 33 063 &#51, 3</td><td>83 53 123 S S</td><td>115 73 163 s s</td></tr>
<tr><td>20 14 024 DC4 (device control 4)</td><td>52 34 064 4 4</td><td>84 54 124 T T</td><td>116 74 164 t t</td></tr>
<tr><td>21 15 025 NAK (negative acknowledge)</td><td>53 35 065 5 5</td><td>85 55 125 U U</td><td>117 75 165 u u</td></tr>
<tr><td>22 16 026 SYN (synchronous idle)</td><td>54 36 066 6 6</td><td>86 56 126 V V</td><td>118 76 166 &#l 18; v</td></tr>
<tr><td>23 17 027 ETB (end of trans block)</td><td>55 37 067 7 7</td><td>87 57 127 W W</td><td>119 77 167 w w</td></tr>
<tr><td>24 18 030 CAN (cancel)</td><td>56 38 070 8 8</td><td>88 58 130 X X</td><td>120 78 170 x x</td></tr>
<tr><td>25 19 031 EM (end of medium)</td><td>57 39 071 9 9</td><td>89 59 131 Y Y</td><td>121 79 171  y</td></tr>
<tr><td>26 IA 032 SUB (substitute)</td><td>58 3A 072 : :</td><td>90 5A 132 Z Z</td><td>122 7A 172 &#122 z</td></tr>
<tr><td>27 IB 033 ESC (escape)</td><td>59 3B 073 ; :</td><td>91 5B 133 [[</td><td>123 7B 173 &#123 (</td></tr>
<tr><td>28 1C 034 ES (file separator)</td><td>60 3C 074 < <</td><td>92 5C 134 \</td><td>124 7C 174 &#124 |</td></tr>
<tr><td>29 ID 035 GS (group separator)</td><td>61 3D 075 = =</td><td>93 5D 135]]</td><td>125 7D 175 &#125)</td></tr>
<tr><td>30 IE 036 RS (record separator)</td><td>62 3E 076 &062; ></td><td>94 5E 136 ^ ^</td><td>126 7E 176 &#126 ~</td></tr>
<tr><td>31 IF 037 US (unit separator)</td><td>63 3F 077 ? ?</td><td>95 5F 137 _ _</td><td>127 7F 177 &#127 DEL</td></tr>
</table>

Figure 4.3 ASCII code

Table 4.9 8421 code

Decimal	Formed By	Weight			
		$2^3 = 8$	$2^2 = 4$	$2^1 = 2$	$2^0 = 1$
0	$8 \times 0 + 4 \times 0 + 2 \times 0 + 1 \times 0 = 0$	0	0	0	0
1	$8 \times 0 + 4 \times 0 + 2 \times 0 + 1 \times 1 = 1$	0	0	0	1
2	$8 \times 0 + 4 \times 0 + 2 \times 1 + 1 \times 0 = 2$	0	0	1	0
3	$8 \times 0 + 4 \times 0 + 2 \times 1 + 1 \times 1 = 3$	0	0	1	1
4	$8 \times 0 + 4 \times 1 + 2 \times 0 + 1 \times 0 = 4$	0	1	0	0
5	$8 \times 0 + 4 \times 1 + 2 \times 0 + 1 \times 1 = 5$	0	1	0	1
6	$8 \times 0 + 4 \times 1 + 2 \times 1 + 1 \times 0 = 6$	0	1	1	0
7	$8 \times 0 + 4 \times 1 + 2 \times 1 + 1 \times 1 = 7$	0	1	1	1
8	$8 \times 1 + 4 \times 0 + 2 \times 0 + 1 \times 0 = 8$	1	0	0	0
9	$8 \times 1 + 4 \times 0 + 2 \times 0 + 1 \times 1 = 9$	1	0	0	1

Example 4.35

Convert 4567_{10} to BCD_{8421}.

Solution

From Table 4.9, we can write,

$$(4567)_{10} = (0100\ 0101\ 0110\ 0111)_{BCD8421}$$

Example 4.36

Give the BCD equivalent of the decimal number 68.23.

Solution

From Table 4.9, we can write,

$$(68.23)_{10} = (0110\ 1000.0010\ 0011)_{BCD8421}$$

Table 4.10 2421 code

Decimal	Formed By	Weight			
		2	4	2	1
0	$2 \times 0 + 4 \times 0 + 2 \times 0 + 1 \times 0 = 0$	0	0	0	0
1	$2 \times 0 + 4 \times 0 + 2 \times 0 + 1 \times 1 = 1$	0	0	0	1
2	$2 \times 0 + 4 \times 0 + 2 \times 1 + 1 \times 0 = 2$	0	0	1	0
3	$2 \times 0 + 4 \times 0 + 2 \times 1 + 1 \times 1 = 3$	0	0	1	1
4	$2 \times 0 + 4 \times 1 + 2 \times 0 + 1 \times 0 = 4$	0	1	0	0
5	$2 \times 1 + 4 \times 0 + 2 \times 1 + 1 \times 1 = 5$	1	0	1	1
6	$2 \times 1 + 4 \times 1 + 2 \times 0 + 1 \times 0 = 6$	1	1	0	0
7	$2 \times 1 + 4 \times 1 + 2 \times 0 + 1 \times 1 = 7$	1	1	0	1
8	$2 \times 1 + 4 \times 1 + 2 \times 1 + 1 \times 0 = 8$	1	1	1	0
9	$2 \times 1 + 4 \times 1 + 2 \times 1 + 1 \times 1 = 9$	1	1	1	1

Note

Weighted binary codes follow positional weighting principle where each position of the number represents a specific weight.

2421 Code

The 2421 weighted code has weights 2, 4, 2, and 1. In this code, a decimal number is represented using four bits. The maximum weight in this code is 2 + 4 + 2 + 1 = 9. Therefore, the 2421 code can represent decimal numbers from 0 to 9, as shown in Table 4.10.

Similarly, in the 4221 coding, each digit is represented as a four-bit group, and each bit represents 4, 2, 2, and 1, instead of 8, 4, 2, and 1. For example, 7 in 4221 can be written as 1101, because $4 \times 1 + 2 \times 1 + 2 \times 0 + 1 \times 1 = 7$.

4.9.5 Gray Code

The gray code is a minimum change code, in which only one bit in the code changes from one code to the next. It is a non-weighted code. These codes are also known as *single-distance codes*.

The gray code of a number is obtained from its binary code. To derive the gray code of a number, the following steps are used:

- Copy the MSB of the binary code as the MSB of the gray code.
- Add the MSB and the bit next to the MSB to get the corresponding bit for the gray code, and discard the carry.
- Repeat the process.

For example, let us calculate the gray code of 7.

Decimal 7 = Binary 0111

Now gray code of 7 is obtained as follows:

- MSB of gray code 7 is 0 (because MSB of binary 7 is 0)

Now, other bits can be calculated as:

- 0 + 1 = 1
- 1 + 1 = 0 (discard the carry)
- 1 + 1 = 0 (discard the carry)

Hence, gray code for 7 = 0100.

4.9.6 Unicode

ASCII, which is the most widely used encoding scheme, is a seven-bit code that can support only 128 character definitions. These 128 characters can be used easily for English characters, numbers, and punctuation symbols but there is negligible or no support for the characters in other languages of the world. Therefore, organizations started creating their own encoding schemes for other languages' characters, thereby defeating the concept of a universal or standard code for information exchange. Moreover, each new scheme was of different length, and programs were supposed to determine which encoding scheme they would be using.

The only solution to this problem was to have a new encoding scheme that could unify all the different encoding schemes to minimize confusion between the different schemes. This led to the development of Unicode, which can represent characters (including punctuation marks, diacritics, mathematical symbols, technical symbols, and arrows) as integers. It has several character encoding forms such as the following:

UTF-8 This uses only eight bits to encode English characters. This format is widely used in e-mail and on the Internet.

UTF-16 This uses 16 bits to encode the most commonly used characters. A 16-bit Unicode can represent more than 65,000 characters. Moreover, any Unicode character represented in the UTF-16 form can be converted to the UTF-8 form and vice versa without losing information.

UTF-32 This uses 32 bits to encode the characters. A 32-bit Unicode can represent more than 100,000 characters.

Note

UTF stands for Unicode Transformation Format.

Besides representing the characters of different languages, UTF also reserves some codes for private use, which hardware and software vendors can assign internally for their own characters and symbols.

Nowadays, Unicode is widely used to represent text for computer processing, as it provides a consistent way of encoding multilingual characters. This makes it convenient to exchange text files internationally.

Table 4.11 illustrates how coding is done in the ASCII, EBCDIC, XS3, 4221, gray, and Unicode coding techniques.

Table 4.11 Decimal numbers (0–9) represented in different codes

Digit	Binary	ASCII	EBCDIC	XS3	4221	Gray code	Unicode
0	0000	0011 0000	1111 0000	0011	0000	0000	U + 0030
1	0001	0011 0001	1111 0001	0100	0001	0001	U + 0031
2	0010	0011 0010	1111 0010	0101	0010	0011	U + 0032
3	0011	0011 0011	1111 0011	0110	0011	0010	U + 0033
4	0100	0011 0100	1111 0100	0111	1000	0110	U + 0034
5	0101	0011 0101	1111 0101	1000	0111	0111	U + 0035
6	0110	0011 0110	1111 0110	1001	1100	0101	U + 0036
7	0111	0011 0111	1111 0111	1010	1101	0100	U + 0037
8	1000	0011 1000	1111 1000	1011	1110	1100	U + 0038
9	1001	0011 1001	1111 1001	1100	1111	1101	U + 0039

POINTS TO REMEMBER

- Computers are electronic machines that operate using binary logic. These devices use two different voltage levels to represent the two values (0V for logic 0 and +5V for logic 1).
- The number of unique digits used to form numbers within a number system is called radix of that system. Decimal number system has a radix of 10, binary has a radix of 2, octal has a radix of 8, and hexadecimal has a radix of 16.
- To convert a decimal number into its binary/octal/hexadecimal equivalent, simply divide the decimal number by 2/8/16 and then write down the remainders.
- To convert a binary/octal/hexadecimal number into its decimal equivalent, multiply the place holder value by the digit, and then add all the products.
- Signed number representation is required to encode negative numbers in the binary number system.
- The two's complement is the most popular method of representing signed numbers in the binary number system.
- Binary coded decimal (BCD) is a technique of encoding decimal numbers. In unpacked BCD representation, only one decimal number is represented per byte. In packed BCD representation, two decimal numbers are stored in a single byte.
- ASCII is a seven-bit character code that was introduced by ANSI and is used by personal and workstation computers.
- EBCDIC is an eight-bit character encoding technique used on IBM mainframe operating systems. It is considered to be an obsolete coding system, but is still used in some equipment to allow for continued use of software written many years ago that requires an EBCDIC communication environment.
- In the excess-3 coding technique, each decimal digit is the four-bit binary equivalent with 3 (0011) added.
- In a weighted code, position of each digit represents a specific weight. In the 8421 system, the LSB has a weight of $2^0 = 1$, the next bit has a weight $2^1 = 2$, the next bit has a weight of $2^2 = 4$, and the MSB has a weight of $2^3 = 8$.
- Gray code is a minimum change code, in which only one bit changes from one code to the next.
- Unicode is a character encoding industry standard which provides support for characters from other languages of the world. The different variants are: UTF-8, UTF-16, and UTF-32.

EXERCISES

Fill in the Blanks

1. Computers are electronic machines that operate on ________ logic.
2. ________ bits make one word.
3. 0 – 1 = ________.
4. In the ________ technique, the MSB is used to denote the sign of a number.
5. In ________, a number is stored in the lower nibble, and the higher nibble is not relevant to the value of the represented number.
6. ASCII codes can support ________ characters.
7. EBCDIC is a ________ bit character encoding technique.
8. The hexadecimal number system uses digits from ________ to ________.
9. The octal number system was used in the ________ system.
10. Working from right to left, the columns in the hexadecimal number system are ________.

Review Questions

1. What is binary language?
2. Why do computers understand only binary language?
3. Explain the process of converting a binary number into decimal with an example.
4. Describe the general procedure to convert a number from any base system into its decimal equivalent. Explain using examples the conversion of numbers from any three base systems to the decimal system.
5. How can two numbers be subtracted only through addition? Explain with the help of an example.
6. How are signed numbers represented in the binary form?
7. Two's complement is the most popular technique to represent signed numbers. Justify the statement.
8. Differentiate between packed and unpacked BCD representation.
9. How is the 8421 code different from the 4221 code?
10. Give the gray code for the decimal number 13.
11. Convert the following numbers into the decimal number system.
    (a) $(1011\ 0101)_2$
    (b) $(5674)_8$
    (c) $(A1E2)_{16}$
    (d) 0000 1001 (unpacked BCD)
    (e) 1000 0001 (packed BCD)
12. Convert the decimal 987654 into octal and hexadecimal number systems.
13. Convert 1001 0010 1110 into the hexadecimal number system.
14. Convert 89CD into the binary number system.
15. Subtract:
    (a) 10101011 – 01111
    (b) 11100001 – 11110111
    (c) 1010101010 – 111101
16. Add:
    (a) 10101011 + 0111111
    (b) 11100001 + 1111110111
    (c) 1010101010 + 111101
17. Multiply:
    (a) 10111 × 1011
    (b) 1111000 × 100
    (c) 1111101 × 1111
18. Divide:
    (a) 10111110/1011
    (b) 1111000/100
    (c) 1111101101/1111

SCAN THE PAGE TO KNOW MORE

5 Boolean Algebra and Logic Gates

TAKEAWAYS

- Boolean algebra
- Truth tables
- Laws of Boolean algebra
- Venn diagrams
- Logic gates
- Universal gates
- Canonical forms
- Karnaugh map (K-Map)

5.1 BOOLEAN ALGEBRA

As already discussed in Chapter 4, computers understand only binary numbers, in which only the digits 0 and 1 are used. These binary computer systems work on propositional logic, wherein a proposition is a declarative sentence which may be true or false. Propositions may also be stated as functions of other propositions that are connected by three basic logical connectives—AND, OR, and NOT. For example,

I will do postgraduation if I get admission in MSc or MCA.

This statement functionally connects the proposition 'I will do postgraduation' to two propositions—'if I get admission in MSc' and 'if I get admission in MCA'. This scenario can be represented as shown in Figure 5.1.

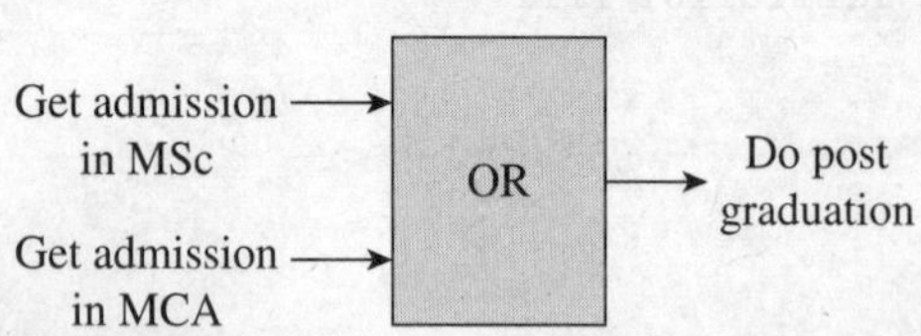

Figure 5.1 Statement and simple propositions

From this discussion, we can conclude that with the OR connective the corresponding output is true if either one of the inputs is true; otherwise, it is false.

We can make this proposition a little more complex by saying 'I will do postgraduation if I do not get a job and if I get admission either in MSc or in MCA'. Before preparing the block diagram for this preposition, we must first state it in a well-structured way to understand how it is composed. The proposition can be given as follows:

Do postgraduation = (NOT (Get a job)) AND ((Get admission in MSc) OR (Get admission in MCA))

The proposition can be represented diagrammatically as shown in Figure 5.2.

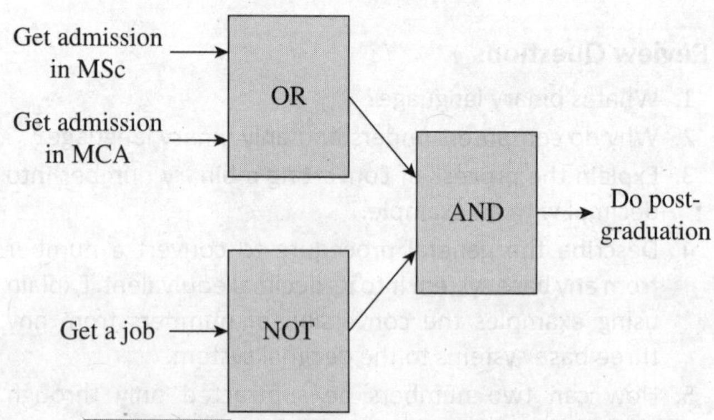

Figure 5.2 Statement and complex propositions

Thus, we see that a complex proposition can be easily stated in terms of binary variables and binary operators (OR, AND, and NOT). It is for this purpose that the mathematician George Boole developed Boolean algebra in 1854.

In Boolean algebra, a system has either of two states—*true* (T) or *false* (F). The following are the salient points of Boolean algebra:

- Value '1' means true.
- Value '0' means false.
- A *Boolean expression* is a combination of Boolean variables and Boolean operators. Boolean expressions that are logically equivalent to one another are called equivalent expressions.
- A *Boolean function* has one or more input variables and generates an output based on the values of these input variables. The result may be 0 or 1.
- Boolean operators take certain inputs and produce an output based on a predetermined table of results (also known as a *truth table*).

- Boolean operator AND (conjunction or intersection) is used as a '·' and in some texts as '∩'. For example, $A \cdot B$ or $A \cap B$ means *A and B*. The AND operator takes two (or more) inputs and returns a 1 only when both (or all) inputs are 1.
- Boolean operator OR (disjunction or union) is used as a '+' and in some texts as '∪'. For example, $A + B$ or $A \cup B$ means *A or B*. The OR operator takes two (or more) inputs and returns a 1 when any or all of the inputs are 1.
- Boolean operator NOT (negation) is used as a "' and in some texts as '–'. It simply negates the value of the operator. For example, *A*' means NOT *A*. If the input is 1, the output will be 0 and vice versa.

Precedence Rules of Boolean Operators

Like arithmetic operators, Boolean operators have an order of precedence and parentheses can be used to group operands to change the order of evaluation. If there are several operators in an expression with the same precedence then they are evaluated left to right. The following table lists Boolean operators in the order of precedence from highest to lowest.

Operator
!
&&
||

For example, in the expression, *A* || *B* && *C*, first *B* && *C* will be evaluated and then *A* will be OR'ed with the result. Let us learn this concept through more examples.

In the expression *A* && *B* || *C* && *D*, first *A* && *B* will be performed followed by *C* && *D* followed by OR between the two results.

In the expression *A* && *B* && *C* || *D*, first *A* && *B* will be evaluated followed by && with *C* followed by || with *D*.

In the expression !*A* && *B* || *C*, first !*A* will be performed followed by && followed by ||.

Boolean algebra forms the basis of digital systems. It is extensively used to design digital circuits and is applied in digital logic, computer programming, set theory, and statistics.

5.2 TRUTH TABLES

A truth table is used to describe a Boolean function of *n* input variables. It lists all possible values of input combinations of the function and the output that will be produced based on these input combinations. Such a table provides a useful visual tool for defining the input–output reltionship of binary variables in a Boolean function.

A Boolean function of *n* variables has 2^n rows of possible input combinations. Each row specifies the output of the Boolean function for a different combination. The truth tables for the three Boolean operators are shown in Table 5.1.

Table 5.1 Truth tables for Boolean operators

AND

A	B	$Z = A \cdot B$
0	0	0
0	1	0
1	0	0
1	1	1

OR

A	B	$Z = A + B$
0	0	0
0	1	1
1	0	1
1	1	1

NOT

A	$Z = A'$
0	1
1	0

A truth table can also be used to represent one or more Boolean functions. For example, Table 5.2 represents the truth table for the Boolean function $Z = A \cup (B \cap C)$.

Table 5.2 Truth table for Boolean function $Z = A \cup (B \cap C)$

A	B	C	$B \cap C$	$Z = A \cup (B \cap C)$
0	0	0	0	0
0	0	1	0	0
0	1	0	0	0
0	1	1	1	1
1	0	0	0	1
1	0	1	0	1
1	1	0	0	1
1	1	1	1	1

5.3 BASIC LAWS OF BOOLEAN ALGEBRA

The laws of Boolean algebra can be divided into two categories—laws applicable on a single variable and laws applicable on multiple variables (Figure 5.3).

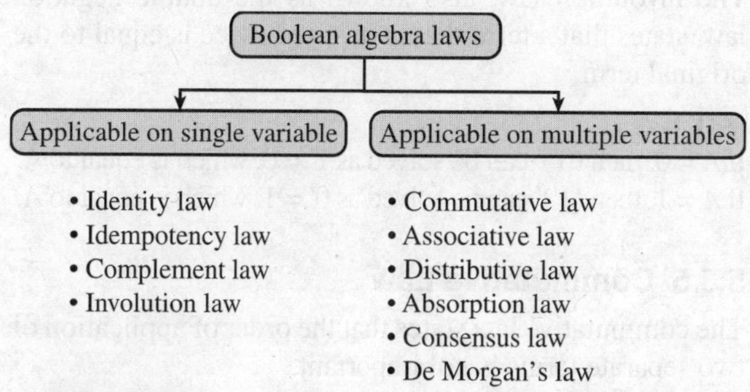

Figure 5.3 Classification of laws of Boolean algebra

5.3.1 Identity Law

The identity law states that a term OR'ed with a 0 or AND'ed with a 1 will always equal that term. Similarly, a term OR'ed with a 1 is always 1 and a term AND'ed with a 0 will always result in 0.

1. $\boldsymbol{A + 0 = A}$
   If $A = 0$, then $0 + 0 = 0$, which is equal to A.
   If $A = 1$, then $1 + 0 = 1$, which is again equal to A.
2. $\boldsymbol{A + 1 = 1}$
   If $A = 0$, then $0 + 1 = 1$.
   If $A = 1$, then $1 + 1 = 1$.
3. $\boldsymbol{A \cdot 0 = 0}$
   If $A = 0$, then $0 \cdot 0 = 0$.
   If $A = 1$, then $1 \cdot 0 = 0$.
4. $\boldsymbol{A \cdot 1 = A}$
   If $A = 0$, then $0 \cdot 1 = 0$, which is equal to A.
   If $A = 1$, then $1 \cdot 1 = 1$, which is again equal to A.

5.3.2 Idempotency Law

The idempotency law states that a term AND'ed with itself or OR'ed with itself is equal to that term.

1. $\boldsymbol{A + A = A}$
   If $A = 0$, then $0 + 0 = 0$, which is equal to A.
   If $A = 1$, then $1 + 1 = 1$, which is again equal to A.
2. $\boldsymbol{A \cdot A = A}$
   If $A = 0$, then $0 \cdot 0 = 0$, which is equal to A.
   If $A = 1$, then $1 \cdot 1 = 1$, which is again equal to A.

5.3.3 Complement Law

The complement law states that a term AND'ed with its complement always results in 0 and a term OR'ed with its complement always results in 1.

1. $\boldsymbol{A + A' = 1}$
   If $A = 0$, then $0 + 1 = 1$.
   If $A = 1$, then $1 + 0 = 1$.
2. $\boldsymbol{A \cdot A' = 0}$
   If $A = 0$, then $0 \cdot 1 = 0$.
   If $A = 1$, then $1 \cdot 0 = 0$.

5.3.4 Involution Law

The involution law, also known as the double negation law, states that a term that is inverted twice is equal to the original term.

$(A')' = A$
If $A = 0$, then $(0')'$ can be solved as $1' = 0$, which is equal to A.
If $A = 1$, then $(1')'$ can be solved as $0' = 1$, which is equal to A.

5.3.5 Commutative Law

The commutative law states that the order of application of two separate terms is not important.

1. $\boldsymbol{A + B = B + A}$

The truth table of the Boolean functions proves this law, as shown in Table 5.3.

Table 5.3 Truth table for Boolean functions $A + B$ and $B + A$

A	B	$A + B$	$B + A$
0	0	0	0
0	1	1	1
1	0	1	1
1	1	1	1

2. $\boldsymbol{A \cdot B = B \cdot A}$

   Table 5.4 shows the truth table of the Boolean functions, which proves this law.

Table 5.4 Truth table for Boolean fuctions $A \cdot B$ and $B \cdot A$

A	B	$A \cdot B$	$B \cdot A$
0	0	0	0
0	1	0	0
1	0	0	0
1	1	1	1

5.3.6 Associative Law

The associative law allows removal of brackets from an expression and regrouping of the variables.

1. $\boldsymbol{A + (B + C) = (A + B) + C}$

   The truth table of the Boolean functions, shown in Table 5.5, proves this law.

Table 5.5 Truth table for Boolean functions $A + (B + C)$ and $(A + B) + C$

A	B	C	$A + (B + C)$	$(A + B) + C$
0	0	0	0	0
0	0	1	1	1
0	1	0	1	1
0	1	1	1	1
1	0	0	1	1
1	0	1	1	1
1	1	0	1	1
1	1	1	1	1

2. $\boldsymbol{A \cdot (B \cdot C) = (A \cdot B) \cdot C}$

   The truth table of the Boolean functions, shown in Table 5.6, proves this law.

Table 5.6 Truth table for Boolean functions $A \cdot (B \cdot C)$ and $(A \cdot B) \cdot C$

A	B	C	$A \cdot (B \cdot C)$	$(A \cdot B) \cdot C$
0	0	0	0	0
0	0	1	0	0
0	1	0	0	0
0	1	1	0	0
1	0	0	0	0
1	0	1	0	0
1	1	0	0	0
1	1	1	1	1

5.3.7 Distributive Law

The distributive law enables multiplication or factoring out of an expression.

1. $A(B + C) = A \cdot B + A \cdot C$

   The truth table of the Boolean functions, shown in Table 5.7, proves this law.

Table 5.7 Truth table for Boolean functions $A \cdot (B + C)$ and $A \cdot B + A \cdot C$

A	B	C	$B+C$	$A \cdot (B+C)$	$A \cdot B$	$A \cdot C$	$A \cdot B + A \cdot C$
0	0	0	0	0	0	0	0
0	0	1	1	0	0	0	0
0	1	0	1	0	0	0	0
0	1	1	1	0	0	0	0
1	0	0	0	0	0	0	0
1	0	1	1	1	0	1	1
1	1	0	1	1	1	0	1
1	1	1	1	1	1	1	1

2. $A + (B \cdot C) = (A + B) \cdot (A + C)$

   RHS $= (A + B) \cdot (A + C)$
   $= A \cdot A + A \cdot B + A \cdot C + B \cdot C$ (Opening the brackets and multiplying)
   $= A + A \cdot B + A \cdot C + B \cdot C$ (Since $A \cdot A = A$)
   $= A \cdot (1 + B) + A \cdot C + B \cdot C$
   $= A + A \cdot C + B \cdot C$ (Since $1 + B = 1$ and $A \cdot 1 = A$)
   $= A(1 + C) + B \cdot C$
   $= A + B \cdot C =$ LHS (Since $1 + C = 1$ and $A \cdot 1 = A$)

Let us prove this law using the truth table of the Boolean functions (Table 5.8).

Table 5.8 Truth table for Boolean functions $A + (B \cdot C)$ and $(A + B) \cdot (A + C)$

A	B	C	$B \cdot C$	$A + B \cdot C$	$A+B$	$A+C$	$(A+B) \cdot (A+C)$
0	0	0	0	0	0	0	0
0	0	1	0	0	0	1	0
0	1	0	0	0	1	0	0
0	1	1	1	1	1	1	1
1	0	0	0	1	1	1	1
1	0	1	0	1	1	1	1
1	1	0	0	1	1	1	1
1	1	1	1	1	1	1	1

5.3.8 Absorption Law

The absorption law permits the reduction of a complicated expression into a simpler one by absorbing like terms.

1. $A + A \cdot B = A$

   LHS $= A + A{\cdot}B$
   $= A \cdot 1 + A \cdot B$ (Since $A \cdot 1 = A$)
   $= A(1 + B)$
   $= A \cdot 1$ (Since $1 + B = 1$)
   $= A =$ RHS

2. $A \cdot (A + B) = A$

   LHS $= A \cdot (A + B)$
   $= A \cdot A + A{\cdot}B$
   $= A + A \cdot B$ (Since $A \cdot A = A$)
   $= A \cdot 1 + A \cdot B$ (Since $A \cdot 1 = A$)
   $= A \cdot (1 + B)$
   $= A \cdot 1$ (Since $1 + B = 1$)
   $= A =$ RHS (Since $A \cdot 1 = A$)

3. $A + A' \cdot B = A + B$

   LHS $= A + A' \cdot B$
   $= (A + A') \cdot (A + B)$ (Applying distributive law i.e. $A + B \cdot C = (A + B) \cdot (A + C)$)
   $= 1 \cdot (A + B)$ (Since $A + A' = 1$)
   $= A + B =$ RHS

4. $A \cdot (A' + B) = A \cdot B$

   LHS $= A \cdot (A' + B)$
   $= A \cdot A' + A \cdot B$
   $= 0 + A \cdot B$ (Since $A \cdot A' = 0$)
   $= A \cdot B =$ RHS (Since $A + 0 = A$)

5.3.9 Consensus Law

The consensus law is the conjunction of all the unique literals of the terms, excluding the literal that is not negated in one term but negated in the other.

1. $A \cdot B + A' \cdot C + B \cdot C = A \cdot B + A' \cdot C$

   LHS $= A \cdot B + A' \cdot C + B \cdot C$
   $= A \cdot B + A' \cdot C + B \cdot C \cdot 1$ (Since $A \cdot 1 = A$)
   $= A \cdot B + A' \cdot C + B \cdot C\,(A + A')$
   $= A \cdot B + A' \cdot C + A \cdot B \cdot C + A' \cdot B \cdot C$
   $= A \cdot B + A \cdot B \cdot C + A' \cdot C + A' \cdot B \cdot C$

$= A \cdot B(1 + C) + A' \cdot C(1 + B)$
$= A \cdot B + A' \cdot C = \text{RHS}$ (Since $1 + C = 1$ and $1 + B = 1$)

2. $\boldsymbol{(A + B)(A' + C)(B + C) = (A + B)(A' + C)}$

LHS $= (A + B)(A' + C)(B + C)$
$= (A \cdot A' + A' \cdot B + A \cdot C + B \cdot C)(B + C)$
$= (A' \cdot B + A \cdot C + B \cdot C)(B + C)$
(Since $A \cdot A' = 0$)
$= A' \cdot B \cdot B + A \cdot B \cdot C + B \cdot B \cdot C + A' \cdot B \cdot C + A \cdot C \cdot C + B \cdot C \cdot C$
$= A' \cdot B + A \cdot B \cdot C + B \cdot C + A' \cdot B \cdot C + A \cdot C + B \cdot C$ (Since $A \cdot A = A$)
$= A' \cdot B + B \cdot C(A + A') + B \cdot C + A \cdot C$ (Since $A + A = A$)
$= A' \cdot B + B \cdot C + A \cdot C$ (Since $A + A' = 1$)

RHS $= (A + B)(A' + C)$
$= A \cdot A' + A' \cdot B + A \cdot C + B \cdot C$
$= A' \cdot B + A \cdot C + B \cdot C$ (Since $A \cdot A' = 0$)

Therefore, LHS = RHS.

5.3.10 De Morgan's Laws

The two laws are as follows:

1. $\boldsymbol{(A + B)' = A' \cdot B'}$

   The first law states that the complement of the union of two terms is the intersection of their complements.

   Let us prove this law using the truth table of the Boolean functions (Table 5.9).

Table 5.9 Truth table for Boolean functions $(A + B)'$ and $A' \cdot B'$

A	B	$A + B$	$(A + B)'$	A'	B'	$A' \cdot B'$
0	0	0	1	1	1	1
0	1	1	0	1	0	0
1	0	1	0	0	1	0
1	1	1	0	0	0	0

2. $\boldsymbol{(A \cdot B)' = A' + B'}$

   De Morgan's second law states that the complement of the intersection of two terms is the union of their complements.

   Let us prove this law using the truth table of the Boolean functions (Table 5.10).

Table 5.10 Truth table for Boolean functions $(A \cdot B)'$ and $(A' + B')$

A	B	$A \cdot B$	$(A \cdot B)'$	A'	B'	$A' + B'$
0	0	0	1	1	1	1
0	1	0	1	1	0	1
1	0	0	1	0	1	1
1	1	1	0	0	0	0

Duality Principle

The duality property states that all binary expressions remain valid when symbols in expressions are interchanged with their duals, i.e. when the following two steps are performed:

Step 1: Swap OR and AND operators.
Step 2: Replace all 1's by 0's and 0's by 1's.

For example, consider the expression $0 \cdot 1 = 0$. The dual of this expression is $1 + 0 = 1$

Similarly, the dual of expression $1 \cdot 1 = 1$ is $0 + 0 = 0$.

5.4 VENN DIAGRAMS

A Venn diagram can be used to represent Boolean operations using shaded overlapping regions. In the Venn diagrams that are presented in this section, there is one circular region for each variable. The interior and exterior of a region of a particular variable corresponds to values 1 (true) and 0 (false), respectively. The Venn diagrams corresponding to AND, OR, and NOT operations are shown in Figure 5.4. Here, the shaded area indicates the value 1 of the operation and the non-shaded area denotes the value 0.

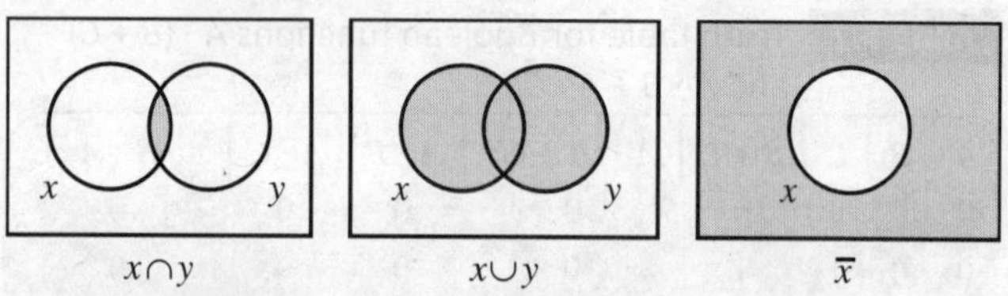

Figure 5.4 Venn diagrams for conjunction (AND), disjunction (OR), and complement (NOT)

The following points can be observed from Figure 5.4:

- For the AND operation, the region common to both circles is shaded to indicate that $x \cap y$ is 1 when both variables are 1. The non-shaded area indicates that $x \cap y$ is 0 for the other three combinations of variables x and y.
- For the OR operation, the regions that lie inside either or both the circles are shaded.
- For the NOT operation, the Venn diagram represents complement x' by shading the region *not* inside the circle.

Venn diagrams are useful to understand and visualize the following laws of Boolean algebra.

Absorption Law: $\boldsymbol{x \cap (x \cup y) = x}$

Shade the portion for $x \cup y$. Next, shade the portion for x. Then shade the area that is common in both the diagrams. The resultant shaded area will be the whole of circle x (Figure 5.5).

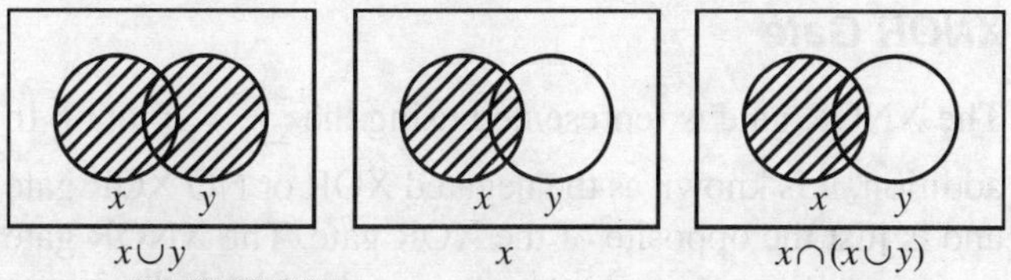

Figure 5.5 Venn diagrams for absorption law

Double Negation Law: (x′)′ = x

First, shade the circle *x*. Then shade the area not in *x*. This will give the region for *x*′. Next shade the area that is not in *x*′, which will be the whole of circle *x* (Figure 5.6).

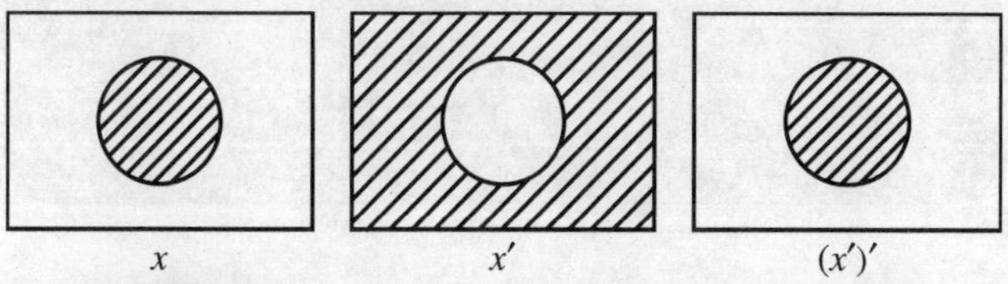

Figure 5.6 Venn diagrams for double negation law

De Morgan's Law: x′ ∩ y′ = (x ∪ y)′

To visualize De Morgan's law, start with the left-hand side (LHS) and shade the area that is neither in *x* nor in *y*. Then, for the right-hand side (RHS), shade the area corresponding to $x \cup y$, which is the area in either or both the circles. Finally, shade the area that is not in the region of $x \cup y$. It can be seen from Figure 5.7 that it is the same area that we had shaded for the LHS.

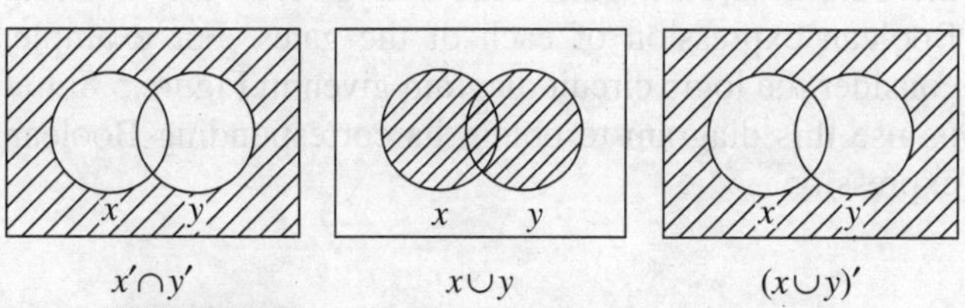

Figure 5.7 Venn diagrams for De Morgan's law

5.5 LOGIC GATES

We have seen that computers work on binary digits, which form the heart of digital electronics. In digital electronics, we are not concerned about electrical signals; rather, we just need to understand the difference between two states: *on* (1) and *off* (0). Moreover, in digital electronics, operations are performed using logic gates, which are also known as Boolean gates. These gates work only on the logic that comprises either a 0 or 1. There are different types of Boolean gates, each of which follows a different set of rules. In this section, we will discuss Boolean gates and in the next section we will see how Boolean expressions can be represented using these gates in digital electronics.

AND Gate

The AND gate is represented with the  symbol. This gate accepts two inputs and gives an output. The output will be 1 if and only if both the inputs are 1, and will be a 0 otherwise. The truth table of the AND gate is given in Table 5.11. The expression involving an AND operation can be written as $\text{Input}_1 \cap \text{Input}_2$ or $\text{Input}_1 \cdot \text{Input}_2$.

Table 5.11 Truth table of AND gate

Input_1	Input_2	Output
0	0	0
0	1	0
1	0	0
1	1	1

OR Gate

The OR gate is represented with the 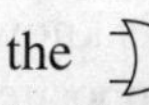 symbol. This gate accepts two inputs and gives an output. The output will be 1 if any of the two inputs is 1. That is, it gives a 0 output only when both the inputs are 0. The truth table of the OR gate is given in Table 5.12. The expression involving an OR operation can be written as $\text{Input}_1 \cup \text{Input}_2$ or $\text{Input}_1 + \text{Input}_2$.

Table 5.12 Truth table of OR gate

Input_1	Input_2	Output
0	0	0
0	1	1
1	0	1
1	1	1

NOT Gate

The NOT gate is represented by the 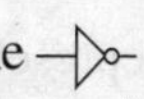 symbol. Unlike the AND and OR gates, the NOT gate accepts just one input. The output produced by a NOT gate is just the opposite of the input given. For example, if the input is 1 the output is 0, and vice versa. The expression involving a NOT operation can be written as NOT Input, or as ~Input, or as Input′.

Table 5.13 shows the truth table of this gate.

Table 5.13 Truth table of NOT gate

Input	Output
0	1
1	0

NAND Gate

The NAND gate is represented using the 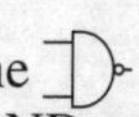 symbol. In addition, it is known as the negated AND or NO AND gate. It is just the opposite of the AND gate. The NAND gate accepts two inputs and returns a 0 if both the inputs are 1, else returns a 1. The truth table of the NAND gate is given in Table 5.14. The expression involving a NAND operation can be written as $Input_1 \mid Input_2$ or $\overline{Input_1 \cdot Input_2}$.

Table 5.14 Truth table of NAND gate

$Input_1$	$Input_2$	Output
0	0	1
0	1	1
1	0	1
1	1	0

NOR Gate

The NOR gate is represented using the 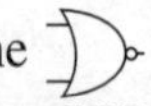 symbol. In addition, it is known as the negated OR or NO OR gate. It is just the opposite of the OR gate. The NOR gate accepts two inputs and returns a 1 only if both the inputs are 0. The truth table of the NOR gate is given in Table 5.15. The expression involving a NOR operation can be written as $Input_1 – Input_2$ or $\overline{Input_1 + Input_2}$.

Table 5.15 Truth table of NOR gate

$Input_1$	$Input_2$	Output
0	0	1
0	1	0
1	0	0
1	1	0

XOR Gate

The XOR gate is represented using the  symbol. The X in the XOR gate stands for *exclusive*. This means that the output of this gate will be 1 if only one of the inputs is 1, but not both. As can be seen in Table 5.16 the output is 0 if both the inputs are 1 or 0. In general, the output of the XOR gate is 1 when the number of its high inputs is odd. This also means that the output will be 1 if the inputs are different. The expression involving an XOR operation can be written as $Input_1 \oplus Input_2$.

Table 5.16 Truth table of XOR gate

$Input_1$	$Input_2$	Output
0	0	0
0	1	1
1	0	1
1	1	0

XNOR Gate

The XNOR gate is represented using the  symbol. In addition, it is known as the negated XOR or NO XOR gate and is just the opposite of the XOR gate. The XNOR gate accepts two inputs and returns a 1 only if both the inputs are same and a 0 otherwise. The expression involving an XNOR operation can be written as $\overline{Input_1 \oplus Input_2}$. The truth table of the XNOR gate is given in Table 5.17.

Table 5.17 Truth table of XNOR gate

$Input_1$	$Input_2$	Output
0	0	1
0	1	0
1	0	0
1	1	1

5.6 LOGIC DIAGRAMS AND BOOLEAN EXPRESSIONS

A logic diagram is a pictorial representation of a combination of logic gates to specify a Boolean expression. Therefore, we can directly obtain Boolean expressions by analysing circuit diagrams or vice versa.

Let us first convert a logic circuit diagram to a Boolean expression. In order to do this, we will first list the inputs at the correct place and then process the inputs through the gates by considering one gate at a time. Then we will write the output of each gate. This will give us the resulting Boolean expression of each of the gates. For example, consider the logic circuit diagram given in Figure 5.8. Let us use this diagram to obtain its corresponding Boolean expression.

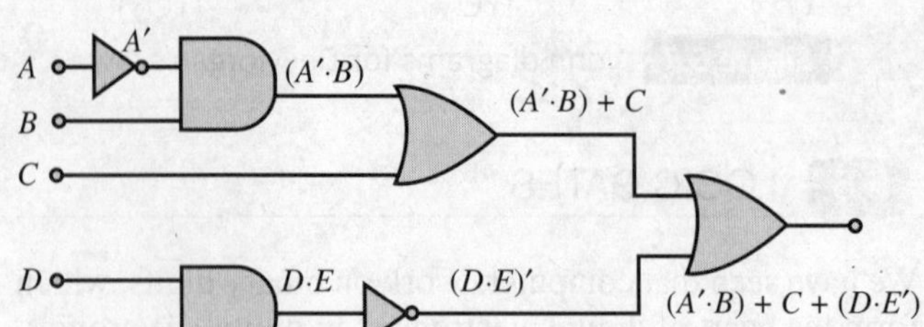

Figure 5.8 Conversion of logic circuit diagram into Boolean expression

Converting a Boolean expression into its equivalent logic diagram is a little difficult since it requires a good understanding of the order of operations, which is as follows:

- Parentheses
- NOT
- AND
- OR

Now, let us draw the circuit diagram for the Boolean expression $Y = (A + B \cdot C) + (B' + C)$ (Figure 5.9). First, we consider the parentheses $(A + B \cdot C)$. Within these parentheses, we will first perform the AND operation followed by the OR operation.

Now, consider the second parentheses $(B' + C)$. Within these parentheses, we will first perform the NOT operation followed by the OR operation.

Finally, the OR operation between the two parentheses is performed in Figure 5.9(e). Note that in Figure 5.9(f), the same figure has been redrawn with single inputs for each input variable.

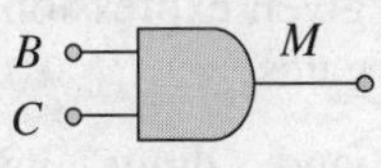

(a) AND operation

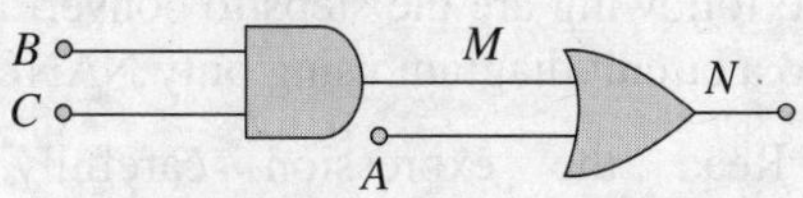

(b) OR operation of the first parentheses

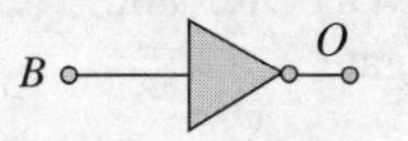

(c) NOT operation

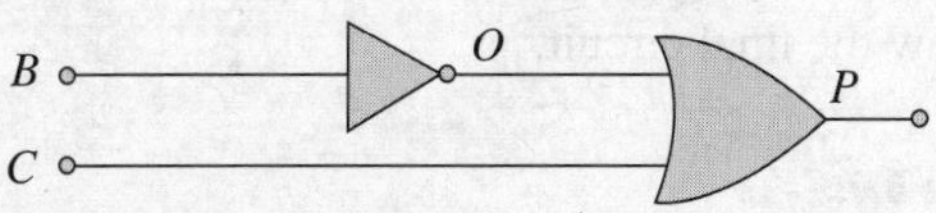

(d) OR operation of the second parentheses

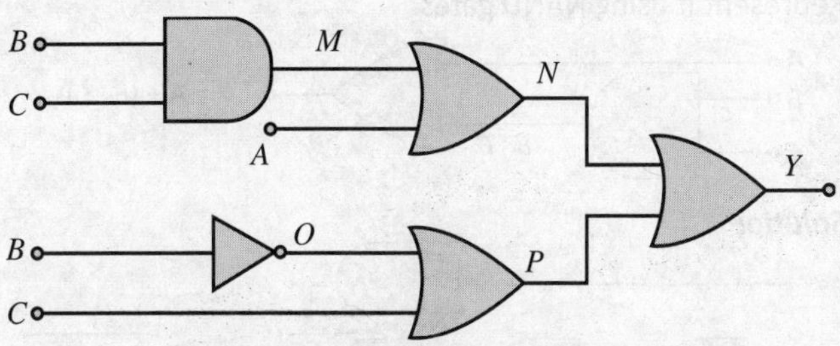

(e) OR operation of the two parentheses

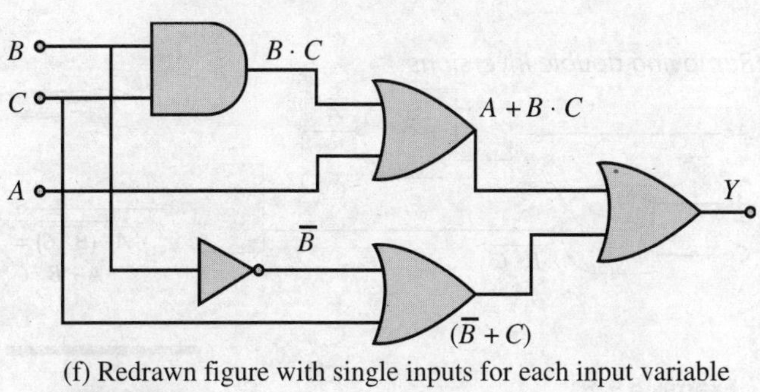

(f) Redrawn figure with single inputs for each input variable

Figure 5.9 Conversion of Boolean expression into logic diagram

Example 5.1

Represent $Y = A + \overline{B}$ using logic gates.

Solution

$Y = A + \overline{B}$

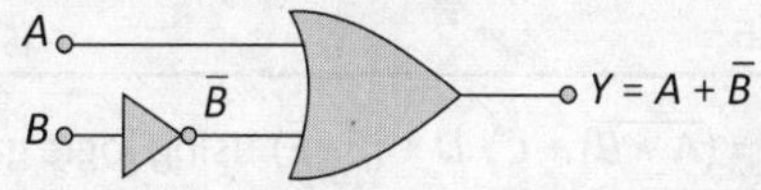

Example 5.2

Represent $Y = \overline{A \cdot B}$ using logic gates.

Solution

$Y = \overline{A \cdot B}$

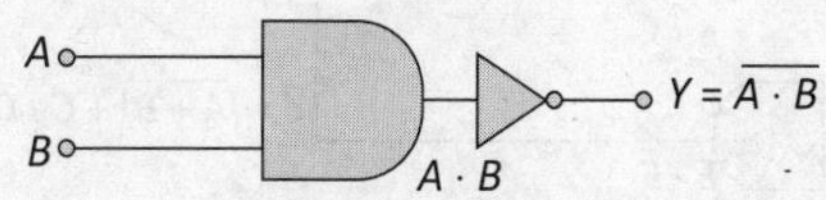

(or)

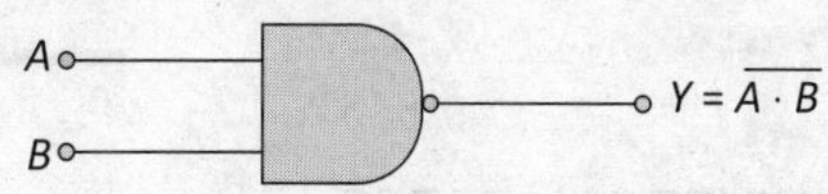

Example 5.3

Represent $Y = (A \cdot B) + C$ using logic gates.

Solution

$Y = (A \cdot B) + C$

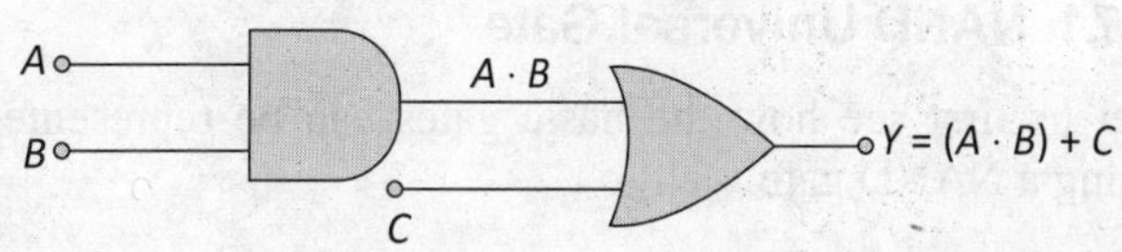

Example 5.4

Represent $Y = (\overline{A + B}) \cdot C$ using logic gates.

Solution

$Y = (\overline{A + B}) \cdot C$

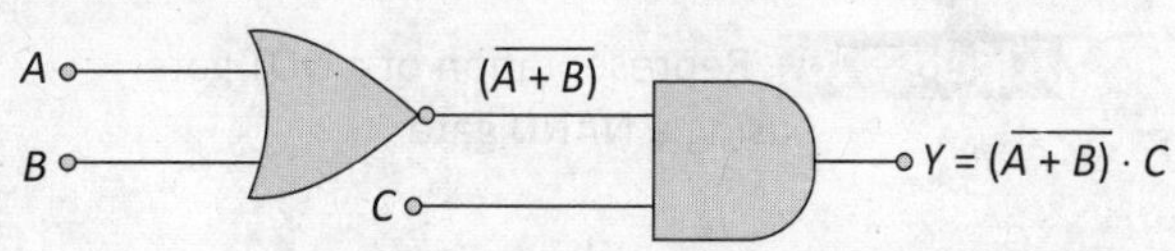

Example 5.5

Represent $Y = (\bar{A} \cdot B) + (C \cdot \bar{D})$ using logic gates.

Solution

$Y = (\bar{A} \cdot B) + (C \cdot \bar{D})$

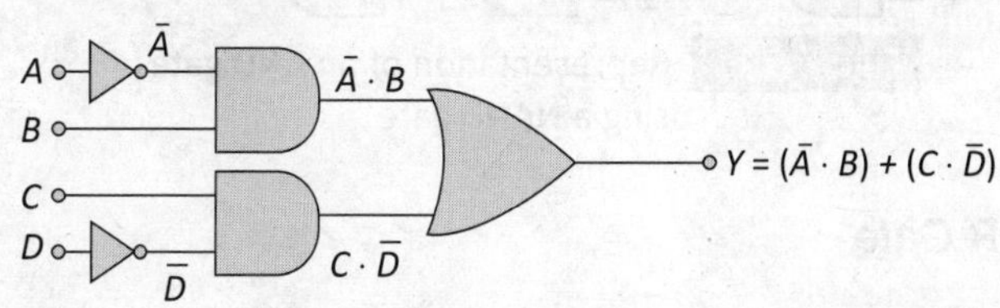

Example 5.6

Represent $Y = (\overline{A + B}) + C \cdot D + (E \cdot \overline{F})$ using logic gates.

Solution

$Y = (\overline{A + B}) + C \cdot D + (E \cdot \overline{F})$

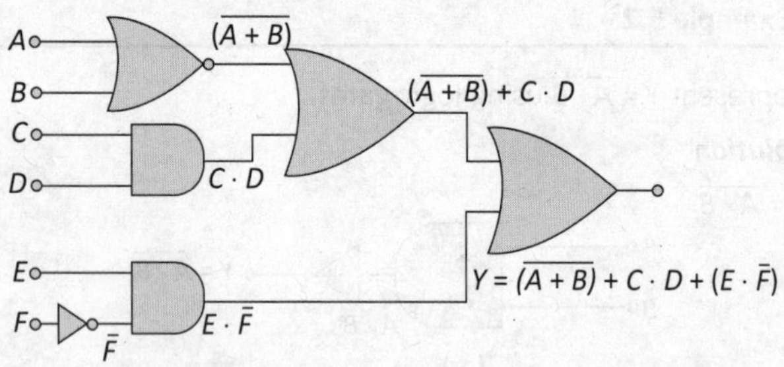

5.7 UNIVERSAL GATES

Universal gates are those gates that can be used for implementing any Boolean function without using any other type of gate. The two important universal gates are NAND and NOR gates.

5.7.1 NAND Universal Gate

Let us first see how the basic gates can be represented using a NAND gate.

NOT Gate

A NOT gate can be obtained by joining the inputs of a NAND gate (Figure 5.10).

Figure 5.10 Representation of a NOT gate using a NAND gate

AND Gate

An AND gate can be implemented by complementing the output of a NAND gate with a NOT gate to get a NOT NAND, that is, AND output (Figure 5.11).

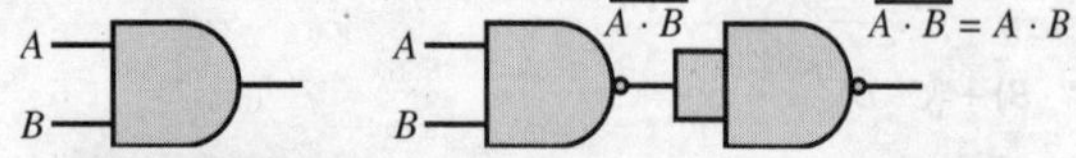

Figure 5.11 Representation of an AND gate using a NAND gate

OR Gate

An OR gate can be implemented using a NAND gate as shown in Figure 5.12.

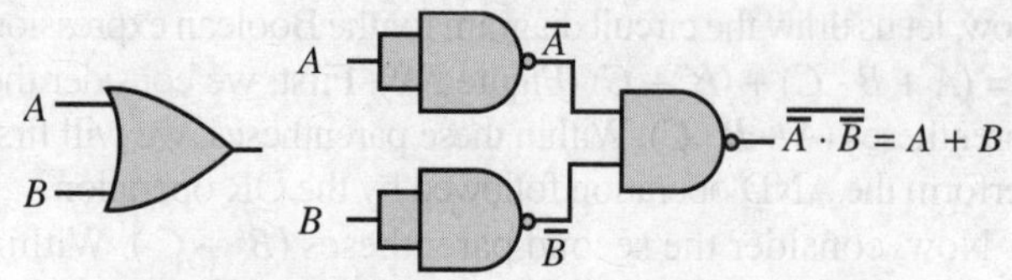

Figure 5.12 Representation of an OR gate using a NAND gate

Converting a Boolean Expression into a Circuit Diagram using NAND Gates

The following are the steps to convert a given expression into a circuit diagram using only NAND gates:

- Read the expression carefully and draw its corresponding circuit diagram.
- Replace every AND, OR, and NOT gate with its equivalent NAND gate.
- Redraw the circuit.
- Identify and remove double inversions (i.e., back-to-back inverters, if any).
- Redraw the final circuit.

Example 5.7

$Y = A + (B \cdot C)$ has been represented using AND and OR gates. Represent it using NAND gates.

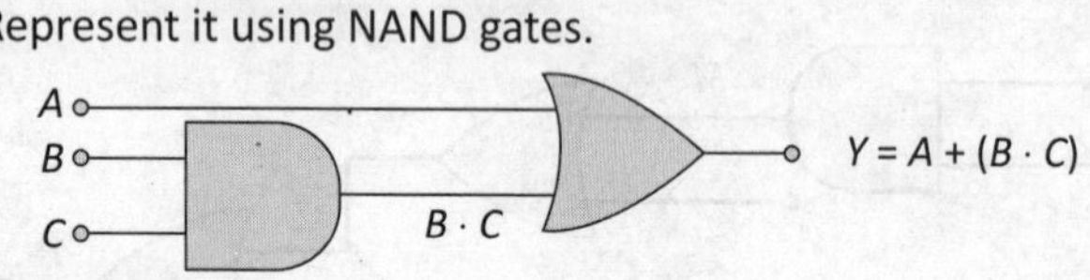

Solution

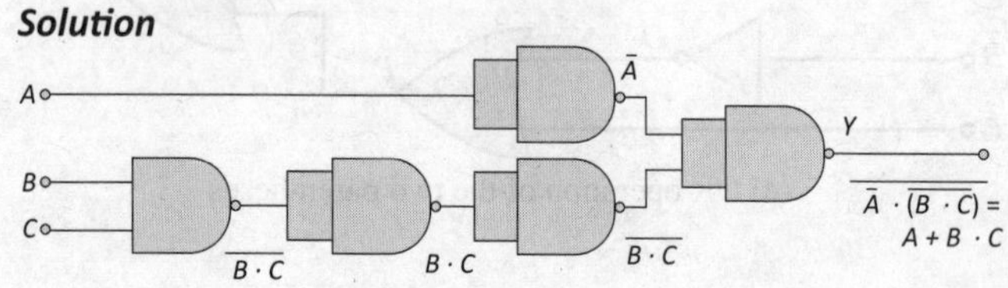

Removing double inversions

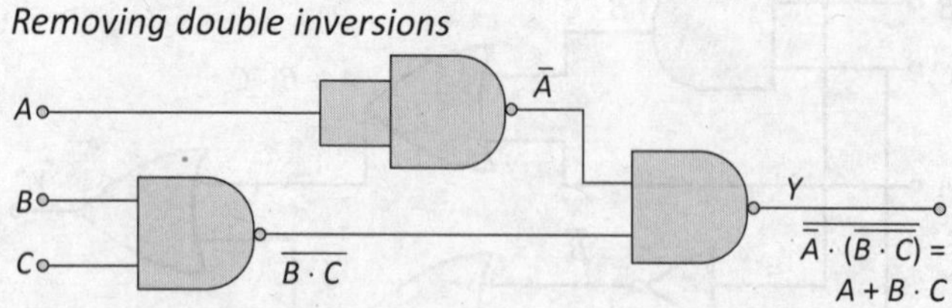

Example 5.8

Represent the expression $Y = (A+B)\cdot(C+D)$ using only NAND gates.

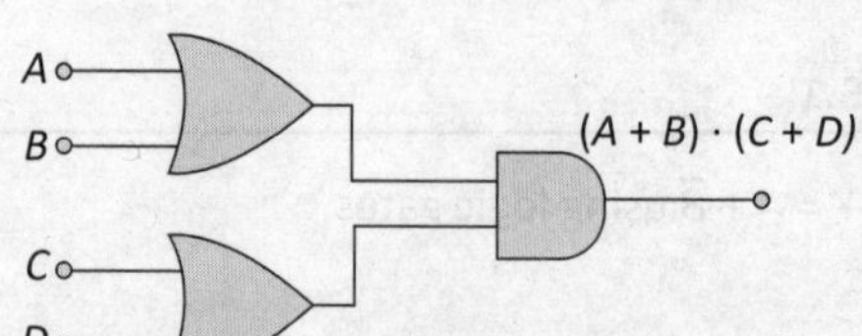

Solution

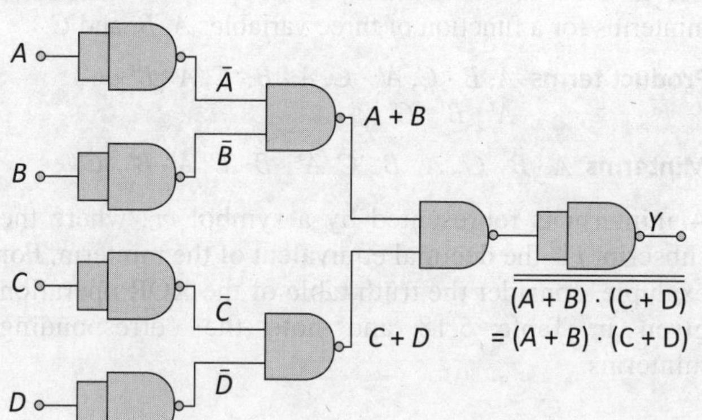

5.7.2 NOR Universal Gate

Let us see now how the basic gates can be represented using a NOR gate.

NOT Gate

A NOT gate is implemented by joining the inputs of a NOR gate. This is because a NOR gate is equivalent to an OR gate leading to a NOT gate (Figure 5.13).

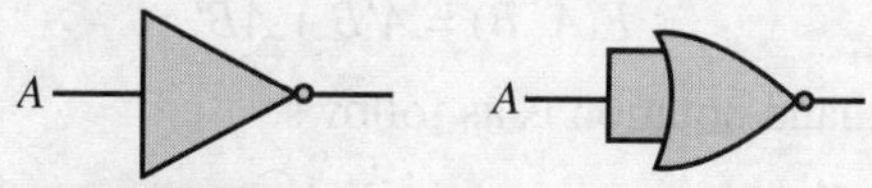

Figure 5.13 Representation of a NOT gate using a NOR gate

OR Gate

An OR gate can be obtained by complementing the output of a NOR gate with a NOT gate to get a NOT NOR, that is, OR output (Figure 5.14).

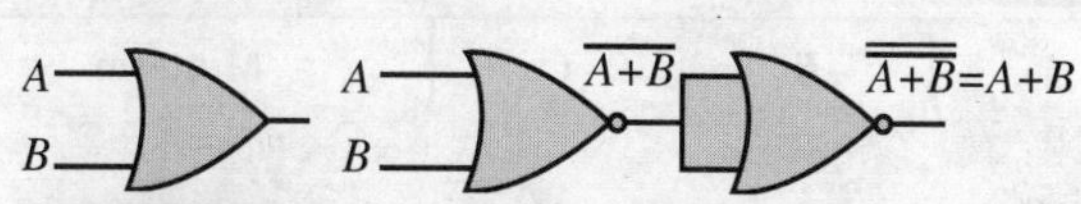

Figure 5.14 Representation of an OR gate using a NOR gate

AND Gate

From the truth tables, we can observe that an AND gate gives the output as 1 when both the inputs are 1, whereas a NOR gate outputs 1 only when both the inputs are 0. This means that an AND gate can be implemented by inverting the inputs to a NOR gate (Figure 5.15).

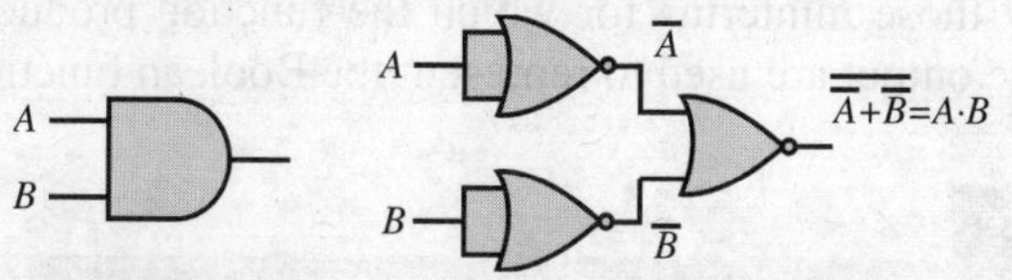

Figure 5.15 Representation of an AND gate using a NOR gate

Converting a Boolean Expression into a Circuit Diagram using NOR Gates

The following are the steps to convert a given expression into a circuit diagram using only NOR gates:

- Read the expression carefully and draw its corresponding circuit diagram.
- Replace every AND, OR, and NOT gate with its equivalent NOR gate.
- Redraw the circuit.
- Identify and remove double inversions (i.e., back-to-back inverters, if any).
- Redraw the final circuit.

Example 5.9

$Y = \overline{(A \cdot B) + C}$ has been represented using AND, OR, and NOT gates. Represent it using the universal NOR gate.

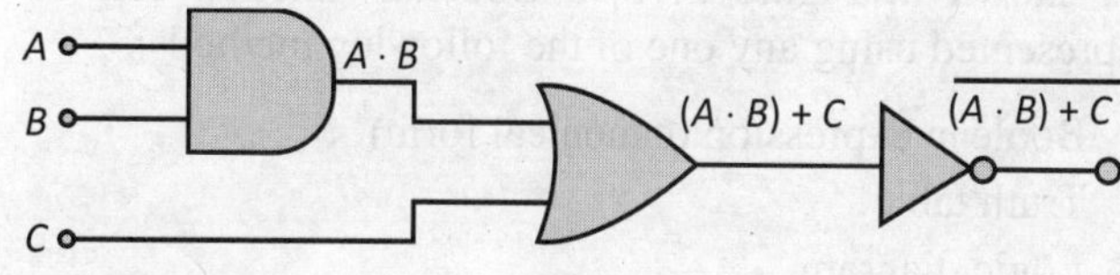

Solution

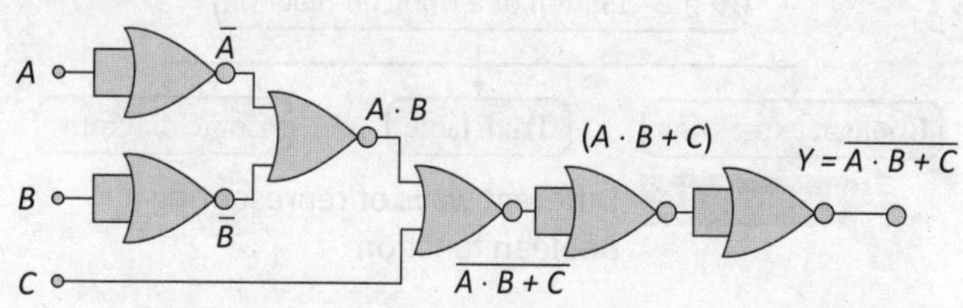

Removing double inversions

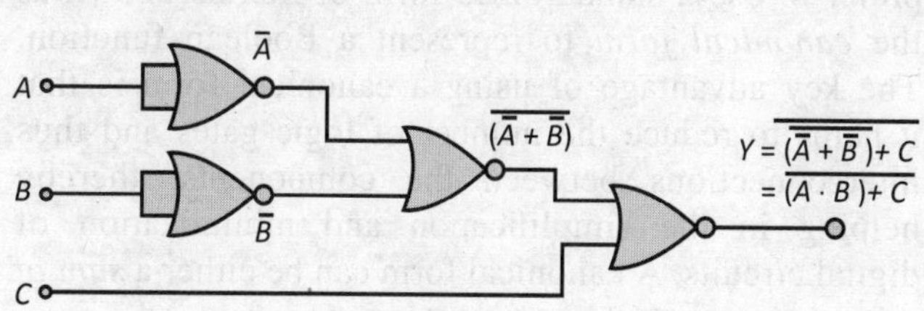

Example 5.10

Represent the expression $Y = (A+B)\cdot(C+D)$ using only NOR gates.

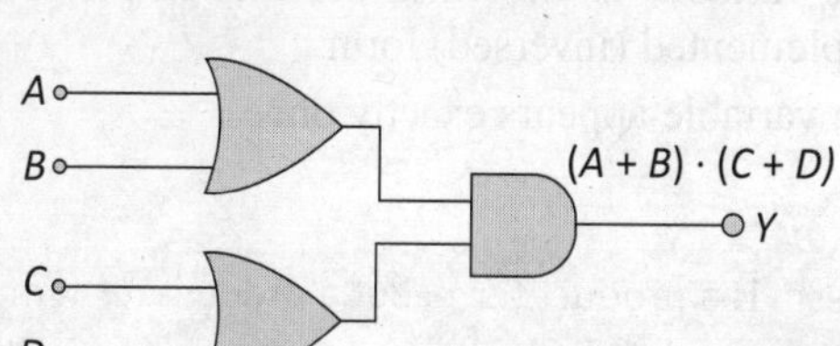

Solution

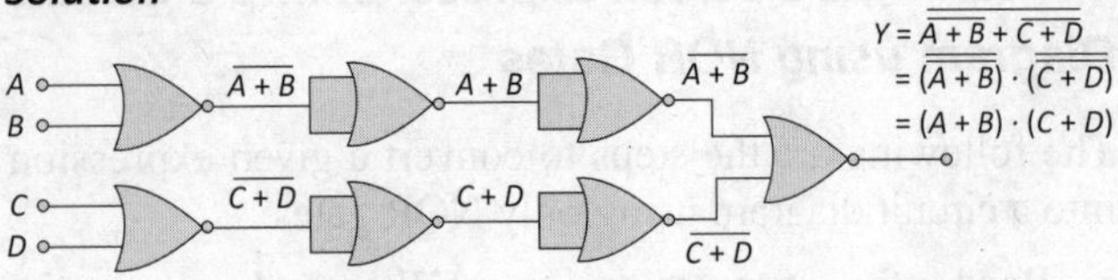

Removing double inversions

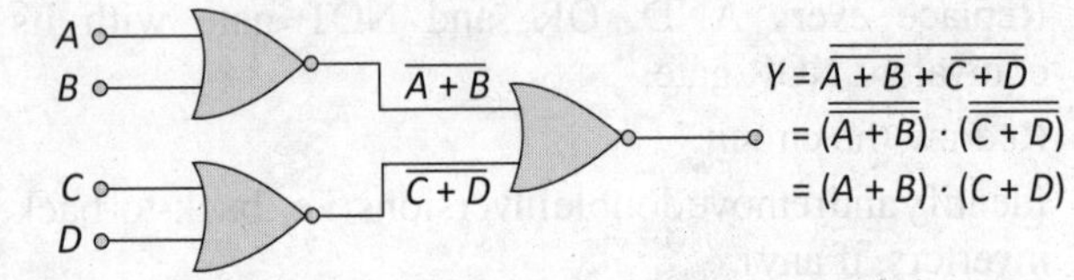

5.8 REPRESENTATIONS OF BOOLEAN FUNCTIONS

As shown in Figure 5.16, a Boolean function can be represented using any one of the following methods:

- Boolean expression (canonical form)
- Truth table
- Logic diagram

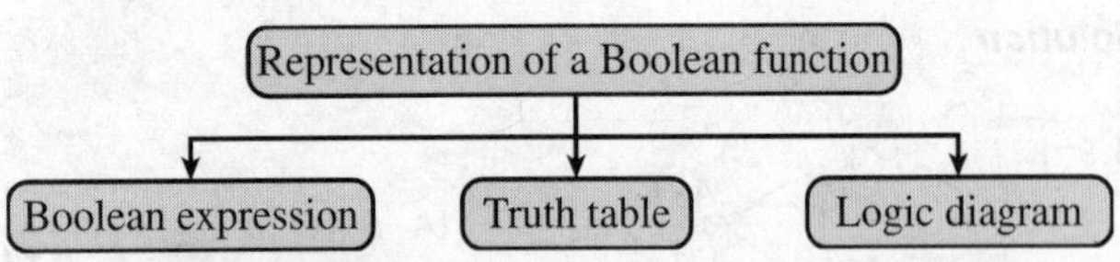

Figure 5.16 Different ways of representing a Boolean function

In Boolean algebra, a variable or a complemented variable is called a *literal*. Designers of logical circuits prefer to use a standardized form of literals known as the *canonical form* to represent a Boolean function. The key advantage of using a canonical form is that it helps to reduce the number of logic gates and thus interconnections between the components, thereby helping in the simplification and minimization of digital circuits. A canonical form can be either a *sum of minterms* or a *product of maxterms*.

5.8.1 Minterm

A *minterm* is a canonical product (or a canonical sum of products—SOP) term and has the following features:

- It includes all the variables of a function.
- Each variable is in either the un-complemented or complemented (inversed) form.
- Each variable appears exactly once.

Note

A minterm is a product term, but a product term may or may not be a minterm.

Let us look at some examples of product terms and minterms for a function of three variables *A*, *B*, and *C*:

Product terms $A, B \cdot C, A' \cdot C, A \cdot B \cdot C, A \cdot B' \cdot C,$
$A' \cdot B' \cdot C'$

Minterms $A \cdot B \cdot C', A \cdot B \cdot C, A' \cdot B \cdot C, A \cdot B' \cdot C'$

A minterm is represented by a symbol m_j, where the subscript *j* is the decimal equivalent of the minterm. For example, consider the truth table of the XOR operation given in Table 5.18 and note the corresponding minterms.

Table 5.18 Truth table of XOR operation

A	*B*	*A* XOR *B*	Minterm
0	0	0	–
0	1	1	$m_1 = A'B$
1	0	1	$m_2 = AB'$
1	1	0	–

By looking at the truth table, we can say that the XOR function can be represented as a sum of the minterms or the canonical SOP form as follows:

$$F(A, B) = A'B + AB'$$

The shorthand notation is as follows:

$$F(A, B) = m_1 + m_2 \text{ or } F(A, B) = \Sigma m(1, 2)$$

A Boolean function with *n* variables has 2^n minterms, as each variable can be in either the complemented or un-complemented form. Thus, a three-variable function, $F(A, B, C)$, has $2^3 = 8$ minterms as shown in Table 5.19.

Table 5.19 Minterms of a three-variable function

A	*B*	*C*	Minterm
0	0	0	$m_0 = A'B'C'$
0	0	1	$m_1 = A'B'C$
0	1	0	$m_2 = A'BC'$
0	1	1	$m_3 = A'BC$
1	0	0	$m_4 = AB'C'$
1	0	1	$m_5 = AB'C$
1	1	0	$m_6 = ABC'$
1	1	1	$m_7 = ABC$

Only those minterms for which the function produces 1 as the output are used to represent the Boolean functions.

Note

A Boolean function can be represented as a *sum of minterms*; *f* = Σ(minterms).

Note that the sum of minterms form is unique for any function. We can convert any SOP expression into the canonical SOP form using the following steps:

- Determine the product terms of the expression.
- Ensure that each product term has all the variables used in the Boolean expression.
- If there is a product term in which one or more variables are missing, then multiply that term with the sum of the missing variables and their complement.
- Expand the Boolean expression and delete the repeated terms from the expression.

Example 5.11

Convert $F(A, B, C) = AB' + BC' + AC'$ to the canonical SOP form.

Solution

Multiply each term with the sum of the missing variable and its complement. Therefore,

$F(A, B, C) = AB' (C + C') + BC' (A + A') + AC' (B + B')$

$= AB'C + AB'C' + ABC' + A'BC' + ABC' + AB'C'$

$= AB'C + AB'C' + ABC' + A'BC'$ (Because $A + A = A$)

$= 101 + 100 + 110 + 010$

$= m_5 + m_4 + m_6 + m_2$

Therefore, the canonical SOP form of the given Boolean expression can be given as follows:

$F(A, B, C) = m_5 + m_4 + m_6 + m_2$ or $F(A, B, C) = \Sigma m(2, 4, 5, 6)$

Example 5.12

Convert $AB + AC$ to the canonical SOP form.

Solution

$F(A,B,C) = AB(C+C') + AC(B+B')$

$= ABC + ABC' + ABC + AB'C$

$= ABC + ABC' + AB'C$ (Because $A+A=A$)

$= 111 + 110 + 101$

$= m_7 + m_6 + m_5$

Therefore, $F(A,B,C) = m_7 + m_6 + m_5 = \Sigma m(7,6,5)$

5.8.2 Maxterm

A *maxterm* is a canonical sum (or a canonical product of sums—POS) term and has the following features:

- It includes all the variables of a function.
- Each variable is in either the un-complemented or complemented (inversed) form.
- Each variable appears exactly once.
- A function with n variables has 2^n maxterms.
- Each maxterm is false for exactly one combination of input variables.

Note

A maxterm is a sum term, but a sum term may or may not be a maxterm.

Let us consider some examples of sum terms and maxterms for a function of three variables A, B, and C:

Sum terms $A, A + B, B + C, A' + B, A' + B'$

Maxterms $A + B + C, A + B' + C, A' + B + C, A' + B' + C'$

A maxterm is represented by a symbol M_j, where the subscript j is the decimal equivalent of the maxterm. For example, consider the truth table of the XOR operation given in Table 5.20 and note the corresponding maxterms.

Table 5.20 Truth table of XOR operation

A	B	A XOR B	Maxterms
0	0	0	$M_0 = A + B$
0	1	1	–
1	0	1	–
1	1	0	$M_3 = A' + B'$

Only those input combinations for which the function produces 0 as the output are considered to find the product of maxterms.

It should be noted that for M_0 we have written $M_0 = A + B$ and not $A' + B'$. This is because any minterm m_i is the complement of the corresponding maxterm M_i, that is, $m_i' = M_i$. It is possible to check this. $(A' \cdot B')' = A + B$. Therefore, in a maxterm, 0 will be represented in the un-complemented form and 1 will be represented in the complemented form.

By looking at the truth table, we can say that the XOR function can be represented as the product of the maxterms or the canonical POS form as follows:

$$F(A, B) = (A + B) \cdot (A' + B')$$

The shorthand notation is as follows:

$$F(A, B) = M_0 \cdot M_3 \text{ or } F(A, B) = \Pi M(0, 3)$$

Therefore, $A' \cdot B + A \cdot B'$ and $(A + B) \cdot (A' + B')$ are equivalent expressions for the XOR function.

Note

A Boolean function can be represented as a product of maxterms; $f = \Pi M$(maxterms)

We can convert any POS expression into the canonical POS form using the following steps:

- Determine the sum terms of the expression.
- Ensure that each sum term has all the variables used in the Boolean expression.
- If there is a sum term in which one or more variables are missing, then add that term with the product of the missing variables and their complement.
- Expand the Boolean expression and delete the repeated terms from the expression.

Example 5.13

Convert $F(A, B, C) = (A + B')(B + C')$ to the canonical POS form.

Solution

Add each term with the product of the missing variable and its complement. Therefore,

$$F(A, B, C) = [(A + B') + (C \cdot C')][(B + C') + (A \cdot A')]$$
$$= (A + B' + C \cdot C')(B + C' + A \cdot A')$$

Using the distributive law, we can write

$$F(A, B, C) = (A + B' + C)(A + B' + C')(B + C' + A)(B + C' + A')$$
$$= (A + B' + C)(A + B' + C')(A + B + C')(A' + B + C')$$
$$= (010)(011)(001)(101)$$
$$= (M_2)(M_3)(M_1)(M_5)$$

Therefore, the canonical SOP form of the given Boolean expression can be given as

$$F(A, B, C) = M_2 \cdot M_3 \cdot M_1 \cdot M_5 \text{ or } F(A, B, C) = \Pi M(1, 2, 3, 5)$$

Example 5.14

Convert $(A + B)(A + C)$ to the canonical POS form.

Solution

$$F(A,B,C) = [(A + B) + (C \cdot C')]\ [(A + C) + (B \cdot B')]$$
$$= (A + B + C)\ (A + B + C')\ (A + B + C)\ (A + B' + C)$$
$$= (A + B + C)\ (A + B + C')\ (A + B' + C) \quad (\text{Because } A \cdot A = A)$$
$$= (000)\ (001)\ (010)$$
$$= (M_0)\ (M_1)\ (M_2)$$

Therefore, $F(A,B,C) = \Pi M(0,1,2)$

5.9 SIMPLIFICATION OF BOOLEAN EXPRESSIONS USING KARNAUGH MAP

Karnaugh map (K-map) is a tool to represent Boolean functions of up to six variables. It is a pictorial method to minimize Boolean expressions without using Boolean algebra theorems and equations, thereby making the process of minimization simpler, faster, and efficient.

An n-variable K-map has 2^n cells where each cell corresponds to an n-variable truth table value. The cells in a K-map are arranged in such a way that adjacent cells correspond to truth rows that differ in position by only one bit (logical adjacency).

K-maps can be easily used to represent expressions that involve two to four variables. Expressions with five to six variables are comparatively difficult but achievable, but expressions with seven or more variables are extremely difficult (if not impossible) to minimize using a K-map.

Consider the truth table of two variables and observe the K-map for this truth table (Table 5.21). A cell of the K-map contains a 1 if the output value for A and B in the truth table has a 1.

Table 5.21 Truth table and K-map for two variables

A	*B*	Output *Y*
0	0	1
0	1	1
1	0	0
1	1	0

A \ *B*	0	1
0	1	1
1	0	0

Table 5.22 Truth table and K-map for three variables

A	*B*	*C*	Output *Y*
0	0	0	1
0	0	1	1
0	1	0	0
0	1	1	0
1	0	0	0
1	0	1	1
1	1	0	1
1	1	1	0

A \ *BC*	00	01	11	10
0	1	1	0	0
1	0	1	0	1

Table 5.23 Truth table and K-map for four variables

A	*B*	*C*	*D*	Output *Y*
0	0	0	0	0
0	0	0	1	1
0	0	1	0	0
0	0	1	1	0
0	1	0	0	0
0	1	0	1	1
0	1	1	0	0
0	1	1	1	0
1	0	0	0	0
1	0	0	1	1
1	0	1	0	0
1	0	1	1	0
1	1	0	0	0
1	1	0	1	1
1	1	1	0	0
1	1	1	1	0

AB \ *CD*	00	01	11	10
00	0	1	0	0
01	0	1	0	0
11	0	1	0	0
10	0	1	0	0

Also observe the truth tables of three (Table 5.22) and four (Table 5.23) variables and observe the K-map for these tables.

Rules for Minimization

The following are the rules for minimizing an expression using a K-map.

Rule I Form groups of cells in such a way that a group should not include a cell with a zero value.

A\B	0	1
0	1	1
1	0	0

A\B	0	1
0	1	1
1	0	0

Wrong: This is not a group.

Rule II Groups may be formed either horizontally or vertically. They cannot be formed diagonally.

A\B	0	1
0	1	1
1	0	0

A\B	0	1
0	0	1
1	0	1

A\B	0	1
0	0	1
1	1	0

Wrong: This is not a group.

Rule III Groups should contain one, two, four, eight, or generally 2^n cells.

A\B	0	1
0	1	1
1	0	0

Group of two 1s

A\BC	00	01	11	10
0	1	1	1	1
1	0	0	0	1

Group of four 1s

A\BC	00	01	11	10
0	0	1	1	1
1	1	0	0	0

Wrong: Group of three 1s

Rule IV Groups must be as large as possible.

A\BC	00	01	11	10
0	1	1	0	0
1	1	1	0	0

A\BC	00	01	11	10
0	1	1	0	0
1	1	1	0	0

Wrong: Groups should be as large as possible

Rule V Groups may overlap.

A\BC	00	01	11	10
0	1	1	1	1
1	1	1	0	0

Overlapping groups

A\BC	00	01	11	10
0	1	1	1	1
1	1	1	0	0

Wrong: Non-overlapping groups

Rule VI Groups can be wrapped around the table. For example, the leftmost cell in a row can be grouped with the rightmost cell in that row. Similarly, the topmost cell in a column may be grouped with the bottommost cell in that column.

AB\CD	00	01	11	10
00	0	0	0	1
01	0	1	1	0
11	0	1	1	0
10	1	0	0	1

Topmost cell

Rightmost cell

Leftmost cell

Bottommost cell

Rule VII The number of groups should be as small as possible (provided any of the earlier stated rules are not violated).

A\BC	00	01	11	10
0	1	1	0	0
1	1	1	1	1

A\BC	00	01	11	10
0	1	1	0	0
1	1	1	1	1

Wrong: Too many groups.

Example 5.15

Consider the expression $Y = A' \cdot B' + A \cdot B' + A' \cdot B$. Plot a K-map to minimize the expression.

Solution

A\B	0	1
0	1	1
1	1	0

Group I

Group II

In group I, there is an entry 1 when $A = 0$ and $B = 0$ and when $A = 0$ and $B = 1$, which means that the output is 1 when $A = 0$

or $A' = 1$. That is, the output is independent of the input value of B.

Similarly, in group II, there is a 1 when $A = 0$ and $B = 0$ and when $A = 1$ and $B = 0$, which means that the output is 1 when $B = 0$ or $B' = 1$. Thus, the output is independent of the input value of A. Hence, the minimized form of this expression can be given as $A' + B'$.

Therefore, $Y = A' + B'$.

Example 5.16

Consider the expression $Y = A' \cdot B' \cdot C' + A' \cdot B' \cdot C + A' \cdot B \cdot C + A' \cdot B \cdot C'$ and minimize it using a K-map.

Solution

In the group of 1s, we see that the output is independent of the values of B and C. This is because there is a 1 when B = 0 as well as when B = 1. Similarly, there is a 1 when C = 0 as well as when C = 1. However, the output is 1 only when A = 0 or A' = 1.

Therefore, $Y = A'$.

A \ BC	00	01	11	10
0	1	1	1	1
1	0	0	0	0

Example 5.17

Consider the expression $Y = A' \cdot B' \cdot C + A' \cdot B \cdot C + A \cdot B' \cdot C + A \cdot B \cdot C$ and minimize it using a K-map.

Solution

The group of 1s is independent of the value of A (as output is 1 when A = 0 or A = 1). Similarly, the output is also independent of the value of B. However, the output is 1 when the value of C is 1.

Hence, the result is $Y = C$.

A \ BC	00	01	11	10
0	0	1	1	0
1	0	1	1	0

Example 5.18

Consider the expression $Y = A' \cdot B' \cdot C' + A' \cdot B + A \cdot B \cdot C' + A \cdot C$ and minimize it using K-map.

Solution

$A' \cdot B' \cdot C' + A' \cdot B + A \cdot B \cdot C' + A \cdot C$ can be expanded as:

$$A' \cdot B' \cdot C' + A' \cdot B \cdot (C + C') + A \cdot B \cdot C' + A \cdot C\ (B + B')$$

$$A' \cdot B' \cdot C' + A' \cdot B \cdot C + A' \cdot B \cdot C' + A \cdot B \cdot C' + A \cdot B \cdot C + A \cdot B' \cdot C$$

Hence, the K-map can be drawn as

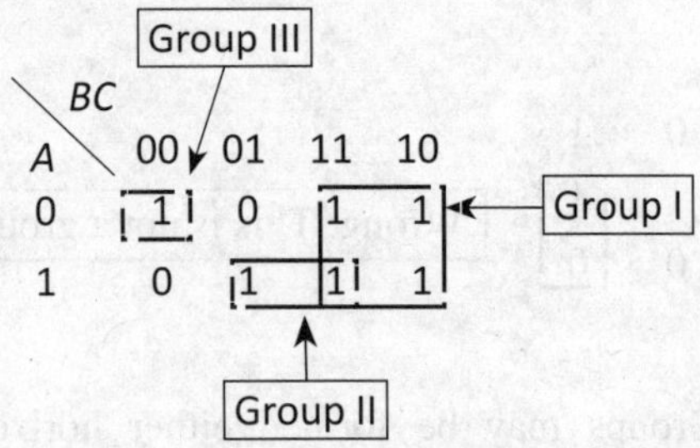

In group I, the output is independent of C and A as whether the value of A or C is 0 or 1 the output is always 1. So, the first group minimizes to B.

In group II, the output is independent of B as the output is 1 when A = 1 and C = 1. Therefore, group II minimizes to AC.

In group III, the output is independent of B. The output is a 1 when $A = 0$ ($\overline{A} = 1$) and $C = 0$ ($\overline{C} = 1$). Therefore, group III minimizes to $\overline{A}\,\overline{C}$.

Hence, $Y = B + AC + \overline{A}\,\overline{C}$.

Example 5.19

Consider the expression $Y = \overline{A}B\overline{C}D + \overline{A}BC\overline{D} + AB\overline{C}D + ABCD + ABC\overline{D} + A\overline{BC}D + A\overline{B}CD + \overline{A}BCD$ and minimize it using K-map.

Solution

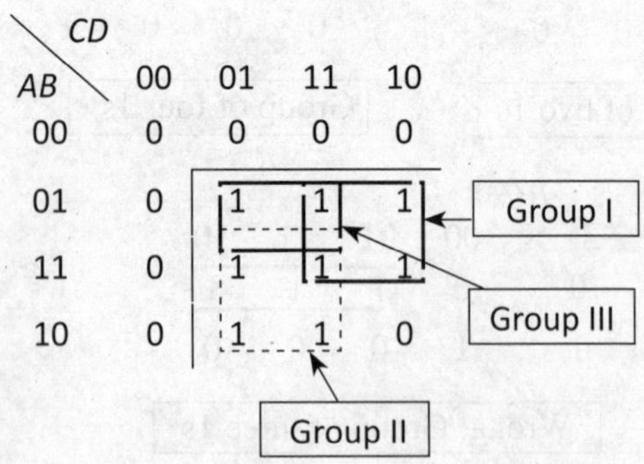

In group I, the output is independent of A and D. The output is 1 when both B and C are equal to 1. Hence, group I minimizes to BC.

In group II, the output is independent of B and C. The output is 1 when A = 1 and D = 1. Hence, group II minimizes to AD.

In group III, the output is independent of C. The output is 1, when A = 0, B = 1, and D = 1. Therefore, group III minimizes to $\overline{A}BD$.

Hence, $Y = BC + AD + \overline{A}BD$

POINTS TO REMEMBER

- Computers understand only binary numbers, in which only the digits 0 and 1 are used. A complex proposition can be easily stated in terms of binary variables and binary operators (OR, AND, and NOT).
- Boolean operators take certain inputs and produce an output based on a predetermined table of results (also known as a truth table). A truth table lists all the possible values of input combinations of the function and the output that will be produced based on these input combinations.
- A Venn diagram can be used to represent Boolean operations using shaded overlapping regions.
- A logic gate or a Boolean gate is an electronic circuit, which acts as a basic building block of any digital system.
- NAND and NOR gates are known as universal gates because they can be used to implement all other logic gates.
- A variable or a complemented variable is called a *literal*. Designers of logical circuits prefer to use a standardized form of literals called the *canonical form* to represent a Boolean function. This helps them to reduce the number of logic gates for simplification and minimization of digital circuits. A canonical form can be either a *sum of minterms* or a *product of maxterms*.
- Karnaugh map (K-map) is a tool to represent Boolean functions of upto six variables. An *n*-variable K-map has 2^n cells where each cell corresponds to an *n*-variable truth table value.

EXERCISES

Fill in the Blanks

1. Computers understand ______ language.
2. Binary computers work on ______ logic.
3. ______ represent Boolean operations using shaded overlapping regions.
4. ______ is a visual tool for defining the input–output relationship of binary variables in a Boolean function.
5. $A + 0 = A$ is an example of ______ law.
6. A variable or a complemented variable is called a ______.
7. A ______ is a canonical sum term.
8. In a maxterm, ______ will be represented in the uncomplemented form.
9. A logic diagram is used to specify a ______.
10. ______ and ______ gates are known as universal gates.

Review Questions

1. What is Boolean algebra? Give its applications.
2. Explain Boolean laws using Venn diagrams.
3. Draw the Venn diagram for the Boolean expression $(A \cup B)' \cap C$.
4. Explain the utility of a truth table as a visualization tool in Boolean algebra.
5. Draw the truth table for $Z = A \cap (B \cup C)$.
6. Prove the validity of the consensus and absorption laws.
7. How are Boolean functions represented?
8. Differentiate between a minterm and a maxterm.
9. Give the minterms and maxterms for the Boolean AND operation.
10. Explain the steps to convert an SOP expression into its canonical SOP form with the help of an example.
11. Convert $F(A, B, C) = A'B + B'C + A'C$ to the canonical SOP form.
12. Explain the steps to convert a POS expression into the canonical POS form with the help of an example.
13. Convert $F(A, B, C) = (A' + B')(B' + C)$ to the canonical POS form.
14. What are logic diagrams? How are they useful?
15. Draw the logic diagram for the Boolean expression $Y = (A \cdot B + C' \cdot D) + (A' + D)$.
16. Implement the following expressions using logic gates:
    (a) $Y = (A \cdot B) + (C \cdot D) \cdot E$
    (b) $Y = A + (C + D) \cdot (A \cdot B)$
17. Implement the expressions given in Question 16 using NAND gates.
18. Implement the expressions given in Question 16 using NOR gates.
19. Write a short note on K-maps.
20. Draw a K-map and simplify the Boolean expression given by $f(x, y, z) = \Sigma m(0, 2, 3, 4, 6, 7)$.

SCAN THE PAGE TO KNOW MORE

6 Computer Software

TAKEAWAYS

- System software
- BIOS
- Operating systems
- Utility software
- Translators
- Application software
- Pre-written software
- Customized software
- Productivity software
- Microsoft Office
- Command interpreter
- Mobile operating systems
- Generations of programming languages

6.1 INTRODUCTION TO COMPUTER SOFTWARE

When we talk about a computer, we actually mean the following two parts:

- The first is the computer hardware, which performs all the computation and calculation work that computers are known for.
- The second part is the computer software, which instructs the hardware what to do and how to do it.

Figure 6.1 illustrates these parts.

If we think of a computer as a living being, then the hardware would be the body that performs actions such as seeing with the eyes, lifting objects, and filling the lungs with air. The software would be the intelligence that helps in interpreting the images that are seen through the eyes, instructing the arms how to lift objects, and instructing the body to fill the lungs with air.

Since the computer hardware is a digital machine, it can understand only two basic values—*on* and *off*. The on and off concept forms the basis of *binary language*. Computer software was developed to convert binary language into a form that is useful to tell the computer hardware what to do.

Computer hardware cannot think and make decisions on its own. Hence, it cannot be used to analyse a given set of data and find a solution on its own. The hardware needs a software (a set of programs) to instruct what has to be done. A program is a set of instructions that is arranged in a sequence to guide a computer to find a solution for a given problem. The process of writing a program is called *programming*.

Computer software is written by programmers using a programming language. The programmer writes a set of instructions (program) using a specific programming language. Such programs are known as the *source code*. Another computer program called a *compiler* is then used on the source code, to transform the instructions into a language that the computer can understand. The result is an executable computer program, which is another name for software.

Examples of computer software include the following:

- *Driver software*, which allows a computer to interact with hardware devices such as printers, scanners, and video cards.
- *Educational software*, which includes programs and games that help in teaching and providing drills to help memorize facts. Educational software can be used in

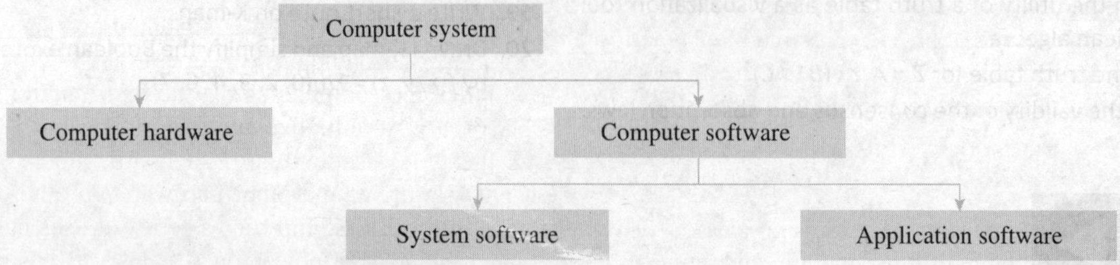

Figure 6.1 Parts of a computer system

diverse areas, from teaching computer-related activities like typing to subjects like chemistry.

- *Media players* and *media development software*, which are specifically designed to play and/or edit digital media files such as music and videos.
- *Productivity software*, which is an older term used to denote any program that allows the user to be more productive in a business sense. Examples of such software include word processors, database management utilities, and presentation software.
- *Operating systems software*, which helps in coordinating system resources and allows execution of other programs. Some examples of operating systems are Windows, Mac OS X, and Linux.
- *Computer games*, which are widely used as a form of entertainment software that has many genres.

6.2 CLASSIFICATION OF COMPUTER SOFTWARE

Computer software can be broadly classified into two groups, namely application software and system software.

- Application software is designed for users to solve a particular problem. It is generally what we think of when we refer to a computer program. Examples of application software include spreadsheets, database systems, desktop publishing software, program development software, games, and web browsers. Simply put, application software represents programs that allow users to do something besides merely run the hardware.
- On the contrary, system software, provides a general programming environment in which programmers can create specific applications to suit their needs. This environment provides new functions that are not available at the hardware level and performs tasks related to executing the application program. System software represents programs that allow the hardware to run properly. It acts as an interface between the hardware of the computer and the application software that users need to run on the computer. Figure 6.2 illustrates the relationship between application software and system software.

Table 6.1 lists the differences between system and application softwares.

6.2.1 System Software

System software is computer software designed to operate computer hardware and to provide and maintain a platform for running application software. Some of the most widely used system software are discussed in this section.

Computer BIOS and Device Drivers

Basic Input/Output System (BIOS) and device drivers provide basic functionality to operate and control the hardware connected to or built into the computer.

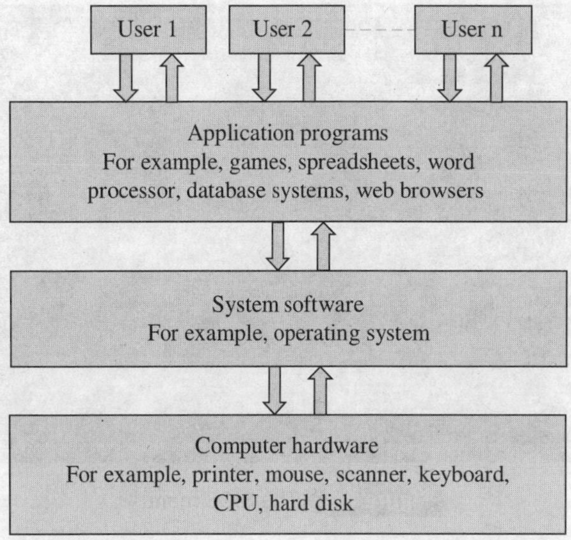

Figure 6.2 Relationship among hardware, system software, and application software

Table 6.1 Differences between system and application software

System software	Application software
It is a collection of programs that enable users to interact with hardware components efficiently.	It is a collection of programs written for a specific application, such as a library system, inventory control system, and so on.
It controls and manages the hardware.	It uses the services provided by the system software to interact with hardware components.
It is machine-dependent.	It is machine independent.
The programmer must understand the architecture of the machine and hardware details to write system software.	In most cases, the programmer ignores the architecture of the machine and hardware details to write application software.
It interacts with the hardware directly.	It interacts with the hardware indirectly through system calls provided by system software.
Writing system software is a complicated task.	Writing application programs is relatively easy.
Examples include compilers and operating systems.	Examples include Microsoft Word and Microsoft Paint.

BIOS is built into the computer and is the first code run by the computer when it is switched on. The key role of BIOS is to load and start the operating system (OS).

When the computer starts, the first function that BIOS performs is to initialize and identify system devices such as the video display card, keyboard, mouse, hard disk, CD/DVD drive, and other hardware. In other words, the code in the BIOS chip runs a series of tests called POST, which stands for power on self test, to ensure that the system devices are working correctly.

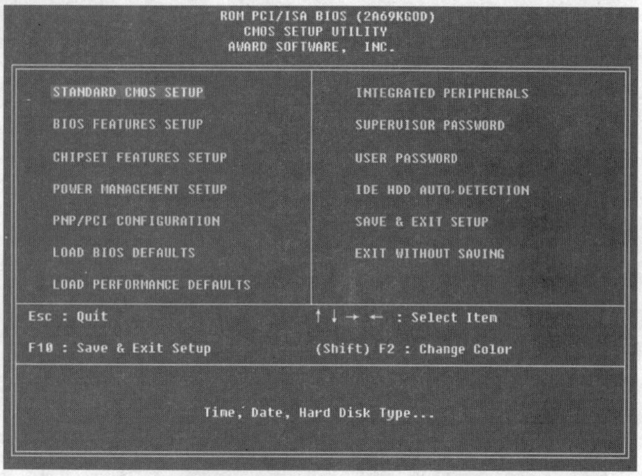

Figure 6.3 The BIOS menu

The BIOS chip then locates the software held on a peripheral device such as a hard disk or a CD, and loads and executes that software, giving it control of the computer. This process is known as *booting*.

BIOS is stored on a ROM chip built into the system. It also has a user interface similar to a menu, which can be accessed by pressing a certain key on the keyboard when the PC starts. A BIOS screen is shown in Figure 6.3.

The BIOS menu enables the user to configure hardware, set the system clock, enable or disable system components, and, most importantly, select the devices which are eligible to be a potential boot device and set various password prompts.

In summary, BIOS performs the following functions:

- Initializes system hardware
- Initializes system registers
- Initializes power management system
- Tests RAM
- Tests all the serial and parallel ports
- Initializes CD/DVD disk drive and hard disk controllers
- Displays system summary information

Operating System

The primary goal of an operating system is to make the computer system (or any other device in which it is installed, such as a cell phone) convenient and efficient to use. The operating system offers generic services to support user applications.

From the point of view of users, the primary consideration is always convenience. Users should find it easy to launch an application and work on it. For example, we use icons, which give us an idea about which application they launch. We have different icons for launching a web browser, an e-mail application, or even a document preparation application. In other words, it is the human–computer interface that helps to identify and launch an application. The interface hides a lot of details of the instructions that performs all these tasks.

Similarly, if we examine the programs that help us in using input devices such as the keyboard/mouse, all the complex details of the character-reading program are hidden from the user. We, as users, simply press buttons to perform the input operation regardless of the complexity of the details involved. The details are handled by the operating system.

An operating system ensures that system resources (such as CPU, memory, I/O devices, and so on) are utilized efficiently. For example, there may be many service requests on a web server, and each user request needs to be serviced. Similarly, there may be many programs residing in the main memory. The system needs to determine which programs are active and which need to wait for some I/O operation, since the programs that need to wait can be suspended temporarily from engaging the processor. Hence, it is important for an operating system to have a control policy and algorithm to allocate system resources.

Utility Software

Utility software is used to analyse, configure, optimize, and maintain the computer system. Utility programs may be requested by application programs during their execution for multiple purposes. Some examples of utility programs include the following:

- *Disk defragmenters* can be used to detect computer files whose contents are broken across several locations on the hard disk, and the fragments can be moved to one location in order to increase efficiency.
- *Disk checkers* can be used to scan the contents of a hard disk to find files or areas that are either corrupt in some way, or were not correctly saved, and eliminate/repair them in order to make the hard drive operate more efficiently.
- *Disk cleaners* can be used to locate files that are either not required for computer operation, or take up considerable amounts of space. Disk cleaners help the user to decide what to delete when their hard disk is full.
- *Disk space analysers* are used for visualizing disk space usage by obtaining the size of all folders (including subfolders) and files in a folder or drive.
- *Disk partitions* are used to divide an individual drive into multiple logical drives, each with its own file system. Each partition is then treated as an individual drive.
- *Backup* utilities can be used to make a copy of all information stored on a disk. In case a disk failure occurs, backup utilities can be used to restore the entire disk. Even if a file gets deleted accidentally, the backup utility can be used to restore the deleted file.
- *Disk compression* can be used to enhance the capacity of the disk by compressing/uncompressing the contents of a disk.
- *File managers* can be used to provide a convenient method of performing routine data management tasks, such as deleting, renaming, cataloguing, moving, copying, merging, generating, and modifying data sets.

- *System profilers* can be used to provide detailed information about the software installed and hardware attached to the computer.
- *Anti-virus* utilities are used to scan the computer for viruses.
- *Data compression* utilities are used to compress files to a smaller size.
- *Cryptographic* utilities are used to encrypt and decrypt files.
- *Launcher applications* are used as a convenient access point for application software.
- *Registry cleaners* are used to clean and optimize the Windows registry by deleting old registry keys that are no longer in use.
- *Network* utilities are used to analyse the computer's network connectivity, configure network settings, and check data transfer or log events.
- *Command line interface (CLI)* and *graphical user interface (GUI)* are used to interface the operating system with other software.

Translators

In this section we shall discuss the functions of translators which are computer programs used to translate a code written in one programming language to a code in another language that the computer understands.

Compiler A *compiler* is a special type of program that transforms source code written in a programming language (the *source language*) into machine language comprising just two digits, 1 and 0 (the *target language)*. The resultant code is known as the *object code*. The object code is the one that will be used to create an executable program. Therefore, a compiler is used to translate the source code from a high-level programming language to a lower level language (e.g., assembly language or machine code).

If the source code contains errors, then the compiler will not be able to execute its intended task. Errors that limit the compiler in understanding a program are called *syntax errors*. Syntax errors are similar to spelling mistakes or typing mistakes. Another type of error is the logical error, which occurs when a program does not function accurately. Logical errors are much harder to locate and correct.

The work of a compiler is simply to translate human-readable source code into computer-executable machine code. It can locate syntax errors in the program (if any), but cannot fix it. Until and unless the syntactical error is rectified, the source code cannot be converted into object code.

Interpreter Similar to the compiler, the *interpreter* also executes instructions written in a high-level language. Basically, a program written in a high-level language can be executed in any of the two ways—first, by compiling the program, and second, by passing the program through an interpreter.

While the compiler translates instructions written in a high-level programming language directly into machine language, the interpreter, on the other hand, translates the instructions into an intermediate form, which it then executes.

Usually, a compiled program executes faster than an interpreted program. However, the big advantage of an interpreter is that it does not need to go through the compilation stage during which machine instructions are generated. This process can be time-consuming if the program is long. Moreover, the interpreter can immediately execute high-level programs.

In summary, compilers and interpreters both achieve similar purposes, but are inherently different in how they achieve that purpose.

Assembler Since computers can execute only codes written in machine language, a special program called *assembler* is required to convert the code written in assembly language into an equivalent code in machine language, which contains only 0s and 1s. An assembler takes an assembly language program as an input and gives a code in machine language (also called an object code) as output. There is a one-to-one correspondence between the assembly language code and the machine language code. However, if there is an error, the assembler gives a list of errors. The object file is created only when the assembly language code is free from errors. The object file can be executed as and when required.

> **Note**
>
> An assembler only translates an assembly program into machine language, the result of which is an object file that can be executed. However, the assembler itself does not execute the object file.

Linker

A linker, also called *link editor and binder*, is a program that combines object modules to form an executable program. Generally, in case of a large program, the programmers prefer to break the code into smaller modules, as this simplifies the programming task. Eventually, when the source code of all the modules has been converted into object code, these modules need to be put together. This is the job of the linker. Usually, the compiler automatically invokes the linker as the last step in compiling a program.

Loader

A *loader* is a special type of program that is part of an operating system and which copies programs from a storage device to the main memory, where they can be executed.

Debugger

Debugging is a necessary step in software development process. Since it is very common for real world applications to have thousands of lines of code, the possibility of having errors in them cannot be ruled out. Therefore, identifying bugs (errors) and removing them as early as possible is very important.

Debugging tools, commonly known as *debuggers*, are used to identify coding errors at different stages of software (or program) development. These days, many programming language packages have a facility for checking the code for errors while it is being written.

A debugger is a program that runs other programs allowing users to exercise some degree of control over their programs so that they can examine them when things go wrong. A debugger helps the programmer to discover the following things:

- Which statement or expression was being executed when the error occurred?
- If an error occurred during the execution of a function, what parameters were passed to it while it was called?
- What is the value of variables at different lines in the program?
- What is the result of evaluating an expression?
- What is the sequence of statements actually executed in a program?

When a program crashes, debuggers show the position of the error in the program. Many debuggers allow programmers to run programs in a step-by-step mode. They also allow them to stop on specific points at which they can examine the value of certain variables.

6.2.2 Application Software

Application software is a type of computer software that employs the capabilities of a computer directly to perform a user-defined task. This is in contrast with system software, which is involved in integrating a computer's capabilities, but does not directly apply them in the performance of tasks that benefit the user.

To understand application software better, consider an analogy where hardware would depict the relationship of an electric light bulb (an application) to an electric power generation plant (a system).

The power plant merely generates electricity, which is not by itself of any real use until harnessed through an application such as the electric light, which performs a service that actually benefits the user.

Typical examples of software applications are word processors, spreadsheets, media players, education software, CAD, CAM, data communication software, statistical and operational research software, etc. Multiple applications bundled together as a package are sometimes referred to as an *application suite*.

Note

Shrink-wrap and click-wrap software

Any licensed software, whether system software or application software, comes in a CD-ROM placed inside a box.

The software is bundled with a license agreement or other terms and conditions, which the customer can read only after opening the box. The box containing the CD-ROM and the agreement is wrapped with a plastic film that is shrunk by heat to form a seal on a tight-fitting package. This bundled software is known as *shrink-wrap* software.

Once the customer buys the software and opens the package, he is bound by the license agreements and other terms and conditions specified in the document. However, in recent times, the trend is shifting towards electronic delivery of software, using the Internet. This is called *click-wrap* software. Agreements for such software are found only on the Internet as a part of the installation process. All in all, click-wrap software is the electronic equivalent of shrink-wrap software.

6.3 ACQUIRING COMPUTER SOFTWARE

When we buy a computer, we are just purchasing the hardware. Now, we know that in the absence of required software, the computer is just a useless box. Therefore, buying a computer is just not enough; to make the computer functional and useful, we need to acquire some software, which can be acquired in three ways as follows:

6.3.1 Buying pre-written software

Nowadays, many pre-written software packages are already available in the market. We just need to find one that best meets our requirements. Here, requirement means two things. First, compatibility with the available hardware and the operating system, and second, the list of desired features, duration of warranty, cost, etc.

6.3.2 Having customized software

If any pre-written software package does not meet the individual's or the organization's requirements, then the next option is to have a customized software package. The organization can create a customized software package either in-house, if the organization has a software development team or outsource it to a different organization.

In-house development of customized software When customized software is created by the software development team in the same organization, the following steps are performed:

- The development team studies the user's requirements and plans for the functional modules of the software keeping in consideration if any pre-written software meets requirements partially. If there exists such a software package, then it can be used and enhanced to fully meet user's requirements, otherwise the software has to be written from scratch.
- The modules planned in the previous step are coded, tested, and documented. The complete software when ready is deployed in the user's machine and then software maintenance activities get started.

Outsourcing the customized software When the customized software is to be created by a different organization, then the following steps are performed:

- Requirements are enlisted.
- Different software development companies are contacted to give an estimate of time, effort, and money involved in creating the software.
- The best software vendor is selected based on the cost quoted by them, their reputation in the market, and their proposal.

The selected software development organization works closely with user(s) and develops a software package as per their preference. When developing a customized software package, it is not necessary that the software will be created from scratch. Many a time, pre-written software that partially meets user's requirements can be enhanced to deliver the final customized software. This would help to reduce the time, effort, and money involved to create the software package.

Note

When the user orders both hardware and software from the same vendor, the vendor develops software on the chosen hardware and delivers the combination of hardware and software to the user. This is called a turnkey solution or an end-to-end solution.

6.3.3 Downloading public domain software

Some software are available on the Internet that the users can download free of cost. If such available software meets user's requirements, they can be easily downloaded. The basic idea behind such software is that its creators want their software to become popular among people. Such type of software is known as public domain software or freeware or shareware. It is also often referred as community-supported software as authors do not support the product directly but users of the software support and help each other.

While some public domain software packages are available free of cost on the Internet with full set of supported features, others are either available with only limited features as the rest of the features can be purchased, or with a full set of features but only for a limited time period known as the trial period.

Some public domain software, also known as open source software that is equally popular among user community, allows its users to download, view, modify, and distribute modified source codes to others. However, there are special licensing systems for open source software so that it can be promoted and at the same time there are copyright protection schemes for the original and subsequent authors of such software.

Note

All open source software are not always free and not all free software are always open source.

6.4 PRODUCTIVITY SOFTWARE

Productivity software is any software that is used to attain something productive, especially in the office or home, as opposed to game software or entertainment software.

Word processing programs, spreadsheet applications, and graphic design software are all examples of productivity software. These are the tools people use to create and produce documents, presentations, databases, charts, graphs, calendars, labels, to-do lists, etc.

Today, there are hundreds of productivity software packages available in the market, but undoubtedly the Microsoft Office package dominates the industry. This may be true because the Windows operating system, which is also produced by Microsoft, is the most widely used operating system, and many computer vendors include full or trial versions of Microsoft Office on new Windows PCs. In addition to this, Microsoft Office gives users the functionality they need to do their jobs.

However, some users prefer to use specialized software dedicated to a specific purpose. For example, they may want word processing software that formats documents in the appropriate style automatically. There are hundreds of specialized productivity software applications available that cater to practically any format one can imagine.

In this section, we will read about different productivity software such as the Microsoft Office package, graphics design software, multimedia software, and database management software.

6.4.1 Introduction to Microsoft Office

Microsoft Office, released by Microsoft on 19 November 1990, is a suite of inter-related applications for the Microsoft Windows and Mac OS X operating systems. Initially, it included Microsoft Word, Microsoft Excel, and Microsoft PowerPoint. However, over the years, the Microsoft Office suite has grown substantially with shared features, such as a common spell checker, OLE data integration, and the Microsoft Visual Basic for applications scripting language. Although the latest version of Microsoft Office is MS Office 2013, in this chapter we will learn to use 2007 edition.

Microsoft Word

Word processors are software packages that enable users to create, edit, print, and save documents for future retrieval and reference. The key advantage of using a word processor is that it allows users to make changes to a document without retyping the entire document. Microsoft Word is the world's leading word processing application. Users can create a variety of documents such as letters, memos, resumes, forms, or any document that

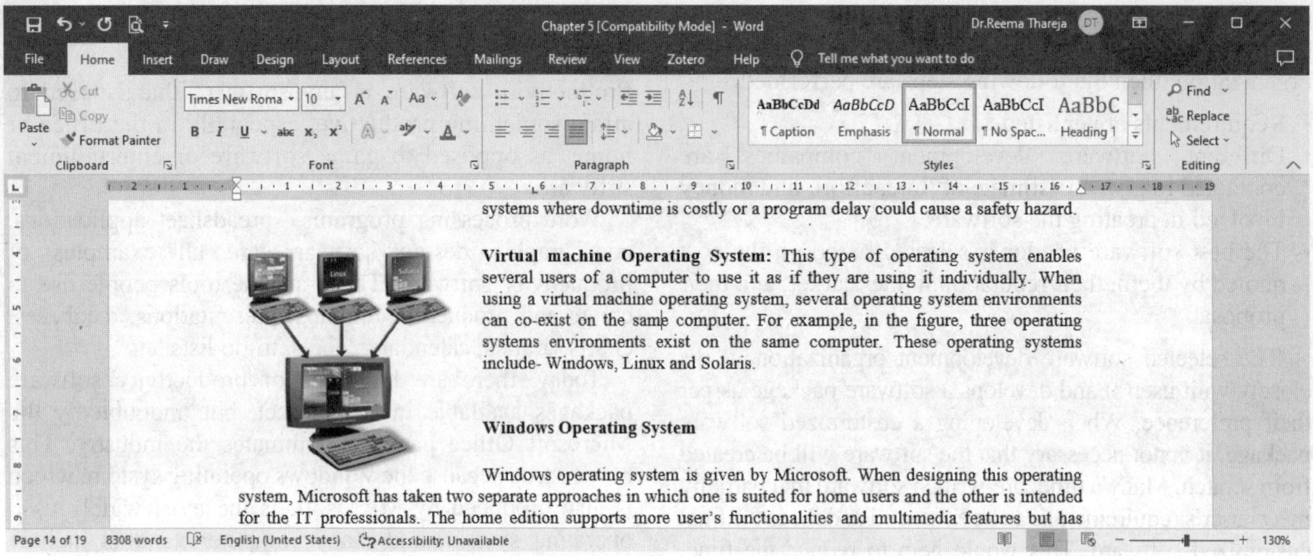

Figure 6.4 Microsoft Word window

can be typed and printed. A screenshot of this application is shown in Figure 6.4.

Microsoft Word enables users to do the following:

- Create documents and edit them later (if required) by adding more text, modifying existing text, deleting/moving some part of the text, etc.
- Change the size of margins to reformat the text in the document.
- Format documents by indenting or double-spacing the text.
- Change the size and type of fonts.
- Insert page numbers, headers, and footers.
- Check spellings and correct them automatically if required.
- Display the word count and other statistics.
- Format the text in columnar style.
- Insert tables in the text.
- Find and replace text.
- Cut, copy, and paste portions of text from one location in the document to another.
- Insert graphs, pictures, and charts into the docment.
- Send the same letter to multiple recipients using the mail-merge facility.
- Add macros so that users can attach specific functions to some function/special keys, a tool bar, or a menu.
- Provide online help on any command.

Before we discuss the functionalities of Microsoft Word, let us first look at the different toolbars available in the application window. Figure 6.5 shows the Menu bar. A click on any menu expands and lists various functions that are available within that menu.

The next is the Quick Access Bar, shown in Figure 6.6, which contains commands that are frequently used. Once a command is added on the toolbar, users can quickly use it in just a single point click. Users can easily add or remove commands from the Quick Access Toolbar.

Figure 6.5 Menu bar

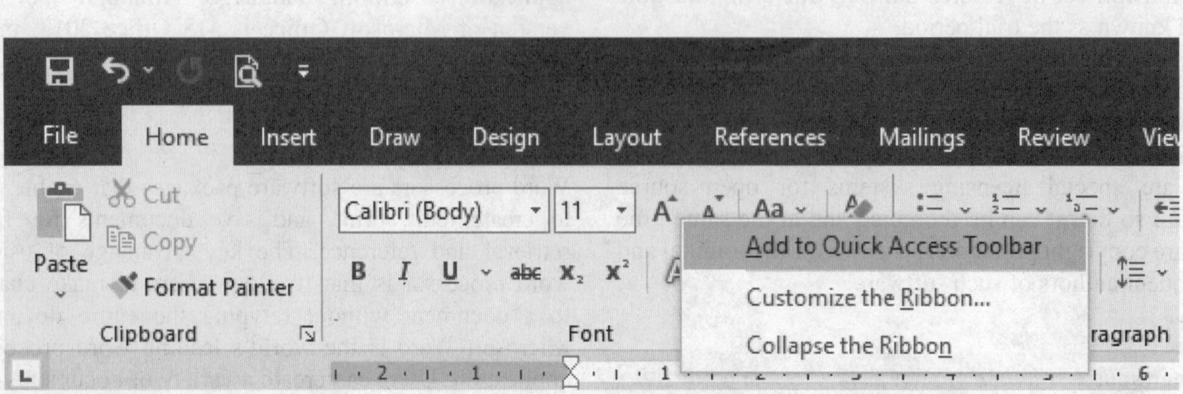

Figure 6.6 Quick Access Toolbar

Adding a command to the Quick Access Toolbar On the ribbon, select the command to be added to the Quick Access Toolbar. Right-click the command, and then select Add to Quick Access Toolbar on the shortcut menu.

Removing a command from the Quick Access Toolbar Right-click the command to be removed from the Quick Access Toolbar. Select Remove from Quick Access Toolbar on the shortcut menu.

Finally, the formatting toolbar, shown in Figure 6.7, contains shortcut buttons for formatting the text. It has buttons for choosing the font style, font name, font size; buttons to make the text bold, italicized, or underlined; buttons for left, right, centre, or justified alignment; buttons to number or bullet the paragraph; and buttons to colour the font and its background.

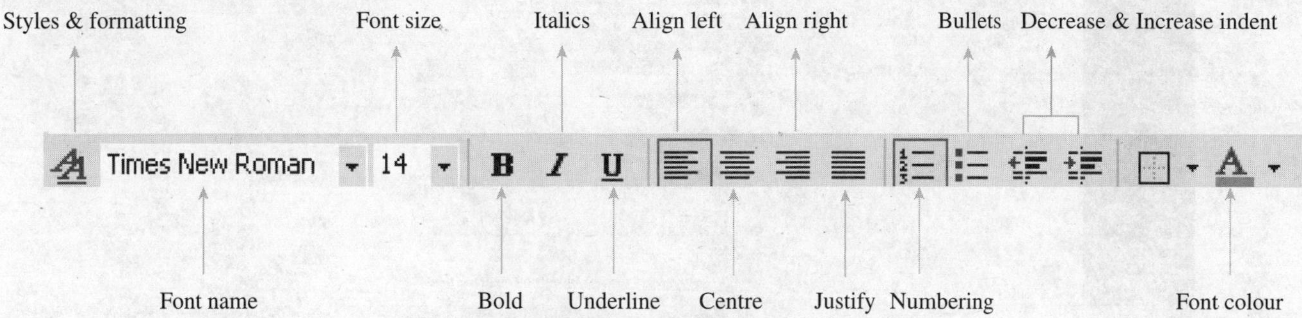

Figure 6.7 Formatting toolbar

Creating a file If MS Word is already open, there are two ways to create a new document. Click the new button on the Quick Access Bar, or click *New* on the File menu (see Figure 6.8).

Saving a file When one has completed working with a document or just wants to store the work before continuing, it is necessary to save the file. This can be done by either choosing File → Save from the Menu bar or clicking the Save button on the Quick Access Toolbar (if option is available) to open the Save As dialog box, shown in Figure 6.9.

The first time a newly created file is saved, the Word application prompts you to enter a location and a name for it. You can click locations like OneDrive - Personal, This PC or use the Browse option if it is any other folder., as shown in Figure 6.10. OneDrive is a cloud storage location, provided for free by Microsoft. Saving files in this location has several benefits. Users can access files from any Internet-connected computer. This also help users to share links to their OneDrive files with others for collaboration. Moreover, these files are safe and secure and users do not have to worry about backups.

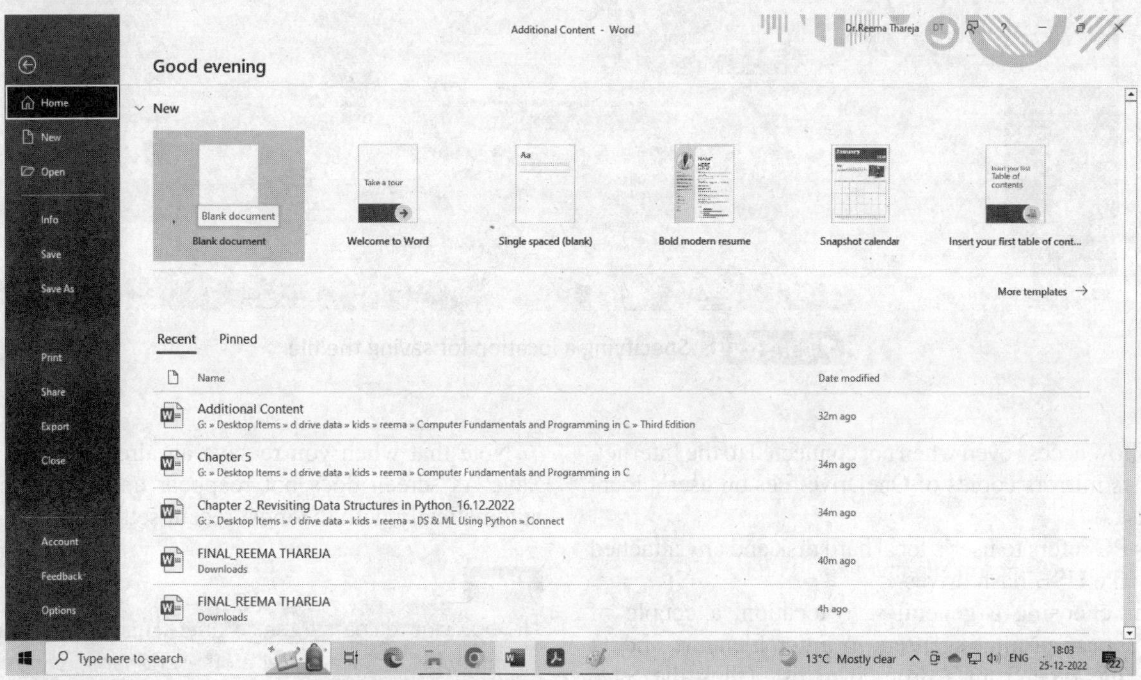

Figure 6.8 Creating a new file in Microsoft Word

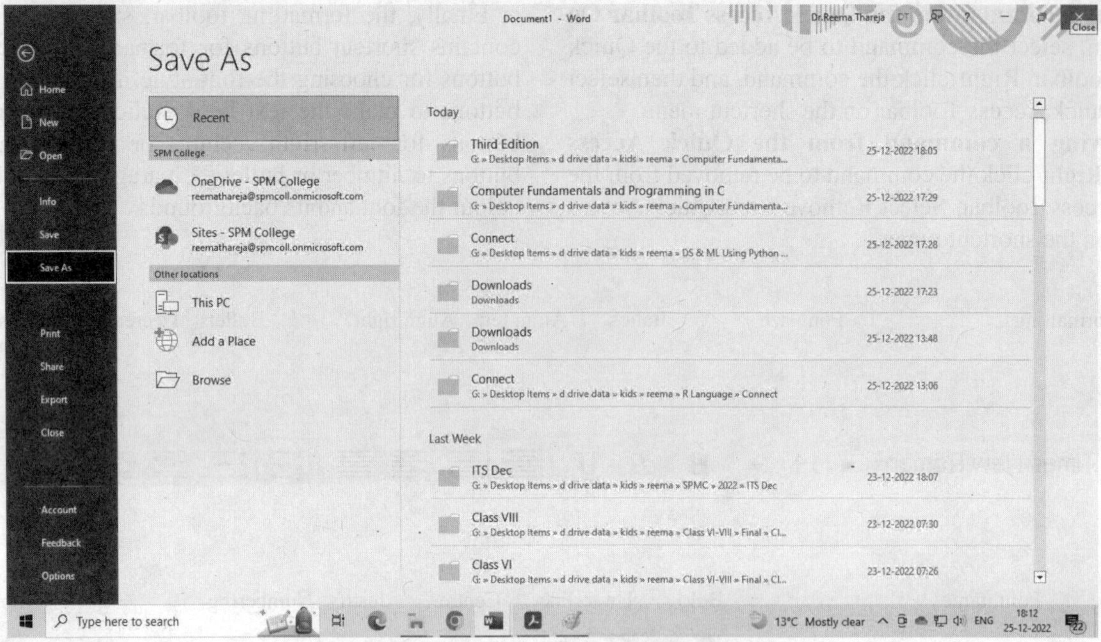

Figure 6.9 Saving a file in Microsoft Word

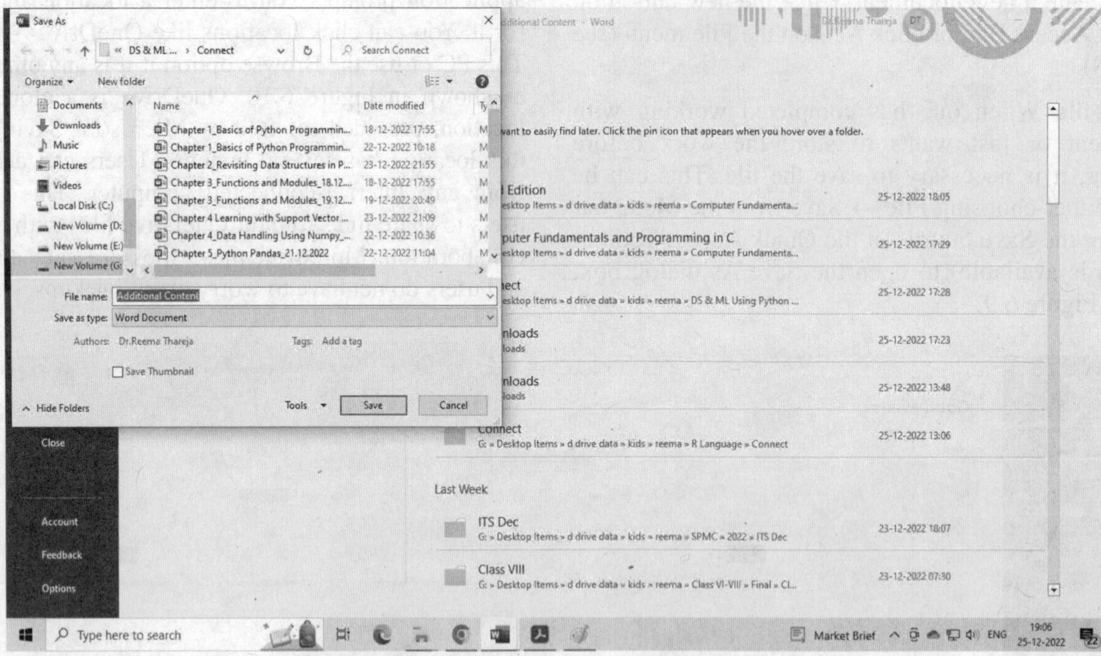

Figure 6.10 Specifying a location for saving the file

To allow access even when not connected to the Internet, Windows mirrors copies of OneDrive files on user's local hard disk.

This PC refers to user's local hard disk and any attached drives, like USB flash drives.

After choosing a general save location, a couple of boxes appear prompting users to enter filename and to choose file type from a drop-down list. Click the Save button.

Note that when you re-save an already saved file, the Save As screen does not reappear and the file is saved automatically with the most recent settings.

Note

If you want to change the settings (such as the location or file type) or save under a different name, choose File → Save As to make the Save As controls appear.

Note

File names can be up to 256 characters long and can contain uppercase and lowercase letters and spaces. However, they cannot contain punctuation marks other than underscores and hyphens.

Closing a file Removing a document from the document window is achieved by choosing File → Close or clicking the *Close* button (the cross sign on the upper right corner of the document window) on the document window. If a document that has been changed since it was last saved is closed, a prompt appears to save the changes.

Opening an existing file To open an existing file, the following steps are to be followed (Figure 6.11):

1. In the Microsoft Word program, click File → Open.
2. In the *Look in* list, click the drive, folder location that contains the file to be opened.
3. In the folder list, locate and open the folder that contains the file.
4. Click the file, and then click *Open*.

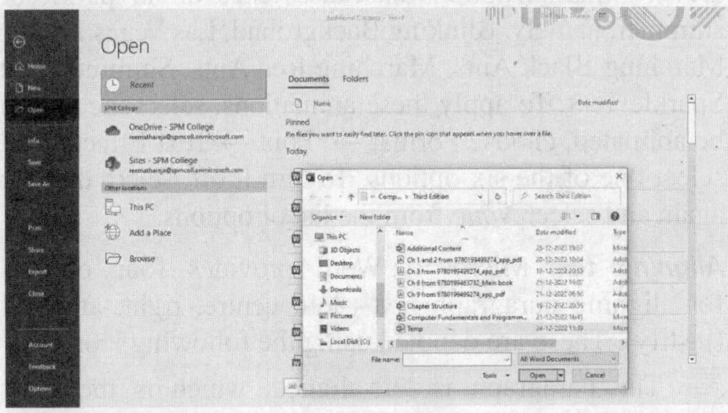

Figure 6.11 Opening an existing file in Microsoft Word

Printing a document Previewing the document before printing gives one the chance to see how the pages break and whether there are any layout problems that will make the document look less than its best. Microsoft Word offers two ways to see how a document will look when it is printed:

- *Print Layout* view (View → Print Layout)—In this view, one is able to enter text, insert graphics, and work in columns while seeing how the printed document will turn out.
- *Print Preview* allows one to view multiple pages of the document at once, zoom in and out of pages easily, adjust margins, and shrink the document by one page to prevent a small carryover from appearing on a page by itself. To open Print Preview, click the *Print Preview* button on the Quick Access Toolbar or choose File → Print Preview.

The dream of a paperless office may not be a long way from reality. In the meantime, however, we are still expected to generate a hard-copy of most documents we write. A few tricks can make all the difference in producing a printed document that reflects the professional appearance one would like to convey. There are two ways to print a document, depending on how much control one needs:

- If one needs to specify print settings, choose File → Print from the Menu bar to open the Print dialog box, shown in Figure 6.12, which allows one to select a printer, choose the number of copies, and specify what should be printed. Clicking the *Options* button at the bottom of the dialog box opens a page where one can select the print quality and other settings.
- To send a document to the printer immediately, using the default print options (and without opening a dialog box), click the *Print* button on the Quick Access Toolbar. This is convenient in most of the applications.

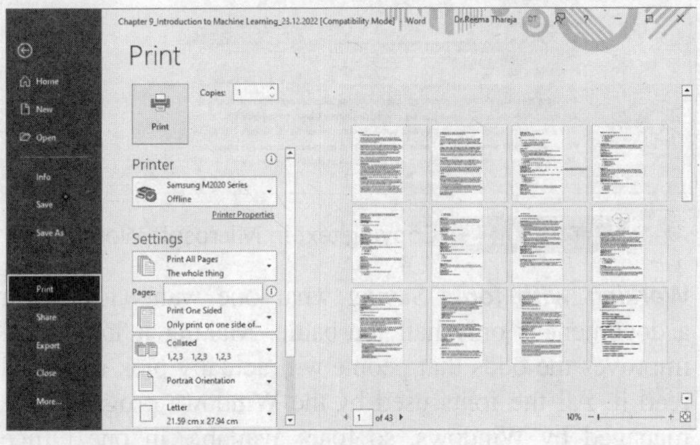

Figure 6.12 Printing a file in Microsoft Word

Editing a document Power users are those who use the minimum number of steps to complete a task. They are not just proficient, but also efficient, particularly with skills that are used frequently in Microsoft Word. Knowing several ways to select and replace text lets one streamline many of the other tasks that can be accomplished with the documents.

Selecting text To select a piece of text, press the *Shift* key and, with the help of arrow keys select the text, or simply drag the mouse over the text. Once finished with working on the selected text, clicking somewhere in the document deselects the text.

Correcting mistakes The easiest way to correct mistakes is to select the text that requires correction and type the text for replacement. Pressing any key will immediately delete the selected text. To correct mistakes that one makes while typing, one of the following methods can be used:

- Using the *Backspace* or *Delete* keys
- Clicking the *Undo* button on the Quick Access Toolbar

Copying and moving text The most commonly used method of moving and copying text is through the use of the Cut, Copy, and Paste features on the Quick Access

Toolbar and Menu bar. The user finds it easy to move and copy text by using the following methods:

- Select the text to be copied or to be cut.
- Right click on the selected text and click on Copy.
- Place the cursor at the position where the text has to be pasted.
- Right click at that position and click on Paste option.

Figure 6.13 shows the screenshot for copying the selected text.

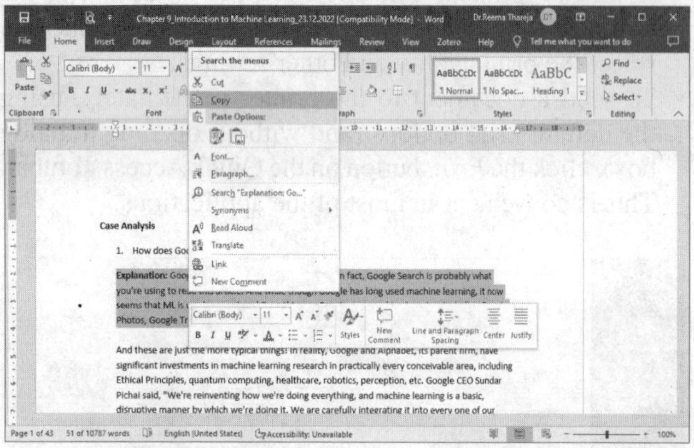

Figure 6.13 Copying text in Microsoft Word

Working with fonts Saying what one wants to say in a document is only half the battle. Making it look good improves the odds that people will actually pick it up and read it. All the fonts used by the Windows programs are managed by Windows, so fonts available in one Office application will be available in all the others. The Formatting toolbar includes buttons and drop-down menus that lets the user choose a font, font size, effects such as bold, italics, and underline, and font colour. If one needs font options that are not available on the toolbar, open the Font dialog box shown in Figure 6.14, by choosing Format → Font.

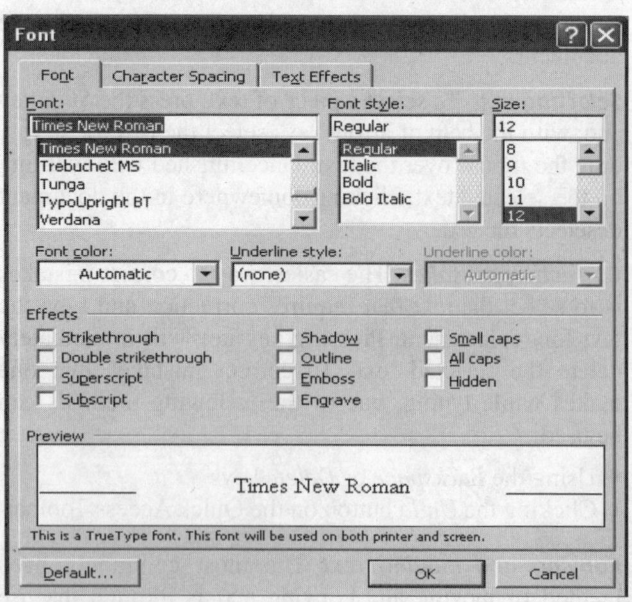

Figure 6.14 Using the Font tab in Microsoft Word

Microsoft Word's Font dialog box has three page tabs: *Font*, *Character Spacing*, and *Text Effects*. On the Font page, one can select font attributes and see how a font will look by noting the changes in the preview as the desired styles, sizes, underlining, colours, and effects are applied.

There are 11 effects that one can apply from the Font dialog box. The strikethrough and double strikethrough options can be used to show proposed deletions in a contract or bylaws. The user may apply superscript and subscript styles to place special characters in formulae (H_2O or Πr^2), and use outline, emboss, and engrave to stylize the text so that it stands out.

Character spacing Character spacing is used to adjust the distance between characters. For example, one can spread a title such as MEMORANDUM across a page without having to add two or three spaces between the characters (MEMORANDUM). Character spacing is commonly used in advanced desktop publishing when the characters are to be sized and scaled precisely.

Animation Animation is a text enhancement feature designed for documents that will be read onscreen. There are six animation options that causes text to blink, sparkle, or shimmer, namely, Blinking Background, Las Vegas Lights, Marching Black Ants, Marching Red Ants, Shimmer, and Sparkle Text. To apply these animations, select the text to be animated, choose Format → Font → Text Effects, and select one of the six options. To turn it off, select the text again and select *None* from the list of options.

Aligning text Microsoft Word provides four options for aligning paragraph text—left, centre, right, and full (justify). These are denoted using the following icons:

The paragraph is left-aligned, which is the most common alignment type. It means that text lines up with the left margin and leaves a ragged edge at the right margin. Left-aligned text is considered the easiest to read.

The paragraph is centred. This style is generally used for headings and desktop publishing creations. Centred text is equally positioned between the left and right margins.

The paragraph is right-aligned. Right alignment is used in headers and footers and other text that needs to be put off to the side. It means that text lines up with the right margin and leaves a ragged edge at the left margin. Right-aligned text is the hardest to read.

The paragraph is justified or fully aligned. Justified text appears formal because the text lines up evenly with the left and right margins. It is often used in documents with columns of text. Sometimes the paragraph looks unbalanced because too much space has to be inserted between the characters.

To align text, select the text and click on one of the alignment buttons on the Formatting toolbar.

Creating lists Microsoft Word makes it easy to create bulleted and numbered lists. If a list begins with a number, Microsoft Word will automatically number the following paragraphs when Enter is pressed.

To apply numbering to existing text, select the paragraphs and click the Numbering button on the Formatting toolbar. Use the Bullets button to bullet existing paragraphs of text. To automatically number or bullet text as content is typed in, do the following:

- Type the number 1 and a period, followed by a space, and then enter text for the item. For bullets, begin with an asterisk and a space.
- Press Enter. Microsoft Word will automatically number the next item 2, or bullet the next item.
- Continue entering text and pressing the Enter key to create numbered or bulleted points.
- When the list is complete, press Enter twice to turn automatic numbering or bullets off.

One can also begin numbering by clicking the Numbering button before typing the first paragraph. To use letters rather than numbers in automatic numbering, type A rather than 1 to begin. Word will number the second and succeeding paragraphs B, C, D, and so on. If the first paragraph is numbered 'I', Word will use Roman numerals to number the paragraphs.

Spelling and grammar Spell-checking software has been in use for a long time. When one runs *Spelling and Grammar* or has the *Check spelling as you type* option turned on, Microsoft Word checks each word against its dictionaries. When a word is not found, it is flagged for verification. As shown in Figure 6.15, right-clicking on a red-underlined word provides options to select a word from a list of choices, namely Ignore All, Add, or choosing from a list of AutoCorrect entries.

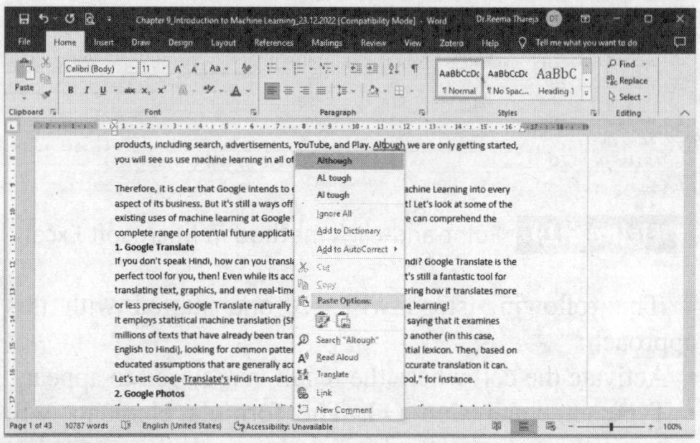

Figure 6.15 Using the AutoCorrect feature in Microsoft Word

- Ignore this occurrence of the word.
- Ignore All occurrences of the word in this document.
- Add the word to the custom dictionary, so that Microsoft Office will recognize it the next time it is used.
- Change the word by choosing one of the suggested corrections or by editing the word manually.
- Change all occurrences of the word in this document by choosing one of the suggested corrections or by editing the word manually.
- AutoCorrect the word (after choosing or entering a correction) and add it to the AutoCorrect dictionary.

Finding and replacing text One of the fastest ways to make repetitive changes throughout a long document is to use *Find and Replace*. *Find* helps the user to locate a text string, and *Replace* substitutes the new text for the existing string. The following steps are used to find and replace text:

- Click on Find command in the Home Tab to open the Find and Replace dialog box.
- Enter the characters to be searched for in the *Find What* text box. Click *Find Next.*
- Close the *Find* dialog box (see Figure 6.16) and click the *Next Find/Go To* button at the bottom of the vertical scroll bar. Browse through each of the occurrences of the text string.

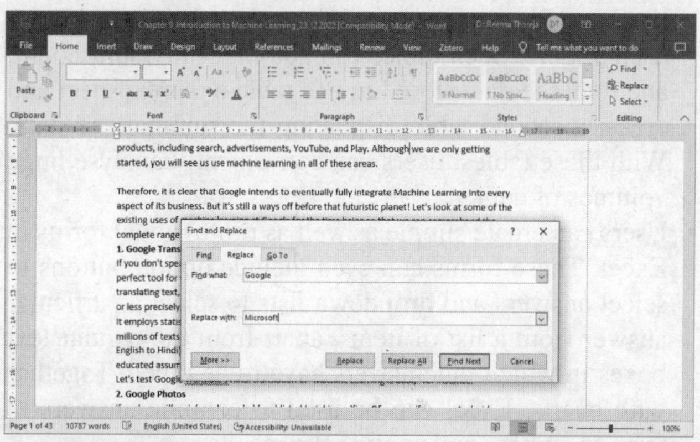

Figure 6.16 Finding and replacing text in Microsoft Word

Using Replace To replace text, open the *Find* dialog box and click the *Replace* tab. Enter the text required to be found in the *Find What* text box and the text to replace it with in the *Replace With* text box. One can choose to replace one occurrence at a time by clicking *Find Next* and then *Replace*, or, if the user is very sure of what he/she is doing, choosing *Replace All* would complete all the replacements in one step. When Microsoft Word is finished, it opens a dialog box that indicates the total number of replacements made.

Microsoft Excel

A spreadsheet software is one in which data is stored into rows and columns, or 'cells' that can be formatted in various fonts or colours. Microsoft Excel (see Figure 6.17) is an example of a spreadsheet software which is used to store, organize, and manipulate data. The stored data can also be converted into graphs for analysis.

It includes a number of simple as well as complex formulae and functions to calculate variables in the data and is therefore widely used in finance to automatically calculate variables such as profit, loss, or expenditure.

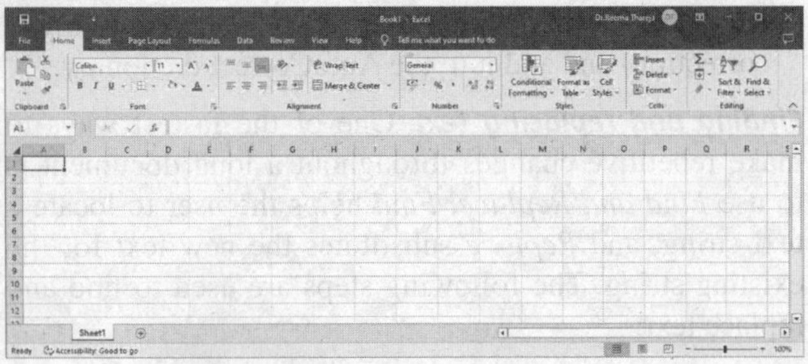

Figure 6.17 Microsoft Excel window

Microsoft Excel is widely used for the following applications:

- Excel is used to manage data records and name lists in a tabular fashion. With Excel, users can easily sort the list and filter it like a database tool.
- Excel is an excellent analytical tool, widely used in business. Pivot table is one of the main features which is used widely. Such tables can automatically sort, count, and total the data stored in one table or spreadsheet and create a second table displaying the summarized data. With these tables, users can conveniently analyse huge volumes of data.
- Users can create simple as well as professional forms in Excel. These forms can even include option buttons to select answers and dropdown lists to select a particular answer from a list of items, apart from the regular text boxes in which the answers have to be typed. Together with charts, Excel can be used to compile answers to tests or quizzes and analyse the results.
- Many small and large organizations use Excel as the primary tool for corporate budgeting.
- Excel is widely used for managing inventories in many companies. Using well-designed forms, pre-defined functions and formulae, and pivot tables, users can get a good detailed analysis of stock movement and inventory level at any point in time.
- Finding the profit breakeven point is not simple. However, with Excel, it can be calculated easily and accurately in just a few seconds.

Excel application window The Excel application window as shown in Figure 6.18 includes the standard title bar and command bars. Below the command bars is a strip that contains the name box and the formula bar. The Excel status bar displays information about current selections, commands, or operations. The right end of the status bar displays NUM if the keyboard's Num Lock is on.

Workbooks and worksheets When Excel is launched, the Excel application window opens with a new Excel workbook. A workbook is a multi-page Excel document. Each page in the workbook is called a worksheet, and the active worksheet is displayed in the document window. The sheet tabs are used to move to another worksheet and the navigation buttons are used to scroll through the sheet tabs.

Worksheet components Each worksheet is divided into columns, rows, and cells, separated by grid lines, as shown in Figure 6.18. Columns are vertical divisions. The first column is named A, and the letter A appears in the column heading. The horizontal rows are numbered. Each worksheet has 256 columns and 65,536 rows. A cell is the intersection of a row and a column. Each cell has a unique address composed of the cell's column and row. For example, the cell in the upper-left corner of the worksheet is cell A1. When data is entered, it is always placed in the active cell.

To enter data in a cell, first activate the cell, and then begin typing the data. As soon characters are entered, an insertion point appears in the cell, the text appears in the cell and the formula bar, and the formula bar buttons are activated.

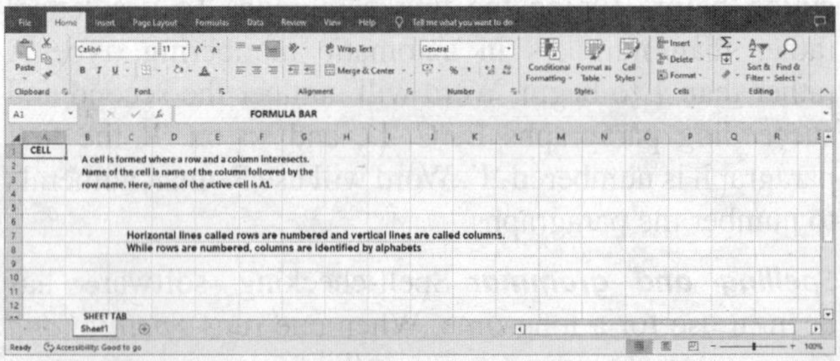

Figure 6.18 Components of a Microsoft Excel worksheet

Point-and-click formulae Point-and-click (see Figure 6.19) is a highly reliable method that Excel is known for.

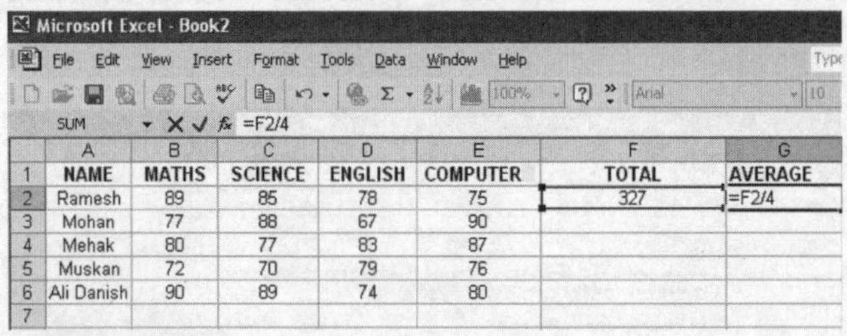

Figure 6.19 Point-and-click method in Microsoft Excel

The following steps will get one started with this approach:

- Activate the cell where the result is required to appear.
- Type an equal sign (=). The formula elements will begin appearing in the formula bar as they are typed or selected.
- Click the first cell to be included in the formula.
- Type an operator.
- Click the next cell in the formula.
- Repeat Steps 4 and 5 until the entire formula is entered.
- Finish the entry by pressing Enter.

Filling formulae In the previous example, the formula for each student's total marks is the same—marks obtained in Maths + Science + English + Computer. Since one working formula has already been created, all one needs to do is fill it to the other cells.

There is a square box in the lower-right corner of the cell called the fill handle. As the mouse is moved towards the lower-right corner of cell, the mouse pointer changes shape to a black cross to let the user know that the mouse can be used for a fill operation.

Filling is a form of copying. Begin by activating the cell that has the formula to be copied. Move the mouse pointer toward the fill handle until the mouse pointer changes to the fill pointer shape.

Press the mouse button and drag the fill handle down to select the cells to which the formula is to be copied. Release the mouse button, and the formula will be filled in the other cells. Figures 6.20(a) and (b) illustrate this operation.

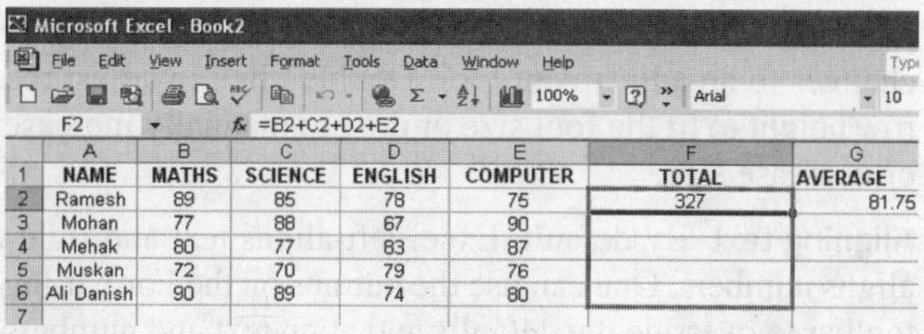

	A	B	C	D	E	F	G
1	NAME	MATHS	SCIENCE	ENGLISH	COMPUTER	TOTAL	AVERAGE
2	Ramesh	89	85	78	75	327	81.75
3	Mohan	77	88	67	90		
4	Mehak	80	77	83	87		
5	Muskan	72	70	79	76		
6	Ali Danish	90	89	74	80		

(a)

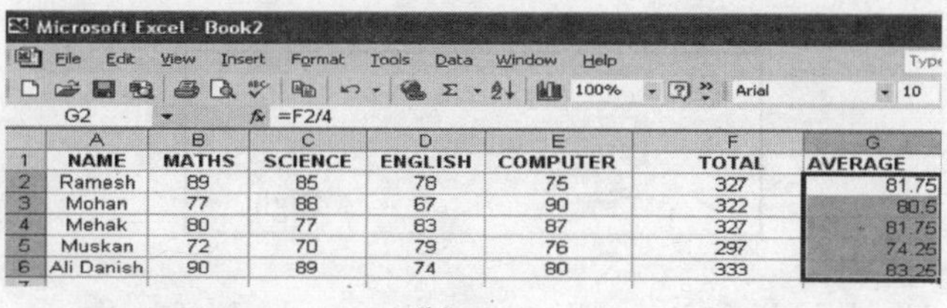

	A	B	C	D	E	F	G
1	NAME	MATHS	SCIENCE	ENGLISH	COMPUTER	TOTAL	AVERAGE
2	Ramesh	89	85	78	75	327	81.75
3	Mohan	77	88	67	90	322	80.5
4	Mehak	80	77	83	87	327	81.75
5	Muskan	72	70	79	76	297	74.25
6	Ali Danish	90	89	74	80	333	83.25

(b)

Figure 6.20 Filling formula operation (a) Before filling (b) After filling

Excel can also fill the destination cells with a value from a source cell and increase this value in each successive cell in the series, based on the step value that is specified. For instance, if one cell contains the number 10, or the date 02/14/07, the user can use Excel to utilize these values to fill the other cells and automatically add 2 to each successive cell value, or seven days to each succeeding cell date.

Excel will even fill the cells based on the series of values in successive cells. Let's say a user selects three cells, with successive values of 3, 6, and 9, and three more blank cells after them. Excel can recognize the series and automatically fill the three selected blank cells with 12, 15, and 18 (the next values in the series where $n = n + 3$).

For using the AutoFill feature, the starting fill value is selected based on one of following three approaches:

- *One cell:* A single cell is selected if the user needs to fill cells based on the contents of one cell, which will increase according to a step value that is specified.
- *Series of cells:* A set of adjoining cells containing a series of values is selected for using those values to continue in other blank cells.
- *Formula cell:* A cell containing a formula is chosen if the user wants to fill other cells with the formula.

When creating a series with the fill handle, just drag in one direction at a time. For example, you can fill the series left to right of the cell that contains the initial values, or from above or below the cell containing the initial values.

When the fill handle is dragged, Excel either creates a series in all of the cells that you select or copies the entire range with the initial value. For example, when you use the fill handle, Excel will either copy an initial value into every cell or a sequential series (such as 10, 11, 12, and so on), by selecting the Fill Series command on the AutoFill Options shortcut menu.

This is shown in Figure 6.21.

> **Note**
>
> Note: You cannot fill a series diagonally. Series can be filled only horizontally or vertically.

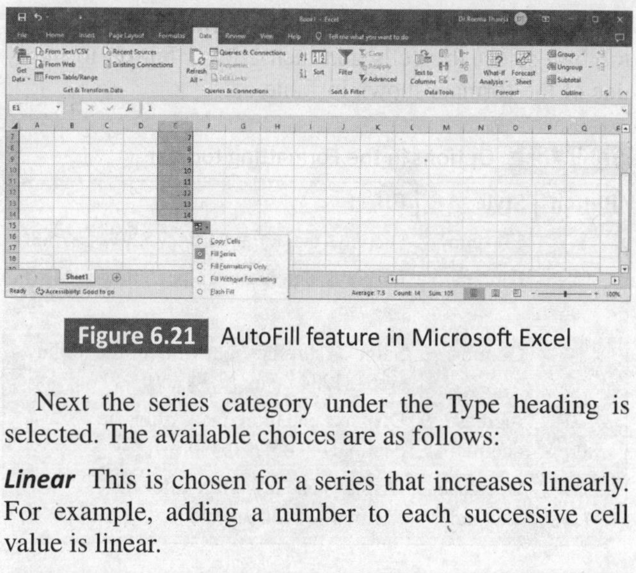

Figure 6.21 AutoFill feature in Microsoft Excel

Next the series category under the Type heading is selected. The available choices are as follows:

Linear This is chosen for a series that increases linearly. For example, adding a number to each successive cell value is linear.

Growth This is selected for a series that increases geometrically or exponentially. For instance, multiplying each successive cell value by the preceding cell value is growth.

Date This is used for dates to be incremented. In addition, the date interval to be used is selected in the Date Unit area. The choices are Day, Weekday, Month, and Year.

AutoFill This is used for formulae or other series types. It determines what series type to use based on the cells selected. This option is the same as filling by dragging the fill handle.

For linear or growth series types, the trend box is checked or a step value and/or stop value is filled, based on the following:

Trend This box is checked if a range of cells with progressive values is selected. Excel will determine what the trend is and fill the blank cells accordingly.

Step value The value that should be used in incrementing the Linear or Growth series of values is entered here.

Stop value This is an optional field which specifies the maximum value to be reached in the series.

Formatting numbers Excel lets the user present numbers in a variety of formats. Formatting is used to identify numbers as currency or percents and to make numbers easier to read by aligning decimal points in a column. Formatting can be effected in the selected cells with three tools:

- Formatting toolbar
- Format Cells dialog box
- Shortcut menu

When a user formats a number, its appearance changes, not its numeric value. The default format for numbers, General, does not display zeros that have no effect on the value of the number. For example, if one enters 10.50, 10.5 has the same numeric value, so Excel does not display the extra or trailing zero.

Using the Formatting toolbar To format cells with the toolbar, select the cells and then click a button to apply one of the formats shown in Table 6.2.

Table 6.2 Options in the Formatting toolbar

Button	Style	Effect
$	Currency	Displays the dollar sign—75.30 as $75.30
%	Percent	Displays a number as a percentage—45 as 45%
,	Comma	Same as currency, but without the dollar sign—12345.6 as 12,345.60
←.0 .00	Increase decimal	Displays one more place after the decimal—0.45 as 0.450
.00 →.0	Decrease decimal	Displays one less place after the decimal—0.450 as 0.45

Using the Format Cells dialog box Excel has more numeric formats, which can be selected from the Format Cells dialog box. Select the cells to be formatted. Then open the dialog box by clicking Format → Cells from the Menu bar. The format cells dialog box has separate pages for Number, Alignment, Font, Border, Patterns, and Protection, as shown in Figure 6.22.

Adjusting column width and row height By default, Excel columns are slightly more than eight characters wide. If the data in a worksheet is wider than the column, the column width may need to be adjusted so that it becomes wide enough to contain the data. One can adjust the column width manually by dragging the column border to AutoFit the column width to the existing data.

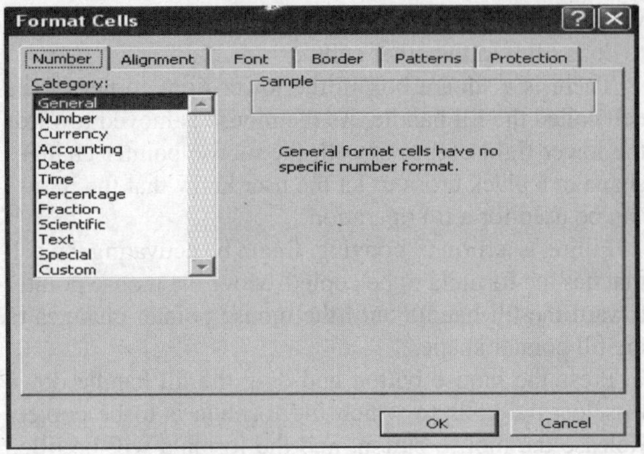

Figure 6.22 Format Cells dialog box

The row height can be adjusted in a similar manner. If the pointer is moved to the lower edge of a row heading, it changes to an adjustment tool. Double-click to adjust the row height to fit the font size or drag to manually increase or decrease size.

Aligning text By default, Excel left-aligns text and right-aligns numbers. One can use the buttons on the Formatting toolbar to override the defaults and align text and numbers at the left, centre, and right within the cells as follows:

Left
Center
Right

The default settings reflect some standard rules for aligning text and numbers:

- Columns of text should be left-aligned because we are used to reading left-aligned text.
- Columns of numbers should be kept in the default (right) alignment and formatted so that the decimal points are aligned.
- Column labels should appear over the contents of the column. If the column is filled with numbers, the heading should be right-aligned or centred. Labels for text columns should be left-aligned or centred.

Rotating text The rotation tools are used to orient text vertically or to rotate text to a specific orientation. These steps guide the user through the process:

- Select the cell containing the words to be rotated, select Format → Cells, and click the Alignment tab in the Format Cells dialog box. Choose one of the following options:
  - To orient text vertically, click the box with the vertical word 'Text' in it.
  - To rotate text to another orientation, either use the Degrees spin box or drag the Text indicator in the rotation tool.
- Click OK to apply the rotation.

Merge, Shrink to Fit, and Wrap Text These actions can be performed by following these steps:

- Select the title and several additional cells below the title.
- Select Format Cells and check one or all of the following options in the Format Cells dialog box:
  - Click the Merge Cells check box to merge the cells.
  - Shrink to Fit reduces the size of the type within selected cells so the contents fit.
  - Wrap Text wraps the contents of a cell if it exceeds the cell's boundaries.

Borders and colour Effective use of fonts can help make worksheets easier to understand. Borders and colour provide further ways to highlight information in a worksheet. A border is a line drawn around a cell or group of cells. Fill colour is used to highlight the background of part of a worksheet and font colour is applied to text.

Using functions and references Excel includes hundreds of other functions that one can use to calculate results used in statistics, finance, engineering, math, and other fields. Functions are formulae, so all functions begin with the equal sign (=). This is followed by the function name, one or more arguments separated by commas, and this entire expression is enclosed in parentheses.

Before entering a function, the cell in which the result is to be displayed should be activated. The '+' in the formula bar is clicked to open the formula palette. The Name box (to the left of the formula bar) changes to a Function box, displaying the name of a last function that was used (SUM).

A list of functions in the formula palette of Microsoft Excel is shown in Figure 6.23.

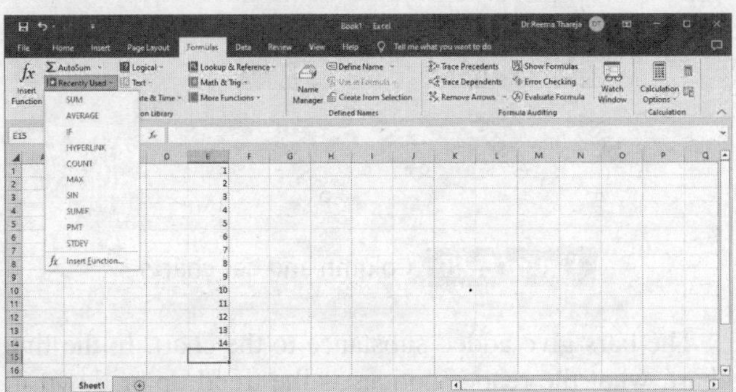

Figure 6.23 List of functions in the formula palette of Microsoft Excel

If the required function is on the list, it is selected, and Excel moves the function to the formula bar and the formula palette. The formula palette (see Figure 6.24) expands to include a description of the function and one or more text boxes for the function's arguments.

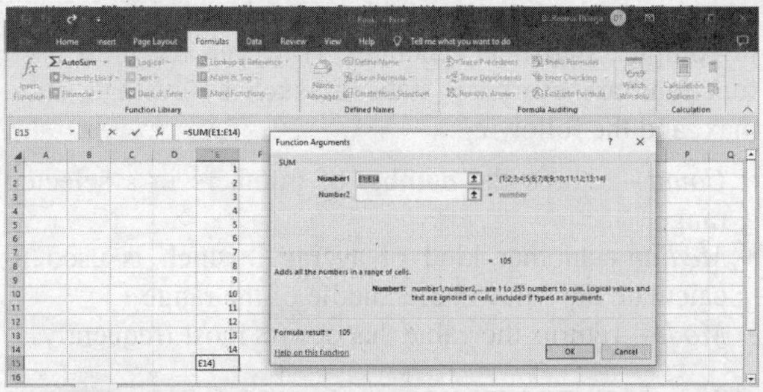

Figure 6.24 Function arguments in the formula palette of Microsoft Excel

After all the required arguments have been selected, OK is clicked to finish the entry and close the Formula Palette. As with any formula, the results of the function are displayed in the active cell. The function itself is displayed in the formula bar when the cell is active.

If the required function is not listed in the Function box, More Functions at the bottom of the list is chosen to open the Insert Function dialog box, as shown in Figure 6.25.

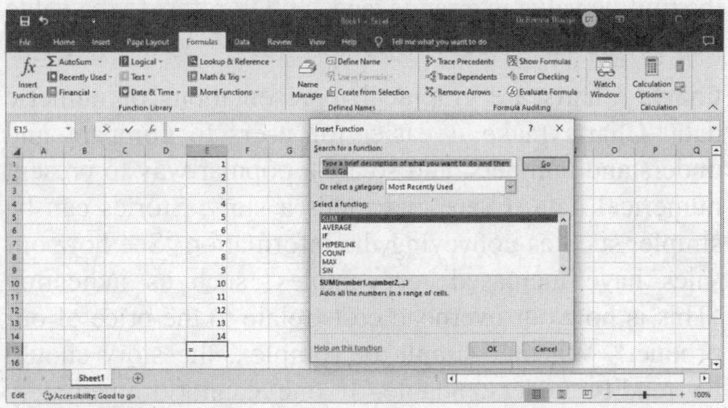

Figure 6.25 Searching for a function in Microsoft Excel

One can search for a function or select a function category. Depending on the category selected, the corresponding list of the functions will be displayed in the textbox. Click on OK to choose the selected function and return to the Formula Palette.

These steps summarize the method to use Excel functions:

- Activate the cell where the result of the function needs to appear.
- Click the = button on the formula bar.
- Choose a function from the Function box drop-down list; or, if the function does not appear on the list, choose More Functions to open the Insert Function dialog box. Choose a category and the specific function. Click OK to return to the Formula Palette.
- In the Formula Palette, select the Number 1 text box. That is, select the cells to include in the argument.
- Click the OK button to complete the entry.

Working with statistical tables Excel includes a fistful of complex statistical functions. However, the most used functions are everyday statistics such as average, min, max, and the following:

- *Count*—returns the number of numbers in a selected range
- *Median*—another kind of average, which is used to calculate the value in the middle of the range
- *Mode*—returns the value that occurs most frequently.

Using COUNT, MEDIAN, and MODE: The COUNT function indicates the numbers of cells that are present in a selected range. If the user has a small worksheet, this can be easily counted but its difficult for large worksheets, and the problem is compounded when some cells in a column are blank.

AVERAGE returns a value called the arithmetic mean—the total of all the values in a range divided by the number of values in the range. When we talk about averages—bowling scores, test grades, speed on several typing tests—we are referring to the arithmetic mean.

However, there are two other types of averages: MEDIAN and MODE. MEDIAN indicates which value is the middle value in a range, and MODE refers to the value that occurs most frequently.

Charts Charts are graphical representations of numeric data. Charts make it easier for users to compare and understand numbers, and so are a popular way to present numerical data. Every chart tells a story. Stories can be simple, such as conveying the information 'See how our sales have increased' or complex, such as indicating 'This is how our overhead costs relate to the price of our product'. Whether simple or complex, the story should be readily understandable. If one cannot immediately understand what a chart means, then it is not a well presented chart. Charts are constructed with data points, which are individual numbers in a worksheet.

Understanding chart types Excel comes with a wide variety of charts capable of graphically representing most standard types of data analysis, and even some more exotic numeric interpolations. The type of data being used and presented determines the type of chart to be used to plot the data on. Excel has charts in the following categories:

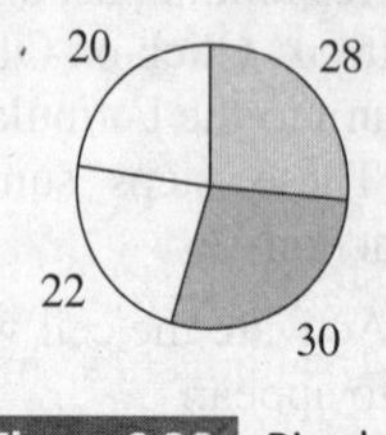

Figure 6.26 Pie chart

- *Pie charts*: These work best for displaying how much each part contributes to a total value (see Figure 6.26).
- *Series charts*: More than one data series can be charted in a series chart. This lets one compare the data points in the series, such as January vs February, or the sale of Reynolds pens vs Flair pens. There are several types of series charts. A user can give the same set of data a very different look by simply changing the chart type.
- *Line and area charts*: These show data points connected with lines, indicating upward or downward trends in value, as shown in Figure 6.27.

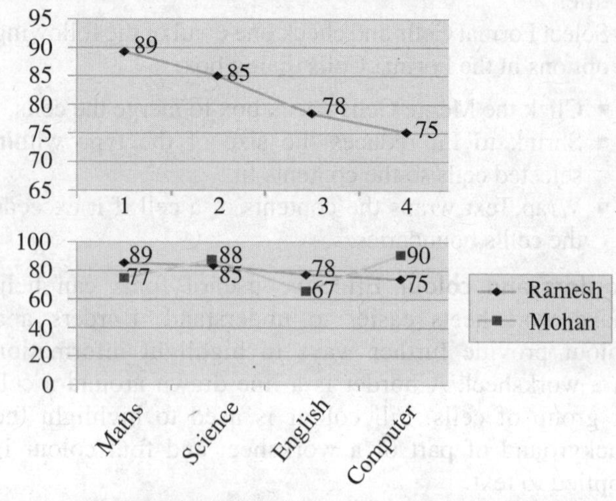

Figure 6.27 Line and area charts

The series chart shown in the second figure is a line chart showing the relationship between marks obtained by two students in different subjects. Line charts are available in a 2D version (as shown) or in a 3D version, which is sometimes called a *ribbon chart*. An area chart is a line chart with the area below the line filled.

- *Column and bar charts*: These compare values across categories, with results presented vertically in column charts and horizontally in bar charts. Figure 6.28 shows the same information presented as a bar chart.

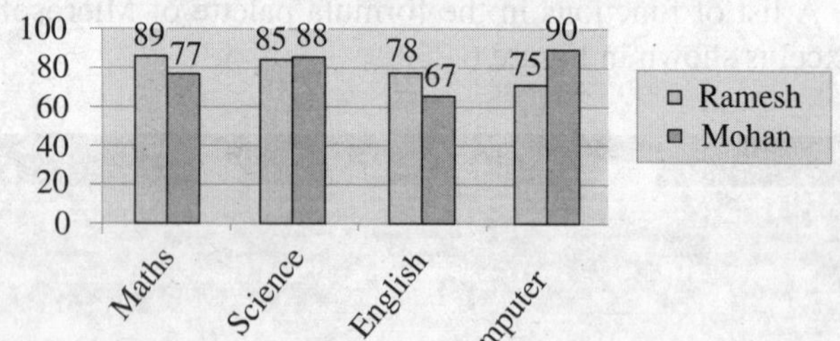

Figure 6.28 Column and bar charts

The bars give added substance to the chart. In the line chart, what the reader notices is the trend up or down in each line and the gaps between the lines. The bar chart not only makes the data seem more substantial, it also makes the differences between the destinations even clearer. The horizontal line is called the x-axis, and the vertical line is the y-axis.

- *Specialty charts*: Excel includes a number of charts suitable for presenting scientific, statistical, and financial data. Scatter charts are used to present experimental results. Surface and contour charts are good for presenting 3D and 2D changes in data. Radar charts show data values in relation to a single metric. Stock charts present values from three to five series of data, including open, high, low, close, and volume trading information.

Creating a chart The easiest way to create a chart is by using the chart wizard. Begin the chart creation process by selecting the data to be used in the chart. With the expectation of the chart's title, everything else that appears in the chart should be selected somewhere in the worksheet.

Step 1: Enter the data in the spreadsheet.

Step 2: Click on the Insert Tab.

Step 3: Select the type of chart. You can use "Recommended Charts" option to allow Excel suggest you a chart based on the data stored.

Step 4: Excel automatically draws the chart and inserts it into the spreadsheet.

Once drawn, you can format the chart- change the colors, labels etc. a chat is formatted by click in the chart. You can add different styles, elements and colors by clicking on suitable options in the commands present in Chart Design Tab. A window that appears on the right also help you format the chart area.

It is always recommended to add chart elements for better understanding. Some important elements are.

Titles: titles for the chart and axes

Axes: Display or hide axes

Gridlines: Display gridlines and display or hide the third dimension of a 3D chart

Legend: Display and place a legend

Data Labels: Display text or values as data labels

Data Table: Show the selected range from the worksheet as part of the chart

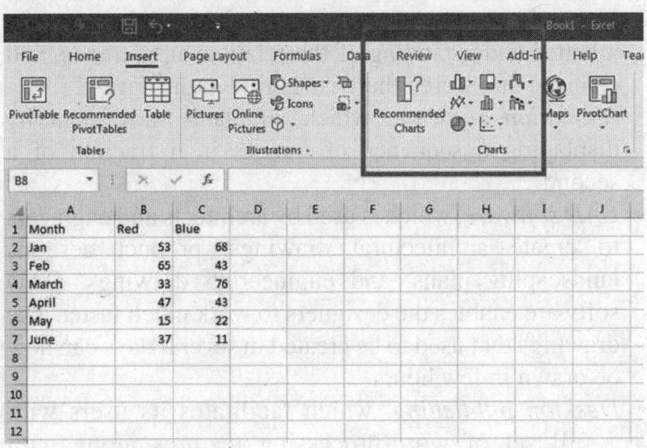

Figure 6.29 Chart wizard in Microsoft Excel

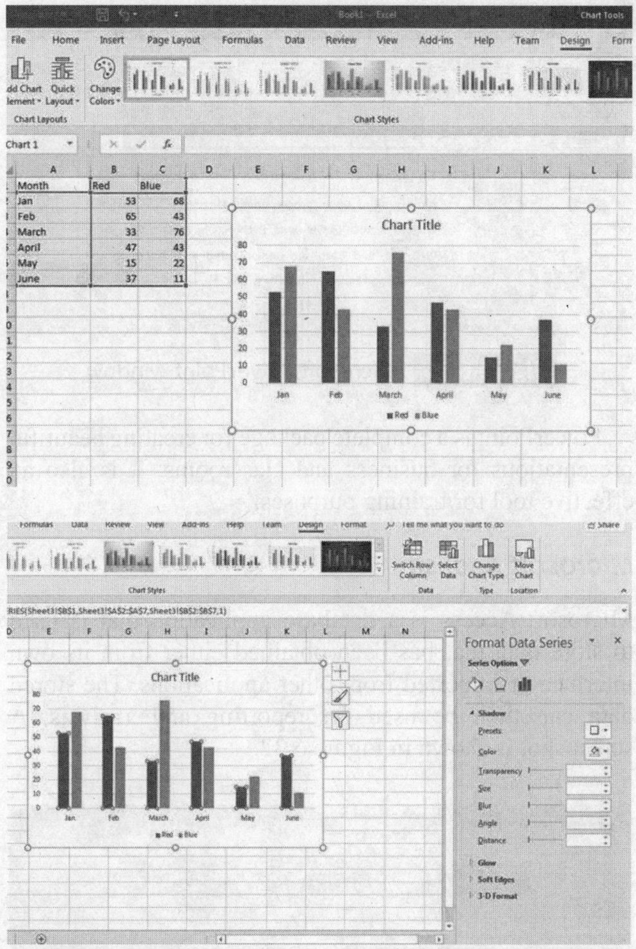

Figure 6.30 Specifying chart options in Microsoft Excel

Microsoft PowerPoint

Microsoft PowerPoint is used to create multimedia presentations and slide shows. Similar to Microsoft Word, it also includes the tools to format text and incorporate design templates. Users can create presentations by using any design template that is available with the program. Many more free add-ins and templates are available online from Microsoft and a host of other websites. Figure 6.31 shows a screenshot of this tool.

When designing presentations using Microsoft PowerPoint, users can add effects on slide transitions and add sound clips, images, animations, or video clips to make the presentation even more interesting for the target audience.

In addition to slide shows, PowerPoint also offers printing options to facilitate the users to provide handouts and outlines for the audience as well as notes pages for the speaker to refer to during presentations.

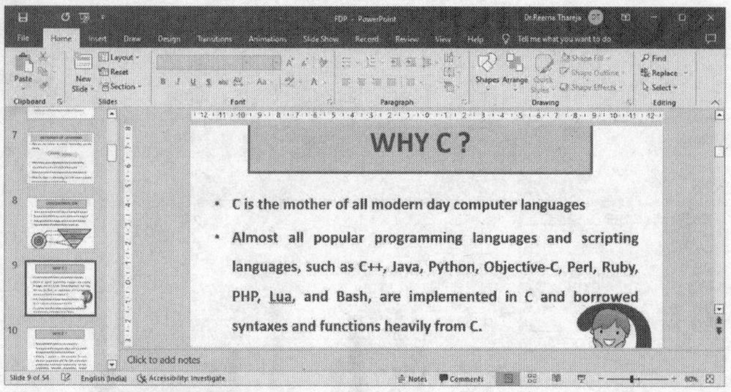

Figure 6.31 Microsoft PowerPoint window

PowerPoint is a complete package for creating beautiful presentations for business and classrooms. It is also an effective tool for training purposes.

Microsoft Access

Microsoft Access is a database application that is used to store data that has been obtained either from its own interface or imported from other applications. The stored data can then be used for reporting and analysis. A screenshot is shown in Figure 6.32.

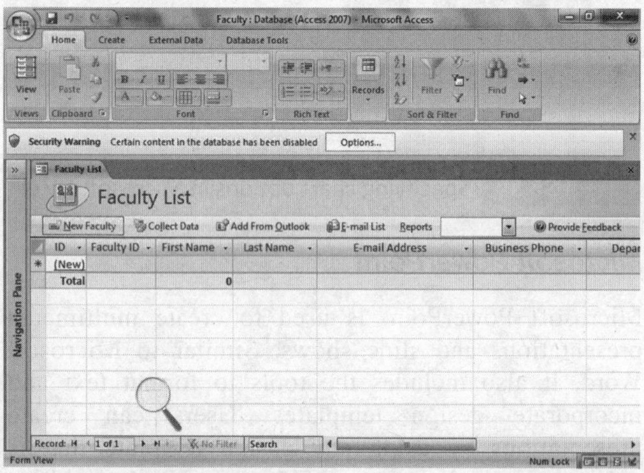

Figure 6.32 Microsoft Access window

Microsoft Access can be used as a front-end, with another application being used as the back-end tables, such as Microsoft SQL Server and non-Microsoft products such as Oracle and Sybase. Similarly, some products (such as Visual Basic, ASP.NET) can act as the front-end and can use Microsoft Access tables as the back-end.

Microsoft Access is equipped with a query interface, forms to input and display data, and reports for printing. Tables designed in Access support a variety of standard field types, indices, record locking, and referential integrity features. In addition to this, Access supports the use of macros to automate repetitive tasks.

Microsoft Access is equally popular among non-programmers as well as professional developers. While non-programmers can create visually pleasing and relatively advanced solutions with very little or no code, professional programmers, on the other hand, can create complex databases and place them on the network to enable multiple users to share and update data without overwriting each other's work.

Microsoft Access is particularly appropriate for meeting end-user database needs and for rapid application development. Access users enjoy its ease of use to create highly focused applications.

6.5 GRAPHICS SOFTWARE

Graphics software, or image editing software, is a program that allows users to create and edit digital images and illustrations. Examples of such software include Adobe Photoshop, Adobe Illustrator, Paint Shop Pro, Microsoft Paint, etc.

Most graphics programs have the ability to import and export one or more graphics file formats. Some of the graphics applications are the following:

- *Paint programs*, which enable users to create rough freehand drawings. The images are stored as bitmaps and can easily be edited as and when required.
- *Illustration/Design/Draw programs*, which provide users more advanced features than paint programs. They are particularly used for drawing curved lines. Such programs store images in vector-based formats. These programs also allow users to draw circles, arcs, and other shapes smoothly and properly connected to each other. Moreover, the program enables the users to move, copy, delete, rotate, tilt, flip horizontally/vertically, and increase/decrease the size of objects.
- *Presentation software,* using which users can create bar charts, pie charts, graphics, slide shows and reports. The charts are usually based on numerical data imported from spreadsheet applications. Presentation software is widely used by analysts and decision makers to gain a better understanding of the relationships, trends, and changes that were otherwise buried in the data.
- *Animation software*, which simulates movement by displaying a sequence of images in a fraction of a second.
- *CAD software*, which is used by architects and engineers to create architectural drawings, product designs, landscaping plans, and engineering drawings. CAD software enables the designers to work much faster. The drawings that used to be created in several days can now be drawn in few hours.
- *Desktop publishing,* which facilitates its users with a full set of word-processing features along with a fine control over placement of text and graphics. Using such an application, the users can easily create newsletters, advertisements, books, and other types of documents.

6.6 MULTIMEDIA SOFTWARE

Multimedia is a comprehensive term that means different types of media. It includes a combination of text, audio, still images, animation, video, and interactive content forms.

Multimedia content can be broadly divided into two groups, linear and non-linear. While the linear active content progresses without any navigational control for the viewer (like in case of cinema presentation), non-linear content, on the other hand, supports user's interaction to control progress (as in case of computer games).

Multimedia presentations can be live or recorded. In a recorded presentation, the user can interact via a navigation system but in a live multimedia presentation, interaction is possible only through the presenter or performer.

Nowadays, multimedia is widely applied in areas such as advertisements, education, entertainment, engineering, medicine, mathematics, business, and scientific research.

Multimedia is used for creating exciting advertisements to attract the attention of the target audience. It is also used in business to design training programs. In the entertainment industry, multimedia is used to create special effects in movies and animations. It is also used in computer games and some video games that are a popular pastime.

Edutainment, which combines education with multimedia entertainment, is now emerging as a trend in school as well as higher education. This has made learning theories simpler than ever before. Moreover, visually impaired people or those with other kinds of disabilities can pursue their careers by using training programs specially designed for them.

Multimedia is used by engineers and researchers for modelling and simulation. For example, a scientist can look at a molecular model of a particular substance and manipulate it to arrive at a new substance. Even in medicines, doctors are now trained by observing a virtual surgery.

6.7 DATABASE MANAGEMENT SOFTWARE

Database management software (DBMS) is a collection of programs which helps users to store, edit, and extract data from a database. Today, different types of DBMSs are available in the market, such as Microsoft Access, FileMaker, DB2, SQL Server, and Oracle, to name a few. While some types of DBMS can run on personal computers, others run on huge systems such as mainframes.

The use of a DBMS has become so common that it has now become a part of our everyday life. It is used in computerized library systems, automated teller machines, flight reservation systems, computerized parts inventory systems, etc. All these applications call for the creation of a series of rights or privileges that can be associated with a specific user. This means that it is possible to designate one or more database administrators who control each function, as well as provide other users with various levels of administration rights.

From a technical point of view, DBMSs can differ widely based on the way they organize the underlying data in the database. A DBMS can be relational, network, flat, or hierarchical. The internal organization of the data can affect the speed and flexibility with which the information can be extracted.

Information from a database is extracted in the form of a *query*, which is a stylized question. Consider the following query:

```
SELECT ALL FROM STUDENTS WHERE MARKS > 90
```

The query requests all records from the table `STUDENTS` that have marks greater than 90. The set of rules for constructing queries is known as *query language*. The most commonly used query language is structured query language (SQL).

The information from a database can be presented to the users in a variety of formats. For example, many DBMSs include a *report writer program* that outputs the data in the form of a report. Many DBMSs also include a graphics component to display the information in the form of graphs and charts. DBMS facilitates its users to control data access, enforce data integrity, manage concurrency, and restore the database from backups.

6.8 OPERATING SYSTEMS

An operating system is a collection of system programs that control the operations of the computer system. An operating system has the following main objectives.

- *Manages the computer hardware*: The OS controls and efficiently utilizes hardware components such as CPU, memory, and I/O devices.
- *Provides a user interface*: The OS enables users to easily interact with the computer hardware. For example, the Windows operating system displays icons, using which the users can interact with the system.
- *Process management*: The OS enables a user to execute more than one job at the same time to enhance productivity. Multiple processes being executed at the same time calls for efficient utilization of the system's resources by the operating system.
- *Memory management*: Finding vacant spaces in the primary memory, loading the appropriate data and programs in the located space, executing them, and removing them from the memory is all done by the operating system.
- *File management*: The OS allows users to create, copy, delete, and rename files.
- *Security management*: The OS protects stored information from malicious users. It ensures that the data and files stored cannot be accessed by unauthorized users.

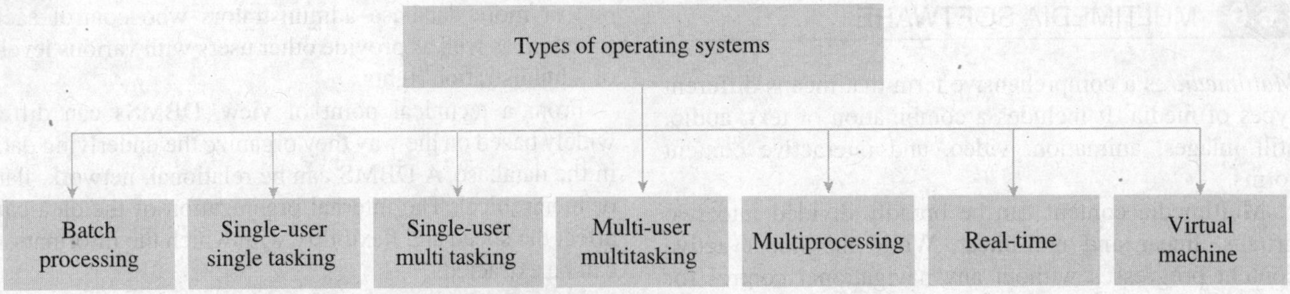

Figure 6.33 Types of operating systems

6.8.1 Types of Operating Systems

Based on the usage and requirements, operating systems can be classified into different categories, as shown in Figure 6.33.

Batch processing operating system This is an OS that allows very limited or no interaction between the user and processor during the execution of work. Data and programs that need to be processed are bundled and collected as a 'batch' and executed together.

Batch processing operating systems perform very well when a large amount of data has to be processed, and either the data or the processing is similar in nature. Batch processing is performed automatically without any user intervention.

For example, an organization uses batch processing to automate its payrolls. The process would identify each employee, calculate his/her monthly salary (with tax deductions), and print the corresponding pay slip. Batch processing is useful for this purpose since these procedures are repeated for every employee each month.

Single-user single-tasking operating system As the name indicates, this operating system allows only one program to execute at a time. It is designed to manage the computer to enable a single user to do a single job effectively at any point of time. The Palm OS for Palm handheld computers is an example of a modern single-user, single-tasking operating system.

Single-user multitasking operating system This operating system allows a single user to perform several tasks simultaneously. This is the operating system that we usually use in our desktop and laptop computers. These operating systems enhance the productivity of the users as they can complete more than one job at the same time.

For example, when we are typing a document in Microsoft Word while listening to a song and downloading a file from the Internet, we are actually doing three jobs at the same time with the help of a multitasking operating system. Microsoft's Windows and Apple's Mac OS platforms are both examples of such operating systems.

Multi-user multitasking operating system A multi-user operating system enables multiple users on different computers to access a single system (with one operating system). In simple terms, it allows more users to connect to the main computer (which has only one CPU and one OS) to perform more than one job at a time. Hence, users on multiple terminals can access the same data and application programs that are stored on the main computer (Figure 6.34).

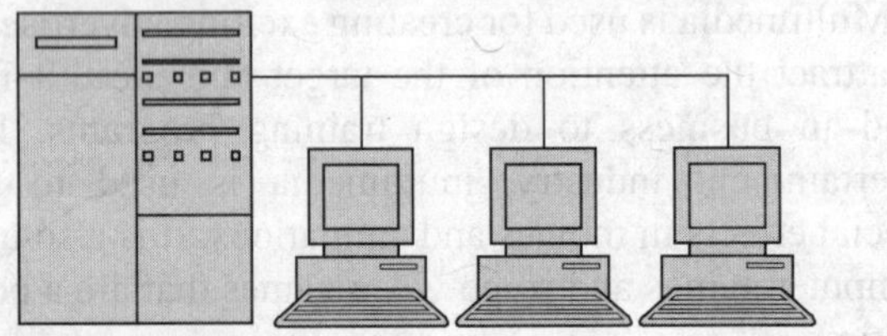

Figure 6.34 Main computer and its terminals

Multi-user multitasking operating systems are quite complicated as they must efficiently manage the jobs and resources required by the different users connected to it. The users will typically be at terminals or computers that access the main system through a network. In a multi-user operating system, each user is accessing the same OS at different machines. This type of system is often used on mainframes and similar machines. However, if the main system fails, it can affect several users.

Multiprocessing Multiprocessing means using two or more processors (CPUs) within a single computer system. It refers to the coordinated processing of programs by more than one processor. In a multiprocessing system, a complex program can be divided into smaller parts and then executed concurrently by multiple processors in parallel.

However, the term *multiprocessing* should not be confused with *multiprogramming* which means the interleaved execution of two or more programs by a single processor. Today, most of the modern computers support multiprogramming. Moreover, a system can be both multiprocessing and multiprogramming, only one of the two, or neither of the two.

Real-time operating system A real-time operating system (RTOS) is basically used to control machinery, scientific instruments, and industrial systems. It has very little user-interface capability and does not support end-user utilities.

Similar to other operating systems, RTOS also manages the hardware resources of a computer and host applications that run on the computer. However, unlike other operating systems, an RTOS is specially designed to run applications with very precise timing and a high degree of reliability. This is particularly useful in measurement and automation systems where downtime is costly or a program delay could cause a safety hazard.

Virtual machine operating system This type of operating system enables several users of a computer to use it as if they are using it individually. When using a virtual machine operating system, several operating system environments can co-exist on the same computer. For example, in Figure 6.35, three operating system environments exist on the same computer. These operating systems include Windows, Linux, and Solaris.

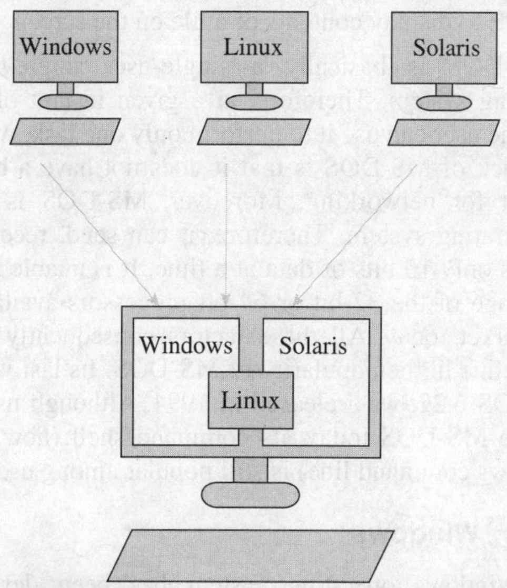

Figure 6.35 Virtual machine operating system

6.8.2 Command Interpretation

The command interpretation module or command interpreter of the operating system provides a set of commands that users can execute. This set of commands is often called system calls. When a user executes a system call, the command interpreter interprets the instructions and allocates system's resources to handle user's request. The command interpreter also provides an easy-to-use intuitive interface to the users, thereby hiding internal complexities and fulfilling operating system's objective of ease of use.

The user interface of command interpreter can be broadly classified into two groups—CLI and GUI which are explained as follows:

Note

Command interpreter is the interface between the user and the operating system.

Command line interface (CLI) is a way by which users can interact with a program by typing commands at the prompt. Such an interface makes use of only the keyboard to issue commands. Although CLI has been widely replaced by GUI, many computer users still prefer CLI because of the following advantages:

- They provide a more concise and powerful means to control a program or operating system.
- Programs with CLI can be easily automated through scripting.
- This interface is very valuable for some type of operations. For example, if we have to rename 100 files in Windows that is based on GUI, then it will take a long time but with CLI the same operation can be performed in a few seconds.
- When sharing resources over the network, CLI is widely used as some networking devices can only be manipulated using a command line interface.
- A CLI is stable in the sense that once a user has learned to execute commands, the procedure will never change as compared to GUI. Even if new commands are introduced, the original ones will always remain the same.

Graphical user interface (GUI) is an interface that makes use of the following graphical components to allow users to easily interact with the computer or system:

Pointer A pointer is a small-angled arrow that enables the users to select commands and objects on the screen.

Pointing device A device such as mouse or trackball that enables the user to select objects on the screen.

Icons Icons are small pictures that represent commands, files, or windows. Users can execute commands or open an application by moving the pointer to the icon and clicking the mouse button. Common examples of icons that we use are small rectangles for files, file folders for directories, a trash can to indicate a place where we dispose unwanted files, and direction buttons on web browsers that help users to navigate to the previous page or next page.

Menus Menu is a GUI element that displays a list of available commands. Users can execute commands by selecting a choice from the menu.

Window A window is a rectangular portion of the screen that displays applications, menus, icons, files, etc. GUI facilitates the users to work in multiple windows simultaneously where each window displays a different application, or each window can display different files that have been opened or created by the same application.

The advantages of GUI are as follows:

- With well-designed GUIs, users can get rid of the burden of learning complex commands to perform even small operations.
- The interface is intuitive. Therefore, users take less time to learn and work with the system. For example, it is far simpler to move a file from one directory to another by dragging its icon with the mouse than remembering and

typing the complete command without any mistake to perform the same operation.

- GUIs ease the task of transferring data from one application to another. However, the two applications must be running the same GUI. For example, we can easily incorporate a pie chart created in MS-Excel into a document created using MS-Word.
- GUI gives users an immediate visual feedback of the effect of user's action. For example, when a file is deleted, the icon of that file immediately disappears, thereby notifying the user that the file has been removed from its current location.

6.9 POPULAR OPERATING SYSTEMS

MS-DOS, Windows family of operating systems, Unix, Linux, and Mac OS X are some of examples of commonly used operating systems. Each operating system has specific characteristics. Here, we will discuss the features of MS-DOS, Windows family of operating systems, Unix, and Linux.

6.9.1 Microsoft DOS

Microsoft DOS is a non-graphical command line operating system, which was released by Microsoft in August 1981. It was the first widely installed operating system in personal computers in the 1980s. MS-DOS was not only one of the most powerful operating systems of that time but was also easy to load and install. It requires neither much memory nor a very sophisticated computer to run on.

Since MS-DOS supports a CLI (refer Figure 6.36), users need to remember the commands and know where

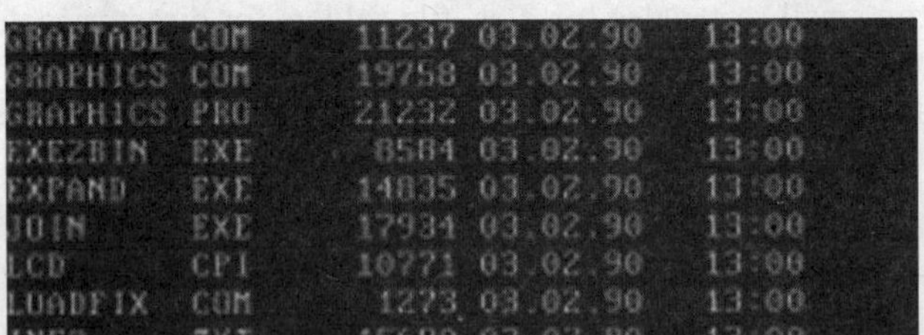

Figure 6.36 MS-DOS

the programs and data are stored. The *command.com* module of the MS-DOS command mode interprets the command and executes it. As compared to the operating systems of today, MS-DOS has relatively a very small number of commands.

The following are some of the frequently used commands:

- CD to change the current directory
- COPY to copy a file
- DEL to delete a file
- DIR to list directory contents
- EDIT to start an editor to create or edit text files
- FORMAT to format a disk
- HELP to display information about a command
- MKDIR to create a new directory
- RD to remove a directory
- REN to rename a file
- TYPE to display contents of a file on the screen

MS-DOS is basically a single-user single-tasking operating system. Therefore, at a given instant of time, only one user can use it to perform only one task. Another drawback of MS-DOS is that it does not have a built-in support for networking. Moreover, MS-DOS is a 16-bit operating system. Therefore, it can send, receive, or process only 16 bits of data at a time. It is unable to take advantage of the 32-bit or 64-bit processors available in the market today. All these factors consequently led to the decline in the popularity of MS-DOS. Its last version, MS-DOS 6.22, was released in 1994. Although users do not use MS-DOS today, its command shell (now called Windows command line) is still popular among users.

6.9.2 Windows

The Windows operating system has been developed by Microsoft. When designing this operating system, Microsoft has taken two separate approaches in which one is suited for home users and the other is intended for the IT professionals. The home edition supports more user functionalities and multimedia features but has limited support for security and networking. The professional edition, on the other hand, is well suited for server environment, has limited multimedia features but offers enhanced networking capability and security.

The first version of Windows (version 1.0) which was released in November 1985 was not very popular as it lacked functionality compared to the Apple operating system. After two years, version 2.0 was released, which achieved slightly more popularity than its predecessor. Then, in January 1988, version 2.03 was released which offered a totally different look that resulted in Apple filing a lawsuit against Microsoft with accusations of infringement.

In 1990, version 3.0 was released which became the first edition to reach commercial success by selling two million copies within the first six months.

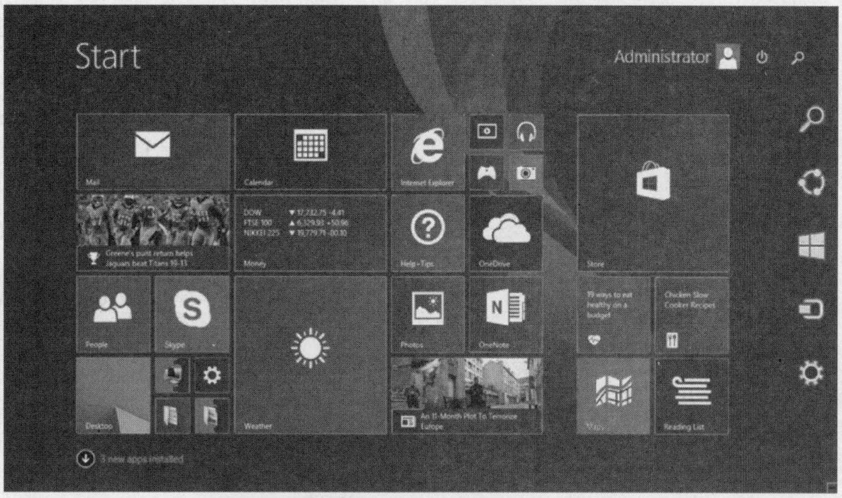

Figure 6.37 Windows 8 Start screen

Windows 3.0 had highly improved user interface along with new multitasking capabilities. Later, in March 1992, version 3.1 was released, which offered the operating system a facelift. In July 1993, Windows NT was released and became the first operating system to be designed for a professional platform.

In August 1995, Windows 95 was released, meant to replace Windows 3.1. This operating system provided support for pre-emptive multi-tasking and offered a consumer solution with significant changes to the user interface. It was the first operating system by Microsoft that used the plug-and-play system. Windows 95 revolutionized the desktop platform and achieved mass popularity.

Later, Windows 98 was released in June 1998. However, it was criticized for being slower and less reliable than its predecessor. Hence, many of these issues were addressed a year later with the release of Windows 98 Second Edition.

In February 2000, Microsoft brought out another professional operating system known as Windows 2000, the consumer version of which was released as Windows ME in September of that year.

October 2001 witnessed the release of Windows XP, which was based on the NT kernel and managed to retain the extreme functionality of its home-based predecessors. XP became very popular among the masses and was available in two different editions, home and professional. Windows XP was succeeded by Windows Vista, which included several new features with an emphasis on security.

Windows 7, which is meant for use on PCs such as desktops, laptops, notebooks, tablet PCs and media centre PC, was released in October 2009. It offers a range of new features and is compatible with applications and hardware supported by Windows Vista.

Windows 8 was released by Microsoft in 2012 and was specifically designed to be used on PCs and tablets. The first differentiating feature of Windows 8 was its Start screen that is the first screen displayed after a user logs into Windows 8 (see Figure 6.37). The Start screen is the main interface that is used to launch programs, search for files, and browse the web. Programs that are designed for the Start screen interface are called *apps*.

Windows 8 contains tiles that represent different programs that can be launched by simply clicking on the tile. The tiles also contain information widgets that are used to display real-time information directly on the Start screen. For example, users can quickly see the data related to weather, e-mail, articles, etc.

While a square tile is used to quickly launch an application, the rectangle tile is used to display real-time information. The Start screen has a number of pages, where each page has different tiles. If there is no place for a tile on one page, then it can be added to other pages. Users can move the tiles from one page to another and organize them in categories.

Note

Output of an *app* can be redirected to a projector by pressing the Window Key and the P key together

Some of the features of Windows 8 are as follows:

Windows Apps and the Microsoft Store Microsoft has introduced a new Windows Store from where users can either download or purchase apps.

Note

When a user purchases an app he can install it on four other computers running on Windows 8

User's settings travels with them In Windows 8, users are given an option to either create a local account or a Microsoft account. With a local account, a user can only logon to his/her local computer and his/her information will not be synchronized with other computers he/she may use. On the other hand, with a Microsoft account, Windows 8 will synchronize certain data, such as app settings, profile pictures, and passwords to the Microsoft Cloud. This information will be automatically synchronized to other computers that the user uses with the same Microsoft account. This gives a uniform experience that travels with users from computer to computer.

Note

To create a Microsoft account, you need to register your email address as a Microsoft account at Live.com

The Charms Bar It is a small menu that appears when you hover mouse over the bottom right corner or the upper right of the screen or by pressing the **Windows + C** key simultaneously. This menu contains five options – Search, Share, Start, Devices, and Settings (see Figure 6.37).

Search By clicking on the search option, users can search through apps, files, and settings for items that match the keyword.

Share Users can share data from one app with another app, program, or service by clicking on this option. For example, when using the Weather app users can take a screenshot and share it with others.

Start Start option displays the classic Windows desktop on the computer's screen.

Devices This option helps users to specify on what device he/she would like to play the app. For example, users can select a device that a particular app will display its content on.

Settings Users can configure the settings of the app they are currently using by either clicking on the settings option or by pressing the **Windows + I** key simultaneously. For example, users can change the volume, shutdown or restart the computer, change language, enable notifications, and monitor network connections.

Note

To access the Start Menu, users must hover the mouse over the lower left corner of the desktop or by right clicking on Start Screen.

Windows 10 is a new and an exciting operating system for organizations and their employees which was released in July 2015.

Windows 10 was purposely developed to bridge the gap between touch (tablets, smartphones) and non-touch devices (laptops and desktops). With Windows 10, all the apps that were designed to run on touch devices could also run on a desktop (Figure 6.38). Windows 10 combines the best features of old and new features into a cohesive package, thereby correcting nearly all of the shortcomings of Windows 8.

Note

The upgrade process of Windows 10 is almost free for most Windows 7 and 8 users.

Some features of Windows 10 include:

One converged Windows platform Windows 10 has a universal app platform with a single security model, and

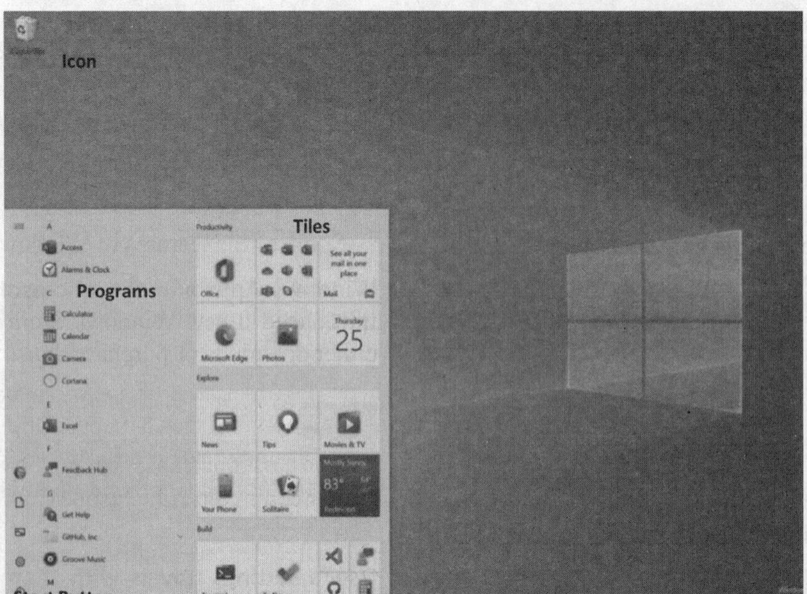

Figure 6.38 Windows 10 Start screen

the same deployment and management approach to render a unified experience across varied devices, ranging from smartphones to the industry devices.

Designed the way people work As the Start menu of Windows 7 is back in Windows 10, the desktop of Windows 10 is quite familiar to the users. Therefore, there is virtually no learning curve required as the Start menu has been expanded to provide one-click access to the functions and files that are used frequently.

Secure Windows 10 has powerful security and identity protection features that are easy to manage. For example, it allows users to create identities for accessing devices, apps, and sites to protect the computer against security breach, data theft, or phishing.

Windows 10 not only secures data that is stored in the computer but also protects it while it is being transferred – tablet or PC to USB drive, email, or cloud. For this, it provides an additional layer of protection at the application and file level.

Supports continuous innovation Windows 10 provides great compatibility with all the existing apps. Moreover, Windows 10 is automatically updated whenever a new update is available. Users can choose the way in which their Windows is updated – through Windows Update or in a managed environment.

An open app store for business Windows 10 has a single app store that is open for business. It also enables organizations to create a customized store that includes their choice of apps.

Live tiles Colourful and animated tiles were first introduced in Windows 8. They included shortcuts for various apps and informative widgets. The Start menu of Windows 10 is a miniaturized version of the full screen Start menu of Windows 8. If you don't like tiles, you can unpin them and use them from your computer, leaving only a narrow column of frequently used apps.

Note

Windows 10 is a flexible, adaptable, and customizable operating system. It is a good mix of menus of Windows 7 and customizable Live Tiles from Windows 8.

Windows 11 offers flexibility of multiple windows and the ability to snap apps side by side. Features like Snap Layouts, Snap Groups and Desktops have been introduced to organize windows and optimize the screen in a layout that is visually clean. Users can also create separate Desktops for each part of their life and customize them accordingly. For example, imagine having a Desktop for work, gaming or school.

Another feature, Chat from Microsoft Teams has been integrated in the taskbar that help users to instantly connect through text, chat, voice or video with their contacts. If the other person being connected to has not downloaded the Teams app, then messages can still be exchanged via two-way SMS.

The most exciting feature of Windows 11 is that users can now use Android apps on Windows. Users can find Android apps in the Microsoft Store and download them through the Amazon Appstore.

6.9.3 UNIX

The UNIX operating system was first developed in the 1960s, and since then it has been under constant development. UNIX is a stable, multi-user, multi-tasking operating system for servers, desktops, and laptop computers.

Similar to Windows, UNIX also supports a GUI to provide an easy-to-use environment. UNIX is made up of three parts—the kernel, the shell, and the files/processes.

Kernel The kernel of UNIX is the hub of the operating system as it allocates CPU time and memory to programs and handles communications when a system call is invoked.

Shell The shell acts as an interface between the user and the kernel. When a user logs in, the login program authenticates the user by verifying the username and password, and then starts a program called the shell. The shell is a command line interpreter (CLI). It interprets the commands typed by the user and executes them with the help of the kernel. The commands are nothing but programs, and when they terminate, the shell displays another prompt (which is a % symbol).

Let us take an example to see how the shell and kernel work together to execute the commands typed by the user. When the user types `rm myfile` (which means removing the file `myfile`), the shell searches the file containing the program `rm`, and then uses system calls to request the kernel to execute the program `rm` on `myfile`.

Files and processes Everything in UNIX is either considered to be a file or a process. A process is a program under execution and a file is a collection of data. Users can create their own files using a text editor. Example of files include a document, the text of a program written in some high-level programming language, a directory containing information about its contents which may contain other directories (subdirectories), and ordinary files.

The advantages of using the UNIX operating system are as follows:

- It is flexible and can be easily installed on different types of computers (such as supercomputers, microcomputers, mainframes, and so on).
- It is far more stable than Windows and thus requires less maintenance.
- It offers more security features than the Windows operating system.
- The processing power of UNIX is greater than that of Windows.

- It is the most widely used operating system for web servers. Almost 90 percent of the web servers have UNIX installed on them.

6.9.4 Linux

Linux is a very powerful, free, open-source operating system based on UNIX. It was originally created by Linus Torvalds with the assistance of developers from around the globe. Users can download Linux for free from the Internet and also make changes to it. The advantages of Linux include the following:

Low cost Linux is available for free on the Internet, so users need not spend huge amounts of money to obtain licenses. Moreover, users can also edit its source code to develop a customized operating system.

Stability Linux is a stable operating system. It rarely freezes or slows down and has continuous up-times of hundreds of days or more.

Performance Linux gives very high performance on various networks. It can handle large numbers of users simultaneously.

Networking Linux is widely used in networks as it provides a strong support for network functionality. Any computer with Linux can easily be connected to another computer to form a client–server model. Moreover, Linux is known to perform tasks such as network backup faster than any other operating system.

Flexibility Linux is a flexible operating system as it can be used for high-performance server applications, desktop applications, and embedded systems. The user has the option to install only the needed components for a particular use.

Compatibility Linux is a Unix-based operating system and is therefore compatible with it. This means that it can run all common Unix software packages and can process all common file formats.

Fast and easy to install Linux comes with user-friendly installation.

Better use of hard disk Linux uses its resources well, even when the hard disk is almost full.

Multitasking Linux is a multitasking operating system, so it can execute several jobs simultaneously.

Security Linux is a secure operating system as it supports many options for file ownership and permissions.

In summary, Linux is a popular operating system used by home and office users. It is mainly used for high-performance business and in web servers. Moreover, Linux can be installed on a wide variety of computers ranging from mobile phones, tablet computers, routers, and video game consoles, to desktop computers, mainframes, and supercomputers. Today, Linux is the most popular server operating system, and runs the ten fastest supercomputers in the world.

6.10 MOBILE OPERATING SYSTEMS

In the past, mobile phones were seen as devices that could be used for making phone calls and for sending text messages. With passage of time, mobile phones have evolved into smartphones that are much closer to handheld computers. Besides making calls and sending text messages, smartphones allow users to send emails, play games, watch the news, make video calls, and much more.

Like computers, smartphones also have an operating system to support advance functions that were once supported by only computers. While some operating systems are open source software others are proprietary.

Note

An open source OS lays no restrictions on what you can download on it, or who can develop apps for it. It is entirely customizable.

A mobile operating system (or mobile OS) is a set of data and programs that is specifically designed to run on mobile devices such as smartphones, PDAs, tablet computers, wearable devices, and other handheld devices. The mobile OS is an operating system (system software), which provides a platform on which other applications can run. It manages all the hardware and optimizes the efficiency of the application software in the device. For example, it manages mobile multimedia functions, Internet connectivity, Bluetooth, Wi-Fi, camera, music player, voice recorder, etc., in a mobile device.

Some commonly used mobile operating systems are the iOS, Android, Windows Phone, and so on.

In this section we will discuss some popular mobile operating systems.

Android Android is Google's operating system which is used on mobile devices. Android devices can install a range of apps from Google Play, which is an official app market. These days, Android is being used on mobile devices manufactured by leading smartphone manufacturers such as Samsung, HTC, Motorola, and many others. Currently, Android is one of the top operating systems.

Android OS is an open source operating system powered by the Linux kernel. Users can use this OS to develop apps as it poses very little restriction on its licensing. Android also allows its users to customize multiple home screens with useful widgets and apps that give a quicker, easier access to the content and functions that they use frequently. Android is a multitasking OS in which users can close programs by simply swiping them away. Users can download a wide range of apps from the Android Market.

Note

Open source is the opposite of proprietary. A proprietary design means it is owned by a company and would not allow any other company to duplicate its product.

BlackBerry OS It is a proprietary mobile OS developed by BlackBerry Limited to be used on BlackBerry mobile devices. The BlackBerry OS is popular amongst corporate users as it offers synchronization with business software when used with the BlackBerry Enterprise Server.

iPhone OS It is developed by Apple to be used on its iPhone devices. It is popularly referred as iOS and is supported by Apple devices such as iPhone, iPad, iPad 2 and iPod Touch. The iOS is also proprietary software and can be used only on Apple's own manufactured devices. It was introduced on 29 June 2007 when the first iPhone was developed and the latest version being used is the iOS 6. Unlike Android, the main focus of iOS has been on performance rather than appearance.

The Apple iOS is a multi-touch, multitasking operating system. It comes with the Safari web browser for Internet use, an iPod application for playing music and Apple's Mail for managing emails. Users can download different applications currently available on the App Store directly on their mobile device.

Windows Mobile Windows Mobile is Microsoft's mobile OS which is used in smartphones and mobile devices with or without touchscreens. Microsoft had announced Windows Phone 7 in 2010. Its colourful and user-friendly interface has made it in demand all over the world. Window Phone is recognizable from its tile-based interface dubbed Metro, which features removable and interchangeable squares sections on the home screen, each with its own purpose and function.

Windows Phone has a pre-installed mobile-optimized version of the Internet Explorer for accessing the web, and a program called Exchange that provides secure corporate e-mail accounts.

6.11 PROGRAMMING LANGUAGES

A programming language is a language specifically designed to express computations that can be performed using the computer. Programming languages are used to create programs that control the behaviour of a system, to express algorithms, or as a mode of human communication.

Usually, programming languages have a vocabulary of syntax and semantics for instructing a computer to perform specific tasks. The term *programming language* usually refers to high-level languages, such as BASIC, C, C++, COBOL, FORTRAN, Ada, and Pascal, to name a few. Each of these languages has a unique set of keywords (words that it understands) and a special syntax for organizing program instructions.

While high-level programming languages are easy for humans to read and understand, the computer only understands the machine language, which consists of only numbers. Each different type of central processing unit (CPU) has its own unique machine language.

In between the machine languages and high-level languages, there is another type of language known as the assembly language. Assembly languages are similar to machine languages, but they are much easier to program in, because they allow a programmer to substitute names for numbers.

However, irrespective of the language used by the programmer, the programs that are written using any programming language has to be converted into the machine language so that the computer can understand it. There are two ways to do this: *compiling* or *interpreting* the program.

The question of which language is best depends on the following factors:

- The type of computer on which the program has to be executed
- The type of program
- The expertise of the programmer

For example, FORTRAN is particularly a good language for processing numerical data, but it does not lend itself very well to organizing large programs. Pascal can be used for writing well-structured and readable programs, but it is not as flexible as the C programming language. C++ goes one step ahead of C by incorporating powerful object-oriented features, but it is complex and difficult to learn.

6.12 GENERATION OF PROGRAMMING LANGUAGES

We now know that programming languages are the primary tools for creating a software. Today, hundreds of programming languages exist in the market, some more used than others, and each claiming to be the best. However, back in the 1940s, when computers were being developed, there was just one language—the machine language.

The concept of generations of programming languages (also known as levels) is closely connected to the advances in technology that brought about the different generations of computers. The four generations of programming languages include—machine language, assembly language, high-level language (also known as third generation language or 3GL), and very high-level language (also known as fourth generation language or 4GL).

6.12.1 First Generation: Machine Language

Programming of the first stored-program computer systems was performed in machine language (Figure 6.39). This is the lowest level of programming language and also the only language that computers understand. All the commands and data values are expressed using 1s and 0s, corresponding to the 'on' and 'off' electrical states in a computer.

In the 1950s, each computer had its own native language, and programmers had primitive systems for combining numbers to represent instructions such as *add* and *subtract*. Although there were similarities between

MACHINE LANGUAGE

This is an example of a machine language program that will add two numbers and find their average. It is in hexadecimal notation instead of binary notation because that is how the computer presented the code to the programmer.

```
                                        000 0000A  0000
                                        000 0000F  0008
                                        000 0000B  0008
                                                   0008
                                                   0058
                                                   00Θ0
FF55   CF   FF54   CF   FF53   CF   C1  00A9
       FF24   CF   FF27   CF   D2   C7  00CC
                                                   00E4
                                                   010D
                                                   013D
```

Figure 6.39 A machine language program

the machine languages, a computer could not understand programs written in another machine language.

In a machine language, all instructions, memory locations, numbers, and characters are represented in strings of 1s and 0s. Although machine language programs are typically displayed with the binary numbers represented in octal (base-8) or hexadecimal (base-16), these programs are not easy for humans to read, write, or debug.

The main advantage of the machine language is that the code can be executed very quickly and efficiently, since it is directly executed by the CPU.

However, on the downside, the machine language is difficult to learn and is far more difficult to correct if errors occur. Moreover, if you want to add some instructions into the memory at some location, then all the instructions after the insertion point would have to be moved down to make room in the memory to accommodate the new instructions.

Last but not the least, code written in machine language is not portable and transferable to a different computer. It needs to be completely rewritten since the machine language for one computer could be significantly different from that of another computer. Architectural considerations make portability a tough issue to resolve.

6.12.2 Second Generation: Assembly Language

The second generation programming languages (2GL) include the assembly language. They are symbolic programming languages that use symbolic notation to represent machine language instructions. These languages are closely connected to the machine language and the internal architecture of the computer system on which they are used. Since they are so close to the machines, they are also called low-level languages. Nearly all computer systems have an assembly language available for use.

Assembly language, developed in the mid-1950s, was a great leap forward. It used symbolic codes, also known as *mnemonic* codes, which are easy-to-remember abbreviations, rather than numbers. Examples of these codes include ADD for addition, CMP for compare, MUL for multiply, etc.

Assembly language programs consist of a series of individual statements or instructions to instruct the computer what to do. Basically, an assembly language statement consists of a label, an operation code (opcode), and one or more *operands*.

Labels are used to identify and refer to instructions in the program. The opcode is a mnemonic that specifies the operation that has to be performed, such as *move, add, subtract,* or *compare*. The operand specifies the register or the location in main memory where the data to be processed is located.

However, as with the machine language, the statement or instruction in the assembly language will vary from machine to machine, because the language is directly related to the internal architecture of the computer, and is not designed to be machine independent. This makes the code written in assembly language less portable, as the code written to be executed on one machine will not run on machines from a different or sometimes even the same manufacturer.

No doubt, the code written in assembly language will be very efficient in terms of execution time and main memory usage, as the language is also closely connected to the machine language.

Programs written in assembly language require a translator, often known as an assembler, to convert them into machine language. This is because the computer will understand only the language of 1s and 0s. It will not understand mnemonics such as ADD, CMP, SUB and so on.

The following instructions are a part of assembly language code to illustrate addition of two numbers.

```
MOV AX,4     Stores the value 4 in the AX
    register of CPU
MOV BX,6     Stores the value 6 in the BX
    register of CPU
ADD AX,BX      Add the contents of AX and BX
    registers. Store the result in AX register
```

Although assembly languages are much better to work with as compared to machine languages, they still require the programmer to think on the machine's level. Even today, some programmers still use assembly language to write parts of applications where speed of execution is critical, like video games, but most programmers today have switched to third generation programming languages (3GLs) or fourth generation programming languages (4GLs) to do the same.

6.12.3 Third Generation: High-level Language

A 3GL is a refinement of the 2GL. The 2GLs brought logical structure to software. The third generation was introduced to make the languages more programmer-friendly.

The 3GLs spurred the great increase in data processing that occurred in the 1960s and 1970s. In these languages, the program statements are not closely related to the internal characteristics of the computer and are therefore often referred to as high-level languages.

Generally, a statement written in a high-level programming language will expand into several machine language instructions. This is in contrast to assembly languages, where one statement normally generates one machine language instruction. The 3GLs made programming easier, efficient, and less error-prone.

High-level languages fall somewhere between natural languages and machine languages. The 3GL includes languages such as FORTRAN and COBOL, which made it possible for scientists and businesspeople to write programs using familiar terms instead of obscure machine instructions.

The first widespread use of high-level languages in the early 1960s changed programming into something quite different from what it had been. Programs were written in an English-like manner, making them more convenient to use and giving the programmer more time to address a client's problems.

Although 3GLs relieve the programmer of demanding details, they do not provide the flexibility available in low-level languages. However, a few high-level languages such as C and FORTH combine some of the flexibility of assembly languages with the power of high-level languages, but these languages are not well suited to the beginning programmer.

While some high-level languages were specifically designed to serve a specific purpose (such as controlling industrial robots or creating graphics), other languages were flexible and were considered to be general-purpose languages. Most of the programmers preferred to use general-purpose high-level languages such as BASIC, FORTRAN, PASCAL, COBOL, C++, or Java to write the code for their applications.

Again, a translator is needed to translate the instructions written in a high-level language into computer-executable machine language. Such translators are commonly known as *interpreters* and *compilers*. Each high-level language has many compilers, and there is one for each type of computer.

For example, the machine language, generated by one computer's C compiler is not the same as the machine language of some other computer. Therefore, it is necessary to have a C compiler for each type of computer on which the C program has to be executed.

The 3GLs make it easier to write and debug a program and give the programmer more time to think about its overall logic. The programs written in such languages are portable between machines. For example, a program written in standard C can be compiled and executed on any computer that has a standard C compiler.

6.12.4 Fourth Generation: Very High-level Language

With each generation, programming languages have become easier to use and more like natural languages. However, 4GLs are a little different from their prior generation because they are basically non-procedural. When writing code using a procedural language, the programmer has to tell the computer how a task is done—add this, compare that, do this if the condition is true, and so on, in a very specific step-by-step manner. In striking contrast, while using a non-procedural language, the programmers define only what they want the computer to do, without supplying all the details of how it has to be done.

Although there is no standard rule that defines what a fourth generation language is, certain characteristics of such a language include the following:

- The code comprising instructions are written in English-like sentences.
- They are non-procedural, so users concentrate on the 'what' instead of the 'how' aspect of the task.
- The code is easier to maintain.
- The 4GL code enhances the productivity of programmers, as they have to type fewer lines of code to get something done. It is said that a programmer becomes 10 times more productive when he or she writes the code using a 4GL than a 3GL.

A typical example of a 4GL is the query language that allows a user to request information from a database with precisely worded English-like sentences. A query language is used as a database user interface and hides the specific details of the database from the user. For example, when working with structured query language (SQL), the programmer just needs to remember a few rules of *syntax* and *logic*, but it is much easier to learn than COBOL or C.

Let us take an example in which a report has to be generated that displays the total number of students enrolled in each class and in each semester in a school. Using a 4GL, the request would look similar to this:

```
TABLE FILE ENROLLMENT
SUM STUDENTS BY SEMESTER BY CLASS
```

Hence, we can see that a 4GL is much simpler to learn and work with. The same code, if written in the C language or any other 3GL, would require multiple lines of code to do the same task.

4GLs are still evolving, which makes it difficult to define or standardize them. The only downside of a 4GL is that it does not make efficient use of the machine's resources. However, the benefit of executing a program fast and easily far outweighs the extra costs of running it.

6.12.5 Fifth Generation Programming Language

The 5GLs are centered on solving problems using constraints given to the program, rather than using an algorithm written by a programmer. Most constraint-based and logical programming languages and some declarative languages form a part of the fifth generation languages. 5GLs are widely used in artificial intelligence (AI) research. Typical examples of 5GLs include programming in logic (Prolog), official production system, version 5 (OPS5), and Mercury.

Another aspect of a 5GL is that it contains visual tools to help in developing a program. A good example of a 5GL is visual basic (VB).

Hence, taking a forward leap from the 4GLs, 5GLs are designed to make the computer solve a given problem without the programmer. While working with a 4GL, the programmer has to write specific code to perform a task, but with 5GL, the programmer only needs to worry about what problems need to be solved and what conditions need to be met, without worrying about how to implement a routine or algorithm to solve them.

Generally, 5GLs were built upon list programming (Lisp), many originating on the Lisp machine, such as ICAD. There are many frame languages, such as KL-ONE.

In the 1990s, 5GLs were considered to be the wave of the future, and some predicted that they would replace all other languages for system development (except the low-level languages). In 1982–93, Japan had invested much research and money into their fifth generation computer systems project, hoping to design a massive computer network of machines using these tools. However, when larger programs were built, the flaws of the approach became more apparent. Researchers began to observe that, starting from a set of constraints defining a particular problem, deriving an efficient algorithm to solve is very difficult . All these things could not be automated and still require the insight of a programmer.

However, today, the 5GLs are back as a possible level of computer language. Software vendors across the globe currently claim that their software meets the visual programming requirements of the 5GL concept.

POINTS TO REMEMBER

- A computer has two parts—hardware, which does all the physical work computers are known for, and software, which tells the hardware what to do and how to do it.
- Computer software is written by computer programmers using a programming language.
- Application software is designed to solve a particular problem for users.
- System software represents programs that allow the hardware to run properly. System software acts as an interface between the hardware of the computer and the application software that users need to run on the computer.
- The key role of BIOS is to load and start the operating system. The code in the BIOS chip runs a series of tests called POST to ensure that the system devices are working correctly. BIOS is stored on a ROM chip built into the system.
- Utility software is used to analyse, configure, optimize, and maintain the computer system.
- A compiler is a special type of program that transforms source code written in a programming language (the source language) into machine language comprising of just two digits, 1 and 0 (the target language). The resultant code is known as the object code.
- The interpreter takes one statement of high-level language code, translates it into the machine level code, executes it, and then takes the next statement and repeats the process until the entire program is translated.
- An assembler takes an assembly language program as input and gives a code in machine language (also called object code) as output.
- A linker is a program that combines object modules to form an executable program.
- A loader is a special type of program that copies programs from a storage device to main memory, where they can be executed.
- Software can be acquired in three ways—(a) by buying pre-written software, or (b) by developing a customized software, or (c) by downloading public domain software.
- Microsoft Office is a suite of inter-related applications for the Microsoft Windows and Mac OS X operating systems. The popular applications include Microsoft Word, Microsoft Excel, and Microsoft PowerPoint.
- An operating system is a collection of system programs that control the operations of the computer system. MS-DOS, Windows family of operating systems, Unix, Linux, and Mac OS X are some of examples of commonly used operating systems.
- The command interpretation module or command interpreter of the operating system provides a set of commands that users can execute.
- The user interface of command interpreter can be broadly classified into two groups—CLI and GUI.
- A mobile operating system (or mobile OS) is a set of data and programs that is specifically designed to run on mobile devices such as smartphones, PDAs, tablet computers, wearable devices, and other handheld devices. Some commonly used mobile operating systems are the iOS, Android, and Windows Phone.

- Programming languages are used to create programs that control the behaviour of a system, to express algorithms, or as a mode of human communication.
- Every programming language has a vocabulary of syntax and semantics for instructing a computer to perform specific tasks.
- While high-level programming languages are easy for the humans to read and understand, the computer actually understands the machine language, which consists of only numbers.
- The second generation of programming languages includes the assembly language. Assembly languages are symbolic programming languages that use symbolic notation to represent machine language instructions.
- An assembly language statement consists of a label, an operation code, and one or more *operands*. Labels are used to identify and refer instructions in the program. The operation code (opcode) is a mnemonic that specifies the operation that has to be performed, such as *move*, *add*, *subtract*, or *compare*. The operand specifies the register or the location in the main memory, where the data to be processed is located.
- 3GLs fall between natural languages and machine languages. They include languages such as FORTRAN and COBOL, which made it possible for scientists and businesspeople to write programs using familiar terms instead of obscure machine instructions.
- While working with 4GLs, the programmers define only what they want the computer to do, without supplying all the details of how it has to be done.
- 5GLs are centred on solving problems using constraints given to the program, rather than using an algorithm written by a programmer. They are widely used in AI research.

GLOSSARY

Application software Software that employs the capabilities of a computer directly to perform a user-defined task

Compiler Software that transforms source code written in a programming language into machine language comprising of just two digits, 1 and 0

Linker Software that combines object modules to form an executable program

Loader Software that copies programs from a storage device to the main memory, where they can be executed

Productivity software Software that is used to attain something productive, especially in the office or at home, as opposed to game or entertainment software

Program A set of instructions arranged in a sequence to guide a computer to find a solution for the given problem

System software Software that acts as an interface between the hardware of the computer and the application software that users need to run on the computer

Command line interface Command line interface (CLI) is a type of interface in which users interact with a program by typing commands at the prompt

Freeware Public domain software available on the Internet which can be easily downloaded

Graphical user interface Graphical user interface (GUI) is a type of user interface that enables users to interact with programs in more ways than typing. A *GUI* offers graphical icons and visual indicators to display the information and actions available to a user. The actions are performed by direct manipulation of the graphical elements.

Translator A computer program, which translates a code written in one programming language to a code in another language that the computer understands

Turnkey solution When the user orders both hardware and software from the same vendor, the vendor develops software on the chosen hardware and delivers the combination of hardware and software to the user. This is called a turnkey solution or an end-to-end solution.

Proprietary software A software owned by a company or an individual. The owner almost always imposes major restrictions on its use and distribution.

EXERCISES

Fill in the Blanks

1. _____ instructs the hardware what to do and how to do it.
2. The hardware needs a _____ to instruct what has to be done.
3. The process of writing a program is called _____.
4. _____ is used to write computer software.
5. _____ transforms source code into binary language.
6. _____ allows a computer to interact with additional hardware devices such as printers, scanners, and video cards.
7. _____helps in coordinating system resources and allows other programs to execute.

8. _____ provides a platform for running application software.
9. ____ can be used to encrypt and decrypt files.
10. ______ is a software package that enables its users to create, edit, print, and save documents for future retrieval and reference.
11. ______ is used by architects and engineers to create architectural drawings.
12. _____ is used to design newsletters, advertisements, books, and other types of documents.
13. ____ is used to store, edit, and extract data from a database.
14. Information from a database is extracted in the form of a ______.
15. Adobe Photoshop is an example of ______ software.
16. Command interpreter is the interface between the ______ and the ______.
17. ______ is a good language for processing numerical data.
18. Assembly language statement consists of a ______, ______, and one or more ______.
19. ______ is used to convert assembly-level program into machine language.
20. ______ and ______ are used to translate the instructions written in high-level language into computer-executable machine language.

Multiple-choice Questions

1. BIOS is stored in
   (a) RAM (b) ROM
   (c) hard disk (d) none of these
2. Which of the following languages should not be used for organizing large programs?
   (a) C (b) C++
   (c) COBOL (d) FORTRAN
3. Which of the following languages is a symbolic language?
   (a) Machine language (b) C
   (c) Assembly language (d) All of these
4. Which of the following languages does not need any translator?
   (a) Machine language (b) 3GL
   (c) Assembly language (d) 4GL
5. Choose the odd one out from the following:
   (a) Compiler (b) Interpreter
   (c) Assembler (d) Linker
6. Which one of the following is a utility software?
   (a) Word processor (b) Anti virus
   (c) Desktop publishing tool (d) Compiler
7. POST is performed by the
   (a) operating system (b) assembler
   (c) BIOS (d) linker
8. Printer, monitor, keyboard, and mouse are examples of
   (a) operating system (b) computer hardware
   (c) firmware (d) device drivers
9. Windows Vista, Linux, and UNIX are examples of
   (a) operating systems (b) computer hardware
   (c) firmware (d) device drivers
10. Which among the following is an excellent analytical tool?
    (a) Microsoft Word (b) Microsoft Excel
    (c) Microsoft Access (d) Microsoft PowerPoint
11. Which interface makes use of the graphical components to allow users to easily interact with the computer system?
    (a) CPU (b) CLI
    (c) GUI (d) CUI
12. Which of the following versions of Windows operating system introduced live tiles?
    (a) Windows 7 (b) Windows 8
    (c) Windows 8.1 (d) Windows 10
13. To which generation does COBOL belong?
    (a) First generation (b) Second generation
    (c) Third generation (d) Fourth generation
14. Which generation language concentrates on the 'what' instead of the 'how' aspect of the task?
    (a) First generation (b) Second generation
    (c) Third generation (d) Fourth generation
15. Choose the 5GLs from the following:
    (a) Prolog (b) OPS5
    (c) Mercury (d) All of these

State True or False

1. Computer hardware does all the physical work computers are known for.
2. The computer hardware cannot think and make decisions on its own.
3. The term software refers to a set of instructions arranged in a sequence to guide a computer to find a solution for the given problem.
4. A word processor is an example of an educational software.
5. Desktop publishing system is a system software.
6. BIOS defines the firmware interface.
7. Pascal cannot be used for writing well-structured programs.
8. Assembly language is a low-level programming language.
9. Microsoft Excel is an example of a word processor.
10. Microsoft PowerPoint is used to create multimedia presentations and slide shows.
11. Microsoft Access can be used as a front-end as well as back-end application.
12. Multimedia software is used to create and edit digital images and illustrations.

13. Microsoft DOS is a non-graphical command line operating system
14. iOS is an open source operating system.
15. C and Pascal can be used for writing well-structured and readable programs.
16. Code written in machine language is highly portable.

Review Questions

1. Broadly classify the computer system into two parts. In addition, make a comparison between a human body and the computer system, thereby explaining which part performs what function.
2. Differentiate between computer hardware and software.
3. Define programming.
4. Define source code.
5. What is booting?
6. What criteria are used to select the language in which a program will be written?
7. Explain the role of the operating system.
8. Give some examples of computer software.
9. Differentiate between source code and object code.
10. Why are compilers and interpreters used? Is there any difference between a compiler and an interpreter?
11. What is application software? Give examples.
12. What is BIOS?
13. What do you understand by utility software? Is it a mandatory software for users?
14. Differentiate between syntax errors and logical errors.
15. Can a program written in a high-level language execute without a linker?
16. Write a short note on graphics software.
17. Give the significance of multimedia software in today's scenario.
18. What do you understand by DBMS?
19. How is application software different from system software?
20. Give a brief description of the Microsoft Office package.
21. Write a short note on the different operating systems.
22. Classify the operating systems based on their capabilities.
23. Define the term programming language. Give certain examples of such languages.
24. State the factors that a user would consider to choose a particular programming language.
25. What is machine language? Do we still use it?
26. Write a short note on assembly languages.
27. Code written in machine language is efficient and fast to execute. Comment.
28. How is a third generation programming language better than its predecessors?
29. Explain the significance of an assembler, interpreter, and compiler.
30. 4GL code enhances the productivity of the programmers. Justify.

LAB ACTIVITY 5: MANAGING ACCOUNTS IN WINDOWS 10

Windows 10 allows users to have multiple accounts on their computers, so that they can easily share their computers with their friends and family. At any time, users can add or remove these accounts as and when required.

Activity I: Creating a New Local User in Windows 10

Creating an account for a person also creates a Microsoft account for him/her. This allows those person(s) to transfer their account to another computer. Follow the instructions given below to create a new local user.

Step 1: Open the Settings app from the Start menu.

Step 2: Click on Accounts.

Step 3: Click on Family & other users.

Step 4: Click on Add someone else to this PC. See Figure E.1.

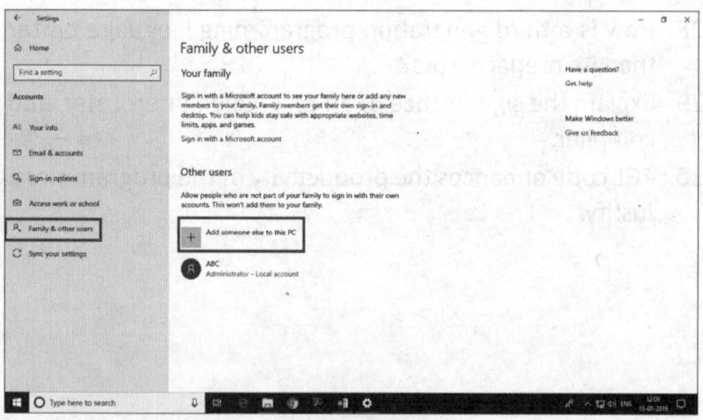

Figure E.1

Step 5: Click on I don't have this person's sign-in information.

Step 6: Click on Add a user without a Microsoft account.

Step 7: Enter his/her username, password, and password hint.

Step 8: Click on Next.

Activity II: Making a Local User an Administrator in Windows 10

By default, a new local user added to your computer will be just a standard user having only limited access to the computer. To give any user full access, you can make the user an administrator by following the steps given below.

Step 1: Open the Settings app from the Start menu.

Step 2: Click on Accounts.

Step 3: Click on Family & other users.

Step 4: Click on the account you wish to change.

Step 5: Click on the Change account type button. See Figure E.2.

Step 6: Click on the drop-down menu.

Step 7: Click on Administrator.

Step 8: Click on the OK button.

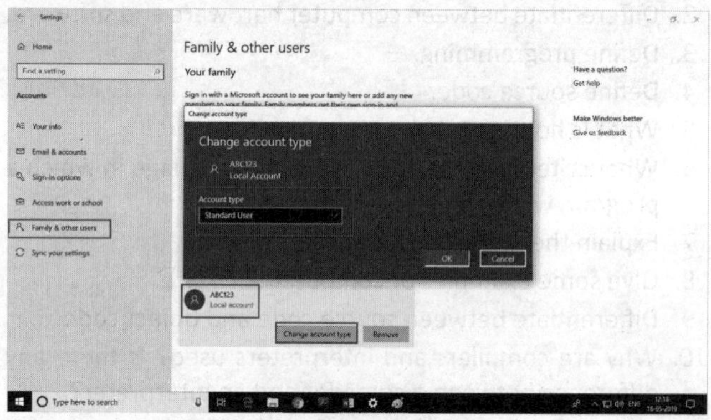

Figure E.2

Activity III: Removing a Local User in Windows 10

Step 1: Open the Settings app from the Start menu.

Step 2: Click on Accounts.

Step 3: Click on Family & other users.

Step 4: Click on the account you wish to remove.

Step 5: Click on the Remove button. See Figure E.3.

Step 6: Click on the Delete account and data button.

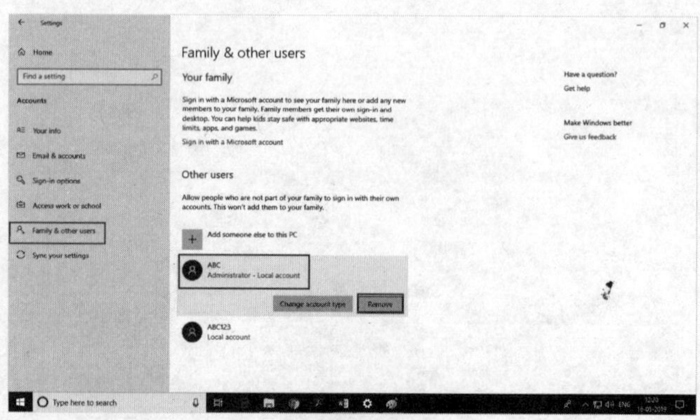

Figure E.3

7 Computer Networks and the Internet

TAKEAWAYS

- Network topologies
- Types of networks
- Connecting media
- Connecting devices
- Computer networks
- Wireless networks
- Data transmission mode
- OSI model
- TCP/IP model
- Internet
- Internet protocol address
- Domain name system
- Uniform resource locator
- Internet services

7.1 INTRODUCTION TO COMPUTER NETWORKS

A computer network, simply referred to as a network, is a collection of computers and devices interconnected to facilitate sharing of resources such as printers, information, and electronic documents.

7.1.1 Advantages of Computer Networks

The advantages of interconnecting computing devices are discussed in the following subsections.

File Sharing

The key benefit of a computer network is that it facilitates its users to share files, and to access files that are stored on a remote computer. Users can sit at their workstation and easily access files stored on other workstations that are connected to the same network, provided they are authorized to do so. This saves the time required to copy a file from one system to another by using a storage device such as a pen drive or a CD-ROM. Moreover, users can access or update the information stored in a database, making it up-to-date and accurate. Hence, network file sharing among computers gives more flexibility and allows users to share photos, music files, and documents with others working on other connected computers. However, the most important advantage of network file sharing is that it allows multiple users to collaborate on the same project through the network.

Resource Sharing

Computer networks facilitate the users to share the limited and otherwise expensive resources among a number of computing devices. For example, in a computer lab, there may be 30 computers but only one or two printers. In order to allow every computer to use the printer, there are two options. First, to buy an individual printer for every computer, so that each computer has a printer attached to it. The second and more viable option is to use the already available printers and connect all the computers and printers in the lab via a network, so that every computer has access to the printer.

Increased Storage Capacity

Attaching a number of computers to the network enables sharing of files. Files stored on one computer can easily be accessed by another computer. A standalone computer may have limited storage capacity, but when several computers are connected together, the storage memory of all these computers can be made available for each computer.

Increased Cost Efficiency

The software packages available in the market are costly and take time for installation. Computer networks are a feasible cost-efficient solution as they allow software to be stored or installed on one computer which can then be shared among other computers connected on the same network.

Load Sharing

If one computer is designated to carry out all the jobs, then it is very likely that the computer will slow down, thereby taking hours to complete all the jobs. Hence, a better option is to transfer the extra jobs to another machine (connected on the same network) for execution. This greatly improves the performance of the system.

Facilitating Communication

Using a network, users can communicate efficiently and easily through electronic mail (e-mail) and instant messaging, thereby allowing the exchange of important messages in a speedy manner without wasting paper.

However, on the downside, the problems associated with computer networks are as follows:

- If the server fails, the application cannot be accessed and can lead to data loss.
- If the server is hacked, it can lead to misuse of data.
- When the number of computers and computing devices exceed the permissible number, the performance and efficiency of the system can decrease considerably.
- Network management is a difficult and tedious job.

7.2 TYPES OF NETWORKS

These days, different types of networks are widely used, both in homes and in businesses. These networks are categorized based on their scale and scope, preferences for networking industries, and their design and implementation issues. In this section, we shall discuss these network types that include local area network (LAN), wide area network (WAN), metropolitan area network (MAN), campus area network or corporate area network (CAN), and personal area network (PAN).

Of these, LAN and WAN are the original categories of area networks, and the others have gradually emerged over many years as a result of advancement in technology.

7.2.1 Local Area Network

LAN was first invented for communication between two computers. However, later, with growth in technology, it was used to connect computers and devices in a limited geographical area such as homes, schools, computer laboratories, office buildings, or a closely positioned group of buildings (Figure 7.1). Owing to the limited scope and cost of operation, LANs are typically owned, controlled, and managed by a single person or organization.

A LAN can be one of two types—*wired* or *wireless*. While a wired LAN may use the ethernet cable to physically connect all computers on the network, the wireless LAN, on the other hand, uses radio waves for communication and eliminates the need for wires.

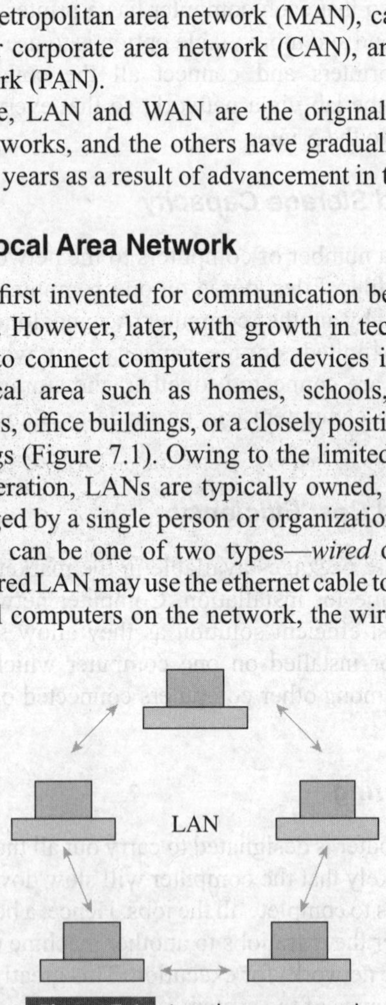

Figure 7.1 Local area network

LANs are the preferred networks because they have higher data transfer rates, smaller geographic range, and there is no need for leased telecommunication lines.

7.2.2 Wide Area Network

As indicated by the name, WANs (Figure 7.2) span a large geographic area such as a city, country, or even intercontinental distances, using a communication channel that combines many types of media such as telephone lines, cables, and air waves. A WAN often uses transmission facilities provided by common carriers, such as telephone companies. It can be created by linking LANs together.

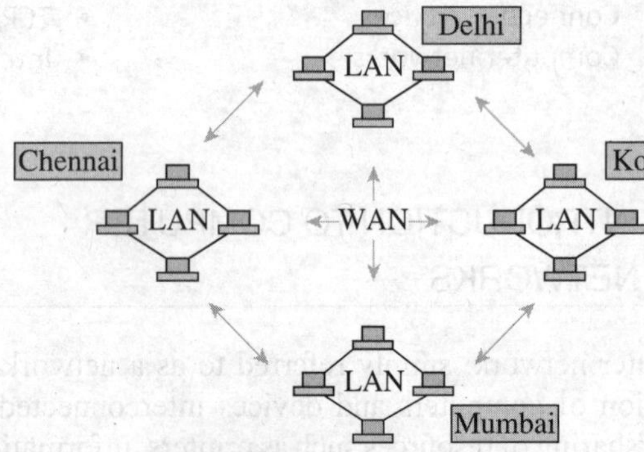

Figure 7.2 Wide area network

The Internet is the largest WAN, spanning the Earth. A WAN is a geographically dispersed collection of LANs. A LAN can be easily connected to a WAN by using a special network device called *router*. WANs and LANs can be easily distinguished from each other in several important ways. Most WANs (such as the Internet) are not owned by any one individual or organization, but rather exist under collective or distributed ownership and management. WANs generally utilize different and much more expensive networking equipment than LANs.

The Internet is a public WAN, but organizations can also form private WANs, which are basically two or more LANs connected to each other. For example, a company with offices in Delhi, Kolkata, Chennai, and Mumbai might have a LAN set up at each office. These individual LANs can be connected through leased telephone lines to ease communication, thereby forming a WAN.

7.2.3 Metropolitan Area Network

A MAN is a network that interconnects computers and other devices in a geographical area or region larger than that covered by even a large LAN, but smaller than the area covered by a WAN. A MAN (Figure 7.3) may interconnect networks in a city, a campus, or a community to form a single larger network (which may then be connected to a WAN). It may be formed by interconnecting several LANs by bridging them with backbone lines with the help of

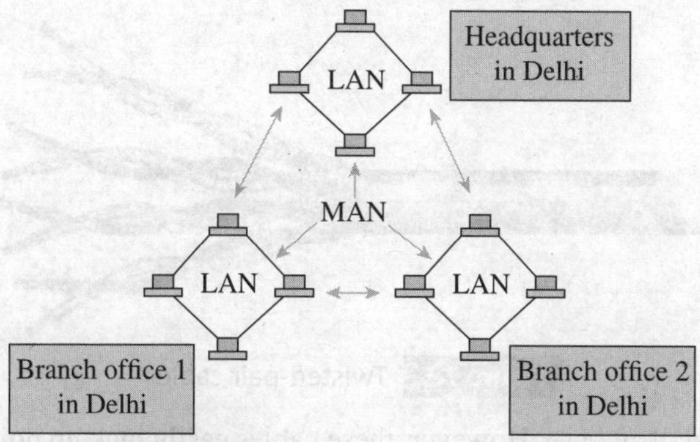

Figure 7.3 Metropolitan area network

fibre optic cables. In areas where cabling is not possible to connect all LANs to form a MAN, wireless alternatives such as microwave, radio, or infrared laser links can be used.

MANs use technologies adopted from both LANs and WANs. A MAN can be distinguished from a LAN or WAN in the following ways:

- The size of the network lies in between that of a LAN and a WAN. A MAN typically covers an area of 5–50 square km. Many MANs can cover an area the size of a city, although in some cases they may be as small as a group of buildings.
- A MAN (as with a WAN) is usually not owned by a single individual or an organization. It is generally owned by either a consortium of users or by a network service provider who sells the service to the users.
- A MAN is a high-speed network that allows sharing of regional resources.

Though the MAN is not a very widely used network, it has its own importance for some government bodies and organizations on larger scale.

7.2.4 Campus/Corporate Area Network

A CAN is a computer network created by interconnecting LANs within a limited geographical area. The network is almost entirely owned by the campus of an enterprise, university, government, military bases, etc. The size of the area that CANs covers is larger than that of LANs and smaller than that of MANs or WANs.

CANs are typically designed for the particular place that hits the highest point level. For example, in case of a university having multiple labs, or multiple buildings, it is called the campus area network and in case of an organization with multiple offices or multiple departments in the buildings it is termed as the corporate area network.

These days, CANs are mostly formed using the wireless communication mediums rather than cables and wirings because wireless communication has become more economical than the use of long wires and cables. CANs are economical, beneficial, and easy to implement in the specific locality. Therefore, they are widely used by universities and other corporate organizations to work from any block and receive the same speed of data transfer.

7.2.5 Personal Area Network

A PAN is a computer network designed for communication between computer devices such as mobile computers and cell phones that are close to one person. The scope or the reach of a PAN is a few metres (less than 10 metres). PANs are basically used to communicate with the personal devices themselves or for connecting to a higher-level network and the Internet. PANs can either be wired with computer buses such as universal serial bus (USB) and FireWire or be wireless with network technologies such as infrared and Bluetooth. Bluetooth PANs are also called *piconets*.

PANs can be used to transfer files including e-mails, calendar appointments, digital photos, and music. These days, PANs are also used to enable wearable computer devices to communicate with other nearby computers and exchange digital information using the electrical conductivity of the human body as a data network. For example, two people can wear business-card-sized transmitters and receivers to exchange information by shaking hands. We all know that the human body is a good conductor of electricity. When two people shake hands, an electric field passes tiny currents and the electric circuit becomes complete, thereby enabling each person's data, such as e-mail addresses and phone numbers, to be transferred to the other person's laptop computer or a similar device. Interestingly, even the clothes of a person can be used to transfer data.

7.2.6 Peer-to-Peer Networks

Peer-to-peer or P2P network is a type of network in which each computer has the same capabilities and responsibilities. This is in contrast to a client–server or master–slave architecture in which some computers have higher capabilities (called server) than others (clients). Though P2P networks are simple, they may give low performance under heavy loads.

In a P2P network (Figure 7.4), either party can initiate communication. These networks are widely used on the Internet to share files, printers, and other devices among different users. To exchange files, users must first download a P2P networking program (e.g., Gnutellanet). Then they must enter the address of the computer to which they want to connect. Once the connection is established, files can be exchanged between the two computers. On the Internet, P2P networks handle high volume of file sharing traffic by distributing the load across many computers. Other benefits of distribution of resources across peers include the following:

- Higher storage and access capacity
- Improved reliability due to the availability of multiple peer systems
- Improved security by distributing partial secrets across peers

A client–server system having a centralized server to manage and control the network and to provide services to the clients

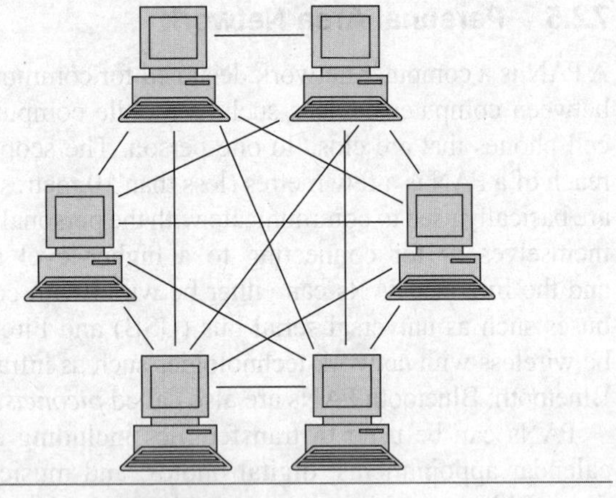

Figure 7.4 P2P network

suffers from inefficient allocation of resources and limited scalability. In future, if more clients want to connect to the server, it will incur additional costs and consume more bandwidth from the system. This inefficiency is overcome in P2P systems.

7.3 PHYSICAL COMPONENTS OF A NETWORK

The three primary physical components of a network include the following:

- Connecting media—includes both wired and wireless media through which the signals are sent from one computer to another.
- Connecting devices—includes different devices such as switches, routers, hubs, bridges, which are used to connect the computers
- Network topologies—defines the layout of the network

7.4 WIRED MEDIA

Computers and other computing devices can be connected by different kinds of media such as twisted-pair cables, coaxial cables, and optical fibres.

7.4.1 Twisted-pair Wires

Twisted-pair wires, which consist of copper wires that are twisted into pairs, are the most widely used medium for telecommunication. Figure 7.5 shows a bunch of twisted-pair cables enclosed in plastic insulation. While ordinary telephone wires consist of two insulated copper wires twisted into pairs, computer networking cables, on the other hand, consist of four pairs of copper cables that can be utilized for both voice and data transmission.

The twisted wires help to reduce crosstalk and electromagnetic induction. The transmission speed of twisted-pair cable varies from two million bits per second (bps) to 100 million bps. They are cheap and easy to

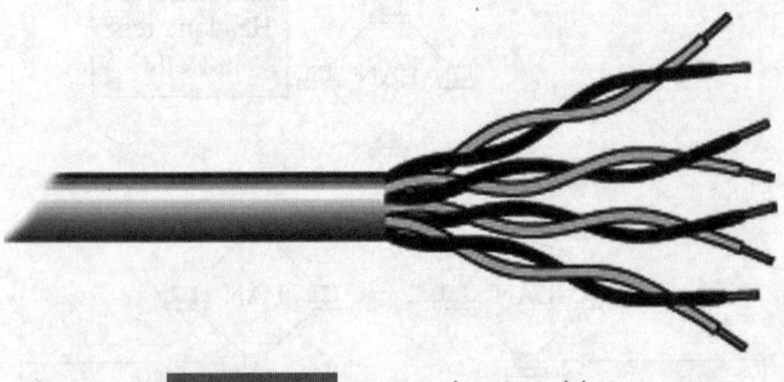

Figure 7.5 Twisted-pair cables

install and use. However, these cables easily pick up noise signals, and thus become prone to error when their length extends beyond 100 metres.

7.4.2 Coaxial Cables

Coaxial cables are a highly preferred connecting medium for cable television systems and for connecting the computers within an office building or within short distances to form a network. The coaxial cable consists of a single copper conductor at its centre, encapsulated inside a plastic layer that provides insulation between the conductor and a braided metal shield (refer Figure 7.6). The metal shield blocks any interference from the outside environment and is again protected by an outer shield of plastic material.

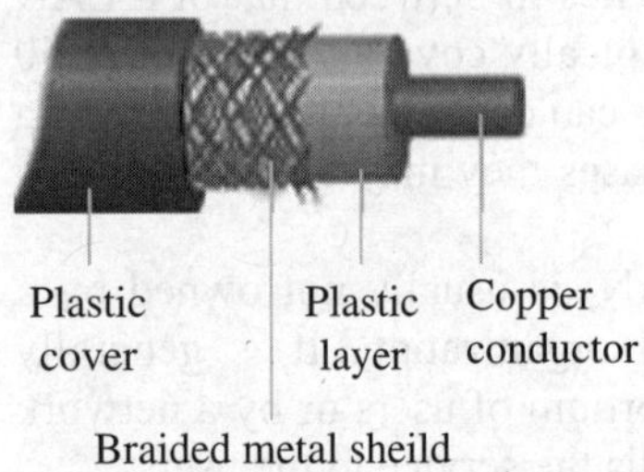

Figure 7.6 Coaxial cable

The coaxial cable is highly resistant to signal interference and can support greater cable lengths between network devices than twisted-pair cables. Its transmission speed varies from 200 million to more than 500 million bps. However, the downside of this cable is that it is difficult to install.

7.4.3 Fibre Optic Cables

The fibre optic cable (shown in Figure 7.7) is constructed in several layers. The core is the actual glass, or fibre conductor, which is covered with a refractive coating called cladding that causes the light to travel in a controlled path along the entire length of the glass core. The next layer is a protective covering or an insulating jacket made of teflon or polyvinyl chloride (PVC) to protect the core and coating from any kind of damage. It also prevents light from escaping the assembly.

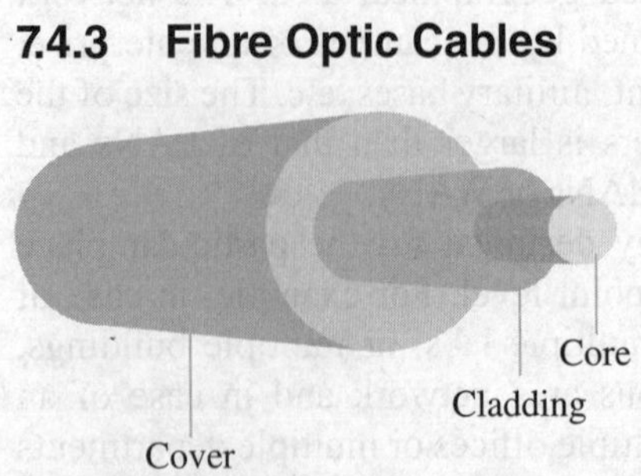

Figure 7.7 Fibre optic cable

Optical fibre cables carry data as pulses of light. They transmit light that can travel over extended distances. Fibre optic cables are not affected by electromagnetic radiation and are thus best suited for certain environments that contain large amounts of electrical interference. The transmission speed of an optical fibre cable is hundreds of times more than that of coaxial cables, and thousands of times more than that of twisted-pair wires. This capacity has helped broaden communication possibilities by including services such as videoconferencing and other interactive services. Moreover, these days, the trend is moving towards using coloured light rather than white light. Initially, only one message could be carried in a stream of white light impulses, but with this technology, multiple signals can be carried simultaneously.

7.5 WIRELESS MEDIA

The wireless technologies that connect computers and other devices to form a network include terrestrial microwave, communication satellites, cellular systems, and infrared systems.

7.5.1 Terrestrial Microwaves

Terrestrial microwaves use earth-based transmitters and receivers. Microwave antennas are usually placed on the top of buildings, towers, hills, and mountain peaks, and resemble satellite dishes. Terrestrial microwaves use the low-gigahertz range, which limits all communications to the line-of-sight. Two relay stations are separated by approximately 40 km. A terrestrial microwave communication setup is shown in Figure 7.8.

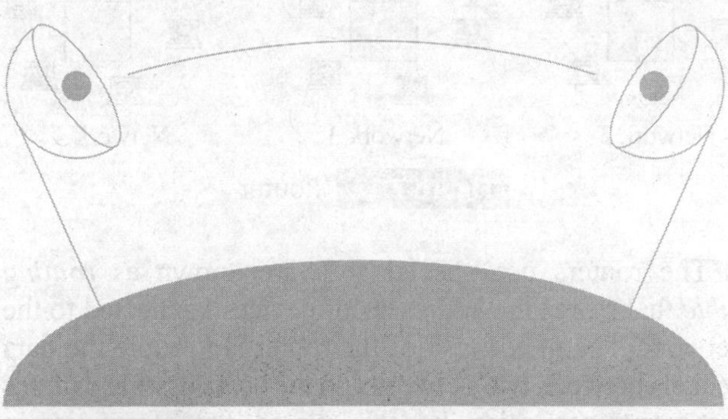

Figure 7.8 Terrestrial microwave communication

7.5.2 Satellite Communication

In satellite communication (depicted in Figure 7.9), signals are transferred between the sender and the receiver using a satellite that is stationed in space, typically 35,400 km (for geosynchronous satellites) above the equator. In this process, the signal, which is basically a beam of modulated microwaves, is sent towards the satellite. The satellite amplifies the received signal and transmits it back to the receiver's antenna present on the earth's surface.

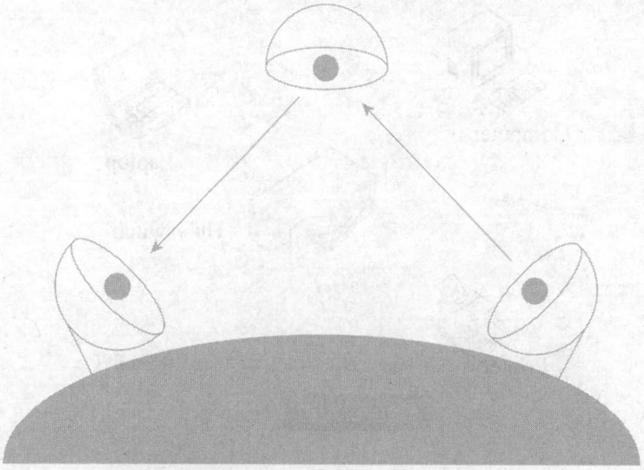

Figure 7.9 Satellite communication

This means that all the transfer of signal happens in space. Satellites can be used to relay voice, data, and TV signals.

7.5.3 Infrared Communication

Infrared light is widely used by TV and video cassette recorder (VCR) remote controls. In computers, infrared technology enables computing devices to communicate via short-range wireless signals. Infrared signals are used to transfer digital data. Infrared communication has become an alternative to cables and provides a point-to-point, low-cost way to connect computers with each other or with other devices and appliances. Moreover, cellular phones are also equipped with infrared ports to enable them to be connected to a computer for dial-up networking connections. Note that infrared signals can only be transmitted within small distances (not more than 10 metres face-to-face) without any object in the line of transmission.

7.6 NETWORKING DEVICES

Computer networking devices are communication devices that enable the users to create a network. These devices are also known as network equipment, intermediate systems (IS) or interworking unit (IWU). In this section, we will read about commonly used networking devices.

7.6.1 Hub

A hub (shown in Figure 7.10) is a device to which different devices are connected so that they can communicate with each other. Every computer on the network is directly connected with the hub. When data packets arrive at a hub, it broadcasts them to all the devices connected to it. Hence, every device picks the message but only the destined device processes the packet and all other computers just discard them.

A hub is not an intelligent device; its main function is to amplify the signal and broadcast them to all the devices connected to it.

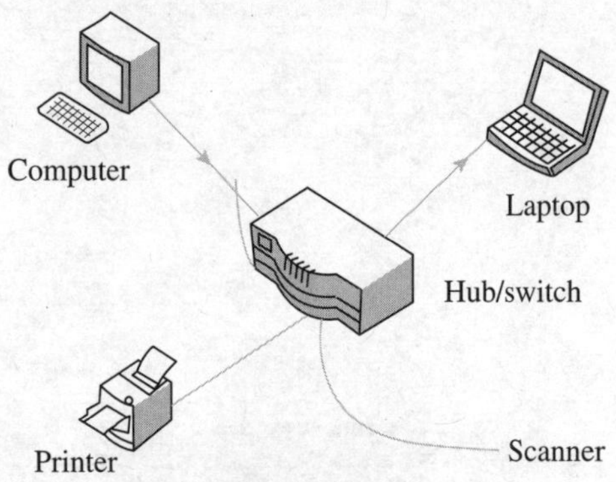

Figure 7.10 Hub

7.6.2 Repeater

Network repeaters are electronic devices that regenerate incoming electrical, wireless, or optical signals. Without a repeater, the data can only span a limited distance before the quality of the signal degrades. Repeaters attempt to preserve signal integrity by removing unwanted noise from the incoming signal, restoring the weak/distorted signal, thereby extending the distance over which data can safely travel.

A repeater connects two segments of the network cable. It regenerates the signals before sending it to the other segments, but this regeneration requires a small amount of time. This can cause a propagation delay, which can affect network communication, especially when there are several repeaters in a row. To avoid such a long delay, many network architectures limit the number of repeaters that can be used in a row.

7.6.3 Switch

A switch is a device that can be used in all places where a hub is used. However, it is much better than the hub because a switch has a switching table within it. The switching table stores the address of every computer or device connected to it and sends the data only to the destined device rather than broadcast the data to all the devices connected to it. Therefore, the switch is considered to be an intelligent device as it selects the devices among many devices connected to it to forward the data.

7.6.4 Bridge

A bridge is a device that connects two or more LANs (refer Figure 7.11). When a bridge receives data from one LAN to forward it to another LAN, it first regenerates (or amplifies) the signals and then forwards the data to the other LAN. Amplification ensures that the devices on the network receive accurate information. Otherwise, the signals become weaker as they travel, and a 1 sent by the transmitting device may be interpreted as a 0 by the receiving device.

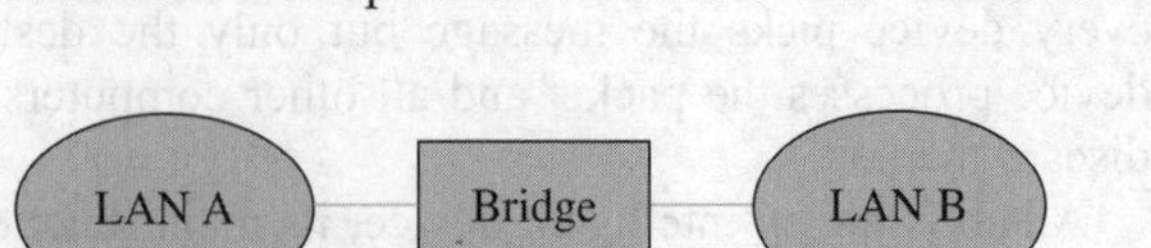

Figure 7.11 Bridge

A bridge reads the address of the receiving device specified on the data packet to identify the destination of the packet. It then forwards the packet only to the network to which the receiving device is connected, thereby reducing the traffic on other network segments. Bridges can be programmed to reject packets from particular networks. However, bridges do not normally allow connection of networks with different architectures.

7.6.5 Router

A router (shown in Figure 7.12) is an intelligent device that routes data to destination computers. It is basically used to connect two logically and physically different networks, two LANs, two WANs, and a LAN with WAN.

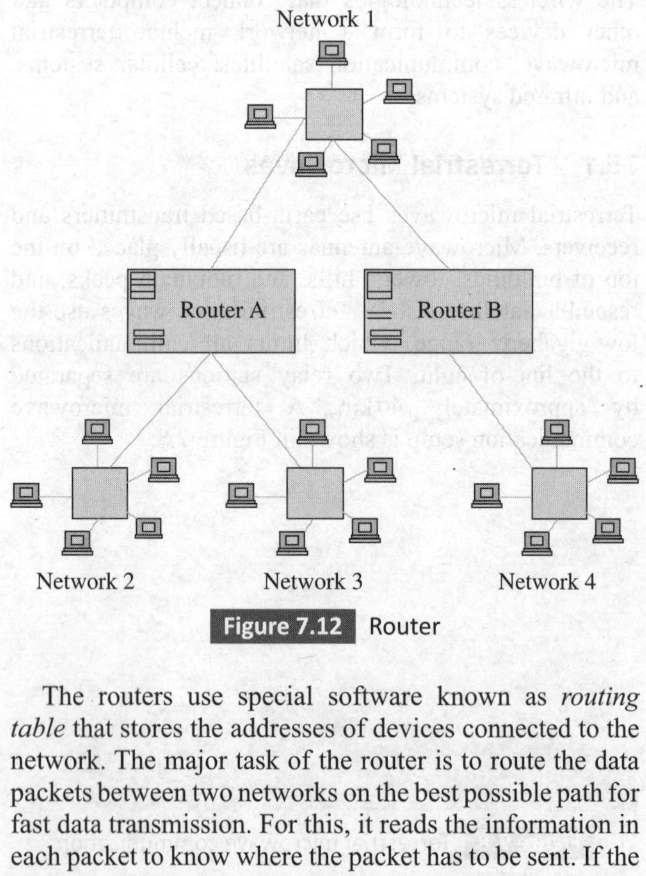

Figure 7.12 Router

The routers use special software known as *routing table* that stores the addresses of devices connected to the network. The major task of the router is to route the data packets between two networks on the best possible path for fast data transmission. For this, it reads the information in each packet to know where the packet has to be sent. If the packet is destined for an immediate network it has access to, it will forward the packet to the appropriate network so that it can reach the destination device. However, if the packet is destined for another network, the router will forward the packet to another router.

Figure 7.13 shows four networks connected with the help of two routers. If a packet reaches Router A to be sent on a device on Network 2, Router A simply forwards that packet to Network 2 so that it can reach the destination device. However, if the packet is meant for a device on

Network 4, Router A sends the packet to Router B so that it can pass it to Network 4, which is directly connected to it.

7.6.6 Gateway

A gateway, shown in Figure 7.13, is a very complicated networking device that is basically used to connect two or more dissimilar networks that use entirely different protocols (a set of rules that must be followed to exchange information). For example, if you know only English but want to talk to a person who knows only French, then you need a translator to facilitate your communication. The gateway acts as a translator between two dissimilar networks. It accepts data formatted by one network and converts it into a format that can be accepted by the other network.

Figure 7.13 Gateway

A gateway can be implemented in either software or hardware. The other key role that a gateway performs is to provide security to the network. It can be used to monitor incoming/outgoing traffic to check for any malicious activity within the network, which can be harmful to network integrity.

7.6.7 Network Interface Card

One can use the phone service through a telephone device. Similarly, one can use the network services through a network interface card (NIC), also known as the network adapter or the LAN card. That is, no computer can communicate to other devices without a properly installed and configured LAN card. The communication cables that connect different devices to form a network are connected via this card.

An NIC acts as the liaison for the computer to send and receive data on the LAN. Every LAN follows a set of protocols. The most common protocol being used is the ethernet and a lesser used protocol is token ring. Hence, when forming a LAN, an NIC must be installed in each computer on the network, and all NICs in the network must support the same protocol.

NICs are available in two varieties—wired and wireless. While most modern desktop computers use a wired NIC, the laptops, on the other hand, come with both wired and wireless LAN cards.

However, if your computer does not have an NIC, then you may use a USB-based adaptor that can be plugged into the USB port of the computer. This is a portable adaptor and is again available in two varieties—wired and wireless.

7.7 NETWORK TOPOLOGIES

Topology refers to the schematic description of the arrangement of a network. That is, *network topology* refers to the actual geometric layout of computers and other devices connected to the network. There are different network topologies; each suited to specific tasks and having its own advantages and disadvantages. Some of these topologies are explained in this section.

7.7.1 Bus Topology

In a bus topology (Figure 7.14), each computer or server is connected to a single cable. Hence, all the nodes (computers and other devices) share the same communication channel. When a node wants to send a message to another node, it creates a message and adds the address of the recipient to it. Then, it checks whether the line is free or not. If the line is free, it places the message on the line (transmission channel); else, it waits until the channel becomes available.

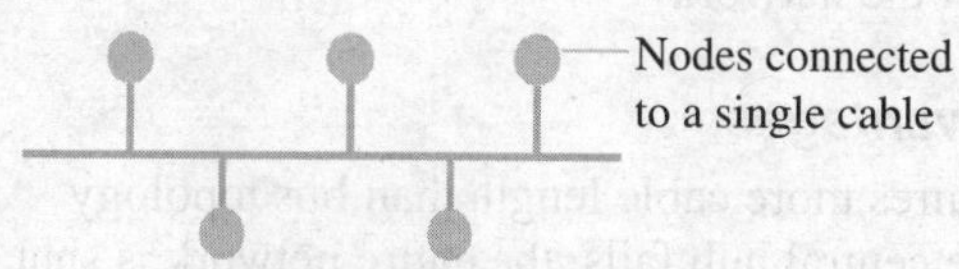

Figure 7.14 Bus topology

When the message is placed on the line, each and every node connected to it checks the destination address mentioned on it. If the node's address does not match the intended address, it ignores the message. The message is picked up and opened only by the addressee. The receiving device also sends an acknowledgement to the sending device before it frees the line.

Advantages

- Easy to install and to connect a new device to the network
- Requires less cable length than the star topology
- Inexpensive as only one cable is required
- Failure of a single node does not affect the network

Disadvantages

- Failure in the cable results in shutting down of the entire network.
- In case of network shutdown, it becomes very difficult to identify the problem.
- As the number of nodes increases, the speed of the network slows down.

7.7.2 Star Topology

The star topology (Figure 7.15) is considered the easiest topology to design and implement. In this topology, each node is connected to a central hub (or server) with a point-to-point connection. All traffic that traverses the

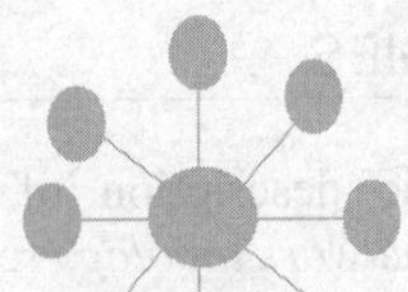

Figure 7.15 Star topology

network passes through the central hub. That is, it is the host node that controls communication between other nodes.

The hub acts as a signal repeater. When a node has to send a message to another node connected to the network, it will first have to send that message to the hub. The hub will regenerate the message (since signals become weak due to noise) and then send it to the destination node.

Advantages

- Easy to install
- New nodes can be connected easily
- Network does not get disturbed when a device is added or removed from it
- Easy to detect faults
- Failure of any other node (except the hub) does not affect the network

Disadvantages

- Requires more cable length than bus topology
- If the central hub fails, the entire network is shut down
- More expensive than bus topology because of the cost of hubs, cables, etc

7.7.3 Ring Topology

In a ring topology (Figure 7.16), all the nodes are connected to each other in the shape of a closed loop, so that every node is connected directly to two other nodes, one on either side of it. In a ring network, messages travel through the ring in a circular fashion in the same direction (either clockwise or counter-clockwise). A failure in any cable or device breaks the loop and can cause the network to shut down.

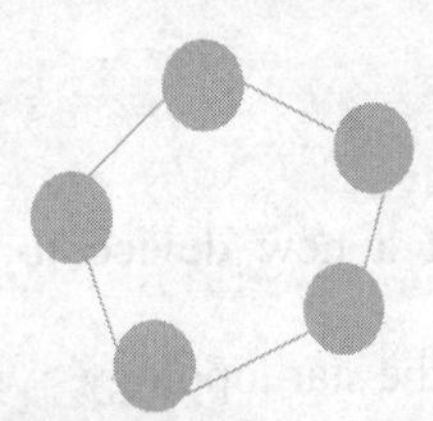

Figure 7.16 Ring topology

In a ring topology, each device acts as a repeater to keep the signal strong as it travels. Each device incorporates a receiver for the incoming signal and a transmitter to send the data to the next device connected to it in the ring. A node receives the data/message from any of its two adjacent nodes. Then, it checks the destination address. If the message is addressed to it, it accepts the data and processes it; otherwise, it just regenerates the signals and passes it to the next node in sequence. In this topology, every computer takes turns to communicate with the other nodes connected to the network.

Advantages

- Best suited for networks that do not have a hub
- More reliable than star topology as the communication does not depend on a single hub
- Easy to install
- Can span over larger distances
- Every node has equal chance to transmit data

Disadvantages

- Causes delay in communication which is directly proportional to the number of nodes in the network. Hence, adding new nodes will just increase the delay caused.
- In case of network failure, difficult to diagnose the fault
- If one node fails, the entire network is shut down because the ring is not complete.
- Difficult to add or remove nodes from the network

7.7.4 Mesh topology

In a mesh network (Figure 7.17), also known as a completely connected network, every node is connected to every other node on the network using a separate physical link. Mesh topology involves the concept of routes. Unlike other topologies, in a mesh network, a message can take any of the several possible paths from the source to the destination. For example, if a message has to be sent from A to B via C, then if node C fails, then the message can be sent to B via any other node in the network.

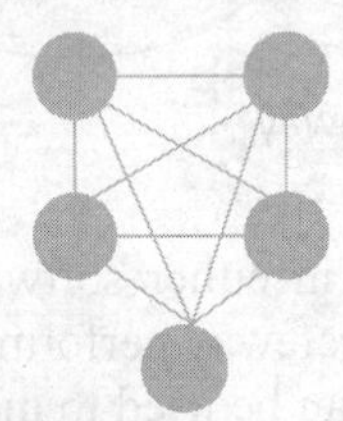

Figure 7.17 Mesh topology

Advantages

- Failure of a node does not affect the entire network; only the communication with that particular node is affected.
- Communication is fast as there is a direct link between the nodes.
- Each connection can have its own data load, so the traffic problem is eliminated.
- Ensures security of data because every message travels along a dedicated link
- It is easy to detect network errors.

Disadvantages

- It is the most expensive network as, for *n* nodes, $n \times (n-1)/2$ physical links (cables) are required.
- It is difficult to install.

7.7.5 Hybrid Topology

We have discussed the star, ring, bus, and mesh topologies. Each of these has its own advantages and disadvantages. Hence, in the real world, a pure star, pure ring, or pure bus is rarely used. Rather, a combination of two or more topologies is preferred.

Hence, hybrid network topology (shown in Figure 7.18) uses a combination of two or more topologies in such a way that the resulting network does not exhibit one of the standard topologies (e.g., bus, star, and ring). Two very commonly used hybrid network topologies include the *star–ring* and the *star–bus* networks. However, the exact configuration of a hybrid network depends on the needs and structure of the organization where it is deployed.

Consider an example of a hybrid network: an organization has two departments where one department has connected its computers using the bus topology and the other department is using the ring topology. Now, the networks of the two departments can be connected by a central hub, thereby using the star topology.

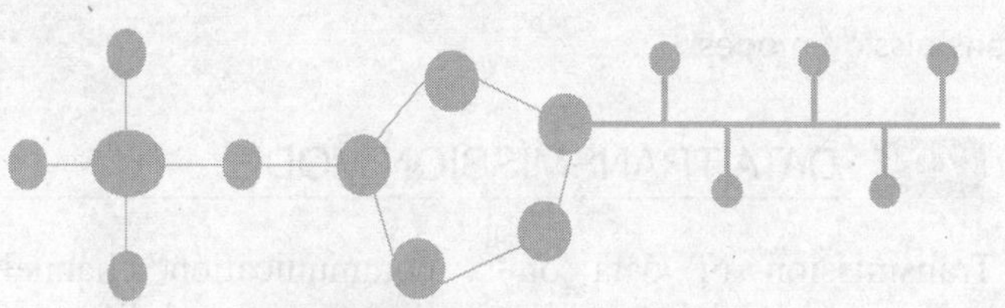

Figure 7.18 Hybrid topology

7.8 WIRELESS NETWORKS

A wireless network uses any of the wireless media to connect computers on a network. Cellular phone networks and Wi-Fi local networks are examples of wireless networks. Wireless LANs use high-frequency radio signals, infrared light beams, or lasers to communicate with remote computers. For longer distances, wireless communication is also done through cellular telephone technology, microwave transmission, or by satellites. Wireless networks enable laptop computers or other portable devices to connect to the LAN. They are also preferred in older buildings where it may be difficult or impossible to install additional cables.

A wireless network is a cost-effective means to access the Internet. When we take our laptop either at hotels, airports, or other public places and access the Internet, we are actually working through a wireless network.

Wi-Fi

Wi-Fi is a wireless networking technology which provides wireless Internet and network connections. WiFi Alliance, which owns the Wi-Fi registered trademark, is a global, non-profit organization that helps to ensure standards and interoperability for Wi-Fi networks. Wi-Fi networks use the Ethernet protocol.

Wireless Access Point

A wireless access point (WAP) is a device that allows wireless devices to connect to a wired network using Wi-Fi. The access point in such a scenario can be a router. To understand the importance of a WAP, let us first understand how a Wi-Fi network operates. Like walkie-talkies, cell phones, radios, and televisions, a wireless network uses radio waves for a two-way communication in the following manner.

- *Step 1*: A computer's wireless adapter receives user's data and translates it into a radio signal.
- *Step 2*: The radio signal is then transmitted through the antenna.
- *Step 3*: A wireless router receives the radio signal and decodes it.
- *Step 4*: The router sends the decoded data to the Internet through a physical and wired connection.

At the receiver's site, the same set of process takes place but in reverse. The router receives the data from the Internet through a wired connection. It translates data into radio signals and transmits it to the sender's wireless adapter. If many computers are present each with their own wireless adapter, then all these computers can use a single router to connect to the Internet. However, if the router fails or if too many users access high-bandwidth applications at the same time, then users may either suffer from electromagnetic interference or may get disconnected.

Wi-Fi Hotspots

An area with an accessible wireless network is called a Wi-Fi hotspot. Wi-Fi hotspots that we often use at a public space such as cafes and airports may be either free or may demand a small fee for use. To use a Wi-Fi hotspot, users must have a wireless adapter that plugs into the PC card slot or universal serial bus (USB) port. However, many new laptops and desktops come with built-in wireless transmitters. Even the mobile devices are Wi-Fi-enabled to allow users to access the wireless network from any location.

Once the wireless adapter is installed, the computer in a Wi-Fi hotspot will automatically discover existing networks. It will then inform the user about the existing network and seek permission to connect to it.

Bluetooth

Bluetooth is a wireless technology for exchanging data by using low-power radio communication. It is often used to link phones, wireless headsets, computers, and other devices over short distances, typically up to 30 feet (10 metres). Bluetooth operates in 2.4 Hz of frequency range and allows devices to communicate at less than 1 Mbps. Though some consider it to be a good replacement to Wi-Fi networks, Bluetooth networking is not only slower but also limited in range, and supports fewer devices.

Today, Bluetooth is commonly used in the following applications:

- It is used in devices such as baby monitors, garage-door openers, GPS receivers, bar code scanners, traffic control devices, medical equipment, modems, watches, and the new generation cordless phones. These devices come with in-built support for Bluetooth or a Bluetooth dongle can be used to make a device ready for data exchange using Bluetooth.

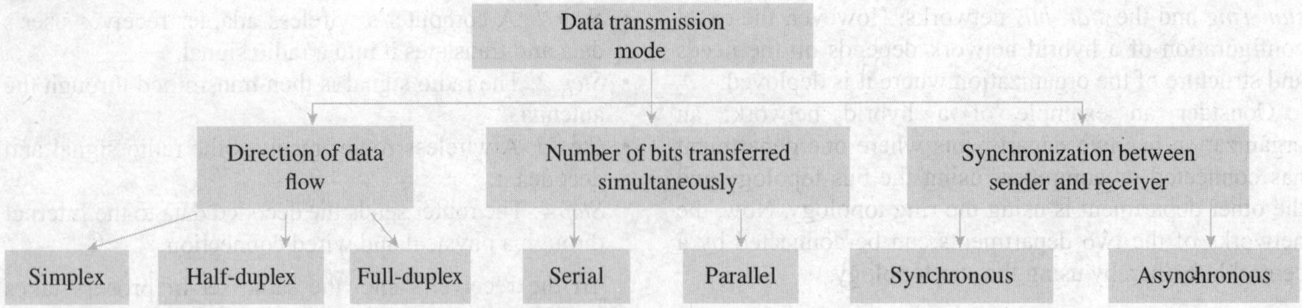

Figure 7.19 Data transmission modes

- It is used for controlling a hands-free headset from a mobile phone.
- It is used for controlling a Bluetooth-compatible car stereo system from a mobile phone.
- It is used for creating a network of PCs in a confined space where little bandwidth is required.
- It is used for enabling wireless communication between the input and output devices of a computer.
- It is used in the control of and communication between devices where infrared system is used.
- It is used in low bandwidth applications that prefer cable-free connection.
- It is used for advertising products by using Bluetooth-enabled hoardings to send advertisements to other discoverable Bluetooth devices.
- It is used for tracking and identifying the location of objects in real-time location systems. The objects have an embedded tag, which sends wireless signals to readers that receive and process those signals.

Limitations of Wireless Networks

The limitations of wireless networks are as follows.

Interference Electromagnetic interference is a common problem in wireless networks which degrades a signal. It can occur either due to other networks or because of devices that generate radio waves that are within or close to the radio bands used for communication.

Absorption Wireless networks suffer due to absorption of electromagnetic waves by some materials, thereby preventing them from reaching the receiver.

Reflection Materials that are either metallic or conductive cause reflection, which may prevent the signals from being properly received.

Multi-path fading Reflection can cause a signal to take different routes before reaching the receiver. At certain locations, the signal may get cancelled out, leading to multi-path fading.

Hidden node problem This problem occurs when a computer is visible from a wireless access point but seems unavailable from other computers communicating with that WAP.

7.9 DATA TRANSMISSION MODE

Transmission of data on a communication channel between two machines can take place in several different ways as shown in Figure 7.19. This transmission can be characterized by the following features:

- Direction of data flow
- Number of bits sent simultaneously
- Synchronization between the sending and receiving devices

7.9.1 Simplex, Half-duplex, and Full-duplex Connections

The data transmission mode refers to the direction of flow of data. Based on this characteristic, a connection can be further classified into three categories—simplex, half-duplex, and full-duplex.

In the *simplex mode*, data flows in only one direction, from the sending device to the receiving device. A simplex connection is often desirable where the data need not flow in both directions. For example, the computer can send a message to the printer, but the printer need not send any data or message to the computer.

In the real world, simplex mode of data transmission is not very popular because most of the communications require bi-directional exchange of data. However, this mode of communication is used in business, at certain point-of-sale terminals in which sales data is entered without the need for a corresponding reply. It is also used in radio and TV transmissions.

In a simplex transmission, only one device transmits data, and all other connected devices can only receive data. Hence, this type of transmission is similar to a one-way traffic, as data flows only in one direction. Note that in simplex transmission, the roles of the sending and receiving devices cannot be reversed. That is, the device which has assumed the role of sending data can only send and not receive. Similarly, the receiver can only receive data but can never send it. Figure 7.20 depicts the simplex transmission.

In the *half-duplex mode*, also known as an alternating connection or semi-duplex, there is only one

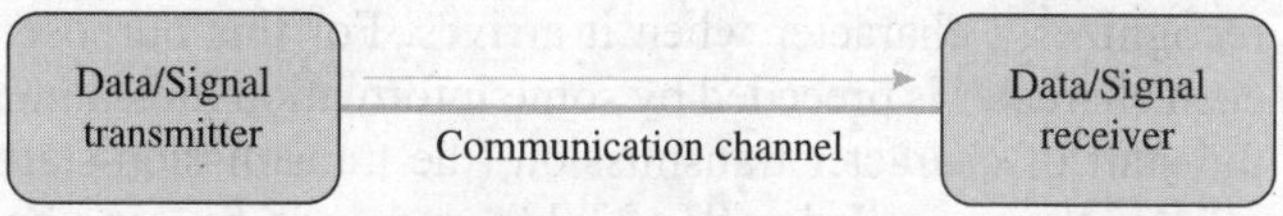

Figure 7.20 Simplex mode

communication channel (a wire or a cable) to carry data. However, both the devices can be either a transmitter or a receiver. That is, devices can share the channel but only one of them can transmit at a time. While one device is transmitting the data/signals, the other will be in receiving mode, and vice versa. This is shown in Figure 7.21.

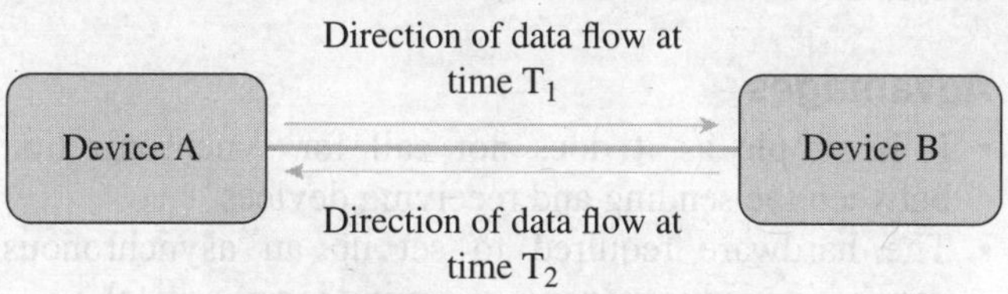

Figure 7.21 Half-duplex mode

In the half-duplex mode, the data is sent and received alternatively. Hence, it can be thought of as a one-lane bridge, where vehicles can come from both the directions, but not at the same time. Vehicles on one side must wait until traffic coming from the opposite direction has crossed the bridge. In the real world, the half-duplex mode is utilized in web browsing. The user sends a request to download a particular web page, then that page is downloaded and displayed to the user.

In a *full-duplex mode*, data flows in both the directions simultaneously as shown in Figure 7.22. That is, each end of the line can transmit and receive the data/signals at the same time. The number of communication channels in a full-duplex connection can either be one or two. Two separate communication channels can carry data in both directions and can be thought of as the combination of two simplex lines, one in each direction. However, if there is only one single communication channel, then the bandwidth of the channel is divided into two for each direction of data transmission. A full-duplex connection can be thought of as a two-lane bridge where vehicles can simultaneously travel in both the directions but only in their respective lanes.

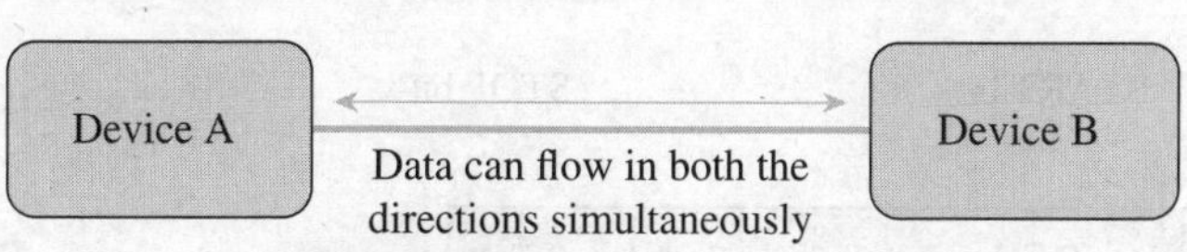

Figure 7.22 Full-duplex mode

In the real world, the full-duplex data transmission mode is widely applied in telephone systems, where both the caller and the receiver can talk at the same time.

7.9.2 Serial and Parallel Transmissions

The term *transmission mode* also refers to the number of bits that can be simultaneously transmitted over the communication channels. Based on this definition, connections can be classified as serial or parallel connections. Since modern-day computers can process several bits of data at the same time, the basic connections on a computer are parallel connections.

Parallel Connection

In a parallel connection, n bits are simultaneously transmitted over the communication channels. These n bits are concurrently transmitted through separate communication lines. As an analogy, parallel transmission can be thought of as a multi-lane highway where a number of automobiles can travel at the same time.

If one has seen the inside of a CPU, it may be observed that the data bus has 32 lanes (in case of 32-bit computers). This is because, in a computer, binary data flows from one unit to another using the parallel mode. Hence, all the 32 bits of data are transferred simultaneously on 32-lane connections. Similarly, in a networked environment, parallel transmission may be used to transfer data from a computer to the printer. Parallel mode of transmission (shown in Figure 7.23) is undoubtedly a very fast data transmission mode.

The communication channels in a parallel connection may contain either of the following:

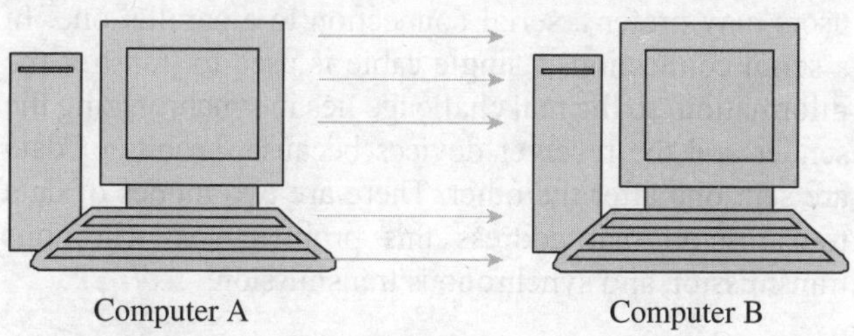

Figure 7.23 Parallel communication between computers

- n physical lines so that each bit is sent on a physical line. Parallel cables are made up of several wires in a single cable. However, closeness of conductive wires in a single cable can result in interference, particularly at high speeds, thereby degrading the signal quality.
- One physical line that is divided into several sub-channels. This is done by dividing the bandwidth of the line so that each bit is sent at a different frequency.

Serial Connection

In a serial connection, the data is sent one bit at a time over the transmission channel. However, since most processors process data in parallel, the device that sends the data must convert the parallel data into serial form before sending it to the receiver. Similarly, on receiving the serial data, the receiver must convert it into parallel data, so that it can be processed further.

In serial data transmission, bits of data are transmitted sequentially through a single communication channel as shown in Figure 7.24. An analogy would be the flow of

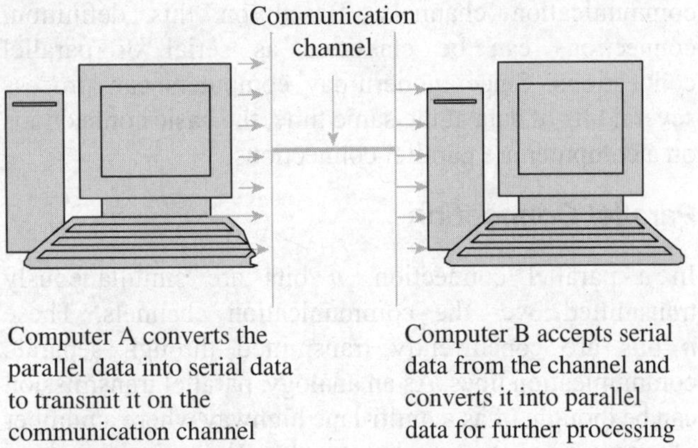

Figure 7.24 Serial communication between computers

traffic on a one-lane residential street. Serial transmission is undoubtedly slower than parallel transmission because data is sent sequentially in a bit-by-bit manner. In the real world, serial transmission mode is used while working with a serial mouse.

7.9.3 Synchronous and Asynchronous Data Transmission Modes

Parallel connections may result in interference, and hence users may prefer a serial connection to a parallel one. In a serial connection, a single cable is used to transmit the information, so the real challenge lies in synchronizing the sender and the receiver devices because the bits of data are sent one after the other. There are two modes of data transmission that address this problem—asynchronous transmission and synchronous transmission.

Asynchronous Transmission

In the asynchronous mode of transmission, the sender transmits the data character by character (or byte by byte) to the receiver at any point of time. This mode of transmission is best suited for connecting input devices, printers, modems, fax machines, etc., to the computer, as data is sent to the receiver at irregular intervals of time.

However, since the data arrives abruptly at any time, it is very essential to ensure that the receiving device recognizes a character when it arrives. For this purpose, each character is preceded by some information indicating the start of character transmission (the transmission-start information is called a *START bit*) and ends by sending the end-of-transmission information (called a *STOP bit*). Figure 7.25 shows the asynchronous mode of transmission.

Basically, an asynchronous line that is idle (not being used) is identified with the value 1. The devices connected to the network first check whether the line is idle or disconnected. If the line is free or idle, the sending device first sends a start bit that has a value 0. Thus, when the line switches from a value of 1 to a value of 0, the receiver is alerted about the arrival of a character.

Advantages

- It is simple as it does not call for synchronization between the sending and receiving devices.
- The hardware required to set up an asynchronous connection is inexpensive as timing is not critical.
- An asynchronous connection can be set up very fast and is therefore very well suited for applications where messages are generated at irregular intervals like data entry from the keyboard.

Disadvantage

Overhead is involved in sending the control bits (START bit, STOP bit), which actually do not carry any information.

Synchronous Transmission

In synchronous transmission, the sender and the receiver are synchronized with each other using a clock. In this transmission mode, characters or bytes are grouped together to form a data block. Then, a header and trailer are added to the data block to form a frame.

The header contains useful information that is needed by the receiving device to synchronize its clock with the sender's clock. It is followed by the block of data containing a variable number of bits, which is again followed by a trailer. The trailer is used to terminate the message and contains an end-of-file (EOF) character followed by a check character that helps detect any transmission error. This is shown in Figure 7.26.

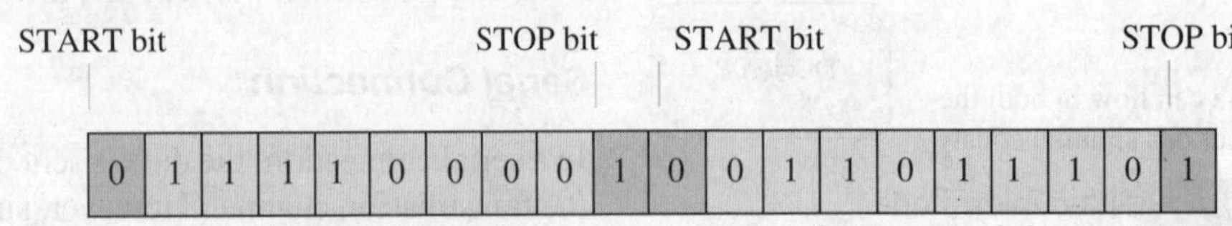

Figure 7.25 Asynchronous transmission

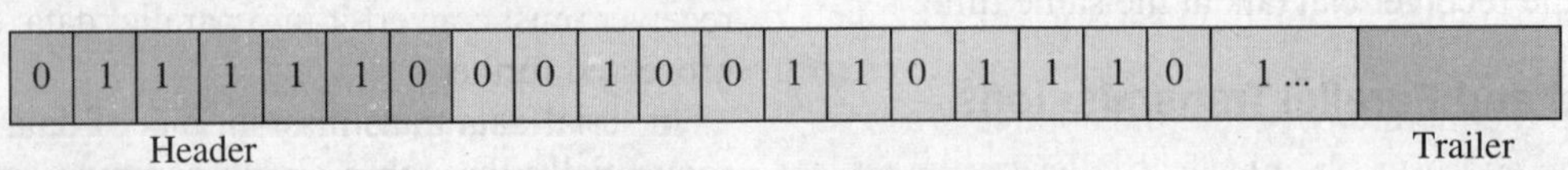

Figure 7.26 Synchronous transmission

Synchronous transmission is more efficient and faster than its asynchronous counterpart. It is best suited for communication between two devices that have a buffer (small area of memory) to store the individual characters to form a data block of length 80 or 132 characters.

Advantages

- There is lower overhead as there is no need to send START and STOP bits for every single character.
- It enjoys higher throughput because of the lower overhead.

Disadvantages

- The sending and the receiving devices must have a buffer area to assemble the blocks of data.
- It is more complex than asynchronous mode of transmission.
- The hardware required is more expensive.
- For error-free transmission, the clocks of the receiving and sending devices must be synchronized.

7.10 OPEN SYSTEM INTERCONNECTION MODEL

The Open System Interconnection (OSI) model given by the International Standards Organization (ISO) in 1984 is an abstract model that provides a networking framework of standards to enable diverse equipment and applications from different vendors to communicate with each other. When a vendor's device adheres to the standards set by the OSI model, it can be easily connected to other devices produced by other vendors. Correspondingly, the further a vendor departs from those standards, higher is the difficulty in connecting its devices with devices of other vendors. Incompatibility with set standards not only makes devices difficult to connect but also makes them expensive to design and less marketable than other devices following the norms.

The OSI model divides the complex task of computer-to-computer communication (also known as internetworking) into a series of seven layers (Figure 7.27). These seven layers are functionally independent of each other. Therefore, any change made in one layer does not affect the function of any other layer. While providing services to the layers above it, they receive services from the layers below it. During implementation, the upper layers consisting of layers 7, 6, and 5 are implemented using software while the lower layers, that is, layers 4, 3, 2, and 1, are implemented using both hardware and software.

In the OSI model, data is transferred from one layer to the next. It starts from the application layer of the sending device and goes until the physical layer. The data then travels over the channel to the next computer and moves back up the hierarchy. While the application layer is closest to the end-user, the physical layer on the other hand is closest to the physical network medium (wires).

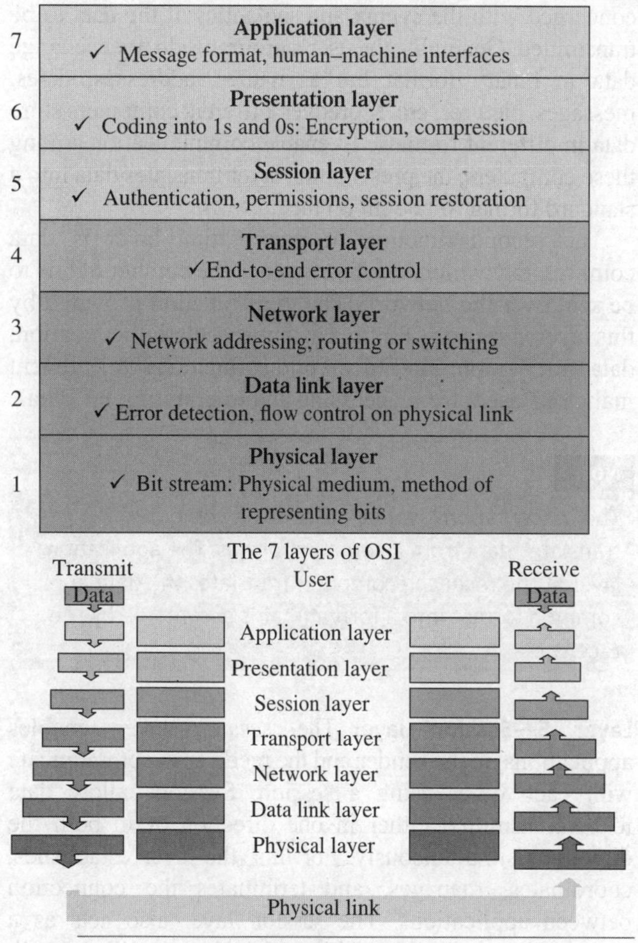

Figure 7.27 OSI model

Hence, the OSI model simplifies the entire process of network communication by dividing it into logical smaller pieces and makes network designs more extensible as new services can easily be added in a layered architecture than in a monolithic one.

Layer 7—Application layer The application layer provides services to support end-user applications such as e-mail, file transfer, user interface, database access, remote printer access, and so on. The commonly used protocols in this layer include HTTP, WWW, FTP, TELNET, and SMTP.

It is the responsibility of the application layer to hide the underlying incompatibilities and complexities of network communication to enable a smooth transfer between systems. Web browser is an example of application layer that provides user's applications access to the network through the layers below it.

> **Note**
>
> The application layer acts as a window for end-users' applications to access network services.

Layer 6—Presentation layer The presentation layer, also called the syntax layer, acts as a translator between the application program and the network format. This layer is concerned with the syntax and semantics of the data to be transmitted. Generally, the user's programs do not exchange data in binary format but as names, addresses, dates, messages, pictures, etc. Moreover, different computers store data in different formats. To enable communication among these computers, the presentation layer translates data into a standard format to be sent on the network.

The second function of presentation layer is data compression, which is done to reduce the number of bits to be sent over the network. The third function provided by this layer is security. For this, it implements authentication, data encryption, and decryption functions to prevent malicious users from accessing and interpreting the data.

Note

The presentation layer at the sending computer translates data from a common format. The application layer at the receiving computer translates the data in common format into a format that is acceptable by the receiver.

Layer 5—Session layer The session layer enables applications on the sender and the receiver to communicate with each other using a session. Sessions allow data to be transmitted either in one direction or in both the directions simultaneously. For this, the layer establishes, coordinates, manages, and terminates the connection between applications. The session layer also acts as a dialogue controller to decide which device will transmit the information. Additionally, the layer synchronizes data transmission and adds checkpoints in it. This is useful especially when a large amount of data has to be transferred. For example, if the user is downloading a file of 500MB, then the session layer may insert checkpoints after every 100MB of data. Now if the system crashes when already 250MB of data is transferred, then the sender will send data only after first 200MB. In the absence of this checkpoint, the entire 250 MB of data has to be transferred again.

Note

The session layer establishes and terminates connection, provides data synchronization, controls dialogues, and inserts checkpoints.

Layer 4—Transport layer The transport layer is responsible for reliable data transfer between two systems. This layer not only transfers data but also provides error and flow control mechanisms to ensure complete and reliable data transfer. It enables the receiver to receive accurate data in the right sequence without any data loss or duplication. The basic functionalities that the transport layer provides include the following:

- At the sender's site, it accepts data from the session layer, breaks it into smaller units (if there is a large message and the network accepts only smaller size messages), and sends them to the network layer.
- The transport layer at the destination station reassembles the smaller units in the right sequence to form the message.
- It provides reliable delivery of messages.
- The transport layer at the receiver sends acknowledgment to the sender when it receives the message.
- The transport layer at the receiver informs the sender to temporarily stop sending messages when no message buffers are vailable at the receiver.
- It performs data multiplexing.
- If there is an error in the message received, the transport layer asks the sender to re-send that data.

Note

The transport layer provides error control, flow control, and reliable transfer of data.

Layer 3—Network layer The network layer is in charge of all of the addressing issues. It accepts data packets (smaller units of message), determines the best path or route, and sends the packets on that route so that it can either reach the receiver or reach a device that is closer to the receiver. The network layer manages network problems like data congestion, which occurs when there are too many packets present in a network.

The network layer creates a logical path for transmitting data from the sender to the receiver. It controls the operation of the subnet (a part of the network) and decides the optimal path for the data based on network conditions, priority of service, and other factors.

Note

The main job of the network layer is routing and data transmission.

Layer 2—Data link layer The data link layer converts data packets into a stream of 1s and 0s. It is also responsible for error control, flow control, and reliable data transfer. The data link layer is divided into two sub-layers as follows:

- Media access control (MAC) controls how a computer on the network can access data and have permissions to transmit it.
- Logical link control (LLC) performs error control and flow control functions. In case of errors, the data link layer asks the sender to retransmit the data.

Note that the transport layer also provides error and flow control. Generally, if the sender and the receiver are both on the same network, then error and flow control by the transport layer is not required. These features can be supported by the data link layer itself. But when the two devices are on different networks, then error and flow control must be implemented at the data link layer as well as at the transport layer.

Note

The data link layer converts packets into a stream of bits and provides error control and flow control mechanisms.

Layer 1—Physical layer The physical layer converts the raw stream of bits into electric signals, optical signals, or electromagnetic signals depending on whether the underlying network uses a cable circuit (using coaxial cable), fibre-optic circuit, or a microwave circuit, respectively.

The physical layer is concerned with all the physical aspects of data transmission. For this, it performs the following tasks:

- It establishes, maintains, and terminates physical connections between computers.
- It decides how many volts should be used to represent 0 and 1.
- It decides how many bits should be transmitted in a second.
- It decides the mode of data transmission (simplex, half-duplex, or full-duplex).
- It defines physical and electrical specifications for devices to interface to the network, like the shape and layout of pins in connectors, broadcast frequencies, and specifications of the cable.

Note

The physical layer transmits (on sender) and receives (on receiver) data from the physical media.

7.11 TRANSMISSION CONTROL PROTOCOL/INTERNET PROTOCOL MODEL

The transmission control protocol/Internet protocol (TCP/IP) is a suite of protocols used as the basic communication language or protocol of the Internet. As shown in Figure 7.28, each layer of the TCP/IP model corresponds to one or more layers of the OSI model. Table 7.1 summarizes the types of services performed and protocols used at each layer within the TCP/IP model.

Note that at the application layer users access web applications such as email or page download to generate

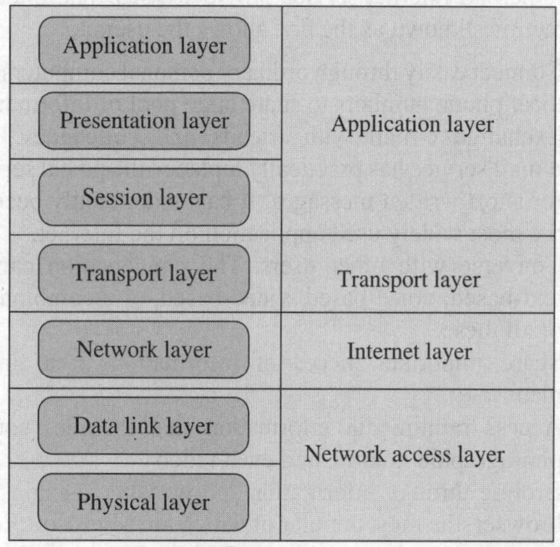

Figure 7.28 TCP/IP model

Table 7.1 Function of layers in the TCP/IP model

Layer	Function	Protocol
Application	Provides users with an interface to communicate. This interface could be the web browser. This layer sends and receives data from the transport layer	HTTP, TELNET, FTP, TFTP, SNMP, DNS, SMTP
Transport	Facilitates transport of data segments across the network. It is responsible for host-to-host delivery. While transmitting, transport layer receives data from application layer and sends data to the Internet layer. But while receiving, it accepts data from Internet layer and passes it to the application layer.	TCP for connection-oriented and reliable communication User datagram protocol (UDP) for connection-less and unreliable communication
Internet	Packages data into IP datagrams, which contain source and destination address. Forwards the datagrams on the best route available. While receiving data, the Internet layer receives data from the network access layer and passes it to the transport layer. While sending data, it does the opposite.	IP, ARP, RARP, ICMP
Network access	Provides access to the physical network Specifies details of how data is physically sent through the network. Concerned about electrical, mechanical, and physical details of the network interface. While transmitting data, it sends data to the physical network after receiving it from the Internet layer. While receiving, it accepts data from the network and passes it to the Internet layer.	Ethernet, token ring, FDDI, frame relay

data. This data at the transport layer is chopped into smaller units called segments. At the Internet layer, segments are packed into IP datagrams. These datagrams are then chopped at the network access layer to form frames that are transmitted across the networks.

7.12 INTERNET

The Internet is a global network that connects billions of computers all over the world. It is a network of networks. The Internet links different organizations, academic institutions, government offices, and home users to share information among a large group of users.

Each computer on the Internet is called a *host*. To connect to the Internet, the user must gain access through a commercial Internet service provider (ISP). The Internet, sometimes known as the *net*, allows the users to:

- Connect easily through ordinary personal computers and local phone numbers to share huge pool of information
- Exchange e-mail with friends and colleagues. The e-mail service has practically replaced the postal service for short written messages. It has undoubtedly become the most widely used application on the Internet.
- Converse with other users. The conversation can be text-based, voice-based, video-based, or a combination of all these.
- Share important pieces of information in a timely manner
- Access multimedia information that includes sound, photographic images, and even video
- Browse through information and websites using a web browser, the most popular of which are Microsoft Edge, Netscape Navigator, Opera, Google Chrome, Mozilla Firefox, and Safari

An additional feature of the Internet is that it lacks a central authority that controls it. Although there are different governing boards that work to establish policies and standards, the Internet is bound by few rules and answers to no single organization.

7.12.1 History

The roots of the Internet can be traced to the year 1969 when the Advanced Research Projects Agency (ARPA) of the US government formed the very first network, which was widely known as the Advanced Research Projects Agency Network (ARPANET). This network was initially created to interconnect computers so that the users in the research organizations and universities could communicate with each other and share information.

However, it was in the year 1989 that the US government lifted restrictions on the use of the Internet and allowed it to be used for commercial purposes as well. Since then, the Internet has grown rapidly to become the world's largest network that connects thousands of networks, billions of computers, hundreds of countries across the world.

7.13 INTERNET PROTOCOL ADDRESS

When you have to send a letter to your friend, you always mention the residence address of your friend so that it can reach her. This residence address is unique. If you want to talk to your friend, you need to dial her telephone number, which is again unique. Similarly, if you have to send a message over the Internet, you need some addressing mechanism so that the message can reach the correct destination.

Internet protocol address or IP address is, therefore, a unique address allotted to computing devices such as computers, routers, printers, scanners, modems, smartphones, tablets, and so on that are connected with the Internet. This address facilitates unique identification of devices for communication to take place.

Features

The following are the features of IP address:

- An IP address is divided into four parts where each part is separated from the other using a dot.
- Each part of the address contains a number ranging from 0–255.
- For example, 79.121.10.190 is a valid IP address.
- Without IP addresses, sending and receiving data over the Internet would be impossible.

7.13.1 Types of IP Addresses

There are two categories of IP addresses—static or dynamic and public or private.

Static and dynamic Internet protocol addresses As the name suggests, static IP addresses never change and dynamic IP addresses keep changing dynamically whenever users log on to the network. Many a time, dynamic IP addresses are issued using a leasing system. Therefore, the allocated IP address remains valid for a limited time. When the lease expires, the computer automatically requests a new lease. Similarly, when there is an IP address conflict, a request for another IP address is sent to the ISP automatically. The entire process of requesting IP addresses is automated and is therefore hidden from the users. Table 7.2 shows the differences between static and dynamic IP addresses.

7.14 DOMAIN NAME SYSTEM

When you want to talk to a friend, you do not type his number. You may be having several friends and memorizing everyone's number is just not possible. Therefore, you save all important phone numbers along with their names in your phonebook. To connect with your friend, instead of dialling his 10-digit cell number, you just search for his name in the phonebook and click the *Call* button. Although you use the name, your call is not connected based on name. The name is converted into a number which is then used to establish the connection.

Table 7.2 Differences between static and dynamic IP address

Static IP address	Dynamic IP address
This IP address is permanent.	This IP address is temporary and changes dynamically.
A computer retains its static address every time it is connected to the Internet.	A computer is allotted a new dynamic IP address every time it is connected to the Internet.
It is a reliable way to facilitate communication between remote devices.	It is not a reliable way to facilitate communication between remote devices.
This address reveals technical information about the continent, country, and city in which the computer is located.	Dynamic IP address does not reveal any such detail.
There are limited static addresses.	It can support a large number of users who do not require the same IP address always.
It is allotted to devices that connect to the Internet using a broadband connection.	It is allotted to devices using a dial-up connection to connect to the Internet.
Email servers and other web servers must have a static IP address.	It is not suitable for servers.
It is preferable for applications such as voice over IP, online gaming, and other applications that need to locate and connect to a particular computer on the Internet.	It is preferable for applications that work fine with temporary and one-time IP addresses.
It is less safe and requires extra security mechanism.	It is safe to use.
A user can configure his static IP address himself.	Dynamic IP address is allotted by the ISP server. This allocation is transparent from the user.

Coming back to the Internet, we have seen that every device has a unique IP address. To connect with a particular device you need to specify its address. However, we do not really type the IP address. For example, if we want to connect to google.com, we just type www.google.com. Then where is the IP address and how are we able to access the website? The answer to this question is the Domain Name System (DNS). Similar to the phonebook service, the Internet has a corresponding DNS service that translates domain names into IP addresses (for example, www.google.com into 74.125.224.72). This means that every time we use the Internet, we always use the DNS.

The DNS system works as a network of DNS servers. As maintaining a central database of all the computers on the Internet along with their names and IP address is quite unpractical, the DNS distributes the responsibility of storing domain names and their corresponding IP addresses to authoritative name servers. These name servers are responsible for the domain they support. The authoritative name servers may even delegate authority to other sub-domain servers. Besides providing speedy mapping, this authority delegation process ensures distributed and fault-tolerant service to Internet users.

In such a networked DNS environment, if one DNS server does not know the IP address of a particular domain name, it asks another server for the same. The process is repeated until a proper match between IP address and domain name is found.

Note

DNS is a service that automatically converts domain names into IP addresses.

Some commonly used domains are as follows:

gov Government agencies

edu Educational institutions

org Non-profit organizations

mil Military

com Commercial business

net Network organizations

int International organizations

Some country domains are as follows:

ca Canada

th Thailand

fr France

jp Japan

in India

us Unites States of America

uk United Kingdom

Other domain names include .museum (for museums), .info (informational websites), .name (personal websites), .pro (for professionals), .aero (for aeronautical companies), .coops (for co-operative organizations), .jobs (for job posting), and .mobl (for mobile communication networks).

Like our full names in which the general name or surname comes on the right and our specific name comes on the left, domain names are also organized from right to left, with general domains to the right, and specific domains to the left. For example, in the domain name www.google.com, there are three domain names, each separated by a dot. Here, .com is a general domain and google is a sub-domain, and www is a sub-domain prefix for the World Wide Web.

7.15 UNIFORM RESOURCE LOCATOR OR UNIVERSAL RESOURCE LOCATOR

A uniform resource locator (URL) specifies the unique address for a file that is accessible on the Internet. It is provided by the user in the address bar. For example, when you type www.google.com, after pressing the Enter key,

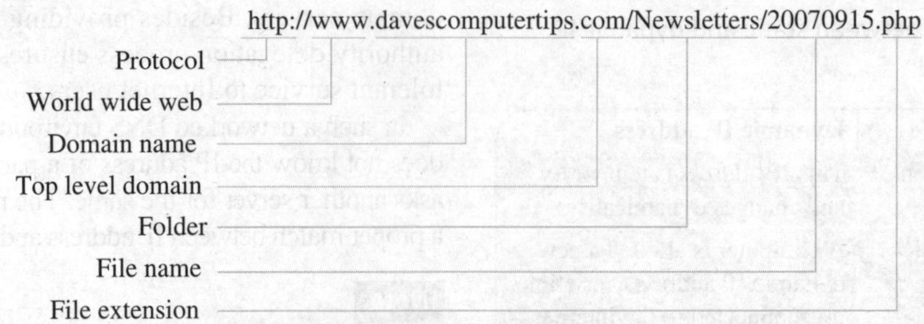

Figure 7.29 Uniform resource locator

there is a long sequence of characters in the address bar. This is the URL. This means that to access any page on the Internet, we need to provide its URL.

The file on the Internet that we want to access can be a web page, an audio file, video file, or image with extensions .htm, .php, .mp4, .avi, .jpg, .bmp, .gif, .asp, .cgi, .xml, etc.

The syntax for a URL is as follows:

Protocol://domain-name/path

where protocol specifies the name of the protocol to be used to access the file resource. Commonly used protocols are http, https, ftp, telnet, news, gopher, mailto, etc. This field specifies how to connect.

Domain name identifies the name of the website. This means that the domain field identifies where to connect.

Path is a hierarchical description that indicates the location of the file. It indicates to the web server what to connect.

For example, when we just write http://www.google.com, http is the protocol, www.google.com is the domain name, and by default, the home page which is saved as index.htm is displayed to the user. Refer to Figure 7.29 which shows another sample URL.

If we provide the URL as, http://www.example.com/Student/ABC.TXT, then http is used to fetch the file AB.TXT from Student directory stored in the computer on which the website www.example.com is hosted.

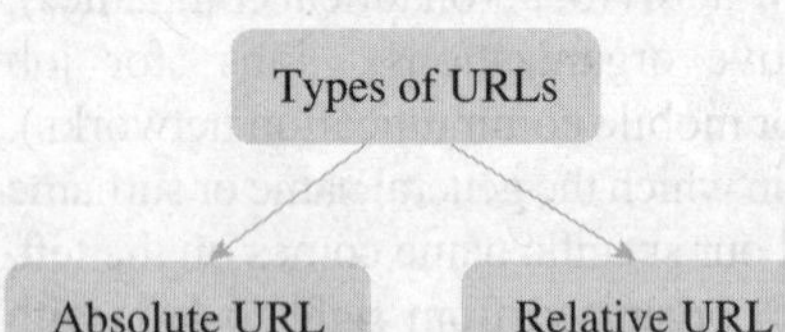

Figure 7.30 Types of URLs

There are basically two types of URLs as shown in Figure 7.30. While an absolute URL specifies the complete URL containing all three fields (protocol, domain, and path), relative URLs, on the other hand, contain only the one field which is the domain name.

Many a time, you must have observed a complex URL as the one given here, especially when you log in to your email account or search for a string on google.

http://www.google.com/cgi-bin/search.cgi?q=computer%20fundamentals

Although it seems complex, it is actually very simple to interpret. In the query, http is the protocol, www.google.com is the domain, and search.cgi is a file in the cgi-bin directory. Anything following the question mark (?) in a URL is a pair of variable(s) and its value(s). In the URL, q?computer%20fundamentals means that q is a variable name, and computer%20fundamentals is the value of q. Since blank spaces are not allowed in a URL, blank space has been written as %20. Spaces can also be written as a +(plus) sign. In the query, the user is trying to search computer fundamentals on Google.

These values are sent by the user's computer to Google's server. Google will find relevant pages and will display the result on the user's screen. Similarly, when we log in to our email account, we supply two values to the server—username and password. In such a situation, multiple variables are separated with an ampersand (&) sign as shown here:

http://www.gmail.com/config/passwd.cgi?u=erree&p=s2ejmd3

In the URL, there are two different variables—u with value erree and p with value s2ejmd3.

Note

A domain name is not the same as URL because it is just a small part of the entire URL.

Note

IPv5 is an experimental protocol for Unix-based systems and was never released to be used by the general public. All odd-numbered versions are developed for experimental purposes.

7.16 INTERNET SERVICES

Today, the Internet has become a part of not only the big organizations, universities, and offices, but has become the need of home users (like students) all over the world. In this era, life without the Internet has become unimaginable. In this section, we will read in detail about these services.

7.16.1 Electronic Mail

An e-mail is a means of transmission of messages electronically over communication networks. These messages may vary from notes entered using the keyboard to electronic

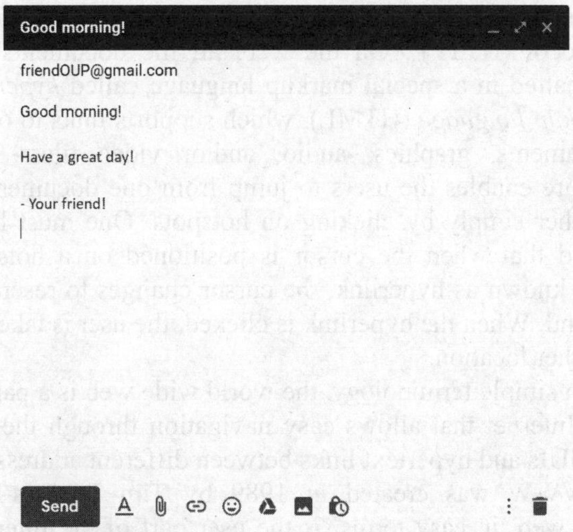

Figure 7.31 Composing an e-mail

files stored on disk. Companies that are fully computerized make extensive use of an e-mail because it is fast, flexible, and reliable. Figure 7.31 shows an e-mail application.

E-mail is one of the most widely used services on the Internet. Anyone who has an e-mail account can send an e-mail (like a letter) to any other person who also has an e-mail account (provided the e-mail address of the recipient is known). Usually, the structure of the e-mail can be given as: *username@domain name*.

For example, if a user has created an e-mail account in Gmail, then the e-mail address is *username*@gmail.com, where *username* is his/her Gmail screen name.

Using an e-mail is rather straightforward. If one has an e-mail account, he/she can just click on the option 'Compose e-mail' (or similar options corresponding to the browser being used). Thereafter, the user will be prompted to enter the following fields:

To In this field, the e-mail address of the recipient should be typed.

Subject In this field, anything illustrating the content of the message can be keyed in. However, the length of this field is limited.

Body This field contains the content of the message. Most e-mail systems include a basic text editor for composing messages, but uses may also edit messages using any other editor of their choice.

CC and BCC Filling these fields is optional. However, similar to the *To* field, these fields also contain e-mail addresses of recipients. While CC stands for carbon copy, BCC, on the other hand, means blind carbon copy. When a user wishes to send the same e-mail message to multiple recipients, he/she can add the extra e-mail addresses in the CC field, separating each address with a comma. BCC works just like CC, except the e-mail addresses in BCC are not revealed to the other recipients. For example, if a user sends an e-mail To: Goransh and BCC: Radhika, then Radhika will be able to see Goransh's e-mail address, but Goransh will not see Radhika's e-mail address.

Moreover, there are also options for attachments and forwards. The attachment option enables the users to attach files to the e-mail. The forward option is used to forward (make a copy) of a message received from someone and mail it to someone else.

The messages are stored in electronic mailboxes until the recipient fetches them. After reading the message, the receiver may save it, delete it, forward it to someone else, or reply to it. All in all, e-mail is a good alternative to the traditional paper-based letters. It is much faster and easier to use as there is no need to buy envelopes and stamps, and involves no queuing in the post office.

7.16.2 File Transfer Protocol

File transfer protocol (FTP) is one of the oldest applications of the Internet, which is basically used for transferring files from one computer to another, such as from a user's personal computer to a web server. It is the preferred method of exchanging files because it is faster and reliable. It is usually used to

- enable the users to share files, computer programs, and/ or data
- enhance the use of remote computers
- provide authentication and security to the stored files and programs
- transfer data reliably and efficiently

The FTP program can be invoked either by typing the FTP commands on a simple command line interface (CLI) such as the MS-DOS prompt window or with a commercial program that offers a graphical user interface (GUI). Even the web browser can make FTP requests to download the selected programs.

7.16.3 Chatting

Chatting is a very popular service of the Internet that allows two or more online users to come together to talk using an instant messenger. Chatting helps users to stay connected with concerned people in business or family who live many miles away.

To chat with users on the Internet, every user must have an account with a username and password to enter the website. Chatting involves the exchange of typed-in messages between a group of users who take part from anywhere on the Internet. The chatting program also enables the users to arrange a private chat between two parties who meet initially in a group chat.

These days, even the business organizations are using chatting services to host online business meetings, or to answer any queries of customers or provide them online support and assistance.

Whether a business chat or a personal chat, it can be ongoing or scheduled for a particular time and duration. Most chats are focused on a particular topic of interest and some involve guest experts or celebrities to talk to other online people who want to join the chat.

7.16.4 Internet Conferencing

The evolution of the Internet has changed the way in which business houses arrange conferences among the concerned parties. These days, organizations are increasingly switching to the Internet conferencing to reduce the extra costs involved in travelling and making telephone calls, thereby resulting in better time management and enhanced productivity.

Internet conferencing is quite similar to traditional teleconferencing. The difference is that, during an Internet conference call, the participants will sit in their respective offices while being connected to each other through the Internet. Many Internet conferencing software packages allow as many as 25 online participants to participate in the web meeting.

Today, there are a number of software packages available on the Internet that can be easily downloaded to host a conference call at little or no cost. To start an Internet conference call, the users need a computer with an Internet connection, related software, a webcam, and a microphone (to see and hear what the remote or distant participants are saying). During the conference, users can share information, files, video, and audio clips.

7.16.5 Electronic Newspaper

An online newspaper, shown in Figure 7.32, also known as a web newspaper or an electronic newspaper, is a newspaper on the Internet, which is either published separately or as an online version of a printed periodical.

Figure 7.32 Electronic newspaper

Source: Oleksiy Mark/Shutterstock/OUP Picture Bank

With the online newspapers, users can read the full coverage of breaking news in a timely manner. The credibility and strong brand recognition of well-established newspapers, and the close relationships they have with advertisers, plus the savings in overhead costs has led to the movement away from the printing process.

7.16.6 World Wide Web

The technical definition of the world wide web (WWW) or simply web, can be given as 'all the resources and users on the Internet that are using the hypertext transfer protocol (HTTP)'. On the web, all the documents are formatted in a special markup language called *hypertext markup language* (HTML), which supports links to other documents, graphics, audio, and/or video files. This feature enables the users to jump from one document to another simply by clicking on hotspots. One must have noted that when the cursor is positioned on a hotspot, also known as hyperlink, the cursor changes to resemble a hand. When the hyperlink is clicked, the user is taken to another location.

In simple terminology, the world wide web is a part of the Internet that allows easy navigation through the use of GUIs and hypertext links between different addresses.

WWW was created in 1989 by Tim Berners-Lee. The web, in easy terms, is the user part of the Internet. Users make use of the Web to communicate and access information for business and recreational purposes. There are several applications called *web browsers* that make it easy to access the web. Some popular web browsers are Mozilla Firefox, Opera, Google Chrome, Netscape Navigator, and Microsoft's Internet Explorer.

Many a times, we think that the Internet and the world wide web are the same, but this notion is not correct. The Internet and the web work together. While the Internet provides the underlying structure, the web, on the other hand, utilizes that structure to offer content, documents, multimedia, etc. For example, the Internet is like the highway, and the web is like a truck that uses that highway to get from place to place.

> **Note**
>
> Hypertext is a method of instant cross-referencing. On websites, certain words or phrases appear in a different colour than the rest, and are often underlined. When such words or phrases are selected, the users are transferred to the site or page that is relevant to this word or phrase. Sometimes there are buttons, images, or portions of images that are 'clickable'.

7.16.7 Online Shopping

Online shopping means buying goods and/or services from merchants who sell on the Internet. The popularity of the web gave an excellent opportunity to merchants to sell their products to people who surf the Internet. Shoppers can now visit web stores 24 × 7 as per their convenience, that too while sitting in their home, office, or even while travelling.

Consumers buy a variety of products from online stores ranging from books, clothing, household appliances, toys, hardware, software, and health insurance policies.

The number of people who want to shop online is increasing day-by-day. This is mainly because when a customer shops at a brick-and-mortar store, he or she has to drive to the store, find a parking place, and walk throughout the store until he or she locates the products that are needed. Even after selecting all the products, the customer has to wait in long queues to get the billing done. In striking contrast, online shopping is very convenient. With online shopping, a shopper logs onto the Internet, visits the store's website, and selects the products. Once all the products have been selected, the user can click the option to calculate the invoice and pay for the purchase using their debit/credit card. Figure 7.33 shows an electronics shopping cart used by an online shopping portal.

Figure 7.33 Electronic shopping cart
Source: Bloomua/Shutterstock/OUP Picture Bank

7.16.8 Search Engine

The World Wide Web stores enormous amount of information on an amazing variety of topics in hundreds of millions of pages. Finding information from this huge source is extremely difficult. The information we need is often stored in different names in different sites. Therefore, a special site called a search engine (e.g., Google, Yahoo, MSN Search, and Bing) is used to help people find information stored on various sites. Each of these search engines has its own abilities and features but they all help to minimize the time required to find information. Search engines use automated software called robots, bots, or spiders that travel along the Web searching all documents and files to create a searchable index of the files and documents containing the keyword. The search engine then applies a predetermined algorithm that ranks the pages according to their importance. It then displays the search results to users in the form of a list commonly called *hits*. Most of the times, the search results obtained from one search engine may not match those obtained from another search engine. This is because each search engine applies its own technique to search and rank the pages; therefore, it is always beneficial to use more than one search engine on a regular basis. Some sites such as *Yahoo*, *Search*, and *EasySearcher* not only use their search engine but also give the results from simultaneous searches of other search indexes. The following are some useful tips to search for information on the World Wide Web.

- *Use precise and specific keywords*: For example, if you want to know about kidneys, then do not type *body parts* as the keyword as this would get too much general information about our body parts and not enough specific hits about kidney.
- *If required, use two or more keywords*: However, write the most important keywords first. For example, if information is required about the functions of kidneys then write both the words in the same order.
- *Write correct spellings of the keyword*: Wrong spellings can give unexpected results. For example, if information on *bear* is required, spelling the word as *beer* will give entirely different results.
- *Use more than one search engine*: Each search engine gives different results. This is because different search engines look through different websites on the Internet to create their databases. When searching using a particular search engine, only a small proportion of the total sites available is considered. Therefore, searching for the same information using different search engines gives better results.

For getting better search results, while specifying keywords users must keep in mind the following points:

- *Use AND*: If you have to search for more than one keyword and all of them do not form a phrase, then specify the keywords using a '+' sign or writing AND between them. This will instruct the search engine to return web pages that contain all the keywords. For example, if information on functions of kidneys is required, then the user must either type *kidney + functions* or type *kidney AND functions*.
- *Use OR*: If there is more than one keyword and users want information on any of the keywords, then they must use OR in between the keywords given in parentheses. For example, if a user wants information about Delhi or NCR, then he/she should type (*Delhi OR NCR*). This would return web pages that contain either keyword.
- *Use NOT*: If users want to limit the search result by indicating keywords that should not be a part of result, then they must use the NOT or – symbol. For example, if a user wants information about Delhi but not NCR, then he/she must either type *Delhi NOT NCR* or type *Delhi – NCR*.
- *Use quotation marks*: When there are multiple keywords that form a phrase, enclose the keywords in quotation marks. The search engine will then return the pages that have the keywords in the exact order of the words in quotations. For example, if the user is looking for a book on *Computer Fundamentals and Programming in C*, then he/she must type the complete title in quotation marks. This would give pages that contain the full phrase together. Otherwise, information on *Computer Fundamentals* (only) and *Programming in C* (only) will also be displayed.
- *Combine symbols, if required*: For example, if the user wants information about government universities in Delhi but not in NCR, then he must type *government universities + Delhi – NCR*.

POINTS TO REMEMBER

- A computer network, simply known as a network, is a collection of computers and devices interconnected to facilitate sharing of resources, information, and electronic documents and among interconnected devices.
- The three primary physical components of a computer network are connecting media, network devices, and network topologies.
- The wireless technologies that connect computers and other devices to form a network include terrestrial microwave, communication satellites, cellular systems, and infrared systems.
- The topology of a network refers to the schematic description of the arrangement of a network. That is, it refers to the actual geometric layout of computers and other devices connected to the network.
- Wireless LANs use high frequency radio signals, infrared light beams, or lasers to communicate with remote computers.
- Wi-Fi is a wireless networking technology which provides wireless Internet and network connections.
- Bluetooth is a wireless technology for exchanging data by using low-power radio communication.
- Transmission of data through a communication channel between two machines can take place in different ways depending on the direction of the data flow, number of bits sent simultaneously, and synchronization between the sending and the receiving devices.
- OSI model simplifies the entire process of network communication (by dividing it into logical smaller pieces) and makes network designs more extensible as new services can easily be added in a layered architecture than in a monolithic one.
- Transmission Control Protocol (TCP) is a protocol that works at the transport layer and is used with the IP protocol, which is used to send data packets between sender and receiver devices.
- The Internet is a global network that connects billions of computers all over of the world.
- Internet protocol address is a unique address allotted to computing devices such as computers, routers, printers, scanners, modems, smartphones, tablets, and so on that are connected to the Internet.
- Domain name system (DNS) is a service that automatically converts domain names into IP addresses.
- While an absolute uniform resource locator (URL) specifies the complete URL containing all three fields—protocol, domain, and path, relative URLs, on the other hand, contain only one field—the domain name.
- Electronic mail (email) means the transmission of messages over communication networks.
- Internet chat allows two or more online users to come together to talk using an instant messenger.
- With online newspaper, users can read the full coverage of breaking news in a timely manner.
- Online shopping means buying goods and/or services from merchants who sell on the Internet.

GLOSSARY

Bridge A device that connects two or more LANs. When a bridge receives data from one LAN to forward to another, it first regenerates (or amplifies) the signals and then forwards the data.

Browser It is a software that enables the users to access the web.

Bus topology It is a network topology in which each computer or server is connected to a single cable and all the nodes share the same communication channel.

CAN It stands for campus area network and interconnects LANs within a limited geographical area. CAN is almost entirely owned by the campus of an enterprise, university, government, military base, etc.

Chat An Internet service that enables users to communicate with other people in real-time. The user types message using his or her keyboard. The message then appears on the screen of the other person. Similarly, the message typed by the other person appears on the user's screen.

Client program A program that requests information from another computer on the network. The client program accesses and displays the retrieved information to the user. For example, the web browser is a client program that accesses and displays web pages.

Computer network It is a collection of computers and devices interconnected to facilitate sharing of resources, information, and electronic documents among interconnected devices.

Download To make a copy of a file from another computer to your computer. For example, the user may copy a song from another computer on the Internet to his or her computer.

E-mail It is a communications system designed to enable the users to send and receive electronic messages across a network.

FTP Short form of file transfer protocol. It is basically a program that enables users to transfer files from one computer to another.

Gateway It is a device which connects two or more dissimilar networks that use entirely different protocols.

Gopher A program that organizes information on the Internet by using a system of menus. Items in the menus can be linked to other documents, or to other information services.

Host Any computer on a network.

HTML HTML stands for hypertext markup language and is used to create hypertext documents for use on the web.

HTTP It stands for hyper text transfer protocol. It is a protocol that defines a set of rules to exchange documents on the web.

Hub It is a network device that connects devices to enable them to communicate with each other.

Hybrid topology It is a topology that uses a combination of any two or more topologies in such a way that the resulting network does not exhibit one of the standard topologies.

Hypertext It is a hypertext document is one that includes links to other documents on the web.

Internet The Internet is a network of networks. It connects several networks all around the world to enable them to exchange information with each other. For this purpose, all the computers on the Internet use a common set of rules (protocol) for communication. Therefore, the Internet uses a set of protocols called transmission control protocol/Internet protocol (TCP/IP).

Internet service provider A commercial service that sells access to the Internet to individuals. Users connect to the ISP through a modem. While some ISPs only offer a basic connection to the Internet, others, on the other hand, sell a variety of value-added services such as discussion forums, tech support, software libraries, news, weather reports, stock prices, plane reservations, and even electronic shopping malls.

LAN It stands for local area network and connects devices in a limited geographical area. Owing to their limited scope and cost of operation, LANs are typically owned, controlled, and managed by a single person or organization.

Link A word, picture, or other area of a web page that users can click on to move to another spot in the same document or to another document. Links (words) may be underlined and usually appear in a contrasting text colour. When the user clicks on the link, the colour of the text changes.

MAN It stands for metropolitan area network and interconnects computers and other devices in a geographic area or region larger than that covered by even a large LAN but smaller than the area covered by a WAN.

Mesh topology It is a topology in which each node is connected to every other node on the network using a separate physical link.

Network Two or more computers or computing devices when connected with each other to share information and/or resources forms a network.

Network topology The schematic description of the arrangement of a network.

Newsgroup An Internet service in which readers can post messages or articles for other people to read. Other people can also reply to articles that they read on a newsgroup. It enables people with similar interests to communicate with each other.

Node Each computer connected to a network is called a node.

PAN It stands for personal area network and is designed for communication between devices such as mobile computers, cell phones, and PDAs that are close to one person. The scope or the reach of a PAN is a few metres (less than 10 metres).

Ping It is a message sent to check if a server is running.

Protocol A set of standardized rules that should be followed to exchange information among computers. There are different types of protocols for different kinds of communication. For example, HTTP specifies the rules for exchanging information on the WWW. FTP defines the rules to copy files from one computer to another across a network.

Repeater A network device that regenerates incoming electrical, wireless, or optical signals. Without a repeater, the data can only span a limited distance before the quality of the signal degrades.

Ring topology A topology in which all the nodes are connected to each other in the shape of a closed loop, so that every node is connected directly to two other nodes, one on either side of it.

Router An intelligent network device that routes data to destination computers. It is basically used to connect two logically and physically different networks, two LANs, two WANs, and a LAN with a WAN.

Server A program that provides information or services to other programs. For example, the web browser is a client that uses services like e-mail from the server.

Star topology A topology in which each node is connected to a central hub (or server) with a point-to-point connection.

Switch It is a switch is an intelligent network device that sends the data to the destined device.

Upload It is just the opposite of download and means transferring a file, picture, document, and/or audio/video clip from one's computer to some other computer.

URL A uniform resource locator (URL) specifies the addresses for webpages. That is, a URL uniquely identifies a webpage. URLs have three parts: Protocol name, server name, and a directory path. For example, consider the URL http://wings.avkids.com/SPIT/index.html. Here, 'http://' is the name of the protocol, 'wings.avkids.com' is the server's name, and '/SPIT/index.html' is the location of the file on the server.

WAN It stands for wide area network and spans a large geographical area such as a city, country, or even intercontinental distances, using a communications channel that combines many types of media such as telephone lines, cables, and air waves.

Wireless access point (WAP) It is a device that allows wireless devices to connect to a wired network using Wi-Fi

Webpage It is a document on the web that can contain text, pictures, movies, sounds, or links to other pages.

Website It is a collection of web pages on the web having to do with a particular topic or organization.

Wi-Fi It stands for wireless fidelity and usually means a form of wireless data communication.

Wi-Fi hotspot It is an area with an accessible wireless network

World Wide Web An interconnected set of hypertext documents located throughout the Internet.

EXERCISES

Fill in the Blanks

1. A ______ cable is a highly preferred connecting media for cable television systems.
2. The ______ of the fibre optic cable causes light to travel in a controlled path along the entire length of the glass core.
3. The geosynchronous satellites are positioned at a distance of______ kms above the equator.
4. The ______ mode of data transmission is utilized in web browsing.
5. In a ______ connection, *n* bits are simultaneously transmitted over the communication channel.
6. START and STOP bits are sent in ______ mode of transmission.
7. In synchronous transmission, the sender and the receiver are synchronized using a ______.
8. The______ refers to the actual geometric layout of computing devices connected to the network.
9. In the ______ topology, each node is connected to a central hub.
10. A mesh network of *n* nodes requires ______ physical links.
11. LANs are based on ______ technology.
12. Bluetooth PANs are also called ______.
13. Router uses special software known as ______.
14. The ______ is a network of networks.
15. The WWW was created by ______.
16. Wi-Fi networks use the ______ protocol.
17. ______ is a device that allows wireless devices to connect to a wired network using Wi-Fi.
18. Bluetooth operates in ______ of frequency range and allows devices to communicate at less than ______
19. ______ is an example of application layer
20. ______ layer acts as a translator between the application program and the network format.

Multiple-choice Questions

1. Which mode of data transmission is used in point-of-sale terminals?
   (a) Simplex (b) Half-duplex
   (c) Full-duplex (d) Serial
2. Which connection can be thought of as a two-lane bridge?
   (a) Synchronous (b) Half-duplex
   (c) Full-duplex (d) Parallel
3. Which mode of transmission is best suited for connecting input devices, printers, modems, fax machines, etc., to the computer?
   (a) Synchronous (b) Asynchronous
   (c) Full-duplex (d) Parallel
4. In which topology do the nodes share the same communication channel?
   (a) Ring (b) Star
   (c) Bus (d) Mesh
5. Which topology is best suited for a network that does not have a hub?
   (a) Ring (b) Star
   (c) Bus (d) Mesh
6. In which topology has every node an equal chance to transmit data?
   (a) Ring (b) Star
   (c) Bus (d) Mesh
7. Which device is used to connect a LAN to a WAN?
   (a) Hub (b) Switch
   (c) Bridge (d) Router

8. The underlying technology of WAN may include which of the following?
   (a) Frame Relay (b) X.25
   (c) ATM (d) All of these
9. Which of the following acts as the liaison for the computer to send and receive data on the LAN?
   (a) Hub (b) Gateway
   (c) Bridge (d) NIC
10. A program that requests information from another computer on the network is known as_______.
   (a) hub (b) server
   (c) client (d) host
11. HTTP, WWW, FTP, TELNET, and SMTP are used in which layer of OSI?
   (a) Physical (b) Network
   (c) Application (d) Presentation
12. Which layer decides the optimal route for data transmission?
   (a) Physical (b) Network
   (c) Session (d) Data Link
13. IP, ARP, RARP, ICMP protocols are used in the ______ layer of TCP/IP model
   (a) Application (b) Transport
   (c) Internet (d) Network Access

State True or False

1. Twisted-pair cables are free from noise and other electrical interference.
2. The satellite amplifies the received signal before transmitting it back to the earth-based antenna.
3. Infrared signals can be transmitted within small distances not more than 10 metres without any object in the line of transmission.
4. In duplex mode, there must be two communication channels between the sender and the receiver.
5. In a computer, binary data flows from one unit to another using parallel mode.
6. Bus topology requires less cable length than star topology.
7. Each node in a star topology acts as a signal repeater.
8. In ring topology, every node is connected to every other node on the network.
9. The Internet is the largest PAN.
10. Hub broadcasts a message to every device on the network.
11. Bridge is an intelligent network device.
12. A gateway provides security to the network.
13. The Internet and the world wide web are the same.
14. A server is a program that provides information or services to other programs.
15. Cellular phone network is an example of wireless networks.
16. Router is an example of WAP.
17. Bluetooth technology can be used to connect devices in a range of 100 meters.
18. Session layer is responsible for data compression.
19. Error and flow control are done by both transport and data link layer.

Review Questions

1. Define the term network. Give its key advantages.
2. What do you understand by the term connecting media? Illustrate it in detail with respect to wired networks.
3. Why are fibre optic cables better than twisted-pair and coaxial cables?
4. Write a short note on wireless network technologies.
5. What are the limitations of using infrared communication?
6. Differentiate among simplex, half-duplex, and full-duplex modes of data transmission.
7. How is parallel transmission better than serial transmission? Is there any consideration for transmitting the data in parallel?
8. Explain the synchronous and asynchronous modes of data transmission.
9. What is topology? Discuss key topologies used to form a network.
10. Differentiate between a MAN and a WAN.
11. Write a short note on the different types of area networks.
12. Which device will you prefer to form a network—hub or a switch? Justify your answer.
13. Explain the role of repeaters. How are they helpful?
14. How can a bridge help in controlling traffic on network segments?
15. In what situation must the network have a gateway?
16. What is NIC?
17. Write an essay on the Internet and its services.
18. Why is online shopping not very popular among the masses?
19. What are the layers in OSI model? Write the utility of each layer.
20. Write a brief note on TCP/IP Model.
21. Differentiate between static and dynamic IP address.
22. What do you understand by the term URL?
23. Explain the significance of DNS.

8 Designing Efficient Programs

TAKEAWAYS

- Programming paradigms
- Design of efficient programs
- Algorithms
- Flowcharts
- Pseudocodes
- Types of errors
- Testing
- Debugging

8.1 PROGRAMMING PARADIGMS

A programming paradigm is a fundamental style of programming that defines how the structure and basic elements of a computer program will be built. The style of writing programs and the set of capabilities and limitations that a particular programming language has depends on the programming paradigm it supports. While some programming languages strictly follow a single paradigm, others may draw concepts from more than one. The sweeping trend in the evolution of high-level programming languages has resulted in a shift in programming paradigm. These paradigms, in sequence of their application, can be classified as follows:

- Monolithic programming—emphasizes on finding a solution
- Procedural programming—lays stress on algorithms
- Structured programming—focuses on modules
- Object-oriented programming—emphasizes on classes and objects
- Logic-oriented programming—focuses on goals usually expressed in predicate calculus
- Rule-oriented programming—makes use of 'if-then-else' rules for computation
- Constraint-oriented programming—utilizes invariant relationships to solve a problem

Each of these paradigms has its own strengths and weaknesses and no single paradigm can suit all applications. For example, for designing computation-intensive problems, procedure-oriented programming is preferred; for designing a knowledge base, rule-based programming would be the best option; and for hypothesis derivation, logic-oriented programming is used. In this book, we will discuss only the first four paradigms.

8.1.1 Monolithic Programming

Programs written using monolithic programming languages such as assembly language and BASIC consist of global data and sequential code. The global data can be accessed and modified (knowingly or mistakenly) from any part of the program, thereby posing a serious threat to its integrity. A sequential code is one in which all instructions are executed in the specified sequence. In order to change the sequence of instructions, jump statements or 'goto' statements are used. Figure 8.1 shows the structure of a monolithic program. As the name suggests, monolithic programs have just one program module as such programming languages do not support the concept of subroutines. Therefore, all the actions required to complete a particular task are embedded within the same application itself. This not only makes the size of the program large but also makes it difficult to debug and maintain. For all these reasons, monolithic programming language is used only for very small and simple applications where reusability is not a concern.

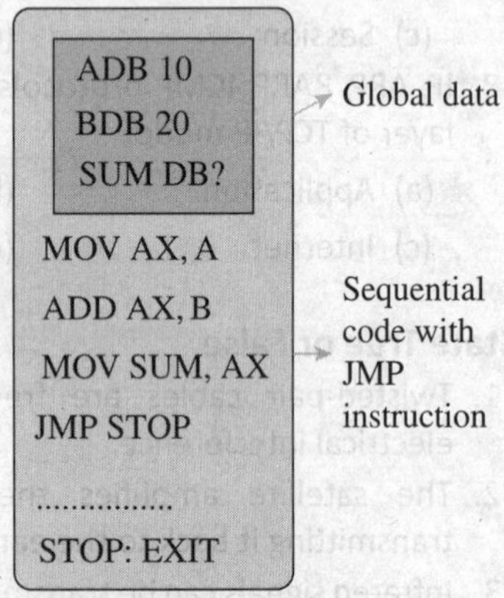

Figure 8.1 Structure of a monolithic program

8.1.2 Procedural Programming

In procedural languages, a program is divided into subroutines that can access global data. To avoid repetition of code, each subroutine performs a well-defined task. A subroutine that needs the service provided by another

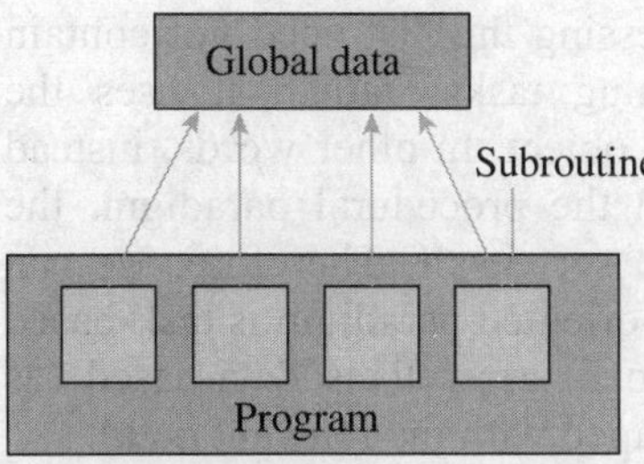

Figure 8.2 Structure of a procedural program

subroutine can call that subroutine. Therefore, with 'jump', 'goto', and 'call' instructions, the sequence of execution of instructions can be altered. Figure 8.2 shows the structure of a procedural language. FORTRAN and COBOL are two popular procedural programming languages.

Advantages

- The only goal is to write correct programs
- Programs are easier to write as compared to monolithic programming

Disadvantages

- No concept of reusability
- Requires more time and effort to write programs
- Programs are difficult to maintain
- Global data is shared and therefore may get altered (mistakenly)

8.1.3 Structured Programming

Structured programming, also referred to as modular programming, was first suggested by mathematicians, Corrado Bohm and Guiseppe Jacopini in 1966. It was specifically designed to enforce a logical structure on the program to make it more efficient and easier to understand and modify. Structured programming was basically defined to be used in large programs that require large development team to develop different parts of the same program. Structured programming employs a top-down approach in which the overall program structure is broken down into separate modules. This allows the code to be loaded into memory more efficiently and also be reused in other programs. Modules are coded separately and once a module is written and tested individually, it is then integrated with other modules to form the overall program structure (refer to Fig. 8.3). Structured programming is, therefore, based on modularization which groups related statements together into modules. Modularization makes it easier to write, debug, and understand the program. Ideally, modules should not be longer than a page. It is always easy to understand a series of 10 single-page modules than a single 10-page program. For large and complex programs, the overall program structure may further require the need to break the modules into subsidiary pieces. This process continues until an individual piece of code can be written easily. Almost every modern programming language similar to C, Pascal, etc., supports the concepts of structured programming. In addition to the techniques of structured programming for writing modules, it also focuses on structuring its data. In structured programming, the program flow follows a simple sequence and usually avoids the use of 'goto' statements. Besides sequential flow, structured programming also supports selection and repetition as mentioned here.

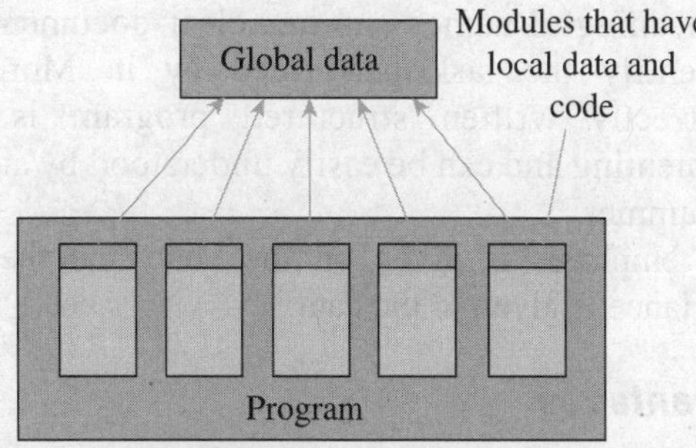

Figure 8.3 Structured program

- Selection allows for choosing any one of a number of statements to execute, based on the current status of the program. Selection statements contain keywords such as 'if', 'then', 'end if', or 'switch' that help to identify the order as a logical executable.
- In repetition, a selected statement remains active until the program reaches a point where there is a need for some other action to take place. It includes keywords such as 'repeat', 'for', or 'do... until'. Essentially, repetition instructs the program as to how long it needs to continue the function before requesting further instructions.

Advantages

- The goal of structured programming is to write correct programs that are easy to understand and change.
- Modules enhance programmers' productivity by allowing them to look at the big picture first and focus on details later.
- With modules, many programmers can work on a single, large program, with each working on a different module.
- A structured program takes less time to be written than other programs. Modules or procedures written for one program can be reused in other programs as well.
- Each module performs a specific task.
- Each module has its own local data.
- A structured program is easy to debug because each procedure is specialized to perform just one task and every procedure can be checked individually for the presence of any error. In striking contrast, unstructured programs consist of a sequence of instructions that are not grouped for specific tasks. Their logic is cluttered with details and, therefore, difficult to follow.
- Individual procedures are easy to change as well as understand. In a structured program, every procedure

has meaningful names and has clear documentation to identify the task performed by it. Moreover, a correctly written structured program is self-documenting and can be easily understood by another programmer.

- More emphasis is given on the code and the least importance is given to the data.

Disadvantages

- Not data-centred
- Global data is shared and therefore may get inadvertently modified
- Main focus is on functions

8.1.4 Object-oriented Programming (OOP)

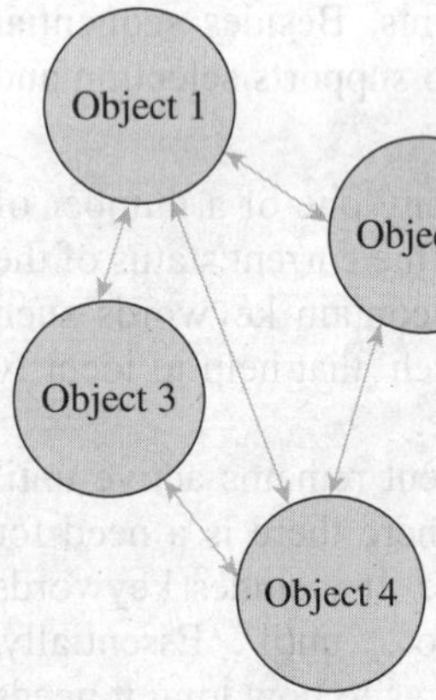

Objects of a program interact by sending messages to each other

Figure 8.4 Object-oriented paradigm

With the increase in size and complexity of programs, there was a need for a new programming paradigm that could help to develop maintainable programs. To implement this, the flaws in previous paradigms had to be corrected. Consequently, OOP was developed. It treats data as a critical element in the program development and restricts its flow freely around the system. We have seen that monolithic, procedural, and structured programming paradigms are task-based as they focus on the actions the program should accomplish. However, the object-oriented paradigm is task-based and data-based. In this paradigm, all the relevant data and tasks are grouped together in entities known as objects (refer to Fig. 8.4). For example, consider a list of numbers. The procedural or structured programming paradigm considers this list as merely a collection of data. Any program that accesses this list must have some procedures or functions to process this list. For example, to find the largest number or to sort the numbers in the list, we need specific procedures or functions to do the task. Therefore, the list is a passive entity as it is maintained by a controlling program rather than having the responsibility of maintaining itself. However, in the object-oriented paradigm, the list and the associated operations are treated as one entity known as an object. In this approach, the list is considered an object consisting of the list, along with a collection of routines for manipulating the list. In the list object, there may be routines for adding a number to the list, deleting a number from the list, sorting the list, etc. The major difference between OOP and traditional approaches is that the program accessing this list need not contain procedures for performing tasks; rather, it uses the routines provided in the object. In other words, instead of sorting the list as in the procedural paradigm, the program asks the list to sort itself. Therefore, we can conclude that the object-oriented paradigm is task-based (as it considers operations) as well as data-based (as these operations are grouped with the relevant data).

The striking features of OOP include the following:

- Programs are data centred.
- Programs are divided in terms of objects and not procedures.
- Functions that operate on data are tied together with the data.
- Data is hidden and not accessible by external functions.
- New data and functions can be easily added as and when required.
- Follows a bottom-up approach for problem solving.

In the forthcoming chapters, we are going to study C programming language which supports both procedural as well as structured programming.

8.2. EXAMPLE OF A STRUCTURED PROGRAM

Imagine that your institute wants to create a program to manage the names and addresses of a list of students. For this, you would need to break down the program into the following modules:

- Enter new names and addresses
- Modify existing entries
- Sort entries
- Print the list

Now, each of these modules can be further broken down into smaller modules. For example, the first module can be subdivided into modules such as follows:

- Prompt the user to enter new data
- Read the existing list from the disk
- Add the name and address to the existing list
- Save the updated list to the disk

Similarly, 'Modify existing entries' can be further divided into modules such as follows:

- Read the existing list from disk
- Modify one or more entries
- Save the updated list to disk

Observe that the two sub-modules—'Read the existing list from disk' and 'Save the updated list to disk' are common to both the modules. Hence, once these sub-modules are written, they can be used in both the modules, which require the same tasks to be performed. The structured programming method results in a hierarchical or layered program structure, which is depicted in Figure 8.5.

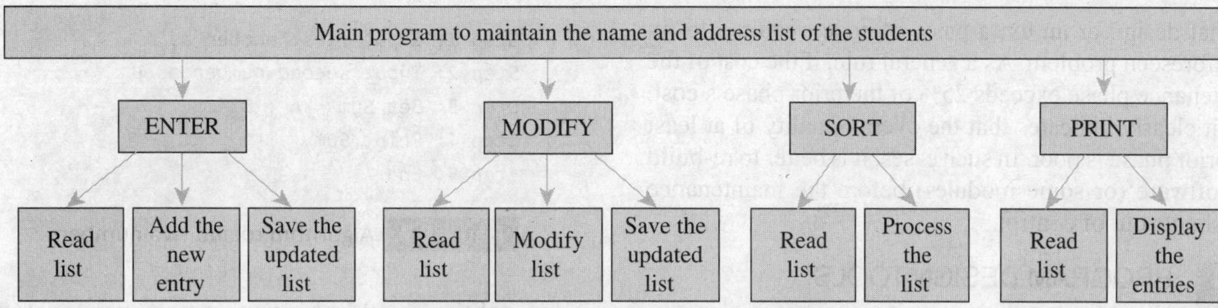

Figure 8.5 Layered program structure

8.3 DESIGN AND IMPLEMENTATION OF EFFICIENT PROGRAMS

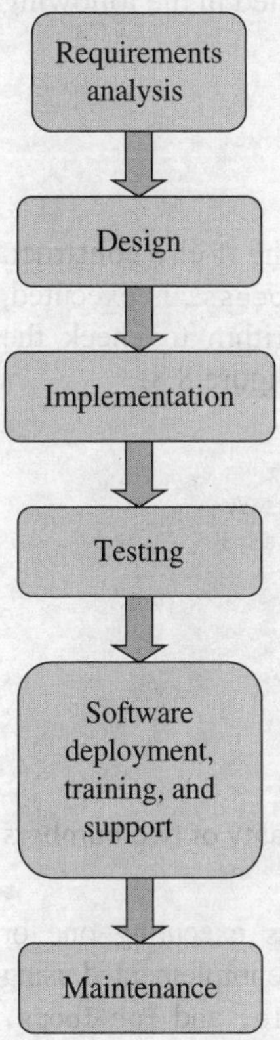

Figure 8.6 Phases in software development life cycle

The design and development of correct, efficient, and maintainable programs depend on the approach adopted by the programmer to perform various activities that need to be performed during the development process. The entire program or software (collection of programs) development process is divided into a number of phases, where each phase performs a well-defined task. Moreover, the output of one phase provides the input for its subsequent phase.

The phases in the software development life cycle (SDLC) process is shown in Figure 8.6.

The phases in the SDLC process can be summarized as follows:

Requirements analysis In this phase, the user's expectations are gathered to know why the program/software has to be built. Then, all the gathered requirements are analysed to arrive at the scope or the objective of the overall software product. The last activity in this phase includes documenting every identified requirement of the users in order to avoid any doubts or uncertainty regarding the functionality of the programs.

The functionality, capability, performance, and availability of hardware and software components are all analysed in this phase.

Design The requirements documented in the previous phase acts as an input to the design phase. In the design phase, a plan of actions is made before the actual development process can start. This plan will be followed throughout the development process. Moreover, in the design phase, the core structure of the software/program is broken down into modules. The solution of the program is then specified for each module in the form of algorithms or flowcharts. The design phase, therefore, specifies how the program/software will be built.

Implementation In this phase, the designed algorithms are converted into program code using any of the high-level languages. The particular choice of language will depend on the type of program, such as whether it is a system or an application program. While C is preferred for writing system programs, Visual Basic might be preferred for writing an application program. The program codes are tested by the programmer to ensure their correctness.

This phase is also called construction or code generation phase as the code of the software is generated in this phase. While constructing the code, the development team checks whether the software is compatible with the available hardware and other software components that were mentioned in the Requirements Specification Document created in the first phase .

Testing In this phase, all the modules are tested together to ensure that the overall system works well as a whole product. Although individual pieces of codes are already tested by the programmers in the implementation phase, there is always a chance for bugs to creep into the program when the individual modules are integrated to form the overall program structure. In this phase, the software is tested using a large number of varied inputs, also known as test data, to ensure that the software is working as expected by the user's requirements that were identified in the requirements analysis phase.

Software deployment, training, and support After the code is tested and the software or the program has been approved by the users, it is installed or deployed in the production environment. This is a crucial phase that is often ignored by most developers. Program designers and developers spend a lot of time to create software but if nobody in an organization knows how to use it or fix up certain problems, then no one would like to use it. Moreover, people are often resistant to change and avoid venturing into an unfamiliar area, so as a part of the deployment phase, it has become very crucial to have training classes for the users of the software.

Maintenance Maintenance and enhancements are ongoing activities that are done to cope with newly discovered problems or new requirements. Such activities may take a long time to complete as the requirement may call for the addition of new code that does not fit the original design or an extra piece of code, required to fix an unforeseen problem. As a general rule, if the cost of the maintenance phase exceeds 25% of the prior phase's cost, then it clearly indicates that the overall quality of at least one prior phase is poor. In such cases, it is better to re-build the software (or some modules) before the maintenance cost shoots out of control.

8.4 PROGRAM DESIGN TOOLS: ALGORITHMS, FLOWCHARTS, PSEUDOCODES

This section will deal with different tools, which are used to design solution(s) of a given problem at hand.

8.4.1 Algorithms

The typical meaning of an algorithm is a formally defined procedure for performing some calculation. If a procedure is formally defined, then it must be implemented using some formal language, and such languages are known as *programming languages*. The algorithm gives the logic of the program, that is, a step-by-step description of how to arrive at a solution.

In general terms, an algorithm provides a blueprint to writing a program to solve a particular problem. It is considered to be an effective procedure for solving a problem in a finite number of steps. That is, a well-defined algorithm always provides an answer, and is guaranteed to terminate.

Algorithms are mainly used to achieve *software reuse*. Once we have an idea or a blueprint of a solution, we can implement it in any high-level language, such as C, C++, Java, and so on. In order to qualify as an algorithm, a sequence of instructions must possess the following characteristics:

- Be precise
- Be unambiguous
- Not even a single instruction must be repeated infinitely.
- After the algorithm gets terminated, the desired result must be obtained.

Control Structures Used In Algorithms

An algorithm has a finite number of steps and some steps may involve decision-making and repetition. Broadly speaking, an algorithm may employ three control structures, namely, sequence, decision, and repetition.

Sequence Sequence means that each step of the algorithm is executed in the specified order. An algorithm to add two numbers is given in Figure 8.7. This algorithm performs the steps in a purely sequential order.

Decision Decision statements are used when the outcome of the process depends on some condition. For example, `if x = y, then print "EQUAL"`. Hence, the general form of the `if` construct can be given as follows:

```
IF condition then process
```

```
Step 1: Input first number as A
Step 2: Input second number as B
Step 3: Set Sum = A + B
Step 4: Print Sum
Step 5: End
```

Figure 8.7 Algorithm to add two numbers

A condition in this context is any statement that may evaluate either to a true value or a false value. In the preceding example, the variable x can either be equal or not equal to y. However, it cannot be both true and false. If the condition is true then the process is executed.

A decision statement can also be stated in the following manner:

```
IF condition
  then process1
ELSE process2
```

This form is commonly known as the if-else construct. Here, if the condition is true then `process1` is executed, else `process2` is executed. An algorithm to check the equality of two numbers is shown in Figure 8.8.

```
Step 1: Input first number as A
Step 2: Input second number as B
Step 3: IF A = B
            Print "Equal"
        ELSE
            Print "Not equal"
        [END of IF]
Step 4: End
```

Figure 8.8 Algorithm to test the equality of two numbers

Repetition Repetition, which involves executing one or more steps for a number of times, can be implemented using constructs such as the `while`, `do-while`, and `for loops`. These loops execute one or more steps until some condition is true. Figure 8.9 shows an algorithm that prints the first 10 natural numbers.

```
Step 1: [initialize] Set I = 1, N = 10
Step 2: Repeat Steps 3 and 4 while I <= N
Step 3: Print I
Step 4: SET I = I + 1
        [END OF LOOP]
Step 5: End
```

Figure 8.9 Algorithm to print the first 10 natural numbers

Example 8.1

Write an algorithm for interchanging/swapping two values.

Solution

```
Step 1: Input first number as A
Step 2: Input second number as B
Step 3: Set temp = A
Step 4: Set A = B
Step 5: Set B = temp
Step 6: Print A, B
Step 7: End
```

Example 8.2

Write an algorithm to find the larger of two numbers.

Solution

```
Step 1: Input first number as A
Step 2: Input second number as B
Step 3: IF A > B
          Print A
        ELSE IF A < B
          Print B
        ELSE
          Print "The numbers are equal"
        [END OF IF]
Step 4: End
```

Example 8.3

Write an algorithm to find whether a number is even or odd.

Solution

```
Step 1: Input number as A
Step 2: IF A % 2 = 0
          Print "Even"
        ELSE
          Print "Odd"
        [END OF IF]
Step 3: End
```

Example 8.4

Write an algorithm to print the grade obtained by a student using the following rules:

Marks	Grade
Above 75	O
60-75	A
50-60	B
40-50	C
Less than 40	D

Solution

```
Step 1: Enter the marks obtained as M
Step 2: IF M > 75
          Print "O"
Step 3: IF M >= 60 and M < 75
          Print "A"
Step 4: IF M >= 50 and M < 60
          Print "B"
Step 5: IF M >= 40 and M < 50
          Print "C"
        ELSE
          Print "D"
        [END OF IF]
Step 6: End
```

Example 8.5

Write an algorithm to find the sum of first N natural numbers.

Solution

```
Step 1: Input N
Step 2: Set I = 1, sum = 0
Step 3: Repeat Steps 4 and 5 while I <= N
Step 4: Set sum = sum + I
Step 5: Set I = I + 1
        [END OF LOOP]
Step 6: Print sum
Step 7: End
```

8.4.2 FLOWCHARTS

A flowchart is a graphical or symbolic representation of a process. It is basically used to design and document virtually complex processes to help the viewers to visualize the logic of the process, so that they can gain a better understanding of the process and find flaws, bottlenecks, and other less obvious features within it.

When designing a flowchart, each step in the process is depicted by a different symbol and is associated with a short description. The symbols in the flowchart (refer Figure 8.10) are linked together with arrows to show the flow of logic in the process.

The symbols used in a flowchart include the following:

- *Start and end symbols* are also known as the terminal symbols and are represented as circles, ovals, or rounded rectangles. Terminal symbols are always the first and the last symbols in a flowchart.
- *Arrows* depict the flow of control of the program. They illustrate the exact sequence in which the instructions are executed.
- *Generic processing step,* also called as an activity, is represented using a rectangle. Activities include instructions such as `add a to b, save the result`. Therefore, a processing symbol represents arithmetic and data movement instructions. When more than one process has to be executed simultaneously, they can be placed in the same processing box. However,

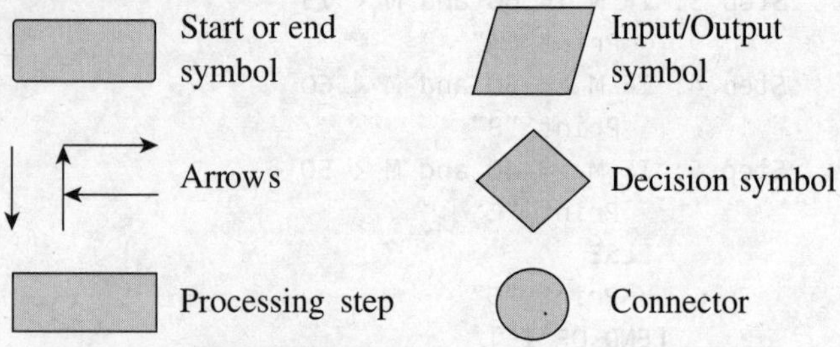

Figure 8.10 Symbols of flowchart

their execution will be carried out in the order of their appearance.

- *Input/Output symbols* are represented using a parallelogram and are used to get inputs from the users or display the results to them.
- A *conditional or decision symbol* is represented using a diamond. It is basically used to depict a Yes/No question or a True/False test. The two symbols coming out of it, one from the bottom point and the other from the right point, corresponds to Yes or True, and No or False, respectively. The arrows should always be labelled. A decision symbol in a flowchart can have more than two arrows, which indicates that a complex decision is being taken.
- *Labelled connectors* are represented by an identifying label inside a circle and are used in complex or multi-sheet diagrams to substitute for arrows. For each label, the 'outflow' connector must have one or more 'inflow' connectors. A pair of identically labelled connectors is used to indicate a continued flow when the use of lines becomes confusing.

Significance of Flowcharts

A flowchart is a diagrammatic representation that illustrates the sequence of steps that must be performed to solve a problem. It is usually drawn in the early stages of formulating computer solutions. It facilitates communication between programmers and users. Once a flowchart is drawn, programmers can make users understand the solution easily and clearly.

Flowcharts are very important in the programming of a problem as they help the programmers to understand the logic of complicated and lengthy problems. Once a flowchart is drawn, it becomes easy for the programmers to write the program in any high-level language. Hence, the flowchart has become a necessity for better documentation of complex programs.

A flowchart follows the top-down approach in solving problems.

Example 8.6

Draw a flowchart to calculate the sum of the first 10 natural numbers.

Solution

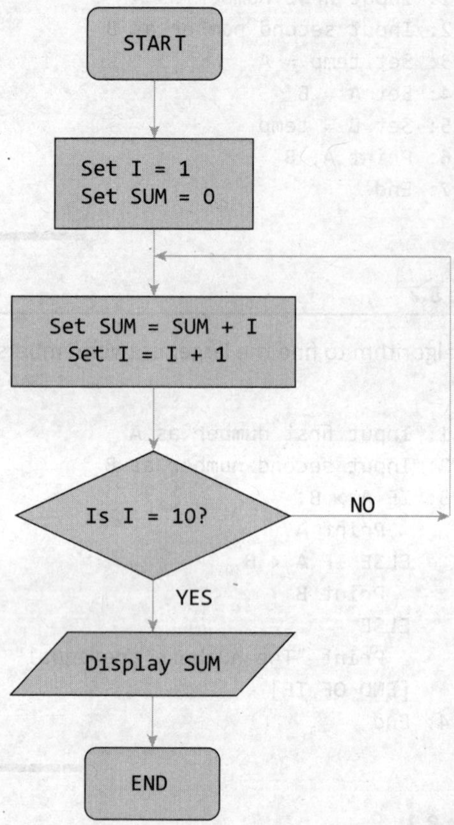

Example 8.7

Draw a flowchart to add two numbers.

Solution

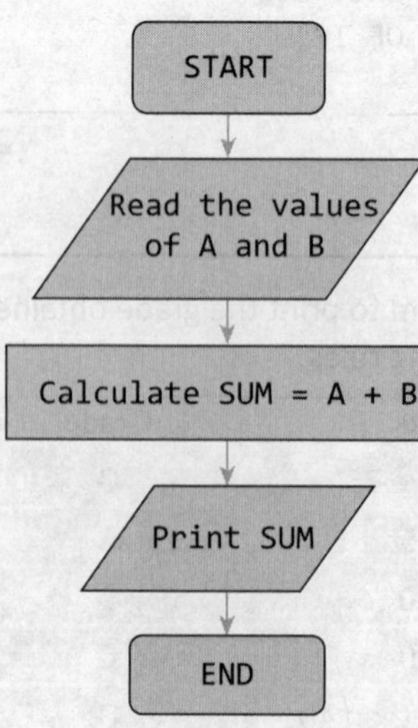

Example 8.8

Draw a flowchart to calculate the salary of a daily wager.

Solution

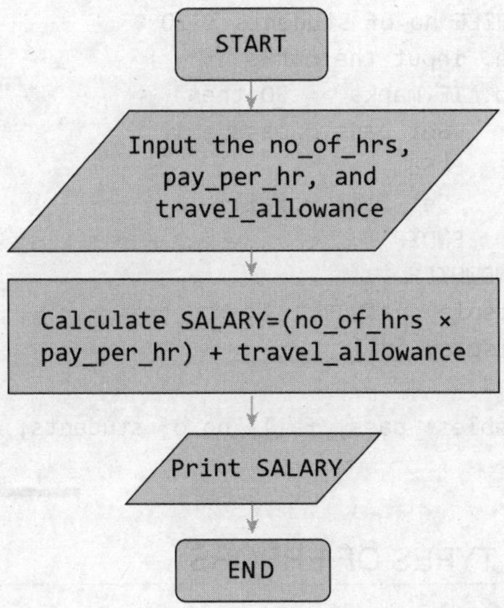

Example 8.9

Draw a flowchart to determine the largest of three numbers.

Solution

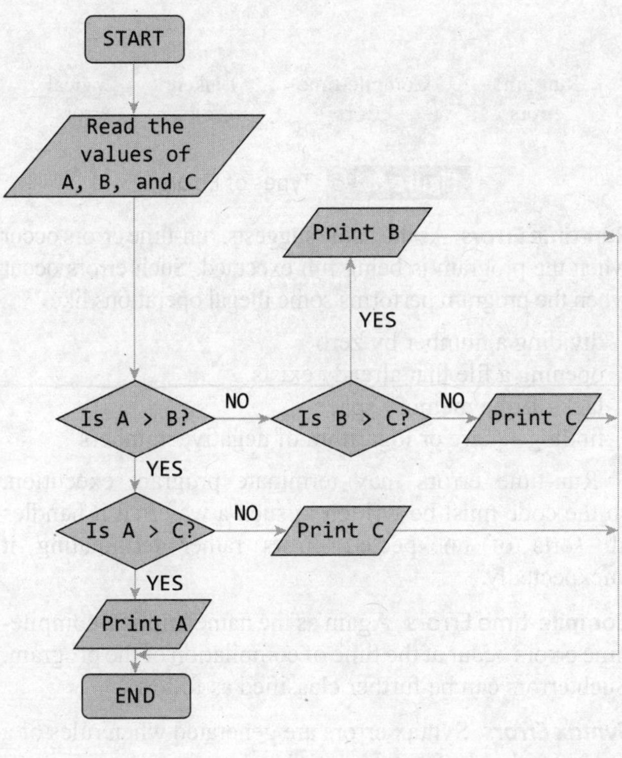

Advantages

- They are very good communication tools to explain the logic of a system to all concerned. They help to analyse the problem in a more effective manner.
- They are also used for program documentation. They are even more helpful in the case of complex programs.
- They act as a guide or blueprint for the programmers to code the solution in any programming language. They direct the programmers to go from the starting point of the program to the ending point without missing any step in between. This results in error-free programs.
- They can be used to debug programs that have error(s). They help the programmers to easily detect, locate, and remove mistakes in the program in a systematic manner.

Limitations

- Drawing flowcharts is a laborious and a time-consuming activity. Just imagine the effort required to draw a flowchart of a program having 50,000 statements in it!
- Many a times, the flowchart of a complex program becomes complex and clumsy.
- At times, a little bit of alteration in the solution may require complete redrawing of the flowchart.
- The essentials of what is done may get lost in the technical details of how it is done.
- There are no well-defined standards that limit the details that must be incorporated into a flowchart.

8.4.3 Pseudocodes

Pseudocode is a compact and informal high-level description of an algorithm that uses the structural conventions of a programming language. It facilitates designers to focus on the logic of the algorithm without getting bogged down by the details of language syntax. An ideal pseudocode must be complete, describing the entire logic of the algorithm, so that it can be translated straightaway into a programming language.

It is basically meant for human reading rather than machine reading, so it omits the details that are not essential for humans. Such details include variable declarations, system-specific code, and subroutines.

Pseudocodes are an outline of a program that can easily be converted into programming statements. They consist of short English phrases that explain specific tasks within a program's algorithm. They should not include keywords in any specific computer language.

The sole purpose of pseudocodes is to enhance human understandability of the solution. They are commonly used in textbooks and scientific publications for documenting algorithms, and for sketching out the program structure before the actual coding is done. This helps even non-programmers to understand the logic of the designed solution. There are no standards defined for writing a pseudocode, because a pseudocode is not an executable program. Flowcharts can be considered as graphical alternatives to pseudocodes, but require more space on paper.

Example 8.10

Write a pseudocode for calculating the price of a product after adding the sales tax to its original price.

Solution

```
1. Read the price of the product
2. Read the sales tax rate
3. Calculate sales tax = price of the item ×;
   sales tax rate
4. Calculate total price = price of the product
   + sales tax
5. Print total price
6. End
Variables: price of the item, sales tax rate,
   sales tax, total price
```

Example 8.11

Write a pseudocode to calculate the weekly wages of an employee. The pay depends on wages per hour and the number of hours worked. Moreover, if the employee has worked for more than 30 hours, then he or she gets twice the wages per hour, for every extra hour that he or she has worked.

Solution

```
1. Read hours worked
2. Read wages per hour
3. Set overtime charges to 0
4. Set overtime hrs to 0
5. IF hours worked > 30 then
   a. Calculate overtime hrs = hours worked -
      30
   b. Calculate overtime charges = overtime
      hrs × (2 × wages per hour)
   c. Set hours worked = hours worked -
      overtime hrs
   ENDIF
6. Calculate salary = (hours worked × wages
   per hour) + overtime charges
7. Display salary
5. End
Variables: hours worked, wages per hour,
   overtime charges, overtime hrs, salary
```

Example 8.12

Write a pseudocode to read the marks of 10 students. If marks is greater than 50, the student passes, else the student fails. Count the number of students passing and failing.

Solution

```
1. Set pass to 0
2. Set fail to 0
3. Set no of students to 1
4. WHILE no of students ≤ 10
   a. input the marks
   b. IF marks >= 50 then
        Set pass = pass + 1
      ELSE
        Set fail = fail + 1
      ENDIF
   ENDWHILE
5. Display pass
6. Display fail
7. End
Variables: pass, fail, no of students, marks
```

8.5 TYPES OF ERRORS

While writing programs, very often we get errors in our programs. These errors if not removed will either give erroneous output or will not let the compiler to compile the program. These errors are broadly classified under four groups as shown in Figure 8.11.

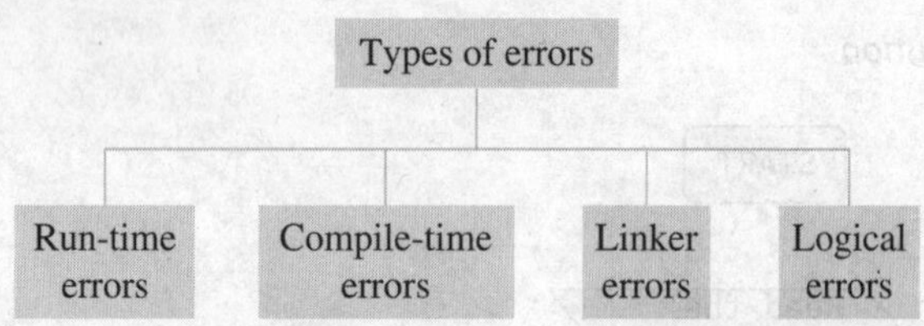

Figure 8.11 Types of Errors

Run-time Errors As the name suggests, run-time errors occur when the program is being run executed. Such errors occur when the program performs some illegal operations like

- dividing a number by zero
- opening a file that already exists
- lack of free memory space
- finding square or logarithm of negative numbers

Run-time errors may terminate program execution, so the code must be written in such a way that it handles all sorts of unexpected errors rather terminating it unexpectedly.

Compile-time Errors Again as the name implies, compile-time errors occur at the time of compilation of the program. Such errors can be further classified as follows:

Syntax Errors Syntax errors are generated when rules of a programming language are violated.

Semantic Errors Semantic errors are those errors which may comply with rules of the programming language but are not meaningful to the compiler.

Logical Errors Logical errors are errors in the program code that result in unexpected and undesirable output which is obviously not correct. Such errors are not detected by the compiler, and programmers must check their code line by line or use a debugger to locate and rectify the errors. Logical errors occur due to incorrect statements.

Linker Errors These errors occur when the linker is not able to find the function definition for a given prototype.

8.6 TESTING AND DEBUGGING APPROACHES

Testing is an activity that is performed to verify correct behaviour of a program. It is specifically carried out with an intent to find errors. Ideally testing should be conducted at all stages of program development. However, in the implementation stage, the following three types of tests can be conducted:

Unit Tests Unit testing is applied only on a single unit or module to ensure whether it exhibits the expected behaviour.

Integration Tests These tests are a logical extension of unit tests. In this test, two units that have already been tested are combined into a component and the interface between them is tested. The guiding principle is to test combinations of pieces and then gradually expanding the component to include other modules as well. This process is repeated until all the modules are tested together. The main focus of integration testing is to identify errors that occur when the units are combined.

System Tests System testing checks the entire system. For example, if our program code consists of three modules then each of the module is tested individually using unit tests and then system test is applied to test this entire system as one system.

Debugging, on the other hand, is an activity that includes execution testing and code correction. The main aim of debugging is locating errors in the program code. Once the errors are located, they are then isolated and fixed to produce an error-free code. Different approaches applied for debugging a code includes:

Brute-Force Method In this technique, a printout of CPU registers and relevant memory locations is taken, studied, and documented. It is the least efficient way of debugging a program and is generally done when all the other methods fail.

Backtracking Method It is a popular technique that is widely used to debug small applications. It works by locating the first symptom of error and then tracing backward across the entire source code until the real cause of error is detected. However, the main drawback of this approach is that with increase in number of source code lines, the possible backward paths become too large to manage.

Cause Elimination In this approach, a list of all possible causes of an error is developed. Then relevant tests are carried out to eliminate each of them. If some tests indicate that a particular cause may be responsible for an error then the data are refined to isolate the error.

Example 8.13

Let us take a problem, collect its requirement, design the solution, implement it in C and then test our program.

Marks	Grade
Above 75	O
60-75	A
50-60	B
40-50	C
Less than 40	D

Problem Statement To develop an automatic system that accepts marks of a student and generates his/her grade.

Requirements Analysis Ask the users to enlist the rules for assigning grades. These rules are:

Design In this phase, write an algorithm that gives a solution to the problem.

```
Step 1: Enter the marks obtained as M
Step 2: If M > 75 then print "O"
Step 3: If M >= 60 and M < 75 then print "A"
Step 4: If M >= 50 and M < 60 then print "B"
Step 5: If M >= 40 and M < 50 then print "C"
        else
        print "D"
Step 6: End
```

Implementation Write the C program to implement the proposed algorithm.

```
#include <stdio.h>

int main()
{ int marks;
  char grade;

  printf("\n Enter the marks of the student:");
  scanf("%d", &marks);
  if (marks<0 || marks >100)
  {   printf("\n Not Possible");
      exit(1);
  }
  if(marks>=75)
    grade = 'O';
  else if(marks>=60 && marks<75)
    grade = 'A';
  else if(marks>=50 && marks<60)
    grade = 'B';
  else if(marks>=40 && marks<50)
```

```
        grade = 'C';
    else
        grade = 'D';
    printf("\n GRADE = %c", grade);
  }
```

Test Case ID	Input	Expected Output	Actual Output
1	–12	Not Possible	Not Possible
2	112	Not Possible	Not Possible
3	32	D	D
4	46	C	C
5	54	B	B
6	68	A	A
7	91	O	O
8	40	C	C
9	50	B	B
10	60	A	A
11	75	O	O
12	100	O	O
13	0	D	D

Test The above program is then tested with different test data to ensure that the program gives correct output for all relevant and possible inputs. The test cases are shown in the table given below.

Note in the above table, we have identified test cases for the following,

1. "Not Possible" Combinations
2. A middle value from each range
3. Boundary values for each range

POINTS TO REMEMBER

- Programs written using monolithic programming languages such as assembly language and BASIC consist of global data and sequential code.
- In procedural languages, a program is divided into subroutines that can access global data.
- Structured programming employs a top-down approach in which the overall program structure is broken down into separate modules.
- Object-oriented programming treats data as a critical element in the program development and restricts its flow freely around the system.
- The entire program or software (collection of programs) development process is divided into a number of phases, where each phase performs a well-defined task.
- During requirements analysis, users' expectations are gathered to know why the program/software has to be built.
- In the design phase, a plan of action is made.
- In the implementation phase, the designed algorithms are converted into program code using any of the high-level languages.
- In the testing phase, all the modules are tested together to ensure that the overall system works well as a whole product.
- After the code is tested and the software or the program has been approved by the users, it is then installed or deployed in the production environment.
- Maintenance and enhancements are ongoing activities that are done to cope with newly discovered problems or new requirements.
- The different tools which are available to design solution(s) of a given problem are: algorithms, flowcharts, and pseudocodes.
- Algorithms give the logic of the program, that is, a step-by-step description of how to arrive at a solution. They are implemented using programming languages.
- A flowchart is a diagrammatic representation that illustrates the sequence of steps that must be performed to solve a problem. They are usually drawn in the early stages of formulating computer solutions. They facilitate communication between programmers and users.
- Pseudocode is a compact and informal high-level description of an algorithm that uses the structural conventions of an algorithm. It facilitates the designers to focus on the logic of the algorithm without getting bogged down by the details of language syntax.

GLOSSARY

Algorithm A formally defined procedure for performing some calculation. It provides a blueprint to writing a program that solves a particular problem.

Compile-time errors These are errors that occur at the time of compilation of the program

Debugging An activity that includes execution testing and code correction. The mainaim of debugging is to locate errors in the program code.

Flowchart A flowchart is a graphical or symbolic representation of a process.

Programming paradigm A fundamental style of programming that defines how the structure and basic elements of a computer program will be built.

Pseudocode Pseudocode is a compact and informal high-level description of an algorithm that uses the structural conventions of a programming language.

Runtime errors These are errors that occur when the program is being executed.

Structured programming Structured programming is a programming approach that employs a top-down approach in such a way that the overall program structure is broken down into separate modules. This allows the code to be loaded into the memory more efficiently and also be reused in other programs.

Testing An activity performed to verify the correct behaviour of a program. It is specifically carried out with the intent to find errors.

EXERCISES

Fill in the Blanks

1. ____ and ____ statements are used to change the sequence of execution of instructions.
2. ________ paradigm supports bottom-up approach of problem-solving.
3. FORTRAN and COBOL are two popular ____ programming languages.
4. ____ is a formally defined procedure for performing some calculation.
5. ________ statements are used when the outcome of the process depends on some condition.
6. Repetition can be implemented using constructs such as ______, ______, and ______.
7. The ______ symbol is always the first and the last symbol in a flowchart.
8. ______ is a form of structured English that describes algorithms.
9. ______ is used to express algorithms and as a mode of human communication.
10. In the ______ phase, a plan of actions is made.
11. Algorithms and flowcharts are designed in the ______ phase.
12. In the ______ phase, designed algorithms are converted into program code.
13. User's expectations are gathered in the ______ phase.
14. ______ errors may terminate program execution.
15. Debugging is an activity that includes ______ and ______.

Multiple-choice Questions

1. Which programming paradigm utilizes invariant relationships to solve a problem?
   (a) Rule-based (c) Structured
   (b) Constraint-based (d) Object-oriented
2. Which is the preferred paradigm for designing a knowledge base?
   (a) Rule-based (b) Constraint-based
   (c) Structured (d) Object-oriented
3. Which type of programming does not support subroutines?
   (a) Monolithic (b) Structured
   (c) Rule-based (d) Object-oriented
4. C and Pascal belong to which type of programming language?
   (a) Monolithic (b) Structured
   (c) Logic-oriented (d) Object-oriented
5. Which paradigm holds data as a priority?
   (a) Monolithic (b) Structured
   (c) Logic-oriented (d) Object-oriented
6. Which among the following is an ongoing activity in software development?
   (a) Requirements analysis (b) Implementation
   (c) User training (d) Maintenance
7. The functionality, capability, performance, availability of hardware and software components are all analysed in which phase?
   (a) Requirements analysis (b) Design
   (c) Implementation (d) Testing
8. In which phase are algorithms, flowcharts, and pseudocodes prepared?
   (a) Requirements analysis (b) Design
   (c) Implementation (d) Testing
9. Algorithms should be
   (a) precise (b) unambiguous
   (c) clear (d) all of these
10. To check whether a given number is even or odd, you will use which type of control structure?
    (a) Sequence (b) Decision
    (c) Repetition (d) All of these

11. Which one of the following is a graphical or symbolic representation of a process?
    (a) Algorithm (b) Flowchart
    (c) Pseudocode (d) Program
12. In a flowchart, which symbol is represented using a rectangle?
    (a) Terminal (b) Decision
    (c) Activity (d) Input/Output
13. Which of the following details are omitted in pseudocodes?
    (a) Variable declaration (b) System specific code
    (c) Subroutines (d) All of these
14. Trying to open a file that already exists, will result in which type of error?
    (a) Run time (b) Compile time
    (c) Linker error (d) Logical error
15. Which of the following errors is generated when rules of a programming language are violated?
    (a) Syntax error (b) Semantic error
    (c) Linker error (d) Logical error

State True or False

1. In monolithic paradigm, global data can be accessed and modified from any part of the program.
2. Monolithic programs have two modules.
3. Monolithic programs are easy to debug and maintain.
4. Structured programming is based on modularization.
5. Object-oriented programming supports modularization.
6. Structured programming heavily uses goto statements.
7. Modules enhance the programmer's productivity.
8. A structured program takes more time to be written than other programs.
9. An algorithm solves a problem in a finite number of steps.
10. Repetition means that each step of the algorithm is executed in the specified order.
11. Terminal symbol depicts the flow of control of the program.
12. Labelled connectors are square in shape.
13. Flowcharts are drawn in the early stages of formulating computer solutions.
14. The main focus of pseudocodes is on the details of the language syntax.
15. In the deployment phase, all the modules are tested together to ensure that the overall system works well as a whole product.
16. Maintenance is an ongoing activity.
17. Algorithms are implemented using a programming language.
18. Logical errors are detected by the compiler.

Review Questions

1. What do you understand by the term 'programming paradigm'?
2. Discuss any three programming paradigms in detail.
3. How is structured programming better than monolithic programming?
4. Describe the special characteristics of monolithic programming.
5. Explain how functional abstraction is achieved in structured programming.
6. Which programming paradigm is data-based and why?
7. What are the advantages of modularization?
8. Briefly explain the phases in software development project
9. Define an algorithm. How is it useful in the context of software development?
10. Explain sequence, repetition, and decision statements? In addition, give the keywords used in each type of statement.
11. With the help of an example explain the use of a flowchart.
12. How is a flowchart different from an algorithm? Do we need to have both of them for developing a program?
13. What do you understand by the term pseudocode?
14. Differentiate between algorithm and pseudocodes.
15. Testing is an unavoidable phase in software development life cycle. Comment.
16. What are the different types of errors which frequently occur in programs?
17. Differentiate between syntax and semantic errors.
18. Differentiate between unit test, integration test, and system test.
19. What are the different techniques for debugging a computer program?
20. Suppose you are given a problem to find all composite numbers in range provided by users. Perform all the phases of software development on this problem.

LAB ACTIVITY 6: FINDING THE IP ADDRESSES OF DIFFERENT DEVICES

Activity I: Finding the IP Address of a PC

To find the IP address of your PC that has Windows installed on it, follow the steps given below:

Step 1: Click on the Start button and type cmd to open the Command Prompt window.

Step 2: In the Command Prompt window, type ipcong and press Enter. The IP address will be displayed. See Figure F.1.

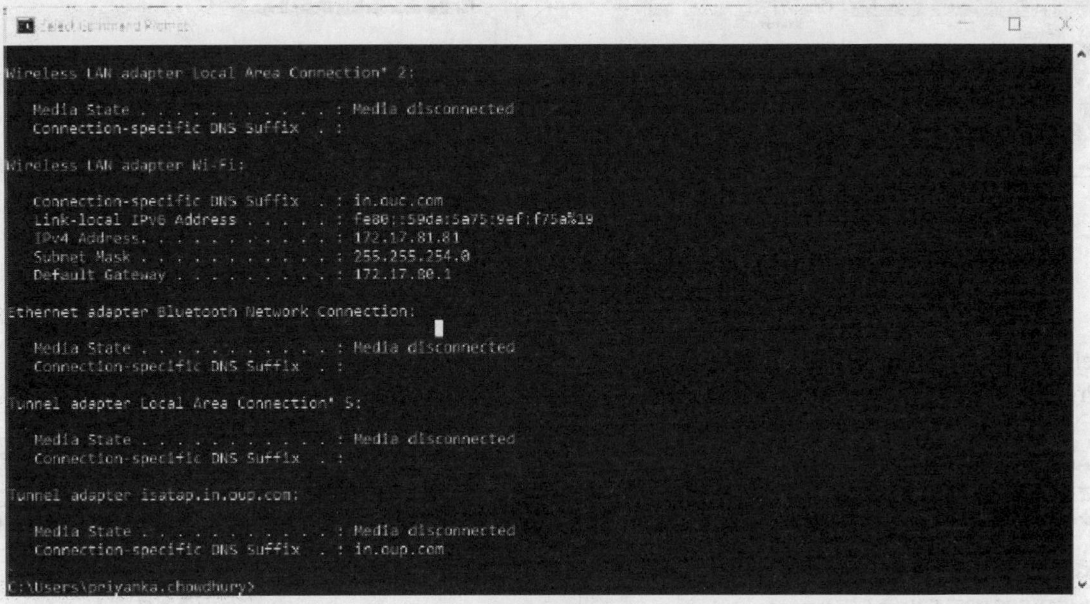

Figure F.1

Activity II: Finding the IP Address of a Printer

To know the IP address of your printer or fax, follow the steps given below:

Step 1: Click on the Start button and select Control Panel.

Step 2: In the Control Panel, click on Devices and Printers.

Step 3: Right-click the printer name followed by a left click on Printer Properties.

Step 4: Click on the Ports tab, and widen the rst column which displays IP addresses of the printers.

Activity III: Changing the IP Address of a Windows Computer

Step 1: Click on the Start button and select Control Panel.

Step 2: In the Control Panel, click on Network and Sharing Center.

Step 3: Click on Change adapter settings. See Figure F.2.

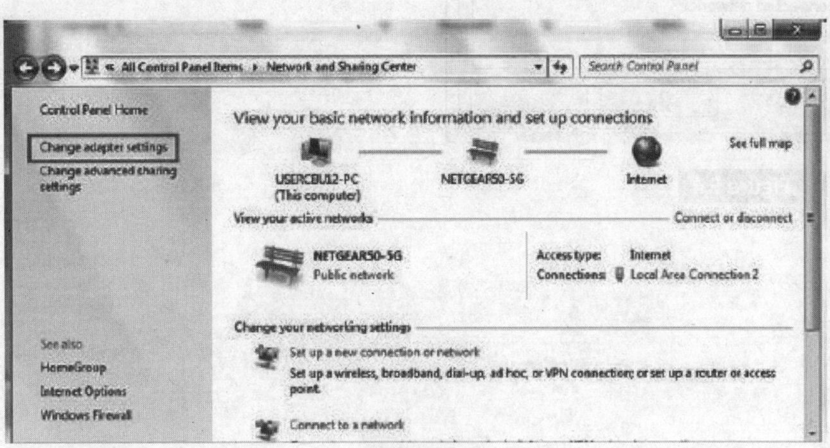

Figure F.2

Step 4: Right-click on Local Area Connection and select Properties. See Figure F.3.

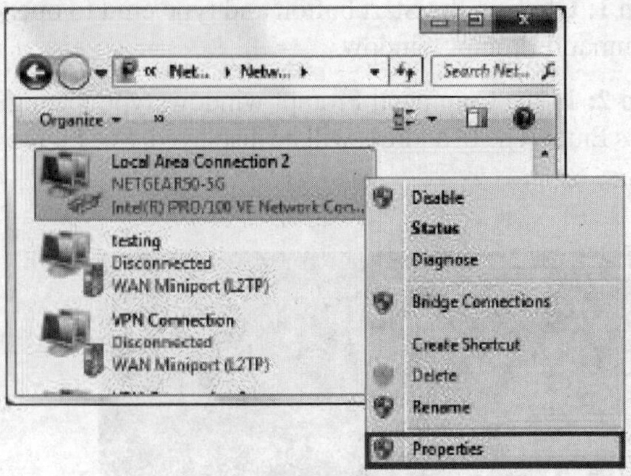

Figure F.3

Step 5: Select Internet Protocol Version 4 (TCP/IPv4) and click on Properties. See Figure F.4.

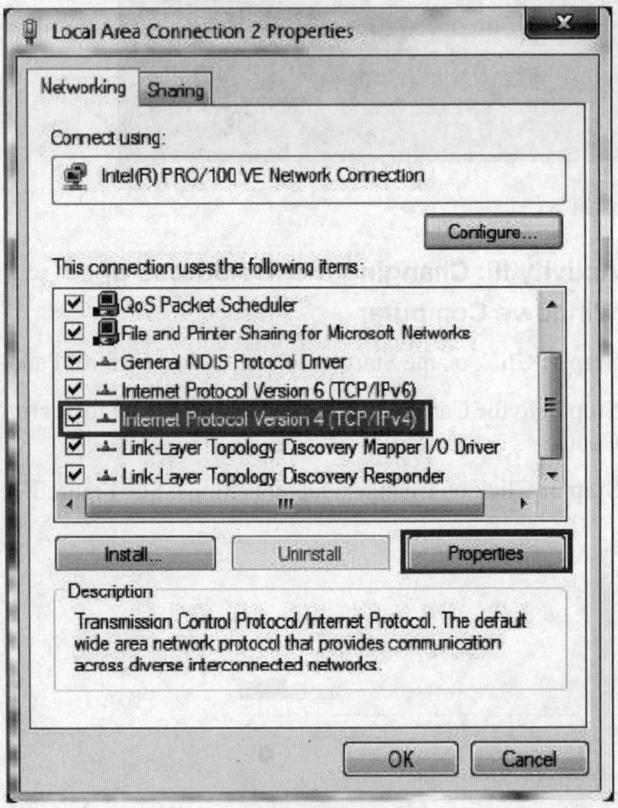

Figure F.4

Step 6: Make the desired changes and then click on OK. See Figure F.5. Close the Local Area Connection properties window.

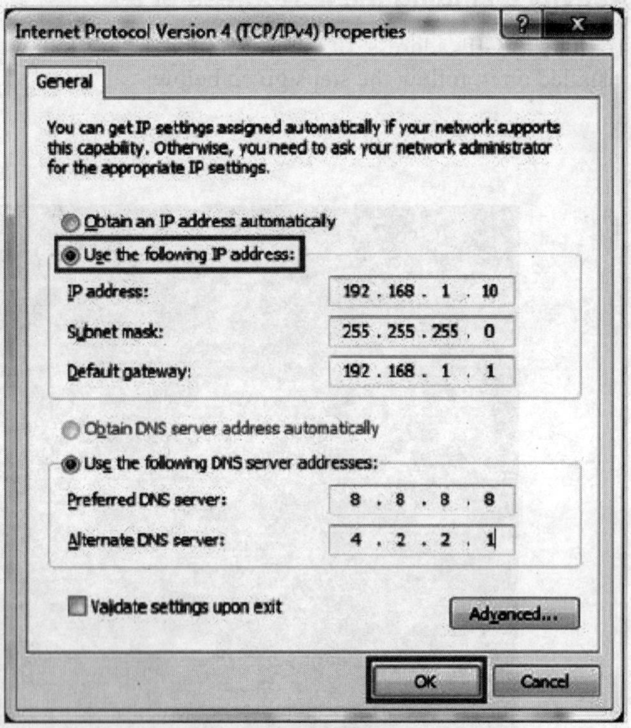

Figure F.5

LAB ACTIVITY 7: WORKING WITH WEB BROWSERS

Activity I: Adding Favorites in Microsoft Edge

Favorites, also known as Bookmarks in Chrome, are links to websites that help you to easily get back to your favorite websites. To create a bookmark in Microsoft Edge, follow the steps given below:

Step 1: Open Microsoft Edge.

Step 2: Type the URL of the website in the address bar for which you want to create a bookmark.

Step 3: Click on ☆ in the top-right edge of Microsoft Edge to open the Favorites menu (see Figure G.1).

Step 4: Click on the Add button to save the current page as a favorite. You can save the page in the Favorites folder or create a new folder.

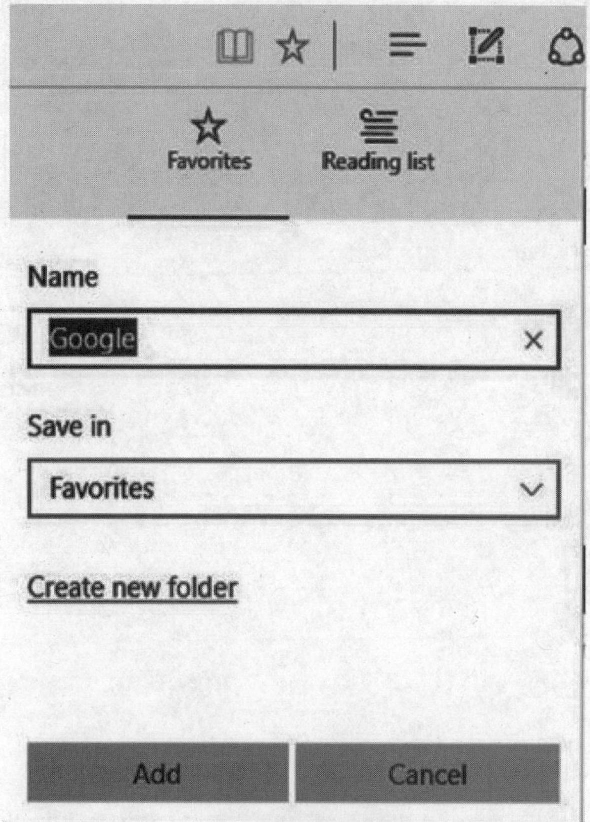

FIGURE G.1

Activity II: Viewing History in Google Chrome

Every web browser maintains a history of web pages, that is, the list of pages that you have visited today, yesterday, or even a week before. To view history in Google Chorme, follow the steps given below:

Step 1: Click on at the top right corner in Google Chrome window.

Step 2: Click on History. A list of date-wise recently closed windows will be displayed. Click on any link to view that page (see Figure G.2).

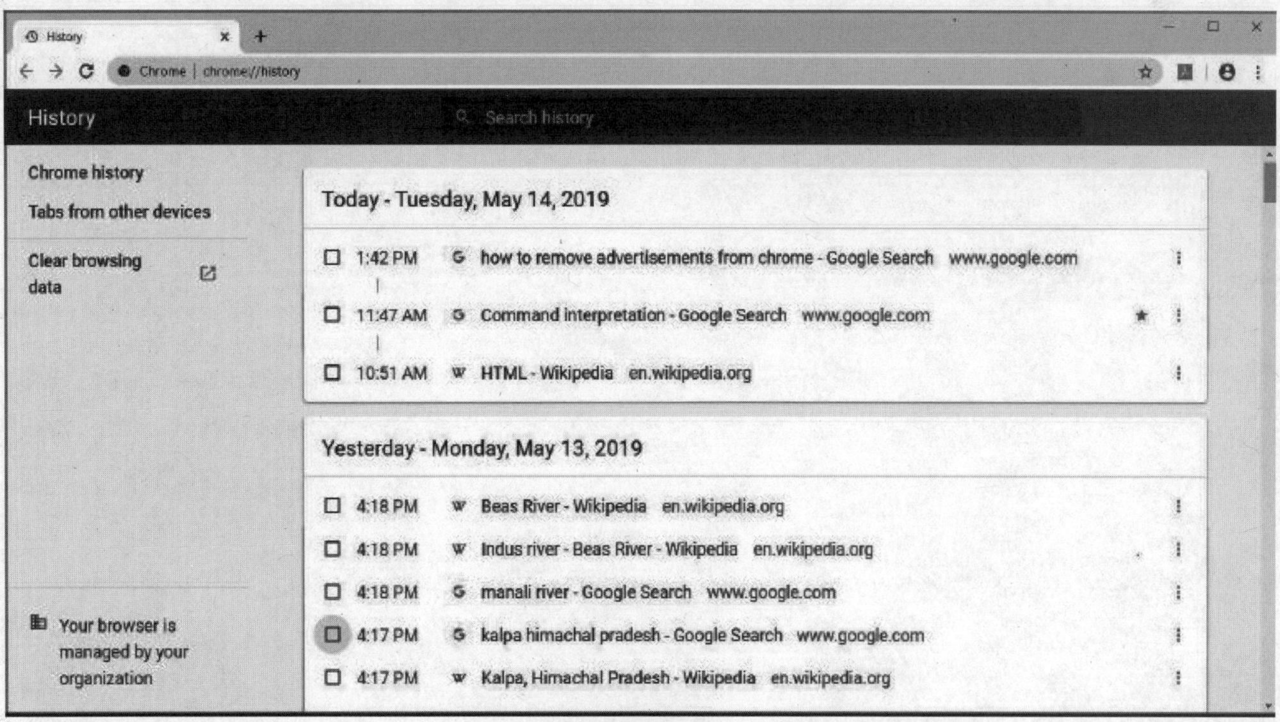

Figure G.2

PART II

PROGRAMMING IN C

9 Introduction to C

TAKEAWAYS

- Writing a C program
- Compiling and executing a C program
- Adding comments to a program
- Tokens, character set and keywords
- Identifiers
- Basic data types
- Variables and constants
- Input/Output statements
- Operators
- Operator precedence chart
- Type conversion and typecasting

9.1 INTRODUCTION

The programming language C was developed in the early 1970s by Dennis Ritchie at Bell Laboratories to be used by the UNIX operating system. It was named 'C' because many of its features were derived from an earlier language called 'B'. Although C was designed for implementing system software, it was later on widely used for developing portable application software.

C is one of the most popular programming languages. It is being used on several different software platforms. In a nutshell, there are a few computer architectures for which a C compiler does not exist.

It is a good idea to learn C because few other programming languages such as C++ and Java are also based on C which means you will be able to learn them more easily in the future.

9.1.1 Background

Like many other modern languages, C is derived from ALGOL (the first language to use a block structure). Although ALGOL was not accepted widely in the United States, it was widely used in Europe. ALGOL's introduction in the 1960s led the way for the development of structured programming concepts.

Before C, several other programming languages were developed. For example, in 1967 Martin Richards developed a language called BCPL (Basic Combined Programming Language). BCPL was basically a type-less (had no concept of data types) language which facilitated direct access of memory. This made it useful for system programmers. Then in 1970, Ken Thompson developed a language called B, which was used to develop the first version of UNIX. C was developed by Dennis Ritchie in 1972 that took concepts from ALGOL, BCPL, and B. In addition to the concepts of these languages, C also supports the concept of data types. Since UNIX operating system was also developed at Bell Laboratories along with C language, C and UNIX are strongly associated with each other.

For many years, C was mainly used in academic institutions, but with the release of different C compilers for commercial use and popularity of UNIX, C was widely accepted by computer professionals.

C (also known as Traditional C) was documented and popularized in the book *The C Programming Language* by Brian W. Kernighan and Dennis Ritchie in 1978. This book was so popular that the language came to be known as 'K & R C'. The tremendous growth of C language resulted in the development of different versions of the language that were similar but incompatible with each other. Therefore, in the year 1983, the American National Standards Institute (ANSI) started working on defining the standard for C. This standard was approved in December 1989 and came to be known as ANSI C. In 1990, the International Standards Organization (ISO) adopted the ANSI standard. This version of C came to be known as C89. In 1995, some minor changes were made to C89; the new modified version was known as C95. Figure 9.1 shows the taxonomy of C language. During 1990s, C++ and Java programming languages became popular among the users so the Standardization Committee of C felt that a few features of C++/Java if added to C would enhance its usefulness. So, in 1999 when some significant changes were made to C95, the modified version came to be known as C99. Some of the changes made in the C99 version are as follows:

- Extension to the character types, so that they can support even non-English characters
- Boolean data type
- Extension to the integer data type
- Inclusion of type definitions in the `for` statement
- Inclusion of imaginary and complex types
- Addition of //, better known as C++ style line comment

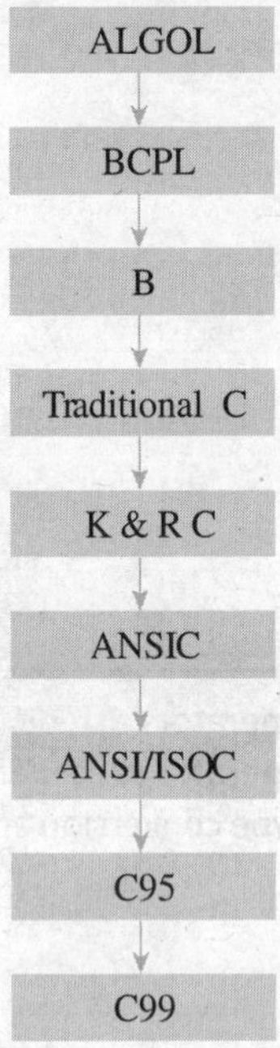

Figure 9.1 Taxonomy of C language

In 2007, work began on another revision of the C standard, informally called "C1X". The new version was officially published in 2011 and added numerous new features to C and the library, including type generic macros, anonymous structures, improved Unicode support, atomic operations, multi-threading, and bounds-checked functions. It also made some portions of the C99 library optional, and improved compatibility with C++. Later, the C17 version was published in June 2018. It introduced no new language features but simply corrected technical defects in C11. C2x is an informal name for the next (after C17) major C language standard revision. It is expected to be published in 2023 and would therefore be called C23.

9.1.2 Characteristics of C

C is a robust language whose rich set of built-in functions and operators can be used to write complex programs. The C compiler combines the features of assembly languages and high-level languages, which makes it best suited for writing system software as well as business packages. Some basic characteristics of C language that define the language and have led to its popularity as a programming language are listed below. In this book, we will learn all these aspects.

- C is a high-level programming language, which enables the programmer to concentrate on the problem at hand and not worry about the machine code on which the program would be run.
- Small size—C has only 32 keywords. This makes it relatively easy to learn as compared to other languages.
- C makes extensive use of function calls.
- C is well suited for structured programming. In this programming approach, C enables users to think of a problem in terms of functions/modules where the collection of all the modules makes up a complete program. This feature facilitates ease in program debugging, testing, and maintenance.
- Unlike PASCAL it supports loose typing (as a character can be treated as an integer and vice versa).
- Structured language as the code can be organized as a collection of one or more functions.
- Stable language. ANSI C was created in 1983 and since then it has not been revised.
- Quick language as a well written C program is likely to be as quick as or quicker than a program written in any other language. Since C programs make use of operators and data types, they are fast and efficient. For example, a program written to increment a value from 0–15000 using BASIC would take 50 seconds whereas a C program would do the same in just 1 second.
- Facilitates low level (bitwise) programming.
- Supports pointers to refer computer memory, arrays, structures, and functions.
- Core language. C is a core language as many other programming languages (like C++, Java, Perl, etc.) are based on C. If you know C, learning other computer languages becomes much easier.
- C is a portable language, i.e., a C program written for one computer can be run on another computer with little or no modification.
- C is an extensible language as it enables the user to add his own functions to the C library.
- C is often treated as the second best language for any given programming task. While the best language depends on the particular task to be performed, the second best language, on the other hand, will always be C.

9.1.3 Uses of C

C is a very simple language that is widely used by software professionals around the globe. The uses of C language can be summarized as follows:

- C language is primarily used for system programming. The portability, efficiency, the ability to access specific hardware addresses, and low runtime demand on system resources make it a good choice for implementing operating systems and embedded system applications.
- C has been so widely accepted by professionals that compilers, libraries, and interpreters of other programming languages are often written in C.
- For portability and convenience reasons, C is sometimes used as an intermediate language for implementation of other languages. Examples of compilers which use C this way are BitC, Gambit, the Glasgow Haskell Compiler, Squeak, and Vala.
- Basically, C was designed as a programming language and was not meant to be used as a compiler target language. Therefore, although C can be used as an intermediate language it is not an ideal option. This led to the development of C-based intermediate languages such as C--.
- C is widely used to implement end-user applications.

9.2 STRUCTURE OF A C PROGRAM

A C program is composed of preprocessor commands, a global declaration section, and one or more functions (Figure 9.2).

The preprocessor directives contain special instructions that indicate how to prepare the program for compilation. One of the most important and commonly used preprocessor commands is *include* which tells the compiler that to execute the program, some information is needed from the specified header file.

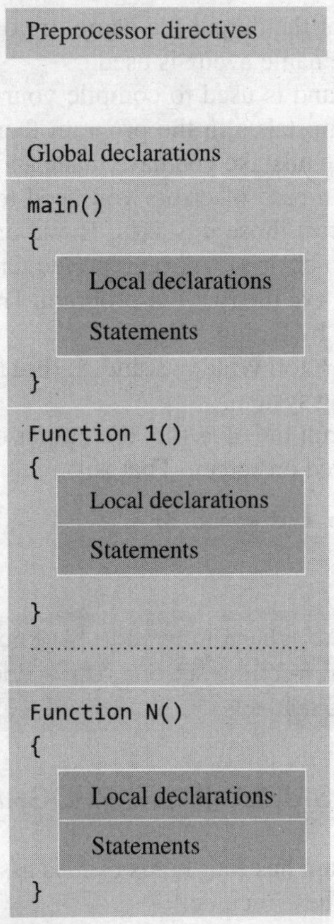

Figure 9.2 Structure of a C program

In this section we will omit the global declaration part and will revisit it in the chapter on Functions.

A C program contains one or more functions, where a function is defined as a group of C statements that are executed together. The statements in a C function are written in a logical sequence to perform a specific task. The `main()` function is the most important function and is a part of every C program. The execution of a C program begins at this function.

All functions (including `main()`) are divided into two parts—the declaration section and the statement section. The declaration section precedes the statement section and is used to describe the data that will be used in the function. Note that data declared within a function are known as local declaration as that data will be visible only within that function. Stated in other terms, the life-time of the data will be only till the function ends. The statement section in a function contains the code that manipulates the data to perform a specified task.

From the structure given above we can conclude that a C program can have any number of functions depending on the tasks that have to be performed, and each function can have any number of statements arranged according to specific meaningful sequence.

> **Note**
>
> Programmers can choose any name for functions. It is not mandatory to write `Function1`, `Function2`, etc., but with an exception that every program must contain one function that has its name as `main()`.

9.3 WRITING THE FIRST C PROGRAM

To write a C program, we first need to write the code. For this, open a text editor. If you are a Windows user you may use Notepad and if you prefer working on UNIX/Linux you can use *emacs* or *vi*. Once the text editor is opened on your screen, type the following statements:

```
#include <stdio.h>
int main()
{
  printf("\n Welcome to the world of C ");
  return 0;
}
```

Output

```
Welcome to the world of C
```

`#include <stdio.h>`

This is a preprocessor command that comes as the first statement in our code. All preprocessor commands start with symbol hash (#). The `#include` statement tells the compiler to include the standard input/output library or header file (`stdio.h`) in the program. This file has some in-built functions. By simply including this file in our code we can use these functions directly. The standard input/output header file contains functions for input and output of data such as reading values from the keyboard and printing the results on the screen.

`int main()`

Every C program contains a `main()` function which is the starting point of the program. `int` is the return value of the `main()` function. After all the statements in the program have been written, the last statement of the program will return an integer value to the operating system. The concepts will be clear to us when we read the chapter on Functions. So even if you do not understand certain things, do not worry.

> **Programming Tip:**
> If you do not place a parenthesis after `main`, a compiler error will be generated.

{ } The two curly brackets are used to group all the related statements of the `main` function. All the statements between the braces form the function body. The function body contains a set of instructions to perform the given task.

```
printf("\n Welcome to the
world of C ");
```

The `printf` function is defined in the `stdio.h` file and is used to print text on the screen. The message that has to be displayed on the screen is enclosed within double quotes and put inside brackets.

> **Programming Tip:**
> Placing a semi-colon after the parenthesis of `main` function will generate a compiler error.

The message is quoted because in C a text (also known as a string or a sequence of characters) is always put between inverted commas. '`\n`' is an escape sequence and represents a newline character. It is used to print the message on a new line on the screen. Like the newline character, the other escape sequences supported by C language are shown in Table 9.1.

Table 9.1 Escape sequences

Escape sequence	Purpose	Escape sequence	Purpose
\a	Audible signal	\?	Question mark
\b	Backspace	\\	Back slash
\t	Tab	\'	Single quote
\n	Newline	\"	Double quote
\v	Vertical tab	\0	Octal constant
\f	New page\ Clear screen	\x	Hexadecimal constant
\r	Carriage return		

> **Note**
> Escape sequences are actually non-printing control characters that begin with a backslash (\).

```
return 0;
```

This is a return command that is used to return the value 0 to the operating system to give an indication that there were no errors during the execution of the program.

> **Note**
> Every statement in the `main` function ends with a semi-colon (;).

Now that you have written all the statements using the text editor, save the text file as `first.c`. If you are a Windows user then open the command prompt by clicking `Start-<Run` and typing 'command' and clicking `Ok`.

Using the command prompt, change to the directory in which you had saved your file and then type:

```
C:\<tc first.c
```

In case you are working on UNIX/Linux operating system, then exit the text editor and type

```
$cc first.c -ofirst
```

The `-o` is for the output file name. If you leave out the `-o` then the file name `a.out` is used.

This command is used to compile your C program. If there are any mistakes in the program then the compiler will tell you the mistake you have made and on which line you made it. In case of errors you need to re-open your .c file and correct those mistakes. However, if everything is right then no error(s) will be reported and the compiler will create an . exe file for your program. This `.exe` file can be directly run by typing

'`hello.exe`' for Windows and '`./hello`' for UNIX/Linux operating system.

When you run the `.exe` file, the output of the program will be displayed on screen. That is,

```
Welcome to the world of C
```

> **Note**
> The `printf` and `return` statements have been indented or moved away from the left side. This is done to make the code more readable.

9.4 FILES USED IN A C PROGRAM

Every C program has four kinds of files associated with it (Figure 9.3). These include:

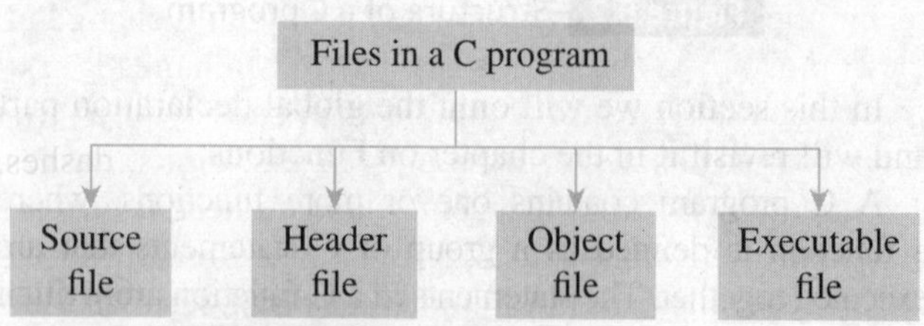

Figure 9.3 Files in a C program

9.4.1 Source Code Files

The source code file contains the source code of the program. The file extension of any C source code file is '`.c`'. This file contains C source code that defines the `main` function and maybe other functions. The `main()` function is the starting point of execution when you successfully compile and run the program. A C program in general may include even other source code files (with the file extension `.c`).

9.4.2 Header Files

When working with large projects, it is often desirable to separate out certain subroutines from the `main()` function of the program. There also may be a case that the same subroutine has to be used in different programs. In the latter case, one option is to copy the code of the desired subroutine from one program to another. But copying the code is often tedious as well as error prone and makes maintainability more difficult.

So, another option is to make subroutines and store them in a different file known as header file. The advantages of header files can be realized in the following cases:

- The programmer wants to use the same subroutines in different programs. For this, he simply has to compile the source code of the subroutines once, and then link to the resulting object file in any other program in which the functionalities of these subroutines are required.
- The programmer wants to change or add subroutines, and have those changes reflected in all the other programs. In this case, he just needs to change the source file for the subroutines, recompile its source code, and then re-link programs that use them. This way time can be saved as compared to editing the subroutines in every individual program that uses them.

Programming Tip:
Missing the inclusion of appropriate header files in a C program will generate an error. Such a program may compile but the linker will give an error message as it will not be able to find the functions used in the program.

Thus, we see that using a header file produces the same results as copying the header file into each source file that needs it. Also when a header file is included, the related declarations appear in only one place. If in future we need to modify the subroutines, we just need to make the changes in one place, and programs that include the header file will automatically use the new version when recompiled later. There is no need to find and change all the copies of the subroutine that has to be changed.

Conventionally, header files names ends with a '`.h`' extension and names can use only letters, digits, dashes, and underscores. Although some standard header files are automatically available to C programmers, in addition to those header files, the programmer may have his own user-defined header files.

Standard Header Files In the program that we have written till now, we used `printf()` function that has not been written by us. We do not know the details of how this function works. Such functions that are provided by all C compilers are included in standard header files. Examples of these standard header files include:

- `string.h` : for string handling functions
- `stdlib.h` : for some miscellaneous functions
- `stdio.h` : for standardized input and output functions
- `math.h` : for mathematical functions
- `alloc.h` : for dynamic memory allocation

All the header files are referenced at the start of the source code file that uses one or more functions from that file.

9.4.3 Object Files

Object files are generated by the compiler as a result of processing the source code file. Object files contain compact binary code of the function definitions. Linker uses these object files to produce an executable file (`.exe` file) by combining the object files together. Object files have a '`.o`' extension, although some operating systems including Windows and MS-DOS have a '`.obj`' extension for the object file.

9.4.4 Binary Executable Files

The binary executable file is generated by the linker. The linker links the various object files to produce a binary file that can be directly executed. On Windows operating system, the executable files have a '`.exe`' extension.

9.5 COMPILING AND EXECUTING C PROGRAMS

C is a compiled language. So once a C program is written, you must run it through a C compiler that can create an executable file to be run by the computer. While the C program is human-readable, the executable file, on the other hand, is a machine-readable file available in an executable form.

The mechanical part of running a C program begins with one or more program source files, and ends with an executable file, which can be run on a computer.

The programming process starts with creating a source file that consists of the statements of the program written in C language. This source file usually contains ASCII characters and can be produced with a text editor, such as Windows notepad, or in an Integrated Design Environment.

The source file is then processed by a special program called a compiler.

Note
Every programming language has its own compiler.

The compiler translates the source code into an object code. The object code contains the machine instructions for the CPU, and calls to the operating system API (Application Programming Interface).

However, even the object file is not an executable file. Therefore, in the next step, the object file is processed with another special program called a linker. While there is a different compiler for every individual language, the same linker is used for object files regardless of the original language in which the new program was written. The output of the linker is an executable or runnable file. The process is shown in Figure 9.4.

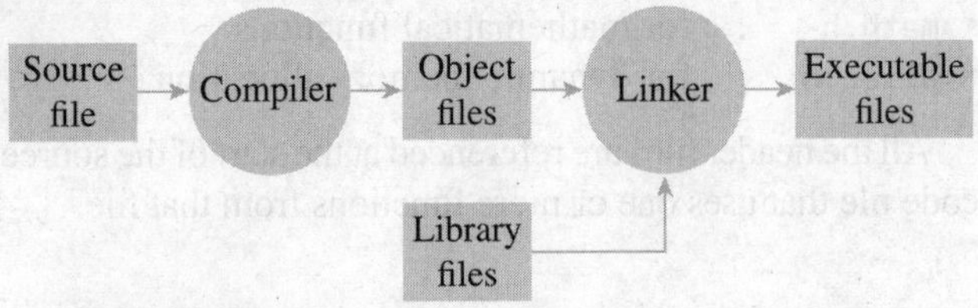

Figure 9.4 Overview of compilation and execution process

In C language programs, there are two kinds of source files. In addition to the main (.c) source file, which contains executable statements there are also header (.h) source files. Since all input and output in C programs is done through library functions, every C program therefore uses standard header files. These header files should be written as part of the source code for modular C programs.

The compilation process shown in Figure 9.5 is done in two steps. In the first step, the preprocessor program reads the source file as text, and produces another text file as output. Source code lines which begin with the # symbol are actually not written in C but in the preprocessor language. The output of the preprocessor is a text file which does not contain any preprocessor statements. This file is ready to be processed by the compiler. The linker combines the object file with library routines (supplied with the compiler) to produce the final executable file.

In modular programming, the source code is divided into two or more source files. All these source files are compiled separately thereby producing multiple object files. These object files are combined by the linker to produce an executable file (Figure 9.6).

9.6 USING COMMENTS

Many a time the meaning or the purpose of the program code is not clear to the reader. Therefore, it is a good programming practice to place some comments in the code to help the reader understand the code clearly. Comments are just a way of explaining what a program does. It is merely an internal program documentation. The compiler ignores the comments when forming the object file. This means that the comments are non-executable statements. C supports two types of comments.

- // is used to comment a single statement. This is known as a *line comment*. A line comment can be placed anywhere on the line and it does not require to be specifically ended as the end of the line automatically *ends the line*.
- /* is used to comment multiple statements. A /* is ended with */ and all statements that lie within these characters are commented. This type of comment is known as *block comment*.

Programming Tip:
Not putting the */ after the termination of the block comment is a compiler error.

Note that commented statements are not executed by the compiler. Rather, they are ignored by the compiler as they are simply added in the program to make the code understandable by the programmer to other people who

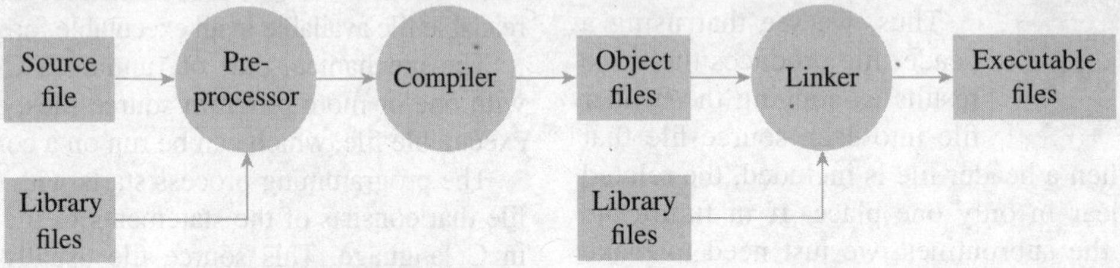

Figure 9.5 Preprocessing before compilation

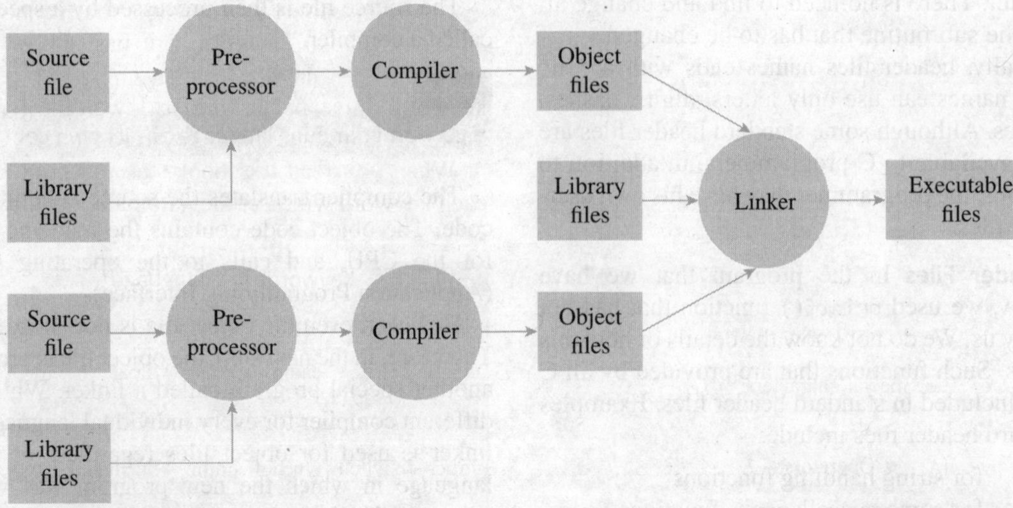

Figure 9.6 Modular programming—the complete compilation and execution process

read it. It is a good habit to always put a comment at the top of a program that tells you what the program does. This will help in defining the usage of the program the moment someone opens it.

Commented statements can be used anywhere in the program. You can also use comments in between your code to explain a piece of code that is a bit complicated. The code given below shows the way in which we can make use of comments in our first program.

```
/* Author: Reema Thareja
   Description: To print 'Welcome to the
    world of C' on the screen */
#include <stdio.h>
int main()
{
   printf("\n Welcome to the world of C ");
    // prints message
   return 0; // returns a value 0 to the
     operating system
}
```

Output

```
Welcome to the world of C
```

Since comments are not executed by the compiler, they do not affect the execution speed and the size of the compiled program. Therefore, using comments liberally in your programs aids other users in understanding the operations of the program as well as in debugging and testing.

9.7 C TOKENS

Tokens are the basic building blocks in C language. You may think of a token as the smallest individual unit in a C program. This means that a program is constructed using a combination of these tokens. There are six main types of tokens in C. They are shown in Figure 9.7.

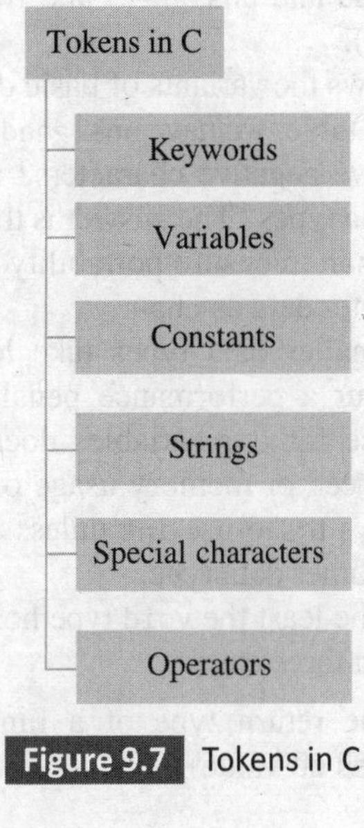

Figure 9.7 Tokens in C

9.8 CHARACTER SET IN C

Like in natural languages, computer languages also use a character set that defines the fundamental units used to represent information. In C, a character means any letter from English alphabet, a digit or a special symbol used to represent information. These characters when combined together form tokens that act as basic building blocks of a C program. The character set of C can therefore be given as:

a. English alphabet: Include both lower case (`a - z`) as well as upper case (`A - Z`) letters
b. Digits: Include numerical digits from `0` to `9`
c. Special characters: Include symbols such as `~, @, %, ^, &, *,{, }, <, >, =, _, +, -, $, /, (, ), \, ;, :, [, ], ', ", ?, ., !, |`
d. White space characters: These characters are used to print a blank space on the screen. They are shown in Figure 9.8.
e. Escape sequence: Escape sequences have already been discussed in Section 2.3.

White space character	Meaning
\b	Blank space
\t	Horizontal tab
\v	Vertical return
\r	Carriage return
\f	Form feed
\n	New line

Figure 9.8 White space characters in C

9.9 KEYWORDS

Like every computer language, C has a set of reserved words often known as keywords that cannot be used as an identifier. All keywords are basically a sequence of characters that have a fixed meaning. By convention all keywords must be written in lowercase (small) letters. Table 9.2 shows the list of keywords in C.

When you read this book, the meaning and utility of each keyword will become automatically clear to you.

Table 9.2 Keywords in C language

auto	break	case	char	const	continue	default
double	else	enum	extern	float	for	goto
int	long	register	return	short	signed	sizeof
struct	switch	typedef	union	unsigned	void	volatile
do	if	static	while			

9.10 IDENTIFIERS

Identifiers, as the name suggests, help us to identify data and other objects in the program. Identifiers are basically the names given to program elements such as variables, arrays, and functions. Identifiers may consist of sequence of letters, numerals, or underscores.

9.10.1 Rules for Forming Identifier Names

Some rules have to be followed while forming identifier names. They are as follows:

- Identifiers cannot include any special characters or punctuation marks (like #, $, ^, ?, ., etc.) except the underscore '_'.
- There cannot be two successive underscores.
- Keywords cannot be used as identifiers.
- The case of alphabetic characters that form the identifier name is significant. For example, 'FIRST' is different from 'first' and 'First'.
- Identifiers must begin with a letter or an underscore. However, use of underscore as the first character must be avoided because several compiler-defined identifiers in the standard C library have underscore as their first character. Hence, inadvertently duplicated names may cause definition conflicts.
- Identifiers can be of any reasonable length. They should not contain more than 31 characters. They can actually be longer than 31, but the compiler looks at only the first 31 characters of the name.

Programming Tip:
C is a case sensitive language. If you type `printf` function as `Printf`, then an error will be generated.

Although it is a good practice to use meaningful identifier names, it is not compulsory. Good identifiers are descriptive but short. To cut short the identifier, you may use abbreviations. C allows identifiers (names) to be up to 63 characters long. If a name is longer than 63 characters, then only the first 31 characters are used.

As a general practice, if the identifier is a little long, then you may use an underscore to separate the parts of the name or you may use capital letters for each part.

Examples of valid identifiers include:

```
roll_number, marks, name, emp_number,
basic_pay, HRA, DA, dept_code, DeptCode,
RollNo, EMP_NO
```

Examples of invalid identifiers include:

```
23_student, %marks, @name, #emp_number,
basic.pay, -HRA, (DA), &dept_code, auto
```

Note

C is a case-sensitive language. Therefore `rno`, `Rno`, `RNo`, `RNO` are considered as different identifiers.

9.11 BASIC DATA TYPES IN C

C language provides very few basic data types. Table 9.3 lists the basic data types, their size, range, and usage for a C programmer on a 16-bit computer. In addition to this, we also have variants of `int` and `float` data types.

Table 9.3 Basic data types in C

Data type	Keyword used	Size in bytes	Range	Use
Character	char	1	–128 to 127	To store characters
Integer	int	2	–32768 to 32767	To store integer numbers
Floating point	float	4	3.4E–38 to 3.4E+38	To store floating point numbers
Double	double	8	1.7E–308 to 1.7E+308	To store big floating point numbers
Valueless	void	0	Valueless	—

The `char` data type is of one byte and is used to store single characters. Note that C does not provide any data type for storing text. This is because text is made up of individual characters.

You will be surprised to see that the range of `char` is given as –128 to 127. `char` is supposed to store characters not numbers, so why this range? The answer is that, in memory characters are stored in their ASCII codes. For example, the character 'A' has the ASCII code 65. In memory we will not store 'A' but 65 (in binary number format).

In addition, C also supports four modifiers—two sign specifiers (`signed` and `unsigned`) and two size specifiers (`short` and `long`).

Table 9.4 shows the variants of basic data types. As can be seen from the table, we have `unsigned char` and `signed char`. Do we have negative characters? No, then why do we have such data types? The answer is that we use `signed` and `unsigned char` to ensure portability of programs that store non-character data as `char`.

While the smaller data types take less memory, the larger types incur a performance penalty. Although the data type we use for our variables does not have a big impact on the speed or memory usage of the application, we should always try to use `int` unless there is a special need to use any other data type.

Last but not the least the `void` type holds no value. It is primarily used in three cases:

- To specify the return type of a function (when the function returns no value)

Table 9.4 Detailed list of data types

Data type	Size in bytes	Range
char	1	–128 to 127
unsigned char	1	0 to 255
signed char	1	–128 to 127
int	2	–32768 to 32767
unsigned int	2	0 to 65535
signed int	2	–32768 to 32767
short int	2	–32768 to 32767
unsigned short int	2	0 to 65535
signed short int	2	–32768 to 32767
long int	4	–2147483648 to 2147483647
unsigned long int	4	0 to 4294967295
signed long int	4	–2147483648 to 2147483647
float	4	3.4E–38 to 3.4E+38
double	8	1.7E–308 to 1.7E+308
long double	10	3.4E–4932 to 1.1E+4932

- To specify the parameters of the function (when the function accepts no arguments from the caller)
- To create generic pointers. We will read about generic pointers in the chapter on Pointers.

We will discuss the `void` data type in detail in the coming chapters.

Note

Unsigned `int/char` keeps the sign bit free and makes the entire word available for storage of the non-negative numbers.

Sign bit is the leftmost bit of a memory word which is used to determine the sign of the content stored in that word. When it is 0, the value is positive and when it is 1, the value is negative.

9.11.1 How are Float and Double Stored?

In computer memory, float and double values are stored in mantissa and exponent forms where the exponent represents power of 2 (not 10). The number of bytes used to represent a floating point number generally depends on the precision of the value. While float is used to declare single-precision values, double is used to represent double-precision values.

Floating-point numbers use the IEEE (Institute of Electrical and Electronics Engineers) format to represent mantissa and exponents. According to the IEEE format, a floating point value in its binary form is known as a *normalized form*. In the normalized form, the exponent is adjusted in such a way that the binary point in the mantissa always lies to the right of the most significant non-zero digit.

Example 9.1

Convert the floating point number 5.32 into an IEEE normalized form.

2 | 5 | R		$0.32 \times 2 = 0.64$ | 0	
2 | 2 | 1	Write the remainders in the reverse order of generation	$0.64 \times 2 = 1.28$ | 1	Write the whole numbers in the same order of generation
2 | 1 | 0		$0.28 \times 2 = 0.56$ | 0	
0 | 1		$0.56 \times 2 = 1.12$ | 1	

Thus, the binary equivalent of 5.32 = 101.0101.
The normalized form of this binary number is obtained by adjusting the exponent until the decimal point is to the right of the most significant 1.
Therefore, the normalized binary equivalent = 1.010101×2^2.

Moreover, the IEEE format for storing floating point numbers uses a sign bit, mantissa, and the exponent (Figure 9.9). The sign bit denotes the sign of the value. If the value is positive, the sign bit contains 0 and in case the value is negative it stores 1.

Sign bit	Exponent	Mantissa

Figure 9.9 IEEE format for storing floating point numbers

Generally, exponent is an integer value stored in unsigned binary format after adding a positive bias. In other words, because exponents are stored in an unsigned form, the exponent is biased by half its possible value. For type `float`, the bias is 127; for type `double`, it is 1023. You can compute the actual exponent value by subtracting the bias value from the exponent value. Finally, the normalized binary equivalent is stored in such a way that lower byte is stored at higher memory address. For example, `ABCD` is actually stored as `DCBA`.

9.12 VARIABLES

A *variable* is defined as a meaningful name given to a data storage location in computer memory. When using a variable, we actually refer to address of the memory where the data is stored. C language supports two basic kinds of variables—numeric and character.

9.12.1 Numeric Variables

Numeric variables can be used to store either integer values or floating point values. While an integer value is a whole number without a fraction part or decimal point, a floating point value can have a decimal point.

Numeric variables may also be associated with modifiers, such as `short`, `long`, `signed`, and `unsigned`. The difference between signed and unsigned numeric variables is that signed variables can be either negative or positive but unsigned variables can only be positive. Therefore, by using an unsigned variable we can increase the maximum positive range. When we do not specify the `signed/unsigned` modifier, C language automatically takes it as a signed variable. To declare an unsigned variable, the `unsigned` modifier must be explicitly added during the declaration of the variable.

9.12.2 Character Variables

Character variables are just single characters enclosed within single quotes. These characters could be any character from the ASCII character set—letters (`'a'`, `'A'`), numerals (`'2'`), or special characters (`'&'`). In C, a number that is given in single quotes is not the same as a number without them. This is because `2` is treated as an integer value but `'2'` is a considered character not an integer.

9.12.3 Declaring Variables

Each variable to be used in the program must be declared. To declare a variable, specify the data type of the variable followed by its name. The data type indicates the kind of values that the variable will store. Variable names should always be meaningful and must reflect the purpose of their usage in the program. The memory location of the variable is of importance to the compiler only and not to the programmer. Programmers must only be concerned with accessing data through their symbolic names. In C, variable declaration always ends with a semicolon, for example:

```
int emp_num;
float salary;
char grade;
double balance_amount;
unsigned short int acc_no;
```

In C variables can be declared at any place in the program but two things must be kept in mind. First, variables should be declared before using them. Second, variables should be declared closest to their first point of use to make the source code easier to maintain.

C allows multiple variables of the same type to be declared in one statement. So the following statement is legal in C.

```
float temp_in_celsius, temp_in_farenheit;
```

In C variables are declared at three basic places as follows:

- When a variable is declared inside a function it is known as a *local variable*.
- When a variable is declared in the definition of function parameters it is known as a *formal parameter* (we will study this in the chapter on Functions).
- When the variable is declared outside all functions, it is known as a *global variable*.

Note

A variable cannot be of type `void`.

9.12.4 Initializing Variables

While declaring variables, we can also initialize them with some value. For example,

```
int emp_num = 7;
float salary = 2156.35;
char grade = 'A';
double balance_amount = 100000000;
```

The initializer applies only to the variable defined immediately before it. Therefore, the statement

```
int count, flag = 1;
```

initializes the variable `flag` and not `count`. If you want both the variables to be declared in a single statement then write,

```
int count = 0, flag = 1;
```

When variables are declared but not initialized they usually contain garbage values (there are exceptions to this that we will study later).

9.13 CONSTANTS

Constants are identifiers whose values do not change. While values of variables can be changed at any time, values of constants can never be changed. Constants are used to define fixed values like mathematical constant pi or the charge on an electron so that their value does not get changed in the program even by mistake.

A constant is an explicit data value specified by the programmer. The value of the constant is known to the compiler at the compile time. C allows the programmer to specify constants of integer type, floating point type, character type, and string type (Figure 9.10).

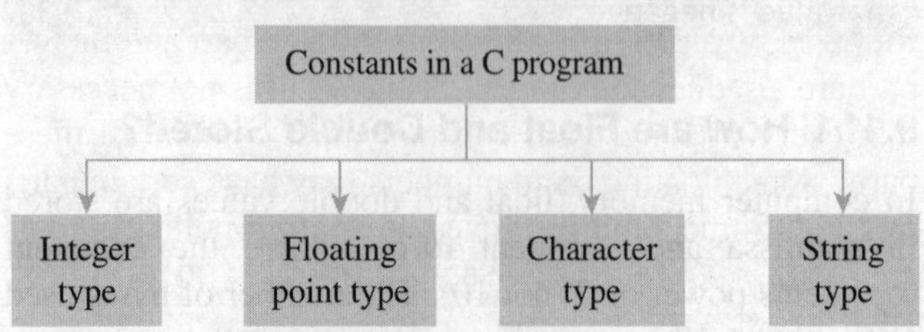

Figure 9.10 Constants in C

9.13.1 Integer Constants

A constant of integer type consists of a sequence of digits. For example, `1, 34, 567, 8907` are valid integer constants.

A literal integer like 1234 is of type int by default. For a long integer constant the literal is succeeded with either 'L' or 'l' (like 1234567L). Similarly, an unsigned int literal is written with a 'U' or 'u' suffix (e.g. 12U). Therefore, 1234L, 1234l, 1234U, 1234u, 1234LU, 1234ul are all valid integer constants.

Integer literals can be expressed in decimal, octal, or hexadecimal notation. By default an integer is expressed in decimal notation. Decimal integers consist of a set of digits, 0 through 9, preceded by an optional - or + sign. Examples of decimal integer constants include: 123, -123, +123, and 0.

While writing integer constants, embedded spaces, commas, and non-digit characters are not allowed. Therefore, integer constants given below are totally invalid in C.

```
123 456
12,34,567
$123
```

An integer constant preceded by a zero (0) is an octal number. Octal integers consist of a set of digits, 0 through 7. Examples of octal integers include

```
012   0   01234
```

Similarly, an integer constant is expressed in hexadecimal notation if it is preceded with 0x or 0X. Hexadecimal numbers contain digits from 0-9 and letters A through F, which represent numbers 10 through 15. For example, decimal 72 is equivalent to 0110 in octal notation and 0x48 in hexadecimal notation. Examples of hexadecimal integers are 0X12, 0x7F, 0xABCD, 0X1A3B.

Note

In C, a decimal integer constant is treated as an unsigned long if its magnitude exceeds that of signed long. An octal or hexadecimal integer that exceeds the limit of int is taken to be unsigned. If even this limit is exceeded, it is taken as long; and in case this limit is exceeded, it is treated as unsigned long.

9.13.2 Floating Point Constants

Integer numbers are inadequate to express numbers that have a fractional part. A floating point constant consists of an integer part, a decimal point, a fractional part, and an exponent field containing an e or E (e means exponent) followed by an integer where the fraction part and integer part are a sequence of digits. However, it is not necessary that every floating point constant must contain all these parts. Some floating point numbers may have certain parts missing. Some valid examples of floating point numbers are: 0.02, -0.23, 123.456, +0.34 123, 0.9, -0.7, +0.8 etc.

A literal like 0.07 is treated as of type double by default. To make it a float type literal, you must specify it using suffix F or f. Consider some valid floating point literals given below. (Note that suffix L is for long double.)

```
0.02F  0.34f  3.141592654L  0.002146  2.146E-3
```

A floating point number may also be expressed in scientific notation. In this notation, the mantissa is either a floating point number or an integer and exponent is an integer with an optional plus or minus sign. Therefore, the numbers given below are valid floating point numbers

```
0.5e2  14E-2  1.2e+3  2.1E-3  -5.6e-2
```

Thus, we see that scientific notation is used to express numbers that are either very small or very large. For example,

```
120000000 = 1.2E8  and  -0.000000025 = -2.5E-8
```

9.13.3 Character Constants

A character constant consists of a single character enclosed in single quotes. For example, 'a' and '@' are character constants. In computers, characters are stored using machine's character set using ASCII codes. All escape sequences mentioned in Table 9.1 are also character constants.

9.13.4 String Constants

A string constant is a sequence of characters enclosed in double quotes. So "a" is not the same as 'a'. The characters comprising the string constant are stored in successive memory locations. When a string constant is encountered in a C program, the compiler records the address of the first character and appends a null character ('\0') to the string to mark the end of the string. Thus, length of a string constant is equal to number of characters in the string plus 1 (for the null character). Therefore, the length of string literal "hello" is 6.

9.13.5 Declaring Constants

To declare a constant, precede the normal variable declaration with const keyword and assign it a value. For example,

```
const float pi = 3.14;
```

The const keyword specifies that the value of pi cannot change.

However, another way to designate a constant is to use the pre-processor command define. Like other preprocessor commands, define is preceded with a # symbol. Although #define statements can be placed anywhere in a C program, it is always recommended that these statements be placed at the beginning of the program to make them easy to find and modify at a later stage. Look at the example given below which defines the value of pi using define.

```
#define pi 3.14159
#define service_tax 0.12
```

In these examples, the value of pi will never change but service tax may change. Whenever the value of the service tax is altered, it needs to be corrected only in the define statement.

When the preprocessor reformats the program to be compiled by the compiler, it replaces each defined name (like `pi`, `service_tax`) in the source program with its corresponding value. Hence, it just works like the Find-and-Replace command available in a text editor.

Let us take a look at some rules that need to be applied to a `#define` statement which defines a constant.

Rule 1: Constant names are usually written in capital letters to visually distinguish them from other variable names which are normally written in lower case characters. Note that this is just a convention and not a rule.

Rule 2: No blank spaces are permitted between the # symbol and `define` keyword.

Rule 3: Blank space must be used between `#define` and constant name and between constant name and constant value.

Rule 4: `#define` is a pre-processor compiler directive and not a statement. Therefore, it does not end with a semi-colon.

9.14 INPUT/OUTPUT STATEMENTS IN C

Before performing input and output in C programs, let us first understand the concept from scratch. This section deals with the basic understanding of the streams involved in accepting input and printing output in C programs.

9.14.1 Streams

A stream is the source of data as well as the destination of data. Streams are associated with a physical device such as a monitor or a file stored on the secondary memory. C uses two forms of streams—text and binary, as shown in Figure 9.11.

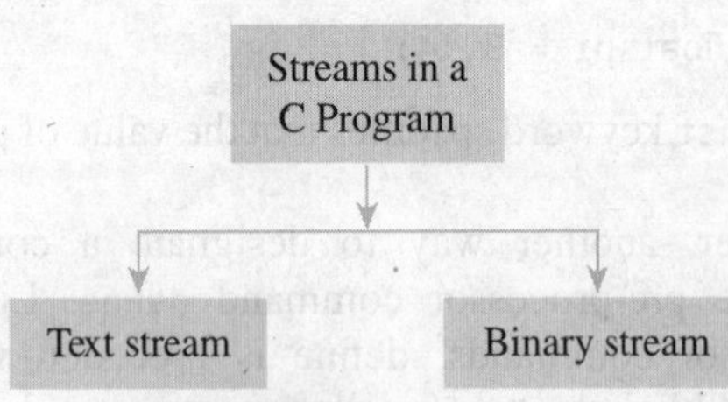

Figure 9.11 Streams in C

In a text stream, sequence of characters is divided into lines with each line being terminated with a new-line character (`\n`). On the other hand, a binary stream contains data values using their memory representation.

We can do input/output from the keyboard/monitor or from any file but in this chapter we will assume that the source of data is the keyboard and destination of the data is the monitor (Figure 9.12). File handling, i.e., handling input and output via C programs, will be discussed later as a separate chapter.

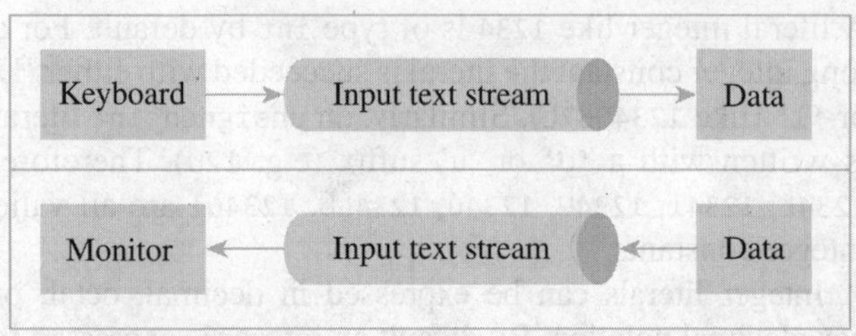

Figure 9.12 Input and output streams in C

9.14.2 Formatting Input/Output

C language supports two formatting functions `printf` and `scanf`. `printf` is used to convert data stored in the program into a text stream for output to the monitor, and `scanf` is used to convert the text stream coming from the keyboard to data values and stores them in program variables. In this section, we will discuss these functions.

Background

The most fundamental operation in a C program is to accept input values from a standard input device (keyboard) and output the data produced by the program to a standard output device (monitor). So far we had been assigning values to variables using the assignment operator =. For example,

```
int a = 3;
```

But what if we want to assign value to variable that is inputted by the user at run-time? This is done by using the `scanf` function that reads data from the keyboard. Similarly, for outputting results of the program, `printf` function is used that sends results to a terminal. Like `printf` and `scanf`, there are different functions in C that can carry out the input/output operations. These functions are collectively known as Standard Input/Output Library. A program that uses standard input/output functions must contain the following statement at the beginning of the program:

```
#include <stdio.h>
```

9.14.3 printf()

The `printf` function (stands for print formatting) is used to display information required by the user and also prints the values of the variables. For this, the `printf` function takes data values, converts them to a text stream using formatting specifications in the control string and passes the resulting text stream to the standard output. The control string may contain zero or more conversion specifications, textual data, and control characters to be displayed (Figure 9.13).

Each data value to be formatted into the text stream is described using a separate conversion specification in the control string. The specification in the control string describes the data value's type, size and specific format information as shown in Figure 9.13.

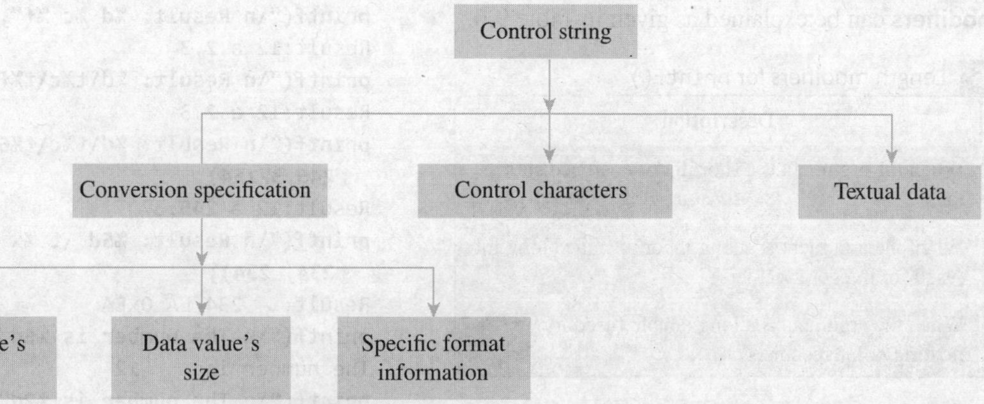

Figure 9.13 printf() function in C

The syntax of printf function can be given as

```
printf ("control string", variable list);
```

The function accepts two parameters—control string and variable list. The control string may also contain the text to be printed like instructions to the user, captions, identifiers, or any other text to make the output readable. In some printf statements you may find only a text string that has to be displayed on screen (as seen in the first program in this chapter). The control characters can also be included in the printf statement. These control characters include \n, \t, \r, \a, etc.

The parameter control string in the printf() function is nothing but a C string that contains the text that has to be written on to the standard output device. After the control string, the function can have as many additional arguments as specified in the control string.

Note that there must be enough arguments, otherwise the result will be completely unpredictable. However, if by mistake you specify more number of arguments, the excess arguments will simply be ignored. The prototype of the control string can be given as follows.

```
%[flags][width][.precision][length modifier]
   type specifier
```

Each control string must begin with a % sign. The % character specifies how the next variable in the list of variables has to be printed. After % sign follows:

Flags is an optional argument which specifies output justification such as numerical sign, trailing zeros or octal, decimal, or hexadecimal prefixes. Table 9.5 shows the different types of flags with their description.

Table 9.5 Flags in printf() function

Flags	Description
–	Left-justify within the given field width
+	Display the data with its numeric sign (either + or –)
#	Used to provide additional specifiers like o, x, X, 0, 0x, or 0X for octal and hexadecimal values, respectively, for values different than zero
0	The number is left-padded with zeros (0) instead of spaces

Note that when data is shorter than the specified width then by default the data is right justified. To left justify the data use minus sign (–) in the flags field.

When the data value to be printed is smaller than the width specified, then padding is used to fill the unused spaces. By default, the data is padded with blank spaces. If zero is used in the flag field then the data is padded with zeros. One thing to remember here is that zero flag is ignored when used with left justification because adding zeros after a number changes its value.

Width is an optional argument which specifies the minimum number of positions in the output. If data needs more space than specified, then printf overrides the width specified by the user. However, if the number of output characters is smaller than the specified width, then the output would be right justified with blank spaces to the left. Width is a very important field especially when you have to align output in columns. However, if the user does not mention any width then the output will take just enough room for data.

Precision is an optional argument which specifies the maximum number of characters to print.

- For integer specifiers (d, i, o, u, x, X): precision flag specifies the minimum number of digits to be written. However, if the value to be written is shorter than this number, the result is padded with leading zeros. Otherwise, if the value is longer, it is not truncated.
- For character strings, precision specifies the maximum number of characters to be printed.
- For floating point numbers, the precision flag specifies the number of decimal places to be printed.

Its format can be given as .m, where m specifies the number of decimal digits. When no precision modifier is specified, printf prints six decimal positions.

When both width and precision fields are used, width must be large enough to contain the integral value of the number, the decimal point and the number of digits after the decimal point. Therefore, a conversion specification %7.3f means print a floating point value of maximum 7 digits where 3 digits are allotted for the digits after the decimal point.

Length modifiers can be explained as given in Table 9.6.

Table 9.6 Length modifiers for `printf()`

Length	Description
h	When the argument is a short int or unsigned short int
l	When the argument is a long int or unsigned long int (used for integer specifiers)
L	When the argument is a long double (used for floating point specifiers)

Type specifiers are used to define the type and the interpretation of the value of the corresponding argument (Table 9.7).

Table 9.7 Type specifiers for `printf()`

Type	Qualifying input
c	For single characters
d	For integer values
f	For floating point numbers
E, e	Floating point numbers in exponential format
G, g	Floating point numbers in the shorter of e format
o	For octal numbers
s	For a sequence of (string of) characters
u	For unsigned integer values
X, x	For hexadecimal values

Note that if the user specifies a wrong specifier then unpredictable things will be seen on the screen and the error might propagate to other values in the `printf()` list.

The most simple `printf` statement is

```
printf ("Welcome to the world of C language");
```

When executed, the function prompts the message enclosed in the quotation to be displayed on the screen.

Note

The minimum field width and precision specifiers are usually constants. However, they may also be provided by arguments to `printf()`. This is done by using the * modifier as shown in the printf statement below.

```
printf("%*.*f", 10, 4, 1234.34);
```

Here, the minimum field width is 10, the precision is 4, and the value to be displayed is 1234.34.

Example 9.2

```
printf("\n Result: %d%c%f", 12, 'a', 2.3);
Result:12a2.3
printf("\n Result: %d %c %f", 12, 'a', 2.3);
Result:12 a 2.3
printf("\n Result: %d\t%c\t%f", 12, 'a', 2.3);
Result:12 a 2.3
printf("\n Result: %d\t%c\t%6.2f", 12, 'a',
   245.37154);
Result:12 a 245.37
printf("\n Result: %5d \t %x \t %#x", 234,
   234, 234);
Result:   234 EA OxEA
printf("\n The number is %6d", 12);
The number is     12
printf("\n The number is %2d", 1234);
The number is 1234
printf("\n The number is %6d", 1234);
The number is   1234
printf("\n The number is
%-6d", 1234);
The number is 1234
// 2 _ indicates
2 white spaces
printf("\n The number is
%06d", 1234);
The number is 001234
printf("\n The price of this item is %09.2f
   rupees", 123.456);
The price of this item is 000123.45 rupees
printf("\n This is \'so\' beautiful");
This is 'so' beautiful
printf("\n This is \"so\" beautiful");
This is "so" beautiful
printf("\n This is \\ so beautiful ");
This is \ so beautiful
printf("\n a = |%-+7.2f| b = %0+7.2f c =
   %-0+8.2f", 1.2, 1.2, 1.2);
a = +1.20    b = 0001.20 c = 1.20
```

Programming Tip: Not placing a comma after the format string in a read or write statement is a compiler error.

(Note that in this example, - means left justify, + means display the sign, 7 specifies the width, and 2 specifies the precision.)

```
printf("\n %7.4f \n %7.2f \n %-7.2f \n %f
   \n %10.2e \n %11.4e \n %-10.2e \n %e",
   98.7654, 98.7654, 98.7654, 98.7654,
   98.7654, 98.7654, 98.7654, 98.7654);
98.7654
  98.77
98.77
98.7654
  9.88e+01
9.8765e+01
9.88e+01
9.876540e+01

char ch = 'A';
printf("\n %c \n %3c \n %5c", ch, ch, ch);
A
  A
    A
```

> **Programming Tip:**
> Placing an address operator with a variable in the printf statement will generate a run-time error.

```
char str[] = "Good Morning";
printf("\n %s", str);
printf("\n %20s", str);
printf("\n %20.10s", str);
printf("\n %.7s", str);
printf("\n %-20.10s",
 str);
printf("\n %7s", str);
```

```
Good Morning
        Good Morning
          Good Morni
Good Mo
Good Morni
Good Morning
```

(Note that in the last printf statement the complete string "Good Morning" is printed. This is because if data needs more space than specified, then printf function overrides the width specified by the user.)

9.14.4 scanf()

The scanf() function stands for scan formatting and is used to read formatted data from the keyboard. The scanf function takes a text stream from the keyboard, extracts and formats data from the stream according to a format control string and then stores the data in specified program variables. The syntax of the scanf() function can be given as:

```
scanf("control string", arg1, arg2, arg3,
  ..........argn);
```

The *control string* specifies the type and format of the data that has to be obtained from the keyboard and stored in the memory locations pointed by arguments arg1, arg2,…, argn, i.e., the arguments are actually the variable addresses where each piece of data is to be stored.

The prototype of the control string can be given as:

```
%[*][width][modifier]type
```

Here * is an optional argument that suppresses assignment of the input field, i.e., it indicates that data should be read from the stream but ignored (not stored in the memory location).

Width is an optional argument that specifies the maximum number of characters to be read. However, fewer characters will be read if the scanf function encounters a white space or an inconvertible character because the moment scanf function encounters a white space character it will stop processing further.

Modifier is an optional argument that can be h, l, or L for the data pointed by the corresponding additional arguments. Modifier h is used for short int or unsigned short int, l is used for long int, unsigned long int, or double values. Finally, L is used for long double data values.

Type specifies the type of data that has to be read. It also indicates how this data is expected to be read from the user. The type specifiers for scanf function are same as given for printf() function in Table 9.7.

The scanf function ignores any blank spaces, tabs, and newlines entered by the user. The function simply returns the number of input fields successfully scanned and stored.

We will not discuss functions in detial in this chapter. So understanding scanf function in depth will be a bit difficult here, but for now just understand that the scanf function is used to store values in memory locations associated with variables. For this, the function should have the address of the variables. The address of the variable is denoted by an '&' sign followed by the name of the variable.

> **Note**
> Whenever data is read from the keyboard, there is always a return character from a previous read operation. So we should always code at least one white space character in the conversion specification in order to flush that white space character. For example, to read two or more data values together in a single scanf statement, we must insert a white space between two fields as shown below:
>
> `scanf("%d %c", &i, &ch);`

Now let us quickly summarize the rules to use a scanf function in our C programs.

Rule 1: The scanf function works until:

(a) the maximum number of characters has been processed,
(b) a white space character is encountered, or
(c) an error is detected.

Rule 2: Every variable that has to be processed must have a conversion specification associated with it. Therefore, the following scanf statement will generate an error as num3 has no conversion specification associated with it.

```
scanf("%d %d", &num1, &num2, &num3);
```

Rule 3: There must be a variable address for each conversion specification. Therefore, the following scanf statement will generate an error as no variable address is given for the third conversion specification.

```
scanf("%d %d %d", &num1, &num2);
```

Remember that the ampersand operator (&) before each variable name specifies the address of that variable name.

Rule 4: An error will be generated if the format string is ended with a white space character.

Rule 5: The data entered by the user must match the character specified in the control string (except white space or a conversion specification), otherwise an error will be generated and scanf will stop its processing. For example, consider the following scanf statement.

```
scanf("%d / %d", &num1, &num2);
```

Here, the slash in the control string is neither a white space character nor a part of conversion specification, so the users must enter data of the form 21/46.

Rule 6: Input data values must be separated by spaces.

Rule 7: Any unread data value will be considered as a part of the data input in the next call to scanf.

Rule 8: When the field width specifier is used, it should be large enough to contain the input data size.

Look at the code given below that shows how we input values in variables of different data types.

```
int num;
scanf("%d ", &num);
```

The scanf function reads an integer value (because the type specifier is %d) into the address or the memory location pointed by num.

```
float salary;
scanf("%f ", &salary);
```

The scanf function reads a floating point number (because the type specifier is %f) into the address or the memory location pointed by salary.

```
char ch;
scanf("%c ", &ch);
```

The scanf function reads a single character (because the type specifier is %c) into the address or the memory location pointed by ch.

```
char str[10];
scanf("%s ", str);
```

The scanf function reads a string or a sequence of characters (because the type specifier is %s) into the address or the memory location pointed by str. Note that in case of reading strings, we do not use the & sign in the scanf function. This will be discussed in the chapter on Strings.

> **Programming Tip:**
> A compiler error will be generated if the read and write parameters are not separated by commas.

Look at the following code which combines reading of variables of different data types in one single statement.

```
int num;
float fnum;
char ch;
char str[10];
scanf("%d %f %c %s", &num, &fnum, &ch, str);
```

Look at the scanf statement given below for the same code. The statement ignores the character variable and does not store it (as it is preceded by *).

```
scanf("%d %f %*c %s", &num, &fnum, &ch, str);
```

Remember that if an attempt is made to read a value that does not match the expected data type, the scanf function will not read any further and would immediately return the values read.

9.14.5 Examples of printf/scanf

Look at the following codes that show how we output values of variables of different data types.

```
int num;
scanf("%d ", &num);
printf("%d", num);
```

The printf function prints an integer value (because the type specifier is %d) pointed by num on the screen.

```
float salary;
scanf("%f ", &salary);
printf(".2%f", salary);
```

The printf function prints the floating point number (because the type specifier is %f) pointed by salary on the screen. Here, the control string specifies that only two digits must be displayed after the decimal point.

> **Programming Tip:**
> A float specifier cannot be used to read an integer value.

```
char ch;
scanf("%c ", &ch);
printf("%c", ch);
```

The printf function prints a single character (because the type specifier is %c) pointed by ch on the screen.

```
char str[10];
scanf("%s ", str);
```

The printf function prints a string or a sequence of characters (because the type specifier is %s) pointed by str on the screen.

```
scanf("%2d %5d", &num1, &num2);
```

The scanf statement will read two integer numbers. The first integer number will have two digits while the second can have a maximum of 5 digits.

Look at the following code which combines all the print statements in one single statement.

```
int num;
float fnum;
char ch;
char str[10];
double dnum;
short snum;
long int lnum;
printf("\n Enter the values : (");
scanf("%d %f %c %s %e %hd %ld", &num, &fnum,
   &ch, str, &dnum, &snum, &lnum);
printf("\n num = %d \n fnum = %.2f \n ch =
   %c \n str = %s \n dnum = %e \n snum = %hd
   \n lnum = %ld", num, fnum, ch, str, dnum,
   snum, lnum);
```

Note

In the printf statement, '\n', is called the newline character and is used to print the succeeding text on the new line. The following output will be generated on execution of the printf() function.

```
Enter the values
2 3456.443 a abcde 24.321E-2 1 12345678
num = 2
fnum = 3456.44
ch = a
str = abcde
dnum = 0.24321
snum = 1
lnum = 12345678
```

Remember one thing that scanf terminates as soon as it encounters a white space character so if you enter the string as abc def, then only abc is assigned to str.

1. Find the output of the following program.

```
#include <stdio.h>
int main()
{
  int a, b;
  printf("\n Enter two four digit numbers :");
  scanf("%2d %4d", &a, &b);
  printf("\n The two numbers are : %d and
   %d", a, b);
  return 0;
}
```

Output

```
Enter two four digit numbers : 1234 5678
The two numbers are : 12 and 34
```

Programming Tip:
Using an incorrect specifier for the data type being read or written will generate a run-time error.

Here, variable a is assigned value 12 because it is specified as %2d, so it will accept only the first two digits. The rest of the number will be assigned to b. The value 5678 that is unread will be assigned to the first variable in the next call to the scanf function.

Note

The %n specifier is used to assign the number of characters read till the point at which the %n is encountered to the variable pointed to by the corresponding argument. The following code fragment illustrates its use.

```
int count;
printf("Hello %n World!", &count);
printf("%d", count);
```

The output would be—Hello World! 6 because 6 is the number of characters read before the %n modifier.

2. Write a program to demonstrate the use of printf statement to print values of variables of different data types.

```
#include <stdio.h>
int main()
{
  // Declare and initialize variables
  int num = 7;
  float amt = 123.45;
  char code = 'A';
  double pi = 3.1415926536;
  long int population_of_
   india = 10000000000;
   char msg[] = "Hi";

  // Print the values of variables
  printf("\n NUM = %d \n AMT = %f \n CODE
   = %c \n PI = %e \n POPULATION OF INDIA
   = %ld \n MESSAGE = %s", num, amt, code,
   pi, population_of_india, msg);
  return 0;
}
```

Output

```
NUM = 7
AMT = 123.450000
CODE = A
PI = 3.141590e+00
POPULATION OF INDIA = 10000000000
MESSAGE = Hi
```

3. Write a program to demonstrate the use of printf and scanf statements to read and print values of variables of different data types.

```
#include <stdio.h>
int main()
{
  int num;
  float amt;
  char code;
  double pi;
  long int population_of_india;
  char msg[10];

printf("\n Enter the value of num : ");
  scanf("%d", &num);
  printf("\n Enter the value of amt : ");
  scanf("%f", &amt);
  printf("\n Enter the value of pi : ");
  scanf("%e", &pi);
  printf("\n Enter the population of
   India : ");
  scanf("%ld", &population_of_india);
  printf("\n Enter the value of code : ");
  scanf("%c", &code);
  printf("\n Enter the message : ");
  scanf("%s", msg);
```

```
    printf("\n NUM = %d \n AMT = %f \n PI = %e
     \n POPULATION OF INDIA = %ld \n CODE =
     %c \n MESSAGE = %s", num, amt, pi,
     population_of_india, code, msg);
    return 0;
}
```

Output

```
Enter the value of num : 5
Enter the value of amt : 123.45
Enter the value of pi : 3.14159
Enter the population of India : 12345
Enter the value of code : c
Enter the message : Hello
NUM = 5
AMT = 123.450000
PI = 3.141590e+00
POPULATION OF INDIA = 12345
CODE = c
MESSAGE = Hello
```

4. Write a program to calculate the area of a triangle using Hero's formula.

```
#include <stdio.h>
#include <math.h>
int main()
{
    float a, b, c, area, S;
    printf("\n Enter the length of the three
     sides of the triangle : ");
    scanf("%f %f %f", &a, &b, &c);
    S = ( a + b + c)/2;

    /* sqrt is a mathematical function defined
     in math.h header file */
    area = sqrt(S*(S-a)*(S-b)*(S-c));
    printf("\n Area = %f", area);
    return 0;
}
```

Output

```
Enter the length of the three sides of the
  triangle : 12 16 20
Area = 96
```

5. Write a program to calculate the distance between two points.

```
#include <stdio.h>
#include <math.h>

int main()
{
    int x1, x2, y1, y2;
    float distance;
    printf("\n Enter the x and y coordinates of
     the first point : ");
    scanf("%d %d", &x1, &y1);
    printf("\n Enter the x and y coordinates of
     the second point :");
    scanf("%d %d", &x2, &y2);

    /* sqrt and pow are mathematical functions
     defined in math.h header file */
    distance = sqrt(pow((x2-x1), 2)
              +pow((y2-y1), 2));
    printf("\n Distance = %f", distance);
    return 0;
}
```

Output

```
Enter the x and y coordinates of the first
   point : 2 5
Enter the x and y coordinates of the second
   point : 3 7
Distance = 2.236068
```

9.14.6 Detecting Errors During Data Input

When the `scanf` function completes reading all the data values, it returns the number of values that are successfully read. This return value can be used to determine whether there was any error while reading the input. For example, the statement,

```
scanf("%d %f %c", &a, &b, &c);
```

will return 3 if the user enters, say,

```
12 12.34 A
```

It will return 1 if the user enters erroneous data like

```
12 ABC 12.34
```

This is because a string was entered while the user was expecting a floating point value. So, the `scanf` function reads only first data value correctly and then terminates as soon as it encounters a mismatch between the type of data expected and the type of data entered.

9.15 OPERATORS IN C

An operator is a symbol that specifies the mathematical, logical, or relational operation to be performed. C language supports different types of operators, which can be used with variables and constants to form expressions. These operators can be categorized into the following major groups:

- Arithmetic operators
- Relational operators
- Equality operators
- Logical operators
- Unary operators
- Conditional operators
- Bitwise operators
- Assignment operators

- Comma operator
- `sizeof` operator

In this section, we will discuss all these operators.

9.15.1 Arithmetic Operators

Consider three variables declared as,

```
int a=9, b=3, result;
```

We will use these variables to explain arithmetic operators. Table 9.8 shows the arithmetic operators, their syntax, and usage in C language.

Table 9.8 Arithmetic operators

Operation	Operator	Syntax	Comment	Result
Multiply	*	a * b	result = a * b	27
Divide	/	a / b	result = a/b	3
Addition	+	a + b	result = a + b	12
Subtraction	–	a – b	result = a – b	6
Modulus	%	a % b	result = a % b	0

In Table 9.8, `a` and `b` (on which the operator is applied) are called operands. Arithmetic operators can be applied to any integer or floating-point number. The addition, subtraction, multiplication, and division (`+, -, *,/`) operators perform the usual arithmetic operations in C programs, so you are already familiar with these operators.

However, the operator `%` must be new to you. The modulus operator (`%`) finds the remainder of an integer division. This operator can be applied only to integer operands and cannot be used on float or double operands. Therefore, the code given below generates a compiler error.

```
#include <stdio.h>
int main()
{
float c = 20.0;
printf("\n Result = %f", c % 5);
/* WRONG. Modulus operator is being applied to
   a float operand */

return 0;
}
```

While performing modulo division, the sign of the result is always the sign of the first operand (the dividend). Therefore,

```
16 % 3 = 1        -16 % 3 = -1
16 % -3 = 1       -16 % -3 = -1
```

When both operands of the division operator (`/`) are integers, the division is performed as an integer division. Integer division always results in an integer result. So, the result is always rounded-off by ignoring the remainder. Therefore,

```
9/4 = 2    and    -9/4 = -3
```

From the above observation, we can conclude two things. If `op1` and `op2` are integers and the quotient is not an integer, then we have two cases:

- If `op1` and `op2` have the same sign, then `op1/op2` is the largest integer less than the true quotient.
- If `op1` and `op2` have opposite signs, then `op1/op2` is the smallest integer greater than the true quotient.

Note that it is not possible to divide any number by zero. This is an illegal operation that results in a run-time division-by-zero exception, thereby terminating the program.

Except for modulus operator, all other arithmetic operators can accept a mix of integer and floating point numbers. If both operands are integers, the result will be an integer. If one or both operands are floating point numbers, then the result will be a floating point number.

All the arithmetic operators bind from left to right. As in mathematics the multiplication, division, and modulus operators have higher precedence over the addition and subtraction operators, i.e., if an arithmetic expression consists of a mix of operators, then multiplication, division, and modulus will be carried out first in a left to right order, before any addition and subtraction could be performed. For example,

```
3 + 4 * 7
= 3 + 28
= 31
```

6. Write a program to perform addition, subtraction, division, integer division, multiplication, and modulo division on two integer numbers.

```
#include <stdio.h>
int main()
{

 int num1, num2;
 int add_res=0, sub_res=0, mul_res=0,
   idiv_res=0, modiv_res=0;
 float fdiv_res=0.0;
 printf("\n Enter the first number : ");
 scanf("%d", &num1);
 printf("\n Enter the second number : ");
 scanf("%d", &num2);

 add_res = num1 + num2;
 sub_res = num1 - num2;
 mul_res = num1 * num2;
 idiv_res = num1/num2;
 modiv_res = num1%num2;
 fdiv_res = (float)num1/num2;
 printf("\n %d + %d = %d", num1, num2, add_res);
```

```
printf("\n %d - %d = %d", num1, num2, sub_
  res);
printf("\n %d × %d = %d", num1, num2, mul_res);
printf("\n %d / %d = %d (Integer Division)",
  num1, num2, idiv_res);
printf("\n %d %% %d = %d (Moduluo Division)",
  num1, num2, modiv_res);
printf("\n %d / %d = %.2f (Normal Division)",
  num1, num2, fdiv_res);
return 0;
}
```

Output

```
Enter the first number : 9
Enter the second number : 7
9 + 7 = 16
9 - 7 = 2
9 * 7 = 63
9 / 7 = 1 (Integer Division)
9 % 7 = 2 (Moduluo Division)
9 / 7 = 1.29 (Normal Division)
```

7. Write a program to subtract two long integers.

```
#include <stdio.h>
int main()
{
  long int num1= 1234567, num2, diff=0;
  printf("\n Enter the number: ");
  scanf("%ld", &num2);
  diff = num1 - num2;
  printf("\n Difference = %ld", diff);
  return 0;
}
```

Output

```
Enter the number: 1234
Difference = 1233333
```

9.15.2 Relational Operators

A relational operator, also known as a comparison operator, is an operator that compares two values. Expressions that contain relational operators are called *relational expressions*. Relational operators return true or false value, depending on whether the conditional relationship between the two operands holds or not.

For example, to test if x is less than y, relational operator < is used as `x < y`. This expression will return `true(1)` if x is less than y; otherwise the value of the expression will be `false(0)`.

Relational operators can be used to determine the relationships between the operands. These relationships are illustrated in Table 9.9.

The relational operators are evaluated from left to right. The operands of a relational operator must evaluate to a number. Characters are considered valid operands since they are represented by numeric values in the computer system. So, if we say, `'A' < 'B'`, where A is 65 and B is 66 then the result would be 1 as `65 < 66`.

When arithmetic expressions are used on either side of a relational operator, then first the arithmetic expression will be evaluated and then the result will be compared. This is because arithmetic operators have a higher priority over relational operators.

However, relational operators should not be used for comparing strings as this will result in comparing the address of the string and not their contents. You must be wondering why so? The answer to this question will be clear to you in the later chapters. A few examples of relational operators are as follows:

Table 9.9 Relational operators

Operator	Meaning	Example
<	Less than	3 < 5 gives 1
>	Greater than	7 > 9 gives 0
<=	Less than or equal to	100 <= 100 gives 1
>=	Greater than equal to	50 >= 100 gives 0

If `x=1, y=2,` and `z = 3,` then

Expressions that evaluate to TRUE Note that these expressions are true because their value is not zero.	*Expressions that evaluate to* FALSE Note that these expressions are false because their value is zero.
(x) (x + y) (z * 9) (z + 10 - 5 * x) (z - x + y)	(x - 1) (!(z)) (0 * y) (y == 1) (y % 2)

Note

Although blank spaces are allowed between an operand and an operator, no space is permitted between the components of an operator (like > = is not allowed, it should be >=). Therefore, writing x==y is correct but writing x = = y is not acceptable in C language.

8. Write a program to show the use of relational operators.

```
#include <stdio.h>
int main ()
{
  int x=10, y=20;
  printf("\n %d < %d = %d", x, y, x<y);
  printf("\n %d == %d = %d", x, y, x==y);
  printf("\n %d != %d = %d", x, y, x!=y);
  printf("\n %d > %d = %d", x, y, x>y);
  printf("\n %d >= %d = %d", x, y, x>=y);
```

```
    printf("\n %d <= %d = %d", x, y, x<=y);
    return 0;
}
```

Output

```
10 < 20 = 1
10 == 20 = 0
10 != 20 = 1
10 > 20 = 0
10 >= 20 = 0
10 <= 20 = 1
```

9.15.3 Equality Operators

C language supports two kinds of equality operators to compare their operands for strict equality or inequality. They are equal to (==) and not equal to (!=) operators. The equality operators have lower precedence than the relational operators.

The equal-to operator (==) returns true (1) if operands on both the sides of the operator have the same value; otherwise, it returns false (0). On the contrary, the not-equal-to operator (!=) returns true(1) if the operands do not have the same value; else it returns false (0). Table 9.10 summarizes equality operators.

Table 9.10 Equality operators

Operator	Meaning
==	Returns 1 if both operands are equal, 0 otherwise
!=	Returns 1 if operands do not have the same value, 0 otherwise

9.15.4 Logical Operators

C language supports three logical operators—logical AND (&&), logical OR (||), and logical NOT (!). As in case of arithmetic expressions, the logical expressions are evaluated from left to right.

Logical AND

Logical AND operator is a binary operator, which simultaneously evaluates two values or relational expressions. If both the operands are true, then the whole expression evaluates to true. If both or one of the operands is false, then the whole expression evaluates to false. The truth table of logical AND operator is given in Table 9.11.

Table 9.11 Truth table of logical AND

A	B	A &&B
0	0	0
0	1	0
1	0	0
1	1	1

For example,

```
(a < b) && (b > c)
```

The expression to the left is (a < b) and that on the right is (b > c). The whole expression is true only if both expressions are true, i.e., if b is greater than both a and c.

Logical OR

Logical OR returns a false value if both the operands are false. Otherwise it returns a true value. The truth table of logical OR operator is given in Table 9.12.

Table 9.12 Truth table of logical OR

A	B	A || B
0	0	0
0	1	1
1	0	1
1	1	1

For example,

```
(a < b) || (b > c)
```

The expression to the left is (a < b) and that on the right is (b > c). The whole expression is true if either b is greater than a or b is greater than c or b is greater than both a and c.

Logical NOT

The logical NOT operator takes a single expression and negates the value of the expression. That is, logical NOT produces a 0 if the expression evaluates to a non-zero value and produces a 1 if the expression produces a zero. In other words, it just reverses the value of the expression. The truth table of logical NOT operator is given in Table 9.13.

Table 9.13 Truth table of Logical NOT

A	! A
0	1
1	0

For example,

```
int a = 10, b;
b = !a;
```

Now the value of b = 0. This is because value of a = 10. !a = 0. The value of !a is assigned to b, hence, the result.

Logical expressions operate in a short cut fashion and the evaluation is stopped when it is known for sure what the final outcome would be. For example, in a logical expression involving logical AND, if the first operand is false, then the second operand is not evaluated as it is for sure that the result will be false. Similarly, for a logical expression involving logical OR, if the first operand is true, then the second operand is not evaluated as it is for sure that the result will be true.

But this approach has a side effect. For example, consider the following expression:

```
(x > 9) && (y + 1)
```

OR

```
(x > 9) || (y + 1)
```

In the above logical AND expression if the first operand is false then the entire expression will not be evaluated and thus the value of y will never be incremented. Same is the case with the logical OR expression. If the first expression is true then the second will never be evaluated and value of y will never be incremented.

9.15.5 Unary Operators

Unary operators act on single operands. C language supports three unary operators: unary minus, increment, and decrement operators.

Unary Minus

Unary minus (–) operator is strikingly different from the binary arithmetic operator that operates on two operands and subtracts the second operand from the first operand. When an operand is preceded by a minus sign, the unary operator negates its value. For example, if a number is positive then it becomes negative when preceded with a unary minus operator. Similarly, if the number is negative, it becomes positive after applying the unary minus operator. For example,

```
int a, b = 10;
a = -(b);
```

The result of this expression is a = -10 because variable b has a positive value. After applying unary minus operator (-) on the operand b, the value becomes –10, which indicates it as a negative value.

Increment Operator (++) and Decrement Operator (- -)

The increment operator is a unary operator that increases the value of its operand by 1. Similarly, the decrement operator decreases the value of its operand by 1. For example, --x is equivalent to writing x = x - 1.

The increment/decrement operators have two variants—**prefix** and **postfix**. In a prefix expression (++x or --x), the operator is applied before an operand is fetched for computation and, thus, the altered value is used for the computation of the expression in which it occurs. On the contrary, in a postfix expression (x++ or x--) an operator is applied after an operand is fetched for computation. Therefore, the unaltered value is used for the computation of the expression in which it occurs.

Therefore, an important point to note about unary increment and decrement operators is that x++ is not same as ++x. Similarly, x-- is not same as --x. Both x++ and ++x increment the value of x by 1. In the former case, the value of x is returned before it is incremented, whereas, in the latter case, the value of x is returned after it is incremented. For example,

```
int x = 10, y;
y = x++;
```

is equivalent to writing

```
y = x;
x = x + 1;
```

whereas,

```
y = ++x;
```

is equivalent to writing

```
x = x + 1;
y = x;
```

The same principle applies to unary decrement operators. The unary operators have a higher precedence than the binary operators. If in an expression we have more than one unary operator then unlike arithmetic operators, they are evaluated from right to left.

When applying the increment or decrement operator, the operand must be a variable. This operator can never be applied to a constant or an expression.

Note

When postfix ++ or – – is used with a variable in an expression, then the expression is evaluated first using the original value of the variable and then the variable is incremented or decremented by one.

Similarly, when prefix ++ or – – is used with a variable in an expression, then the variable is first incremented or decremented and then the expression is evaluated using the new value of the variable.

9. Write a program to illustrate the use of unary prefix increment and decrement operators.

```
#include <stdio.h>
int main()
{
    int num = 3;
    // Using unary prefix increment operator
    printf("\n The value of num = %d", num);
    printf("\n The value of ++num = %d", ++num);
    printf("\n The new value of num = %d", num);

    // Using unary prefix decrement operator
    printf("\n\n The value of num = %d", num);
```

```
    printf("\n The value of --num = %d", --num);
    printf("\n The new value of num = %d", num);
    return 0;
  }
```

Output

```
The value of num = 3
The value of ++num = 4
The new value of num = 4
The value of num = 4
The value of --num = 3
The new value of num = 3
```

10. Write a program to illustrate the use of unary postfix increment and decrement operators.

```
#include <stdio.h>
int main()
{
  int num = 3;
  // Using unary postfix increment operator
  printf("\n The value of num = %d", num);
  printf("\n The value of num++ = %d", num++);
  printf("\n The new value of num = %d", num);
  // Using unary postfix decrement operator
  printf("\n\n The value of num = %d", num);
  printf("\n The value of num = %d", num--);
  printf("\n The new value of num = %d", num);
  return 0;
}
```

Output

```
The value of num = 3
The value of num++ = 3
The new value of num = 4
The value of num = 4
The value of num-- = 4
The new value of num = 3
```

9.15.6 Conditional Operator

The conditional operator or the ternary (`?:`) is just like an **`if-else`** statement that can be used within expressions. Such an operator is useful in situations in which there are two or more alternatives for an expression. The syntax of the conditional operator is

```
exp1 ? exp2 : exp3
```

`exp1` is evaluated first. If it is true, then `exp2` is evaluated and becomes the result of the expression, otherwise `exp3` is evaluated and becomes the result of the expression. For example,

```
large = (a > b) ? a : b
```

The conditional operator is used to find the larger of two given numbers. First `exp1`, that is `(a > b)` is evaluated. If `a` is greater than `b`, then `large = a`, else `large = b`. Hence, `large` is equal to either `a` or `b` but not both.

Hence, conditional operator is used in certain situations, replacing `if-else` condition phrases. Conditional operator makes the program code more compact, more readable, and safer to use, as it is easier to check any error (if present) in one single line itself. Conditional operator is also known as ternary operator as it is neither a unary nor a binary operator; it takes *three* operands.

An expression using conditional operator can be used as an operand of another conditional operation. That means C allows you to have nested conditional expressions. Consider the expression given below which illustrates this concept.

```
int a = 5, b = 3, c= 7, small;
small = ( a < b ? ( a < c ? a : c) :
  (b < c ? b : c));
```

11. Write a program to find the largest of three numbers using ternary operator.

```
#include <stdio.h>
int main()
{
  int num1, num2, num3, large;
  printf("\n Enter the first number: ");
  scanf("%d", &num1);
  printf("\n Enter the second number: ");
  scanf("%d", &num2);
  printf("\n Enter the third number: ");
  scanf("%d", &num3);
  large = num1>num2?(num1>num3?num1:num3):
  (num2>num3?num2:num3);
  printf("\n The largest number is: %d", large);
  return 0;
}
```

Output

```
Enter the first number: 12
Enter the second number: 34
Enter the third number: 23
The largest number is:  34
```

9.15.7 Bitwise Operators

As the name suggests, bitwise operators are those operators that perform operations at bit level. These operators include: bitwise AND, bitwise OR, bitwise XOR, and shift operators. The bitwise operators expect their operands to be integers and treat them as a sequence of bits.

Bitwise AND

Like boolean AND (&&) bitwise AND operator (&) performs operation on bits instead of bytes, chars, integers, etc. When we use the bitwise AND operator, the bit in the first operand is ANDed with the corresponding bit in the second operand. The truth table is same as we had seen in logical AND operation. The bitwise AND operator compares each bit of its first operand with the corresponding bit of its second operand. If both bits are 1, the corresponding bit in the result is 1 and 0 otherwise. For example,

```
10101010 & 01010101 = 00000000
```

In a C program, the & operator is used as follows.

```
int a = 10, b = 20, c=0;
c = a&b;
```

Bitwise OR

When we use the bitwise OR operator (|), the bit in the first operand is ORed with the corresponding bit in the second operand. The truth table is same as we had seen in logical OR operation. The bitwise-OR operator compares each bit of its first operand with the corresponding bit of its second operand. If one or both bits are 1, the corresponding bit in the result is 1 and 0 otherwise. For example,

```
10101010 & 01010101 = 11111111
```

In a C program, the | operator is used as follows.

```
int a = 10, b = 20, c=0;
c = a|b
```

Bitwise XOR

The bitwise XOR operator (^) performs operation on individual bits of the operands. When we use the bitwise XOR operator, the bit in the first operand is XORed with the corresponding bit in the second operand. The truth table of bitwise XOR operator is shown in Table 9.14.

Table 9.14 Truth table of bitwise XOR

A	B	A ^ B
0	0	0
0	1	1
1	0	1
1	1	0

The bitwise XOR operator compares each bit of its first operand with the corresponding bit of its second operand. If one of the bits is 1, the corresponding bit in the result is 1 and 0 otherwise. For example,

```
10101010 ^ 01010101 = 11111111
```

In a C program, the ^ operator is used as follows:

```
int a = 10, b = 20, c=0;
c = a^b
```

Bitwise NOT

The bitwise NOT, or complement, is a unary operator that performs logical negation on each bit of the operand. By performing negation of each bit, it actually produces the 1's complement of the given binary value. Bitwise NOT operator sets the bit to 1 if it was initially 0 and sets it to 0 if it was initially 1. For example,

```
~10101011 = 01010100
```

Note

Bitwise operators are used for testing the bits or shifting them left or right. Always remember that bitwise operators cannot be applied to float or double variables.

Shift Operator

C supports two bitwise shift operators. They are shift-left (<<) and shift-right (>>). These operations are simple and are responsible for shifting bits either to the left or to the right. The syntax for a shift operation can be given as

```
operand op num
```

where the bits in operand are shifted left or right depending on the operator (left if the operator is << and right if the operator is >>) by the number of places denoted by num.

For example, if we have `x = 0001 1101`, then

```
x << 1 produces 0011 1010
```

When we apply a left-shift, every bit in x is shifted to the left by one place. So, the MSB (most significant bit) of x is lost, and the LSB of x is set to 0.

Therefore, if we have `x = 0001 1101`, then

```
x << 4 produces 1101 0000.
```

If you observe carefully, you will notice that shifting once to the left multiplies the number by 2. Hence, multiple shifts of 1 to the left, results in multiplying the number by 2 over and over again.

On the contrary, when we apply a shift-right operator, every bit in x is shifted to the right by one place. So, the LSB (least significant bit) of x is lost, the MSB of x is set to 0. For example, if we have `x = 0001 1101`, then

```
x >> 1 produces = 0000 1110
```

Similarly, if we have `x = 0001 1101`, then

```
x >> 4 produces 0000 0001.
```

If you observe carefully, you will notice that shifting once to the right divides the number by 2. Hence, multiple shifts of 1 to the right, results in dividing the number by 2 over and over again.

12. Write a program to show use of bitwise operators.

```
#include <stdio.h>
void main()
{
  int a=27, b= 39;
```

```
    printf("\n a & b = %d", a&b);
    printf("\n a | b = %d", a|b);
    printf("\n ~a = %d", ~a);
    printf("\n ~b = %d", ~b);
    printf("\n a ^ b = %d", a^b);
    printf("\n a << 1 = %d", a<<1);
    printf("\n b >> 1 = %d", b>>1);
}
```

Output

```
a & b = 3
a | b = 63
~a = -28
~b = -40
a ^ b = 60
a << 1 = 54
b >> 1 = 19
```

9.15.8 Assignment Operators

In C, the assignment operator is responsible for assigning values to the variables. While the equal sign (=) is the fundamental assignment operator, C language also supports other assignment operators that provide shorthand ways to represent common variable assignments.

When an equal sign is encountered in an expression, the compiler processes the statement on the right side of the sign and assigns the result to the variable on the left side. For example,

```
int x;
x = 10;
```

assigns the value 10 to variable x. If we have,

```
int x = 2, y = 3, sum = 0;
sum = x + y;
then sum = 5.
```

The assignment operator has right-to-left associativity, so the expression

```
a = b = c = 10;
```

is evaluated as

```
(a = (b = (c = 10)));
```

First 10 is assigned to c, then the value of c is assigned to b. Finally, the value of b is assigned to a.

The operand to the left of the assignment operator must always be a variable name. C does not allow any expression, constant, or function to be placed to the left of the assignment operator. Therefore, the statement a + b = 0; is invalid in C language.

To the right of the assignment operator you may have an arbitrary expression. In that case, the expression would be evaluated and the result would be stored in the location denoted by the variable name.

Other Assignment Operators

C language supports a set of shorthand assignment operators of the form

```
variable op = expression
```

where op is a binary arithmetic operator. Table 9.15 shows the list of other assignment operators that are supported by C.

The advantage of using shorthand assignment operators are as follows:

- Shorthand expressions are easier to write as the expression on the left side need not be repeated.
- The statements involving shorthand operators are easier to read as they are more concise.
- The statements involving shorthand operators are more efficient and easy to understand.

13. Write a program to demonstrate the use of assignment operators.

```
#include <stdio.h>
int main()
{
    int num1 = 3, num2 = 5;
    printf("\n Initial value of num1 = %d and
     num2 = %d", num1, num2);
    num1 += num2 * 4 - 7;
    printf("\n After the evaluation of the
     expression num1 = %d and num2 = %d",
     num1, num2);
    return 0;
}
```

Output

```
Initial value of num1 = 3 and num2 = 5
After the evaluation of the expression num1
   = 16 and num2 = 5
```

9.15.9 Comma Operator

The comma operator in C takes two operands. It works by evaluating the first and discarding its value, and then evaluates the second and returns the value as the result of the expression. Comma separated operands when chained together are evaluated in left-to-right sequence with the right most value yielding the result of the expression. Among all the operators, the comma operator has the lowest precedence.

Therefore, when a comma operator is used, the entire expression evaluates to the value of the right expression. For example, the following statement first increments a, then increments b and then assigns the value of b to x.

```
int a=2, b=3, x=0;
x = (++a, b+=a);
```

Now, the value of x = 6.

Table 9.15 Assignment Operators

Operator	Syntax	Equivalent to	Meaning	Example

/=	variable /= expression	variable = variable / expression	Divides the value of a variable by the value of an expression and assigns the result to the variable.	float a = 9.0;
				float b = 3.0;
				a /= b;

\=	variable \= expression	variable = variable \ expression	Divides the value of a variable by the value of an expression and assigns the integer result to the variable.	int a = 9;
				int b = 3;
				a \= b;

*=	variable *= expression	variable = variable * expression	Multiplies the value of a variable by the value of an expression and assigns the result to the variable.	int a = 9;
				int b = 3;
				a *= b;

+=	variable += expression	variable = variable + expression	Adds the value of a variable to the value of an expression and assigns the result to the variable.	int a = 9;
				int b = 3;
				a += b;

–=	variable –= expression	variable = variable – expression	Subtracts the value of the expression from the value of the variable and assigns the result to the variable.	int a = 9;
				int b = 3;
				a –= b;

&=	variable &= expression	variable = variable & expression	Performs the bitwise AND between the value of variable and value of the expression and assigns the result to the variable.	int a = 10;
				int b = 20;
				a &= b;

^=	variable ^= expression	variable = variable ^ expression	Performs the bitwise XOR between the value of variable and value of the expression and assigns the result to the variable.	int a = 10;
				int b = 20;
				a ^= b;

<<=	variable <<= amount	variable = variable << amount	Performs an arithmetic left shift (amount times) on the value of a variable and assigns the result back to the variable.	int a = 9;
				int b = 3;
				a <<= b;

>>=	variable >>= amount	variable = variable >> amount	Performs an arithmetic right shift (amount times) on the value of a variable and assigns the result back to the variable.	int a = 9;
				int b = 3;
				a >>= b;

9.15.10 `sizeof` Operator

The `sizeof` operator is a unary operator used to calculate the size of data types. This operator can be applied to all data types. When using this operator, the keyword `sizeof` is followed by a type name, variable, or expression. The operator returns the size of the variable, data type, or expression in bytes, i.e., the `sizeof` operator is used to determine the amount of memory space that the variable/expression/data type will take.

When a type name is used, it is enclosed in parentheses, but in case of variable names and expressions they can be specified with or without parentheses. A `sizeof` expression returns an unsigned value that specifies the space in bytes required by the data type, variable, or expression. For example, `sizeof(char)` returns `1`, i.e., the size of a character data type. If we have,

```
int a = 10;
unsigned int result;
result = sizeof(a);
```

Then `result = 2`, which is the space required to store the variable a in memory. Since a is an integer, it requires 2 bytes of storage space.

9.15.11 Operator Precedence Chart

C operators have two properties: *priority* and *associativity*. When an expression has more than one operator then it is the relative priorities of the operators with respect to each other that determine the order in which the expression will be evaluated. Associativity defines the direction in which the operator acts on the operands. It can be either left-to-right or right-to-left. Priority is given precedence over associativity to determine the order in which the expressions are evaluated. Associativity is then applied, if the need arises.

Table 9.16 lists the operators that C language supports in the order of their *precedence* (highest to lowest). *Associativity* indicates the order in which the operators of equal precedence in an expression are evaluated.

You must be wondering why the priority of the assignment operator is so low. This is because the action of assignment is performed only when the entire computation is done. It is not uncommon for a programmer to forget the priority of the operators while writing any program. So it is recommended that you use the parentheses operator to override default priorities. From Table 9.16 you can see that the parenthesis operator has the highest priority. So any operator placed within the parenthesis will be evaluated before any other operator.

Table 9.16 Operator precedence

Operator	Associativity	Operator	Associativity
() [] . —>	left-to-right	&	left-to-right
++(postfix) − −(postfix)	right-to-left	^	left-to-right
++(prefix) − −(prefix) +(unary) – (unary) ! ~ (type) *(indirection) &(address) sizeof	right-to-left	|	left-to-right
* / %	left-to-right	&&	left-to-right
+ −	left-to-right	||	left-to-right
<< >>	left-to-right	?:	right-to-left
< <= > >=	left-to-right	= += −= *= /= %= &= ^= |= <<= >>=	right-to-left
== !=	left-to-right	,(comma)	left-to-right

Example 9.3

Evaluating expressions using the precedence chart

1.
```
x = 3 * 4 + 5 * 6
  = 12 + 5 * 6
  = 12 + 30
  = 42
```

2.
```
x = 3 * (4 + 5) * 6
  = 3 * 9 * 6
  = 27 * 6
  = 162
```

3.
```
x = 3 * 4 % 5 / 2
  = 12 % 5 / 2
  = 2 / 2
  = 1
```

4.
```
x = 3 * (4 % 5) / 2
  = 3 * 4 / 2
  = 12 / 2
  = 6
```

5.
```
x = 3 * 4 % (5 / 2)
  = 3 * 4 % 2
  = 12 % 2
  = 0
```

6.
```
x = 3 * ((4 % 5) / 2)
  = 3 * (4 / 2)
  = 3 * 2
  = 6
```

Take the following variable declarations,

```
int a = 0, b = 1, c = -1;
float x = 2.5, y = 0.0;
```

If we write,

```
a = b = c = 7;
```

Since the assignment operator works from right-to-left, `c = 7`. Then since `b = c`, therefore `b = 7`. Now `a = b`, so `a = 7`.

7. `a += b -= c *= 10`

This is expanded as

```
a = a + (b = b - (c = c * 10))
  = a + (b = 1 - (-10))
  = a + (b = 11)
  = 0 + 11
  = 11
```

8. `--a * ( 5 + b) / 2 - c++ * b`

```
  = --a * 6 / 2 - c++ * b
  = --a * 6 / 2 - -1 * b
```

(Value of c has been incremented but its altered value will not be visible for the evaluation of this expression)

```
  = -1 * 6 / 2 - -1 * 1
```

(Value of a has been incremented and its altered value will be used for the evaluation of this expression)

```
  = -1 * 3 - -1 * 1
  = -3 - -1 * 1
  = -3 - -1
  = -2
```

9. `a * b * c`

`= (a * b) * c` (because associativity of * is from left-to-right)

```
  = 0
```

10. `a && b`

```
  = 0
```

11. `a < b && c < b`

```
  = 1
```

12. `b + c || ! a`

```
  = ( b + c) || (!a)
  = 0 ||1
  = 1
```

13. `x * 5 && 5 || ( b / c)`

```
  = ((x * 5) && 5) || (b / c)
  = (12.5 && 5) || (1/-1)
  = 1
```

14. `a <= 10 && x >= 1 && b`

```
  = ((a <= 10) && (x >= 1)) && b
  = (1 && 1) && 1
  = 1
```

15. `!x || !c || b +.c`

```
  = ((!x) || (!c)) || (b + c)
  = (0 || 0) || 0
  = 0
```

16. `x * y < a + b || c`

```
  = ((x * y) < (a + b)) || c
  = (0 < 1) || -1
  = 1
```

17. `(x > y) + !a || c++`

```
  = ((x > y) + (!a)) || (c++)
  = (1 + 1) || 0
  = 1
```

14. Write a program to calculate the area of a circle.

```
#include <stdio.h>
int main()
{
  float radius;
  double area, circumference;
  printf("\n Enter the radius of the
    circle: ");
  scanf("%f", &radius);
  area = 3.14 * radius * radius;
  circumference = 2 * 3.14 * radius;
  printf("AREA = %.2le", area);
  printf("\n CIRCUMFERENCE = %.2e",
    circumference);
  return 0;
}
```

Output

```
Enter the radius of the circle: 7
AREA = 153.86
CIRCUMFERENCE = 4.40e+01
```

15. Write a program to print the ASCII value of a character.

```
#include <stdio.h>
int main()
{
  char ch;
  printf("\n Enter any character: ");
  scanf("%c", &ch);
  printf("\n The ASCII value of %c is:
  %d",ch,ch);
  return 0;
}
```

Output

```
Enter any character: A
The ASCII value of A is: 65
```

16. Write a program to read a character in upper case and then print it in lower case.

```
#include <stdio.h>
int main()
{
  char ch;
  printf("\n Enter any character in upper
    case: ");
  scanf("%c", &ch);
  printf("\n The character in lower case is:
  %c", ch+32);
  return 0;
}
```

Output

```
Enter any character: A
The character in lower case is: a
```

17. Write a program to print the digit at ones place of a number.

```
#include <stdio.h>
 int main()
{
  int num, digit_at_ones_place;
  printf("\n Enter any number: ");
  scanf("%d", &num);
  digit_at_ones_place = num % 10;
  printf("\n The digit at ones place of %d is
  %d", num, digit_at_ones_place);
  return 0;
}
```

Output

```
Enter any number: 123
The digit at ones place of 123 is 3
```

18. Write a program to swap two numbers using a temporary variable.

```
#include <stdio.h>
int main()
{
  int num1, num2, temp;
  printf("\n Enter the first number: ");
  scanf("%d",&num1);
  printf("\n Enter the second number: ");
  scanf("%d",&num2);
  temp = num1;
  num1 = num2;
  num2 = temp;
  printf("\n The first number is %d", num1);
  printf("\n The second number is %d", num2);
  return 0;
}
```

Output

```
Enter the first number : 3
Enter the second number : 5
The first number is 5
The second number is 3
```

19. Write a program to swap two numbers without using a temporary variable.

```
#include <stdio.h>
int main()
{
  int num1, num2;
  printf("\n Enter the first number: ");
  scanf("%d",&num1);
  printf("\n Enter the second number: ");
  scanf("%d",&num2);
  num1 = num1 + num2;
  num2 = num1 - num2;
  num1 = num1 - num2;
  printf("\n The first number is %d", num1);
  printf("\n The second number is %d", num2);
  return 0;
}
```

Output

```
Enter the first number: 3
Enter the second number: 5
The first number is 5
The second number is 3
```

20. Write a program to convert degrees Fahrenheit into degrees celsius.

```
#include <stdio.h>
int main()
{
  float fahrenheit, celsius;
  printf("\n Enter the temperature in
  fahrenheit: ");
  scanf("%f", &fahrenheit);
  celsius = (0.56) * (fahrenheit - 32);
  printf("\n Temperature in degrees celsius
  = %f", celsius);
  return 0;
}
```

Output

```
Enter the temperature in fahrenheit: 32
Temperature in degree celsius = 0
```

21. Write a program that displays the size of every data type.

```
#include <stdio.h>
int main()
{
  printf("\n The size of short integer is:
  %d", sizeof(short int));
  printf("\n The size of unsigned integer is:
  %d", sizeof(unsigned int));
  printf("\n The size of signed integer is:
  %d", sizeof(signed int));
  printf("\n The size of integer is: %d",
  sizeof(int));
  printf("\n The size of long integer is:
  %d", sizeof(long int));

  printf("\n The size of character is: %d",
  sizeof(char));
```

```
printf("\n The size of unsigned character is:
 %d", sizeof(unsigned char));
printf("\n The size of signed character is:
 %d", sizeof(signed char));

printf("\n The size of floating point number
 is: %d", sizeof(float));
printf("\n The size of double number is:
 %d", sizeof(double));
return 0;
}
```

Output

```
The size of short integer is: 2
The size of unsigned integer is: 2
The size of signed integer is: 2
The size of integer is: 2
The size of long integer is: 2

The size of character is: 1
The size of unsigned character is: 1
The size of signed character is: 1

The size of floating point number is: 4
The size of double number is: 8
```

22. Write a program to calculate the total amount of money in the piggybank, given the coins of Rs 10, Rs 5, Rs 2, and Re 1.

```
#include <stdio.h>
int main()
{
  int num_of_10_coins, num_of_5_coins,
   num_of_2_coins, num_of_1_coins;
  float total_amt = 0.0;
  printf("\n Enter the number of Rs10 coins
   in the piggybank: ");
  scanf("%d", &num_of_10_coins);
  printf("\n Enter the number of Rs5 coins
   in the piggybank: ");
  scanf("%d", &num_of_5_coins);
  printf("\n Enter the number of Rs2 coins
   in the piggybank: ");
  scanf("%d", &num_of_2_coins);
  printf("\n Enter the number of Re1 coins
   in the piggybank: ");
  scanf("%d", &num_of_1_coins);

  total_amt = num_of_10_coins * 10 + num_of_
   5_coins * 5 + num_of_2_coins * 2 + num_of_
   1_coins;

  printf("\n Total amount in the piggybank =
   %f", total_amt);
  return 0;
}
```

Output

```
Enter the number of Rs10 coins in the
  piggybank: 10
Enter the number of Rs5 coins in the
  piggybank: 23
Enter the number of Rs2 coins in the
  piggybank: 43
Enter the number of Re1 coins in the
  piggybank: 6
Total amount in the piggybank = 307
```

23. Write a program to calculate the bill amount for an item given its quantity sold, value, discount, and tax.

```
#include <stdio.h>
int main()
{
  float total_amt, amt, sub_total, discount_amt,
   tax_amt, qty, val, discount, tax;
  printf("\n Enter the quantity of item
   sold: ");
  scanf("%f", &qty);
  printf("\n Enter the value of item: ");
  scanf("%f", &val);
  printf("\n Enter the discount percentage: ");
  scanf("%f", &discount);
  printf("\n Enter the tax: ");
  scanf("%f", &tax);

  amt = qty * val;
  discount_amt = (amt * discount)/100.0;
  sub_total = amt - discount_amt;
  tax_amt = (sub_total * tax) /100.0;
  total_amt = sub_total + tax_amt;
  printf("\n\n\n ************* BILL
   *************");
  printf("\n Quantity Sold: %f", qty);
  printf("\n Price per item: %f", val);
  printf("\n -------------");
  printf("\n Amount: %f", amt);
  printf("\n Discount: - %f", discount_amt);
  printf("\n Discounted Total: %f", sub_total);
  printf("\n Tax: + %f", tax_amt);
  printf("\n -------------");
  printf("\n Total Amount %f", total_amt);
  return 0;
}
```

Output

```
Enter the quantity of item sold: 20
Enter the value of item: 300
Enter the discount percentage: 10
Enter the tax: 12
************* BILL **************
```

```
Quantity Sold :            20
Price per item :          300
------------------------------------
  Amount :                6000
  Discount :         -     600
  Discounted Total :      5400
  Tax :              +     648
------------------------------------
  Total Amount            6048
```

9.16 TYPE CONVERSION AND TYPECASTING

Till now we have assumed that all the expressions involved data of the same type. But what happens when expressions involve two different data types, like multiplying a floating point number and an integer. Such type of situations are handled either through type conversion or typecasting.

Type conversion or typecasting of variables refers to changing a variable of one data type into another. Type conversion is done implicitly, whereas typecasting has to be done explicitly by the programmer. We will discuss both of them here.

9.16.1 Type Conversion

Type conversion is done when the expression has variables of different data types. To evaluate the expression, the data type is promoted from lower to higher level where the hierarchy of data types (from higher to lower) can be given as: double, float, long, int, short, and char. Figure 9.14 shows the conversion hierarchy of data types.

Type conversion is automatically done when we assign an integer value to a floating point variable. Consider the code given below in which an integer data type is promoted to float. This is known as *promotion* (when a lower level data type is promoted to a higher type).

```
float x;
int y = 3;
x = y;
```

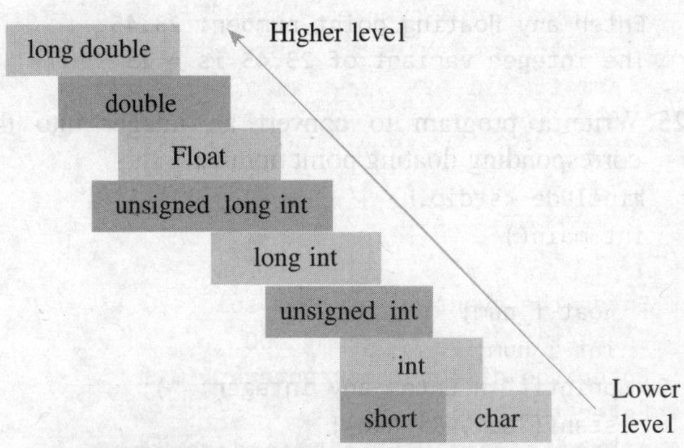

Figure 9.14 Conversion hierarchy of data types

Now, x = 3.0, as automatically integer value is converted into its equivalent floating point representation. In some cases, when an integer is converted into a floating point number, the resulting floating point number may not exactly match the integer value. This is because the floating point number format used internally by the computer cannot accurately represent every possible integer number. So even if the value of `x = 2.99999995`, you must not worry. The loss of accuracy because of this feature would be always insignificant for the final result. Let us summarize how promotion is done:

- `float` operands are converted to `double`.
- `char` or `short` operands whether signed or unsigned are converted to `int`.
- If any one operand is `double`, the other operand is also converted to `double`. Hence, the result is also of type `double`.
- If any one operand is `long`, the other operand is also converted to `long`. Hence, the result is also of type `long`.

Figure 9.15 exhibits type conversions in an expression.

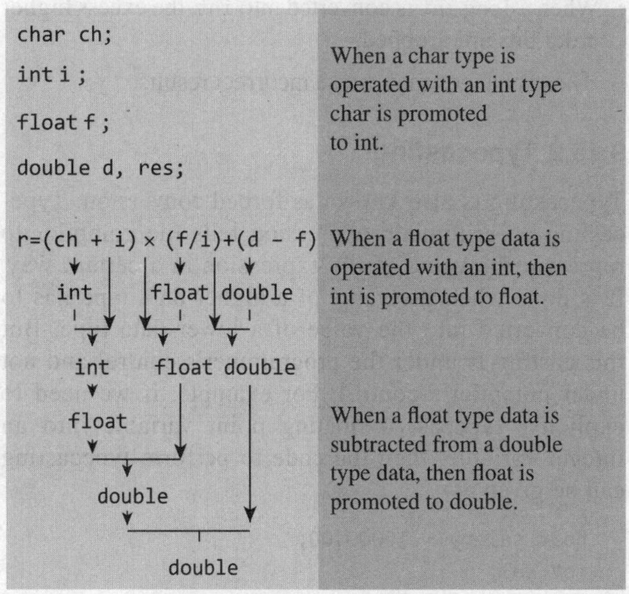

Figure 9.15 Type conversion

Consider the following group of statements:

```
float f = 3.5;
int i;
i = f;
```

The statement `i = f` results in `f` to be demoted to type `int`, i.e., the fractional part of `f` will be lost and `i` will contain `3` (not `3.5`). In this case demotion takes place, i.e., a higher level data type is converted into a lower type. Whenever demotion occurs, some information is lost. For example, in this case the fractional part of the floating point number is lost.

Similarly, if we convert an `int` to a `short int` or a `long int` to `int`, or `int` to `char`, the compiler just drops the extra bits (Figure 9.16).

Note

No compile time warning message is generated when information is lost while demoting the type of data.

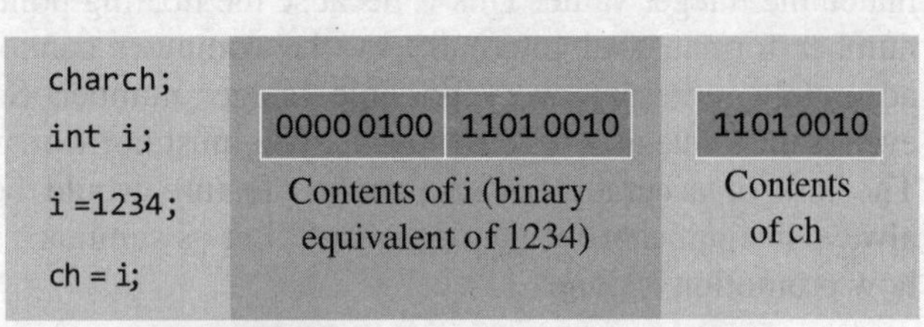

Figure 9.16 Implicit conversion example

Thus we can observe the following changes are unavoidable when performing type conversions.

- When a `float` value is converted to an `int` value, the fractional part is truncated.
- When a `double` value is converted to a `float` value, rounding of digits is done.
- When a `long int` is converted into `int`, the excess higher order bits are dropped.

These changes may cause incorrect results.

9.16.2 Typecasting

Typecasting is also known as forced conversion. Typecasting an arithmetic expression tells the compiler to represent the value of the expression in a certain way. It is done when the value of a higher data type has to be converted into the value of a lower data type. But this casting is under the programmer's control and not under compiler's control. For example, if we need to explicitly typecast a floating point variable into an integer variable, then the code to perform typecasting can be given as:

```
float salary = 10000.00;
int sal;
sal = (int) salary;
```

When floating point numbers are converted to integers (as in type conversion), the digits after the decimal are truncated. Therefore, data is lost when floating-point representations are converted to integral representations. So in order to avoid such type of inaccuracies, `int` type variables must be typecast to `float` type.

As we see in the code above, typecasting can be done by placing the destination data type in parentheses followed by the variable name that has to be converted. Hence, we conclude that typecasting is done to make a variable of one data type to act like a variable of another type.

We can also typecast integer values to its character equivalent (as per ASCII code) and vice versa. Typecasting is also done in arithmetic operations to get correct result. For example, when dividing two integers, the result can be of `float` type. Also when multiplying two integers the result can be of `long int`. So to get correct precision value, typecasting can be done. For instance:

```
int a = 500, b = 70 ;
float res;
res = (float) a/b;
```

Let us look at some more examples of typecasting.

- `res = (int)9.5;`
  `9.5` is converted to `9` by truncation and then assigned to `res`.
- `res = (int)12.3 / (int)4.2;`
  It is evaluated as `12/4` and the value `3` is assigned to `res`.
- `res = (double)total/n;`
  `total` is converted to `double` and then division is done in floating point mode.
- `res = (int)(a+b);`
  The value of `a+b` is converted to integer and then assigned to `res`.
- `res = (int)a + b;`
  `a` is converted to `int` and then added with `b`.
- `res = cos((double)x);`
  It converts `x` to `double` before finding its cosine value.

---

24. Write a program to convert a floating point number into the corresponding integer.

```
#include <stdio.h>
int main()
{
  float f_num;
  int i_num;
  printf("\n Enter any floating point number: ");
  scanf("%f", &f_num);
  i_num = (int)f_num;
  printf("\n The integer variant of %f is =
  %d", f_num, i_num);
  return 0;
}
```

Output

```
Enter any floating point number: 23.45
The integer variant of 23.45 is = 23
```

25. Write a program to convert an integer into the corresponding floating point number.

```
#include <stdio.h>
int main()
{
  float f_num;
  int i_num;
  printf("\n Enter any integer: ");
  scanf("%d", &i_num);
  f_num = (float)i_num;
```

```
  printf("\n The floating point variant of
   %d is = %f", i_num, f_num);
  return 0;
}
```

Output

```
Enter any integer: 12
The floating point variant of 12 is = 12.00000
```

26. Write a program to calculate a student's result based on two examinations, one sports event, and three activities conducted. The weightage of activities = 30%, sports = 20%, and examination = 50%.

```
#include <stdio.h>
#define ACTIVITIES_WEIGHTAGE 30
#define SPORTS_WEIGHTAGE 20
#define EXAMS_WEIGHTAGE 50
#define EXAMS_TOTAL 200
#define ACTIVITIES_TOTAL 60
#define SPORTS_TOTAL 50
int main()
{
  int exam_score1, activities_score1,
   sports_score;
  int exam_score2, activities_score2,
   activities_score3;
  float exam_total, activities_total;
  float total_percent, exam_percent,
   sports_percent, activities_percent;
  printf("\n Enter the score obtained in two
   examinations (out of 100): ");
  scanf("%d %d", &exam_score1, &exam_score2);
  printf("\n Enter the score obtained in
   sports events (out of 50): ");
  scanf("%d", &sports_score);
  printf("\n Enter the score obtained in
   three activities (out of 20): ");
  scanf("%d %d %d", &activities_score1,
   &activities_score2, &activities_score3);
  exam_total = exam_score1 + exam_score2;
  activities_total = activities_score1 +
   activities_score2 + activities_score3;
  exam_percent = (float)exam_total * EXAMS_
   WEIGHTAGE / EXAMS_TOTAL;
  sports_percent = (float)sports_score *
   SPORTS_WEIGHTAGE / SPORTS_TOTAL;
  activities_percent = (float)activities_total
   * ACTIVITIES_WEIGHTAGE / ACTIVITIES_TOTAL;

  total_percent = exam_percent + sports_
   percent + activities_percent;

  printf("\n\n **********************
   RESULT **************************");
  printf("\n Total percent in examintaion :
   %f", exam_percent);
  printf("\n Total percent in activities :
   %f", activities_percent);
  printf("\n Total percent in sports :
   %f", sports_percent);
  printf("\n --------------------------------
   -------------------------");
  printf("\n Total percentage : %f",
   total_percent);
  return 0;
}
```

Output

```
Enter the score obtained in two examinations
   (out of 100): 78 89
Enter the score obtained in sports events
   (out of 50): 34
Enter the score obtained in three activities
   (out of 20): 19 18 17
****************** RESULT *****************
Total percent in examintaion: 41.75
Total percent in activities : 27
Total percent in sports      : 13
------------------------------------------
Total percentage      : 82
```

POINTS TO REMEMBER

- C was developed in the early 1970s by Dennis Ritchie at Bell Laboratories.
- A C program is composed of preprocessor commands, a global declaration section, and one or more functions.
- A function is defined as a group of C statements that are executed together.
- The execution of a C program begins at `main()` function.
- Every word in a C program is either a keyword or an identifier. C has a set of reserved words known as keywords that cannot be used as an identifier.
- The basic data types supported by C language are: char, int, float, and double.
- A variable is defined as a meaningful name given to a data storage location in computer memory. When using a variable, we actually refer to address of the memory where the data is stored.
- The difference between signed and unsigned numeric variables is that signed variables can be either negative or positive but unsigned variables can only be positive. By default, C takes a signed variable.

- The statement `return 0;` returns value 0 to the operating system to give an indication that no errors were encountered during the execution of the program.
- Modulus operator (%) can be applied only to integer operands and not to `float` or `double` operands.
- The conditional operator or the ternary (?:) is just like an if–else statement that can be used within expressions. Conditional operator is also known as ternary operator as it takes *three* operands.
- The bitwise NOT, or complement, produces the 1's complement of the given binary value.
- The comma operator evaluates the first expression and discards its value, and then evaluates the second and returns the value as the result of the expression.
- `sizeof` is a unary operator used to calculate the size of data types. This operator can be applied to all data types.
- While type conversion is done implicitly, typecasting has to be done explicitly by the programmer. Typecasting is done when the value of a higher data type has to be converted to a lower data type.

GLOSSARY

ANSI C American National Standards Institute's definition of the C programming language. It is the same as the ISO definition.

Constant A value that cannot be changed.

C tokens All the permissible characters that C language supports when combined together form tokens that act as the basic building blocks of a program.

Data type Defines the type of values that a data can take. For example, int, char, float.

Escape sequence Control codes that comprise of combinations of a backslash followed by letters or digits which represent non-printing characters.

Expression A sequence of operators and operands that may yield a single value as the result of its computation.

Executable program Program which will run in the environment of the operating system or within an appropriate run time environment.

Floating-point number Number that comprises a decimal place and exponent.

Format specification A string which controls the manner in which input or output of values has to be done.

Identifier The names used to refer to stored data values as in case of constants, variables, or functions.

Integer A number that has no fractional part.

Keyword A word which has a predefined meaning to a C compiler and therefore must not be used for any other purpose.

Library file The file which comprises of compiled versions of commonly used functions that can be linked to an object file to make an executable program.

Library function A function whose source code is stored in an external library file.

Linker The tool that connects object code and libraries to form a complete, executable program.

Operator precedence The order in which operators are applied to operands during the evaluation of an expression.

Preprocessor A processor that manipulates the initial directives of the source file. The source file contains instructions that specify how the source file shall be processed and compiled.

Preprocessor directive Instructions in the source file that specify how the file shall be processed and compiled.

Program A text file that contains the source code to be compiled.

Runtime error A program that is encountered when a program is executed.

Source code A text file that contains the source code to be compiled.

Statement A simple statement in C language that is followed by a semicolon.

Syntax error An error or mistake in the source code that prevents the compiler from converting it into object code.

Variable An identifier (and storage) for a data type. The value of a variable may change as the program runs.

EXERCISES

Fill in the Blanks

1. C was developed by ________.
2. ________ is a group of C statements that are executed together.
3. Execution of the C program begins at ________.
4. In memory characters are stored as ________.
5. The statement `return 0;` returns 0 to the ________.
6. ________ finds the remainder of an integer division.
7. ________ operator reverses the value of the expression.
8. `sizeof` is a ________ operator used to calculate the size of data types.
9. ________ is also known as forced conversion.
10. The `scanf()` function returns ________.
11. ________ function prints data on the monitor.
12. ________ establishes the original value for a variable.
13. Character constants are quoted using ________.
14. A C program ends with a ________.
15. ________ file contains mathematical functions.
16. ________ causes the cursor to move to the next line.
17. Floating point values denote ________ values by default.
18. A variable can be made constant by declaring it with the qualifier ________ at the time of initialization.
19. The sign of the result is positive in modulo division if ________.
20. Associativity of operators defines ________.
21. ________ can be used to change the order of evaluation expressions.
22. ________ operator returns the number of bytes occupied by the operand.
23. The ________ specification is used to read/write a short integer.
24. The ________ specification is used to read/write a hexadecimal integer.
25. To print the data left-justified, ________ specification is used.

Multiple-choice Questions

1. The operator which compares two values is
   (a) assignment (b) relational
   (c) unary (d) equal
2. Which operator is used to simultaneously evaluate two expressions with relational operators?
   (a) AND (b) OR
   (c) NOT (d) All of these
3. Ternary operator operates on how many operands?
   (a) 1 (b) 2
   (c) 3 (d) 4
4. Which operator produces the 1s complement of the given binary value?
   (a) Logical AND (b) Bitwise AND
   (c) Logical OR (d) Bitwise NOT
5. Which operator has the lowest precedence?
   (a) sizeof (b) unary
   (c) assignment (d) comma
6. Short integer has which conversion character associated with it
   (a) %c (b) %d
   (c) %hd (d) %f
7. Which of the following is not a character constant?
   (a) 'A' (b) "A"
   (c) ' ' (d) '*'
8. Which of the following is not a floating point constant?
   (a) 20 (b) -4.5
   (c) 'a' (d) pi
9. Identify the valid variable name.
   (a) Initial.Name (b) A+B
   (c) $amt (d) Floats
10. Which operator cannot be used with float operands?
    (a) + (b) −
    (c) % (d) *
11. Identify the erroneous expression.
    (a) x=y=2, 4; (b) res = ++a * 5;
    (c) res = /4; (d) res = a++ −b *2

State True or False

1. We can have only one function in a C program.
2. Header files are used to store program's source code.
3. Keywords are case sensitive.
4. Variable first is same as First.
5. An identifier can contain any valid printable ASCII character.
6. Signed variables can increase the maximum positive range.
7. Commented statements are not executed by the compiler.
8. $amount is a valid identifier in C.
9. Comments cannot be nested.
10. The equality operators have higher precedence than the relational operators.
11. Shifting once to the left multiplies the number by 2.
12. printf("%d", scanf("%d", &num)); is a valid C statement.
13. 1,234 is a valid integer constant.
14. A printf statement can generate only one line of output.
15. stdio.h is used to store the source code of the program.
16. The closing brace of main() is the logical end of the program.
17. The declaration section gives instructions to the computer.
18. Declaration of variables can be done anywhere in the program.

19. Underscore can be used anywhere in the variable name.
20. void is a data type in C.
21. The scanf() function can be used to read only one value at a time.
22. All arithmetic operators have same precedence.
23. The modulus operator can be used only with integers.

Review Questions

1. What are header files? Why are they important? Can we write a C program without using any header file?
2. What are variables?
3. Explain the difference between declaration and definition.
4. How is memory reserved using a declaration statement?
5. What does the data type of a variable signify?
6. Give the structure of a C program.
7. What do you understand by identifiers and keywords?
8. Write a short note on basic data types that the C language supports.
9. Why do we need signed and unsigned char?
10. Explain the terms variables and constants. How many type of variables are supported by C?
11. Why do we include <stdio.h> in our programs?
12. Write a short note on operators available in C language.
13. Give the operator precedence chart.
14. Evaluate the expression: (x > y) + ++a || !c
15. Differentiate between typecasting and type conversion.
16. Write short notes on printf and scanf functions.
17. Explain the utility of #define and #include statements.
18. Find errors in the following declaration statements.

```
Int n;
float a b;
double = a, b;
complex a b;
a,b : INTEGER
long int a;b;
```

19. Find error(s) in the following code.

```
int a = 9;
float y = 2.0;
a = b % a;
printf("%d", a);
```

20. Find error(s) in the following scanf statement.

```
scanf("%d%f", &marks, &avg);
```

Programming Exercises

1. Write a program to read an integer. Then display the value of that integer in decimal, octal, and hexadecimal notation.
2. Write a program that prints a floating point value in exponential format with the following specifications:
   (a) Correct to two decimal places;
   (b) Correct to four decimal places; and
   (c) Correct to eight decimal places.
3. Write a program to read 10 integers. Display these numbers by printing three numbers in a line separated by commas.
4. Write a program to print the count of even numbers between 1 and 200. Also print their sum.
5. Write a program to count number of vowels in a text.
6. Write a program to read the address of a user. Display the result by breaking it into multiple lines.
7. Write a program to read two floating point numbers. Add these numbers and assign the result to an integer. Finally display the value of all the three variables.
8. Write a program to read a floating point number. Display the rightmost digit of the integral part of the number.
9. Write a program to calculate simple interest and compound interest.
10. Write a program to calculate salary of an employee, given his basic pay (to be entered by the user), HRA = 10% of the basic pay, TA = 5% of basic pay. Define HRA and TA as constants and use them to calculate the salary of the employee.
11. Write a program to prepare a grocery bill. For that enter the name of the items purchased, quantity in which it is purchased, and its price per unit. Then display the bill in the following format.

```
************** B I L L **************
Item   Quantity      Price      Amount
_____________________________________
Total Amount to be paid
_____________________________________
```

12. Write a C program using printf statement to print BYE in the following format.

```
BBB     Y   Y    EEEE
B  B     Y Y     E
BBB       Y      EEEE
B  B      Y      E
BBB       Y      EEEE
```

Find the output of the following codes.

1.

```
#include <stdio.h>
int main()

    int x=3, y=5, z=7;
    int a, b;
    a = x * 2 + y / 5 - z * y;
    b = ++x * (y - 3) / 2 - z++ * y;
    printf("\n a = %d", a);
    printf("\n b = %d", b);
    return 0;
}
```

2.

```
#include <stdio.h>
int main()
{
    int a, b =3;
    char c = 'A';
    a = b + c;
    printf("\n a = %d", a);
    return 0;
}
```

3.

```
#include <stdio.h>
```

```
int main()
{
  int a;
  printf("\n %d", 1/3 + 1/3);
  printf("\n %f", 1.0/3.0 + 1.0/3.0);
  a = 15/10.0 + 3/2;
  printf("\n %d", a);
  return 0;
}
```

4. #include <stdio.h>

```
int main()
{
  int a = 4;
  printf("\n %d", 10 + a++);
  printf("\n %d", 10 + ++a);
  return 0;
}
```

5. #include <stdio.h>

```
int main()
{
  int a = 4, b = 5, c= 6;
  a = b == c;
  printf("\n a = %d", a);
  return 0;
}
```

6. #include <stdio.h>

```
int main()
{
  int a=1, b=2, c=3, d=4, e=5, res;
  res = a + b /c - d * e;
  printf("\n Result = %d", res);
  res = (a + b) /c - d * e;
  printf("\n Result = %d",res);
  res = a + ( b / (c -d)) * e;
  printf("\n Result = %d",res);
  return 0;
}
```

7. #include <stdio.h>

```
int main()
{
  int a = 4, b = 5;
  printf("\n %d", (a > b)? a: b);
   return 0;
}
```

8. #include <stdio.h>

```
int main()
{
  int a = 4, b = 12, c= -3, res;
  res = a > b && a < c;
  printf("\n %d", res);
  res = a == c || a < b;
  printf("\n %d", res);
  res = b >10 || b && c < 0 || a > 0;
  printf("\n %d", res);
  res = (a/2.0 == 0.0 && b/2.0 !=
  0.0) || c < 0.0;
  printf("\n %d", res);
  return 0;
}
```

9. #include <stdio.h>

```
int main()
{
  int a = 20, b = 5, result;
  float c = 20.0, d= 5.0;
  printf("\n 10 + a / 4 * b = %d",
   10 + a / 4 * b);
  printf("\n c / d * b + a - b = %d",
   c / d * b + a - b);
  return 0;
}
```

10. #include <stdio.h>

```
int main()
{
  int a, b;
  printf("\n a = %d \t b = %d \t a + b =
   %d", a, b, a+b);
  return 0;
}
```

11. #include <stdio.h>

```
int main()
{
  printf("\n %d", 'F');
  return 0;
}
```

12. #include <stdio.h>

```
int main()
{
  int n = 2;
  n = !n;
  printf("\n n = %d", n);
  return 0;
}
```

13. #include <stdio.h>

```
int main()
{
  int a = 100, b = 3;
  float c;
  c = a/b;
  printf("\n c = %f", c);

  return 0;
}
```

14. #include <stdio.h>

```
int main()
{
  int n = -2;
  printf("\n n = %d", -n);
  return 0;
}
```

15. #include <stdio.h>

```
int main()
{
  int a = 2, b = 3, c, d;
  c = a++;
  d = ++b;
  printf("\n c = %d d = %d", c, d);
  return 0;
}
```

16. #include <stdio.h>
```
int main()
{
  int _ = 30;
  printf("\n _ = %d", _);
  return 0;
}
```

17. #include <stdio.h>
```
int main()
{
  int a = 2, b = 3, c, d;
  a++;
  ++b;
  printf("\n a = %d b = %d", a, b);
  return 0;
}
```

18. #include <stdio.h>
```
int main()
{
  int a = 2, b = 3;
  printf("\n %d", ++(a - b));
  return 0;
}
```

19. #include <stdio.h>
```
int main()
{
  int a = 2, b = 3;
  printf("\n %d", ++a - b);
  return 0;
}
```

20. #include <stdio.h>
```
int main()
{
  int a = 2, b = 3;
  printf("\n a * b = %d", a*b);
  printf("\n a / b = %d", a/b);
  printf("\n a % b = %d", a%b);
  printf("\n a && b = %d", a &&b);
  return 0;
}
```

21. #include <stdio.h>
```
int main()
{
  int a = 2;
  a = a + 3*a++;
  printf("\n a= %d", a);
  return 0;
  }
```

22. #include <stdio.h>
```
int main()
{
  int result;
  result = 3 + 5 - 1 * 17 % -13;
  printf("%d", result);
  result = 3 * 2 + ( 15 / 4 % 7);
  printf("%d", result);
  result = 18 / 9 / 3 * 2 * 3 *
   5 % 10 / 4;
  printf("%d", result);
  return 0;
}
```

23. #include <stdio.h>
```
int main()
{
  int n = 2;
  printf("\n %d %d %d", n++, n, ++n);
  return 0;
}
```

24. #include <stdio.h>
```
int main()
{
  int a = 2, b = 3, c=4;
  a=b==c;
  printf("\n a = %d",a);
  return 0;
}
```

25. #include <stdio.h>
```
int main()
{
  int num = 070;
  printf("\n num = %d", num);
  printf("\n num = %o", num);
  printf("\n num = %x", num);
  return 0;
}
```

26. #include <stdio.h>
```
int main()
{
  printf("\n %40.27s Welcome to
   C programming");
  printf("\n %40.20s Welcome to
   C programming");
  printf("\n %40.14s Welcome to
   C programming");
  printf("\n %-40.27s Welcome to
   C programming");
  printf("\n %-40.20s Welcome to
   C programming");
  printf("\n %-40.14s Welcome to
   C programming");
  return 0;
}
```

27. #include <stdio.h>
```
int main()
```

```
{
  int a = -21, b = 3;
  printf("\n %d", a/b + 10);
  b = -b;
  printf("\n %d", a/b + 10);
  return 0;
}
```

28. #include <stdio.h>

```
int main()
{
  int a;
  float b;
  printf("\n Enter four digit number: ");
  scanf("%2d", &a);
  printf("\n Enter any floating point
   number: ");
  scanf("%f", &b);
  printf("\n The numbers are : %d
   and %f", a, b);
  return 0;
}
```

29. #include <stdio.h>

```
int main()
{
  char a, b, c;
  printf("\n Enter three characters : ");
  scanf("%c %c %c", &a, &b, &c);
  a++; b++; c++
  printf("\n a = %c b = %c and d =
    %c", a, b, c);
  return 0;
}
```

30. #include <stdio.h>

```
int main ()
{
  int x=10, y=20, res;
  res = y++ + x++;
  res += ++y + ++x;
  printf("\n x = %d  y = %d  RESULT =
  %d", x,y, res);
  return 0;
}
```

31. #include <stdio.h>

```
int main ()
{
  int x=10, y=20, res;
  res = x+++y;
  printf("\n x = %d  y = %d  RESULT = %d",
    x,y, res);
  return 0;
}
```

ANNEXURE 1

Writing, Compiling, and Executing a C Program in Unix and Linux

To execute a C program, first make sure that the C compiler gcc is installed on your machine. This is done by writing ***$ whereis cc*** or ***$ which cc*** command in the command shell. If gcc is present then the complete path of the compiler will be displayed on screen. In case the compiler is present, follow the steps given below to write and execute the program.

Step 1: Open the Vim editor and type the program. For this first type the following command in the command shell.

$ vim firstprog.c

Now when the editor gets opened type the program given below.

```
#include <stdio.h>
void main()
{
  printf("Welcome to the World of
   Programming");
}
```

Step 2: Compile the program using cc or gcc command. The command will create the *a.out* file.

$ cc firstprog.c

Step 3: Execute the C program. The program can be executed in two ways. First, by executing the *a.out* to see the output. Second, by renaming it to another file and executing it as shown below.

$ ./a.out

or

$ mv a.out firstprogram

$ ./firstprogram

This will print `Welcome to the World of Programming` on the screen.

Writing, Compiling, and Executing a C Program in Ubuntu

Step1: Open a text editor to write the C program. You can choose Vim, or gedit, or any other editor available to you.

Step 2: Type the code as shown below and save it in a file (for example, firstprog.c).

```
#include <stdio.h>
void main()
{
  printf("Welcome to the World of
   Programming");
}
```

Step 3: Compile the program using gcc, which is a compiler that is installed by default in Ubuntu. For compiling, write the following command

gcc firstprog.c –o firstprogram

In the above command, gcc is the compiler; *firstprog.c* is the name of the file to be compiled and the name following *–o* specifies the filename of the output. When you execute this command, the compiler will generate an executable file in case there are no syntax or semantic errors in the program. If there are errors, the compiler will notify you about the errors and you will then have to fix them before re-compiling the code.

Step 4: Execute the program by typing the command given below.

./firstprogram

10 Decision Control and Looping Statements

TAKEAWAYS

- Decision control statements
- Conditional branching statements
- Iterative statements
- for, while, do-while loops
- Nested loops
- break, continue, and goto statements

10.1 INTRODUCTION TO DECISION CONTROL STATEMENTS

Till now we know that the code in a C program is executed sequentially from the first line of the program to its last line, i.e., the second statement is executed after the first, the third statement is executed after the second, and so on.

Although this is true, but in some cases we want only selected statements to be executed. Such type of conditional processing extends the usefulness of programs. It allows the programmers to build programs that determine which statements of the code should be executed and which should be ignored.

C supports two types of decision control statements that can alter the flow of a sequence of instructions. These include conditional type branching and unconditional type branching. Figure 10.1 shows the categorization of decision control statements in C language.

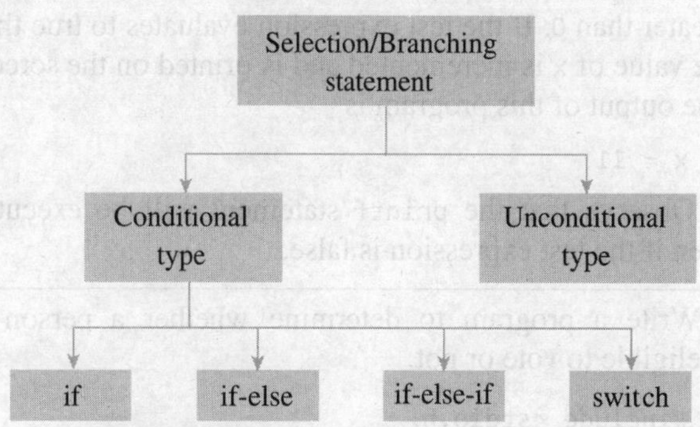

Figure 10.1 Decision control statements

10.2 CONDITIONAL BRANCHING STATEMENTS

The conditional branching statements help to jump from one part of the program to another depending on whether a particular condition is satisfied or not. These decision control statements include:

- if statement
- if–else statement
- if–else–if statement
- switch statement

10.2.1 `if` Statement

The `if` statement is the simplest form of decision control statements that is frequently used in decision-making. The general form of a simple `if` statement is shown in Figure 10.2.

The `if` block may include one statement or *n* statements enclosed within curly brackets. First, the test expression is evaluated. If the test expression is true, the statement of `if` block (statement 1 to *n*) are executed otherwise these statements will be skipped and the execution will jump to statement *x*.

> **Programming Tip:** Properly indent the statements that are dependent on the previous statements.

The statement in an `if` block is any valid C language statement and the test expression is any valid C language expression that may include logical operators. Note

SYNTAX OF IF STATEMENT

```
if (test expression)
{
   statement 1;
   ..........
   statement n;
}
statement x;
```

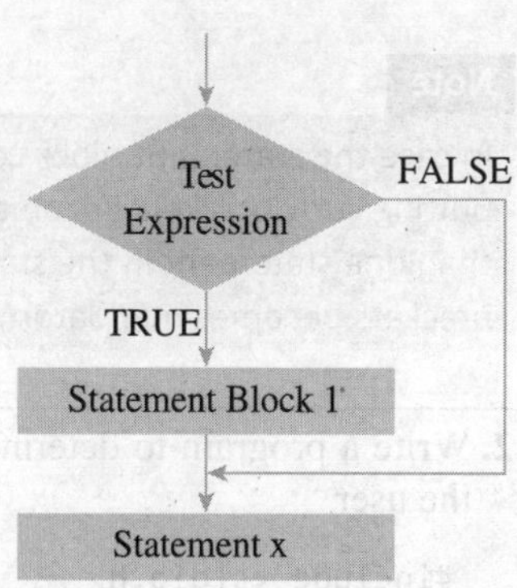

Figure 10.2 `if` statement construct

that there is no semicolon after the test expression. This is because the condition and statement should be put together as a single statement.

```
#include <stdio.h>
int main()
{
  int x=10;  // Initialize the value of x
  if ( x>0)  // Test the value of x
  x++;       // Increment x if it is > 0
  printf("\n x = %d", x);
    // Print the value of x
  return 0;
}
```

Output

```
x = 11
```

In the above code, we take a variable `x` and initialize it to `10`. In the test expression we check if the value of `x` is greater than `0`. If the test expression evaluates to true then the value of `x` is incremented and is printed on the screen. The output of this program is

```
x = 11
```

Observe that the `printf` statement will be executed even if the test expression is false.

---

1. Write a program to determine whether a person is eligible to vote or not.

```
#include <stdio.h>
int main()
{
  int age;
  printf("\n Enter the age: ");
  scanf("%d", &age);
  if(age >= 18)
  printf("\n You are eligible to vote");

  return 0;
}
```

Output

```
Enter the age: 28
You are eligible to vote
```

Note

In case the statement block contains only one statement, putting curly brackets becomes optional. If there is more than one statement in the statement block, putting curly brackets becomes mandatory.

---

2. Write a program to determine the character entered by the user.

```
#include <stdio.h>
#include <ctype.h>
int in()
{
  char ch;
  printf("\n Press any key: ");
  scanf("%c", &ch);
  if(isalpha(ch)>0)
    printf("\n The user has entered a
    character");
  if(isdigit(ch)>0)
    printf("\n The user has entered a digit");
  if(isprint(ch)>0)
    printf("\n The user has entered a
    printable character");
  if(ispunct(ch)>0)
    printf("\n The user has entered a
    punctuation mark");
  if(isspace(ch)>0)
    printf("\n The user has entered a white
    space character");

  return 0;
}
```

Output

```
Press any key: 3
The user has entered a digit
```

Now let us write a program to detect errors during data input. But before doing this we must remember that when the `scanf()` function completes its action, it returns the number of items that are successfully read. We can use this returned value to test if any error has occurred during data input. For example, consider the following function:

```
scanf("%d %f %c", &a, &b, &c);
```

If the user enters:

```
1 1.2 A
```

then the `scanf()` function will return 3, since three values have been successfully read. But had the user entered,

```
1 abc A
```

then the `scanf()` function will immediately terminate when it encounters `abc` as it was expecting a floating point value and will print an error message. So after understanding this concept, let us write a program code to detect an error in data input.

```
#include <stdio.h>
main()
{
  int num;
  char ch;
  printf("\n Enter an int and a char value:
  ");
  // Check the return value of scanf()
  if(scanf("%d %c", &num, &ch)==2)
```

```
    printf("\n Data read successfully");
    else
    printf("\n Error in data input");
  }
```

Output

```
  Enter an int and a char value: 2 A
  Data read successfully
```

10.2.2 `if-else` Statement

We have studied that the `if` statement plays a vital role in conditional branching. Its usage is very simple. The test expression is evaluated. If the result is true, the statement(s) followed by the expression is executed else if the expression is false, the statement is skipped by the compiler.

Programming Tip:
Align the matching if-else clauses vertically.

But what if you want a separate set of statements to be executed if the expression returns a zero value? In such cases, we use an `if-else` statement rather than using simple `if` statement. The general form of a simple `if-else` statement is shown in Figure 10.3.

In the syntax shown, we have written statement block. A statement block may include one or more statements. According to the `if-else` construct, first the test expression is evaluated. If the expression is true, statement block 1 is executed and statement block 2 is skipped. Otherwise, if the expression is false, statement block 2 is executed and statement block 1 is ignored. Now in any case after the statement block 1 or 2 gets executed, the control will pass to statement *x*. Therefore, statement *x* is executed in every case.

3. Write a program to find whether the given number is even or odd.

```
#include <stdio.h>

int main()
{
  int num;

  printf("\n Enter any number: ");
  scanf("%d",&num);
  if(num%2 == 0)
  printf("\n %d is an even number", num);
  else
  printf("\n %d is an odd number", num);
  return 0;
}
```

Output

```
Enter any number: 11
11 is an odd number
```

4. Write a program to enter any character. If the entered character is in lower case then convert it into upper case and if it is a lower case character then convert it into upper case.

```
#include <stdio.h>

int main()
{
  char ch;

  printf("\n Enter any character: ");
  scanf("%c", &ch);
  if(ch >='A' && ch<='Z')
  printf("\n The entered character is in upper
  case. In lower case it is: %c", (ch+32));
  else
  printf("\n The entered character is in lower
  case. In upper case it is: %c", (ch-32));
  return 0;
}
```

Output

```
Enter any character: a
The entered character is in lower case. In
upper case it is: A
```

```
SYNTAX OF IF-ELSE STATEMENT

if (test expression)
{
   statement block 1;
}
else
{
   statement block 2;
}
statement x;
```

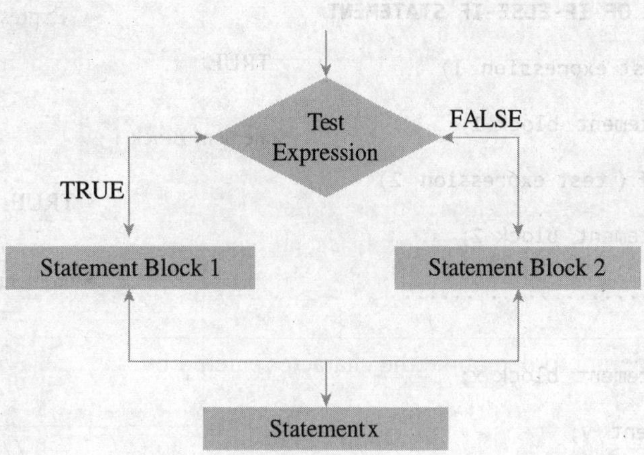

Figure 10.3 if-else statement construct

5. Write a program to enter a character and then determine whether it is a vowel or not.

```
#include <stdio.h>

int main()
{
  char ch;

  printf("\n Enter any character: ");
  scanf("%c", &ch);
  if(ch =='a' ||ch =='e' ||ch=='i' ||ch=='o'
    ||ch=='u' || ch=='A' ||ch=='E' ||ch=='I'
    ||ch=='O' ||ch=='U' )
    printf("\n %c is a vowel", ch);
  else
    printf("\n %c is not a vowel");

  return 0;
}
```

Output

```
Enter any character: v
v is not a vowel
```

6. Write a program to find whether a given year is a leap year or not.

```
#include <stdio.h>

int main()
{
  int year;

  printf("\n Enter any year: ");
  scanf("%d",&year);
  if(((year%4 == 0) && ((year%100 !=0)) ||
    (year%400 == 0)))
    printf("\n Leap Year");
  else
    printf("\n Not a Leap Year");
  return 0;
}
```

Output

```
Enter any year: 1996
Leap Year
```

Pitfall A very common pitfall while using `if` statements is to use assignment operator (`=`) instead of comparison operator (`==`). For example, consider the statement

```
if(a = 10)
  printf("%d", a);
```

Here, the statement does not test whether `a` is equal to `10` or not. Rather the value `10` is assigned to `a` and then the value is returned to the `if` construct for testing. Since the value of `a` is non-zero, the `if` construct returns a `1`.

Programming Tip: Do not use floating point numbers for checking for equality in a test expression.

The compiler cannot detect such kinds of errors and thus the programmer should carefully use the operators. The program code given below shows the outcome of mishandling the assignment and the comparison operators.

```
#include <stdio.h>
main()
{
  int x = 2, y = 3;
  if(x = y)
    printf("\n EQUAL");
  else
    printf("\n NOT EQUAL");
}
```

Output

```
EQUAL
```

```
#include <stdio.h>
main()
```

SYNTAX OF IF-ELSE-IF STATEMENT

```
if ( test expression 1)
{
  statement block 1;
}
else if ( test expression 2)
{
  statement block 2;
}
........................
else
{
  statement block x;
}
statement y;
```

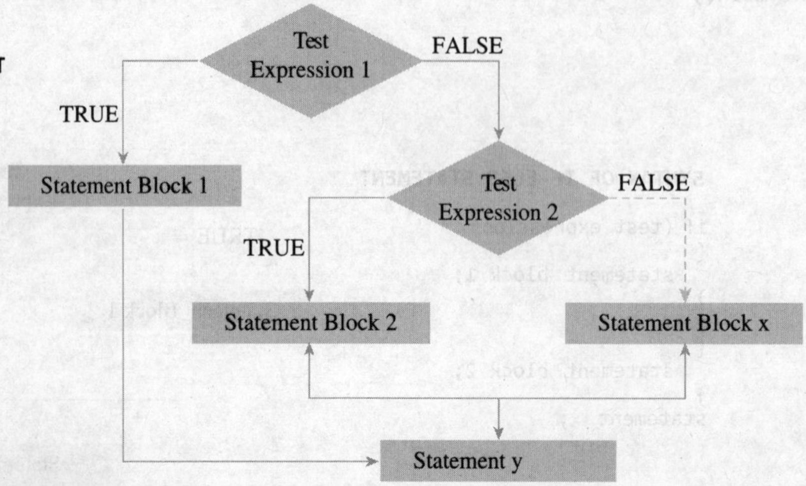

Figure 10.4 if–else–if statement construct

```
{
  int x = 2, y = 3;
  if(x == y)
    printf("\n EQUAL");
  else
    printf("\n NOT EQUAL");
}
```

Output

```
NOT EQUAL
```

10.2.3 `if-else-if` Statement

C language supports `if-else-if` statements to test additional conditions apart from the initial test expression. The `if-else-if` construct works in the same way as a normal `if` statement. `if-else-if` construct is also known as nested `if` construct. Its construct is given in Figure 10.4.

Programming Tip:
Braces must be placed on separate lines so that the block of statements can be easily identified.

It is not necessary that every `if` statement should have an `else` block as C supports simple `if` statements. After the first test expression or the first `if` branch, the programmer can have as many `else-if` branches as he wants depending on the expressions that have to be tested. For example, the following code tests whether a number entered by the user is negative, positive, or equal to zero.

7. Write a program to demonstrate the use of nested `if` structure.

```
#include <stdio.h>
int main()
{
  int x, y;
  printf("\n Enter two numbers: ");
  scanf("%d %d", &x, &y);
  if(x == y)
    printf("\n The two numbers are equal");
  else if(x > y)
    printf("\n %d is greater than %d", x, y);
  else
    printf("\n %d is smaller than %d", x, y);
  return 0;
}
```

Output

```
Enter two numbers: 12 23
12 is smaller than 23
```

8. Write a program to test whether a number entered is positive, negative, or equal to zero.

```
#include <stdio.h>
int main()
{
  int num;
  printf("\n Enter any number: ");
  scanf("%d", &num);
  if(num==0)
  printf("\n The number is
  equal to zero");
  else if(num>0)
  printf("\n The number is
  positive");
  else
  printf("\n The number is
  negative");
  return 0;
}
```

Programming Tip:
Keep the logical expressions simple and short. For this, you may use nested if statements.

Output

```
Enter any number: 0
The number is equal to zero
```

In the above program to test whether a number is positive or negative, if the first test expression evaluates to a true value then rest of the statements in the code will be ignored and after executing the `printf` statement which displays `"The number is equal to zero"`, the control will jump to `return 0` statement.

9. A company decides to give bonus to all its employees on Diwali. A 5% bonus on salary is given to the male workers and 10% bonus on salary to the female workers. Write a program to enter the salary and sex of the employee. If the salary of the employee is less than Rs 10,000 then the employee gets an extra 2% bonus on salary. Calculate the bonus that has to be given to the employee and display the salary that the employee will get.

```
#include <stdio.h>
int main()
{
  char ch;
  float sal, bonus, amt_to_be_paid;
  printf("\n Enter the sex of the employee
  (m or f): ");
  scanf("%c", &ch);
  printf("\n Enter the salary of the
  employee: ");
  scanf("%f", &sal);
  if(ch == 'm')
    bonus = 0.05 * sal;
  else
    bonus = 0.10 * sal;
  if (sal < 10000)
    bonus += 0.20 * sal;
  amt_to_be_paid = sal + bonus;
  printf("\n Salary = %f", sal);
  printf("\n Bonus = %f", bonus);
  printf("\n ***************************");
  printf("\n Amount to be paid: %f", amt_to_
  be_paid);
```

```
    return 0;
}
```

Output

```
Enter the sex of the employee (m or f): f
Enter the salary of the employee: 12000
Salary = 12000
Bonus = 1200
**************************
Amount to be paid: 13200
```

Consider the following code which shows usage of the `if-else-if` statement.

Note

The AND operand (&&) is used to form a compound relation expression. In C, the following expression is invalid.

```
if (60 ≤ marks ≤ 75)
```

The correct way to write is as follows:

```
if ((marks ≥ 60) && (marks ≤ 75))
```

10. Write a program to display the examination result.

```
#include <stdio.h>
int main()
{
  int marks;
  printf("\n Enter the marks obtained: ");
  scanf("%d", &marks);
  if ( marks >= 75)
    printf("\n DISTINCTION");
    else if ( marks >= 60 &&
    marks <75)
      printf("\n FIRST
    DIVISION");
    else if ( marks >= 50 &&
    marks < 60)
      printf("\n SECOND
    DIVISION");
    else if ( marks >= 40 &&
    marks < 50)
    printf("\n THIRD DIVISION");
  else
    printf("\n FAIL");
  return 0;
}
```

Programming Tip: Try to use the most probable condition first so that unnecessary tests are eliminated and the efficiency of the program is improved.

Output

```
Enter the marks obtained: 55
SECOND DIVISION
```

11. Write a program to calculate tax, given the following conditions:

- if income is less than 1,50,000 then no tax
- if taxable income is in the range 1,50,001–300,000 then charge 10% tax
- if taxable income is in the range 3,00,001–500,000 then charge 20% tax
- if taxable income is above 5,00,001 then charge 30% tax

```
#include <stdio.h>

#define MIN1 150001
#define MAX1 300000
#define RATE1 0.10
#define MIN2 300001
#define MAX2 500000
#define RATE2 0.20
#define MIN3 500001
#define RATE3 0.30

int main()
{
  double income, taxable_income, tax;

  printf("\n Enter the income: ");
  scanf("%lf", &income);
  taxable_income = income - 150000;
  if(taxable_income <= 0)
    printf("\n NO TAX");
  else if(taxable_income >= MIN1 && taxable_
   income < MAX1)
   tax = (taxable_income - MIN1) * RATE1;
  else if(taxable_income >= MIN2 && taxable_
    income < MAX2)
    tax = (taxable_income - MIN2) * RATE2;
  else
    tax = (taxable_income - MIN3) * RATE3;
  printf("\n TAX = %lf", tax);

  return 0;
}
```

Output

```
Enter the income: 900000
TAX = 74999.70
```

12. Write a program to find the greatest of three numbers.

```
#include <stdio.h>

int main()
{
  int num1, num2, num3, big=0;

  printf("\n Enter the first number: ");
  scanf("%d", &num1);
  printf("\n Enter the second number: ");
  scanf("%d", &num2);
  printf("\n Enter the third number: ");
  scanf("%d", &num3);
  if(num1>num2)
  {
  if(num1>num3)
    printf("\n %d is greater than %d and %d",
    num1, num2, num3);
```

```
   else
      printf("\n %d is greater than %d and %d",
      num3, num1, num2);

   }
   else if(num2>num3)
      printf("\n %d is greater than %d and %d",
      num2, num1, num3);
   else
   printf("\n %d is greater than %d and %d",
   num3, num1, num2);
   return 0;
   }
```

Programming Tip: It is always recommended to indent the statements in the block by at least three spaces to the right of the braces.

Output

```
Enter the first number: 12
Enter the second number:
23
Enter the third number: 9
23 is greater than 12 and 9
```

13. Write a program to input three numbers and then find largest of them using && operator.

```
#include <stdio.h>

int main()
{
   int num1, num2, num3;

   printf("\n Enter the first number: ");
   scanf("%d", &num1);
   printf("\n Enter the second number: ");
   scanf("%d", &num2);
   printf("\n Enter the third number: ");
   scanf("%d", &num3);
   if(num1>num2 && num1>num3)
      printf("\n %d is the largest number", num1);
   if(num2>num1 && num2>num3)
      printf("\n %d is the largest number",
   num2);
   else
      printf("\n %d is the largest number", num3);

   return 0;
}
```

Output

```
Enter the first number: 12
Enter the second number: 23
Enter the third number: 9
23 is the largest number
```

14. Write a program to enter the marks of a student in four subjects. Then calculate the total, aggregate, and display the grades obtained by the student.

```
#include <stdio.h>
int main()
{
   int marks1, marks2, marks3, marks4,
   total = 0;
   float avg =0.0;

   printf("\n Enter the marks in
   Mathematics: ");
   scanf("%d", &marks1);
   printf("\n Enter the marks in Science: ");
   scanf("%d", &marks2);
   printf("\n Enter the marks in Social
     Science: ");
   scanf("%d", &marks3);
   printf("\n Enter the marks in Computer
     Science: ");
   scanf("%d", &marks4);
   total = marks1 + marks2 + marks3 + marks4;
   avg = (float) total/4;
   printf("\n TOTAL = %d", total);
   printf("\n AGGREGATE = %.2f", avg);
   if(avg >= 75)
     printf("\n DISTINCTION");
   else if(avg>=60 && avg<75)
     printf("\n FIRST DIVISION");
   else if(avg>=50 && avg<60)
     printf("\n SECOND DIVISION");
   else if(avg>=40 && avg<50)
     printf("\n THIRD DIVISION");
   else
     printf("\n FAIL");
   return 0;
}
```

Output

```
Enter the marks in Mathematics: 90
Enter the marks in Science: 91
Enter the marks in Social Science: 92
Enter the marks in Computer Science: 93
TOTAL = 366
AGGREGATE = 91.00
DISTINCTION
```

15. Write a program to calculate the roots of a quadratic equation.

```
#include <stdio.h>
#include <math.h>

void main()
{
   int a, b, c;
   float D, deno, root1, root2;

   printf("\n Enter the values of a, b,
     and c :");
   scanf("%d %d %d", &a, &b, &c);
   D = (b * b) - (4 * a * c);
```

```
    deno = 2 * a;
    if(D > 0)
    {
      printf("\n REAL ROOTS");
      root1 = (-b + sqrt(D)) / deno;
      root2 = (-b - sqrt(D)) / deno;
      printf("\n ROOT1 = %f \t ROOT 2 = %f",
        root1, root2);
    }
    else if(D == 0)
    {
      printf("\n EQUAL ROOTS");
      root1 = -b/deno;
      printf("\n ROOT1 = %f \t ROOT 2 = %f",
      root1, root1);
    }
    else
      printf("\n IMAGINARY ROOTS");

  }
```

Output

```
Enter the values of a, b, and c : 3 4 5
IMAGINARY ROOTS
```

Let us now summarize the rules for using `if`, `if-else`, and `if-else-if` statements.

Rule 1: The expression must be enclosed in parentheses.

Rule 2: No semicolon is placed after the `if/if-else/if-else-if` statement. Semicolon is placed only at the end of statements in the statement block.

Rule 3: A statement block begins and ends with a curly brace. No semicolon is placed after the opening/closing braces.

Dangling Else Problem

With nesting of `if-else` statements, we often encounter a problem known as *dangling else problem.* This problem is created when there is no matching else for every `if` statement. In such cases, C always pairs an `else` statement to the most recent unpaired `if` statement in the current block. Consider the following code which shows such a scenario.

> **Programming Tip:**
> While forming the conditional expression, try to use positive statements rather than using compound negative statements.

```
if(a > b)
if(a > c)
  printf("\n a is greater than b and c");
else
  printf("\n a is not greater than b and c");
```

The problem is that both the outer `if` statement and the inner `if` statement might conceivably own the `else` clause. So the programmer must always see that every `if` statement is paired with an appropriate `else` statement.

Comparing Floating Point Numbers

We should never use floating point numbers for testing equality. This is because floating point numbers are just approximations, so it is always better to use floating point numbers for testing 'approximately equal' rather than testing for exactly equal.

We can test for approximate equality by subtracting the two floating point numbers (that are to be tested) and comparing their absolute value of the difference against a very small number, **epsilon**. For example, consider the code given below which compares two floating point numbers. Note that epsilon is chosen by the programmer to be small enough so that the two numbers can be considered equal.

```
#include <stdio.h>
#include <math.h>
#define EPSILON 1.0e-5
int main()
{
  double num1 = 10.0, num2 = 9.5;
  double res1, res2;
  res1 = num2 / num1 * num1;
  res2 = num2;
  /* fabs() is a C library function that
  returns the floating point absolute value */
  if(fabs(res2 - res1) < EPSILON)
    printf("EQUAL");
  else
    printf("NOT EQUAL");
  return 0;
}
```

Also note that adding a very small floating point value to a very large floating point value or subtracting floating point numbers of widely differing magnitudes may not have any effect. This is because adding/subtracting two floating point numbers that differ in magnitude by more than the precision of the data type used will not affect the larger number.

10.2.4 switch case

A `switch` case statement is a multi-way decision statement that is a simplified version of an `if-else` block that evaluates only one variable. The general form of a `switch` statement is shown in Figure 10.5.

> **Programming Tip:**
> It is always recommended to use default label in a switch statement.

Table 10.1 compares general form of a `switch` statement with that of an `if-else` statement.

Here, statement blocks refer to statement lists that may contain zero or more statements. *These statements in the block are not enclosed within opening and closing braces.*

Syntax of Switch Statement

```
switch ( variable )
{
case  value1:
  Statement  Block 1;
  break;
case  value2:
  Statement  Block 2;
  break;
.......................
case  value N:
  Statement  Block N;
  break;
default:
  Statement  Block D;
  break;
}
Statement  X;
```

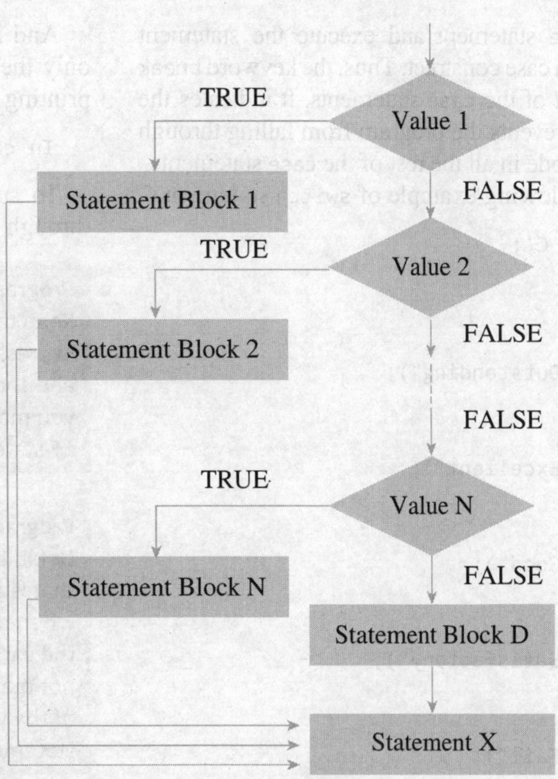

Figure 10.5 The switch statement construct

Table 10.1 Comparison between the switch and if-else construct

Generalized switch statement	Generalized if-else statement

switch(x) {
case 1: // do this
case 2: // do this
case 3: // do this
....
default: //do this
}
	if(exp1)
	{
	// do this
	}
	else if(exp2)
	{
	// do this
	}
	else if(exp3)
	{
	// do this
	}

The power of nested `if-else` statements lies in the fact that it can evaluate more than one expression in a single logical structure. Switch statements are mostly used in two situations:

- When there is only one variable to evaluate in the expression
- When many conditions are being tested for

When there are many conditions to test, using the `if` and `else-if` constructs becomes a bit complicated and confusing. Therefore, `switch case` statements are often used as an alternative to long `if` statements that compare a variable to several *integral* values (integral values are those values that can be expressed as an integer, such as the value of a char). Switch statements are also used to handle the input given by the user.

We have already seen the syntax of the `switch` statement. The `switch case` statement compares the value of the variable given in the `switch` statement with the value of each case statement that follows. When the value of the `switch` and the `case` statement matches, the statement block of that particular case is executed.

Did you notice the keyword `default` in the syntax of the switch case statement? `default` is also a case that is executed when the value of the variable does not match with any of the values of the `case` statement, i.e., the `default` case is executed when no match is found between the values of `switch` and `case` statements and thus there are no statements to be executed. Although the `default` case is optional, it is always recommended to include it as it handles any unexpected cases.

> **Programming Tip:**
> C supports decision control statements that can alter the flow of a sequence of instructions.
> A `switch-case` statement is a multi-way decision statement that is a simplified version of an `if-else` block that evaluates only one variable.

In the syntax of the `switch case` statement, we have used another keyword `break`. The `break` statement must be used at the end of each case because if it is not used, then the case that matched and all the following cases will be executed. For example, if the value of `switch` statement matched with that of `case 2`, then all the statements in `case 2` as well as rest of the cases including `default` will be executed. The `break` statement tells the compiler to jump out of the `switch case` statement and execute the statement following the switch case construct. Thus, the keyword `break` is used to break out of the `case` statements. It indicates the end of a case and prevents the program from falling through and executing the code in all the rest of the `case` statements.

Consider the following example of `switch` statement.

```
char grade = 'C';
switch(grade)
{
case 'O':
  printf("\n Outstanding");
  break;
case 'A':
  printf("\n Excellent");
  break;
case 'B':
  printf("\n Good");
  break;
case 'C':
  printf("\n Satisfactory");
  break;
case 'F':
  printf("\n Fail");
  break;
default:
  printf("\n Invalid Grade");
  break;
}
```

Output

```
Satisfactory
```

16. Write a program to demonstrate the use of switch statement without a break.

```
#include <stdio.h>
int main()
{
int option = 1;
switch(option)
{
  case 1: printf("\n In case 1");
  case 2: printf("\n In case 2");
  default: printf("\n In case default");
}
return 0;
}
```

Output

```
In case 1
In case 2
In case default
```

Had the value of option been 2, then the output would have been

```
In case 2
In case default
```

And if option was equal to 3 or any other value then only the default case would have been executed, thereby printing

```
In case default
```

To summarize the `switch case` construct, let us go through the following rules:

Programming Tip:
Keep the logical expressions simple and short. For this, you may use nested `if` statements.

Programming Tip:
Default is also a case that is executed when the value of the variable does not match with any of the values of case statements.

- The control expression that follows the keyword `switch` must be of integral type (i.e., either an integer or any value that can be converted to an integer).
- Each case label should be followed with a constant or a constant expression.
- Every case label must evaluate to a unique constant expression value.
- Case labels must end with a colon.
- Two case labels may have the same set of actions associated with them.
- The `default` label is optional and is executed only when the value of the expression does not match with any labelled constant expression. It is recommended to have a `default` case in every `switch case` statement.
- The `default` label can be placed anywhere in the `switch` statement. But the most appropriate position of `default` case is at the end of the `switch case` statement.
- There can be only one `default` label in a switch statement.
- C permits nested switch statements, i.e., a switch `statement` within another `switch` statement.

17. Write a program to determine whether an entered character is a vowel or not.

```
#include <stdio.h>
int main()
{
  char ch;
  printf("\n Enter any character: ");
  scanf("%c", &ch);
  switch(ch)
  {
    case 'A':
    case 'a':
      printf("\n % c is vowel", ch);
      break;
    case 'E':
    case 'e':
      printf("\n % c is vowel", ch);
      break;
    case 'I':
    case 'i':
      printf("\n % c is vowel", ch);
```

```
    break;
  case 'O':
  case 'o':
    printf("\n % c is vowel", ch);
    break;
  case 'U':
  case 'u':
    printf("\n % c is vowel", ch);
    break;
  default: printf("%c is not a vowel", ch);
  }
  return 0;
}
```

Output

```
Enter any character: E
E is vowel
```

Note that there is no break statement after case A, so if the character 'A' is entered, then the control will execute the statements given in case 'a'.

18. Write a program to enter a number from 1–7 and display the corresponding day of the week using switch case statement.

```
#include <stdio.h>

int main()
{
  int day;

  printf("\n Enter any number from 1 to 7: ");
  scanf("%d",&day);

  switch(day)
  {
  case 1: printf("\n SUNDAY");
  break;
  case 2: printf("\n MONDAY");
  break;
  case 3: printf("\n TUESDAY");
  break;
  case 4: printf("\n WEDNESDAY");
  break;
  case 5: printf("\n THURSDAY");
  break;
  case 6: printf("\n FRIDAY");
  break;
  case 7: printf("\n SATURDAY");
  break;
  default: printf("\n Wrong Number");
  }
  return 0;
}
```

Output

```
Enter any number from 1 to 7: 5
THURSDAY
```

19. Write a program that accepts a number from 1 to 10. Print whether the number is even or odd using a switch case construct.

```
#include <stdio.h>
void main()
{
  int num;
  printf("\n Enter any number (1 to 10): ");
  scanf("%d", &num);
  switch(num)
  {
  case 1:
  case 3:
  case 5:
  case 7:
  case 9:
    printf("\n ODD");
    break;
  case 2:
  case 4:
  case 6:
  case 8:
  case 10:
    printf("\n EVEN");
  default:
    printf("\n INVALID INPUT");
    break;
  }
}
```

OR

```
#include <stdio.h>
void main()
{
  int num, rem;
  printf("\n Enter any number (1 to 10): ");
  scanf("%d", &num);
  rem = num%2;
  switch(rem)
  {
  case 0:
    printf("\n EVEN");
    break;
  case 1:
    printf("\n ODD");
    break;
  }
}
```

Output

```
Enter any number from 1 to 10: 7
ODD
```

Advantages of Using a switch case *Statement*

Switch case statement is preferred by programmers due to the following reasons:

- Easy to debug
- Easy to read and understand
- Ease of maintenance as compared with its equivalent `if-else` statements
- Like `if-else` statements, `switch` statements can also be nested
- Executes faster than its equivalent `if-else` construct

10.3 ITERATIVE STATEMENTS

Iterative statements are used to repeat the execution of a list of statements, depending on the value of an integer expression. C language supports three types of iterative statements also known as looping statements. They are:

- while loop
- do-while loop
- for loop

In this section, we will discuss all these statements.

10.3.1 `while` Loop

The `while` loop provides a mechanism to repeat one or more statements while a particular condition is true. Figure 10.6 shows the syntax and general form of representation of a `while` loop.

In the `while` loop, the condition is tested before any of the statements in the statement block is executed. If the condition is true, only then the statements will be executed otherwise if the condition is false, the control will jump to statement *y*, which is the immediate statement outside the `while` loop block.

Programming Tip:
Iterative statements are used to repeat the execution of a list of statements, depending on the value of an integer expression.

From the flowchart, it is clear that we need to constantly update the condition of the `while` loop. It is this condition which determines when the loop will end. The `while` loop will execute as long as the condition is true. Note if the condition is never updated and the condition never becomes false then the computer will run into an infinite loop which is never desirable.

Programming Tip:
Check that the relational operator is not mistyped as an assignment operator.

A `while` loop is also referred to as a top-checking loop since control condition is placed as the first line of the code. If the control condition evaluates to false, then the statements enclosed in the loop are never executed.

For example, look at the following code which prints first 10 numbers using a `while` loop.

```
#include <stdio.h>
int main()
{
  int i = 1;    //  initialize loop variable
  while(i<=10)  //  test the condition
  {        //  execute the loop statements
   printf(" %d", i);
   i = i + 1;  // condition updated
  }

 return 0;
}
```

Output

```
1 2 3 4 5 6 7 8 9 10
```

Initially `i = 1` and is less than 10, i.e., the condition is true, so in the `while` loop the value of `i` is printed and the condition is updated so that with every execution of the loop, the terminating condition becomes approachable. Let us look at some more programming examples that illustrate the use of `while` loop.

20. Write a program to calculate the sum of first 10 numbers.

```
#include <stdio.h>
int main()
{
  int i = 1, sum = 0;
  while(i<=10)
  {
```

Syntax of While Loop

```
statement  x;
while  (condition)
{
 statement block;
}
statement  y;
```

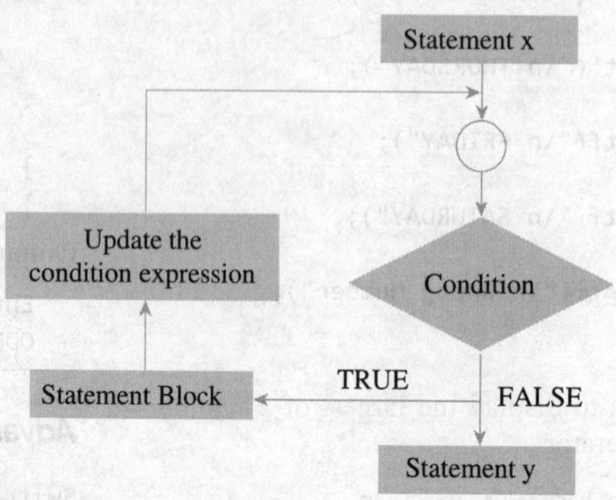

Figure 10.6 The `while` loop construct

```
    sum = sum + i;
    i = i + 1; // condition updated
  }
  printf("\n SUM = %d", sum);
  return 0;
}
```

Output

```
SUM = 55
```

21. Write a program to print 20 horizontal asterisks (*).

```
#include <stdio.h>
int main()
{
  int i=1;
  while (i<=20)
  {
    printf("*");
    i++;
  }
  return 0;
}
```

Output

```
********************
```

22. Write a program to calculate the sum of numbers from *m* to *n*.

```
#include <stdio.h>
int main()
{
  int n, m, sum =0;

  printf("\n Enter the value of m: ");
  scanf("%d", &m);

  printf("\n Enter the value of n: ");
  scanf("%d", &n);

  while(m<=n)
  {
    sum = sum + m;
    m = m + 1;
  }
  printf("\n SUM = %d", sum);
  return 0;
}
```

Output

```
Enter the value of m: 7
Enter the value of n: 11
SUM = 45
```

23. Write a program to display the largest of 5 numbers using ternary operator.

```
#include <stdio.h>
int main()
{
  int i=1, large = -32768, num;

  while(i<=5)
  {
    printf("\n Enter the number: ");
    scanf("%d",&num);
    large = num>large?num:large;
    i++;
  }
  printf("\n The largest of five numbers
  entered is: %d", large);
  return 0;
}
```

Output

```
Enter the number : 29
Enter the number : 15
Enter the number : 17
Enter the number : 19
Enter the number : 25
The largest of five numbers entered is: 29
```

24. Write a program to read the numbers until –1 is encountered. Also count the negative, positive, and zeros entered by the user.

```
#include <stdio.h>

int main()
{
  int num;
  int negatives=0, positives=0, zeros=0;

  printf("\n Enter -1 to exit.");
  printf("\n\n Enter any number: ");
  scanf("%d",&num);

  while(num != -1)
  {
    if(num>0)
      positives++;
    else if(num<0)
      negatives++;
    else
      zeros++;
    printf("\n\n Enter any number: ");
    scanf("%d",&num);
  }
  printf("\n Count of positive numbers entered
  = %d", positives);
  printf("\n Count of negative numbers entered
  = %d", negatives);
  printf("\n Count of zeros entered = %d",
  zeros);
```

```
    return 0;
}
```

Output

```
Enter -1 to exit
Enter any number: -12
Enter any number: 108
Enter any number: -24
Enter any number: 99
Enter any number: -23
Enter any number: 101
Enter any number: -1
Count of positive numbers entered = 3
Count of negative numbers entered = 3
Count of zeros entered = 0
```

25. Write a program to calculate the average of numbers entered by the user.

```
#include <stdio.h>
int main()
{
    int num, sum = 0, count = 0;
    float avg;
    printf("\n Enter any number. Enter -1 to
      STOP: ");
    scanf("%d", &num);
          while(num != -1)
          {
          count++;
          sum = sum + num;
          printf("\n Enter any
          number. Enter -1 to
          STOP: ");
          scanf("%d", &num);
          }
        avg = (float)sum/count;
        printf("\n SUM = %d", sum);
        printf("\n AVERAGE = %.2f",
        avg);
        return 0;
}
```

> **Programming Tip:** Placing a semicolon after the while/for loop in not a syntax error. So it will not be reported by the compiler. However, it is considered to be a logical error as it changes the output of the program.

Output

```
Enter -1 to exit
Enter any number. Enter -1 to STOP: 23
Enter any number. Enter -1 to STOP: 13
Enter any number. Enter -1 to STOP: 3
Enter any number. Enter -1 to STOP: 53
Enter any number. Enter -1 to STOP: 4
Enter any number. Enter -1 to STOP: 63
Enter any number. Enter -1 to STOP: -23
Enter any number. Enter -1 to STOP: -6
Enter any number. Enter -1 to STOP: -1
SUM = 130
AVERAGE = 16.25
```

Thus, we see that `while` loop is very useful for designing interactive programs in which the number of times the statements in the loop have to be executed is not known in advance. The program will execute until the user wants to stop by entering `-1`.

Now look at the code given below which results in an infinite loop. The code given below is supposed to calculate the average of first 10 numbers, but since the condition never becomes false, the output will not be generated and the intended task will not be performed.

```
#include <stdio.h>
int main()
{
  int i = 0, sum =0;
  float avg = 0.0;

  while(i<=10)
  {
    sum = sum + i;
  }
  avg = (float) sum/10;
  printf("\n The sum of first 10 numbers = %d",
   sum);
  printf("\n The average of first 10 numbers =
   %f", avg);
  return 0;
}
```

10.3.2 do-while Loop

The `do-while` loop is similar to the `while` loop. The only difference is that in a `do-while` loop, the test condition is evaluted at the end of the loop. Now that the test condition is evaluted at the end, this clearly means that the body of the loop gets executed at least one time (even if the condition is false). Figure 10.7 shows the syntax and general form of representation of a `do-while` loop.

Note that the test condition is enclosed in parentheses and followed by a semicolon. The statements in the statement block are enclosed within curly brackets. The curly brackets are optional if there is only one statement in the body of the `do-while` loop.

Like the `while` loop, the `do-while` loop continues to execute whilst the condition is true. There is no choice whether to enter the loop or not because the loop will be executed at least once irrespective of whether the condition is true or false. Hence, entry in the loop is automatic. There is only one choice: to continue or to exit. The `do-while` loop will continue to execute while the condition is true and when the condition becomes false, the control will jump to statement following the `do-while` loop.

Similar to the `while` loop, the `do-while` is an indefinite loop as the loop can execute until the user wants to stop. The number of times the loop has to be executed can thus be determined at the run time. However, unlike the `while` loop, the `do-while` loop is a bottom-checking loop, since the control expression is placed after the body of the loop.

The major disadvantage of using a `do-while` loop is that it always executes at least once, even if the user enters

Syntax of do-while Loop

```
statement x;
do
{
statement block;
}while (condition);

statement y;
```

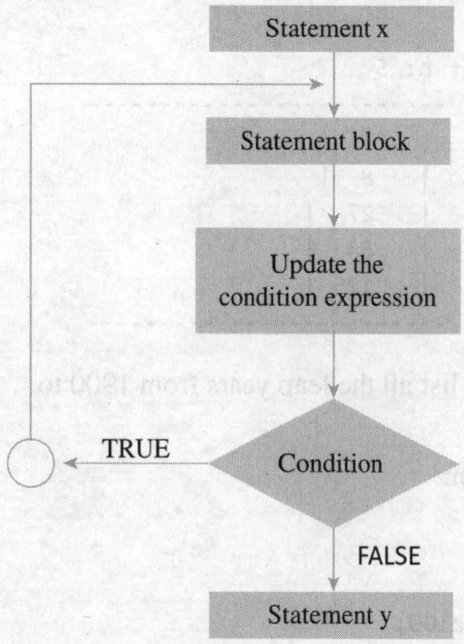

Figure 10.7 do-while construct

some invalid data. One complete execution of the loop takes place before the first comparison is actually done. However, do-while loops are widely used to print a list of options for a menu-driven programs. For example, look at the following code.

```
#include <stdio.h>
int main()
{
int i = 1;
do
{
  printf("\n %d", i);
  i = i + 1;
} while(i<=10);
return 0;
}
```

What do you think will be the output? The code will print numbers from 1 to 10.

26. Write a program to calculate the average of first *n* numbers.

> **Programming Tip:**
> Do not forget to place a semicolon at the end of the do-while statement.

```
#include <stdio.h>
int main()
{
  int n, i = 1, sum = 0;
  float avg = 0.0;
  printf("\n Enter the value of n: ");
  scanf("%d", &n);
  do
  {
    sum = sum + i;
    i = i + 1;
  } while(i<=n);
  avg = (float) sum/n;
  printf("\n The sum of first %d numbers = %d",
    n, sum);
  printf("\n The average of first %d numbers =
    %.2f", n, avg);
  return 0;
}
```

Output

```
Enter the value of n: 18
The sum of first 18 numbers = 171
The average of first 18 numbers = 9.00
```

27. Write a program using a do-while loop to display the square and cube of first *n* natural numbers.

```
#include <stdio.h>

int main()
{
  int i, n;

  printf("\n Enter the value of n: ");
  scanf("%d", &n);
  printf("\n ---------------------------");
  i=1;
  do
  {
      printf("\n | \t %d \t |
      \t %d \t | \t %ld \t |", i,
      i*i, i*i*i);
        i++;
      } while(i<=n);
      printf("\n ----------------
      -----------");
      return 0;
      }
```

> **Programming Tip:**
> Avoid using do-while loop for implementing pre-test loops and use the do-while loop for post-test loops.

Output

```
Enter the value of n: 5
------------------------------------------
|   1   |   1     |   1  |
|   2   |   4     |   8  |
|   3   |   9     |   27  |
|   4   |   16    |   64  |
|   5   |   25    |   125 |
------------------------------------------
```

28. Write a program to list all the leap years from 1900 to 1920.

```
#include <stdio.h>

int main()
{
  int m=1900, n=2100;

  do
{
  if(((m%4 == 0) && (m%100!=0))||(m%400==0)))
  printf("\n %d is a leap year",m);
  m = m+1;
}while(m<=n);
return 0;
}
```

Programming Tip:
If you want that the body of the loop must get executed at least once, then use the do-while loop.

Output

```
1904 is a leap year
1908 is a leap year
1912 is a leap year
1916 is a leap year
1920 is a leap year
...
2096 is a leap year
```

29. Write a program to read a character until a `*` is encountered. Also count the number of upper case, lower case, and numbers entered.

```
#include <stdio.h>

int main()
{
  char ch;
  int lowers = 0, uppers = 0, numbers = 0;

  printf("\n Enter any character: ");
  scanf("%c", &ch);

  do
{
  if(ch >='A' && ch<='Z')
    uppers++;
  if(ch >='a' && ch<='z')
    lowers++;
  if(ch >='0' && ch<='9')
    numbers++;

  fflush(stdin);
  /* The function is used to clear the
   standard input file. */
  printf("\n Enter another character. Enter *
   to exit.");
  scanf("%c", &ch);
  } while(ch != '*');

  printf("\n Total count of lower case
   characters entered = %d", lowers);
  printf("\n Total count of upper case
   characters entered = %d", uppers);
  printf("\n Total count of numbers entered =
   %d", numbers);
  return 0;
}
```

Output

```
Enter any character: O
Enter another character. Enter * to exit. x
Enter another character. Enter * to exit. F
Enter another character. Enter * to exit. o
Enter another character. Enter * to exit. R
Enter another character. Enter * to exit. d
Enter another character. Enter * to exit. *

Total count of lower case characters entered
  = 3
Total count of upper case characters entered
  = 3
Total count of numbers entered = 0
```

30. Write a program to read the numbers until –1 is encountered. Also calculate the sum and mean of all positive numbers entered and the sum and mean of all negative numbers entered separately.

```
#include <stdio.h>

int main()
{
  int num;
  int sum_negatives=0, sum_positives=0;
  int positives = 0, negatives = 0;
  float mean_positives = 0.0, mean_negatives =
   0.0;

  printf("\n Enter -1 to exit");
  printf("\n\n Enter any number: ");
  scanf("%d",&num);

  do
  {
```

```
    if(num>0)
    {
      sum_positives += num;
      positives++;
    }
    else if(num<0)
    {
      sum_negatives += num;
      negatives++;
    }

  printf("\n\n Enter any number: ");
  scanf("%d",&num);
  } while(num != -1);

  mean_positives = (float)sum_positives/
    positives;
  mean_negatives = (float) sum_negatives/
    negatives;

  printf("\n Sum of all positive numbers
     entered = %d", sum_positives);
  printf("\n Mean of all positive numbers
     entered = %.2f", mean_positives);

  printf("\n Sum of all negative numbers
     entered = %d", sum_negatives);
  printf("\n Mean of all negative numbers
     entered = %.2f", mean_negatives);
  return 0;
}
```

Output

```
Enter -1 to exit
Enter any number: 9
Enter any number: 8
Enter any number: 7
Enter any number: -6
Enter any number: -5
Enter any number: -4
Enter any number: -1
Sum of all positive numbers entered = 24
Mean of all positive numbers entered = 8.00
Sum of all negative numbers entered = -15
Mean of all negative numbers entered = -5.00
```

10.3.3 for Loop

Like the `while` and `do-while` loops, the `for` loop provides a mechanism to repeat a task until a particular condition is true. `For` loop is usually known as a determinate or definite loop because the programmer knows exactly how many times the loop will repeat. The number of times the loop has to be executed can be determined mathematically by checking the logic of the loop. The syntax and general form of a `for` loop is given in Figure 10.8.

When a `for` loop is used, the loop variable is initialized only once. With every iteration of the loop, the value of the loop variable is updated and the condition is checked. If the condition is true, then the statement block of the loop is executed, else the statements comprising the statement block of the `for` loop are skipped and the control jumps to the immediate statement following the `for` loop body.

Syntax of for Loop

```
for (initialization;  condition;
       increment/decrement/update)
{
statement block;
}
statement y;
```

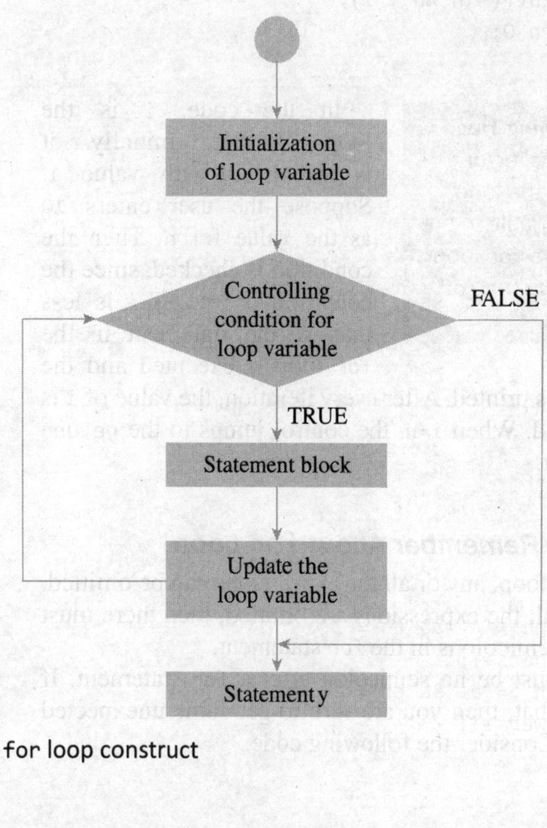

Figure 10.8 for loop construct

In the syntax of the for loop, initialization of the loop variable allows the programmer to give it a value. Second, the condition specifies that while the conditional expression is true the loop should continue to repeat itself. With every iteration, the condition when the loop would terminate should be approachable. So, with every iteration, the loop variable must be updated. Updating the loop variable may include incrementing the loop variable, decrementing the loop variable or setting it to some other value like, `i +=2`, where `i` is the loop variable.

Note that every section of the for loop is separated from the other with a semicolon. It is possible that one of the sections may be empty, though the semicolons still have to be there. However, if the condition is empty, it is evaluated as true and the loop will repeat until something else stops it.

The for loop is widely used to execute a single or a group of statements a limited number of times. Another point to consider is that in a for loop, condition is tested before the statements contained in the body are executed. So if the condition does not hold true, then the body of the for loop is not executed.

Look at the following code which prints the first *n* numbers using a for loop.

```
#include <stdio.h>
int main()
{
  int i, n;
  printf("\n Enter the value of n :");
  scanf("%d", &n);
  for(i=1;i<=n;i++)
    printf("\n %d", i);
  return 0;
}
```

> **Programming Tip:**
> It is a logical error to update the loop control variable in the body of the for loop as well as in the for statement.

In the code, i is the loop variable. Initially, it is initialized with value 1. Suppose the user enters 10 as the value for n. Then the condition is checked, since the condition is true as i is less than n, the statement in the for loop is executed and the value of i is printed. After every iteration, the value of i is incremented. When i=n, the control jumps to the return 0 statement.

Points to Remember About for *Loop*

- In a for loop, any or all the expressions can be omitted. In case all the expressions are omitted, then there must be two semicolons in the for statement.
- There must be no semicolon after a for statement. If you do that, then you are sure to get some unexpected results. Consider the following code.

```
#include <stdio.h>
int main()
{
  int i;
  for(i=0;i<10;i++);
    printf(" %d", i);
  return 0;
}
```

In this code, the loop initializes i to 0 and increments its value. Since a semicolon is placed after the loop, it means that loop does not contain any statement. So even if the condition is true, no statement is executed. The loop continues till i becomes 10 and the moment i=10, the statement following the for loop is executed and the value of i (10) is printed on the screen.

When we place a semicolon after the for statement, then the compiler will not generate any error message. Rather it will treat the statement as a null statement. Usually such type of null statement is used to generate time delays. For example, the following code produces no output and simply delays further processing.

```
#include <stdio.h>
int main()
{
  int i;
  for(i=10000;i>0;i--);
    printf(" %d", i);
  return 0;
}
```

- Multiple initializations must be separated with a comma operator as shown in the following code segment.

```
#include <stdio.h>
int main()
{
  int i, sum;
  for(i=0, sum=0;i<10;i++)
    sum += i;
  printf(" %d", sum);
  return 0;
}
```

- If there is no initialization to be done, then the initialization statement can be skipped by giving only a semicolon. This is shown in the following code.

> **Programming Tip:**
> Although we can place the initialization, testing and updating the loop control variable outside the for loop, we must try to avoid it as much as possible.

```
#include <stdio.h>
int main()
{
  int i=0;
  for(;i<10;i++)
    printf("%d", i);
  return 0;
}
```

- Multiple conditions in the test expression can be tested by using logical operators (&& or ||).
- If the loop controlling variable is updated within the statement block, then the third part can be skipped. This is shown in the code given below.

```
#include <stdio.h>
int main()
{
  int i=0;
  for(;i<10;)
  {
    printf(" %d", i);
    i = i + 1;
  }
return 0;
}
```

- Multiple statements can be included in the third part of the for statement by using the comma operator. For example, the for statement given below is valid in C.

```
for(i=0, j=10;i<j; i++, j--)
```

- The controlling variable can also be incremented/ decremented by values other than 1. This is shown in the code below which prints all odd numbers from 1 to 10.

```
#include <stdio.h>
int main()
{
  int i;
  for(i=1;i<=10;i+=2)
    printf(" %d", i);
  return 0;
}
```

- If the for loop contains nothing but two semicolons, that is no initialization, condition testing, and updating of the loop control variable then the for loop may become an infinite loop if no stopping condition is specified in the body of the loop. For example, the following code will infinitely print C Programming on the computer screen.

Programming Tip: Although placing an arithmetic expression in initialization and updating section of the for loop is permissible, try to avoid them as they may cause some round-off and/or truncation errors.

```
#include <stdio.h>
int main()
{
    for(;;)
  printf(" C Programming");
  return 0;
}
```

- Never use a floating point variable as the loop control variable. This is because floating point values are just approximations and therefore may result in imprecise values and thus inaccurate test for termination. For example, the following code will result in an infinite loop because of inaccuracies of floating point numbers.

```
#include <stdio.h>
int main()
{
  float i;
  for(i=100;i>=10;)
  {
    printf(" %f", i);
   i = (float)i/10;
  }
  return 0;
}
```

Selecting an appropriate loop Loops can be entry-controlled (also known as pre-test) or exit-controlled (also known as post-test). While in an entry-controlled loop, condition is tested before the loop starts, an exit-controlled loop, on the other hand, tests the condition after the loop is executed. If the condition is not met in entry-controlled loop, then the loop will never execute. However, in case of post-test, the body of the loop is executed unconditionally for the first time.

If your requirement is to have a pre-test loop, then choose either for loop or while loop. In case, you need to have a post-test loop then choose a do-while loop.

Look at Table 10.2 which shows a comparison between a pre-test loop and a post-test loop.

Table 10.2 Comparison of pre-test and post-test loops

Feature	Pre-test loop	Post-test loop
Initialization	1	1
Number of tests	N+1	N
Statements executed	N	N
Loop control variable update	N	N
Minimum iterations	0	1

When we know in advance the number of times the loop should be executed, we use a counter-controlled loop. The counter is a variable that must be initialized, tested, and updated for performing the loop operations. Such a counter-controlled loop in which the counter is assigned a constant or a value is also known as a definite repetition loop.

When we do not know in advance the number of times the loop will be executed, we use a sentinel-controlled loop. In such a loop, a special value called the sentinel value is used to change the loop control expression from true to false. For example, when data is read from the user, the user may be notified that when they want the execution to stop, they may enter -1. This value is called a *sentinel value*. A sentinel-controlled loop is often useful for indefinite repetition loops.

If your requirement is to have a counter-controlled loop, then choose for loop, else if you need to have a sentinel-controlled loop, then go for either a while loop or a `do-while` loop. Although a sentinel-controlled loop can be implemented using `for` loop, `while`, and `do-while` loops offer better option.

10.4 NESTED LOOPS

C allows its users to have nested loops, i.e., loops that can be placed inside other loops. Although this feature will work with any loop such as `while`, `do-while`, and `for`, it is most commonly used with the `for` loop, because this is easiest to control. A `for` loop can be used to control the number of times that a particular set of statements will be executed. Another outer loop could be used to control the number of times that a whole loop is repeated.

In C, loops can be nested to any desired level. However, loops should be properly indented so that a reader can easily determine which statements are contained within each `for` statement. To see the benefit of nesting loops, we will see some programs that exhibit the use of nested loops.

31. Write a program to print the following pattern.

```
Pass 1- 1 2 3 4 5
Pass 2- 1 2 3 4 5
Pass 3- 1 2 3 4 5
Pass 4- 1 2 3 4 5
Pass 5- 1 2 3 4 5
```

```
#include <stdio.h>
int main()
{
  int i, j;
  for(i=1;i<=5;i++)
  {
    printf("\n Pass %d- ",i);
    for(j=1;j<=5;j++)
      printf(" %d", j);
  }
return 0;
}
```

32. Write a program to print the following pattern.

```
**********
**********
**********
**********
**********
```

```
#include <stdio.h>
int main()
{
 int i, j;
 for(i=1;i<=5;i++)
 {
   printf("\n");
   for(j=1;j<=10;j++)
     printf("*");
 }
 return 0;
}
```

33. Write a program to print the following pattern.

```
*
**
***
****
*****
```

```
#include <stdio.h>
int main()
{
  int i, j;
  for(i=1;i<=5;i++)
  {
    printf("\n");
    for(j=1;j<=i;j++)
      printf("*");
  }
return 0;
}
```

34. Write a program to print the following pattern.

```
1
12
123
1234
12345
```

```
#include <stdio.h>
int main()
{
  int i, j;
  for(i=1;i<=5;i++)
  {
    printf("\n");
    for(j=1;j<=i;j++)
      printf("%d", j);
  }
return 0;
}
```

35. Write a program to print the following pattern.

```
1
22
333
4444
55555
```

```
#include <stdio.h>
int main()
{
  int i, j;
  for(i=1;i<=5;i++)
  {
    printf("\n");
    for(j=1;j<=i;j++)
```

```
    printf("%d", i);
  }
return 0;
}
```

36. Write a program to print the following pattern.

```
0
12
345
6789
```

```
#include <stdio.h>
int main()
{
  int i, j, count=0;
  for(i=1;i<=4;i++)
  {
    printf("\n");
    for(j=1;j<=i;j++)
      printf("%d", count++);
  }
 return 0;
}
```

37. Write a program to print the following pattern.

```
A
AB
ABC
ABCD
ABCDE
ABCDEF
```

```
#include <stdio.h>
int main()
{
  char i, j;
  for(i=65;i<=70;i++)
  {
    printf("\n");
    for(j=65;j<=i;j++)
      printf("%c", j);
  }
return 0;
}
```

38. Write a program to print the following pattern.

```
        1
      1 2
    1 2 3
  1 2 3 4
1 2 3 4 5
```

```
#include <stdio.h>
#define N 5
int main()
{
  int i, j, k;
  for(i=1;i<=N;i++)
  {
    for(k=N;k>=i;k--)
      printf(" ");
    for(j=1;j<=i;j++)
      printf("%d", j);
    printf("\n");
  }
return 0;
}
```

39. Write a program to print the following pattern.

```
        1
      1 2 1
    1 2 3 2 1
  1 2 3 4 3 2 1
1 2 3 4 5 4 3 2 1
```

```
#include <stdio.h>
#define N 5
int main()
{
  int i, j, k, l;
  for(i=1;i<=N;i++)
  {
    for(k=N;k>=i;k--)
      printf(" ");
    for(j=1;j<=i;j++)
      printf("%d", j);
    for(l=j-2;l>0;l--)
      printf("%d", l);
    printf("\n");
  }
return 0;
}
```

40. Write a program to print the following pattern.

```
1
2 2
3 3 3
4 4 4 4
5 5 5 5 5
```

```
#include <stdio.h>
#define N 5
int main()
{
  int i, j, k, count=5, c;
  for(i=1;i<=N;i++)
  {
    for(k=1;k<=count;k++)
      printf(" ");
      for(j=1;j<=i;j++)
        printf("%2d", i);
        printf("\n");
        c--;
  }
return 0;
}
```

41. Write a program to print the multiplication table of *n*, where *n* is entered by the user.

```
#include <stdio.h>
int main()
{
  int n, i;
  printf("\n Enter any number: ");
  scanf("%d", &n);

  printf("\n Multiplication table of %d", n);
  printf("\n ************************");
  for(i=0;i<=20;i++)
  printf("\n %d X %d = %d", n, i, (n * i));
  return 0;
}
```

Output

```
Enter any number: 2
Multiplication table of 2
************************
2 X 0 = 0
2 X 1 = 2
…..
2 X 20 = 40
```

42. Write a program using for loop to print all the numbers from *m* to *n*, thereby classifying them as even or odd

```
#include <stdio.h>

int main()
{
  int i, m, n;

  printf("\n Enter the value of m: ");
  scanf("%d", &m);
  printf("\n Enter the value n: ");
  scanf("%d", &n);
  for(i=m;i<=n;i++)
  {
    if(i%2 == 0)
      printf("\n %d is even",i);
    else
      printf("\n %d is odd", i);
  }
return 0;
}
```

Output

```
Enter the value of m: 5
Enter the value of n: 7
5 is odd
6 is even
7 is odd
```

43. Write a program using for loop to calculate the average of first *n* natural numbers.

```
#include <stdio.h>
int main()
{
  int n, i, sum =0;
  float avg = 0.0;

  printf("\n Enter the value of n: ");
  scanf("%d", &n);
  for(i=1;i<=n;i++)
    sum = sum + i;
  avg = (float) sum/n;
  printf("\n The sum of first n natural numbers
   = %d", sum);
  printf("\n The average of first n natural
   numbers = %.2f", avg);
  return 0;
}
```

Output

```
Enter the value of n: 10
The sum of first n natural numbers = 55
The average of first n natural numbers = 5.50
```

44. Write a program using for loop to calculate factorial of a number.

```
#include <stdio.h>

int main()
{
  int fact = 1, num;

  printf("\n Enter the number: ");
  scanf("%d",&num);
  if(num == 0)
    fact = 1;
  else
  {
    for(int i=1; i<=num;i++)
    fact = fact * i;
  }
printf("\n Factorial of %d is: %d ", num,
  fact);
return 0;
}
```

Output

```
Enter the number: 5
Factorial of 5 is: 120
```

45. Write a program to classify a given number as prime or composite.

```
#include <stdio.h>

int main()
{
  int flag = 0, i, num;

  printf("\n Enter any number: ");
```

```
  scanf("%d", &num);
  for(i=2; i<num/2;i++)
  {
   if(num%i == 0)
   {
    flag =1;
    break;
   }
  }
 if(flag == 1)
  printf("\n %d is a composite number", num);
 else
  printf("\n %d is a prime number", num);
 return 0;
 }
```

Output

```
Enter the number: 5
5 is a prime number
```

46. Write a program using do-while loop to read the numbers until –1 is encountered. Also count the number of prime numbers and composite numbers entered by the user

```
#include <stdio.h>

int main()
{
  int num, i;
  int primes=0, composites=0, flag=0;
  printf("\n Enter -1 to exit");
  printf("\n\n Enter any number:");
  scanf("%d",&num);
  do
  {
  for(i=2;i<=num/2;i++)
  {
  if(num%i==0)
    {
     flag=1;
     break;
    }
  }
 if(flag==0)
  primes++;
 else
  composites++;

 flag=0;
 printf("\n\n Enter any number: ");
 scanf("%d",&num);
 } while(num != -1);
 printf("\n Count of prime numbers entered =
   %d", primes);
 printf("\n Count of composite numbers entered
   = %d", composites);
 return 0;
 }
```

Output

```
 Enter -1 to exit
 Enter any number: 5
 Enter any number: 10
 Enter any number: 7
 Enter any number: -1
 Count of prime numbers entered = 2
 Count of composite numbers entered = 1
```

47. Write a program to calculate pow(x,n) i.e., to calculate x^n.

```
#include <stdio.h>

#include <math.h>
int main()
{
 int i, num, n;
 long int result =1;

 printf("\n Enter the number: ");
 scanf("%d", &num);
 printf("\n Till which power to
  calculate: ");
 scanf("%d", &n);
 for(i=1;i<=n;i++)
   result = result * num;
   printf("\n pow(%d, %d) = %ld", num, n,
  result);
 return 0;
}
```

Output

```
Enter the number: 2
Till which power to calculate: 5
pow(2, 5) = 32
```

48. Write a program to print the reverse of a number.

```
#include <stdio.h>

int main()
{
 int num, temp;

 printf("\n Enter the number: ");
 scanf("%d", &num);
 printf("\n The reversed number is: ");
 while(num != 0)
{
 temp = num%10;
 printf("%d",temp);
 num = num/10;
}
return 0;
}
```

Output

```
Enter the number: 123
The reversed number is: 321
```

49. Write a program to enter a number and then calculate the sum of its digits.

```
#include <stdio.h>

int main()
{
  int num, temp, sumofdigits = 0;

  printf("\n Enter the number: ");
  scanf("%d", &num);

  while(num != 0)
{
  temp = num%10;
  sumofdigits += temp;
  num = num/10;
}
printf("\n The sum of digits = %d",
  sumofdigits);
return 0;
}
```

Output

```
Enter the number: 123
The sum of digits = 6
```

50. Write a program to enter a decimal number. Calculate and display the binary equivalent of this number.

```
#include <stdio.h>

#include <math.h>

int main()
{
  int decimal_num, remainder, binary_num = 0,
  i = 0;

  printf("\n Enter the decimal number: ");
  scanf("%d", &decimal_num);
  while(decimal_num != 0)
  {
    remainder = decimal_num%2;
    binary_num += remainder*pow(10,i);
    decimal_num = decimal_num/2;
    i++;
  }
printf("\n The binary equivalent = %d",
  binary_num);
return 0;
}
```

Output

```
Enter the decimal number: 7
The binary equivalent = 111
```

51. Write a program to enter a decimal number. Calculate and display the octal equivalent of this number

```
#include <stdio.h>

#include <math.h>

int main()
{
  int decimal_num, remainder, octal_num = 0,
   i = 0;

  printf("\n Enter the decimal number: ");
  scanf("%d", &decimal_num);
  while(decimal_num != 0)
  {
    remainder = decimal_num%8;
    octal_num += remainder*pow(10,i);
    decimal_num = decimal_num/8;
    i++;
  }
printf("\n The octal equivalent = %d", octal_
  num);
return 0;
}
```

Output

```
Enter the decimal number: 18
The octal equivalent = 22
```

52. Write a program to enter a binary number. Calculate and display the decimal equivalent of this number.

```
#include <stdio.h>

#include <math.h>

int main()
{
  int decimal_num = 0, remainder, binary_num,
    i = 0;

  printf("\n Enter the binary number: ");
  scanf("%d", &binary_num);
  while(binary_num != 0)
  {
    remainder = binary_num%10;
    decimal_num += remainder*pow(2,i);
    binary_num = binary_num/10;
    i++;
  }
printf("\n The decimal equivalent = %d",
  decimal_num);
return 0;
}
```

Output

```
Enter the binary number : 111
The decimal equivalent = 7
```

53. Write a program to enter an octal number. Calculate and display the decimal equivalent of this number.

```
#include <stdio.h>

#include <math.h>

int main()
{
  int decimal_num= 0, remainder, octal_num,
  i = 0;

  printf("\n Enter the octal number: ");
  scanf("%d", &octal_num);
  while(octal_num != 0)
  {
    remainder = octal_num%10;
    decimal_num += remainder*pow(8,i);
    octal_num = octal_num/10;
    i++;
  }
 printf("\n The decimal equivalent = %d",
   decimal_num);
 return 0;
 }
```

Output

```
Enter the octal number: 22
The decimal equivalent = 18
```

54. Write a program to enter a hexadecimal number. Calculate and display the decimal equivalent of this number.

```
#include <stdio.h>

#include <math.h>

int main()
{
  int decimal_num= 0, remainder, hex_num, i
   =0;

  printf("\n Enter the hexadecimal number: ");
  scanf("%d", &hex_num);
  while(hex_num != 0)
  {
    remainder = hex_num%10;
    decimal_num += remainder*pow(16,i);
    hex_num = hex_num/10;
    i++;
  }
 printf("\n The decimal equivalent = %d",
   decimal_num);
 return 0;
 }
```

Output

```
Enter the hexadecimal number: 39
The decimal equivalent = 57
```

55. Write a program to calculate GCD of two numbers.

```
#include <stdio.h>

int main()
{
  int num1, num2, temp;
  int dividend, divisor, remainder;

  printf("\n Enter the first number: ");
  scanf("%d", &num1);
  printf("\n Enter the second number: ");
  scanf("%d", &num2);

  if(num1>num2)
  {
    dividend = num1;
    divisor = num2;
  }
  else
  {
    dividend = num2;
    divisor = num1;
  }

 while(divisor)
 {
  remainder = dividend%divisor;
  dividend = divisor;
  divisor = remainder;
 }
 printf("\n GCD of %d and %d is = %d", num1,
   num2, dividend);
 return 0;
 }
```

Output

```
Enter the first number: 64
Enter the second number: 14
GCD of 64 and 14 is = 2
```

56. Write a program to sum the series $1 + \frac{1}{2} + \frac{1}{3} + \cdots + \frac{1}{n}$.

```
#include <stdio.h>

int main()
{
  int n, i;
  float sum=0.0, a;

  printf("\n Enter the value of n: ");
  scanf("%d", &n);
  for(i=1;i<=n;i++)
  { a=(float)1/i;
    sum = sum +a;
  }
 printf("\n The sum of series 1/1 + 1/2 + ....
   + 1/%d = %.2f",n,sum);
```

```
return 0;
}
```

Output

```
Enter the value of n: 5
The sum of series 1/1 + 1/2 + .... + 1/5 =
  2.28
```

57 Write a program to sum the series $\frac{1}{1^2}+\frac{1}{2^2}+\cdots+\frac{1}{3^2}$.

```
#include <stdio.h>
#include <math.h>

int main()
{
  int n, i;
  float sum=0.0, a;

  printf("\n Enter the value of n: ");
  scanf("%d", &n);
  for(i=1;i<=n;i++)
  { a = (float)1/pow(i,2);
    sum = sum +a;
  }
printf("\n The sum of series 1/1² + 1/ 2² + ….
   1/%d² = %.2f",n,sum);
return 0;
}
```

Output

```
Enter the value of n: 5
The sum of series 1/1² + 1/ 2² + …. 1/5² = 1.46
```

58. Write a program to sum the series $\frac{1}{2}+\frac{2}{3}\cdots+\frac{n}{(n+1)}$.

```
#include <stdio.h>

int main()
{
  int n, i;
  float sum=0.0, a;

  printf("\n Enter the value of n: ");
  scanf("%d", &n);
  for(i=1;i<=n;i++)
  { a= (float) i/(i+1);
    sum = sum +a;
  }
printf("\n The sum of series 1/2 + 2/3 +
  ....%d/%d = %f",n,n+1,sum);
return 0;
}
```

Output

```
Enter the value of n :5
The sum of series 1/2 + 2/3 + ....5/6 =
  2.681+E
```

59. Write a program to sum the series $\frac{1}{1}+\frac{2^2}{2}+\frac{3^3}{3}+\cdots$

```
#include <stdio.h>

#include <math.h>
int main()
{
  int n, NUM, i;
  float sum=0.0;

  printf("\n Enter the value of n: ");
  scanf("%d", &n);
  for(i=1;i<=n;i++)
  {
    NUM = pow(i,i);
    sum += (float)NUM/i;
  }
printf("\n 1/1 + 4/2 + 27/3 + .... = %.2f",
  sum);
return 0;
}
```

Output

```
Enter the value of n:5
1/1 + 4/2 + 27/3 + .... = 701.00
```

60. Write a program to calculate sum of cubes of first *n* numbers.

> **Programming Tip:**
> It is a logical error to skip the updating of loop control variable in the while/do-while loop. Without an update statement, the loop will become an infinite loop.

```
#include <stdio.h>

#include <math.h>

int main()
{
  int i, n;
  int term, sum = 0;

  printf("\n Enter the
value of n: ");

  scanf("%d", &n);
  for(i=1;i<=n;i++)
  {
    term = pow(i,3);
    sum += term;
  }
  printf("\n 1³ + 2³ + 3³ + ... = %d", sum);
  return 0;
}
```

Output

```
Enter the value of n:5
1³ + 2³ + 3³ + ... = 225
```

61. Write a program to calculate sum of squares of first *n* even numbers.

```
#include <stdio.h>
```

```
#include <math.h>
int main()
{
  int i, n;
  int term, sum = 0;

  printf("\n Enter the value of n: ");
  scanf("%d", &n);
  for(i=1;i<=n;i++)
  {
    if(i%2 == 0)
    { term = pow(i,2);
      sum += term;
    }
  }
printf("\n 2² + 4² + 6² +... = %d", sum);
return 0;
}
```

Output

```
Enter the value of n: 5
2² + 4² + 6² + ... = 20
```

62. Write a program to find whether the given number is an Armstrong number or not.

```
#include <stdio.h>

#include <math.h>
int main()
{
  int num, sum=0, r, n;

  printf("\n Enter the number: ");
  scanf("%d", &num);
  n=num;
  while(n>0)
  {
    r=n%10;
    sum += pow(r,3);
    n=n/10;
  }
 if(sum==num)
   printf("\n %d is an Armstrong number", num);
 else
   printf("\n %d is not an Armstrong number",
   num);
 return 0;
}
```

Output

```
Enter the number : 432
432 is not an armstrong number
```

63. Write a program using for loop to calculate the value of an investment, given the initial value of investment and the annual interest. Calculate the value of investment over a period of time.

```
#include <stdio.h>
int main()
{
  double initVal, futureVal, ROI;
  int yrs, i;
  printf("\n Enter the investment value: ");
  scanf("%lf", &initVal);
  printf("\n Enter the rate of interest: ");
  scanf("%lf", &ROI);
  printf("\n Enter the number of years for
   which investment has to be done: ");
  scanf("%d", &yrs);
  futureVal=initVal;
  printf("\n YEAR \t\t VALUE");
  printf("\n ___________________");
  for(i=1;i<=yrs;i++)
  {
    futureVal = futureVal * (1 + ROI/100.0);
    printf("\n  %d \t %lf", i, futureVal);
  }
return 0;
}
```

Output

```
Enter the investment value: 20000
Enter the rate of interest: 12
Enter the number of years for which investment
   has to be done: 5
YEAR     VALUE
_____________________

1    22400.00
2    25088.00
3    28098.56
4    31470.38
5    35246.83
```

64. Write a program to generate calendar of a month given the start day of the week and the number of days in that month.

```
#include <stdio.h>
int main()
{
  int i, j, startDay, num_of_days;
  printf("\n Enter the starting day of the
   week (1 to 7): ");
  scanf("%d", &startDay);
  printf("\n Enter the number of days in that
   month: ");
  scanf("%d", &num_of_days);
  printf(" Sun Mon Tue Wed Thurs Fri Sat\n");
  printf("\n ______________________________");
  for(i=0;i<startDay-1;i++)
```

```
    printf("   ");
   for(j=1;j<=num_of_days;j++)
   {
     if(i>6)
     {
       printf("\n");
       i=1;
     }
     else
       i++;
     printf("%2d ", j);
   }
  return 0;
  }
```

Output

```
  Enter the starting day of the week (1 to 7): 5
  Enter the number of days in that month : 31
  Sun  Mon  Tue  Wed  Thurs  Fri  Sat
  1    2    3    4    5      6    7
```

10.5 BREAK AND CONTINUE STATEMENTS

In this section, we discuss break and continue statements.

10.5.1 break Statement

In C, the break statement is used to terminate the execution of the nearest enclosing loop in which it appears. We have already seen its usage in the switch statement. The break statement is widely used with for loop, while loop, and do-while loop. When the compiler encounters a break statement, the control passes to the statement that follows the loop in which the break statement appears. Its syntax is quite simple, just type keyword break followed with a semicolon.

> **Programming Tip:**
> The break statement is used to terminate the execution of the nearest enclosing loop in which it appears.

```
  break;
```

In switch statement if the break statement is missing then every case from the matched case label till the end of the switch, including the default, is executed. This example given below shows the manner in which break statement is used to terminate the statement in which it is embedded.

```
  #include <stdio.h>
  int main()
  {
    int i = 1;
    while(i<=10)
    {
      if (i==5)
        break;
```

```
while(...)
{
.....
if(condition)
break ;
.....
}
.......
```

Transfers control out of the loop while

```
do
{
.....
if(condition)
break ;
.....
}while( ...);
.......
```

Transfers control out of the do-while loop

```
for(...)
{
.....
if(condition)
break ;
.....
}
.......
```

Transfers control out of the for loop

```
for(...)
{
  .......
  for(...)
  {
  .......
  if(condition)
  break ;
  .......
  }
  .........
}
```

Transfers control out of inner for loop

Figure 10.9 break statement

```
      printf("\n %d", i);
      i = i + 1;
    }
  return 0;
  }
```

Note that the code is meant to print first 10 numbers using a while loop, but it will actually print only numbers from 1 to 4. As soon as i becomes equal to 5, the break statement is executed and the control jumps to the statement following the while loop.

Hence, the break statement is used to exit a loop from any point within its body, bypassing its normal termination expression. When the break statement is encountered inside a loop, the loop is immediately terminated, and program control is passed to the next statement following the loop. Figure 10.9 shows the transfer of control when the break statement is encountered.

10.5.2 continue Statement

> **Programming Tip:**
> When the compiler encounters a continue statement, then rest of the statements in the loop are skipped and the control is unconditionally transferred to the loop-continuation portion of the nearest loop.

Like the break statement, the continue statement is used in the body of a loop. When the compiler encounters a continue statement then the rest of the statements in the loop are skipped and the control is unconditionally transferred to the loop-continuation portion of the nearest enclosing loop.

Its syntax is quite simple, just type keyword `continue` followed with a semicolon.

```
continue;
```

Again like the `break` statement, the `continue` statement cannot be used without an enclosing `for`, `while`, or `do-while` statement. When the `continue` statement is encountered in the `while` and `do-while` loops, the control is transferred to the code that tests the controlling expression. However, if placed within a `for` loop, the `continue` statement causes a branch to the code that updates the loop variable. For example, look at the following code.

```
#include <stdio.h>
int main()
{
int i;
for(i=1; i<= 10; i++)
{
  if (i==5)
    continue;
  printf("\t %d", i);
}
return 0;
}
```

The code given here is meant to print numbers from `1` to 10. But as soon as `i` becomes equal to 5, the `continue` statement is encountered, so rest of the statements in the `for` loop are skipped and the control passes to the expression that increments the value of `i`. The output of this program would thus be

> **Programming Tip:**
> As far as possible, try not to use goto, break, and continue statements as they violate the rules of structured programming.

```
1  2  3  4  6  7  8  9  10
```

(Note that there is no `5` in the series. It could not be printed, as `continue` causes skipping of the statement that printed the value of `i` on screen).

Figure 10.10 illustrates the use of `continue` statement in loops.

Hence, we conclude that the `continue` statement is somewhat the opposite of the `break` statement. It forces the next iteration of the loop to take place, skipping any code in between itself and the test condition of the loop. The `continue` statement is usually used to restart a statement sequence when an error occurs. Look at the program code given below that demonstrates the use of `break` and `continue` statements.

```
while (...)
{
.....
if(condition)
continue;
.....
}
.......
Transfers control
to the condition
expression of the
while loop
```

```
do
{
.....
if(condition)
continue ;
.....
}while( ... );
.......
Transfers control
to the condition
expression of the
do-while loop
```

```
for(...)
{
.....
if(condition)
continue ;
.....
}
.......
Transfers control
to the condition
expression of the
for loop
```

```
for(...)
{
............
for(...)
{
.......
if(condition)
continue;
.......
}
.......
}
Transfers control
to the condition
expression of the
inner for loop
```

Figure 10.10 continue statement

65. Write a program to calculate square root of a number.

```
#include <stdio.h>
#include <math.h>
int main()
{
int num;
do
{
printf("\n Enter any number. Enter 999 to
   stop: ");
scanf("%d", &num);
if(num == 999)
break;     // quits the loop
if (num < 0)
{
printf("\n Square root of negative numbers is
   not defined");
continue;  // skips the following statements
}
printf("\n The square root of %d is %f", num,
   sqrt(num));
}while(1);
return 0;
}
```

10.6 goto STATEMENT

The `goto` statement is used to transfer control to a specified `label`. However, the `label` must reside in the same function and can appear only before one statement in the same function. The syntax of `goto` statement is shown in Figure 10.11.

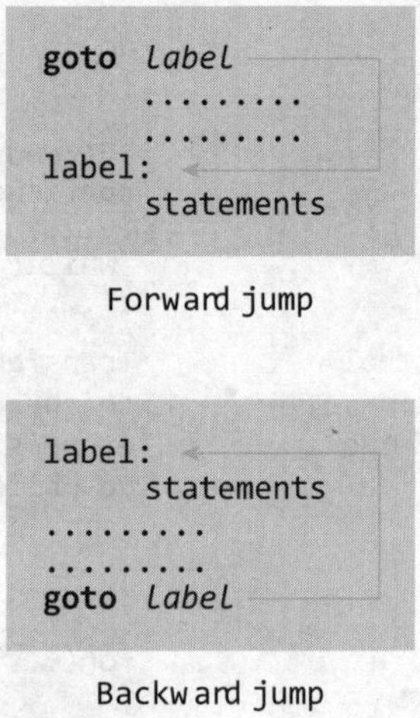

Figure 10.11 goto statement

Here, `label` is an identifier that specifies the place where the branch is to be made. `Label` can be any valid variable name that is followed by a colon (`:`). The `label` is placed immediately before the statement where the control has to be transferred.

The `label` can be placed anywhere in the program either before or after the `goto` statement. Whenever the `goto` statement is encountered the control is immediately transferred to the statements following the `label`. Therefore, `goto` statement breaks the normal sequential execution of the program. If the `label` is placed after the `goto` statement, then it is called a *forward jump* and in case it is located before the `goto` statement, it is said to be a *backward jump*.

The `goto` statement is often combined with the `if` statement to cause a conditional transfer of control.

```
IF condition THEN goto label
```

In this book, we will not use the `goto` statement because computer scientists usually avoid this statement in favour of the 'structured programming' paradigm. Some scientists think that the `goto` statement should be abolished from higher-level languages because they complicate the task of analysing and verifying the correctness of programs (particularly those involving loops).

Moreover, structured program theory proves that the availability of the `goto` statement is not necessary to write programs, as combination of sequence, selection, and repetition constructs is sufficient to perform any computation. The code given below demonstrates the use of a `goto` statement. The program calculates the sum of all positive numbers entered by the user.

> **Programming Tip:**
> Follow proper indentation for better clarity, readability, and understanding of the loops.

```
#include <stdio.h>
int main()
{
int num, sum=0;
read:   // label for goto statement
printf("\n Enter the number. Enter 999 to end:
  ");
scanf("%d", &num);
if (num != 999)
{
  if(num < 0)
    goto read;  //jump to label- read
  sum += num;
  goto read;  // jump to label- read
}
printf("\n Sum of the numbers entered by the
  user is = %d", sum);
return 0;
}
```

Conclusion

- It is not necessary to use `goto` statement as it can always be eliminated by rearranging the code.
- Using the `goto` statement violates the rules of structured programming.
- It is a good programming practice to use `break`, `continue`, and `return` statements in preference to `goto` whenever possible.
- `Goto` statements make the program code complicated and render the program unreadable.

> **Note**
> One must avoid the use of `break`, `continue`, and `goto` statements as much as possible as they are techniques used in unstructured programming.

In structured programming, you must prefer to use `if` and `if-else` constructs to avoid such statements. For example, look at the following code which calculates the sum of numbers entered by the user. The first version uses the `break` statement. The second version replaces `break` by `if-else` construct.

```
// Uses break statement
#include <stdio.h>
int main()
{
 int num, sum=0;
 while(1)
 {
   printf("\n Enter any number. Enter -1 to
   stop: ");
   scanf("%d", &num);
     if(num==-1)
       break;  // quit the loop
   sum+=num;
 }
printf("\n SUM = %d", sum);
return 0;
```

```
}
/* Same program without using break statement */
#include <stdio.h>
int main()
{
   int num, sum=0, flag=1;
   // flag will be used to exit from the loop
   while(flag==1)  // loop control variable
   {
      printf("\n Enter any number. Enter -1 to
      stop: ");
      scanf("%d", &num);
      if(num!=-1)
         sum+=num;
      else
         flag=0;   // to quit the loop
   }
printf("\n SUM = %d", sum);
return 0;
}
```

Now let us see how we can eliminate continue statement from our programs. Let us first write a program that calculates the average of all non-zero numbers entered by the user using the continue statement. The second program will do the same job but without using continue.

```
#include <stdio.h>
int main()
{
int num, sum=0, flag=1, count=0;
float avg;
// flag will be used to exit from the loop
while(flag==1)
{
printf("\n Enter any number. Enter -1 to
   stop: ");
scanf("%d", &num);
if(num==0)
   continue; // skip the following statements
if(num!=-1)
{
      sum+=num;
      count++;
   }
   else
flag=0;
// set loop control variable to jump out of loop
}
printf("\n SUM = %d", sum);
avg = (float) sum/count;
printf("\n Average = %f", avg);
return 0;
}
// Same program without using continue statement
#include <stdio.h>
int main()
{
int num, sum=0, flag=1, count=0;
float avg;
// flag will be used to exit from the loop
while(flag==1)
{
printf("\n Enter any number. Enter -1 to stop:
   ");
scanf("%d", &num);
if(num!=0)
{
   if(num!=-1)
   {
      sum+=num;
      count++;
   }
   else
      flag=0;
   }
}
printf("\n SUM = %d", sum);
avg = (float) sum/count;
printf("\n Average = %f", avg);
return 0;
}
```

POINTS TO REMEMBER

- C was developed in the early 1970s by Dennis Ritchie at Bell Laboratories.
- A C program is composed of preprocessor commands, a global declaration section, and one or more functions.
- A function is defined as a group of C statements that are executed together.
- The execution of a C program begins at `main()` function.
- Every word in a C program is either a keyword or an identifier. C has a set of reserved words known as keywords that cannot be used as an identifier.
- The basic data types supported by C language are: char, int, float, and double.
- A variable is defined as a meaningful name given to a data storage location in computer memory. When using a variable, we actually refer to address of the memory where the data is stored.
- The difference between signed and unsigned numeric variables is that signed variables can be either negative or positive but unsigned variables can only be positive. By default, C takes a signed variable.
- C supports conditional type branching and unconditional type branching. The conditional branching statements help to jump from one part of the program to another depending on whether a particular condition is satisfied or not.

- With nesting of if-else statements, we often encounter a problem known as dangling else problem. This problem is created when there is no matching else for every if statement. In such cases, C always pairs an else statement with the most recent unpaired if statement in the current block.
- Switch case statements are often used as an alternative to long if statements that compare a variable to several integral values. Switch statements are also used to handle the input given by a user.
- Default is a case that is executed when the value of the variable does not match with any of the values of case statements.
- Iterative statements are used to repeat the execution of a list of statements, depending on the value of an integer expression.
- The while/do-while/for loops provide a mechanism to repeat one or more statements while a particular condition is true. In the do-while loop, the test condition is tested at the end of the loop while in case of for and while loops the test condition is tested before entering the loop.
- The break statement is used to terminate the execution of the nearest enclosing loop in which it appears.
- The continue statement is used to transfer control to the loop-continuation part of the nearest enclosing loop.
- The goto statement is used to transfer control to a specified label. However, the label must reside in the same function and can appear before only one statement in the same function.

GLOSSARY

Conditional branching Conditional branching statements are used to jump from one part of the program to another depending on whether a particular condition is satisfied or not.

continue statement When the compiler encounters a continue statement then the rest of the statements in the loop are skipped and the control is unconditionally transferred to the loop-continuation portion of the nearest enclosing loop.

Dangling else problem Problem encountered with nesting of if-else statements which is created when there is no matching else for every if statement.

do-while loop A form of iterative statement in which the test condition is evaluated at the end of the loop.

for loop The mechanism used to repeat a task until a particular condition is true. for loop is usually known as a determinate or definite loop because the programmer knows exactly how many times the loop will repeat.

goto statement It is used to transfer control to a specified label.

if statement Simplest form of decision control statement that is frequently used in decision-making.

if-else-if statement Decision control statement that works in the same way as a normal if statement. It is also known as nested if construct.

if-else statement Decision control statement in which first the test expression is evaluated. If the expression is true, if block is executed and else block is skipped. Otherwise, if the expression is false, else block is executed and if block is ignored.

Iterative statement Statement used to repeat the execution of a list of statements, depending on the value of an integer expression.

Nested loop Loops placed inside other loops.

switch case statement A switch case statement is a multi-way decision statement that is a simplified version of an if-else block that evaluates only one variable.

while loop The mechanism used to repeat one or more statements while a particular condition is true.

EXERCISES

Fill in the Blanks

1. Dangling else problem occurs when ________.
2. The switch control expression must be of ________ type.
3. In a do-while loop, if the body of the loop is executed n times, the test condition is evaluated ________ times.
4. The ____________statement is used to skip statements in a loop.
5. A loop that always satisfies the test condition is known as a ____________ loop.
6. In a counter-controlled loop, ____________ variable is used to count the number of times the loop will execute.
7. ____________ statements help to jump from one part of the program to another depending on whether a particular condition is satisfied or not.
8. ____________ statements are used to repeat the execution of a list of statements.
9. In ____________ loop, the entry is automatic and there is only a choice to continue it further or not.

10. When we do not know in advance the number of times the loop will be executed, we use a ____________loop.
11. The ____________statement is used to transfer control to a specified label.
12. ____________statement violates the rules of structured programming.

Multiple-choice Questions

1. Which type of statement helps to jump from one part of the program to another depending on whether a particular condition is satisfied or not?
   (a) Conditional branching (b) Loops
   (c) Iterative (d) None of these
2. A statement block consists of how many statements?
   (a) 0 (b) 1
   (c) n (d) None of these
3. Dangling else problem can arise in which of the following statement(s)?
   (a) Conditional branching (b) Loops
   (c) Iterative (d) None of these
4. Which among the following is a multi-way decision statement?
   (a) if-else (b) if-else-if
   (c) switch (d) do-while loop
5. Case labels must end with which token?
   (a) , (b) :
   (c) ; (d) /
6. The default label can be placed at which position in the switch statement?
   (a) Beginning (b) End
   (c) Middle (d) Anywhere
7. The statements in the statement block are encapsulated within a ____?
   (a) () (b) {}
   (c) [] (d) <>
8. Which statement is used to terminate the execution of the nearest enclosing loop in which it appears?
   (a) break (b) continue
   (c) default (d) case
9. When the ______ statement is encountered then the rest of the statements in the loop are skipped.
   (a) break (b) continue
   (c) default (d) case

State True or False

1. Decision control statements are used to repeat the execution of a list of statements.
2. The expression in a selection statement can have no side effects.
3. An expression in an `if` statement must be enclosed within parentheses.
4. No two case labels can have the same value.
5. The case labelled constant can be a constant or a variable.
6. The `if-else` statement requires integral values in its expressions.
7. There can be only one default case in the `switch-case` statement
8. The `do-while` loop checks the test expression and then executes the statements placed within its body.
9. In a `while` loop, if the body is executed n times, then the test expression is executed (n + 1) times.
10. The number of times the loop control variable is updated is equal to the number of times the loop iterates.
11. In the `for` loop, the value of the loop control variable must be less than that of its ending value.
12. It is necessary to have initialization, testing, and updating expressions within the `for` statement.
13. In a pre-test loop, the test condition is checked after the body of the loop.
14. Post-test loops get executed at least for one time.
15. In a `while` loop, the loop control variable is initialized in the body of the loop.
16. The loop control variable may be updated before or after the loop iterates.
17. Counter-controlled loop must be designed as pre-test loops.
18. The `do-while` loop is a post-test loop.
19. The `for` loop and `while` loop are pre-test loops.
20. Every case label must evaluate to a unique constant expression value.
21. Two case labels may have the same set of actions associated with them.
22. The default label can be placed anywhere in the `switch` statement.
23. C does not permit nested `switch` statements.
24. When we place a semicolon after the `for` statement, the compiler will generate an error message.

Review Questions

1. What are decision control statements? Explain in detail.
2. Compare the use of `if-else` construct with that of conditional operator.
3. Explain the importance of a `switch case` statement. In which situations is a `switch case` desirable? Also give its limitations.
4. How is comma operator useful in a `for` loop? Explain with the help of relevant examples.
5. Write a short note on goto statement. As a programmer would you prefer to use this statement? Justify your answer.
6. With the help of an example explain the dangling `if-else` problem.
7. Why floating point numbers should not be used for equality in expressions?

8. Explain the usefulness of default statement in switch case statement.
9. Give the points of similarity and differences between a while loop and a do-while loop.
10. Distinguish between the break and the continue statements.
11. Write a short note on iterative statements that C language supports.
12. Enter two integers as dividend and divisor. If the divisor is greater than zero then divide the dividend by the divisor. Assign their result to an integer variable rem and their quotient to a floating point number quo.
13. When will you prefer to work with a switch statement?
14. What is a null statement? How can it be useful in our programs?
15. In what situation will you prefer to use for, while, and do while loops?
16. Can we use a for loop when the number of iterations is not known in advance? If yes, give a program that illustrates how this can be done.
17. Change the following for loop into a while loop. Also convert the for loop into a do-while loop.

```
int i;
for(i=10;i>0;i--)
printf("%d", i);
```

18. Change the following do-while loop into a for loop. Also rewrite the code by changing the do-while loop into a for loop.

```
int num;
printf("\n Enter any number. Enter 999 to
    stop : ");
scanf("%d", &num);
do
{
printf("%d", x);
printf("\n Enter any number. Enter 999 to stop
    : ");
scanf("%d", &num);
}while(num != 999);
```

19. Change the following while loop into a do-while loop. Also convert the while loop into a for loop.

```
int num;
printf("\n Enter any number. Enter 999 to stop
    : ");
scanf("%d", &num);
while(num != 999)
{
printf("%d", x);
printf("\n Enter any number. Enter 999 to stop
    : ");
scanf("%d", &num);
}
```

20. The following for loops are written to print numbers from 1 to 10. Are these loops correct? Justify your answer.

```
(a) int i;
    for(i=0;i<10;i++)
    printf("%d", i);
(b) int i, num;
    for(i=0;i<10;i++)
    {
    num = i+1;
    printf("%d", num);
    }
(c) int i;
    for(i=1;i<=10;i++)
    {
    printf("%d", i);
    i++
    }
```

Programming Exercises

1. Write a program to read a floating point number and an integer. If the value of the floating point number is greater than 3.14 then add 10 to the integer.
2. Write a program to print the prime factors of a number.
3. Write a program to test if a given number is a power of 2.
   Hint: A number x is a power of 2 if x != 0 and x & (x - 1)) == 0
4. Write a program to print the Floyd's triangle.
5. Write a program to read two numbers. Then find out whether the first number is a multiple of the second number.
6. Write a program using switch case to display a menu that offers 5 options: read three numbers, calculate total, calculate average, display the smallest, and display the largest value.
7. Write a program to display the sin(x) value where x ranges from 0 to 360 in steps of 15.
8. Write a program to display the cos(x) and tan(x) values where x ranges from 0 to 360 in steps of 15.
9. Write a program to calculate electricity bill based on the following information:

Consumption unit	Rate of charge
0 – 150	Rs 3 per unit
151 – 350	Rs 100 plus Rs 3.75 per unit exceeding 150 units
351 – 450	Rs 250 plus Rs 4 per unit exceeding 350 units
451 – 600	Rs 300 plus Rs 4.25 per unit exceeding 450 units
Above 600	Rs 400 plus Rs 5 per unit exceeding 600 units

10. Write a program to read an angle from the user and then display its quadrant.
11. Write a program that accepts the current date and the date of birth of the user. Then calculate the age of the user and display it on the screen. Note that the date should be displayed in the format specified as dd/mm/yy.
12. A class has 50 students. Every student is supposed to give three examinations. Write a program to read the marks obtained by each student in all three examinations. Calculate and display the total marks and average of each student in the class.
13. Write a program in which the control variable is updated in the statements of the `for` loop.
14. Write a program which demonstrates the use of `goto`, `break`, and `continue` statements.
15. Write a program that displays all the numbers from 1 to 100 that are not divisible by 2 as well as by 3.
16. Write a program to calculate parking charges of a vehicle. Enter the type of vehicle as a character (like c for car, b for bus, etc.) and number of hours then calculate charges as given below:
    - Truck/Bus – 20 Rs per hour
    - Car – 10 Rs per hour
    - Scooter/ Cycle/ Motor cycle – 5 Rs per hour
17. Modify the above program to calculate the parking charges. Read the hours and minutes when the vehicle enters the parking lot. When the vehicle is leaving, enter its leaving time. Calculate the difference between the two timings to calculate the number of hours and minutes for which the vehicle was parked. Finally calculate the charges based on following rules and then display the result on the screen.

Vehicle name	Rate till 3 hours	Rate after 3 hours
Truck/Bus	20	30
Car	10	20
Cycle/ Motor cycle/ Scooter	5	10

18. Write a program to read month of the year as an integer. Then display the name of the month.
19. Write a program to print the sum of all odd numbers from 1 to 100.
20. Write an interactive program to read an integer. If it is positive then display the corresponding binary representation of that number. The user must enter 999 to stop. In case the user enters a negative number then ignore that input and ask the user to re-enter any different number.
21. Write a program to print 20 asterisks.
22. Write a program that accepts any number and prints the number of digits in that number.
23. Write a program to generate the following pattern:

```
* * * * *
*       *
*       *
*       *
* * * * *
```

24. Write a program to generate the following pattern:

```
$ * * * *
* $     *
*   $   *
*     $ *
* * * * $
```

25. Write a program to generate the following pattern:

```
$ * * * $
* $   $ *
*   $   *
* $   $ *
$ * * * $
```

26. Write programs to implement the following sequence of numbers.

```
1, 8, 27, 64,...
-5, -2, 0, 3, 6, 9, 12, ...
-2, -4, -6, -8, -10, -12, ...
1, 4, 7, 10, ...
```

27. Write a program that reads integers until the user wants to stop. When the user stops entering numbers, display the largest of all the numbers entered.
28. Write a program to print the sum of the following series.

$-x + x^2 - x^3 + x^4 + \ldots$

$1 + (1+2) + (1+2+3) + \ldots$

$1 - x + x^2/2! - x^3/3! + \ldots$

29. Write a program to print the following pattern.

```
*
* *
* * *
* * * *
* * * * *
* * * *
* * *
* *
*
```

30. Write a program to print the following pattern.

```
1
2 1 2
3 2 1 2 3
```

31. Write a program to read a 5 digit number and then display the number in the following format. For example the user entered 12345, the result should be

```
12345        1
2345         12
345          123
45           1234
5            12345
```

Find the output of the following codes.

1.
```
include <stdio.h>
int main()
{
int a = 2, b = 3, c = 4;
if( c!= 100)
  a = 10;
else
  b = 10;
 if(a + b > 10)
  c = 12;
  a = 20;
  b = ++c;
printf(" \n a = %d \t b = %d \t c = %d" , a, b,
  c);
return 0;
}
```
2.
```
#include <stdio.h>
int main()
{
int a = 2, b = 3, c = 4;
if(b==2)
  a=10;
else
  c=10;
printf("\n a = %d \t b = %d \t c = %d", a, b,
  c);
return 0;
}
```
3.
```
#include <stdio.h>
int main()
{
int a = 2, b = 3, c = 4;
if(a&&b)
  c=10;
else
  c=20;
printf("\n a = %d \t b = %d \t c = %d" , a, b,
  c);
return 0;
}
```
4.
```
#include <stdio.h>
int main()
{
int a = 2, b = 3, c = 4;
if(a || b || c)
  c=10;
else
  c=20;
printf("\n a = %d \t b = %d \t c = %d", a, b,
  c);
return 0;
}
```
5.
```
#include <stdio.h>
int main()
{
int a = 2, b = 3, c = 4;
if(a)
if(b)
  c=10;
else
  c=20;
printf(" \n a = %d \t b = %d \t c = %d", a, b,
  c);
return 0;
}
```
6.
```
#include <stdio.h>
int main()
{
int a = 2, b = 3, c = 4;
if(a == 0 || b >= c && c > 0)
if(a && b)
  c=10;
else
  c=20;
printf(" \n a = %d \t b = %d \t c = %d", a, b,
  c);
return 0;
}
```
7.
```
#include <stdio.h>
int main()
{
int a = 2, b = 3, c = 4;
if(a==b)
  c++;
printf(" \n a = %d \t b = %d \t c = %d" , a, b,
  c);
return 0;
}
```
8.
```
#include <stdio.h>
int main()
{
int a = 2, b = 3, c = 4;
if(a = b < c)
  {
  c++;
  a--;
  }
++b;
printf(" \n a = %d \t b = %d \t c = %d", a, b,
  c);
return 0;
}
```
9.
```
switch(ch)
{
case 'a':
case 'A':
  printf("\n A");
case 'b':
case 'B':
  printf("\n B");
```

```
default:
printf("\n DEFAULT");
}
```

10.
```
switch(ch)
{
case 'a':
case 'A':
  printf("\n A");
case 'b':
case 'B':
  printf("\n B");
  break;
default:
  printf("\n DEFAULT");
}
```

11.
```
switch(ch)
{
case 'a':
case 'A':
  printf("\n A");
  break;
case 'b':
case 'B':
  printf("\n B");
  break;
default:
  printf("\n DEFAULT");
}
```

12.
```
#include <stdio.h>
void main()
{
int num = 10;
printf("\n %d", a>100);
}
```

13.
```
#include <stdio.h>
void main()
{
printf("HELLO");
if (-1)
  printf("WORLD");
}
```

14.
```
#include <stdio.h>
void main()
{
int a = 3;
if(a < 10)
  printf("\n LESS");
if(a < 20)
  printf("\n LESS");
if(a < 30)
  printf("\n LESS");
}
```

15.
```
#include <stdio.h>
void main()
{
int a=10, b=20, c=30, d=40;
if( c < d)
if ( c < b)
  printf("\n c");
else if(a < c)
  printf("\n a");
if(a > b)
  printf("\n b");
else
  printf("\n d");
}
```

16.
```
#include <stdio.h>
void main()
{
char ch = 'Y';
switch(ch)
{
default:
  printf("\n YES OR NO");
case 'Y':
  printf("YES");
  break;
case 'N':
  printf("NO");
  break;
}
}
```

17.
```
#include <stdio.h>
int main()
{
int num=10;
for(num++num++num++)
printf("%d", num);
return 0;
}
```

18.
```
#include <stdio.h>
int main()
{
int num=10;
for(;--num;)
printf(" %d", num);
return 0;
}
```

19.
```
#include <stdio.h>
int main()
{
int num=10;
for(;!num;num++)
printf(" %d", num);
return 0;
}
```

20.
```
#include <stdio.h>
int main()
{
float PI = 3.14, area;
```

```
int r = 7;
while(r>=0)
{
area = PI * r * r;
printf("\n Area = %f", area);
}
return 0;
}
```

21. #include <stdio.h>
```
void main()
{
int i=0, n=10;
while(i==0)
{
if(n<10)
break;
n--;
}
printf("\n i=%d and n=%d", i,n);
}
```

22. #include <stdio.h>
```
void main()
{
int i=0;
do
  {
  printf("\n %d",i);
  i++;
  }while(i<=0);
printf("\n STOP");
}
```

23. #include <stdio.h>
```
void main()
{
int i, j;
for(i=0;i<=10;i++)
{
printf("\n");
for(j=0;j<=i0;j++)
printf(" ");
printf("\n %d", j);
}
}
```

24. #include <stdio.h>
```
void main()
{
int num = 10;
printf("\n %d", a>10);
}
```

25. #include <stdio.h>
```
void main()
{
printf("HELLO");
if (!1)
  printf("WORLD");
}
```

26. #include <stdio.h>
```
void main()
{
int x=-1;
unsigned int y=1;
if(x < y)
  printf("\n SMALL");
else
  printf("\n LARGE");
}
```

27. #include <stdio.h>
```
void main()
{
char ch = -63;
int num = -36;
unsigned int unum = -18;
if(ch > num)
{
  printf("A");
  if(ch > unum)
    printf("B");
  else
    printf("C");
}
else
{
  printf("D");
  if(num < unum)
  printf("E");
  else
  printf("F");
}
}
```

28. #include <stdio.h>
```
int main()
{
int num=10;
for(;++num;num-=2)
printf(" %d", num);
return 0;
}
```

29. #include <stdio.h>
```
int main()
{
int num=10;
for(;;)
printf("HI!!");
return 0;
}
```

30. #include <stdio.h>
```
int main()
{
int num=10;
```

```
for(num++ num<=100; num=100)
printf("%d", num);
return 0;
}
```

31.
```
#include <stdio.h>
int main()
{
while(1);
printf("Hi");
return 0;
}
```

32.
```
#include <stdio.h>
int main()
{
int i=0;
char c ='0';
while(i<10)
{
printf("%c", c + i);
i++;
}
return 0;
}
```

33.
```
#include <stdio.h>
void main()
{
int i=0;
do
{
if(i>10)
continue;
i++;
}while(i<20);
printf("\n i=%d", i);
}
```

34.
```
#include <stdio.h>
void main()
{
int i=1;
for(;i<=1;i++)
{
printf("\n %d",i);
printf("\n STOP");
}
}
```

35.
```
#include <stdio.h>
void main ()
{
int i, j;
for(i=10;i>=0;i--)
{
printf("\n");
for(j=i;j>=0;j--)
printf("%d", j);
}
}
```

Find errors in the following codes.

(a)
```
#include <stdio.h>
void main()
{
int i=1;
while(i<=10)
  {
  i=1;
  printf("%d", i);
  i++;
  }
}
```

(b)
```
include <stdio.h>
 void main()
{
int i;
for(i=0,i<=10;i++)
printf("%d", i);
}
```

(c)
```
#include <stdio.h>
void main()
{
int i=1;
do
{
  printf("%d", i);
  i++;
}while(i=10)
}
```

(d)
```
#include <stdio.h>
void main()
{
int i,j;
for(i=1,j=0;i+j<=10;i++)
printf("%d", i);
j+=2;
}
```

Give the functionality of the following loops.

(a)
```
int i=1, sum=0;
while(i!=10)
{
sum +=i;
i = i+2;
}
```

(b)
```
int i, sum=0;
for (i=1;i<=10)
sum+=i;
```

(c)
```
int i;
for (i=1;i<=10;i++)
i--;
```

(d)
```
int i=10;
do
{ printf("%d", i);
} while(i>0);
```

(e)
```
int i=10;
```

```
   do
   { printf("%d", i);
   } while(i<5);
(f) int i=1, n=10, sum=0;
   while(i<=n)
   {
   sum+=i;
   i++
   }
(g) int i, sum=0;
   for (i=1;;i++)
   sum+=i;
(h) int i=10;
   while(i-->0)
   printf("%d", i);
(i) int i;
   for (i=10;i>5;i-=2)
   printf("%d", i);
(j) int i;
   for (i=10;i>5;)
   printf("%d", i);
```

CASE STUDY 1: Chapters 9 and 10

We have learnt the basics of programming in C language and concepts to write decision-making programs, let us now apply our learning to write some useful programs.

ROMAN NUMERALS

Roman numerals are written as combinations of seven letters. These letters include:

I = 1	C = 100
V = 5	D = 500
X = 10	M = 1000
L = 50	

If smaller numbers follow larger numbers, the numbers are added. Otherwise, if a smaller number precedes a larger number, the smaller number is subtracted from the larger. For example, to convert 1,100 in Roman numerals, you would write M for 1000 and then a C after it for 100. Therefore, 1100 = MC in Roman numerals. Some more examples include:

- VII = 5 + 2= 7
- IX = 10 – 1 = 9
- XL = 50 – 10 = 40
- CX= 100 + 0 = 11
- MCMLXXXIV = 1000 + (1000 – 100) + 50 + 30 + (5 – 1) = 1984

Roman Numeral Table

1	I	14	XIV	27	XXVII	150	CL
2	II	15	XV	28	XXVIII	200	CC
3	III	16	XVI	29	XXIX	300	CCC
4	IV	17	XVII	30	XXX	400	CD
5	V	18	XVIII	31	XXXI	500	D
6	VI	19	XIX	40	XL	600	DC
7	VII	20	XX	50	L	700	DCC
8	VIII	21	XXI	60	LX	800	DCCC
9	IX	22	XXII	70	LXX	900	CM
10	X	23	XXIII	80	LXXX	1000	M
11	XI	24	XXIV	90	XC	1600	MDC
12	XII	25	XXV	100	C	1700	MDCC
13	XIII	26	XXVI	101	CI	1900	MCM

1. Write a program to show the Roman number representation of a given number.

```
#include <stdio.h>

main()
{
  int number;
  int ones, tens, hundreds, thousand;

  printf("\n Enter any number
(1-3000): ");
  scanf("%d",&number);

  if(number==0||number>3000)
      printf ("\n INVALID NUMBER");
  thousand = number/1000;
  hundreds = ((number/100)%10);
  tens = ((number/10)%10);
  ones = ((number/1)%10);

  if (thousand ==1)
      printf("M");
  else if (thousand ==2)
      printf("MM");
  else if (thousand ==3)
      printf("MMM");

  if (hundreds == 1)
      printf("C");
  else if (hundreds == 2)
      printf("CC");
  else if (hundreds == 3)
      printf("CCC");
  else if (hundreds == 4)
      printf("CD");
  else if (hundreds ==5)
      printf("D");
  else if (hundreds == 6)
      printf("DC");
  else if (hundreds == 7)
      printf("DCC");
  else if (hundreds ==8)
      printf("DCCC");
  else if (hundreds == 9)
      printf("CM");

  if (tens == 1)
      printf("X");
  else if (tens == 2)
      printf("XX");
  else if (tens == 3)
      printf("XXX");
  else if (tens == 4)
      printf("XL");
  else if (tens ==5)
      printf("L");
  else if (tens == 6)
      printf("LX");
  else if (tens == 7)
      printf("LXX");
  else if (tens ==8)
      printf("LXXX");
  else if (tens == 9)
      printf("XC");
```

```
if (ones == 1)
    printf("I");
else if (ones == 2)
    printf("II");
else if (ones == 3)
    printf("III");
else if (ones == 4)
    printf("IV");
else if (ones ==5)
    printf("V");
else if (ones == 6)
    printf("VI");
else if (ones == 7)
    printf("VII");
else if (ones ==8)
    printf("VIII");
else if (ones == 9)
    printf("IX");

}
```

Output

```
Enter any number (1-3000): 139
CXXXIX
```

An algorithm to calculate the day of the week:

1. *Centuries*: Use the centuries table given below to calculate the century.
2. *Years*: We know that there are 365 days in a year, that is, 52 weeks plus 1 day. Each year starts on the day of the week after that starting the preceding year. Each leap year has one more day than a common year.

   If we know on which day a century starts (from above), and we add the number of years elapsed since the start of the century, plus the number of leap years that have elapsed since the start of the century, we get the day of the week on which the year starts. Where *year* is the last two digits of the year.
3. *Months*: Use the months table to find the day of the week a month starts.
4. *Day of the month*: Once we know on which day of the week the month starts, we simply add the day of the month to find the final result.

Centuries table

1700 – 1799	4
1800 – 1899	2
1900 – 1999	0
2000 – 2099	6
2100 – 2199	4
2200 – 2299	2
2300 – 2399	0
2400 – 2499	6
2500 – 2599	4
2600 – 2699	2

Months table

January	1 (in leap year 6)
February	4 (in leap year 2)
March	4
April	0
May	2
June	5
July	0
August	3
September	6
October	1
November	4
December	6

Days table

Sunday	1
Monday	2
Tuesday	3
Wednesday	4
Thursday	5
Friday	6
Saturday	7

EXAMPLE I

Let us calculate the day of April 24, 1982.

1. Find the century value of 1900s from the centuries table: 0
2. Last two digits give the value of year: 82
3. Divide the 82 by 4: 82/4 = 20.5 and drop the fractional part: 20
4. Find the value of April in the months table: 6
5. Add all numbers from steps 1–4 to the day of the month (in this case, 24): 0 + 82 + 20 + 6 + 24 = 132.
6. Divide the result of step 5 by 7 and find the remainder: 132/7 = 18 remainder 6
7. Look up the day's table for the remainder obtained. 6 = Saturday.

That the values in the century table, months table, and days table are pre-determined. We will only be using them to calculate the day of a particular date.

2. Write a program to find out the day for a given date.

```
#include <stdio.h>
#include <stdlib.h>

main()
{
  int dd,mm,yy,year,month,day,i,n;

    printf("\n Enter the date: ");
    scanf("%d %d %d",&dd,&mm,&yy);
    if( dd>31 || mm>12)
    {
        printf(" INVALID INPUT ");

        exit(0);
    }
    year = yy-1900;
```

```
    year = year/4;
    year = year+yy-1900;
    switch(mm)
    {
        case 1:
        case 10:
            month = 1;
            break;
        case 2:
        case 3:
        case 11:
            month = 4;
            break;
        case 7:
        case 4:
            month = 0;
            break;
        case 5:
            month = 2;
            break;
        case 6:
            month = 5;
            break;
        case 8:
            month = 3;
            break;
        case 9:
        case 12:
            month = 6;
            break;
    }
    year = year+month;
    year = year+dd;
    day  = year%7;
    switch(day)
    {
        case 0:
            // Since 7%7 = 0, case 0 means it's a
  Saturday
            printf("\n  SATURDAY");
            break;
        case 1:
            printf("\n SUNDAY");
            break;
        case 2:
            printf("\n MONDAY");
            break;
        case 3:
            printf("\n TUESDAY");
            break;
        case 4:
            printf("\n WEDNESDAY");
            break;
        case 5:
            printf("\n THURSDAY");
            break;
        case 6:
            printf("\n FRIDAY");
            break;
    }
    return 0;
}
```

Output

```
Enter the date:  29 10 1981
THURSDAY
```

11 Functions

TAKEAWAYS

- Using functions
- Function declaration
- Function definition
- Function call
- Call-by-value and call-by-reference
- Scope of variables
- Storage classes
- Recursive functions
- Tower of Hanoi

11.1 INTRODUCTION

C enables programmers to break up a program into segments commonly known as *functions*, each of which can be written more or less independently of the others. Every function in the program is supposed to perform a well-defined task. Therefore, the code of one function is completely insulated from the other functions.

Every function interfaces to the outside world in terms of how information is transferred to it and how results generated by it are transmitted back. This interface is specified by the function name. For example, look at Figure 11.1 which explains how the `main()` function calls another function to perform a well-defined task.

```
main()
{
...........
...........
func1();
...........
...........
return 0;
}
```

```
func1()
{
 Statement Block;
}
```

Figure 11.1 The `main()` function calls `func1()`

From the figure, we can see that `main()` calls a function named `func1()`. Therefore, `main()` is known as the *calling function* and `func1()` is known as the *called function*. The moment the compiler encounters a function call, instead of executing the next statement in the calling function, the control jumps to the statements that are part of the called function. After the called function is executed, the control is returned back to the calling function.

It is not necessary that the `main()` function can call only one function, it can call as many functions as it wants and as many times as it wants. For example, a function call placed within a `for` loop, `while` loop, or `do-while` loop can call the same function multiple times until the condition holds true.

Another point is that it is not only the `main()` function that can call other functions. A function can call any other function. For example, look at Figure 11.2 which shows one function calling another, and this function in turn calling some other function. From this we see that every function encapsulates a set of operations and when called it returns information to the calling function.

11.1.1 Why are Functions Needed?

Let us analyse the reasons for segmenting a program into fuctions as it is an important aspect of programming.

- Dividing a program into separate well-defined functions facilitates each function to be written and tested separately. This simplifies the process of getting the total program to work. Figure 11.3 shows that the `main()` function calls other functions for dividing the entire code into smaller sections (or functions). This approach is referred to as the *top-down* approach.
- Understanding, coding, and testing multiple separate functions is far easier than doing it for one big function.
- If a big program has to be developed without the use of any function other than `main()` function, then there will be countless lines in the `main()` function and maintaining this program will be very difficult. A large program size is a serious issue in micro-computers where memory space is limited.
- All the libraries in C contain a set of functions that the programmers are free to use in their programs. These

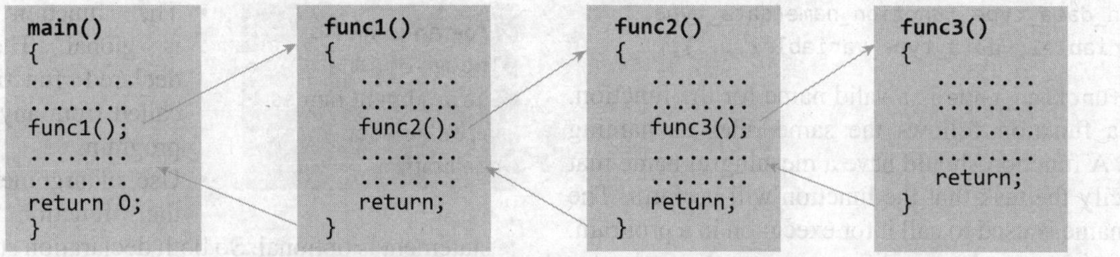

Figure 11.2 Functions calling another functions

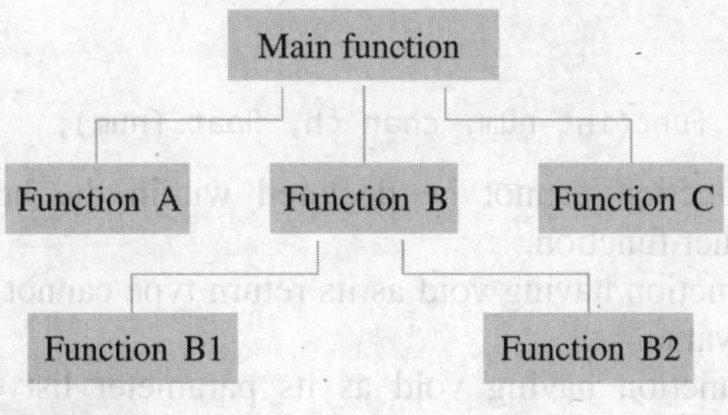

Figure 11.3 Top-down approach of solving a problem

functions have been pre-written and pre-tested, so the programmers can use them without worrying about their code details. This speeds up program development, by allowing the programmer to concentrate only on the code that he has to write.

- When a big program is broken into comparatively smaller functions, then different programmers working on that project can divide the workload by writing different functions.
- Like C libraries, programmers can also write their functions and use them at different points in the main program or in any other program that needs its functionalities.

Consider a program that executes a set of instructions repeatedly *n* times, though not continuously. In case the instructions had to be repeated continuously for *n* times, they can be placed within a loop. But if these instructions have to be executed abruptly from anywhere within the program code, then instead of writing these instructions wherever they are required, a better idea is to place these instructions in a function and call that function wherever required. Figure 11.4 explains this concept.

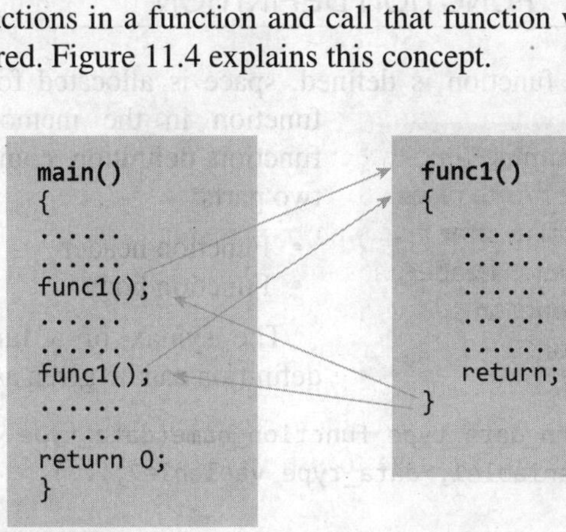

Figure 11.4 Function func1() called twice from main()

11.2 USING FUNCTIONS

In the second chapter, we have discussed that when we execute a C program, the operating system calls the `main()` function of the program which marks the entry point for the execution. When the program is executed, the `main()` function returns some value to the operating system.

Any function (including `main()`) can be compared to a black box that takes in input, processes it, and then produces the result. However, we may also have a function that does not take any inputs at all, or the one that does not return anything at all.

While using functions we will be using the following terminologies:

- A function *f* that uses another function *g* is known as the *calling function* and g is known as the *called function.*
- The inputs that a function takes are known as *arguments/parameters.*
- When a called function returns some result back to the calling function, it is said to *return* that result.
- The calling function may or may not pass *parameters* to the called function. If the called function accepts arguments, the calling function will pass parameters, else it will not do so.
- *Function declaration* is a declaration statement that identifies a function with its name, a list of arguments that it accepts, and the type of data it returns.
- *Function definition* consists of a function header that identifies the function, followed by the body of the function containing the executable code for that function.

11.3 FUNCTION DECLARATION/ FUNCTION PROTOTYPE

Before using a function, the compiler must know about the number of parameters and the type of parameters that the function expects to receive and the data type of the value that it will return to the calling function. Placing the function declaration statement prior to its use enables the compiler to make a check on the arguments used while calling that function.

The general format for declaring a function that accepts some arguments and returns some value as a result can be given as:

```
return_data_type function_name(data_type
   variable1, data_type variable2,...);
```

Here, `function_name` is a valid name for the function. Naming a function follows the same rules as naming variables. A function should have a meaningful name that must specify the task that the function will perform. The function name is used to call it for execution in a program. Every function must have a different name that indicates the particular job that the function does.

`return_data_type` specifies the data type of the value that will be returned to the calling function as a result of the processing performed by the called function.

`data_type variable1, data_type variable2, ...` is a list of variables of specified data types. These variables are passed from the calling function to the called function. They are also known as *arguments* or *parameters* that the called function accepts to perform its task. Table 11.1 shows examples of valid function declarations in C.

Table 11.1 Valid function declarations

Function declaration	Use of the function
Return data type ↓ char convert_to_uppercase (char ch);	Converts a character to upper case. The function receives a character as an argument, converts it into upper case and returns the converted character back to the calling function.
Function name ↓ float avg (int a, int b);	Calculates average of two integer numbers a and b received as arguments. The function returns a floating point value.
int find_largest (int a, int b, int c); ↑ Data type of variable	Finds the largest of three numbers—a, b, and c received as arguments. An integer value which is the largest of the three numbers is returned to the calling function.
double multiply (float a, float b); ↑ Variable 1	Multiplies two floating point numbers a and b that are received as arguments and returns a double value.
void swap (int a, int b);	Swaps or interchanges the value of integer variables a and b received as arguments. The function returns no value, therefore the return type is void.
void print(void);	The function is used to print information on screen. The function neither accepts any value as argument nor returns any value. Therefore, the return type is void and the argument list contains void data type.

Things to remember about function declaration:

- After the declaration of every function, there should be a semicolon. If the semicolon is missing, the compiler will generate an error message.

> **Programming Tip:** Though optional, use argument names in the function declaration.

- The function declaration is global. Therefore, the declared function can be called from any point in the program.
- Use of argument names in the function declaration statement is optional. So both declaration statements are valid in C.

```
int func(int, char, float);
```

or

```
int func(int num, char ch, float fnum);
```

- A function cannot be declared within the body of another function.
- A function having void as its return type cannot return any value.
- A function having void as its parameter list cannot accept any value. So the function declared as

```
void print(void);
```

or

```
void print();
```

does not accept any input/arguments from the calling function.

- If the function declaration does not specify any return type, then by default, the function returns an integer value. Therefore, when a function is declared as

```
sum(int a, int b);
```

Then the function sum accepts two integer values from the calling function and in turn returns an integer value to the caller.

- Some compilers make it compulsory to declare the function before its usage while other compilers make it optional. However, it is a good practice to always declare the function before its use as it allows error checking on the arguments in the function call.

11.4 FUNCTION DEFINITION

When a function is defined, space is allocated for that function in the memory. A function definition comprises two parts:

> **Programming Tip:** It is an error to place a semicolon after the function header in the function definition.

- Function header
- Function body

The syntax of a function definition can be given as:

```
return_data_type function_name(data_type
   variable1, data_type variable2,...)
{
   .........
```

```
    statements
    ......
    return(variable);
}
```

The number of arguments and the order of arguments in the function header must be same as that given in the function declaration statement.

Programming Tip: The parameter list in the function definition as well as function declaration must match.

While `return_data_type function_name(data_type variable1, data_type variable2,..)` is known as the function header, the rest of the portion comprising of program statements within { } is the function body which contains the code to perform the specific task.

The function header is same as function declaration. The only difference between the two is that a function header is not followed by a semicolon. The list of variables in the function header is known as the *formal parameter list*. The parameter list may have zero or more parameters of any data type. The function body contains instructions to perform the desired computation in a function.

The function definition itself can act as an implicit function declaration. So the programmer may skip the function declaration statement in case the function is defined before being used.

Programming Tip: A function can be defined either before or after `main()`.

> **Note**
>
> The argument names in the function declaration and function definition need not be the same. However, the data types of the arguments specified in function declaration must match with those given in function definition.

11.5 FUNCTION CALL

The function call statement invokes the function. When a function is invoked the compiler jumps to the called function to execute the statements that are part of that function. Once the called function is executed, the program control passes back to the calling function.

Function call statement has the following syntax:

```
function_name(variable1, variable2, ...);
```

When the function declaration is present before the function call, the compiler can check if the correct number and type of arguments are used in the function call and the returned value, if any, is being used reasonably.

Function definitions are often placed in separate header files which can be included in other C source files that wish to use these functions. For example, the header file `stdio.h` contains the definition of `scanf` and `printf` functions. We simply include this header file and call these functions without worrying about the code to implement their functionality.

> **Note**
>
> List of variables used in function call is known as actual parameter list. The actual parameter list may contain variable names, expressions, or constants.

11.5.1 Points to Remember While Calling Functions

The following points are to be kept in mind while calling functions:

- Function name and the number and type of arguments in the function call must be same as that given in the function declaration and function header of the function definition.
- If the parameters passed to a function are more than what it is specified to accept then the extra arguments will be discarded.
- If the parameters passed to a function are less than what it is specified to accept then the unmatched arguments will be initialized to some garbage value.
- Names (and not the types) of variables in function declaration, function call, and header of function definition may vary.
- If the data type of the argument passed does not match with that specified in the function declaration then either the unmatched argument will be initialized to some garbage value or a compile time error will be generated.
- Arguments may be passed in the form of expressions to the called function. In such cases, arguments are first evaluated and converted to the type of formal parameter and then the body of the function gets executed.
- The parameter list must be separated with commas.
- If the return type of the function is not `void`, then the value returned by the called function may be assigned to some variable as shown in the following statement.

```
variable_name = function_
    name(variable1, variable2, ...);
```

Programming Tip: A logical error will be generated if the arguments in the function call are placed in the wrong order.

Let us now try writing a program using function.

1. Write a program to add two integers using functions.

```
#include <stdio.h>
// FUNCTION DECLARATION
int sum(int a, int b);
int main()
{
  int num1, num2, total = 0;
```

```
    printf("\n Enter the first number: ");
    scanf("%d", &num1);
    printf("\n Enter the second number: ");
    scanf("%d", &num2);
    total = sum(num1, num2);
      // FUNCTION CALL
    printf("\n Total = %d", total);
    return 0;
  }

  // FUNCTION DEFINITION
  int sum (int a, int b)      // FUNCTION HEADER
  {                           // FUNCTION BODY
    int result;
    result = a + b;
    return result;
  }
```

Output

```
Enter the first number: 20
Enter the second number: 30
Total = 50
```

The variables declared within the function and its parameters are local to that function. The programmer may use same names for variables in other functions. This eliminates the need for thinking and keeping unique names for variables declared in all the functions in the program.

Programming Tip:
It is an error to use void as the return type when the function is expected to return a value to the calling function.

In the `sum()` function, we have declared a variable `result` just like any other variable. Variables declared within a function are called *automatic local variables* because of two reasons.

- First, they are local to the function. So, their effect (in terms of scope, lifetime, or accessibility) is limited to the function. Any change made to these variables is visible only in that function.
- Second, they are automatically created whenever the function is called and cease to exist after control exits the function.

Note

A function cannot be used on the left side of an assignment statement. Therefore writing, `func(10) = 100;` is invalid in C, where `func` is a function that accepts an integer value.

11.6 return STATEMENT

The `return` statement terminates the execution of the called function and returns control to the calling function.

Programming Tip:
It is an error to use a return statement in a function that has void as its return type.

When the `return` statement is encountered, the program execution resumes in the calling function at the point immediately following the function call. Refer Figure 11.2 in which the control passes from the called function to the calling function when the return statement is encountered.

A `return` statement may or may not return a value to the calling function. The syntax of `return` statement can be given as

```
return <expression>;
```

Here `expression` is placed in between angular brackets because specifying an expression is optional. The value of `expression`, if present, is returned to the calling function. However, in case `expression` is omitted, the return value of the function is undefined.

The expression, if present, is converted to the type returned by the function. A function that has `void` as its return type cannot return any value to the calling function. So in a function that has been declared with return type `void`, a `return` statement containing an expression generates a warning and the expression is not evaluated.

For functions that have no `return` statement, the control automatically returns to the calling function after the last statement of the called function is executed. In other words an implicit return takes place upon execution of the last statement of the called function, and control automatically returns to the calling function.

Note

The programmer may or may not place the expression in a return statement within parentheses.
By default, the return type of a function is int.

Programming Tip:
When the value returned by a function is assigned to a variable, then the returned value is converted to the type of the variable receiving it.

A function may have more than one `return` statement. For example, consider the program given below.

```
#include <stdio.h>
int check_relation(int a,
int b);
int main()
{
   int a=3, b=5, res;
   res = check_relation(a, b);
   if(res==0) // Test the returned value
      printf("\n EQUAL");
   if(res==1)
      printf("\n a is greater than b");
   if(res==-1)
      printf("\n a is less than b");
   return 0;
}
int check_relation(int a, int b)
```

```
{
  if(a==b)
      return 0;
  else if(a>b)
      return 1;
  else
      return -1;
}
```

> **Programming Tip:** An error is generated when the function does not return data of the specified type.

Output

```
a is less than b
```

In the aforegiven program there are multiple `return` statements, but only one of them will get executed depending upon the condition. The `return` statement, like the break statement, is used to cause a premature termination of the function.

An expression appearing in a `return` statement is converted to the return type of the function in which the statement appears. If no implicit conversion is possible, the `return` statement is invalid. Since the return type of the function `check_relation()` is int, so the result either `0`, `1`, or `-1` is evaluated as an integer.

> **Programming Tip:** A function that does not return any value cannot be placed on the right side of the assignment operator.

We have mentioned earlier that the variables declared inside the function cease to exist after the last statement of the function is executed. So how can we return the value of sum to the program that adds two integers using a function? The answer to this question is that a copy of the value being returned is made automatically and this copy is available to the return point in the program.

11.6.1 Using Variable Number of Arguments

Some functions have a variable number of arguments and data types that cannot be known at the compile time. Typical examples of such functions include the `printf()` and `scanf()` functions. ANSI C offers a symbol called ellipsis to handle such functions. The ellipsis consists of three periods (...). It can be used as:

```
int func(char ch, ...);
```

The function declaration statement given above states that `func` is a function that has an arbitrary number and type of arguments. However, one must ensure that both the function declaration and function definition should use the ellipsis symbol.

11.7 PASSING PARAMETERS TO FUNCTIONS

When a function is called, the calling function may have to pass some values to the called function. We have been doing this in the programming examples given so far. We will now learn the technicalities involved in passing arguments/parameters to the called function.

There are two ways in which arguments or parameters can be passed to the called function. They include:

- **Call by value** in which values of variables are passed by the calling function to the called function. The programs that we have written so far call functions using call-by-value method of passing parameters.
- **Call by reference** in which address of variables are passed by the calling function to the called function.

11.7.1 Call by Value

Till now, we had been calling functions and passing arguments to them using call-by-value method. In the call-by-value method, the called function creates new variables to store the value of the arguments passed to it. Therefore, the called function uses a copy of the actual arguments to perform its intended task.

If the called function is supposed to modify the value of the parameters passed to it, then the change will be reflected only in the called function. In the calling function no change will be made to the value of the variables. This is because all the changes were made to the copy of the variables and not to the actual variables.

> **Programming Tip:** It is legal to have multiple return statements in C.

To understand this concept, consider the code given below. The `add()` function accepts an integer variable `num` and adds `10` to it. In the calling function, the value of `num = 2`. In `add()`, the value of `num` is modified to `12` but in the calling function the change is not reflected.

```
#include <stdio.h>
void add(int n);
int main()
{
  int num = 2;
  printf("\n The value of num before calling
   the function = %d", num);
  add(num);
  printf("\n The value of num after calling
   the function = %d", num);
  return 0;
}

void add(int n)
{
  n = n + 10;
  printf("\n The value of num in the called
   function = %d", n);
}
```

Output

```
The value of num before calling the function = 2
The value of num in the called function = 12
The value of num after calling the function = 2
```

Since the called function uses a copy of `num`, the value of `num` in the calling function remains untouched. This concept can be more clearly understood from Figure 11.5.

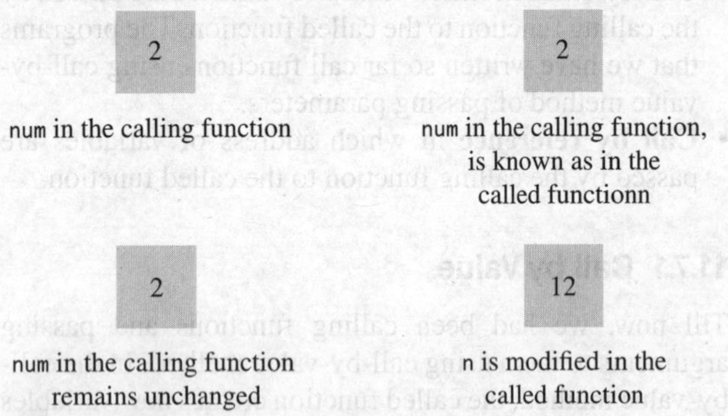

Figure 11.5 Call-by-value method of argument passing

In the aforegiven program, the called function could not directly modify the value of the argument that was passed to it. In case the value has to be changed, then the programmer may use the `return` statement. This is shown in the following code.

```
#include <stdio.h>
int add (int n);
int main()
{
  int num = 2;
  printf("\n The value of num before calling
   the function = %d", num);
  num = add(num);
  printf("\n The value of num after calling
   the function = %d", num);
  return 0;
}

int add(int n)
{
  n = n + 10;
  printf("\n The value of num in the called
   function = %d", n);
  return n;
}
```

Output

```
The value of num before calling the function = 2
The value of num in the called function = 12
The value of num after calling the function = 12
```

The following points are to be noted while passing arguments to a function using the call-by-value method.

- When ablrguments are passed by value, the called function creates new variables of the same data type as the arguments passed to it.
- The values of the arguments passed by the function are copied into the newly created variables.
- Arguments are called by value when the called function does not need to modify the values of the original variables in the calling function.
- Values of the variables in the calling function remain unaffected when the arguments are passed using call-by-value technique.

Therefore, call-by-value method of passing arguments to a function must be used only in two cases:

- When the called function does not need to modify the value of the actual parameter. It simply uses the value of the parameter to perform its task.
- When you want that the called function should only temporarily modify the value of the variables and not permanently. So although the called function may modify the value of the variables, these variables remain unchanged in the calling function.

> **Programming Tip:**
> Using call-by-value method of passing values is preferred to avoid inadvertent changes to variables of the calling function in the called function.

Pros and Cons

The biggest advantage of using the call-by-value technique to pass arguments to the called function is that arguments can be variables (e.g., `x`), literals (e.g., `6`), or expressions (e.g., `x + 1`). The disadvantage is that copying data consumes additional storage space. In addition, it can take a lot of time to copy, thereby resulting in performance penalty, especially if the function is called many times.

11.7.2 Call by Reference

When the calling function passes arguments to the called function using call-by-value method, the only way to return the modified value of the argument to the caller is explicitly using the `return` statement. A better option when a function wants to modify the value of the argument is to pass arguments using call-by-reference technique. In call by reference, we declare the function parameters as references rather than normal variables. When this is done any changes made by the function to the arguments it receives are visible in the calling function.

To indicate that an argument is passed using call by reference, an asterisk (`*`) is placed after the type in the parameter list. This way, changes made to the parameter in the called function will then be reflected in the calling function.

Hence, in call-by-reference method, a function receives an implicit reference to the argument, rather than a copy of its value. Therefore, the function can modify the value of the variable and that change will be reflected in the calling function as well. The following program uses this concept.

To understand this concept, consider the code given below.

```
#include <stdio.h>
void add (int *n);
int main()
{
  int num = 2;
```

```
    printf("\n The value of num before
     calling the function = %d", num);
    add(&num);
    printf("\n The value of num after calling
     the function = %d", num);
    return 0;
  }

  void add(int *n)
  {
    *n = *n + 10;
    printf("\n The value of num in the called
     function = %d", *n);
  }
```

Output

```
The value of num before calling the function = 2
The value of num in the called function = 12
The value of num after calling the function = 12
```

Advantages

The advantages of using the call-by-reference technique of passing arguments are as follows:

- Since arguments are not copied into new variables, it provides greater time and space efficiency.
- The called function can change the value of the argument and the change is reflected in the calling function.
- A `return` statement can return only one value. In case we need to return multiple values, pass those arguments by reference.

Disadvantages

However, the side-effect of using this technique is that when an argument is passed using call by address, it becomes difficult to tell whether that argument is meant for input, output, or both.

Now let us write a few programs that use both the call-by-value and the call-by-reference mechanisms.

2. Write a function to swap the value of two variables.

```
#include <stdio.h>
void swap_call_by_val(int, int);
void swap_call_by_ref(int *, int *);
int main()
  {
    int a=1, b=2, c=3, d=4;
    printf("\n In main(), a = %d and b = %d",
      a, b);
    swap_call_by_val(a, b);
    printf("\n In main(), a = %d and b = %d",
      a, b);
    printf("\n\n In main(), c = %d and d =
      %d", c, d);
    swap_call_by_ref(&c, &d);
      // address of the variables is passed
    printf("\n In main(), c = %d and d =
      %d", c, d);
    return 0;
  }
void swap_call_by_val(int a, int b)
  {
    int temp;
    temp = a;
    a = b;
    b = temp;
    printf("\n In function (Call By Value
      Method) a = %d and b = %d", a, b);
  }
void swap_call_by_ref(int *c, int *d)
  {
    int temp;
    temp = *c;
      // * operator used to refer to the value
    *c = *d;
    *d = temp;
    printf("\n In function (Call By Reference
      Method) c = %d and d = %d", *c, *d);
  }
```

Output

```
In main(), a = 1 and b = 2
In function (Call By Value Method) a = 2 and
b = 1
In main(), a = 1 and b = 2

In main(), c = 3 and d = 4
In function (Call By Reference Method) c = 4
and d = 3
In main(), c = 4 and d = 3
```

3. Write a program to find biggest of three integers using functions.

```
#include <stdio.h>
int greater(int a, int b, int c);

int main()
{
  int num1, num2, num3, large;
  printf("\n Enter the first number: ");
  scanf("%d", &num1);
  printf("\n Enter the second number: ");
  scanf("%d", &num2);
  printf("\n Enter the third number: ");
  scanf("%d", &num3);

  large = greater(num1, num2, num3);
  printf("\n Largest number = %d", large);
  return 0;
  }

  int greater(int a, int b, int c)
  {
```

```
    if(a>b && a>c)
      return a;
    if(b>a && b>c)
      return b;
    else
      return c;
  }
```

Output

```
Enter the first number : 45
Enter the second number: 23
Enter the third number : 34
Largest number = 45
```

4. Write a program to calculate area of a circle using function.

```
#include <stdio.h>
float cal_area(float r);
int main()
{
    float area, radius;
    printf("\n Enter the radius of the
      circle: ");
    scanf("%f", &radius);
    area = cal_area(radius);
    printf("\n Area of the circle with radius
      %f = %f", radius, area);
    return 0;
}
float cal_area(float radius)
{
    return (3.14 * radius * radius);
}
```

Output

```
Enter the radius of the circle: 7
Area of the circle with radius 7 = 153.83
```

5. Write a program to convert time to minutes.

```
#include <stdio.h>
int convert_time_in_mins(int hrs, int
   minutes);
int main()
{
    int hrs, minutes, total_mins;
    printf("\n Enter hours and minutes: ");
    scanf("%d %d", &hrs, &minutes);
    total_mins = convert_time_in_mins(hrs,
      minutes);
    printf("\n Total minutes = %d", total_
      mins);
    return 0;
}

int convert_time_in_mins(int hrs, int mins)
{
    mins = hrs*60 + mins;
    return mins;
}
```

Output

```
Enter hours and minutes: 4 30
Total minutes = 270
```

6. Write a program to calculate *P(n/r)*.

```
#include <stdio.h>
int Fact(int);
int main()
{
    int n, r;
    float result;
    printf("\n Enter the value of n: ");
    scanf("%d", &n);
    printf("\n Enter the value of r: ");
    scanf("%d", &r);
    result = (float)Fact(n)/Fact(r);
    printf("\n P(n/r): P(%d)/(%d) = %.2f", n,
      r, result);
    return 0;
}
int Fact(int num)
{
    int f=1, i;
    for(i=num;i>=1;i--)
      f = f*i;
    return f;
}
```

Output

```
Enter the value of n: 4
Enter the value of r: 2
P(n/r): P(4)/(2) = 12.00
```

7. Write a program to calculate *C(n/r)*.

```
#include <stdio.h>
int Fact(int);
int main()
{
    int n, r;
    float result;
    printf("\n Enter the value of n: ");
    scanf("%d", &n);
    printf("\n Enter the value of r: ");
    scanf("%d", &r);
    result = (float)Fact(n)/(Fact(r)*Fact(n-r));
    printf("\n C(n/r) : C(%d)/(%d) = %.2f", n,
      r, result);
    return 0;
}
int Fact(int num)
{
    int f=1, i;
```

```
for(i=num;i>=1;i--)
    f = f*i;
  return f;
}
```

Output

```
Enter the value of n: 4
Enter the value of r: 2
C(n/r): C(4)/(2) = 6.00
```

8. Write a program to sum the series—1/1! + 1/2! + 1/3! + ….. + 1/*n*!.

```
#include <stdio.h>
int Fact(int);
int main()
{
    int n, f, i;
    float result=0.0;
    printf("\n Enter the value of n: ");
    scanf("%d", &n);
    for(i=1;i<=n;i++)
    {
      f=Fact(i);
      result += 1/(float)f;
    }
      printf("\n The sum of the series 1/1! +
        1/2! + 1/3!... = %.1f", result);
    return 0;
}
int Fact(int num)
{
    int f=1, i;
    for(i=num;i>=1;i--)
      f = f*i;
    return f;
}
```

Output

```
Enter the value of n: 2
The sum of the series 1/1! + 1/2! +
  1/3!... = 1.5
```

9. Write a program to sum the series—1/1! + 4/2! + 27/3! + ….

```
#include <stdio.h>
#include <math.h>
int Fact(int);
int main()
{
    int n, i, NUM, DENO;
    float sum=0.0;
    printf("\n Enter the value of n");
    scanf("%d",&n);
    for(i=1;i<=n;i++)
    {
        NUM = pow(i,i);
        DENO = Fact(i);
        sum += (float)NUM/DENO;
    }
    printf("\n 1/1! + 4/2! + 27/3! + ....=
     %.2f", sum);
    return 0;
}
int Fact(int n)
{
    int f=1, i;
    for(i=n;i>=1;i--)
      f=f*i;
    return f;
}
```

Output

```
Enter the value of n: 3
1/1! + 4/2! + 27/3! + ....= 7.50
```

11.8 SCOPE OF VARIABLES

In C, all constants and variables have a defined scope. By scope we mean the accessibility and visibility of the variables at different points in the program. A variable or a constant in C has four types of scope: block, function, program, and file.

11.8.1 Block Scope

We have studied that a statement block is a group of statements enclosed within opening and closing curly brackets { }. If a variable is declared within a statement block then as soon as the control exits that block, the variable will cease to exist. Such a variable also known as a local variable is said to have a *block scope*.

So far we had been using local variables. For example, if we declare an integer *x* inside a function, then that variable is unknown to the rest of the program (i.e., outside that function).

> **Programming Tip:**
> It is an error to use the name of a function argument as the name of a local variable.

Blocks of statements may be placed one after the other in a program; such blocks that are placed at the same level are known as *parallel blocks*. However, a program may also contain a nested block, like a `while` loop inside `main()`. If an integer *x* is declared and initialized in `main()`, and then re-declared and re-initialized in a `while` loop, then the integer variable *x* will occupy different memory slots and will be considered as different variables. The following code reveals this concept:

```
#include <stdio.h>
int main()
{
  int x = 10;
  int i=0;
  printf("\n The value of x outside the
     while loop is %d", x);
  while (i<3)
  {
    int x = i;
    printf("\n The value of x inside the
      while loop is %d", x);
    i++;
  }

  printf("\n The value of x outside the
     while loop is %d", x);
  return 0;
}
```

Output

```
The value of x outside the while loop is 10
The value of x inside the while loop is 0
The value of x inside the while loop is 1
The value of x inside the while loop is 2
The value of x outside the while loop is 10
```

Programming Tip: Try to avoid variable names that hides variables in outer scope.

You may get an error message while executing this code. This is because some C compilers make it mandatory to declare all the variables first before you use them, i.e., they permit declaration of variables right after the curly brackets of `main()` starts.

Hence, we can conclude two things:

- Variables declared with same names as those in outer block mask the outer block variables while executing the inner block.
- In nested blocks, variables declared outside the inner blocks are accessible to the nested blocks, provided these variables are not re-declared within the inner block.

Note

In order to avoid error, a programmer must use different names for variables not common to inner as well as outer blocks.

11.8.2 Function Scope

Function scope indicates that a variable is active and visible from the beginning to the end of a function. In C, only the `goto` label has function scope. In other words function scope is applicable only with `goto` label names. This means that the programmer cannot have the same label names inside a function.

Using `goto` statements is not recommended as it is not considered to be a good programming practice. We will not discuss the `goto` statement in detail here but we will take a look at an example code that demonstrates the function scope.

```
int main()
{
  .
  .
  loop:    /* A goto label has function
    scope */
  .
  .
  .
  goto loop;  /* the goto statement */
  .
  .
  return 0;
}
```

In this example, the label `loop` is visible from the beginning to the end of the `main()` function. Therefore, there should not be more than one label having the same name within the `main()` function.

11.8.3 Program Scope

Till now we have studied that variables declared within a function are local variables. These local variables (also known as internal variables) are automatically created when they are declared in the function and are usable only within that function. The local variables are unknown to other functions in the program. Such variables cease to exist after the function in which they are declared is exited and are re-created each time the function is called.

Programming Tip: A global variable can be used from anywhere in the program whereas the local variable ceases to exist outside the function in which it is declared.

However, if you want a function to access some variables which are not passed to it as arguments, then declare those variables outside any function blocks. Such variables are commonly known as *global variables* and can be accessed from any point in the program.

Lifetime Global variables are created at the beginning of program execution and remain in existence throughout the period of execution of the program. These variables are known to all the functions in the program and are accessible to them for usage. Global variables are not limited to a particular function so they exist even when a function calls another function. These variables retain their value so that they can be used from every function in the program.

Place of Declaration The global variables are declared outside all the functions including `main()`. Although there is no specific rule that states where the global variables must be declared, it is always recommended to declare them on top of the program code.

Name Conflict If we have a variable declared in a function that has same name as that of the global variable, then the function will use the local variable declared within it and ignore the global variable. However, the programmer must not use names of global variables as the names of local variables, as this may lead to confusion and erroneous result.

Note

If a global variable is not initialized during its declaration then it is automatically initialized to zero by default.

Consider the following program.

```
#include <stdio.h>
int x = 10;
void print();
int main()
{
  printf("\n The value of x in the main()
     = %d", x);
  int x = 2;
  printf("\n The value of local variable x
     in the main() = %d", x);
  print();
  return 0;
}
void print()
{
  printf("\n The value of x in the print()
     = %d", x);
}
```

Output

```
The value of x in the main() = 10
The value of local variable x in the main() = 2
The value of x in the print() = 10
```

From the code we see that local variables overwrite the value of global variables. In big programs use of global variables is not recommended until it is very important to use them because there is a big risk of confusing them with any local variables of the same name.

Note

Functions are considered to be self-contained and independent modules. So they need to be isolated from the rest of the code, but using global variables goes against this idea behind creating independent functions.

11.8.4 File Scope

When a global variable is accessible until the end of the file, the variable is said to have *file scope*. To allow a variable to have file scope, declare that variable with the static keyword before specifying its data type:

```
static int x = 10;
```

A global static variable can be used anywhere from the file in which it is declared but it is not accessible by any other file. Such variables are useful when the programmer writes his own header files.

11.9 STORAGE CLASSES

Storage class defines the scope (visibility) and lifetime of variables and/or functions declared within a C program. In addition to this, the storage class gives the following information about the variable or the function.

- The storage class of a function or a variable determines the part of memory where storage space will be allocated for that variable or function (whether the variable/function will be stored in a register or in RAM).
- It specifies how long the storage allocation will continue to exist for that function or variable.
- It specifies the scope of the variable or function, i.e., the storage class indicates the part of the C program in which the variable name is visible or the part in which it is accessible. In other words, whether the variable/function can be referenced throughout the program or only within the function, block, or source file where it has been defined.
- It specifies whether the variable or function has internal, external, or no linkage.
- It specifies whether the variable will be automatically initialized to zero or to any indeterminate value.

C supports four storage classes: `automatic`, `register`, `external`, and `static`. The general syntax for specifying the storage class of a variable can be given as:

```
<storage_class_specifier> <data type>
   <variable name>
```

11.9.1 `auto` Storage Class

The auto storage class specifier is used to explicitly declare a variable with *automatic storage*. It is the default storage class for variables declared inside a block. For example, if we write

```
auto int x;
```

then *x* is an integer that has automatic storage. It is deleted when the block in which *x* is declared is exited.

The `auto` storage class can be used to declare variables in a block or the names of function parameters. However, since the variable names or names of function parameters by default have automatic storage, the `auto` storage class specifier is therefore treated as redundant while declaring data.

Important things to remember about variables declared with `auto` storage class are as follows:

- All local variables declared within a function belong to automatic storage class by default.
- They should be declared at the start of the program block, right after the opening curly bracket {.
- Memory for the variable is automatically allocated upon entry to a block and freed automatically upon exit from that block.
- The scope of the variable is local to the block in which it is declared. These variables may be declared within a nested block.
- Every time the block (in which the automatic variable is declared) is entered, the variable is initialized with the values declared.
- The `auto` variables are stored in the primary memory of the computer.
- If `auto` variables are not initialized at the time of declaration, then they contain some garbage value.

The following code uses an `auto` integer that is local to the function in which it is defined.

```
#include <stdio.h>
void func1()
{
  int a=10;
  printf("\n a = %d", a);
    // auto integer local to func1()
}
void func2()
{
    int a=20;
    printf("\n a = %d", a);
      // auto integer local to func2()
}
void main()
{
    int a=30;// auto integer local to main()
    func1();
    func2();
    printf("\n a = %d", a);
}
```

Output

```
a = 10
a = 20
a = 30
```

11.9.2 `register` Storage Class

When a variable is declared using `register` as its storage class, it is stored in a CPU register instead of RAM. Since the variable is stored in a register, the maximum size of the variable is equal to the register size. One drawback of using a register variable is that they cannot be operated using the unary `'&'` operator because it does not have a memory location associated with it. A register variable is declared in the following manner:

```
register int x;
```

Register variables are used when quick access to the variable is needed. It is not always necessary that the register variable will be stored in the register. Rather, the register variable might be stored in a register depending on the hardware and implementation restrictions.

Hence, programmers can only suggest to the compiler to store those variables in the registers which are used repeatedly or whose access times are critical. However, for the compiler, it is not an obligation to always accept such requests. In case the compiler rejects the request to store the variable in the register, the variable is treated as having the storage class specifier auto.

Like `auto` variables, `register` variables also have automatic storage duration. That is, each time a block is entered, the `register` variables defined in that block are accessible and the moment that block is exited, the variables become no longer accessible for use. Now let us have a look at the following code that uses a `register` variable.

```
#include <stdio.h>
int exp(int a, int b);
int main()
{
    int a=3, b=5, res;
    res = exp(a, b);
    printf("\n %d to the power of %d = %d",
      a, b, res);
    return 0;

}
int exp(int a, int b)
{
    register int res=1;
    int i;
    for(i=1;i<=b;i++)
      res = res*a;
    return res;
}
```

Output

```
3 to the power of 5 = 243
```

11.9.3 `extern` Storage Class

A large C program can be broken down into smaller programs. When these smaller programs are compiled, they are joined together to form a large program. However, these smaller programs may need to share certain variables for processing. For such situations C language provides an external storage class that is specified using the keyword `extern`.

The `extern` storage class is used to give a reference of a global variable that is visible to all the program files. Such global variables are declared like any other variable in one of the program files. When there are multiple files in a program and you need to use a particular function or variable in a file apart from which it is declared, then use the `extern` keyword. To declare a variable *x* as `extern` write,

```
extern int x;
```

External variables may be declared outside any function in a source code file as any other variable is declared. But usually external variables are declared and defined at the beginning of a source file.

Memory is allocated for external variables when the program begins execution, and remains allocated until the program terminates. External variables may be initialized while they are declared. However, the initializer must be a constant expression. The compiler will initialize its value only once during the compiler time. In case the `extern` variable is not initialized, it will be initialized to zero by default.

External variables have global scope, i.e., these variables are visible and accessible from all the functions in the program. However, if any function has a local variable with the same name and type as that of the `global` or `extern` variable, then references to the name will access the local variable rather than the `extern` variable. Hence extern variables are overwritten by local variables.

Let us now write a program in which we will use the `extern` keyword.

```
// FILE 1.C

#include <stdio.h>
#include <FILE2.C>
  // Programmer's own header file
int x;
void print(void);
int main()
{
  x = 10;
  printf("\n x in FILE1 = %d", x);
  print();
  return 0;
}
// END OF FILE1.C
// FILE2.C
#include <stdio.h>
extern int x;
void print()
{
  printf("\n x in FILE 2 = %d", x);
}
main()
{
// Statements
}
// END OF FILE2.C
```

Output

```
x in FILE1 = 10
x in FILE2 = 10
```

In the program, we have used two files—`File1` and `File2`. `File1` has declared a global variable *x*. `File1` also includes `File2` which has a `printf` function that uses the external variable *x* to print its value on the screen.

Note

The `extern` specifier tells the compiler that the variable has already been declared elsewhere and therefore it should not allocate storage space for that variable again. During compilation of the program, the linker will automatically resolve the reference problem.

In a multi-file program, the global variable must be declared only once (in any one of the files) without using the `extern` keyword. This is because otherwise the linker will have a conflict as to which variable to use and therefore in such a situation it raises a warning message.

11.9.4 `static` Storage Class

While `auto` is the default storage class for all local variables, `static` is the default storage class for all global variables. Static variables have a lifetime over the entire program, i.e., memory for the `static` variables is allocated when the program begins running and is freed when the program terminates. To declare an integer *x* as `static`, write

```
static int x = 10;
```

Here *x* is a local static variable. Static local variables when defined within a function are initialized at the runtime. The difference between an `auto` variable and a `static` variable is that the `static` variable when defined within a function is not re-initialized when the function is called again and again. It is initialized just once and further calls of the function share the value of the `static` variable. Hence, the `static` variable inside a function retains its value during various calls.

When a `static` variable is not explicitly initialized by the programmer, then it is automatically initialized to zero when memory is allocated for it. Although `static` automatic variables exist even after the block in which they are defined terminates, their scope is local to the block in which they are defined.

`Static` storage class can be specified for `auto` as well as `extern` variables. For example we can write,

```
static extern int x;
```

When we declare a variable as `extern static` variable, then that variable is accessible from all the functions in this source file.

Note

`static` variables can be initialized while they are being declared. But this initialization is done only once at the compile time when memory is being allocated for the static variable. Further, the value with which the static variable is initialized must be a constant expression.

Look at the following code which clearly differentiates between a `static` variable and a normal variable.

```
#include <stdio.h>
void print(void);
```

Table 11.2 Comparison of storage classes

FEATURE	STORAGE CLASS			
	auto	extern	register	static
Accessibility	Accessible within the function or block in which it is declared.	Accessible within all program files that are a part of the program.	Accessible within the function or block in which it is declared.	Local: Accessible within the function or block in which it is declared. Global: Accessible within the program in which it is declared.
Storage	Main memory	Main memory	CPU register	Main memory
Existence	Exists when the function or block in which it is declared is entered. Ceases to exist when the control returns from the function or the block in which it was declared.	Exists throughout the execution of the program.	Exists when the function or block in which it is declared is entered. Ceases to exist when the control returns from the function or the block in which it was declared.	Local: Retains value between function calls or block entries.Global: Preserves value in program files.
Default value	Garbage	Zero	Garbage	Zero

```
int main()
{
  printf("\n First call of print()(");
  print();
  printf("\n\n Second call of print()(");
  print();
  printf("\n\n Third call of print()(");
  print();
  return 0;
}

void print()
{
  static int x;
  int y = 0;
  printf("\n Static integer variable, x =
     %d", x);
  printf("\n Integer variable, y = %d", y);
  x++;
  y++;
}
```

Output

```
First call of print()
Static integer variable, x = 0
Integer variable, y = 0

Second call of print()
Static integer variable, x = 1
Integer variable, y = 0

Third call of print()
Static integer variable, x = 2
Integer variable, y = 0
```

11.9.5 Comparison of Storage Classes

Table 11.2 compares the key features of all the storage classes.

11.10 RECURSIVE FUNCTIONS

A *recursive function* is defined as a function that calls itself to solve a smaller version of its task until a final call is made which does not require a call to itself. Every recursive solution has two major cases:

- *Base case,* in which the problem is simple enough to be solved directly without making any further calls to the same function.
- *Recursive case,* in which first the problem at hand is divided into simpler sub-parts. Second the function calls itself but with sub-parts of the problem obtained in the first step. Third, the result is obtained by combining the solutions of simpler sub-parts.

Therefore, recursion is defining a large and complex problem in terms of smaller and more easily solvable problems. In recursive function, a complex problem is defined in terms of simpler problems and the simplest problem is given explicitly.

To understand recursive functions, let us take an example of calculating factorial of a number. To calculate $n!$, we multiply the number with factorial of the number that is 1 less than that number. In other words, $n! = n \times (n-1)!$

Let us say we need to find the value of 5!.

$$5! = 5 \times 4 \times 3 \times 2 \times 1$$
$$= 120$$

This can be written as

$5! = 5 \times 4!$, where $4! = 4 \times 3!$

Therefore,

$5! = 5 \times 4 \times 3!$

Similarly, we can also write,

$5! = 5 \times 4 \times 3 \times 2!$

Expanding further

$5! = 5 \times 4 \times 3 \times 2 \times 1!$

We know, $1! = 1$

Therefore, the series of problems and solutions can be given as shown in Figure 11.6.

PROBLEM	SOLUTION
5!	5 × 4 × 3 × 2 × 1 !
= 5 × 4!	= 5 × 4 × 3 × 2 × 1
= 5 × 4 × 3 !	= 5 × 4 × 3 × 2
= 5 × 4 × 3 × 2 !	= 5 × 4 × 6
= 5 × 4 × 3 × 2 × 1 !	= 5 × 24
	= 120

Figure 11.6 Recursive factorial function

Programming Tip: Every recursive function must have at least one base case. Otherwise, the recursive function will generate an infinite sequence of calls thereby resulting in an error condition known as an infinite stack.

Now if you look at the problem carefully, you can see that we can write a recursive function to calculate the factorial of a number. Every recursive function must have a base case and a recursive case. For the factorial function,

- **Base case** is when $n = 1$, because if $n = 1$, the result will be 1 as $1! = 1$.
- **Recursive case** of the factorial function will call itself but with a smaller value of n, this case can be given as

$$\text{factorial}(n) = n \times \text{factorial}(n - 1)$$

Look at the following code which calculates the factorial of a number recursively.

```
#include <stdio.h>
int Fact(int);
int main()
{
    int num, factorial;
    printf("\n Enter the number: ");
    scanf("%d", &num);
    factorial = Fact(num);
    printf("\n Factorial of %d = %d", num,
       factorial);
    return 0;
}
int Fact(int n)
{
   if(n==1)
     return 1;
   else
     return (n * Fact(n-1));
}
```

From the aforegiven example, let us analyse the basic steps of a recursive program.

Step 1: Specify the base case which will stop the function from making a call to itself.

Step 2: Check to see whether the current value being processed matches with the value of the base case. If yes, process and return the value.

Step 3: Divide the problem into smaller or simpler sub-problems.

Step 4: Call the function from the sub-problems.

Step 5: Combine the results of the sub-problems.

Step 6: Return the result of the entire problem.

Note

The base case of a recursive function acts as the terminating condition. So, in the absence of an explicitly defined base case, a recursive function would call itself indefinitely.

11.10.1 Greatest Common Divisor

The greatest common divisor (GCD) of two numbers (integers) is the largest integer that divides both the numbers. We can find the GCD of two numbers recursively by using the *Euclid's algorithm* that states

$$\text{GCD}(a, b) = \begin{cases} b, \text{ if } b \text{ divides } a \\ \text{GCD}(b, a \bmod b), \text{ otherwise} \end{cases}$$

GCD can be implemented as a recursive function because if b does not divide a, then we call the same function (GCD) with another set of parameters that are smaller and simpler than the original ones. Here we assume that $a > b$. However if $a < b$, then interchange a and b in the aforegiven formula.

Working

Assume $a = 62$ and $b = 8$

GCD(62, 8)
  rem = 62 % 8 = 6
  GCD(8, 6)
    rem = 8 % 6 = 2
    GCD(6, 2)
      rem = 6 % 2 = 0
    Return 2
  Return 2
Return 2

10. Write a program to calculate GCD using recursive functions.

```
#include <stdio.h>
int GCD(int, int);
int main()
{
  int num1, num2, res;
  printf("\n Enter the two numbers: ");
  scanf("%d %d", &num1, &num2);
  res = GCD(num1, num2);
  printf("\n GCD of %d and %d = %d", num1,
     num2, res);
  return 0;
}

int GCD(int x, int y)
{
  int rem;
  rem = x%y;
  if(rem==0)
    return y;
  else
    return (GCD(y, rem));
}
```

Output

```
Enter the two numbers: 62 8
GCD of 62 and 8 = 2
```

11.10.2 Finding Exponents

We can find exponent of a number using recursion. To find x^y, the base case would be when $y = 0$, as we know that any number raised to the power 0 is 1. Therefore, the general formula to find x^y can be given as

$$\text{EXP}(x, y) = \begin{cases} 1, \text{ if } y == 0 \\ x \times \text{EXP}(x^{y-1}), \text{ otherwise} \end{cases}$$

Working

exp_rec(2, 4) = 2 × exp_rec(2, 3)
exp_rec(2, 3) = 2 × exp_rec(2, 2)
exp_rec(2, 2) 2 × exp_rec(2, 1)
exp_rec(2, 1) = 2 × exp_rec(2, 0)
exp_rec(2, 0) = 1
exp_rec(2, 1) = 2 × 1 = 2
exp_rec(2, 2) = 2 × 2 = 4
exp_rec(2, 3) = 2 × 4 = 8
exp_rec(2, 4) = 2 × 8 = 16

11. Write a program to calculate exp(x,y) using recursive functions.

```
#include <stdio.h>
int exp_rec(int, int);
int main()
{
  int num1, num2, res;
  printf("\n Enter the two numbers: ");
  scanf("%d %d", &num1, &num2);
  res = exp_rec(num1, num2);
  printf ("\n RESULT = %d", res);
  return 0;
}
int exp_rec(int x, int y)
{
  if( y==0)
    return 1;
  else
    return (x * exp_rec(x, y-1));
}
```

Output

```
Enter the two numbers: 5 3
RESULT = 125
```

11.10.3 Fibonacci Series

The Fibonacci series can be given as:

0 1 1 2 3 5 8 13 21 34 55 ……

That is, the third term of the series is the sum of the first and second terms. Similarly, fourth term is the sum of second and third terms, and so on. Now we will design a recursive solution to find the nth term of the Fibonacci series. The general formula to do so can be given as:

$$\text{FIB}(n) = \begin{cases} 0, \text{ if } n = 0 \\ 1, \text{ if } n = 1 \\ \text{FIB } (n-1) + \text{FIB } (n-2), \text{ otherwise} \end{cases}$$

As per the formula, FIB(0) = 0 and FIB(1) = 1 and, FIB(2) = FIB(1) + FIB(0) = 1 + 0 = 1. So we have two base cases. This is necessary because every problem is divided into two smaller problems.

12. Write a program to print the Fibonacci series using recursion.

```
#include <stdio.h>
int Fibonacci(int);
int main()
{
  int n, i = 0, res;
  printf("Enter the number of terms\n");
  scanf("%d",&n);
  printf("Fibonacci series\n");
  for(i = 0; i < n; i++ )
  {
    res = Fibonacci(i);
    printf("%d\t",res);
  }
  return 0;
}
```

```
int Fibonacci(int n)
{
    if ( n == 0 )
        return 0;
    else if ( n == 1 )
        return 1;
    else
        return ( Fibonacci(n-1) +
    Fibonacci(n-2) );
}
```

Output

```
Enter the number of terms 5
Fibonacci series
0  1  1  2  3
```

11.11 TYPES OF RECURSION

Recursion is a technique that breaks a problem into one or more sub-problems that are similar to the original problem. Any recursive function can be characterized based on:

- whether the function calls itself directly or indirectly (*direct or indirect recursion*),
- whether any operation is pending at each recursive call (*tail-recursive* or not), and
- the structure of the calling pattern (*linear or tree-recursive*).

In this section, we will discuss all these types of recursions.

11.11.1 Direct Recursion

A function is said to be *directly* recursive if it explicitly calls itself. For example, consider Figure 11.7.

```
int Func(int  n)
{
    if(n==0)
        return  n;
    else
        return(Func(n-1));
}
```

Figure 11.7 Direct recursion

Here, `Func()` calls itself for all positive values of *n*, so it is said to be a directly recursive function.

11.11.2 Indirect Recursion

A function is said to be *indirectly* recursive if it contains a call to another function which ultimately calls it. Look at the functions given in Figure 11.8. These two functions are indirectly recursive as they both call each other.

```
int Func1(int  n)
{
    if(n==0)
        return  n;
    else
        return  Func2(n);
}
```

```
int Func2(int  x)
{
    return  Func1(x-1);
}
```

Figure 11.8 Indirect recursion

11.11.3 Tail Recursion

A recursive function is said to be *tail* recursive if no operations are pending to be performed when the recursive function returns to its caller. When the called function returns, the returned value is immediately returned from the calling function. Tail recursive functions are highly desirable because they are much more efficient to use as the amount of information that has to be stored on the system stack is independent of the number of recursive calls.

For example, the factorial function that we have written is a non-tail-recursive function (Figure 11.9), because there is a pending operation of multiplication to be performed on return from each recursive call.

```
int Fact(int  n)
{
    if(n==1)
        return  1;
    else
        return  (n * Fact(n-1));
}
```

Figure 11.9 Non-tail recursive function

Whenever there is a pending operation to be performed, the function becomes non-tail recursive. In such a non-tail recursive function (Figure 11.10), information about each pending operation must be stored, so the amount of information directly depends on the number of calls.

However, the same factorial function can be written in a tail-recursive manner as shown in Figure 11.10.

In the code, `Fact1` function preserves the syntax of `Fact(n)`. Here the recursion occurs in the `Fact1` function and not in `Fact` function. Carefully observe that `Fact1` has no pending operation to be performed on return from recursive calls. The value computed by the recursive call is simply returned without any modification. So in this case, the amount of information to be stored on the system stack is constant (just the values of *n* and `res` need to be stored) and is independent of the number of recursive calls.

```
int Fact(n)
{
    return Fact1(n, 1);
}
int Fact1(int n, int res)
{
    if (n==1)
        return res;
    else
        return Fact1(n-1, n*res);
}
```

Figure 11.10 Tail-recursive function

Converting Recursive Functions to Tail Recursive

A non-tail recursive function can be converted into a tail-recursive function by using an *auxiliary parameter* as we did in case of the Factorial function. The auxiliary parameter is used to form the result. When we use such a parameter, the pending operation is incorporated into the auxiliary parameter so that the recursive call no longer has a pending operation. We generally use an auxiliary function while using the auxiliary parameter. This is done to keep the syntax clean and to hide the fact that auxiliary parameters are needed.

11.11.4 Linear and Tree Recursion

Recursive functions can also be characterized depending on the way in which recursion grows, i.e., in a linear fashion or forming a tree structure (Figure 11.11).

In simple words, a recursive function is said to be *linearly* recursive when the pending operation (if any) does not make another recursive call to the function. For example, observe the last line of recursive factorial function. The factorial function is linearly recursive as the pending operation involves only multiplication to be performed and does not involve another recursive call to Fact.

On the contrary, a recursive function is said to be *tree* recursive (or *non-linearly* recursive) if the pending operation makes another recursive call to the function. For example, the Fibonacci function `Fib` in which the pending operations recursively calls the `Fib` function.

11.12 TOWER OF HANOI

The tower of Hanoi is one of the main applications of recursion. It says, 'if you can solve $n - 1$ cases, then you can easily solve the nth case'.

Look at Figure 11.12 which shows three rings mounted on pole A. The problem is to move all these rings from pole A to pole C while maintaining the same order. The main issue is that the smaller disk must always come above the larger disk.

```
int Fibonacci(int  num)
{
  if(num == 0)
    return 0;
  else if(num == 1)
    return 1;
  else
    return ( Fibonacci  (num - 1) + Fibonacci(num  - 2));
}
Observe the series of function calls. When the function
returns, the pending operation in turn calls the function
  Fibonacci(7) = Fibonacci (6) + Fibonacci (5)
  Fibonacci(6) + Fibonacci (5) + Fibonacci (4)
  Fibonacci(5) = Fibonacci (4) + Fibonacci (3)
  Fibonacci(4) = Fibonacci (3) + Fibonacci (2)
  Fibonacci(3) = Fibonacci (2) + Fibonacci (1)
  Fibonacci(2) = Fibonacci (1) + Fibonacci (0)
Now we have, Fibonacci(2) = 1 + 0 =1
  Fibonacci(3) = 1 + 1 = 2
  Fibonacci(4) = 2 + 1 = 3
  Fibonacci(5) = 3 + 2 = 5
  Fibonacci(6) = 3 + 5 = 8
  Fibonacci(7) = 5 + 8 = 13
```

Figure 11.11 Tree recursion

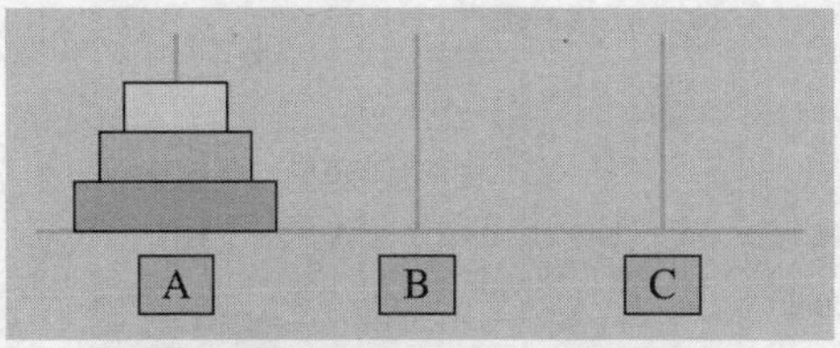

Figure 11.12 Tower of Hanoi

We will be doing this using a spare pole. In our case, A is the source pole, C is the destination pole, and B is the spare pole. To transfer all the three rings from A to C, we will first shift the upper two rings ($n - 1$ rings) from the source pole to the spare pole. We move the first two rings from pole A to B using C as the spare pole as shown in Figure 11.13.

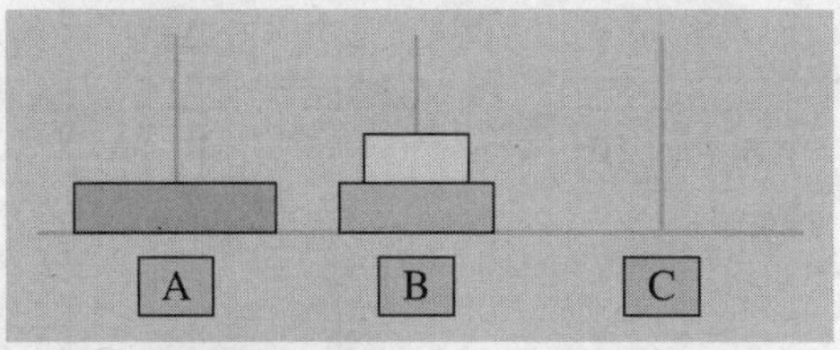

Figure 11.13 Move rings from A to B

Now that $n - 1$ rings have been removed from pole A, the nth ring can be easily moved from the source pole (A) to the destination pole (C). Figure 11.14 shows this step.

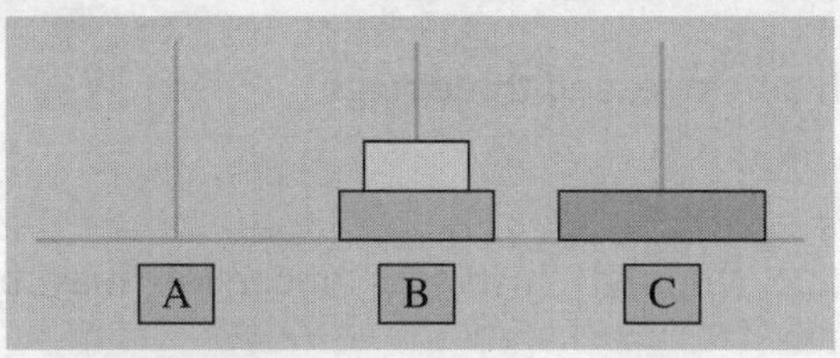

Figure 11.14 Move rings from A to C

The final step is to move the $n - 1$ rings from B to C using A as the spare pole. This is shown in Figure 11.15.

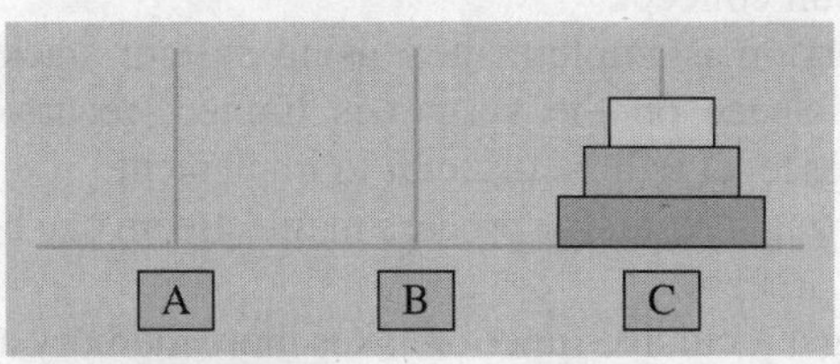

Figure 11.15 Move rings from B to C

To summarize, the solution to our problem of moving n rings from A to C using B as spare can be given as:

Base case: if $n = 1$

- Move the ring from A to C using B as spare

Recursive case:

- Move $n - 1$ rings from A to B using C as spare
- Move the one ring left on A to C using B as spare
- Move $n - 1$ rings from B to C using A as spare

The following code implements the solution of the Tower of Hanoi problem.

```
#include <stdio.h>
void move(int, char, char, char);
int main()
{
  int n;
  printf("\n Enter the number of rings: ");
  scanf("%d", &n);
  move(n,'A', 'C', 'B');
  return 0;
}

void move(int n, char source, char dest, char
   spare)
{
   if (n==1)
     printf("\n Move from %c to
       %c",source,dest);
   else
   {
      move(n-1,source,spare,dest);
      move(1,source,dest,spare);
      move(n-1,spare,dest,source);
   }
}
```

Let us look at the Tower of Hanoi problem in detail using the aforegiven program. Figure 11.16 explains the working of the program using one, then two, and finally three rings.

11.13 RECURSION VS ITERATION

Recursion is more of a top-down approach to problem-solving in which the original problem is divided into smaller sub-problems. On the contrary, iteration follows a bottom-up approach that begins with what is known and then constructing the solution step by step.

Recursion is an excellent way of solving complex problems especially when the problem can be defined in recursive terms. For such problems, a recursive code can be written and modified in a much simpler and clearer manner.

However, recursive solutions are not always the best solutions. In some cases, recursive programs may require substantial amount of run-time overhead. Therefore, when implementing a recursive solution, there is a trade-off involved between the time spent in constructing and maintaining the program and the cost incurred in running-time and memory space required for the execution of the program.

Whenever a recursive function is called, some amount of overhead in the form of a run time stack is always involved. Before jumping to the function with a smaller parameter, the original parameters, the local variables, and the return address of the calling function are all stored on

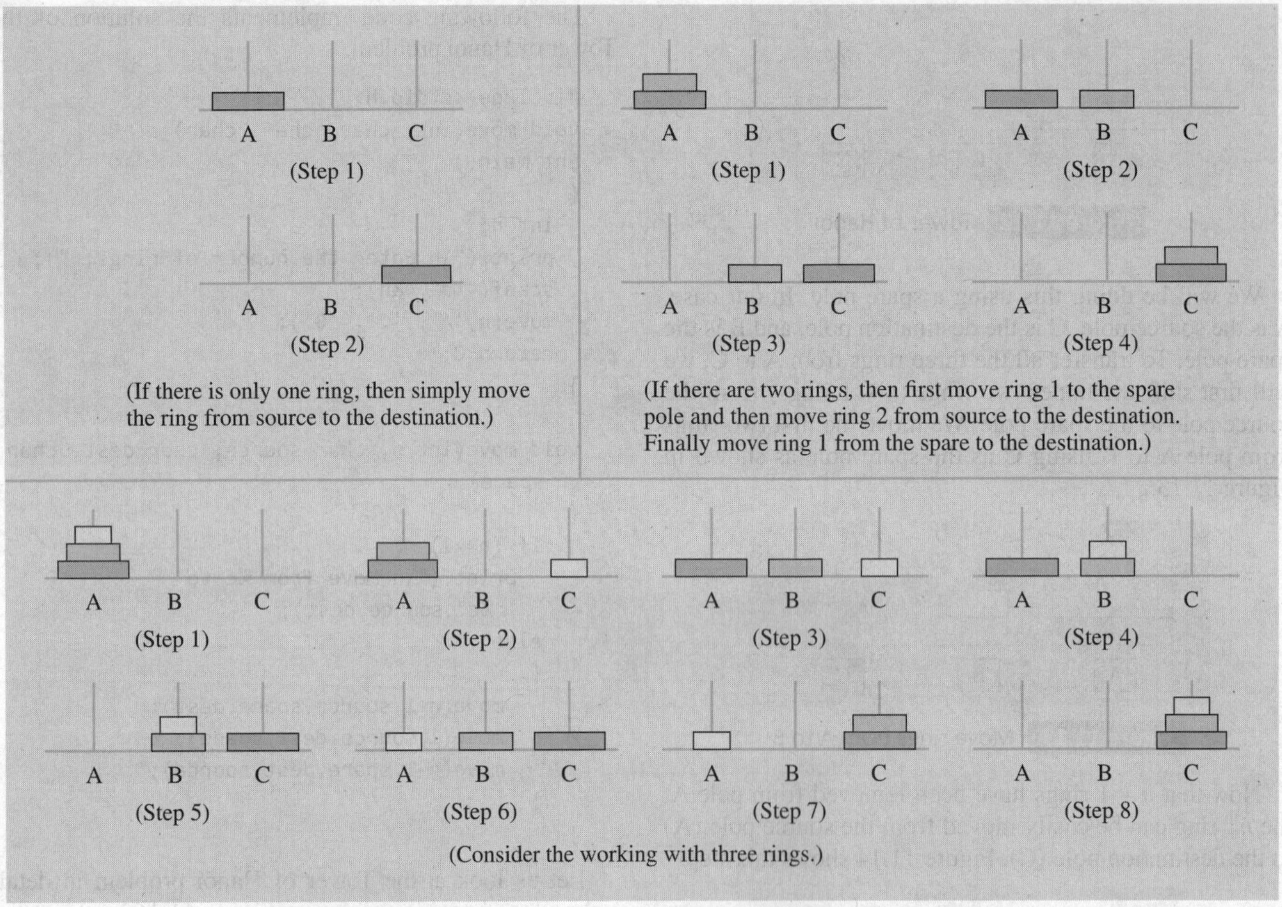

Figure 11.16 Working of Tower of Hanoi with one, two, and three rings

the system stack. Therefore, while using recursion a lot of time is needed to first push all the information on the stack when the function is called and then time is again involved in retrieving the information stored on the stack once the control passes back to the calling function.

To conclude, one must use recursion only to find solution to a problem for which no obvious iterative solution is known. To summarize the concept of recursion, let us briefly discuss the pros and cons of recursion.

The advantages of using a recursive program include the following:

- Recursive solutions often tend to be shorter and simpler than non-recursive ones.
- Code is clearer and easier to use.
- Recursion works similar to the original formula to solve a problem.
- Recursion follows a divide and conquer technique to solve problems.
- In some (limited) instances, recursion may be more efficient.

The drawbacks/disadvantages of using a recursive program include the following:

- For some programmers and readers, recursion is a difficult concept.
- Recursion is implemented using system stack. If the stack space on the system is limited, recursion to a deeper level will be difficult to implement.
- Aborting a recursive process in midstream can be a very slow process.
- Using a recursive function takes more memory and time to execute as compared to its non-recursive counterpart.
- It is difficult to find bugs, particularly while using global variables.

The advantages of recursion pays off for the extra overhead involved in terms of time and space required.

POINTS TO REMEMBER

- Every function in a program is supposed to perform a well-defined task. The moment the compiler encounters a function call, the control jumps to the statements that are part of the called function. After the called function is executed, the control is returned back to the calling function.
- All the libraries in C contain a set of functions that have been prewritten and pre-tested, which the programmers can use without worrying about the code details. This speeds up program development.
- While function declaration statement identifies a function with its name, the list of arguments that it accepts and the type of data it returns, the function definition, on the other hand, consists of a function header that identifies the function, followed by the body of the function containing the executable code for that function.
- `main()` is the function that is called by the operating system and, therefore, it is supposed to return the result of its processing to the operating system.
- Placing the function declaration statement prior to its use enables the compiler to make a check on the arguments used while calling that function.
- A function having void as its return type cannot return any value. Similarly, a function having void as its parameter list cannot accept any value.
- When a function is defined, space is allocated for that function in the memory. A function definition comprises of two parts: function header and function body.
- Call-by-value method passes values of the variables to the called function. Therefore, the called function uses a copy of the actual arguments to perform its intended task. This method is used when the function does not need to modify the values of the original variables in the calling function.
- In call-by-reference method, address of the variable is passed by the calling function to the called function. Hence, in this method, a function receives an implicit reference to the argument, rather than a copy of its value. This allows the function to modify the value of the variable and that change will be reflected in the calling function as well.
- Scope means the accessibility and visibility of the variables at different points in the program. A variable or a constant in C has four types of scope: block, function, program, and file scope.
- Storage class defines the scope (visibility) and lifetime of variables and/or functions declared within a C program.
- The auto storage class is the default storage class for variables declared inside a block. The scope of the variable is local to the block in which it is declared. When a variable is declared using register as its storage class, it is stored in a CPU register instead of RAM. Extern is used to give a reference of a global variable that is visible to all the program files. Static is the default storage class for global variables.
- A recursive function is defined as a function that calls itself to solve a smaller version of its task until a final call is made which does not require a call to itself. Recursive functions are implemented using system stack.

GLOSSARY

Argument A value passed to the called function by the calling function.

Block A sequence of definitions, declarations, and statements, enclosed within curly brackets.

Divide and conquer Solving a problem by dividing it into two or more smaller instances. Each of these smaller instances is recursively solved, and the solutions are combined to produce a solution for the original problem.

Formal parameter List of the variables in the function header.

Iteration Solving a problem by repeatedly working on successive parts of the problem.

Recursion An algorithmic technique where a function calls itself with a smaller version of the task in order to solve that task.

Recursion termination The point at which base condition is met and a recursive algorithm stops calling itself and begins to return values.

Tail recursion A form of recursion in which the last operation of a function is a recursive call.

EXERCISES

Fill in the Blanks

1. ________ provides an interface to use the function.
2. After the function is executed, the control passes back to the ________.
3. A function that uses another function is known as the ________.
4. The inputs that the function takes are known as ________.
5. `main()` is called by the ________.
6. Function definition consists of ________ and ________.
7. In ________ method, address of the variable is passed by the calling function to the called function.
8. Function scope is applicable only within ________.
9. Function that calls itself is known as a ________ function.
10. Recursive functions are implemented using ________.
11. ________ function is defined as a function that calls itself.
12. The function `int func();` takes ________ arguments.
13. ________ variables can be accessed from all functions in the program.
14. The execution of a program starts at ________.
15. By default, the return type of a function is ________.
16. Variable declared inside a function is known as ________.

Multiple-choice Questions

1. The function that is invoked is known as
   (a) calling function (b) caller function
   (c) called function (d) invoking function
2. Function declaration statement identifies a function with its
   (a) name (b) arguments
   (c) data type of return value (d) all of these
3. Which return type cannot return any value to the caller?
   (a) int (b) float
   (c) void (d) double
4. Memory is allocated for a function when the function is
   (a) declared (b) defined
   (c) called (d) returned
5. Which keyword allows a variable to have file scope?
   (a) auto (b) static
   (c) register (d) extern
6. The default storage class of global variables is
   (a) auto (b) static
   (c) register (d) extern
7. Which variable retains its value in-between function calls?
   (a) auto (b) static
   (c) register (d) extern
8. The default storage class of a local variable is
   (a) auto (b) static
   (c) register (d) extern

State True or False

1. The calling function must always pass parameters to the called function.
2. Function header is used to identify the function.
3. The name of a function is global.
4. No function can be declared within the body of another function.
5. The function call statement invokes the function.
6. Auto variables are stored inside CPU registers.
7. Extern variables are initialized by default.
8. The default storage class of local variables is `extern`.
9. Recursion follows a divide-and-conquer technique to solve problems.
10. Local variables overwrite the value of global variables.
11. A C function can return only one value.
12. A function must have at least one argument.
13. A function can be declared and defined before `main()`.
14. A function can be defined in `main()`.
15. Variable names in the function definition must match with those specified in the function declaration.
16. Specifying variable names in the function declaration is optional.
17. `main()` is a user-defined function.

Review Questions

1. Define a function. Why are they needed?
2. Explain the concept of making function calls.
3. Differentiate between function declaration and function definition.
4. Differentiate between formal parameters and actual parameters.
5. How many types of storage classes C language supports? Why do we need different types of such classes?
6. Give the features of each storage class.
7. Explain the concept of recursive functions with example.
8. Differentiate between an iterative function and a recursive function. Which one will you prefer to use and in what circumstances?
9. What will happen when the actual parameters are less than formal parameters in a function?
10. What will happen when data type of a variable in the function declaration does not match with the corresponding variable in the function header?
11. What will happen when a function returns a value that does not match with the return type of the function?
12. Explain the Tower of Hanoi problem.

13. Differentiate between call by value and call by reference using suitable examples.
14. What do you understand by scope of a variable? Explain in detail with suitable examples.
15. Why function declaration statement is placed prior to function definition?

Programming Exercises

1. Write a program to calculate factorial of a number using recursion. Also write a non-recursive function to do the same job.
2. Write a program using function that calculates the hypotenuse of a right-angled triangle.
3. Write a function that accepts a number *n* as input and returns the average of numbers from 1 to *n*.
4. Write a function to reverse a string using recursion.
5. Write a function is_prime that returns 1 if the argument passed to it is a prime number and a 0 otherwise.
6. Write a function that accepts an integer between 1 and 12 to represent the month number and displays the corresponding month of the year (For example if month = 1, then display JANUARY).
7. Write a function is_leap_year which takes the year as its argument and checks whether the year is a leap year or not and then displays an appropriate message on the screen.
8. Write a program to concatenate two strings using recursion.
9. Write a program to read an integer number. Print the reverse of this number using recursion
10. Write a program to swap two variables that are defined as global variables.
11. Write a program to compute `F(x, y)` where
    `F(x, y) = F(x-y, y) + 1 if y?x`
    `And F(x, y) = 0 if x<y`
12. Write a program to compute F(n, r) where
    `F(n, r) can be recursively defined as`
    `F(n, r) = F(n-1, r) + F(n-1, r-1)`
13. Write a program to compute Lambda(n) for all positive values of n where Lambda(n) can be recursively defined as
    `Lambda(n) = Lambda(n/2) + 1 if n>1`
    `AND Lambda(n) = 0 if n =1`
14. Write a program to compute `F(M, N)` where
    `F(M, N) can be recursively defined as`
    `F(M,N) = 1 if M=0 or M?N?1`
    `AND F(M,N) = F(M-1,N) +`
    `F(M-1, N-1) otherwise`
15. Write a menu driven program to add, subtract, multiply, and divide two integers using functions.
16. Write a program to find the smallest of three integers using functions.
17. Write a program to calculate area of a triangle using function.
18. Write a program to find whether a number is divisible by two or not using functions.
19. Write a program to illustrate call-by-value technique of passing arguments to a function.
20. Write a program to illustrate call-by-reference technique of passing arguments to a function.
21. Write a program to swap two integers using call-by-value method of passing arguments to a function.
22. Write a program using function to calculate x to the power of y, where y can be either negative or positive.
23. Write a program using function to calculate compound interest given the principal, rate of interest, and number of years.
24. Write a program to swap two integers using call-by-reference method of passing arguments to a function.
25. Write a program to calculate factorial of a number (a) using recursion (b) without using recursion.
26. Write a program to convert the given string "hello world" to "dlrow olleh" without using recursion.
27. Write a program to find HCF of two numbers (a) using recursion (b) without using recursion.
28. Write a program to calculate x^y (a) using recursion (b) without using recursion.
29. Write a program to print the Fibonacci series (a) using recursion (b) without using recursion.
30. Write a program using functions to perform calculator operations.
31. Write a function that converts temperature given in Celsius into Fahrenheit.
32. Write a function that prints the conversion table of Degrees Fahrenheit into Degrees Celsius ranging from 32-212 degrees Celsius.
33. Write a function to draw the following pattern on the screen

```
********
!      !
!      !
!      !
********
```

34. Write a function to print a table of binomial coefficients which is given by the formula-
    `B(m, x) = m!/ (x! (m-x)!) where m > x`
    `Hint:B(m,0) = 1, B(0,0) = 1 and`
    `B(m,x) = B(m, x-1) * [( m - x + 1)/x]`
35. Write a program to evaluate
    $f(x) = x - x^3/3! + x^5/5! - x^7/7! + \ldots.$

Find the output of the following codes

1.

```
#include <stdio.h>
int func();
main()
{
    printf("%d", func());
    printf("%d", func());
```

```
    printf("%d", func());
    printf("%d", func());
    return 0;
}
int func()
{
    int counter=0;
    return counter;
}
```

2.
```
#include <stdio.h>
int func();
int counter = 5;
main()
{
    printf("%d", func());
    printf("%d", func());
    printf("%d", func());
    printf("%d", func());
    return 0;
}
int func()
{
    return counter++;
}
```

3.
```
#include <stdio.h>
int add(int, int);
main()
{
    int a=2, b=3;
    printf("%d %d %d", a, b, add(a, b));
    return 0;
}
int add(int a, int b)
{
    int c;
    c = a+b;
}
```

4.
```
#include <stdio.h>
int func(int);
main()
{
    int a=2;
    printf("%d", func(a));
    return 0;
}
int func(int a)
{
    if(a>1)
        return func(--a) + 10;
    else
        return 0;
}
```

5.
```
#include <stdio.h>
void func(int);
main()
{
    int a=127;
    printf("%d", a);
    func(a);
    return 0;
}
void func(int a)
{
    a++;
    printf("%d", a);
}
```

6.
```
#include <stdio.h>
void func(int);
auto int a;
main()
{
    int a=10;
    printf("%d", a);
    func(a);
    return 0;
}
void func(int a)
{
    a++;
    printf("%d", a);
}
```

7.
```
#include <stdio.h>
static int add(int val)
{
    static int sum;
    sum += val;
    return sum;
}
main()
{
    int i, n=10;
    for(i=0;i<10;i++)
        add(i);
    printf("\n SUM = %d", add(0));
    return 0;
}
```

8.
```
#include <stdio.h>
void func(int);
int a=10;
main()
{
    int a=2;
    printf("%d", a);
    func(a);
    printf("%d", a);
    return 0;
}
void func(int a)
{
    a=20;
}
```

9.
```
#include <stdio.h>
void func(char);
main()
{
    char ch=256;
    func(ch);
    return 0;
}
void func(char a)
{
        printf("%d", a);
}
```

10.
```
#include <stdio.h>
int a;
static int func()
{
      return a++;
}
main()
{
    a=10;
    printf("%d", func());
    a *= 10;
    printf("%d", func());
    return 0;
}
```

11.
```
#include <stdio.h>
int prod(int x, int y)
{
    return (x*y);
}
main()
{
    int x=2, y=3, z;
    z = prod(x,prod(x,y));
    printf("%d", z);
    return 0;
}
```

ANNEXURE 2

User Defined Header Files

At times programmers may need a function that provides additional processing capabilities and may want to create a separate source code file to contain that function. This would help to segregate the function from rest of the main source code. In such a situation, the user may create a user-defined header file so that the compiler knows how to call this function.

For example, if we want the factorial function to be stored in a user-defined header file, then write the code of the factorial function in a file and save it as `fact.h`. Then in the main program file, we will include the `fact.h` file and call the function in the same way as we call other functions. Look at the code given below which illustrates this concept.

```
int factorial(int num)
{
    long int f=1;
    for(;num >= 1;num--)
        f = f * num;
    return f;
}

// Contents for the main file
#include <stdio.h>
#include "fact.h"
int main()
{
    int num, f;
    printf("\n Enter any number: ");
    scanf("%d", &num);
    f = factorial(num);
    printf("\n FACTORIAL of %d = %d",
        num, f);
    return 0;
}
```

In the above code, a user-defined header file-fact.h has been used. The name of the header file has been enclosed within quotes to tell the compiler not to look along the standard library path, but to look in the same path as the source file.

When you compile the file that contains the source code, that is the file contains `main()`, the compiler will compile it into object code. As long as the C program is syntactically correct, the object code will be created.

The linker will combine the object code and library files, and create an executable file. It is the header file that links the definition of the function with the implementation.

12 Arrays

TAKEAWAYS

- Array declaration
- Operations on arrays
- Linear and binary search
- Passing arrays to functions
- Operations on 2D arrays
- Two-dimensional arrays
- Array length
- Multidimensional arrays
- Array implementation of sparse matrices
- Application of arrays

12.1 INTRODUCTION

We will explain the concept of arrays using an analogy. Take a situation in which we have 20 students in a class and we have been asked to write a program that reads and prints the marks of all these 20 students. In this program, we will need 20 integer variables with different names, as shown in Figure 12.1.

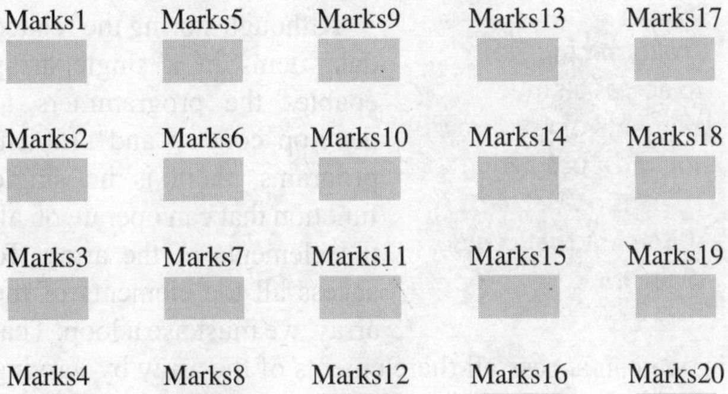

Figure 12.1 Twenty variables for 20 students

Now to read values for these 20 different variables, we must have 20 read statements. Similarly, to print the value of these variables, we need 20 write statements. If it is just a matter of 20 variables, then it might be acceptable for the user to follow this approach. But would it be possible to follow this approach if we have to read and print marks of the students

- in the entire course (say 100 students)
- in the entire college (say 500 students)
- in the entire university (say 10000 students)

The answer is no, definitely not! To process large amount of data, we need a data structure known as *array*. An array is a collection of similar data elements. These data elements have the same data type. The elements of the array are stored in consecutive memory locations and are referenced by an index (also known as the subscript). *Subscript* is an ordinal number which is used to identify an element of the array. Some examples where the concept of an array can be used include lists of the following:

- Temperatures recorded on every day of the month
- Employees in a company
- Students in a class
- Products sold
- Customers

12.2 DECLARATION OF ARRAYS

We have already seen that every variable must be declared before it is used. The same concept is true in case of array variables also. An array must be declared before being used. Declaring an array means specifying three things:

- Data type—what kind of values it can store, for example `int, char, float, double`
- Name—to identify the array
- Size—the maximum number of values that the array can hold

Arrays are declared using the following syntax:

```
type name[size];
```

> **Programming Tip:**
> To declare and define an array, you must specify its name, type, and size.

Here the type can be either `int, float, double, char,` or any other valid data type. The number within brackets indicates the size of the array, i.e., the maximum number of elements that can be stored in the array. The size of the array is a constant and must have a value at compilation time. For example, if we write,

```
int marks[10];
```

1st element	2nd element	3rd element	4th element	5th element	6th element	7th element	8th element	9th element	10th element
marks[0]	marks[1]	marks[2]	marks[3]	marks[4]	marks[5]	marks[6]	marks[7]	marks[8]	marks[9]

Figure 12.2 Memory representation of an array of 10 elements

The above statement declares `marks` to be an array containing 10 elements. In C, the array index (also known as subscript) starts from zero. This means that the array marks will contain 10 elements in all. The first element will be stored in marks[0], the second element in `marks[1]`, and so on. Therefore, the last element, i.e., the 10th element will be stored in `marks[9]`. Note that `0, 1, 2, 3` written within square brackets are subscripts/index. In memory, the array will be stored as shown in Figure 12.2.

> **Programming Tip:**
> In an array of size n, the index ranges from 0 to n – 1.

Points to Remember

- Note that C does not allow declaring an array whose number of elements is not known at the compile time. Therefore, the following array declarations are illegal in C.

```
int arr[];
int n, arr[n];
```

- Generally it is a good programming practice to define the size of an array as a symbolic constant as shown in the following code.

```
#include <stdio.h>
#define N 100
main()
 {
 int arr[N];
 ..........
 }
```

- The size of the array can be specified using an expression. However, the components of the expression must be available for evaluation of the expression when the program is compiled. Therefore, the following array declarations are valid in C language.

```
#include <stdio.h>
#define N 100
main()
 {
 int i=10;
 int arr[N+10], my_arr[i-5*10];
 ..........
 }
```

> **Note**
> C array indices start from 0. So for an array with N elements, the index of the last element is N – 1.

- C never checks the validity of the array index— neither at compile time nor at run time. So even if you declare an array as

```
int arr[N];
```

The C compiler will not raise any error but the result of running such code is totally unpredictable. Even if you declare an array of 10 elements and later on by mistake try to access the 11th element, no error will be generated. But the results will be unpredictable as the memory occupied by the (so-called) 11th element may be storing data of another object.

12.3 ACCESSING THE ELEMENTS OF AN ARRAY

For accessing an individual element of the array, the array subscript must be used. For example, to access the fourth element of the array, we must write `arr[3]`. The subscript/index must be an integral value or an expression that evaluates to an integral value.

> **Programming Tip:**
> To access all the elements of the array, you must use a loop. There is no single statement that can do the work.

Although storing the related data items in a single array enables the programmers to develop concise and efficient programs, there is no single function that can operate on all the elements of the array. To access all the elements of the array, we must use a loop. That is, we can access all the elements of the array by varying the value of the subscript into the array. But note that the subscript must be an integral value or an expression that evaluates to an integral value. As shown in Figure 12.2, the first element of the array `marks[10]` can be accessed by writing, `marks[0]`. Now to process all the elements of the array, we will use a loop as shown in Figure 12.3.

```
// Set each element of the array to -1

int i, marks[10];
for(i=0;i<10;i++)
        marks[i] = -1;
```

Figure 12.3 Code to initialize each element of the array to –1

The code accesses every individual element of the array and sets its value to –1. In the `for` loop, first the value of `marks[0]` is set to –1, then the value of the index `(i)` is incremented and the next value, i.e., marks[1] is set to –1. The procedure is continued until all the 10 elements of the array are set to –1.

Note

There is no single statement that can read, access, or print all the elements of the array. To do this, we have to do it using a for/while/do-while loop to execute the same statement with different index values.

12.3.1 Calculating the Address of Array Elements

You must be wondering that how C knows where an individual element of the array is located in the memory. The answer is that the array name is a symbolic reference to the address of the first byte of the array. When we use the array name, we are actually referring to the first byte of the array.

The subscript or the index represents the offset from the beginning of the array to the element being referenced. With just the array name and the index, C can calculate the address of any element in the array.

Since an array stores all its data elements in consecutive memory locations, storing just the base address, i.e, the address of the first element in the array is sufficient. The address of other data elements can simply be calculated using the base address. The formula for doing this calculation is:

```
Address of data element, A[k] = BA(A) + w(k -
   lower_bound)
```

Here, A is the array, k is the index of the element for which we have to calculate the address, BA is the base address of the array A, w is the word size of one element in memory (for example, size of int is 2), and lower_bound is the index of the first element in the array.

Example 12.1

Given an array int marks[] = {99, 67, 78, 56, 88, 90, 34, 85}. Calculate the address of marks[4] if base address = 1000.

Solution

	99	67	78	56	88	90	34	85
marks	[0]	[1]	[2]	[3]	**[4]**	[5]	[6]	[7]
	1000	1002	1004	1006	**1008**	1010	1012	1014

We know that storing an integer value requires 2 bytes, therefore, word size is 2 bytes.

```
Address(Marks[4])  = 1000 + 2(4 - 0)
                   = 1000 + 2(4) = 1008
```

Example 12.2

Given an array, float avg[] = {99.0, 67.0, 78.0, 56.0, 88.0, 90.0, 34.0, 85.0}. Calculate the address of avg [4] if base address = 1000.

	99.0	67.0	78.0	56.0	88.0	90.0	34.0	85.0
avg	[0]	[1]	[2]	[3]	**[4]**	[5]	[6]	[7]
	1000	1004	1008	1012	**1016**	1020	1024	1028

We know that storing a floating point number requires 4 bytes, therefore, word size is 4 bytes.

```
Address(Avg[4])   = 1000 + 4(4 - 0)
                  = 1000 + 4(4) = 1016
```

Note

When we write arr[i], the compiler interprets it as the contents of memory slot which is i slots away from the beginning of the array arr.

12.3.2 Calculating the Length of an Array

Length of the array is given by the number of elements stored in it. The general formula to calculate the length of the array is:

```
Length = upper_bound - lower_bound + 1
```

where upper_bound is the index of the last element and lower_bound is the index of the first element in the array.

Usually, lower_bound is zero but this is not a compulsion as we can have an array whose index may start from any non-zero value.

Example 12.3

Let Age[5] be an array of integers such that

```
Age[0] = 2    Age[1] = 5    Age[2] = 3
Age[3] = 1    Age[4] = 7
```

Solution

Show the memory representation of the array and calculate its length.

Memory representation of the array Age is as given

2	5	3	1	7
Age[0]	Age[1]	Age[2]	Age[3]	Age[4]

Length = upper_bound - lower_bound + 1
Here, lower_bound = 0, upper_bound = 4
Therefore, length = 4 - 0 + 1 = 5

12.4 STORING VALUES IN ARRAYS

When we declare an array, we are just allocating space for the elements; no values are stored in the array. There are three ways to store values in an array—first, to initialize the array element at the time of declaration; second, to input value for every individual element at the run time; third to assign values to the individual elements. This is shown in Figure 12.4.

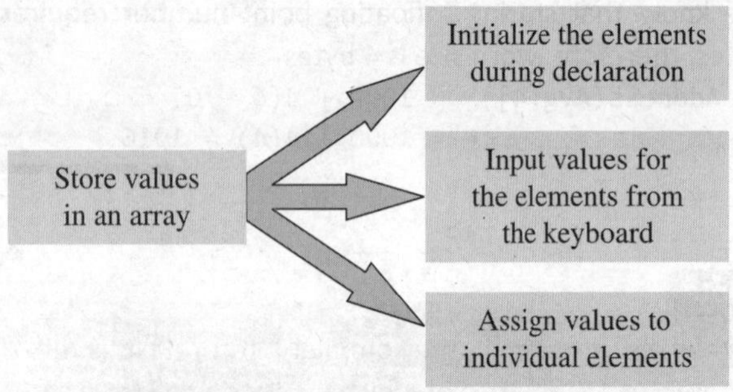

Figure 12.4 Storing values in an array

12.4.1 Initializing Arrays during Declaration

Elements of the array can also be initialized at the time of declaration as other variables. When an array is initialized, we need to provide a value for every element in the array. Arrays are initialized by writing,

> **Programming Tip:**
> By default, the elements of the array are not initialized. They may contain some garbage value, so before using the array you must initialize the array or read some meaningful data into it.

```
type array_name[size] =
{list of values};
```

The values are written within curly brackets and every value is separated by a comma. It is a compiler error to specify more number of values than the number of elements in the array. When we write,

```
int marks[5] = {90, 82,
78, 95, 88};
```

an array with name `marks` is declared that has enough space to store 5 elements. The first element, i.e., `marks[0]` is assigned with the value `90`. Similarly, the second element of the array, i.e., `marks[1]` is assigned `82`, and so on.

While initializing the array at the time of declaration, the programmer may omit the size of the array. For example,

```
int marks[] = {98, 97, 90};
```

The above statement is absolutely legal. Here, the compiler will allocate enough space for all initialized elements. If the number of values provided is less than the number of elements in the array, the un-assigned elements are filled with zeros. Figure 12.5 illustrates initialization of arrays.

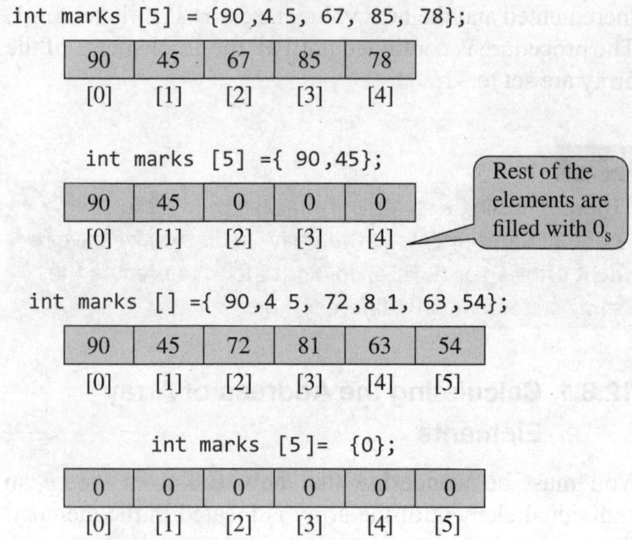

Figure 12.5 Initialization of array elements

> **Note**
> If we have more initializers than the declared size of the array, then a compile time error will be generated. For example, the following statement will result in a compiler error.
>
> `int marks [3] = {1,2,3,4};`

12.4.2 Inputting Values from the Keyboard

An array can be filled by inputting values from the keyboard. In this method, a `while/do-while` or a `for loop` is executed to input the value for each element of the array. For example, look at the code shown in Figure 12.6.

```
// Input value of each element of the array

int i, marks[10];
for(i=0;i<10;i++)
        scanf("%d", &marks[i]);
```

Figure 12.6 Code for inputting each element of the array

In the code, we start with the index `i` at `0` and input the value for the first element of the array. Since the array can have 10 elements, we must input values for elements whose index varies from `0` to `9`. Therefore, in the `for` loop, we test for condition (`i<10`) which means the number of elements in the array.

12.4.3 Assigning Values to Individual Elements

The third way is to assign values to individual elements of the array by using the assignment operator. Any value that evaluates to the data type of the array can be assigned to the individual array element. A simple assignment statement can be written as:

```
marks[3] = 100;
```

Here, `100` is assigned to the fourth element of the array which is specified as `marks[3]`.

We cannot assign one array to another array, even if the two arrays have the same type and size. To copy an array, you must copy the value of every element of the first array into the element of the second array. Figure 12.7 illustrates the code to copy an array.

```
// Copy an array at the individual element level

int i, arr1[10], arr2[10];
arr[1] = {0,1,2,3,4,5,6,7,8,9};
for(i=0;i<10;i++)
      arr2[i] = arr1[i];
```

Figure 12.7 Code to copy an array at the individual element level

In Figure 12.7, the code accesses each element of the first array and simultaneously assigns its value to the corresponding element of the second array. Finally, the index value `i` is incremented to access the next element in succession. Therefore, when this code is executed, `arr2[0] = arr1[0]`, `arr2[1] = arr1[1]`, `arr2[2] = arr1[2]`, and so on.

We can also use a loop to assign a pattern of values to the array elements. For example, if we want to fill an array with even integers starting (from 0), then we will write the code as shown in Figure 12.8.

```
// Fill an array with even numbers

int i, arr[10];
for(i=0;i<10;i++)
      arr[i] = i*2;
```

Figure 12.8 Code for filling an array with even numbers

In the code, we assign to each element a value equal to twice of its index, where index starts from zero. So after executing this code we will have, `arr[0] = 0`, `arr[1] = 2`, `arr[2] = 4`, and so on.

12.5 OPERATIONS ON ARRAYS

There are a number of operations that can be preformed on arrays. These operations include the following:

- Traversing an array
- Inserting an element in an array
- Deleting an element from an array
- Merging two arrays
- Searching an element in an array
- Sorting an array in ascending or descending order

We will study all these operations in detail in this section.

12.5.1 Traversing an Array

Traversing an array means accessing each and every element of the array for a specific purpose.

If `A` is an array of homogeneous data elements, then traversing the data elements can include printing every element, counting the total number of elements, or performing any process on these elements. Since an array is a linear data structure (because all its elements form a sequence), traversing its elements is very simple and straightforward. The algorithm for array traversal is given in Figure 12.9.

```
Step 1: [INITIALIZATION]  SET I = lower_bound
Step 2: Repeat Steps 3 to 4 while I< = upper_bound
Step 3: Apply Process to A[I]
Step 4: SET  I = I + 1
           [END OF LOOP]
Step 5: EXIT
```

Figure 12.9 Algorithm for array traversal

In Step 1, we initialize index `i` to the `lower_bound` of the array. In Step 2, a `while` loop is executed. Steps 3 and 4 form part of the loop. Step 3 processes the individual array element as specified by the array name and index value. Step 4 increments the index value so that the next array element could be processed. The `while` loop in Step 2 is executed until all the elements in the array are processed. In other words, the `while` loop will be executed until `i` is less than or equal to the `upper_bound` of the array.

Example 12.4

Assume that there is an array Marks[ ], such that the index of the array specifies the roll number of the student and the value of a particular element denotes the marks obtained by the student. For example, if it is given Marks[4] =78, then the student whose roll number is 4 has obtained 78 marks in the examination. Now, write an algorithm to:

(a) Find the total number of students who have secured 80 or more marks.

(b) Print the roll number and marks of all the students who have got distinction.

Solution

(a) **Step 1:** `[Initialization] Set Count = 0, I = lower_bound`

Step 2: `Repeat for I = lower_bound to upper_bound`
`IF Marks[I] >= 80, then: Set Count = Count + 1`
`[End of IF]`
`Set I = I + 1`
`[END OF LOOP]`

Step 3: `Exit`

(b) **Step 1:** `[Initialization] Set I = lower_bound`

```
Step 2: Repeat for I = lower_bound to upper_
bound
    IF Marks[I] >= 75, Write: I,
       Marks[I]
    [End of IF]
    Set I = I + 1
    [END OF LOOP]
  Step 3:  Exit
```

1. Write a program to read and display n numbers using an array.

```
#include <stdio.h>
int main()
{
  int i=0, n, arr[20];

  printf("\n Enter the number of elements:");
  scanf("%d", &n);

  printf("\n Enter the elements");

  for(i=0;i<n;i++)
   {
    printf("\n Arr[%d] = ", i);
    scanf("%d", &arr[i]);
   }
  printf("\n The array elements are\n");
  for(i=0;i<n;i++)
  printf("Arr[%d] = %d\t", i, arr[i]);
  return 0;
}
```

Output

```
Enter the number of elements: 5
Enter the elements
Arr[0] = 1
Arr[1] = 2
Arr[2] = 3
Arr[3] = 4
Arr[4] = 5
The array elements are
Arr[0] = 1    Arr[1] = 2    Arr[2] = 3
Arr[3] = 4    Arr[4] = 5
```

2. Write a program to read and display n random numbers using an array.

```
#include <stdio.h>
#include <stdlib.h>
#define MAX 10
int main()
  {
  int arr[MAX], i,RandNo;
  for(i=0;i< MAX;i++)
  {
   /* Scale the random number in the range
         0 to MAX-1 */
    RandNo = rand() % MAX;
    // rand() is a pre-defined function
    arr[i] = RandNo;
   }
  printf("\n The contents of the array are:
      \n");
  for(i=0;i<MAX;i++)
    printf("\t %d", arr[i]);
  return 0;
}
```

Output

```
The contents of the array are:
6  0  8  4  7  1  0  2  7  3
```

3. Write a program to print the position of the smallest of n numbers using arrays.

```
#include <stdio.h>
int main()
{
  int i, n, arr[20], small, pos;
  printf("\n Enter the number of elements in
         the array: ");
  scanf("%d", &n);
  printf("\n Enter the elements:");
  for(i=0;i<n;i++)
    scanf("%d",&arr[i]);
  small=arr[0];    pos=0;
  for(i=1;i<n;i++)
  {
    if(arr[i]<small)
    {
      small = arr[i];
      pos = i;
    }
  }
  printf("\n The smallest element is : %d",
         small);
  printf("\n The position of the smallest
         element in the array is: %d", pos);
  return 0;
}
```

Output

```
Enter the number of elements in the array: 5
Enter the elements: 1 2 3 4 5
The smallest element is: 1
The position of the smallest element in the
array is: 0
```

4. Write a program to interchange the largest and the smallest number in the array.

```
#include <stdio.h>
int main()
{
  int i, n, arr[20], temp;
  int small, small_pos;
  int large, large_pos;
```

```
printf("\n Enter the number of elements :");
scanf("%d", &n);

for(i=0;i<n;i++)
{
  printf("\n Enter the value of element
        %d: ",i);
  scanf("%d",&arr[i]);
}
small=arr[0];
small_pos=0;
large=arr[0];
large_pos=0;
for(i=1;i<n;i++)
{
  if(arr[i]<small)
  {
    small = arr[i];
    small_pos = i;
  }
  if(arr[i]>large)
  {
    large = arr[i];
    large_pos = i;
  }
}
printf("\n The smallest of these numbers
        is : %d", small);
printf("\n The position of the smallest
        number in the array is: %d",small_
        pos);
printf("\n The largest of these numbers
       is: %d", large);
printf("\n The position of the largest
        number in the array is: %d",large_
        pos);
temp = arr[large_pos];
arr[large_pos] =arr[small_pos];
arr[small_pos] = temp;
printf("\n The new array is: ");
for(i=0;i<n;i++)
  printf(" \n %d ", arr[i]);
return 0;
}
```

Output

```
Enter the number of elements: 5
Enter the value of element 0:1
Enter the value of element 1:2
Enter the value of element 2:3
Enter the value of element 3:4
Enter the value of element 4:5
The smallest of these numbers is : 1
The position of the smallest number in the
  array is: 0
The largest of these numbers is: 5
The position of the largest number in the
  array is: 4
The new array is:
5 2 3 4  1
```

5. Write a program to find the second largest number using an array of n numbers.

```
#include <stdio.h>
int main()
{
  int i, n, arr[20],  pos, large, second_
  large;

  printf("\n Enter the number of elements
   in the array: ");
  scanf("%d", &n);

  for(i=0;i<n;i++)
  {
    printf("\n Enter the number: ");
    scanf("%d",&arr[i]);
  }
  large=arr[0];pos=0;
  for(i=1;i<n;i++)
  {
    if(arr[i]>large)
    {
      large = arr[i];
       pos = i;
    }
  }
  second_large=arr[n-pos-1];
  for(i=0;i<n;i++)
  {
    if(i != pos)
    {
      if(arr[i]>second_large)
        second_large = arr[i];
    }
  }
  printf("\n The numbers you entered are: ");
  for(i=0;i<n;i++)
    printf("%d  ", arr[i]);
  printf("\n The largest of these numbers is:
  %d",large);
  printf("\n The second largest of these
  numbers is: %d",second_large);
  return 0;
}
```

Output

```
Enter the number of elements in the array: 5
Enter the number: 1
Enter the number: 2
Enter the number: 3
Enter the number: 4
```

```
Enter the number: 5
The numbers you entered are:
1 2 3 4  5
The largest of these numbers is: 5
The second largest of these numbers is: 4
```

6. Write a program to enter n number of digits. Form a number using these digits.

```
#include <stdio.h>
#include <math.h>
int main()
{
  int number=0, digit[10], numofdigits,i;

  printf("\n Enter the number of digits: ");
  scanf("%d", &numofdigits);

  for(i=0;i<numofdigits;i++)
  {
    printf("\n Enter the %dth digit: ", i);
    scanf("%d", &digit[i]);
  }
  i=0;
  while(i<numofdigits)
  {
    number = number + digit[i] * pow(10,i);
    i++;
  }
  printf("\n The number is: %d", number);
  return 0;
}
```

Output

```
Enter the number of digits: 3
Enter the 0th digit: 3
Enter the 1th digit: 4
Enter the 2th digit: 5
The number is: 543
```

7. Write a program to find whether the array of integers contains a duplicate number.

```
#include <stdio.h>
int main()
{
  int array[10], i, n, j, flag=0;

  printf("\n Enter the size of the array:");
  scanf("%d", &n);
  printf("\n Enter the elements:");
  for(i=0;i<n;i++)
  {
    scanf("%d", &array[i]);
  }
  for(i=0;i<n;i++)
  {
    for(j= i+1;j<n;j++)
    {
      if(array[i] == array[j] && i!=j)
      {
        flag=1;
        printf("\n Duplicate numbers found
          at location %d and %d",
          i, j);
      }

    }
  }
  if(flag==0)
  printf("\n No Duplicate");
  return 0;
}
```

Output

```
Enter the size of the array: 5
Enter the elements: 1 2 3 4 5
No Duplicate
```

8. Write a program to read marks of 10 students in the range of 0–100. Then make 10 groups: 0–10, 10–20, 20–30, etc. Count the number of values that falls in each group and display the result.

```
#include <stdio.h>
int main()
{
  int marks[50], i;
  int group[10]={0};
  printf("\n Enter the marks of 10 students
  : \n");
  for(i=0;i<10;i++)
  {
    printf("\n MARKS[%d] = ", i);
    scanf("%d", &marks[i]);
    ++group[(int)(marks[i])/10];
  }
  printf("\n ************************");
  printf("\n GROUP \t\t FREQUENCY");
  for(i=0;i<10;i++)
    printf("\n  %d \t\t %d", i, group[i]);
  return 0;
}
```

Output

```
Enter the marks of 10 students:
MARKS[0] = 95
MARKS[1] = 88
MARKS[2] = 67
MARKS[3] = 78
MARKS[4] = 81
MARKS[5] = 98
MARKS[6] = 55
MARKS[7] = 45
```

```
MARKS[8] = 72
MARKS[9] = 90
************************
GROUP   FREQUENCY
0       0
1       0
2       0
3       0
4       1
5       1
6       1
7       2
8       2
9       3
```

9. Modify the above program to display frequency histograms of each group.

```
#include <stdio.h>
int main()
{
  int marks[10], i, index;
  int group[10]={0};
  printf("\n Enter the marks of 10 students
  : \n");
  for(i=0;i<10;i++)
  {
    printf("\n MARKS[%d] = ", i);
    scanf("%d", &marks[i]);
    ++group[(int)(marks[i])/10];
  }
  printf("\n ************************");
  i=0;
  printf("\n FREQUENCY HISTOGRAM");
  for(index=0;index<10;index++)
  {
    printf("\n GROUP %d | ",index);
    for(i=0;i<group[index];i++)
      printf(" *");
  }
  return 0;
}
```

Output

```
Enter the marks of 10 students:
MARKS[0] = 95
MARKS[1] = 88
MARKS[2] = 67
MARKS[3] = 78
MARKS[4] = 81
MARKS[5] = 98
MARKS[6] = 55
MARKS[7] = 45
MARKS[8] = 72
MARKS[9] = 90
************************
FREQUENCY HISTOGRAM
GROUP 0 |
GROUP 1 |
GROUP 2 |
GROUP 3 |
GROUP 4 | *
GROUP 5 | *
GROUP 6 | *
GROUP 7 | * *
GROUP 8 | * *
GROUP 9 | * * *
```

10. Write a program to read a sorted list of floating point values and then calculate and display the median of the values.

```
#include <stdio.h>
int main()
{
  int i, j, n;
  float median, values[10];
  printf("\n Enter the size of the array: ");
  scanf("%d" &n);
  printf("\n Enter the values: ");
  for(i=0;i<n;i++)
    scanf("%f", &values[i]);
  if(n%2==0)
    median = (values[n/2] + values[n/2+1])/2.0;
  else
    median = values[n/2 + 1];
  printf("\n MEDIAN = %.2f", median);
  return 0;
}
```

Output

```
Enter the size of the array: 5
Enter the values:
12 34 56 78 89
MEDIAN = 56.00
```

12.5.2 Inserting an Element in an Array

Inserting an element in an array means adding a new data element to an already existing array. If the element has to be insertion at the end of the existing array, then the task of insertion is quite simple. We just have to add 1 to the `upper_bound` and assign the value. Here we assume that the memory space allocated for the array is still available. For example, if an array is declared to contain 10 elements, but currently it is having only 8 elements, then obviously there is space to accommodate two more elements. But if it already has 10 elements, then we will not be able to add another element to it.

Figure 12.10 shows an algorithm to insert a new element to the end of the array.

In Step 1, we increment the value of the `upper_bound`. In Step 2, the new value is stored at the position pointed by `upper_bound`.

```
Step 1: Set upper_bound = upper_bound+1
Step 2: Set A[upper_bound] = VAL
Step 3: EXIT
```

Figure 12.10 Algorithm to append a new element to an existing array

For example, if we have an array that is declared as

```
int marks[60];
```

The array is declared to store marks of all the students in the class. Now suppose there are 54 students and a new student comes and is asked to give the same test. The marks of this new student would be stored in `marks[55]`. Assuming that the student secured 68 marks, we will assign the value as,

```
marks[55] = 68;
```

However, if we have to insert an element in the middle of the array, then this is not a trivial task. On an average, we might have to move as much as half of the elements from their position in order to accommodate space for the new element.

For example, consider an array whose elements are arranged in ascending order. Now, if a new element has to be added, it will have to be added probably somewhere in the middle of the array. To do this, we will have to first find the location where the new element will be inserted and then move all the elements (that have a value greater than that of the new element) one space to the right so that space can be created to store the new value.

Example 12.5

`Data[]` is an array that is declared as `int Data[20];` and contains the following values:

```
Data[] = {12, 23, 34, 45, 56, 67, 78, 89, 90,
  100};
```

(a) Calculate the length of the array.
(b) Find the upper bound and lower bound.
(c) Show the memory representation of the array.
(d) If a new data element with value 75 has to be inserted, find its position.
(e) Insert the new data element and then show the memory representation of the array.

Solution

(a) Length of the array = number of elements
Therefore, length of the array = 10
(b) By default, `lower_bound = 0` and `upper_bound = 9`
(c)

12	23	34	45	56	67	78	89	90	100
Data [0]	[1]	[2]	[3]	[4]	[5]	[6]	[7]	[8]	[9]

(d) Since the elements of the array are stored in ascending order, the new data element will be stored after 67, i.e., at the 6th location. So, all the array elements from the 6th position will be moved one location towards the right to accommodate the new value.
(e)

12	23	34	45	56	67	75	78	89	90	100
Data [0]	[1]	[2]	[3]	[4]	[5]	[6]	[7]	[8]	[9]	[10]

Algorithm to Insert an Element in the Middle of an Array

The algorithm INSERT will be declared as `INSERT (A, N, POS, VAL)`. The arguments are

(a) `A`, the array in which the element has to be inserted
(c) `N`, the number of elements in the array
(d) `POS`, the position at which the element has to be inserted and
(e) `VAL`, the value that has to be inserted.

In the algorithm given in Figure 12.11, in Step 1, we first initialize `I` with the total number of elements in the array.

```
Step 1: [INITIALIZATION] SET I = N
Step 2: Reapeat Steps 3 and 4 while I > = POS
Step 3:                 SET A [I +1] = A[I]
                        SET A [I +1] = A[I]
        [END OF LOOP]
Step 4: SET N = N + 1
Step 6: SET A [POS] = VAL
Step 7: EXIT
```

Figure 12.11 Algorithm to insert a new element at a specified position

In Step 2, a `while` loop is executed which will move all the elements that have index greater than `POS` one position towards right to create space for the new element. In Step 5, we increment the total number of elements in the array by 1 and finally in Step 6, the new value is inserted at the desired position.

Now, let us visualize this algorithm by taking an example. Initial `Data[]` is given as shown in Figure 12.12.

Calling `INSERT (Data, 6, 3, 100)` will lead to the following processing in the array:

11. Write a program to insert a number at a given location in an array.

```
#include <stdio.h>
int main()
{
  int i, n, num, pos, arr[10];

  printf("\n Enter the number of elements in
  the array: ");
```

45	23	34	12	56	20	20
Data[0]	Data[1]	Data[2]	Data[3]	Data[4]	Data[5]	Data[6]

45	23	34	12	56	56	20
Data[0]	Data[1]	Data[2]	Data[3]	Data[4]	Data[5]	Data[6]

45	23	34	12	12	56	20
Data[0]	Data[1]	Data[2]	Data[3]	Data[4]	Data[5]	Data[6]

45	23	34	100	12	56	20
Data[0]	Data[1]	Data[2]	Data[3]	Data[4]	Data[5]	Data[6]

Figure 12.12 Inserting a new value in an existing array

```
    scanf("%d", &n);
    printf("\n Enter the values:");
    for(i=0;i<n;i++)
    {
      scanf("%d", &arr[i]);
    }
    printf("\n Enter the number to be
    inserted: ");
    scanf("%d", &num);
    printf("\n Enter the position at which the
     number has to be added: ");
    scanf("%d", &pos);

    for(i=n-1;i>=pos;i--)
      arr[i+1] = arr[i];
    arr[pos] = num;
    n++;
    printf("\n The array after insertion of
    %d is: ", num);

    for(i=0;i<n;i++)
      printf("\t %d", arr[i]);
    return 0;
}
```

Output

```
Enter the number of elements in the array: 5
Enter the values: 1 2 3 4 5
Enter the number to be inserted: 7
Enter the position at which the number has
to be added: 3
The array after insertion of 7 is:
1 2 3 7 4 5
```

12. Write a program to insert a number in an array that is already sorted in ascending order.

```
#include <stdio.h>
int main()
{
  int i, n, j, num, arr[10];

  printf("\n Enter the number of elements
  in the array: ");
  scanf("%d", &n);
  printf("\n Enter the array elements:");
  for(i=0;i<n;i++)
      scanf("%d", &arr[i]);
  printf("\n Enter the number to be inserted: ");
  scanf("%d", &num);
  for(i=0;i<n;i++)
  {
    if(arr[i] > num)
    {
      for(j = n-1; j>=i; j--)
        arr[j+1] = arr[j];
      arr[i] = num;
      break;
    }
  }
  n++;
  printf("\n The array after insertion of
  %d is: ", num);
  for(i=0;i<n;i++)
    printf("\t %d", arr[i]);
  return 0;
}
```

Output

```
Enter the number of elements in the array: 5
Enter the array elements: 1 2 3 4 5
Enter the number to be inserted: 6
The array after insertion of 6 is:
1 2 3 4 5 6
```

12.5.3 Deleting an Element from an Array

Deleting an element from an array means removing a data element from an already existing array. If the element has to be deleted from the end of the existing array, then the task of deletion is quite simple. We just have to subtract 1 from the upper_bound. Figure 12.13 shows an algorithm to delete an element from the end of the array.

```
Step 1: SET upper_bound  = upper_bound  - 1
Step 2: EXIT
```

Figure 12.13 Algorithm to delete the last element of an array

For example, if we have an array that is declared as

```
int marks[];
```

The array is declared to store marks of all the students in the class. Now suppose there are 54 students and the student with roll number 54 leaves the course. The marks of this student was therefore stored in `marks[54]`. We just have to decrement the `upper_bound`. Subtracting 1 from the `upper_bound` will indicate that there are 53 valid data in the array.

However, if we have to delete the element from the middle of the array, then this task is not trivial. On an average, we might have to move as much as half of the elements from their position in order to occupy the space of the deleted element.

For example, consider an array whose elements are arranged in ascending order. Now, if an element has to be deleted from somewhere middle of the array. To do this, we will first find the location from where the element has to be deleted and then move all the elements (that have a value greater than that of the element) one location towards the left so that location vacated by the deleted element is occupied by the next element and so on.

Example 12.6

`Data[]` is an array that is declared as `int Data[10];` and contains the following values:

```
Data[] = {12, 23, 34, 45, 56, 67, 78, 89, 90, 100};
```

(a) If a data element with value 56 has to be deleted, find its position.

(b) Delete the data element and give the memory representation of the array.

Solution

12	23	34	45	56	67	78	89	90	100

(a) Since the elements of the array are stored in ascending order, we will compare the value that has to be deleted with the value of every element in the array. As soon as `VAL = Data[I]`, where `I` is the index or subscript of the array, we will get the position from which the element has to be deleted. For example, if we see this array, here `VAL = 56. Data[0] = 12` which is not equal to 56. Like this, we will compare and finally get the value of `POS = 4.`

(b)

12	23	34	45	67	78	89	90	100
Data [0]	[1]	[2]	[3]	[4]	[5]	[6]	[7]	[8]

Algorithm to Delete an Element From the Middle of an Array

The algorithm `DELETE` will be declared as `DELETE(A, N, POS)`. The arguments are as follows:

(a) `A`, the array from which the element has to be deleted

(b) `N`, the number of elements in the array

(c) `POS`, the position from which the element has to be deleted

Figure 12.14 shows the algorithm in which we first initialize `I` with the position from which the element has to be deleted. In Step 2, a `while` loop is executed which will move all the elements that have index greater than `POS` one location towards left to occupy the location vacated by the deleted element. When we say that we are deleting an element, we are actually overwriting the element with the value of its successive element. In Step 5, we decrement the total number of elements in the array by 1.

```
Step 1: [INITIALIZATION]   SET I = POS
Step 2: Repeat Steps 3 and 4 while I <= N - 1
Step 3: SET A [I] = A [I + 1]
Step 4: SET I = I + 1
           [END OF LOOP]
Step 5: SET N = N - 1
Step 6: EXIT
```

Figure 12.14 Algorithm to delete an element from the middle of an array

Now, let us visualize this algorithm by taking an example and having a look at Figure 12.15.

45	23	34	12	56	20
Data[0]	Data[1]	Data[2]	Data[3]	Data[4]	Data[5]

(a)

45	23	12	12	56	20
Data[0]	Data[1]	Data[2]	Data[3]	Data[4]	Data[5]

(b)

45	23	12	56	56	20
Data[0]	Data[1]	Data[2]	Data[3]	Data[4]	Data[5]

(c)

45	23	12	56	20	20
Data[0]	Data[1]	Data[2]	Data[3]	Data[4]	Data[5]

(d)

45	23	12	56	20
Data[0]	Data[1]	Data[2]	Data[3]	Data[4]

(e)

Figure 12.15 Deleting an element from an array

Initial `Data[]` is given as shown in Figure 12.15.

Calling `DELETE (Data, 6, 2)` will lead to the following processing in the array:

13. Write a program to delete a number from a given location in an array.

```
#include <stdio.h>
int main()
{
  int i, n, pos, arr[10];

  printf("\n Enter the size of the array:");
  scanf("%d", &n);
  printf("\n Enter the elements of the array : ");
  for(i=0;i<n;i++)
    scanf("%d", &arr[i]);
  printf("\n Enter the position from which
  the number has to be deleted: ");
  scanf("%d", &pos);

  for(i= pos; i<n-1;i++)
    arr[i] = arr [i+1];
  n--;
  printf("\n The array after deletion is:");
  for(i=0;i<n;i++)
    printf("\n Arr[%d] = %d", i, arr[i]);
  return 0;
}
```

Output

```
Enter the size of the array: 5
Enter the elements of the array:
1 2 3 4 5
Enter the position from which the number has
to be deleted: 3
The array after deletion is:
Arr[0] = 1
Arr[1] = 2
Arr[2] = 3
Arr[3] = 5
```

14. Write a program to delete a number from an array that is already sorted in ascending order.

```
#include <stdio.h>
int main()
{
  int i, n, j, num, arr[10];
  printf("\n Enter the number of elements
  in the array : ");
  scanf("%d", &n);
  printf("\n Enter the elements:");
  for(i=0;i<n;i++)
    scanf("%d", &arr[i]);
  printf("\n Enter the number to be deleted
  : ");
  scanf("%d", &num);

  for(i=0;i<n;i++)
  {
    if(arr[i] == num)
    {
      for(j=i; j<n-1;j++)
        arr[j] = arr[j+1];
    }
  }
  printf("\n The array after deletion is:
  ");
  for(i=0;i<n-1;i++)
    printf("\t%d", arr[i]);
  return 0;
}
```

Output

```
Enter the number of elements in the array: 5
Enter the elements: 1 2 3 4 5
Enter the number to be deleted: 3
The array after deletion is: 1 2 4 5
```

12.5.4 Merging Two Arrays

Merging two arrays in a third array means first copying the contents of the first array into the third array and then copying the contents of the second array into the third array. Hence, the merged array contains contents of the first array followed by the contents of the second array.

If the arrays are unsorted then merging the arrays is very simple as one just needs to copy the contents of one array into another. But merging is not a trivial task when the two arrays are sorted and the merged array also needs to be sorted. Let us first discuss the merge operation on unsorted arrays. This operation is shown in Figure 12.16.

Array 1	90	56	89	77	69							
Array 2	45	88	76	99	12	58	81					
Array 3	90	56	89	77	69	45	88	76	99	12	58	81

Figure 12.16 Merging of two unsorted arrays

15. Write a program to merge two unsorted arrays.

```
#include <stdio.h>
int main()
{
  int arr1[10], arr2[10], arr3[20];
  int i, n1, n2, m, index=0;
  printf("\n Enter the number of elements
  in array 1: ");
  scanf("%d", &n1);
  printf("\n Enter the elements of the first
  array");
  for(i=0;i<n1;i++)
    scanf("%d", &arr1[i]);
```

```
printf("\n Enter the number of elements in
array 2: ");
scanf("%d", &n2);
printf("\n Enter the elements of the second
array");
for(i=0;i<n2;i++)
  scanf("%d", &arr2[i]);
m = n1+n2;
for(i=0;i<n1;i++)
{
  arr3[index] = arr1[i];
  index++;
}
for(i=0;i<n2;i++)
{
  arr3[index] = arr2[i];
  index++;
}
printf("\n\n The merged array is");
for(i=0;i<m;i++)
  printf("\t Arr[%d] = %d", i, arr3[i]);
return 0;
}
```

Output

```
Enter the number of elements in array 1: 3
Enter the elements of the first array
10 20 30
Enter the number of elements in array 2: 3
Enter the elements of the second array
15 25 35
The merged array is
Arr[0] = 10  Arr[1] = 20  Arr[2] = 30
Arr[3] = 15  Arr[4] = 25  Arr[5] = 35
```

If we have two sorted arrays and the resultant merged array also needs to be a sorted one, then the task of merging the arrays becomes a little difficult. The task of merging can be explained using Figure 12.17.

Array 1- | 20 | 30 | 40 | 50 | 60 |

Array 2- | 15 | 22 | 31 | 45 | 56 | 62 | 78 |

Array 3- | 15 | 20 | 22 | 30 | 31 | 40 | 45 | 50 | 56 | 60 | 62 | 78 |

Figure 12.17 Merging of two sorted arrays

The figure shows how the merged array is formed using two sorted arrays. Here, we first compare the 1st element of array 1 with the 1st element of array 2, put the smaller element in the merged array. Since 20 > 15, we put 15 as the first element in the merged array. We then compare the 2nd element of the second array with the 1st element of the first array. Since 20 < 22, now 20 is stored as the second element of the merged array. Next, 2nd element of the first array is compared with the 2nd element of the second array. Since 30 > 22, we store 22 as the third element of the merged array. Now, we will compare the 2nd element of the first array with 3rd element of the second array. As 30 < 31, we store 30 as the 4th element of the merged array. This procedure will be repeated until elements of both the arrays are placed in the right location in the merged array.

16. Write a program to merge two sorted arrays.

```
#include <stdio.h>
int main()
{
  int arr1[10], arr2[10], arr3[20];
  int i, n1, n2, m, index=0;
  int index_first = 0, index_second = 0;
  printf("\n Enter the number of elements in
  array1: ");
  scanf("%d", &n1);
  printf("\n Enter the elements of the first
  array");
  for(i=0;i<n1;i++)
    scanf("%d", &arr1[i]);

  printf("\n Enter the number of elements in
  array2 : ");
  scanf("%d", &n2);
  printf("\n Enter the elements of the second
  array");
  for(i=0;i<n2;i++)
    scanf("%d", &arr2[i]);
  m = n1+n2;
  while(index_first < n1 && index_second < n2)
  {
    if(arr1[index_first]<arr2[index_second])
    {
      arr3[index] = arr1[index_first];
      index_first++;
    }
    else
    {
      arr3[index] = arr2[index_second];
      index_second++;
    }
    index++;
  }

/* if elements of the first array are over and
 the second array has some elements */

  if(index_first == n1)
  {
    while(index_second<n2)
    {
      arr3[index] = arr2[index_second];
      index_second++;
```

```
            index++;
        }
    }
    /* if elements of the second array are over
       and the first array has some elements */

    else if(index_second == n2)
    {
        while(index_first<n1)
        {
            arr3[index] = arr1[index_first];
            index_first++;
            index++;
        }
    }
    printf("\n\n The contents of the merged
    array are");
    for(i=0;i<m;i++)
        printf("\n Arr[%d] = %d", i, arr3[i]);
    return 0;
}
```

Output

```
Enter the number of elements in array1: 3
Enter the elements of the first array
10 20 30
Enter the number of elements in array2: 3
Enter the elements of the second array
15 25 35
The contents of the merged array are
Arr[0] = 10  Arr[1] = 15  Arr[2] = 20
Arr[3] = 25  Arr[4] = 30  Arr[5] = 35
```

12.5.5 Searching for a Value in an Array

Searching means to find whether a particular value is present in the array or not. If the value is present in the array then search is said to be successful and the search process gives the location of that value in the array. Otherwise, if the value is not present in the array, the search process displays the appropriate message and in this case search is said to be unsuccessful.

There are two popular methods for searching the array elements. One is *linear search* and the second is *binary search*. The algorithm that should be used depends entirely on how the values are organized in the array. For example, if the elements of the array are arranged in ascending order, then binary search should be used as it is more efficient for sorted list. We will discuss these two methods in detail in this section.

Linear Search

Linear search, also called *sequential search*, is a very simple method used for searching an array for a particular value. It works by comparing every element of the array one by one in sequence until a match is found. Linear search is mostly used to search an unordered list of elements (array in which data elements are not sorted). For example, if an array `A[]` is declared and initialized as

```
int A[] = {10, 8, 2, 7, 3, 4, 9, 1, 6, 5};
```

and the value to be searched is `VAL = 7`, then searching means to find whether the value `7` is present in the array or not. If yes, then the search is successful and it returns the position of occurrence of `VAL`. Here, `POS = 3` (index starting from 0). Figure 12.18 illustrates this concept.

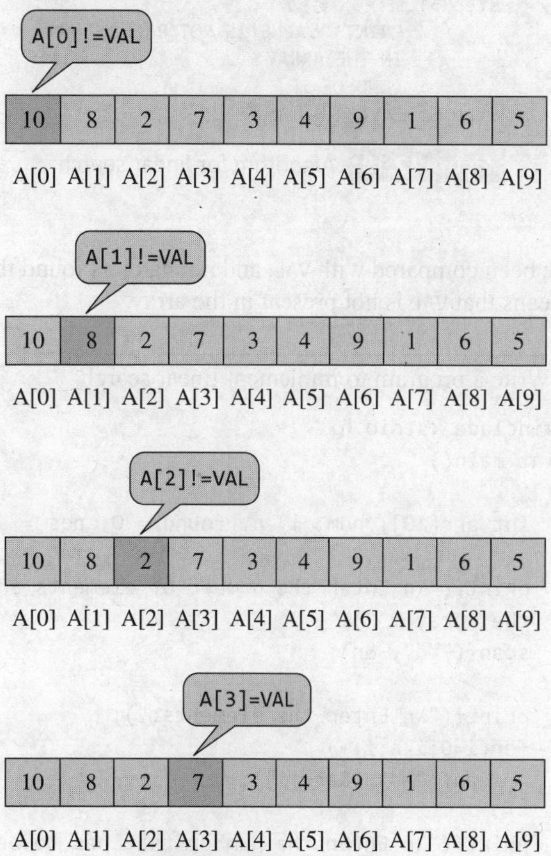

Figure 12.18 Linear search

Obviously, the best case of linear search is when `VAL` is equal to the first element of the array. In this case, only one comparison will be made.

Likewise, the worst case will happen when either `VAL` is not present in the array or it is equal to the last element of the array. In both the cases, *n* comparisons will be made. However, the performance of the linear search algorithm (Figure 12.19) can be improved by using a sorted array.

In Step 1 and Step 2 of the algorithm, we initialize the value of `POS` and `I`. In Step 3, a `while` loop is executed that would be executed until `I` is less than `N` (total number of elements in the array). In Step 4, a check is made to see if a match is found between the current array element and `VAL`. If a match is found, then the position of the array element is printed else the value of `I` is incremented to match the next element with `VAL`. However, if all the array elements

```
LINEAR_SEARCH(A, N, VAL)

Step 1: [INITIALIZE] SET POS = -1
Step 2: [INITIALIZE] SET I = 1
Step 3:      Repeat Step 4 while I<=N
Step 4:           IF A[I] = VAL
                       SET POS = I
                       PRINT POS
                       Go to Step 6
                  [END OF IF]
             SET I = I+1
             [END OF LOOP]
Step 5: IF POS = -1
             PRINT "VALUE IS NOT PRESENT
             IN THE ARRAY "
             [END OF IF]
Step 6: EXIT
```

Figure 12.19 Algorithm for linear search

have been compared with VAL, and no match is found then it means that VAL is not present in the array.

17. Write a program to implement linear search.

```
#include <stdio.h>
int main()
{
  int arr[10], num, i, n, found = 0, pos = -1;

  printf("\n Enter the number of elements in
  the array : ");
  scanf("%d", &n);

  printf("\n Enter the elements:");
  for(i=0;i<n;i++)
    scanf("%d", &arr[i]);

  printf("\n Enter the number that has to be
  searched : ");
  scanf("%d", &num);

  for(i=0;i<n;i++)
  {
    if(arr[i] == num)
    {
      found =1;
      pos=i;
      printf("\n %d is found in the array
        at position = %d", num, i);
      break;
    }
  }
  if (found == 0)
    printf("\n %d does not exist in the
      array", num);
  return 0;
}
```

Output

```
Enter the number of elements in the array: 5
Enter the elements: 1 2 3 4 5
Enter the number that has to be searched: 7
7 does not exist in the array
```

Binary Search

We have seen that the linear search algorithm is very slow. If we have an array with 1 million entries then to search a value from that array, we would need to make 1 million comparisons in the worst case. However, if the array is sorted, we have a better and efficient alternative known as binary search.

Binary search is a searching algorithm that works efficiently with a *sorted list*. The algorithm finds the position of a particular element in the array. The mechanism of binary search can be better understood by using the analogy of a telephone directory. When we are searching for a particular name in the directory, we will first open the directory from the middle and then decide whether to look for the name in the first part of the directory or in the second part of the directory. Again we will open some page in the middle and the whole process will be repeated until we finally find the name.

Now let us consider how this mechanism will be applied to search for a value in a sorted array. Given an array that is declared and initialized as

```
int A[] = {0, 1, 2, 3, 4, 5, 6, 7, 8, 9, 10};
```

and the value to be searched is VAL = 9. The algorithm (Figure 12.20) will proceed in the following manner.

BEG = 0, END = 10, MID = (0 + 10)/2 = 5

Now, VAL = 9 and A[MID] = A[5] = 5

A[5] is less than VAL, therefore, we will now search for the value in the latter half of the array. So, we change the values of BEG and MID.

Now, BEG = MID + 1 = 6, END = 10, MID = (6 + 10)/2 =16/2 = 8

Now, VAL = 9 and A[MID] = A[8] = 8

A[8] is less than VAL, therefore, we will now search for the value in the latter half of the array. So, again we change the values of BEG and MID.

Now, BEG = MID + 1 = 9, END = 10, MID = (9 + 10)/2 = 9

Now VAL = 9 and A[MID] = 9.

In this algorithm we see that BEG and END are the beginning and ending positions of the segment that we are looking to search for the element. MID is calculated as (BEG + END)/2. Initially, BEG = lower_bound and END = upper_bound. The algorithm will terminate when A[MID] = VAL. When the algorithm ends, we will set POS = MID. POS is the position at which the value is present in the array.

However, if VAL is not equal to A[MID], then the values of BEG, END, and MID will be changed depending on whether VAL is smaller or greater than A[MID].

```
BINARY_SEARCH(A, lower_bound, upper_bound, VAL)

Step 1: [INITIALIZE] SET BEG = lower_bound, END = upper_bound, POS = -1
Step 2: Repeat Steps 3 and 4 while BEG <= END
Step 3:         SET MID = (BEG + END)/2
Step 4:         IF A[MID] = VAL, then
                     POS = MID
                     PRINT POS
                     Go to Step 6
                ELSE IF A[MID] > VAL, then
                     SET END = MID - 1
                ELSE
                     SET BEG = MID + 1
                [END OF IF]
       [END OF LOOP]
Step 5: IF POS = -1, then
            PRINT "VAL IS NOT PRESENT IN THE ARRAY"
       [END OF IF]
Step 6: EXIT
```

Figure 12.20 Algorithm for binary search

(a) If `VAL < A[MID]`, then `VAL` will be present in the left segment of the array. So, the value of `END` will be changed as, `END = MID - 1`

(b) If `VAL > A[MID]`, then `VAL` will be present in the right segment of the array. So, the value of `BEG` will be changed as, `BEG = MID + 1`

Finally, if `VAL` is not present in the array, then eventually `END` will be less than `BEG`. When this happens, the algorithm will terminate and the search will be unsuccessful.

Figure 12.20 shows the algorithm for binary search.

In Step 1, we initialize the value of variables—`BEG`, `END` and `POS`. In Step 2, a `while` loop is executed until `BEG` is less than or equal to `END`. In Step 3, value of `MID` is calculated. In Step 4, we check if the value of `A[MID]` is equal to `VAL` (item to be searched in the array). If a match is found then value of `POS` is printed and the algorithm exits. However, if a match is not found and if the value of `A[MID]` is greater than `VAL`, then the value of `END` is modified otherwise if `A[MID]` is less than `VAL`, then value of `BEG` is altered. In Step 5, if the value of `POS = -1`, then it means `VAL` is not present in the array and an appropriate message is printed on the screen before the algorithm exits.

18. Write a program to implement binary search.

```
#include <stdio.h>
int main()
{
  int arr[10], num, i, n, pos = -1, beg, end,
  mid, found =0;

  printf("\n Enter the number of elements in
  the array: ");
  scanf("%d", &n);
  printf("\n Enter the elements: ");
  for(i=0;i<n;i++)
  {
    scanf("%d", &arr[i]);
  }
  printf("\n Enter the number that has to be
  searched: ");
  scanf("%d", &num);

  beg = 0, end = n-1;
  while(beg <= end)
  {
    mid = (beg + end)/2;
    if (arr[mid] == num)
    {
    printf("\n %d is present in the array
      at position = %d", num, mid);
    found=1;
    break;
    }
    else if (arr[mid]>num)
      end = mid-1;
    else
      beg = mid+1;
  }
  if ( beg > end && found == 0)
    printf("\n %d does not exist in the
      array", num);
  return 0;
}
```

Output

```
Enter the number of elements in the array: 5
Enter the elements: 1 2 3 4 5
Enter the number that has to be searched: 7
7 does not exist in the array
```

12.6 PASSING ARRAYS TO FUNCTIONS

Like variables of other data types, we can also pass an array to a function. While in some situations, you may want to pass individual elements of the array, and in other situations you may want to pass the entire array. In this section, we will discuss both these cases. Look at Figure 12.21 which will make the concept easier to understand.

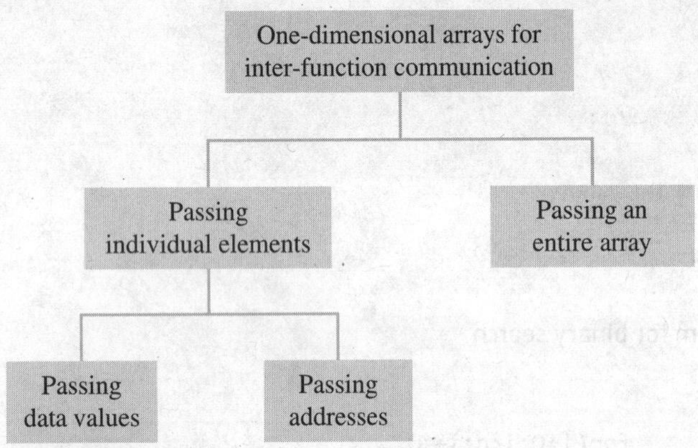

Figure 12.21 One-dimensional arrays for inter-function communication

Passing Individual Elements

The individual elements of an array can be passed to a function by passing either their data values or their addresses.

Passing Data Values

The individual elements can be passed in the same manner as we pass variables of any other data type. The condition is just that the data type of the array element must match with the type of the function parameter. Figure 12.22 shows the code to pass an individual array element by passing data value.

In the example given, only one element of the array is passed to the called function. This is done by using the index expression. So `arr[3]` actually evaluates to a single

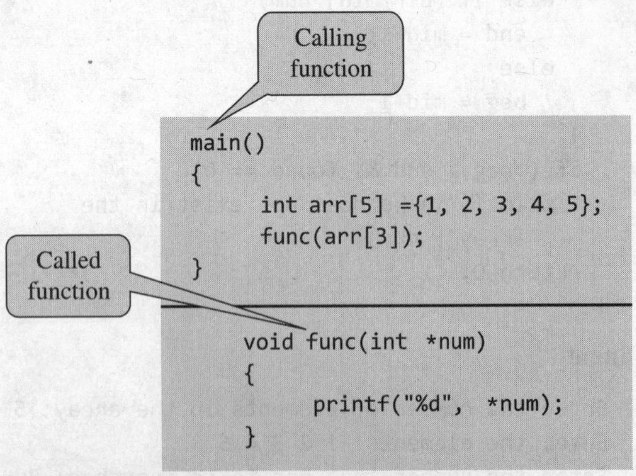

Figure 12.22 Passing value of individual array elements to a function

integer value. The called function hardly bothers whether a normal integer variable is passed to it or an array value is passed.

Passing Addresses

Like ordinary variables, we can pass the address of an individual array element by preceding the indexed array element with the address operator (&). Therefore, to pass the address of the fourth element of the array to the called function, we will write `&arr[3]`.

However, in the called function the value of the array element must be accessed using the indirection (`*`) operator (Figure 12.23).

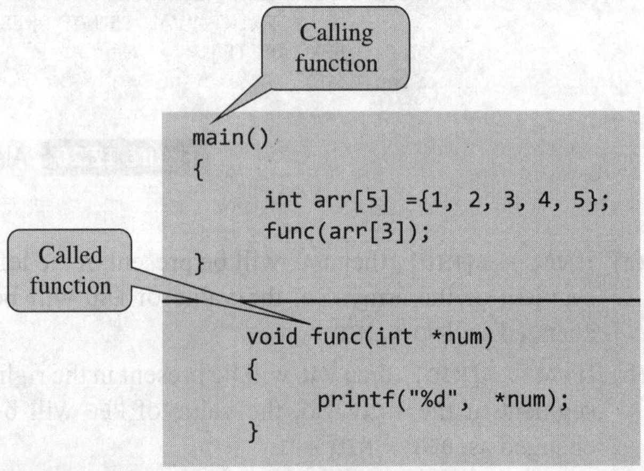

Figure 12.23 Passing address of individual array elements to function

Passing the Entire Array

We have studied that in C the array name refers to the first byte of the array in memory. The address of rest of the elements in the array can be calculated using the array name and the index value of the element. Therefore, when we need to pass an entire array to a function, we can simply pass the name of the array. Figure 12.24 illustrates the code which passes the entire array to the called function.

> **Programming Tip:**
> When an entire array is to be sent to the called function, the calling function just needs to pass the name of the array.

In cases where we do not want the called function to make any changes to the array, the array must be received as a constant array by the called function. This prevents any type of unintentional modifications of the array elements. To declare the array as a constant array, simply add the keyword `const` before the data type of the array.

19. Write a program to read and print an array of n numbers.

```
#include <stdio.h>
void read_array( int arr[], int);
void display_array( int arr[], int);
```

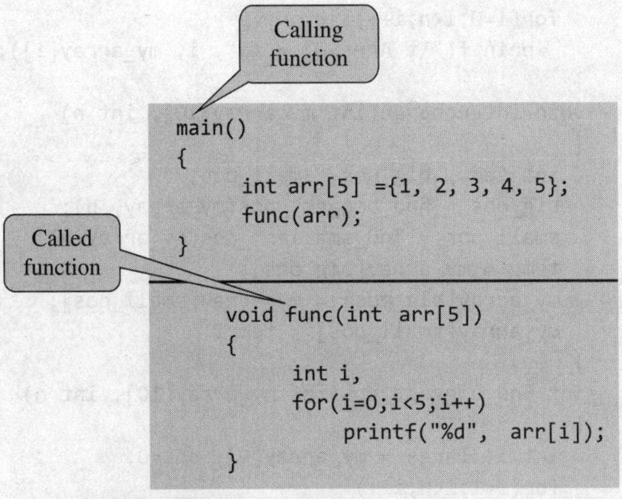

Figure 12.24 Passing entire array to function

```
int main()
{
  int num[10], n;
  printf("\n Enter the size of the array:");
  scanf("%d", &n);
  read_array(num, n);
  display_array(num, n);
  return 0;
}
void read_array(int arr[10], int n)
{
  int i;
  printf("\n Enter the elements of the
  array:");
  for(i=0;i<n;i++)
  {
    scanf("%d", &arr[i]);
  }
}
void display_array(int arr[10], int n)
{
  printf("\n The elements of the array are :");
  for(int i=0;i<n;i++)
    printf("\t %d", arr[i]);
}
```

Output

```
Enter the size of the array: 5
Enter the elements of the array: 1 2 3 4 5
The elements of the array are: 1 2 3 4 5
```

20. Write a program to merge two integer arrays. Also display the merged array in reverse order.

```
#include <stdio.h>
void read_array(int my_array[], int);
void display_array(int my_array[], int);
void merge_array(int my_array3[], int, int
my_array1[], int, int my_array2[], int);
void reverse_array(int my_array[], int);
int main()
{
  int arr1[10], arr2[10], arr3[20], n, m, t;

  printf("\n Enter the number of elements in
  the first array: ");
  scanf("%d", &m);
           read_array(arr1, m);
           printf("\n Enter the
           number of elements in the
           second array: ");
           scanf("%d", &n);
           read_array(arr2, n);
           t = m + n;
           merge_array(arr3, t, arr1,
           m, arr2, n);

           printf("\n The merged
           array is : ");
           display_array(arr3, t);

           printf("\n The merged
           array in reverse order is:
           ");
           reverse_array(arr3, t);
           return 0;
           }
         void read_array(int my_
         array[10], int n)
{
  int i;
  for(i=0;i<n;i++)
    scanf("%d", &my_array[i]);
}
void merge_array(int my_array3[], int t, int
  my_array1[], int m, int my_array2[], int n)
{
  int i, j=0;
  for(i=0; i<m; i++)
  {
    my_array3[j] = my_array1[i];
    j++;
  }
  for(i=0; i<n; i++)
  {
    my_array3[j] = my_array2[i];
    j++;
  }
}
void display_array(int my_array[], int n)
{
  int i;
  for(i=0;i<n;i++)
    printf("\n Arr[%d] = %d", i,
      my_array[i]);
}
void reverse_array(int my_array[], int m)
```

Programming Tip:
While using arrays, we must check for validity of the index because such checks are not made by the compiler. An invalid index when used with an assignment operator may destroy the data of another part of the program and thus cause it to fail later. While initializing the array, if we provide more initializers than the number of elements in the array, a compiler error will be generated.

```
{
  int i, j;
  for(i=m-1, j=0;i>=0;i--, j++)
    printf("\n arr[%d] = %d", j,
      my_array[i]);
}
```

Output

```
Enter the number of elements in the first
array: 3
10 20 30
Enter the number of elements in the second
array: 3
15 25 35
The merged array is:
Arr[0] = 10  Arr[1] = 20  Arr[2] = 30
Arr[3] = 15  Arr[4] = 25  Arr[5] = 35
The merged array in reverse order is:
Arr[0] = 35    Arr[1] = 25    Arr[2] = 15
Arr[3] = 30    Arr[4] = 20    Arr[5] = 10
```

21. Write a program to interchange the largest and the smallest number in an array.

```
#include <stdio.h>
void read_array(int my_array[], int);
void display_array(int my_array[], int);
void interchange(int arr[], int);
int find_biggest_pos(int my_array[10], int n);
int find_smallest_pos(int my_array[10], int n);

int main()
{
  int arr[10], n;

  printf("\n Enter the size of the array:");
  scanf("%d", &n);
  read_array(arr, n);
  printf("\n The elements of the array
  are\n");
  display_array(arr, n);
  interchange(arr, n);
  printf("\n The elements of the array after
  interchange are\n");
  display_array(arr, n);
  return 0;
}
void read_array(int my_array[10], int n)
{
  int i;
  printf("\n Enter the elements");
  for(i=0;i<n;i++)
    scanf("%d", &my_array[i]);
}
void display_array(int my_array[10], int n)
{
  int i;
  printf("n");
  for(i=0;i<n;i++)
    printf("\t Arr[%d] = %d", i, my_array[i]);
}
void interchange(int my_array[10], int n)
{
  int temp, big_pos, small_pos;
  big_pos = find_biggest_pos(my_array, n);
  small_pos = find_smallest_pos(my_array,n);
  temp = my_array[big_pos];
  my_array[big_pos] = my_array[small_pos];
  my_array[small_pos] = temp;
}
int find_biggest_pos(int my_array[10], int n)
{
  int i, large = my_array[0], pos=0;
  for(i=1;i<n;i++)
  {
    if (my_array[i] > large)
    {
      large = my_array[i];
      pos=i;
    }
  }
  return pos;
}
int find_smallest_pos(int my_array[10], int n)
{
  int i, small = my_array[0], pos=0;
  for(i=1;i<n;i++)
  {
    if (my_array[i] < small)
    {
      small = my_array[i];
      pos=i;
    }
  }
  return pos;
}
```

Output

```
Enter the size of the array: 5
Enter the elements 1 2 3 4 5
The elements of the array are
Arr[0] = 1  Arr[1] = 2  Arr[2] = 3
Arr[3] = 4  Arr[4] = 5
The elements of the array after interchange are
Arr[0] = 5  Arr[1] = 2  Arr[2] = 3
Arr[3] = 4  Arr[4] = 1
```

Note

If a function receives an array that does not change it, then the array should be received as a constant array. This would ensure that the contents of the array are not accidentally changed. To declare an array as constant, prefix its type with the const keyword, as shown below.

```
int sum(const int arr[ ], int n);
```

12.7 TWO-DIMENSIONAL ARRAYS

Till now we have read only about one-dimensional arrays. A one-dimensional array is organized linearly and only in one direction. But at times, we need to store data in the form of matrices or tables. Here the concept of one-dimensional array is extended to incorporate two-dimensional data structures. A two-dimensional array is specified using two subscripts where one subscript denotes row and the other denotes column. C considers the two-dimensional array as an array of one-dimensional arrays. Figure 12.25 shows a two-dimensional array which can be viewed as an array of arrays.

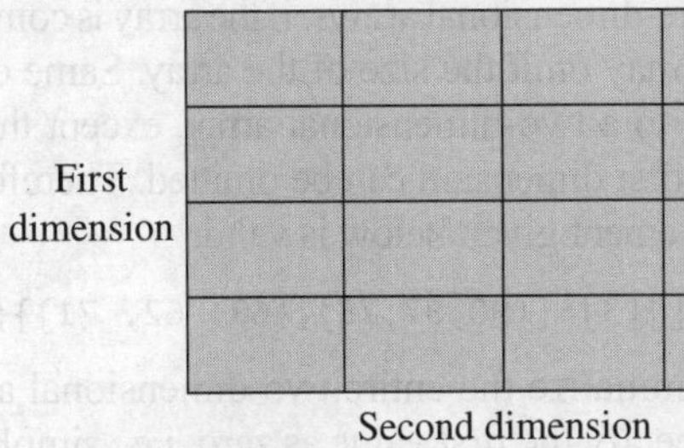

Figure 12.25 Two-dimensional array

12.7.1 Declaring Two-dimensional Arrays

Similar to one-dimensional arrays, two-dimensional arrays must be declared before being used. The declaration statement tells the compiler the name of the array, the data type of each element in the array, and the size of each dimension. A two-dimensional array is declared as

```
data_type array_name[row_size][column_size];
```

Therefore, a two-dimensional `m × n` array is an array that contains `m × n` data elements and each element is accessed using two subscripts, `i` and `j` where `i<= m` and `j<= n`.

For example, if we want to store the marks obtained by 3 students in 5 different subjects, then we can declare a two-dimensional array as

```
int marks[3][5];
```

A two-dimensional array called `marks` is declared that has `m(3)` rows and `n(5)` columns. The first element of the array is denoted by `marks[0][0]`, the second element as `marks[0][1]`, and so on. Here, `marks[0][0]` stores the marks obtained by the first student in the first subject, `marks[1][0]` stores the marks obtained by the second student in the first subject, and so on.

Note

Each dimension of the two-dimensional array is indexed from zero to its maximum size minus one. The first index selects the row and the second selects the column.

The pictorial form of a two-dimensional array is given in Figure 12.26.

Hence, we see that a 2D array is treated as a collection of 1D arrays. To understand this, we can also see the representation of a two-dimensional array as shown in Figure 12.27.

Although Figure 12.27 shows a rectangular picture of a two-dimensional array, these elements will be actually stored sequentially in memory. Since computer memory is basically one-dimensional, a multidimensional array cannot be stored in memory as a grid.

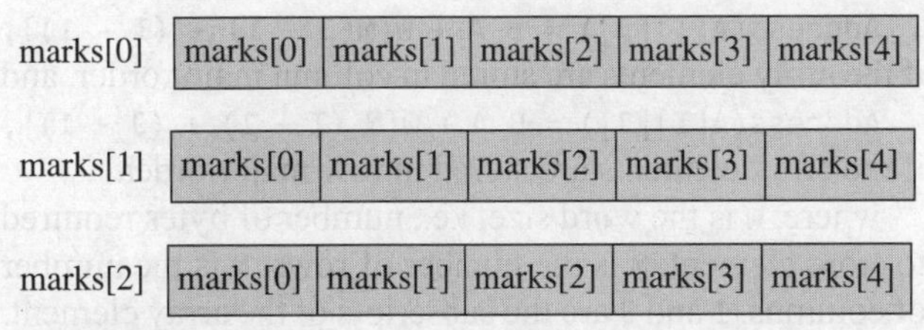

Figure 12.27 Representation of two-dimensional array marks[3][5] as individual 1D arrays

There are two ways of storing a two-dimensional array in memory. The first way is *row major order* and the second is *column major order*. Let us see how the elements of a 2D array are stored in row major order. Here, the elements of the first row are stored before the elements of the second and third row, i.e., the elements of the array are stored row by row where n elements of the first row will occupy the first n locations. This is illustrated in Figure 12.28.

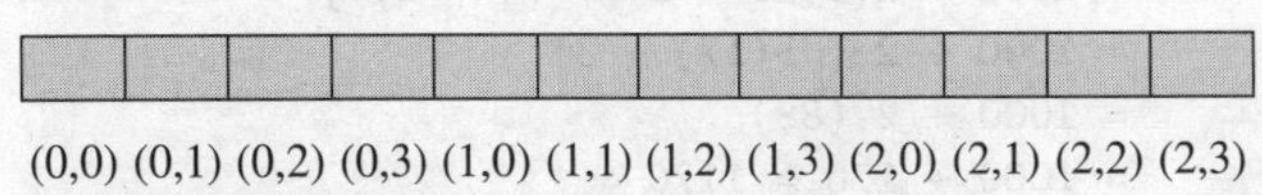

Figure 12.28 Elements of a 3 × 4 2D array in row major order

Rows / Columns	Column 0	Column 1	Column 2	Column 3	Column 4
Row 0	marks[0][0]	marks[0][1]	marks[0][2]	marks[0][3]	marks[0][4]
Row 1	marks[1][0]	marks[1][1]	marks[1][2]	marks[1][3]	marks[1][4]
Row 2	marks[2][0]	marks[2][1]	marks[2][2]	marks[2][3]	marks[2][4]

Figure 12.26 Two-dimensional array

When we store the elements in a column major order, the elements of the first column are stored before the elements of the second and third column, i.e., the elements of the array are stored column by column where m elements of the first column will occupy the first m locations. This is illustrated in Figure 12.29.

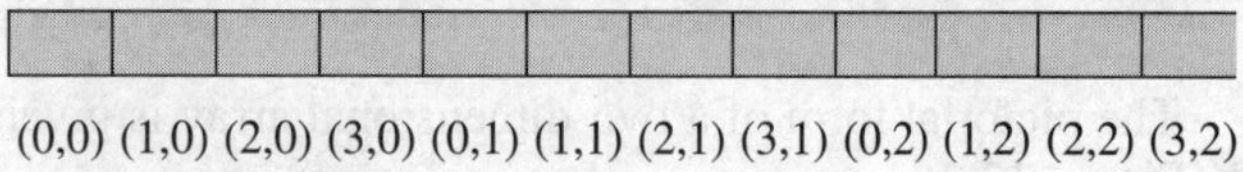

Figure 12.29 Elements of a 4 × 3 2D array in column major order

In one-dimensional arrays, we have seen that computer does not keep track of the address of every element in the array. It stores only the address of the first element and calculates the addresses of other elements from the base address (address of the first element). Same is the case with a two-dimensional array. Here also, the computer stores the base address and the address of the other elements is calculated using the following formula.

```
Address(A[I][J]) = B_A + w{M(J - 1) + (I - 1)},
```

if the array elements are stored in column major order, and

```
Address(A[I][J]) = B_A + w{N (I - 1) + (J - 1)},
```

if the array elements are stored in row major order.

where, `w` is the word size, i.e., number of bytes required to store element, `M` is the number of rows, `N` is the number of columns, `I` and `J` are the subscripts of the array element, and `B_A` is the base address.

Example 12.7

Consider a 20 × 5 two-dimensional array `Marks` which has `base address` = 1000 and the word size = 2. Now compute the address of the element `Marks[18, 4]` assuming that the elements are stored in row major order.

Solution

```
Address(A[I][J])
  = Base_Address + w{N (I - 1) + (J - 1)}
Address(Marks[18,4])
  = 1000 + 2{5(18 – 1) + (4 – 1) }
  = 1000 + 2 { 5(17) + 3}
  = 1000 + 2 (88)
  = 1000 + 176 = 1176
```

12.7.2 Initializing Two-dimensional Arrays

Like in case of other variables, declaring a two-dimensional array only reserves space for the array in the memory. No values are stored in it. A two-dimensional array is initialized in the same way as a one-dimensional array. For example,

```
int marks[2][3] = {90, 87, 78, 68, 62, 71};
```

The initialization of a two-dimensional array is done row by row. The above statement can also be written as

```
int marks[2][3]={{90,87,78},{68, 62, 71}};
```

The given two-dimensional array has 2 rows and 3 columns. Here, the elements in the first row are initialized first and then the elements of the second row are initialized. Therefore,

```
marks[0][0] = 90  marks[0][1] = 87
marks[0][2] = 78  marks[1][0] = 68
marks[1][1] = 62  marks[1][2] = 71
```

Therefore, in the aforegiven example, each row is defined as a one-dimensional array of three elements that are enclosed in braces. Commas are used to separate the elements in the row as well as to separate the elements of two rows.

In case of one-dimensional arrays, if the array is completely initialized, we may omit the size of the array. Same concept can be applied to a two-dimensional array, except that only the size of the first dimension can be omitted. Therefore, the declaration statement given below is valid.

```
int marks[][3]={{90,87,78},{68, 62, 71}};
```

In order to initialize the entire two-dimensional array to zero, simply specify the first value as zero, i.e., simply write

```
int marks[2][3] = {0};
```

If some values are missing in the initializer then it is automatically set to zero. For example, the statement given below will initialize the values in the first row but the elements of the second row will be initialized to zero.

```
int marks[2][3] ={ {50, 60, 70}};
```

Individual elements of a two-dimensional array can be initialized using the assignment operator as shown below.

```
marks[1][2] = 79;
marks[1][2] = marks[1][1] + 10;
```

In order to input the values from the keyboard, you must use the following code.

```
for(i=0;i<2;i++)
  for(j=0;j<2;j++)
    scanf("%d", &arr[i][j]);
```

Note

An un-initialized array contains unpredictable contents.

12.7.3 Accessing the Elements of Two-dimensional Arrays

The elements of a 2D array are stored in contiguous memory locations. While accessing the elements, remember that the last subscript varies most rapidly whereas the first varies least rapidly.

In case of one-dimensional arrays we used a single `for` loop to vary the index `i` in every pass, so that all the elements could be scanned. Since a two-dimensional array contains two subscripts, we will use two `for` loops to scan the elements. The first `for` loop will scan each row in the

2D array and the second `for` loop will scan individual columns for every row in the array.

Look at the programs given below which use two `for` loops to access the elements of a 2D array.

22. Write a program to print the elements of a 2D array.

```
#include <stdio.h>
int main()
{
  int arr[2][2] = {12, 34, 56,32};
  int i, j;
  for(i=0;i<2;i++)
  {
    printf("\n");
    for(j=0;j<2;j++)
      printf("%d\t", arr[i][j]);
  }
  return 0;
}
```

Output

```
12  34
56  32
```

23. Write a program to generate Pascal's triangle.

```
#include <stdio.h>
int main()
{
  int arr[7][7]={0};
  int row=2, col, i, j;
  arr[0][0] = arr[1][0] = arr[1][1] = 1;
  while(row < 7)
  {
    arr[row][0] = 1;
    for(col = 1;col <= row;col++)
    arr[row][col] = arr[row-1][col-1] +
      arr[row-1][col];
    row++;
  }
  for(i=0;i<7;i++)
  {
    printf("\n");
    for(j=0;j<=i;j++)
      printf("\t %d", arr[i][j]);
  }
  return 0;
}
```

Output

```
1
1  1
1  2  1
1  3  3  1
1  4  6  4  1
1  5  10  10  5  1
1  6  15  20  15  6  1
```

24. In a small company there are 5 salesmen. Each salesman is supposed to sell 3 products. Write a program using a two-dimensional array to print (i) the total sales by each salesman and (ii) total sales of each item.

```
#include <stdio.h>
int main()
{
  int sales[5][3], i, j, total_sales=0;
  //INPUT DATA
  printf("\n ENTER THE DATA");
  printf("\n *****************");
  for(i=0;i<5;i++)
  {
    printf("\n Enter the sales of 3 items
          sold by salesman %d: ", i);
    for(j=0;j<3;j++)
      scanf("%d", &sales[i][j]);
  }
  // PRINT TOTAL SALES BY EACH SALESMAN
  for(i=0;i<5;i++)
  {
    total_sales = 0;
    for(j=0;j<3;j++)
      total_sales += sales[i][j];
    printf("\n Total Sales By Salesman %d
          = %d",i, total_sales);
  }
  // TOTAL SALES OF EACH ITEM
  for(i=0;i<3;i++)  // for each item
  {
    total_sales=0;
    for(j=0;j<5;j++)  // for each salesman
      total_sales += sales[j][i];
    printf("\n Total sales of item %d
          = %d", i, total_sales);
  }
  return 0;
}
```

Output

```
ENTER THE DATA
*****************
Enter the sales of 3 items sold by saleman
0: 23 23 45
Enter the sales of 3 items sold by salesman
1: 34 45 63
Enter the sales of 3 items sold by salesman
2: 36 33 43
Enter the sales of 3 items sold by salesman
3: 33 52 35
Enter the sales of 3 items sold by salesman
4: 32 45 64
Total Sales By Salesman 0 = 91
Total Sales By Salesman 1 = 142
Total Sales By Salesman 2 = 112
```

```
Total Sales By Salesman 3 = 120
Total Sales By Salesman 4 = 141
Total sales of item 0 = 158
Total sales of item 1 = 198
Total sales of item 2 = 250
```

25. In a class there are 10 students. Each student is supposed to appear in 3 tests. Write a program using two-dimensional arrays to print

(i) the marks obtained by each student in different subjects.

(ii) total marks and average obtained by each student.

(iii) store the average of each student in a separate 1D array so that it can be used to calculate the class average.

```
#include <stdio.h>
int main()
{
  int marks[10][3], i, j;
  int total_marks[10]={0};
  float class_avg=0.0, total_avg = 0.0;
  float avg[10];

  //INPUT DATA
  printf("\n ENTER THE DATA");
  for(i=0;i<10;i++)
  {
  printf("\n Enter the marks of student %d
       in 3 subjects : ", i);
    for(j=0;j<3;j++)
      scanf("%d", &marks[i][j]);
  }

  // CALCULATE TOTAL MARKS OF EACH STUDENT
  for(i=0;i<10;i++)
  {
    for(j=0;j<3;j++)
      total_marks[i] += marks[i][j];
  }
  // CALCULATE AVERAGE OF EACH STUDENT
  for(i=0;i<10;i++)
  {
    for(j=0;j<3;j++)
      avg[i] = (float)total_marks[i]/3.0;
  }
  // CALCULATE CLASS AVERAGE
  for(i=0;i<10;i++)
    total_avg += avg[i];
  class_avg = (float)total_avg/10;
  // DISPLAY RESULTS
  printf("\n\n STUD NO.\t MARKS IN 3 SUBJECTS
  \t TOTAL MARKS \t AVERAGE");
  for(i=0;i<10;i++)
  { printf("\n %4d", i);
    for(j=0;j<3;j++)
      printf(" %d", marks[i][j]);
    printf("%4d \t%.2f", total_marks[i],
       avg[i]);
  }
  printf("\n\n CLASS AVERAGE = %.2f", class_
  avg);
  return 0;
}
```

Output

```
ENTER THE DATA
Enter the marks of student 0 in 3 subjects:
78 89 90
Enter the marks of student 1 in 3 subjects:
98 87 76
Enter the marks of student 2 in 3 subjects:
67 78 89
Enter the marks of student 3 in 3 subjects:
90 87 65
Enter the marks of student 4 in 3 subjects:
56 87 97
Enter the marks of student 5 in 3 subjects:
45 67 89
Enter the marks of student 6 in 3 subjects:
66 77 88
Enter the marks of student 7 in 3 subjects:
76 87 98
Enter the marks of student 8 in 3 subjects:
67 88 66
Enter the marks of student 9 in 3 subjects:
66 75 78
STUD NO    MARKS IN 3      TOTAL    AVERAGE
            SUBJECTS                  MARKS
   0       78  89  90       257      85.67
   1       98  87  76       261      87.00
   2       67  78  89       234      78.00
   3       90  87  65       242      80.67
   4       56  87  97       240      80.00
   5       45  67  89       201      67.00
   6       66  77  88       231      77.00
   7       76  87  98       261      87.00
   8       67  88  66       221      73.67
   9       66  75  78       210      73.00

CLASS AVERAGE = 78.90
```

26. Write a program to read a two-dimensional array `marks` which stores marks of 5 students in 3 subjects. Write a program to display the highest marks in each subject.

```
#include <stdio.h>
int main()
{
  int marks[5][3], i, j, max_marks;
  for(i=0;i<5;i++)
  {
    printf("\n Enter the marks obtained by
         student %d",i);
```

```
    for(j=0;j<3;j++)
    {
      printf("\n marks[%d][%d] = ", i, j);
      scanf("%d", &marks[i][j]);
    }
  }
  for(j=0;j<3;j++)
  {
    max_marks = marks[0][j];
    for(i=1;i<5;i++)
    {
      if(marks[i][j]>max_marks)
      max_marks = marks[i][j];
    }
  printf("\n The highest marks obtained
          in the subject %d= %d", j,
          max_marks);
  }
  return 0;
}
```

Output

```
Enter the marks obtained by student 0
marks[0][0] = 89
marks[0][1] = 76
marks[0][2] = 100
Enter the marks obtained by student 1
marks[1][0] = 99
marks[1][1] = 90
marks[1][2] = 89
Enter the marks obtained by student 2
marks[2][0] = 67
marks[2][1] = 76
marks[2][2] = 56
Enter the marks obtained by student 3
marks[3][0] = 88
marks[3][1] = 77
marks[3][2] = 66
Enter the marks obtained by student 4
marks[4][0] = 67
marks[4][1] = 78
marks[4][2] = 89
The highest marks obtained in the subject 0
= 99
The highest marks obtained in the subject 1
= 90
The highest marks obtained in the subject 2
= 100
```

12.8 OPERATIONS ON TWO-DIMENSIONAL ARRAYS

Two-dimensional arrays can be used to implement the mathematical concept of matrices. In mathematics, a matrix is a grid of numbers, arranged in rows and columns. Thus, using two-dimensional arrays, we can perform the following operations on an $m \times n$ matrix.

Transpose Transpose of a $m \times n$ matrix A is given as a $n \times m$ matrix B where,

$$B_{i,j} = A_{j,i}$$

Sum Two matrices that are compatible with each other can be added together thereby storing the result in the third matrix. Two matrices are said to be compatible when they have the same number of rows and columns. Elements of the matrices can be added by writing:

$$C_{i,j} = A_{i,j} + B_{i,j}$$

Difference Two matrices that are compatible with each other can be subtracted thereby storing the result in the third matrix. Two matrices are said to be compatible when they have the same number of rows and columns. Elements of the matrices can be subtracted by writing:

$$C_{i,j} = A_{i,j} - B_{i,j}$$

Product Two matrices can be multiplied with each other if the number of columns in the first matrix is equal to the number of rows in the second matrix. Therefore, $m \times n$ matrix A can be multiplied with a $p \times q$ matrix if $n = p$. Elements of the matrices can be multiplied by writing:

$$C_{i,j} = \Sigma A_{i,k}B_{k,j} \text{ for } k=1 \text{ to } k < n$$

27. Write a program to read and display a 3 × 3 matrix.

```
#include <stdio.h>
int main()
{
  int i, j, mat[3][3];

  printf("\n Enter the elements of the
  matrix ");
  printf("\n ************************");
  for(i=0;i<3;i++)
  {
    for(j=0;j<3;j++)
       scanf("%d",&mat[i][j]);
  }
  printf("\n The elements of the matrix are ");
  printf("\n ************************");
  for(i=0;i<3;i++)
  {
    printf("\n");
    for(j=0;j<3;j++)
    printf("\t %d", mat[i][j]);
  }
  return 0;
}
```

Output

```
Enter the elements of the matrix
************************
1 2 3 4 5 6 7 8 9
The elements of the matrix are
************************
1 2 3
4 5 6
7 8 9
```

28. Write a program to transpose a 3 × 3 matrix.

```
#include <stdio.h>
int main()
{
  int i, j, mat[3][3], transposed_mat[3][3];
  printf("\n Enter the elements of the
  matrix");
  printf("\n ************************");
  for(i=0;i<3;i++)
  {
    for(j=0;j<3;j++)
    {
      scanf("%d", &mat[i][j]);
    }
  }
  printf("\n The elements of the matrix are ");
  printf("\n ************************");
  for(i=0;i<3;i++)
  {
    printf("\n");
    for(j=0;j<3;j++)
    printf("\t %d", mat[i][j]);
  }
  for(i=0;i<3;i++)
  {
    for(j=0;j<3;j++)
       transposed_mat[i][j] = mat[j][i];
  }
  printf("\n The elements of the transposed
  matrix are ");
  printf("\n ************************");

  for(i=0;i<3;i++)
  {
    printf("\n");
    for(j=0;j<3;j++)
    printf("\t %d",transposed_mat[i][j]);
  }
  return 0;
}
```

Output

```
Enter the elements of the matrix
************************
1 2 3 4 5 6 7 8 9
The elements of the matrix are
************************
1 2 3
4 5 6
7 8 9
The elements of the transposed matrix are
************************
1 4 7
2 5 8
7 8 9
```

29. Write a program to input two $m \times n$ matrices and then calculate the sum of their corresponding elements and store it in a third $m \times n$ matrix.

```
#include <stdio.h>
int main()
{
  int i, j;
  int rows1, cols1, rows2, cols2, rows_sum,
  cols_sum;
  int mat1[5][5], mat2[5][5], sum[5][5];

  printf("\n Enter the number of rows in the
  first matrix: ");
  scanf("%d",&rows1);

  printf("\n Enter the number of columns in
  the first matrix: ");
  scanf("%d",&cols1);

  printf("\n Enter the number of rows in the
  second matrix: ");
  scanf("%d",&rows2);
  printf("\n Enter the number of columns in
  the second matrix:");
  scanf("%d",&cols2);

  if(rows1 != rows2 || cols1 != cols2)
  {
    printf("\n The number of rows and columns
        of both the matrices must be equal");
    exit();
  }
  rows_sum = rows1;
  cols_sum = cols1;

  printf("\n Enter the elements of the first
  matrix");
  printf("\n ************************");

  for(i=0;i<rows1;i++)
  {
    for(j=0;j<cols1;j++)
      scanf("%d",&mat1[i][j]);
  }
```

```
    printf("\n Enter the elements of the second
    matrix");
    printf("\n *************************");

    for(i=0;i<rows2;i++)
    {
      for(j=0;j<cols2;j++)
         scanf("%d",&mat2[i][j]);
    }
    for(i=0;i<rows_sum;i++)
    {
      for(j=0;j<cols_sum;j++)
        sum[i][j] = mat1[i][j] + mat2[i][j];
    }
    printf("\n The elements of the resultant
    matrix are");
    printf("\n *************************");

    for(i=0;i<rows_sum;i++)
    {
      printf("\n");
      for(j=0;j<cols_sum;j++)
         printf("\t %d", sum[i][j]);
    }
    return 0;
  }
```

Output

```
Enter the number of rows in the first
matrix: 2
Enter the number of columns in the first
matrix: 2
Enter the number of rows in the second
matrix: 2
Enter the number of columns in the second
matrix: 2
Enter the elements of the first matrix
*************************
1 2 3 4
Enter the elements of the second matrix
*************************
5 6 7 8
The elements of the resultant matrix are
*************************
6  8
10 12
```

30. Write a program to multiply two $m \times n$ matrices.

```
#include <stdio.h>
int main()
{
  int i, j, k;
  int rows1, cols1, rows2, cols2, res_rows,
  res_cols;
  int mat1[5][5], mat2[5][5], res[5][5];
  printf("\n Enter the number of rows in the
  first matrix: ");
  scanf("%d",&rows1);

  printf("\n Enter the number of columns in
  the first matrix: ");
  scanf("%d",&cols1);

  printf("\n Enter the number of rows in the
  second matrix: ");
  scanf("%d",&rows2);

  printf("\n Enter the number of columns in
  the second matrix:");
  scanf("%d",&cols2);

  if(cols1 != rows2)
  {
    printf("\n The number of columns in
        the first matrix must be equal
        to the number of rows in the
        second matrix");
    exit();
  }
  res_rows = rows1;
  res_cols = cols2;

  printf("\n Enter the elements of the first
  matrix");
  printf("\n *************************");

  for(i=0;i<rows1;i++)
  {
    for(j=0;j<cols1;j++)
      scanf("%d",&mat1[i][j]);
  }
  printf("\n Enter the elements of the second
  matrix");
  printf("\n *************************");
  for(i = 0; i < rows2;i++)
  {
    for(j = 0; j < cols2;j++)
      scanf("%d",&mat2[i][j]);
  }
  for(i = 0; i < res_rows;i++)
  {
    j=0;
    for(j= 0; j < res_cols;j++)
    {

      res[i][j]=0;
      for(k = 0; k < res_cols; k++)
         res[i][j] += mat1[i][k] * mat2[k]
                 [j];
    }
  }
```

```
    printf("\n The elements of the product
    matrix are");
    printf("\n *************************");

    for(i=0;i<res_rows;i++)
    {
      printf("\n");
      for(j = 0; j < res_cols;j++)
      printf("\t %d",res[i][j]);
    }
    return 0;
}
```

Output

```
Enter the number of rows in the first
  matrix: 2
Enter the number of columns in the first
matrix: 2
Enter the number of rows in the second
matrix: 2
Enter the number of columns in the second
matrix: 2
Enter the elements of the first matrix
*************************
1 2 3 4
Enter the elements of the second matrix
*************************
5 6 7 8
The elements of the product matrix are
*************************
19    22
43    50
```

12.9 PASSING TWO-DIMENSIONAL ARRAYS TO FUNCTIONS

There are three ways of passing two-dimensional arrays to functions. First, we can pass individual elements of the array. This is exactly same as passing elements of a one-dimensional array. Second, we can pass a single row of the two-dimensional array. This is equivalent to passing the entire one-dimensional array to a function. This has already been discussed in the previous section. Third, we can pass the entire two-dimensional array to the function. Refer Figure 12.30 which shows the three ways of using two-dimensional arrays for inter-function communication.

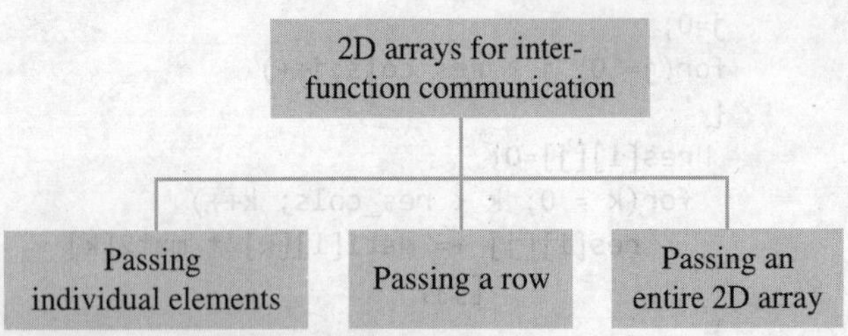

Figure 12.30 Two-dimensional arrays for inter-function communication

12.9.1 Passing a Row

A row of a two-dimensional array can be passed by indexing the array name with the row number. When we send a single row of a two-dimensional array, then the called function receives a one-dimensional array. Figure 12.31 illustrates how a single row of a two-dimensional array is passed to the called function.

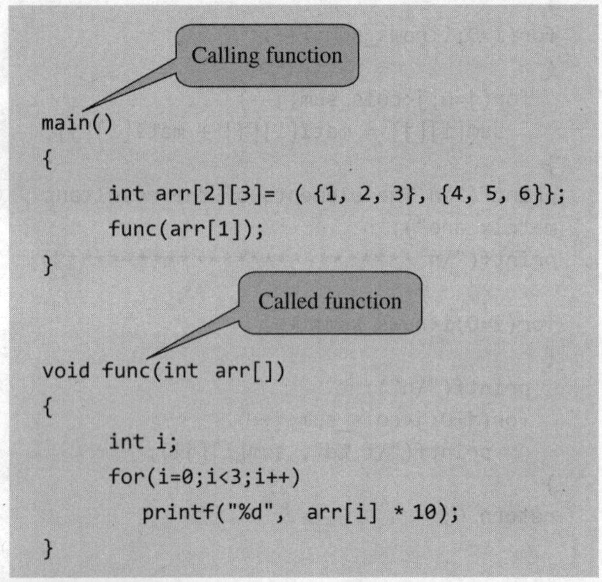

Figure 12.31 Passing a single row of a 2D array

12.9.2 Passing an Entire 2D Array

To pass a two-dimensional array to a function, we use the array name as the actual parameter. However, the parameter in the called function must indicate that the array has two dimensions.

31. Write a menu-driven program to read and display an $m \times n$ matrix. Also find the sum, transpose, and product of two $m \times n$ matrices.

> **Programming Tip:**
> A compiler error will be generated if you omit the array size in the parameter declaration for any array dimension other than the first.

```
#include <stdio.h>
void read_matrix(int mat[2][2], int, int);
void sum_matrix(int mat1[2]
[2], int mat2[2][2], int,
int);
void mul_matrix(int mat1[2]
[2], int mat2[2][2], int,
int);
void transpose_matrix(int
mat2[2][2], int, int);
void display_matrix(int
mat[2][2], int r, int c);
int main()
{
  int option, row, col;
  int mat1[2][2], mat2[2][2];
```

```
do
{

  printf("\n ******* MAIN MENU ********");
  printf("\n 1. Read the two matrices");
  printf("\n 2. Add the matrices");
  printf("\n 3. Multiply the matrices");
  printf("\n 4. Transpose the matrix");
  printf("\n 5. EXIT");

  printf("\n\n Enter your option: ");
  scanf("%d", &option);
  switch(option)
  {
   case 1:
        printf("\n Enter the number of
            rows and columns of
            the matrix: ");
        scanf("%d %d", &row, &col);
     printf("\n Enter the first
            matrix: ");
        read_matrix(mat1, row, col);
        printf("\n Enter the second
            matrix: ");
        read_matrix(mat2, row, col);
        break;
   case 2:
        sum_matrix(mat1, mat2, row,
           col);
        break;
   case 3:
        if(col == row)
        mul_matrix(mat1, mat2, row,
           col);
        else
        printf("\n To multiply two
           matrices, number of
           columns in the first
           matrix must be equal to
           number of rows in the
           second matrix");
        break;
   case 4:
        transpose_matrix(mat1, row, col);
        break;
  }
 }
 while(option != 5);
 return 0;
}
void read_matrix(int mat[2][2], int r, int c)
{
 int i, j;
 for(i = 0;i < r;i++)
 { printf("\n");
  for(j = 0;j < c;j++)
  {
   printf("\t mat[%d][%d] = ",i,j);
   scanf("%d", &mat[i][j]);
  }
 }
}
void sum_matrix(int mat1[2][2], int mat2[2]
 [2], int r, int c)
{
 int i, j, sum[2][2];
 for(i=0;i<r;i++)
 {
  for(j=0;j<c;j++)
  sum[i][j] = mat1[i][j] + mat2[i][j];
 }
 display_matrix(sum, r, c);
}
void mul_matrix(int mat1[2][2], int mat2[2]
  [2], int r, int c)
{
 int i, j, k, prod[2][2];
 for(i=0;i<r;i++)
 {
  for(j=0;j<c;j++)
  {
  prod[i][j] = 0;
  for(k=0;k<c;k++)
  prod[i][j] += mat1[i][k] * mat2[k][j];
  }
 }
 display_matrix(prod, r, c);
}
void transpose_matrix(int mat[2][2], int r,
 int c)
{
 int i, j, tp_mat[2][2];
 for(i=0;i<r;i++)
 {
  for(j=0;j<c;j++)
    tp_mat[j][i] = mat[i][j];
 }
 display_matrix(tp_mat, r, c);
}

void display_matrix(int mat[2][2], int r,
 int c)
{
 int i, j;
 for(i=0;i<r;i++)
 {
  printf("\n");
  for(j=0;j<c;j++)
    printf("\t mat[%d][%d] = %d", i, j,
        mat[i][j]);
 }
}
```

Output

```
******* MAIN MENU ********
1. Read the two matrices
2. Add the matrices
3. Multiply the matrices
4. Transpose the matrix
5. EXIT
Enter your option: 1
Enter the number of rows and columns of the
matrix: 2 2
Enter the first matrix:
mat[0][0] = 1  mat[0][1] = 2
mat[1][0] = 3  mat[1][1] = 4
Enter the second matrix :
mat[0][0] = 2  mat[0][1] = 3
mat[1][0] = 4  mat[1][1] = 5
******* MAIN MENU ********
1. Read the two matrices
2. Add the matrices
3. Multiply the matrices
4. Transpose the matrix
5. EXIT
Enter your option: 2
mat[0][0] = 3  mat[0][1] = 5
mat[1][0] = 7  mat[1][1] = 9
.......
```

32. Write a program to fill a square matrix with value zero on the diagonals, 1 on the upper right triangle, and –1 on the lower left triangle.

```
#include <stdio.h>
void read_matrix(int mat[5][5], int);
void display_matrix(int mat[5][5], int);
int main()
{
  int row;
  int mat[5][5];
  printf("\n Enter the number of rows and
  columns of the matrix ");
  scanf("%d", &row);
  read_matrix(mat, row);
  display_matrix(mat, row);
  return 0;
}

void read_matrix(int mat[5][5], int r)
{
  int i, j;
  for(i = 0;i < r;i++)
  {
    for(j = 0;j < r;j++)
    {
      if(i==j)
        mat[i][j] = 0;
      else if(i>j)
        mat[i][j] = -1;
      else
        mat[i][j] = 1;
    }
  }
}
void display_matrix(int mat[5][5], int r)
{
  int i, j;
  for(i=0;i<r;i++)
  {
    printf("\n");
    for(j=0;j<r;j++)
      printf("\t %d", mat[i][j]);
  }
}
```

Output

```
Enter the number of rows and columns of the
matrix: 2
 0    1
-1    0
```

33. Write a program to check whether a matrix is symmetric or not.

Hint: A matrix is symmetric if it is equal to its transpose.

```
#include <stdio.h>
int isSymmetric(int a[3][3], int n)
{
  int i, j, flag;
  for(i = 0; i < n; i++)
  {
    for(j = 0; j < n; j++)
    {
      if(i != j && a[i][j] == a[j][i])
        flag = 1;
    }
  }
  if(flag == 1)
    return 1;
  else return 0;
}

void main()
{
  int arr[3][3], i, j, n, flag;
  printf("\n Enter the number of rows and
    columns: ");
  scanf("%d", &n);
  printf("\n Enter the elements of the array: ");
  for(i = 0; i < n; i++)
  {
    for(j = 0; j < n; j++)
    {  printf("arr[%d][%d] = ", i, j);
       scanf("%d", & arr[i][j]);
    }
  }
  flag = isSymmetric(arr, n);
```

```
    if(flag == 1)
        printf("\n The array is symmetric");
    else
        printf("\n The array is not symmetric");
}
```

12.10 MULTIDIMENSIONAL ARRAYS

A multidimensional array in simple terms is an array of arrays. Like we have one index in a one-dimensional array, two indices in a two-dimensional array, in the same way we have n indices in an n-dimensional array or multidimensional array. Conversely, an n-dimensional array is specified using n indices. An n-dimensional $m_1 \times m_2 \times m_3 \times \ldots m_n$ array is a collection $m_1 * m_2 * m_3 * \ldots * m_n$ elements. In a multidimensional array, a particular element is specified by using n subscripts as $A[I_1][I_2][I_3]\ldots[I_n]$, where,

$I_1 <= M_1 \quad I_2 <= M_2 \quad I_3 <= M_3 \quad \ldots \quad I_n <= M_n$

A multidimensional array can contain as many indices as needed and the requirement of the memory increases with the number of indices used. However, practically speaking we will hardly use more than three indices in any program. Figure 12.32 shows a three-dimensional array. The array has three pages, four rows, and two columns.

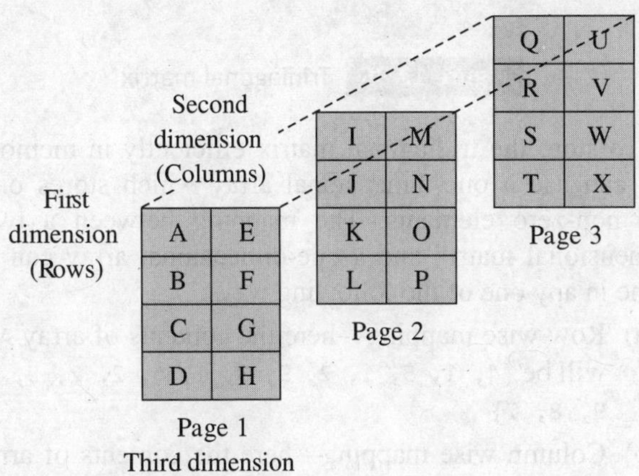

Figure 12.32 Three-dimensional array

A multidimensional array is declared and initialized similar to one- and two-dimensional arrays.

Example 12.8

Consider a three-dimensional array defined as int A[2][2][3]. Calculate the number of elements in the array. Also show the memory representation of the array in row major order and column major order.

Note

A three-dimensional array consists of pages. Each page in turn contains m rows and n columns.

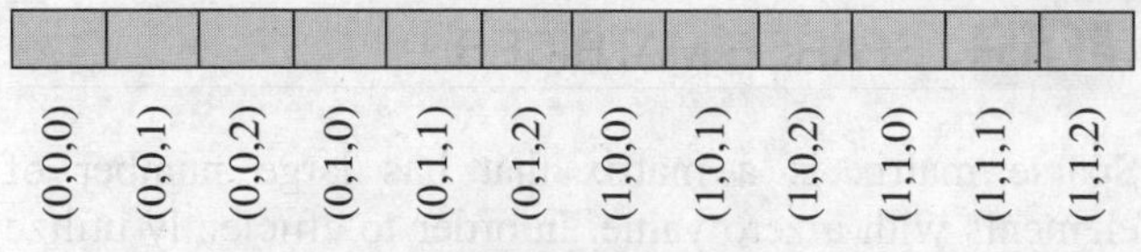

(a) Row major order

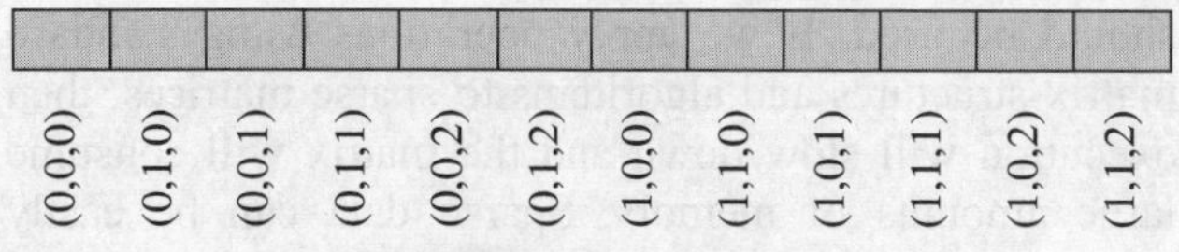

(b) Column major order

The three dimensional array will contain 2 × 2 × 3 = 12 elements.

34. Write a program to read and display a 2 × 2 × 2 array.

```
#include <stdio.h>
int main()
{
    int array[2][2][2], i, j, k;
    printf("\n Enter the elements of the
            matrix");
    for(i = 0;i < 2;i++)
    {
        for(j = 0;j < 2;j++)
        {
            for(k = 0;k < 2;k++)
            {
                scanf("%d", &array[i][j][k]);
            }
        }
    }
    printf("\n The matrix is: ");
    for(i = 0;i < 2;i++)
    {
        printf("\n\n");
        for(j = 0;j < 2;j++)
        {
            printf("\n");
            for(k = 0;k < 2;k++)
            printf("\tarr[%d][%d]
            [%d] = %d", i, j, k, array[i][j][k]);
        }
    }
    return 0;
}
```

Output

```
Enter the elements of the matrix
1 2 3 4 5 6 7 8
The matrix is:
arr[0][0][0] = 1        arr[0][0][1] = 2
arr[0][1][0] = 3        arr[0][1][1] = 4
arr[1][0][0] = 5        arr[1][0][1] = 6
arr[1][1][0] = 7        arr[1][1][1] = 8
```

12.11 SPARSE MATRICES

Sparse matrix is a matrix that has large number of elements with a zero value. In order to efficiently utilize the memory, specialized algorithms and data structures that take advantage of the sparse structure of the matrix should be used. If we apply operations using standard matrix structures and algorithms to sparse matrices, then execution will slow down and the matrix will consume large amounts of memory. Sparse data can be easily compressed which in turn can significantly reduce memory usage.

There are two types of sparse matrices. In the first type of sparse matrix, all elements above the main diagonal have a zero value. This type of sparse matrix is also called a *lower triangular matrix* because if you see it pictorially, all the elements with a non-zero value appear below the diagonal. In a lower triangular matrix, $A_{i,j} = 0$ where $i < j$. An $n \times n$ lower triangular matrix A has one non zero element in the first row, two non-zero elements, in the second row and likewise, n non-zero elements in the nth row. Figure 12.33 shows a lower triangular matrix.

1				
5	3			
2	7	-1		
3	1	4	2	
-9	2	-8	1	7

Figure 12.33 Lower triangular matrix

To store the lower triangular matrix efficiently in memory, we can use a one-dimensional array which stores only the non-zero elements. The mapping between a two-dimensional-matrix and a one-dimensional array can be done in any one of the following ways:

(a) Row-wise mapping—here the contents of array `A[]` will be `{1, 5, 3, 2, 7, -1, 3, 1, 4, 2, -9, 2, -8, 1, 7}`

(b) Column-wise mapping—here the contents of array `A[]` will be `{1, 5, 2, 3, -9, 3, 7, 1, 2, -1, 4, -8, 2, 1, 7}`

Like a lower triangular matrix, we also have an *upper triangular matrix* in which $A_{i,j} = 0$ where `i>j`. An $n \times n$ upper triangular matrix A has n non-zero elements in the first row, `n-1` non-zero elements in the second row and likewise, `1` non-zero element in the `nth` row. Figure 12.34 shows an upper triangular matrix.

In the second variant of a sparse matrix, elements with a non-zero value can appear only on the diagonal or immediately above or below the diagonal. This type of matrix is also called a *tridiagonal matrix*. Hence in a tridiagonal matrix, $A_{i,j} = 0$ where `|i - j|> 1`.

1	2	3	4	5
	3	6	7	8
		-1	9	1
			9	3
				7

Figure 12.34 Upper triangular matrix

In a tridiagonal matrix, if elements are present on

(a) the main diagonal, it contains non-zero elements for `i=j`. In all, there will be `n` elements.

(b) below the main diagonal, it contains non-zero elements for `i=j+1`. In all, there will be `n-1` elements.

(c) above the main diagonal, it contains non-zero elements for `i=j-1`. In all, there will be `n-1` elements.

Figure 12.35 shows a tridiagonal matrix.

4	1				
5	1	2			
	9	3	1		
		4	2	2	
			5	1	9
				8	7

Figure 12.35 Tridiagonal matrix

To store the tridiagonal matrix efficiently in memory, we can use a one-dimensional array which stores only the non-zero elements. The mapping between a two-dimensional matrix and a one-dimensional array can be done in any one of the following ways:

(a) Row wise mapping—here the contents of array `A[]` will be `{4, 1, 5, 1, 2, 9, 3, 1, 4, 2, 2, 5, 1, 9, 8, 7}`

(b) Column wise mapping—here the contents of array `A[]` will be `{4, 5, 1, 1, 9, 2, 3, 4, 1, 2, 5, 2, 1, 8, 9, 7}`

(c) Diagonal wise mapping—here the contents of array `A[]` will be `{5, 9, 4, 5, 8, 4, 1, 3, 2, 1, 7, 1, 2, 1, 2, 9}`

12.11.1 Array Representation of Sparse Matrices

Let us see how we can represent a sparse matrix. Consider the sparse matrix given below.

$$\begin{bmatrix} 0 & 2 & 0 \\ 0 & 0 & 4 \\ 0 & 0 & 0 \end{bmatrix}$$

Out of 9 elements, the matrix has only two non-zero elements. This sparse matrix can be represented using the matrix given below.

$$\begin{bmatrix} 3 & 3 & 2 \\ 0 & 1 & 2 \\ 1 & 2 & 4 \end{bmatrix}$$

- The first row gives the number of rows (3), number of columns (3), and number of non-zero elements (2) in the sparse matrix.
- The second row specifies the location and value of first non-zero element. The first non-zero value 2 is at (0, 1) location.
- Similarly, third row specifies the location and value of the next non-zero element, i.e. value 4 at (1, 2) location.

This means that in the array representation of the sparse matrix, number of rows will be one more than the number of non-zero values.

35. Write a program that shows the array representation of a sparse matrix.

```
#include <stdio.h>

void sparse_mat(int mat[3][3], int, int, int);
void main()
{  int i, j, rows, cols, num_values = 0;
  int mat[3][3];
  printf("\n Enter the number of rows : ");
  scanf("%d",&rows);
  printf("\n Enter the number of columns:");
  scanf("%d",&cols);
  printf("\n Enter the elements of array:");
  for(i=0;i<rows;i++)
  { for(j=0;j<cols;j++)
    {
      scanf("%d", &mat[i][j]);
    }
  }
  printf("\n The sparse matrix is : \n");
  for(i=0;i<rows;i++)
  {
      printf("\n");
    for(j=0;j<cols;j++)
      printf("%d", mat[i][j]);

  }
  for(i=0;i<rows;i++)
  {  for(j=0;j<cols;j++)
    {  if(mat[i][j]!=0)
         num_values++;
    }
  }
  sparse_mat(mat, num_values, rows, cols);
}
void sparse_mat(int mat[3][3], int num_values,
   int rows, int cols)
{ int new_mat[5][3], i, j, temp_index =1;
  new_mat[0][0] = rows;
  new_mat[0][1] = cols;
  new_mat[0][2] = num_values;
  for(i=1;i<=rows;i++)
  { for(j=1;j<=cols;j++)
    {  if(mat[i-1][j-1] != 0)
      {  new_mat[temp_index][0] = i-1;
         new_mat[temp_index][1] = j-1;
         new_mat[temp_index][2] = mat[i-1]
    [j-1];
    temp_index++;
      }
    }
  }
  printf("\n\n The new matrix is : \n");
  for(i=0;i<=num_values;i++)
  { printf("\n");
    for(j=0;j<3;j++)
      printf(" %d", new_mat[i][j]);
  }
}
```

Output

```
Enter the number of rows : 2
Enter the number of columns : 2
Enter the elements of array : 1 0 0 0
The sparse matrix is :
1 0
0 0
The new matrix is :
2 2 1
0 0 1
```

Note

For better performance, memory for the new matrix must be allocated using dynamic memory allocation which will be discussed later in this book. We may also represent the sparse matrix using a linked list.

12.12 APPLICATIONS OF ARRAYS

- Arrays are widely used to implement mathematical vectors, matrices, and other kinds of rectangular tables.
- Many databases include one-dimensional arrays whose elements are records.
- Arrays are also used to implement other data structures such as strings, stacks, queues, heaps, and hash tables. We will read about few of these data structures in the subsequent chapters.
- Arrays can be used for sorting elements in ascending or descending order.

POINTS TO REMEMBER

- An array is a collection of similar data elements of the same data type.
- The elements of the array are stored in consecutive memory locations and are referenced by an index (also known as the subscript). Subscript is an ordinal number which is used to identify an element of the array.
- Declaring an array means specifying three things: data type, name, and its size.
- The name of the array is a symbolic reference to the address of the first byte of the array. Therefore, whenever we use the array name, we are actually referring to the first byte of that array. The index specifies an offset from the beginning of the array to the element being referenced.
- A two-dimensional array is specified using two subscripts where first subscript denotes row and the second denotes column. C considers the two-dimensional array as an array of one-dimensional arrays.
- A multidimensional array is an array of arrays. Like we have one index in a one-dimensional array, two indices in a two-dimensional array, in the same way we have n indices in an n-dimensional or multidimensional array. Conversely, an n-dimensional array is specified using n indices.
- Sparse matrix is a matrix that has large number of elements with a zero value. There are two types of sparse matrices.
- In the first type of sparse matrix, all elements above the main diagonal have a zero value. This type of sparse matrix is called a lower triangular matrix.
- In the second variant of a sparse matrix, elements with a non-zero value can appear only on the diagonal or immediately above or below the diagonal. This type of sparse matrix is called a tridiagonal matrix.

GLOSSARY

Array Collection of similar data elements

Array index Location of an item in an array

Binary search Searching method in which a sorted array is searched by repeatedly dividing the search interval in half. Begin with an interval covering the whole array. If the value of the search key is less than the item in the middle of the interval, narrow the interval to the lower half. Otherwise narrow it to the upper half. Repeatedly check until the value is found or the interval is empty

k-dimensional array An array with exactly *k* orthogonal axes or *k* dimensions

Linear search Searching method in which an array is searched by checking elements one at a time

Lower triangular matrix A matrix A_{ij} forms a lower triangular matrix when $A_{ij} = 0$ for $i < j$

Matrix A two-dimensional array in which the first index is the row and the second index is the column

One-dimensional array An array with one dimension or one subscript/index

Subscript An ordinal number, which is used to identify an element of the array

Sparse matrix A matrix that has relatively few non-zero elements

Three-dimensional array An array with three dimensions or three subscripts/indices

Two-dimensional array An array with two dimensions or two subscripts/indices

Upper triangular matrix A matrix A_{ij} forms an upper triangular matrix when $A_{ij} = 0$ for $i > j$

EXERCISES

Fill in the Blanks

1. An array is a ________.
2. Every element in an array is accessed using a ________.
3. An expression that evaluates to an ________ value may be used as an index.
4. The elements of an array are stored in ________ memory locations.
5. An n-dimensional array contains ________ subscripts.
6. Name of the array acts as a ________.
7. Declaring an array means specifying ________, ________, and ________.
8. The subscript or the index represents the offset from the beginning of the array to ________.
9. ________ is the address of the first element in the array.
10. Length of the array is given by the number of ________.

11. __________ means accessing each element of the array for a specific purpose.
12. Performance of the linear search algorithm can be improved by using a __________.
13. A multi-dimensional array in simple terms is an __________.
14. arr[3] = 10; initializes the __________ element of the array with value 10.
15. The __________ search locates the value by starting at the beginning of the array and moving towards its end.

Multiple Choice Questions

1. If an array is declared as arr[] = {1,3,5,7,9}; then what is the value of sizeof(arr[3])?
   (a) 1 (b) 2
   (c) 3 (d) 8
2. If an array is declared as arr[] = {1,3,5,7,9}; then what is the value of arr[3]?
   (a) 1 (b) 7
   (c) 9 (d) 5
3. If an array is declared as double arr[50], how many bytes will be allocated to it?
   (a) 50 (b) 100
   (c) 200 (d) 400
4. If an array is declared as int arr[50], how many elements can it hold?
   (a) 49 (b) 50
   (c) 51 (d) 0
5. If an array is declared as int arr[5][5], how many elements can it store?
   (a) 5 (b) 25
   (c) 10 (d) 0
6. In linear search, when VAL is equal to the first element of the array, which case is it?
   (a) worst case (b) average case
   (c) best case (d) amortized case
7. Given an integer array, arr[], the ith element can be accessed by writing
   (a) (arr+i) (b) *(i + arr)
   (c) arr[i] (d) all of these

State True or False

1. An array is used to refer to multiple memory locations having the same name.
2. An array need not be declared before being used.
3. An array contains elements of the same data type.
4. A loop is used to access all the elements of the array.
5. All the elements of an array are automatically initialized to zero when the array is declared.
6. An array stores all its data elements in non-consecutive memory locations.
7. To copy an array, you must copy the value of every element of the first array into the element of the second array.
8. Lower bound is the index of the last element of the array.
9. Merged array contains contents of the first array followed by the contents of the second array.
10. Binary search is also called sequential search.
11. Linear search is performed on a sorted array.
12. Binary search is the best search algorithm for all types of arrays.
13. It is possible to pass an entire array as a function argument.
14. arr[i] is equivalent to writing *(arr+i).
15. Array name is equivalent to the address of its last element.
16. When an array is passed to a function, C passes the value for each element.
17. When an array is passed to a function, it is always passed by call-by-reference method.
18. Linear search can be used to search a value in any array.
19. Linear search is recommended for small arrays.
20. A two-dimensional array is nothing but an array of one-dimensional arrays.
21. A two-dimensional array contains data of two different types.
22. A char type variable can be used as a subscript in an array.
23. By default, the first subscript of the array is zero.
24. A long int value can be used as an array subscript.
25. The maximum number of dimensions that an array can have is 4.

Review Questions

1. Why are arrays needed?
2. What does array name signify?
3. How is an array represented in memory?
4. How is a two-dimensional array represented in memory?
5. How can one-dimensional and two-dimensional arrays be used for inter-function communication?
6. How are multidimensional arrays useful?
7. What happens when an array is initialized with
   (a) fewer initializers as compared to its size?
   (b) more initializers as compared to its size?
8. Explain sparse matrix.
9. Why does storing of sparse matrices need extra consideration? How are sparse matrices stored efficiently in the computer's memory?
10. For an array declared as int arr[50], calculate the address of arr[35], if Base(arr) = 1000 and w=2.
11. Consider a 10 × 5 two-dimensional array `Marks` which has base address = 2000 and the number of words per memory location of the array = 2. Now compute the address of the element- `Marks[8, 5]` assuming that the elements are stored in row major order.
12. Given an array, int arr[] = (9, 18, 27, 36, 45, 54, 63, 72, 81, 90, 99). Trace the steps of binary search algorithm to find value 90 and 17 in the array.

13. Which technique of searching an element in the array do you prefer to use and in which situation?
14. Consider a 10 × 10 two-dimensional array which has base address = 1000 and the number of memory locations per element of the array = 2. Now compute the address of the element arr[8][5] assuming that the elements are stored in row major order. Then calculate the same assuming the elements are stored in column major order.

Programming Exercises

1. Write a program which deletes all duplicate elements in an array.
2. Write a program that tests the equality of two one-dimensional arrays.
3. Write a program that reads an array of 100 integers. Display all pairs of elements whose sum is 50.
4. Write a program to input an array of 10 numbers and swap the value of the largest and smallest number.
5. Write a program to interchange second element with the second last element.
6. Write a program that calculates the sum of squares of the elements.
7. Write a program to calculate the number of duplicate entries in the array.
8. Write a program to arrange the values of an array in such a way that even numbers precede the odd numbers.
9. Given a sorted array of integers, write a program to calculate the sum, mean, variance, and standard deviation of the numbers in the array.
10. Write a program to compute the sum and mean of the elements of a two-dimensional array.
11. Write a program that computes the sum of elements that are stored on the main diagonal of a matrix using pointers.
12. Write a program to count the total number of non-zero elements in a two-dimensional array.
13. Write a program to read and display an array of 10 floating point numbers using functions.
14. Write a program to read an array of 10 floating point numbers. Display the mean of these numbers till two decimal places.
15. Write a program to read an array of 10 floating point numbers. Display the smallest number and its position in the array.
16. Write a program to input the elements of a two-dimensional array. Then from this array make two arrays: one that stores all odd elements of the two-dimensional array and the other stores all even elements of the array.
17. Write a program to merge two integer arrays. Also display the merged array in reverse order.
18. Write a program to transpose a 3 × 3 × 3 matrix.
19. Write a program to multiply two m × n matrices.
20. Write a menu driven program to add, subtract, and transpose two matrices.
21. Write a program that reads a matrix and displays the sum of its diagonal elements.
22. Write a program that reads a matrix and displays the sum of the elements above the main diagonal.
    Hint: Calculate sum of elements of array A, where for an element A_{ij}, $i < j$
23. Write a program that reads a matrix and displays the sum of the elements below the main diagonal.
    Hint: Calculate sum of elementsof array A ,where for an element A_{ij}, $i > j$
24. Write a program that reads a square matrix of size n × n. Write a function `int is_Upper_Triangular(int a[][], int n)` that returns 1 if the matrix is upper triangular.
    Hint: Array A is upper triangular if A_{ij}= 0 for $i > j$
25. Write a program that reads a square matrix of size n × n. Write a function `int is_Lower_Triangular(int a[][], int n)` that returns 1 if the matrix is lower triangular.
    Hint: Array A is lower triangular if A_{ij}= 0 for $i < j$
26. Write a program that reads a square matrix of size n × n. Write a function `int isSymmetric(int a[][], int n)` that returns 1 if the matrix is upper triangular.
    Hint: Array A is symmetric if A_{ij}= A_{ji} for all values of i and j
27. Write a program to calculate XA + YB where A and B are matrices and X = 2, and Y = 3.
28. Write a program to read an array of 10 floating point numbers. Display the position of the second largest number.
29. Write a program to enter five single digit numbers in an array. Form a number using the array elements.
30. Write a program to find whether number 3 is present in the array arr[]= {1,2,3,4,5,6,7,8}.
31. Write a program to read a sorted floating point array. Update the array to insert a new number.
32. Write a program to read a floating point array. Update the array to delete the number from the specified location.
33. Modify the linear search program so that it operates on a sorted array.
34. Write a program to build an array of 100 random numbers in the range 1 to 100. Perform the following operations on the array.
    (a) Count the number of elements that are completely divisible by 3.
    (b) Display the elements of the array by displaying a maximum of ten elements in one line.
    (c) Display only the even elements of the array by displaying a maximum of ten elements in one line.
    (d) Count the number of odd elements.
    (e) Find the smallest element in the array.
    (f) Find the position of the largest value in the array.
35. Write a program to read two floating point arrays. Merge these arrays and display the resultant array.
36. Write a program to read two sorted floating point arrays. Merge these arrays and display the resultant array.
37. Write a program to read and display a p*q*r array.
38. Write a program to initialize all diagonal elements of a two-dimensional array to zero.

39. Consider an array MARKS[20][5] which stores the marks obtained by 20 students in 5 subjects. Now write a program to
    (a) find the average marks obtained in each subject
    (b) find the average marks obtained by every student
    (c) find the number of students who have scored below 50 in their average
    (d) display the scores obtained by every student

Find the output of the following codes.

1.
```
#include <stdio.h>
main()
{
  int i, arr[10];
  for(i=0;i<10;i++)
    arr[i*2] = 1;
  for(i=0;i<10;i++)
    arr[i*2+1] = -1;
  for(i=0;i<10;i++)
    printf("\t %d", arr[i]);
  return 0;
}
```

2.
```
#include <stdio.h>
main()
{
  int arr[]={0,1,2,0,1,2,0,1,2};
  printf("\\n %d",arr[3]);
  printf("\\n %d",arr[arr[3]]);
  printf("\\n %d",arr[arr[3]+arr[1]]);
  printf("\\n %d", arr[arr[arr[arr[1]]]]);
  return 0;
}
```

3.
```
#include <stdio.h>
main()
{
  int arr1[]={0,1,2,0,1,2,0,1,2,0};
  int i, arr2[10];
  for(i=0;i<10;i++)
    arr2[i] = arr1[9-i];
  for(i=0;i<10;i++)
    printf("\t %d", arr2[i]);
  return 0;
}
```

Identify errors, if any, in the following declaration statements.

(a) int marks(10);
(b) int marks[10, 5];
(c) int marks[10],[5];
(d) int marks[10];
(e) int marks[ ];
(f) int marks[10] [5];
(g) int marks[9+1][6-1];

Identify errors, if any, in the following initialization statements.

(a) int marks[ ] = {0,0,0,0};
(b) int marks[2][3] = {10,20,30,40};
(c) int marks[2,3] = {10, 20,30},{40,50,60}};
(d) int marks[10] = {0};

CASE STUDY 2: Chapter 12

INTRODUCTION TO SORTING

The term *sorting* means arranging the elements of the array in some relevant order which may be either ascending or descending, i.e., if `A` is an array, then the elements of `A` are arranged in sorted order (ascending order) in such a way that, `A[0] < A[1] < A[2] < ... < A[N-1]`.

For example, if we have an array that is declared and initialized as,

```
int A[] = {21, 34, 11, 9, 1, 0, 22};
```

Then the sorted array (ascending order) can be given as, `A[] = {0, 1, 9, 11, 21, 22, 34}`.

A *sorting algorithm* is defined as an algorithm that puts elements of a list in a certain order (that can be either numerical, lexicographical, or any user-defined order). Efficient sorting algorithms are widely used to optimize the use of other algorithms like search and merge algorithms which require sorted lists to work correctly. There are two types of sorting:

- *Internal sorting* which deals with sorting the data stored in computer's memory.
- *External sorting* which deals with sorting the data stored in files. External sorting is applied when there is voluminous data that cannot be stored in computer's memory.

In this section we will discuss only about internal sorting.

BUBBLE SORT

Bubble sort is a very simple method that sorts the array elements by repeatedly moving the largest element to the highest index position of the array (in case of arranging elements in ascending order). In bubble sorting, consecutive adjacent pairs of elements in the array are compared with each other. If the element at the lower index is greater than the element at the higher index, the two elements are interchanged so that the smaller element is placed before the bigger one. This process is continued till the list of unsorted elements gets exhausted.

This procedure of sorting is called bubble sorting because the smaller elements 'bubble' to the top of the list. At the end of the first pass, the largest element in the list will be placed at the end of the list. Bubble sort is also referred to as sinking sort.

Note

If the elements are to be sorted in descending order, then with each pass the smallest element is moved to the highest index of the array.

Bubble Sort Example

To discuss bubble sort, let us consider an array that has the following elements:

```
A[] = {30, 52, 29, 87, 63, 27, 19, 54}
```

Pass 1:

(a) Compare 30 and 52. Since 30 < 52, then no swapping is done.

(b) Compare 52 and 29. Since 52 > 29, swapping is done. 30, **29, 52**, 87, 63, 27, 19, 54

(c) Compare 52 and 87. Since 52 < 87, no swapping is done.

(d) Compare, 87 and 63. Since, 87 > 63, swapping is done. 30, 29, 52, **63, 87**, 27, 19, 54

(e) Compare 87 and 27. Since 87 > 27, swapping is done. 30, 29, 52, 63, **27, 87**, 19, 54

(f) Compare 87 and 19. Since 87 > 19, swapping is done. 30, 29, 52, 63, 27, **19, 87**, 54

(g) Compare 87 and 54. Since 87 > 54, swapping is done. 30, 29, 52, 63, 27, 19, **54, 87**

Observe that after the end of the first pass, the largest element is placed at the highest index of the array. All the other elements are still unsorted.

Pass 2:

(a) Compare 30 and 29. Since 30 > 29, swapping is done. **29, 30**, 52, 63, 27, 19, 54, 87

(b) Compare 30 and 52. Since 30 < 52, no swapping is done.

(c) Compare 52 and 63. Since 52 < 63, no swapping is done.

(d) Compare 63 and 27. Since 63 > 27, swapping is done. 29, 30, 52, **27, 63**, 19, 54, 87

(e) Compare 63 and 19. Since 63 > 19, swapping is done. 29, 30, 52, 27, **19, 63**, 54, 87

(f) Compare 63 and 54. Since 63 > 54, swapping is done. 29, 30, 52, 27, 19, **54, 63**, 87

Observe that after the end of the second pass, the second largest element is placed at the second highest index of the array. All the other elements are still unsorted.

Pass 3:

(a) Compare 29 and 30. Since 29 < 30, no swapping is done.

(b) Compare 30 and 52. Since 30 < 52, no swapping is done.

(c) Compare 52 and 27. Since 52 > 27, swapping is done. 29, 30, **27, 52**, 19, 54, 63, 87

(d) Compare 52 and 19. Since 52 > 19, swapping is done. 29, 30, 27, **19, 52**, 54, 63, 87

(e) Compare 52 and 54. Since 52 < 54, no swapping is done.

Observe that after the end of the third pass, the third largest element is placed at the third highest index of the array. All the other elements are still unsorted.

Pass 4:

(a) Compare 29 and 30. Since 29 < 30, no swapping is done.

(b) Compare 30 and 27. Since 30 > 27, swapping is done. 29, **27, 30**, 19, 52, 54, 63, 87

(c) Compare 30 and 19. Since 30 > 19, swapping is done. 29, 27, **19, 30**, 52, 54, 63, 87

(d) Compare 30 and 52. Since 30 < 52, no swapping is done.

Observe that after the end of the fourth pass, the fourth largest element is placed at the fourth highest index of the array. All the other elements are still unsorted.

Pass 5:

(a) Compare 29 and 27. Since 29 > 27, swapping is done.
27, 29, 19, 30, 52, 54, 63, 87

(b) Compare 29 and 19. Since 29 > 19, swapping is done.
27, **19, 29**, 30, 52, 54, 63, 87

(c) Compare 29 and 30. Since 29 < 30, no swapping is done.

Observe that after the end of the fifth pass, the fifth largest element is placed at the fifth highest index of the array. All the other elements are still unsorted.

Pass 6:

(a) Compare 27 and 19. Since 27 > 19, swapping is done.
19, 27, 29, 30, 52, 54, 63, 87

(b) Compare 27 and 29. Since 27 < 29, no swapping is done.

Observe that after the end of the sixth pass, the sixth largest element is placed at the sixth largest index of the array. All the other elements are still unsorted.

Pass 7:

(a) Compare 19 and 27. Since 19 < 27, no swapping is done.

Observe that the entire list is sorted now.

1. Write a program to enter n numbers in an array. Redisplay the array with elements being sorted in ascending order.

```
#include <stdio.h>
int main()
{
  int i, n, temp, j, arr [10];
  printf("\n Enter the number of elements in
    the array: ");
  scanf("%d", &n);
  printf("\n Enter the elements ");
  for(i = 0;i < n;i++)
    scanf("%d", &arr [i]);
  for(i = 0;i < n-1;i++)
  {
    for(j = 0;j < n-i-1;j++)
    {
      if(arr [j] > arr [j+1])
      {
      temp = arr [j];
      arr [j] = arr [j+1];
      arr [j+1] = temp;
      }
    }
  }
  printf("\n The array sorted in ascending
    order is: \n");
  for(i = 0;i < n;i++)
    printf("\t %d", arr[i]);
  return 0;
}
```

Output

```
Enter the number of elements in the array: 6
Enter the elements 27 72 36 63 45 54
The array sorted in ascending order is:
27 36 45 54 63 72
```

INSERTION SORT

Insertion sort is a very simple sorting algorithm, in which the sorted array (or list) is built one element at a time. We all are familiar with this technique of sorting as we usually use it for ordering a deck of cards while playing bridge.

The main idea behind insertion sort is that it inserts each item into its proper place in the final list. To save memory, most implementations of the insertion sort algorithm work by moving the current data element past the already sorted values and repeatedly interchanging it with the preceding value until it is in its correct place.

Technique

Insertion sort works as follows:

- The array of values to be sorted is divided into two sets. One that stores sorted values and the other contains unsorted values.
- The sorting algorithm will proceed until there are elements in the unsorted set.
- Suppose there are *n* elements in the array. Initially the element with index 0 (assuming LB = 0) is in the sorted set, rest of the elements are in the unsorted set.
- The first element of the unsorted partition has array index 1 (if LB = 0).
- During each iteration of the algorithm, the first element in the unsorted set is picked up and inserted into the correct position in the sorted set.

Insertion Sort Example

Consider an array of integers given below. Sort the values in the array using insertion sort.

39	9	45	63	18	81	108	54	72	36

39	9	45	63	18	81	108	54	72	36

A[0] is the only element in sorted list

Pass 1:	9	39	45	63	18	81	108	54	72	36
Pass 2:	9	39	45	63	18	81	108	54	72	36
Pass 3:	9	39	45	63	18	81	108	54	72	36
Pass 4:	9	18	39	45	63	81	108	54	72	36

Pass 5:	9	18	39	45	63	81	108	54	72	36
Pass 6:	9	18	39	45	63	81	108	54	72	36
Pass 7:	9	18	39	45	54	63	81	108	72	36
Pass 8:	9	18	39	45	54	63	72	81	108	36
Pass 9:	9	18	36	39	45	54	63	72	81	108

Initially, A[0] is the only element in the sorted set. In Pass 1, A[1] will be placed either before or after A[0], so that the array A is sorted. In pass 2, A[2] will be placed either before A[0], in-between A[0] and A[1] or after A[1], so that the array is sorted. In pass 3, A[3] will be placed in its proper place so that the array A is sorted. In Pass N–1, A[N–1] will be placed in its proper place so that the array A is sorted.

To insert the element A[K] in the sorted list A[0], A[1], ..., A[K-1], we need to compare A[K] with A[K-1], then with A[K-2], then with A[K-3] until we meet an element A[J] such that A[J] <= A[K].

In order to insert A[K] in its correct position, we need to move each element A[K-1], A[K-2], ..., A[J+1] by one position and then A[K] is inserted at the (J+1)th location.

2. Write a program to sort an array using insertion sort algorithm.

```
#include <stdio.h>
void insertion_sort(int arr[],int n);
void main()
{
  int arr[10], i, n;
  printf("\n Enter the number of elements in
    the array: ");
  scanf("%d", &n);
  printf("\n Enter the elements of the
  array");
  for(i = 0;i < n;i++)
  {
    scanf("%d", &arr[i]);
  }
  insertion_sort(arr,n);
  printf("\n The sorted array is: \n");
  for(i = 0;i < n;i++)
    printf("%d\t", arr[i]);
}
void insertion_sort(int arr[], int n)
{
  int i, j, temp;
  for(i = 1;i < n;i++)
  {
    temp = arr[i];
    j = i-1;
    while((temp < arr[j]) && (j>=0))
    {
    arr[j+1] = arr[j];
    j--;
    }
    arr[j+1] = temp;
  }
}
```

Output

```
Enter the number of elements in the array: 6
Enter the elements of the array 27 72 36 63
45 54
The sorted array is:
27 36 45 54 63 72
```

SELECTION SORT

Selection sort is generally the preferred choice for sorting files with very large objects (records) and small keys. Although selection sort performs worse than insertion sort algorithm it is noted for its simplicity, and also has performance advantages over more complicated algorithms in certain situations.

Technique

Consider an array ARR with N elements. The selection sort makes N–1 passes to sort the entire array and works as follows. First find the smallest value in the array and place it in the first position. Then find the second smallest value in the array and place it in the second position. Repeat this procedure until the entire array is sorted. Therefore,

In pass 1, find the position POS of the smallest value in the array and then swap ARR[POS] and ARR[0]. Thus, ARR[0] is sorted.

In pass 2, find the position POS of the smallest value in sub-array of N–1 elements. Swap ARR[POS] with ARR[1]. Now, A[0] and A[1] is sorted.

In pass 3, find the position POS of the smallest value in sub-array of N–2 elements. Swap ARR[POS] with ARR[2]. Now ARR[0], ARR[1] and ARR[2] is sorted.

In pass N–1, find the position POS of the smaller of the elements ARR[N-2] and ARR[N-1]. Swap ARR[POS] and ARR[N-2] so that ARR[0], ARR[1], … , ARR[N-1] is sorted.

Selection Sort Example

Sort the array given below using selection sort

39	9	81	45	90	27	72	18

PASS	POS	ARR[0]	ARR[1]	ARR[2]	ARR[3]	ARR[4]	ARR[5]	ARR[6]	ARR[7]
1	1	9	39	81	45	90	27	72	18
2	7	9	18	81	45	90	27	72	39
3	5	9	18	27	45	90	81	72	39
4	7	9	18	27	39	90	81	72	45
5	7	9	18	27	39	45	81	72	90
6	6	9	18	27	39	45	72	81	90
7	6	9	18	27	39	45	72	81	90

The advantages of the selection sort algorithm are as follows:

- Simple and easy to implement
- Can be used for small data sets
- 60 per cent more efficient than bubble sort algorithm

The disadvantage is that it is inefficient for large data sets. Insertion sort is considered to be better than selection sort and bubble sort.

3. Write a program to sort an array using selection sort algorithm.

```
#include <stdio.h>
int smallest(int arr[], int k, int n);
void selection_sort(int arr[], int n);
void main()
{
  int arr[10], i, n;
  printf("\n Enter the number of elements in
the array: ");
  scanf("%d", &n);
  printf("\n Enter the elements of the array");
  for(i = 0;i < n;i++)
  {
    scanf("%d", &arr[i]);
  }
  selection_sort(arr, n);
  printf("\n The sorted array is: \n");
  for(i = 0;i< n;i++)
    printf("%d\t", arr[i]);
}
int smallest(int arr[], int k, int n)
{
  int pos = k, small=arr[k], i;
  for(i = k+1;i < n;i++)
  {
    if(arr[i]< small)
    {
    small = arr[i];
    pos = i;
    }
  }
  return pos;
}
void selection_sort(int arr[],int n)
{
  int k, pos, temp;
  for(k = 0;k < n;k++)
  {
    pos = smallest(arr, k, n);
    temp = arr[k];
    arr[k] = arr[pos];
    arr[pos] = temp;
  }
}
```

Output

```
Enter the number of elements in the array: 6
Enter the elements of the array 27 72 36
63 45 54
The sorted array is:
27 36 45 54 63 72
```

13 Strings

TAKEAWAYS

- Reading and writing strings
- Suppressing input
- Operations on strings
- String and character functions
- Arrays of strings

13.1 INTRODUCTION

Nowadays, computers are widely used for word processing applications such as creating, inserting, updating, and modifying textual data. Besides this we need to search for a particular pattern within a text, delete it, or replace it with another pattern. So there is actually a lot we as users do to manipulate the textual data.

> **Programming Tip:** Character constants are enclosed in single quotes. String constants are enclosed in double quotes.

In C language, a string is a null-terminated character array. This means that after the last character, a null character (`'\0'`) is stored to signify the end of the character array. For example, if we write

```
char str[] = "HELLO";
```

We are declaring a character array that has five usable characters namely, `H, E, L, L,` and `O`. Apart from these characters, a null character (`'\0'`) is stored at the end of the string. So, the internal representation of the string becomes `HELLO'\0'`. To store a string of length 5, we need 5 + 1 locations (1 extra for the null character). The name of the character array (or the string) is a pointer to the beginning of the string. Figure 13.1 shows the difference between character storage and string storage.

If we declare `str` as,

```
char str[5] = "HELLO";
```

Then the null character will not be appended automatically to the character array. This is because `str` can hold only 5 characters and the characters in `HELLO` have already filled the locations allocated to it.

> **Note**
> When the compiler assigns a character string to a character array, it automatically appends a null character to the end of the string. Therefore, the size of the string should be equal to maximum number of characters in the string plus one.

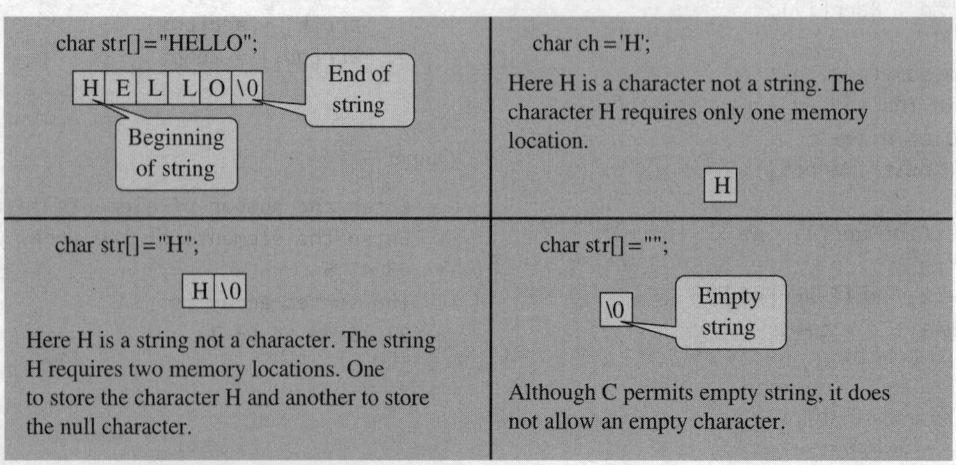

Figure 13.1 Difference between character storage and string storage

> **Programming Tip:** When allocating memory space for a character array, reserve space to hold the null character also.

Like we use subscripts (also known as index) to access the elements of an array, similarly subscripts are also used to access the elements of the character array. The subscript starts with a zero (`0`). All the characters of a string array are stored in successive memory locations. Figure 13.2 shows how `str[]` is stored in memory.

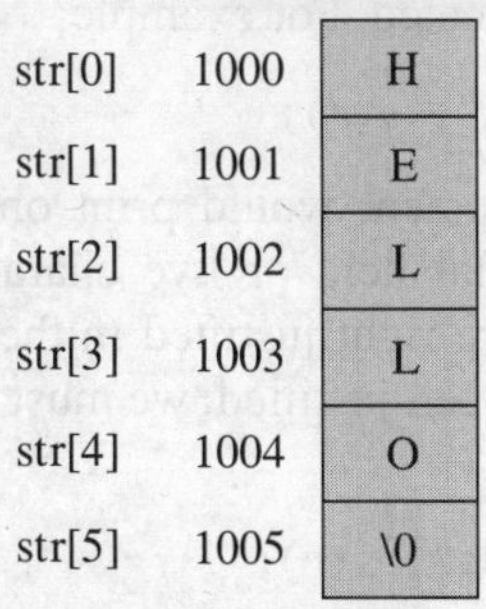

Figure 13.2 Memory representation of a character array

Thus we see that a string is a sequence of characters. In Figure 13.2, `1000, 1001, 1002,` and so on are the memory addresses of individual characters. From the figure, we see that `H` is stored at memory location `1000` but in reality the ASCII codes of characters are stored in memory and not the character itself, i.e., at address `1000, 72` will be stored since the ASCII code for `H` is `72`.

```
char str[] = "HELLO";
```

The aforegiven statement declares a constant string as we have assigned value to it while declaring the string. However, the general form of declaring a string is

```
char str[size];
```

When we declare the string in this way, we can store `size -1` characters in the array because the last character would be the null character. For example, `char mesg[100];` can store a maximum of `99` usable characters.

Till now we have seen one way of initializing strings. The other way to initialize a string is to initialize it as an array of characters, like

```
char str[] = {'H', 'E', 'L', 'L', 'O', '\0'};
```

In this example, we have explicitly added the null character. Further, observe that we have not mentioned the size of the string (or the character array). Here, the compiler will automatically calculate the size based on the number of elements initialized. So, in this example 6 memory slots will be reserved to store the string variable, `str`.

We can also declare a string with size much larger than the number of elements that are initialized. For example, consider the statement below:

```
char str[10] = "HELLO";
```

In such cases, the compiler creates a character array of size 10, stores the value `"HELLO"` in it and finally terminates the value with a null character. Rest of the elements in the array are automatically initialized to `NULL`. Figure 13.3 shows the memory representation of such a string.

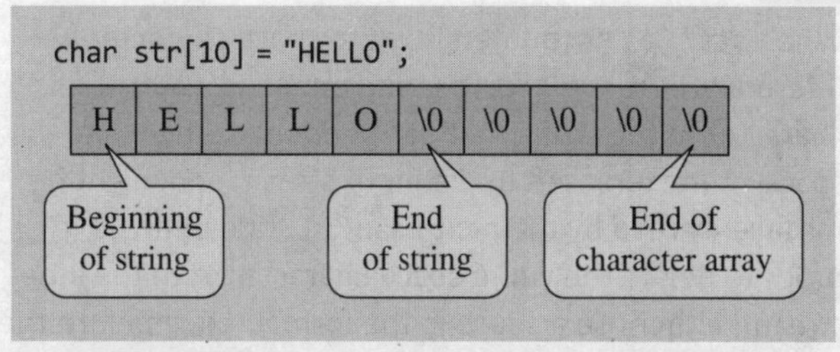

Figure 13.3 Memory representation of a string

Consider the following declaration:

```
char str[3];
str = "HELLO";
```

The above declaration is illegal in C and would generate a compile time error because of two reasons. First, the array is initialized with more elements than it can store. Second, initialization cannot be separated from declaration.

> **Note**
>
> An array name cannot be used as the left operand of an assignment operator. Therefore, the following statement is illegal in C.
>
> ```
> char str2, str1[]="HI";
> str2 = str1;
> ```

13.1.1 Reading Strings

If we declare a string by writing

```
char str[100];
```

Then `str` can be read by using three ways:

1. using `scanf` function
2. using `gets()` function
3. using `getchar()`, `getch()` or `getche()` function repeatedly

Strings can be read using `scanf()` by writing

```
scanf("%s", str);
```

Although the syntax of `scanf()` function is well known and easy to use, the main pitfall with this function is that the function terminates as soon as it finds a blank space. For example, if the user enters `Hello World`, then `str` will contain only `Hello`. This is because the moment a blank space is encountered, the string is terminated by the `scanf()` function. You may also specify a field width to indicate the

> **Programming Tip:** Using & operand with a string variable in the scanf statement generates an error.

maximum number of characters that can be read in. Remember that extra characters are left unconsumed in the input buffer.

Unlike `int(%d)`, `float(%f)`, and `char(%c)`, `%s` format does not require ampersand before the variable name.

> **Note**
>
> When `scanf()` encounters a white space character, it terminates reading further and appends a null character to the string that has been read. The white space character is left in the input stream and might be mistakenly read by the next `scanf()` statement. So in order to delete the white space character from the input stream, either use a space in the format string before the next conversion code or FLUSH the input stream by using the `fflush` function by writing `fflush(stdin)`.

The next method of reading a string is by using `gets()` function. The string can be read by writing

```
gets(str);
```

`gets()` is a simple function that overcomes the drawbacks of the `scanf()` function. The `gets()` function takes the starting address of the string which will hold the input. The string inputted using `gets()` is automatically terminated with a null character.

Last but not the least, strings can also be read by calling the `getchar()` function repeatedly to read a sequence of single characters (unless a terminating character is entered) and simultaneously storing it in a character array as shown below.

```
i=0;
ch = getchar(); // Get a character
while(ch != '*')
{
  str[i] = ch;
    // Store the read character in str
  i++;
  ch = getchar();  // Get another character
}
str[i] = '\0';
// terminate str with null character
```

> **Programming Tip:**
> A compile time error will be generated if a string is assigned to a character variable.

Note that in this method, you have to deliberately append the characters with a null character. The other two functions automatically do this.

13.1.2 Writing Strings

Strings can be displayed on screen using three ways:

1. using `printf()` function
2. using `puts()` function
3. using `putchar()`function repeatedly

A string can be displayed using `printf()` by writing

```
printf("%s", str);
```

We use the conversion character `'s'` to output a string. We may also use width and precision specifications along with `%s` (as discussed in Chapter 2). The width specifies the minimum output field width. If the string is short, extra space is either left padded or right padded. A negative width left pads short string rather than the default right justification. The precision specifies the maximum number of characters to be displayed. If the string is long, the extra characters are truncated. For example,

```
printf("%5.3s", str);
```

The above statement would print only the first three characters in a total field of five characters. Also these three characters are right justified in the allocated width. To make the string left justified, we must use a minus sign. For example,

```
printf("%-5.3s", str);
```

> **Note**
>
> When the field width is less than the length of the string, the entire string will be printed. Also if the number of characters to be printed is specified as zero, then nothing is printed on the screen.

The next method of writing a string is by using `puts()` function. The string can be displayed by writing

```
puts(str);
```

`puts()` is a simple function that overcomes the drawbacks of the `printf()` function. The `puts()` function writes a line of output on the screen. It terminates the line with a newline character (`'\n'`). It returns an `EOF (-1)` if an error occurs and returns a positive number on success.

Last but not the least, strings can also be written by calling the `putchar()` function repeatedly to print a sequence of single characters.

```
i=0;
while(str[i] != '\0')
{
  putchar(str[i]);
    // Print the character on the screen
  i++;
}
```

> **Note**
>
> Note one interesting point from the given fragment.
>
> ```
> char str = "Hello";
> printf("\n %s", str); // prints Hello
> printf("\n %s", &str); // prints Hello
> printf("\n %s", &str[2]); // prints llo
> ```
>
> This is possible because a string is an array of characters.

13.1.3 Summary of Functions Used to Read and Write Characters

Table 13.1 contains a list of functions that are used to read characters from the keyboard and write characters to the screen.

1. Write a program to display a string using printf().

```
#include <stdio.h>
int main()
{
    char str[] = "Introduction to C";
    printf("\n |%s|", str);
    printf("\n |%20s|", str);
    printf("\n |%-20s|", str);
    printf("\n |%.4s|", str);
    printf("\n |%20.4s|", str);
    printf("\n |%-20.4s|", str);
      return 0;
}
```

Output

```
|Introduction to C|
|   Introduction to C|
|Introduction to C   |
|Intr|
|                Intr |
|Intr                 |
```

Table 13.1 Functions to read and write characters

Function	Operation
getchar()	Used to read a character from the keyboard; waits for carriage return (enter key). It returns an integer, in which the low-order byte contains the character. getchar() can be used to input any key, including RETURN, TAB, and ESC.
getche()	Similar to getch(). The only difference is that getche() echoes the character on screen.
putchar()	Used to write a character to the screen. It accepts an integer parameter of which only the low-order byte is output to the screen. Returns the character written, or EOF (-1) if an error occurs.

The printf() function in UNIX supports specification of variable field width or precision, i.e., if we write,

```
printf("\n %*.s*, w, p, str);
```

Then the printf() statement will print first p characters of str in the field width of w.

2. Write a program to print the following pattern.

```
H
H E
H E L
H E L L
H E L L O
H E L L O
H E L L
H E L
H E
H
```

```
#include <stdio.h>
int main()
{
   int i, w, p;
   char str[] = "HELLO";
   printf("\n");
   for(i=0;i<5;i++)
   {
     p = i+1;
     printf("\n %-5.*s", p, str);
   }
   printf("\n");
   for(i=4;i>=0;i--)
   {
     p = i+1;
     printf("\n %-5.*s", p, str);
   }
     return 0;
}
```

sprintf() *Function*

The library function sprintf() is similar to printf(). The only difference is that the formatted output is written to a memory area rather than directly to a standard output (screen). sprintf() is useful in situations when formatted strings in memory have to be transmitted over a communication channel or to a special device.

The syntax of sprintf() can be given as

```
int sprintf( char * buffer, const char *
   format [ , argument , ...] );
```

Here, buffer is the place where string needs to be stored. The arguments command is an ellipsis so you can put as many types of arguments as you want. Finally, format is the string that contains the text to be printed. The string may contain format tags.

```
#include < stdio.h>
main()
{
   char buf[100];
   int num = 10;
```

```
    sprintf(buf, "num = %3d", num);
}
```

13.2 SUPPRESSING INPUT

The `scanf()` function can be used to read a field without assigning it to any variable. This is done by preceeding that field's format code with a `*`. For example, consider the example below:

```
scanf("%d*c%d", &hr, &min);
```

The time can be read as `9:05`. Here the colon would be read but not assigned to anything. Therefore, assignment suppression is particularly useful when part of what is input needs to be suppressed.

13.2.1 Using a Scanset

The ANSI standard added the new scanset feature to the C language. *Scanset* is used to define a set of characters which may be read and assigned to the corresponding string. Scanset is defined by placing the characters inside square brackets prefixed with a `%`, as shown in the example below:

```
%["aeiou"]
```

When we use the above scanset, `scanf()` will continue to read characters and put them into the string until it encounters a character that is not specified in the scanset. For example, consider the code given below.

```
#include <stdio.h>
int main()
{
   char str[10];
   printf("\n Enter string: " );
   scanf("%[aeiou]", str );
   printf( "The string is: %s", str);
   return 0;
}
```

The code will stop accepting a character as soon as the user enters a character that is not a vowel.

However, if the first character in the set is a ^ (caret symbol), then `scanf()` will accept any character that is not defined by the scanset. For example, if you write

```
scanf("%[^aeiou]", str);
```

Then, `str` will accept characters other than those specified in the scanset, i.e., it will accept any non-vowel character. However, the caret and the opening bracket can be included in the scanset anywhere. They have a predefined meaning only when they are included as the first character of the scanset. So if you want to accept a text from the user that contains caret and opening bracket then make sure that they are not the first characters in the scanset. This is shown in the following example.

```
scanf("%[0123456789.^[]()_+-$%&*]", str );
```

In the given example, `str` can accept any character enclosed in the opening and closing square brackets (including ^ and [).

The user can also specify a range of acceptable characters using a hyphen. This is shown in the statement given below:

```
scanf("%[a-z]", str );
```

Here, `str` will accept any character from small `a` to small `z`. Always remember that scansets are case sensitive. However, if you want to accept a hyphen then it must either be the first or the last character in the set.

Example 13.1

To better understand scanset, try the following code with different inputs

```
#include <stdio.h>
int main()
{
   char str[10];
   printf("\n Enter string: " );
   scanf("%[A-Z]", str );
     // Reads only upper case characters
   printf( "The string is : %s", str);
   return 0;
}
```

A major difference between scanset and the string conversion codes is that scanset does not skip leading white spaces. If the white space is a part of the scanset, then scanset accepts any white space character, otherwise it terminates if a white space character is entered without being specified in the scanset.

Scanset may also terminate if a field width specification is included and the maximum number of characters that can be read has been reached. For example, the statement given below will read maximum 10 vowels. So the `scanf` statement will terminate if 10 characters have been read or if a non-vowel character is entered.

```
scanf("%10[aeiou]", str );
```

`sscanf()` *Function*

The `sscanf` function accepts a string from which to read input. It accepts a template string and a series of related arguments. The `sscanf` function is similar to scanf function except that the first argument of `sscanf` specifies a string from which to read, whereas scanf can only read from standard input. Its syntax is given as

```
sscanf(const char *str, const char
    *format,[p1, p2, ...]);
```

Here sscanf() reads data from str and stores them according to the parameter format into the locations given by the additional arguments. Locations pointed by each additional argument are filled with their corresponding type of value specified in the format string.

Consider the example given below:

```
sscanf(str, "%d", &num);
```

Here, sscanf takes three arguments. The first is str that contains data to be converted. The second is a string containing a format specifier that determines how the string is converted. Finally, the third is a memory location to place the result of the conversion. When the sscanf function completes successfully, it returns the number of items successfully read.

Similar to scanf(), sscanf() terminates as soon as it encounters a space, i.e., it continues to read till it comes across a blank space.

13.3 STRING TAXONOMY

In C, we can store a string either in fixed-length format or in variable-length format as shown in Figure 13.4.

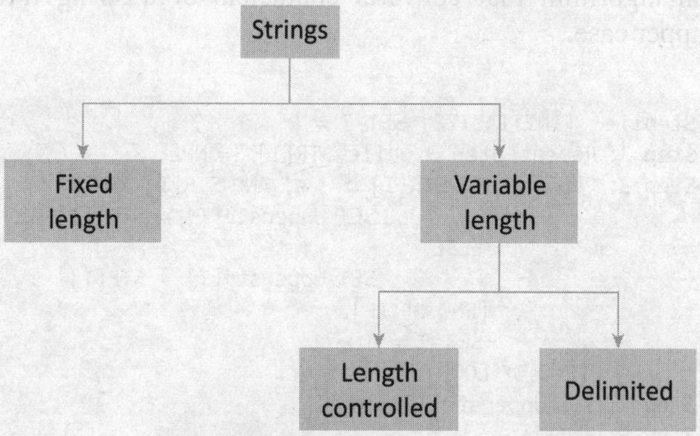

Figure 13.4 String taxonomy

Fixed-length strings When storing a string in a fixed-length format, you need to specify an appropriate size for the string variable. If the size is too small, then you will not be able to store all the elements in the string. On the other hand, if the string size is large, then unnecessarily memory space will be wasted.

Variable-length strings A better option is to use a variable length format in which the string can be expanded or contracted to accommodate the elements in it. For example, if you declare a string variable to store the name of a student. If a student has a long name of say 20 characters, then the string can be expanded to accommodate 20 characters. On the other hand, a student name has only 5 characters, then the string variable can be contracted to store only 5 characters. However, to use a variable-length string format you need a technique to indicate the end of elements that are a part of the string. This can be done either by using length-controlled string or a delimiter.

Length-controlled strings In a length-controlled string, you need to specify the number of characters in the string. This count is used by string manipulation functions to determine the actual length of the string variable.

Delimited strings In this format, the string is ended with a delimiter. The delimiter is then used to identify the end of the string. For example, in English language every sentence is ended with a full-stop (.). Similarly, in C we can use any character such as comma, semicolon, colon, dash, null character, etc. as the delimiter of a string. However, null character is the most commonly used string delimiter in the C language.

You must be having some confusion when we use the term string and character array. Basically a string is stored in an array of characters. If we are using the null character as the string delimiting character then we treat the part of the array from the beginning to the null character as the string and ignore the rest. Figure 13.5 illustrates this concept.

```
char str[10];
gets(str);
```

If the user enters HELLO, then array of characters can be given as

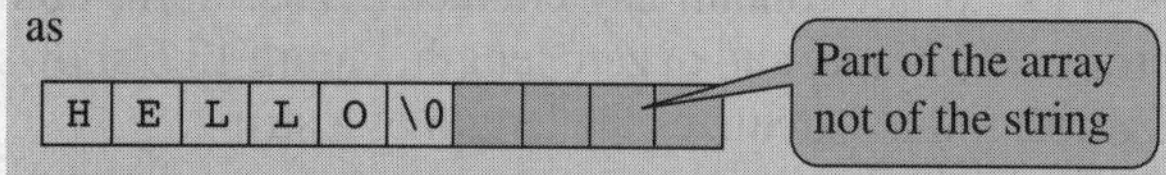

Although the array has 10 locations, only the first 6 locations will be treated as a string.

Figure 13.5 Delimited string

Note

In C, a string is a variable length array of characters that is delimited by the null character.

13.4 OPERATIONS ON STRINGS

In this section, we will learn about different operations that can be performed on character arrays. But before we start with these operations, we must understand the way arithmetic operators can be applied to characters.

In C, characters can be manipulated in the same way as we do with numbers. When we use a character constant or a character variable in an expression, it is automatically converted into an integer value, where the value depends on the local character set of the system. For example, if we write

```
int i;
char ch = 'A';
i = ch;
printf("%d", i);

// Prints 65, ASCII value of ch is 'A'
```

C also enables programmers to perform arithmetic operations on character variables and character constants. So, if we write

```
int i;
char ch = 'A';
i = ch + 10;
printf("%d", i);
// Prints 75, ASCII value of ch that is 'A' + 10
```

Character variables and character constants can be used with relational operators as shown in the example below,

```
char ch = 'C';
if(ch >= 'A' && ch <= 'Z')
printf("The character is in upper case");
```

13.4.1 Finding the Length of a String

The number of characters in the string constitutes the length of the string. For example, `LENGTH("C PROGRAMMING IS FUN")` will return `19`. Note that even blank spaces are counted as characters in the string.

`LENGTH("\0") = 0` and `LENGTH("") = 0` because both the strings do not contain any character. Therefore, both the strings are empty and of zero length. Figure 13.6 shows an algorithm that calculates the length of a string.

```
Step 1: [INITIALIZE] SET I = 0
Step 2: Repeat Step 3 while STR [I]! = NULL
Step 3:       SET I = I + 1
        [END OF LOOP]
Step 4: SET LENGTH = I
Step 5: END
```

Figure 13.6 Algorithm to calculate the length of a string

In this algorithm, `I` is used as an index of the string `STR`. To traverse each and every character of `STR` we increment the value of `I`. Once the null character is encountered, the control jumps out of the `while` loop and length is initialized with the value of `I`. This is because the number of characters in the string constitutes its length.

Note

There is a library function strlen(s1) that returns the length of s1. It is defined in string.h.

3. Write a program to find the length of a string.

```
#include <stdio.h>
int main()
{
  char str[100], i = 0, length;
  printf("\n Enter the string :");
  gets(str);
  while(str[i] != '\0')
    i++;
  length = i;
  printf("\n The length of the string is :
  %d", length);
  return 0;
}
```

Output

```
Enter the string : HELLO
The length of the string is : 5
```

13.4.2 Converting Characters of a String into Upper Case

We have already seen that in memory the ASCII codes are stored instead of the real value. The ASCII code for `A-Z` varies from `65` to `91` and the ASCII code for `a-z` ranges from `97` to `123`. So if we have to convert a lower case character to upper case, then we just need to subtract `32` from the ASCII value of the character. Figure 13.7 shows an algorithm that converts characters of a string into upper case.

```
Step1:   [INITIALIZE] SET I = 0
Step 2: Repeat Step 3 while STR[I] != NULL
Step 3:         IF STR[I] >= 'a' AND STR[I] <= 'z'
                     SET Upperstr[I] = STR [I]-32
                ELSE
                     SET Upperstr[I] = STR[I]
                [END OF IF]
                SET I = I + 1
        [END OF LOOP]
Step 4: SET Upperstr[I] = NULL
Step 5: EXIT
```

Figure 13.7 Algorithm to convert characters of a string into upper case.

Note

There is a library function toupper() that converts a character into upper case. It is defined in ctype.h

In the algorithm, we initialize `I` to zero. Using `I` as the index of `STR`, we traverse each character from Step 2 to 3. If the character is already in upper case, then it is copied in `Upperstr` else the lower case character is converted into upper case by subtracting `32` from its ASCII value. The upper case character is then stored in `Upperstr`. Finally, when all the characters have been traversed a null character is appended to `Upperstr` (as done in Step 4).

4. Write a program to convert characters of a string to upper case.

```
#include <stdio.h>
int main()
{
  char str[100], upper_str [100];
  int i=0, j=0;
  printf("\n Enter the string:");
  gets(str);
  while(str[i] != '\0')
  {
    if(str[i]>='a' && str[i]<='z')
      upper_str[j] = str[i] -32;
    else
      upper_str[j] = str[i];
    i++; j++;
  }
  upper_str[j] = '\0';
  printf("\n The string converted into upper
  case is : ");
  puts(upper_str);
  return 0;
}
```

Output

```
Enter the string: hello
The string converted into upper case is: HELLO
```

13.4.3 Converting Characters of a String Into Lower Case

If we have to convert an upper case character into lower case, then we just need to add `32` to its ASCII value. Figure 13.8 shows an algorithm that converts characters of a string into lower case.

Note

In C, there is a library function tolower() that converts a character into lower case. It is defined in ctype.h

```
Step 1:   [INITIALIZE] SET I = 0
Step 2: Repeat Step 3 while STR[I] != NULL
Step 3:        IF STR[I] >= 'A' AND STR[I] <= 'Z'
                       SET Lowerstr[I] = STR [I] + 32
               ELSE
                       SET Lowerstr[I] = STR [I]
               [END OF IF]
               SET I = I + 1
         [END OF LOOP]
Step 4: SET Lowerstr[I] = NULL
Step 5: EXIT
```

Figure 13.8 Algorithm to convert characters of a string into lower case

In the algorithm, we initialize `I` to `zero`. Using `I` as the index of `STR`, we traverse each character from Step 2 to 3. If the character is already in lower case, then it is copied in `Lowerstr` else the upper case character is converted into lower case by adding `32` to its ASCII value. The lower case character is then stored in `Lowerstr`. Finally, when all the characters have been traversed a null character is appended to `Lowerstr` (as done in Step 4).

5. Write a program to convert characters of a string into lower case.

```
#include <stdio.h>
int main()
{
  char str[100], lower_str [100];
  int i = 0, j = 0;
  printf("\n Enter the string :");
  gets(str);
  while(str[i] != '\0')
  {
    if(str[i]>='A' && str[i]<='Z')
      lower_str[j] = str[i] + 32;
    else
      lower_str[j] = str[i];
    i++; j++;
  }
  lower_str[j] = '\0';
  printf("\n The string converted into lower
  case is : ");
  puts(lower_str);
  return 0;
}
```

Output

```
Enter the string : HeLLo
The string converted into lower case is: hello
```

13.4.4 Concatenating Two Strings to Form a New String

If `S1` and `S2` are two strings, then *concatenation* operation produces a string which contains characters of `S1` followed by the characters of `S2`. Figure 13.9 shows an algorithm that concatenates two strings.

```
Step 1: [INITIALIZE] I = 0 and J = 0
Step 2: Repeat Steps 3 to 4 while str1 [i]! = NULL
Step 3:          SET new_str[J] = str1[I]
Step 4:          Set I = I+1 and J = J+1
           [END of LOOP]
Step 5: SET I=0
Step 6: Repeat Steps 6 to 7 while str2[i]! = NULL
Step 7:          SET new_str[J] = str2 [I]
Step 8:          Set I = I+1 and J = J+1
           [END of LOOP]
Step 9: SET new_str[J] = NULL
Step 10: EXIT
```

Figure 13.9 Algorithm to concatenate two strings

In this algorithm, we first initialize the two counters I and J to zero. To concatenate the strings, we have to copy the contents of the first string followed by the contents of the second string in a third string, new_str. Steps 2 to 4 copies the contents of the first string in new_str. Likewise, Steps 6 to 8 copies the contents of the second string in new_str. After the contents have been copied, a null character is appended at the end of new_str.

6. Write a program to concatenate two strings.

```
#include <stdio.h>
int main()
{
  char str1[100], str2[100], str3[100];
  int i=0, j=0;
  printf("\n Enter the first string : ");
  gets(str1);
  printf("\n Enter the second string : ");
  gets(str2);
  while(str1[i] != '\0')
  {
    str3[j] = str1[i];
    i++;
    j++;
  }
  i=0;
  while(str2[i] != '\0')
  {
    str3[j] = str2[i];
    i++;
    j++;
  }
  str3[j] = '\0';
  printf("\n The concatenated string is:");
  puts(str3);
    return 0;
}
```

Output

```
Enter the first string : Hello,
Enter the second string: How are you?
The concatenated string is: Hello, How are you?
```

13.4.5 Appending a String to Another String

Appending one string to another string involves copying the contents of the source string at the end of the destination string. For example, if S1 and S2 are two strings, then appending S1 to S2 means we have to add the contents of S1 to S2. Here S1 is the source string and S2 is the destination string. The append operation would leave the source string S1 unchanged and destination string S2 = S2 + S1. Figure 13.10 shows an algorithm that appends two strings.

```
Step 1:  [INITIALIZE] SET I=0 and J=0
Step 2: Repeat Step 3 while Dest_Str[I] != NULL
Step 3:   SET I + I + 1
          [END OF LOOP]
Step 4: Repeat Steps 5 to 7 while Source_Str[J] != NULL
Step 5:   Dest_Str[I] = Source_Str[J]
Step 6:   SET I = I+1
Step 7:   SET J = J+1
        [END OF LOOP]
Step 8: SET Dest_Str[J] = NULL
Step 9: EXIT
```

Figure 13.10 Algorithm to append a string to another string

Note

There is a library function strcat(s1, s2) that concatenates s2 to s1. It is defined in string.h.

In this algorithm, we first traverse through the destination string to reach its end, i.e., reach the position where a null character is encountered. The characters of the source string are then copied into the destination string starting from that position. Finally, a null character is added to terminate the destination string.

7. Write a program to append a string to another string

```
#include <stdio.h>
int main()
{
  char Dest_Str[100], Source_Str[50];
  int i = 0, j = 0;
  printf("\n Enter the source string : ");
  gets(Source_Str);
  printf("\n Enter the destination string:");
  gets(Dest_Str);
  while(Dest_Str[i] != '\0')
    i++;
  while(Source_Str[j] != '\0')
  {
    Dest_Str[i] = Source_Str[j];
    i++;
    j++;
  }
  Dest_Str[i] = '\0';
  printf("\n After appending, the destination
  string is: ");
  puts(Dest_Str);
  return 0;
}
```

Output

```
Enter the source string: How are you?
Enter the destination string: Hi,
```

```
After appending, the destination string is:
Hi, How are you?
```

13.4.6 Comparing Two Strings

If S1 and S2 are two strings then comparing two strings will give either of these results:

(a) S1 and S2 are equal
(b) S1 > S2, when in dictionary order S1 will come after S2
(c) S1 < S2, when in dictionary order S1 precedes S2

To compare the two strings, each and every character is compared from both the strings. If all the characters are same then the two strings are said to be equal. Figure 13.11 shows an algorithm that compares two strings.

Note

There is a library function strcmp (s1, s2) that compares s2 with s1. It is defined in string.h.

```
Step 1:  [INITIALIZE] SET I = 0,SAME = 0
Step 2: SET Len1= Length(STR1),  Len2= Length(STR2)
Step 3: IF len1 != len2, then
          Write "Strings Are Not Equal"
        ELSE
          Repeat while I<Len1
            IF STR1[I] = STR2[I]
                SET I = I + 1
            ELSE
                Go to Step 4
            [END OF IF]
          [END OF LOOP]
        IF I = Len1
            SET SAME = 1
            Write "Strings are equal"
        [END OF IF]
Step 4: IF SAME = 0
          IF STR1[I] > STR2[I],then
            Write "String 1 is greaterthan String2"
          ELSE IF STR1[I] < STR2[I], then
            Write "String 2 is greater than String1"
          [END OF IF]
        [END OF IF]
Step 5: EXIT
```

Figure 13.11 Algorithm to compare two strings

In this algorithm, we first check whether the two strings are of same length. If not, then there is no point in moving ahead as it straightaway means that the two strings are not same. However, if the two strings are of the same length, then we compare character by character to check if all the characters are same. If yes, then variable SAME is set to 1 else if SAME = 0, then we check which string precedes the other in dictionary order and print the corresponding message.

8. Write a program to compare two strings.

```
#include <stdio.h>
#include <string.h>
int main()
{
  char str1[50], str2[50];
  int i=0, len1 = 0, len2 = 0, same = 0;
  printf("\n Enter the first string : ");
  gets(str1);
  printf("\n Enter the second string : ");
  gets(str2);
  len1 = strlen(str1);
  len2 = strlen(str2);
  if(len1 == len2)
  {
   while(i<len1)
   {
   if(str1[i] == str2[i])
     i++;
   else break;
   }
   if(i==len1)
  {
   same=1;
   printf("\n The two strings are equal");
  }
  }
  if(len1!=len2)
   printf("\n The two strings are not
   equal");
  if(same == 0)
  {
  if(str1[i]>str2[i])
   printf("\n String1 is greater than
   string2");
  else if(str1[i]<str2[i])
   printf("\n String2 is greater than
   string1");
  }
  return 0;
}
```

Output

```
Enter the first string: Hello
Enter the second string: Hello
The two strings are equal
```

13.4.7 Reversing a String

If S1= "HELLO", then reverse of S1 = "OLLEH". To reverse a string we just need to swap the first character with the last, second character with the second last character, so on and so forth. Figure 13.12 shows an algorithm that reverses a string.

Note

There is a library function strrev(s1) that reverses all the characters in the string except the null character. It is defined in string.h.

```
Step 1: [INITIALIZE] SET I=0, J=Length(STR)-1
Step 2: Repeat Steps 3 and 4 while I < J
Step 3:      SWAP (STR(I), STR(J))
Step 4:      SET I = I + 1, J = J - 1
        [END OF LOOP]
Step 5: EXIT
```

Figure 13.12 Algorithm to reverse a string

In Step 1, I is initialized to zero and J is initialized to the length of the string – 1. In Step 2, a while loop is executed until all the characters of the string are accessed. In Step 3, we swap the ith character of STR with its jth character. (As a result, the first character of STR will be interchanged with the last character, the second character will be interchanged with the second last character of STR, and so on). In Step 4, the value of I is incremented and J is decremented to traverse STR in the forward and backward direction, respectively.

9. Write a program to reverse the given string.

```
#include <stdio.h>
#include <string.h>
int main()
{
  char str[100], reverse_str[100], temp;
  int i = 0, j = 0;
  printf("\n Enter the string: ");
  gets(str);
  j=strlen(str)-1;
  while(i<j)
  {
    temp = str[j];
    str[j] = str[i];
    str[i] = temp;
    i++;
    j--;
  }
  printf("\n The reversed string is: ");
  puts(str);
    return 0;
}
```

Output

```
Enter the string: Hi there
The reversed string is: ereht iH
```

13.4.8 Extracting a Substring from Left

In order to extract a substring from the main string we need to copy the content of the string starting from the first position to the nth position where n is the number of characters to be extracted.

For example, if S1 = "Hello World", then Substr_Left(S1, 7) = Hello W

Figure 13.13 shows an algorithm that extracts the first *n* characters from a string.

```
Step 1:  [INITIALIZE] SET I = 0
Step 2: Repeat Steps 3 to 4 while STR[I]! = NULL AND
        I < N
Step 3:     SET Substr[I] = STR[I]
Step 4:     SET I = I + 1
        [END OFLOOP]
Step 5: SET Substr[I] = NULL
Step 6: EXIT
```

Figure 13.13 Algorithm to extract first *n* characters from a string

In Step 1, we initialize the index variable I with zero. In Step 2, a while loop is executed until all the characters of STR have been accessed and I is less than N. In Step 3, the Ith character of STR is copied in the Ith character of Substr. In Step 4, the value of I is incremented to access the next character in STR. In Step 5, Substr is appended with a null character.

10. Write a program to extract the first *n* characters of a string.

```
#include <stdio.h>
int main()
{
  char str[100], substr[100];
  int i=0, n;
  printf("\n Enter the string: ");
  gets(str);
  printf("\n Enter the number of characters to
  be copied: ");
  scanf("%d", &n);
  i = 0;
  while(str[i] != '\0' && i< n)
  {
    substr[i] = str[i];
    i++;
  }
  substr [i] = '\0';
  printf("\n The substring is: ");
  puts(substr);
    return 0;
}
```

Output

```
Enter the string: Hi there
Enter the number of characters to be copied: 2
The substring is: Hi
```

13.4.9 Extracting a Substring from Right of the String

In order to extract a substring from the right side of the main string we need to first calculate the position from the left. For example, if `S1 = "Hello World"` and we have to copy 7 characters starting from the right, then we have to actually start extracting characters from the 4th position. This is calculated by total number of characters – *n*.

For example, if `S1 = "Hello World"`, then `Substr_Right(S1, 7) = o World`

Figure 13.14 shows an algorithm that extracts *n* characters from the right of a string.

```
Step 1: [INITIALIZE] SET I = 0, J = Length(STR) - N
Step 2: Repeat Steps 3 to 4 while STR[J]!= NULL
Step 3:      SET Substr [I] = STR[J]
Step 4:      SET I = I + 1, J = J + 1
       [END OF LOOP]
Step 5: SET Substr [I] = NULL
Step 6: EXIT
```

Figure 13.14 Algorithm to extract n characters from the right of a string

In Step 1, we initialize the index variable `I` to zero and `J` to `Length(STR) – N`, so that `J` points to the character from which the string has to be copied in the substring. In Step 2, a `while` loop is executed until the null character in `STR` is accessed. In Step 3, the `J`th character of `STR` is copied in the `I`th character of `Substr`. In Step 4, the value of `I` and `J` are incremented. In Step 5, `Substr` is appended with a null character.

11. Write a program to extract the last *n* characters of a string.

```
#include <stdio.h>
int main()
{
  char str[100], substr[100];
  int i=0, j=0, n;
  printf("\n Enter the string : ");
  gets(str);
  printf("\n Enter the number of characters to
  be copied: ");
  scanf("%d", &n);
  j = strlen(str) - n;
  while(str[j] != '\0')
  {
    substr[i] = str[j];
    i++, j++;
  }
  substr [i] = '\0';
  printf("\n The substring is : ");
  puts(substr);
  return 0;
}
```

Output

```
Enter the string : Hi there
Enter the number of characters to be copied : 5
The substring is : there
```

13.4.10 Extracting a Substring from the Middle of a String

To extract a substring from a given string requires information about three things. The main string, the position of the first character of the substring in the given string, and the number of characters/length of the substring. For example, if we have a string,

```
str[] = "Welcome to the world of programming";
```

then,

```
SUBSTRING(str, 15, 5) = world
```

Figure 13.15 shows an algorithm that extracts the substring from a middle of a string.

```
Step 1: [INITIALIZE] Set I = M, J = 0
Step 2: Repeat Steps 3 to 6 while str[I]!=NULL and N>0
Step 3:      SET substr[J] = str[I]
Step 4:      SET I = I + 1
Step 5:      SET J = J + 1
Step 6:      SET N = N - 1
       [END OF LOOP]
Step 7: SET substr[J] = NULL
Step 8: EXIT
```

Figure 13.15 Algorithm to extract a substring from the middle of a string

In this algorithm, we initialize a loop counter `I` to `M`, i.e., the position from which the characters have to be copied. Steps 3 to 6 are repeated until `N` characters have been copied. With every character copied, we decrement the value of `N`. The characters of the string are copied into a string called `substr`. At the end a null character is appended to `substr` to terminate the string.

12. Write a program to extract a substring from a given string.

```
#include <stdio.h>
int main()
{
  char str[100], substr[100];
  int i=0, j=0, n, m;
```

```
printf("\n Enter the main string: ");
gets(str);
printf("\n Enter the position from which to
start the substring: ");
scanf("%d", &m);
printf("\n Enter the length of the
 substring: ");
scanf("%d", &n);
i=m;
while(str[i] != '\0' &&  n>0)
{
  substr[j] = str[i];
  i++;
  j++;
  n--;
}
substr[j] = '\0';
printf("\n The substring is : ");
puts(str);
return 0;
}
```

Output

```
Enter the main string : Hi there
Enter the position from which to start the
substring: 1
Enter the length of the substring: 7
The substring is : i there
```

13.4.11 Inserting a String in Another String

The insertion operation inserts a string `S` in the main text `T` at `k`th position. The general syntax of this operation is: `INSERT(text, position, string)`. For example, `INSERT("XYZXYZ", 3, "AAA") = "XYZAAAXYZ"`

Figure 13.16 shows an algorithm to insert a string in a given text at the specified position.

```
Step 1: [INITIALIZE] SET I=0,J=0 and K=0
Step 2: Repeat Step 3 while text[I] ! = NULL
Step 3: IF I = pos,then
     Repeat while str[K] ! = NULL
        new_str[j] = str[k]
        SET J = J+1
        SET K = K+1
     [END OF INNER LOOP]
       ELSE
        new_str[[J] = text[I]
        SET J = J+1
        [END OF IF]
     SET I = I+1
  [END OF OUTER LOOP]
Step 4: SET new_str[J] = NULL
Step 5: EXIT
```

Figure 13.16 Algorithm to insert a string in a given text at the specified position

> **Programming Tip:**
> A program must include stdio.h for standard I/O operations, ctype.h for character handling functions, string.h for string functions, and stdlib.h for other general utility functions.

This algorithm first initializes the indexes in the string to zero. From Steps 3 to 4, the contents of `new_str` are built. If `I` is exactly equal to the position at which the substring has to be inserted into the text, then the inner loop copies the contents of the substring into the `new_str`. Otherwise, the contents of the text are copied into it.

13. Write a program to insert a string in the main text.

```
#include <stdio.h>
int main()
{
  char text[100], str[20], ins_text[100];
  int i=0, j=0, k=0,pos;
  printf("\n Enter the main text : ");
  gets(text);
  printf("\n Enter the string to be inserted
  : ");
  gets(str);
  printf("\n Enter the position at which the
  string has to be inserted: ");
  scanf("%d", &pos);
  while(text[i]!='\0')
  {
  if(i==pos)
  {
  while(str[k]!='\0')
  {
  ins_text[j]=str[k];
  j++;
  k++;
  }
  }
  else
  {
  ins_text[j]=text[i];
  j++;
  }
  i++;
 }
 ins_text[j]='\0';
 printf("\n The new string is: ");
 puts(ins_text);
 return 0;
}
```

Output

```
Enter the main text: How you?
```

```
Enter the string to be inserted: are
Enter the position at which the string has to
be inserted: 6
The new string is: How are you?
```

13.4.12 Indexing

Index operation returns the position in the string where the string pattern first occurs. For example,

```
INDEX("Welcome to the world of programming",
"world") = 15
```

However, if the pattern does not exist in the string, the `INDEX` function returns `0`. Figure 13.17 shows an algorithm to find the index of the first occurrence of a string within a given text.

```
Step 1:  [INITIALIZE] SET I = 0 and
              MAX = LENGTH(text) - LENGTH(str) +1
Step 2:  Repeat Steps 3 to 6 while I <= MAX
Step 3:  Repeat Step 4 for K = 0 to Length(str)
Step 4:      IF str[K] ! = text[I+K], then GOTO step6
         [END of inner loop]
Step 5:  SET INDEX = I. Gotostep8
Step 6:  SET I = I+1
         [END OF OUTER LOOP]
Step 7:  SET INDEX = -1
Step 8:  EXIT
```

Figure 13.17 Algorithm to find the index of the first occurrence of a string within a given text

In this algorithm, `MAX` is initialized to `LENGTH(text)` – `Length(str) + 1`. Take for example, if a text contains- `"Welcome To Programming"` and the string contains `"World"`. In the main text we will look for at the most `22 - 5 + 1 = 18` characters because after that there is no scope left for the string to be present in the text.

Steps 3 to 6 are repeated until each and every character of the text has been checked for the occurrence of the string within it. In the inner loop, in Step 3, we check `n` characters of string with `n` characters of text to find if the characters are same. If it is not the case, then we move to Step 6, where `I` is incremented. If the string is found, index is initialized with `I` else set to `-1`. For example, if

```
TEXT = W E L C O M E  T O  T H E  W O R L D
STRING = C O M E
```

In the first pass of the inner loop, we will compare `WORLD` with `WELC` character by character. As soon as `E` and `O` do not match, the control will move to Step 6 and then `ELCO` will be compared with `WORLD`. In the next pass, `COME` will be compared with `COME`.

We will write the programming code of indexing operation in the operations that follows.

13.4.13 Deleting a String from the Main String

The deletion operation deletes a substring from a given text. We write it as, `DELETE(text, position, length)`. For example,

```
DELETE("ABCDXXXABCD", 4, 3) = "ABCDABCD"
```

Figure 13.18 shows an algorithm to delete a substring from a given text.

```
Step 1: [INITIALIZE] SET I=0 and J=0
Step 2: Repeat Steps 3 to 6 while text[I] ! = NULL
Step 3: IF I=M,then
                Repeat while N>0
                      SET I = I+1
                      SET N = N-1
                [END OFLOOP]
        [END OF IF]
Step 4: SET new_str[J] = text[I]
Step 5: SET J = J + 1
Step 6: SET I = I + 1
        [END OF LOOP]
Step 7: SET new_str[J] = NULL
Step 8: EXIT
```

Figure 13.18 Algorithm to delete a substring from a text

In this algorithm, we first initialize indexes to `zero`. Steps 3 to 6 are repeated until all the characters of the text are scanned. If `I` is exactly equal to `M`, the position from which deletion has to be done, then the index of the text is incremented and `N` is decremented. `N` is the number of characters that have to be deleted starting from position `M`. However, if `I` is not equal to `M`, then the characters of the text are simply copied into `new_str`.

Deletion operation can also be used to delete a string from a given text. To do this, we first find the first index at which the string occurs in the text. Then we delete `N` number of characters from the text, where `N` is the number of characters in the string.

14. Write a program to delete a substring from a text.

```
#include <stdio.h>
int main()
{
  char text[200], str[20], new_text[200];
  int i=0, j=0, k, n=0, copy_loop=0;
  printf("\n Enter the main text: ");
  gets(text);
  printf("\n Enter the string to be deleted: ");
  gets(str);
  while(text[i]!='\0')
  {
      j=0, k=i;
      while(text[k]==str[j] && str[j]!='\0')
      {
      k++;
```

```
        j++;
      }
      if(str[j]=='\0')
        copy_loop=k;
      new_text[n] = text[copy_loop];
      i++;
      copy_loop++;
      n++;
    }
    new_text[n]='\0';
    printf("\n The new string is: ");
    puts(new_text);
    return 0;
}
```

Output

```
Enter the main text: Hello, how are you?
Enter the string to be deleted: , how are you?
The new string is: Hello
```

13.4.14 Replacing a Pattern with Another Pattern in a String

Replacement operation is used to replace the pattern P1 by another pattern P2. This is done by writing, REPLACE(text, pattern1, pattern2)

For example, ("AAABBBCCC", "BBB", "X") = AAAXCCC ("AAABBBCCC", "X", "YYY")= AAABBBCC.

In the second example, there is no change as 'X' does not appear in the text. Figure 13.19 shows an algorithm to replace a pattern P1 with another pattern P2 in the text.

```
Step 1: [INITIALIZE] SET POS = INDEX(TEXT,P1)
Step 2: SET TEXT = DELETE(TEXT,POS,LENGTH(P1))
Step 3: INSERT(TEXT, POS,P2)
Step 4: EXIT
```

Figure 13.19 Algorithm to replace a pattern P_1 with another pattern P_2 in the text

The algorithm is very simple, where we first find the position POS, at which the pattern occurs in the text, then delete the existing pattern from that position, and insert a new pattern there. String matching refers to finding occurrences of a pattern string within another string.

15. Write a program to replace a pattern with another pattern in the text.

```
#include <stdio.h>
int main()
{
  char str[200], pat[20], new_str[200],
  rep_pat[100];
  int i=0, j=0, k, n=0, copy_loop=0,
  rep_index=0;
  printf("\n Enter the string: ");
  gets(str);
  printf("\n Enter the pattern to be replaced:
  ");
  gets(pat);
  printf("\n Enter the replacing pattern: ");
  gets(rep_pat);
  while(str[i]!='\0')
  {
  j=0,k=i;
    while(str[k]==pat[j] && pat[j]!='\0')
    {
      k++;
      j++;
    }
    if(pat[j]=='\0')
    {
      copy_loop=k;
      while(rep_pat[rep_index] !='\0')
      {
        new_str[n] = rep_pat[rep_index];
        rep_index++;
        n++;
      }
    }
    new_str[n] = str[copy_loop];
    i++;
    copy_loop++;
    n++;
  }
  new_str[n]='\0';
  printf("\n The new string is: ");
  puts(new_str);
  return 0;
}
```

Output

```
Enter the string: How ARE you?
Enter the pattern to be replaced: ARE
Enter the replacing pattern: are
The new string is : How are you?
```

13.5 MISCELLANEOUS STRING AND CHARACTER FUNCTIONS

In this section, we will discuss some character and string manipulation functions that are part of header files—ctype.h, string.h, and stdlib.h.

13.5.1 Character Manipulation Functions

Table 13.2 illustrates some character functions contained in ctype.h.

Table 13.2 Functions in `ctype.h`

Function	Usage	Example
isalnum(int c)	Checks whether character c is an alphanumeric character	isalpha('A');
isalpha(int c)	Checks whether character c is an alphabetic character	isalpha('z');
iscntrl(int c)	Checks whether character c is a control character	scanf("%d", &c);iscntrl(c);
isdigit(int c)	Checks whether character c is a digit	isdigit(3);
isgraph()	Checks whether character c is a graphic or printing character. The function excludes the white space character	isgraph('!');
isprint(int c)	Checks whether character c is a printing character. The function includes the white space character	isprint('@');
islower(int c)	Checks whether the character c is in lower case	islower('k');
isupper(int c)	Checks whether the character c is in upper case	isupper('K');
ispunct(int c)	Checks whether the character c is a punctuation mark	ispunct('?');
isspace(int c)	Checks whether the character c is a white space character	isspace(' ');
isxdigit(int c)	Checks whether the character c is a hexadecimal digit	isxdigit('F');
tolower(int c)	Converts the character c to lower case	tolower('K') returns k
toupper(int c)	Converts the character c to upper case	tolower('k') returns K

13.5.2 String Manipulation Functions

In this section we will look at some commonly used string functions present in the `string.h` and `stdlib.h` header files.

`strcat` *Function*

Syntax:

```
char *strcat(char *str1, const char *str2);
```

> **Programming Tip:**
> Before using string copy and concatenating functions, ensure that the destination string has enough space to store all the elements so that memory overwriting does not take place.

The `strcat` function appends the string pointed to by `str2` to the end of the string pointed to by `str1`. The terminating null character of `str1` is overwritten. The process stops when the terminating null character of `str2` is copied. The argument `str1` is returned. Note that `str1` should be big enough to store the contents of `str2`.

```
#include <stdio.h>
#include <string.h>
int main()
{
  char str1[50] = "Programming";
  char str2[] = "In C";
  strcat(str1, str2);
  printf("\n str1: %s", str1);
  return 0;
}
```

Output

```
str1: Programming In C
```

`strncat` *Function*

Syntax:

```
char *strncat(char *str1, const char *str2,
size_t n);
```

This function appends the string pointed to by `str2` to the end of the string pointed to by `str1` up to `n` characters long. The terminating null character of `str1` is overwritten. Copying stops when `n` characters are copied or the terminating null character of `str2` is copied. A terminating null character is appended to `str1` before returning to the calling function.

```
#include <stdio.h>
#include <string.h>
int main()
{
  char str1[50] = "Programming";
  char str2[] = "In C";
  strncat(str1, str2, 2);
  printf("\n str1: %s", str1);
  return 0;
}
```

Output

```
str1: Programming In
```

`strchr` *Function*

Syntax:

```
char *strchr(const char *str, int c);
```

The `strchr ( )` function searches for the first occurrence of the character `c` (an unsigned char) in the string pointed to by the argument `str`. The function returns a pointer pointing to the first matching character, or `NULL` if no match is found.

```
#include <stdio.h>
#include <string.h>
int main()
{
  char str[50] = "Programming In C";
  char *pos;
```

```
  pos = strchr(str, 'n');
  if(pos)
    printf("\n n is found in str at position
    %d", pos);
  else
    printf("\n n is not present in the
    string");
  return 0;
}
```

Output

```
n is found in str at position 9
```

strrchr *Function*

Syntax:

```
char *strrchr(const char *str, int c);
```

The strrchr ( ) function searches for the first occurrence of the character c (an unsigned char) beginning at the rear end and working towards the front in the string pointed to by the argument str, i.e., the function searches for the last occurrence of the character c and returns a pointer pointing to the last matching character, or NULL if no match is found.

```
#include <stdio.h>
#include <string.h>
int main()
{
  char str[50] = "Programming In C";
  char *pos;
  pos = strrchr(str, 'n');
  if(pos)
    printf("\n The last position of n is:
    %d", pos);
  else
    printf("\n n is not present in the
    string");
  return 0;
}
```

Output

```
The last position of n is: 13
```

strcmp *Function*

Syntax:

```
int strcmp(const char *str1, const char
*str2);
```

The strcmp function compares the string pointed to by str1 to the string pointed to by str2. The function returns zero if the strings are equal. Otherwise, it returns a value less than zero or greater than zero if str1 is less than or greater than str2 respectively.

```
#include <stdio.h>
#include <string.h>
int main()
{
  char str1[10] = "HELLO";
  char str2[10] = "HEY";
  if(strcmp(str1,str2)==0)
    printf("\n The two strings are
    identical");
  else
    printf("\n The two strings are not
    identical");
  return 0;
}
```

Output

```
The two strings are not identical
```

strncmp *Function*

Syntax:

```
int strncmp(const char *str1, const char
*str2, size_t n);
```

This function compares at most the first n bytes of str1 and str2. The process stops comparing after the null character is encountered. The function returns zero if the first n bytes of the strings are equal. Otherwise, it returns a value less than zero or greater than zero if str1 is less than or greater than str2, respectively.

```
#include <stdio.h>
#include <string.h>
int main()
{
  char str1[10] = "HELLO";
  char str2[10] = "HEY";
  if(strncmp(str1,str2,2)==0)
    printf("\n The two strings are
   identical");
  else
    printf("\n The two strings are not
   identical");
  return 0;
}
```

Output

```
The two strings are identical
```

strcpy *Function*

Syntax:

```
char *strcpy(char *st r1, const char *str2);
```

This function copies the string pointed to by str2 to str1 including the null character of str2. It returns the argument str1. Here str1 should be big enough to store the contents of str2.

```
#include <stdio.h>
```

```
#include <string.h>
int main()
{
  char str1[10], str2[10] = "HELLO";
  strcpy(str1,str2);
  printf("\n str1: %s", str1);
  return 0;
}
```

Output

```
HELLO
```

strncpy *Function*

Syntax:

```
char *strncpy(char *str1, const char *str2,
size_t n);
```

This function copies up to n characters from the string pointed to by str2 to str1. Copying stops when n characters are copied. However, if the null character in str2 is reached then the null character is continually copied to str1 until n characters have been copied. Finally, a null character is appended to str1. However, if n is zero or negative then nothing is copied.

> **Programming Tip:**
> Do not use string functions on a character array that is not terminated with a null character.

```
#include <stdio.h>
#include <string.h>
int main()
{
  char str1[10], str2[10] = "HELLO";
  strncpy(str1,str2, 2);
  printf("\n str1: %s", str1);
  return 0;
}
```

Output

```
HE
```

> **Note**
> To copy the string str2 in str1, a better way is to write
>
> `strncpy(str1, str2, sizeof(str1)-1);`
>
> This would enforce the copying of only that many characters for which str1 has space to accommodate.

strlen *Function*

Syntax:

```
size_t strlen(const char *str);
```

This function calculates the length of the string str up to but not including the null character, i.e., the function returns the number of characters in the string.

```
#include <stdio.h>
#include <string.h>
int main()
{
  char str[] = "HELLO";
  printf("\n Length of str is: %d",
  strlen(str));
  return 0;
}
```

Output

```
Length of str is: 5
```

strstr *Function*

Syntax:

```
char *strstr(const char *str1, const char
*str2);
```

This function is used to find the first occurrence of string str2 (not including the terminating null character) in the string str1. It returns a pointer to the first occurrence of str2 in str1. If no match is found, then a null pointer is returned.

```
#include <stdio.h>
#include <string.h>
int main()
{
  char str1[] = "HAPPY BIRTHDAY TO YOU";
  char str2[] = "DAY";
  char *ptr;
  ptr = strstr(str1, str2);
  if(ptr)
    printf("\n Substring Found");
  else
    printf("\n Substring Not Found");
  return 0;
}
```

Output

```
Substring Found
```

strspn *Function*

Syntax:

```
size_t strspn(const char *str1, const char *str2);
```

The function returns the index of the first character in str1 that doesn't match any character in str2.

```
#include <stdio.h>
#include <string.h>
int main()
{
  char str1[] = "HAPPY BIRTHDAY TO YOU";
  char str2[] = "HAPPY BIRTHDAY JOE";
  printf("\n The position of first character in
  str2 that does not match with that in str1
  is %d", strspn(str1,str2));
```

```
    return 0;
}
```

Output

```
The position of first character in str2 that
does not match with that in str1 is 15
```

strcspn *Function*

Syntax:

```
size_t strcspn(const char *str1, const char
*str2);
```

The function returns the index of the first character in `str1` that matches any of the characters in `str2`.

```
#include <stdio.h>
#include <string.h>
int main()
{
  char str1[] = "PROGRAMMING IN C";
  char str2[] = "IN";
  printf("\n The position of first character in
  str2 that matches with that in str1 is %d",
  strcspn(str1,str2));
  return 0;
}
```

Output

```
The position of first character in str2 that
matches with that in str1 is 8
```

strpbrk *Function*

Syntax:

```
char *strpbrk(const char *str1, const char
*str2);
```

The function `strpbrk()` returns a pointer to the first occurrence in `str1` of any character in `str2`, or `NULL` if none are present. The only difference between `strpbrk()` and `strcspn` is that `strcspn()` returns the index of the character and `strpbrk()` returns a pointer to the first occurrence of a character in `str2`.

```
#include <stdio.h>
#include <string.h>
int main()
{
  char str1[] = "PROGRAMMING IN C";
  char str2[] = "AB";
  char *ptr = strpbrk(str1,str2);
  if(ptr==NULL)
    printf("\n No character matches in the two
    strings");
  else
    printf("\n Character in str2 matches with
    that in str1");
  return 0;
}
```

Output

```
No character matches in the two strings
```

strtok *Function*

Syntax:

```
char *strtok( char *str1, const char
   *delimiter );
```

The `strtok()` function is used to isolate sequential tokens in a null-terminated string, `str`. These tokens are separated in the string using delimiters. The first time that `strtok` is called, `str` should be specified; subsequent calls, wishing to obtain further tokens from the same string, should pass a null pointer instead. However, the delimiter must be supplied each time, though it may change between calls.

The `strtok()` function returns a pointer to the beginning of each subsequent token in the string, after replacing the token itself with a null character. When all tokens are left, a null pointer is returned.

```
#include <stdio.h>
#include <string.h>
main ()
{
  char str[] = "Hello, to, the, world of,
  programming";
  char delim[] = ",";
  char result[20];
  result = strtok(str, delim);
  while(result!=NULL)
  {
    printf("\n %s", result);
    result = strtok(NULL, delim);
  }
  return 0;
}
```

Output

```
Hello
to
the
world of
programming
```

strtol *Function*

Syntax:

```
long strtol(const char *str, char **end, int
base);
```

The `strtol` function converts the string pointed by `str` to a `long` value. The function skips leading white space characters and stops when it encounters the first non-numeric character. `strtol` stores the address of the first invalid character in str in *end. If there were no digits at all, then the strtol function will store the original value of str in *end. You may pass NULL instead of *end if you do not want to store the invalid characters anywhere.

Finally, the third argument base specifies whether the number is in hexadecimal, octal, binary, or decimal representation.

```
#include <stdio.h>
#include <stdlib.h>
main ()
{
  long num;
  num = strtol("12345 Decimal Value", NULL, 10);
  printf("\n%ld", num);
  num = strtol("65432 Octal Value", NULL, 8);
  printf("\n%ld", num);
  num = strtol("10110101 Binary Value", NULL, 2);
  printf("\n%ld", num);
  num = strtol("A7CB4 Hexadecimal Value", NULL,
    16);
  printf("\n%ld", num);
  return 0;
}
```

Output

```
12345
27418
181
687284
```

strtod *Function*

Syntax:

```
double strtod(const char *str, char **end);
```

The function accepts a string str that has an optional plus ('+') or minus sign ('-') followed by either:

- a decimal number containing a sequence of decimal digits optionally consisting of a decimal point, or
- a hexadecimal number consisting of a "0X" or "0x" followed by a sequence of hexadecimal digits optionally containing a decimal point.

In both cases, the number may be optionally followed by an exponent ('E' or 'e' for decimal constants or a 'P' or 'p' for hexadecimal constants), followed by an optional plus or minus sign, followed by a sequence of decimal digits. For decimal and hexadecimal constants, the exponent indicates the power of 10 and 2, respectively, by which the number should be scaled.

```
#include <stdio.h>
#include <stdlib.h>
main ()
{
  double num;
  num = strtod("123.345abcdefg", NULL);
  printf("%lf", num);
  return 0;
}
```

Output

```
123.345000
```

atoi() *Function*

Till now you must have understood that the value 1 is an integer and '1' is a character. So there is a huge difference when we write the two statements given below

```
int i=1;     // here i =1
int i='1';    /* here i =49, the ASCII value
  of character 1*/
```

Similarly, 123 is an integer number but '123' is a string of digits. What if you want to operate some integer operations on the string '123'? For this, C provides a function atoi that converts a given string into its corresponding integer.

The atoi() function converts a given string passed to it as an argument into an integer. The atoi() function returns that integer to the calling function. However, the string should start with a number. atoi() will stop reading from the string as soon as it encounters a non-numerical character. atoi() is included in the stdlib.h file. So before using this function in your program, you must include this header file. The syntax of atoi() can be given as,

```
int atoi(const char *str);
```

Example `i = atoi("123.456");`
`RESULT: i = 123.`

atof() *Function*

The atof() function converts the string that it accepts as an argument into a double value and then returns that value to the calling function. However, the string must start with a valid number. One point to remember is that the string can be terminated with any non-numerical character, other than "E" or "e". The syntax of atof() can be given as,

```
double atof(const char *str);
```

Example `x = atof("12.39 is the answer");`
`RESULT: x = 12.39`

atol() *Function*

The atol() function converts the string into a long int value. The atol function returns the converted long value to the calling function. Like atoi, the atol() function will read from a string until it finds any character that should not be in a long. Its syntax can be given as,

```
long atol(const char *str);
```

Example `x = atol("12345.6789");`
`RESULT: x = 12345L.`

Note

The atoi(), atof(), and atol() functions are a part of stdlib.h header file.

13.6 ARRAYS OF STRINGS

Till now we have seen that a string is an array of characters. For example, if we say char `name[] = "Mohan"`, then name is a string (character array) that has five characters.

Now suppose that there are 20 students in a class and we need a string that stores names of all the 20 students. How can this be done? Here, we need a string of strings or an array of strings. Such an array of strings would store 20 individual strings. An array of strings is declared as,

```
char names[20][30];
```

Here, the first index that specifies the number of strings that are needed and the second index specifies the length of every individual string. So here, we allocate space for 20 names where each name can be a maximum of 30 characters long. The general syntax for declaring a two-dimensional array of strings can be given as

```
<data type> <array_name> [row_size][column_
size];
```

Let us see the memory representation of an array of strings. If we have an array declared as

```
char name[5][10] = {"Ram", "Mohan", "Shyam",
"Hari", "Gopal"};
```

Then in memory the array is stored as shown in Figure 13.20.

Name[0]	R	A	M	'\0'						
Name[1]	M	O	H	A	N	'\0'				
Name[2]	S	H	Y	A	M	'\0'				
Name[3]	H	A	R	I	'\0'					
Name[4]	G	O	P	A	L	'\0'				

Figure 13.20 Memory representation of a 2D character array

By declaring the array names, we allocate 50 bytes. But the actual memory occupied is 27 bytes. Thus we see, more than half of the memory allocated lies wasted. Figure 13.21 shows an algorithm to process an individual string from an array of strings.

```
Step 1: [Initialize] SET I=0
Step 2: Repeat Step 3 while I<N
Step 3: Apply Process to NAMES[I]
        [END OF LOOP]
Step 4: EXIT
```

Figure 13.21 Algorithm to process an individual string from an array of strings

Programming Tip: When accessing elements of a character array, make sure that the elements are within the array boundaries.

In Step 1, we initialize the index variable `I` to `zero`. In Step 2, a `while` loop is executed until all the strings in the array are accessed. In Step 3, each individual string is processed.

16. Write a program to read and print the names of n students of a class.

```
#include <stdio.h>
int main()
{
  char names[5][10];
  int i, n;
  printf("\n Enter the number of students:");
  scanf("%d", &n);
  for(i=0;i<n;i++)
  {
    printf("\n Enter the name of
      student %d: ", i+1);
    gets(names[i]);
  }
  printf("\n Names of the students are:\n");
  for(i = 0;i < n;i++)
    puts(names[i]);
    return 0;
}
```

Output

```
Enter the number of students: 3
Enter the name of student 1: Aditya
Enter the name of student 2: Goransh
Enter the name of student 3: Sarthak
Names of the students are: Aditya Goransh
Sarthak
```

17. Write a program to sort names of students.

```
#include <stdio.h>
int main()
{
  char names[5][10], temp[10];
  int i, n, j;
  printf("\n Enter the number of students: ");
  scanf("%d", &n);
  for(i=0;i<n;i++)
  {
    printf("\n Enter the name of the  student
    %d: ", i+1);
    gets(names[i]);
  }
```

```
        for(i = 0;i < n;i++)
        {
          for(j = 0;j < n-i-1;j++)
          {
          if(strcmp(names[j], names[j+1])>0)
          {
            strcpy(temp, names[j]);
            strcpy(names[j], names[j+1]);
            strcpy(names[j+1], temp);
          }
          }
        }
        printf("\n Names of
         the students are: ");
        for(i=0;i<n;i++)
           puts(names[i]);
             return 0;
    }
```

Programming Tip: Strings cannot be manipulated with arithmetic or other operators available in C boundaries.

Output

```
Enter the number of students: 3
Enter the name of student 1: Sarthak
Enter the name of student 2: Goransh
Enter the name of student 3: Aditya
Names of the students are: Aditya Goransh
Sarthak
```

18. Write a program to read and print the text until a * is encountered. Also count the number of characters in the text entered.

```
#include <stdio.h>
int main()
{
  char str[100];
  int i=0;
  printf("\n Enter * to end");
  printf("\n Enter the text: ");
  scanf("%c", &str[i]);
  while(str[i] != '*')
  {
    i++;
    scanf("%c", &str[i]);
  }
  str[i] = '\0';
  printf("\n The text is: ");
  i=0;
  while(str[i] != '\0')
  {
    printf("%c", str[i]);
    i++;
  }
  printf("\n The count of characters is:
   %d",i);
  return 0;
}
```

Output

```
Enter * to end
Enter the text: Hi there*
The text is: Hi there
The count of characters is: 8
```

19. Write a program to read a sentence. Then count the number of words in the sentence.

```
#include <stdio.h>
int main()
{
  char str[200];
  int i=0, count=0;
  printf("\n Enter the sentence: ");
  gets(str);
  while(str[i] != '\0')
  {
    if(str[i] == ' ' && str[i+1] != ' ')
    count++;
    i++;
  }
  printf("\n The total count of words is: %d",
  count+1);
  return 0;
}
```

Output

```
Enter the sentence: How are you
The total count of words is: 3
```

20. Write a program to read multiple lines of text until a * is entered. Then count the number of characters, words, and lines in the text.

```
#include <stdio.h>
int main()
{
  char str[200];
  int i=0, word_count = 0, line_count =0,
   char_count = 0;
  printf("\n Enter a * to end");
  printf("\n Enter the text: ");
  scanf("%c", &str[i]);
  while(str[i] != '*')
  {
    i++;
    scanf("%c", &str[i]);
  }
  str[i] = '\0';
  i=0;
  while(str[i] != '\0')
  {
```

```
    if(str[i] == '\n' || i==79)
      line_count++;
    if(str[i] == ' ' && str[i+1] != ' ')
      word_count++;
    char_count++;
    i++;
  }
  printf("\n The total count of words is: %d",
  word_count+1);
  printf("\n The total count of lines is: %d",
  line_count+1);
  printf("\n The total count of characters is:
  %d", char_count);
  return 0;
}
```

Output

```
Enter the text: Hi there*
The total count of words is: 2
The total count of lines is: 1
The total count of characters is: 8
```

21. Write a program to copy n characters of a string from the mth position in another string.

```
#include <stdio.h>
int main()
{
  char str[1000], copy_str[1000];
  int i=0, j=0, m, n;
  printf("\n Enter the text: ");
  gets(str);
  printf("\n Enter the position from which to
  start: ");
  scanf("%d", &m);
  printf("\n Enter the number of characters to
  be copied: ");
  scanf("%d", &n);
  i = m;
  while(str[i] != '\0' && n>0)
  {
    copy_str[j] = str[i];
    i++;
    j++;
    n--;
  }
  copy_str[j] = '\0';
  printf("\n The copied text is: ");
  puts(copy_str);
  return 0;
}
```

Output

```
Enter the text: How are you?
Enter the position from which to start: 2
Enter the number of characters to be copied: 5
The copied text is: w are
```

22. Write a program to enter a text that has commas. Replace all the commas with semi colons and then display the text.

```
#include <stdio.h>
int main()
{
  char str[1000], copy_str[1000];
  int i=0;
  printf("\n Enter the text: ");
  gets(str);
  while(str[i] != '\0')
  {
    if(str[i] ==',')
      copy_str[i] = ';';
    else
      copy_str[i] = str[i];
    i++;
  }
  copy_str[i] = '\0';
  printf("\n The copied text is: ");
  i=0;
  while(copy_str[i] != '\0')
  {
    printf("%c", copy_str[i]);
    i++;
  }
  return 0;
}
```

Output

```
Enter the text: Hello, How are you
The copied text is: Hello; How are you
```

23. Write a program to enter a text that contains multiple lines. Rewrite this text by printing line numbers before the text of the line starts.

```
#include <stdio.h>
int main()
{
  char str[1000];
  int i=0, linecount = 1;
  printf("\n Enter a * to end");
  printf("\n **************");
  printf("\n Enter the text: ");
  scanf("%c", &str[i]);
  while(str[i] != '*')
  {
    i++;
    scanf("%c", &str[i]);
  }
  str[i] = '\0';
```

```
    i=0;
    while(str[i] != '\0')
    {
      if(linecount == 1 && i == 0)
        printf("\n %d\t", linecount);
      if(str[i] == '\n')
      {
        linecount++;
        printf("\n %d\t", linecount);
      }
      printf("%c", str[i]);
      i++;
    }
    return 0;
}
```

Output

```
Enter a * to end
**************
Enter the text:
Hello
how
are You?*
1  Hello
2  how
3  are you?
```

24. Write a program to enter a text that contains multiple lines. Display the n lines of text starting from the mth line.

```
#include <stdio.h>
int main()
{
  char str[1000];
  int i = 0, j, m, n, linecount = 0;
  clrscr();
  printf("\n Enter a * to end ");
  printf("\n Enter the text: ");
  scanf("%c", &str[i]);
  while(str[i]!='*')
    { i++;
      scanf("%c", &str[i]);
    }
  str[i] = '\0';
  printf("\n Enter the line number from which
  to copy : ");
  scanf("%d", &m);
  printf("\n Enter the line number till which
  to copy : ");
  scanf("%d", &n);
  i=0;
  while(str[i] != '\0')
  {
   if(linecount == m )
   {
     j = i;
     while(n>0)
     {
       printf("%c", str[j]);
       j++;
       if(str[j] == '\n')
       {
       n--;
       linecount++;
       printf("%d \t", linecount);
       }
     }
   }
   else
   {
     i++;
     if(str[i] == '\n')
     linecount++;
   }
  }
  return 0;
}
```

Output

```
Enter a * to end
Enter the text : Hello
how
are you?
*
Enter the line number from which to copy: 1
Enter the line number till which to copy: 2
Hello 1
how 2
```

25. Write a program to enter a text. Then enter a pattern and count the number of times the pattern is repeated in the text.

```
#include <stdio.h>
int main()
{
  char str[200], pat[20];
  int i=0, j=0, found=0, k, count=0;
  printf("\n Enter the string: ");
  gets(str);
  printf("\n Enter the pattern: ");
  gets(pat);
   while(str[i]!='\0')
   {
     j=0, k=i;
  while(str[k]==pat[j] && pat[j]!='\0')
     {
       k++;
       j++;
     }
     if(pat[j]=='\0')
     {
       found=1;
```

```
        count++;
    }
    i++;
    }
    if(found==1)
        printf("\n PATTERN FOUND %d TIMES",
        count);
    else
        printf("\n PATTERN NOT FOUND");
  return 0;
}
```

Output

```
Enter the string: She sells sea shells on the
sea shore
Enter the pattern: sea
PATTERN FOUND 2 TIMES
```

26. Write a program to find whether a given string is a palindrome or not.

```
#include <stdio.h>
int main()
{
  char str[100];
  int i = 0, j, length = 0;
  printf("\n Enter the string: ");
  gets(str);
  while(str[i] != '\0')
  {
    length++;
    i++;
  }
  i=0;
  j = length - 1;
  while(i <= length/2)
  {
    if(str[i] == str[j])
    {
    i++;
    j--;
    }
    else
    break;
  }
  if(i>=j)
    printf("\n PALINDROME");
  else
    printf("\n NOT A PALINDROME");
  return 0;
}
```

Output

```
Enter the string: madam
PALINDROME
```

27. Write a program to implement a quiz program.

```
#include <stdio.h>
#include <string.h>
main()
{
  char quest[5][100];
  char option1[3][20],option2[3][20],
  option3[3][20],option4[3][20],
  option5[3][20];
  int response[5], correct_ans[5], option, i,
  marks;
  strcpy(quest[0],"Name the capital of
  India");
  strcpy(option1[0],"1. Mumbai");
  strcpy(option1[1],"2. New Delhi");
  strcpy(option1[2],"3. Chennai");
  correct_ans[0] = 1;
  strcpy(quest[1],"Name the national bird of
  India");
  strcpy(option2[0],"1. Peacock");
  strcpy(option2[1],"2. Sparrow");
  strcpy(option2[2],"3. Parrot");
  correct_ans[1]=0;
  strcpy(quest[2],"Name the first Prime
  Minister of India");
  strcpy(option3[0],"1. M D Gandhi");
  strcpy(option3[1],"2. S D Sharma");
  strcpy(option3[2],"3. J L Nehru");
  correct_ans[2]=2;
  strcpy(quest[3],"Name the first female
  President of India");
  strcpy(option4[0],"1. Pratibha Patil");
  strcpy(option4[1],"2. Sonia Gandhi");
  strcpy(option4[2],"3. Indira Gandhi");
  correct_ans[3] = 0;
  strcpy(quest[4],"Name the youngest Prime
  Minister of India");
  strcpy(option5[0],"1. Rajiv Gandhi");
  strcpy(option5[1],"2. Sanjay Gandhi");
  strcpy(option5[2],"3. Rahul Gandhi");
  correct_ans[4] = 0;
  do
  {
    printf("\n\n\n\n QUIZ PROGRAM");
    printf("\n******************");
    printf("\n 1. Display Questions");
    printf("\n 2. Display Correct Answers");
    printf("\n 3. Display Result");
    printf("\n 4. EXIT");
    printf("\n ************************");
    printf("\n\n\n Enter your option: ");
    scanf("%d", &option);
    switch(option)
    {
    case 1:
```

```
printf("\n %s \n", quest[0]);
for(i=0;i<3;i++)
  printf("\n %s", option1[i]);
  printf("\n\n Enter your answer number:
  ");
  scanf("%d", &response[0]);
  printf("\n %s \n", quest[1]);
for(i=0;i<3;i++)
  printf("\n %s", option2[i]);
  printf("\n\n Enter your answer number:
  ");
  scanf("%d", &response[1]);
  printf("\n %s \n", quest[2]);
for(i=0;i<3;i++)
 printf("\n %s", option3[i]);
 printf("\n\n Enter your answer number: ");
 scanf("%d", &response[2]);
 printf("\n %s \n", quest[3]);
for(i=0;i<3;i++)
 printf("\n %s", option4[i]);
 printf("\n\n Enter your answer number: ");
 scanf("%d", &response[3]);
 printf("\n %s \n", quest[4]);
for(i=0;i<3;i++)
 printf("\n %s", option5[i]);
 printf("\n\n Enter your answer number: ");
 scanf("%d", &response[4]);
break;
case 2:
  printf("\n\n CHECK THE CORRECT ANSWERS");
  printf("\n ************************");
  printf("\n %s \n
%s",quest[0],option1[correct_ans[0]]);
  printf("\n\n %s \n
%s",quest[1],option2[correct_ans[1]]);
  printf("\n\n %s \n
%s",quest[2],option3[correct_ans[2]]);
  printf("\n\n %s \n
%s",quest[3],option4[correct_ans[3]]);
  printf("\n\n %s \n
%s",quest[4],option5[correct_ans[4]]);
  break;
  case 3:
  marks = 0;
  for(i = 0;i <= 4;i++)
  {
  if(correct_ans[i]+1 == response[i])
  marks++;
  }
  printf("\n Out of 5 you score %d", marks);
  break;
  }
 }while(option!=4);
 return 0;
}
```

POINTS TO REMEMBER

- A string is a null-terminated character array.
- A string is terminated with a null character ('\0') to signify the end of the character array.
- A string is a character array in which individual characters can be accessed using a subscript that starts from zero.
- All the characters of a string array are stored in successive memory locations.
- Strings can be read by using three ways—using scanf() function, using gets() function, or using getchar() function repeatedly.
- scanf function terminates as soon as it finds a blank space.
- gets() takes the starting address of the string which will hold the input. The string inputted using gets() is automatically terminated with a null character.
- Strings can also be read by calling getchar() repeatedly to read a sequence of single characters (unless a terminating character is entered).
- Strings can be displayed on the screen using three ways—using printf() function, using puts() function or using putchar() function repeatedly.
- In printf(), the width specifies the minimum output field width. If the string is short, extra space is either left padded or right padded. The precision specifies the maximum number of characters to be displayed. A negative width left pads short string rather than the default right justification. If the string is long, the extra characters are truncated.
- The number of characters in the string constitutes the length of the string.
- Appending one string to another string involves copying the contents of the source string at the end of the destination string.
- To extract a substring from a given string requires information about three things—the main string, the position of the first character of the substring in the given string, and length of the substring.
- Index operation returns the position in the string where the string pattern first occurs.
- Replacement operation is used to replace the pattern P1 by another pattern P2.

GLOSSARY

Scanset It is used to define a set of characters which may be read and assigned to a string. It is defined by placing the characters inside square brackets preceded with a %.

String An array of characters terminated by a null character.

String matching Finding occurrences of a *pattern* string within another *string*.

String taxonomy A string can be stored either in fixed-length or in variable-length format.

EXERCISES

Fill in the Blanks

1. Strings are ________.
2. Every string is terminated with a ________.
3. If a string is given as "AB CD", the length of this string is ________.
4. The subscript of a string starts with ________.
5. Characters of a string are stored in ________ memory locations.
6. char mesg[100]; can store maximum ________ characters.
7. ________ function terminates as soon as it finds a blank space.
8. LENGTH("") = ________.
9. The ASCII code for A-Z varies from ________.
10. toupper() is used to ________.
11. S1>S2, means ________.
12. The function to reverse a string is ________.
13. If S1 = "GOOD MORNING", then Substr_Left (S1, 7) =
14. INDEX("Welcome to the world of programming", "world") = ________.
15. ________ returns the position in the string where the string pattern first occurs.
16. The atoi() function is present in ________ header file.
17. strncat(str1, str2,n) is used to ________.
18. strcmp(str1, str2) returns 1 if ________.
19. ________ function computes the length of a string.
20. Besides printf(), ________ function can be used to print a line of text on the screen.

Multiple-choice Questions

1. LENGTH("\0") =
   (a) -1 (b) 0
   (c) 1 (d) None of these
2. ASCII code for a–z ranges from
   (a) 0–26 (b) 35–81
   (c) 97–123 (d) None of these
3. Insert("XXXYYYZZZ", 1, "PPP") =
   (a) PPPXXXYYYZZZ (b) XPPPXXYYYZZZ
   (c) XXXYYYZZZPPP
4. Delete("XXXYYYZZZ", 4,3) =
   (a) XXYZ (b) XXXYYZZ
   (c) XXXYZZ
5. If str[] = "Welcome to the world of programming", then SUBSTRING(str, 15, 5) =
   (a) world (b) programming
   (c) welcome (d) none of these
6. strcat() is defined in which of the header files?
   (a) ctype.h (b) stdio.h
   (c) string.h (d) math.h
7. A string can be read using which function?
   (a) gets() (b) scanf()
   (c) getchar() (d) All of these
8. Replace("XXXYYYZZZ", "XY", "AB") =
   (a) XXABYYZZZ (b) XABYYYZZZ
   (c) ABXXXYYYZZ
9. The index of U in Oxford University Press is?
   (a) 5 (b) 6
   (c) 7 (d) 8
10. s1 = "HI", s2 = "HELLO", s3 = "BYE". How can we concatenate the three strings?
    (a) strcat(s1,s2,s3)
    (b) strcat(s1(strcat(s2,s3)))
    (c) strcpy(s1, strcat(s2,s3))
11. strlen("Oxford University Press") is ?
    (a) 22 (b) 23
    (c) 24 (d) 25
12. Which function adds a string to the end of another string?
    (a) stradd() (b) strcat()
    (c) strtok() (d) strcpy()

State True or False

1. A string "Hello World" can be read using scanf().
2. Initializing a string as char str[]="HELLO"; is incorrect as a null character has not been explicitly added.
3. A string when read using scanf() needs an ampersand character.
4. `gets()` takes the starting address of the string which will hold the input.
5. `gets()` and `scanf()` automatically append a null character at the end of the string read from the keyboard.
6. The `scanf()` function can be used to read a line of text that includes white space characters.
7. The `tolower()` function is defined in ctype.h header file.
8. Arithmetic operators can be applied to string variables.
9. String variables can be present either on the left or on the right side of the assignment operator.
10. If `S1` and `S2` are two strings, then concatenation operation produces a string which contains characters of `S2` followed by the characters of `S1`.
11. Appending one string to another string involves copying the contents of the source string at the end of the destination string.
12. S1<S2, when in dictionary order S1 precedes S2
13. If S1 = "GOOD MORNING", then Substr_Right(S1, 5) = MORNING.
14. Replace ("AAABBBCCC", "X", "YYY")= AAABBBCC.
15. When a string is initialized during its declaration, the string must be explicitly terminated with a null character.
16. strcmp("and", "ant") will return a positive value.
17. Assignment operator can be used to copy the contents of one string into another.

Review Questions

1. What are strings? Discuss some operations that can be performed on strings.
2. Explain how strings are represented in main memory.
3. How are strings read from the standard input device? Explain the different functions used to perform string input operation.
4. Explain how strings can be displayed on the screen.
5. Explain the syntax of printf() and scanf().
6. Write a short note on operations that can be performed on strings.
7. Differentiate between gets() and scanf().
8. Give the drawbacks of getchar() and scanf(). Which function can be used to overcome the shortcomings of getchar() and scanf()?
9. How can putchar() be used to print a string?
10. Differentiate between a character and a string.
11. Differentiate between a character array and a string.
12. List all the substrings that can be formed from the string "ABCD".
13. What do you understand by pattern matching? Give an algorithm for it.
14. Write a short note on arrays of strings.
15. How is an array of strings represented in the memory?
16. Explain with an example how an array of strings is stored in main memory.
17. If Substring function is given as SUBSTRING(string, position, length) then, find S(5,9) if S = "Welcome to world of C Programming".
18. If Index function is given as INDEX(text, pattern), then find the index(T, P) where T = "Welcome to world of C Programming" and P = "of".

Programming Exercises

1. Write a program in C to concatenate first n characters of a string to another string.
2. Write a program in C that compares first n characters of one string with first n characters of another string.
3. Write a program that reads your name and then displays the ASCII value of each character in your name on a separate line.
4. Write a program in C that removes leading and trailing spaces from a string.
5. Write a program to read a word and re-write its characters in alphabetical order.
6. Write a program that accepts an integer value from 0 to 999. Display the value of the number read in words. That is, if the user enters 753, then print Seven Hundred Fifty Three.
7. Write a program to insert a word before a given word in the text.
8. Write a program to (a) read a name and then display it in abbreviated form, (b) Janak Raj Thareja should be displayed as JRT; (c) Janak Raj Thareja should be displayed as J.R. Thareja.
9. Write a program in C that replaces a given character with another character in the string.
10. Write a program to display the word Hello in the following format:

```
H
H E
H E L
H E L L
H E L L O
```

11. Write a program to display the given string array in reverse order.
12. Write a program to count the number of characters, words, and lines in the given text.
13. Write a program to count the number of digits, upper case characters, lower case characters, and special characters in a given string.
14. Write a program to count the total number of occurrences of a given character in the string.
15. Write a program to accept a text. Count and display the number of times the word "the" appears in the text.
16. Write a program to find the last instance of occurrence of a sub-string within a string.

17. Write a program to insert a sub-string in the middle of a given string.
18. Write a program to input an array of strings. Then reverse the string in the format shown below.
"HAPPY BIRTHDAY TO YOU" should be displayed as "YOU TO BIRTHDAY HAPPY".
19. Write a program to append a given string in the following format.
"GOOD MORNING MORNING GOOD"
20. Write a program to input a text of at least two paragraphs. Interchange the first and second paragraphs and then re-display the text on screen.
21. Write a program to input a text of at least two paragraphs. Construct an array PAR such that PAR[i] contains the location of the ith paragraph in TEXT.
22. Write a program to find the length of "GOOD MORNING".
23. (a) Write a program to convert the given string "GOOD MORNING" to "good morning".
(b) Write a program to convert the given string "hello world" to "HELLO WORLD".
24. Write a program to concatenate two given strings "Good Morning" and "World". Display the resultant string.
25. Write a program to append two given strings "Good Morning" and "World". Display the resultant string.
26. Write a program to check whether the two given strings "Good Morning" and "GOOD MORNING" are same.
27. Write a program to convert the given string "hello world" to "dlrow olleh".
28. Write a menu driven program that demonstrates the use of string functions present in the string.h header file.
29. Write a menu driven program that demonstrates the use of character handling functions present in the ctype.h header file.
30. Write a program to extract the string "od Mo" from the given string "Good Morning".
31. Write a program to insert "University" in the given string "Oxford Press" so that the string should read as "Oxford University Press".
32. Write a program to delete "University" from the given string "Oxford University Press" so that the string should read as "Oxford Press".
33. Write a menu driven program to read a string, display the string, merge two strings, copy n characters from the mth position, calculate the length of the string.
34. Write a program to copy the last n characters of a character array in another character array. Also convert the lower case letters into upper case letters while copying.
35. Write a program to simulate the strcpy function.
36. Write a program to read and display names of employees in a department.
37. Write a program to sort the names of employees alphabetically.
38. Write a program to read a short story. Display the n lines of story starting from the mth line.
39. Write a program to read a short story. Rewrite the story by printing the line number before the starting of each line.
40. Write a program to display a list of candidates. Prompt 100 users to cast their vote. Finally display the winner in the elections.
41. Write a program to delete the last character of a string.
42. Write a program to delete the first character of a string.
43. Write a program to insert a new name in the string array STUD[][], assuming that names are sorted alphabetically.
44. Write a program to delete a name in the string array STUD[][], assuming that names are sorted alphabetically.
45. In a class there are 20 students. Each student is supposed to appear in three tests and two quizzes throughout the year. Make an array that stores the names of all these 20 students. Make five arrays that store marks of three subjects as well as scores of two quizzes for all the students. Calculate the average and total marks of each student. Display the result.

Find the output of the following codes.

1.
```
main()
{
    char str1[]= {'H','I'};
    char str2[] = {'H',  'I',  '\0'};
    if(strcmp(str1, str2) == 0)
      printf("\n The strings are equal");
    else
      printf("\n Strings are not equal");
}
```
2.
```
main()
{
    char str[]= "Programming in C";
    int i;
    while(str[i]!='\0')
    {
      if(i%2==0)
        printf("%c", str[i]);
      i++;
    }
}
```
3.
```
main()
{
    char str[]="GGOD MORNING";
    printf("\n %20.10s", str);
    printf("\n %s", str[0]);
    printf("\n %s", &str[5]);
}
```
4.
```
main()
{
    char ch = 'k';
    printf("%c", ch+10);
}
```

```
5. main()
   {
     char str1[]= "Programming";
     char str2[] = "Is Fun";
     strcpy(str1, str2);
     printf("\n %s", str1);
   }
6. main()
   {
     char str1[]= "Programming";
     char str2[] = "Is Fun";
     strncpy(str1, str2, 3);
     printf("\n %s", str1);
   }
7. main()
   {
     char str1[]= "Programming";
     char str2[] = "Project";
     printf("%d", strncmp(str1, str2, 3));
   }
8. main()
   {
     char str[]= "Oxford University Press";
     printf("%s", strstr(str, "Uni"));
   }
```

Find errors in the following codes.

```
1. main()
   {
     char str1[]="Programming";
     char str2[] = "In C;
     str1 = str2;
     printf("\n str1 = %s", str1);
   }
2. main()
   {
     char str[]={'H','e','l','l','o'};
     printf("\n str = %s", str);
   }
3. main()
   {
     char str[5]="HELLO";
     printf("\n str = %s", str);
   }
4. main()
   {
     char str[10];
     strncpy(str1, "HELLO", 3);
     printf("\n str = %s", str);
   }
5. main()
   {
     char str[10];
     strcpy(str, "Hello there");
     printf("\n str = %s", str);
   }
6. main()
   {
     char str[]= "Hello there";
     if(strstr(str, "Uni")==0)
       printf("\n Substring Found");
   }
7. main()
   {
     char str1[10], str2[10];
     gets(str1, str2);
     printf("\n str1 = %s and str2 = %s", str1,
     str2);
   }
```

14 Pointers

TAKEAWAYS

- Pointer expressions
- Pointer arithmetic
- Null and generic pointers
- Pointers with functions
- Pointers with arrays
- Pointers with strings
- Arrays of pointers
- Pointers with 2D and 3D arrays
- Function pointers
- Pointers to pointers
- Dynamic memory allocation

14.1 UNDERSTANDING THE COMPUTER'S MEMORY

Every computer has a primary memory. All data and programs need to be placed in the primary memory for execution. RAM (Random Access Memory), which is a part of the primary memory, is a collection of memory locations (often known as cells) and each location has a specific address. Each memory location is capable of storing 1 byte of data (though new computers are able to store 2 bytes of data but in this book we have been talking about locations storing 1 byte of data). Therefore, a `char` type data needs just 1 memory location, an `int` type data needs 2 memory locations. Similarly, `float` and `double` type data need 4 and 8 memory locations, respectively.

In general, the computer has three areas of memory each of which is used for a specific task. These areas of memory include—stack, heap, and global memory.

Stack A fixed size of memory called system stack is allocated by the system and is filled as needed from the bottom to the top, one element at a time. These elements can be removed from the top to the bottom by removing one element at a time, i.e., the last element added to the stack is removed first.

When a program has used the variables or data stored in the stack, it can be discarded to enable the stack to be used by other programs to store their data. We have already read a little bit on the system stack in Chapter 11 when we discussed recursion.

Note

System stack is the section of memory that is allocated for automatic variables within functions.

Heap It is a contiguous block of memory that is available for use by programs when the need arises. A fixed size heap is allocated by the system and is used by the system in a random fashion.

The addresses of the memory locations in heap that are not currently allocated to any program for use are stored in a free list. When a program requests a block of memory, the dynamic allocation technique (discussed at the end of this chapter) takes a block from the heap and assigns it to the program. When the program has finished using the block, it returns the memory block to the heap and the addresses of the memory locations in that block are added to the free list.

Compared to heaps, stacks are faster but smaller and expensive. When a program begins execution with the `main()` function, all variables declared within `main()` are allocated space on the stack. Moreover, all the parametres passed to a called function are stored on the stack.

Global memory The block of code that is the `main()` program (along with other functions in the program) is stored in the global memory. The memory in the global area is allocated randomly to store the code of different functions in the program in such a way that one function is not contiguous to another function. Besides the function code, all global variables declared in the program are stored in the global memory area.

Other memory layouts C provides some more memory areas such as text segment, BSS, and shared library segment.

- The text segment is used to store the machine instructions corresponding to the compiled program. This is generally a read-only memory segment.
- BSS (Block Started by Symbol) is used to store un-initialized global variables.
- Shared library segment contains the executable image of shared libraries that are being used by the program.

14.2 INTRODUCTION TO POINTERS

Every variable in C language has a name and a value associated with it. When a variable is declared, a specific block of memory within the computer is allocated to hold the value of that variable. The size of the allocated block depends on the type of the data. Let us write a program to find the size of the various data types on your system. (Note the size of integer may vary from one system to another. In 32 bit systems, integer variable is allocated 4 bytes while on 16 bit systems it is allocated 2 bytes.)

1. Write a program to find the size of various data types on your system.

```
#include <stdio.h>
int main()
{
  printf("\n The size of short integer is :
  %d", sizeof(short int));
  printf("\n The size of unsigned integer is:
  %d", sizeof(unsigned int));
  printf("\n The size of signed integer is:
  %d", sizeof(signed int));
  printf("\n The size of integer is: %d",
  sizeof(int));
  printf("\n The size of long integer is: %d",
  sizeof(long int));

  printf("\n The size of character is: %d",
  sizeof(char));
  printf("\n The size of unsigned character
  is: %d", sizeof(unsigned char));
  printf("\n The size of signed character is:
  %d", sizeof(signed char));

  printf("\n The size of floating point number
  is: %d", sizeof(float));
  printf("\n The size of double number is:
  %d", sizeof(double));
  return 0;
}
```

Output

```
The size of short integer is: 2
The size of unsigned integer is: 2
The size of signed integer is: 2
The size of integer is: 2
The size of long integer is: 4
The size of character is: 1
The size of unsigned character is: 1
The size of signed character is: 1
The size of floating point number is: 4
The size of double number is: 8
```

Consider the statement below:

```
int x = 10;
```

When this statement executes, the compiler sets aside 2 bytes of memory to hold the value 10. It also sets up a symbol table in which it adds the symbol x and the relative address in memory where those 2 bytes are set aside.

Thus, every variable in C has a value and a memory location (commonly known as address) associated with it. Some texts use the term *rvalue* and *lvalue* for the value and the address of the variable, respectively.

The rvalue appears on the right side of the assignment statement (10 in the above statement) and cannot be used on the left side of the assignment statement. Therefore, writing `10 = k;` is illegal. If we write

```
int x, y;
x = 10;
y = x;
```

then in this code we have two integer variables x and y. Compiler reserves memory for integer variable x and stores rvalue 10 in it. When we say y = x, then x is interpreted as its rvalue (since it is on the right hand side of the assignment operator '='). Here x refers to the value stored at the memory location set aside for x, in this case 10. After this statement is executed, the rvalue of y is also 10.

You must be wondering why we are discussing addresses and lvalues? Actually pointers are nothing but memory addresses. A *pointer* is a variable that contains the memory location of another variable. Therefore, a pointer is a variable that represents the location of a data item, such as a variable or an array element. Pointers are frequently used in C language as they have a number of useful applications. These applications include:

- to pass information back and forth between a function and its reference point
- enable programmers to return multiple data items from a function via function arguments
- provide an alternate way to access individual elements of the array
- to pass arrays and strings as function arguments
- enable references to functions. So with pointers, programmers can even pass functions as argument to another function
- to create complex data structures such as trees, linked lists, linked stacks, linked queues, and graphs
- for dynamic memory allocation of a variable

14.3 DECLARING POINTER VARIABLES

Programming Tip: The data type of the pointer variable and the variable to which it points must be the same.

A pointer provides access to a variable by using the address of that variable. A pointer variable is therefore a variable that stores the address of another variable. The general syntax of declaring pointer variables can be given as below:

```
data_type *ptr_name;
```

Here, data_type is the data type of the value that the pointer will point to. For example,

```
int *pnum;
char *pch;
float *pfnum;
```

In each of the aforegiven statements, a pointer variable is declared to point to a variable of the specified data type. Although all these pointers, pnum, pch, and pfnum point to different data types, they will occupy the same amount of space in memory. But how much space they occupy will depend on the platform where the code is going to run. To verify this, execute the following code and observe the result.

```
#include <stdio.h>
main()
{
  int *pnum;
  char *pch;
  float *pfnum;
  double *pdnum;
  long *plnum;
   printf("\n Size of integer pointer = %d",
   sizeof(pnum));
  printf("\n Size of character pointer = %d",
  sizeof(pch));
  printf("\n Size of float pointer = %d",
  sizeof(pfnum));
  printf("\n Size of double pointer = %d",
  sizeof(pdnum));
  printf("\n Size of long pointer = %d",
  sizeof(plnum));
}
```

Output

```
Size of integer pointer = 2
Size of character pointer = 2
Size of float pointer = 2
Size of double pointer = 2
Size of long pointer = 2
```

Now let us declare an integer pointer variable and start using it in our program code.

```
int x= 10;
int *ptr;
ptr = &x;
```

In the above statement, ptr is the name of pointer variable. The '*' informs the compiler that ptr is a pointer variable and the int specifies that it will store the address of an integer variable.

Programming Tip:
A pointer variable can store only the address of a variable.

An integer pointer variable, therefore, *points* to an integer variable. In the last statement, ptr is assigned the address of x. The & operator retrieves the lvalue (address) of x, and assigns it to the pointer ptr.

Consider the memory cells given in Figure 14.1.

				10					
1000	1001	1002	1003	1004	1005	1006	1007	1008	1009

Figure 14.1 Memory representation

Now, since x is an integer variable, it will be allocated 2 bytes. Assuming that the compiler assigns it memory locations 1003 and 1004, we say the value of x = 10 and the address of x (written as &x) is equal to 1003, i.e., the starting address of x in the memory. When we write, ptr = &x, then ptr = 1003.

Note

In C, pointers are not allowed to store actual memory addresses, but only the addresses of variables of a given type. Therefore writing a statement like int *ptr = 1000; is absolutely illegal in C.

We can *dereference* a pointer, i.e., refer to the value of the variable to which it points, by using unary '*' operator (also known as *indirection operator*) as *ptr, i.e., *ptr = 10, since 10 is value of x. Therefore, * is equivalent to writing *value at address*. Look at the code below which shows the use of pointer variable.

Programming Tip:
As the address of a memory location is a constant, it cannot be changed in the program code.

```
#include <stdio.h>
int main()
{
  int num, *pnum;
  pnum = &num;
  printf("\n Enter the number: ");
  scanf("%d", &num);
  printf("\n The number that was entered is:
  %d", *pnum);
  printf("\n The address of number in memory
  is: %p", &num);
  return 0;
}
```

Output

```
Enter the number: 10
The number that was entered is: 10
The address of number in memory is: FFDC
```

Note

%p control string prints the argument as a memory address in hexadecimal form. %u prints memory address in decimal form.

Programming Tip:
A pointer variable cannot be assigned value of the variable to which it points.

Can you tell what will be the value of `*(&num)`? Yes it is equivalent to `num`. The indirection and the address operators are inverse of each other, so when combined in an expression, they cancel each other.

We can also assign values to variables using pointer variables and modify their values. The code given below shows this.

```
#include <stdio.h>
int main()
{
  int num, *pnum;
  pnum = &num;
  *pnum = 10;
  printf("\n *pnum = %d", *pnum);
  printf("\n num = %d", num);
  *pnum  = *pnum + 1;
  // increments the value of num
  printf("\n After increment *pnum = %d",
  *pnum);
  printf("\n After increment num = %d", num);
  return 0;
}
```

Output

```
*pnum = 10
num = 10
After increment *pnum = 11
After increment num = 11
```

Now can you predict the output of the following code?

```
#include <stdio.h>
int main()
{
  int num, *pnum1, *pnum2;
  pnum1 = &num;
  *pnum1 = 10;
  pnum2 = pnum1;
  printf("\n Value of num using all three
   variables (num, *pnum1, *pnum2) = %d %d
   %d", num, *pnum1, *pnum2);
  printf("\n Address of num using all three
   variables (&num, pnum1, pnum2) = %x %x %x",
   num, pnum1, pnum2);
  return 0;
}
```

While the first `printf` statement will print the value of `num`, the second `printf` statement will print the address of `num`. These are just three different ways to refer to the value and address of the same variable.

Note
Any number of pointers can point to the same address.

Programming Tip:
It is an error to assign address of a variable to another variable of the same type. The variable to which the address is being assigned must be declared as a pointer variable.

The address of a variable is the address of the first byte occupied by that variable. Basically, address of the variable is the relative location of the variable with respect to the program's memory space. Although the address of a variable cannot be changed, the variable's address may change during different program runs, i.e., if you try to print the address of `num` today, it may print `4010`. Next time when you run the program, it may print the address as `FA12`.

One point to remember always is that both the data type of the pointer variable and the variable whose address it will store must be of the same type. Therefore, the following code is not valid.

```
int x = 10;
float y = 2.0;
int *px;
float *py;
px = &y;  //INVALID
py = &x;//INVALID
```

Also note that it is not necessary that the pointer variable will point to the same variable throughout the program. It can point to any variable as long as the data type of the pointer variable is same as that of the variable it points to. The following code illustrates this concept.

```
#include <stdio.h>
int main()
{
  int a=3, b=5;
  int *pnum;
  pnum = &a;
  printf("\n a = %d", *pnum);
  pnum = &b;
  printf("\n b = %d", *pnum);
  return 0;
}
```

Output

```
a = 3
b = 5
```

Note
Using an un-initialized pointer can cause unpredictable results.

14.4 POINTER EXPRESSIONS AND POINTER ARITHMETIC

Like other variables, pointer variables can also be used in expressions. For example, if `ptr1` and `ptr2` are pointers, then the following statements are valid.

```
int num1=2, num2= 3, sum=0, mul=0, div=1;
int *ptr1, *ptr2;
ptr1 = &num1;
ptr2 = &num2;
sum = *ptr1 + *ptr2;
mul = sum * *ptr1;
*ptr2 +=1;
div = 9 + *ptr1/*ptr2 - 30;
```

In C, the programmer may add or subtract integers from pointers.We can also subtract one pointer from the other. We can also use short hand operators with the pointer variables as we use with other variables.

Programming Tip: A pointer variable that is declared but not initialized contains garbage value. Hence, a pointer variable must not be used before it is assigned any variable's address.

C also allows to compare pointers by using relational operators in the expressions. For example, `p1 > p2`, `p1 == p2`, and `p1! = p2` are all valid in C.

When using pointers, unary increment (`++`) and decrement (`--`) operators have greater precedence than the dereference operator (`*`). Both these operators have a special behaviour when used as suffix. In that case the expression is evaluated with the value it had before being increased. Therefore, the expression

```
*ptr++
```

is equivalent to `*(ptr++)` as ++ has greater operator precedence than `*`. Therefore, the expression will increase the value of `ptr` so that it now points to the next memory location. This means the statement `*ptr++` does not perform the intended task. Therefore, to increment the value of the variable whose address is stored in `ptr`, you should write

```
(*ptr)++
```

Now, let us consider another C statement

```
int num1=2, num2=3;
int *p = &num1, *q=&num2;
*p++ = *q++;
```

Programming Tip: It is an error to subtract two pointer variables.

What will `*p++ = *q++` do? Because `++` has a higher precedence than `*`, both p and q are increased, but because the increment operators (`++`) are used as postfix and not prefix, the value assigned to `*p` is `*q` before both p and q are increased. Then both are increased. So the statement is equivalent to writing:

```
*p = *q;
++p; ++q;
```

Let us now summarize the rules for pointer operations:

- A pointer variable can be assigned the address of another variable (of the same type).
- A pointer variable can be assigned the value of another pointer variable (of the same type).
- A pointer variable can be initialized with a null value.
- Prefix or postfix increment and decrement operators can be applied on a pointer variable.
- An integer value can be added or subtracted from a pointer variable.
- A pointer variable can be compared with another pointer variable of the same type using relational operators.
- A pointer variable cannot be multiplied by a constant.
- A pointer variable cannot be added to another pointer variable.

2. Write a program to print Hello World, using pointers.

```
#include <stdio.h>
int main()
{
    char *ch = "Hello World";
    printf("%s", ch);
    return 0;
}
```

Output

```
Hello World
```

3. Write a program to add two floating point numbers. The result should contain only two digits after the decimal.

```
#include <stdio.h>
int main()
{
    float num1, num2, sum = 0.0;
    float *pnum1 = &num1, *pnum2 = &num2,
     *psum = &sum;
    printf("\n Enter the two numbers: ");
    scanf("%f %f", pnum1, pnum2);
    // pnum1 = &num1;
    *psum = *pnum1 + *pnum2;
    printf("\n %f + %f = %.2f", *pnum1,
     *pnum2, *psum);
    return 0;
}
```

Output

```
Enter the two numbers: 2.5 3.4
2.5 + 3.4 = 5.90
```

4. Write a program to calculate area of a circle.

```
#include <stdio.h>

int main()
{
    double radius, area = 0.0;
    double *pradius = &radius, *parea = &area;
    printf("\n Enter the radius of the circle: ");
    scanf("%lf", pradius);
    *parea = 3.14 * (*pradius) * (*pradius);
    printf("\n The area of the circle with
     radius %.2lf = %.2lf", *pradius, *parea);
```

```
    return 0;
}
```

Output

```
Enter the radius of the circle: 7
The area of the circle with radius 7.00 = 153.83
```

5. Write a program to convert a floating point number into an integer.

```
#include <stdio.h>
int main()
{
    float fnum, *pfnum = &fnum;
    int num, *pnum = &num;
    printf("\n Enter the floating point no.: ");
    scanf("%f", &fnum);
    *pnum = (int)*pfnum;
    printf("\n The integer equivalent of %.2f
     = %d", *pfnum, *pnum);
    return 0;
}
```

Output

```
Enter the floating point no.: 3.4
The integer equivalent of 3.40 = 3
```

6. Write a program to print a character. Also print its ASCII value and rewrite the character in upper case.

```
#include <stdio.h>

int main()
{
    int ch, *pch = &ch;

    printf("\n Enter the character: ");
    scanf("%c", &ch);
    printf("\n The char entered is: %c", *pch);
    printf("\n ASCII value of the char is: %d",
     *pch);
    printf("\n The char in upper case is: %c",
     *pch - 32);

    return 0;
}
```

Output

```
Enter the character: z
The char entered is: z
ASCII value of the char is: 122
The char in upper case is: Z
```

7. Write a program using pointer variables to read a character until * is entered. If the character is in upper case, print it in lower case and vice versa. Also count the number of upper and lower case characters entered.

```
#include <stdio.h>
int main()
{
    char ch, *pch = &ch;
    int upper = 0, lower = 0;

    printf("\n Enter the character: ");
    scanf("%c", pch);
    while(*pch != '*')
    {
    if(*pch >= 'A' && *pch <= 'Z')
    {
        *pch += 32;
        upper++;
    }
    if(*pch >= 'a' && *pch <= 'z')
    {
        *pch -= 32;
        lower++;
    }
    printf("%c", *pch);
    printf("\n Enter the character: ");
    scanf("%c", pch);
    }
    printf("\n Total number of upper case
     characters = %d", upper);
    printf("\n Total number of lower case
     characters = %d", lower);

    return 0;
}
```

Output

```
Enter the character: A
a
Enter the character: b
B
Enter the character: c
C
Enter the character: *
Total number of upper case characters = 1
Total number of lower case characters = 2
```

8. Write a program to test whether a number is positive, negative, or equal to zero.

```
#include <stdio.h>
int main()
{
    int num, *pnum = &num;
    printf("\n Enter any number: ");
    scanf("%d", pnum);
    if(*pnum>0)
      printf("\n The number is positive");
    else
    {
    if(*pnum<0)
      printf("\n The number is negative");
    else
```

```
    printf("\n The number is equal to zero");
  }
  return 0;
}
```

Output

```
Enter any number: -1
The number is negative
```

9. Write a program to display the sum and average of numbers from m to n.

```
#include <stdio.h>
int main()
{
  int range;
  int m, *pm = &m;
  int n, *pn = &n;
  int sum = 0, *psum = &sum;
  float avg, *pavg = &avg;
  printf("\n Enter the starting and ending
   limit of the numbers to be summed:");
      scanf("%d %d", pm, pn);
      range = n - m ;
  while(*pm <= *pn)
  {
  *psum = *psum + *pm;
  *pm = *pm + 1;
  }
  printf("\n Sum of numbers = %d", *psum);
  *pavg = (float)*psum / range;
  printf("\n Average of numbers = %.2f",
   *pavg);
  return 0;
}
```

Output

```
Enter the starting and ending limit of the
  numbers to be summed: 0 10
Sum of numbers = 55
Average of numbers = 5.50
```

10. Write a program to print all even numbers from m to n.

```
#include <stdio.h>

int main()
{
  int m, *pm = &m;
  int n, *pn = &n;
  printf("\n Enter the starting and ending
   limit of the numbers: ");
  scanf("%d %d", pm, pn);
  while(*pm <= *pn)
  {
      if(*pm %2 == 0)
        printf("\n %d is even", *pm);
            (*pm)++;
  }
  return 0;
}
```

Output

```
Enter the starting and ending limit of the
   numbers: 0 10
0 is even
2 is even
4 is even
6 is even
8 is even
10 is even
```

11. Write a program to read numbers until –1 is entered. Also display whether the number is prime or composite.

```
#include <stdio.h>
int main()
{
  int num, *pnum = &num;
  int i, flag = 0;
  printf("\n ***** ENTER -1 TO EXIT *****);
  printf("\n Enter any number: ");
  scanf("%d", pnum);
  while(*pnum != -1)
  {
  if(*pnum == 1)
  printf("\n %d is neither prime nor
   composite", *pnum);
  else if(*pnum == 2)
  printf("\n %d is prime", *pnum);
  else
  {
  for(i=2; i<*pnum/2; i++)
  {
  if(*pnum/i == 0)
  flag =1;
  }
    if(flag == 0)
  printf("\n %d is prime", *pnum);
  else
  printf("\n %d is composite", *pnum);
  }
  printf("\n Enter any number: ");
  scanf("%d", pnum);
  }
  return 0;
}
```

Output

```
***** ENTER -1 TO EXIT *****
Enter any number: 3
3 is prime
Enter any number: 1
1 is neither prime nor composite
Enter any number: -1
```

14.5 NULL POINTERS

We have seen that a pointer variable is a pointer to some other variable of the same data type. However, in some cases we may prefer to have *null* pointer which is a special pointer that does not point to any value. This means that a null pointer does not point to any valid memory address.

To declare a null pointer you may use the predefined constant `NULL`, which is defined in several standard header files including `<stdio.h>`, `<stdlib.h>`, and `<string.h>`. After including any of these files in your program, write

```
int *ptr = NULL;
```

You can always check whether a given pointer variable stores address of some variable or contains a `NULL` by writing:

```
if (ptr == NULL)
{
  Statement block;
}
```

You may also initialize a pointer as a null pointer by using a constant 0, as shown below.

```
int ptr;
ptr = 0;
```

Programming Tip:
It is a logical error to dereference a null pointer.

This is a valid statement in C, as `NULL` which is a preprocessor macro typically has the value, or replacement text, `0`. However, to avoid ambiguity it is always better to use `NULL` to declare a null pointer.

A function that returns pointer values can return a null pointer when it is unable to perform its task.

Null pointers are used in situations where one of the pointers in the program points to different locations at different times. In such situations it is always better to set it to a null pointer when it doesn't point anywhere valid, and to test to see if it's a null pointer before using it.

Note

A run time error is generated if you try to dereference a null pointer.

14.6 GENERIC POINTERS

A *generic pointer* is a pointer variable that has `void` as its data type. The void pointer, or the generic pointer, is a special type of pointer that can be used to point to variables of any data type. It is declared like a normal pointer variable but using the `void` keyword as the pointer's data type. For example,

Programming Tip:
A compiler error will be generated if you assign a pointer of one type to a pointer of another type without a cast.

```
void *ptr;
```

In C, since you cannot have a variable of type `void`, the void pointer will therefore not point to any data and thus cannot be dereferenced. You need to type cast a void pointer (generic pointer) to another kind of pointer before using it.

Programming Tip:
A pointer variable of type void * cannot be dereferenced.

Generic pointers are often used when you want a pointer to point to data of different types at different times. For example, look at the code given below.

```
#include <stdio.h>
int main()
{
  int x=10;
  char ch = 'A';
  void *gp;
  gp = &x;
  printf("\n Generic pointer points to the
   integer value = %d", *(int*)gp);
  gp = &ch;
  printf("\n Generic pointer now points to the
   character = %c", *(char*)gp);
  return 0;
}
```

Output

```
Generic pointer points to the integer value
   = 10
Generic pointer now points to the character
   = A
```

It is always recommended to avoid using generic pointers unless absolutely necessary, as they effectively allow you to avoid type checking.

14.7 PASSING ARGUMENTS TO FUNCTION USING POINTERS

We have already seen call-by-value method of passing parametres to a function. Using call-by-value method, it is impossible to modify the actual parameters when you pass them to a function. Furthermore, the incoming arguments to a function are treated as local variables in the function and those local variables get a *copy* of the values passed from their calling function.

Programming Tip:
While using pointers to pass arguments to a function, the calling function must pass addresses of the variables as arguments and the called function must dereference the arguments to use them in the function body for processing.

Pointers provide a mechanism to modify data declared in one function using code written in another function. In other words: If data is declared in `func1()` and we want to write code in `func2()` that modifies the data in `func1()`, then we must pass the addresses of the variables to `func2()`.

The calling function sends the addresses of the variables and the called function declares those incoming arguments as pointers. In order to modify the variables sent by the calling function, the called function must dereference the pointers that were passed to it. Thus, passing pointers to a function avoids the overhead of copying data from one function to another. Hence, to use pointers for passing arguments to a function, the programmer must do the following:

- Declare the function parametres as pointers
- Use the dereferenced pointers in the function body
- Pass the addresses as the actual argument when the function is called.

Note

It is an error to return a pointer to a local variable in the called function, because when the function terminates , its memory may be allocated to a different program.

Let us write some programs that pass pointer variables as parameters to functions.

12. Write a program to add two integers using functions

```
#include <stdio.h>

void sum (int *a, int *b, int *t);
int main()
{
  int num1, num2, total;
  printf("\n Enter the first number: ");
  scanf("%d", &num1);
  printf("\n Enter the second number: ");
  scanf("%d", &num2);
  sum(&num1, &num2, &total);
  printf("\n Total = %d", total);

  return 0;
}
void sum (int *a, int *b, int *t)
{
  *t = *a + *b;
}
```

Output

```
Enter the first number: 2
Enter the second number: 3
Total = 5
```

13. Write a program, using functions, to find the biggest of three integers.

```
#include <stdio.h>
int greater(int *a, int *b, int *c, int
    *large);
int main()
{
  int num1, num2, num3, large;
  printf("\n Enter the first number: ");
  scanf("%d", &num1);
  printf("\n Enter the second number: ");
  scanf("%d", &num2);
  printf("\n Enter the third number: ");
  scanf("%d", &num3);
  greater(&num1, &num2, &num3, &large);
  return 0;
}
int greater (int *a, int
*b, int *c, int *large)
{
  if(*a > *b && *a > *c)
  *large = *a;
  if(*b > *a && *b > *c)
  *large = *b;
  else
  *large = *c;
  printf("\n Largest number = %d", *large);
}
```

Programming Tip: A compiler error will be generated if you use pointer arithmetic with multiply, divide or modulo operators.

Output

```
Enter the first number: 1
Enter the second number: 7
Enter the third number: 9
Largest number = 9
```

14. Write a program to calculate area of a triangle.

```
#include <stdio.h>
void read(float *b, float *h);
void calculate_area (float *b, float *h,
  float *a);
int main()
{
  float base, height, area;
  read(&base, &height);
  calculate_area(&base, &height, &area);
  printf("\n Area of the triangle with base
   %.1f and height %.1f = %.2f", base, height,
   area);
  return 0;
}
void read(float *b, float *h)
{
  printf("\n Enter the base of the
   triangle: ");
  scanf("%f", b);
  printf("\n Enter the height of the
   triangle: ");
  scanf("%f", h);
}
void calculate_area (float *b, float *h,
  float *a)
{
```

```
    *a = 0.5 * (*b) * (*h);
}
```

Output

```
Enter the base of the triangle: 10
Enter the height of the triangle: 5
Area of the triangle with base 10.0 and
   height 5.0 = 25.00
```

We know that functions usually return only one value, but pointers can be used to return more than one value to the calling function. This is done by allowing the arguments to be passed by addresses which enables the function to alter the values pointed to and thus helps to return more than one value.

14.8 POINTERS AND ARRAYS

The concept of array is very much bound to the one of the pointers. An array occupies consecutive memory locations. Consider Figure 14.2. For example, if we have an array declared as

`int arr[] = {1, 2, 3, 4, 5};` then in memory it would be stored as shown in Figure 14.2.

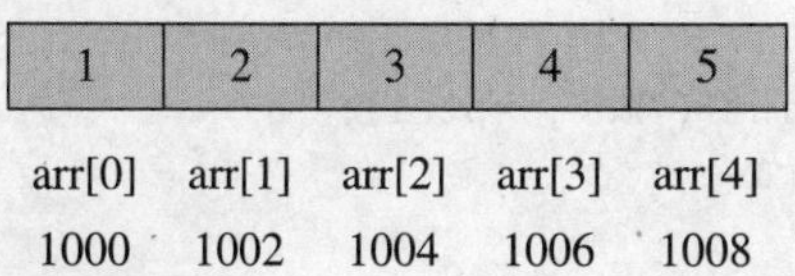

Figure 14.2 Memory representation of `arr[]`

Array notation is a form of pointer notation. The name of the array is the starting address of the array in memory. It is also known as the base address. In other words, base address is the address of the first element in the array or the address of `arr[0]`. Now let us use a pointer variable as given in the statement below.

```
int *ptr;
ptr = &arr[0];
```

> **Programming Tip:**
> The name of the array is actually a pointer that points to the first element of the array.

Here, `ptr` is made to point to the first element of the array. Execute the code given below and observe the output which will make the concept clear to you.

```
main()
{
  int arr[]={1,2,3,4,5};
  printf("\n Address of array = %p %p %p",
   arr, &arr[0], &arr);
}
```

Similarly, writing `ptr = &arr[2]`, makes `ptr` to point to the third element of the array that has index 2. Figure 14.3 shows `ptr` pointing to the third element of the array.

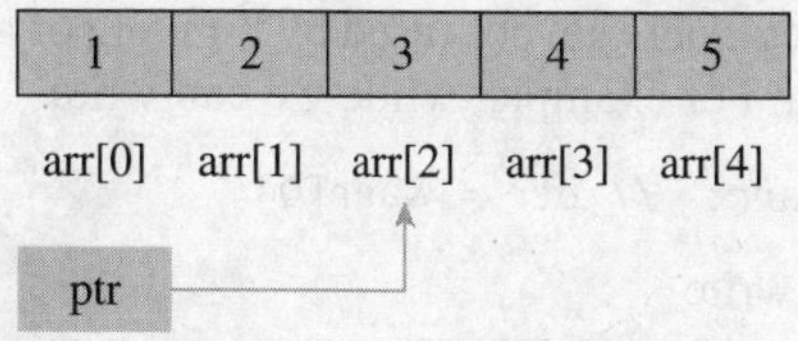

Figure 14.3 `ptr` pointing to the third element of the array

If pointer variable `ptr` holds the address of the first element in the array, then the address of successive elements can be calculated by writing `ptr++`.

```
int *ptr = &arr[0];
ptr++;
printf("\n The value of the second element of
   the array is %d", *ptr);
```

The `printf()` function will print the value 2 because after being incremented `ptr` points to the next location. One point to note here is that if x is an integer variable, then `x++` adds `1` to the value of x. But `ptr` is a pointer variable, so when we write `ptr +i`, then adding `i` gives a pointer that points `i` elements further along an array than the original pointer.

> **Programming Tip:**
> An error is generated if an attempt is made to change the address of the array.

Since `++ptr` and `ptr++` are both equivalent to `ptr +1`, incrementing a pointer using the unary ++ operator, increments the address it stores by the amount given by sizeof(type) where *type* is the data type of the variable it points to (i.e., `2` for an integer). For example, consider Figure 14.4.

If `ptr` originally points to `arr[2]`, then `ptr++` will point to the next element, i.e., `arr[3]`. This is shown in Figure 14.4.

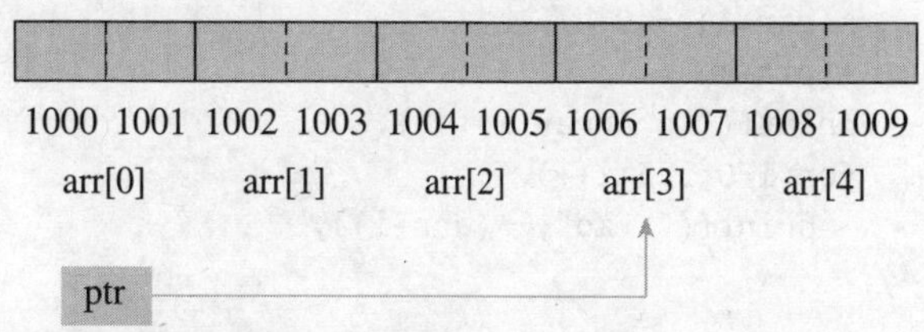

Figure 14.4 `ptr` pointing to the fourth element of the array

Had this been a character array, every byte in the memory would have been used to store an individual character. `ptr++` would then add only 1 byte to the address of `ptr`.

When using pointers, an expression like `arr[i]` is equivalent to writing `*(arr+i)`. If `arr` is the array name, then the compiler implicitly takes

```
arr = &arr[0]
```

To print the value of the third element of the array, we can straightaway use the expression `*(arr+2)`. Note that `arr[i] = *(arr + i)`

Many beginners get confused by thinking of array name as a pointer. For example, while we can write

```
ptr = arr;  // ptr = &arr[0]
```

we cannot write

```
arr = ptr;
```

This is because while ptr is a variable, arr is a constant. The location at which the first element of arr will be stored cannot be changed once arr[] has been declared. Therefore, an array name is often known to be a constant pointer.

Programming Tip: When an array is passed to a function, we are actually passing a pointer to the function. Therefore, in the function declaration you must declare a pointer to receive the array name.

To summarize, the name of an array is equivalent to the address of its first element, as a pointer is equivalent to the address of the element that it points to. Therefore, arrays and pointers use the same concept.

Note

arr[i], i[arr], *(arr+i), *(i+arr) gives the same value.

Look at the following code and understand the result of executing them.

```
main()
{
   int arr[]={1,2,3,4,5};
   int *ptr, i;
   ptr=&arr[2];
   *ptr = -1;
   *(ptr+1) = 0;
   *(ptr-1) = 1;
   printf("\n Array is: ");
   for(i=0;i<5;i++)
     printf("  %d", *(arr+i));
}
```

Output

```
Array is:   1  1  -1  0  5
```

In C we can add or subtract an integer from a pointer to get a new pointer, pointing somewhere other than the original position. C also permits addition and subtraction of two pointer variables. For example, look at the code given below.

```
main()
{
   int arr[]={1,2,3,4,5,6,7,8,9};
   int *ptr1, *ptr2;
   ptr1 = arr;
   ptr2 = ptr1+2;
   printf("%d", ptr2 -ptr1);
}
```

Output

```
2
```

In the code, ptr1 and ptr2 are pointers pointing to the elements of the same array. We may subtract two pointers as long as they point to the same array. Here, the output is 2 because there are two elements between ptr1 and ptr2. Both the pointers must point to the same array or one past the end of the array, otherwise this behaviour cannot be defined.

Moreover, C also allows pointer variables to be compared with each other. Obviously, if two pointers are equal, then they point to the same location in the array. However, if one pointer is less than the other, it means that the pointer points to some element nearer to the beginning of the array.

15. Write a program to display an array of given numbers.

```
#include <stdio.h>
main()
{
  int arr[]={1,2,3,4,5,6,7,8,9};
  int *ptr1, *ptr2;
  ptr1 = arr;
  ptr2 = &arr[8];
  while(ptr1<=ptr2)
  {
    printf("%d", *ptr1);
    ptr1++;
  }
}
```

Output

```
1 2 3 4 5 6 7 8 9
```

16. Write a program to read and display an array of n integers.

```
#include <stdio.h>
int main()
{
  int i, n;
  int arr[10], *parr = arr;
  printf("\n Enter the number of elements: ");
  scanf("%d", &n);
   printf("\n Enter the elements: ");
  for(i = 0; i < n; i++)
  scanf("%d", parr+i);
    printf("\n The elements entered are: ");
  for(i=0; i < n; i++)
  printf("\t %d", *(parr+i));
  return 0;
}
```

Output

```
Enter the number of elements: 5
Enter the elements: 1 2 3 4 5
The elements entered are: 1 2 3 4 5
```

Table 14.1 summarizes pointer arithmetic.

Table 14.1 Pointer arithmetic

Operation	Condition	Declaration	Description
Assignment	Pointers must be of same type	int *ptr1, *ptr2;	If we write *ptr1 = *ptr2, then both the pointers point to the same location
Addition of an integer		int i, *ptr;	If we write, ptr + i, then ptr will point to ith object after its initial position
Subtraction of an integer		int i, *ptr;	If we write ptr – i, then ptr will point to ith object before its initial position
Comparison of pointers	Pointers should point to elements of the same array	int *ptr1, *ptr2;	If we write ptr1 < ptr2, then it would return 1 if ptr1 points to an element that is near to the beginning of the array, i.e., the element comes before the element pointed by ptr2
Subtraction of pointers	Pointers should point to elements of the same array	int *ptr1, *ptr2;	If we write ptr1 – ptr2, then it returns the number of elements between ptr1 and ptr2 (provided ptr1 > ptr2)
Addition of pointers is illegal in C. Therefore, ptr1+ptr2 is not valid in C.			

Note

An object is a named region of storage; an lvalue is an expression referring to an object.

17. Write a program to find mean of *n* numbers using arrays.

```
#include <stdio.h>
int main()
{
  int i, n, arr[20], sum = 0;
  int *pn = &n, *parr = arr, *psum = &sum;
  float mean = 0.0, *pmean = &mean;
  printf("\n Enter the number of elements:");
  scanf("%d", pn);
  for(i = 0; i < *pn; i++)
  {
     printf("\n Enter the number: ");
     scanf("%d", (parr + i));
  }
  for(i=0; i < *pn; i++)
     *psum += *(arr + i);
  *pmean = (float)*psum / *pn;
  printf("\n The numbers you entered are: ");
  for(i=0; i < *pn; i++)
     printf("%d ", *(arr + i));
  printf("\n The sum is: %d", *psum);
  printf("\n The mean is: %.2f", *pmean);
  return 0;
}
```

Output

```
Enter the number of elements: 5
Enter the number: 1
Enter the number: 2
Enter the number: 3
Enter the number: 4
Enter the number: 5
The numbers you entered are:
1 2 3 4 5
The sum is: 15
The mean is: 3.00
```

18. Write a program to find the largest of *n* numbers using arrays. Also display its position.

```
#include <stdio.h>
int main()
{
  int i, n, arr[20], large = -32768, pos = 0;
  int *pn = &n, *parr = arr, *plarge = &large,
   *ppos = &pos;
  printf("\n Enter the number of elements in
   the array: ");
  scanf("%d", pn);
  for(i = 0; i < *pn;i++)
  {
     printf("\n Enter the number: ");
     scanf("%d", parr+i);
  }
  for(i = 0; i < *pn; i++)
  {
     if(*(parr+i) > *plarge)
  {
  *plarge = *(parr+i);
  *ppos = i;
  }
  }
  printf("\n The numbers you entered are: ");
  for(i = 0; i < *pn;i++)
     printf("%d ", *(parr+i));
  printf("\n The largest of these numbers is:
   %d", *plarge);
```

```
  printf("\n The position of the largest
   number in the array is: %d", *ppos);
  return 0;
}
```

Output

```
Enter the number of elements in the array: 5
Enter the number: 1
Enter the number: 2
Enter the number: 3
Enter the number: 4
Enter the number: 5
The numbers you entered are:
1 2 3 4 5
The largest of these numbers is: 5
The position of the largest number in the
   array is: 4
```

14.9 PASSING AN ARRAY TO A FUNCTION

An array can be passed to a function using pointers. For this, a function that expects an array can declare the formal parameter in either of the two following ways:

`func(int arr[]);` OR `func(int *arr);`

When we pass the name of the array to a function, the address of the zeroth element of the array is copied to the local pointer variable in the function. Observe the difference; unlike ordinary variables the values of the elements are not copied, only the address of the first element is copied.

When a formal parameter is declared in a function header as an array, it is interpreted as a pointer to a variable and not as an array. With this pointer variable you can access all the elements of the array by using the expression, `array_name + index`. To find out how many elements are there in the array, you must pass the size of the array as another parameter to the function. So for a function that accepts an array as parameter, the declaration should be as follows.

```
func(int arr[], int n);  OR
func(int *arr, int n);
```

Look at the following program which illustrates the use of pointers to pass an array to a function.

19. Write a program to read and print an array of n numbers, then find out the smallest number. Also print the position of the smallest number.

```
#include <stdio.h>
void read_array(int *arr, int n);
void print_array(int *arr, int n);
void find_small(int *arr, int n, int *small,
   int *pos);
int main()
{
   int num[10], n, small=32767, pos;
   printf("\n Enter the size of the array: ");
   scanf("%d", &n);
   read_array(num, n);
   print_array(num, n);
   find_small(num, n, &small, &pos);
   printf("\n The smallest number in the array
    is %d at position %d", small, pos);
   return 0;
}
void read_array(int *arr, int n)
{
   int i;
    printf("\n Enter the array elements: ");
   for(i=0;i<n;i++)
     scanf("%d", &arr[i]);
}
void print_array(int *arr, int n)
{
   int i;
    printf("\n The array elements are: ");
   for(i=0;i<n;i++)
     printf("\t %d", arr[i]);
}
void find_small(int *arr, int n, int *small,
   int *pos)
{
int i;
   for(i=0;i<n;i++)
   {
      if(*(arr+i)< *small)
      {
      *small = *(arr+i);
      *pos = i;
      }
   }
}
```

Output

```
Enter the size of the array: 5
Enter the array elements: 1 2 3 4 5
The array elements are: 1 2 3 4 5
The smallest number in the array is 1 at
   position 0
```

It is not necessary to pass the whole array to a function. We can also pass a part of the array known as a sub-array. A pointer to a sub-array is also an array pointer. For example, if we want to send the array starting from the third element then we can pass the address of the third element and the size of the sub-array, i.e., if there are 10 elements in the array, and we want to pass the array starting from the third element, then only eight elements would be a part of the sub-array. So the function call can be written as

```
func(&arr[2], 8);
```

14.10 DIFFERENCE BETWEEN ARRAY NAME AND POINTER

When memory is allocated to an array, its base address is fixed and it cannot be changed during program execution. In other words, an array name is an address constant. Therefore, its value cannot be changed. To ensure that the address of the array does not get changed even inadvertently, C does not allow array names to be used as an lvalue. Hence, array names cannot appear on the left side of the assignment operator.

However, you may declare a pointer variable of appropriate type that points to the first element of the array and use it as lvalue. Figure 14.5 shows two sets of codes. The first code gives an error as the array name is being used as an lvalue for the ++ operator. The second code shows the correct way of doing the same thing.

```
main()
{
        int arr[5], i;
        for(i=0;i<5;i++)
        {
              *arr=0;
              arr++;          //ERROR
        }
        for( i = 0; i < 5;i++)
              printf("\n  %d", *(arr+i));
}
```

```
main()
{
        int arr[5], i, *parr;
        parr = arr;
        for( i = 0; i < 5;i++)
        {
              *parr=0;
              parr++;
        }
        for( i = 0; i < 5;i++)
              printf("\n  %d", *(arr+i));
}
```

Figure 14.5 Difference between array name and pointer

Second thing to remember is that an array cannot be assigned to another array. This is because an array name cannot be used as the lvalue.

```
int arr1[]={1,2,3,4,5};
int arr2[5];
arr2 = arr1;  // ERROR
```

But one pointer variable can be assigned to another pointer variable of the same type. Therefore, the following statements are valid in C.

```
int arr1[]={1,2,3,4,5};
int *ptr1, *ptr2;
ptr1 = arr1;
ptr2 = ptr1;
```

When we write `ptr2 = ptr1`, we are not copying the data pointed to. Rather, we are just making two pointers point to the same location. This is shown in Figure 14.6.

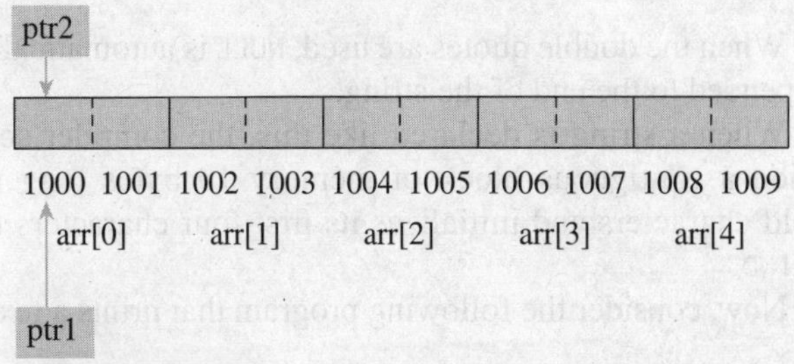

Figure 14.6 Pointers pointing to the same location

Third point of difference lies with the return value of the address operator. The address operator returns the address of the operand. But when an address operator is applied to an array name, it gives the same value as the array reference without the operator. Therefore, `arr` and `&arr` give the same value. However, this is not true for a pointer variable.

Last but not the least, the `sizeof` operator when applied to an array name returns the number of bytes allocated for the array. But in case of a pointer variable, the `sizeof` operator returns the number of bytes used for the pointer variable (machine dependent). Look at the following code which illustrates this concept.

```
main()
{
  int arr[]={1,2,3,4,5};
  int *ptr;
  ptr=arr;
  printf("\n Size of array = %d", sizeof(arr));
  printf("\n Size of pointer variable = %d",
    sizeof(ptr));
}
```

Output (On Turbo C)

```
Size of array = 10
Size of pointer variable = 2
```

14.11 POINTERS AND STRINGS

In C, strings are treated as arrays of characters that are terminated with a binary zero character (written as `'\0'`). Consider, for example,

```
char str[10];
str[0] = 'H';
str[1] = 'i';
str[2] = '!':
str[3] = '\0';
```

C language provides two alternate ways of declaring and initializing a string. First, you may write:

```
char str[10] = {'H', 'i', '!', '\0'};
```

But this also takes more typing than is convenient. So, C permits:

```
char str[10] = "Hi!";
```

When the double quotes are used, `NULL` is automatically appended to the end of the string.

When a string is declared like this, the compiler sets aside a contiguous block of memory 10 bytes long to hold characters and initializes its first four characters to `Hi!\0`.

Now, consider the following program that prints a text.

```
#include <stdio.h>
int main()
{
  char str[] = "Hello";
  char *pstr;
  pstr = str;
  printf("\n The string is: ");
  while(*pstr != '\0')
  {
    printf("%c", *pstr);
    pstr++;
  }
  return 0;
}
```

Output

```
The string is: Hello
```

In this program, we declare a character pointer `*pstr` to show the string on the screen. We then *point* the pointer `pstr` to `str`. Then we print each character of the string in the `while` loop. Instead of using the `while` loop, we could have straightaway used the function `puts()` as shown below.

```
puts(pstr);
```

The function prototype for `puts()` is as follows:

```
int puts(const char *s);
```

Here the `const` modifier is used to assure the user that the function will not modify the contents pointed to by the source pointer. The address of the string is passed to the function as an argument.

The parameter passed to `puts()` is a pointer which is the address to which it points to, or, simply, an address. Thus writing `puts(str);` means passing the address of `str[0]`.

Similarly, when we write `puts(pstr);` we are passing the same address, because we have written `pstr = str;`

Consider another program which reads a string and then scans each character to count the number of upper and lower case characters entered.

```
#include <stdio.h>
int main()
{
  char str[100], *pstr;
  int upper = 0, lower = 0;
  printf("\n Enter the string: ");
  gets(str);
  pstr = str;

  while(*pstr != '\0')
  {
    if(*pstr >= 'A' && *pstr <= 'Z')
      upper++;
    else if(*pstr >= 'a' && *pstr <= 'z')
      lower++;
    pstr++;
  }
  printf("\n Total number of upper case
   characters = %d", upper);
  printf("\n Total number of lower case
   characters = %d", lower);
  return 0;
}
```

Output

```
Enter the string: How are you
Total number of upper case characters = 1
Total number of lower case characters = 8
```

20. Write a program to read and print a text. Also count the number of characters, words, and lines in the text.

```
#include <stdio.h>
int main()
{
  char str[100], *pstr;
  int chars = 0, lines = 0, words = 0;
  printf("\n Enter the string: ");
  pstr = str;
  while(*pstr != '\0')
  {
    if(*pstr == '\n')
      lines++;
    if(*pstr == ' ' && *(pstr + 1) != ' ')
      words++;
    chars++;
    pstr++;
  }
  printf("\n The string is: ");
  puts(str);
  printf("\n Number of characters = %d",
   chars);
  printf("\n Number of lines = %d", lines +1);
  printf("\n Number of words = %d", words +1);
  return 0;
}
```

Output

```
Enter the string: How are you
Number of characters = 11
Number of lines = 1
Number of words = 3
```

21. Write a program to copy a character array in another character array.

```
#include <stdio.h>

int main()
{
  char str[100], copy_str[100];
  char *pstr, *pcopy_str;
  int i = 0;

  pstr = str;
  pcopy_str = copy_str;
  printf("\n Enter the string: ");
   gets(str);
  while(*pstr != '\0')
  {
     *pcopy_str = *pstr;
     pstr++, pcopy_str++;
  }
  *pcopy_str = '\0';
  printf("\n The copied text is: ");
  pcopy_str = copy_str;
  while(*pcopy_str != '\0')
  {
     printf("%c", *pcopy_str);
     pcopy_str++;
  }

  return 0;
}
```

Output

```
Enter the string: C Programming
The copied text is: C Programming
```

22. Write a program to copy n characters of a character array from the mth position in another character array.

```
#include <stdio.h>
int main()
{
  char str[100], copy_str[100];
  char *pstr, *pcopy_str;
  int m, n, i = 0;
  pstr = str;
  pcopy_str = copy_str;
  printf("\n Enter the string: ");
  gets(pstr);
  printf("\n Enter the position from which to
   start: ");
  scanf("%d", &m);
  printf("\n Enter the number of characters to
   be copied: ");
  scanf("%d", &n);
  pstr = pstr + m;
  i=0;
  while(*pstr != '\0' && i <n)
  {
     *pcopy_str = *pstr;
     pcopy_str++;
     pstr++;
     i++;
  }
  *pcopy_str = '\0';
  printf("\n The copied text is: ");
  puts(copy_str);
  return 0;
}
```

Output

```
Enter the string: How are you
Enter the position from which to start: 2
Enter the number of characters to be
  copied: 5
The copied text is: w are
```

23. Write a program to copy the last n characters of a character array in another character array.

```
#include <stdio.h>
#include <string.h>
int main()
{
  char str[100], copy_str[100];
  char *pstr, *pcopy_str;
  int i = 0, n;
  pstr = str;
  pcopy_str = copy_str;
  printf("\n Enter the string:");
  gets(str);
  printf("\n Enter the number of characters to
   be copied (from the end): ");
  scanf("%d", &n);
  pstr = pstr + strlen(str) – n;
  while(*pstr != '\0')
  {
     *pcopy_str = *pstr;
     pstr++; pcopy_str++;
  }
  *pcopy_str = '\0';
  printf("\n The copied text is: ");
  puts(copy_str);
  return 0;
}
```

Output

```
Enter the string: Hi there
Enter the number of characters to be copied
   (from the end): 5
The copied text is: there
```

24. Write a program to read a text, delete all the semi-colons it has, and finally replace all '.' with a ','.

```
#include <stdio.h>
int main()
{
```

```
    char str[100], copy_str[100];
    char *pstr, *pcopy_str;
    pstr = str;
    pcopy_str = copy_str;
    printf("\n Enter the string: ");
    gets(str);
    while(*pstr != '\0')
    {
       if(*pstr != ';')
       { } // do nothing
       else if (*pstr == '.')
         *pcopy_str = ',';
       else
         *pcopy_str = *pstr;
       pstr++; pcopy_str++;
    }
    *pcopy_str = '\0';
    printf("\n The new text is: ");
    pcopy_str = copy_str;
    while(*pcopy_str != '\0')
    {
       printf("%c", *pcopy_str);
       pcopy_str++;
    }
    return 0;
  }
```

Output

```
Enter the string: Programming in C; is a book
   written by; Reema Thareja.
The new text is: Programming in C is a book
   written by Reema Thareja,
```

25. Write a program to reverse a string.

```
#include <stdio.h>
int main()
{
   char str[100], copy_str[100];
   char *pstr, *pcopy_str;
   pstr = str;
   pcopy_str = copy_str;
   printf("\n Enter * to end");
   printf("\n Enter the string: ");
   scanf("%c", pstr);
   while(*pstr != '*')
   {
      pstr++;
      scanf("%c", pstr);
   }
   *pstr = '\0';
   pstr--;
   while (pstr >= str)
   {
      *pcopy_str = *pstr;
      pcopy_str++;
      pstr--;
   }
   *pcopy_str = '\0';
   printf("\n The new text is: ");
   pcopy_str = copy_str;
   while(*pcopy_str != '\0')
   {
      printf("%c", *pcopy_str);
      pcopy_str++;
   }
   return 0;
}
```

Output

```
Enter * to end
Enter the string: Learning C++
The new text is: ++C gninraeL
```

26. Write a program to concatenate two strings.

```
#include <stdio.h>
int main()
{
   char str1[100], str2[100], copy_str[200];
   char *pstr1, *pstr2, *pcopy_str;
   pstr1 = str1;
   pstr2 = str2;
   pcopy_str = copy_str;
   printf("\n Enter the first string: ");
   gets(str1);
   printf("\n Enter the second string: ");
   gets(str2);
   while(*pstr1 != '\0')
   {
      *pcopy_str = *pstr1;
      pcopy_str++, pstr1++;
   }
   while(*pstr2 != '\0')
   {
      *pcopy_str = *pstr2;
      pcopy_str++, pstr2++;
   }
   *pcopy_str = '\0';
   printf("\n The new text is: ");
   pcopy_str = copy_str;
   while(*pcopy_str != '\0')
   {
      printf("%c", *pcopy_str);
      pcopy_str++;
   }
   return 0;
}
```

Output

```
Enter the first string: Programming in C by
Enter the second string: Reema Thareja
The new text is: Programming in C by Reema
   Thareja
```

14.12 ARRAYS OF POINTERS

An array of pointers can be declared as

```
int *ptr[10];
```

The above statement declares an array of 10 pointers where each of the pointer points to an integer variable. For example, look at the code given below.

```
int *ptr[10];
int p = 1, q = 2, r = 3, s = 4, t = 5;
ptr[0] = &p;
ptr[1] = &q;
ptr[2] = &r;
ptr[3] = &s;
ptr[4] = &t
```

Can you tell what will be the output of the following statement?

```
printf("\n %d", *ptr[3]);
```

The output will be 4 because `ptr[3]` stores the address of integer variable `s` and `*ptr[3]` will therefore print the value of `s` that is `4`. Now look at another code in which we store the address of three individual arrays in the array of pointers.

```
main()
{
  int arr1[]={1,2,3,4,5};
  int arr2[]={0,2,4,6,8};
  int arr3[]={1,3,5,7,9};
  int *parr[3] = {arr1, arr2, arr3};
  int i;
  for(i = 0;i<3;i++)
    printf("%d", *parr[i]);
}
```

Output

```
1 0 1
```

Surprised with this output? Try to understand the concept. In the `for` loop, `parr[0]` stores the base address of `arr1` (or, `&arr1[0]`). So writing `*parr[0]` will print the value stored at `&arr1[0]`. Same is the case with `*parr[1]` and `*parr[2]`.

Now consider an array of character pointers that point to strings.

```
char *ptr[3];
```

In the `ptr` array, each element is a character pointer. Therefore, we can assign character pointers to the elements of the array. For example,

```
ptr[0] = str;
```

Another way to initialize an array of characters with three strings can be given as,

```
char *ptr[3] = {"Janak",Raj",Paul"};
```

Here, `ptr[0]` is `Janak`, `ptr[1]` is `Raj`, and `ptr[2]` is `Paul`.

The memory layout of `ptr` can be given as shown in Figure 14.7. It requires only 15 bytes to store the three strings.

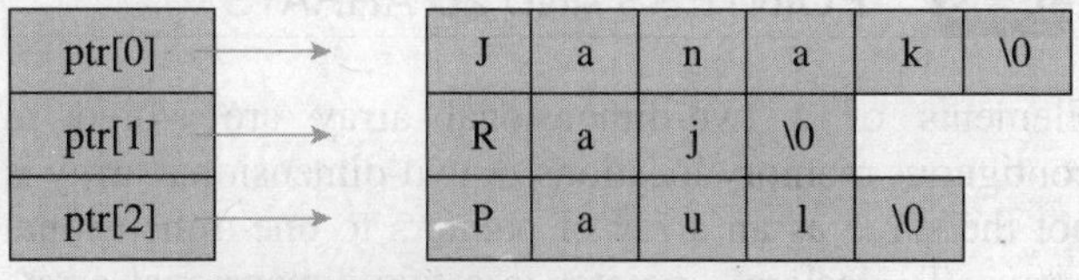

Figure 14.7 Memory layout of ptr

However, `char str[3][10] = {"Janak", "Raj", "Paul"};` will behave in the same way as an array of characters. The only difference is the memory layout (Figure 14.8). While the array of pointers needs only 15 bytes of storage, `str` will reserve 30 bytes in memory, despite the fact that some memory locations will be reserved but not utilized.

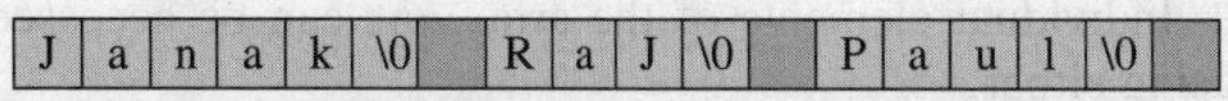

The grey locations represent the uninitialized memory cells

Figure 14.8 Memory layout

Look at the following program that uses an array of character pointers to display the name of the day corresponding to the number.

```
#include <stdio.h>
char *day_of_week(int);
main()
{
  int day_num;
  char *day;
  printf("\n Enter the day from 1 to 7:");
  scanf("%d", &day_num);
  day = day_of_week(day_num);
  if(day)
    printf("%s", day);
  else
    printf("\n Invalid Day");

}
char *day_of_week(int day)
{
  char *week_day[7] = {"SUNDAY", "MONDAY",
   "TUESDAY", "WEDNESDAY", "THURSDAY",
   "FRIDAY", "SATURDAY"};
  if(day>=1 || day<=7)
    return week_day[day-1];
  else
    return NULL;
}
```

Output

```
Enter the day from 1 to 7: 3
TUESDAY
```

An array of pointers whose elements point to arrays of varying sizes is called a *ragged array*. Therefore, array of pointers week_day and ptr in the above discussion are better known as ragged arrays.

14.13 POINTERS AND 2D ARRAYS

Elements of a two-dimensional array are stored in contiguous memory locations. A two-dimensional array is not the same as an array of pointers to one-dimensional arrays. To declare a pointer to a two-dimensional array, you may write

```
int **ptr;
```

Here int **ptr is an array of pointers (to one-dimensional arrays), while int mat[5][5] is a 2D array. They are not the same type and are not interchangeable.

Consider a two-dimensional array declared as

```
int mat[5][5];
```

Individual elements of the array mat can be accessed using either:

```
mat[i][j] or
*(*(mat + i) + j) or
*(mat[i]+j);
```

To understand more fully what is going on, let us replace

```
*(multi + row) with X so the expression
*(*(mat + i) + j) becomes *(X + col)
```

Using pointer arithmetic, we know that the address pointed to by (i.e., value of) X + col + 1 must be greater than the address X + col by an amount equal to sizeof(int).

Since mat is a two-dimensional array, we know that in the expression multi + row as used above, multi + row + 1 must increase in value by an amount equal to that needed to *point to* the next row, which in this case would be an amount equal to cols * sizeof(int).

Thus, in case of a two-dimensional array, in order to evaluate expression (for a row major 2D array), we must know a total of 4 values:

1. The address of the first element of the array, which is given by the name of the array, i.e., mat in our case
2. The size of the type of the elements of the array, i.e., size of integers in our case
3. The specific index value for the row
4. The specific index value for the column

Note that

```
int (*ptr)[10];
```

declares ptr to be a pointer to an array of 10 integers. This is different from

```
int *ptr[10];
```

which would make ptr the name of an array of 10 pointers to type int. You must be thinking how pointer arithmetic works if you have an array of pointers. For example:

```
int * arr[10] ;
int ** ptr = arr ;
```

In this case, arr has type int **. Since all pointers have the same size, the address of ptr + i can be calculated as:

```
addr(ptr + i) = addr(ptr) + [sizeof(int *) * i]
              = addr(ptr) + [2 * i]
```

Since arr has type int **,

```
arr[0] = &arr[0][0],
arr[1] = &arr[1][0], and in general,
arr[i] = &arr[i][0].
```

According to pointer arithmetic, arr + i = & arr[i], yet this skips an entire row of 5 elements, i.e., it skips complete 10 bytes (5 elements each of 2 bytes size). Therefore, if arr is address **1000**, then arr + 2 is address **1010**. To summarize, &arr[0][0], arr[0], arr, and &arr[0] point to the base address.

```
&arr[0][0] + 1 points to arr[0][1]
arr[0] + 1 points to arr[0][1]
arr + 1 points to arr[1][0]
&arr[0] + 1 points to arr[1][0]
```

To conclude, a two-dimensional array is not the same as an array of pointers to 1D arrays. Actually a two-dimensional array is declared as:

```
int (*ptr)[10] ;
```

Here ptr is a pointer to an array of 10 elements. The parentheses are not optional. In the absence of these parentheses, ptr becomes an array of 10 pointers, not a pointer to an array of 10 integers.

Note

Pointer to a one-dimensional array can be declared as

```
int arr[]={1,2,3,4,5};
int *parr;
parr = arr;
```

Similarly, pointer to a two-dimensional array can be declared as

```
int arr[2][2]={{1,2},{3,4}};
int (*parr)[2];
parr=arr;
```

Look at the code given below which illustrates the use of a pointer to a two-dimensional array.

```
#include <stdio.h>
main()
```

```
{
  int arr[2][2]={{1,2},{3,4}};
  int i, j, (*parr)[2];
  parr = arr;
  for(i = 0; i < 2; i++)
  {
    for(j = 0; j < 2 ;j++)
      printf(" %d", (*(parr+i))[j]);
  }
}
```

Output

```
1 2 3 4
```

The golden rule to access an element of a two-dimensional array can be given as

```
arr[i][j] = (*(arr+i))[j] = *((*arr+i))+j)
  = *(arr[i]+j)
```

Therefore,

```
arr[0][0] = *(arr)[0] = *((*arr)+0)
  = *(arr[0]+0)
arr[1][2] = (*(arr+1))[2] = *((*(arr+1))+2)
  = *(arr[1]+2)
```

If we declare an array of pointer using `data_type *array_name[SIZE];` Here SIZE represents the number of rows and the space for columns that can be dynamically allocated.	If we declare a pointer to an array using, `data_type (*array_name)[SIZE];` Here SIZE represents the number of columns and the space for rows that may be dynamically allocated.

27. Write a program to read and display a 3 × 3 matrix.

```
#include <stdio.h>
int main()
{
  int i, j, mat[3][3];
  printf("\n Enter elements of the matrix");
  printf("\n ************************");
  for(i=0;i<3;i++)
  {
    for(j=0;j<3;j++)
  {
  printf("\n mat[%d][%d] = ",i,j);
  scanf("%d", &mat[i][j]);
  }
  }
  printf("\n Elements of the matrix are");
  printf("\n ************************");
  for(i=0;i<3;i++)
  {
    printf("\n");
    for(j = 0; j < 3; j++)
  printf("\t mat[%d][%d] = %d",i,j, *(*(mat +
   i)+j));
  }
  return 0;
}
```

OR

```
#include <stdio.h>
int main()
{
  int i, j, mat[3][3];
  printf("\n Enter elements of the matrix");
  printf("\n ************************");
  for(i=0;i<3;i++)
  {
    for(j=0;j<3;j++)
    {
    printf("\n mat[%d][%d] = ",i,j);
    scanf("%d", (*(mat + i)+j));
    }
  }
  printf("\n The elements of the matrix are
   ");
  printf("\n ************************");
  for(i=0;i<3;i++)
  {
    printf("\n");
    for(j=0;j<3;j++)
    printf("\t mat[%d][%d] = %d",i,j,
      *(*(mat + i)+j));
  }
  return 0;
}
```

OR

```
#include <stdio.h>
void display(int (*)[3]);
int main()
{
  int i, j, mat[3][3];

  printf("\n Enter elements of the matrix");
  printf("\n ************************");
  for(i=0;i<3;i++)
  {
    for(j = 0; j < 3; j++)
    {
    printf("\n mat[%d][%d] =",i,j);
    scanf("%d", &mat[i][j]);
    }
  }
  display(mat);
}
void display(int (*mat)[3])
{
  int i, j;
  printf("\n Elements of the matrix are");
```

```
    printf("\n *************************");
    for(i = 0; i < 3; i++)
    {
        printf("\n");
        for(j=0;j<3;j++)
        printf("\t mat[%d][%d] = %d",i,j,
         *(*(mat + i)+j));
    }
    return 0;
}
```

Output

```
Enter elements of the matrix
*******************************
1 2 3 4 5 6 7 8 9
Elements of the matrix are
*******************************
1 2 3
4 5 6
7 8 9
```

Note

A double pointer cannot be used as a 2D array. Therefore, it is wrong to declare: 'int **mat' and then use 'mat' as a 2D array. These are two very different data types used to access different locations in memory. So running such a code may abort the program with a 'memory access violation' error.

A 2D array is not equivalent to a double pointer. A 'pointer to pointer of T' can't serve as a '2D array of T'. The 2D array is equivalent to a pointer to row of T, and this is very different from pointer to pointer of T.

When a double pointer that points to the first element of an array is used with the subscript notation ptr[0][0], it is fully dereferenced two times and the resulting object will have an address equal to the value of the first element of the array.

14.14 POINTERS AND 3D ARRAYS

In this section, we will see how pointers can be used to access a three-dimensional array. We have seen that pointer to a one-dimensional array can be declared as

```
int arr[]={1,2,3,4,5};
int *parr;
parr = arr;
```

Similarly, pointer to a two-dimensional array can be declared as

```
int arr[2][2]={{1,2},{3,4}};
int (*parr)[2];
parr = arr;
```

A pointer to a three-dimensional array can be declared as

```
int arr[2][2][2]={1,2,3,4,5,6,7,8};
int (*parr)[2][2];
parr = arr;
```

We can access an element of a three-dimensional array by writing,

```
arr[i][j][k] = *(*(*(arr+i)+j)+k)
```

Look at the code given below which illustrates the use of a pointer to a three-dimensional array.

```
#include <stdio.h>

main()
{
  int i,j,k;
  int arr[2][2][2];
  int (*parr)[2][2]= arr;

  printf("\n Enter the elements of a 2 × 2 × 2
   array: ");
  for(i = 0; i < 2; i++)
  {
    for(j = 0; j < 2; j++)
    {
      for(k = 0; k < 2; k++)
        scanf("%d", &arr[i][j][k]);
    }
  }
  printf("\n The elements of the 2 × 2 × 2
   array are: ");
  for(i = 0; i < 2; i++)
  {
    for(j = 0; j < 2; j++)
    {
      for(k = 0; k < 2; k++)
        printf("%d", *(*(*(parr+i)+j)+k));
    }
  }

  return 0;
}
```

Output

```
Enter the elements of a 2 × 2 × 2 array: 1 2 3
 4 5 6 7 8
The elements of the 2 × 2 × 2 array are: 1 2 3
 4 5 6 7 8
```

Note

In the `printf` statement, you could also have used `*(*(*(arr+i)+j)+k))` instead of `*(*(*(parr+i)+j)+k))`.

14.15 FUNCTION POINTERS

C allows operations with pointers to functions. We have seen earlier in this chapter that every function code along with its variables is allocated some space in the memory. Thus, every function has an address. *Function pointers* are pointer variables that point to the address of a function. Like other pointer variables, function pointers can be declared, assigned values, and used to access the functions they point to.

This is a useful technique for passing a function as an argument to another function. In order to declare a pointer to a function we have to declare it like the prototype of the function except that the name of the function is enclosed between parentheses `()` and an asterisk `(*)` is inserted before the name. The syntax of declaring a function pointer can be given as

```
return_type(*function_pointer_name)(argument_
    list);
```

Look at the declaration below in which we declare a pointer to a function that returns an integer value and accepts two arguments—one of type `int` and the other of type `float`.

```
int (*func)(int a, float b);
```

Because of precedence, if you do not put the function name within parenthesis, you will end up declaring a function returning a pointer as shown:

```
/* function returning pointer to int */
int *func(int a, float b);
```

14.15.1 Initializing a Function Pointer

As in case of other pointer variables, a function pointer must be initialized prior to use. If we have declared a pointer to the function, then that pointer can be assigned the address of the correct function just by using its name. Like in the case of an array, a function name is changed into an address when it's used in an expression. It is optional to use the address operator (`&`) in front of the function name.

For example, if `fp` is a function pointer and we have a function `add()` with prototype given as

```
int add(int, int);
```

Then writing `fp = add;` initializes the function pointer `fp` with the address of `add()`.

14.15.2 Calling a Function Using a Function Pointer

When a pointer to a function is declared, it can be called using one of two forms:

```
(*func)(1,2);
```

OR

```
func(1,2);
```

Look at the program given below which makes use of a pointer to a function.

```
#include <stdio.h>
void print(int n);
void (*fp)(int);
main()
{
  fp = print;
  (*fp)(10);
  fp(20);
  return 0;
}
void print(int value)
{
  printf("\n %d", value);
}
```

Output

```
10
20
```

Now let us write another code that illustrates how the contents of `fp` can be changed at run time to point to two different functions during program execution.

```
#include <stdio.h>
float (*func)(float, float);
float add(float, float);
float sub(float, float);
main()
{
  func = add;
  // function pointer points to add
  printf("\n Addition = %.2f", func(9.5,
   3.1));
  func = sub;
  // function pointer points to sub
  printf("\n Subtraction = %.2f", func(9.5,
   3.1));
}
float add(float x, float y)
{
  return (x + y);
}
float sub(float x, float y)
{
  return (x - y);
}
```

Output

```
Addition = 12.60
Subtraction = 6.40
```

A function pointer can be declared and initialized to `NULL` as shown below:

```
int (*fp)(int) = NULL;
```

14.15.3 Comparing Function Pointers

Comparison operators such as == and != can be used the same way as usual. Consider the code given below which checks if `fp` actually contains the address of the function `print(int)`.

```
if(fp >0){ // check if initialized
   if(fp == print)
      printf("\n Pointer points to print");
   else
      printf("\n Pointer not initialized!");
}
```

14.15.4 Passing a Function Pointer as an Argument to a Function

A function pointer can be passed as the calling argument of a function. This is in fact necessary if you want to pass a pointer to a callback function. The following code shows how to pass a pointer to a function which returns an `int` and accepts two `int` values.

Note that in the program below, the function `operate` calls the functions `add` and `subtract` with the following line:

```
result = (*operate_fp) (num1, num2);
#include <stdio.h>
int add(int, int);
int sub(int, int);
int operate(int (*operate_fp) (int, int), int,
   int);
main()
{
  int result;
  result = operate(add, 9, 7);
  printf ("\n Addition = %d", result);
  result = operate(sub, 9, 7);
  printf ("\n Subtraction = %d", result);
  return 0;
}
int add (int a, int b)
{
  return (a + b);
}
int sub (int a, int b)
{
  return (a - b);
}
int operate(int (*operate_fp) (int, int), int
   a, int b)
{
  int result;
  result = (*operate_fp) (a,b);
  return result;
}
```

Output

```
Addition = 16
Subtraction = 2
```

14.16 ARRAY OF FUNCTION POINTERS

When an array of function pointers is declared, the appropriate function is selected using an index. The code given below shows the way to define and use an array of function pointers in C.

Step 1: Use `typedef` keyword so that `fp` can be used as type

```
typedef int (*fp)(int, int);
```

Step 2: Define the array and initialize each element to `NULL`. This can be done in two ways:

```
/* with 10 pointers to functions which return
   an int and take two ints */
1. fp funcArr[10] = {NULL};
2. int (*funcArr[10])(int, int) = {NULL};
```

Step 3: Assign the function's address—`Add` and `Subtract`

```
funcArr1[0] = funcArr2[1] = Add;
funcArr[0] = &Add;
funcArr[1] = &Subtract;
```

Step 4: Call the function using an index to address the function pointer

```
printf("%d\n", funcArr[1](2, 3));
  // short form
printf("%d\n", (*funcArr[0])(2, 3));
  // correct way
```

28. Write a program, that uses an array of function pointers, to add, subtract, multiply, or divide two given numbers.

```
#include <stdio.h>
  int sum(int a, int b);
  int subtract(int a, int b);
  int mul(int a, int b);
  int div(int a, int b);

  int (*fp[4]) (int a, int b);

  int main(void)
  {
    int result;
    int num1, num2, op;
    fp[0] = sum;
    fp[1] = subtract;
    fp[2] = mul;
    fp[3] = div;
```

```
    printf("\n Enter the numbers: ");
    scanf("%d %d", &num1, &num2);
    do
  {
    printf("\n 0: Add \n 1: Subtract \n
  2: Multiply \n 3: Divide \n 4. EXIT\n");
     printf("\n\n Enter the operation: ");
     scanf("%d", &op);
    result = (*fp[op]) (num1, num2);
    printf("\n Result = %d", result);
  } while(op!=4);
    return 0;
  }
  int sum(int a, int b)
  {
    return a + b;
  }
  int subtract(int a, int b)
  {
    return a - b;
  }
  int mul(int a, int b)
  {
    return a * b;
  }
  int div(int a, int b)
  {
    if(b)
         return a / b;
    else
         return 0;
  }
```

Output

```
Enter the numbers: 2 3
0: Add
1: Subtract
2: Multiply
3: Divide
4. EXIT
Enter the operation: 0
Result = 5
Enter the operation: 4
```

14.17 POINTERS TO POINTERS

In C language you are also allowed to use pointers that point to pointers. The pointers in turn point to data (or even to other pointers). To declare pointers to pointers, just add an asterisk (`*`) for each level of reference.

For example, if we have:

```
int x = 10;
int *px; //pointer to an integer
int **ppx; /* pointer to a pointer to an
  integer */
px = &x;
ppx = &px;
```

Assume that the memory location of these variables is as shown in Figure 14.9.

Now if we write,

```
printf("\n %d", **ppx);
```

then it will print `10`, the value of `x`.

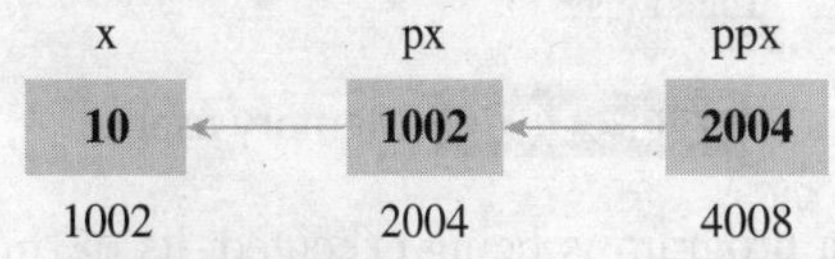

Figure 14.9 Pointer to pointer

14.18 MEMORY ALLOCATION IN C PROGRAMS

C supports three kinds of memory allocation through the variables in C programs:

Static allocation When we declare a static or global variable, static allocation is done for the variable. Each static or global variable is allocated a fixed size of memory space. The number of bytes reserved for the variable cannot change during execution of the program. Till now we have been using this technique to define variables, arrays, and pointers.

Automatic allocation When we declare an automatic variable, such as a function argument or a local variable, automatic memory allocation is done. The space for an automatic variable is allocated when the compound statement containing the declaration is entered, and is freed when it exits from a compound statement.

Dynamic allocation A third important kind of memory allocation is known as *dynamic allocation.* In the following sections we will read about dynamic memory allocation using pointers.

14.19 MEMORY USAGE

Before jumping into dynamic memory allocation, let us first understand how memory is used. Conceptually, memory is divided into two—program memory and data memory (Figure 14.10).

The program memory consists of memory used for `main()` and other called functions in the program, whereas data memory consists of memory needed for permanent definitions such as global data, local data, constants, and dynamic memory data. The way in which `C` handles the memory requirements is a function of the operating system and the compiler.

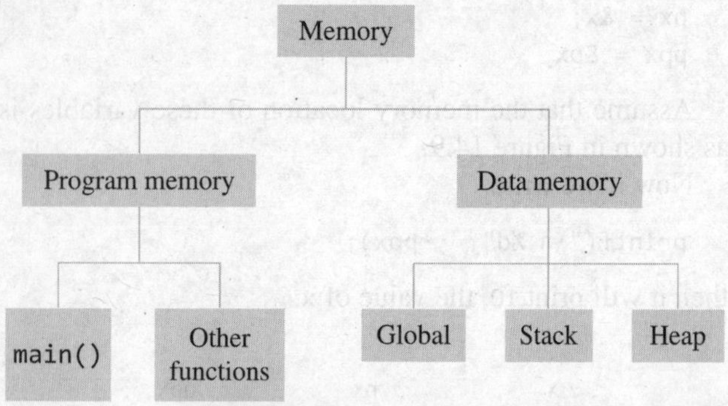

Figure 14.10 Memory usage

When a program is being executed, its `main()` and all other functions are always kept in the memory. However, the local variables of the function are available in the memory only when they are active. When we studied recursive functions, we have seen that the system stack is used to store a single copy of the function and multiple copies of the local variables.

Apart from the stack, we also have a memory allocation known as heap. Heap memory is unused memory allocated to the program and available to be assigned during its execution. When we dynamically allocate memory for variables, heap acts as a memory pool from which memory is allocated to those variables.

However, this is just a conceptual view of memory and implementation of the memory is entirely in the hands of system designers.

14.20 DYNAMIC MEMORY ALLOCATION

The process of allocating memory to the variables during execution of the program or at run time is known as *dynamic memory allocation*. C language has four library routines which allow this function.

Till now whenever we needed an array we had declared a static array of fixed size, say

```
int arr[100];
```

When this statement is executed, consecutive space for 100 integers is allocated. It is not uncommon that we may be using only 10% or 20% of the allocated space, thereby wasting rest of the space. To overcome this problem and to utilize the memory efficiently C language provides a mechanism of dynamically allocating memory so that only the amount of memory that is actually required is reserved. We reserve space only at the run time for the variables that are actually required. Dynamic memory allocation gives best performance in situations in which we do not know memory requirements in advance.

C provides four library routines to automatically allocate memory at the run time. These routines are shown in Table 14.2.

When we have to dynamically allocate memory for variables in our programs then pointers are the only way to go. When we use `malloc()` for dynamic memory allocation, then you need to manage the memory allocated for variables yourself.

Table 14.2 Memory allocation/de-allocation functions

Function	Task
`malloc()`	Allocates memory and returns a pointer to the first byte of allocated space
`calloc()`	Allocates space for an array of elements and initializes them to zero. Like `malloc()`, `calloc()` also returns a pointer to the memory
`free()`	Frees previously allocated memory
`realloc()`	Alters the size of previously allocated memory

14.20.1 Memory Allocation Process

In computer science, the free memory region is called the heap. The size of heap is not constant as it keeps changing when the program is executed. In the course of program execution, some new variables are created and some variables cease to exist when the block in which they were declared is exited. For this reason it is not uncommon to encounter memory overflow problems during dynamic allocation process. When an overflow condition occurs, the memory allocation functions mentioned above will return a null pointer.

14.20.2 Allocating a Block of Memory

Let us see how memory is allocated using `malloc()`. `malloc` is declared in `<stdlib.h>`, so we include this header file in any program that calls `malloc`. The `malloc` function reserves a block of memory of specified size and returns a pointer of type `void`. This means that we can assign it to any type of pointer. The general syntax of `malloc()` is

```
ptr =(cast-type*)malloc(byte-size);
```

where `ptr` is a pointer of type `cast-type`. `malloc()` returns a pointer (of cast type) to an area of memory with size `byte-size`. For example,

```
arr=(int*)malloc(10*sizeof(int));
```

> **Programming Tip:**
> To use dynamic memory allocation functions, you must include the header file stdlib.h.

This statement is used to dynamically allocate memory equivalent to 10 times the area of `int` bytes. On successful execution of the statement the space is reserved and the address of the first byte of memory allocated is assigned to the pointer `arr` of type `int`.

The `calloc()` function is another function that reserves memory at the run time. It is normally used to request multiple blocks of storage each of the same size and then sets all bytes to `zero`. `calloc()` stands for contiguous memory allocation and is primarily used to allocate memory for arrays. The syntax of calloc() can be given as

```
ptr=(cast-type*) calloc(n,elem-size);
```

The aforegiven statement allocates contiguous space for n blocks each size of elements size bytes. The only difference between malloc() and calloc() is that when we use calloc(), all bytes are initialized to zero. calloc() returns a pointer to the first byte of the allocated region.

When we allocate memory using malloc() or calloc(), a null pointer will be returned if there is not enough space in the system to allocate. It is a *not a pointer* marker; therefore, it is not a pointer you can use. Thus, whenever you allocate memory using malloc() or calloc(), you must check the returned pointer before using it. If the program receives a null pointer, it should at the very least print an error message and exit, or perhaps figure out some way of proceeding without the memory it asked for. But in any case, the program cannot go on to use the null pointer it got back from malloc()/calloc().

A call to malloc, with an error check, typically looks something like this:

```
int *ip = malloc(100 * sizeof(int));
if(ip == NULL)
{
  printf("\n Memory could not  be allocated");
  return;
}
```

29. Write a program to read and display values of an integer array. Allocate space dynamically for the array.

```
#include <stdio.h>

#include <stdlib.h>
main()
{
  int i, n;
  int *arr;

  printf("\n Enter the number of elements ");
  scanf("%d", &n);
  arr = (int *)malloc(n  *  sizeof(int));
  if(arr == NULL)
  {
    printf("\n Memory Allocation Failed");
    exit(0);
  }
  for(i = 0;i < n;i++)
  {
    printf("\n Enter the value %d of the
      array: ", i);
    scanf("%d", &arr[i]);
  }
  printf("\n The array contains \n");
  for(i = 0;i < n;i++)
    printf("%d", arr[i]);
    // another way is to write *(arr+i)
  return 0;
}
```

Now let us also see how we can allocate memory using the calloc function. The calloc() function accepts two parametres—num and size, where num is the number of elements to be allocated and size is the size of elements. The following program demonstrates the use of calloc() to dynamically allocate space for an integer array.

```
#include <stdio.h>
#include <stdlib.h>
main ()
{
  int i,n;
  int *arr;
  printf ("\n Enter the number of elements:
  ");
  scanf("%d",&n);
  arr = (int*) calloc(n,sizeof(int));
  if (arr==NULL)
    exit (1);
  printf("\n Enter the %d values to be stored
   in the array", n);
  for (i = 0; i < n; i++)
      scanf ("%d",&arr[i]);
  printf ("\n You have entered: ");
  for(i = 0; i < n; i++)
    printf ("%d",arr[i]);
  free(arr);
  return 0;
}
```

14.20.3 Releasing the Used Space

When a variable is allocated space during the compile time, then the memory used by that variable is automatically released by the system in accordance with its storage class. But when we dynamically allocate memory then it is our responsibility to release the space when it is not required. This is even more important when the storage space is limited. Therefore, if we no longer need the data stored in a particular block of memory and we do not intend to use that block for storing any other information, then as a good programming practice we must release that block of memory for future use, using the free function. The general syntax of free() is,

```
free(ptr);
```

where ptr is a pointer that has been created by using malloc() or calloc(). When memory is de-allocated using free(), it is returned back to the free list within the heap.

14.20.4 To Alter the Size of Allocated Memory

At times the memory allocated by using `calloc()` or `malloc()` might be insufficient or in excess. In both the situations we can always use `realloc()` to change the memory size already allocated by `calloc()` and `malloc()`. This process is called *reallocation of memory*. The general syntax for `realloc()` can be given as

```
ptr = realloc(ptr,newsize);
```

The `realloc()` function allocates new memory space of size specified by `newsize` to the pointer variable `ptr`. It returns a pointer to the first byte of the memory block. The allocated new block may or may not be at the same region. Thus, we see that `realloc()` takes two arguments. The first is the pointer referencing the memory and the second is the total number of bytes you want to reallocate. If you pass zero as the second argument, it will be equivalent to calling `free()`. Like `malloc()` and `calloc()`, `realloc` returns a void pointer if successful, else a null pointer is returned.

If `realloc()` was able to make the old block of memory bigger, it returns the same pointer. Otherwise, if `realloc()` has to go elsewhere to get enough contiguous memory then it returns a pointer to the new memory, after copying your old data there. However, if `realloc()` can't find enough memory to satisfy the new request at all, it returns a null pointer. So again you must check before using that the pointer returned by `realloc()` is not a null pointer.

```
/*Example program for reallocation*/
#include < stdio.h>
#include < stdlib.h>
#define NULL 0
main()
{
  char *str;
  /*Allocating memory*/
  str = (char *)malloc(10);
  if(str==NULL)
  {
    printf("\n Memory could not be
    allocated");
    exit(1);
  }
  strcpy(str,"Hi");
  printf("\n STR = %s", str);
  /*Reallocation*/
  str = (char *)realloc(str,20);
  if(str==NULL)
  {
    printf("\n Memory could not be
      reallocated");
    exit(1);
  }
  printf("\n STR size modified.\n");
  printf("\n STR = %s\n", str);
  strcpy(str,"Hi there");
  printf("\n STR = %s", str);
  /*freeing memory*/
  free(str);
  return 0;
}
```

Note

With `realloc()`, you can allocate more bytes without losing your data.

Dynamically Allocating a 2D Array

We have seen how `malloc()` can be used to allocate a block of memory which can simulate an array. Now we can extend our understanding further to do the same to simulate multidimensional arrays.

If we are not sure of the number of columns that the array will have, then we will first allocate memory for each row by calling `malloc`. Each row will then be represented by a pointer. Look at the code below which illustrates this concept.

```
#include <stdlib.h>
#include <stdio.h>
main()
{
  int **arr, i, j, ROWS, COLS;
  printf("\n Enter the number of rows and
   columns in the array: ");
  scanf("%d %d", &ROWS, &COLS);
  arr = (int **)malloc(ROWS * sizeof(int *));
  if(arr == NULL)
  {
    printf("\n Memory could not be
      allocated");
    exit(-1);
  }
  for(i=0; i<ROWS; i++)
  {
    arr[i] = (int *)malloc(COLS *
      sizeof(int));
    if(arr[i] == NULL)
    {
      printf("\n Memory Allocation Failed");
      exit(-1);
    }
  }
  printf("\n Enter the values of the array:
  ");
  for(i = 0; i < ROWS; i++)
  {
    for(j = 0; j < COLS; j++)
      scanf("%d", &arr[i][j]);
  }
```

```
    printf("\n The array is as follows: ");
    for(i = 0; i < ROWS; i++)
    {
      for(j = 0; j < COLS; j++)
        printf("%d", arr[i][j]);
    }
    for(i = 0; i < ROWS; i++)
      free(arr[i]);
    free(arr);
    return 0;
}
```

Here, arr is a pointer-to-pointer-to-int: at the first level it points to a block of pointers, one for each row. We first allocate space for rows in the array. The space allocated to each row is big enough to hold a pointer-to-int, or int *. If we successfully allocate it, then this space will be filled with pointers to columns (number of ints). This can be better understood from Figure 14.11.

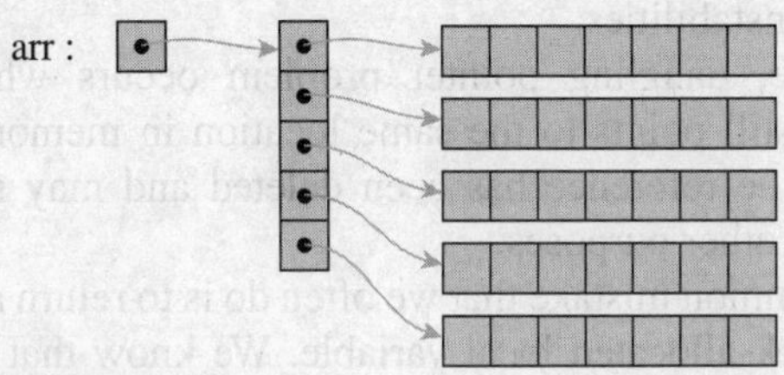

Figure 14.11 Memory allocation for a two-dimensional array

Once the memory is allocated for the two-dimensional array, we can use subscripts to access its elements. When we write, arr[i][j], it means we are looking for the ith pointer pointed to by arr, and then for the jth int pointed to by that inner pointer.

When we have to pass such an array to a function, then the prototype of the function will be written as

```
func(int **arr, int ROWS, int COLS);
```

In the aforegiven declaration, func accepts a pointer-to-pointer-to-int and the dimensions of the arrays as parametres, so that it will know how many rows and columns there are.

Look at the code given below which illustrates another way of dynamically allocating space for a 2D array.

```
#include <stdlib.h>
#include <stdio.h>
main()
{
  int **arr, i, j, ROWS, COLS;
  printf("\n Enter the number of rows and
   columns in the array: ");
  scanf("%d %d", &ROWS, &COLS);
  arr = (int *)malloc(ROWS * COLS *
  sizeof(int));
  if(arr == NULL)
  {
    printf("\n Memory could not be
      allocated");
    exit(-1);
  }
  printf("\n Enter the values of the array: ");
  for(i = 0; i < ROWS; i++)
  {
    for(j = 0; j < COLS; j++)
      scanf("%d", &arr[i][j]);
  }
  printf("\n The array is as follows: ");
  for(i = 0; i < ROWS; i++)
  {
    for(j = 0; j < COLS; j++)
      printf("%d", arr[i][j]);
  }
  for(i = 0; i < ROWS; i++)
    free(arr[i]);
  free(arr);
  return 0;
}
```

Note

To dynamically allocate space for a 3-D array, arr[10][20][30], perform the following steps

1. `int ***arr;`
2. `arr = (int ***) malloc(10* sizeof(int **));`
3. `for(i=0;i<10;i++) arr[i] = (int **) malloc(20*sizeof(int *));`
4. `for(i=0;i<10;i++) {for(j=0; j<20;j++) arr[i][j] = (int *)malloc(30 * sizeof(int));`

14.21 DRAWBACKS OF POINTERS

Although pointers are very useful in C they are not free from limitations. If used incorrectly, pointers can lead to bugs that are difficult to unearth. For example, if you use a pointer to read a memory location but that pointer is pointing to an incorrect location then you may end up reading a wrong value. An erroneous input always leads to an erroneous output, therefore however efficient your program code may be, the output will always be wrong. Same is the case when writing a value to a particular memory location.

Consider a scenario in which the program code is supposed to read the account balance of a customer, add new amount to it, and then re-write the modified value to that location. If the pointer is pointing to the account balance of some other customer then the account balance of the wrong customer will be updated.

Let us try to find some common errors encountered when using pointers.

```
int x, *px;
x = 10;
*px = 20;
```

Error un-initialized pointer. px is pointing to an unknown memory location. Hence it will overwrite that location's contents and store 20 in it. Such a pointer is called a *wild pointer*. A pointer which is not initialized with any address is called a wild pointer. It may contain any garbage address and thus dereferencing a wild pointer can be dangerous.

```
int x, *px;
x = 10;
px = x;
ERROR: It should be px = &x;
int x = 10, y = 20, *px, *py;
px = &x, py = &y;
if(px < py)     // it should be *px and *py
  printf("\n px is less than py");
else
  printf("\n py is less than px");
```

Look at another code given below.

```
#include <stdio.h>
main()
{
  char *str1, *str2;
  printf("\n Enter the string: ");
  gets(str1);
  while(*str1!='\0')
  {
    *str2 = *str1;
    str2++, str1++;
  }
  *str2='\0';
  printf("\n String is: ");
  while(*str2!='\0')
  {
    printf("%c", *str2);
    str2++;
  }
}
```

Error str2 will not be printed because str2 has moved ahead of its starting location and before displaying the string, it has not been initialized with its starting address.

Memory leak Memory leakage occurs when memory is allocated but not released when it is no longer required. This causes an application to unnecessarily consume memory thereby reducing the memory available for other applications. Although in small programs it is not a big concern but when dealing with large projects, memory leakage may result in slowing down the application or crashing the application when the computer memory resource limits are reached.

For example, if a function dynamically allocates memory for 100 double values and forgets to free the memory and in worst case if that function is called several times within the code then ultimately the system may crash.

Dangling pointer Dangling pointers arise when an object is deleted or de-allocated, without modifying the value of the pointer. As a result, the pointer still points to the memory location of the de-allocated memory.

Once the memory is de-allocated, the system may reallocate that block of freed memory to another process. In case the program then dereferences the (now) dangling pointer, *unpredictable behaviour may result*, as the memory may now contain completely different data.

This problem can become worse when the program writes data to memory pointed by a dangling pointer causing a silent corruption of unrelated data, leading to bugs that can be extremely difficult to find. Moreover, if the overwritten data is bookkeeping data used by the system's memory allocator, the corruption can even cause system instabilities.

Hence, dangling pointer problem occurs when the pointer still points to the same location in memory even though the reference has been deleted and may now be used for other purposes.

A common mistake that we often do is to return address of a stack-allocated local variable. We know that once a called function returns, the space for these variables gets de-allocated and technically they have garbage values. Look at the code below which illustrates how we get a dangling pointer when a called function returns.

```
char *func(void)
{
    Char ch='A';
    /* ... */
    return &ch;
}
```

The aforegiven program returns the address of ch. So the calling function may access its value. Any functions called thereafter will overwrite the stack storage allocated for ch with other values and the pointer would no longer work correctly. Therefore, if a pointer to ch must be returned it must be declared as static.

Consider the code below which illustrates another dangling pointer problem.

```
#include <stdio.h>
#include <string.h>
void main()
{
  char *ptr = (char *)malloc(10);
  strcpy(ptr, "WELCOME");
  printf("%s",ptr);
  free (ptr);   /* ptr now becomes a dangling
   pointer */
```

```
    ptr = NULL;   /* ptr is no more a dangling
     pointer */
  }
```

Output

```
  WELCOME
```

Here `ptr` becomes a dangling pointer. A solution to the above is to assign `0(NULL)` to `ptr` immediately before exiting the block in which it is declared. An alternative solution would be to somehow guarantee that `ptr` will not be used again without further initialization.

Memory corruption Memory corruption often occurs when due to programming errors, the content of a memory location gets modified unintentionally. When the program uses the contents of the corrupted memory, it either results in program crash or in strange and bizarre results.

Memory corruption is one of the most difficult programming errors to trace mainly because of two reasons:

- The source of the memory corruption and its manifestation may be far apart. Therefore, it may become hard to correlate the cause and the effect of the problem.
- Symptoms of memory corruption problem may appear under unusual conditions thereby making it even harder to consistently reproduce the error.

Memory corruption errors can be broadly classified into following categories:

1. *Using un-initialized memory*: An un-initialized memory contains garbage value. Hence, using the contents of an un-initialized memory can lead to unpredictable program behaviour.
2. *Using un-owned memory*: A common programming mistake is to use pointers for accessing and modifying memory that is not owned by the program. This situation may arise when the pointer happens to be a null pointer or a dangling pointer. Using such a pointer to write to a memory location is a serious programming flaw as it may lead to crash of another program or even the operating system.
3. *Using beyond allocated memory (buffer overflow)*: If the elements of the array are accessed in a loop, with incorrect terminating condition, memory beyond the array bounds may be manipulated. Buffer overflow is a common programming flaw exploited by computer viruses causing serious threat to computer security.
4. *Faulty de-allocation of memory*: Memory leaks and freeing of un-allocated memory can also result in memory corruption.

These days, memory debuggers such as *Purify*, *Valgrind*, and *Insure++* are widely used for detecting memory corruption errors.

POINTS TO REMEMBER

- All data and programs need to be placed in the primary memory for execution.
- A pointer is a variable that contains the memory address of another variable.
- The '&' operator retrieves the lvalue (address) of the variable. We can dereference a pointer, i.e., refer to the value of the variable to which it points by using unary '*' operator.
- The address of a memory location is a pointer constant, therefore it cannot be changed in the program code.
- Unary increment and decrement operators have greater precedence than the dereference operator (*).
- Null pointer is a special pointer value that is known not to point anywhere. This means that a null pointer does not point to any valid memory address. To declare a null pointer you may use the predefined constant NULL. You may also initialize a pointer as a null pointer by using the constant 0.
- A generic pointer is a pointer variable that has 'void' as its data type. The generic pointer can be used to point to variables of any data type.
- When the memory for an array is allocated, its base address is fixed and it cannot be changed during program execution.
- When we dynamically allocate memory for variables, heap acts as a memory pool from which memory is allocated to those variables. The process of allocating memory to the variables during execution of the program or at run time is known as dynamic memory allocation.
- `malloc()`, `calloc()`, and `realloc` returns a void pointer if successful, else a `NULL` is returned.
- Memory leakage occurs when memory is allocated but not released when it is no longer required.

GLOSSARY

Dereference To look up a value referred to. Usually, the 'value referred to' is the value pointed to by a pointer. Therefore, 'dereference a pointer' means to see what it points to. In C, a pointer is dereferenced either using the unary * operator or the array subscripting operator [].

Function pointer It is a pointer to any function type.

Lvalue An expression that appears on the left-hand sign of an assignment operator, hence, something that can perhaps be assigned to. An lvalue specifies something that has a location, as opposed to a transient value.

Null pointer A pointer value which is not the address of any object or function. A null pointer points to nothing.

Null pointer constant It is an integral constant expression with value 0 (or such an expression cast to void *), that represents a null pointer.

Pointer It is a variable that stores addresses.

Rvalue An expression that appears on the right-hand sign of an assignment operator. Generally, rvalue can participate in an expression or be assigned to some other variable.

EXERCISES

Fill in the Blanks

1. Size of character pointer is ______.
2. Allocating memory at run time is known as ______.
3. A pointer to a pointer stores ______ of another ______ variable.
4. ______ pointer does not point to any valid memory address.
5. The size of memory allocated for a variable depends on its ______.
6. On 16-bit systems, integer variable is allocated ______ bytes.
7. The ______ appears on the right side of the assignment statement.
8. Pointers are nothing but ______.
9. ______ enable programmers to return multiple values from a function via function arguments.
10. The ______ operator informs the compiler that the variable is a pointer variable.
11. Data and programs need to be placed in the ______ for execution.
12. When compared with heaps, ______ are faster but also smaller and expensive.
13. All variables declared within main() are allocated space on the ______.
14. Shared libraries segment contains ______.
15. The `malloc()` function returns ______.
16. When memory is de-allocated using `free()`, it is returned back to the ______ within the ______.
17. The `malloc()`, `calloc()`, and `realloc` functions return ______ if successful, else ______ is returned.
18. The `realloc()` function is used to ______.
19. A two-dimensional array is a ______.
20. An un-initialized memory contains ______.
21. The only integer value that can be assigned to a pointer variable is ______.
22. ______ can be used as parameter declaration to declare an array of integers passed to a function.
23. Dynamically allocated memory can be referred using ______.
24. ______ function returns memory to the heap.
25. Ragged array is implemented using an array of pointers to ______.

Multiple-choice Questions

1. The operator * signifies a
   (a) referencing operator (b) dereferencing operator
   (c) address operator (d) none of these
2. *(&num) is equivalent to writing
   (a) &num (b) *num
   (c) num (d) none of these
3. Pointers are used to create complex data structures like
   (a) trees (b) linked list
   (c) stack (d) queue
   (e) all of these
4. While declaring pointer variables, which operator do we use?
   (a) address (b) arrow
   (c) indirection (d) dot
5. Which operator retrieves the lvalue of a variable?
   (a) & (b) *
   (c) -> (d) None of these
6. The code of the main() program is stored in memory in
   (a) stack (b) heap
   (c) global (d) bss
7. For dynamically allocated variables, memory is allocated from which memory area?
   (a) Stack (b) Heap
   (c) Global (d) BSS

8. The `malloc()` function is declared in which header file
   (a) stdio.h (b) stdlib.h
   (c) conio.h (d) iostream.h
9. Which function is used to request memory and set all allocated bytes to zero?
   (a) `malloc()` (b) `calloc()`
   (c) `realloc()` (d) `free()`

State True or False

1. A pointer is a variable.
2. The & operator retrieves the lvalue of the variable.
3. Array name can be used as a pointer.
4. Unary increment and decrement operators have greater precedence than the dereference operator.
5. The generic pointer can be pointed at variables of any data type.
6. A function pointer cannot be passed as a function's calling argument.
7. On 32-bit systems, integer variable is allocated 4 bytes.
8. Lvalue cannot be used on the left side of the assignment statement.
9. Pointers provide an alternate way to access individual elements of the array.
10. Pointer is a variable that represents the contents of a data item.
11. A fixed size of stack is allocated by the system and is filled as needed from the top to bottom.
12. All the parameters passed to the called function will be stored on the stack.
13. When the memory for an array is allocated, its base address is fixed and it cannot be changed during program execution.
14. An array can be assigned to another array.
15. Memory leakage occurs when memory is allocated but not released when it is no longer required.
16. `mat[i][j]` is equivalent to `*(*(mat + i) + j)`.
17. Dangling pointers arise when an object is deleted or de-allocated, without modifying the value of the pointer.
18. It is possible to add two pointer variables.
19. Pointer constants cannot be changed.
20. The value of a pointer is always an address.
21. `*ptr++` will add 1 to the value pointed by `ptr`.
22. Pointers of different types can be assigned to each other without a cast.
23. Adding 1 to a pointer variable will make it point 1 byte ahead of the memory location to which it is currently pointing.
24. Any arithmetic operator can be used to modify the value of a pointer.
25. Only one call to `free()` is enough to release the entire array allocated using `calloc()`.
26. Ragged arrays consume less memory space.

Review Questions

1. Explain the difference between a null pointer and a void pointer.
2. Write a short note on pointers.
3. Compare pointer and array name.
4. Explain the result of the following code:
```
int num1 = 2, num2 = 3;
int *p = &num1, *q = &num2;
*p++ = *q++;
```
5. What do you understand by a null pointer?
6. What is an array of pointers? How is it different from a pointer to an array?
7. Write a short note on pointer arithmetic.
8. How are generic pointers different from other pointer variables?
9. What do you understand by the term pointer to a function?
10. Differentiate beween ptr++ and *ptr++.
11. How are arrays related to pointers?
12. Briefly explain array of pointers.
13. Give the advantages of using pointers.
14. Can we have an array of function pointers? If yes, illustrate with the help of a suitable example.
15. Explain the term dynamic memory allocation.
16. Differentiate between `malloc()`, `calloc`, and `realloc()`.
17. Write a short note on pointers to pointers.
18. Differentiate between a function returning pointer to `int` and a pointer to function returning `int`.
19. Differentiate between pointer to constants and constant to pointers.
20. Explain the call by address technique of passing parameters to function.
21. How are pointers used on two-dimensional arrays?
22. How can you declare a pointer variable?
23. Differentiate between a variable address and a variable's value. How can we access a variable's address and its value using pointers?
24. Give a brief summary of different memory areas available to the programmer.
25. What do you understand by dereferencing a pointer variable?
26. Write a short note on pointer expressions and pointer arithmetic.
27. What will *p++ = *q++ do?
28. Write a short note on pointer and a three-dimensional array.
29. How can a pointer be used to access individual elements of an array? Illustrate with an example.
30. Can we assign a pointer variable to another pointer variable? Justify your answer with the help of an example.
31. What will happen if we add or subtract an integer to or from a pointer variable?

32. Is it possible to compare two pointer variables? Illustrate using an example.
33. Can we subtract two pointer variables?
34. With the help of an example explain how an array can be passed to a function? Is it possible to send just a single element of the array to a function?
35. Can array names appear on the left side of the assignment operator? Why?
36. Differentiate between an array name and an array pointer.
37. How can you have array of function pointers? Illustrate with an example.
38. Briefly discuss memory allocation schemes in C language.
39. Write a short note on `realloc()`. Give a program to explain its usage.
40. With the help of an example, explain how pointers can be used to dynamically allocate space for two-dimensional and three-dimensional arrays.
41. Write a short note on wild pointers.
42. Give a brief description of memory leakage problem with the help of an example.
43. What is a dangling pointer?
44. Explain memory corruption with the help of suitable examples.
45. Differentiate between `*(arr+i)` and `(arr+i)`.
46. How can we access the value pointed by a pointer to a pointer?

Programming Exercises

1. Write a program to print 'Hello World' using pointers.
2. Write a program to enter a lowercase character. Print this character in uppercase and also display its ASCII value.
3. Write a program to subtract two integer values.
4. Write a program to calculate area of a circle.
5. Write a program to convert 3.14 into its integral equivalent.
6. Write a program to find smallest of three integer values.
7. Write a program to input a character and categorize it as a vowel or a consonant.
8. Write a program to input 10 values in an array. Categorize each value as positive, negative, or equal to zero.
9. Write a program to input a character. If it is in uppercase print in lowercase and vice versa.
10. Write a program to display the sum and average of numbers from 100 to 200.
11. Write a program to print all odd numbers from 100 to 200.
12. Write a program to input 10 values in an array. Categorize each value as prime or composite.
13. Write a program to subtract two floating point numbers using functions.
14. Write a program to calculate the area of a circle.
15. Write a program to add two integers using functions. Use call by address technique of passing parameters.
16. Using a program, explain how pointer variables can be used to access strings.
17. Write a program to print "Good Morning" using pointers.
18. Write a program to print the lowercase characters into uppercase and vice versa in the given string "gOOd mORninG".
19. Write a program to copy "University" from the given string "Oxford University Press" in another string.
20. Write a program to copy last five characters from the given string "Oxford University Press" in another string.
21. Write a menu-driven program to perform various string operations using pointers.
22. Write a program to read and print a floating point array. The space for the array should be allocated at the run time.
23. Write a program to demonstrate working of `calloc()`.
24. Write a function to calculate roots of a quadartic equation. The function must accept arguments and return result using pointers.
25. Write a program using pointers to insert a value in an array.
26. Write a program using pointers to search a value from an array.
27. Write a function that accepts a string using pointers. In the function, delete all the occurrences of a given character and display the modified string on the screen.
28. Write a program to reverse a string using pointers.
29. Write a program to compare two arrays using pointers.

Find the output of the following codes.

1.
```
main()
{
    int arr[]={1,2,3,4,5};
    int *ptr, i;
    ptr = arr+4;
    for(i = 4; i >= 0;i--)
       printf("\n %d", *(ptr-i));
}
```
2.
```
main()
{
    int arr[]={1,2,3,4,5};
    int *ptr, i;
    ptr = arr+4;
    for(i = 0; i < 5; i++)
       printf("\n %d", *(ptr-i));
}
```
3.
```
#include <stdio.h>
main()
{
    int val=3;
    int *pval=&val;
    printf("%d %d", ++val, *pval);
}
```

4.
```
#include <stdio.h>
main()
{
  int val=3;
  int *pval=&val;
  printf("%d %d", val, *pval++);
}
```
5.
```
#include <stdio.h>
main()
{
  int val=3;
  int *pval=&val;
  printf("%d %d", val, ++*pval);
}
```
6.
```
#include <stdio.h>
main()
{
  int arr[]={1,2,3,4,5};
  printf("%d", ++*arr);
}
```
7.
```
#include <stdio.h>
main()
{
  int arr[]={1,2,3,4,5};
  int *parr = arr+2;
  printf("%d %d", ++*parr-1, 1+*parr);
}
```
8.
```
#include <stdio.h>
main()
{
  int num = 5, *ptr=&num, x=*ptr;
  printf("%d %d %d", ++num, x+2, *ptr--);
}
```
9.
```
#include <stdio.h>
main()
{
  int num=5, *ptr=&num;
  printf("\n %d", *&num);
  printf("\n %d", *&*&num);
  printf("\n %d", *&ptr);
  printf("\n %d", **&ptr);
  printf("\n %d", &**&ptr);
}
```
10.
```
main()
{
  int num=5, *ptr=&num, x=*ptr;
  printf("%d %d", num, x+2, (*ptr)--);
}
```
11.
```
#include <stdio.h>
main()
{
  int arr[]={1,2,3,4,5}, i, k = 3;
  for(i=0;i<10;i++)
    *(arr+i)=i;
  printf("%d", *(arr+k-1));
}
```
12.
```
#include <stdio.h>
main()
{
  int arr[]={1,2,3,4,5};
  int i=1,j=2;
  printf("\n %d", *(arr+1+i));
  printf("\n %d", *(arr+*(arr+1)));
  printf("\n %d", *(arr+i)+*(arr+j));
  printf("\n %d", *(arr+j));
}
```
13.
```
main()
{
  char str[]="ABCDEFGH", *pstr=str;
  pstr++;
  while(*pstr!='H')
    printf("%c", *pstr++);
}
```
14.
```
main()
{
  char str[]="ABCDEFGH";
  printf("%d", (&str[3]-&str[0]));
}
```
15.
```
main()
{
  char *str="ABCDEFGH";
  (*str++);
  printf("%s", str);
}
```
16.
```
main()
{
  char *str="ABCDEFGH";
  str++;
  printf("%s", str);
}
```
17.
```
main()
{
  char *str="AbcDefGh";
  int i=0;
  while(*str)
  {
    if(isupper(*str++))
      i++;
  }
  printf("%d", i);
}
```
18.
```
main()
{
  printf("Hello World"+3);
}
```
19.
```
main()
{
  int arr[][2]={1,2,3,4,5,6,7,8,9};
  printf("%d", sizeof(arr));
}
```

20.
```
main()
{
  int arr[2][3]={1,2,3,4,5,6,7,8,9};
  printf("%d", sizeof(arr[1]));
}
```

21.
```
main()
{
  int arr[5], *parr=arr;
  while(parr < &arr[5])
  {
    *parr = parr-arr;
    printf("%d", *parr);
    parr++;
  }
}
```

22.
```
main()
{
  char *str = "Hello World";
  str[5]='!';
  printf("%s", str);
}
```

23.
```
main()
{
  char *str1 = "Hello World";
  char str2[20] = "Hello World";
  char str3[] = "Hello World";
  printf(" %d %d %d", sizeof(str1),
   sizeof(str2), sizeof(str3));
}
```

24.
```
main()
{
  register int num = 3, *ptr = &num;
  printf("%d",*ptr);
}
```

25.
```
#include <stdio.h>
void func(int (*parr)[3]);
main()
{
  int arr[2][3] = {1,2,3,4,5,6};
  func(arr);
  func(arr + 1);
}
void func(int (*parr)[3])
{
  int i;
  for(i = 0; i < 2; i++)
    printf("%d", (*parr)[i]);
}
```

Find errors if any in the following statements.

1. `int ptr, *ptr;`
2. `int num, *ptr=num;`
3. `int *ptr=10;`
4. `int num, **ptr=#`
5. `int *ptr1, *ptr2, *ptr3=*ptr1+*ptr2;`
6. `int *ptr; scanf("%d", &ptr);`

ANNEXURE 3

Deciphering Pointer Declarations

The *right–left* rule is a widely used rule for creating as well as deciphering C declarations. Before starting, let us first understand the meaning of different symbols and the way in which they are read.

Symbol	Read as	Location
*	pointer to	placed on the left side
[]	array of	placed on the right side
()	function returning	placed on the right side

The following are the steps to decipher the declaration:

Step 1: Find the identifier and read as 'identifier is'.

Step 2: Read the symbols on the right of the identifier. For example, if you find '( )', then you know that it is a function declaration. So you can now say, 'identifier is function returning'. Or if you encounter a '[ ]', then read it as 'identifier is array of'.

Continue moving right until you either run out of symbols or you encounter a right parenthesis.

Step 3: Now, check the symbols to the left of the identifier. If it is not a symbol given in the table, then just say it. For example if you encounter `int`, then just say it as it is. Otherwise, translate it into English using the above table. Continue going left until you either run out of symbols or you encounter a left parenthesis.

Step 4: Repeat Steps 2 and 3 until the entire declaration is completely deciphered.

Consider some examples:

```
int *ptr[];
```

Step 1: Find the identifier. Here, the identifier is `ptr`. So we can say,

```
'ptr is'
```

Step 2: Identify the symbols on the right side of the identifier until you run out of symbols or encounter a right parenthesis. Here, the symbol is []. So we can say

```
'ptr is array of'
```

Step 3: Move to left of the identifier until you run out of symbols or encounter a left parenthesis. Here, the symbol is `*`. So we can say,

```
ptr is array of pointer to
```

Step 4: Continue moving left. Here, you find `int`. So say,

```
ptr is array of pointer to int.
```

Now decipher the following declaration

```
int *(*func())();
```

Step 1: Find the identifier. Here, the identifier is `func`. So we can say,

```
func is
```

Step 2: Identify the symbols on the right side of the identifier until you run out of symbols or encounter a right parenthesis. Here, the symbol is (). So say

```
func is function returning
```

Step 3: Move to left of the identifier until you run out of symbols or encounter a left parenthesis. Here, the symbol is `*`. So say,

```
func is function returning pointer to
```

Step 4: Can't move left anymore because of the left parenthesis, so now move to right. Here, you will encounter a symbol (). So say,

```
func is function returning pointer to function
   returning
```

Step 5: Can't move right anymore as all symbols have exhausted so move to left. Here you will encounter a '`*`'. So say,

```
func is function returning pointer to function
   returning pointer to
```

Step 6: Continue moving left. Here you will find `int`. So say,

```
func is function returning pointer to function
   returning pointer to int.
```

Some declarations also contain array size and function parameters. So if you encounter a symbol as '[10]', then read it as 'array (size 10)'. If you encounter, something like '(int *, char)', then read it as 'function expecting (int *, char) and returning...'. Now consider such an example and decipher the following declaration:

```
int (*(*func)(int *, char))[3][5];
```

Use the steps illustrated above and check your answer.

```
func is pointer to function expecting (int
   *,char) and
returning pointer to array (size 3) of array
   (size 5) of int.
```

Some Illegal Declarations in C

It is quite possible that you end up with some illegal declarations using this rule. So, you must be very clear about what is legal in C and what is not allowed in the language. For example, consider a declaration as shown:

```
int *((*func)())[][];
```

This can be deciphered as `func is pointer to function returning array of array of pointer to int`. But did you notice that a function cannot return an array, but only a pointer to an array. Therefore, this declaration is illegal.

Let us look as some more illegal combinations in C language:

```
[]()-C does not permit an array of functions
()()-A function cannot return a function
()[]-A function cannot return an array
```

The table given below lists the declaration, meaning, and its remarks as valid or invalid.

Declaration	Meaning	Remarks
float num;	num is a float	Valid
char *ch;	ch is a pointer to char	Valid
int arr[];	arr is an array of int	Valid
float func();	func is a function returning float	Valid
int **ptr;	ptr is a pointer to pointer to int	Valid
char (*ptr)[];	ptr is a pointer to array of char	Valid
char (*ptr)();	ptr is a pointer to function returning char	Valid
float *ptr[];	ptr is array of pointers to float	Valid
int mat[][];	mat is an array of array of int	Valid
int func[]()	func is an array of function returning int	Invalid
float *func();	func is a function returning pointer to float	Valid
float func()[];	func is a function returning array of float	Invalid
float func()();	func is a function returning function returning float	Invalid
int ***ptr;	ptr is a pointer to pointer to pointer to int	Valid
int (**ptr)[];	ptr is a pointer to pointer to array of int	Valid
float (**func)();	func is a pointer to pointer to a function returning float	Valid
char *(*ptr)[];	ptr is a pointer to array of pointer to char	Valid
float (*ptr)[][];	ptr is a pointer to array of array of float	Valid
float (*ptr)[]();	ptr is a pointer to array of function returning float	Invalid
char *(*(ptr)();	ptr is a pointer to function returning a pointer to char	Valid
char (*ptr)()[];	ptr is a pointer to function returning an array of char	Invalid
int (*ptr)()();	ptr is a pointer to function returning function returning int	Invalid
float **ptr[];	ptr is an array of pointer to pointer to int	Valid
char (*ptr[])[];	ptr is array of pointers to array of char	Valid
char (*ptr[])();	ptr is array of pointer to function returning char	Valid
float *ptr[][];	ptr is array of array of pointer to float	Valid
int arr[][][];	arr is array of array of array of int	Valid
int arr[][]();	arr is array of array of function returning int	Invalid
float *arr[]();	arr is array of function returning pointer to float	Invalid
int arr[]()[];	arr is array of function returning array of int	Invalid
float **func();	func is a function returning pointer to float pointer (or pointer to float)	Valid
char *func()[];	func is a function returning array of char pointer	Invalid
float (*func())[];	func is a function returning pointer to array of float	Valid
float (*func())();	func is a function returning pointer to function returning float	Valid
char func()[][];	func is a function returning array of array of char	Invalid
char func()[]();	func is a function returning array of array of function returning char	Invalid
char *func()();	func is a function returning function returning char pointer	Invalid

CASE STUDY 3: Chapters 13 and 14

In C language, a string is a null-terminated character array and a pointer is a variable that contains the memory location of another variable. Therefore, a pointer is a variable that represents the location of a data item such as a variable or an array element.

Pointers provide an alternate way to access individual elements of the array and they are used to pass arrays and strings as function arguments. We will utilize all these concepts to write a program that performs various operations on a string (using pointers).

1. Write a menu-driven program to read the following operations: 1. Read a string, 2. Display the string, 3. Merge two strings, 4. Copy n characters from the mth position, 5. Calculate the length of the string, 6. Count the number of upper case, lower case, numbers and special characters, 7. Count the number of words, lines, and characters, 8. Replace, with; 9. Exit.

```
#include <stdio.h>
#include <string.h>

void read_str(char *my_str);
void display_str(char *my_str);
void merge_str(char *my_str1, char *my_str2,
  char *my_str3);
void copy(char my_str1[], int m, int n);
int cal_len(char my_str[]);
void count(char my_str[]);
void count_wlc(char my_str[]);
void replace_str(char *my_str);
int main()
{
 char str1[100], str2[100], merged_str[200],
  copy_str[100];
 int option, m, n, length=0;

 do
 {
  printf("\n 1. Enter the string");
  printf("\n 2. Display the string");
  printf("\n 3. Merge two strings");
  printf("\n 4. Copy n characters from mth
   position");
  printf("\n 5. Calculate length of the
   string");
  printf("\n 6. Count the number of upper
   case, lower case, numbers, and special
   characters");
  printf("\n 7. Count the number of words,
   lines, and characters");
  printf("\n 8. Replace, with ;");
  printf("\n 9. EXIT");

  printf("\n\n Enter your option: ");
  scanf("%d", &option);
  switch(option)
  {
   case 1:
    read_str(str1);
    break;
   case 2:
    display_str(str1);
    break;
   case 3:
    read_str(str2);
    merge_str(str1, str2, merged_str);
    break;
   case 4:
    printf("\n Enter the position from which
 to copy the text: ");
    scanf("%d", &m);
   printf("\n Enter the number of characters
 to be copied: ");
    scanf("%d", &n);
    copy(str1, m, n);
    break;
   case 5:
    length = cal_len(str1);
   printf("\n The length of the string is:
%d", length);
    break;
   case 6:
    count(str1);
    break;
   case 7:
    count_wlc(str1);
    break;
   case 8:
    replace_str(str1);
    break;
  }
 }while (option != 9);
 return 0;
}

void read_str( char *my_str)
{
 printf("\n Enter the string: ");
 gets(my_str);
}

void display_str(char *my_str)
{

 printf("\n The string is: ");
 while(*my_str != '\0')
 {
  printf("%c", *my_str);
  my_str++;
 }
}

void merge_str(char *my_str1, char *my_str2,
  char *my_str3)
```

```
{
  strcpy(my_str3,my_str1);
  strcat(my_str3, my_str2);
  display_str(my_str3);
}

void copy(char my_str1[], int m, int n)
{
  int i = 0;
  char *pstr;
  printf("\n The copied string is: ");
  while(i < n || my_str1[m]!='\0')
  {
    *pstr = my_str1[m];
    m++;i++;
    printf("%c",*pstr);
  }
}

int cal_len(char my_str[])
{
  char *str = my_str;
  int len = 0;
  while(*str != '\0')
  {
    str++;
    len++;
  }
  return len;

}

void count(char my_str[])
{
  char *pstr = my_str;
  int upper_case = 0, lower_case = 0, numbers
   = 0, spcl_char = 0;
  while (*pstr != '\0')
  {
    if (*pstr >= 'A' && *pstr <= 'Z')
      upper_case++;
    else if (*pstr >= 'a' && *pstr <= 'z')
      lower_case++;
    else if (*pstr >= '0' && *pstr <= '9')
      numbers++;
    else
      spcl_char++;
    pstr++;
  }
   printf("\n  Upper  case  characters  =  %d",
  upper_case);
   printf("\n  Lower  case  characters  =  %d",
  lower_case);
  printf("\n Numbers = %d", numbers);
  printf("\n Special characters = %d", spcl_char);
}

void count_wlc(char my_str[])
{
  char *pstr = my_str;
  int words =0, lines =0, characters = 0;
  while(*pstr != '\0')
  {
   if (*pstr == '\n')
     lines++;
   if (*pstr == ' ' && *(my_str+1) != ' ')
     words++;
   characters++;
   pstr++;
  }
  printf("\n Number of words = %d", words+1);
  printf("\n Number of lines = %d", lines+1);
   printf("\n  Number  of  characters  =  %d",
 characters);
}

void replace_str(char my_str[])
{
  char *pstr=my_str;
  while (*pstr != '\0')
  {
   if(*pstr == ',')
     *pstr = ';';
   pstr++;
  }
  display_str(my_str);
}
```

Output

```
1. Enter the string
2. Display the string
3. Merge two strings
4. Copy n characters from mth position
5. Calculate length of the string
6. Count the number of upper case, lower case,
   numbers, and special characters
7.  Count  the  number  of  words,  lines,  and
   characters
8. Replace, with;
9. EXIT
Enter your option: 1
Enter the string: Hi

1. Enter the string
2. Display the string
3. Merge two strings
4. Copy n characters from mth position
5. Calculate length of the string
6. Count the number of upper case, lower case,
   numbers and special characters
7. Count the number of words, lines and characters
8. Replace, with;
9. EXIT
Enter your option: 3
Enter the string: there
The string is: Hi there
```

15 Structure, Union, and Enumerated Data Type

TAKEAWAYS

- Structure declaration, initialization, and access
- Nested structures
- Arrays of unions
- Structures and functions
- Self-referential structures
- Unions
- Arrays of structures
- Unions within structures
- Structure within unions
- Enumerated data type

15.1 INTRODUCTION

A structure is a user-defined data type that can store related information (even of different data types) together. It is similar to records and can be used to store information about an entity. The major difference between a structure and an array is that an array contains related information of the same data type.

A structure is, therefore, a collection of variables under a single name. The variables within a structure are of different data types and each has a name that is used to select it from the structure.

15.1.1 Structure Declaration

A structure is declared using the keyword `struct` followed by the structure name. All the variables of the structure are declared within the structure. A structure type is generally declared by using the following syntax:

```
struct struct-name
{
   data_type var-name;
   data_type var-name;
   ...
};
```

Programming Tip: Do not forget to place a semicolon after the definition of structures and unions.

For example, if we have to define a structure for a student, then the related information probably would be: `roll_number`, `name`, `course`, and `fees`. This structure can be declared as:

```
struct student
{
   int r_no;
   char name[20];
   char course[20];
   float fees;
};
```

Now, the structure has become a user-defined data type. Each variable name declared within a structure is called a member of the structure. The structure declaration, however, does not allocate any memory or consume storage space. It just gives a template that conveys to the C compiler how the structure should be laid out in memory and gives details of the member names. Like any other data type, memory is allocated for the structure when we declare a variable of the structure. For example, we can define a variable by writing

```
struct student stud1;
```

Here, `struct student` is a data type and `stud1` is a variable. Look at another way of declaring variables. In the following syntax, the variable is declared at the time of structure declaration.

```
struct student
{
  int r_no;
  char name[20];
  char course[20];
  float fees;
}stud1, stud2;
```

In this declaration we declare two variables `stud1` and `stud2` of the type `student`. So if you want to declare more than one variable of the structure, then separate the variables using a comma.

When we declare variables of the structure, separate memory is allocated for each variable. This is shown in Figure 15.1.

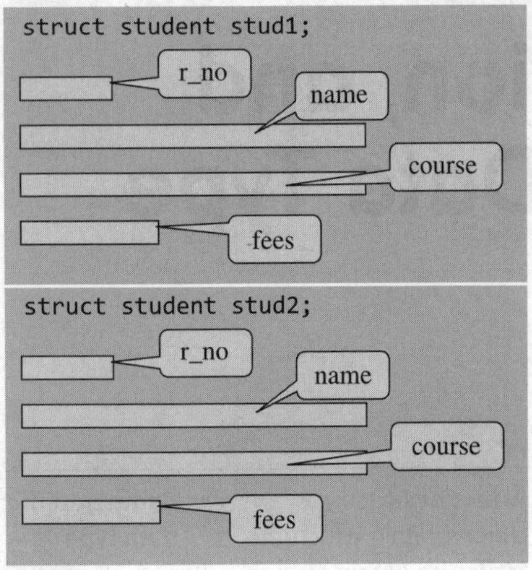

Figure 15.1 Memory allocation for structure variables

Let us see some more structure declarations.

Example 15.1

Declare a structure to store information about a point in the coordinate system.

Solution

```
struct point
{
  int x,y;
};
```

Example 15.2

Declare a structure to store customer information.

Solution

```
struct customer
{
  int cust_id;
  char name[20];
  char address[20];
  long int phone_num;
  int DOB;
};
```

Example 15.3

Declare a structure to store information of a particular date.

Solution

```
struct date
{
  int day;
  int month;
  int year;
};
```

Example 15.4

Declare a structure to store information of a particular book.

Programming Tip:
Use different member names for different structures for clarity.

Solution

```
struct BOOK
{
  char title[20];
  char author[20];
  int pages;
  float price;
  int yr_of_publication;
};
```

Example 15.5

Declare a structure to create an inventory record.

Solution

```
struct inventory
{
  char prod_name[20];
  float price;
  int stock;
};
```

Note

Structure type and variable declaration of a structure can be either local or global depending on their placement in the code.

Last but not the least, structure member names and names of the structure follow the same rules as laid down for the names of ordinary variables. However, care should be taken to ensure that the name of structure and the name of a structure member should not be the same. Moreover, structure name and its variable name should also be different.

15.1.2 `Typedef` Declarations

Programming Tip:
C does not allow declaration of variables at the time of creating a typedef definition. So variables must be declared in an independent statement.

The `typedef` (derived from type definition) keyword enables the programmer to create a new data type name from an existing data type. By using `typedef`, no new data is created, rather an alternate name is given to a known data type.

The general syntax of using the `typedef` keyword is given as:

```
typedef existing data_type new data_type
```

Note that `typedef` statement does not occupy any memory, it simply defines a new type. For example, if we write

```
typedef int INTEGER;
```

then `INTEGER` is the new name of data type `int`. To declare variables using the new data type name, precede the variable name with the data type name (new). Therefore, to define an integer variable, we may now write

```
INTEGER num=5;
```

When we precede a `struct` name with `typedef` keyword, then the `struct` becomes a new type. It is used to make the construct shorter with more meaningful names for types already defined by C or for types that you have declared. A `typedef` declaration is a synonym for the type. For example, writing

```
typedef struct student
{
    int r_no;
    char name[20];
    char course[20];
    float fees;
};
```

Now that you have preceded the structure's name with the keyword `typedef`, `student` becomes a new data type. Therefore, now you can straightaway declare variables of this new data type as you declare variables of type `int`, `float`, `char`, `double`, etc. To declare a variable of structure `student` you will just write

```
student stud1;
```

Note that we have not written `struct student stud1`.

15.1.3 Initialization of Structures

A structure can be initialized in the same way as other data types are initialized. *Initializing a structure* means assigning some constants to the members of the structure. When the user does not explicitly initialize the structure, then C automatically does that. For `int` and `float` members, the values are initialized to zero and character and string members are initialized to `'\0'` by default (in the absence of any initialization done by the user).

The initializers are enclosed in braces and are separated by commas. However, care must be taken to see that the initializers match their corresponding types in the structure definition.

The general syntax to initialize a structure variable is given as follows:

```
struct struct_name
{
    data_type member_name1;
    data_type member_name2;
    data_type member_name3;
    .......................
}struct_var = {constant1, constant2,
   constant 3,...};
```

OR

Programming Tip:
It is an error to assign a structure of one type to a structure of another type.

```
struct struct_name
{
    data_type member_name1;
    data_type member_name2;
    data_type member_name3;
    ......................
};
struct struct_name struct_var = {constant1,
constant2, constant 3,...};
```

For example, we can initialize a `student` structure by writing

```
struct student
{
 int r_no;
 char name[20];
 char course[20];
 float fees;
}stud1 = {01, "Rahul", "BCA", 45000};
```

or by writing

```
struct student stud1 = {01, "Rahul", "BCA",
45000};
```

Figure 15.2 illustrates how the values will be assigned to the individual fields of the structure.

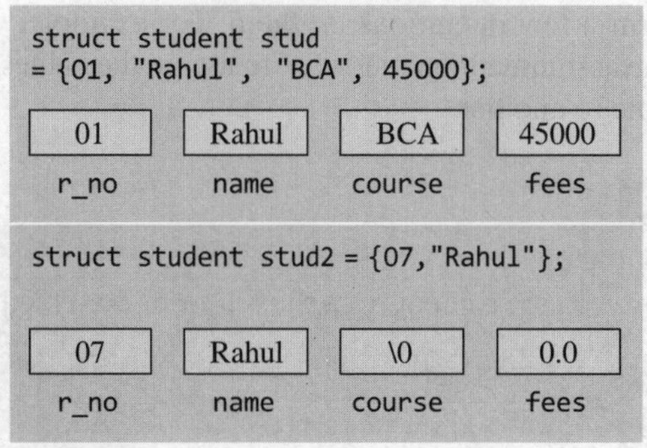

Figure 15.2 Assigning values to structure members

When all the members of a structure are not initialized, it is called partial initialization. In case of partial initialization, first few members of the structure are initialized and those that are uninitialized are assigned default values.

15.1.4 Accessing the Members of a Structure

Programming Tip:
A member of the structure cannot be accessed directly using its name. Rather you must use the structure name followed by the dot operator before specifying the member name.

Each member of a structure can be used just like a normal variable, but its name will be a bit longer. A structure member variable is generally accessed using a `'.'` (dot) operator. The syntax of accessing a structure or a member of a structure can be given as follows:

```
struct_var.member_name
```

The dot operator is used to select a particular member of the structure. For example, to assign value to the individual data members of the structure variable `stud1`, we may write

```
stud1.r_no = 01;
stud1.name = "Rahul";
stud1.course = "BCA";
stud1.fees = 45000;
```

To input values for data members of the structure variable `stud1`, we may write

```
scanf("%d", &stud1.r_no);
scanf("%s", stud1.name);
```

Similarly, to print the values of structure variable `stud1`, we may write

```
printf("%s", stud1.course);
printf("%f", stud1.fees);
```

Memory is allocated only when we declare variables of the structure. In other words, memory is allocated only when we instantiate the structure. In the absence of any variable, structure definition is just a template that will be used to reserve memory when a variable of type `struct` is declared.

Once the variables of a structure are defined, we can perform a few operations on them. For example, we can use the assignment operator `'='` to assign the values of one variable to another.

Note

Of all the operators ->, ., (), and [] have the highest priority. This is evident from the following statement:

```
stud1.fees++ will be interpreted as (stud1.
   fees)++
```

15.1.5 Copying and Comparing Structures

We can assign a structure to another structure of the same type. For example, if we have two structure variables `stud1` and `stud2` of type `struct student` given as

Programming Tip: An error will be generated if you try to compare two structure variables.

```
struct student stud1 =
{01, "Rahul", "BCA",
45000};
struct student stud2;
```

Then to assign one structure variable to another we will write,

```
stud2 = stud1;
```

This statement initializes the members of `stud2` with the values of members of `stud1`. Therefore, now the values of `stud1` and `stud2` can be given as shown in Figure 15.3.

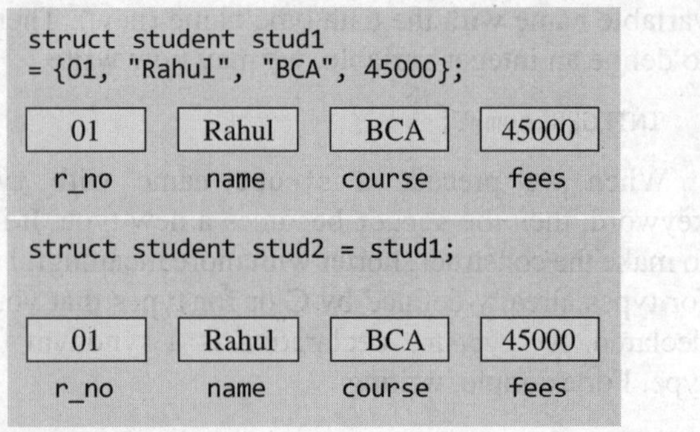

Figure 15.3 Copying values of structure variables

C does not permit comparison of one structure variable with another. However, individual members of one structure can be compared with individual members of another structure. When we compare one structure member with another structure's member, the comparison will behave like any other ordinary variable comparison. For example, to compare the fees of two students, we will write

```
if(stud1.fees > stud2.fees)
  // Fees of stud1 is greater than stud2
```

15.1.6 Finding the Size of a Structure

In this section, we will read about three different ways through which we can find the number of bytes a structure will occupy in the memory.

Simple Addition

In this technique, we will make a list of all data types and add the memory required by each. For example, let's consider a simple structure of an employee.

```
struct Employee
{ intemp_ID;
  char name[20];
  double salary;
  char designation[20];
  float experience;
};
```

Now, Size = size of `emp_ID` + size of `name` + size of `salary` + size of `designation` + size of `experience`

Size of `emp_ID` = 2
Size of `name` = 20 × size of character
Size of `salary` = 8
Size of `designation` = 20 × size of character
Size of `experience` = 4

Therefore, Size =

$= 2 + 20 \times 1 + 8 + 20 \times 1 + 4$
$= 2 + 20 + 8 + 20 + 4$
$= 54$ bytes

Using sizeof Operator

As discussed earlier, `sizeof` operator is used to calculate the size of a data type, variable, or an expression. To use this operator simply write, `sizeof (struct_name);`

For example, the code given below prints the size of structure `Employee`.

```
#include <stdio.h>
typedef struct Employee
{ int emp_ID;
  char name[20];
  double salary;
  char designation[20];
  float experience;
};
void main()
{
  struct Employee e;
  printf("\n %d", sizeof(e));
}
```

Output

```
54
```

Note

Syntax of sizeof operator is similar to that of a function but sizeof is not a library function. It is an operator in C.

Subtracting the Addresses

In this technique, we use an array of structure variables. Then we subtract the address of first element of next consecutive variable from the address of the first element of preceding structure variable. For example, the code below finds the size of structure `Employee`.

```
#include <stdio.h>
typedef struct Employee
{ int emp_ID;
  char name[20];
  double salary;
  char designation[20];
  float experience;
};

void main()
{
  struct Employee e[5];
  int start, end, len;

  /* address of the first element of first
   employee */
  start = &e[0].emp_ID;
  /* address of the first element of second
   employee */
  end = &e[1].emp_ID;

  len = end - start;
  printf("\n Size of the structure = %d",
   len);
}
```

Output

```
Size of the structure = 54
```

---

1. Write a program using structures to read and display the information about a student.

```
#include <stdio.h>
int main()
{
  struct student
  {
    int roll_no;
    char name[80];
    float fees;
    char DOB[80];
  };
  struct student stud1;
  printf("\n Enter the roll number: ");
  scanf("%d", &stud1.roll_no);
  printf("\n Enter the name: ");
  scanf("%s", stud1.name);
  printf("\n Enter the fees: ");
  scanf("%f", &stud1.fees);
  printf("\n Enter the DOB: ");
  scanf("%s", stud1.DOB);
  printf("\n *******STUDENT'S DETAILS
  *******");
  printf("\n ROLL No. = %d", stud1.roll_no);
  printf("\n NAME = %s", stud1.name);
  printf("\n FEES = %f", stud1.fees);
  printf("\n DOB = %s", stud1.DOB);
  return 0;
}
```

Output

```
Enter the roll number: 01
Enter the name: Rahul
Enter the fees: 45000
Enter the DOB: 25-09-1991
*******STUDENT'S DETAILS *******
ROLL No. = 01
NAME = Rahul
FEES = 45000.00
DOB = 25-09-1991
```

2. Write a program, using structures to find the largest of three numbers.

```
#include <stdio.h>
int main()
{
  struct numbers
  {
    int a, b, c;
    int largest;
  };
  struct numbers num;
  printf("\n Enter the three numbers: ");
  scanf("%d %d %d", &num.a, &num.b, &num.c);
  if (num.a > num.b && num.a > num.c)
    num.largest = num.a;
  if (num.b > num.a && num.b > num.c)
    num.largest = num.b;
  if (num.c > num.a && num.c > num.b)
    num.largest = num.c;
  printf("\n The largest number is: %d", num.
  largest);
  return 0;
}
```

Output

```
Enter the three numbers: 7 9 1
The largest number is: 9
```

3. Write a program to read, display, add, and subtract two complex numbers.

```
#include <stdio.h>
int main()
{
  typedef struct complex
  {
    int real;
    int imag;
  }COMPLEX;
  COMPLEX c1, c2, sum_c, sub_c;
  int option;
  do
  {
    printf("\n ***** MAIN MENU *****");
    printf("\n 1. Read the complex nos.");
    printf("\n 2. Display the complex nos.");
    printf("\n 3. Add the complex nos.");
    printf("\n 4. Subtract the complex nos.");
    printf("\n 5. EXIT");
    printf("\n Enter your option: ");
    scanf("%d", &option);
    switch(option)
    {
    case 1:
      printf("\n Enter the real and imaginary
        parts of the first complex number: ");
      scanf("%d %d", &c1.real, &c1.imag);
      printf("\n Enter the real and imaginary
        parts of the second complex number: ");
      scanf("%d %d", &c2.real, &c2.imag);
      break;
    case 2:
      printf("\n The first complex number is:
        %d + %di", c1.real, c1.imag);
      printf("\n The second complex number is:
        %d + %di", c2.real, c2.imag);
      break;
    case 3:
      sum_c.real = c1.real + c2.real;
      sum_c.imag = c1.imag + c2.imag;
      printf("\n The sum of two complex numbers
        is: %d + %di", sum_c.real, sum_c.imag);
      break;
    case 4:
      sub_c.real = c1.real - c2.real;
      sub_c.imag = c1.imag – c2.imag;
      printf("\n The difference between two
        complex numbers is: %d + %di",
        sub_c.real, sub_c.imag);
      break;
    }
  }while(option != 5);
  return 0;
}
```

Output

```
***** MAIN MENU ******
1. Read the complex nos
2. Display the complex nos.
3. Add the complex nos.
4. Subtract the complex nos.
5. EXIT
Enter your option: 1
Enter the real and imaginary parts of the first
complex number: 2 3
Enter the real and imaginary parts of the
second complex number: 4 5
***** MAIN MENU ******
1. Read the complex nos.
2. Display the complex nos.
3. Add the complex nos.
4. Subtract the complex nos.
5. EXIT
Enter your option: 3
The sum of two complex numbers is: 6 + 8i
```

4. Write a program to enter two points and then calculate the distance between them.

```
#include <stdio.h>
```

```
#include <math.h>
int main()
{
  typedef struct point
  {
    int x, y;
  }POINT;
  POINT p1, p2;
  float distance;
  printf("\n Enter the coordinates of the first
    point: ");
  scanf("%d %d", &p1.x, &p1.y);
  printf("\n Enter the coordinates of the
    second point: ");
  scanf("%d %d", &p2.x, &p2.y);
  distance = sqrt(pow((p1.x - p2.x), 2) +
    pow((p1.y - p2.y), 2));
  printf("\n The coordinates of the first point
    are: %dx %dy", p1.x, p1.y);
  printf("\n The coordinates of the second
    point are: %dx %dy", p2.x, p2.y);
  printf("\n Distance between p1 and p2 = %f",
    distance);
  return 0;
}
```

Output

```
Enter the coordinates of the first point: 2 3
Enter the coordinates of the second point: 9 9
The coordinates of the first point are: 2x 3y
The coordinates of the second point are: 9x 9y
Distance between p1 and p2 = 9.219544
```

15.2 NESTED STRUCTURES

A structure can be placed within another structure, i.e., a structure may contain another structure as its member. A structure that contains another structure as its member is called a *nested structure*.

Let us now see how we declare nested structures or structures that contain structures. Although it is possible to declare a nested structure with one declaration, it is not recommended. The easier and clearer way is to declare the structures separately and then group them in a high-level structure. When you do this, take care to check that nesting is done from inside out (from lowest level to the most inclusive level), i.e., to say, declare the innermost structure, then the next level structure, working towards the outer (most inclusive) structure.

```
typedef struct
{
  char first_name[20];
  char mid_name[20];
  char last_name[20];
}NAME;
typedef struct
{
  int dd;
  int mm;
  int yy;
}DATE;

typedef struct student
{
  int r_no;
  NAME name;
  char course[20];
  DATE DOB;
  float fees;
};
```

In this example, we see that the structure student contains two other structures—NAME and DATE. Both these structures have their own fields. The structure NAME has three fields: first_name, mid_name, and last_name. The structure DATE also has three fields: dd, mm, and yy, which specify the day, month, and year of the date. To assign values to the structure fields, we will write

```
student stud1;
stud1.name.first_name = "Janak";
stud1.name.mid_name = "Raj";
stud1.name.last_name = "Thareja";
stud1.course = "BCA";
stud1.DOB.dd = 15;
stud1.DOB.mm = 09;
stud1.DOB.yy = 1990;
stud1.fees = 45000;
```

In case of nested structures, we use the dot operator in conjunction with the structure variables to access the members of the innermost as well as the outermost structures. The use of nested structures is illustrated in the following program:

5. Write a program to read and display information of a student using a structure within a structure.

```
#include <stdio.h>
int main()
{
  struct DOB
  {
    int day;
    int month;
    int year;
  };
  struct student
  {
    int roll_no;
    char name[100];
    float fees;
    struct DOB date;
  };
```

```
    struct student stud1;
    printf("\n Enter the roll number: ");
    scanf("%d", &stud1.roll_no);
    printf("\n Enter the name: ");
    scanf("%s", stud1.name);
    printf("\n Enter the fees: ");
    scanf("%f", &stud1.fees);
    printf("\n Enter the DOB: ");
    scanf("%d %d %d", &stud1.date.day,
     &stud1.date.month, &stud1.date.year);
    printf("\n ***** STUDENT'S DETAILS *****");
    printf("\n ROLL No. = %d", stud1.roll_no);
    printf("\n NAME = %s", stud1.name);
    printf("\n FEES = %f", stud1.fees);
    printf("\n DOB = %d - %d - %d", stud1.date.
     day, stud1.date.month, stud1.date.year);
    return 0;
}
```

Output

```
Enter the roll number: 01
Enter the name: Rahul
Enter the fees: 45000
Enter the DOB: 25 09 1991
***** STUDENT'S DETAILS *****
ROLL No. = 01
NAME = Rahul
FEES = 45000.00
DOB = 25-09-1991
```

15.3 ARRAYS OF STRUCTURES

In the aforegiven examples, we have seen how to declare a structure and assign values to its data members. Now we will discuss how to declare an array of a structure. For this purpose, let us first analyse, where we would need array of structures.

In a class, we do not have just one student. But there may be at least 30 students. So the same definition of the structure can be used for all the 30 students. This would be possible when we create an array of the structure. An array of a structure is declared in the same way as we declare an array of a built-in data type.

> **Programming Tip:**
> It is an error to omit array subscripts when referring to individual structures of an array of structures.

Another example where an array of structures is desirable is in case of an organization. An organization has a number of employees. So, defining a separate structure for every employee is not a viable solution. So here we can have a common structure definition for all the employees. This can again be done by declaring an array of the structure employee.

The general syntax for declaring an array of a structure can be given as

```
struct struct_name
{
  data_type member_name1;
  data_type member_name2;
  data_type member_name3;
  ......................
};
struct struct_name struct_var[index];
```

Consider the given structure definition.

```
struct student
{
 int r_no;
 char name[20];
 char course[20];
 float fees;
};
```

A student array can be declared simply by writing

```
student stud[30];
```

Now, to assign values to the ith student of the class, we will write,

```
stud[i].r_no = 09;
stud[i].name = "RASHI";
stud[i].course = "MCA";
stud[i].fees = 60000;
```

In order to initialize the array of structure variables at the time of declaration, you should write as follows:

```
student stud[3] = {{01, "Aman", "BCA",
45000},{02, "Aryan", "MCA", 60000}, {03,
"John", "BCA", 45000}};
```

6. Write a program to read and display the information of all the students in the class.

```
#include <stdio.h>
int main()
{
 struct student
 {
   int roll_no;
   char name[80];
   int fees;
   char DOB[80];
 };
 struct student stud[50];
 int n, i;
 printf("\n Enter the number of students: ");
 scanf("%d", &n);
 for(i = 0;i < n;i++)
 {
   printf("\n Enter the roll number: ");
```

```
    scanf("%d", &stud[i].roll_no);
    printf("\n Enter the name: ");
    gets(stud[i].name);
    printf("\n Enter the fees: ");
    scanf("%d", &stud[i].fees);
    printf("\n Enter the DOB: ");
    gets(stud[i].DOB);
    }
  for(i = 0;i < n;i++)
  {
    printf("\n ********DETAILS OF STUDENT %d
      ********", i+1);
    printf("\n ROLL No. = %d", stud[i].
      roll_no);
    printf("\n NAME = %s", stud[i].name);
    printf("\n FEES = %d", stud[i].fees);
    printf("\n DOB = %s", stud[i].DOB);
  }
  return 0;
}
```

Output

```
Enter the number of students: 2
Enter the roll number: 1
Enter the name: kirti
Enter the fees: 5678
Enter the DOB: 9 9 91
Enter the roll number: 2
Enter the name: kangana
Enter the fees: 5678
Enter the DOB: 27 8 91
********DETAILS OF STUDENT 1********
ROLL No. = 1
NAME = kirti
FEES = 5678
DOB = 9 9 91
********DETAILS OF STUDENT 2********
ROLL No. = 2
NAME = kangana
FEES = 5678
DOB = 27 8 91
```

7. Write a program to read and display the information of all the students in the class. Then edit the details of the ith student and redisplay the entire information.

```
#include <stdio.h>
#include <string.h>
int main()
{
  struct student
  {
    int roll_no;
    char name[80];
    int fees;
    char DOB[80];
  };
  struct student stud[50];
  int n, i, rolno, new_rolno;
  int new_fees;
  char new_DOB[80], new_name[80];
  printf("\n Enter the number of students: ");
  scanf("%d", &n);
  for(i = 0;i < n;i++)
  {
    printf("\n Enter the roll number: ");
    scanf("%d", &stud[i].roll_no);
    printf("\n Enter the name: ");
    gets(stud[i].name);
    printf("\n Enter the fees: ");
    scanf("%d", stud[i].fees);
    printf("\n Enter the DOB: ");
    gets(stud[i].DOB);
  }
  for(i = 0;i < n;i++)
  {
    printf("\n ********DETAILS OF STUDENT
      %d********", i+1);
    printf("\n ROLL No. = %d", stud[i].
      roll_no);
    printf("\n NAME = %s", stud[i].name);
    printf("\n FEES = %d", stud[i].fees);
    printf("\n DATE OF BIRTH = %s",
     stud[i].  DOB);
  }
   printf("\n Enter the roll no. of the
     student whose record has to be edited: ");
   scanf("%d", &rolno);
   printf("\n Enter the new roll number: ");
   scanf("%d", &new_rolno);
   printf("\n Enter the new name: ");
   scanf("%s", new_name);
   printf("\n Enter the new fees: ");
   scanf("%d", &new_fees);
   printf("\n Enter the new date of birth: ");
   scanf("%s", new_DOB);
   stud[rolno-1].roll_no = new_rolno;
   strcpy(stud[rolno-1].name, new_name);
   stud[rolno-1].fees = new_fees;
   strcpy(stud[rolno-1].DOB,new_DOB);
   for(i=0;i<n;i++)
   {
    printf("\n ********DETAILS OF STUDENT
      %d********", i+1);
    printf("\n ROLL No. = %d", stud[i].
      roll_no);
    printf("\n NAME = %s", stud[i].name);
    printf("\n FEES = %d", stud[i].fees);
    printf("\n DATE OF BIRTH = %s",
      stud[i].DOB);
   }
  return 0;
}
```

Output

```
Enter the number of students: 2
Enter the roll number: 1
Enter the name: kirti
Enter the fees: 5678
Enter the DOB: 9 9 91
Enter the roll number: 2
Enter the name: kangana
Enter the fees: 5678
Enter the DOB: 27 8 91
********DETAILS OF STUDENT 1********
ROLL No. = 1
NAME = kirti
FEES = 5678
DOB = 9 9 91
********DETAILS OF STUDENT 2********
ROLL No. = 2
NAME = kangana
FEES = 5678
DOB = 27 8 91
Enter the roll no. of the student whose record
   has to be edited: 2
Enter the new roll number: 2
Enter the new name: kangana khullar
Enter the new fees: 7000
Enter the new date of birth: 27 8 92
********DETAILS OF STUDENT 1********
ROLL No. = 1
NAME = kirti
FEES = 5678
DOB = 9 9 91
********DETAILS OF STUDENT 2********
ROLL No. = 2
NAME = kangana
FEES = 7000
DOB = 27 8 92
```

15.4 STRUCTURES AND FUNCTIONS

For structures to be fully useful, we must have a mechanism to pass them to functions and return them. A function may access the members of a structure in three ways as shown in Figure 15.4.

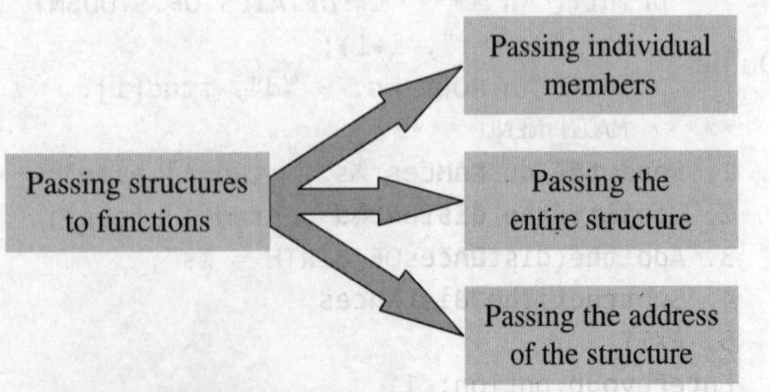

Figure 15.4 Passing structures to functions

15.4.1 Passing Individual Members

To pass any individual member of the structure to a function we must use the direct selection operator to refer to the individual members for the actual parameters. The called program does not know if the two variables are ordinary variables or structure members. Look at the following code that illustrates this concept.

```
#include <stdio.h>
typedef struct
{
  int x;
  int y;
}POINT;
void display(int, int);
int main()
{
  POINT p1 = {2, 3};
  display(p1.x, p1.y);
  return 0;
}
void display(int a, int b)
{
  printf("The coordinates of the point are: %d
  %d", a, b);
}
```

Output

```
The coordinates of the point are: 2 3
```

15.4.2 Passing the Entire Structure

Just like any other variable, we can pass an entire structure as a function argument. When a structure is passed as an argument, it is passed using the call by value method, i.e., a copy of each member of the structure is made. This is a very inefficient method especially when the structure is very big or the function is called frequently. In such a situation, passing and working with pointers may be more efficient.

The general syntax for passing a structure to a function and returning a structure can be given as

```
struct struct_name func_name(struct struct_
  name struct_var);
```

This syntax can vary as per need. For example, in some situations we may want a function to receive a structure but return a void or value of some other data type. The following code passes a structure to the function using the call-by-value method.

```
#include <stdio.h>
typedef struct
{
  int x;
  int y;
}POINT;
void display(POINT);
```

```
main()
{
  POINT p1 = {2, 3};
  display(p1);
  return 0;
}
void display(POINT p)
{
  printf("%d %d", p.x, p.y);
}
```

8. Write a program to read, display, add, and subtract two distances. Distance must be defined using kms and metres.

```
#include <stdio.h>
typedef struct distance
{
  int kms;
  int metres;
}DISTANCE;
DISTANCE add_distance(DISTANCE, DISTANCE);
DISTANCE subtract_distance(DISTANCE,
   DISTANCE);
DISTANCE d1, d2, d3, d4;
int main()
{
  int option;
    do
  {
  printf("\n ***** MAIN MENU *****");
  printf("\n 1. Read the distances ");
  printf("\n 2. Display the distances");
  printf("\n 3. Add the distances");
  printf("\n 4. Subtract the distances");
  printf("\n 5. EXIT");
  printf("\n Enter your option: ");
  scanf("%d", &option);
  switch(option)
  {
  case 1:
  printf("\n Enter the first distance in
    kms and metres: ");
  scanf("%d %d", &d1.kms, &d1.metres);
  printf("\n Enter the second distance in
    kms and metres: ");
  scanf("%d %d", &d2.kms, &d2.metres);
  break;
  case 2:
  printf("\n The first distance is: %d
    kms %d metres", d1.kms, d1.metres);
  printf("\n The second distance is: %d
    kms %d metres", d2.kms, d2.metres);
  break;
  case 3:
  d3 = add_distance(d1, d2);
  printf("\n The sum of two distances
    is: %d kms %d metres", d3.kms, d3.metres);
  break;
  case 4:
  d4 = subtract_distance(d1, d2);
  printf("\n The difference between two
   distances is: %d kms %d metres", d4.kms,
   d4.metres);
  break;
  }
  }while(option != 5);
  return 0;
}
DISTANCE add_distance(DISTANCE d1, DISTANCE d2)
{
  DISTANCE sum;
  sum.metres = d1.metres + d2. metres;
  sum.kms = d1.kms + d2.kms;
  if(sum.metres >= 1000)
  {
    sum.metres = sum.metres%1000;
    sum.kms += 1;
  }
  return sum;
}
DISTANCE subtract_distance(DISTANCE d1,
   DISTANCE d2)
{
  DISTANCE sub;
  if(d1.kms > d2.kms)
  {
    sub.metres = d1.metres – d2. metres;
    sub.kms = d1.kms – d2.kms;
  }
  else
  {
    sub.metres = d2.metres – d1. metres;
    sub.kms = d2.kms – d1.kms;
  }
  if(sub.metres < 0)
  {
    sub.kms = sub.kms - 1;
    sub.metres = sub.metres + 1000;
  }
  return sub;
}
```

Output

```
***** MAIN MENU *****
1. Read the distances
2. Display the distances
3. Add the distances
4. Subtract the distances
5. EXIT
Enter your option: 1
Enter the first distance in kms and metres: 5 300
```

```
Enter the second distance in kms and metres:
3 400
***** MAIN MENU *****
1. Read the distances
2. Display the distances
3. Add the distances
4. Subtract the distances
5. EXIT
Enter your option: 3
The sum of two distances is: 8 kms 700 metres
```

9. Write a program to read, display, add, and subtract two time variables defined using hours, minutes, and seconds.

```
#include <stdio.h>
typedef struct
{
  int hr;
  int min;
  int sec;
}TIME;
TIME t1, t2, t3, t4;
TIME subtract_time(TIME, TIME);
TIME add_time(TIME, TIME);
int main()
{
  int option;
  do
  {
    printf("\n **** MAIN MENU ****");
    printf("\n 1. Read time ");
    printf("\n 2. Display time");
    printf("\n 3. Add");
    printf("\n 4. Subtract");
    printf("\n 5. EXIT");
    printf("\n Enter your option: ");
    scanf("%d", &option);
    switch(option)
    {
    case 1:
    printf("\n Enter the first time in
      hrs, mins, and secs: ");
    scanf("%d %d %d", &t1.hr, &t1.min, &t1.sec);
    printf("\n Enter the second time in
      hrs, mins, and secs: ");
    scanf("%d %d %d", &t2.hr, &t2.min, &t2.sec);
    break;
    case 2:
    printf("\n The first time is: %d hr %d min
      %d sec", t1.hr, t1.min, t1.sec);
    printf("\n The second time is: %d hr %d
      min %d sec", t2.hr, t2.min, t2.sec);
    break;
    case 3:
    t3 = add_time(t1, t2);
    printf("\n The sum of the two time
      values is: %d hr %d min %d sec", t3.hr,
      t3.min, t3.sec);
    break;
    case 4:
    t4 = subtract_time(t1, t2);
    printf("\n The difference in time
      is: %d hr %d min %d sec", t4.hr, t4.min,
      t4.sec);
    break;
  }
  }while(option != 5);
  return 0;
}
TIME add_time(TIME t1, TIME t2)
{
  TIME sum;
  sum.sec = t1.sec + t2.sec;
  while(sum.sec >= 60)
  {
    sum.sec -=60;
    sum.min++;
  }
  sum.min = t1.min + t2.min;
  while(sum.min >= 60)
  {
    sum.min -=60;
    sum.hr++;
  }
  sum.hr = t1.hr + t2.hr;
  return sum;
}
TIME subtract_time(TIME t1, TIME t2)
{
  TIME sub;
  if(t1.hr > t2.hr)
  {
    if(t1.sec < t2.sec)
    {
    t1.sec += 60;
    t1.min--;
    }
    sub.sec = t1.sec - t2.sec;
    if(t1.min < t2.min)
    {
    t1.min += 60;
    t1.hr--;
    }
    sub.min = t1.min - t2.min;
    sub.hr = t1.hr - t2.hr;
  }
  else
  {
    if(t2.sec < t1.sec)
    {
    t2.sec += 60;
```

```
        t2.min--;
        }
        sub.sec = t2.sec - t1.sec;
        if(t2.min < t1.min)
        {
        t2.min += 60;
        t2.hr--;
        }
        sub.min = t2.min - t1.min;
        sub.hr = t2.hr - t1.hr;
    }
    return sub;
}
```

Output

```
**** MAIN MENU ****
1. Read time
2. Display time
3. Add
4. Subtract
5. EXIT
Enter your option: 1
Enter the first time in hrs, mins, and secs:
2 30 20
Enter the second time in hrs, mins, and secs:
3 20 30
**** MAIN MENU ****
1. Read time
2. Display time
3. Add
4. Subtract
5. EXIT
Enter your option: 3
The sum of the two time values is: 5 hr 50 min
   50 sec
```

Let us summarize some points that must be considered while passing a structure to a function.

- If the called function is returning a copy of the entire structure then its return type must be declared as `struct` followed by the structure name.
- The structure variable used as parameter in the function declaration must be the same as that of the actual argument in the called function (and that should be the name of the `struct` type).
- When a function returns a structure then in the calling function the returned structure must be assigned to a structure variable of the same type.

Programming Tip: Using pointers to pass a structure to a function is more efficient than using the call-by-value method.

15.4.3 Passing Structures Through Pointers

Passing large structures to functions using the call-by-value method is very inefficient. Therefore, it is preferred to pass structures through pointers. It is possible to create a pointer to almost any type in C, including user-defined types. It is extremely common to create pointers to structures. As in other cases, a pointer to a structure is never itself a structure, but merely a variable that holds the address of a structure. The syntax to declare a pointer to a structure can be given as follows:

```
struct struct_name
{
  data_type member_name1;
  data_type member_name2;
  data_type member_name3;
  .......................
}*ptr;
```

OR

```
struct struct_name *ptr;
```

For our student structure, we can declare a pointer variable by writing

```
struct student *ptr_stud, stud;
```

The next thing to do is to assign the address of `stud` to the pointer using the address operator (`&`) as we would do in case of any other pointer. So to assign the address, we will write

```
ptr_stud = &stud;
```

To access the members of the structure, one way is to write

```
/* get the structure, then select a member */
            (*ptr_stud).roll_no;
```

Programming Tip: The selection operator (->) is a single token, so do not place any white space between them.

Since parentheses have a higher precedence than `*`, writing this statement would work well. But this statement is not easy for a beginner to work with. So C introduces a new operator to do the same task. This operator is known as the pointing-to operator (`->`). Here it is being used:

```
/* the roll_no in the structure ptr_stud
  points to */
ptr_stud -> roll_no = 01;
```

This statement is far easier than its alternative.

10. Write a program, using a pointer to a structure to initialize the members of the structure.

```
#include <stdio.h>
struct student
{
  int r_no;
  char name[20];
  char course[20];
```

```
    int fees;
};

int main()
{
    struct student stud1, stud2, *ptr_stud1,
    *ptr_stud2;
    ptr_stud1 = &stud1;
    ptr_stud2 = &stud2;
    ptr_stud1 -> r_no = 01;
    strcpy(ptr_stud1 -> name, "Rahul");
    strcpy(ptr_stud1 -> course, "BCA");
    ptr_stud1 -> fees = 45000;

    printf("\n Enter the details of the second
      student:");
    printf("\n Enter the Roll Number =");
    scanf("%d", &ptr_stud2 -> r_no);
    printf("\n Enter the Name = ");
    gets(ptr_stud2 -> name);
    printf("\n Enter the Course = ");
    gets(ptr_stud2 -> course);
    printf("\n Enter the Fees = ");
    scanf("%d", &ptr_stud2 -> fees);

    printf("\n DETAILS OF FIRST STUDENT");
    printf("\n ROLL NUMBER = %d", ptr_stud1 ->
      r_no);
    printf("\n NAME = %s", ptr_stud1 -> name);
    printf("\n COURSE = %s", ptr_stud1 ->
      course);
    printf("\n FEES = %d", ptr_stud1 -> fees);
    printf("\n\n\n\n DETAILS OF SECOND
    STUDENT");
    printf("\n ROLL NUMBER = %d", ptr_stud2 ->
      r_no);
    printf("\n NAME = %s", ptr_stud2 -> name);
    printf("\n COURSE = %s", ptr_stud2 ->
      course);
    printf("\n FEES = %d", ptr_stud2 -> fees);

    return 0;
}
```

Output

```
Enter the details of the second student:
Enter the Roll Number = 02
Enter the Name = Aditya
Enter the Course = MCA
Enter the Fees = 60000

DETAILS OF FIRST STUDENT
ROLL NUMBER = 01
NAME = Rahul
COURSE = BCA
FEES = 45000
DETAILS OF SECOND STUDENT
ROLL NUMBER = 02
NAME = Aditya
COURSE = MCA
FEES = 60000
```

11. Write a program, using a pointer to a structure, to initialize the members of the structure using an alternative technique.

```
#include <stdio.h>
struct student
{
    int r_no;
    char name[20];
    char course[20];
    float fees;
};

int main()
{
    struct student *ptr_stud1;
    struct student stud1 = {01, "Rahul", "BCA",
      45000};
    ptr_stud1 = &stud1;
    printf("\n DETAILS OF STUDENT");
    printf("\n ROLL NUMBER = %d", ptr_stud1 ->
      r_no);
    printf("\n NAME = %s ", ptr_stud1 -> name);
    printf("\n COURSE = %s", ptr_stud1
      -> course);
    printf("\n FEES = %.2f", ptr_stud1 -> fees);
    return 0;
}
```

Output

```
DETAILS OF STUDENT
ROLL NUMBER = 01
NAME = Rahul
COURSE = BCA
FEES = 45000.00
```

12. Write a program, using an array of pointers to a structure, to read and display the data of a student.

```
#include <stdio.h>
#include <stdlib.h>
typedef struct student
{
int r_no;
char name[20];
char course[20];
int fees;
};
struct student *ptr[10];
int main()
```

```
{
int i;
for(i=0;i<2;i++)
{
ptr[i] = (struct student *)
   malloc(sizeof(struct student));
printf("\n Enter the data for student %d
   ",i+1);
printf("\n ROLL NO.:");
scanf("%d", &ptr[i] -> r_no);
printf("\n NAME: ");
fflush(stdin);
gets(ptr[i] -> name);
printf("\n COURSE:");
gets(ptr[i] -> course);
printf("\n FEES:");
scanf("%d", &ptr[i] -> fees);
}
printf("\n DETAILS OF STUDENTS");
for(i=0;i<2;i++)
{
printf("\n ROLL NUMBER = %d",ptr[i] -> r_no);
printf("\n NAME = %s", ptr[i] ->name);
printf("\n COURSE = %s", ptr[i] ->course);
printf("\n FEES = %d", ptr[i] ->fees);
}
return 0;
}
```

Output

```
Enter the data for student 1
ROLL NO.: 01
NAME: Rahul
COURSE: BCA
FEES: 45000
Enter the data for student 2
ROLL NO.:02
NAME:Priya
COURSE:BCA
FEES:25000
DETAILS OF STUDENTS
ROLL NUMBER = 01
NAME = Rahul
COURSE = BCA
FEES = 45000
ROLL NUMBER = 02
NAME = Priya
COURSE = BCA
FEES = 25000
```

13. Write a program to read, display, add, and subtract two heights. Height should be given in feet and inches.

```
#include <stdio.h>

typedef struct
{
  int ft;
  int inch;
}HEIGHT;

HEIGHT h1, h2, h3;
HEIGHT add_height(HEIGHT *, HEIGHT *);
HEIGHT subtract_height(HEIGHT *, HEIGHT *);
int main()
{
  int option;
  do
  {
    printf("\n *** MAIN MENU ***");
    printf("\n 1. Read height ");
    printf("\n 2. Display height");
    printf("\n 3. Add");
    printf("\n 4. Subtract");
    printf("\n 5. EXIT");
    printf("\n Enter your option: ");
    scanf("%d", &option);
    switch(option)
    {
    case 1:
    printf("\n Enter the first height in feet
     and inches: ");
    scanf("%d %d", &h1.ft, &h1.inch);
    printf("\n Enter the second height in feet
     and inches: ");
    scanf("%d %d", &h2.ft, &h2.inch);
    break;
    case 2:
    printf("\n The first height is: %d ft %d
     inch", h1.ft, h1.inch);
    printf("\n The second height is: %d ft %d
     inch", h2.ft, h2.inch);
    break;
    case 3:
    h3 = add_height(&h1, &h2);
    printf("\n The sum of two heights is: %d
     ft %d inch", h3.ft, h3.inch);
    break;
    case 4:
    h3 = subtract_height(&h1, &h2);
    printf("\n The difference of two heights
     is: %d ft %d inch", h3.ft, h3.inch);
    break;}
    }
  while(option != 5);
```

```
  return 0;
}
HEIGHT add_height(HEIGHT *h1, HEIGHT *h2)
{
  HEIGHT sum;
  sum.inch = h1 -> inch + h2 -> inch;
  while(sum.inch > 12)
  {
    sum.inch -= 12;
    sum.ft++;
  }
  sum.ft = h1 -> ft + h2 -> ft;
  return sum;
}
HEIGHT subtract_height(HEIGHT *h1, HEIGHT *h2)
{
  HEIGHT sub;
  if(h1 -> ft > h2 -> ft)
  {
    if(h1 -> inch < h2 -> inch)
    {
    h1 -> inch += 12;
    h1 -> ft--;
    }
    sub.inch = h1 -> inch - h2 -> inch;
    sub.ft = h1 -> ft - h2 -> ft;
  }
  else
  {
    if(h2 -> inch < h1 -> inch)
    {
    h2 -> inch += 12;
    h2 -> ft--;
    }
    sub.inch = h2 -> inch - h1 -> inch;
    sub.ft = h2 -> ft - h1 -> ft;
  }
  return sub;
}
```

Output

```
*** MAIN MENU ***
1. Read height
2. Display height
3. Add
4. Subtract
5. EXIT
Enter your option: 1
Enter the first height in feet and inches: 2 3
Enter the second height in feet and inches: 4 5
*** MAIN MENU ***
1. Read height
2. Display height
3. Add
4. Subtract
5. EXIT
Enter your option: 3
The sum of two heights is: 6 ft 8 inch
```

14. Write a program that passes a pointer to a structure to a function.

```
#include <stdio.h>
typedef struct student
{
  int r_no;
  char name[20];
  char course[20];
  int fees;
};

void display(struct student *);
int main()
{
  struct student *ptr;
  ptr = (struct student *)malloc(sizeof
   (struct student));
  printf("\n Enter the data for the student ");
  printf("\n ROLL NO.: ");
  scanf("%d", &ptr -> r_no);
  printf("\n NAME: ");
  gets(ptr -> name);
  printf("\n COURSE: ");
  gets(ptr -> course);
  printf("\n FEES: ");
  scanf("%d", &ptr -> fees);
  display(ptr);
  return 0;
}

void display(struct student *ptr)
{
  printf("\n DETAILS OF STUDENT");
  printf("\n ROLL NUMBER = %d", ptr -> r_no);
  printf("\n NAME = %s", ptr -> name);
  printf("\n COURSE = %s", ptr -> course);
  printf("\n FEES = %d", ptr -> fees);
}
```

Output

```
Enter the data for the student
ROLL NO.: 01
NAME: Rahul
COURSE: BCA
FEES: 45000

DETAILS OF STUDENT
ROLL NUMBER = 01
NAME = Rahul
COURSE = BCA
FEES = 45000.00
```

15. Write a program to illustrate the use of arrays within a structure.

```
#include <stdio.h>
typedef struct student
{
  char name[20];
  int roll_no;
  int marks[3];
};

void display(struct student* s)
{
  int i;
  printf("\n NAME = %s \n ROLL NO =
    %d\n", s -> name, s -> roll_no);
  printf("\n MARKS = ");
  for(i = 0;i < 3;i++)

    printf(" %d", s -> marks[i]);
}
int main()
{
  struct student *s[2];
  int i,j;
  for(i = 0;i < 2;i++)
  {
    s[i]=(struct student*)
    malloc(sizeof(struct student));
    printf("\n\n Enter the name of student
     %d: ", i+1);
    gets(s[i] -> name);
    printf("\n Enter the roll number of
     student %d: ", i+1);
    scanf("%d", &s[i] -> roll_no);
    printf("\n Enter the marks obtained in
     three subjects by student %d: ", i+1);
    for(j = 0;j < 3;j++)
      scanf("%d",&s[i] -> marks[j]);
    }
  printf("\n \n\n *****DETAILS*****");
  for(i=0;i<2;i++)
    display(s[i]);
  return 0;
}
```

Output

```
Enter the name of student 1: Goransh
Enter the roll number of student 1: 01
Enter the marks obtained in three subjects by
student 1: 99 100 99
Enter the name of student 2: Pranjal
Enter the roll number of student 2: 02
Enter the marks obtained in three subjects by
student 2: 90 100 89
*****DETAILS*****
NAME    = Goransh
ROLL NO = 01
MARKS   = 99 100 99
NAME    = Pranjal
ROLL NO = 02
MARKS   = 90 100 89
```

15.5 SELF-REFERENTIAL STRUCTURES

Self-referential structures are those structures that contain a reference to data of its same type, i.e., in addition to other data, a self-referential structure contains a pointer to a data that is of the same type as that of the structure. For example, consider the structure node given as follows:

```
struct node
{
  int val;
  struct node *next;
};
```

Here the structure node will contain two types of data—an integer `val` and `next`, which is a pointer to a node. You must be wondering why we need such a structure. Actually, self-referential structure is the foundation of other data structures. Their purpose will be clear to you when you study linked list representation of data structures.

> **Programming Tip:**
> It is an error to use a structure/union variable as a member of its own struct type structure or union type union, respectively.

15.6 UNIONS

Similar to structures, a union is a collection of variables of different data types. The only difference between a structure and a union is that in case of unions, you can only store information in one field at any one time.

To better understand a union, think of it as a chunk of memory that is used to store variables of different types. When a new value is assigned to a field, the existing data is replaced with the new data.

Thus unions are used to save memory. They are useful for applications that involve multiple members, where values need not be assigned to all the members at any one time.

15.6.1 Declaring a Union

The syntax for declaring a union is the same as that of declaring a structure. The only difference is that instead of using the keyword struct, the keyword union would be used. The syntax for union declaration can be given as

```
union union-name
{
  data_type var-name;
  data_type var-name;
  ..................
};
```

Programming Tip: Variable of a structure or a union can be declared at the time of structure/union definition by placing the variable name after the closing brace and before the semicolon.

Again, the typedef keyword can be used to simplify the declaration of union variables.

The most important thing to remember about a union is that the size of a union is the size of its largest field. This is because sufficient number of bytes must be reserved to store the largest sized field.

15.6.2 Accessing a Member of a Union

A member of a union can be accessed using the same syntax as that of a structure. To access the fields of a union, use the dot operator (.), i.e., the union variable name followed by the dot operator followed by the member name.

15.6.3 Initializing Unions

Programming Tip: It is an error to initialize any other union member except the first member.

A striking difference between a structure and a union is that in case of a union, the fields share the same memory space, so fresh data replaces any existing data. Look at the following code and observe the difference between a structure and union when their fields are to be initialized.

```
#include <stdio.h>
typedef struct POINT1
{
  int x, y;
};

typedef union POINT2
{
  int x;
  int y;
};
int main()
{
  struct POINT1 P1 = {2,3};
  // POINT2 P2 ={4,5}; Illegal with union
  union POINT2 P2;
  P2.x = 4;
  P2.y = 5;
  printf("\n The co-ordinates of P1 are %d
    and %d", P1.x, P1.y);
  printf("\n The co-ordinates of P2 are %d
    and %d", P2.x, P2.y);
  return 0;
}
```

Output

```
The co-ordinates of P1 are 2 and 3
The co-ordinates of P2 are 5 and 5
```

In this code, POINT1 is a structure name and POINT2 is a union name. However, both the declarations are almost same (except the keywords—struct and union); in main(), you see a point of difference while initializing values. The fields of a union cannot be initialized all at once.

Look at the output carefully. For the structure variable the output is fine but for the union variable the answer does not seem to be correct.

Programming Tip: The size of a union is equal to the size of its largest member.

To understand the concept of union, execute the following code. The code given below just re-arranges the printf statements. You will be surprised to see the result.

```
#include <stdio.h>
typedef struct POINT1
{
  int x, y;
};

typedef union POINT2
{
  int x;
  int y;
};
int main()
{
  struct POINT1 P1 = {2,3};
  union POINT2 P2;
  printf("\n The co-ordinates of P1 are %d and
  %d", P1.x, P1.y);
  P2. x = 4;
  printf("\n The x co-ordinate of P2 is %d",
   P2.x);
  P2.y = 5;
  printf("\n The y co-ordinate of P2 is %d",
   P2.y);
  return 0;
}
```

Output

```
The co-ordinates of P1 are 2 and 3
The x co-ordinate of P2 is 4
The y co-ordinate of P2 is 5
```

Here although the output is correct, the data is still over-written in memory.

15.7 ARRAYS OF UNION VARIABLES

Like structures we can also have an array of union variables. However, because of the problem of new data overwriting existing data in the other fields, the program may not display the accurate results.

```
#include <stdio.h>
union POINT
{
  int x, y;
};

int main()
{
  int i;
  union POINT points[3];
  points[0].x = 2;
  points[0].y = 3;
  points[1].x = 4;
  points[1].y = 5;
  points[2].x = 6;
  points[2].y = 7;
  for(i=0;i<3;i++)
     printf("\n Co-ordinates of Point[%d]
        are %d and %d", i, points[i].x,
  points[i].y);
  return 0;
}
```

Output

```
Co-ordinates of Point[0] are 3 and 3
Co-ordinates of Point[1] are 5 and 5
Co-ordinates of Point[2] are 7 and 7
```

15.8 UNIONS INSIDE STRUCTURES

You must be wondering, why do we need unions? In general, unions can be very useful when declared inside a structure. Consider an example in which you want a field of a structure to contain a string or an integer, depending on what the user specifies. The following code illustrates such a scenario.

```
#include <stdio.h>
struct student
{
  union
  {
    char name[20];
    int roll_no;
  };
  int marks;
};
int main()
{
  struct student stud;
  char choice;
  printf("\n You can enter the name or roll
   number of the student");
  printf("\n Do you want to enter the name? (Y
   or N): ");
  gets(choice);
  if(choice=='y' || choice=='Y')
  {
    printf("\n Enter the name: ");
    gets(stud.name);
  }
  else
  {
    printf("\n Enter the roll number: ");
    scanf("%d", &stud.roll_no);
  }
  printf("\n Enter the marks: ");
  scanf("%d", &stud.marks);
  if(choice=='y' || choice=='Y')
    printf("\n Name: %s ", stud.name);
  else
    printf("\n Roll Number: %d ", stud.roll_no);
  printf("\n Marks: %d", stud.marks);
  return 0;
}
```

Now in this code, we have a union embedded within a structure. We know, the fields of a union will share memory, so in the main program we ask the user which data he/she would like to store and depending on his/her choice the appropriate field is used.

Note

Pointing to unions, passing unions to functions, and passing pointers to unions to functions are all done in the same way as that of structures.

15.9 STRUCTURES INSIDE UNIONS

C also allows users to have a structure within a union. The program given below illustrates the use of structures within a union. There are two structure variables in the union. The size of the union will be the size of the structure variable which is larger of the two. During run-time, programmer will choose to enter name or roll number of the student and the corresponding action will thus be taken.

```
#include <stdio.h>
typedef struct a
{ int marks;
  char name [20];
};
typedef struct b
```

```
{ int marks;
  int roll_no;
};

typedef union Student
{ struct a A;
  struct b B;
};
main()
{
  union Student s;
  char ch;
  printf("\n Do you want to enter name or roll
    number of the student : (N/R)- ");
  scanf("%c", &ch);
  if(ch == 'R')
  {
    printf("\n Enter the roll number : ");
    scanf("%d", &s.B.roll_no);
    printf("\n Enter the marks : ");
    scanf("%d", &s.B.marks);
  }
  else
  {
    printf("\n Enter the name : ");
    gets(s.A.name);
    printf("\n Enter the marks : ");
    scanf("%d", &s.A.marks);
  }
    printf("\n ****** STUDENT'S DETAILS
    ******");
    if(ch == 'N')
    {
      printf("\n NAME : ");
      puts(s.A.name);
      printf("\n MARKS : %d", s.A.marks);
    }
    else
    {
      printf("\n ROLL NO : %d", s.B.roll_no);
      printf("\n MARKS : %d", s.B.marks);
    }
}
```

Output

```
Do you want to enter name or roll number of
the student : (N/R)- R
Enter the roll number : 12
Enter the marks : 99
****** STUDENT'S DETAILS ******
ROLL NO : 12
MARKS : 99
```

15.10 ENUMERATED DATA TYPE

The enumerated data type is a user-defined type based on the standard integer type. An enumeration consists of a set of named integer constants. In other words, in an enumerated type, each integer value is assigned an identifier. This identifier (which is also known as an enumeration constant) can be used as a symbolic name to make the program more readable.

To define enumerated data types, we use the keyword `enum`, which is the abbreviation for `ENUMERATE`. Enumerations create new data types to contain values that are not limited to the values that fundamental data types may take. The syntax of creating an enumerated data type can be given as follows:

```
enum enumeration_name {identifier1,
  identifier2, …, identifiern };
```

The `enum` keyword is basically used to declare and initialize a sequence of integer constants. Here, `enumeration_name` is optional. Consider the following example, which creates a new type of variable called `COLORS` to store colour constants.

```
enum COLORS {RED, BLUE, BLACK, GREEN, YELLOW,
   PURPLE, WHITE};
```

Note that no fundamental data type is used in the declaration of `COLORS`. After this statement, `COLORS` has become a new data type. Here, `COLORS` is the name given to the set of constants. In case you do not assign any value to a constant, the default value for the first one in the list—`RED` (in our case) has the value of 0. The rest of the undefined constants have a value 1 more than its previous one. That is, if you do not initialize the constants, then each one would have a unique value. The first would be zero and the rest would count upwards. So, in our example,

```
RED = 0, BLUE = 1, BLACK = 2, GREEN = 3,
YELLOW = 4, PURPLE = 5, WHITE = 6
```

If you want to explicitly assign values to these integer constants then you should specifically mention those values shown as follows:

```
enum COLORS {RED = 2, BLUE, BLACK = 5, GREEN
  = 7, YELLOW, PURPLE, WHITE = 15};
```

As a result of this statement, now `RED = 2, BLUE = 3, BLACK = 5, GREEN = 7, YELLOW = 8, PURPLE = 9, WHITE = 15`.

Look at the code which illustrates the declaration and access of enumerated data types.

```
#include <stdio.h>
int main()
{ enum {RED=2, BLUE, BLACK=5, GREEN=7, YELLOW,
PURPLE, WHITE=15};
  printf("\n RED = %d", RED);
  printf("\n BLUE = %d", BLUE);
  printf("\n BLACK = %d", BLACK);
  printf("\n GREEN = %d", GREEN);
```

```
    printf("\n YELLOW = %d", YELLOW);
    printf("\n PURPLE = %d", PURPLE);
    printf("\n WHITE = %d", WHITE);
    return 0;
}
```

Output

```
RED = 2
BLUE = 3
BLACK = 5
GREEN = 7
YELLOW = 8
PURPLE = 9
WHITE = 15
```

Note

The value of an enumerator constant is always of the type `int`. Therefore, the storage associated with an enumeration variable is the storage required for a single `int` value. The enumeration constant or a value of the enumerated type can be used anywhere in the program where the C language permits an integer expression.

The following rules apply to the members of an enumeration list:

- An enumeration list may contain duplicate constant values. Therefore, two different identifiers may be assigned the same value, say 3.
- The identifiers in the enumeration list must be different from other identifiers in the same scope with the same visibility including ordinary variable names and identifiers in other enumeration lists.
- Enumeration names follow the normal scoping rules. So every enumeration name must be different from other enumeration, structure, and union names with the same visibility.

Note

If we create an enumerated type without enumeration_name, it is known as an anonymous enumerated type. For example, enum {OFF, ON}; declares an enumerated type that has two constants OFF with a value 0 and ON with a value 1.

15.10.1 enum Variables

We have seen that enumerated constants are basically integers, so programs with statements such as `int fore_color = RED;` is considered to be a legal statement in C.

In extension to this, C also permits the user to declare variables of an enumerated data type in the same way as we create variables of other basic data types. The syntax for declaring a variable of an enumerated data type can be given as

```
enumeration_name variable_name;
```

So to create a variable of `COLORS`, we may write

```
enum COLORS bg_color;
```

This declares a variable called `bg_color`, which is of the enumerated data type, COLORS. Another way to declare a variable can be as illustrated in the following statement.

```
enum COLORS {RED, BLUE, BLACK, GREEN, YELLOW,
   PURPLE, WHITE}bg_color, fore_color;
```

15.10.2 Using the Typedef Keyword

C also permits to use the `typedef` keyword for enumerated data types. For example, if we write

```
typedef enum COLORS color;
```

Then, we can straightaway declare variables by writing

```
color forecolor = RED;
```

15.10.3 Assigning Values to Enumerated Variables

Once the enumerated variable has been declared, values can be stored in it. However, an enumerated variable can hold only declared values for the type. For example, to assign the colour black to the background colour, we will write,

```
bg_color = BLACK;
```

An important thing to note here is that once an enumerated variable has been assigned a value, we can store its value in another variable of the same type. The following statements illustrate this concept.

```
enum COLORS bg_color, border_color;
bg_color = BLACK;
border_color = bg_color;
```

15.10.4 Enumeration Type Conversion

Enumerated types can be implicitly or explicitly cast. For example, the compiler can implicitly cast an enumerated type to an integer when required. However, when we implicitly cast an integer to an enumerated type, the compiler will either generate an error or a warning message.

To understand this, answer one question. If we write

```
enum COLORS{RED, BLUE, BLACK, GREEN, YELLOW,
  PURPLE, WHITE};
enum COLORS c;
c = BLACK + WHITE;
```

Here, c is an enumerated data type variable. If we write `c = BLACK + WHITE`, then logically, it should be `2 + 6 = 8`, which is basically a value of type int. However, the left-hand side of the assignment operator is of the type `enum COLORS`. So the statement would report an error. To remove the error, you can do either of two things. First, declare c to be an int. Second, cast the right-hand side in the following manner

```
c = enum COLORS(BLACK + WHITE);
```

To summarize,

```
enum COLORS(RED, BLUE, BLACK, GREEN, YELLOW,
PURPLE, WHITE};
enum COLORS c;
c = BLACK;  //valid in C
c = 2;      // illegal in C
c = (enum COLORS)2;  // Right way
```

15.10.5 Comparing Enumerated Types

C also allows using comparison operators on enumerated data type. Look at the following statements, which illustrate this concept.

```
bg_color = (enum COLORS)6;
if(bg_color == WHITE)
  fore_color = BLUE;
fore_color = BLACK;
if(bg_color == fore_color)
  printf("\n NOT VISIBLE");
```

Since enumerated types are derived from integer type, they can be used in a switch case statement. The following code demonstrates the use of the enumerated type in a switch case statement.

```
enum {RED, BLUE, BLACK, GREEN, YELLOW, PURPLE,
WHITE}bg_color;
switch(bg_color)
{
  case RED:
  case BLUE:
  case GREEN:
     printf("\n It is a primary color");
     break;
  case default:
     printf("\n It is not a primary color");
     break;
}
```

15.10.6 Input/Output Operations on Enumerated Types

Since enumerated types are derived types, they cannot be read or written using formatted input/output functions available in the C language. When we read or write an enumerated type, we read/write it as an integer. The compiler would implicitly do the type conversion as discussed earlier. The following statements illustrate this concept.

```
enum COLORS(RED, BLUE, BLACK, GREEN, YELLOW,
PURPLE, WHITE};
enum COLORS c;
scanf("%d", &c);
printf("\n Color = %d", c);
```

16. Write a program to display the name of the colours using an enumerated type.

```
#include <stdio.h>
enum COLORS {RED, BLUE, BLACK, GREEN, YELLOW,
  PURPLE, WHITE};
int main()
{
  enum COLORS c;
  char *color_name[] = {"RED", "BLUE",
  "BLACK", "GREEN", "YELLOW", "PURPLE",
  "WHITE"};
  for(c = RED; c <= WHITE; c++)

   printf("\n %s", color_name[c]);
  return 0;
}
```

OR

```
#include <stdio.h>
#include <stdlib.h>
enum COLORS {red, blue, black, green, yellow,
  purple, white};
int main()
{
  enum COLORS c;
  c = rand()%7;
  switch(c)
  {
    case red: printf("\n RED"); break;
    case blue: printf("\n BLUE"); break;
    case black: printf("\n BLACK"); break;
    case green: printf("\n GREEN"); break;
    case yellow: printf("\n YELLOW");
   break;
    case purple: printf("\n PURPLE");
   break;
    case white: printf("\n WHITE"); break;
  }
  return 0;
```

Output

```
GREEN
```

POINTS TO REMEMBER

- Structure is basically a user-defined data type that can store related information (even of different data types) together. The major difference between a structure and an array is that an array contains related information of the same data type.
- A structure is declared using the keyword `struct` followed by a structure name. The structure definition, however, does not allocate any memory or consume storage space. It just gives a template that conveys to the C compiler how the structure is laid out in memory and gives details of the member names. Like any other data type, memory is allocated for the structure when we declare a variable of the structure.
- When we precede a `struct` name with `typedef` keyword, then the `struct` becomes a new data type.
- When the user does not explicitly initialize the structure C automatically does this. For `int` and float members, the values are initialized to zero and character and string members are initialized to `'\0'` by default.
- A structure member variable is generally accessed using a `'.'` (dot operator).
- A structure can be placed within another structure. That is, a structure may contain another structure as its member. Such a structure is called a nested structure.
- Self-referential structures are those that contain a reference to data of its same type. That is, a self-referential structure, in addition to other data, contains a pointer to data that is of the same type as that of the structure.
- A union is a collection of variables of different data types in which memory is shared among these variables. The size of a union is equal to the size of its largest member.
- The only difference between a structure and a union is that in case of unions information can only be stored in one member at a time.

GLOSSARY

Enumerated data type An enumeration consists of a set of named integer constants.

Nested structure A structure placed within another structure, i.e., a structure that contains another structure as its member.

Self-referential structures Structures that contain a reference to data of its same type. A self-referential structure, in addition to other data, contains a pointer to a data that is of the same type as that of the structure.

Structure Structure is a user-defined data type that can store related information (even of different data types) together.

Structure initialization Initializing a structure means assigning some constants to the members of the structure. When the user does not explicitly initialize the structure C automatically does this. For `int` and `float` members, the values are initialized to zero and character and string members are initialized to the `'\0'` by default.

Typedef declaration When we precede a `struct` name with `typedef` keyword, then `struct` becomes a new data type. It is used to make the construct shorter with more meaningful names for types already defined by C or for types that you have declared. A `typedef` declaration is a synonym for the type.

Union A union is a collection of fields of different data types in which information can be stored in one field at a time.

EXERCISES

Fill in the Blanks

1. Structure is a ________ data type.
2. A structure is similar to ________.
3. ________ contains related information of the same data type.
4. ________ contains related information of the same or different data type(s).
5. Memory is allocated for a structure when ________ is done.
6. ________ is just a template that will be used to reserve memory when a variable of type `struct` is declared.

7. A ________ is a collection of variables under a single name.
8. A structure is declared using the keyword `struct` followed by a ________.
9. When we precede a `struct` name with ________, then `struct` becomes a new data type.
10. For `int` and `float` structure members, the values are initialized to ________.
11. `Character` and `string` structure members are initialized to ________ by default.
12. A structure member variable is generally accessed using a ________.
13. A structure placed within another structure is called a ________.
14. ________ structures contain a reference to data of their same type.
15. The keyword `typedef` is used to ________.
16. ________ is a collection of data under one name in which memory is shared among the members.
17. The selection operator is used to ________.
18. ________ permits sharing of memory among different types of data.

Multiple-choice Questions

1. A data structure that can store related information together is
   (a) array (b) string
   (c) structure (d) all of these
2. A data structure that can store related information of different data types together is
   (a) array (b) string
   (c) structure (d) all of these
3. Memory for a structure is allocated at the time of
   (a) structure definition
   (b) structure variable declaration
   (c) structure declaration
   (d) function declaration
4. A structure member variable is generally accessed using the
   (a) address operator (b) dot operator
   (c) comma operator (d) ternary operator
5. A structure can be placed within another structure and is known as
   (a) self-referential structure
   (b) nested structure
   (c) parallel structure
   (d) pointer to structure
6. A union member variable is generally accessed using the
   (a) address operator (b) dot operator
   (c) comma operator (d) ternary operator
7. Typedef can be used with which of these data types?
   (a) `struct` (b) `union`
   (c) `enum` (d) All of these
8. The enumerated type is derived from which data type?
   (a) `int` (b) `float`
   (c) `double` (d) `char`

State True or False

1. Structures contain related information of the same data type.
2. A `struct` type is a primitive data type.
3. Structure declaration reserves memory for the structure.
4. Initializing a structure means assigning some constants to the members of the structure.
5. When the user does not explicitly initialize the structure C automatically does this.
6. The dereference operator is used to select a particular member of a structure.
7. New variables can be created using the `typedef` keyword.
8. Memory is allocated for a structure only when we declare variables of the structure.
9. A nested structure contains another structure as its member.
10. C permits copying of one structure variable to another.
11. Unions and structures are initialized in the same way.
12. A structure cannot have a union as its member.
13. C permits nested unions.
14. In an enumerated type, an integer value can be assigned to only one enumeration constant.
15. Declaring an enumerated type automatically creates a variable.
16. The identifiers in an enumerated type are automatically assigned values.
17. A field in a structure can itself be a structure.
18. No two members of a union should have the same name.
19. No two identifiers in an enumerated type must have the same value.
20. A union can have another union as its member.
21. A union can be a member of a structure.

Review Questions

1. What is the advantage of using structures?
2. Differentiate between a structure and a union.
3. How is a structure name different from a structure variable?
4. Structure declaration reserves memory for the structure. Comment on this statement with valid justifications.
5. Differentiate between a structure and an array.
6. Write a short note on structures and interprocess communication.

7. Explain the utility of typedef keyword in structures.
8. Explain with an example how structures are initialized.
9. Is it possible to create an array of structures? Explain with the help of an example.
10. What do you understand by a union?
11. Differentiate between a union and a structure.
12. Explain how members of a union are accessed using a program code.
13. In which applications unions can be useful?
14. Write a short note on nested structures.

Programming Exercises

1. Write a program using structures to read and display the information about an employee.
2. Write a program to find the smallest of three numbers using structures.
3. Write a program to calculate the distance between the given points (6,3) and (2,2).
4. Write a menu-driven program to add and subtract 5+6i and 4-2i.
5. Write a program to read and display the information about an employee using nested structures.
6. Write a program to read and display the information about the entire faculty of a particular department.
7. Write a program to read and display the information about all the employees in a department. Edit the details of the ith employee and redisplay the information.
8. Write a program to add and subtract distances 6 km and 300 m and 4 km and 700 m.
9. Write a program to add and subtract heights 6'2" and 5'4".
10. Write a program to add and subtract 10 hr 20 min 50 sec and 5 hr 30 min 40 sec.
11. Write a program that uses a structure called date that has it passed to an isLeapYear function to determine if the year is a leap year.
12. Write a program using pointer to structure to initialize the members in the structure. Use functions to print the student's information.
13. Write a program using pointer to structure to initialize the members in the structure using an alternative technique.
14. Define a structure date containing three integers—day, month, and year. Write a program using functions to read data, to validate the date entered by the user, and then print the date on the screen. For example, if you enter 29,2,2010 then that is an invalid date as 2010 is not a leap year. Similarly 31,6,2007 is invalid as June does not have 31 days.
15. Using the structure definition of the above program, write a function to increment that. Make sure that the incremented date is a valid date.
16. Modify the above program to add a specific number of days to the given date.
17. Using the structure definition of question 14, write a function to compare two date variables.
18. Write a program to define a structure vector. Then write functions to read data, print data, add two vectors, and scale the members of a vector by a factor of 10.
19. Write a program to define a structure for a hotel that has members' name, address, grade, number of rooms, and room charges. Write a function to print the names of a hotel in a particular grade. Also write a function to print names of a hotel that have room charges less than the specified value.
20. Write a program to define a union and a structure both having exactly the same members. Using the sizeof operator, print the size of structure variable as well as union variable and comment on the result.
21. Declare a structure time that has three fields—hr, min, sec. Create two variables start_time and end_time. Input their values from the user. Then while start_time does not reach the end-time, display GOOD DAY on the screen.
22. Declare a structure fraction that has two fields—numerator and denominator. Create two variables and compare them using function. Return 0 if the two fractions are equal, −1 if the first fraction is less than the second and 1 otherwise. You may convert a fraction into a floating point number for your convenience.
23. Declare a structure POINT. Input the co-ordinates of a point variable and determine the quadrant in which it lies. The following table can be used to determine the quadrant

Quadrant	X	Y
1	Positive	Positive
2	Negative	Positive
3	Negative	Negative
4	Positive	Negative

24. Write a program to calculate the area of one of the geometric figure—circle, rectangle, or a triangle. Write a function to calculate the area. The function must receive one parameter which is a structure that contains the type of figure and the size of the components needed to calculate the area must be a part of a union. Note that a circle requires just one component, rectangle requires two components, and a triangle requires the size of three components to calculate the area.
25. Write a program to create a structure with information given below. Then read and print the data.

    Employee[10]

    (a) Emp_Id

    (b) Name

    (i) First Name

    (ii) Middle Name

    (iii) Last Name

    (c) Address

    (i) Area

    (ii) City

    (iii) State

(d) Age
(e) Salary
(f) Designation

26. Declare a structure(s) that represents the following hierarchical information:
(a) Student
(b) Roll Number
(c) Name
   (i) First name
   (ii) Middle Name
   (iii) Last Name
(d) Sex
(e) Date of Birth
   (i) Day
   (ii) Month
   (iii) Year
(f) Marks
   (i) English
   (ii) Mathematics
   (iii) Computer Science

27. Define a structure to store the name, an array marks[] which stores marks of five different subjects and a character grade. Write a program to display the details of the student whose name is entered by the user. Use the structure definition of question 26 to make an array of student. Display the name of the students who have secured less than 40% of aggregate.
28. Modify question 27 to print each student's average marks, class average (that includes average of all the students' marks).
29. Make an array of students as illustrated in question 26 and write a program to display the details of the student with the given DOB.
30. Make an array of students as illustrated in question 26 and write a program to delete the record of the student with the given last name.

Find the output of the following codes.

1.
```
main()
{
typedef struct values
{
    int i;
    float f;
}v;
v.i = 2;
v.f = 2.3;
printf("\n %d %f", v.i, v.f);
}
```

2.
```
typedef struct values
{
    int i;
    float f;
}v;
main()
{
v.i = 2;
v.f = 2.3;
printf("\n %d %f", v.i, v.f);
}
```

3.
```
typedef struct values
{
    int i;
    float f;
}v;
main()
{
static values v = {5, 2.3};
printf("\n %d %f", v.i, v.f);
}
```

4.
```
typedef struct first
{
    int i;
    float f;
};
struct second
{
    int i;
    float f;
};
main()
{
    struct first f = {7,4.5};
    struct second s = {4,3.4};
    int diff;
    diff = f.i - s.i;
      printf("\n %d", diff);
}
```

5.
```
typedef struct values
{
    int i;
    int val[10];
}v = {1,2,3,4,5,6,7,8,9}, *ptr = &v;
main()
{
printf("\n %d %d", v.i, ptr -> i);
printf("\n %d %d %d", v.val[3],
ptr -> val[3], *(v.val+3));
}
```

6.
```
typedef struct values
{
    int i;
    float f;
};
void change(values *v, int a, float b)
{
    v -> i = a;
    v -> f = b;
}
main()
```

```
{
values val = {2, 3.4};
printf("\n %d %f", val.i, val.f);
change(&val, 5, 7.9);
printf("\n %d %f", val.i, val.f);
}
```

Find errors in the following structure definitions.

1.
```
struct
{
    int item_code;
    float price;
}
```
2.
```
struct product
{
    char prod_name[20];
    float price;
}product p[10];
```

Find errors in the following statements.

1.
```
struct student
{
    char name[20];
    int id;
}name = "Ram", 9;
```
2.
```
union student
{
    char name[20];
    int id;
}s = {'Ram",01};
```

ANNEXURE 4

Bit Fields in Structure

C facilitates the users to store integer members in memory spaces smaller than what the compiler would ordinarily allow. These space-saving structure members are called *bit fields.* In addition to this, C also permits the users to explicitly declare the width in bits. Bit fields are generally used in developing application programs that force a data structure to correspond to a fixed hardware representation and are unlikely to be portable.

Therefore, besides having declarators for members of a structure or union, a structure declarator can also be a specified number of bits, generally known as a bit field. A bit field is interpreted as an integral type. The syntax for specifying a bit field can be given as

```
type-specifier declarator: constant-
expression
```

In the syntax, the `constant-expression` is used to specify the width of the field in bits. The `type-specifier` for the `declarator` must be *unsigned int*, *signed int*, or *int*, and the `constant-expression` must be a non-negative integer value. If the value of the constant expression is zero, the declaration has no *declarator*.

Key Points About Bit Fields

- C does not permit arrays of bit fields, pointers to bit fields, and functions returning bit fields.
- C permits ordinary member variables along with bit fields as structure members.
- The *declarator* is optional and is used to name the bit field.
- Bit fields can only be declared as part of a structure.
- The `address-of` operator (&) cannot be applied to bit-field components. This means that you cannot use `scanf` to read values into a bit field. To read a value, you may use a temporary variable and then assign its value to the bit field.
- Bit fields that are not named cannot be referenced, and their contents at run time are unpredictable. However, they can be used as dummy fields, for alignment purposes.
- Bit fields must be long enough to contain the bit pattern. Therefore, the following statement is invalid in C language.

```
short num: 15
```

- When a value that is out of range is assigned to a bit field, the lower-order bit pattern is preserved and the appropriate bits are assigned.
- Although the maximum bit field length is 64 bits, for portability reasons, do not use bit fields that are greater than 32 bits in size.
- Bit fields with a length of 0 must be unnamed.

Let us look at a structure that has bit fields.

```
struct
{
  unsigned short a: 2;
  unsigned short b: 1;
  int c: 7;
  unsigned short d: 4;
};
```

In the aforegiven structure, the size of the structure is 2 bytes. Bit fields have the same semantics as the integer type. This means a bit field is used in expressions in exactly the same way as a variable of the same base type would be used, regardless of how many bits are in the bit field.

The C99 standard requires the allowable data types for a bit field to include qualified and unqualified signed int and unsigned int in addition to the following types:

- int
- short, signed short, and unsigned short
- char, signed char, and unsigned char
- long, signed long, and unsigned long
- long long, signed long long, and unsigned long long

Note

In all implementations, the default integer type for a bit field is unsigned.

Drawbacks

Bit fields are basically used to represent single bit flags, with each flag stored in a separate bit. However, bit members in structs have practical drawbacks.

- First, the ordering of bits in memory is architecture-dependent and memory padding rules vary from compiler to compiler. Moreover, many C compilers that are used today generate inefficient code for reading and writing bit members.
- Second, bit fields can require a surprising amount of run-time code to manipulate the values and therefore, the programs may end up using more space than they save.

SLACK BYTE

In order to store any type of data in a structure, there is a minimum fixed byte which must be reserved by the memory. This minimum byte, which is usually machine-dependent, is known as that *word boundary*. For example, TURBO C is based on the 8086 microprocessor and has two-byte word boWundary. So any data type reserves at least two bytes of memory space. To understand it clearly, consider the following structure.

```
struct employee
```

```
{
   char grade;
   int id;
   int emp_code;
   float salary;
   char promotion_due;
};
```

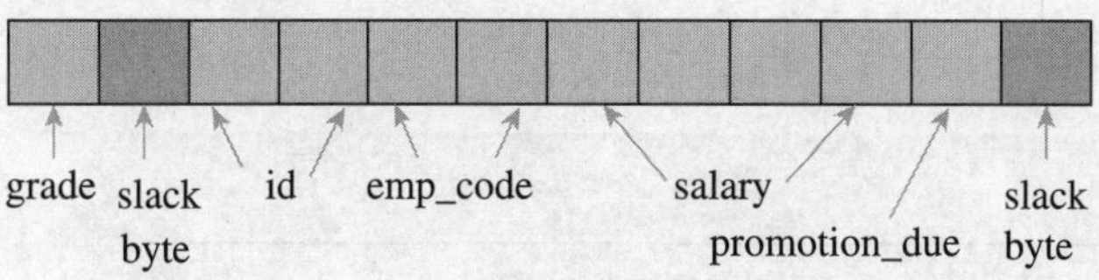

In the figure, `char grade` will reserve two bytes but stores the data only in the first byte since size of `char` is one byte. Now `int id` has a size of two bytes and will search for two bytes but there is only one byte available so it will again reserve the next two byte of memory space. That one byte will be useless as it will not be used to store any data. Such a useless byte is known as *slack byte* and the structure is called an *unbalanced structure*.

Converting an unbalanced structure into a balanced structure

Now consider the same structure in which the sequence of fields has been altered.

```
struct employee_m
{
   char grade;
   char promotion_due;
   int id;
   int emp_code;
   float sal;
};
```

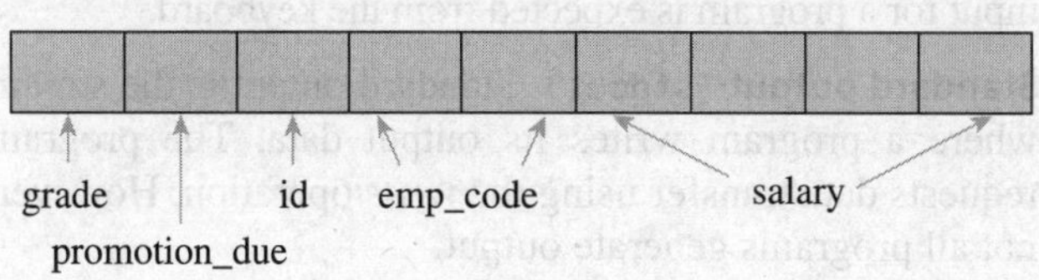

First `char grade` will reserve two bytes and stores the data only in the first byte. Now `char promotion_due` will search for one byte and since one byte is available it will store the data in that byte. Now `int id` will reserve two bytes and stores the data in the two bytes allocated to it. Similarly, `int emp_code` will reserve two bytes to store the data and `float salary` will reserve four bytes to do the same. Note that by re-arrangement of the fields, there is no slack byte, and we have saved the wastage of memory and structure `employee_m` is a balanced structure.

To understand the concept with clarity, execute the following code.

```
main()
{
struct employee
{
   char grade;
   int id;
   int emp_code;
   float salary;
   char promotion_due;
};
struct employee_m
{
   char grade;
   char promotion_due;
   int id;
   int emp_code;
   float sal;
};
printf("\n Size of employee =
   %d",sizeof(struct employee));
printf("\n Size of employee_m =
   %d",sizeof(struct employee_m));
}
```

Output

```
Size of employee = 20
Size of employee_m = 16
```

Hence, slack byte is useful for speed optimization as it aligns bytes so that they can be read from the structure faster.

16 Files

TAKEAWAYS

- Streams in C
- Reading data from files
- Writing data to files
- Error handling
- Command line arguments
- Random access of data
- Renaming files
- Creating temporary files

16.1 INTRODUCTION TO FILES

A *file* is a collection of data stored on a secondary storage device like hard disk. Till now, we had been processing data that was entered through the computer's keyboard. But this task can become very tedious especially when there is a huge amount of data to be processed. A better solution, therefore, is to combine all the input data into a file and then design a C program to read this data from the file whenever required.

Broadly speaking, a file is basically used because real-life applications involve large amounts of data and in such applications the console-oriented I/O operations pose two major problems:

- First, it becomes cumbersome and time-consuming to handle huge amount of data through terminals.
- Second, when doing I/O using terminal, the entire data is lost when either the program is terminated or computer is turned off. Therefore, it becomes necessary to store data on a permanent storage device (e.g. hard disks) and read whenever required, without destroying the data.

In order to use files, we have to learn file input and output operations, i.e., how data is read from or written to a file. Although file I/O operations are almost same as terminal I/O, the only difference is that when doing file I/O, the user must specify the name of the file from which data should be read/written.

16.1.1 Streams in C

In C, the standard streams are termed as pre-connected input and output channels between a text terminal and the program (when it begins execution). Therefore, *stream is a logical interface to the devices that are connected to the computer.*

Stream is widely used as a logical interface to a file where a file can refer to a disk file, the computer screen, keyboard, etc. Although files may differ in the form and capabilities, all streams are the same.

The three standard streams (Figure 16.1) in C language are as follows:

- standard input (`stdin`)
- standard output (`stdout`)
- standard error (`stderr`)

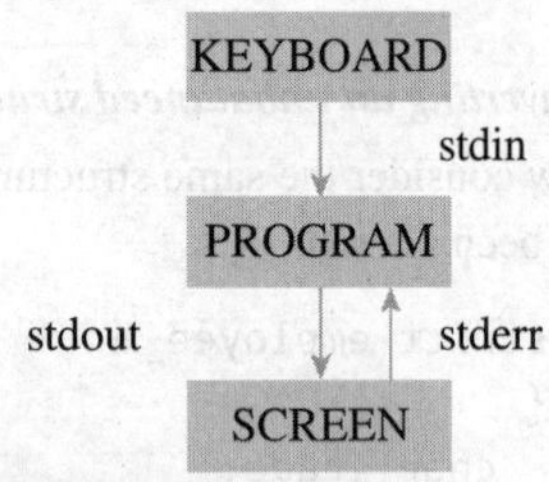

Figure 16.1 Standard streams

Standard input (`stdin`) Standard input or the stream from which the program receives its data. The program requests transfer of data using the *read* operation. However, not all programs require input. Generally, unless redirected, input for a program is expected from the keyboard.

Standard output (`stdout`) Standard output is the stream where a program writes its output data. The program requests data transfer using the *write* operation. However, not all programs generate output.

Standard error (`stderr`) Standard error is basically an output stream used by programs to report error messages or diagnostics. It is a stream independent of standard output and can be redirected separately. No doubt, the *standard output* and *standard error* can also be directed to the same destination.

A stream is linked to a file using an *open* operation and dissociated from a file using a *close* operation.

16.1.2 Buffer Associated with File Streams

When a stream linked to a disk file is created, a buffer is automatically created and associated with the stream. A buffer is nothing but a block of memory that is used for temporary storage of data that has to be read from or written to a file.

Buffers are needed because disk drives are block-oriented devices as they can operate efficiently when data has to be read/written in blocks of certain size. An ideal buffer size is hardware-dependent.

The buffer acts as an interface between the stream (which is character-oriented) and the disk hardware (which is block-oriented). When the program has to write data to the stream, it is saved in the buffer till it is full. Then the entire contents of the buffer are written to the disk as a block. This is shown in Figure 16.2.

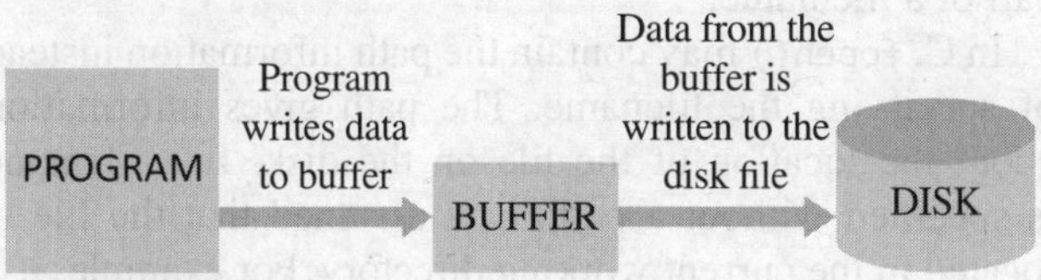

Figure 16.2 Buffers associated with streams

Similarly, when reading data from a disk file, the data is read as a block from the file and written into the buffer. The program reads data from the buffer. The creation and operation of the buffer is automatically handled by the operating system. However, C provides some functions for buffer manipulation. The data resides in the buffer until the buffer is flushed or written to a file.

16.1.3 Types of Files

In C, the types of files used can be broadly classified into two categories—ASCII text files and binary files.

ASCII Text Files

A *text file* is a stream of characters that can be sequentially processed by a computer in forward direction. For this reason, a text file is usually opened for only one kind of operation (reading, writing, or appending) at any given time. Because text files only process characters, they can only read or write data one character at a time. In C, a text stream is treated as a special kind of file.

Depending on the requirements of the operating system and the operation that has to be performed (read/write operation) on the file, newline characters may be converted to or from carriage return/line feed combinations. Besides this, other character conversions may also be done to satisfy the storage requirements of the operating system. However, these conversions occur transparently to process a text file.

In a text file, each line contains zero or more characters and ends with one or more characters that specify the end of line. Each line in a text file can have a maximum of 255 characters. A line in a text file is not a C string, so it is not terminated by a null character. When data is written to a text file, each newline character is converted to a carriage return/line feed character. Similarly, when data is read from a text file, each carriage return/line feed character is converted into newline character.

Programming Tip: The contents of a binary file are not human-readable. If you want the data stored in the file to be human-readable, then store the data in a text file.

Another important thing is that when a text file is used, there are actually two representations of data—internal or external. For example, an `int` value will be represented as 2 or 4 bytes of memory internally, but externally the `int` value will be represented as a string of characters representing its decimal or hexadecimal value. To convert internal representation into external, we can use `printf` and `fprintf` functions. Similarly, to convert an external representation into internal `scanf` and `fscanf` can be used. We will read more about these functions in the coming sections.

Note

In a text file, each line of data ends with a newline character. Each file ends with a special character called the end-of-file (EOF) marker.

Binary Files

A binary file may contain any type of data, encoded in binary form for computer storage and processing purposes. Like a text file, a binary file is a collection of bytes. In C, a byte and a character are equivalent. Therefore, a binary file is also referred to as a character stream with the following two essential differences:

- A binary file does not require any special processing of the data and each byte of data is transferred to or from the disk unprocessed.
- C places no restrictions on the file, and it may be read from, or written to, in any manner the programmer wants.

While text files can be processed sequentially, binary files, on the other hand, can be either processed sequentially or randomly depending on the needs of the application. In C, to process a file randomly, the programmer must move the current file position to an appropriate place in the file before reading or writing data. For example, if a file is used to store records (using structures) of students, then to update a particular record, the programmer must first locate the appropriate record, read the record into memory, update it, and finally write the record back to the disk at its appropriate location in the file.

Note

Binary files store data in the internal representation format. Therefore, an `int` value will be stored in binary form as a 2 or 4 byte value. The same format is used to store data in memory as well as in file. Like text file, binary file also ends with an EOF marker.

In a text file, an integer value 123 will be stored as a sequence of three characters—1, 2, and 3. So each character will take 1 byte and, therefore, to store the integer value 123 we need 3 bytes. However, in a binary file, the `int` value 123 will be stored in 2 bytes in the binary form. This clearly indicates that binary files take less space to store the same piece of data and eliminate conversion between internal and external representations and are thus more efficient than the text files.

16.2 USING FILES IN C

To use files in C, we must follow the steps given below:

- declare a file pointer variable
- open the file
- process the file
- close the file

In this section, we will go through all these steps in detail.

16.2.1 Declaring a File Pointer Variable

There can be a number of files on the disk. In order to access a particular file, you must specify the name of the file that has to be used. This is accomplished by using a file pointer variable that points to a structure `FILE` (defined in `stdio.h`). The file pointer will then be used in all subsequent operations in the file. The syntax for declaring a file pointer is

> **Programming Tip:** An error will be generated if you use the filename to access a file rather than the file pointer.

```
FILE *file_pointer_name;
```

For example, if we write

```
FILE *fp;
```

Then, `fp` is declared as a file pointer.

16.2.2 Opening a File

A file must first be opened before data can be read from it or written to it. In order to open a file and associate it with a stream, the `fopen()` function is used. The prototype of `fopen()` can be given as

```
FILE *fopen(const char *file_name, const char
    *mode);
```

Using the above declaration, the file whose pathname is the string pointed to by `file_name` is opened in the mode specified using the mode. If successful, `fopen()` returns a pointer-to-structure and if it fails, it returns `NULL`.

> **Programming Tip:** A file must be opened before any operation can be performed on it.

File Name

Every file on the disk has a name associated with it. The naming convention of a file varies from one operating system to another. For example, in DOS the file name can have one to eight characters optionally followed by a period and an extension that has one to three characters. However, Windows and UNIX permit filenames having maximum of 256 characters. Windows also lays some restrictions on usage of certain characters in the filenames, i.e., characters such as `/`, `\`, `:`, `*`, `?`, `"`, `<`, `>`, and `!` cannot be part of a file name.

In C, `fopen()` may contain the path information instead of specifying the filename. The path gives information about the location of the file on the disk. If a filename is specified without a path, it is assumed that the file is located in the current working directory. For example, if a file named `Student.DAT` is located on `D` drive in directory `BCA`, then the path of the file can be specified by writing

```
D:\BCA\Student.DAT
```

In C, a backslash character has a special meaning with respect to escape sequences when placed in a string. So in order to represent a backslash character in a C program, you must precede it with another backslash. Hence, the above path will be specified as given below in the C program.

```
D:\\BCA\\Student.DAT
```

File Mode

The second argument in `fopen()` is the *mode*. Mode conveys to C the type of processing that will be done with the file. The different modes in which a file can be opened for processing are given in Table 16.1.

Look at the code given below which opens a file using `fopen()`.

```
FILE *fp;
fp = fopen("Student.DAT", "r");
if(fp==NULL)
{
   printf("\n The file could not be opened");
   exit(1);
}
```

OR

```
char filename[30];
FILE *fp;
gets(filename);
fp = fopen(filename, "r+");
if(fp==NULL)
{
   printf("\n The file could not be opened");
   exit(1);
}
```

Table 16.1 File modes

Mode	Description
r	Open a text file for reading. If the stream (file) does not exist, then an error will be reported.
w	Open a text file for writing. If the stream does not exist, then it is created. If the file already exists, then its contents would be deleted.
a	Append to a text file. If the file does not exist, it is created.
rb	Open a binary file for reading. 'b' indicates binary. By default this will be a sequential file in Media 4 format.
wb	Open a binary file for writing.
ab	Append to a binary file.
r+	Open a text file for both reading and writing. The stream will be positioned at the beginning of the file. When you specify 'r+', you indicate that you want to read the file before you write to it. Thus, the file must already exist.
w+	Open a text file for both reading and writing. The stream will be created if it does not exist, and will be truncated if it exists.
a+	Open a text file for both reading and writing. The stream will be positioned at the end of the file content.
r+b/rb+	Open a binary file for read/write.
w+b/wb+	Create a binary file for read/write.
a+b/ab+	Append a binary file for read/write.

We have already discussed that `fopen()` returns a pointer to `FILE` structure if successful and a `NULL` otherwise. So it is recommended to check whether the file was successfully opened before actually using the file. The `fopen()` function can fail to open the specified file under certain conditions that are listed as follows:

Programming Tip:
An error will be generated if you try to open a file that does not exist.

- Opening a file that is not ready for use
- Opening a file that is specified to be on a non-existent directory/drive
- Opening a non-existent file for reading
- Opening a file to which access is not permitted

16.2.3 Closing a File Using `fclose()`

To close an open file, the `fclose()` function is used which disconnects a file pointer from a file. After `fclose()` has disconnected the file pointer from the file, the pointer can be used to access a different file or the same file but in a different mode. The `fclose()` function not only closes the file, but also flushes all the buffers that are maintained for that file.

If you do not close a file after using it, the system closes it automatically when the program exits. However, since there is a limit on the number of files which can be opened simultaneously, the programmer must close a file when it has been used. The prototype of the `fclose()` function can be given as

Programming Tip:
It is always recommended to close all the opened files when they are not going to be used further in the program.

```
int fclose(FILE *fp);
```

Here, `fp` is a file pointer which points to the file that has to be closed. The function returns an integer value which indicates whether `fclose()` was successful or not. A zero is returned if the function was successful, and a non-zero value is returned if an error occurred.

Note

When `fclose()` is executed, any unwritten buffered data for the stream will be written to the file and any unread buffered data will be discarded.

In addition to `fclose()`, there is a function `fcloseall()` which closes all the streams that are currently opened except the standard streams (such as `stdin, stdout,` and `stderr`). The prototype of `fcloseall()` can be given as

```
int fcloseall(void);
```

`fcloseall()` also flushes any stream buffers and returns the number of streams closed.

If a file's buffer has to be flushed without closing it then use `fflush()` or `flushall()` to flush the buffers of all open streams.

16.3 READING DATA FROM FILES

C provides the following set of functions to read data from a file.

- `fscanf()`
- `fgets()`
- `fgetc()`
- `fread()`

In this section, we will read about these functions.

16.3.1 `fscanf()`

The `fscanf()` function is used to read formatted data from the stream. The syntax of `fscanf()` can be given as

```
int fscanf(FILE *stream, const char *format,…);
```

The `fscanf()` function is used to read data from the `stream` and store them according to the parameter `format` into the locations pointed by the additional arguments. However, these additional arguments must point to the objects that have already occupied memory. These objects are of type as specified by their corresponding format tag within the `format` string.

Similar to the format specifiers used in `scanf()`, in `fscanf()` also the *format specifiers* is a C string that begins with a percentage sign (%). The format specifier is used to specify the type and format of the data that has to be obtained from the stream and stored in the memory locations pointed by the additional arguments. The prototype of a format specifier can be given as

`%[*][width][modifiers]type`, where

* is an optional argument that suppresses assignment of the input field. It indicates that data should be read from the stream and ignored (not stored in the memory location).

width specifies the maximum number of characters to be read. However, fewer characters will be read if the `fscanf` function encounters a white space or an unconvertible character.

modifiers can be `h`, `l`, or `L` for the data pointed by the corresponding additional arguments. Modifier `h` is used for `short int` or `unsigned short int`, `l` is used for `long int`, `unsigned long int`, or `double` values. Finally, `L` is used for `long double` data values.

type specifies the type of data that has to be read. It also indicates how this data is expected to be read from the user.

The type specifiers for `fscanf` function are given in Table 16.2.

Table 16.2 Type specifiers

Type	Qualifying input
C	for single characters
D	for decimal values
e, E, f, g, G	for floating point numbers
O	for octal numbers
S	for a sequence of (string of) characters
U	for unsigned decimal values
x, X	for hexadecimal values

The `fscanf` function has some additional arguments. Each of the additional arguments must point to an object of the type specified by its corresponding `%` tag within the `format` string, in the same order.

Note

The `fscanf` function is similar to the `scanf` function, except that the first argument of `fscanf` specifies a stream from which to read, whereas `scanf` can only read from standard input.

Let us look at an example which illustrates the use of `fscanf()`. Here, we will not give the complete program but just a partial program to demonstrate the use of `fscanf()`.

```
#include <stdio.h>
int main()
{
   FILE *fp;
   char name[80];
   int roll_no;
   fp = fopen("Student.DAT", "r");
   if(fp==NULL)
   {
      printf("\n The file could not be
        opened");
      exit(1);
   }
   printf("\n Enter the name and roll number
     of the student: ");
   // READ FROM KEYBOARD
   fscanf(stdin, "%s %d", name, &roll_no);
   /* read from keyboard */
   printf("\n NAME: %s \t ROLL NUMBER = %d",
     name, roll_no);
   // READ FROM FILE Student.DAT
   fscanf(fp, "%s %d", name, &roll_no);
   printf("\n NAME: %s \t ROLL NUMBER = %d",
     name, roll_no);
   fclose(fp);
   return 0;
}
```

Output

```
Enter the name and roll number of the student:
   01 Zubin
NAME: Zubin ROLL NUMBER = 01
NAME: Goransh ROLL NUMBER = 03
```

Note

If you want to use `fprintf ()` to write on the screen, then specify `stdout` instead of specifying any other file pointer.

16.3.2 fgets()

The `fgets()` function stands for *file get string*. The `fgets()` function is used to get a string from a stream. The syntax of `fgets()` can be given as

```
char *fgets(char *str, int size, FILE
   *stream);
```

The `fgets()` function reads at most one less than the number of characters specified by size (gets `size - 1` characters) from the given stream and stores them in the string `str`. The `fgets()` fuction terminates as soon as it encounters either a newline character, EOF, or any other error. However, if a newline character is encountered it is retained. When all the characters are read without any error, a `'\0'` character is appended to the end of the string.

The gets() and fgets() functions are almost same except that gets() has an infinite size and a stream of stdin. Another difference is that when gets() encounters a newline character, it does not retain it, i.e., the newline character (if any) is not stored in the string.

On successful completion, fgets() will return str. However, if the stream is at EOF, the EOF indicator for the stream will be set and fgets() will return a NULL pointer. In case, fgets() encounters any error while reading, the error indicator for the stream will be set and NULL pointer will be returned. Look at the program code given below which demonstrates the use of fgets().

```
#include <stdio.h>
int main()
{
    FILE *fp;
    char str[80];
    fp = fopen("ABC.DAT", "r");
    if(fp==NULL)
    {
        printf("\n The file could not be opened");
        exit(1);
    }
    /* the file will read 79 characters during
    each iteration and will print them on the
    screen */
    while (fgets(str, 80, fp) != NULL)
        printf("\n %s", str);
    printf("\n\n File Read. Now closing the file");
    fclose(fp);
    return 0;
}
```

Output

```
Abdceweeferrttet gfejjherroiew tjketjer
   fddfgdfgfd
File Read. Now closing the file
```

16.3.3 fgets()

The fgetc() function returns the next character from stream, EOF if the end of file is reached, or if there is an error. The syntax of fgetc() can be given as

```
int fgetc(FILE *stream);
```

fgetc() returns the character read as an int or returns EOF to indicate an error or end of file.

fgetc() reads a single character from the current position of a file (file associated with stream). After reading the character, the function increments the associated file pointer (if defined) to point to the next character. However, if the stream has already reached the end of file, the EOF indicator for the stream is set. Look at the following program code which demonstrates the use of fgets() function.

```
#include <stdio.h>
main()
{
    FILE *fp;
    char str[80];
    int i, ch;
    fp = fopen("Program.C", "r");
    if(fp==NULL)
    {
        printf("\n The file could not be
          opened");
        exit(1);
    }
    // Read 79 characters and store them in str
        ch = fgetc(fp);
    for(i=0; (i < 79) && (feof(fp) == 0); i++)
    {
        str[i] = (char)ch;
        ch = fgetc(stream);
        // reads character by character
    }
    str[i] = '\0';
    // append the string with a null character
    printf("\n %s", str);
    fclose(fp);
}
```

The above program displays either first 79 characters or less characters if the file contains less than 79 characters.

The feof() function is used to detect the end of file. We will read more on this function later in this chapter.

16.3.4 fread()

The fread() function is used to read data from a file. Its syntax can be given as

```
int fread(void *str, size_t size, size_t num,
   FILE *stream);
```

The fread() function reads num number of objects (where each object is size bytes) and places them into the array pointed to by str. The data is read from the given input stream.

Upon successful completion, fread() returns the number of bytes successfully read. The number of objects will be less than num if a read error or end-of-file is encountered. If size or num is 0, fread() will return 0 and the contents of str and the state of the stream remain unchanged. In case of error, the error indicator for the stream will be set.

The fread() function advances the file position indicator for the stream by the number of bytes read.

Note

The fread() function does not distinguish between end-of-file and error. The programmer must use feof and ferror to determine which of the two has occurred.

Look at the program given below which illustrates the use of `fread()`.

```
#include <stdio.h>
main()
{
    FILE *fp;
    char str[11];
    fp = fopen("Letter.TXT", "r+");
    if(fp==NULL)
    {
        printf("\n The file could not be opened");
        exit(1);
    }
    fread(str, 1, 10, fp);
    /* In the str 10 objects of 1 byte are read
    from the file pointd by fp */
    str[10]= '\0';
    printf("\n First 9 characters of the file
      are: %s", str);
        fclose(fp);
}
```

Output

```
First 9 characters of the file are: Hello how
```

Since `fread()` returns the number of bytes successfully read, we can also modify the above program to print the number of bytes read. This would be helpful to know how many characters were read.

```
#include <stdio.h>
main()
{
    FILE *fp;
    char str[80];
    size_t bytes_read;
    fp = fopen("Letter.TXT", "r+");
    if(fp==NULL)
    {
        printf("\n The file could not be opened");
        exit(1);
    }
    bytes_read = fread(str, 1, 79, fp);
    str[bytes_read+1]= '\0';
    /* explicitly store null character at the
    end of str */
    printf("\n First %d characters of the file
      are: %s", bytes_read, str);
        fclose(fp);
}
```

The output will depend on the contents of the file. Assuming 14 characters were read, the output can be given as

```
Hello how r u?
```

This program assumes that you have created a file `Letter.TXT` that contains 14 characters which have been displayed above.

The `fread()` function does not check for overflow in the receiving area of memory. It is the programmer's job to ensure that the memory pointed to by `str` must be large enough to hold the number of objects being read.

If you have opened a stream for updating and later you want to switch from reading to writing or vice versa, you must first use the `fseek()` or `rewind()` function. However, if you have been reading and have reached end-of-file, then you can immediately switch to writing. We will discuss the `fseek()` and `rewind` functions later in this chapter.

16.4 WRITING DATA TO FILES

C provides the following set of functions to read data from a file:

- `fprintf()`
- `fputs()`
- `fputc()`
- `fwrite()`

In this section, we will read about these functions.

16.4.1 fprintf()

The `fprintf()` function is used to write formatted output to stream. The syntax of `fprintf()` can be given as

```
int fprintf (FILE * stream, const char *
   format, ...);
```

The function writes data that is formatted as specified by the format argument to the specified stream. After the format parameter, the function can have as many additional arguments as specified in the format.

The parameter format in `fprintf()` is nothing but a C string that contains the text that has to be written on to the stream. Although not mandatory, `fprintf()` can optionally contain format tags that are replaced by the values specified in subsequent additional arguments and are formatted as requested.

Note

There must be enough arguments for format because if there are not, then result will be completely unpredictable. However, if by mistake you specify more number of arguments, the excess arguments will simply be ignored.

The prototype of the format tag can be given as

```
%[flags][width][.precision][length]specifier
```

Each format specifier must begin with a `%` sign. The `%` sign is followed by:

flags which specifies output justification such as decimal point, numerical sign, trailing zeros, or octal or hexadecimal prefixes. Table 16.3 shows the different types of flags with their description.

Table 16.3 Flags in printf()

Flags	Description
-	Left justify within the given data field width
+	Displays the data with its numeric sign (either + or –)
#	Used to provide additional specifiers such as o, x, X, 0, 0x, or 0X for octal and hexadecimal values, respectively, for values except zero.
0	The number is left-padded with zeros (0) instead of spaces.

width specifies the minimum number of characters to print after being padded with zeros or blank spaces.

precision specifies the maximum number of characters to print.

- For integer specifiers (d, i, o, u, x, X): precision flag specifies the minimum number of digits to be written. However, if the value to be written is shorter than this number, the result is padded with leading zeros. Otherwise, if the value is longer, it is not truncated.
- For character strings, precision specifies the maximum number of characters to be printed.

length field can be explained as given in Table 16.4.

specifier is used to define the type and the interpretation of the value of the corresponding argument.

The fprintf() function may contain some additional parameters as well depending on the format string. Each argument must contain a value to be inserted instead of each % tag specified in the format parameter, if any. In other words, the number of arguments must be equal to the number of % tags that expect a value.

Table 16.4 Length field in printf()

Length	Description
h	When the argument is a short int or unsigned short int
l	When the argument is a long int or unsigned long int for integer specifiers
L	When the argument is a long double (used for floating point specifiers)

Look at the program given below which demonstrates the use of fprintf().

```
#include <stdio.h>
main()
{
    FILE *fp;
    int i;
    char name[20];
    float salary;
    fp = fopen("Details.TXT", "w");
    if(fp==NULL)
    {
        printf("\n The file could not be opened");
        exit(1);
    }
    for(i = 0;i < 10;i++)
    {
        puts("\n Enter your name: ");
        gets(name);
        fflush(stdin);
        puts("\n Enter your salary: ");
        scanf("%f", &salary);
        fprintf(fp, " (%d) NAME: [%-10.10s]
          \t SALARY %5.2f", i, name, salary);
    }
    fclose(fp);
}
```

Programming Tip:
If you open a file for writing using w mode, then the contents of file will be deleted. If a file has to be used for reading as well as writting, it must be opened in w+ mode

Output

```
Enter your name: Aryan
Enter your salary: 50000
Enter your name: Anshita
Enter your salary: 65000
Enter your name: Saesha
Enter your salary: 70000
```

This example asks the user to enter the name and salary of 10 people. Each time the user enters the name and salary, the data read is written to Details.TXT. The names are written on new lines in the file. In this example, we have used three format tags:

- %d to specify a signed decimal integer.
- %-10.10s. Here – indicates that the characters must be left aligned. There can be a minimum of 10 characters as well as a maximum of 10 characters (.10) in the strings.
- %f to specify a floating point number.

Note

If you want to use fprintf () to write on the screen, then specify stdout instead of specifying any other file pointer.

16.4.2 fputs()

The opposite of fgets() is fputs(). The fputs() function is used to write a line to a file. The syntax of fputs() can be given as

```
int fputs(const char *str, FILE *stream);
```

The fputs() function writes the string pointed to by str to the stream pointed to by stream. On successful completion, fputs() returns 0. In case of any error, fputs() returns EOF.

```
#include <stdio.h>
main()
{
    FILE *fp;
    char feedback[100];
    fp = fopen("Comments.TXT", "w");
    if(fp==NULL)
```

```
    {
        printf("\n The file could not be opened");
        exit(1);
    }
    printf("\n Provide feedback on this book: ");
    gets(feedback);
    fflush(stdin);
    // feedback stored
    fputs(feedback, fp);
        fclose(fp);
}
```

Output

```
Provide feedback on this book: good
```

16.4.3 fputc()

The `fputc()` function is just the opposite of `fgetc()` and is used to write a character to the stream.

```
int fputc(int c, FILE *stream);
```

The `fputc()` function will write the byte specified by C (converted to an `unsigned char`) to the output stream pointed to by `stream`. On successful completion, `fputc()` will return the value it has written. Otherwise, in case of error, the function will return `EOF` and the error indicator for the stream will be set.

```
#include <stdio.h>
main()
{
    FILE *fp;
    char feedback[100];
    int i;
    fp = fopen("Comments.TXT", "w");
    if(fp==NULL)
    {
        printf("\n The file could not be
    opened");
        exit(1);
    }
    printf("\n Provide feedback on this book: ");
    gets(feedback);
    for(i = 0;i < feedback[i];i++)
    fputc(feedback[i], fp);
    fclose(fp);
}
```

Output

```
Provide feedback on this book: good
```

Note

The standard file `stdout` is buffered in case the output unit is not the terminal. On the contrary, the standard file `stderr` is usually unbuffered. However, the settings of `stdout` and `stderr` can be changed using `setbuf`.

Programming Tip:
EOF is an integer type defined in `stdio.h` and has a value '–1'.

When an output stream is unbuffered, information appears on the destination device as soon as it is written. When it is buffered, characters are saved internally and then written out as a group. In order to force buffered characters to be output before the buffer is full, use `fflush()`.

16.4.4 fwrite()

The `fwrite()` function is used to write data to a file. The syntax of `fwrite` can be given as

```
int fwrite(const void *str, size_t size,
    size_t count, FILE *stream);
```

The `fwrite()` function will write objects (number of objects will be specified by `count`) of size specified by `size`, from the array pointed to by `str` to the stream pointed to by `stream`.

The file-position indicator for the stream (if defined) will be advanced by the number of bytes successfully written. If an error occurs, the resulting value of the file-position indicator for the stream is unspecified.

On successful completion, the `fwrite()` function returns the number of objects successfully written. The number of objects will be less than `count` if an error is encountered. If `size` or `count` is 0, `fwrite()` will return 0 and the contents of the stream remains unchanged. In case of error, the error indicator for the stream will be set.

```
#include <stdio.h>
#include <string.h>
#include <stdlib.h>
int main(void)
{
    FILE *fp;
    size_t count;
    char str[] = "GOOD MORNING";
    fp = fopen("Welcome.txt", "wb");
    if(fp==NULL)
    {
    printf("\n The file could not be opened");
    exit(1);
    }
    count = fwrite(str, 1, strlen(str), fp);
    printf("\n %d bytes were
        written to the file", count);
  fclose(fp);
        return 0;
}
```

Output

```
13 bytes were written to the file
```

Note

fwrite() can be used to write characters, integers, or structures to a file. However, fwrite() can be used only with files that are opened in binary mode.

16.5 DETECTING THE END-OF-FILE

When reading or writing data to files, we often do not know exactly how long the file is. For example, while reading the file, we usually start reading from the beginning and proceed towards the end of the file. In C, there are two ways to detect EOF:

- While reading the file in text mode, character by character, the programmer can compare the character that has been read with EOF, which is a symbolic constant defined in stdio.h with a value -1. The following statement does that

```
while(1)
{
    c = fgetc(fp);
    // here c is an int variable
    if (c==EOF)
       break;
    printf("%c", c);
}
```

- The other way is to use the standard library function feof() which is defined in stdio.h. The feof() function is used to distinguish between two cases:
    - When a stream operation has reached the end of a file
    - When the EOF error code has returned an error indicator even when the end of the file has not been reached

The prototype of feof() can be given as

```
int feof(FILE *fp);
```

The function takes a pointer to the FILE structure of the stream to check as an argument and returns zero (false) when the end of file has not been reached and a one (true) if the end of file has been reached. Look at the following:

The output assumes that a file Student.DAT already exists and conatins the following data: 1 Aditya 2 Chaitanya 3 Goransh

```
#include <stdio.h>
main()
{
   FILE *fp;
   char str[80];
   fp = fopen("Student.DAT", "r");
   if(fp==NULL)
   {
      printf("\n The file could not be opened");
      exit(1);
   }
   /* The loop continues until fp reaches
         the end-of-file */
   while(!feof(fp))
   {
   fgets(str, 79, fp);
      // Reads 79 bytes at a time
      printf("\n %s", str);
   }
   printf("\n\n File Read. Now closing the
   file");
   fclose(fp);
   return 0;
}
```

Output

```
1 Aditya 2 Chaitanya 3 Goransh
```

16.6 ERROR HANDLING DURING FILE OPERATIONS

It is quite common that an error may occur while reading data from or writing data to a file. For example, an error may arise

- when trying to read a file beyond EOF indicator
- when trying to read a file that does not exist
- when trying to use a file that has not been opened
- when trying to use a file in an inappropriate mode, i.e., writing data to a file that has been opened for reading
- when writing to a file that is write-protected (i.e., trying to write to a read-only file)

If we fail to check for errors, then the program may behave abnormally. Therefore, an unchecked error may result in premature termination of the program or incorrect output.

Programming Tip: An error will be generated if you try to read a file that is opened in w mode and vice versa.

In C, the library function ferror() is used to check for errors in the stream. Its prototype can be given as

```
int ferror (FILE *stream);
```

The ferror() function checks for any errors in the stream. It returns value zero if no errors have occurred and a non-zero value if there is an error. The error indication will last until the file is closed or it is cleared by the clearerr() function. Look at the code given below which uses the ferror().

```
#include <stdio.h>
main()
{
```

```
    FILE *fp;
    char feedback[100];
    int i;
    fp = fopen("Comments.TXT", "w");
    if(fp==NULL)
    {
       printf("\n The file could not be opened");
       exit(1);
    }
    printf("\n Provide feedback on this book: ");
    gets(feedback);
    for(i = 0; i < feedback[i];i++)
       fputc(feedback[i], fp);
    if(ferror(fp))
    {
       printf("\n Error writing in file");
       exit(1);
    }
    fclose(fp);
}
```

When you execute this code and an error occurs while writing the feedback, the program will terminate and a message indicating `Error writing in file` will be displayed on the screen.

16.6.1 clearerr()

The `clearerr()` function is used to clear the end-of-file and error indicators for the stream. Its protoype can be given as

```
void clearerr(FILE *stream);
```

The `clearerr()` function clears the error for the stream pointed to by `stream`. The function is used because error indicators are not automatically cleared; once the error indicator for a specified stream is set, operations on that stream continue to return an error value until `clearerr`, `fseek`, `fsetpos`, or `rewind` is called. Look at the code given below which uses `clearerr()`

```
#include <stdio.h>
#include <stdlib.h>
#include <errno.h>
main()
{
   FILE *fp;
   fp = fopen("Comments.TXT", "w");
   if(fp==NULL)
   {
      perror("OOPS ERROR");
      printf("\n error no = %d", errno);
      exit(1);
   }
   printf("\n Kindly give the feedback on this
     book: ");
   gets(feedback);
   for(i = 0; i < feedback[i];i++)
   {
      fputc(feedback[i], fp);
      if (ferror(fp))
      {
         clearerr(fp);
         break;
         /* clears the error indicators and
           jumps out of for loop */
      }
   }
   // close the file
   fclose(fp);
}
```

16.6.2 perror()

The `perror()` function stands for print error. In case of an error, the programmer can determine the type of error that has occurred using the `perror()` function. The `perror()` function defined in `stdio.h` header file is used to handle errors in C programs. When called, `perror()` displays a message on `stderr` describing the most recent error that occurred during a library function call or system call. The prototype of `perror()` can be given as

```
void perror(char *msg);
```

The `perror()` function takes one argument `msg` which points to an optional user-defined message. This message is printed first, followed by a colon, and the implementation-defined message that describes the most recent error.

If a call to `perror()` is made when no error has actually occurred, then a `No error` will be displayed. The most important thing to remember is that a call to `perror()` does nothing to deal with the error condition. It is entirely up to the program to take action. For example, the program may prompt the user to do something such as terminate the program.

Usually the program's action will be determined by checking the value of `errno` and the nature of the error. In order to use the external constant `errno`, you must include the header file `errno.h`. The program given below illustrates the use of `perror()`. Here we assume that the file `Comments.TXT` does not exist.

```
#include <stdio.h>
#include <stdlib.h>
#include <errno.h>
main()
{
   FILE *fp;
   fp = fopen("Comments.TXT", "w");
   if(fp==NULL)
   {
      perror("OOPS ERROR");
      printf("\n error no = %d", errno);
      exit(1);
   }
```

```
    printf("\n Provide feedback on this book: ");
    gets(feedback);
    for(i=0; i<feedback[i];i++)
       fputc(feedback[i], fp);
    fclose(fp);
}
```

Output

```
OOPS ERROR: No such file or directory
errno =2
```

16.7 ACCEPTING COMMAND LINE ARGUMENTS

C facilitates its programmers to pass command arguments. Command-line arguments are given after the name of a program in command-line operating systems like `DOS` or `Linux`, and are passed in to the program from the operating system.

Till now, no arguments were passed to the `main()` function. But now in order to understand command-line arguments, you must first understand the full declaration of the main function. The `main()` function can accept two arguments,

- The first argument is an integer value that specifies the number of command-line arguments.
- The second argument is a full list of all of the command-line arguments.

The full declaration of `main()` can be given as

```
int main (int arg c, char *argv[])
```

The integer, `arg c` specifies the number of arguments passed to the program from the command line, including the name of the program.

The array of character pointers, `argv` contains the list of all the arguments. `argv[0]` is the name of the program, or an empty string if the name is not available. `argv[1]` to `argv[argc - 1]` specifies the command line argument. In a C program, every element in `argv` can be used as a string. Moreover, elements of `argv` can also be accessed as a two-dimensional array. Note that `argv[argc]` is a `NULL` pointer.

In other words, each element of the array `argv` is a pointer where each pointer points to a string. Thus, `argv[0]` points to a string that contains the first parameter on the command line which is the program's name, `argv[1]` points to the next parameter, and so on. Look at the program given below which illustrates the use of command line arguments.

```
int main(int argc, char *argv[])
{
    int i;
    printf("\n Number of argumnets passed =
      %d",argc);
     for (i = 0; i < argc; i++)
         printf("\n arg[i] = %s",argv[i]);
    return 0;
}
```

In the program, `main()` accepts command line arguments through `argc` and `argv`. In the `main()` function, the value of `argc` is printed which gives the number of arguments passed. Then each argument passed is printed in the `for` loop using the array of pointers, `argv`.

For example when you execute this program from DOS prompt by writing

```
C:\>tc clpro.c Reema Thareja
```

Then `argc = 3`, where `argv[0] = clpro.c argv[1] = Reema` and `argv[2] = Thareja`

1. Write a program to read a file character by character, and display it simultaneously on the screen.

```
#include <stdio.h>
#include <string.h>
main()
{
    FILE *fp;
    int ch;
    char filename[20];
    printf("\n Enter the filename: ");
    fp = fopen(filename, "r");
    if(fp==NULL)
    {
        printf("\n Error Opening the File");
        exit(1);
    }
    ch= fgetc(fp);
    while(ch!=EOF)
    {
        putchar(ch);
        ch = fgetc(fp);
    }
    fclose(fp);
}
```

Output

```
Enter the filename: Letter.TXT
Hello how are you?
```

2. Write a program to count the number of characters and number of lines in a file.

```
#include <stdio.h>
#include <string.h>
main()
{
    FILE *fp;
    int ch, no_of_characters = 0, no_of_lines = 1;
    char filename[20];
    printf("\n Enter the filename: ");
    fp = fopen(filename, "r");
    if(fp==NULL)
```

```
{
    printf("\n Error Opening the File");
    exit(1);
}
ch= fgetc(fp);
while(ch!=EOF)
{
    if(ch=='\n')
        no_of_lines++;
    no_of_characters++;
    ch = fgetc(fp);
}
if(no_of_characters > 0)
printf("\n In the file %s, there are %d
    lines and %d characters", filename, no_of_
    lines, no_of_characters);
else
    printf("\n File is empty");
fclose(fp);
}
```

Output

```
Enter the filename: Letter.TXT
In the file Letter.TXT, there is 1 line and 18
   characters
```

3. Write a program to print the text of a file on screen by printing the text line by line and displaying the line numbers before the text in each line. Use command line argument to enter the filename.

```
#include <stdio.h>
int main(int argc, char *argv[])
{
    FILE *fp1;
    char text[100], ch;
    int line = 1;
    int i = 0;
    if(argc != 2)
    {
        printf("\n Full information is not
            provided. Please provide a filename");
        return 0;
    }
    fp1 = fopen(argv[1], "r");
    if(fp1 == NULL)
    {
        printf("\n File Opening Error");
        return 0;
    }
    i = 0;
    while(feof(fp1) == 0)
    {
        fscanf(fp1, "%c", &ch);
        if (ch == '\n')
        {
            line++;
            text[i] = '\0';
            printf("%d %s", line, text);
            i = 0;
        }
        text[i] = ch;
        i++;
    }
    text[i] = '\0';
    printf("%s", text);
    fclose(fp1);
    return 0;
}
```

Output

```
1 Hello how are you?
```

4. Write a program to compare two files to check whether they are identical or not.

```
#include <stdio.h>
int main()
{
FILE *fp1, *fp2;
int ch1, ch2;
char filename1[20], filename2[20];
printf("\n Enter the name of the first file: ");
gets(filename1);
fflush(stdin);
printf("\n Enter the name of the second file: ");
gets(filename2);
fflush(stdin);
if((fp1=fopen(filename1, "r"))==0)
{
    printf("\n Error opening the first file");
    exit(1);
}
if((fp2=fopen(filename2, "r"))==0)
{
    printf("\n Error opening the second file");
    exit(1);
}
ch1 = fgetc(fp1);
ch2 = fgetc(fp2);
while(ch1!=EOF && ch2!=EOF && ch1==ch2)
{
    /* Reading and comparing the contents
        of two files */
    ch1 = fgetc(fp1);
    ch2 = fgetc(fp2);
}
if(ch1==ch2)
```

```
    printf("\n Files are identical");
    else
    printf("\n Files are not identical");
    fclose(fp1);
    fclose(fp2);
    return 0;
}
```

Output

```
Enter the name of the first filename:
    Comments.TXT
Enter the name of the second filename:
    Letter.TXT
Files are not identical
```

5. Write a program to copy one file into another. Copy one character at a time.

```
#include <stdio.h>
int main()
{
    FILE *fp1, *fp2;
    int ch;
    char filename1[20], filename2[20];
    printf("\n Enter the name of the first file: ");
    gets(filename1);
    fflush(stdin);
    printf("\n Enter the name of the second
      file: ");
    gets(filename2);
    fflush(stdin);
    if((fp1=fopen(filename1, "r"))==0)
    {
        printf("\n Error opening the first file");
        exit(1);
    }
    if((fp2=fopen(filename2, "w"))==0)
    {
        printf("\n Error opening the second file");
        exit(1);
    }
            // Copy from fp1 to fp2
        ch = fgetc(fp1);
        while(ch!=EOF)
    {
        putc(ch, fp2);
        ch = fgetc(fp1);
    }
    printf("\n FILE COPIED");
    fclose(fp1);
    fclose(fp2);
    return 0;
}
```

Output

```
Enter the name of the first filename: Comments.TXT
Enter the name of the second filename:
    User_Comments.TXT
FILE COPIED
```

6. Write a program to copy one file into another. Copy multiple characters simultaneously.

```
#include <stdio.h>
int main()
{
    FILE *fp1, *fp2;
    char filename1[20], filename2[20], str[30];
    printf("\n Enter the name of the first
      filename: ");
    gets(filename1);
    fflush(stdin);
    printf("\n Enter the name of the second
      filename: ");
    gets(filename2);
    fflush(stdin);
    if((fp1=fopen(filename1, "r"))==0)
    {
        printf("\n Error opening the first file");
        exit(1);
    }
    if((fp2=fopen(filename2, "w"))==0)
    {
        printf("\n Error opening the second file");
        exit(1);
    }
    while((fgets(str, sizeof(str),
        fp1))!=NULL)
    fputs(str, fp2);
    fclose(fp1);
    fclose(fp2);
    return 0;
}
```

Output

```
Enter the name of the first filename:
    Comments.TXT
Enter the name of the second filename:
    User_Comments.TXT
FILE COPIED
```

7. Write a program to read a file that contains characters. Encrypt the data in this file while writing it into another file. (e.g., while writing the data in another file you can use the formula ch = ch –2, i.e., if the data contains character 'red' the encrypted data becomes 'pcb').

```
#include <stdio.h>
int main(int argc, char *argv[])
```

```
{
    FILE *fp1, *fp2;
    char ch;
    if(argc != 3)
    {
        printf("\n Full information is not
            provided");
        return 0;
    }
    fp1 = fopen(argv[1], "r");
    if(fp1 == NULL)
    {
        printf("\n File Opening Error");
        return 0;
    }
    fp2 = fopen(argv[2], "w");
    if(fp2 == NULL)
    {
        printf("\n File Opening Error");
        return 0;
    }
    while (feof(fp1) == 0)
    {
        fscanf(fp1, "%c", &ch);
        fprintf(fp2, "%c", ch - 2);
         /*encrypted character is printed on
           the screen */
    }
    printf("\n The encrypted data is written to
      the file");
    fclose(fp2);
    fcloseall();
    return 0;
}
```

Output

```
The encrypted data is written to the file
```

8. Write a program to read a file that contains lower case characters. Then write these characters into another file with all lower case characters converted into upper case (e.g., if the file contains data – 'red' it must be written in another file as 'RED').

```
#include <stdio.h>
int main(int argc, char *argv[])
{
    FILE *fp1, *fp2;
    char ch;
    if(argc != 3)
    {
        printf("\n Full information is not
            provided");
        return 0;
    }
    fp1 = fopen(argv[1], "r");
    if(fp1 == NULL)
    {
        printf("\n File Opening Error");
        return 0;
    }
    fp2 = fopen(argv[2], "w");
    if(fp2 == NULL)
    {
        printf("\n File Opening Error");
        return 0;
    }
    while (feof(fp1) == 0)
    {
        fscanf(fp1, "%c", &ch);
        fprintf(fp2, "%c", ch - 32);
    }
    fcloseall();
    printf("\n File copied with upper case
      characters");
    return 0;
}
```

Output

```
File copied with upper case characters
```

9. Write a program to merge two files into a third file. The names of the files must be entered using command line arguments.

```
#include <stdio.h>
int main(int argc, char *argv[])
{
    FILE *fp1, *fp2, *fp3;
    char ch;
    if(argc != 4)  /* Read three filenames
    from the user */
    {
        printf("\n Full information is not
            provided");
        return 0;
    }
    fp1 = fopen(argv[1], "r");
    if(fp1 == NULL)
    {
        printf("\n File Opening Error");
        return 0;
    }
    fp2 = fopen(argv[2], "r");
    if(fp2 == NULL)
    {
        printf("\n File Opening Error");
```

```
        return 0;
    }
    fp3 = fopen(argv[3], "w");
    if(fp3 == NULL)
    {
        printf("\n File Opening Error");
        return 0;
    }
    while (feof(fp1) != 0)
    {
        fscanf(fp1, "%c", &ch);
        fprintf(fp3, "%c", ch);
    }
    while (feof(fp2) != 0)
    {
        fscanf(fp2, "%c", &ch);
        fprintf(fp3, "%c", ch);
    }
    fcloseall();
    printf("\n File merged");
    return 0;
}
```

Output

```
File merged
```

10. Write a program to read some text from the keyboard and store it in a file.

```
#include <stdio.h>
#include <string.h>
main()
{
    FILE *fp;
    char filename[20], str[100];
    printf("\n Enter the filename: ");
    fp = fopen(filename, "w");
    if(fp==NULL)
    {
        printf("\n Error Opening The File");
        exit(1);
    }
    printf("\n Enter the text: ");
    gets(str);
    fflush(stdin);
    fprintf(fp, "%s", str);
    fclose(fp);
}
```

Output

```
Enter the filename: Greet.TXT
Enter the text: Good Morning
```

11. Write a program to read the details of a student and then print it on the screen as well as write it into a file.

```
#include <stdio.h>
int main()
{
    FILE *fp;
    typedef struct student
    {
        int roll_no;
        char name[80];
        float fees;
        char DOB[80];
    }STUDENT;
    STUDENT stud1;

    fp = fopen("student_details.dat", "w");
    if(fp == NULL)
    {
        printf("\n File Opening Error");
        return 0;
    }
    printf("\n Enter the roll number: ");
    scanf("%d", &stud1.roll_no);
    printf("\n Enter the name: ");
    scanf("%s", stud1.name);
    printf("\n Enter the fees: ");
    scanf("%f", &stud1.fees);
    printf("\n Enter the DOB: ");
    scanf("%s", stud1.DOB);

    // PRINT ON SCREEN

    printf("\n *** STUDENT'S DETAILS ***");
    printf("\n ROLL No. = %d", stud1.roll_no);
    printf("\n NAME = %s", stud1.name);
    printf("\n FEES = %f", stud1.fees);
    printf("\n DOB = %s", stud1.DOB);
    // WRITE TO FILE

    fprintf(fp,"%d %s %f %s", stud1.roll_no,
    stud1.name, stud1.fees, stud1.DOB);

    fclose(fp);
    return 0;
}
```

Output

```
Enter the roll number: 01
Enter the name: Aman
Enter the fees: 45000
Enter the DOB: 20-9-91

*** STUDENT'S DETAILS ***
ROLL No. = 01
NAME = Aman
FEES = 45000
DOB = 20-9-91
```

12. Write a program to read the details of a student from a file and then print it on the screen.

```
#include <stdio.h>
int main()
{
    FILE *fp;
    typedef struct student
    {
        int roll_no;
        char name[80];
        float fees;
        char DOB[80];
    }STUDENT;

    STUDENT stud1;
    fp = fopen("student_details.dat", "r");
    if(fp == NULL)
    {
        printf("\n File Opening Error");
        return 0;
    }
    // READ FROM FILE
    fscanf(fp,"%d %s %f %s", &stud1.roll_no,
    stud1.name, &stud1.fees, stud1.DOB);
    // PRINT ON SCREEN
    printf("\n *** STUDENT'S DETAILS ***");
    printf("\n ROLL No. = %d", stud1.roll_no);
    printf("\n NAME = %s", stud1.name);
    printf("\n FEES = %f", stud1.fees);
    printf("\n DOB = %s", stud1.DOB);

    fclose(fp);
    return 0;
}
```

Output

```
*** STUDENT'S DETAILS ***
ROLL No. = 01
NAME = Aman
FEES = 45000
DOB = 20-9-91
```

13. Write a program to read the details of student until a '–1' is entered and simultaneously write the data to a file.

```
#include <stdio.h>
int main()
{
    FILE *fp;
    typedef struct student
    {
        int roll_no;
        char name[80];
        float fees;
        char DOB[80];
    }STUDENT;
    STUDENT stud1;
    fp = fopen("student_details.dat", "w");
    if(fp == NULL)
    {
        printf("\n File Opening Error");
        return 0;
    }
    printf("\n Enter the roll number: ");
    scanf("%d", &stud1.roll_no);
    while(stud1.roll_no != -1)
    {
        printf("\n Enter the name: ");
        scanf("%s", stud1.name);
        printf("\n Enter the fees: ");
        scanf("%f", &stud1.fees);
        printf("\n Enter the DOB: ");
        scanf("%s", stud1.DOB);
        fprintf(fp,"%d %s %f %s", stud1.roll_
            no, stud1.name, stud1.fees, stud1.
            DOB);
        fflush(stdin);
        printf("\n Enter the roll number: ");
        scanf("%d", &stud1.roll_no);
    }
    fclose(fp);
    return 0;
}
```

Output

```
Enter the roll number: 01
Enter the name: Aman
Enter the fees: 45000
Enter the DOB: 20-9-91
Enter the roll number: 02
Enter the name: Divij
Enter the fees: 45000
Enter the DOB: 29-10-91
Enter the roll number: 03
Enter the name: Saransh
Enter the fees: 45000
Enter the DOB: 2-3-92
Enter the roll number: -1
```

14. Write a program to read characters until a '*' is entered. Simultaneously store these characters in a file.

```
#include <stdio.h>
int main()
```

```
{
    FILE *fp;
    char ch;
    fp = fopen("characters.dat", "w");
    if(fp == NULL)
    {
       printf("\n File Opening Error");
       return 0;
    }
    printf("\n Enter the characters: ");
    scanf("%c", &ch);
    while(ch != '*')
    {
       fprintf(fp, "%c", ch);
       scanf("%c", &ch);
    }
    printf("\n Written to the file");
    fclose(fp);
    return 0;
}
```

Output

```
Enter the characters: abcdef*
Written to the file
```

15. Write a program to count the number of lower case, upper case, numbers, and special characters present in the contents of a file. (Assume that the file contains the following data: 1. Hello, How are you?)

```
#include <stdio.h>
int main(int argc, char *argv[])
{
    FILE *fp;
    int ch, upper_case = 0, lower_case = 0,
    numbers = 0, special_chars = 0;
    if(argc != 2)
    {
       printf("\n Full information is not
          provided");
       return 0;
    }
    fp = fopen(argv[1], "r");
    if(fp == NULL)
    {
       printf("\n File Opening Error");
       return 0;
    }
    int i = 0;
    while(feof(fp) == 0)
    {
       fscanf(fp, "%c", &ch);
       if (ch >= 'A' && ch <= 'Z')
          upper_case++;
       if (ch >= 'a' && ch <= 'z')
          lower_case++;
       if (ch >= '0' && ch <= '9')
          numbers++;
       else
          special_chars++;
    }
    fclose(fp);
    printf("\n Number of upper case
    characters = %d", upper_case);
    printf("\n Number of lower case
    characters = %d", lower_case);
    printf("\n Number of digits = %d",
    numbers);
    printf("\n Number of special characters
      = %d", special_chars);
    return 0;
}
```

Output

```
Number of upper case characters = 2
Number of lower case characters = 12
Number of digits = 1
Number of special characters = 3
```

16. Write a program to write record of students to a file using array of structures.

```
#include <stdio.h>
int main()
{
    FILE *fp;
    typedef struct student
    {
       int roll_no;
       char name[80];
       int marks;
    }STUDENT;
    STUDENT stud1[5];
    int i;
    fp = fopen("student_details.txt", "w");
    if(fp == NULL)
    {
       printf("\n File Opening Error");
       return 0;
    }
    for(i = 0; i < 3;i++)
    {
       printf("\n Enter the roll number: ");
       scanf("%d", &stud1[i].roll_no);
       printf("\n Enter the name: ");
       scanf("%s", stud1[i].name);
       printf("\n Enter the marks: ");
       scanf("%d", &stud1[i].marks);
```

```
    }
    // PRINT ON SCREEN
    for(i = 0;i < 3;i++)
    {
        printf("\n *** STUDENT'S DETAILS ***");
        printf("\n ROLL No. = %d", stud1[i].roll_no);
        printf("\n NAME = %s", stud1[i].name);
        printf("\n MARKS = %d", stud1[i].marks);
        // WRITE TO FILE
        fprintf(fp,"%d %s %d", stud1[i].roll_no,
            stud1[i].name, stud1[i].marks);
    }
    printf("\n Data Written to the file");
    fclose(fp);
    return 0;
}
```

Output

```
***STUDENT'S DETAILS ***
ROLL No. = 01
NAME = Aditya
MARKS = 78
***STUDENT'S DETAILS ***
ROLL No. = 02
NAME = Goransh
MARKS = 100
***STUDENT'S DETAILS ***
ROLL No. = 03
NAME = Sarthak
MARKS = 81
Data Written to the file
```

17. Write a program to append a record to the student's file.

```
#include <stdio.h>
int main()
{
    FILE *fp;
    typedef struct student
    {
        int roll_no;
        char name[80];
        int marks;
    }STUDENT;
    STUDENT stud1;
    fp = fopen("student_details.txt", "a");
    if(fp == NULL)
    {
        printf("\n File Opening Error");
        return 0;
    }
    printf("\n Enter the Roll Number = ");
    scanf("%d", &stud1.roll_no);
    printf("\n Enter the Name = ");
    scanf("%s", stud1.name);
    printf("\n Enter the Marks = ");
    scanf("%d", &stud1.marks);
    fprintf(fp, "\n %d %s %d", stud1.roll_no,
        stud1.name, stud1.marks);
/* After entering the record add a -1 to the
    file to denote the end of records */
    fprintf("fp, %d", -1);
    printf("\n Data Appended");
    fclose(fp);
    return 0;
}
```

Output

```
Enter the Roll Number = 04
Enter the Name = Sanchita
Enter the Marks = 50
Data Appended
```

18. Write a program to read the record of a particular student.

```
#include <stdio.h>
int main()
{
  FILE *fp1;
  typedef struct student
  {
    int roll_no;
    char name[80];
    int marks;
}STUDENT;
STUDENT stud1;
int found =0, rno;
fp1 = fopen("student_details.txt", "r");
if(fp1 == NULL)
{
   printf("\n File Opening Error");
   return 0;
}
printf("\n Enter the roll number of the
   student whose record has to be read: ");
scanf("%d", &rno);
while(1)
{
fscanf(fp1, "%d %s %d", &stud1.roll_no, stud1.
   name, &stud1.marks);
if(stud1.roll_no == -1)
break;
if(stud1.roll_no == rno)
{
   found = 1;
```

```
printf("\n The details of student are");
printf(" %d %s %d", stud1.roll_no,
stud1.name, stud1.marks);
  break;
  }
}
if (found==0)
  printf("\n Record not found in the file");
fclose(fp1);
return 0;
}
```

Output

```
Enter the roll number of the student whose
   record has to be read: 02
The details of student are - 02 Goransh 100
```

19. Write a program to edit the record of a particular student.

```
#include <stdio.h>
int main()
{
   FILE *fp1, *fp2;
   typedef struct student
   {
      int roll_no;
      char name[80];
      int marks;
   }STUDENT;
   STUDENT stud1;
   int found = 0, rno;
   fp1 = fopen("student_details.txt", "r");
   if(fp1 == NULL)
   {
      printf("\n File Opening Error");
      return 0;
   }
   fp2 = fopen("temp.txt", "w");
   if(fp2 == NULL)
   {
      printf("\n File Opening Error");
      return 0;
   }
   printf("\n Enter the roll number of the
      student whose record has to be
      modified: ");
   scanf("%d", &rno);
   while(1)
   {
      fscanf(fp1, "%d", &stud1.roll_no);
      if(stud1.roll_no == -1)
      break;
      if(stud1.roll_no == rno)
      {
      found = 1;
      fscanf(fp1, "%s %d", stud1.name,
         &stud1.marks);
      printf("\n The details of existing
        record are ");
      printf(" %d %s %d", stud1.roll_no,
        stud1.name, stud1.marks);
      printf("\n Enter the modified name of
        the student: ");
      scanf("%s", stud1.name);
      printf("\n Enter the modified marks of
        the student: ");
      scanf("%d", &stud1.marks);
      /* Write the modified record to the
        temporary file */
      fprintf(fp2, "%d %s %d", stud1.roll_no,
        stud1.name, stud1.marks);
      }
      else
      {
        /* Copy the non-matching records to
              the temporary file     */
        fscanf(fp1, "%s %d", stud1.name,
           &stud1.marks);
        fprintf(fp2, "%d %s %d", stud1.roll_no,
           stud1.name, stud1.marks);
      }
   }
   fprintf(fp2,"%d", -1);
   fclose(fp1);
   fclose(fp2);
   if(found==0)
   printf("\n The record with roll number %d
     was not found in the file", rno);
   else
   {
      fp1 = fopen("student_details.txt", "w");
      if(fp1 == NULL)
      {
      printf("\n File Opening Error");
      return 0;
      }
      fp2 = fopen("temp.txt", "r");
      if(fp2 == NULL)
      {
      printf("\n File Opening Error");
      return 0;
      }
      /* Copy the contents of temporary file
        into actual file */
      while(1)
      {
      fscanf(fp2,"%d",&stud1.roll_no);
      if(stud1.roll_no==-1)
      break;
      fscanf(fp2, "%s %d",stud1.name,
        &stud1.marks);
      fprintf(fp1, "%d %s %d", stud1.roll_
        no, stud1.name, stud1.marks);
      }
   }
```

```
    fclose(fp1);
    fclose(fp2);
    printf("\n Record Updated");
    return 0;
}
```

Output

```
Enter the roll number of the student whose
    record has to be modified: 03
The details of exisitng record are - 03
    Sarthak 81
Enter the modified name of the student: Sarthak
Enter the modified marks of the student: 85
Record Updated
```

20. Write a program to delete the record of a particular student.

```
#include <stdio.h>
int main()
{
    FILE *fp1, *fp2;
    typedef struct student
    {
        int roll_no;
        char name[80];
        int marks;
    }STUDENT;
    STUDENT stud1;
    int found =0, rno;
    fp1 = fopen("student_details.txt", "r");
    if(fp1 == NULL)
    {
        printf("\n File Opening Error");
        return 0;
    }
    fp2 = fopen("temp.txt", "w");
    if(fp2 == NULL)
    {
        printf("\n File Opening Error");
        return 0;
    }
    printf("\n Enter the roll number of the
        student whose record has to be
        deleted: ");
    scanf("%d", &rno);
    while(1)
    {
        fscanf(fp1, "%d", &stud1.roll_no);
        if(stud1.roll_no == -1)
        break;
        if(stud1.roll_no == rno)
        {
        found = 1;
        fscanf(fp1, "%s %d", stud1.name,
            &stud1.marks);
        }
        /* The matching record is not copied
            to temp file */
        else
        {
        /* Copy the non-matching records to
            the temporary file */
        fscanf(fp1, "%s %d", stud1.name,
            &stud1.marks);
        fprintf(fp2, "%d %s %d ", stud1.roll_
            no, stud1.name, stud1.marks);
        }
    }
    fprintf(fp2," %d", -1);
    fclose(fp1);
    fclose(fp2);
    if(found==0)
    printf("\n The record with roll number %d
        was not found in the file", rno);
    else
    {
        fp1 = fopen("student_details.txt", "w");
        if(fp1 == NULL)
        {
        printf("\n File Opening Error");
        return 0;
        }
        fp2 = fopen("temp.txt", "r");
        if(fp2 == NULL)
        {
        printf("\n File Opening Error");
        return 0;
        }
        /* Copy the contents of temporary file
            into actual file */
        while(1)
        {
        fscanf(fp2,"%d",&stud1.roll_no);
        if(stud1.roll_no==-1)
        break;
        fscanf(fp2, "%s %d",stud1.name,
            &stud1.marks);
        fprintf(fp1, "%d %s %d ", stud1.roll_
            no, stud1.name, stud1.marks);
        }
    }
    fprintf(fp1, "%d ",-1);
    fclose(fp1);
    fclose(fp2);
    printf("\n Record Deleted");
    /* The programmer may delete the temp
    file which will no longer be required */
    return 0;
}
```

Output

```
Enter the roll number of the student whose
   record has to be deleted: 01
Record Deleted
```

21. Write a program to store records of an employee in employee file. The data must be stored using binary file.

```
#include <stdio.h>
int main()
{
   typedef struct employee
   {
      int emp_code;
      char name[20];
      int hra;
      int da;
      int ta;
   };
   FILE *fp;
   struct employee e[5];
   int i;
   fp = fopen("employee.txt", "wb");
   if(fp==NULL)
   {
      printf("\n Error opening file");
      exit(1);
   }
   printf("\n Enter the details ");
   for(i = 0; i < 2; i++)
   {
      printf("\n\n Enter the employee code:");
      scanf("%d", &e[i].emp_code);
      printf("\n\n Enter the name of the
         employee: ");
      scanf("%s", e[i].name);
      printf("\n\n Enter the HRA, DA, and TA: ");
      scanf("%d %d %d", &e[i].hra, &e[i].da,
         &e[i].ta);
      fwrite(&e[i], sizeof(e[i]), 1, fp);
   }
   fclose(fp);
   return 0;
}
```

Output

```
Enter the details
Enter the employee code: 01
Enter the name of the employee: Gargi
Enter the HRA, DA and TA: 10000 2000 5000
Enter the employee code: 02
Enter the name of the employee: Nikita
Enter the HRA, DA and TA: 10000 2000 5000
```

22. Write a to read the records stored in 'employee.txt' file in binary mode.

```
#include <stdio.h>
int main()
{
   typedef struct employee
   {
      int emp_code;
      char name[20];
      int hra;
      int da;
      int ta;
   };
   FILE *fp;
   struct employee e;
   int i;
   fp = fopen("employee.txt", "rb");
   if(fp==NULL)
   {
      printf("\n Error opening file");
      exit(1);
   }
   printf("\n THE DETAILS OF THE EMPLOYEES ARE ");
   while(1)
   {
      fread(&e, sizeof(e), 1, fp);
      if(feof(fp))
      break;
      printf("\n\n Employee Code: %d", e.emp_code);
      printf("\n\n Name: %s", e.name);
      printf("\n\n HRA, DA, and TA: %d %d
         %d", e.hra, e.da, e.ta);
   }
   fclose(fp);
   return 0;
```

Output

```
THE DETAILS OF THE EMPLOYEES ARE
Employee Code: 01
Name: Gargi
HRA, DA and TA: 10000 5000 2000
Employee Code: 02
Name: Nikita
HRA, DA and TA: 10000 5000 2000
```

23. Write a program to append a record to the employee file (binary file).

```
#include <stdio.h>
int main()
{
   typedef struct employee
   {
      int emp_code;
      char name[20];
      int hra;
      int da;
```

```
    int ta;
  };
  FILE *fp;
  struct employee e;
  int i;
  fp = fopen("employee.txt", "ab");
  if(fp==NULL)
  {
    printf("\n Error opening file");
    exit(1);
  }
  printf("\n\n Enter the employee code:");
  scanf("%d", &e.emp_code);
  printf("\n\n Enter the name of employee: ");
  scanf("%s", e.name);
  printf("\n\n Enter the HRA, DA, and TA:");
  scanf("%d %d %d", &e.hra, &e.da, &e.ta);
  fwrite(&e, sizeof(e), 1, fp);
  fclose(fp);
  printf("\n Record Appended");
  return 0;
}
```

Output

```
Enter the employee code: 06
Enter the name of employee: Tanya
Enter the HRA, DA and TA: 20000 10000 3000
Record Appended
```

24. Write a program to edit the employee record stored in a binary file.

```
#include <stdio.h>
int main()
{
  typedef struct employee
  {
    int emp_code;
    char name[20];
    int hra;
    int da;
    int ta;
  };
  FILE *fp1, *fp2;
  struct employee e;
  int i, ec, found = 0;
  fp1 = fopen("employee.txt", "rb");
  if(fp1==NULL)
  {
    printf("\n Error opening file");
    exit(1);
  }
  fp2 = fopen("temp_emp.txt", "wb");
  if(fp2==NULL)
  {
    printf("\n Error opening file");
    exit(1);
  }
  printf("\n Enter the code of the employee
    whose information has to be edited: ");
  scanf("%d",&ec);
  while(1)
  {
    fread(&e,sizeof(e),1,fp1);
    if(feof(fp1))
    break;
    if(e.emp_code==ec)
    {
    found=1;
    printf("\n The existing record is: %d
      %s %d %d %d", e.emp_code, e.name,
      e.hra, e.ta, e.da);
    printf("\n Enter the modified name: ");
    scanf("%s", e.name);
    printf("\n Enter the modified HRA, TA,
      and DA: ");
    scanf("%d %d %d", &e.hra, &e.ta, &e.da);
    fwrite(&e, sizeof(e),1,fp2);
    }
    else
    fwrite(&e, sizeof(e),1,fp2);
  }
  fclose(fp1);
  fclose(fp2);
  if(found==0)
  printf("\n Record not found");
  else
  {
    fp1 = fopen("employee.txt", "wb");
    if(fp1==NULL)
    {
    printf("\n Error opening file");
    exit(1);
    }
    fp2 = fopen("temp_emp.txt", "rb");
    if(fp2==NULL)
    {
    printf("\n Error opening file");
    exit(1);
    }
    while(1)
    {
    fread(&e, sizeof(e),1,fp2);
    if(feof(fp2))
    break;
    fwrite(&e, sizeof(e), 1, fp1);
    }
  }
  fclose(fp1);
  fclose(fp2);
  printf("\n Record Edited");
```

```
    return 0;
}
```

Output

```
Enter the code of the employee whose
    information has to be edited: 01
The existing record is: 01 Gargi 10000 5000
    2000
Enter the modified name: Gargi
Enter the modified HRA, TA, and DA: 20000 10000
    30000
Record Edited
```

16.8 FUNCTIONS FOR SELECTING A RECORD RANDOMLY

In this section, we will read about functions that are used to randomly access a record stored in a binary file. These functions include `fseek()`, `ftell()`, `rewind()`, `fgetpos()`, and `fsetpos()`.

16.8.1 fseek()

The `fseek()` function is used to reposition a binary stream. The prototype of `fseek()` function which is defined in `stdio.h` can be given as

```
int fseek(FILE *stream, long offset, int
    origin);
```

`fseek()` is used to set the file position pointer for the given stream. The variable offset is an integer value that gives the number of bytes to move forward or backward in the file. The value of offset may be positive or negative, provided it makes sense. For example, you cannot specify a negative offset if you are starting at the beginning of the file. The `origin` value should have one of the following values (defined in `stdio.h`):

- `SEEK_SET`: to perform input or output on `offset` bytes from start of the file
- `SEEK_CUR`: to perform input or output on `offset` bytes from the current position in the file
- `SEEK_END`: to perform input or output on `offset` bytes from the end of the file
- `SEEK_SET`, `SEEK_CUR`, and `SEEK_END` are defined constants with value `0`, `1`, and `2`, respectively.

Programming Tip:
While using `fseek()`, if the third parameter is specified as `SEEK_END`, then you must provide a negative offset, otherwise it will try to access beyond `EOF`.

On successful operation, `fseek()` returns zero and in case of failure, it returns a non-zero value. For example, if you try to perform a seek operation on a file that is not opened in binary mode then a non-zero value will be returned. `fseek()` can be used to move the file pointer beyond a file, but not before the beginning.

Note

If a file has been opened for update and later if you want to switch from reading to writing or vice versa, then you must use `fseek()`.

Table 16.5 gives the interpretation of the `fseek()` fuction.

Table 16.5 Origin field in `fseek()`.

Function Call	Meaning
fseek (fp, 0L, SEEK_SET);	Move to the beginning of the file
fseek (fp, 0L, SEEK_CUR);	Stay at the current position
fseek (fp, 0L, SEEK_END);	Go to the end of the file
fseek (fp, m, SEEK_CUR);	Move forward by m bytes in the file from the current location
fseek (fp, -m, SEEK_CUR);	Move backwards by m bytes in file from the current location
fseek (fp, -m, SEEK_END);	Move backwards by m bytes from the end of the file

The `fseek()` function is primarily used with binary files as it has limited functionality with text files.

25. Write a program to randomly read the nth record of a binary file.

```
#include <stdio.h>
int main()
{
    typedef struct employee
    {
        int emp_code;
        char name[20];
        int hra;
        int da;
        int ta;
    };
    FILE *fp;
    struct employee e;
    int result, rec_no;
    fp = fopen("employee.txt", "rb");
    if(fp==NULL)
    {
        printf("\n Error opening file");
        exit(1);
    }
    printf("\n\n Enter the rec_no you want to
      read: ");
    scanf("%d", &rec_no);
    if(rec_no >= 0)
    {
```

```
    /* from the file pointed by fp read a
       record of the specified record
       starting from the beginning of the
       file*/
    fseek(fp, (rec_no-1)*sizeof(e), SEEK_SET);
    result = fread(&e, sizeof(e), 1, fp);
    if(result == 1)
    {
    printf("\n  EMPLOYEE CODE: %d", e.emp_code);
    printf("\n Name: %s", e.name);
    printf("\n HRA, TA and DA: %d %d %d",
       e.hra, e.ta, e.da);
    }
    else
    printf("\n Record Not Found");
  }
  fclose(fp);
  return 0;
}
```

Output

```
Enter the rec_no you want to read: 06
EMPLOYEE CODE: 06
Name: Tanya
HRA, DA and TA: 20000 10000 3000
```

26. Write a program to print the records in reverse order. The file must be opened in binary mode. Use `fseek()`.

```
#include <stdio.h>
int main()
{
  typedef struct employee
  {
    int emp_code;
    char name[20];
    int hra;
    int da;
    int ta;
  };
  FILE *fp;
  struct employee e;
  int result, i;
  fp =  fopen("employee.txt", "rb");
  if(fp==NULL)
  {
    printf("\n Error opening file");
    exit(1);
  }
  for(i=1;i>=0;i--)
  {
    fseek(fp, i*sizeof(e), SEEK_SET);
    fread(&e, sizeof(e), 1, fp);
    printf("\n  EMPLOYEE CODE: %d", e.emp_code);
    printf("\n Name: %s", e.name);
    printf("\n HRA, TA, and DA: %d %d %d",
       e.hra, e.ta, e.da);
  }
  fclose(fp);
  return 0;
}
```

Output

```
EMPLOYEE CODE: 06
Name: Tanya
HRA, DA and TA: 20000 10000 3000
EMPLOYEE CODE: 05
Name: Ruchi
HRA, DA and TA: 10000 6000 3000
```

27. Write a program to edit a record in binary mode using `fseek()`.

```
#include <stdio.h>
int main()
{
  typedef struct employee
  {
    int emp_code;
    char name[20];
    int hra;
    int da;
  int ta;
  };
  FILE *fp;
  struct employee e;
  int rec_no;
  fp = fopen("employee.txt", "r+");
  if(fp==NULL)
  {
    printf("\n Error opening file");
    exit(1);
  }
  printf("\n Enter record no. to be modified: ");
  scanf("%d", &rec_no);
  fseek(fp, (rec_no-1)*sizeof(e), SEEK_SET);
  fread(&e, sizeof(e), 1, fp);
  printf("\n Enter modified name of the employee: ");
  scanf("%s", e.name);
  printf("\n Enter the modified HRA, TA,
  and DA of the employee: ");
  scanf("%d %d %d", &e.hra, &e.ta, &e.da);
  fwrite(&e, sizeof(e), 1, fp);
  fclose(fp);
    printf("\n Record Edited");
  return 0;
}
```

Output

```
Enter record no. to be modified: 04
Enter modified name of the employee: Ananya
```

```
Enter the modified HRA, TA, and DA of the
   employee: 30000 1000 5000
Record Edited
```

16.8.2 ftell()

The `ftell()`function is used to know the current position of file pointer. It is at this position where the next input or ouput operation will be performed. The syntax of `ftell()`, defined in `stdio.h`, can be given as

```
long ftell (FILE *stream);
```

Here, `stream` points to the file whose file position indicator has to be determined. If successful, `ftell()` function returns the current file position (in bytes) for stream. However, in case of error, `ftell()` returns `-1`.

When using `ftell()`, error can occur because of the following two reasons:

- First, using `ftell()` with a device that cannot store data (e.g., keyboard).
- Second, when the position is larger than that can be represented in a `long` integer. This will usually happen when dealing with very large files.

Look at the program code which illustrates the use of `ftell()`.

```
/*The program writes data to a file, saves the
   number of bytes stored in it in a variable
   n (by using ftell ()) and then re-opens
   the file to read n bytes from the file and
   simultaneously display it on the screen.*/

main()
{
   FILE *fp;
   char c;
   int n;
   fp=fopen("abc","w");
   if(fp==NULL)
   {
      printf("\n Error Opening The File");
      exit(1);
   }
   while((c=getchar())!=EOF)
   putc(c,fp);
   n = ftell(fp);
   fclose(fp);
   fp=fopen("abc","r");
   if(fp==NULL)
   {
      printf("\n Error Opening The File");
      exit(1);
   }
   while(ftell(fp)<n)
   {
      c = fgetc(fp);
      printf("%c", c);
   }
   fclose(fp);
}
Output
abcdefghijkjdqjdh
```

Note

`ftell()` is useful when we have to deal with text files for which position of the data cannot be calculated.

16.8.3 rewind()

`rewind()` is used to adjust the position of file pointer so that the next I/O operation will take place at the beginning of the file. It is defined in `stdio.h` and its prototype can be given as

```
void rewind(FILE *f);
```

`rewind()` is equivalent to calling `fseek()` with following parameters:

```
fseek(f,0L,SEEK_SET);
```

We have seen earlier that if a file is opened for writing and you want to read it later, then you have to close the existing file and reopen it so that data can be read from the beginning of the file. The other alternative is to to use `rewind()`. Look at the program code given below which demonstrates the use of `rewind()`.

```
#include <stdio.h>
int main()
{
   FILE *fp;
   char feedback[80];
   int i=0;
   fp = fopen("comments.txt", "w+");
   if(fp==NULL)
   {
      printf("\n Error Opening The File");
      exit(1);
   }
   printf("\n Provide comments on this book:
      ");
   scanf("%s", feedback);
   while(feedback[i]!='\0')
   {
      fputc(feedback[i], fp);
      i++;
   }
   rewind(fp);
   printf("\n Contents of the file are: ");
   while(feof(fp)==0)
      printf("%c", fgetc(fp));
   fclose(fp);
   return 0;
}
```

Output

```
Provide comments on this book: Good
Contents of the file are: Good
```

However, you must prefer to use `fseek()` equivalent code rather calling `rewind()` because it is impossible to determine if `rewind()` was successful or not.

16.8.4 fgetpos()

The `fgetpos()` function is used to determine the current position of the stream. The prototype of the `fgetpos()` function as given in `stdio.h` is

```
int fgetpos(FILE *stream, fpos_t *pos);
```

Here, `stream` is the file whose current file pointer position has to be determined. `pos` is used to point to the location where `fgetpos()` can store the position information. In simple words, `fgetpos()` stores the file position indicator of the given file stream in the `pos` variable. The `pos` variable is of type `fpos_t` which is defined in `stdio.h` and is basically an object that can hold every possible position in a `FILE`.

On success, `fgetpos()` returns zero and in case of an error a non-zero value is returned. The value of `pos` obtained through `fgetpos()` can be used by the `fsetpos()` function to return to this same position.

16.8.5 fsetpos()

The `fsetpos()` function is used to move the file position indicator of a stream to the location indicated by the information obtained in `'pos'` by making a call to `fgetpos()`. Like `fgetpos()`, `fsetpos()` is defined in `stdio.h` and its prototype can be given as

```
int fsetpos(FILE *stream, const fpos_t pos);
```

Here, `stream` points to the file whose file pointer indicator has to be re-positioned. `pos` points to positioning information as returned by `fgetpos`.

On success, `fsetpos()` returns a zero and clears the `EOF` indicator. In case of failure it returns a non-zero value.

After the successful call to `fsetpos()`, the next operation on a stream in update mode may be input or output. Look at the program code given below which illustrates the use of `fgetpos()` and `fsetpos()` functions.

Programming Tip: An error will be generated if you try to place the file position indicator before the first byte of the file.

Look at the program given below which opens a file and reads bytes at several different locations.

```
#include <stdio.h>
main()
{
   FILE *fp;
   fpos_t pos;
   char text[20];
   fp = fopen("practise.c", "rb");
   if(fp == NULL)
   {
      printf("\n Error opening file");
      exit(1);
   }
   /* Read some data and then check the
   position. */
   fread(text, sizeof(char), 20, fp);
   if(fgetpos(fp, &pos) != 0)
   {
      printf("\n Error in fgetpos()");
      exit(1);
   }
   fread(text, sizeof(char), 20, fp);
   printf("\n 20 bytes at byte %ld: %s",
   pos, text);

   /* Set a new random position and read
   more data */
   pos = 90;
   if(fsetpos(fp, &pos) != 0)
   {
      printf("\n Error in fsetpos()");
      exit(1);
   }
   fread(text, sizeof(char), 20, fp);
   printf("\n 20 bytes at byte %ld: %s", pos,
   text);
   fclose(fp);
}
```

Output

```
20 bytes at byte 20:
ma
20 bytes at byte 90:
return 0;
}
```

Programming Tip: Only use values for `fsetpos()` that are returned from `fgetpos()`.

16.9 DELETING A FILE

The `remove()` function as the name suggests, is used to erase a file. The prototype of `remove()` as given in `stdio.h` can be given as

```
int remove(const char *filename);
```

The `remove()` function will erase the file specified by `filename`. On success, the function will return zero and in case of error, it will return a non-zero value.

If `filename` specifies a directory, then `remove (filename)` is the equivalent of `rmdir(filename)`. Otherwise, if filename specifies the name of a file then `remove(filename)` is the equivalent of `unlink(filename)`. Look at the program given below which deletes the file `"temp.txt"` from the current directory.

```
#include <stdio.h>
main()
{
   remove("temp.txt");
   return 0;
}
```

Note

You may specify the path of the file which has to be deleted as the argument of `remove()`.

16.10 RENAMING A FILE

The `rename()` function, as the name suggests, is used to rename a file. The prototype of the function is

```
int rename(const char *oldname, const char
   *newname)
```

Here, `oldname` specifies the pathname of the file to be renamed and `newname` gives the new pathname of the file.

On success, `rename ()` returns zero. In case of error, it will return a non-zero value and will set the `errno` to indicate the error. When an error occurs neither the file named by `oldname` nor the file named by `newname` shall be changed or created.

Points to remember about `rename()`

- If the `oldname` specifies the pathname of a file that is not a directory, the `newname` shall also not point to the pathname of a directory.
- If the `oldname` specifies the pathname of a directory then the `newname` shall not point to the pathname of a file that is not a directory. In this case, if the directory named by the `newname` already exists then it shall be removed and `oldname` will be renamed to newname.

Look at the program code given below which illustrates the use of `rename()`.

```
#include <stdio.h>
main()
{
   int success=0;
   success = rename("comments.txt",
   "feedback.txt");
   if(success != 0)
   printf("\n The file could not be renamed");
}
```

16.11 CREATING A TEMPORARY FILE

The `tmpfile()` function is used to create a temporary file. The `tmpfile()` function opens the corresponding stream with access parameters set as `"w+"`. The file created with `tmpfile()` will be automatically deleted when all references to the file are closed, i.e., the file created will be automatically closed and erased when the program has been completely executed. The prototype of `tmpfile()` as given in `stdio.h` header file is

```
FILE * tmpfile(void);
```

On success, `tmpfile()` will return a pointer to the stream of the file that is created. In case of an error, the function will return a `NULL` pointer and set `errno` to indicate the error.

The function can be used in the following manner:

```
FILE *tp = tmpfile();
```

Now the file created can be used in the same way as any other text or binary file.

POINTS TO REMEMBER

- A file is a collection of data stored on a secondary storage device such as a hard disk.
- Stream is a logical interface to the devices that are connected to the computer. The three standard streams in C language are standard input (`stdin`), standard output (`stdout`), and standard error (`stderr`).
- When a stream linked to a disk file is created, a buffer is automatically created and associated with the stream.
- A text file is a stream of characters that can be sequentially processed by a computer in forward direction. A binary file is a file which may contain any type of data, encoded in binary form for computer storage and processing purposes. While text files can be processed sequentially, binary files, on the other hand, can be either processed sequentially or randomly.
- A file must be first opened before data can be read from it or written to it. In order to open a file and associate it with a stream, the `fopen()` function is used.
- To close an open file, the `fclose()` function is used which disconnects a file pointer from a file. `fclose()` not only closes the file but also flushes all the buffers that are maintained for that file.
- If you have opened a stream for updating and later you want to switch from reading to writing or vice

versa, you must first use the `fseek()` or `rewind()` function.

- When an output stream is unbuffered, information appears on the destination device as soon as it is written. When it is buffered, characters are saved internally and then written out as a group. In order to force buffered characters to be output on the destination device before the buffer is full, use `fflush()`.
- `fseek()` is used to reposition a binary stream. The `ftell()` function is used to know the current position of file pointer. It is at this position at which the next input or output operation will be performed.
- The `fgetpos()` function is used to determine the current position of the stream. The `rename()` function is used to rename a file. The `remove()` function is used to erase a file.
- The `tmpfile()` function is used to create a temporary file. The `tmpfile()` opens the corresponding stream with access parameters set as "w+". The file created with `tmpfile()` will be automatically deleted when all references to the file are closed.

GLOSSARY

Binary file A binary file is a file which may contain any type of data, encoded in binary form for computer storage and processing purposes.

Buffer A buffer is a block of memory that is used for temporary storage of data, that has to be read from or written to a file.

File A file is a collection of data stored on a secondary storage device like hard disk.

Standard error Standard error is basically an output stream used by programs to report error messages or diagnostics.

Standard input Standard input is the stream from which the program receives its data.

Standard output Standard output is the stream where a program writes its output data.

Stream Stream is a logical interface to the devices that are connected to the computer.

Text file A text file is a stream of characters that can be sequentially processed by a computer in the forward direction.

EXERCISES

Fill in the Blanks

1. ____________ is a collection of data.
2. The standard streams in C are ____________, ____________, and ____________.
3. ____________ are pre-connected input and output channels between a text terminal and the program.
4. A file must be opened in ____________ mode if it is being opened for updating.
5. ____________ function can be used to move the file marker at the beginning of the file.
6. If a file is opened in 'wb' mode then it is a ____________ file opened for writing.
7. Block input in binary file is done using the ____________ function.
8. ____________ is the stream where a program writes its output data.
9. ____________ is a block of memory that is used for temporary storage of data.
10. The creation and operation of the buffer is automatically handled by the ____________.
11. ____________ file can be processed sequentially as well as randomly.
12. ____________ function closes the file and flushes all the buffers that are maintained for that file.
13. To use `fprintf()` to write on the screen, specify ____________ in place of the file pointer.
14. If you have opened a stream for updating and later you want to switch from reading to writing or vice versa, you must first use the ____________ or ____________ function.
15. The symbolic constant EOF is defined in ____________ and has the value ____________.

Multiple-choice Questions

1. Which function gives the current position of the file?
   (a) `fseek()` (b) `fsetpos()`
   (c) `ftell()` (d) `rewind()`

2. Which function is used to perform block output in binary files?

   (a) `fwrite()` (b) `fprintf()`

   (c) `fputc()` (d) `fputs()`

3. Select the standard stream in C.

   (a) `stdin` (b) `stdout`

   (c) `stderr` (d) all of these

4. From which standard stream does a C program read data?

   (a) `stdin` (b) `stdout`

   (c) `stderr` (d) all of these

5. What acts as an interface between stream and hardware?

   (a) file pointer (b) buffer

   (c) `stdout` (d) `stdin`

6. Which function is used to associate a file with a stream?

   (a) `fread()` (b) `fopen()`

   (c) `floes()` (d) `fflush()`

7. Which function returns the next character from stream, EOF if the end of file is reached, or if there is an error?

   (a) `fgetc()` (b) `fgets()`

   (c) `fputc()` (d) `fwrite()`

State True or False

1. You can use a file without opening it.
2. It is mandatory to close all the files before exiting the program.
3. `stderr` is a standard stream in C.
4. An error will be generated if you try to position the file marker beyond EOF.
5. A file can be read if and only if it is opened in "r" mode.
6. Binary files are slower than text files.
7. In text files, the data is stored in internal format of the computer.
8. Text files can store only character data.
9. Standard output is an output stream used by programs to report error messages or diagnostics.
10. Each line in a text file can have a maximum of 80 characters.
11. Binary files store data in a human readable format.
12. `fread()`returns the number of elements successfully read.
13. `fseek()` is used to reposition a binary stream.
14. The `tmpfile()` function opens the corresponding stream with access parameters set as "w+".
15. The value obtained by using `fgetpos()` can be used only with `fsetpos()`.

Review Questions

1. What is a file?
2. Why do we need to store data in files?
3. Define the term stream.
4. Differentiate between a text file and a binary file.
5. Explain the different modes in which a file can be opened in a C program.
6. Under which circumstances does the `fopen()` fail?
7. Why should you close a file after it is used?
8. What is the impact of `fclose()` on buffered data?
9. Differentiate between `gets()` and `fgets()`.
10. What is the difference between a buffered output stream and an unbuffered output stream?
11. Under what circumstances does the `ftell()` fail?
12. Where can `ftell()` be used?
13. Write a short note on `fgetpos()` and `fsetpos()`.
14. What will happen if the argument to `remove()` specifies a directory? Also state its behaviour when the argument is a filename.
15. Give the importance of associating a buffer with the stream.
16. Write a short note on functions that are used to: (a) read data from a file (b) write data to a file.
17. Write a short note on the following functions. For each function, give a program code that demonstrates its usage.

    (a) `fopen()` (b) `fclose()`

    (c) `ferror()` (d) `clearerr()`

18. What do you understand by EOF?
19. How will you check for EOF when reading a file?
20. Why is it not possible to read from a file and write to the same file without resetting the file pointer?
21. Write a short note on error handling while performing operations.
22. Give the importance of `rewind()`.
23. Differentiate between `rewind()` and `fseek()`. Can `fseek()` work as an alternative to `rewind()`? If yes, how?
24. Why do we need `fflush()`?
25. Differentiate between `fscanf()`and `fread()`.

Programming Exercises

1. Write a program that uses a temporary file created using `tmpfile()`.
2. Write a program to write employees details in a file called employee.dat. Then read the record of the nth employee and calculate his salary.
3. Write a program to read the nth record and display it on screen. Repeat the procedure until –1 is entered.
4. Write a program to copy a file using `feof()`.
5. Create a file and store some names in it. Write a program to read the names in the file in the reverse order without re-opening the file.
6. Write a program to read the contents of a binary file.
7. Write a program to read the contents of a text file.
8. Write a program to write some contents into (a) a binary file (b) a text file.
9. Write a program to read a text file using `fscanf()`.
10. Write a program to read a text file using `fgetc()`.

11. Write a program to illustrate the use of `fprintf()`.
12. Write a program to illustrate the use of `fputc()`.
13. Write a program to count the number of characters in a file.
14. Write a program that reads the file name and text of 20 words as command line arguments. Write the text into a file whose name is given as the file name.
15. Write a program to read data from the keyboard and write it to a file. Read the contents stored in the file and display it on the screen.
16. Write a menu-driven program to read, insert, append, delete, and edit a record stored in a binary file.
17. Write a program to read data from a text file and store it in a binary file. Also read the data stored in the binary file and display it on the screen.
18. Write a program to read a text file, convert all the lower case characters into upper case and re-write the upper case characters in the file. Before the end of the program, all the temporary files must be deleted.
19. Modify the above code fragment to allow the user three chances to enter a valid filename. If a valid file name is not entered after three chances, terminate the program.
20. Assume that there are two files—Names1 and Names2 that store sorted names of students who would be participating in Activity1 and Activity2, respectively. Create a file NAMES.TXT which stores the names from both the files. Note that there should be no repetition of names in NAMES.TXT and while writing name into it, ensure that the file is also sorted.
21. Write a program to create a file that stores only integer values. Append the sum of these integers at the end of the file.
22. Write a program that reads a binary file that stores employees records and prints on the screen the number of records that are stored in the file.
23. Write a program to append a binary file at the end of another.
24. Assume that a file INTEGERS.TXT stores only integer numbers. A value '-1' is stored as the last value to indicate EOF. Write a program to read each integer value stored in the file. While reading the value, compute whether the value is even or odd. If it is even then write that value in a file called EVEN.TXT else write it in ODD.TXT. Finally display the contents of the two files— EVEN.TXT and ODD.TXT.

    Hint: You may use getw and putw functions. They are same as `getc()`and `putc()`. The prototypes of `getw()` and `putw()`are

    ```
    int getw(FILE *fp); and putw(int value, FILE
       *fp);
    ```

Find the output of the following codes.

1.
```
main()
{
   FILE *fp;
   char c;
   fp=fopen("abc","w");
   while((c=getchar())!=EOF)
     putc(c,fp);
   printf('\n No. of characters entered =
   %ld", ftell(fp));
   fclose(fp);
}
```

2.
```
main()
{
   FILE *fp;
   char comment[20];
   int i;
   fp=fopen("Feedbacks","w");
   for(i = 0;i < 5;i++)
   {
     fscanf(stdin, "%s", comment);
     fprintf(fp, "%s", comment);
   }
   fclose(fp);
}
```

3.
```
main()
{
   char c;
   FILE *fp;
   fp = fopen("temp","w+b");
   for(c = 'A';c <= 'I'; c++)
     fputc(c, fp);
   fseek(fp, 2, 0);
   c = fgetc(fp);
   printf("%c", c);
   fclose(fp);
}
```

4.
```
main()
{
   char c;
   FILE *fp;
   fp = fopen("temp","w+b");
   for(c = 'A';c <= 'I', c++)
     fwrite(&c, 1, 1, fp);
   rewind(fp);
   fread(&c,1,1,fp);
   printf("%c", c);
   fclose(fp);
}
```

5.
```
main()
{
   char c;
   FILE *fp;
   long int pos;
   fp = fopen("temp","w+b");
   for(c = 'A';c <= 'I'; c++)
     fwrite(&c, 1, 1, fp);
   pos = ftell(fp);
   pos = -3;
```

```
    fseek(fp, pos, SEEK_END);
    fread(&c,1,1,fp);
    printf("%c", c);
    fclose(fp);
  }
```

6.

```
main()
  {
    int i;
    FILE *fp;
    long int pos;
    fp = fopen("temp","w+b");
    for(i = 1;i <= 10;i++)
      fwrite(&i, sizeof(int), 1, fp);
    fseek(fp, sizeof(int)*2, SEEK_SET);
    fread(&i,sizeof(int),1,fp);
    printf("%d", i);
    fclose(fp);
  }
```

7.

```
main()
  {
    int i;
    FILE *fp;
    long int pos;
    fp = fopen("temp","w+b");
    for(i = 1;i <= 10;i++)
      fwrite(&i, sizeof(int), 1, fp);
    fseek(fp, -sizeof(int)*2, SEEK_CUR);
    fread(&i,sizeof(int),1,fp);
    printf("%d", i);
    fclose(fp);
  }
```

17 Preprocessor Directives

TAKEAWAYS

- Preprocessor directives
- #error directive
- Pragma directives
- Predefined macro names
- Conditional directives

17.1 INTRODUCTION

The preprocessor is a program that processes the source code before it passes through the compiler. It operates under the control of preprocessor directive which is placed in the source program before `main()`. Before the source code is passed through the compiler, it is examined by the preprocessor for any preprocessor directives. In case the program has some preprocessor directives, appropriate actions are taken (depending on the directive) and the source program is handed over to the compiler.

Preprocessor directives are lines included in C programs that are not program statements but directives for the preprocessor. The preprocessor directives are always preceded by a hash sign (#) directive. The preprocessor directive is executed before the actual compilation of programs code begins. Therefore, the preprocessor expands all the directives and takes the corresponding action before any code is generated by the program statements.

> **Programming Tip:** Preprocessor directives must start with a hash ( ) sign.

The preprocessor directives are only one line long because as soon as a newline character is found, the preprocessor directive is considered to end. No semicolon (`;`) can be placed at the end of a preprocessor directive. However, the preprocessor directives may contain a comment (which will be simply ignored).

> **Note**
> In order to extend a preprocessor directive to multiple lines, place a backslash character (\) as the last character of the line. This means that the line is continued in the line following it.

Although the preprocessor directive is usually placed before `main()`, practically speaking, it can appear anywhere in the program code. However, if written in between, the directive will be applied only in the remainder of the source file. The advantages of using preprocessor directives in a C program include:

- Program becomes readable and easy to understand.
- Program can be easily modified or updated.
- Program becomes portable as preprocessor directives make it easy to compile the program in different execution environments.
- Due to the aforesaid reasons, the program also becomes more efficient to use.

17.2 TYPES OF PREPROCESSOR DIRECTIVES

We can broadly categorize the preprocessor directives into two groups—conditional and unconditional preprocessor directives. Figure 17.1 shows the categorization of preprocessor directives.

The conditional directives are used to instruct the preprocessor to select whether or not to include a block of code in the final token stream passed to the compiler. Such directives are `#if, #else, #elif, #ifdef, #ifndef,` and `#endif`.

The unconditional directives such as `#define,#line, #undef,#include,#error,`and `#pragma` perform well-defined tasks. In this chapter we will learn about all these directives in detail.

17.3 #define

To define preprocessor macros we use `#define`. The `#define` statement is also known as *macro definition* or simply a macro. There are two types of macros:

- object-like macro and
- function-like macro.

17.3.1 Object-like Macro

An *object-like macro* is a simple identifier which will be replaced by a code fragment. They are usually used to give symbolic names to numeric constants. Object-like macros do not take any argument. It is the same what we have been using to declare constants using #define directive. The general syntax of defining a macro can be given as

```
#define identifier string
```

The preprocessor replaces every occurrence of the identifier in the source code by a string. The macro must start with the keyword #define and should be followed by an identifier and a string with at least one blank space between them. The string may be any text, a statement, or anything. However, the identifier must be a valid C name. The line

```
#define PI 3.14
```

defines a macro named PI as an abbreviation for the token 3.14. If somewhere after this #define directive there comes a C statement of the form

```
area = PI × radius × radius;
```

Then the C preprocessor will recognize and *expand* the macro PI. The C compiler will see the same tokens as it would if you had written

```
area = 3.14 × radius × radius;
```

A macro definition can also include an expression. However, when using expressions for replacement, make sure that the order of evaluation is correct. As a good programming habit, use parenthesis in the expression. For example, consider the following macro definitions:

Programming Tip:
A semicolon (;) should not be placed at the end of a preprocessor directive.

```
#define ROWS 3
#define COLS 3
#define SIZE (ROWS × COLS)
```

Look at the following program which illustrates the use of #define for literal text substitution:

```
#include <stdio.h>
#define INPUT printf("\n Enter a number: ");
  scanf("%d", &num);
#define EQUALS ==
#define PRINT1 printf("\n GREAT")
#define PRINT2 printf("\n TRY AGAIN")
#define START main() {
#define END getch();\
  return 0; }

START
   int num;
   INPUT
   if(num EQUALS 100)
     PRINT1;
   else
     PRINT2;
END
```

Programming Tip:
In order to extend a preprocessor directive to multiple lines, place a backslash character (\) as the last character of the line.

By convention, macro names are written in uppercase. This makes the program easy to read as anyone can tell at a glance which names are macros.

Note

An identifier is never replaced if it appears in a comment, within a string, or as part of a longer identifier.

17.3.2 Function-like Macros

Function-like macros are more complex than object-like macros. They are known as function-like macros because they are used to stimulate functions. When a function is stimulated using a macro, the macro definition replaces the function definition. The name of the macro serves as the header and the macro body serves as the function body. The name of the macro will then be used to replace the function call.

The function-like macro includes a list of parameters. References to such macros look like function calls. We have studied that when a function is called, control passes from the calling function to the called function at run time. However, when a macro is referenced, source code is inserted into the program at compile time. The parameters are replaced by the corresponding arguments, and the text is inserted into the program stream. Therefore, macros are considered to be much more efficient than functions as they avoid the overhead involved in calling a function.

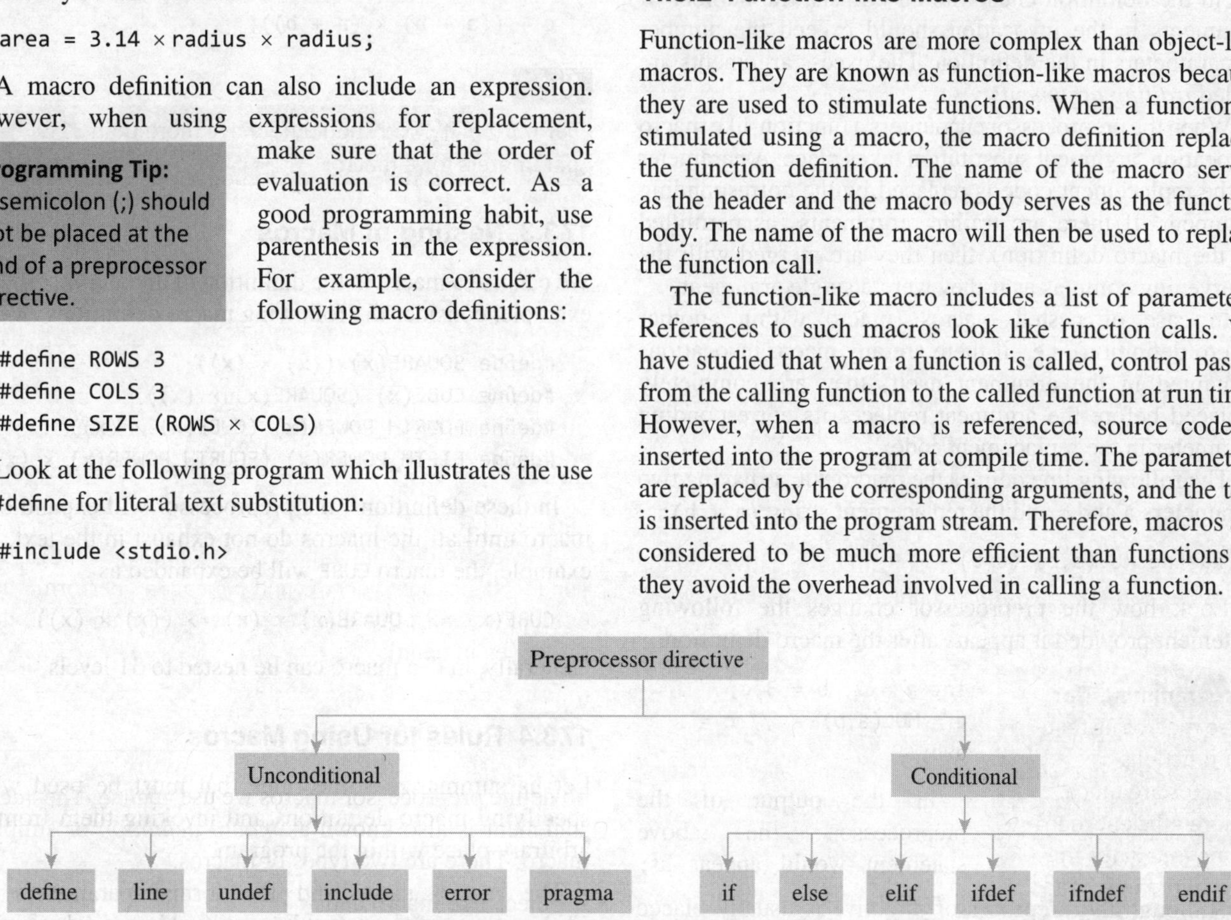

Figure 17.1 Preprocessor directives

> **Programming Tip:** Macro names can be in lowercase characters. But as a convention you must write macro names in uppercase characters.

A function-like macro definition declares the names of formal parameters within parentheses, sepa-rated by commas. In case the function-like macro does not accept any argument, then an empty formal parameter list can be provided.

The syntax of defining a function-like macro can be given as

```
# define identifier(arg1, arg2,...argn) string
```

An `identifier` is followed by a parameter list in parentheses and the replacement `string`. Note that white space cannot separate the identifier (which is the name of the macro) and the left parenthesis of the parameter list. A comma must separate each parameter.

Invoking a Function-like Macro

A function-like macro is invoked by writing the identifier followed by a comma-separated list of arguments in parentheses. However, make sure that the number of arguments should match the number of parameters in the macro definition. One exception to this is if the parameter list in the definition ends with an ellipsis, the number of arguments in the invocation should exceed the number of parameters in the definition. The excess arguments are called *trailing arguments*.

When the preprocessor encounters a function-like macro invocation, argument substitution takes place. A parameter in the replacement code is replaced by the corresponding argument. If there are trailing arguments (as permitted by the macro definition), then they are merged with the intervening commas as if they were a single argument.

In case of nested macros (macro within another macro definition), i.e., if there are any macro invocations contained in the argument itself, they are completely replaced before the argument replaces its corresponding parameter in the replacement code.

The following line defines the macro `MUL` as having two parameters `a` and `b` and the replacement string `(a × b)`:

```
#define MUL(a,b) (a×b)
```

Look how the preprocessor changes the following statement provided it appears after the macro definition.

> **Programming Tip:** Use macros instead of functions as macros are much more efficient than functions since they avoid the overhead involved in calling a function.

```
int a = 2, b = 3,c;
c = MUL(a,b)     // c =
a×b;
```

In the output of the preprocessor, the above statement would appear as: `c = a×b;`

While using function-like macros, you must use parentheses to ensure correct evaluation of replacement text. For example, if a macro `SQUARE` is defined as

```
#define SQUARE(x) (x×x)
```

Then invoking the macro by writing

```
int a = 2, b = 3,c;
c = SQUARE(a);     // c= 2×2;
```

The above statement is fine and would return the value 4. However, had you written the statements given below, you would have got incorrect results. For example, if had you written

```
int a = 2, b = 3,c;
c = SQUARE(a+b);
    // c = 2 + 3 × 2 + 3; so c = 2 + 6 + 3 = 11
```

It is, therefore, very important that you put parentheses around each parameter in the definition to correctly evaluate an expression. So let us redefine our `SQUARE` macro by writing

```
#define SQUARE(x) ((x) × (x))
```

Now a statement like

```
c = SQUARE(a+b);
```

would be expanded as

```
c = ((a + b) × (a + b));
```

> **Note**
> For portability, you should not have more than 31 parameters for a macro.

17.3.3 Nesting of Macros

We can use a macro in the definition of another macro. For example, consider the following macro definitions:

```
#define SQUARE(x) ((x) × (x))
#define CUBE(x) (SQUARE(x) × (x))
#define FOURTH_POWER(x) (CUBE(x) × (x))
#define FIFTH_POWER(x) (FOURTH_POWER(x) × (x))
```

In these definitions, the preprocessor will expand each macro until all the macros do not exhaust in the text. For example, the macro `CUBE` will be expanded as

```
CUBE(x) => SQUARE(x) × (x) => ((x) × (x)) × (x)
```

Generally, in C a macro can be nested to 31 levels.

17.3.4 Rules for Using Macros

Let us summarize some rules that must be used when specifying macro definitions and invoking them from an arbitrary place within the program.

- The macro name and the formal parameters are identifiers, so they must be specified in accordance with the rules for identifiers in the C language.

Programming Tip: Although the preprocessor directive is usually placed before `main()`, it can appear anywhere in the program code. However, if written in between, the directive will be applied only in the remainder of the source file.

- Spaces, tabs, and comments are allowed to be used freely within a `#define` directive. All the spaces, tabs, and comments are replaced by a single space.
- White space between the identifier and the left parenthesis that introduces the parameter list is not allowed.
- When referencing a macro, you may use comments and white-space characters freely. Comments are replaced with a single space. However, white-space characters (except leading and trailing white spaces) are preserved during the substitution.
- The number of arguments in the reference must match the number of parameters in the macro definition.

17.3.5 Operators Related to Macros

In this section, we will read about some operators that are directly or indirectly related to macros in C language.

Operator to Convert to String Literals

The # preprocessor operator which can be used only in a function-like macro definition is used to convert the argument that follows it to a string literal. For example:

```
#include <stdio.h>
#define PRINT(num) printf(#num " = %d", num)
main()
{
  PRINT(20);
}
```

The macro call expands to

```
printf("num" " = %d", num)
```

Finally, the preprocessor will automatically concatenate two string literals into one string. So the above statement will become

```
printf("num = %d", num)
```

Programming Tip: Ensure that there is not more than one # operator in the replacement list of a macro definition because in such a case the order of evaluation of the operators is not defined.

Hence, the unary # operator produces a string from its operand. Consider another macro `MAC` which is defined as

```
#define MAC(x)    #x
```

`MAC("10")` gives a string literal equal to `"10"`. Similarly, `MAC("HI")` would give a string literal `"HI"`.

Rules of using the # operator in a function-like macro definition

The # operator must be used in a function-like macro by following the rules mentioned below:

- A parameter following # operator in a function-like macro is converted into a string literal containing the argument passed to the macro.
- Leading and trailing white-space characters (those that appear before or after) in the argument passed to the macro are deleted.
- If the argument passed to the macro has multiple white-space characters, then they are replaced by a single-space character.
- If the argument passed to the macro contains a string literal and if a \(backslash) character appears within the literal, then on expansion of the macro, a second \ character is inserted before the original \.
- If the argument passed to the macro contains a " (double quotation mark) character, then on expansion of the macro, a \ character is inserted before the ".
- The conversion of an argument into a string literal occurs before macro expansion on that argument.
- If there is more than one # operator in the replacement list of a macro definition, the order of evaluation of the operators is not defined.
- If the result of the macro expansion is not a valid character string literal, the behaviour is undefined.

Merge Operator (##)

At times you need macros to generate new tokens. Using the merge operator you can concatenate two tokens into a third valid token. For example,

```
#include <stdio.h>
#define JOIN(A,B) A##B
main()
{
  int i;
  for(i = 1;i <= 5;i++)
  printf("\n HI JOIN(USER, i): ");
}
The above program would print
HI USER1
HI USER2
HI USER3
HI USER4
HI USER5
```

17.4 #include

An external file containing functions, variables or macro definitions can be included as a part of our program. This avoids the effort to re-write the code that is already written. The `#include` directive is used to inform the preprocessor to treat the contents of a specified file as if those contents had already appeared in the source program at the point where the directive appears.

The `#include` directive can be used in two forms. Both the forms make the preprocessor insert the entire contents of the specified file into the source code of our program. However, the difference between the two is the way in which they search for the specified.

```
#include <filename>
```

This variant is used for system header files. When we include a file using angular brackets, a search is made for the file named `filename` in a standard list of system directories.

```
#include "filename"
```

This variant is used for header files of your own program. When we include a file using double quotes, the preprocessor searches the file named `filename` first in the directory containing the current file, then in the quote directories and then the same directories used for `<filename>`.

Note

The filename can optionally be preceded by a directory specification. For example, you may specify the exact path by writing "c:\students\my_header.h".

Points to Remember

The preprocessor stops searching the directory as soon as it finds a file with the given name.

If a completely unambiguous path for the file is specified between double quotation marks (" "), then the preprocessor searches only that path specification and ignores the standard directories.

If an incomplete path is specified for the filename in double quotes, then the preprocessor first searches the parent file's directory (where a parent file is the one which contains the `#include` directive. For example, if you include a file named `file2` within a file named `file1, file1` is the parent file).

File inclusion can be 'nested', i.e., a `#include` directive can appear in a file named by another `#include` directive. For example, `file1` can include `file2`, and in turn `file2` can include another file named `file3`. In this case, `file1` would be the parent of `file2` and the grandparent of `file3`.

When file inclusion is nested and when compiling is done from the command line, directory searching begins with the directories of the parent file and then proceeds through the directories of any grandparent files.

Note

Nesting of `include` files can continue up to 10 levels.

17.5 #undef

As the name suggests, the `#undef` directive undefines or removes a macro name previously created with `#define`.

Undefining a macro means to cancel its definition. This is done by writing `#undef` followed by the macro name that has to be undefined.

Like definition, undefinition also occurs at a specific point in the source file, and it applies starting from that point. Once a macro name is undefined, the name of the macro ceases to exist (from the point of undefinition) and the preprocessor directive behaves as if it had never been a macro name.

Therefore, the `#undef` directive removes the current definition of macro and all subsequent occurrences of macro name are ignored by the preprocessor.

Note

If you had earlier defined a macro with parameters , then when undefining that macro you do not have to give the parameter list. Simply specify the name of the macro.

You can also apply the `#undef` directive to a macro name that has not been previously defined. This can be done to ensure that the macro name is undefined.

The `#undef` directive when paired with a `#define` directive creates a region in a source program in which the macro has a special meaning. For example, a specific function of the source program can use certain constants to define environment-specific values that do not affect the rest of the program.

The `#undef` directive can also be paired with the `#if` directive to control conditional compilation of the source program. We will read about the `#if` directive later in this chapter.

Consider the following example in which the `#undef` directive removes definitions of a symbolic constant and a macro.

```
#define MAX 10
#define MIN(X,Y) (((X)<(Y))?((X):(Y))
.
.
.
#undef MAX
#undef MIN
```

17.6 #line

Compile the following C program:

```
#include <stdio.h>
main()
{
  int a = 10:
  printf("%d", a);
}
```

The above program has a compile-time error because instead of a semicolon there is a colon that ends the line, `int a = 10`. So when you compile this program an error is generated during the compilation process and the compiler

> **Programming Tip:**
> The filename in the #line directive must be enclosed in double quotes.

will show an error message with references to the name of the file where the error has happened and a line number. This makes it easy to detect the erroneous code and rectify it.

The #line directive enables the users to control the line numbers within the code files as well as the file name that appears when an error takes place. The syntax of #line directive is

```
#line line_number filename
```

Here, line_number is the new line number that will be assigned to the next line of code. The line numbers of successive lines will be increased one by one from this point onwards. The parameter filename is an optional parameter that redefines the file name that will appear in case an error occurs. The filename must be enclosed within double quotes. If no filename is specified, then the compiler will show the original filename. For example:

```
#include <stdio.h>
main()
{
  #line 10 "Error.C"
  int a=10:
  #line 20
  printf("%d, a);
}
```

This code will generate an error that will be shown as error in file "Error.C", lines 10 and 20. Please execute this program with the #line directive and without the #line directive to visualize the difference.

Hence, we see that #line directive can be used to make the compiler provide more meaningful error messages.

> **Note**
> A *preprocessor line control directive* supplies line numbers for compiler messages. It tells the preprocessor to change the compiler's internally stored line number and filename to a given line number and filename.

17.7 #pragma

The #pragma directive is used to control the actions of the compiler in a particular portion of a program without affecting the program as a whole. You can include the pragma directive in your C program from the point where you want them to take effect. The effect of pragma will be applied from the point where it is included to the end of the compilation unit or until another pragma changes its status.

A #pragma directive is an instruction to the compiler and is usually ignored during preprocessing. The syntax of using a pragma directive can be given as

```
#pragma string
```

Here, string can be one of the instructions given to the compiler with any required parameters. Table 17.1 describes some pragma directives.

Table 17.1 Pragma directives

Instruction	Description
COPYRIGHT	To specify a copyright string
COPYRIGHT_DATE	To specify a copyright date for the copyright string
HP_SHLIB_VERSION	To create versions of a shared library routine
LOCALITY	To name a code subspace
OPTIMIZE	To turn the optimization feature on or off
OPT_LEVEL	To set the level of optimization
VERSIONID	To specify a version string

Pragma COPYRIGHT

The syntax of pragma COPYRIGHT can be given as

```
#pragma COPYRIGHT "string"
```

Here, string specifies the set of characters included in the copyright message in the object file.

If no date is specified using pragma COPYRIGHT_DATE, then the current year is used in the copyright message. For example, if we write

```
#pragma COPYRIGHT "JRT Software Ltd"
```

Then the following string is placed in the object code (assuming the current year is 2011):

© Copyright JRT Software Ltd, 2011. All rights reserved. No part of this program may be photocopied, reproduced, or transmitted without prior written consent of JRT Software Ltd.

Pragma COPYRIGHT_DATE

The syntax of pragma COPYRIGHT_DATE can be given as

```
#pragma COPYRIGHT_DATE "string"
```

Here, the string is a date which will be used by the COPYRIGHT pragma.

For example, consider the pragma given below

```
#pragma COPYRIGHT_DATE "1999-2011"
#pragma COPYRIGHT "JRT Software Ltd."
```

The above pragma will place the following string in the object code:

© Copyright JRT Software Ltd, 1999–2011. All rights reserved. No part of this program may be photocopied, reproduced, or transmitted without prior written consent of JRT Software Ltd.

Pragma OPTIMIZE

The syntax of using the pragma OPTIMIZE can be given as

```
#pragma OPTIMIZE ON
#pragma OPTIMIZE OFF
```

The pragma OPTIMIZE is basically used to turn on/off optimization in sections of a source program. However, when using this pragma you must specify one of the optimization options on the aCC command (while giving the command to compile the program), otherwise this pragma is ignored. Also remember that the pragma OPTIMIZE cannot be used within a function.

For example,

```
aCC +O2 Prog.C /* Set optimization to level 2
   for Prog.C */
#pragma OPTIMIZE OFF
void Func1()
{        /* Turn off optimization for this
   function */
     .....
}

#pragma OPTIMIZE ON
void Func2()
{        // Restore optimization to level 2
   ...
}
```

Pragma OPT_LEVEL

The syntax for pragma OPT_LEVEL which is used to set the optimization level to 1,2,3, or 4 can be given as

```
#pragma OPT_LEVEL 1
#pragma OPT_LEVEL 2
#pragma OPT_LEVEL 3
#pragma OPT_LEVEL 4
```

Like the OPTIMIZE pragma, even this pragma cannot be used within a function. Finally, OPT_LEVEL 3 and 4 are allowed only at the beginning of a file.

For example,

```
aCC -O prog.C
#pragma OPT_LEVEL 1
void Func1()
{     // Optimize Func1() at level 1
   ...
}
#pragma OPT_LEVEL 2
void Func2()
{        // Optimize Func2() at level 2
   ...
}
```

Note

The kind of optimization done by the operating system at each level is beyond the scope of this book.

Pragma HP_SHLIB_VERSION

The syntax for HP_SHLIB_VERSION pragma which is used to create different versions of a shared library routine can be given as

```
#pragma HP_SHLIB_VERSION ["]date["]
```

Here, the date argument is of the form month/year, optionally enclosed in quotes. The month must be specified using any number from 1 to 12. The year can be specified as either the last two digits of the year (99 for 1999) or a full year specification (1999). Here the two-digit year codes from 00 to 40 are used to represent the years from 2000 to 2040, respectively.

Note

The version number applies to all global symbols defined in the module's source file.

This pragma should be used only if incompatible changes are made to a source file.

Pragma LOCALITY

The syntax of pragma locality which is used to specify a name to be associated with the code that is written to a re-locatable object module can be given as

```
#pragma LOCALITY "string"
```

Here, string specifies a name to be used for a code subspace. After this directive, all codes following the directive are associated with the name specified in string. The smallest scope of a unique LOCALITY pragma is a function.

Pragma VERSIONID

The syntax of pragma VERSIONID can be given as

```
#pragma VERSIONID "string"
```

Here, string is a string of characters that is placed in the object file. For example, if we write

```
#pragma VERSIONID "JRT Software Ltd.,
   Version 12345.A.01.10"
```

Then this pragma places the characters JRT Software Ltd., Version 12345.A.01.10 into the object file.

Pragma once

The pragma once specifies that the file, in which this pragma directive is specified, will be included (opened) only once by the compiler in a building of a particular file. Its syntax can be given as

```
#pragma once
```

Pragma preprocessor directives are mainly used where each implementation of C supports some features unique to its host machine or operating system. For example, some programs may need to exercise precise control over the memory areas where data is placed or to control the way certain functions receive parameters. In such cases, `#pragma` directive provides machine- and operating-system-specific features for each compiler while retaining overall compatibility with the C language.

17.8 CONDITIONAL DIRECTIVES

A conditional directive is used to instruct the preprocessor to select whether or not to include a block of code in the final token stream passed to the compiler. The preprocessor conditional directives can test arithmetic expressions, or whether a name is defined as a macro, etc.

Although the conditional preprocessor directive resembles an `if` statement, it is important to understand the difference between them. The condition in an `if` statement is tested when the program is executed. So the same C program may behave differently from run to run, depending on the data it is operating on. However, the condition in a preprocessing conditional directive is tested when the program is being compiled. This facilitates the programmer to allow different code to be included in the program depending on the situation at compile time.

However, in today's scenario the distinction is becoming less clear. Modern compilers usually test `if` statements during program compilation in order to check if their conditions are known not to vary at run time, and eliminate code which can never be executed. If you have such a modern compiler then the use of an `if` statement is recommended as the program becomes more readable if you use `if` statements with constant conditions.

Conditional preprocessor directives can be used in the following situations:

- A program may need to use different code depending on the machine or operating system it is to run on. This may be because in certain situations, the code for one operating system becomes erroneous on another operating system. For example, the program might refer to data types or constants that do not exist on the other system. When this happens, it is not enough to avoid executing the invalid code; as even the presence of such data types and constants will make the compiler reject the program. Therefore, in such situations the conditional preprocessing is effective.
- The conditional preprocessor directive is very useful when you want to compile the same source file into two different programs. While one program might make frequent time-consuming consistency checks on its intermediate data, or print the values of those data for debugging, the other program, on the other hand can avoid such checks.
- The conditional preprocessor directives can be used to exclude code from the program whose condition is always false but is needed to keep it as a sort of comment for future reference.

17.8.1 #ifdef

`#ifdef` is the simplest sort of conditional preprocessor directive and is used to check for the existence of macro definitions. Its syntax can be given as

```
#ifdef MACRO
  controlled text
#endif
```

This block is called a conditional group. The controlled text will be included in the output of the preprocessor if and only if `MACRO` is defined. The `#ifdef` is said to be successful if the `MACRO` is defined. The controlled text will be executed only if the `#ifdef` succeeds.

Even if the `#ifdef` directive fails, the controlled text inside it is still run through initial transformations and tokenization. So, the programmer must ensure that the controlled text is lexically valid. For example, all comments and string literals inside a failing conditional group must still end properly.

Note

The kind of optimization done by the operating system at each level is beyond the scope of this book. As the statements under the `controlled text` of the `#ifdef` directive are not enclosed in braces, the `#endif` directive must be used to mark the end of the `#ifdef` block.

The following example defines an array `STACK` if `MAX` is defined for the preprocessor.

```
#ifdef MAX
int STACK[MAX];
#endif
```

In the above example, `STACK` will not be created if `MAX` had not been initially defined.

17.8.2 #ifndef

The `#ifndef` directive is the opposite of `#ifdef` directive. It checks whether the `MACRO` has not been defined or if its definition has been removed with `#undef`. `#ifndef` is successful and returns a non-zero value if the `MACRO` has not been defined. Otherwise in case of failure, that is when the `MACRO` has already been defined, `#ifndef` returns false (0).

Therefore, `#ifndef` directive is used to define code that is to be executed when a particular macro name is not defined. The general format to use `#ifndef` is the same as for `#ifdef`:

```
#ifndef MACRO
  controlled text
#endif
```

Here, `MACRO` and `controlled text` have the same meaning as they have in case of `#ifdef`. Again, the `#endif` directive is needed to mark the end of the `#ifndef` block.

You can also use `#else` directive with `#ifdef` and `#ifndef` directives like

```
#ifdef MACRO
  controlled_text1
#else
  controlled_text2
#endif
```

17.8.3 #if

The `#if` directive is used to control the compilation of portions of a source file. If the specified condition (after the `#if`) has a non-zero value, the controlled text immediately following the `#if` directive is retained in the translation unit.

The `#if` directive in its simplest form consists of

```
#if condition
  controlled text
#endif
```

In the above syntax, `condition` is a C expression of integer type, subject to stringent restrictions, i.e., the condition may contain the following:

- Integer constants (which are all treated as either `long` or `unsigned long`)
- Character constants
- Arithmetic operators for addition, subtraction, multiplication, division, bitwise operators, shift, comparison, and logical operators.
- If an identifier used in the expression is not a macro and has not been currently defined, the compiler treats the identifier as though it were the constant zero.
- Macros which are actually expanded before computation of the expression's value begins
- Defined operator can be used
- The `sizeof` operator is not allowed in `#if` directives.
- Type cast operator is not allowed
- Enumerated data types are not allowed
- The condition must not perform any environmental inquiries and must remain insulated from implementation details on the target computer
- Increment, decrement, and address operators are not allowed

The `controlled text` inside the directive can include other preprocessing directives. However, any statement or any preprocessor directive in the `controlled text` will be executed if that branch of the conditional statement succeeds.

While using the `#if` directive in your program, make sure that each `#if` directive must be matched by a closing `#endif` directive. Any number of `#elif` directives can appear between the `#if` and `#endif` directives, but at most one `#else` directive is allowed. However, the #else directive (if present) must be the last directive before `#endif`.

17.8.4 #else

The `#else` directive can be used within the `controlled text` of a `#if` directive to provide alternative text to be used if the condition is false. The general format of `#else` directive can be given as

```
#if condition
  controlled text1
#else
  controlled text2
#endif
```

If `condition` evaluates to a non-zero value then `controlled text1` becomes active and the `#else` directive acts like a failing conditional and the `controlled text2` is ignored. Similarly, if the `condition` fails or evaluates to zero, then `controlled text2` is considered included and `controlled text1` is ignored.

The `#else` directive is usually used to delimit alternative source text to be compiled if the condition tested for in the corresponding `#if`, `#ifdef`, or `#ifndef` directive is false. However, a `#else` directive is optional.

17.8.5 #elif

The `#elif` directive is used when there are more than two possible alternatives. The `#elif` directive like the `#else` directive is embedded within the `#if` directive and has the following syntax:

```
#if condition
  controlled text1
#elif new_condition
  controlled text2
#else
  controlled text3
#endif
```

Here, when the `if condition` is non-zero then `controlled text1` becomes active and the `#elif` and `#else` directives act like a failing conditional and the `controlled text2` and `controlled text3` are ignored. Similarly, grounds, if the condition fails or evaluates to zero, then `new_condition` is evaluated. If it is true, `controlled text2` is considered included and `controlled text1` and `controlled text3` are ignored. Otherwise, if `condition` and `new_condition` both are false then `#else` directive becomes active and `controlled text3` is included.

The `#elif` directive is same as the combined use of the `else-if` statements. The `#elif` directive is used to delimit alternative source lines to be compiled if `condition` in the corresponding `#if`, `#ifdef`, `#ifndef`, or another `#elif` directive is false and if the `new_condition` in the `#elif` line is true, an `#elif` directive is optional.

```
#define MAX 10
#if OPTION == 1
  int STACK[MAX];
#elif OPTION == 2
```

```
    float STACK[MAX];
  #elif OPTION == 3
    char STACK[MAX];
  #else
    printf("\n INVALID OPTION");
  #endif
```

Note

The `#elif` does not require a matching '`#endif`' of its own. Every `#elif` directive includes a condition to be tested. The text following the `#elif` is processed only if the `#if` condition fails and the `#elif` condition succeeds.

In the above example, we have used more than one `#elif` directives in the same `#if-#endif` group. The text after each `#elif` is processed only if the `#elif` condition succeeds after the original `#if` and any previous `#elif` directives within it have failed.

Note

If the condition specified with `#if` directive is false and if either no `#elif` directives appear or no `#elif` condition evaluates to true, then the preprocessor selects the text block after the `#else` clause. If the `#else` directive is also missing then no controlled text is selected.

17.8.6 #endif

The general syntax of `#endif` preprocessor directive which is used to end the conditional compilation directive can be given as

```
#endif
```

The `#endif` directive ends the scope of the `#if`, `#ifdef`, `#ifndef`, `#else`, or `#elif` directives. The number of `#endif` directives that is required depends on whether the `#elif` or `#else` directive is used. For example, consider the examples given below which, although perform the same task, requires different number of `#endif` directives.

```
#if condition
  Controlled text1
#elif new_condition
  Controlled text2
#endif
```

OR

```
#if condition
  Controlled text1
#else
#if new_condition
  Controlled text2
#endif
#endif
```

17.9 defined OPERATOR

We have seen that we can check the existence of a macro by using `#ifdef` directive. However, there is another way to do the same. The alternative to `#ifdef` directive is to use the `defined` unary operator. The `defined` operator has one of the following forms:

```
defined MACRO

  or

defined (MACRO)
```

The above expression evaluates to 1 if `MACRO` is defined and to 0 if it is not. The `defined` operator helps you to check for macro definitions in one concise line without having to use many `#ifdef` or `#ifndef` directives. For example, consider the following macro checks:

```
#ifdef MACRO1
  #ifdef MACRO2
    controlled text1
#else
  printf("\n MACROS not defined");
#endif
```

OR

```
#if defined (MACRO1) && defined (MACRO2)
  controlled text1
#else
  printf("\n MACROS not defined");
#endif
```

As evident from the above example, the `defined` operator can be combined in any logical expression using the logical operators. However, this operator can only be used in the evaluated expression of an `#if` or `#elif` preprocessor directive.

17.10 #error

The `#error` directive is used to produce compile-time error messages. The syntax of this directive is

```
#error string
```

The error messages include the argument `string`. The `#error` directive is generally used to detect programming inconsistencies and violation of constraints during preprocessing. When `#error` directive is encountered, the compilation process terminates and the message specified in `string` is printed to `stderr`. For example, consider the piece of code given below which illustrates error processing during preprocessing:

```
#ifndef SQUARE
#error MACRO not defined.
#endif

#ifndef VERSION
  #error Version number is not specified.
  #endif

#ifdef WINDOWS
```

```
    ... /* Windows specific code */
#else
    #error "This code works only on WINDOWS
  operating system"
#endif
```

The `#error` directive causes the preprocessor to report a fatal error.

Here the string need not be enclosed within double quotes. It is a good programming practice to enclose the string in double quotes. The `#error` directive is a very important directive mainly because of two reasons:

- First, it helps you to determine whether a given line is being compiled or not.
- Second, when used within a heavily parameterized body of code, it helps to ensure that a particular `MACRO` has been defined.

Besides the `#error` directive, there is another directive—`#warning`, which causes the preprocessor to issue a warning and continue preprocessing. The syntax of `#warning` directive is same as that of `#error`.

```
#warning string
```

Here, `string` is the warning message that has to be displayed. One important place where `#warning` directive can be used is in obsolete header files. You can display a message directing the user to the header file which should be used instead.

17.11 PREDEFINED MACRO NAMES

There are certain predefined macros that are readily available for use by the C programmers. A list of such predefined macros is given in Table 17.2.

```
#include <stdio.h>
 void main(void)
 {
    printf("\n Current File's Path Name:
      %s", __FILE__);
    printf("\n Line Number in the
      current file: %d", __LINE__);
    printf("\n Date of Compilation: %s",
      __DATE__);
    printf("\n Time of Compilation: %s",
      __TIME__);
    #ifdef __STDC__
    printf("\n Your C compiler
      conforms with the ANSI C standard");
    #else
    printf("\n Your C compiler doesn't
      conform with the ANSI C standard");
    #endif
 }
```

Table 17.2 Predefined macros

Macro	Value
LINE	A decimal integer constant which specifies the current line number in the source file being compiled. We have already studied that the line number can be altered with a #line directive.
FILE	A string literal which specifies the name of the source file being compiled.
DATE	Specifies the date of compilation of the current source file. It is a string literal of the form mm dd yyyy.
TIME	A string literal in the form "hh:mm:ss" which is used to specify the time at which the compilation process began.
_ STDC_	Specifies full conformance with ANSI C standard.
TIMESTAMP	A string literal in the form Ddd Mmm Date hh:mm:ss yyyy, where Ddd is the abbreviated day of the week and Date is an integer from 1 to 31. It is used to specify the date and time of the last modification of the current source file.

POINTS TO REMEMBER

- The preprocessor is a program that processes the source code before it passes through the compiler.
- Preprocessor directives are lines included in the C program that are not program statements but directives for the preprocessor. The preprocessor directives are always preceded by a hash sign (#) and are executed before the actual compilation of program code begins.
- To define preprocessor macros, we use #define directive. An object-like macro is a simple identifier which will be replaced by a code fragment. They are usually used to give symbolic names to numeric constants. Function-like macros are used to stimulate functions.
- The merge operator is used to concatenate two tokens into a third valid token.
- The `#include` directive is used to inform the preprocessor to treat the contents of a specified file as if those contents had appeared in the source program at the point where the directive appears.
- `#undef` directive removes a macro name previously created with `#define`. The `#line` directive enables the users to control the line numbers within the code files as well as the file name that appears when an error takes place.

- The #pragma directive is used to control the actions of the compiler in a particular portion of a program without affecting the program as a whole.
- A conditional directive is used to instruct the preprocessor to select whether or not to include a block of code in the final token stream passed to the compiler.
- #ifdef is used to check for the existence of macro definitions. The #ifndef directive is the opposite of #ifdef directive. It checks whether the MACRO has not been defined or if its definition has been removed with #undef. The #if directive is used to control the compilation of portions of a source file.
- The #else directive is used within the controlled text of a #if directive in order to provide alternative text to be used if the condition is false. The #elif directive is used when there are more than two possible alternatives. The #elif directive like the #else directive is embedded within the #if directive.
- The #error directive is used to produce compile-time error messages.

GLOSSARY

Function-like macro It is used to stimulate functions.

Object-like macro It is a simple identifier which will be replaced by a code fragment. They are usually used to give symbolic names to numeric constants.

Preprocessor It is a program that processes the source code before it passes through the compiler.

Preprocessor directives These are lines included in the C program that are not program statements but directives for the preprocessor. They are always preceded by a hash sign (#).

Self-referential macro A macro whose name appears in its definition.

Trailing arguments A function-like macro definition declares the names of formal parameters within parentheses, separated by commas. If the number of arguments in the invocation exceeds the number of parameters in the definition, the excess arguments are called trailing arguments.

EXERCISES

Fill in the Blanks

1. ________ is a program that processes the source code before it passes through the compiler.
2. ________ operates under the control of preprocessor directive.
3. Before the source code is passed through the compiler, it is examined by the preprocessor for any ________.
4. ________ are lines included in the program that are not program statements but directives for the preprocessor.
5. The ________ is also known as a macro.
6. The #define directive is used to ________.
7. ________ is used to give symbolic names to numeric constants.
8. Trailing arguments are ________.
9. ________ preprocessor operator is used to convert the argument that follows it to a string literal.
10. The ________ operator is used to concatenate two tokens into a third valid token.
11. When we include a file using ________, a search is made for the file in a standard list of system directories.
12. File inclusion can be nested to ________ levels.
13. The #undef directive removes a macro name previously created with ________.
14. The ________ directive is used to control the actions of the compiler in a particular portion of a program without affecting the program as a whole.
15. ________ is used to instruct the preprocessor to select whether or not to include a chunk of code in the final token stream passed to the compiler.
16. Each #if directive must be matched by the ________ directive.
17. The #elif directive and the #else directive are embedded within the ________ directive.
18. When ________ directive is encountered, the compilation process terminates.
19. ________ causes the preprocessor to issue a warning and continue preprocessing.
20. ________ specifies full conformance with ANSI C standard.

Multiple-choice Questions

1. The preprocessor directives must be preceded by which symbol?
   (a) * (c) @
   (b) & (d) #
2. In order to extend a preprocessor directive to multiple lines, which character is placed as the last character of the line?
   (a) \ (c) ^
   (b) / (d) !
3. Which directive is used to control the line numbers within the code files as well as the file name that appears when an error takes place?
   (a) #pragma (c) #line
   (b) #define (d) #filename
4. Which directive is used to check for the existence of macro definitions?
   (a) `#if` (c) `#ifdef`
   (b) `#define` (d) `#undef`
5. Choose the operator which can be used in the conditional expression of `#if` directive.
   (a) defined (c) `typecast`
   (b) `sizeof` (d) `address`
6. Which predefined macro is used to specify the date and time of the last modification of the current source file?
   (a) _TIME_ (c) _TIMESTAMP_
   (b) _DATE_ (d) _STDC_

State True or False

1. Preprocessor directives are executable statements in a C program.
2. The preprocessor is executed before the actual compilation of program code begins.
3. Preprocessor directives can only be one line long.
4. Preprocessor directives can appear anywhere in the program.
5. Object-like macros takes one argument.
6. A macro definition can include an expression.
7. It is compulsory to write macro names in uppercase.
8. The # preprocessor operator can be used only in a function-like macro definition.
9. The conversion of an argument into a string literal occurs before macro expansion on that argument.
10. File inclusion cannot be nested.
11. While undefining a macro, you have to specify the parameters, if any.
12. `#ifdef` checks whether the `MACRO` has not been defined or if its definition has been removed with `#undef`.
13. We can use enumerated data types in the expressions of conditional directives.
14. The `#endif` directive is used to end the conditional compilation directive.
15. _TIMESTAMP_ is used to specify the time at which the compilation process began.

Review Questions

1. What do you understand by the term preprocessor directive?
2. Can we have a C program that does not use any preprocessor directive?
3. Why should we incorporate preprocessor directives in our programs? Give at least one example to support your answer.
4. Explain the importance of the #define preprocessor directive.
5. How are trailing arguments, if any, handled by the preprocessor?
6. What happens when the argument passed to the macro has multiple white-space characters?
7. Why should we not use more than one # operator in the replacement list of a macro definition?
8. How can `#include` directive be used in your C program? Illustrate with respect to both the forms available for usage.
9. File inclusion can be nested. Justify this statement with the help of a suitable example.
10. Can the `#undef` directive be applied to a macro name that has not been previously defined? If yes, why?
11. Explain in detail the `#pragma` directive.
12. Write a short note on conditional directives.
13. Compare an `if` statement with the `#if` directive.
14. In which situations will you recommend to use conditional directives in a program?
15. Comment on the restrictions imposed on the conditional expression of `#if` directive.
16. Give the importance of `#error` and `#warning` directives.
17. Give the rules for using macros.
18. Enumerate the rules for using the # operator in a function-like macro definition

18 Introduction to Data Structures

TAKEAWAYS

- Data structures
- Primitive and non-primitive data structures
- Linear and non-linear data structures
- Linked lists
- Stacks
- Queues
- Trees
- Graphs

18.1 INTRODUCTION

A data structure is a group of data elements that are put together under one name, to define a particular way of storing and organizing data in a computer so that it can be used efficiently.

Data structures are used in almost every program or software system. Some common examples of data structures are arrays, linked lists, queues, stacks, binary trees, and graphs. Data structures are widely applied in areas such as:

- Compiler design
- Operating system
- Statistical analysis package
- Database management system (DBMS)
- Numerical analysis
- Simulation
- Artificial intelligence (AI)
- Graphics

When you study DBMS as a subject, you will realize that the major data structure used in the network data model is graphs, in hierarchical data models is trees, and in relational database management systems (RDBMS) is arrays.

Specific data structures are essential ingredients of many efficient algorithms as they enable the programmers to manage huge amounts of data easily and efficiently. Some formal design methods and programming languages emphasize data structures and algorithms as the key organizing factors in software design. This is because representing information is fundamental to computer science. The primary goal of a program or software is not to perform calculations or operations but to store and retrieve information as fast as possible.

Be it any problem at hand, the application of an appropriate data structure provides the most efficient solution. A solution is said to be efficient if it solves the problem within the required resource constraints such as the total space available to store the data and the time allowed to perform each subtask; and the best solution is the one that requires fewer resources than known alternatives.

18.2 CLASSIFICATION OF DATA STRUCTURES

Data structures are generally categorized into two classes: *primitive* and *non-primitive* data structures.

18.2.1 Primitive and Non-primitive Data Structures

Primitive data structures are the fundamental data types which are supported by a programming language. Some basic data types are integer, real, character, and boolean. The terms 'data type', 'basic data type', and 'primitive data type' are often used interchangeably.

Non-primitive data structures are those data structures which are created using primitive data structures. Examples of such data structures include linked lists, stacks, trees, and graphs.

Non-primitive data structures can further be classified into two categories: *linear* and *non-linear* data structures.

18.2.2 Linear and Non-linear Structures

If the elements of a data structure are stored in a linear or sequential order, then it is a linear data structure. Examples include arrays, linked lists, stacks, and queues. Linear data structures can be represented in memory in two different ways. One way is to have to a linear relationship between elements by means of sequential memory locations. The other way is to have a linear relationship between elements by means of links.

However, if the elements of a data structure are not stored in a sequential order, then it is a non-linear data structure. The relationship of adjacency is not maintained between elements of a non-linear data structure. Examples include trees and graphs.

C supports a variety of data structures. We will now introduce all these data structures.

18.3 ARRAYS

An array is a collection of similar data elements. These data elements have the same data type. The elements of the array are stored in consecutive memory locations and are referenced by an index (also known as the subscript).

Arrays are declared using the following syntax:

```
type name[size];
```

For example

```
int marks[10];
```

This statement declares an array `marks` that contains 10 elements. In C, the array index starts from zero. This means that the array `marks` will contain 10 elements in all. The first element will be stored in `marks[0]`, second element in `marks[1]`, and so on. Therefore, the last element, i.e., the 10th element will be stored in `marks[9]`. In memory, the array will be stored as shown in Figure 18.1.

The limitations of arrays are as follows:

- Arrays are of fixed size.
- Data elements are stored in contiguous memory locations which may not be always available.
- Adding and removing elements is difficult because of shifting the elements from their positions.

However, these limitations can be solved by using a linked list. We have already read about arrays in Chapter 12.

18.4 LINKED LISTS

A linked list, in simple terms, is a linear collection of data elements. These data elements are called nodes. Linked lists are data structures that in turn can be used to implement other data structures. Thus, they act as building blocks to implement other data structures such as stacks, queues, and their variations. A linked list can be perceived as a train or a sequence of nodes in which each node contains one or more data fields and a pointer to the next node. In Figure 18.2, we see a linked list in which every node contains two parts—one integer and the other a pointer to the next node.

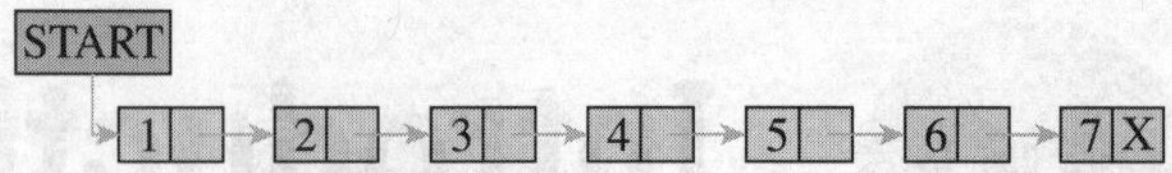

Figure 18.2 A simple linked list

The left part of the node that contains data may include a simple data type, an array, or a structure. The right part of the node contains a pointer to the next node (or address of the next node in the sequence). The last node will have no next node connected to it, so it will store a special value called `NULL`. In Figure 18.2, `NULL` is represented by `X`. However, when we do programming, we usually define `NULL` as `-1`. Hence, a `NULL` pointer denotes the end of the list. Since in a linked list every node contains a pointer to another node which is of the same type, it is also called a *self-referential data type*.

A linked list contains a pointer variable, `START`, which stores the address of the first node in the list. We can traverse the entire list using a single pointer variable `START`. The `START` node will contain the address of the first node; the next part of the first node will in turn store the address of its succeeding node. Using this technique, the individual nodes of the list will form a chain of nodes. If `START = NULL`, this means that the linked list is empty and contains no nodes.

In C, we will implement a linked list using the following code:

```
struct node
{
  int data;
  struct node *next;
};
```

Let us see how a linked list is maintained in memory. In order to form a linked list, we need a structure called node that has two fields—`DATA` and `NEXT`. The `DATA` field will store the information part, and `NEXT` will store the address of the next node in the sequence. Consider Figure 18.3.

From Figure 18.3, we can see that the variable `START` is used to store the address of the first node. Here, in this example, `START = 1`, so the first data is stored at address 1, which is `'H'`. The corresponding variable `NEXT` stores the address of the next node, which is 4. So, we will look at address 4 to fetch the next data item. The second data element obtained from address 4 is `'E'`. Again, we see the corresponding `NEXT`, to go to the next node. From the entry in `NEXT`, we get the next address, that is 7 and fetch

1st element	2nd element	3rd element	4th element	5th element	6th element	7th element	8th element	9th element	10th element
marks[0]	marks[1]	marks[2]	marks[3]	marks[4]	marks[5]	marks[6]	marks[7]	marks[8]	marks[9]

Figure 18.1 Memory representation of an array of 10 elements

'L' as the data. We repeat this procedure until we reach a position, where the NEXT entry contains -1 or NULL, as this would denote the end of the linked list. When we traverse the DATA and NEXT fields in this manner, we will finally see that the linked list in this example stores characters that when put together forms the word 'HELLO'.

START: 1

	Data	Next
1	H	4
2		
3		
4	E	7
5		
6		
7	L	8
8	L	10
9		
10	O	-1

Figure 18.3 START pointing to the first element of a linked list in memory

Note that this figure shows a chunk of memory locations, whose address ranges from 1 to 10. The shaded portion contains data for other applications. Remember that the nodes of a linked list need not be in consecutive memory locations. In our example, the nodes for the linked list are stored at addresses—1, 4, 7, 8, and 10.

Linked Lists Versus Arrays

Both linked lists and arrays are a linear collection of data elements. However, unlike an array, a linked list does not store its nodes in consecutive memory locations. Another point of difference between an array and a linked list is that a linked list does not allow random access of data. Nodes in a linked list can be accessed only in a sequential manner. However, like an array, insertions and deletions can be done at any point in the list in constant time.

Another advantage of linked lists over arrays is that we can add any number of elements in the list. This is not possible in case of an array. For example, if we declare an array as int marks[10], then the array can store a maximum of 10 data elements and not even a single element more than that. There is no such restriction in case of a linked list.

Thus, linked lists provide an efficient way of storing related data and performing basic operations such as insertion, deletion, and updating of information at the cost of the extra space required for storing the address of the next node.

18.4.1 Traversing a Linked List

Traversing a linked list means accessing the nodes of the list in order to perform some processing on them. Remember, a linked list always contains a pointer variable START, which stores the address of the first node of the list. The end of the list is marked by storing NULL or 1 in the NEXT field of the last node. For traversing the linked list, we will also make use of another pointer variable PTR, which will point to the node that is currently being accessed. The algorithm to traverse a linked list is shown in Figure 18.4.

```
Step 1: [INITIALIZE] SET PTR = START
Step 2: Repeat Steps 3 and 4 while PTR != NULL
Step 3:         Apply Process to PTR->DATA
Step 4:         SET PTR = PTR->NEXT
          [END OF LOOP]
Step 5: EXIT
```

Figure 18.4 Algorithm to traverse a linked list

In step 1 of this algorithm, we first initialize PTR with the address of START. So now, PTR points to the first node of the linked list. Then, in step 2, a while loop is executed, which is repeated until PTR processes the last node, that is, until it encounters NULL. In step 3, we apply the process (e.g., print) to the current node, which is the node pointed by PTR. In step 4, we move to the next node by making the PTR variable point to the node whose address is stored in the NEXT field.

Let us now write an algorithm to count the number of nodes in the linked list. To do this, we will traverse each and every node of the list, and while traversing every individual node, we will increment the counter by 1. Once we reach NULL, that is, when all the nodes of the linked list have been traversed, the final value of the counter will be displayed. Figure 18.5 shows the algorithm to print the number of nodes in the linked list.

```
Step 1:[INITIALIZE] SET COUNT = 0
Step 2:[INITIALIZE] SET PTR = START
Step 3: Repeat Steps 4 and 5 while PTR != NULL
Step 4:           SET COUNT = COUNT + 1
Step 5:           SET PTR = PTR->NEXT
          [END OF LOOP]
Step 6: Write COUNT
Step 7: EXIT
```

Figure 18.5 Algorithm to print the number of nodes in a linked list

18.4.2 Searching for a Value in a Linked List

Searching a linked list means finding a particular element in the linked list. As already discussed, a linked list consists of a node which is divided into two parts—the information part, which stores the relevant data, and the NEXT part, which stores the address of the next node in sequence. Hence, obviously, searching means finding whether a given value is present in the information part of the node or not. If it is present, the search algorithm returns the address of the node which contains that value.

Figure 18.6 shows the algorithm to search a linked list.

```
Step 1: [INITIALIZE] SET PTR = START
Step 2: Repeat Step 3 while PTR != NULL
Step 3:         IF VAL = PTR->DATA
                        SET POS = PTR
                        Go To Step 5
                ELSE
                        SET PTR = PTR->NEXT
                [END OF IF]
        [END OF LOOP]
Step 4: SET POS = NULL
Step 5: EXIT
```

Figure 18.6 Algorithm to search a linked list

In step 1, we initialize a pointer variable `PTR` with `START`, which contains the address of the first node. In step 2, a while loop is executed that will compare every node's `DATA` with the `VAL` for which the search is being made. If the search is successful, that is, `VAL` has been found, then the address of that node is stored in `POS`, and the control jumps to the last statement of the algorithm. However, if the search is unsuccessful, `POS` is set to `NULL`, which indicates that the `VAL` is not present in the linked list.

Consider the linked list shown in Figure 18.7. If we have `VAL = 4`, then the flow of the algorithm can be explained as shown in this figure.

18.4.3 Inserting a New Node in a Linked List

In this section, we will see how a new node is added to an already existing linked list. We will take four cases and then see how insertion is done in each case.

Case 1 The new node is inserted at the beginning of the linked list.

Case 2 The new node is inserted at the end of the linked list.

Case 3 The new node is inserted after a given node.

Case 4 The new node is inserted before a given node.

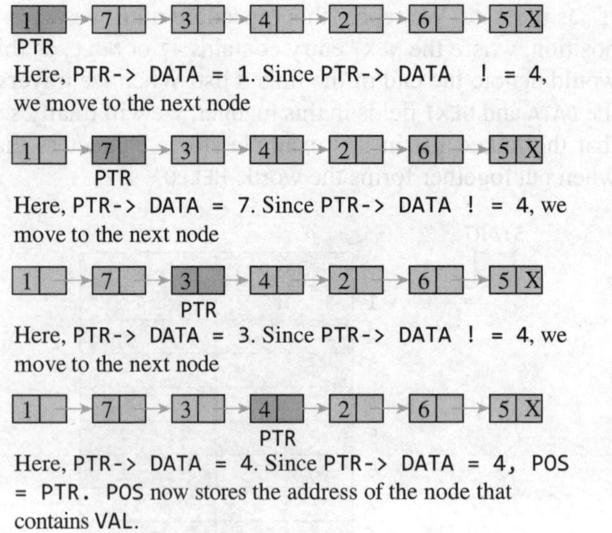

Figure 18.7 Searching a linked list

Before we start with the algorithms to perform insertions in these four cases, let us first discuss an important term, `OVERFLOW`. `OVERFLOW` is a condition that occurs when `AVAIL = NULL`, or no free memory cell is present in the system. In other words, we want to add data to the data structure, but there is no memory space available to do so. When this condition prevails, the programmer must give an appropriate message.

Case 1: The new node is inserted at the beginning of the linked list Consider the linked list shown in Figure 18.8. Suppose we want to add a new node with data 9 and add it as the first node of the list. Then, the following changes will be done in the linked list.

Figure 18.9 shows the algorithm to insert a new node at the beginning of a linked list. In step 1, we first check whether memory is available for the new node. If the free memory has exhausted, then an `OVERFLOW` message is printed. Otherwise, if a free memory cell is available, then we allocate space for the new node. Set its `DATA` part with `VAL`, and its `NEXT` part is initialized with the address

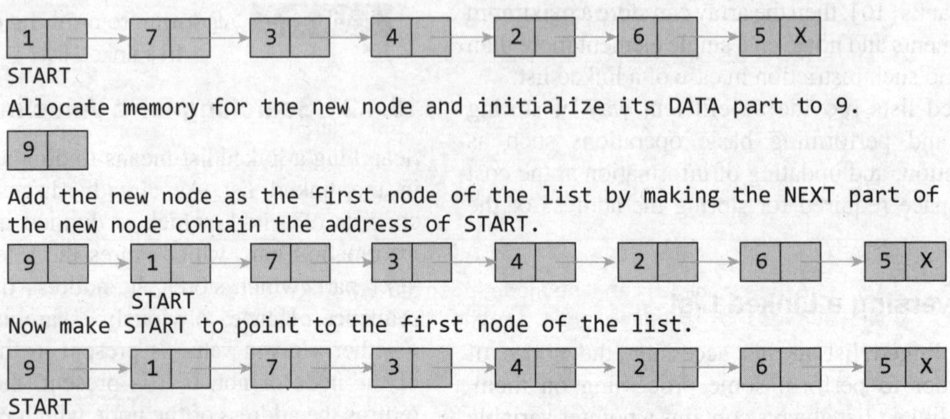

Figure 18.8 Inserting an element at the beginning of a linked list

```
Step 1: IF AVAIL = NULL, then
              Write OVERFLOW
              Go to Step 7
         [END OF IF]
Step 2: SET New_Node = AVAIL
Step 3: SET AVAIL = AVAIL->NEXT
Step 4: SET New_Node->DATA = VAL
Step 5: SET New_Node->Next = START
Step 6: SET START = New_Node
Step 7: EXIT
```

Figure 18.9 Algorithm to insert a new node at the beginning of a linked list

of the first node of the list, which is stored in START. Since the new node is added as the first node of the list, it will now be known as the START node, that is, the START pointer variable will now hold the address of New_Node.

Note the two steps:

```
Step 2: SET New_Node = AVAIL
Step 3: SET AVAIL = AVAIL->NEXT
```

These steps allocate memory for the new node. In C, there are functions like malloc(), alloc(), and calloc(), which does all this automatically on behalf of the user. We have already discussed these functions in Chapter 14.

Case 2: The new node is inserted at the end of the linked list Consider the linked list shown in Figure 18.10. Suppose we want to add a new node with data 9 and add it as the last node of the list. Then, the following changes will be done in the linked list.

Figure 18.11 shows the algorithm to insert a new node at the end of the linked list. In step 1, we first check whether memory is available for the new node. If the free

```
Step 1: IF AVAIL = NULL, then
              Write OVERFLOW
              Go to Step 10
         [END OF IF]
Step 2: SET New_Node = AVAIL
Step 3: SET AVAIL = AVAIL->NEXT
Step 4: SET New_Node->DATA = VAL
Step 5: SET New_Node->Next = NULL
Step 6: SET PTR = START
Step 7: Repeat Step 8 while PTR->NEXT != NULL
Step 8:            SET PTR  = PTR  ->NEXT
        [END OF LOOP]
Step 9: SET PTR->NEXT = New_Node
Step 10: EXIT
```

Figure 18.11 Algorithm to insert a new node at the end of a linked list

memory has exhausted, then an OVERFLOW message is printed. Otherwise, if a free memory cell is available, then we allocate space for the new node. Set its DATA part with VAL, and its NEXT part is initialized with NULL, because this is going to be the last node of the linked list.

In step 6, we take a PTR and initialize it with START. That is, PTR now points to the first node of the linked list. In the while loop, we traverse through the linked list to reach the last node. Once we reach the last node, in step 9, we change the NEXT pointer of the last node to store the address of the new node. Remember that the NEXT field of the new node contains NULL, which signifies the end of the linked list.

Case 3: The new node is inserted after a given node Consider the linked list shown in Figure 18.12. Suppose we want to add a new node with value 9 and add it after

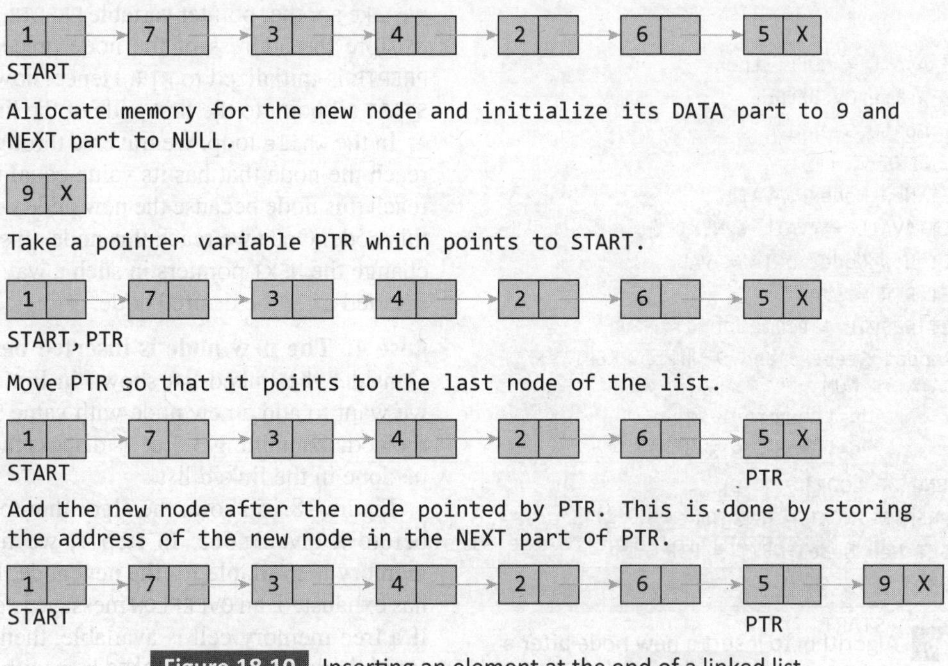

Figure 18.10 Inserting an element at the end of a linked list

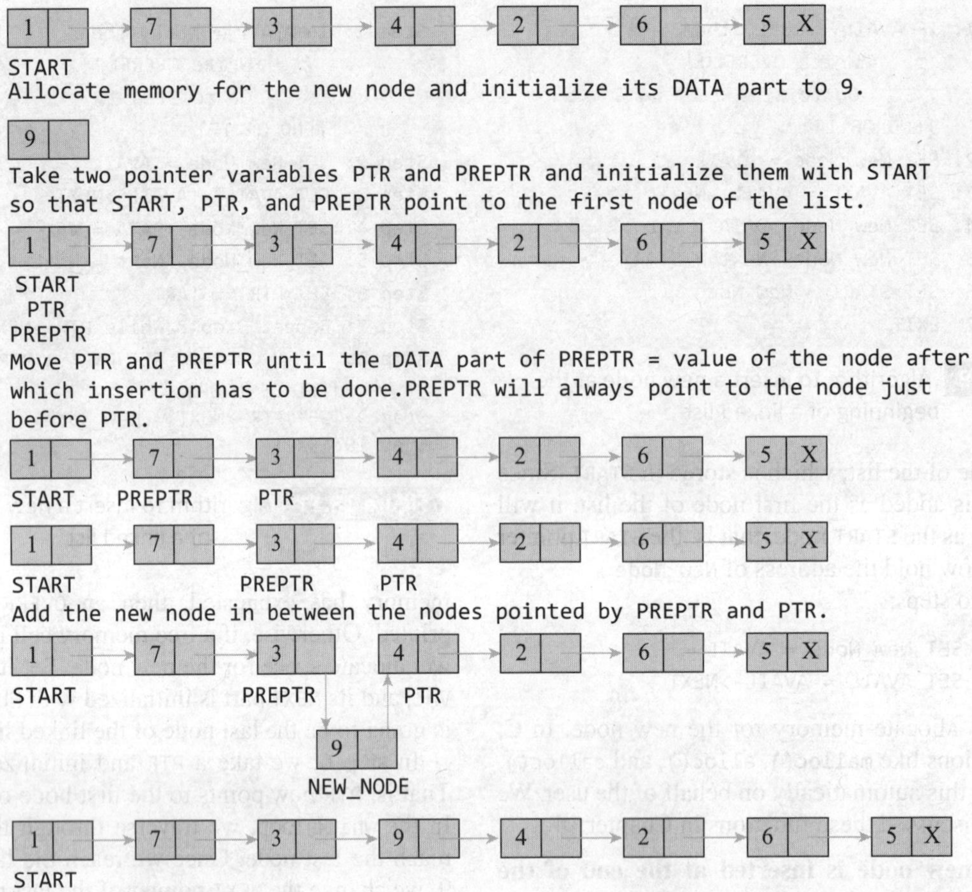

Figure 18.12 Inserting an element after a given node in a linked list

the node containing data 3. Let us look at the changes that will be done in the linked list. The algorithm to add the new node is given in Figure 18.13.

In step 1, we first check whether memory is available for the new node. If the free memory has exhausted, then an OVERFLOW message is printed. Otherwise, if a free memory cell is available, then we allocate space for the new node. Set its DATA part with VAL.

```
Step 1: IF AVAIL = NULL, then
            Write OVERFLOW
            Go to Step 12
        [END OF IF]
Step 2: SET New_Node = AVAIL
Step 3: SET AVAIL = AVAIL ->NEXT
Step 4: SET New_Node->DATA = VAL
Step 5: SET PTR = START
Step 6: SET PREPTR = PTR
Step 7:  Repeat Steps 8 and 9 while PREPTR->
         DATA != NUM
Step 8:          SET PREPTR = PTR
Step 9:          SET PTR = PTR->NEXT
        [END OF LOOP]
Step 10: PREPTR->NEXT = New_Node
Step 11: SET New_Node->NEXT = PTR
Step 12: EXIT
```

Figure 18.13 Algorithm to insert a new node after a node that has value NUM

In step 5, we take a PTR and initialize it with START. That is, PTR now points to the first node of the linked list. Then, we take another pointer variable PREPTR, which will be used to store the address of the node preceding PTR. Initially, PREPTR is initialized to PTR. Hence, now, PTR, PREPTR, and START all point to the first node of the linked list.

In the while loop, we traverse through the linked list to reach the node that has its value equal to NUM. We need to reach this node because the new node will be inserted after this node. Once we reach this node, in steps 10 and 11, we change the NEXT pointers in such a way that a new node is inserted after the desired node.

Case 4: The new node is inserted before a given node Consider the linked list shown in Figure 18.14. Suppose we want to add a new node with value 9 and add it before the node containing 3. Let us discuss the changes that will be done in the linked list.

Figure 18.15 shows the algorithm to insert a new node before a given node. In step 1, we first check whether memory is available for the new node. If the free memory has exhausted, an OVERFLOW message is printed. Otherwise, if a free memory cell is available, then we allocate space for the new node. Set its DATA part with VAL.

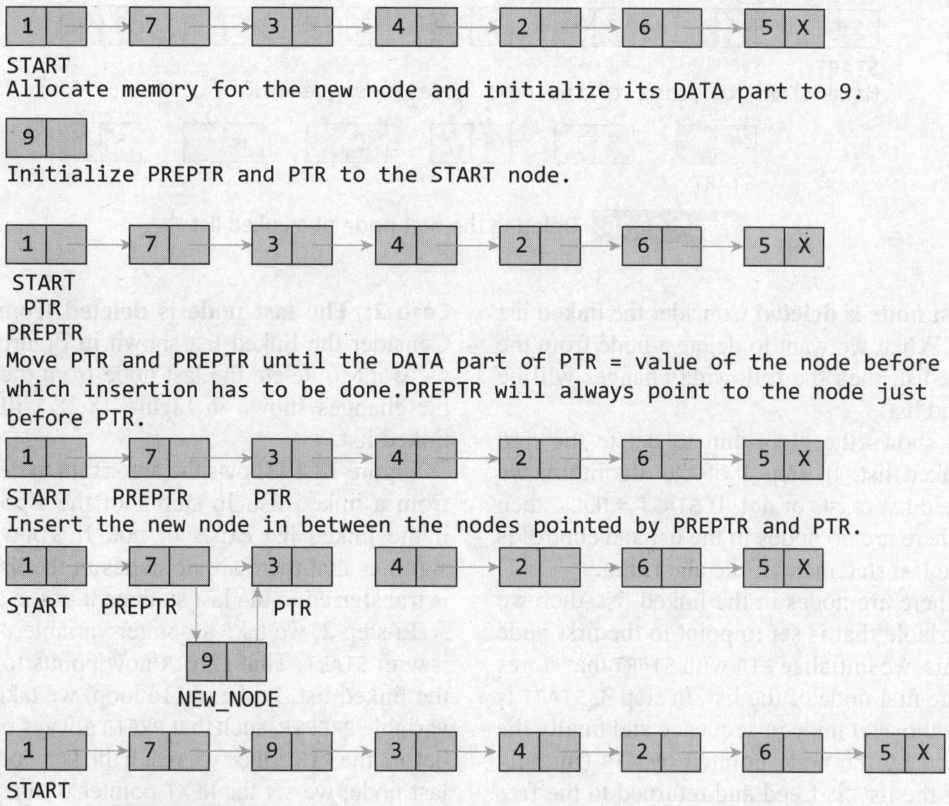

Figure 18.14 Inserting an element before a give node in a linked list

```
Step 1: IF AVAIL = NULL, then
              Write OVERFLOW
              Go to Step 12
        [END OF IF]
Step 2: SET New_Node = AVAIL
Step 3: SET AVAIL = AVAIL->NEXT
Step 4: SET New_Node->DATA = VAL
Step 5: SET PTR = START
Step 6: SET PREPTR = PTR
Step 7:  Repeat Steps 8 and 9 while PTR->
         DATA != NUM
Step 8:         SET PREPTR = PTR
Step 9:         SET PTR = PTR->NEXT
        [END OF LOOP]
Step 10:PREPTR->NEXT = New_Node
Step 11:SET New_Node->NEXT = PTR
Step 12:EXIT
```

Figure 18.15 Algorithm to insert a new node before a node that has value NUM

In step 5, we take a pointer variable PTR and initialize it with START. That is, PTR now points to the first node of the linked list. Then we take another pointer variable PREPTR and initialize it with PTR. Hence, now, PTR, PREPTR, and START all point to the first node of the linked list.

In the while loop, we traverse through the linked list to reach the node that has its value equal to NUM. We need to reach this node because the new node will be inserted before this node. Once we reach this node, in steps 10 and 11, we change NEXT pointers in such a way that new node is inserted before the desired node.

18.4.4 Deleting a Node from a Linked List

In this section, we will discuss how a node is deleted from an already existing linked list. We will take three cases and then see how the deletion is achieved in each case.

Case 1 The first node is deleted.

Case 2 The last node is deleted.

Case 3 The node after a given node is deleted.

Before we start with the algorithms to do deletions in all these three cases, let us first discuss an important term, UNDERFLOW. UNDERFLOW is a condition that occurs when we try to delete a node from a linked list that is empty. This happens when START = NULL, or when we try to delete nodes even when there are no more nodes left.

Note that, when we delete a node from a linked list, then we have to actually free the memory occupied by that node. The memory is returned to the free pool so that it can be used to store other useful programs and data. Hence, whatever be the case of deletion, we always change the AVAIL pointer, so that it now points to the address that has been recently vacated.

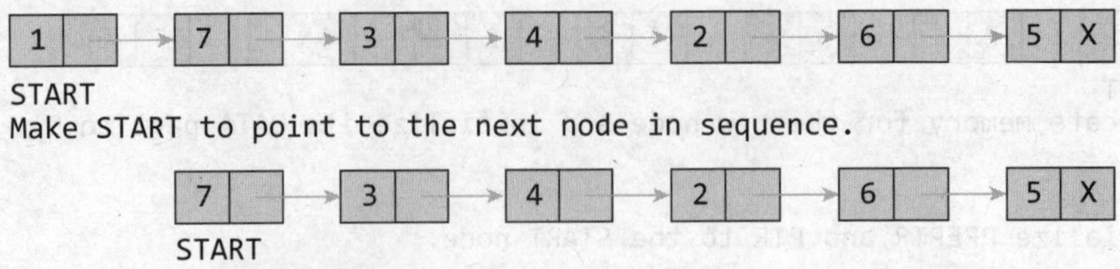

Figure 18.16 Deleting the first node of a linked list

Case 1: The first node is deleted Consider the linked list in Figure 18.16. When we want to delete a node from the beginning of the list, then the following changes will be done in the linked list.

Figure 18.17 shows the algorithm to delete the first node from a linked list. In step 1 of the algorithm, we check if the linked list exists or not. If `START = NULL`, then it signifies that there are no nodes in the list and control is transferred to the last statement of the algorithm.

However, if there are nodes in the linked list, then we use a pointer variable that is set to point to the first node of the list. For this, we initialize `PTR` with `START` that stores the address of the first node of the list. In step 3, `START` is made to point to the next node in sequence and finally the memory occupied by the node pointed by `PTR` (initially the first node of the list) is freed and returned to the free pool.

```
Step 1: IF START = NULL, then
            Write UNDERFLOW
            Go to Step 5
        [END OF IF]
Step 2: SET PTR = START
Step 3: SET START = START->NEXT
Step 4: FREE PTR
Step 5: EXIT
```

Figure 18.17 Algorithm to delete the first node from a linked list

Case 2: The last node is deleted from the linked list Consider the linked list shown in Figure 18.18. Suppose we want to delete the last node from the linked list, then the changes shown in Figure 18.18 will be made in the linked list.

Figure 18.19 shows the algorithm to delete the last node from a linked list. In step 1 of the algorithm, we check if the linked list exists or not. If `START = NULL`, then it signifies that there are no nodes in the list and the control is transferred to the last statement of the algorithm.

In step 2, we take a pointer variable, `PTR` and initialize it with `START`. That is, `PTR` now points to the first node of the linked list. In the `while` loop, we take another pointer variable `PREPTR`, such that `PRETR` always points to one node before the `PTR`. Once we reach the last node and the second last node, we set the `NEXT` pointer of the second last node to `NULL`, so that it now becomes the (new) last node of the linked list. The memory of the previous last node is freed and returned to the free pool.

Case 3: The node after a given node is deleted Consider the linked list shown in Figure 18.20. Suppose we want to delete the node that succeeds the node containing data value 4. Then the following changes will be done in the linked list.

Figure 18.21 shows the algorithm to delete the node after a given node from a linked list. In step 1 of the algorithm, we check if the linked list exists also or not. If `START = NULL`, then it signifies that there are no nodes in

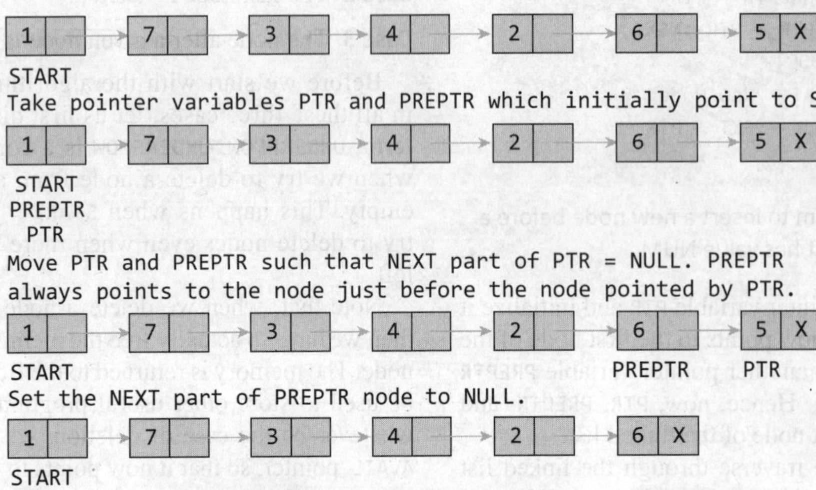

Figure 18.18 Deleting the last node of a linked list

```
Step 1: IF START = NULL, then
            Write UNDERFLOW
            Go to Step  8
        [END OF IF]
Step 2: SET PTR = START
Step 3:  Repeat Steps 4 and 5 while PTR
         ->NEXT != NULL
Step 4:          SET PREPTR = PTR
Step 5:          SET PTR = PTR->NEXT
        [END OF LOOP]
Step 6: SET PREPTR->NEXT = NULL
Step 7: FREE PTR
Step 8: EXIT
```

Figure 18.19 Algorithm to delete the last node from a linked list

the list and the control is transferred to the last statement of the algorithm.

In step 2, we take a pointer variable PTR and initialize it with START. That is, PTR now points to the first node of the linked list. In the while loop, we take another pointer variable PREPTR, such that PREPTR always points to one node before the PTR. Once we reach the node containing VAL and the node succeeding it, we set the NEXT pointer of the node containing VAL to the address contained in the NEXT field of the node succeeding it. The memory of the node succeeding the given node is freed and returned to the free pool.

```
Step 1:  IF START = NULL, then
         Write UNDERFLOW
              Go to Step 10
         [END OF IF]
Step 2: SET PTR = START
Step 3: SET PREPTR = PTR
Step 4:  Repeat Steps 5 and 6 while PREPTR
         ->DATA != NU M
Step 5:  SET PREPTR = PTR
Step 6:  SET PTR = PTR->NEXT
         [END OF LOOP]
Step 7: SET TEMP = PTR
Step 8: SET PREPTR->NEXT = PTR->NEXT
Step 9: FREE TEMP
Step 10:EXIT
```

Figure 18.21 Algorithm to delete the node after a given node from a linked list

1. Write a program to create a linked list and perform insertions and deletions of all cases. Write functions to sort and finally delete the entire list at once.

Solution:

```
#include <stdio.h>
#include <stdlib.h>
```

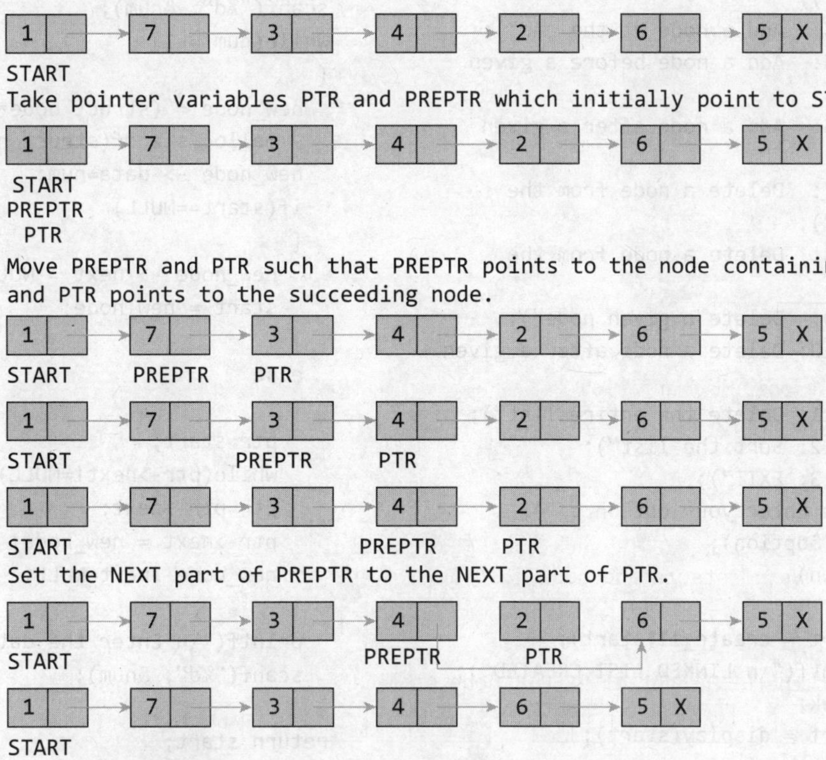

Figure 18.20 Deleting the node after a given node in a linked list

```
#include <malloc.h>
struct node
{
  int data;
  struct node *next;
};
struct node *start = NULL;
struct node *create_ll(struct node *);
struct node *display(struct node *);
struct node *insert_beg(struct node *);
struct node *insert_end(struct node *);
struct node *insert_before(struct node *);
struct node *insert_after(struct node *);
struct node *delete_beg(struct node *);
struct node *delete_end(struct node *);
struct node *delete_node(struct node *);
struct node *delete_after(struct node *);
struct node *delete_list(struct node *);
struct node *sort_list(struct node *);


int main() {
  int option;
  do
  {
    printf("\n\n *****MAIN MENU *****");
    printf("\n 1:  Create a list");
    printf("\n 2:  Display the list");
    printf("\n 3:  Add a node at the
      beginning");
    printf("\n 4:  Add a node at the end");
    printf("\n 5:  Add a node before a given
      node");
    printf("\n 6:  Add a node after a given
      node");
    printf("\n 7:  Delete a node from the
      beginning");
    printf("\n 8:  Delete a node from the
      end");
    printf("\n 9:  Delete a given node");
    printf("\n 10: Delete a node after a given
      node");
    printf("\n 11: Delete the entire list");
    printf("\n 12: Sort the list");
    printf("\n 13: EXIT");
    printf("\n\n Enter your option : ");
    scanf("%d", &option);
    switch(option)
    {
    case 1: start = create_ll(start);
            printf("\n LINKED LIST CREATED");
            break;
    case 2: start = display(start);
            break;
    case 3: start = insert_beg(start);
            break;
    case 4: start = insert_end(start);
            break;
    case 5: start = insert_before(start);
            break;
    case 6: start = insert_after(start);
            break;
    case 7: start = delete_beg(start);
            break;
    case 8: start = delete_end(start);
            break;
    case 9: start = delete_node(start);
            break;
    case 10: start = delete_after(start);
             break;
    case 11: start = delete_list(start);
             printf("\n LINKED LIST DELETED");
             break;
    case 12: start = sort_list(start);
             break;
    }
  }while(option !=13);
  return 0;
}
struct node *create_ll(struct node *start)
{
  struct node *new_node, *ptr;
  int num;
  printf("\n Enter -1 to end");
  printf("\n Enter the data : ");
  scanf("%d", &num);
  while(num!=-1)
  {
    new_node = (struct node*)
      malloc(sizeof(struct node));
    new_node -> data=num;
    if(start==NULL)
    {
      new_node -> next = NULL;
      start = new_node;
    }
    else
    {
      ptr=start;
      while(ptr->next!=NULL)
      ptr=ptr->next;
      ptr->next = new_node;
      new_node->next=NULL;
    }
    printf("\n Enter the data : ");
    scanf("%d", &num);
  }
  return start;
}
```

```
struct node *display(struct node *start)
{
  struct node *ptr;
  ptr = start;
  while(ptr != NULL)
  {
    printf("\t %d", ptr -> data);
    ptr = ptr -> next;
  }
  return start;
}
struct node *insert_beg(struct node *start)
{
  struct node *new_node;
  int num;
  printf("\n Enter the data : ");
  scanf("%d", &num);
  new_node = (struct node *)
   malloc(sizeof(struct node));
  new_node -> data = num;
  new_node -> next = start;
  start = new_node;
  return start;
}
struct node *insert_end(struct node *start)
{
  struct node *ptr, *new_node;
  int num;
  printf("\n Enter the data : ");
  scanf("%d", &num);
  new_node = (struct node *)
   malloc(sizeof(struct node));
  new_node -> data = num;
  new_node -> next = NULL;
  ptr = start;
  while(ptr -> next != NULL)
  ptr = ptr -> next;
  ptr -> next = new_node;
  return start;
}
struct node *insert_before(struct node *start)
{
  struct node *new_node, *ptr, *preptr;
  int num, val;
  printf("\n Enter the data : ");
  scanf("%d", &num);
  printf("\n Enter the value before which the
   data has to be inserted : ");
  scanf("%d", &val);
  new_node = (struct node *)
   malloc(sizeof(struct node));
  new_node -> data = num;
  ptr = start;
  while(ptr -> data != val)
  {
    preptr = ptr;
    ptr = ptr -> next;
  }
  preptr -> next = new_node;
  new_node -> next = ptr;
  return start;
}
struct node *insert_after(struct node *start)
{
  struct node *new_node, *ptr, *preptr;
  int num, val;
  printf("\n Enter the data : ");
  scanf("%d", &num);
  printf("\n Enter the value after which the
   data has to be inserted : ");
  scanf("%d", &val);
  new_node = (struct node *)
   malloc(sizeof(struct node));
  new_node -> data = num;
  ptr = start;
  preptr = ptr;
  while(preptr -> data != val)
  {
    preptr = ptr;
    ptr = ptr -> next;
  }
  preptr -> next=new_node;
  new_node -> next = ptr;
  return start;
}
struct node *delete_beg(struct node *start)
{
  struct node *ptr;
  ptr = start;
  start = start -> next;
  free(ptr);
  return start;
}
struct node *delete_end(struct node *start)
{
  struct node *ptr, *preptr;
  ptr = start;
  while(ptr -> next != NULL)
  {
    preptr = ptr;
    ptr = ptr -> next;
  }
  preptr -> next = NULL;
  free(ptr);
  return start;
}
struct node *delete_node(struct node *start)
{
  struct node *ptr, *preptr;
  int val;
  printf("\n Enter the value of the node which
   has to be deleted : ");
```

```
   scanf("%d", &val);
   ptr = start;
   if(ptr -> data == val)
   {
     start = delete_beg(start);
     return start;
   }
   else
   {
     while(ptr -> data != val)
     {
       preptr = ptr;
       ptr = ptr -> next;
     }
     preptr -> next = ptr -> next;
     free(ptr);
     return start;
   }
 }
 struct node *delete_after(struct node *start)
 {
   struct node *ptr, *preptr;
   int val;
   printf("\n Enter the value after which the
    node has to deleted : ");
   scanf("%d", &val);
   ptr = start;
   preptr = ptr;
   while(preptr -> data != val)
   {
     preptr = ptr;
     ptr = ptr -> next;
   }
   preptr -> next=ptr -> next;
   free(ptr);
   return start;
 }
 struct node *delete_list(struct node *start)
 {
   struct node *ptr;
   if(start!=NULL){
     ptr=start;
     while(ptr != NULL)
     {
       printf("\n %d is to be deleted next",
    ptr -> data);
       start = delete_beg(ptr);
       ptr = start;
     }
   }
   return start;
 }
 struct node *sort_list(struct node *start)
 {
   struct node *ptr1, *ptr2;
   int temp;
   ptr1 = start;
   while(ptr1 -> next != NULL)
   {
     ptr2 = ptr1 -> next;
     while(ptr2 != NULL)
     {
       if(ptr1 -> data > ptr2 -> data)
       {
         temp = ptr1 -> data;
         ptr1 -> data = ptr2 -> data;
         ptr2 -> data = temp;
       }
       ptr2 = ptr2 -> next;
     }
     ptr1 = ptr1 -> next;
   }
   return start;
 }
```

Output

```
*****MAIN MENU *****
1: Create a list
2: Display the list
3: Add a node at the beginning
4: Add the node at the end
5: Add the node before a given node
6: Add the node after a given node
7: Delete a node from the beginning
8: Delete a node from the end
9: Delete a given node
10: Delete a node after a given node
11: Delete the entire list
12: Sort the list
13: Exit
Enter your option : 3
Enter your option : 73
```

18.5 STACKS

Stack is an important data structure which stores its elements in an ordered manner. We will explain the concept of stacks using an analogy. You must have seen a pile of plates where one plate is placed on top of the other, as shown in Figure 18.22. Now, whenever you want

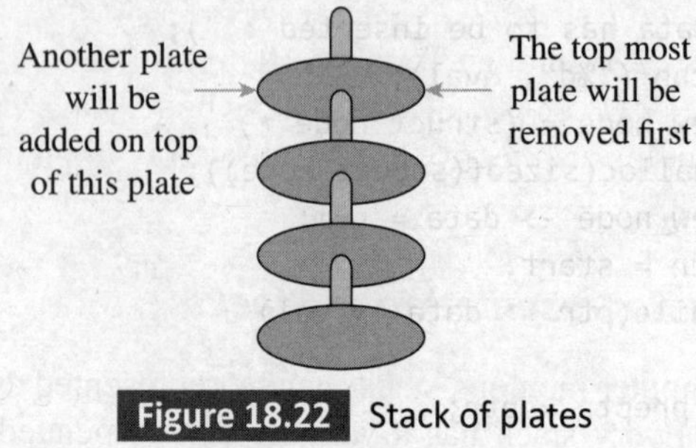

Figure 18.22 Stack of plates

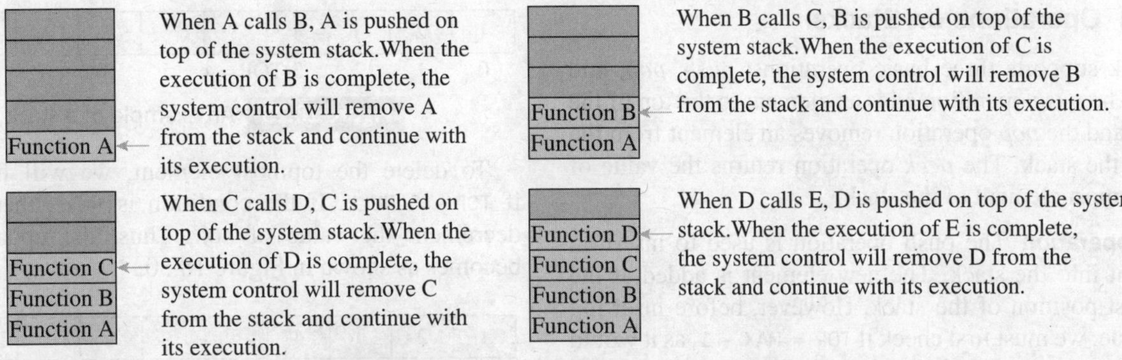

Figure 18.23 System stack in case of function calls

to remove a plate, you will remove the topmost plate first. Hence, you can add and remove an element (plate) only at/from one position, that is, the topmost position.

A stack is a linear data structure which uses the same principle, that is, the elements in a stack are added and removed only from one end, which is called *top*. Hence, a stack is called a last in, first out (LIFO) data structure as the element that is inserted last is the first one to be taken out.

Now the question is, where do we need stacks in computer science? The answer to this question is, in function calls. Consider an example, where we are executing function A. In the course of its execution, function A calls another function B. Now, function B calls another function C, which in turn calls function D. Finally, function D calls another function E.

In order to keep track of the returning point of each active function, a special stack called system stack or call stack is used. Whenever a function calls another function, the calling function is pushed on to the top of the stack. This is because after the called function gets executed, control will be passed back to the calling function. Figure 18.23 depicts this concept.

Now, when function E is executed, function D will be removed from the top of the stack and executed. Once function D gets completely executed, function C will be removed from the stack for execution. The whole procedure will be repeated until all the functions get executed completely. Let us see the stack after each function is executed. This is shown in Figure 18.24.

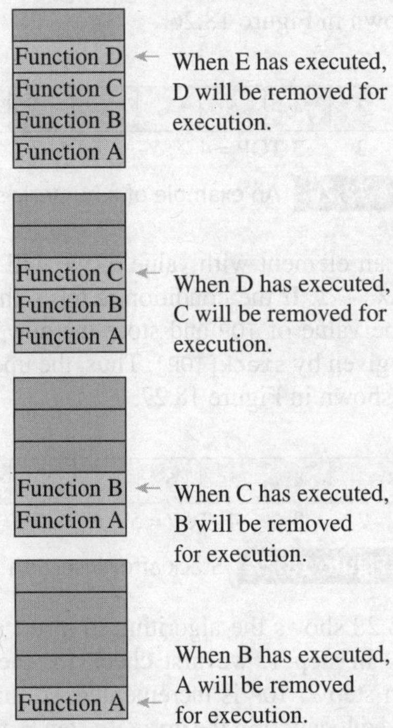

Figure 18.24 System stack when a called function returns to the calling function

Thus, system stacks ensure a proper execution order of functions. Therefore, stacks are frequently used in situations where the order of processing of data is very important, especially when the processing needs to be postponed until other conditions are fulfilled.

Stacks can be implemented using both arrays and linked lists. In this chapter, we will discuss array implementation of stacks.

Array Representation of Stacks

In computer memory, stacks can be represented as a linear array. Every stack has a variable `TOP` associated with it. `TOP` is used to store the address of the topmost element of the stack. It is this position from where the element will be added or deleted. There is another variable, `MAX`, which will be used to store the maximum number of elements that the stack can hold.

If `TOP = NULL`, then it indicates that the stack is empty, and if `TOP = MAX - 1`, then the stack is full. (You must be wondering why we have written `MAX - 1`. Do not forget that array indices start from 0.) Refer to Figure 18.25.

The stack in Figure 18.25 shows that TOP = 4, so insertions and deletions will be done at this position. In this stack, five more elements can still be stored.

AB	AB	ABC	ABCD	ABCDE					
0	1	2	3	TOP = 4	5	6	7	8	9

Figure 18.25 An example of a stack

18.5.1 Operations on Stacks

A stack supports three basic operations: *push*, *pop*, and *peek*. The *push* operation adds an element to the top of the stack, and the *pop* operation removes an element from the top of the stack. The *peek* operation returns the value of the topmost element of the stack.

Push operation The push operation is used to insert an element into the stack. The new element is added at the topmost position of the stack. However, before inserting the value, we must first check if `TOP = MAX - 1`, as it would mean that the stack is full and no further insertions can be done. If an attempt is made to insert a value in a stack that is already full, an `OVERFLOW` message is printed. Consider the stack shown in Figure 18.26.

1	2	3	4	5					
0	1	2	3	TOP = 4	5	6	7	8	9

Figure 18.26 An example of a numeric stack

To insert an element with value 6, we will first check if `TOP = MAX - 1`. If the condition is false, then we will increment the value of `TOP` and store the new element at the position given by `stack[TOP]`. Thus, the updated stack becomes as shown in Figure 18.27.

1	2	3	4	5	6				
0	1	2	3	4	TOP = 5	6	7	8	9

Figure 18.27 Stack after insertion

Figure 18.28 shows the algorithm to insert an element in the stack. In step 1, we first check for the `OVERFLOW` condition. In step 2, `TOP` is incremented, so that it points to the next free location in the array. In step 3, the value is stored in the stack at the location pointed by `TOP`.

```
Step 1: IF TOP = MAX -1, then
                WRITE "OVERFLOW"
                Go to Step 4
        [END OF IF]
Step 2: SET TOP = TOP + 1
Step 3: SET STACK[TOP] = VALUE
Step 4: EXIT
```

Figure 18.28 Algorithm to push an element in a stack

Pop operation The pop operation is used to delete the topmost element from the stack. However, before deleting the value, we must first check if `TOP = NULL`, as it would mean that the stack is empty and therefore no further deletions can be done. If an attempt is made to delete a value from a stack that is already empty, an `UNDERFLOW` message is printed. Consider the stack given in Figure 18.29.

1	2	3	4	5					
0	1	2	3	TOP = 4	5	6	7	8	9

Figure 18.29 An example of a stack

To delete the topmost element, we will first check if `TOP = NULL`. If the condition is false, then we will decrement the value of `TOP`. Thus, the updated stack becomes as shown in Figure 18.30.

1	2	3	4	5					
0	1	2	TOP = 3	4	5	6	7	8	9

Figure 18.30 Stack after deletion

Figure 18.31 shows the algorithm to delete an element from the stack. In step 1, we first check for the `UNDERFLOW` condition. In step 2, the value of the location in the stack pointed by `TOP` is stored in `VAL`. In step 3, `TOP` is decremented.

```
Step 1: IF TOP = NULL, then
                WRITE "UNDERFLOW"
                Go to Step 4
        [END OF IF]
Step 2: SET VAL = STACK[TOP]
Step 3: SET TOP = TOP - 1
Step 4: EXIT
```

Figure 18.31 Algorithm to pop an element from the stack

Peek operation Peek is an operation that returns the value of the topmost element of the stack without deleting it from the stack. The algorithm for the peek operation is given in Figure 18.32.

```
Step 1: IF TOP = NULL, then
                WRITE "STACK IS EMPTY"
                Go TO Step 3
        [END OF IF]
Step 2: RETURN STACK[TOP]
Step 3: EXIT
```

Figure 18.32 Algorithm for peek operation

The peek operation first checks if the stack is empty or if it contains some elements. For this, a condition is checked. If `TOP = NULL`, then an appropriate message is printed; else, the value is returned. Consider the stack given in Figure 18.33.

1	2	3	4	5					
0	1	2	3	TOP = 4	5	6	7	8	9

Figure 18.33 An example of a stack

Here, the peek operation will return 5, as it is the value of the topmost element of the stack.

2. Write a program to perform Push, Pop, and Peek operations on a stack.

Solution:

```
#include <stdio.h>
#include <stdlib.h>
#define MAX 3

int st[MAX], top=-1;
void push(int st[], int val);
int pop(int st[]);
int peek(int st[]);
void display(int st[]);

int main() {
  int val, option;
  do
  {
    printf("\n *****MAIN MENU*****");
    printf("\n 1. PUSH");
    printf("\n 2. POP");
    printf("\n 3. PEEK");
    printf("\n 4. DISPLAY");
    printf("\n 5. EXIT");
    printf("\n Enter your option: ");
    scanf("%d", &option);
    switch(option)
    {
    case 1:
      printf("\n Enter the number to be pushed
        on stack: ");
      scanf("%d", &val);
      push(st, val);
      break;
    case 2:
      val = pop(st);
      if(val != -1)
      printf("\n The value deleted from stack
        is: %d", val);
      break;
    case 3:
      val = peek(st);
      if(val != -1)
      printf("\n The value stored at top of
        stack is: %d", val);
      break;
    case 4:
      display(st);
      break;
    }
  }while(option != 5);
  return 0;
}
void push(int st[], int val)
{
  if(top == MAX-1)
  {
    printf("\n STACK OVERFLOW");
  }
  else
  {
    top++;
    st[top] = val;
  }
}
int pop(int st[])
{
  int val;
  if(top == -1)
  {
    printf("\n STACK UNDERFLOW");
    return -1;
  }
  else
  {
    val = st[top];
    top--;
    return val;
  }
}
void display(int st[])
{
  int i;
  if(top == -1)
  printf("\n STACK IS EMPTY");
  else
  {
    for(i=top;i>=0;i--)
    printf("\n %d",st[i]);
    printf("\n");
  }
}
int peek(int st[])
{
  if(top == -1)
  {
    printf("\n STACK IS EMPTY");
    return -1;
  }
  else
  return (st[top]);
}
```

Output

```
*****MAIN MENU*****
1. PUSH
2. POP
3. PEEK
4. DISPLAY
5. EXIT
Enter your option : 1
Enter the number to be pushed on stack : 500
```

18.6 QUEUES

Let us explain the concept of queues using the analogies given below.

- People using an escalator—those who get on the escalator first will be the first ones to step out of it.
- People waiting for a bus—the first person standing in the line will be the first one to get on to the bus.
- People standing outside the ticketing window of a cinema hall—the first person in the line will get the ticket first and thus will be the first one to move out of it.
- Luggage kept on conveyor belts—the bag that was placed first will be the first to come out at the other end.
- Cars lined up for filling petrol—the car that comes first will be filled first.

In all these examples, we see that the element in the first position is served first. The same is the case with the queue data structure. A queue is a first-in, first-out (FIFO) data structure, in which the element that is inserted first is the first one to be taken out. The elements in a queue are added at one end called the *rear*, and removed from the other end called the *front*.

Queues can be implemented either using arrays or linked lists. In this chapter, we will see how queues are implemented using arrays.

18.6.1 Operations on Queues

Queues can be easily represented using linear arrays. As stated earlier, every queue has `FRONT` and `REAR` variables that will point to the position from where deletions and insertions, respectively, can be performed. Consider the queue shown in Figure 18.34.

12	9	7	18	14	36				
0	1	2	3	4	5	6	7	8	9

Figure 18.34 An example of a queue

Here, `FRONT = 0` and `REAR = 5`. If we want to add one more value in the list, say, another element with value 45, then `REAR` would be incremented by 1 and the value would be stored at the position pointed by `REAR`. The queue after addition would appear as shown in Figure 18.35.

12	9	7	18	14	36	45			
0	1	2	3	4	5	6	7	8	9

Figure 18.35 Queue after insertion of a new element

Here, `FRONT = 0` and `REAR = 6`. Every time a new element has to be added, we will repeat the same procedure.

Now, if we want to delete an element from the queue, then the value of `FRONT` will be incremented. Deletions are done from only this end of the queue. The queue after deletion of an element will be as shown in Figure 18.36.

Here, `FRONT = 1` and `REAR = 6`.

	9	7	18	14	36	45			
0	1	2	3	4	5	6	7	8	9

Figure 18.36 Queue after deletion of an element

However, before inserting an element in the queue, we must check for `OVERFLOW` conditions. An `OVERFLOW` will occur when we try to insert an element into a queue that is already full, when `REAR = MAX - 1`, where `MAX` is the size of the queue, that is, `MAX` specifies the maximum number of elements that the queue can hold. Note we have written `MAX - 1`, because the index starts from 0.

Similarly, before deleting an element from the queue, we must check for the `UNDERFLOW` condition. An `UNDERFLOW` condition occurs when we try to delete an element from a queue that is already empty. If `FRONT = NULL` and `REAR = NULL`, this means that there is no element in the queue.

Figure 18.37 describes the algorithm to insert an element in a queue. In step 1, we first check for the `OVERFLOW` condition. In step 2, we check if the queue is empty. In case the queue is initially empty, then the value of `FRONT` and `REAR` is set to zero, so that the new value can be stored at the zero-th location. Otherwise, if the queue already has some values, then `REAR` is incremented so that it points to the next free location in the array. In step 3, the value is stored in the queue at the location pointed by `REAR`.

```
Step 1: IF REAR=MAX-1, then
                Write OVERFLOW
                Go to Step 4
          [END OF IF]
Step 2: IF FRONT = NULL and REAR = NULL, then
                SET FRONT = REAR = 0
          ELSE
                SET REAR = REAR + 1
          [END OF IF]
Step 3: SET QUEUE[REAR] = NUM
Step 4: EXIT
```

Figure 18.37 Algorithm to insert an element in a queue

Figure 18.38 shows the algorithm to delete an element from a queue. In Step 1, we check for `UNDERFLOW` condition. An `UNDERFLOW` occurs if FRONT = NULL or FRONT > REAR. However, if queue has some values, then FRONT is incremented so that it now points to the next value in the queue.

```
Step 1: IF FRONT = NULL OR FRONT > REAR, then
                Write UNDERFLOW
          ELSE
                SET VAL = QUEUE[FRONT]
                SET FRONT = FRONT + 1
          [END OF IF]
Step 2: EXIT
```

Figure 18.38 Algorithm to delete an element from a queue

3. Write a program to implement a linear queue.

Solution:

```
##include <stdio.h>
```

```
#define MAX 10
int queue[MAX];
int front = -1, rear = -1;
void insert(void);
int delete_element(void);
int peek(void);
void display(void);
int main()
{
  int option, val;
  do
  {
    printf("\n\n ***** MAIN MENU *****");
    printf("\n 1. Insert an element");
    printf("\n 2. Delete an element");
    printf("\n 3. Peek");
    printf("\n 4. Display the queue");
    printf("\n 5. EXIT");
    printf("\n Enter your option : ");
    scanf("%d", &option);
    switch(option)
    {
    case 1:
      insert();
      break;
    case 2:
      val = delete_element();
      if (val != -1)
      printf("\n The number deleted is : %d",
        val);
      break;
    case 3:
      val = peek();
      if (val != -1)
      printf("\n The first value in queue is :
        %d", val);
      break;
    case 4:
      display();
      break;
    }
  }while(option != 5);

  return 0;
}
void insert()
{
  int num;
  printf("\n Enter the number to be inserted
   in the queue : ");
  scanf("%d", &num);
  if(rear == MAX-1)
  printf("\n OVERFLOW");
  else if(front == -1 || rear == -1)
  front = rear = 0;
  else
    rear++;
    queue[rear] = num;
}
int delete_element()
{
  int val;
  if(front == -1 || front>rear)
  {

    printf("\n UNDERFLOW");
    return -1;
  }
  else
  {
    val = queue[front];
    front++;
    if(front > rear)
    front = rear = -1;
    return val;
  }

}
int peek()
{
  if(front==-1 || front>rear)
  {

    printf("\n QUEUE IS EMPTY");
    return -1;
  }
  else
  {
    return queue[front];
  }

}
void display()
{
  int i;
  printf("\n");
  if(front == -1 || front > rear)
  printf("\n QUEUE IS EMPTY");
  else
  {
    for(i = front;i <= rear;i++)
    printf("\t %d", queue[i]);
  }
}
```

Output

```
***** MAIN MENU *****"
1. Insert an element
2. Delete an element
3. Peek
4. Display the queue
5. EXIT
Enter your option : 1
Enter the number to be inserted in the queue
: 50
```

18.7 TREES

A tree is recursively defined as a set of one or more nodes where one node is designated as the root of the tree and all the remaining nodes can be partitioned into non-empty sets each of which is a subtree of the root. In this chapter, we will discuss binary trees in which each note has 0, 1, or at the most 2 children.

In a binary tree every node contains a 'left' pointer which points to the left child, a 'right' pointer which points to the right child, and a data element. The root element is the topmost node in the tree which is pointed by the `root` pointer. If `root = NULL`, it means that the tree is empty.

Figure 18.39 shows a binary tree. In the figure, `R` is the root node and the two trees T_1 and T_2 are called the left and right sub-trees of `R`. If T_1 is non-empty, then T_1 is said to be the left successor of `R`. Likewise, if T_2 is non-empty then, it is called the right successor of `R`.

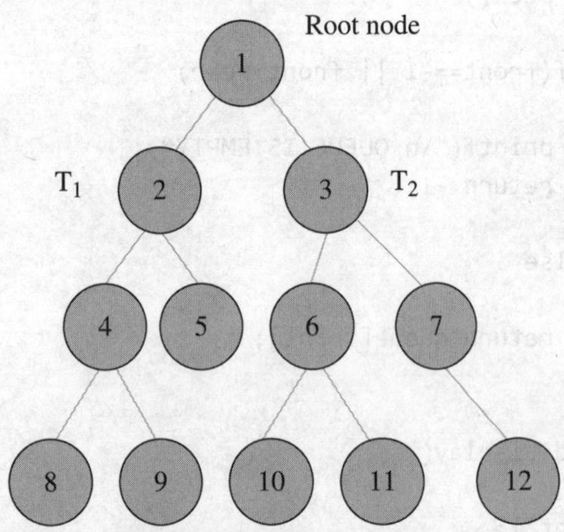

Figure 18.39 Binary tree

In Figure 18.39, node 2 is the left successor and node 3 is the right successor of root node 1. Note that the left sub-tree of root node consists of the nodes 2, 4, 5, 8, and 9. Similarly, the right sub-tree of the root node consists of nodes 3, 6, 7, 10, 11, and 12.

In a binary tree, every node has 0–2 successors. A node that has no successors is called a leaf or terminal node. In the tree in Figure 18.39, root node `R` has two successors 2 and 3. Node 2 has two successor nodes, 4 and 5; node 4 has two successors 8 and 9; node 5 has no successor; node 3 has two successor nodes 6 and 7; node 6 has two successors 10 and 11; and finally, node 7 has only one successor, 12.

A binary tree is recursive by definition as every node in the tree contains a left sub-tree and a right sub-tree. Even the terminal nodes contain an empty left sub-tree and an empty right sub-tree. In Figure 18.39, nodes 5, 8, 9, 10, 11, and 12 have no or zero successors, and are thus said to have empty sub-trees.

Key Terms

- *Parent*: If `N` is any node in `T` that has left successor S_1 and right successor S_2, then `N` is called the parent of S_1 and S_2. Correspondingly, S_1 and S_2 are called the left child and the right child of `N`. Every node other than the root node has a parent.
- *Level number*: Every node in the binary tree is assigned a level number (refer Fig. 18.40). The root node is defined to be at level 0. The left and the right child of the root node have a level number 1. Similarly, every node is at one level higher than its parents. So all child nodes are defined to have level number as parent's level number + 1.

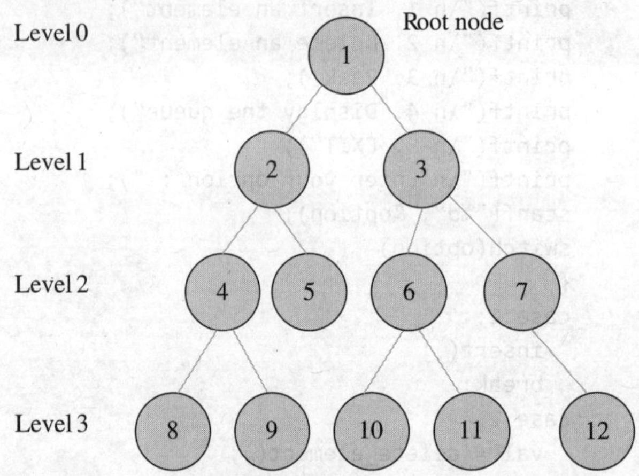

Figure 18.40 Binary tree

- *Degree of a node*: It is equal to the number of children that a node has. The degree of a leaf node is zero. For example, in the tree, degree of node 4 is 2, degree of node 5 is zero and degree of node 7 is 1.
- *Sibling*: All nodes that are at the same level and share the same parent are called siblings (brothers). For example, nodes 2 and 3; nodes 4 and 5; nodes 6 and 7; nodes 8 and 9; and nodes 10 and 11 are siblings.
- *Leaf node*: A node that has no children is called a leaf node or a terminal node. The leaf nodes in the tree are: 8, 9, 5, 10, 11, and 12.
- *Path*: A sequence of consecutive edges. For example, in Fig. 18.40, the path from the root node to the node 8 is given as: 1, 2, 4, and 8.
- *Depth*: The depth of a node `N` is given as the length of the path from the root `R` to the node `N`. The depth of the root node is zero.
- *Height of a tree*: It is the total number of nodes on the path from the root node to the deepest node in the tree. A tree with only a root node has a height of 1. A binary tree of height `h` has at least `h` nodes and at most `2h - 1` nodes. This is because every level will have at least one node and can have at most 2 nodes. So, if every level has two nodes then a tree with height `h` will have at the most `2h - 1` nodes as at level 0, there is only one elementcalled the root. The height of a binary tree with `n` nodes is at least $\log_2(n+1)$ and at most `n`.

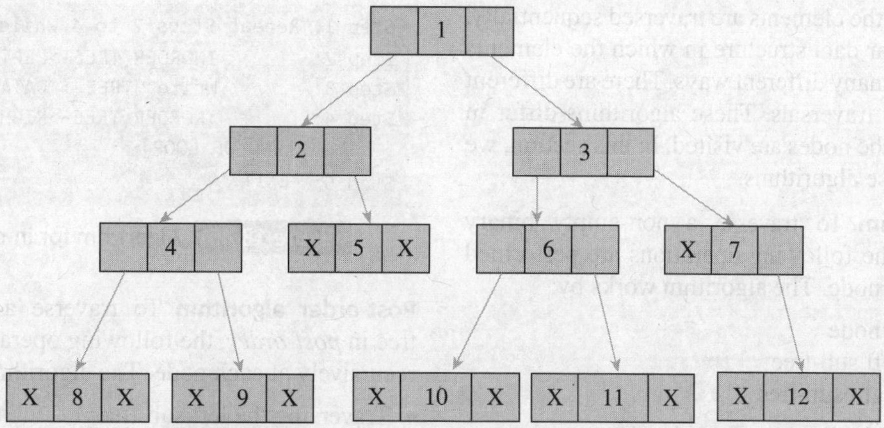

Figure 18.41 Linked representation of a binary tree

- *Ancestor and descendant nodes:* Ancestors of a node are all the nodes along the path from the root to that node. Similarly, descendants of a node are all the nodes along the path from that node to the leaf node.

Binary trees are commonly used to implement binary search trees, expression trees, tournament trees, and binary heaps.

18.7.1 Representation of Binary Trees in Memory

In the computer's memory, a binary tree can be maintained either using a linked representation (as in case of a linked list) or using a sequential representation (as in case of single arrays).

Linked representation of binary trees In the linked representation of binary trees, every node will have three parts: the data element, a pointer to the left node, and a pointer to the right node. Hence, in C, the binary tree is built with a node type given as follows:

```
struct node {
    struct node* left;
    int data;
    struct node* right;
};
```

Every binary tree has a pointer `ROOT`, which will point to the root element (topmost element) of the tree. If `ROOT = NULL`, then it means the tree is empty. The schematic diagram of the linked representation of the binary tree is shown in Figure 18.41.

In this figure, the left field is used to point to the left child of the node or, in technical terms, to store the address of the left child of the node. The middle field is used to store the data. Finally, the right field is used to point to the right child of the node or to store the address of the right child of the node. Empty sub-trees are represented using `X` (meaning `NULL`) in the figure.

Sequential representation of binary trees Sequential representation of binary trees is done using a single or one-dimensional array. Although it is the simplest technique for memory representation, it is very inefficient as it requires a lot of memory space. A sequential binary tree follows the following rules:

- A one-dimensional array, called `TREE`, is used.
- The root of the tree is stored in the first location. That is, `TREE[1]` will store the data of the root element.
- The children of a node `K` will be stored in location `(2*K)` and `(2*K+1)`.
- The maximum size of the array `TREE` is given as (2^h-1), where `h` is the height of the tree.
- An empty tree or sub-tree is specified using `NULL`. If `TREE[1] = NULL`, then the tree is empty.

Figure 18.42 shows a binary tree and its corresponding sequential representation. The tree has 11 nodes, and its height is 4.

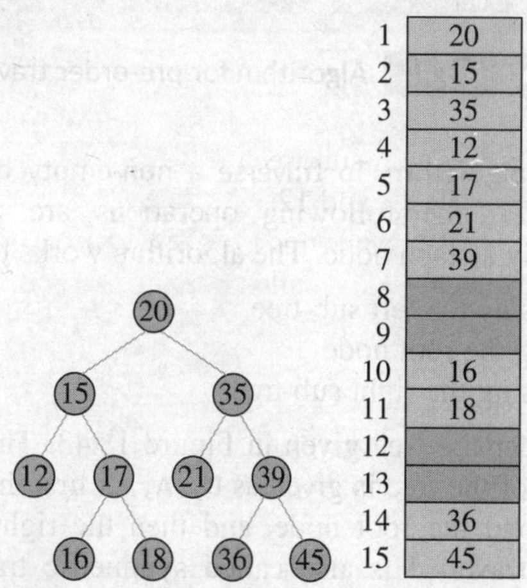

Figure 18.42 Binary tree and its sequential representation

18.7.2 Traversing a Binary Tree

Traversing a binary tree is the process of visiting each node exactly once in a systematic way. Unlike linear data structures in which the elements are traversed sequentially, a tree is a non-linear data structure in which the elements can be traversed in many different ways. There are different algorithms for tree traversals. These algorithms differ in the order in which the nodes are visited. In this section, we will read about these algorithms.

Pre-order algorithm To traverse a non-empty binary tree in pre-order, the following operations are performed recursively at each node. The algorithm works by:

- Visiting the root node
- Traversing the left sub-tree
- Traversing the right sub-tree

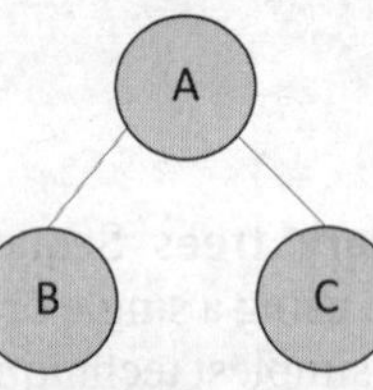

Figure 18.43 Binary tree

Consider the tree given in Figure 18.43.

The pre-order traversal of the tree is given as `A, B, C`; first the root node, second the left sub-tree, and then the right sub-tree. Pre-order traversal is also called depth-first traversal. In this algorithm, the left sub-tree is always traversed before the right sub-tree. The word 'pre' in 'pre-order' specifies that the root node is accessed prior to or before any other nodes in the left and right sub-trees. The pre-order algorithm is also known as node-left-right (NLR) traversal algorithm. The algorithm for pre-order traversal is given as shown in Figure 18.44.

```
Step 1: Repeat Steps 2 to 4 while TREE != NULL
Step 2:              Write TREE->DATA
Step 3:              PREORDER(TREE->LEFT)
Step 4:              PREORDER(TREE->RIGHT)
      [END OF LOOP]
Step 5: EXIT
```

Figure 18.44 Algorithm for pre-order traversal

In-order algorithm To traverse a non-empty binary tree in *in-order*, the following operations are performed recursively at each node. The algorithm works by:

- Traversing the left sub-tree
- Visiting the root node
- Traversing the right sub-tree

Consider the tree given in Figure 18.43. The in-order traversal of the tree is given as `B, A, C`; first the left sub-tree, second the root node, and then the right sub-tree. In-order traversal is also called symmetric traversal. In this algorithm, the left sub-tree is always traversed before the root node and the right sub-tree. The word 'in' in 'in-order' specifies that the root node is accessed in between the left and right sub-trees. The in-order algorithm is also known as LNR (Left-Node-Right) traversal algorithm. The algorithm for in-order travel is shown in Figure 18.45.

```
Step 1: Repeat Steps 2 to 4 while TREE! = NULL
Step 2:         INORDER(TREE->LEFT)
Step 3:         Write "TREE-> DATA"
Step 4:         INORDER(TREE->RIGHT)
          [END OF LOOP]
Step 5:  EXIT
```

Figure 18.45 Algorithm for in-order traversal

Post-order algorithm To traverse a non-empty binary tree in *post-order*, the following operations are performed recursively at each node. The algorithm works by:

- Traversing the left sub-tree
- Traversing the right sub-tree
- Visiting the root node

Consider the tree given in Figure 18.43. The post-order traversal of the tree is given as `B, C, A`; first the left sub-tree, second the right sub-tree, and then the root node. In this algorithm, the left sub-tree is always traversed before the right sub-tree and the root node. The word 'post' in 'post-order' specifies that the root node is accessed after the left and right sub-trees. The post-order algorithm is also known as left-right-node (LRN) traversal algorithm. The algorithm for post-order travel is shown in Figure 18.46.

```
Step 1: Repeat Steps 2 to 4 while TREE != NULL
Step 2:         POSTORDER(TREE->LEFT)
Step 3:         POSTORDER(TREE->RIGHT)
Step 4:         Write "TREE->DATA
          [END OF LOOP]
Step 5: EXIT
```

Figure 18.46 Algorithm for post-order traversal

Level-order traversal In level-order traversal, all the nodes at a level are accessed before going to the next level. This algorithm is also called breadth-first traversal algorithm. Considering the tree given in Figure 18.43, the level order of the tree can be given as: `A, B, and C`.

18.8 GRAPHS

A graph is a data structure that is used to implement the mathematical concept of graphs. It is basically a collection of vertices (also called nodes) and edges that connect these vertices. A graph is often viewed as a generalization of the tree structure, where instead of a having a purely parent-to-child relationship between tree nodes, any kind of complex relationships between the nodes can be represented.

Graphs are widely used to model any situation where entities or things are related to each other in pairs; for example, the following information can be represented by graphs:

- *Family trees* in which the member nodes have an edge from parent to each of their children.

- *Transportation networks* in which nodes are airports, intersections, ports, etc. The edges can be airline flights, one-way roads, shipping routes, etc.

Definition

- A graph G is defined as an ordered set (V, E), where V(G) represents the set of vertices and E(G) represents the edges that connect these vertices.
- Figure 18.47 shows a graph with V(G) = { A, B, C, D, E} and E(G) = { (A, B), (B, C), (A, D), (B, D), (D, E), (C, E) }. Note that there are five vertices or nodes and six edges in the graph.
- A graph can be directed or undirected. In an undirected graph, the edges do not have any direction associated with them. That is, if an edge is drawn between nodes A and B, then the nodes can be traversed from A to B as well as from B to A. Figure 18.47 shows an undirected graph because it does not give any information about the direction of the edges.

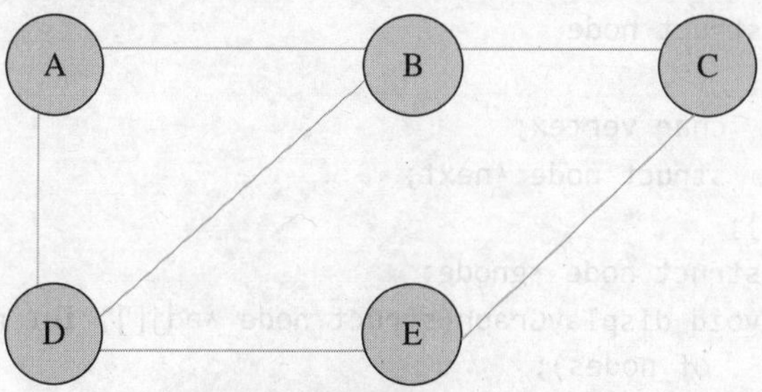

Figure 18.47 Graph

- Look at Figure 18.48, which shows a directed graph. In a directed graph, the edges form an ordered pair. If there is an edge from A to B, then there is a path from A to B, but not from B to A. The edge (A, B) is said to initiate from node A (also known as initial node) and terminate at node B (terminal node).

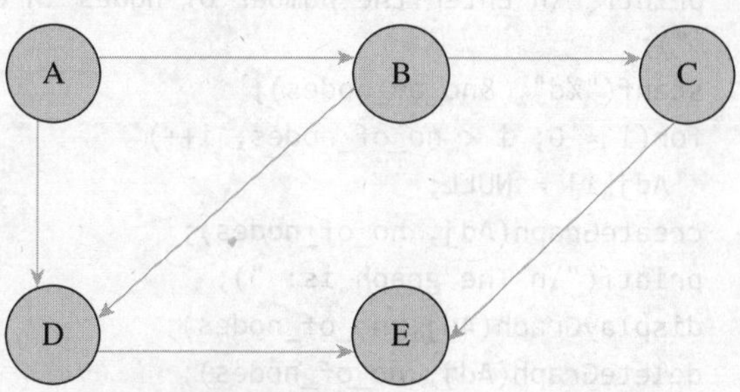

Figure 18.48 Directed graph

Graph Terminology

- *Adjacent nodes or neighbours:* For every edge e = (u, v)that connects nodes u and v; the nodes u and v are the end-points and are said to be the adjacent nodes or neighbours.
- *Degree of a node:* The degree of a node u, deg(u), is the total number of edges containing the node u. If deg(u) = 0, it means that u does not belong to any edge, and such a node is known as an *isolated node*.
- *Path:* A path P, written as P = $(v_0, v_1, v_2, \ldots, v_n)$, of length n from a node u to v is defined as a sequence of (n + 1) nodes. Here, u = v_0, v = v_n, and v_{i-1} is adjacent to v_i for i = 1, 2, 3, …, n.
- *Loop:* An edge that has identical end-points is called a loop. That is, e = (u, u).
- *Size of the graph:* The size of a graph is the total number of edges in it.

Terminology of a Directed Graph

- *Out-degree of a node:* The out-degree of a node u, written as outdeg(u), is the number of edges that originate at u.
- *In-degree of a node*: The in-degree of a node u, written as indeg(u), is the number of edges that terminate at u.
- *Degree of a node:* Degree of a node, written as deg(u), is equal to the sum of in-degree and out-degree of that node. Therefore, deg(u) = indeg(u) + outdeg(u).
- *Source:* A node u is known as a source if it has a positive out-degree but an in-degree = 0.
- *Sink:* A node u is known as a sink if it has a positive in-degree but a zero out-degree.
- *Reachability:* A node v is said to be reachable from node u, if and only if there exists a (directed) path from node u to node v. For example, if you consider the directed graph given in Figure 18.48, you will observe that node D is reachable from node A.

18.8.1 Representation of Graphs

There are two common ways of storing graphs in computer memory. They are:

- Sequential representation by using an adjacency matrix
- Linked representation by using an adjacency list that stores the neighbours of a node using a linked list

In this section, we will discuss both these schemes.

Adjacency matrix representation An adjacency matrix is used to represent the nodes that are adjacent to one another. By definition, we have learnt that two nodes are said to be adjacent if there is an edge connecting them.

In a directed graph G, if node v is adjacent to node u, then surely there is an edge from u to v. That is, if v is adjacent to u, we can get from u to v by traversing one edge. For any graph G having n nodes, the adjacency matrix will have dimensions of n × n.

In an adjacency matrix, the rows and columns are labelled by graph vertices. An entry aij in the adjacency matrix will contain 1, if vertices vi and vj are adjacent to each other. However, if the nodes are not adjacent, aij will be set to zero. To summarize, look at Figure 18.49.

Since an adjacency matrix contains only 0s and 1s, it is called a bit matrix or a Boolean matrix. The entries in the matrix depend on the ordering of the nodes in G. Therefore, a change in the order of nodes will result in

$$a_{ij} = \begin{cases} 1 & \text{if } v_i \text{ is adjacent to } v_j \text{, that is, there is an edge } (v_i, v_j) \\ 0 & \text{otherwise} \end{cases}$$

Figure 18.49 Adjacency matrix entry

a different adjacency matrix. Figure 18.50 shows a graph and its corresponding adjacency matrix.

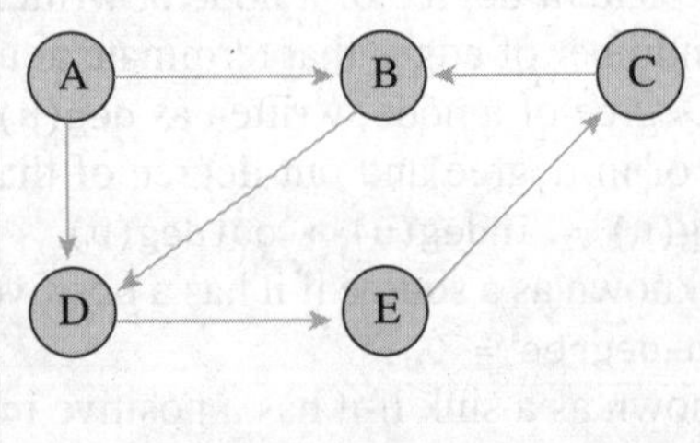

	A	B	C	D	E
A	0	1	0	1	0
B	0	0	0	1	0
C	0	1	0	0	0
D	0	0	0	0	1
E	0	0	1	0	0

Figure 18.50 Directed graph with adjacency matrix

Adjacency list The adjacency list is another way in which graphs can be represented in computer memory. This structure consists of a list of all nodes in G. Furthermore, every node is in turn linked to its own list, which contains the names of all other nodes that are adjacent to itself.

The key advantages of using an adjacency list include:

- It is easy to follow, and clearly shows the adjacent nodes of a particular node.
- It is often used for storing graphs that have a small to moderate number of edges. That is, an adjacency list is preferred for representing sparse graphs in computer memory. Otherwise, an adjacency matrix is a good choice.
- Adding new nodes in G is easy and straightforward when G is represented using an adjacency list. Adding new nodes in an adjacency matrix is a difficult task as the size of the matrix needs to be changed and existing nodes may have to be reordered.

Consider the graph given in Figure 18.51, and see how its adjacency list is stored in memory.

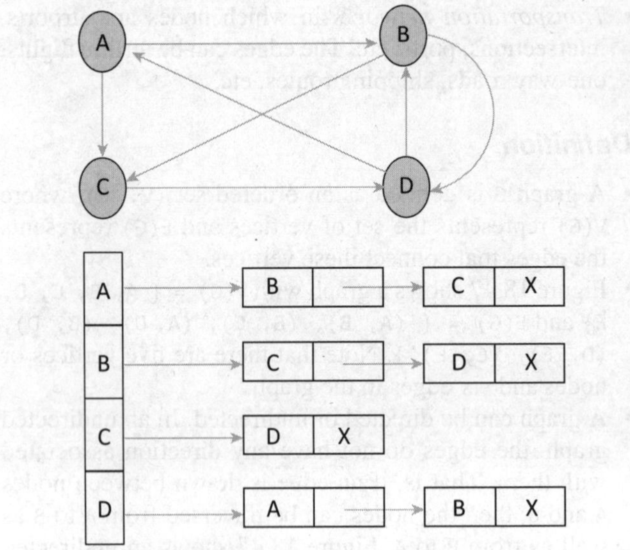

Figure 18.51 Graph G and its adjacency list

4. Write a program to create a graph of n vertices using an adjacency list. Also write the code to read and print its information and finally to delete the graph.

Solution:

```
#include <stdio.h>
#include<stdlib.h>
struct node
{
  char vertex;
  struct node *next;
};
struct node *gnode;
void displayGraph(struct node *adj[], int no_
   of_nodes);
void deleteGraph(struct node *adj[], int no_
   of_nodes);
void createGraph(struct node *adj[], int no_
   of_nodes);
int main()
{
  struct node *Adj[10];
  int i, no_of_nodes;
  printf("\n Enter the number of nodes in G:
  ");
  scanf("%d", &no_of_nodes);
  for(i = 0; i < no_of_nodes; i++)
    Adj[i] = NULL;
  createGraph(Adj, no_of_nodes);
  printf("\n The graph is: ");
  displayGraph(Adj, no_of_nodes);
  deleteGraph(Adj, no_of_nodes);
  return 0;
}
void createGraph(struct node *Adj[], int no_
   of_nodes)
{
  struct node *new_node, *last;
  int i, j, n, val;
  for(i = 0; i < no_of_nodes; i++)
```

```
        {
          last = NULL;
          printf("\n Enter the number of neighbours
        of %d: ", i);
          scanf("%d", &n);
          for(j = 1; j <= n; j++)
          {
            printf("\n Enter the neighbour %d of %d:
            ", j, i);
            scanf("%d", &val);
            new_node = (struct node *)
            malloc(sizeof(struct node));
            new_node -> vertex = val;
            new_node -> next = NULL;
            if (Adj[i] == NULL)
              Adj[i] = new_node;
            else
              last -> next = new_node;
            last = new_node;
          }
        }
}
void displayGraph (struct node *Adj[], int
   no_of_nodes)
{
   struct node *ptr;
   int i;
   for(i = 0; i < no_of_nodes; i++)
   {
     ptr = Adj[i];
     printf("\n The neighbours of node %d
       are:", i);
     while(ptr != NULL)
     {
       printf("\t%d", ptr -> vertex);
       ptr = ptr -> next;
     }
   }
}
void deleteGraph (struct node *Adj[], int
   no_of_nodes)
{
   int i;
   struct node *temp, *ptr;
   for(i = 0; i <= no_of_nodes; i++)
   {
     ptr = Adj[i];
     while(ptr != NULL)
     {
       temp = ptr;
       ptr = ptr -> next;
       free(temp);
     }
     Adj[i] = NULL;
   }
}
```

Output

```
Enter the number of nodes in G: 3
Enter the number of neighbours of 0: 1
Enter the neighbour 1 of 0: 2
Enter the number of neighbours of 1: 2
Enter the neighbour 1 of 1: 0
Enter the neighbour 2 of 1: 2
Enter the number of neighbours of 2: 1
Enter the neighbour 1 of 2: 1
The neighbours of node 0 are: 1
The neighbours of node 1 are: 0 2
The neighbours of node 2 are: 0
```

SUMMARY

- A data structure is a collection of elements that are grouped under one name.
- Data structures can be broadly classified into linear and non-linear data structures. The examples of linear data structures are arrays, linked lists, stacks, and queues. The examples of non-linear data structures are trees and graphs.
- A linked list is a linear collection of nodes.
- Before we insert a new node in a linked list, we need to check for the `OVERFLOW` condition, which occurs when `AVAIL = NULL` or no free memory cell is present in the system.
- Before we delete a node from a linked list, we must first check for the `UNDERFLOW` condition, which occurs when we try to delete a node from a linked list that is empty. This happens when `START = NULL` or when there are no more nodes to delete.
- A stack is a linear data structure in which elements are added and removed only from one end, which is called top. Hence, a stack is called a LIFO data structure as the element that is inserted last is the first one to be taken out.
- A queue is a FIFO data structure in which the element that is inserted first is the first one to be taken out. The elements in a queue are added at one end called rear and removed from the other end called front.
- A tree is a data structure mainly used to store data that is hierarchical in nature. In a binary tree, every node has 0, 1, or at the most 2 successors. A node that has no successors is called the leaf node or the terminal node. Every node other than the root node has a parent.

- Degree of a node is equal to the number of children that a node has. The degree of a leaf node is zero. All nodes that are at the same level and share the same parent are called siblings.
- A graph is basically a collection of vertices (also called nodes) and edges that connect these vertices.
- Degree of a node *u*, deg(*u*), is the total number of edges containing the node *u*. When the degree of a node is zero, it is also called an isolated node. A path P is known as a closed path if the edge has the same end-points.
- Graphs can be represented in memory by using adjacency matrix or adjacency list.

GLOSSARY

Adjacency list A representation of a directed graph with `n` nodes using an array of `n` lists of nodes. List `i` contains vertex `j` if there is an edge from vertex `i` to vertex `j`.

Adjacency matrix A representation of a directed graph using an `n × n` matrix, where `n` is the number of nodes. An entry at `(i,j)` is 1 if there is an edge from vertex `i` to vertex `j`; otherwise, the entry is 0.

Binary tree A tree in which every node can have at most two children.

Depth-first search A search algorithm that considers outgoing edges of a node before any of the node's siblings. That is, extremes are searched first.

Directed graph A graph that has edges represented by ordered pairs of nodes. In a directed graph, each edge can be followed from one vertex to another vertex.

Edge A connection between two nodes of a graph. In a directed graph, an edge goes from one node (source) to another node (destination), thereby making a connection in only one direction.

First-in, first-out A policy in which items are processed in the order of arrival.

Graph A set of nodes connected by edges. That is, a graph is a set of nodes and a binary relation between nodes (adjacency).

In-degree In-degree of a node is equal to the number of in-coming edges of that node in a directed graph.

In-order traversal The traversal technique in which all nodes of a tree are processed by recursively processing the left sub-tree first, then processing the root, and finally the right sub-tree.

Last-in, first-out A policy in which the most recently arrived item is processed first.

Level-order traversal The traversal technique in which all nodes of a tree are processed by depth: first the root and then the children of the root. It is equivalent to a breadth-first search from the root.

Link A reference, pointer, or access handle to another part of the data structure. Usually, it stores the memory address of next node in the list.

Linked list A list in which each node has a link to the next node.

Out-degree The number of out-going edges of a node in a directed graph.

Path A list of nodes of a graph where each node has an edge from it to the next node.

Post-order traversal The traversal technique in which all nodes of a tree are processed by recursively processing all sub-trees and then finally processing the *root*.

Pre-order traversal The traversal technique in which all *nodes* of a tree are processed by processing the root first and then recursively processing all sub-trees.

Queue A collection of items in which the first item added is accessed first.

Sink A node with zero out-degree. That is, a node of a directed graph with no outgoing edges.

Source A node of a directed graph with no incoming edges, that is, a node with zero in-degree.

Stack A collection of items in which only the most recently added item is removed.

Tree A set of notes where a node is designated as the root of the tree and all remaining nodes are partitioned into non-empty sets each of the which is a sub-tree of the root.

EXERCISES

Fill in the Blanks

1. ______ is used to store the address of the first free memory location.
2. Inserting a node in the middle of the singly linked list needs to modify ______ pointers.
3. Deleting a node from the beginning of the singly linked list needs to modify ______ pointers.
4. Data elements in a linked list are known as ______.
5. New nodes are added at the ______ of the queue.
6. A ______ is the appropriate data structure to process batch computer programs submitted to the computer centre.
7. A ______ is the appropriate data structure to process a list of employees that have a contract for a seniority system for hiring and firing.
8. The parent node is also known as the ______ node.
9. The maximum number of nodes at the kth level of binary tree is ______.
10. In a binary tree, every node can have maximum ______ successors.
11. Nodes at the same level that share the same parent are called ______.
12. The height of a binary tree with n nodes is at least ______ and at most ______.
13. ______ node has a zero degree.
14. In-degree of a node is the number of edges that ______ at u.
15. Adjacency matrix is also known as a ______.
16. A path P is known as a ______ path if the edge has the same end-points.

Multiple-choice Questions

1. A linked list is a
   (a) random access structure
   (b) sequential access structure
   (c) Both (a) and (b)
2. An array is a
   (a) random access structure
   (b) sequential access structure
   (c) Both (a) and (b)
3. A stack is a
   (a) LIFO (b) FIFO
   (c) FILO (d) LILO
4. Which function places an element on the stack?
   (a) Pop() (b) Push()
   (c) Peek() (d) isEmpty()
5. Disks piled up one above the other represents a
   (a) stack (b) queue
   (c) linked list (d) array
6. A line in a grocery store represents a
   (a) stack (b) queue
   (c) linked list (d) array
7. In a queue, insertion is done at the
   (a) rear
   (b) front
   (c) back
   (d) top
8. The degree of a leaf node is
   (a) 0
   (b) 1
   (c) 2
   (d) 3
9. The depth of the root node is
   (a) 0
   (b) 1
   (c) 2
   (d) 3
10. A binary tree of height h has at least h nodes and at most ______ nodes.
    (a) $2h$
    (b) 2^h
    (c) 2^{h+1}
    (d) 2^{h-1}
11. Pre-order traversal is also called
    (a) depth-first traversal
    (b) breadth-first traversal
    (c) level-order traversal
    (d) in-order traversal
12. The total number of nodes in the nth level of a binary tree can be given as
    (a) $2n$
    (b) 2^n
    (c) 2^{n+1}
    (d) 2^{n-1}
13. The number of edges that originate at u is called
    (a) in-degree
    (b) out-degree
    (c) degree
    (d) source
14. Total number of edges containing the node u is called
    (a) in-degree
    (b) out-degree
    (c) degree
    (d) None of these

State True or False

1. A linked list is a linear collection of data elements.
2. A linked list can grow and shrink during run-time.
3. A node in a linked list can point to only one node at a time.
4. A node in a singly linked list can reference the previous node.
5. A linked list can store only integer values.
6. A linked list is a random access structure.
7. Every node in a linked list contains an integer part and a pointer.
8. START stores the address of the first node in the list.
9. Underflow is a condition that occurs when we try to delete a node from a linked list that is empty.
10. A queue stores elements in manner such that the first element is at the beginning of the list and the last element is at the end of the list.
11. Pop() is used to add an element on the top of the stack.
12. Nodes that branch into child nodes are called parent nodes.
13. The size of the tree is the number of nodes in the tree.
14. A leaf node does not branch out further.
15. A node that has no successors is called the root node.
16. A binary tree of *n* nodes has exactly *n* - 1 edges.
17. Every node has a parent.
18. Graph is a linear data structure.
19. In-degree of a node is the number of edges leaving that node.
20. The size of a graph is the total number of vertices in it.
21. A node is known as a sink if it has a positive out-degree but an in-degree = 0.

Review Questions

1. Make a comparison between a linked list and a linear array. Which one will you prefer to use and when?
2. What do you understand by stack overflow? Write a program to implement a stack using a linear array that checks for stack overflow condition before inserting elements into it.
3. Differentiate between an array and a stack.
4. How does a linked stack differ from a linear stack?
5. Differentiate between peek() and pop() functions.
6. Give the stack when the following operations are performed on an empty stack:
   - Add `A, B, C, D, E, F`
   - Delete two letters
   - Add G
   - Add H
   - Delete four letters
   - Add `I`
7. Give the queue when the following operations are performed on an empty queue.
   - Add `A, B, C, D, E, F`
   - Delete two letters
   - Add G
   - Add H
   - Delete four letters
   - Add `I`
8. Consider the following queue which has `FRONT = 1` and `REAR = 5`.

	A	B	C	D	E				

   Now perform the following operations on the queue
   - Add F
   - Delete two letters
   - Add G
   - Add H
   - Delete four letters
   - Add `I`
9. Explain the concept of trees. Give its applications.
10. How many binary trees are possible with four nodes?
11. Is it possible to implement binary trees using linear arrays? If yes, explain how?
12. What are the two ways of representing binary trees in memory? Which one do you prefer, and why?
13. Consider the following tree. Now perform the following actions:

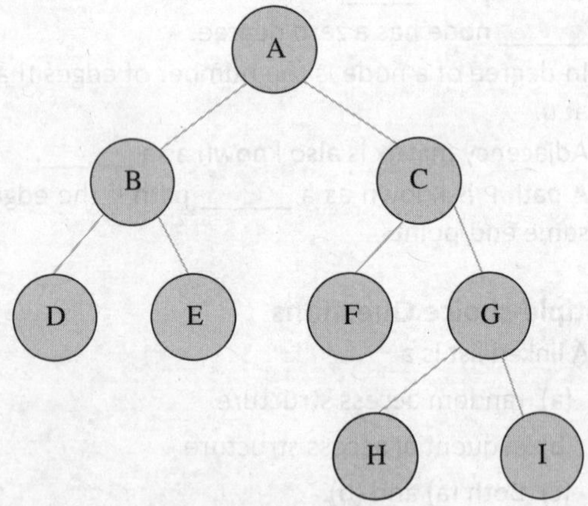

   - Make a list of the leaf nodes
   - Name the leaf nodes
   - Name the non-leaf nodes
   - Name the ancestors of node E
   - Descendants of A
   - Sibling of C
   - Height of the tree
   - Height of sub-tree at E
   - Level of node E
   - Give the in-order traversal of the tree
   - Give the pre-order traversal of the tree
   - Give the post-order traversal of the tree
   - Give the level-order traversal of the tree

14. Give the binary tree having the following memory representation:

ROOT 3

AVAIL 15

	LEFT	DATA	RIGHT
1	–1	8	–1
2	–1	10	–1
3	5	1	8
4			
5	9	2	14
6			
7			
8	20	3	
9	1	4	12
10			
11	–1	7	18
12	–1	9	–1
13			
14	–1	5	–1
15			
16	–1	11	–1
17			
18	–1	12	–1
19			
20	2	6	16

15. Give the memory representation of the following binary tree.

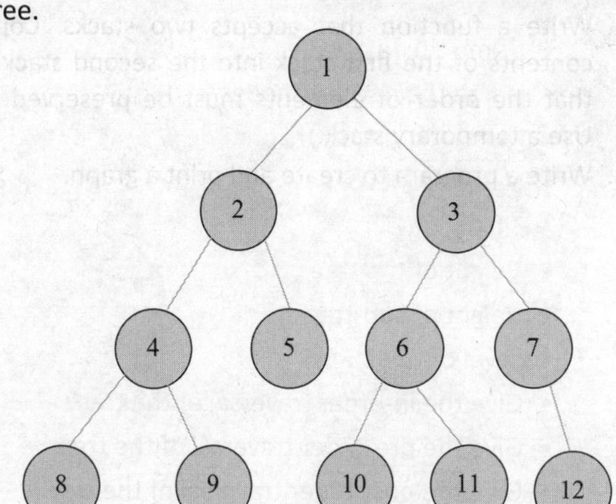

16. Explain the relationship between a linked list structure and a digraph.
17. What is a graph? Explain its key terms.
18. How are graphs represented inside the computer memory? Which method do you prefer, and why?
19. Draw a complete undirected graph having five nodes.
20. Consider the following graph and give the degree of each node.

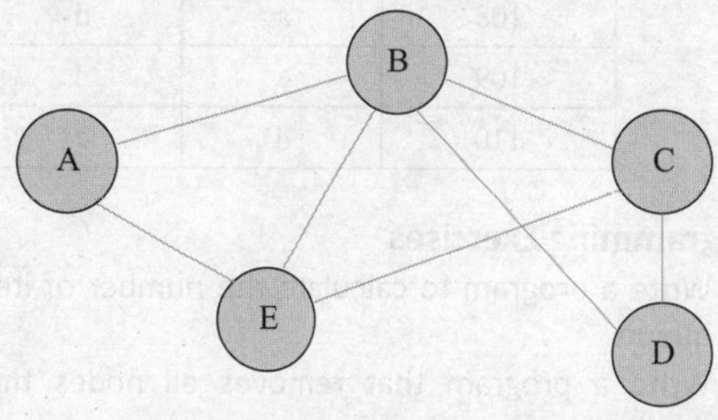

21. Consider the following graph and state all the simple paths from A to D, B to D, and C to D. Also give the in-degree and out-degree of each node. Is there any source or sink in the graph?

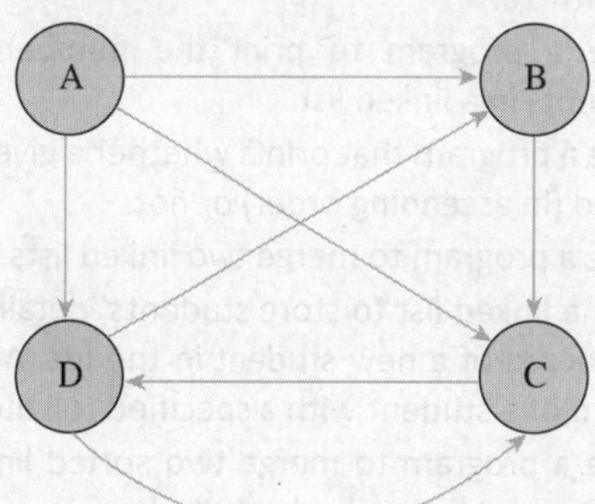

22. Consider the following graph and show its adjacency list in memory.

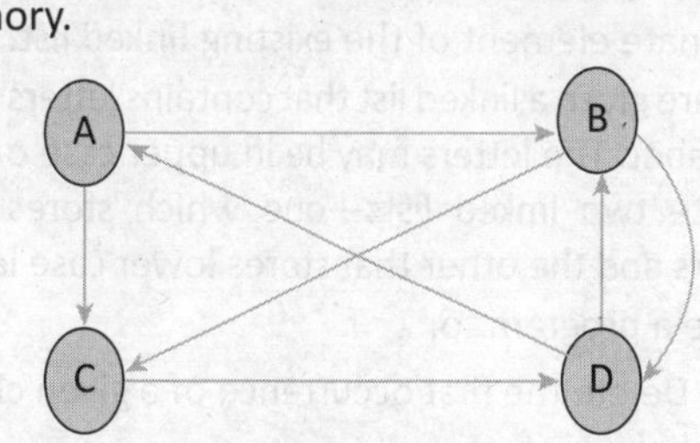

23. Consider the graph given in the previous question and show the changes in the graph as well as its adjacency list when node E and edges (A, E) and (C, E) are added to it. Also, delete edge (B, D) from the graph.
24. Given five cities, (a) New Delhi, (b) Mumbai, (c) Chennai, (d) Bangalore, and (e) Kolkata, a list of flights that connect these cities is given below. Use the given information to construct a graph.

Flight Number	ORIG	DEST
101	b	c
102	c	b

Flight Number	ORIG	DEST
103	e	c
104	c	d
105	b	e
106	e	b
107	e	a
108	a	d
109	e	d
110	d	e

Programming Exercises

1. Write a program to calculate the number of items in a queue.
2. Write a program that removes all nodes that have duplicate information.
3. Write a program to print the total number of occurrences of a given item in a linked list.
4. Write a program to multiply every element of a linked list with 10.
5. Write a program to print the number of non-zero elements in a linked list.
6. Write a program that prints whether a given linked list is sorted (in ascending order) or not.
7. Write a program to merge two linked lists.
8. Form a linked list to store students' details. Then insert the record of a new student in the list. Also delete the record of a student with a specified roll number.
9. Write a program to merge two sorted linked lists. The resultant list must also be sorted.
10. Write a program to create a linked list from an already given list. The new linked list must contain every alternate element of the existing linked list.
11. You are given a linked list that contains letters from English alphabet. The letters may be in upper case or lower case. Create two linked lists—one which stores upper case letters and the other that stores lower case letters.
12. Write a program to:
    a. Delete the first occurrence of a given character in a linked list.
    b. Delete the last occurrence of a given character.
    c. Delete all the occurrences of a given character.
13. Write a program to reverse a linked list using recursion.
14. Write a program to input an *n* digit number. Now, break this number into its individual digits and then store every single digit in a separate node, thereby forming a linked list. For example, if you enter 12345, now there will be five nodes in the list containing nodes with values—1, 2, 3, 4, and 5.
15. Write a program to sum the values of the nodes of a linked list and then calculate the mean.
16. Write a program that prints the minimum and maximum values in a linked list that stores integer values.
17. Write a program to interchange the value of the first element with the last element, second element with second last element, and so on, of a doubly linked list.
18. Write a program to make the first element of singly linked list, the last element of the list.
19. Write a program to count the number of occurrences of a given value in a linked list.
20. Write a program to form a linked list of integer values. Calculate the sum of integers and then display the average of the numbers in the list.
21. Write a program to delete the kth node from a linked list.
22. Write a program to multiply a polynomial with a given number.
23. Write a program that creates a singly linked list. Use a function `isSorted()` that returns 1 if the list is sorted and 0 otherwise.
24. Write a program to implement a stack using a linked list. How is a linked stack better than a linear stack? Do we have underflow and overflow situations in a linked stack?
25. Write a program to implement a simple queue.
26. Write a program to implement a stack that stores names of students in the class.
27. Write a program to create a queue from a stack.
28. Write a program to create a stack from a queue.
29. Write a program to reverse the elements of a queue.
30. Write a program to input two queues and compare their contents.
31. Write a program to input two stacks and compare their contents.
32. Write a function that accepts two stacks. Copy the contents of the first stack into the second stack. Note that the order of elements must be preserved. (Hint: Use a temporary stack.)
33. Write a program to create and print a graph.

APPENDIX A

Bitwise Operations

A.1 BIT LEVEL PROGRAMMING

A C programmer usually does not need to care about operations at the bit level. He has to think only in terms of `int` and `double`, or even higher level data types composed of a combination of these. However, at times it becomes necessary to go to the level of an individual bit. For example, in case of exclusive OR (XOR) encryption or when dealing with data compression, a programmer needs to operate on individual bits of the data and thus needs to do programming at the bit level. Moreover, bit operations can be used to speed up your program.

Thinking About Bits

The byte is the lowest level at which data can be accessed. C does not support bit-type. Therefore, we cannot perform any operation on an individual bit. Even a bitwise operator will be applied to, at a minimum, an entire byte at a time.

We have already studied bitwise NOT, AND, OR, and XOR operators in Chapter 9. To summarize:

- The bitwise NOT (~), or complement, is a unary operator used to perform logical negation on each bit thereby resulting in 1s complement of the given binary value. Bits that are 0s become 1s, and vice versa. For example, `~(1010) = 0101`.
- A bitwise OR (|) takes two bit patterns of equal length, and produces another one of the same length by performing the logical inclusive OR operation on each pair of corresponding bits. In each pair, the result is 1 if the first bit is 1 OR the second bit is 1 OR both bits are 1, otherwise the result is 0.

  `1001 | 0101 = 1101`
- A bitwise exclusive or (`^`) takes two bit patterns of equal length and performs the logical XOR operation on each pair of corresponding bits. In the result, a bit is set to 1 if the two bits are different, and 0 if they are the same.

  The XOR operation is generally used by assembly language programmers as a short-cut to set the value of a register to zero. Performing XOR on a value against itself always results in zero. The XOR operation requires fewer CPU clock cycles when compared with the sequence of operations that has to be performed to load a zero value and save it to the register. The bitwise XOR is also used to toggle flags in a set of bits. For example,

  `1010 ^ 0011 = 1001`
- A bitwise AND (&) takes two bit patterns of equal length and performs the logical AND operation on each pair of corresponding bits. In each pair, the resultant bit is set to 1 if the first bit is 1 and the second bit is 1. Otherwise, it is set to 0. For example:

  `1010 & 0011 = 0010`

  The bitwise AND is commonly used to perform *bit masking*. This is done to isolate part of a string of bits, or to determine whether a particular bit is 1 or 0. For example, to determine if the second bit is 1, you can straightaway do a bitwise AND to it and another bit pattern containing 1 in the second bit. For example,

  `1010 & 0010 = 0010`

  Since the result is 0010 (non-zero), it clearly indicates that the second bit in the original pattern was 1. Such an operation is called *bit masking* because it *masks* the portions that should not be altered or which are not of interest. In this case, the 0 values mask the bits that are not of interest.

  The bitwise AND can also be combined with the bitwise NOT to *clear* bits.

A.2 BITWISE SHIFT OPERATORS

In bitwise shift operations, the bits are moved, or *shifted*, to the left or right. The CPU registers have a fixed number of available bits for storing numerals, so when we perform shift operations; some bits will be '*shifted out*' of the register at one end, while the same number of bits are '*shifted in*' from the other end.

In an *arithmetic shift*, the bits that are shifted out of either end are discarded. There are two types of arithmetic shift: left arithmetic shift and a right arithmetic shift.

In a left arithmetic shift, zeros are shifted in on the right. For example, consider the register with the following bit pattern:

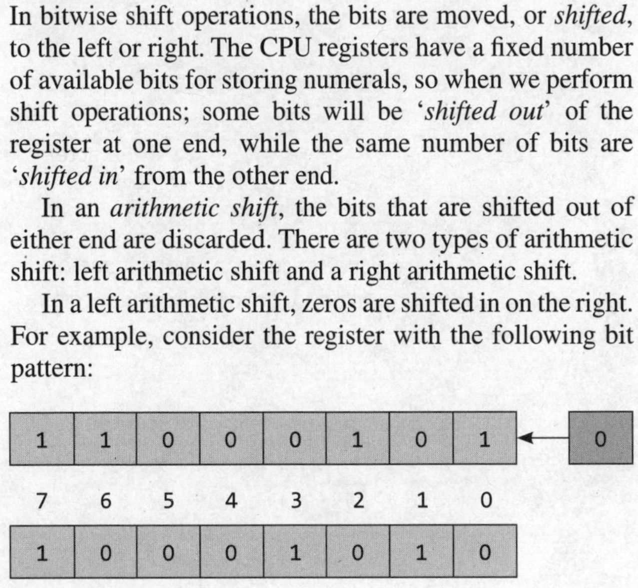

Note that in arithmetic shift left, the leftmost bit was shifted past the end of the register, and a new 0 was shifted into the rightmost position. The general form of doing a left shift can be given as

```
op << n
```

Here, `op` is an integer expression that has to be shifted and `n` is the number of bit positions to be shifted.

For example, if we write

```
unsigned int x = 11000101;
```

Then `x << 2 = 00010100`

If a right arithmetic shift is performed on an unsigned integer then zeros are shifted on the left.

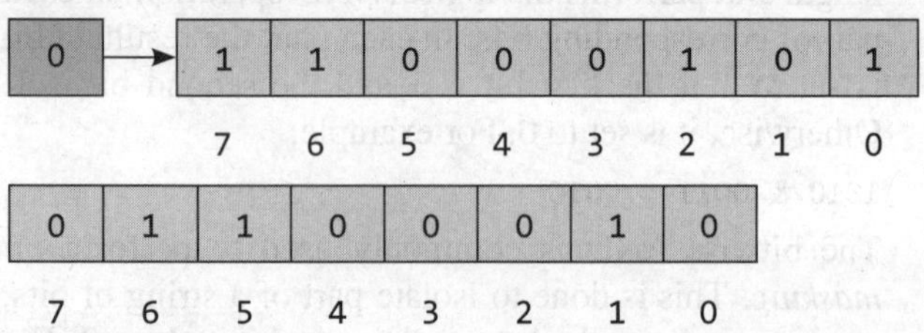

The general form of an arithmetic right shift can be given as `op >> n`.

Here, `op` is an integer expression that has to be shifted and `n` is the number of bit positions to be shifted. For example, if we write

```
unsigned int x = 11000101;
```

Then `x >> 2 = 00110001`

Note that in arithmetic shift right operation, bits in `op` are shifted to right by `n` positions. In this process, the rightmost `n` bits will be lost and zeros will be shifted in the leftmost `n` bits. (This is true for unsigned integers, for signed integers the shift right operation is machine dependent).

Points to remember

- `op` and `n` can be constants or variables.
- `n` cannot be negative.
- `n` should not exceed the number of bits used to represent `op`.
- Left shifting is the equivalent of multiplying by a power of 2.
- Right shift will be the equivalent of integer division by 2.

Note

The left and right shift operators will result in significantly faster code than calculating and then multiplying by a power of two.

Have you wondered what will happen if you shift a number like 128 and store it in a single byte: 10000000? Since, 128 × 2 = 256, and a register is incapable of storing a number that is bigger than a single byte, so it should not be surprising that the result is 00000000.

APPENDIX B

ANSI C Library Functions

<ctype.h>	
int isalnum(int c);	// to check if c is an alphabet or a digit
int isalpha(int c);	// to check if c is an alphabet
int iscntrl(int c);	// to check if c is a control character
int isdigit(int c);	// to check if c is a decimal digit
int isgraph(int c);	// to check if c is a printing character other than space
int islower(int c);	// to check if c is a lower-case character
int isprint(int c);	// to check if c is a printing character including space
int ispunct(int c);	// to check if c is a printing character other than space, letter, or digit
int isspace(int c);	// to check is c if a space, formfeed, newline, carriage return, tab, or vertical tab
int isupper(int c);	// to check if c is an upper-case character
int isxdigit(int c);	// to check if c is a hexadecimal digit
int tolower(int c);	// to convert c into its lower-case equivalent
int toupper(int c);	// to convert c into its upper-case equivalent
<errno.h>	
errno	// object to which certain library functions assign specific positive values when an error occurs
EDOM	// code used for domain errors
ERANGE	// code used for range errors
<limits.h>	
CHAR_BIT	// Specifies the number of bits in a char
CHAR_MAX	// Specifies the maximum value of type char
CHAR_MIN	// Specifies the minimum value of type char
SCHAR_MAX	// Specifies the maximum value of type signed char
SCHAR_MIN	// Specifies the minimum value of type signed char
UCHAR_MAX	// Specifies the maximum value of type unsigned char
SHRT_MAX	// Specifies the maximum value of type short
SHRT_MIN	// Specifies the minimum value of type short
USHRT_MAX	// Specifies the maximum value of type unsigned short
INT_MAX	// Specifies the maximum value of type int
INT_MIN	// Specifies the minimum value of type int
UINT_MAX	// Specifies the maximum value of type unsigned int
LONG_MAX	// Specifies the maximum value of type long
LONG_MIN	// Specifies the minimum value of type long
ULONG_MAX	// Specifies the maximum value of type unsigned long
<math.h>	
double exp(double x);	// Calculates the exponential value of x

double log(double x);	// Calculates the natural logarithm of x
double log10(double x);	// Calculates the base-10 logarithm of x
double pow(double x, double y);	// Calculates the value of x raised to power y
double sqrt(double x);	// Calculates the square root of x
double ceil(double x);	// Calculates the smallest integer not less
than x	
double floor(double x);	// Calculates the largest integer not greater than x
double fabs(double x);	// Calculates the absolute value of x
double ldexp(double x, int n);	// Calculates the x times 2 to the power n
double fmod(double x, double y);	// If y is non-zero, floating-point remainder of x/y, with the same sign as x is returned, else the result is implementation-defined
double sin(double x);	// Calculates the sine of x
double cos(double x);	// Calculates the cosine of x
double tan(double x);	// Calculates the tangent of x
double asin(double x);	// Calculates the arc-sine of x
double acos(double x);	// Calculates the arc-cosine of x
double atan(double x);	// Calculates the arc-tangent of x
double atan2(double y, double x);	// Calculates the arc-tangent of y/x
double sinh(double x);	// Calculates the hyperbolic sine of x
double cosh(double x);	// Calculates the hyperbolic cosine of x
double tanh(double x);	// Calculates the hyperbolic tangent of x
<stddef.h>	
NULL	// Specifies the null pointer constant
offsetof(stype, m)	// gives the offset (in bytes) of member m from start of structure type stype.
size_t	// Specifies the type for objects declared to store the result of the sizeof operator
<stdio.h>	
BUFSIZ	// Specifies the size of the buffer used by setbuf
EOF	// Indicates the end-of-stream or an error
FILENAME_MAX	// Specifies the maximum length of characters to hold a filename
FOPEN_MAX	// Specifies the maximum no. of files you can open simultaneously
L_tmpnam	// Specifies the no. of characters required for a temporary filename
NULL	// Specifies the null pointer constant
SEEK_CUR	// Used in fseek() for specifying the current file position
SEEK_END	// Used in fseek() for specifying the end of file
SEEK_SET	// Used in fseek() for specifying the beginning of a file
TMP_MAX	// Specifies the minimum no. of unique filenames generated
_IOFBF	// Used in setvbuf() for specifying full buffering
_IOLBF	// Used in setvbuf() for specifying line buffering
_IONBF	// Used in setvbuf() for specifying no buffering
stdin	// Specifies the file pointer for standard input stream. Automatically opened when program execution begins.
stdout	// Specifies the file pointer for standard output stream. Automatically opened when program execution begins.
stderr	// Specifies the file pointer for standard error stream. Automatically opened when program execution begins.

FILE	// Specifies the type of object holding information necessary to control a stream
fpos_t	// Specifies the type for objects declared to store file position information
size_t	// Specifies the type for objects declared to store result of sizeof operator
FILE* fopen(const char* filename, const char* mode);	// To open a file filename. It returns a stream, or NULL on failure. mode may be one of the following for text files– r: reading, w: writing, a: append, r+: update (reading and writing), w+: update, discarding previous content (if any), a+: append, reading, and writing at end or one of those strings with b included (after the first character), for binary files.
FILE* freopen(const char* filename, const char* mode, FILE* stream);	// To close a file associated with stream, then opens file filename with specified mode and associates it with stream. It either returns stream or NULL in case of failure.
int fflush(FILE* stream);	// To flush the stream. It returns zero on success or EOF on error. Note that fflush(NULL) flushes all output streams.
int fclose(FILE* stream);	// To close the stream (also flushes it if it is an O/P stream). Returns EOF on error, zero otherwise.
int remove(const char* filename);	// To remove the specified file. Returns non-zero on failure.
int rename(const char* oldname, const char* newname);	// To change name of file oldname to newname. Returns zero on success and a non-zero value on failure.

FILE* tmpfile();	// To create a temporary file (mode "wb+") which will be removed when closed or on normal program termination. The function returns stream or NULL on failure.
int setvbuf(FILE* stream, char* buf, int mode, size_t size);	// To control buffering for stream. mode can be _IOFBF, _IOLBF or _IONBF. The function returns non-zero value on error. However, the function must be called before any other operation on the stream.
void setbuf(FILE* stream, char* buf);	// To control buffering for stream. For null buf, turns off buffering, otherwise it is equivalent to (void)setvbuf(stream, buf, _IOFBF, BUFSIZ).
int fprintf(FILE* stream, const char* format, ...);	// To convert (according to format) and writes output to stream. Returns either the no. of characters written, or negative value on error.
int printf(const char* format, ...);	// printf(f, ...) is equivalent to fprintf(stdout, f, ...)
int sprintf(char* s, const char* format, ...);	// The function is same as fprintf, but the output is written into string s, which must be large enough to hold the output. It terminates the string with '\0' and returns length of s
int vfprintf(FILE* stream, const char* format, va_list arg);	// Same as fprintf but with variable argument list replaced by arg, which must have been initialised by the va_start macro
int vprintf(const char* format, va_list arg);	// Same as printf but with variable argument list replaced by arg, which must have been initialised by the va_start macro
int vsprintf(char* s, const char* format, va_list arg);	// Same as sprintf but with variable argument list replaced by arg, which must have been initialised by the va_start macro

int fscanf(FILE* stream, const char* format, ...);	// To perform formatted input conversion, reading from stream according to the specified format. The function returns no. of items converted and assigned, or EOF if end-of-file or error occurs before any conversion.
int scanf(const char* format, ...);	// scanf(f, ...) is same as fscanf(stdin, f, ...)
int sscanf(char* s, const char* format, ...);	// Same as fscanf but input is read from string s.
int fgetc(FILE* stream);	// Used to return next character from (input) stream or an EOF on end-of-file or error.
char* fgets(char* s, int n, FILE* stream);	// Used to copy characters from input stream stream to s until either n – 1 characters are copied, newline is copied, end-of-file is reached or an error occurs. If no error, s is NULL-terminated. Returns NULL on end-of-file or error, s otherwise.
int fputc(int c, FILE* stream);	// To write the character c to stream. Returns c or EOF on error.
char* fputs(const char* s, FILE* stream);	// To write s, to the output stream. Returns non-negative on success or EOF on error.
int getc(FILE* stream);	// Same as fgetc except that it may be a macro
int getchar(void);	// Same as getc(stdin)
char* gets(char* s);	// To copy characters from stdin into s until either a newline is encountered, end-of-file is reached, or error occurs. Note that it does not copy newline and terminates s with a '\0'. Returns s, or NULL on end-of-file or error. Should not be used because of the potential for buffer overflow.
int putc(int c, FILE* stream);	// Same as fputc except that it may be a macro

int putchar(int c);	// Same as putc(c, stdout)
int puts(const char* s);	// To write s (excluding terminating NUL) and a newline to stdout. Returns a non-negative value on success or EOF on error.
int ungetc(int c, FILE* stream);	// To push c (which must not be EOF), onto the input stream such that it will be returned by the next read. Returns c or EOF on error.
size_t fread(void* ptr, size_t size, size_t nobj, FILE* stream);	// To read (at most) nobj objects of size size from stream stream into ptr and returns number of objects read.
size_t fwrite(const void* ptr, size_t size, size_t nobj, FILE* stream);	// To write to stream stream, nobj objects of size size from array ptr. Returns number of objects written.
int fseek(FILE* stream, long offset, int origin);	// To set file position for stream stream and clears end-of-file indicator. For a binary stream, file position is set to offset bytes from the position indicated by origin: SEEK_SET, SEEK_CUR, or SEEK_END. Returns non-zero on error.
long ftell(FILE* stream);	// Returns current file position for stream or –1 on error
void rewind(FILE* stream);	// Same as fseek(stream, 0L, SEEK_SET);
int fgetpos(FILE* stream, fpos_t* ptr);	// To store current file position for stream in *ptr. Returns non-zero on error.
int fsetpos(FILE* stream, const fpos_t* ptr);	// To set current position of stream to *ptr. Returns non-zero on error.
void clearerr(FILE* stream);	// To clear the end-of-file and other error indicators for stream
int feof(FILE* stream);	// To returns non-zero if end-of-file indicator is set for stream
int ferror(FILE* stream);	// To return non-zero if error indicator is set for stream

void perror(const char* s);	// To print (if non-null) and strerror(errno) to standard error
<stdlib.h>	
EXIT_FAILURE	//Specifies value for status argument to exit indicating failure
EXIT_SUCCESS	//Specifies value for status argument to exit indicating success
RAND_MAX	// Specifies maximum value returned by rand()
NULL	// Specifies Null pointer constant
div_t	// Specifies the return type of div(). Structure having members: int quot, int rem;
ldiv_t	// Specifies the return type of ldiv(). Structure having members: long quot, rem;
size_t	// Specifies type for objects declared to store result of sizeof operator
int abs(int n);	// Returns absolute value of n
long labs(long n);	// Returns absolute value of n
div_t div(int num, int denom);	// Returns quotient and remainder of num/denom
ldiv_t ldiv(long num, long denom);	// Returns quotient and remainder of num/denom
double atof(const char* s);	// Same as strtod(s, (char**)NULL) except that errno is not necessarily set on conversion error
int atoi(const char* s);	// Same as (int) strtol(s, (char**)NULL, 10) except that errno is not necessarily set on conversion error
long atol(const char* s);	// Same as strtol(s, (char**)NULL, 10) except that errno is not necessarily set on conversion error
double strtod(const char* s, char endp);**	// To convert initial characters (ignoring leading white space) of s to type double. If endp non-null, stores pointer to unconverted suffix in *endp.
long strtol(const char* s, char endp, int base);**	// To convert initial characters (ignoring leading white space) of s to type long. If endp non-null, stores pointer to unconverted suffix in *endp. If base lies between 2 and 36, that base is used for conversion; if 0X or 0x implies hexadecimal; 0 implies octal, otherwise decimal assumed.
unsigned long strtoul(const char* s, char endp, int base);**	// Same as strtol except result is unsigned long
void* calloc(size_t nobj, size_t size);	// Returns pointer to allocated space for an array of nobj objects each of size size, or NULL on error
void* malloc(size_t size);	// Returns pointer to allocated space for an object of size size, or NULL on error
void* realloc(void* p, size_t size);	// Returns pointer to allocated space for an object of size size to existing contents of p (if non-null), or NULL on error. On successful operation, old object is deallocated, else remains unchanged.
void free(void* p);	// De-allocates space to which p points (if p is not null)
void abort();	// To abnormally terminate the program
void exit(int status);	// To terminate the program normally. When exit() is called, open files are flushed, open streams are closed and control is returned to environment. status is returned to environment. Zero or EXIT_SUCCESS indicates successful termination and EXIT_FAILURE indicates unsuccessful termination. However, implementations may define other values.

char* getenv(const char* name);	// Returns string associated with name name from implementation's environment, or NULL if no such string exists
void* bsearch(const void* key, const void* base, size_t n, size_t size, int (*cmp)(const void* keyval, const void* datum));	// To search a sorted array base (of n objects each of size size) for item matching key according to comparison function cmp. cmp must return negative value if first argument is less than second, zero if equal and positive if greater. The function either returns a pointer to an item matching key if successful or returns NULL if a match is not found.
void qsort(void* base, size_t n, size_t size, int (*cmp)(const void*, const void*));	// To arrange the elements of an array base (of n objects each of size size) according to comparison function cmp into ascending order cmp must return negative value if first argument is less than second, zero if equal, and positive if greater.
int rand(void);	// To return a pseudo-random number in the range 0 to RAND_MAX
void srand(unsigned int seed);	// To return a new sequence of pseudo-random numbers using the specified seed. Initial seed is 1.
<string.h>	
NULL	// Specifies the Null pointer constant
size_t	// Specifies the type for objects declared to store result of sizeof operator
char* strcpy(char* s, const char* ct);	// Copies ct to s (including '\0') and returns s
char* strncpy(char* s, const char* ct, size_t n);	// Copies atmost n characters of ct to s. If ct is of length less than n then appends a '\0' character to s and returns s.
char* strcat(char* s, const char* ct);	// Concatenates ct to s and returns s
char* strncat(char* s, const char* ct, size_t n);	// To concatenate at most n characters of ct to s. Appends a '\0' character to s and returns it.
int strcmp(const char* cs, const char* ct);	// To compare cs with ct, returning negative value if cs < ct, zero if cs==ct, positive value if cs > ct.
int strncmp(const char* cs, const char* ct, size_t n);	// To compare the first n characters of cs and ct, returning negative value if cs < ct, zero if cs==ct, positive value if cs > ct.
int strcoll(const char* cs, const char* ct);	// To compare cs with ct, returning negative value if cs < ct, zero if cs==ct, positive value if cs > ct.
char* strchr(const char* cs, int c);	// Returns pointer to first occurrence of c in cs, or NULL if not found
char* strrchr(const char* cs, int c);	// Returns pointer to last occurrence of c in cs, or NULL if not found
size_t strspn(const char *str1, const char *str2);	// The function returns the index of the first character in str1 that doesn't match any character in str2
size_t strcspn(const char *str1, const char *str2);	// The function returns the index of the first character in str1 that matches any of the characters in str2.
char *strpbrk(const char *str1, const char *str2);	// The function strpbrk() returns a pointer to the first occurrence in str1 of any character in str2, or NULL if none are present.
char* strstr(const char* cs, const char* ct);	// To return a pointer to first occurrence of ct within cs, or NULL if none is found
size_t strlen(const char* cs);	// To return the length of cs

char* strerror(int n);	// To return a pointer to implementation-defined message string corresponding with error n.
char *strtok(char *str1, const char *delimiter);	// The strtok function is used to isolate sequential tokens in a null-terminated string, str. These tokens are separated in the string using delimiters. The first time that strtok is called, str should be specified; subsequent calls, wishing to obtain further tokens from the same string, should pass a null pointer instead. However, the delimiter must be supplied each time, though it may change between calls.
size_t strxfrm(char* s, const char* ct, size_t n);	// To store in s no more than n characters (including '\0') of a string produced from ct according to a locale-specific transformation. Returns length of entire transformed string.
void* memcpy(void* s, const void* ct, size_t n);	// To copy n characters from ct to s and returns s. In case of object overlap, s may be corrupted.
void* memmove(void* s, const void* ct, size_t n);	// To copy n characters from ct to s and returns s. Inc case of object overlap, s will not be corrupted.
int memcmp(const void* cs, const void* ct, size_t n);	// To compare at most the first n characters of cs and ct, returning negative value if cs < ct, zero if cs == ct, positive value if cs > ct.
void* memchr(const void* cs, int c, size_t n);	// To return a pointer to first occurrence of c in first n characters of cs, or NULL if not found.
void* memset(void* s, int c, size_t n);	// To replace each of the first n characters of s by c and return s

	<time.h>
CLOCKS_PER_SEC	// Specifies the number of clock_t units per second
clock_t	// Specifies an arithmetic type elapsed processor representing time
time_t	// Specifies an arithmetic type representing calendar time
struct tm	// Specifies the components of calendar time:
int tm_sec;	// Gives seconds after the minute
int tm_min;	// Gives minutes after the hour
	<time.h>
int tm_hour;	// Gives hours since midnight
int tm_mday;	// Gives the day of the month
int tm_mon;	// Gives months since January
int tm_year;	// Gives years since 1900
int tm_wday;	// Gives days since Sunday
int tm_yday;	// Gives days since January 1
int tm_isdst;	// Specifies the Daylight Saving Time flag. It is positive if DST is in effect, zero if not in effect, negative if information is not known.
clock_t clock(void);	// Returns elapsed processor time used by program or –1 if not available
time_t time(time_t* tp);	// Returns current calendar time or -1 if not available. If tp ≠ NULL, return value is also assigned to *tp.
double difftime(time_t time2, time_t time1);	// Returns the difference in seconds between time2 and time1
char* asctime(const struct tm* tp);	// Returns the given time as a string of the form: Sun Jan 3 13:08:42 1988\n\0
char* ctime(const time_t* tp);	// Returns string equivalent to calendar time tp converted to local time

struct tm* gmtime(const time_t* tp);	// Returns calendar time *tp converted to Coordinated Universal Time, or NULL if not available	size_t strftime(char* s, size_t smax, const char* fmt, const struct tm* tp);	// Formats *tp into s according to fmt. Places no more than smax characters into s, and returns either no. of characters produced (excluding '\0'), or 0 if greater than smax.
struct tm* localtime(const time_t* tp);	// Returns calendar time *tp converted into local time		

APPENDIX C
Advanced Type Qualifiers and Inline Functions in C

C.1 VOLATILE AND RESTRICT TYPE QUALIFIERS

Type Qualifier: Volatile

In C, a variable or object declared with the volatile keyword will not be optimized by the compiler because the compiler must assume that their values can change at any time.

For example, consider the code given below. Here, the value stored in WAIT is 0. It then starts to poll that value repeatedly until it changes to 255.

```
static int WAIT;
void func (void)
{
  WAIT = 0;
  while (WAIT != 255);
}
```

An optimizing compiler will observe that no other code is changing the value stored in WAIT, and therefore assumes that it will remain equal to 0 at all times. The compiler will then replace the function body with an infinite loop similar to the one that follows:

```
void func_optimized(void)
{
  foo = 0;
  while (true);
}
```

However, func might represent a location that can be changed by other elements of the computer system at any time (for example, a hardware register of a device connected to the CPU). The above code would never detect such a change. So when the volatile keyword is used, the compiler assumes that the current program is the only part of the system that could change the value. The declaration of WAIT must therefore be modified as:

```
static volatile int WAIT;
void bar (void)
{
  WAIT = 0;
  while (WAIT != 255);
}
```

Now, the compiler will not optimize the loop and the system will detect the change when it occurs. The volatile keyword is basically used to allow access to memory-mapped devices and makes use of variables in signal handlers.

Points to remember

- C permits declaration and definition of a volatile or const function only if it is a non-static member function.
- C permits declaration and definition of a function that returns a pointer to a volatile or const function.
- An object can be both const and volatile. Such an object cannot be legitimately modified by its own program but can be modified by some asynchronous process.
- If you put more than one qualifier on a declaration, then the compiler will ignore duplicate type qualifiers.
- The volatile keyword indicates to the compiler that a variable may be modified outside the scope of the program. A volatile variable is normally used in multitasking (threading) systems, when writing drivers with interrupt service routines, or in embedded systems, where the peripheral registers may also be modified by hardware alone.
- When you use the volatile keyword, your program will run slower, because of the extra read operations. Also the program will be larger since the compiler is not allowed to optimize as thoroughly.

When to use the volatile keyword?

A variable must be declared using the volatile type qualifier when:

- a variable is used in more than one context
- a common variable is used in more than one task or thread
- a variable is used both in a task and one or more interrupt service routines
- a variable corresponds to processor-internal registers configured as input

Type Qualifier: Restrict

The restrict type qualifier may only be applied to a pointer. A pointer declaration with the restrict keyword establishes a special association between the pointer and the object it accesses, making the pointer and expressions based on that pointer, the only way to directly or indirectly access the value of that object.

We have studied that a pointer is the address of a memory location. More than one pointer can be used to access the same memory location and modify it during the course of a program. The `restrict` type qualifier indicates to the compiler that if the memory addressed by the `restrict`-qualified pointer is modified, no other pointer will access that same memory. The compiler may choose to optimize code involving `restrict`-qualified pointers in a way that might otherwise result in incorrect behaviour.

Points to remember

- It is a new addition for C99 (the standard from 1999) which is not available in older compilers.
- If a particular piece of memory is not altered then it can be aliased using more than one restricted pointer.
- In the absence of the `restrict` keyword, other pointers can alias the object.
- Caching the value in an object designated through a `restrict`-qualified pointer is safe at the beginning of the block in which the pointer is declared since no pre-existing aliases may also be used to reference that object.

However, the cached value must be restored to the object by the end of the block, where some pre-existing aliases again become available. If new aliases are formed within the block, they can be identified and adjusted to refer to the cached value.

The restrict qualifier and aliasing

The `restrict` qualifier addresses the issue that potential aliasing can inhibit optimizations. Specifically, if a compiler is unable to determine that two different pointers are referencing different objects, then it cannot apply optimizations such as maintaining the values of the objects in registers other than in memory, or reordering loads and stores of these values.

The `restrict` qualifier usually extends two types of aliasing information already specified in the language.

- First, if a single pointer is directly assigned the return value from an invocation of `malloc`, then that pointer is the only way of accessing the allocated object (i.e., another pointer can access that object only by being assigned a value that is based on the value of the first pointer).
- Second you must have observed that there are two versions of an object copying function. This is because on many systems a faster copy is possible if it is known that the source and target arrays do not overlap. The `restrict` qualifier can be used to express the restriction on overlap in a new prototype that is compatible with the original version:

```
void *memcpy(void *restrict s1, const void
    *restrict s2, size_t n);
void *memmove(void * s1, const void * s2,
    size_t n);
```

The `restrict` keyword provides a straightforward implementation of `memcpy` in C, which gives a level of performance that previously required assembly language or other non-standard means.

C.2 INLINE FUNCTIONS IN C

An *inline function* is a programming language construct which instructs the compiler to perform inline expansion on a particular function. For an inline function, the compiler will copy the code from the function definition directly into the code of the calling function rather than creating a separate set of instructions in memory. So, instead of transferring control to and from the calling function and the called function, a modified copy of the function body may be substituted directly for the function call. In this way, the performance overhead of a function call is avoided.

The general format of an inline function is as follows:

```
inline return_data_type function_
    name(arguments)
```

A function is declared inline by using the `inline` function specifier. However, the `inline` specifier is just a request to the compiler that it should perform inline expansion. The compiler is free to ignore the request.

Example C.1

Look at the following inline function which returns the greatest of two integer values.

```
inline int large(int x, int y)
{
    return ((x > y) ? x : y);
}
```

The function may be called in the same way as an ordinary function is called. The statement given below demonstrates how an inline function can be called.

```
int a = 7, b = 9;
int big = large(a, b);
```

Look at another inline function which is used to add two integer values.

```
inline int ADD(int a, int b) {return a + b;}
```

Remember that the `inline` specifier does not change the meaning of the function.

Motivation

When a function is called, the control is transferred from the calling program to the function. After the called function is completely executed, the control is transferred back to the calling program. This concept of function execution may be time consuming since the registers and other processes must be saved before the function gets called.

The extra time and space required may be justified for larger functions but for small functions, the programmer may wish to place the code of the called function in the calling program for it to be executed. This is done by using an inline function.

An inline function reaps the benefits of a function while avoiding its overhead. Inline expansion is used to eliminate the overhead involved in a function call. Inline functions are usually used for functions that are executed frequently. They provide space benefit for very small functions and enable transformation for other optimizations.

In the absence of inline functions, the compiler automatically decides which functions to inline. The programmer has little or no control over which functions are inlined and which are not.

Comparison to macros

Initially in C, inline expansion was accomplished at the source level using parameterized macros. However, C99 opened the way for true inline functions which provided several benefits over macros. These include the following:

- When a macro is invoked, no type checking is performed. However, function calls usually do.
- A macro cannot use the `return` keyword, i.e., a macro cannot return something which is not the result of the last expression invoked inside it.
- Since macros usually use textual substitution, this may cause unintended side-effects and inefficiency due to re-evaluation of arguments and order of operations.
- Compiler errors within macros are often difficult to understand.
- Many constructs are awkward or impossible to express using macros. Moreover, it uses a significantly different syntax. Inline functions, on the other hand, use the same syntax as ordinary functions.
- Debugging a macro is much more difficult than debugging an inlined code.

Advantages

- An inline function generates faster code as it saves the time required to execute function calls.
- Small inline functions (three lines or less) create less code than the equivalent function call, as the compiler does not have to generate code to handle function arguments and a return value.
- Inline functions are subject to code optimizations that are usually not available to normal functions, as the compiler does not perform inter-procedural optimizations.

APPENDIX D

Interview Questions with Solutions

Give the output of the following:

1.
```
#include <stdio.h>
main()
{
  char far *ch;
  printf("\n Size of far pointer is : %d",
  sizeof(ch));
}
```

Ans: 2

****

2.
```
#include <stdio.h>
main()
{
  int arr[10] = {1,2,3,4,5,6};
  printf("%d %d %d %d", arr[0], arr[2], arr[4],
   arr[5], arr[8]);
}
```

Ans: 1 3 5 6 0

When an automatic structure is partially initialized, the remaining elements of the structure are automatically initialized to 0

****

3.
```
#include <stdio.h>
void display(struct stud);
struct student
{
  int roll_no;
  char name[100];
};
main()
{
  struct student s;
  s.roll_no = 10;
  s.name = "ABC";
  display(s);
}
display( struct student s1)
{
  printf("\n %d %s", s.roll_no, s.name);
}
```

Ans: ERROR.

Structure definition must be placed before the display() function

****

4.
```
#include <stdio.h>
main()
{
  struct student
  {
    char name[100];
    int rno;
    float fees;
  };
  struct student s = {"Kamesh"};
  printf("\n %s %d %f", s.name, s.rno, s.fees);
}
```

Ans: Kamesh 0 0.0

When an automatic structure is partially initialized, the remaining elements of the structure are automatically initialized to 0

****

5.
```
#include <stdio.h>
main()
{
  int option = 5;
  switch(option)
  {
    default: printf("Please check your option");
    case 1: printf("\n SUM");
      break;
    case 2: printf("\n SUBTRACT");
      break;
    case 3: printf("\n MULTIPLY");
      break;
  }
}
```

Ans: Please check your option

****

6.
```
#include <stdio.h>
main()
```

```
  {
    int option = 2, i;
    switch(option)
    {
      default: printf("Please check your option");
      case 1: printf("\n SUM");
        break;
      case 2: printf("\n SUBTRACT");
        break;
      case i: printf("\n MULTIPLY");
        break;
    }
  }
```

Ans: Error.

Cannot use i in the case statement

****

```
7. #include <stdio.h>
  main()
  {
    int i = 1;
    for(;;)
    {
      printf("%d", i);
      i++;
      if (i ==5)
        break;
    }
  }
```

Ans: 1 2 3 4

****

```
8. #include <stdio.h>
  main()
  {
    int i = 1;
    while()
    {
      printf("%d", i);
      if (i = =5)
        break;
    }
  }
```

Ans: ERROR, condition in the while loop is a must. The statement should be re-written as while(1)

****

```
9. #include <stdio.h>
  main()
  {
    int num = 10;
    while( num != 100)
    {
     printf("\n %d", num*10);
      if(num == 80)
        goto print_mesg;
    }
  }
  void fun()
  {
    print_mesg:
    printf("\n Hello World");
  }
```

Ans: ERROR, goto cannot take the control outside the function (main() in this case)

****

```
10. #include <stdio.h>
  main()
  {
    int num = 7;
    printf("%d", num++);
    num = num+1;
    printf("%d", ++num);
  }
```

Ans: 7 10

****

```
11. Sum(int num1, int num2)
  {
    int num1 = 20;
    int num2 = 30;
    return (num1 + num2);
  }
```

Ans: Redeclaration of variables – num1 and num2

****

```
12. main()
  {
    int num;
    num = find(7);
    if(num == 1)
      printf("\n Positive");
    else
      printf("\n Negative");
  }
  int find(int n)
  {
    n > 0? return(1) : return(0);
  }
```

Ans: Illegal use of return statement. Rather use it as return (n > 0 ? 1:0);

****

```
13. #include <stdio.h>
  void main()
  {
    int const * num = 7;
```

```
    printf("%d",++(*num));
  }
```

Ans: Error because num is a pointer to a "constant integer" and its value is being changed.

****

```
14. main()
    {
    char str[ ]="abc";
    int i=0;
    while(s[i] != '\0')
    {
    printf("\n%c%c%c%c",str[i],*(str+i),
    *(i+str),i[str]);
    i++;
    }
```

Ans: aaaa

**bbbb

**cccc

Because `str[i]`, `*(i+str)`, `*(str+i)`, `i[str]` are all different ways of accessing the ith element of the array- `str`.

****

```
15. main()
    {
      static int counter = 5;
      printf("%d",counter--);
      if(counter)
        main();
    }
```

Ans: 5 4 3 2 1

Since `static` variables are initialized only once and their values persist between function calls.

****

```
16. main()
    {
    int arr[ ] = {1,2,3,4,5};
    int i,*parr = arr;
    for(i = 0;i < 5;i++) {
      printf(" %d",*arr);
      ++parr; }
    }
```

Ans: 1 1 1 1 1

Because `parr` is being incremented and we are printing the value of `arr`.

****

```
17. main()
    {
    int arr[ ] = {1,2,3,4,5};
    int i,*parr = arr;
    for(i = 0;i < 5;i++) {
      printf(" %d",*parr);
      ++parr; }
    }
```

Ans: 1 2 3 4 5

****

```
18. main()
    {
    int a =-1,b = -1,c = 0, d = 2, res;
    res = a++ && b++ && c++ || d++;
    printf("%d %d %d %d %d", a, b, c, d, res);
    }
```

Ans: 0 0 1 3 1

****

```
19. main()
    {
    char *str;
    printf("%d %d",sizeof(*str), sizeof(str));
    }
```

Ans: 1 2

Since `str` is a pointer to a character type, its value needs 1 byte in memory and the address of this value will be of 2 bytes.

****

```
20. main()
    {
    char str[]="Hello World";
    show(str);
    }
    void show(char *str)
    {
    printf("%s",str);
    }
```

Ans: ERROR. The default argument type and return type of a function is `int`. So a function that has any other type of arguments and/or return type must be declared before it is called. In this case, the return type is `void` and argument type is `char` and there is no declaration statement which gives the details to the compiler in advance. Hence it is an error because the compiler assumes that the function will accept and return an integer value.

****

```
21. main()
    {
    int num = 2;
    printf("c=%d", --2);
    }
```

Ans: ERROR. Unary operator — can be applied to variables and not to constants. Since 2 is a constant, therefore the program generates error.

****

22.
```
#define int char
main()
{
  int num = 65;
  printf("%d",sizeof(num));
}
```

Ans: 1

Because num is actually a char, not an int. See the #define statement.

****

23.
```
main()
{
int res=5;
res = !i > 6;
printf("res = %d", res);
}
```

Ans: res = 0

Because res = 5 in line 1. In line 2, when we write !res, here ! is the negation operator which converts the value of res to Zero. Now, 0 is not > than 5. Therefore the value of res = 0.

****

24.
```
main()
{
char str[] ={'a','b','c','\n','c','\0'};
char *p,*pstr;
p=&str[3];
printf("%d", *p);
pstr=str;
printf("%d", ++*pstr);
}
```

Ans: 10 98

Because p is pointing to the third character in str which is '\n'. The ASCII value of new line character is 10. pstr stores the address of the first character in the str which is 'a'. The value of *pstr is being incremented, therefore it is 98. The ASCII value of a + 1 = 97 + 1 = 98

****

25.
```
main()
{
int arr[2][2][2] = { {1,3,5,7}, {2,4,6,8} };
int *p,*q;
p=&arr[2][2][2];
*q = ***a;
printf("%d %d",*p,*q);
}
```

Ans: Garbage Value 1

Although arr is declared as a 3-D array, the third dimension is not initialized. Therefore, *p will contain garbage value as no value exists for arr[2][2][2]. *q contains the address of the first element in the array, that is 1 in this case.

****

26.
```
main()
{
int num = 5;
 printf("%d %d %d %d %d %d", num++, num--,
 ++num, --num, num);
}
```

Ans: 4 5 5 4 5

Because evaluation is done from right to left.

****

27.
```
#define square(x) x*x
main()
{
int res;
res = 125/square(5);
printf("%d",res);
}
```

Ans: 125

Because when the macro gets expanded

res = 125/5 * 5 = 25 * 5 = 125

****

28.
```
main()
{
char *pstr ="hello",*pstr1;
pstr1=pstr;
while(*pstr != '\0') ++*pstr++;
printf("%s", pstr);
printf("%s", pstr1);
}
```

Ans: efmmp

Evaluate the expression in the following manner (++(*pstr))++. This means the value of pstr is incremented first and then the address of pstr is incremented so that it points to the next character. After the while loop gets executed every character in pstr is incremented and pstr finally points to the null character. Therefore, the first printf statement prints nothing and the second statement prints the modified contents of pstr.

****

```
29. #include <stdio.h>
    #define num 5
    main()
    {
    #define num 100
    printf("%d", num);
    }
```

Ans: 100

A preprocessor directive can be redefined anywhere in the program.

****

```
30. main()
     {
     printf("%p", main);
     }
```

Ans: Address of the `main()` will be printed. `%p` specifies that the address be displayed in hexadecimal numbers.

****

```
31. main()
     {
     char str[]="Hello";
     char pstr = str;
     printf("%c\n",*&*pstr);
     }
```

Ans: H

Because `*pstr = H. &(*pstr) = pstr`. Finally, `*(&(*pstr))=H`

****

```
32. main()
     {
     int arr[2][3]= {{1,2,3},{4,5,6}};
     int i;

     arr[1]=arr[2];

     for (i=0;i<2;i++)
     printf("%d",arr[i]);
     }
```

Ans: ERROR

Because array names are pointer constants, so it cannot be modified.

****

```
33. main()
     {
     int num = scanf("%d", &num);
     printf("%d", num);
     }
```

Ans: 1

Because `scanf` returns the number of items read successfully. In this case, you will be entering only 1 value, so `scanf` reads only 1 item and reports 1.

****

```
34. #include <stdio.h>
    main()
    {
    struct x
    {
    int roll_no=1;
    char name[]="RAM";
    };
    struct x stud;
    printf("%d", s.roll_no);
    printf("%s",s.name);
    }
```

Ans: ERROR

Because you cannot initialize structure members within the structure declaration.

****

```
35. main()
     {
     extern num;
     printf("%d", num);
     }
     int num = -1;
```

Ans: –1

****

```
36. main( )
     {
     int arr[] = {1,2,3,4,5};
     for(j = 0; j < 5; j++)
     {
     printf("%d" ,*arr);
     arr++;
     }
     }
```

Ans: ERROR

`arr` is the name of an array and not a pointer variable so writing `arr++` creates an error

****

```
37. main( )
     {
     void *pv;
     char ch = 'r', *pstr = "music", print_char;
     int num =10;
     pv = &ch;
     print_char = *(char *)pv;
```

```
    printf("%c", print_char);
    pv = &num;
    print_char = *(int *)pv;
    printf("%d", print_char);
    pv = pstr;
    printf("%s",(char *)pv + 2);
    }
```

Ans: r10sic

****

```
38. main()
    {
    int i, n;
    char *str = "bird";
    n = strlen(str);
    *str = str[n];
    for(i = 0; i < n; ++i)
    {
    printf("%s\n",str);
    str++;
    }
    }
```

Ans:

```
(blank space)

ird

rd

d
```

Because the `strlen` function returns 4, i.e, the length of the string. In the next statement the value of the nth location is assigned to the first location. In the `for` loop, the string is printed in each iteration. The only difference is that during each iteration the starting position of the string is incremented. The first iteration prints a blank space because as soon as `printf` statement encounters `'\0'`, it prints nothing and simply increments the pointer value.

****

```
39. main()
    {
    printf("\n HELLO");
    main();
    }
```

Ans: Runtime error will occur because of stack overflow.

****

```
40. main()
    {
    void *pnum, num;
    num = 0;
    pnum = &num;
    printf("%v",num);
    }
```

Ans: ERROR

You can create a variable of `void *` but not of `void`.

****

```
41. main()
    {
    char *str="BIRD";
    char str1[]="BIRD";
    printf("%d %d",sizeof(str), sizeof(str1));
    }
```

Ans: 2 5

****

```
42. main()
    {
    int *pnum;
    {
      int num = 1;
      pnum = &num;
    }
    printf("%d",*pnum);
    }
```

Ans: 1

****

```
   main()
    {
    int num =-5;
    printf("num = %d, -num = %d \n", num,-num);
    }
```

Ans: `num = -5, -num = 5.`

-(-5) becomes 5

****

```
43. main()
    {
    const int num = 5;
    int res = ++num;
    printf("%d", res);
    }
```

Ans: ERROR

The value of a constant cannot be changed.

****

```
44. main()
    {
    register num = 5;
    float fnum = 1.5;
    printf("%d %f", num, fnum);
    }
```

Ans: 5 1.5

Register values are same as other values. The only difference is that the variable declared as register may either be in register or in memory.

****

```
45. main()
    {
    int a = 2, b = 3, res;
    printf("res = %d", a+++b);
    }
```

Ans: 5

Because the expression is evaluated from right to left as a++ + b

****

```
46. struct complex
    {
    int real;
    int imag;
    };
    struct complex c, *pc;
    main()
    {
    pc = &c;
    printf("Complex number is (%d +%di)
     \n",(*pc).real, (*pc).imag);
    }
```

Ans: Complex number is (0 + 0i).

Because when a structure is declared, all its members are automatically initialized to 0.

****

```
47. main()
    {
      int res = f(7);
      printf("%d\n", --res);
    }
    int f(int x)
    {
    return(x++);
    }
```

Ans: 6

The return statement will first return the value of x and then print it. Writing --res, will first decrement and then print the value.

****

```
48. main()
    {
    char ch='a';
     ch = convert(ch);
    printf("%c", ch);
    }
    convert(ch)
    {
    return ch-32;
    }
```

Ans: ERROR

Function declaration error

****

```
49. int arr[] = {1,2,3};
    main()
    {
    int *parr;
    parr = arr;
    printf("%d",*(parr + 5));
    }
```

Ans: Garbage value because array index is out of range.

****

```
50. Mesg1() {
    printf("GOOD");
    }
    Mesg2(){
    printf("Average");
    }
    Mesg3(){
    printf("BAD");
    }
    main()
    {
    int (*pfun[3])();
    pfun[0]=Mesg1;
    pfun[1]=Mesg2;
    pfun[2]=Mesg3;
    pfun[1]();
    }
```

Ans: AVERAGE

Only pfun[1]() is called from main()

****

```
51. main()
    {
    FILE *fp;
    char ch;
    fp = fopen("student.txt","r");
    while((ch = fgetch(fp))!= EOF)
    printf("%c",ch);
    }
```

Ans: Infinite loop because the condition should have been checked against NULL and not EOF

****

```
52. main()
    {
```

```
char *p;
p="%d\n";
p = p+2;
printf("%c", *(p-2));
}
```

Ans: %

****

```
53. IsEqual(int x, int y)
    {
      if(x == y)
        return 1;
      else
        return 0;
      }
      main()
      {
        int fun(), Is Equal();
        printf("%d", fun(IsEqual, 2, 3));
      }
      int fun((*pf)(), int a, int b)
      {
        return((*pf) (a, b));
      }
```

Ans: 0

****

```
54. main()
    {
    static int num=4;
    num = num - 1;
    if(num >= 0){
    main();
    printf("%d",num);
    }
    }
```

Ans: 0 0 0 0

num is a static variable, so its value persists in between function calls. After main() has been called for 4 times, the value of num becomes 0 and the same value is printed.

****

```
55. main()
    {
    char str[]="abcd\0";
    printf("%d", strlen(str));
    }
```

Ans: 4

****

```
56. main()
    {
    char *str="\0";
    if(printf("%s", str))
    printf("GOOD");
    else
    printf("BAD");
    }
```

Ans: GOOD

****

```
57. main()
    {
    int a = a++;
    static int p= p++:
    printf("%d %d", a, p);
    }
```

Ans: Garbage value 1 because a is an int which has not been initialized whereas p is a static int which is initialized to zero by default.

****

```
58. main()
    {
    unsigned int i = 5;
    i = i-1;
    while(i)
    printf("%u ",i);
    }
```

Ans: Infinite loop because 'i' is an unsigned integer, so its value can never be less than 0. As soon as the value gets decremented after reaching 0, 'i' will be assigned positive value like 65535.

****

```
59. main()
    {
    int arr[] = {1,2,3,4,5};
    printf("%d",*arr+1-*arr+3);
    }
```

Ans: 4 because *arr and –*arr cancel out and only 1 + 3 is left

****

```
60. #define mul(x,y) x * y
    main()
    {
    int num1 = 5, num2 = 7, res;
    res = mul(num1 + 2, num2 - 5)
    printf("%d", res);
    }
```

Ans: 14

On macro expansion, the expression becomes

```
5 + 2 * 7 – 5
```

****

```
61. main()
    {
    unsigned int num = 125;
    while(num-->0);
    printf("%d",num);
    }
```

Ans: -1

As soon as num becomes zero, the loop terminates. The post decrement operator subtracts 1 from num which had become 0, hence the result.

****

```
62. main()
    {
    int num = 0;
    while((num--)!= 0)
      num++;
    printf("%d", num);
    }
```

Ans: -1

****

```
63. main()
    {
    float fnum1 = 5, fnum2 = 2.5;
    printf("%f\n", fnum1<<2);
    printf("%lf\n", fnum1%fnum2);
    }
```

Ans: ERROR

Left shift operator does not work for floating point numbers. % is used for integers. For floating point numbers use, fmod().

****

```
64. main()
    {
    unsigned char ch = 0;
    while(ch> = 0) {ch++;}
    printf("%d\n", ch);
    }
```

Ans: Infinite loop because the value of ch will never be negative as it is declared as unsigned.

****

```
65. main()
    {
    unsigned int num = -1;
    if(~0 == num)
    printf("HELLO");
    }
```

Ans: HELLO

Internal representation of 0 is same as that of unsigned –1.

****

```
66. main()
    {
    char *str = "plmno";
    printf("%c",++*(str++);
    }
```

Ans: q

****

```
67. main()
    {
    int num = 2;
    printf("%d",++num == 3);
    }
```

Ans: 1

The expression in the printf statement is evaluated as 3==3, which is true and returns 1.

****

```
68. main()
    {
    int res;
    res = strcmp("abc",abc\0");
    printf("%d", res);
    }
```

Ans: 0

Ending the string constant with \0 explicitly makes no difference. So both abc and abc\0 are same.

****

```
69. main()
    {
    int num = 3;
    int *pnum1 = &num, *pnum2 = &num;
    num += 2;
    *pnum1 += 3;
    *pnum2 += 4;
    printf("%d %d %d", num, *pnum1, *pnum2);
    }
```

Ans: 12 12 12

All the three variables are different names for the same memory location. So any increment to their value results in the same value being updated.

****

70.
```
main()
{
char *str="BAD";
printf("\n sizeof(str) = %d, sizeof(*str) =
 %d, strlen(str) = %d", sizeof(str),
 sizeof(*str), strlen(str));
}
```

Ans:

`sizeof(str) = 2, sizeof(*str) = 1, strlen(str) = 3`

****

71.
```
main()
{
char str[]="BAD";
printf("\n sizeof(str) = %d, strlen(str) =
%d", sizeof(str), strlen(str));
}
```

Ans: `sizeof(str) = 5`

(length of the string + 1 for null character)

`strlen(str) = 3`

****

72.
```
main()
{
char * str = "GOOD";
char * pstr = str;
char ch = 127;
while (*pstr++)
   ch = (*ptr < ch ) ? *ptr : ch;
printf("%d",ch);
}
```

Ans: `0`

The ASCII value of null character is `'0'` which is less than 127.

****

73.
```
main()
{
struct Date;
struct student
{
      char name[30];
      struct Address add;
      struct Date DOB;
}stud;
struct Address
{
      char a[100];
};
struct Date
{
int dd, mm, yy;
};
scanf("%s%s %d %d %d", stud.name, student.
 add.a, &stud.DOB.dd, &stud.DOB.mm, &stud.
 DOB.yy);
printf("%s%s %d %d %d",  stud.name, student.
 add.a, stud.DOB.dd, stud.DOB.mm, stud.DOB.
 yy);
}
```

Ans: `ERROR`

`struct Address` should be defined before being used in `struct` student. Forward declaration is not permissible in C. Same is the case with `struct DOB`.

****

74.
```
main()
{
  char str[4]="GOOD";
  printf("%s", str);
}
```

Ans: `GOOD`

The string does not have space for storing the null character, therefore `str` does not end properly and it continues to print garbage values till it accidentally comes across a NULL character.

****

75.
```
char *f1()
{
    char *temp = "GOOD";
    return temp;
}
char *f2()
{
char temp[] = "BAD";
return temp;
}
main()
{
puts(f1());
printf("%s", f2());
}
```

Ans: `GOOD`

Garbage value

The answer is OK for the first function `f1()` but in case of `f2()`, `temp` is a character array for which memory is allocated in heap and is initialized with `"BAD"`. Temp is created dynamically when the function gets called, and is deleted dynamically when the control passes out of the function. Therefore, `temp` is not visible in `main()`. Hence, garbage value is printed.

APPENDIX E Linux: A Short Guide

Linux is a very powerful multitasking, multi-user operating system based on UNIX. It was originally created by Linus Torvalds, a Finnish-American software engineer, with the assistance of developers from around the globe.

It is an open source operating system since its source code is freely available on the Internet and is free to use.

E.1 COMPONENTS OF LINUX SYSTEM

Linux Operating System has three main components.

Kernel

Kernel is said to be the core part of Linux. It interacts directly with the hardware and is responsible for all major activities. Kernel consists of various modules to provide abstraction to hide low level hardware details from system or application programs. The **Shell** is an interface to kernel that hides complexity of kernel's functions from users. Users type their commands in the shell.

System Library

System libraries contain special functions or programs that when included in user's programs allow them to access Kernel's features. These libraries implement most of the functionalities of the operating system.

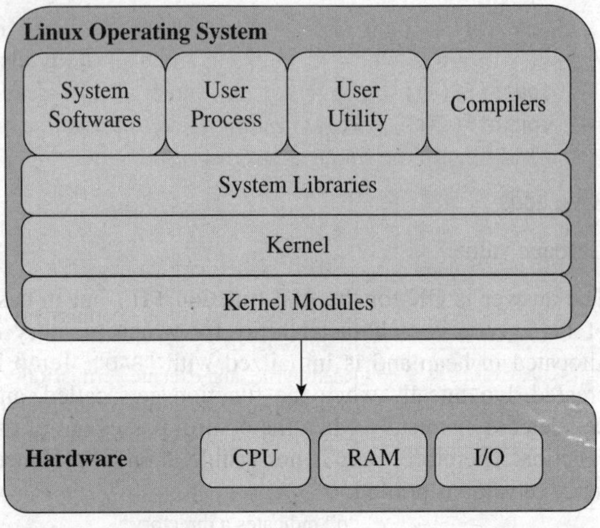

Hardware

The hardware consists of hard disk, CPU, and RAM and the peripheral devices connected to the computer such as I/O devices, and storage devices.

Linux operating system works in either kernel mode or user mode. Kernel component code executes in a special privileged mode called *kernel mode* with full access to all resources of the computer. In this mode, the kernel provides system services to processes and allows a protected access to hardware.

System library contains all the support code which is not required to run in kernel mode. User programs and other system programs that do not require access to system hardware and kernel code works in *user mode*. User programs or utilities (programs that gives users most of the functionalities of an operating systems) use System libraries to access Kernel functions to get system's low level tasks.

E.2 WORKING WITH SHELL IN LINUX

The shell (ex, `BASH`, `Tch`, `ksh`, etc) is the component of Linux that is commonly referred to as "the command line". It is actually a piece of software that provides an interface to the services of a kernel.

> Most modern Linux systems use BASH (Bourne Again Shell) as the default shell.

The command line allows users to execute a wide range of commands. At the command line, users can navigate to perform different tasks like backing up some files to disabling a dying piece of hardware.

For every Linux distribution, the command line prompt looks little different. For example, on one system it may appear as username, the '@' symbol, the machine name, current directory, and some kind of symbol to indicate the end of the prompt (like a dollar sign) as given below.

```
user@linux ~/$
```

In other systems, the prompt may appear as username, a space, the fully qualified domain name of the computer, the complete path of the present working directory followed by a symbol to indicate the end of the prompt (a hash symbol).

```
user linux.box.com/home/user#
```

The prompt differs due to the reasons as given below.

a. default configuration set by the creators of your particular Linux distribution
b. specifically configured by the person who administers the computer.

E.3 DIRECTORY ORIENTED COMMANDS

Command	Description	Example

`cd`	To change directory	If the directory is in the current working directory then specify the name otherwise mention the full path
		`cd marks`
		or `cd /students/marks`
		To move up one directory type,
		`cd..`

`cp`	To copy a directory with all its contents	`cp -r existing_dir new_dir`
`mkdir`	To create a new directory	`mkdir new_dir`
`mv`	To move a directory (rename it)	`mv existing_dir newname_dir`
`pwd`	To display the full path of the current directory	`pwd`
`rmdir`	To remove an existing empty directory	`rmdir`
`rm`	To remove a directory containing other files and directories	Removes all the files and directories with the specified directory `rm -r existing_dir`

E.4 FILE ORIENTED COMMANDS

Command	Description	Example

`cat`	To concatenate files and print on the standard output	To display a file write
		`cat filename.ext`
		To concatenate two files, write
		`cat file1 >> file2`

`touch`	To create new (empty) file
	It is also used to update access and modification times of a file
		To create a new file, write
		`touch filename`
		To update access time, write
		`touch -a filename`
		To update modification time, write
		`touch -m filename`

`cp`	To copy a file	To copy `file1.txt` from current directory to `usr/students` directory write,
		`cp file1.txt usr/students/`
		To copy all C files in the current directory to another directory write
		`cp *.c usr/codes/`

`rm`	To remove or delete a file	`rm filename.txt`
`mv`	To move or rename a file	`mv file1.txt file2.txt`
`wc`	To print the number of newline characters, words and byte counts of file	`wcfile1.txt`
`cmp`	To compare two files byte by byte. If a difference is found, it displays the byte and line number where the first difference is found. In case the files are exactly same then `cmp` returns no output.	`cmp file1.txt file2.txt`

E.5 FILE ACCESS PERMISSIONS COMMANDS

Linux is a multi-user operating system. In such an environment, it is very important to protect one user's files from being accessed by another user(s).Therefore, before discussing the `chmod` command which is used to modify file access rights, let us first understand what we actually mean by the term *file permissions*.

File permissions In Linux, each file or directory is assigned access rights for the owner of the file, the members of a group of related users, and everybody else. These rights can be categorized into three groups –read a file/directory, write to a file/directory, and to execute a file (for example, run the file as a program).

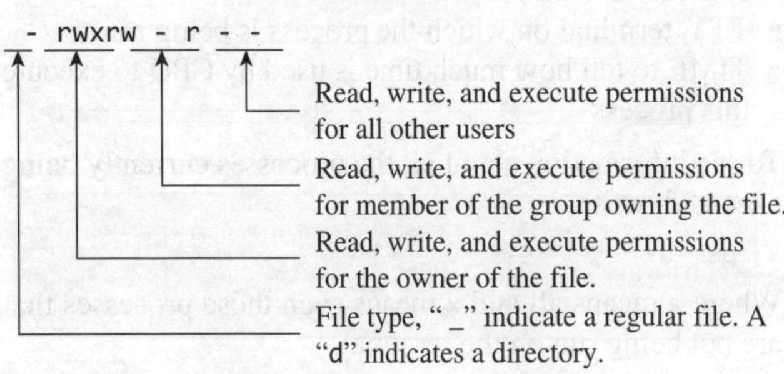

To view the existing permission of a file, just write

```
ls - l file.txt
```

The output would be like, -rwxr-xr-x and other details

To understand this output, separate this access rights byte in groups of three.

You may think of these permissions as a series of bits. A bit is 1 if the permission is given otherwise it is zero. Therefore, the three sets of permissions (owner, group and other) can be expressed as,

```
rwxrwxrwx = 111 111 111 = 7 7 7

rwxrw- r-- = 111 110 100 = 7 6 4

rwx r-x r-- = 111 101 100 = 7 5 4
```

chmod

After having a basic understanding of file permissions, let's now use the chmod command to alter the file permissions.

```
chmod 640 file
```

corresponds to 110100 000 in binary thereby indicating that the owner has only read and write permissions, the group has only read permission and other users have no permissions at all for the file.

Changing file ownership To change the owner, you can use the **chown** command as given below

```
chown new_owner_name file
```

However, to use this command you must be the superuser.

Changing group ownership You can even change the group ownership of a file or directory by using the chgrp command as shown below.

```
chgrp new_group file
```

Note that only the owner of the file can change the group ownership of that file.

E.6 PROCESS ORIENTED COMMANDS

The ps command is one of the most basic commands that is used to view the details of processes (like user id, CPU usage, memory usage, command name, etc.) running on the system. To execute the ps command simply type, ps. You would be shown the following details about the current process.

- Process ID (PID)
- TTY, terminal on which the process is being run
- TIME to tell how much time is used by CPU to execute this process

To see information about all the processes currently being executed, write

```
ps -ax
```

Where a means all and x means even those processes that are not being run on the terminal.

To see all the processes run by a particular user, use the -u option as,

```
ps -u jaya
```

This will display all the processes run by jaya

To display processes sorted by their by CPU or memory usage, use the sort command as given below.

```
ps -aux -sort -pcpu
```

Or, ps -aux -sort -pmem

To display processes by their name or ID use the -C option. For example, to see the details of the processes named abc, write

```
ps -C abc
```

To display the thread of a particular process use the -L option as given below.

ps -L 1234 where 1234 is the PID of the process.

To display the process hierarchy in a tree form, use the pstree command

> ps command can be used to monitor the daily usage of the Linux system.

Command	Description	Example
kill	To kill or terminate a process	kill 1234 where 1234 is the process ID of the process to be terminated
Killall	To terminate all the processes of a particular name	killall getty (where getty is the name of the process)
kill 0	To stop all the processes except your shell	kill 0

E.7 NETWORKING COMMANDS

The following Linux commands help to diagnose any networking problem.

Command	Description	Example
hostname	To find host or domain name and IP address of a host	hostname displays the machine's host hostname -i displays the machine's IP address hostname -d displays the domain name of the machine
ping	To test network connection	ping www.google.com
ifconfig	To get network configuration	ifconfig

Command	Description	Example
netstat	To get details about network connection, routing tables, interfaces, etc.	To display all connections, write `netstat -a` To display only TCP connection, write `netstat -tcp` To display only UDP connection, write `netstat -udp`
nslookup	To find the hostname if IP address is known	`nslookup google.com`
telnet	To communicate with another host	`telnet myhost.com:5555` where `myhost.com` is the host name and `5555` is the port number
finger	To view information about users (login name, terminal name, etc)	`finger`
traceroute	To find the route traversed to reach the network host	`traceroute google.com`

E.8 I/O REDIRECTION

Most command-line programs display the results by sending them to the *standard output* (the screen). To send the standard output to a file, the ">" character is used.

```
ls> file.txt
```

Here, the `ls` command is executed and the results are written in `file.txt`. Since the output has been redirected to a file, no results are displayed on the screen.

Whenever the above command is repeated, the contents of `file.txt` are overwritten by the new output generated by the execution of the command `ls`. If you want the new results to be *appended* to the existing contents of the file, use ">>".

```
ls>> file.txt
```

Many commands accept input from the standard input which is the keyboard. But, like standard output, input can also be redirected so that it is taken from a file instead of the keyboard. For example, to sort a file you need to supply the contents of the file to the `sort` command. This means that the `sort` command is not taking input from the standard input but from the file. In such situations, use the "<" character

```
sort < file.txt
```

If you want to redirect the sorted contents of `file.txt` to another file named `sorted_file.txt`, then write

```
sort < file.txt > sorted_file.txt
```

Pipes One of the most useful applications of Linux I/O redirection is to connect multiple commands together using *pipes*. With pipes, the standard output of one command is fed into the standard input of another. The symbol of pipe is |. For example, if we write

```
cat file.txt | wc
```

Now, the output of `file.txt` file will be sent as input for `wc` command which counts the number of words in that file. Pipes are useful to make a chain of several programs, so that multiple commands can execute at once.

Filters Filter is a class of programs that can be used with pipes. It takes input from the standard input device, performs an operation upon it and then sends the results to standard output. Some common filter programs are given below.

Program	Description
sort	Takes standard input, sorts it and then outputs the result on standard output.
uniq	Stands for unique. It takes a sorted stream of data from standard input and removes duplicate lines of data
grep	Checks each line of input received from the standard input and outputs lines that contain a specified pattern of characters.
fmt	Reads text from standard input, formats it and then displays it on standard output.
pr	Accepts input from the standard input and splits the data into pages with page breaks, headers, and footers in preparation for printing.
head	Displays only the first few lines of its input.
tail	Displays only the last few lines of its input.
tr	Stands for translate. It translates characters, for example, from upper to lower case
awk	A programming language for constructing filters

For example,

```
cat file.txt|fmt|pr|lpr
```

Here, the contents of the file `file.txt` is read and passed to a filter `fmt` which formats the text of the file and then passes it to a filter `pr`, which splits the text into pages and finally gives the results to `lpr`. `lpr` takes input from the standard input and sends it to the printer for printing.

Now can you guess, what is the result of `cat file.txt | sort | uniq | pr | lpr`?

It takes as an input an unsorted file, sorts it, removes duplicate entries, splits into pages and then prints it.

E.8 vi EDITOR

vi stands for visual editor and is the default editor that comes with Linux. It is a full screen editor that works in two modes,

1. *Command mode* which gives commands to perform some actions on the file. In this mode, every character

typed is treated as a command to perform some action.

2. *Insert mode* to enter text into the file. Pressing the Esc key turns off the insert mode.

There are a number of `vi` commands, which are discussed in the table.

Linux and vi are case sensitive.

To start vi editor, type `vi filename`. If the filename exists, then its contents are displayed, otherwise an empty file is opened in which text can be entered.

Command	Description
`:wq`	Quits vi by writing the modified contents
`:q`	Quits vi
`:q!`	Quits vi without saving the changes
`j`	Moves the cursor down one line
`k`	Moves the cursor up one line
`h`	Moves the cursor left one character
`l`	Moves the cursor right one character
`0`	Moves the cursor to the start of current line
`$`	Moves the cursor to the end of current line
`:n`	Moves the cursor to line n
`:0 and :$`	Moves the cursor to first and last line in the file
`^f and ^b`	Moves forward and backward one screen
`U`	Undoes the last action
`i`	Inserts text before the cursor

Command	Description
`I`	Inserts text at the beginning of the current line
`a`	Appends text after cursor
`A`	Appends text to the end of current line
`r`	Replaces single character under cursor
`R`	Replaces characters starting with current cursor position
`x`	Deletes single character under cursor
`Nx`	Deletes n characters starting with the character under cursor
`dw`	Deletes a single word beginning with character under cursor
`dNw`	Deletes N words beginning with character under cursor
`dd`	Deletes the current line
`dNd`	Deletes N lines beginning with the current line
`Yy`	Copies the current line into buffer
`yNy`	Copies N lines into buffer starting from the current line
`P`	Pastes the line(s) in the buffer after the current line
`/string`	Searches forward in file for any occurrence of string
`?string`	Searches backward in file for any occurrence of string
`:.=`	Displays the line number of current line at the bottom of the screen
`:=`	Displays the total number of lines at the bottom of the screen

APPENDIX F Emerging Technologies

F.1 ARTIFICIAL INTELLIGENCE

In 2004, John McCarthy defined Artificial Intelligence (AI) as the science and engineering of making intelligent machines, especially intelligent computer programs. However, much before this definition was coined, the birth of AI was marked by Alan Turing's seminal work, "Computing Machinery and Intelligence" published in 1950. Alan Turing, also known as the "father of computer science" raised questions like "Can machines think?" in this paper. Continuing with his work, he later proposed the "Turing Test", where a human interrogator would try to distinguish between a computer and human text response.

> **Note**
> Few languages that are popularly used to code AI applications are R, Python and Java.

From a layman's view, Artificial Intelligence (AI), simply means the intelligence demonstrated by machines that help them to mimic the actions of humans. AI simulates natural intelligence in machines that are programmed to learn from experiences, adjust to new inputs and perform human-like tasks.

From a researcher's view, AI is a set of algorithms that generates results without having to be explicitly instructed to do so thereby making machines capable of thinking and acting rationally and humanely.

> **Note**
> Most AI examples from chess-playing computers to self-driving cars, heavily depend on deep learning and natural language processing techniques.

AI applications perform specialized tasks by processing large amounts of data and recognizing patterns in it. Besides learning from experience, AI applications can recognize objects, understand and respond to language and make decisions to solve real-world problems. AI perform tasks that normally require human intelligence. The main focus of this technology is to build machines and algorithms which are capable of performing computational tasks that would otherwise require human like brain functions.

While computers execute certain tasks like sorting, computing, memorizing, indexing, finding patterns, etc. far better than humans, they still cannot beat human skills for identifying emotions, recognizing faces, communication and conversation. This is where AI will play a crucial role to enable machines achieve human capabilities.

> **NITI Aayog: National Strategy for Artificial Intelligence has defined AI as,**
> AI refers to the ability of machines to perform cognitive tasks like thinking, perceiving, learning, problem solving and decision making. Initially conceived as a technology that could mimic human intelligence, AI has evolved in ways that far exceed its original conception. With incredible advances made in data collection, processing and computation power, intelligent systems can now be deployed to take over a variety of tasks, enable connectivity and enhance productivity.

How does AI work?

AI systems work effectively when fed with large amounts of labeled training data. This data is thoroughly analyzed to discover correlations and patterns. These patterns are then used to make predictions about future states. For example, a chatbot fed with examples of text chats can learn to converse with humans in real world applications.

AI programming focuses on three cognitive skills: learning, reasoning and self-correction.

Learning processes. AI programs focuse on acquiring data and creating rules for turning that data into actionable information. Rules, also known as algorithms, provide step-by-step instructions to complete a specific task.

Reasoning processes. Success of AI program depends on choosing the right algorithm to reach the desired outcome.

Self-correction processes. AI programs are designed to continually enhance their algorithms to provide the most accurate results.

F.2 METAVERSE

The term 'metaverse' is a combination of two words-'meta' and 'universe' which means an anticipated future iteration of the internet that is often referred to as Web 3.0. The evolution of the internet from Web 2.0 to Web 3.0 will cause a tremendous boost of online 3-D or virtually integrated environments that provide users immersive experience in true sense.

Metaverse is a combination of virtual reality, augmented reality, mixed reality, blockchain technology, Internet of Things (IoT), 5G, **artificial intelligence (AI)** and spatial technologies that is accessed through a browser or headset. It is a device-independent technology that is not owned by a single vendor. Metaverse is an independent virtual economy that uses digital currencies and **nonfungible tokens (NFTs).** It allows users to have real time interactions and experiences across distance.

Basically, metaverse is not just one type of experience. It actually encompasses a continuum of immersive digital experiences that will be available to users in the future to engage them in different activities in digital spaces. For example, a massive virtual reality multiplayer game can be accessed through a VR headset. Similarly, an integrated digital and physical spaces (like location-specific immersive digital content) that are often a need of business users, can be experienced using digital glasses or smartphones.

> Metaverse is not one digital space but a combination of several digital spaces and experiences

Many social media and tech companies like Meta Platforms (formerly known as Facebook) and Microsoft are investing heavily in Social VR to create platforms to allow people to connect socially and work remotely respectively.

F.3 IMMERSIVE EXPERIENCE

Immersive experience is any technology that extends reality or creates a new reality by leveraging the 360 space. While some types of Immersive Experience extend reality by overlaying digital images on a user's environment, others create a new reality by completely immersing users in a digital environment, shutting them out from the rest of the world.

The simplest tool to enjoy immersive content is through smartphones or specialized headsets. On the software side, although a web app or a desktop application can be used, web app is more popular.

Types of Immersive Experiences

360-degree content is an interactive photo or a video recording shot in every direction at the same time. This allows users to change the viewing direction at any moment. Digital twin is a precise virtual model of a real-life object, process, or system. We can even create a digital of an object that does not even exist. Such models can be used to display textual details or to monitor, control, and run simulations.

Figure Experiencing Immersive Experiences

Virtual reality (VR) is a computer simulation that immerses the user inside a virtual world and allows him to interact with the environment. VR stimulates user's senses to make him feel as if her was actually there in that environment.

VR shuts a user completely from the rest of the world while being surrounded by content. Through a head mounted display (HMD), whatever content the user experiences in the headset becomes the reality for him.

360 vs 360 VR: Though the two terms are same, 360 VR is a combination of 360 content with VR mode. It allows users to view the 360 content in a cardboard headset, or sometimes even a mobile 360 VR headset. Users can experience 360 content without the help of an HMD and is best experienced on mobile.

Mobile VR: leverages HMDs that are connected to smartphones. Examples of these are the Samsung Gear VR, Google's Daydream or even Google Cardboard.

True VR: uses headsets with powerful computers or consoles. Examples include HTC Vive, Oculus Rift, Playstation VR, etc. These powerful HMDs use sensors (separate from the HMD) to keep a track of a person's movement and his surroundings. The sensors would then adjust the VR content to whatever is within a user's environment. True VR uses CGI and 3D modelling for content.

360 VR vs In-VR: With 360 VR, users can use their device to explore content by looking in any direction but does not change the content that surrounds the objects. In-VR content takes depth into consideration. This means that when a person is viewing an object, he can move closer to the object or move further away from it. The entire content are adjusted accordingly.

Augmented reality (AR) enhances the user's perception of the real world by adding a computer-simulated layer of information on top of it. While AR adds or hides data from the environment, VR completely replaces the user's perception of the real world.

Using AR, digital images are presented on top of the real world. This means that users who leverage AR are not completely shut off from the world. Instead, AR extends their reality.

For example, Snapchat Filters that overlay digital images onto your face is an application of AR. Another example of AR is Pokemon Go where users can walk around with their mobile phones and find Pokemon that are overlaid on the environment around the user.

Many stores like Target and Ikea have their own AR apps where users can choose a product and place it virtually on anything to see how it looks. For example, you can choose a dress and see how it looks on you. This allow consumers to "try out" a product before even buying it.

Mixed Reality (MR) brings together VR and AR into an enhanced version of AR. Mixed Reality is also referred to as AR 2.0 because it achieves better immersion than AR. MR integrates virtual objects in the real world. It responds to changes in the environment and to user interaction in real-time. Unlike VR, MR does not shut out users from the rest of the world. Instead, the HMD is more like a pair of glasses that overlays digital images on top of your environment (just like AR).

Extended Reality (ER) is used to enhance or completely replace reality.

F.4 ROBOTICS

Robotics is a branch of engineering that involves the conception, design, manufacture, and operation of robots. It is an inter-disciplinary field that includes the study of electronics, computer science, artificial intelligence, mechatronics, nanotechnology and bioengineering.

Science-fiction author Isaac Asimov, had first used the term robotics in the year 1940s. As per him, robots must,

Rule 1: never harm humans.

Rule 2: always follow instructions from humans without violating rule 1.

Rule 3: protect themselves without violating the other rules.

Some important aspects of robot include:

- They have **electrical components** for providing power and control the machinery.
- They have **mechanical construction** and their shape or design depends on the task they are intended to accomplish.
- They are **programmed**. Instructions fed to them help them to determine what, when and how it would do something.

These days, robots are being extensively designed as bots that explore Earth's harshest conditions and assist in almost every facet of healthcare. Though the robotics industry is still evolving, we already have robots that works in the deepest depths of our oceans to the highest heights of outer space. They are being used to do everything that humans could not dream of doing.

Types of Robots

Pre-Programmed Robots operate in a controlled environment to perform simple, monotonous tasks. For example, a mechanical arm on an automotive assembly line that is used to weld a door, or insert a certain part into the engine. This type of robot can perform that task for longer hours, faster and more efficiently than a human.

Humanoid robots look like humans and/or mimic human behaviour. They can perform human-like activities (like running, jumping and carrying objects). Sophia and Atlas are two popular examples of humanoid robots.

Autonomous Robots operate without human operators. They designed to perform tasks in open environments that do not require human supervision. For example, the Roomba vacuum cleaner uses sensors to roam freely throughout a home to clean it.

> Robots are also used for tasks varying from Diffusing Bombs to Performing Surgeries. VR Robots are also becoming popular these days.

Teleoperated Robots are mechanical bots controlled by humans. They are used in extreme geographical conditions, weather, circumstances, etc. for example, human-controlled submarines used to fix underwater pipe leaks during the BP oil spill or drones used to detect landmines on a battlefield are examples of teleoperated robots.

Augmenting Robots either enhance current human capabilities or replace the capabilities a human may have lost. Robotic prosthetic limbs or exoskeletons used to lift hefty weights are examples of such robots.

F.5 BIG DATA

Big data analytics is the process of collecting, organizing, and analysing large sets of data (called *big data*) to discover patterns and other useful information. It can help organizations to better understand the information contained within the data. Big data analysis allows users to evaluate large volumes of transaction data and other data sources that traditional systems would not be able to handle.

Big data is a term used for analysing data sets whose size or type is beyond the ability of traditional relational databases to capture, manage, and process with low-latency (less delay). The special features of data sets used in big data analysis include high volume (large amount), high velocity (frequently changing), or high variety (different types). This data comes from sensors, devices, video/audio, networks, log files, transactional applications, web, and social media. Much of the data is generated in real time and on a very large scale.

Analysing this big data allows data scientists or business users to make better and faster decisions using data that was previously inaccessible or unusable. Big data analytics uses advanced analytics techniques such as text mining, data mining, machine learning, predictive analytics, forecasting, data optimization, and natural language processing. Although these processes are separate, they are integrated for high-performance analytics.

Sophisticated software tools are used for big data analytics. Big data analysis outperforms data warehousing as it can easily handle large amount of unstructured and semi-structured data efficiently. Furthermore, data warehouses may not be able to handle the processing demands posed by sets of big data that are updated frequently or even continually. This is especially important in the case of real-time data on stock trading or analysing the online activities of website visitors or the performance of mobile applications.

Big data analytics environments and technologies including Hadoop, MapReduce, and NoSQL databases can process huge data sets over clustered systems. Big data analysis techniques can analyse large data sets of size ranging from few terabytes to zettabytes.

History and Evolution of Big Data Analytics

The history of big data analysis can be traced back to 1950s when people were not even aware of the term *big data*. In those days, people were analysing business numbers in a basic spreadsheet software to uncover insights and trends in the business.

Later, businesses switched to data warehousing and data mining techniques to gather information, run analytics, and unearth information that could be used for future decisions. However, today businesses have grown to an extent that they are seeking to identify insights for immediate decisions. The ability to work faster and stay agile gives organizations a competitive edge like never before.

F.6 INTERNET OF THINGS

Although the concept was not named until 1999, the Internet of Things has been in development for decades. Internet of Things (IoT) means a system of interrelated computing devices, machines, objects, animals or people that have unique identifiers for identification and also the ability to transfer data over a network without requiring human-to-human or human-to-computer interaction.

If the thing, in the Internet of Things, is a person, then he can have heart monitor implant; if it is an animal, it can have a biochip transponder, if it is an automobile, it can have sensors to generate alert alarms (example, when the pressure in tyre is too low) and if it any other natural or man-made object, then it is assigned an IP address and provided with the ability to transfer data over a network.

The huge availability of address space in IPv6 has led to the development of the Internet of Things. With more IP addresses available, more number of devices can be connected to exchange information with each other.

Today, IoT is being widely used for precision agriculture, building management, healthcare, energy and transportation. The first internet appliance was a Coke machine at Carnegie Melon University in the early 1980s when the programmers succeeded in connecting the machine over the internet to check the status of the machine and determine the availability of a cold drink. This check helped them to save their time as they did not have to go to the machine to buy Coke when it was not available in the machine.

> In simple terminology, IoT is the concept of connecting any devices over the internet.

Later, other devices like cell phones, coffee makers, washing machines, headphones, lamps, wearable devices and almost anything you can think of could be connected. It is interesting to know that the analyst firm Gartner has said that by 2020, there will be over 26 billion connected devices. Other analysts have said that this number will be over 100 billion. So we can conclude that, IoT is a giant network of connected "things" (including people) which will have relationships between people-people, people-things, and things-things.

About the Author

Dr Reema Thareja is Assistant Professor in the Department of Computer Science, Shyama Prasad Mukherji College, University of Delhi. In her 18 years of teaching experience, she has taught several courses including BA, BSc, MSc, BBA, MBA, BCA, and MCA.

Dr Thareja has authored several books in Computer Science and her books have been well accepted across the globe. She has published more than 22 research papers in international journals of repute and filed four patents. She also launched a free mobile app, Jruma, for Apple as well Android devices to promote learning through quizzing and excite users by giving them an opportunity to earn while they learn.

Besides being an author, she is an eminent speaker. Dr Thareja has conducted several Faculty Development Programmes, Seminars, Webinars, and Students' Workshops in India, the UAE, and the USA. She was also invited as a speaker for the Global Virtual Summit in New York.

Dr. Thareja is a Board Member of Studies in Computer Science for two eminent colleges in Vijayawada and a member of Technical Advisory Board of Refactor Academy. Being a member of Computer Society of India, Editorial Board and Elite Speakers group of IMRF have added feathers in her cap. She has received multiple awards and recognitions for her immense contributions in the field of education.